AA

TRAVELLERS' GUIDE
TO EUROPE

Editor: Jackie Rathband
Designer: Gerry McElroy

Gazetteer: compiled by the Publications Research Unit of the Automobile Association
Maps: prepared by the Cartographic Services Unit of the Automobile Association
Cover picture: Rocamadour, Dordogne, France. (Wolverton Colour Library)

Head of Advertisement Sales: Christopher Heard
Tel 0256 20123 (ext 2020)

Advertisement Production: Karen Weeks
Tel 0256 20123 (ext 3525)

Typesetting by Turnergraphic Ltd, Basingstoke

Printed and bound in Great Britain by: William Collins, Glasgow

Every effort is made to ensure accuracy, but the publishers do not hold themselves responsible for any consequences that may arise from errors or omissions. Whilst the contents are believed correct at the time of going to press, changes may have occurred since that time or will occur during the currency of this book.

Published by the Automobile Association, Basingstoke, Hampshire RG21 2EA

ISBN 0 86145 386 7
AA Reference 59598

Contents

European ABC

Motoring and general information

The ABC provides a wide background of motoring regulations and general information and is designed to be read in conjunction with the relevant country section(s).

Motoring laws in Europe are just as wide and complicated as those in the UK but they should cause little difficulty to the average British motorist. He should however, take more care and extend greater courtesy than he would normally do at home, and bear in mind the essentials of good motoring — avoiding any behaviour likely to obstruct traffic, to endanger persons or cause damage to property. It is also important to remember that when travelling in a country the tourist is subject to the laws of that country.

Road signs are mainly international and should be familiar to the British motorist, but in every country there are a few exceptions. One should particularly watch for signs indicating crossings and speed limits. Probably the most unusual aspect of motoring abroad to the British motorist is the universal and firm rule giving priority to traffic coming from the right (except in the Republic of Ireland) and unless this rule is varied by signs, it must be strictly observed.

As well as a current passport, (except for Republic of Ireland, see *Passports* page 18) a tourist temporarily importing a motor vehicle should always carry a full valid national driving licence, even when an International Driving Permit is held, the registration document of the car and evidence of insurance. The proper international distinguishing sign should be affixed to the rear of the vehicle. The appropriate papers must be carried at all times and secured against loss. The practice of spot checks on foreign cars is widespread and to avoid inconvenience or a *police fine,* ensure that your papers are in order and that the international distinguishing sign is of the approved standard design.

Make sure that you have clear all-round vision. See that your seat belts are securely mounted and not damaged, and remember that in most European countries their use is compulsory.

If you are carrying skis, remember that their tips should point to the rear. You must be sure that your vehicle complies with the regulations concerning dimensions for all the countries you intend to pass through (see *ABC* and *Country sections*). This is particularly necessary if you are towing a trailer of any sort. If you are planning to tow a caravan, you will find advice and information in the AA guide *Camping and Caravanning in Europe*.

We know as well as anyone how expensive mechanical repairs and replacement parts can be abroad. While not all breakdowns are avoidable, a vast number of those we deal with occur because the vehicle has not been prepared properly before the start of the journey. A holiday abroad involves many miles of hard driving over roads completely new to you, perhaps without the facilities you have come to take for granted in this country. Therefore you should give serious thought to the business of *preparing your vehicle for a holiday abroad*.

We recommend that your car undergoes a major service by a franchised dealer shortly before your holiday or tour abroad. In addition, it is advisable to carry out your own general check for any audible or visible defects.

It is not practicable to provide a complete list of points to look for but the ABC contains information under the following headings:

Automatic gearboxes
Automatic transmission fluid
Brakes
Cold weather touring
Direction indicators
Electrical
Engine and mechanical
Lights
Spares
Tyres
Warm climate touring

which, if used in conjunction with the manufacturer's handbook, should ensure that no obvious faults are missed.

If AA members would like a thorough check of their car made by one of the AA's experienced engineers, any AA Centre can arrange this at a few days' notice. Our engineer will then submit a written report complete with a list of repairs required. There is a fee for this service. For more information please ask for our leaflet Tech 8.

AA Agents including Port Agents

The Association does not maintain any offices outside Great Britain and Ireland but is represented by allied motoring clubs and other organisations throughout Europe. Additionally it has appointed port agents at the more popular *Belgian, French* and *Spanish* ports whose particular function is to assist and advise motorists embarking and disembarking. European motoring clubs allied to the AA will extend a courtesy service to AA members but this will be commensurate with their facilities. See also *Country sections* for *Belgium, France, Gibraltar* and *Spain.*

Accidents (*See also Country sections*)

The country sections give individual country regulations and information on summoning the emergency services. The international regulations are similar to those in the UK; the following recommendations are usually advisable.

If you are involved in an accident you *must* stop. A warning triangle should be placed on the road at a suitable distance to warn following traffic of the obstruction. The use of hazard warning lights in no way affects the regulations governing the use of warning triangles. Medical assistance should be obtained for persons injured in the accident. If the accident necessitates calling the police, leave the vehicle in the position in which it came to rest; should it seriously obstruct other traffic, mark the position of the vehicle on the road and get the details confirmed by independent witnesses before moving it.

The accident must be reported to the police; if it is required by law; if the accident has caused death or bodily injury; or if the unoccupied vehicle or property has been damaged and there is no one present to represent the interests of the party suffering damage. Notify your insurance company by letter if possible, within 24 hours of the accident; see the conditions of your policy. If a third party is injured, the insurance company or bureau, whose address is given on the back of your Green Card or frontier insurance certificate, should be notified; the company or bureau will, if necessary, pay compensation to the injured party.

Make sure that all the essential particulars are noted, especially details concerning third parties, and co-operate with police or other officials taking on-the-spot notes by supplying your name, address or other personal details as required. It is also a good idea to take photographs of the scene, endeavouring to get good shots of other vehicles involved, their registration plates and any background which might help later enquiries. This record may be useful when completing the insurance company's accident form.

If you are not involved in the accident but feel your assistance as a witness or in any other useful capacity would be helpful, then stop and park your car carefully, well away from the scene. If all the help necessary is at the scene, then do not stop out of curiosity and do not park your car at the site.

Automatic gearboxes

When towing a caravan the fluid in the automatic gearbox becomes hotter and thinner so there is more slip and more heat generated in the gearbox. Many manufacturers recommend the fitting of a gearbox oil cooler. Check with the manufacturer what is suitable for your car.

Automatic transmission fluid

Automatic transmission fluid is not always readily available especially in some of the more remote areas of Western Europe and tourists are advised to carry an emergency supply with them.

BBC World Service

If you wish to receive English language broadcasts whilst travelling abroad, BBC World Service transmissions can be heard in many European countries. A full programme including current affairs, sport and music is available, with world news at approximately every hour. Most car radios operate on medium and long waves and BBC World Service programmes may normally be obtained in north-western Europe by tuning to the following frequencies between the times mentioned.

KHz	Metres	Summer broadcasting times — GMT
1296	231	03.00-03.30, 06.00-06.30, 16.00-18.30, 22.00-23.15
648	463	04.45-05.30, 05.45-10.30, 11.00-16.45, 20.00-03.30
200	1500	02.00-04.30

In some Western European countries it may be possible to receive BBC national services with the exception of Radio 3. For more comprehensive information on BBC transmissions throughout

Europe, write to BBC World Information Centre and Shop, Bush House, Strand, LONDON WC2B 4PH.

Boats

Tourists taking any type of boat by car to France*, German Federal Republic (West Germany), Greece, Italy, Netherlands, Spain*, Switzerland or Yugoslavia are strongly advised to obtain boat registration documentation from the Royal Yachting Association, Queen Street, Gillingham, Dorset SP8 4PQ tel (07476) 4437. A Helmsman's (Overseas) Certificate of Competence is rarely needed, but is advisable for inland waters (except the French canals). The certificate can be obtained from the above address and is free to members of the RYA. Applications should be made well in advance. See also *Carnet de Passages* under *Customs regulations,* page 9, *Identification plate,* page 13 and *Insurance* page 13.

**Boat registration documentation is compulsory for all craft except very small craft under about 10ft. Check with the RYA if you are taking a boat to France.*

Brakes

Car brakes must always be in peak condition. Check especially the level in the brake fluid reservoir and the thickness of the brake lining/pad material. The brake fluid should be completely changed in accordance with the manufacturer's instructions, or at intervals of not more than 18 months or 18,000 miles.

However, it is advisable to change the brake fluid regardless of the foregoing, before departing on a Continental holiday, particularly if the journey includes travelling through a hilly or mountainous area.

Breakdown (*See also Country sections*)

If your car breaks down, endeavour to move it to the side of the road or to a position where it will obstruct the traffic flow as little as possible. Place a warning triangle at the appropriate distance on the road behind the obstruction. Bear in mind road conditions and if near or on a bend the triangle should be placed where it is clearly visible to following traffic. If the car is fitted with hazard warning lights these may be switched on but they will only warn on the straight and will have no effect at bends or rises in the road. If the fault is electrical, the lights may not operate and it is for these reasons that they cannot take the place of a triangle. Having taken these first precautions, seek assistance if you cannot deal with the fault yourself.

Motorists are advised to purchase AA 5-Star Service which provides a wide range of services, insurance and credit vouchers which offer security and peace of mind when travelling in Europe. Cover may be purchased by any motorist although a small additional premium must be paid by non-members. Details and brochures may be obtained from AA Travel Agencies and AA Centres, or by telephoning 021-550 7648.

Note Members who have not purchased AA 5-Star Service prior to departure and who subsequently require assistance may request spare parts or vehicle recovery, but in this case the AA will require a deposit to cover estimated costs and a service fee prior to providing the service. All expenses must be reimbursed to the AA in addition to the service fee.

British Embassies/Consulates

In most countries there is usually more than one British Consulate and degrees of status vary. The functions and office hours of Vice-Consulates and Honorary Consuls are naturally more restricted. Generally Consulates (and consular sections of the Embassy) stand ready to help British travellers overseas, but there are limits to what they can do. A Consulate cannot pay your hotel, medical or any other bills, nor will they do the work of travel agents, information bureaux or police. Any loss or theft of property should be reported to the local police not the Consulate, and a statement obtained confirming the loss or theft. If you still need help, such as the issue of an emergency passport or guidance on how to transfer funds; contact the Consulate. See respective *Country sections* for addresses/locations of British Embassies/Consulates.

Camping and caravanning

Information is given separately in the AA guide *Camping and Caravanning in Europe*, a copy of which may be purchased from most AA Centres.

Caravan and luggage trailers

Carry a list of contents, especially if any valuable or unusual equipment is being carried, as this may be required at a frontier. A towed vehicle should be readily identifiable by a plate in an accessible position showing the name of the maker of the vehicle and his production or serial number. If the vehicle does not have an *identification plate* see page 13. See also *Principal mountain passes* page 37.

Claims against Third Parties

The law and levels of damages in foreign countries are generally different to our own. It is important

to remember this when considering making a claim against another motorist arising out of an accident abroad. Certain types of claims invariably present difficulties, the most common probably being that relating to the recovery of car-hiring charges. Rarely are they recoverable in full and in some countries they may be drastically reduced or not recoverable at all. General damages for pain and suffering are not recoverable in certain countries but even in those countries where they are recoverable the levels are, in most cases, lower than our own.

The negotiation of claims against foreign insurers is extremely protracted and translation of all documents slows down the process. A delay of three months between sending a letter and receiving a reply is not uncommon!

If you have taken out the AA's 5-Star Service cover this includes a discretionary service in respect of certain matters arising abroad requiring legal assistance including the pursuit of uninsured loss claims against third parties arising out of a road accident. In this event, members should seek guidance and/or assistance from the AA.

Cold weather touring

If you are planning a winter tour, make sure that you fit a high-temperature (winter) thermostat and make sure that the strength of your antifreeze mixture is correct for the low temperatures likely to be encountered.

If you are likely to be passing through snow-bound regions, it is important to remember that for many resorts and passes the authorities insist on wheel chains or spiked or studded tyres. However, as wheel chains and spiked or studded tyres can damage the road surface if it is free of snow or ice, there are definite periods when these may be used and in certain countries the use of spiked or studded tyres is illegal. If wheel chains or spiked or studded tyres are compulsory this is usually signposted.

In fair weather, wheel chains or spiked or studded tyres are only necessary on the higher passes, but in severe weather you will probably need them (as a rough guide) at altitudes exceeding 2,000ft.

If you think you will need wheel chains, it is better to take them with you from home. They may be hired from the AA and further details are available from your nearest AA Centre. Information on hiring wheel chains (where such a service exists) in the countries where they are most needed is given in the country sections.

Wheel chains fit over the driven wheels to enable the wheels to grip on snow or icy surfaces. They are sometimes called *snow chains* or *anti-skid chains.* Full-length chains which fit right round the tyre are the most satisfactory, but they must be fitted correctly. Check that the chains do not foul your vehicle bodywork; if your vehicle has front-wheel-drive, then put the steering on full lock while checking. If your vehicle has radial tyres it is essential that you contact the manufacturers of your vehicle and tyres for their recommendations in order to avoid damage to your tyres. Chains should only be used when compulsory or necessary as prolonged use on hard surfaces will damage the tyres. See also *Country sections* for *Andorra, Austria, France, Germany, Italy, Norway, Portugal, Switzerland* and *Yugoslavia.*

Spiked or studded tyres are sometimes called *snow tyres.* They are tyres with rugged treads on to which spikes or studs have been fitted. For the best grip they should be fitted to all wheels. The correct type of spiked or studded winter tyres will generally be more effective than chains. See also *Country sections.*

Note The above comments do not apply where severe winter conditions prevail. It is doubtful whether the cost of preparing a car, normally used in the UK, would be justified for a short period. However, the AA's Technical Services Department will be pleased to advise on specific enquiries.

Compulsory equipment

All countries have differing regulations as to how vehicles circulating on their roads should be equipped but generally domestic laws are not enforced on visiting foreigners. However, where a country considers aspects of safety or other factors are involved, they will impose some regulations on visitors and these will be mentioned in the country sections.

Crash or safety helmets

All countries in this guide (except Belgium where they are strongly recommended) require visiting motorcyclists and their passengers to wear crash or safety helmets.

Credit/Charge cards

Credit/charge cards may be used abroad but their use is subject to the 'conditions of use' set out by the issuing company who, on request, will provide full information. Establishments display the symbols of cards they accept, but it is not possible to produce any detailed lists. However, hotels which accept credit/charge cards are indicated in the gazetteer, see page 50 for further information. See also *Country sections* under *Petrol* for information as to whether credit cards may be used to purchase fuel.

Currency including banking hours

(*See also Country sections*)

There is no limit to the amount of sterling notes you may take abroad. However, it is best to carry only enough currency for immediate expenses.

As many countries have regulations controlling the import and export of currency, you are advised to consult your bank for full information before making final arrangements.

Customs regulations for European countries (other than the UK)

Bona fide visitors to the countries listed in this guide may assume as a general rule that they may *temporarily import personal articles* duty free, providing the following conditions are met:

a that the articles are for personal use and are not to be sold or otherwise disposed of;

b that they may be considered as being in use and in keeping with the personal status of the importer;

c that they are taken out when the importer leaves the country, or

d that the goods stay for no more than 6 months in any 12 month period whichever is the earlier.

All dutiable articles must be declared when you enter a country, otherwise you will be liable to penalties. Should you be taking a large number of personal effects with you, it would be a wise measure to prepare in advance an inventory to present to the Customs authorities on entry. Customs officers may withhold concessions at any time and ask the traveller to deposit enough money to cover possible duty, especially on portable items of apparent high value such as television sets, or radios, cassette recorders, pocket calculators, and musical instruments, etc, all of which must be declared. Any deposit paid (for which a receipt must be obtained) is likely to be high; it is recoverable (but only at the entry point at which it was paid) on leaving the country and exporting the item. Alternatively the Customs may enter the item in the traveller's passport and in these circumstances it is important to remember to get the entry cancelled when the item is exported. Duty and tax free allowances may not apply (except for EEC countries) if the traveller enters the country more than once a month, or if he is under 17 years of age (an alternative age may apply in some countries). However, residents of Channel Islands and Isle of Man do not benefit from EEC allowances due to their fiscal regimes.

A *temporarily imported motor vehicle, caravan, boat* or any other type of *trailer* is subject to strict control on entering a country, attracting Customs duty and a variety of taxes; much depends upon the circumstances and the period of the import and also upon the status of the importer. A person entering a country in which he has no residence, with a private vehicle for holiday or recreational purposes, and intending to export the vehicle within a short period, enjoys special privileges and the normal formalities are reduced to an absolute minimum in the interests of tourism. However, a *Customs Carnet de Passages en Douane* is required to import temporarily certain vehicles, boats and outboard engines into some countries (see *Country sections* for *Belgium, France* and *Luxembourg*). The *Carnet,* for which a charge is made, is a valuable document issued by the AA to its members or as part of the AA 5-Star Service — further information may be obtained from most AA Centres. If you are issued with a *Carnet* you must ensure that it is returned to the AA correctly discharged in order to avoid inconvenience and expense, possibly including payment of customs charges, at a later date. A temporarily imported vehicle, etc, should not:

a be left in the country after the importer has left

b be put at the disposal of a resident of the country;

c be retained in the country longer than the permitted period;

d be lent, sold, hired, given away, exchanged or otherwise disposed of.

A person entering a country with a motor vehicle for a period of generally more than six months (see also *Visa* information page 25) or to take up residence, employment, any commercial activity or with the intention of disposing of the vehicle should seek advice concerning his position well in advance of his departure. Most AA Centres will be pleased to help.

Customs regulations for the United Kingdom

If, when leaving Britain, you export any items of new appearance, as for example watches, items of jewellery, cameras etc, particularly of foreign manufacture, which you bought in the UK, it is a good idea to carry the retailer's receipts with you if they are available. In the absence of such receipts you may be asked to make a written declaration of where the goods were obtained.

The exportation of certain goods *from the United Kingdom* is prohibited or restricted. These include: controlled drugs; most animals, birds and some plants; firearms and ammunition; strategic and technological equipment (including computers); photographic material over 60 years old; and antiques and collectors' items more than 50 years old.

When you *enter the United Kindgom* you will pass through Customs. You must declare everything in excess of the duty and tax free allowance (see below) which you have obtained outside the United Kingdom or on the journey and everything previously obtained free of duty or tax in the United Kingdom. You may not mix allowances between duty-free and non-duty-free sources within each heading except for alcohol which allows for example 1 litre of duty and tax free spirits in addition to 5 litres of duty and tax paid still wine. Currently as a concession only, travellers may use their entitlement of alcoholic drinks not over 22% vol to import table wine in addition to the set table wine allowance. You must also declare any prohibited or restricted goods and goods for commercial purposes. Don't be tempted to hide anything or to mislead the Customs. The penalties are severe and in addition articles which are not properly declared may be forfeited. If articles are hidden in a vehicle, that too becomes liable to forfeiture. The Customs officer is legally entitled to examine your luggage. Please co-operate with him if he asks to examine it. You are responsible for opening, unpacking and repacking your luggage.

Goods obtained duty and tax free in the EEC or duty and tax free on a ship or aircraft, or goods obtained outside the EEC	Duty and tax free allowances	Goods obtained duty and tax paid in the EEC
	Tobacco products	
200	Cigarettes	300
	or	
100	Cigarillos	150
	or	
50	Cigars	75
	or	
250g	Tobacco	400g
	Alcoholic drinks	
2 litres	Still table wine	5 litres
1 litre	Over 22% vol. (eg spirits and strong liqueurs)	1½ litres
	or	
2 litres	Not over 22% vol (eg low strength liqueurs or fortified wines or sparkling wines)	3 litres
	or	
2 litres	Still table wine	3 litres
	Perfume	
50g		75g
	Toilet water	
250cc		375cc
	Other goods	
£28	but no more than: 50 litres of beer 25 mechanical lighters	£207

Note

i The tobacco allowances in the left-hand column are doubled for persons who live outside Europe.

ii Persons under 17 are not entitled to tobacco and drinks allowances.

The importation of certain goods into the United Kingdom is prohibited or restricted. These include controlled drugs such as opium, morphine, heroin, cocaine, cannabis, amphetamines, barbiturates and LSD (lysergide); counterfeit currency; firearms (including gas pistols and similar weapons), ammunition, explosives (including fireworks) and flick knives; horror comics, indecent or obscene books, magazines, films, video tapes and other articles; animals* and birds, whether alive or dead (*eg* stuffed); certain articles derived from endangered species including furskins, ivory, reptile leather and goods made from them; meat and poultry and most of their products (whether or not cooked), including ham, bacon, sausage, pâté, eggs and milk; plants, parts thereof and plant produce, including trees and shrubs, potatoes and certain other vegetables, fruit, bulbs and seeds; wood with bark attached; certain fish and fish eggs, whether live or dead; bees; radio transmitters (*eg* citizens' band radios, walkie-talkies etc) not approved for use in the United Kingdom.

Customs Notice No. 1 is available to all travellers at the point of entry or on the boat and contains useful information of which returning tourists should be aware. Motorists should obtain a copy of Customs Notice No. 15 on the ferry or ship, and display the appropriate red or green sticker that can be found in the notice, on arrival. Advance copies of Customs Notices 1 and 15 can be obtained from HM Customs and Excise, Dorset House, Stamford Street, London SE1 9PS.

***Note:** cats, dogs and other mammals must not be landed unless a British import licence (rabies) has previously been issued.

Dimensions and weight restrictions

For an ordinary private car a height of 4 metres and a width limit of 2.50 metres is generally imposed. However, see *Country sections* for full details. Apart from a laden weight limit imposed on commercial vehicles, every vehicle, private or commercial, has an individual weight limit and as this affects private cars see *Overloading* page 17. See also *Major road tunnels* page 34, as some dimensions are restricted by the shape of tunnels. If you have any doubts consult the AA.

Direction indicators

All direction indicators should be working at between 60 and 120 flashes per minute. Most standard car-flasher units will be overloaded by the extra lamps of a caravan or trailer and a special heavy duty unit or a relay device should be fitted.

Drinking and driving

There is only one safe rule — if you drink, don't drive. The laws are strict and penalties severe.

Driving licence and International Driving Permit

You should carry your national driving licence with you when motoring abroad. If an International Driving Permit is necessary (see *IDP requirements* below) it is recommended that you still carry your national driving licence. In most of the countries covered by this guide a visitor can drive a temporarily imported car or motorcycle without formality for up to three months with a valid full licence (not provisional) issued in the United Kingdom or Republic of Ireland, subject to the minimum age requirements of the country concerned (see *Country sections*). If you should wish to drive a hired or borrowed car in the country you are visiting, make local enquiries.

If your licence is due to expire before your anticipated return, it should be renewed in good time prior to your departure. The Driver and Vehicle Licensing Centre (in Northern Ireland the licensing authority) will accept an application two months before the expiry of your old licence. In the Republic of Ireland licensing authorities will accept an application one month before the expiry of your old licence.

An International Driving Permit (IDP) is an internationally recognised document which enables the holder to drive for a limited period in countries where their national licences are not recognised (see Austrian, Greek and Spanish *Country sections* under *Driving licence*). The permit, for which a statutory charge is made, is issued by the AA to an applicant who holds a valid full British driving licence and who is over 18 years old. It has a validity of 12 months, cannot be renewed, and application forms are available from any AA Travel Agency or AA Centre. The permit cannot be issued to the holder of a foreign licence who must apply to the appropriate authority in the country where the driving licence was issued.

Note Residents of the Republic of Ireland, Channel Islands and the Isle of Man should apply to their local AA Centre for the relevant application form or information as to where it may be obtained.

'E' Card

This card may be displayed in the windscreen of your vehicle to assist the traffic flow across certain frontiers within the European Community. Full conditions of use are given on the card which may be obtained from AA Centres and AA Port Services Centres.

Electrical information

General The public electricity supply in Europe is predominantly AC (alternating current) of 220 volts (50 cycles) but can be as low as 110 volts. In some isolated areas low voltage DC (direct current) is provided. European circular two-pin plugs and screw-type bulbs are usually the rule. Useful electrical adaptors (not voltage transformers) which can be used in Continental shaver points and light bulb sockets are available in the United Kingdom, usually from the larger electrical appliance retailers.

Vehicle Check that all the connections are sound and that the wiring is in good condition. Should any problem arise with the charging system, it is essential to obtain the services of a qualified auto-electrician.

Emergency messages to tourists

In cases of emergency the AA will assist in the passing on of messages to tourists in Austria, Belgium, Denmark, France, Germany, Gibraltar, Greece, Irish Republic, Italy, Luxembourg, Netherlands, Norway, Portugal, Spain, Sweden, Switzerland and Yugoslavia.

The AA can also arrange for messages to be published in overseas editions of the *Daily Mail* and in an extreme emergency (death or serious illness concerning next-of-kin) can arrange to have personal messages broadcast on overseas radio networks. Anyone wishing to use this service should contact their nearest AA Centre.

Before you leave home make sure your relatives understand the procedure to follow should an emergency occur.

If you have reason to expect a message from home, information about which frequencies you should tune in to and at what time such messages are normally broadcast are given in the *Country sections*. If you require further information contact the tourist office or motoring club of the country you are staying in.

No guarantee can be given, either by the AA or by the *Daily Mail,* to trace the person concerned, and no responsibility can be accepted for the authenticity of messages.

Engine and mechanical

Consult your vehicle handbook for servicing intervals. Unless the engine oil has been changed recently, drain and refill with fresh oil and fit a new filter. Deal with any significant leaks by tightening up loose nuts and bolts and renewing faulty joints and seals.

Brands and grades of *engine oil* familiar to the British motorist are usually available in Western Europe but may be difficult to find in remote country areas. When available they will be much more expensive than in the UK and generally packed in 2-litre cans (3½pints). A motorist can usually assess the normal consumption of his car and is strongly advised to carry with him what oil he may require for his trip. If you suspect that there is anything wrong with the engine, however insignificant it may seem, it should be dealt with straight away. Even if everything seems in order, don't neglect such commonsense precautions as checking valve clearances, sparking plugs, and contact breaker points where fitted, and make sure that the distributor cap is sound. The fan belt should be checked for fraying and slackness. If any of the items mentioned previously are showing signs of wear you should replace them.

Any obvious mechanical defects should be attended to at once. Look particularly for play in steering connections and wheel bearings and, where applicable, ensure that they are adequately greased. A car that has covered a high mileage will have absorbed a certain amount of dirt into the fuel system and as breakdowns are often caused by dirt, it is essential that all filters (petrol and air) should be cleaned or renewed.

Owners should think twice about towing a caravan with a car that has already given appreciable service. Hard driving on motorways and in mountainous country puts an extra strain on ageing parts and items such as a burnt-out clutch can be very expensive.

The cooling system should be checked for leaks and the correct proportion of antifreeze and any perished hoses or suspect parts replaced.

Eurocheques

The Eurocheque scheme is a flexible money-transfer system operated by a network of European Banks. All the major UK Banks are part of the Uniform Eurocheque scheme and you will be able to obtain from them a multi-currency cheque book enabling you to write cheques in the currency of the country you are visiting. Approach your Bankers well in advance of your departure for further information.

Ferry crossings

From Britain the shortest sea crossing from a southern port to the Continent would be the obvious but it might not always be the best choice, bearing in mind how it places you on landing for main roads to your destination. Your starting point is important because if you have a long journey to a southern port then a service from an eastern port might be more convenient. Perhaps the Motorail service to the south might save time and possibly an overnight stop? In some circumstances the south-western ports may offer a convenient service and before making bookings it may be worth seeking advice so that the journey can be as economic and as comfortable as possible. Similarly, for crossings to Ireland, there are several departure points along the west coast and much depends on your starting location and ultimate destination for the most convenient ferry service. The AA provides a full information and booking service on all sea, motorail and hovercraft services and instant confirmation is available on many by ringing one of the numbers listed below (Monday to Friday, 09.00-17.00). Ask also if you want information and booking on Continental car-sleeper and ferry services.

The South East 01-930 2462
The West & Wales Bristol (0272) 24417
The Midlands 021-550 7648
The North 061-488 7290
Scotland and Northern Ireland 041-812 2888
Republic of Ireland Dublin (0001) 777004

Fire extinguisher

It is a wise precaution (compulsory in Greece) to equip your vehicle with a fire extinguisher when motoring abroad. An AA Fire Extinguisher may be purchased from your nearest AA Centre.

First-aid kit

It is a wise precaution (compulsory in Austria, Greece and Yugoslavia) to equip your vehicle with a first-aid kit when motoring abroad. An AA First-Aid Kit may be purchased from your nearest AA Centre.

Holiday traffic

For information relating to holiday traffic see *Road conditions* page 22, and the Austrian, French,

German, Spanish and Swiss *Country sections* under the *Roads and holiday traffic* heading.

Horn, use of

In built-up areas the general rule is not to use horns unless safety demands it; in many large towns and resorts, as well as in areas indicated by the international sign (see *inside front cover*), the use of the horn is totally prohibited. See also *Country sections* for *Austria, Gibraltar, Ireland, Italy* and *Luxembourg*.

Identification plate

If a boat, caravan or trailer is taken abroad it must have a unique chassis number for identification purposes. If your boat, caravan or trailer does not have a number an *identification plate* may be purchased from the AA.

Insurance including caravan insurance

Motor insurance is compulsory by law in all the countries covered in this Guide and you are strongly advised to ensure that you are adequately covered for all countries in which you will travel. Temporary policies may be obtained at all frontiers except the Republic of Ireland, but this is a most expensive way of effecting cover. It is best to seek the advice of your insurer regarding the extent of cover and full terms of your existing policy. Some insurers may not be willing to offer cover in the countries that you intend to visit and it may be necessary to seek a new, special policy for the trip from another insurer. Should you have any difficulty, AA Insurance Services will be pleased to help you. *Note* Extra insurance is recommended when visiting Spain (see *Bail Bond* page 347). Third-party insurance is compulsory for certain boats with engines in Italian waters (see *Boats* page 266) and is recommended elsewhere for all boats used abroad. It is compulsory for trailers temporarily imported into Austria (see page 57).

An international motor-insurance certificate or Green Card is recognised in most countries as evidence that you are covered to the minimum extent demanded by law. Compulsory in Andorra, Greece* and Yugoslavia and strongly advised for Italy*, Portugal* and Spain *the AA recommends its use elsewhere.* It will be issued by your own insurer upon payment of the additional premium for extension of your UK policy cover to apply in those countries you intend visiting. It will name all the countries for which it is valid. The document will not be accepted until you have signed it. Green Cards are internationally recognised by police and other authorities and may save a great deal of inconvenience in the event of an accident. If you are towing a caravan or trailer it will need separate insurance, and to be mentioned on your Green Card. Remember, the cover on a caravan or on a trailer associated with a Green Card is normally limited to third-party risks, so a separate policy (see *AA Caravan Plus,* below) is advisable to cover accidental damage, fire or theft.

In accordance with a Common Market Directive, the production and inspection of Green Cards at the frontiers of Common Market countries is no longer a legal requirement and the principle has been accepted by other European countries who are not members of the EEC. However, the fact that Green Cards will not be inspected does not remove the necessity of having insurance cover as required by law in the countries concerned.

Motorists can obtain expert advice through AA Insurance Services for all types of insurance. Several special schemes have been arranged with leading insurers to enable motorists to obtain wide insurance cover at economic premiums. One of these schemes, *AA Caravan Plus,* includes damage cover for caravans and their contents, including personal effects. While detached from the towing vehicle, protection against your legal liability to other persons arising out of the use of the caravan is also provided. Cover is extended to most European countries for up to 60 days without extra charge. *AA Caravan Plus* also provides cover for camping equipment. Full details of *AA Caravan Plus* may be obtained from any AA Centre or direct from AA Insurance Services Ltd, PO Box 2AA, Newcastle upon Tyne NE99 2AA.

Finally, make sure you are covered against damage in transit (*eg* on ferry or motorail). Most comprehensive motor insurance policies provide adequate cover for transit between ports in the UK, but need to be extended to give this cover if travelling outside the UK. You are advised to check this aspect with your insurer before setting off on your journey.

*Although these countries are members of the EEC a Green Card is for the time being still a compulsory requirement or strongly advised as indicated.

International distinguishing sign

An international distinguishing sign of the approved pattern, oval with black letters on a white background, and size (GB at least 6.9in by 4.5in), must be displayed on a vertical surface at the rear of your vehicle (and caravan or trailer if you are towing one). These distinguishing signs signify the country of registration of the vehicle. On the Continent checks are made to ensure that a vehicle's nationality plate is in order. Fines are imposed for failing to display a nationality plate or for not displaying the correct nationality plate, see *Police fines* page 20.

Level crossings

Practically all level crossings are indicated by international signs. Most guarded ones are of the lifting barrier type, sometimes with bells or flashing lights to give warning of an approaching train.

Lights (*See also Country sections*)

For driving abroad (except in the Republic of Ireland) headlights should be adjusted so that the dipped beam does not light the wrong side of the road and dazzle oncoming traffic. The adjustment can be made by fitting headlamp converters (PVC mask sheets) or beam deflectors (clip-on lenses) which may be purchased from your nearest AA Centre. However, beam deflectors must not be used with quartz halogen lamps. It is important to remember to remove the headlamp converters or beam deflectors as soon as you return to the UK.

Dipped headlights should also be used in conditions of fog, snowfall, heavy rain, and when passing through a tunnel, irrespective of its length and lighting. In some countries police will wait at the end of a tunnel to check this requirement. Headlight flashing is used only as a warning of approach or a passing signal at night. In other circumstances it is accepted as a sign of irritation and should be used with caution lest it is misunderstood.

It is a wise precaution (compulsory in Spain and Yugoslavia and recommended in France) to equip your vehicle with a set of replacement bulbs when motoring abroad. An AA Emergency Auto Bulb Kit suitable for most makes of car can be purchased from your nearest AA Centre.

Note Remember to have the lights set to compensate for the load being carried.

Liquefied Petroleum Gas/LPG

The availability of this gas in Europe makes a carefully planned tour, with a converted vehicle, limited but feasible. The gas is retailed by several companies in Europe who will supply information as to where their product may be purchased. LPG is available in all the countries covered by this guide except Portugal and Spain. A motorist regularly purchasing the fuel in UK could possibly obtain lists of European addresses from his retailer.

Hours of opening of filling stations vary from country to country but generally they operate during normal business hours, except for holidays and saints'-days. At weekends LPG users are well advised to fill up on Saturdays and not rely on Sunday opening. It is recommended that a reducer nipple be carried as a precautionary measure. This accessory can normally be obtained from the importer/manufacturer of the LPG unit at minimal cost.

When booking a ferry crossing it is advisable to point out to the booking agent/ferry company that the vehicle runs on a dual fuel system.

Medical treatment

Travellers who are in the habit of taking certain medicines should make sure that they have a sufficient supply to last for their trip since they may be very difficult to get abroad.

Those who suffer from certain diseases (diabetes or coronary artery diseases, for example) should get a letter from their doctor giving treatment details. Some Continental doctors will understand a letter written in English, but it is better to have it translated into the language of the country that it is intended to visit. The AA cannot make such a translation.

Travellers, who for legitimate health reasons carry drugs or appliances (*eg* hypodermic syringe etc) may have difficulty with Customs or other authorities. Others may have a diet problem which would be understood in hotels but for a language problem. The letter which such persons carry should therefore supply treatment details, a statement for Customs, and diet requirements.

The National Health Service is available in the United Kingdom only and medical expenses incurred overseas cannot generally be reimbursed by the United Kingdom Government. There are reciprocal health agreements with most of the countries covered by this guide, but you should not rely exclusively on these arrangements as the cover provided under the respective national schemes is not always comprehensive *eg* any medical care needed as a result of a road accident in the Republic of Ireland is not covered under the reciprocal health agreement. The full costs of medical care must be paid in Andorra, Liechtenstein, Monaco, San Marino and Switzerland. Therefore, as facilities and financial cover can differ considerably between the various countries, you are strongly advised to take out comprehensive and adequate insurance cover before leaving the UK, such as that offered by *Personal Security* under the *AA 5-Star Service*.

Urgently needed medical treatment can be obtained by most visitors, free of charge or at reduced cost, from the health care schemes of those countries with whom the UK has health care arrangements. Details are in leaflet SA30 which is available from local social security offices of the Department of Health and Social Security or from its Leaflets Unit at PO Box 21, Stanmore, Middlesex HA7 1AY. In some of these countries a visitor can obtain urgently needed treatment by showing his UK passport but in some an NHS medical card must be produced and in most European Community countries a certificate of entitlement (E111) is necessary. A form to obtain this certificate is included in the DHSS leaflet. Applicants should allow at least one month for the form to be processed, although in an emergency the E111 can be obtained over the counter of the local DHSS office (residents of the Republic of Ireland should apply to their Regional Health Board for the E111). The DHSS will also supply on request a leaflet SA35 *Notice to Travellers — Health Protection* which gives advice on health precautions and guidance about international vaccination requirements. This may be obtained by writing to the DHSS at the address given below or telephoning ext 6711.

Further information about health care arrangements overseas is obtainable from the Department of Health and Social Security, Alexander Fleming House, Elephant and Castle, London SE1 6BY, *tel* 01-407 5522 ext 6641 (non-EEC countries), ext 6737 (EEC countries).

Minibus

A minibus constructed and equipped to carry 10 or more persons (including the driver) and used outside the UK is subject to the regulations governing international bus and coach journeys. This will generally mean that the vehicle must be fitted with a tachograph and documentation in the form of a waybill, model control document and driver's certificate obtained. Apply to the Bus and Coach Council, Sardinia House, 52 Lincolns Inn Fields, London WC2A 3LZ *tel* 01-831 7546 for waybill and model control document; for other information contact the appropriate authorities as follows:

i in respect of minibus registered in Great Britain (England, Scotland and Wales) contact the local Traffic Area Office of the Department of Transport;

ii in respect of minibus registered in Northern Ireland contact the Department of the Environment for Northern Ireland, Road Transport Department, Upper Galwally, Belfast BT8 4FY.

Residents of the Republic of Ireland should contact the Department of Labour, Mespil Road, Dublin 4 for details about tachographs and the Government Publications Sales Office, Molesworth Street, Dublin 2 for information about documentation.

Note When contacting any of the above authorities, do so well in advance of your departure.

Mirrors

When driving abroad on the right it is essential, as when driving on the left in the UK and Republic of Ireland, to have clear all-round vision. Ideally external rear view mirrors should be fitted to both sides of your vehicle, but certainly on the left to allow for driving on the right.

Motoring Clubs in Europe

The Alliance Internationale de Tourisme (AIT) is the largest confederation of touring associations in the world and it is through this body that the AA is able to offer its members the widest possible touring information service. Its membership consists not of individuals, but of associations or groups of associations having an interest in touring. The Alliance was formed in 1919 — the AA was a founder member and is represented on its Administrative Council and Management Committee. The General Secretariat of the AIT is in Geneva.

Tourists visiting a country where there is an AIT club may avail themselves of its touring advisory services upon furnishing proof of membership of their home AIT club. AA members making overseas trips should, whenever possible, seek the advice of the AA before setting out and should only approach the overseas AIT clubs when necessary.

Motorways (*See also Country sections*)

Most of the countries in this guide have motorways, varying from a few short stretches to a comprehensive system. Tolls are payable on many of them. Motorway leaflets (containing information on tolls etc) for France, Italy, Portugal and Spain are available to AA members. See also *Tolls* page 24.

Orange badge scheme for disabled drivers

Some European countries, operating national schemes of parking concessions for the disabled, have reciprocal arrangements whereby disabled visitors can enjoy the concessions of the host country by displaying the badge of their own scheme. Information, where available, is given in the appropriate *Country section*. However, it should be noted that in some countries responsibility for introducing the concessions rests with individual local authorities and in some cases they may not be generally available. Under these circumstances badge holders should enquire locally, as they should whenever they are in doubt as to their entitlement. As in the UK the arrangements apply only to badge holders themselves and the concessions are not for the benefit of able-bodied friends or relatives. A non-entitled person who seeks to take advantage of the concessions in Europe by wrongfully displaying an orange badge will be liable to whatever penalties apply for unlawful parking in the country in question.

Overloading

This can create safety risks, and in most countries committing such an offence can involve *on-the-spot* fines (see *Police fines* page 20). It would also be a great inconvenience if your car was stopped because of overloading — you would not be allowed to proceed until the load had been reduced. The maximum loaded weight, and its distribution between front and rear axles is decided by the vehicle manufacturer and if your owner's handbook does not give these facts you should seek the advice of the manufacturer direct. There is a public weighbridge in all districts and when the car is fully loaded (not forgetting the passengers, of course) use this to check that the vehicle is within the limits. When loading a vehicle, care should be taken that no lights, reflectors or number plates are masked and that the driver's view is in no way impaired. All luggage loaded on a roof-rack must be tightly secured and should not upset the stability of the vehicle. Any projections beyond the front, rear, or sides of a vehicle that might not be noticed by other drivers must be clearly marked.

Overtaking

When overtaking on roads with two lanes or more in each direction, always signal your intention in good time, and after the manoeuvre, signal and return to the inside lane. Do *not* remain in any other lane. Failure to comply with this regulation, particularly in France, will incur an *on-the-spot* fine (see *Police fines* page 20).

Always overtake on the left (on the right in the Republic of Ireland) and use your horn as a warning to the driver of the vehicle being overtaken (except in areas where the use of the horn is prohibited). Do not overtake whilst being overtaken or when a vehicle behind is preparing to overtake. Do not overtake at level crossings, at intersections, the crest of a hill or at pedestrian crossings. When being overtaken keep well to the right (left in the Republic of Ireland) and reduce speed if necessary — never increase speed. See also *Luxembourg* page 298, *Portugal* page 337, *Spain* page 350 and *Sweden* page 374.

Parking (*See also Country sections*)

Parking is a problem everywhere in Europe and the police are extremely strict with offenders. Heavy fines are inflicted as well as the towing away of unaccompanied offending cars. This can cause inconvenience and heavy charges are imposed for the recovery of impounded vehicles. You should acquaint yourself with local parking regulations and endeavour to understand all relative signs. As a rule always park on the right-hand side of the road (left-hand side in the Republic of Ireland) or at an authorised place. As far as possible park off the main carriageway but not on cycle tracks or tram tracks.

Passengers (*See also Country sections*)

It is an offence in all countries to carry more passengers in a car than the vehicle is constructed to seat, but some have regulations as to how the passengers shall be seated. Where such regulations are applied to visiting foreigners it will be mentioned in the *Country Sections*.

For passenger-carrying vehicles constructed and equipped to carry more than 10 passengers including the driver there are special regulations. See *Minibus* page 16.

Passports

Each person must hold, or be named on, an up-to-date passport valid for all the countries through which it is intended to travel. However, the UK together with the Republic of Ireland, Channel Islands and Isle of Man forms a Common Travel Area. Persons born in the UK do not require a passport when travelling from the UK to the Republic of Ireland; similarly citizens of the Republic of Ireland may travel to the UK without holding a passport.

Passports should be carried at all times and, as an extra precaution, a separate note kept of the number, date and place of issue, There are various types of British passports including the standard or regular passport and the limited British Visitor's Passport. Standard UK passports are issued to British Nationals, ie, British Citizens, British Dependent Territories Citizens, British Overseas Citizens, British Subjects, and British Protected Persons. Normally issued for a period of 10 years, a standard UK passport is valid for travel to all countries in the world. A family passport may cover the holder, spouse and children under 16, but only the first person named on the passport may use it to travel alone. Children under 16 may be issued with a separate passport valid for 5 years and renewable for a further 5 years on application. Full information and application forms in respect of the standard UK passport may be obtained from a main Post Office or from one of the Passport Offices in Belfast, Douglas (Isle of Man), Glasgow, Liverpool, London, Newport (Gwent), Peterborough, St Helier (Jersey) and St Peter Port (Guernsey). Application for a standard passport should be made to the Passport Office appropriate for the area concerned, allowing at least four weeks for passport formalities to be completed, and should be accompanied by the requisite documents and fees.

British Visitor's Passports are issued to British Citizens, British Dependent Territories Citizens or British Overseas Citizens over the age of 8, resident in the UK, Isle of Man or Channel Islands. Valid for one year only and acceptable for travel in Western Europe and West Berlin but not for Yugoslavia, they cannot be used for a business trip or overland travel through the German Democratic Republic to West Berlin. A British Visitor's Passport issued to cover the holder, spouse and children under 16 may only be used by the first person named on the passport to travel alone. Children under 8 cannot have their own Visitor's Passport. Full information and application forms may be obtained from main Post Offices in Great Britain (England, Scotland and Wales) or Passport Offices in the Channel Islands, Isle of Man and Northern Ireland. However, Visitor's Passports or application forms for Visitor's Passports are NOT obtainable from Passport Offices in Great Britain. All applications for a Visitor's Passport must be submitted in person to a main Post Office or Passport Office as appropriate. Provided the documents are in order and the fee is paid the passport is issued immediately.

Irish citizens resident in the Dublin Metropolitan area or in Northern Ireland should apply to the Passport Office, Dublin; if resident elsewhere in the Irish Republic they should apply through the nearest Garda station, Irish citizens resident in Britain should apply to the Irish Embassy in London.

Petrol

In Western Europe, and indeed throughout the world, grades of petrol compare favourably with those in the UK. Internationally-known brands are usually available on main tourist and international routes, but in remote districts familiar brands may not be readily available. The minimum amount of petrol which may be purchased is usually five litres (just over one gallon). It is advisable to keep the petrol tank topped up, particularly in remote areas or if wishing to make an early start when garages may be closed, but when doing this use a lockable filler cap as a security measure. Some garages may close between 12.00 and 15.00hrs for lunch. Generally petrol is readily available and in most of the countries featured in this guide you will find that petrol stations on motorways provide a 24hr service.

In the UK the motorist uses a fuel recommended by the vehicle manufacturer and this is related to a star method (2-Star 90 octane, 3-Star 93 octane and 4-Star 97 octane). Overseas, petrol is graded as *Normal* and *Super* and the local definitions are given in the respective *Country sections* together with the octane ratings. The motorist should be careful to use a grade in the recommended range as many modern engines

designed to run on 4-Star petrol are critical on carburation and ignition settings. Additionally as unleaded petrol is now being sold in some European countries (see *Country sections*) it is important to purchase the correct petrol. If a car designed to run on leaded petrol is filled with unleaded petrol it will do no immediate harm, provided it is the correct octane rating and the next fill is of leaded petrol. However, any queries regarding the performance of a vehicle on an unleaded or lower grade of fuel should be directed to the vehicle manufacturers or their agents. A leaflet containing further information on the subject of *Leaded/Unleaded Fuel in Europe* is available through AA Centres and AA Port Service Centres.

Petrol prices at filling stations on motorways will be higher than elsewhere whilst at self-service pumps it will be slightly cheaper. Although petrol prices are not quoted, the current position can be checked with the AA. Petrol price concessions in the form of petrol coupons are available for Italy (see page 270) and Yugoslavia (see page 416) — check with the AA to ascertain the latest position.

The petrol contained in a vehicle tank may be imported duty-free. In some countries an additional quantity may be imported duty-free in cans whilst others impose duty or forbid the carrying of petrol in cans in a vehicle, see *Country sections* for further information. If you intend carrying a reserve supply of petrol in a can remember that on sea and air ferries and European car-sleeper trains operators insist that spare cans must be empty. ***Note*** A roof-rack laden with luggage increases petrol consumption, which should be taken into consideration when calculating the mileage per gallon.

Photography

Photography in European countries is generally allowed without restriction, with the exception of photographs taken within the vicinity of military or government establishments.

Signs are usually prominent where the use of cameras is prohibited. These are obvious — mostly a picture of a camera crossed by a diagonal line.

Police fines

Some countries impose *on-the-spot* fines for minor traffic offences which vary in amount according to the offence committed and the country concerned. Other countries *eg* France, impose an immediate deposit and subsequently levy a fine which may be greater or lesser than this sum, but which usually matches it. Fines are either paid in cash to the police or at a local post office against a *ticket* issued by the police. They must usually be paid in the currency of the country concerned, and can vary in amount from £3-£690 (approximate amounts). The reason for the fines is to penalise and at the same time keep minor motoring offences out of the courts. Disputing the fine usually leads to a court appearance and delays and additional expense. If the fine is not paid then legal proceedings will usually follow. Some countries immobilise vehicles until a fine is paid and may sell it to pay the penalty imposed.

Once paid, a fine cannot be recovered, but a receipt should always be obtained as proof of payment. Should AA members require assistance in any motoring matter involving local police they should apply to the legal department of the relevant national motoring organisation.

Pollution

Tourists should be aware that pollution of the sea water at European coastal resorts, particularly on the shores of the Mediterranean, represents a severe health hazard. Not many popular resorts wish to admit to this, but many now realise the dangers and erect signs, albeit small ones, forbidding bathing. These signs would read as follows:

	French
No bathing	*Défense de se baigner*
Bathing prohibited	*Il est défendu de se baigner*

	Italian
No bathing	*Vietato bagnàrsi*
Bathing prohibited	*È vietato bagnàrsi*

	Spanish
No bathing	*Prohibido bañarse*
Bathing prohibited	*Se prohibe bañarse*

Postcheques (*See also Country sections*)

National Girobank current account holders who have a cheque guarantee card can use the National Girobank Postcheque service when travelling in all of the countries covered by this guide. The service enables account holders to cash Postcheques, up to the local currency equivalent of about £65, at most post offices. Further information may be obtained from International Division, National Girobank, Bridle Road, BOOTLE, Merseyside GIR 0AA.

Poste restante

If you are uncertain of having a precise address, you can be contacted through the local *poste restante.* Before leaving the United Kingdom, notify your friends of your approximate whereabouts abroad at given times. If you expect mail, call with your passport at the main post office of the town where you are staying. To ensure that the arrival of correspondence will coincide with your stay, your correspondent should check with the Post Office before posting, as delivery times differ throughout Europe, and appropriate allowance must be made. It is most important that the recipient's name be written in full: *eg* Mr Lazarus Perkins, Poste Restante, Turnhout, Belgium. Do not use Esq.

Italy Correspondence can be addressed c/o post office by adding *Fermo in Posta* to the name of the locality. It will be handed over at the local central post office upon identification of the addressee by passport.

Spain Letters should be addressed as follows: name of addressee, *Liste de Correos,* name of town or village, name of province in brackets, if necessary. Letters can be collected from the main post office in the town concerned upon identification of the addressee by passport.

For all other countries letters should be addressed as in the example.

Priority including Roundabouts

(*See also Country sections*)

The general rule is to give way to traffic entering a junction from the right (except in the Republic of Ireland), but this is sometimes varied at roundabouts (see below). This is one aspect of European driving which may cause the British driver the most confusion because his whole training and experience makes it unnatural. Road signs indicate priority or loss of priority and tourists are well advised to make sure that they understand such signs.

Great care should be taken at intersections and tourists should never rely on receiving the right of way, particularly in small towns and villages where local traffic, often slow-moving, such as farm tractors, etc, will assume right of way regardless of oncoming traffic. Always give way to public services and military vehicles. Blind or disabled people, funerals and marching columns must always be allowed right of way. Vehicles such as buses and coaches carrying large numbers of passengers will expect and should be allowed priority.

Generally priority at roundabouts is given to vehicles entering the roundabout unless signposted to the contrary (see *France* page 110). This is a complete reversal of the United Kingdom and Republic of Ireland rule and particular care should be exercised when manoeuvring while circulating in an anti-clockwise direction on a roundabout. It is advisable to keep to the outside lane on a roundabout, if possible, to make your exit easier.

Public holidays

Public holidays, on which banks, offices and shops are closed, vary from country to country, but generally fall into two categories; those which are fixed on the calendar by some national festival or religious date and those which are movable. The latter, usually religious, are based on a movable Easter Sunday, and the actual dates are given in the respective *Country sections.* For information about annual holidays and festivals contact the appropriate Tourist Office, see under *Tourist information* in *Country section* for address.

Radio telephones/Citizens' band radios and transmitters in tourist cars abroad

Many countries exercise controls on the temporary importation and subsequent use of radio transmitters and radio telephones. Therefore if your vehicle contains such equipment, whether fitted or portable, you should approach the AA for guidance.

Registration document

You must carry the original vehicle registration document with you. If the vehicle is not registered in your name, you should have a letter from the owner (for Yugoslavia this must be countersigned by a motoring organisation; for Portugal a special certificate is required, available *free* from the AA) authorising you to use it.

If you are using a UK registered hired or leased vehicle for touring overseas the registration document will not be available and a Hired/Leased Vehicle Certificate (VE103), which may be purchased from the AA, should be used in its place.

If for any reason your registration document has to be sent to the licensing authorities you should bear in mind that, as processing can take some time, the document may not be available in time for your departure. Under these circumstances, a certificate of registration (V379) will normally be issued and can be obtained free of charge from your nearest Local Vehicle

Licensing Office to cover the vehicle for international circulation purposes.

Religious services

Refer to your religious organisations in the British Isles. A directory of British Protestant churches in Europe, North Africa and the Middle East entitled *English Speaking Churches,* can be purchased from Intercon (Intercontinental Church Society), 175 Tower Bridge Road, London SE1 2AQ *tel* 01-407 4588. See also the Belgian, French, Dutch, Spanish and Swiss *Country sections* for details of English-speaking church services in those countries.

Report forms

We would appreciate your comments on accommodation, garages and roads to help us to prepare future publications. Please list your comments on the report forms provided at the back of the guide. The accommodation report form is for your comments on hotels and motels which you have visited, whether they are listed in the guide or not.

Similarly, the garage report form can be used for your reports on garages which you have visited. The road report form can be used for particularly bad stretches and road works.

Road conditions

Main roads are usually in good condition but often not finished to our standards. The camber is often steeper than that usually found in the United Kingdom and edges may be badly corrugated and surfaces allowed to wear beyond the customary limits before being repaired. In France such stretches are sometimes signposted *Chausée déformée.* However, there are extensive motorway systems in France, Germany and Italy, and many miles of such roads in other countries. When roads under repair are closed, you must follow diversion signs — often inadequate — such as *déviation* (French) and *Umleitung* (German). To avoid damage to windscreens or paintwork, drive slowly over loose grit and take care when overtaking.

The months of July and August are the peak of the touring season particularly in Austria, Belgium, France and Germany when the school holidays start, and during this period motorways and main roads are heavily congested. Throughout the summer there is a general exodus from the cities, particularly at weekends when tourists should be prepared for congested roads and consequent hold-ups. See also *Roads* and *Motorways* in *Country sections.*

Road Signs (*See also Inside covers*)

Most road signs throughout Europe are internationally agreed and the majority would be familiar to the British motorist. Watch for road markings — do not cross a solid white or yellow line marked on the road centre. In *Belgium* there are two official languages and signs will be in Flemish or French, see *Roads,* page 79 for further information. In the Basque and Catalonian areas of *Spain* local and national placenames appear on signposts, see page 352 for further information. For *Germany, Greece, Netherlands* and *Yugoslavia* see also *Country sections.*

Rule of the road

In all the countries in this guide except Ireland drive on the right and overtake on the left; in Ireland drive on the left and overtake on the right.

Seat belts

All countries in this guide (except *Italy* where they are *strongly recommended*) require visitors to wear seat belts. If your car is fitted with belts, then in the interest of safety, wear them, otherwise you may run the risk of a police fine.

Spares

The problem of what spares to carry is a difficult one; it depends on the vehicle and how long you are likely to be away. However, you should consider hiring an AA Spares Kit for your car; full information about this service is available from any AA Centre. AA Emergency Windscreens are also available for hire. In addition to the items contained in the spares kit, the following would also prove useful:

- A pair of windscreen wiper blades;
- a torch;
- a length of electrical cable;
- a fire extinguisher;
- an inner tube of the correct type;
- a tow rope;
- a roll of insulating or adhesive tape

Remember that when ordering spare parts for dispatch abroad you must be able to identify them as clearly as possible and by the manufacturer's part numbers if known. When ordering spares, always quote the engine and chassis numbers of your car. See also *Lights,* page 14.

Speed limits (*See also Country sections*)

It is important to observe speed limits at all times. Offenders may be fined and driving licences confiscated on the spot, thus causing great

inconvenience and possible expense. The limits may be varied by road signs and where such signs are displayed the lower limit should be accepted. At certain times limits may also be temporarily varied and information should be available at the frontier. It can be an offence to travel at so slow a speed as to obstruct traffic flow without good reason.

Tolls

Tolls are charged on most motorways in France, Italy, Portugal, Spain and on sections in Austria, Greece and Yugoslavia. Over long distances the toll charges can be quite considerable. It is advisable to weigh the cost against time and convenience (*eg* overnight stops), particularly as some of the all-purpose roads are often fast. Always have some currency of the country in which you are travelling ready to pay the tolls, as travellers' cheques etc, are not acceptable at toll booths. All toll charges quoted in this publication should be used as a guide only as they are subject to change. ***Note*** In Switzerland the authorities charge an annual motorway tax. See under *Motorways* page 388 for further information.

Tourist information

(*See also Country sections*)

National tourist offices are especially equipped to deal with enquiries relating to their countries. They are particularly useful for information on current events, tourist attractions, car hire, equipment hire and information on specific activities such as skin-diving, gliding, horse-riding etc.

The offices in London are most helpful but the local offices overseas merit a visit because they have information not available elsewhere and tourists are advised to visit the office when they arrive at their destination. Hotels etc, will be able to supply the address.

Traffic lights

In principal cities and towns traffic lights operate in a way similar to those in the United Kingdom, although they are sometimes suspended overhead. The density of the light may be so poor that lights could be missed. There is usually only one set on the right-hand side of the road some distance before the road junction, and if you stop too close to the corner the lights will not be visible. Watch out for 'filter' lights which will enable you to turn right at a junction against the main lights. If you wish to go straight ahead do not enter a lane leading to 'filter' lights otherwise you may obstruct traffic wishing to turn. See also the *Country sections* for *Austria, Belgium, France, Germany, Ireland* and *Spain*.

Trams

Trams take priority over other vehicles. Always give way to passengers boarding and alighting. Never position a vehicle so that it impedes the free passage of a tram. Trams must be overtaken on the right except in one-way streets. See also *Country sections* for *Norway* and *Sweden*.

Travellers cheques

We recommend you take Visa Travellers Cheques. You can use them like cash or change them for currency in just about any country in the world. If you should lose them a reverse charge telephone call will put you in touch with Visa's world-wide instant refund service. There are over 60,000 locations in 166 countries so help is never far away. Visa Travellers Cheques are available at any AA Travel Agency and with a cash payment available on demand.

Tyres

Inspect your tyres carefully; if you think they are likely to be more than three-quarters worn before you get back, it is better to replace them before you start out. Expert advice should be sought if you notice uneven wear, scuffed treads or damaged walls, on whether the tyres are suitable for further use. In some European countries, drivers can be fined if tyres are badly worn. The regulations in the UK governing tyres call for a minimum tread depth of 1mm over 75% of the width of the tyre all around the circumference, with the original tread pattern clearly visible on the remainder. European regulations are tougher, a minimum tread depth of 1mm or 1.6mm over the whole width of the tyre around the circumference.

When checking tyre pressures, remember that if the car is heavily loaded the recommended pressures may have to be raised; this may also be required for high-speed driving. Check the recommendations in your handbook but remember pressures can only be checked accurately when the tyres are cold and don't forget the spare tyre.

Using the telephone abroad

(*See also Country sections*)

It is no more difficult to use the telephone abroad than it is at home, it only appears to be so because of unfamiliarity with the language and equipment. In most Continental countries the ringing tone consists of a single tone of about 1-1½ seconds repeated at intervals of between 3 and 10 seconds (depending upon the country). The engaged tone is similar to UK or faster. The information in the *Country sections* will be helpful with elementary principles when making calls from public callboxes, but try to get assistance in case you encounter language difficulties.

International Direct Dial (IDD) calls can be made from many public callboxes abroad thus avoiding the addition of surcharges imposed by most hotels. Types of callboxes from which IDD calls can be made are identified in the *Country sections*. You will need to dial the international code, international country code (for the UK it is 44), the telephone dialling code (omitting the initial '0'), followed by the number. For example to call the AA Basingstoke (0256) 20123 from Italy, dial 00 44 256 20123. Use higher-denomination coins for IDD calls to ensure reasonably lengthy periods of conversation before coin expiry warning. The equivalent of £1 should allow a reasonable period of uninterrupted conversation.

Valuables

Tourists should pay particular attention to the security of their money and items of value while touring. Whenever possible, any excess cash and travellers cheques should be left with the hotel management **against a receipt**. In some areas, children and youths cause a diversion to attract tourists' attention while pickpockets operate in organised gangs. Unusual incidents, which are more likely to occur in crowded markets or shopping centres, should be avoided.

It cannot be stressed too strongly that all valuables should be removed from a parked car even if it is parked in a supervised car park or lock-up garage.

Vehicle excise licence

It is advisable for all vehicles temporarily exported from the UK for a period of 12 months or less to continue to be currently taxed in the UK. If your vehicle excise licence (tax disc) is due to expire whilst you are abroad, you may apply before you leave, by post to any main Post Office for a tax disc to commence up to 42 days in advance of the expiry date of your present disc. You should explain why you want the tax disc in advance and ask for it to be posted to you before you leave, or to an address you will be staying at abroad. However, your application form must always be completed with your UK address.

Visas

A visa is not normally required by United Kingdom and Republic of Ireland passport holders, when visiting Western European countries for periods of three months or less (see *Portugal* page 338). However if you hold a passport of any other nationality, a UK passport not issued in this country, or are in any doubt at all about your position, check with the embassies or consulates of the countries you intend to visit.

Visitors' registration

All visitors to a country must register with local police which is a formality usually satisfied by the completion of a card or certificate when booking into an hotel, camp site or place offering accommodation. If staying with friends or relatives then it is usually the responsibility of the host to seek advice from the police within 24 hours of the arrival of his guests.

For short holiday visits the formalities are very simple but most countries place a time limit on the period that tourists may stay, after which a firmer type of registration is imposed.

Therefore, if you intend staying in any one country for longer than three months (*Portugal* 60 days), you should make the appropriate enquiries before departure from the UK.

Warm-climate touring

In hot weather and at high altitudes, excessive heat in the engine compartment can cause carburation problems. It is advisable, if you are towing a caravan, to consult the manufacturers about the limitations of the cooling system, and the operating temperature of the gearbox fluid if automatic transmission is fitted. See also *Automatic gearboxes* page 5.

Warning triangles/ Hazard warning lights

(*See also Country sections*)

Warning triangles are not required for two-wheeled vehicles. The triangle should be placed on the road behind a stopped vehicle to warn traffic approaching from the rear of an obstruction ahead. Warning triangles should be used when a vehicle has stopped for any reason — not only breakdowns. The triangle should be placed in such a position as to be clearly visible up to 100m (109yds) by day and by night, about 2ft from the edge of the road but not in such a position as to present a danger to on-coming traffic. It should be set about 30m (33yds) behind the obstruction but this distance should be increased up to 100m (109yds) on motorways. An AA Warning Triangle, which complies with the latest international and

European standards, can be hired from the AA or bought in AA Travel Agencies, AA Centres or by mail order.

Although four flashing indicators are allowed in the countries covered by this guide, they in no way affect the regulations governing the use of warning triangles. Generally hazard warning lights should not be used in place of a triangle although they may complement it in use, but see *France* page 112 and *Switzerland* page 390.

Weather information including Winter conditions

Members of the public may telephone or call at one of the Met. Office Weather Centres listed below for information about local, national and continental weather forecasts. The centres ***do not*** provide information about road conditions:

Bristol
The Gaunts House, Denmark Street
☏ (0272) 279298

Cardiff
Southgate House, Wood Street ☏ (0222) 397020

Glasgow
33 Bothwell Street ☏ 041-248 3451

Leeds
Oak House, Park Lane ☏ (0532) 451990

London
284-286 High Holborn ☏ 01-836 4311

Manchester
Exchange Street, Stockport ☏ 061-477 1060

Newcastle upon Tyne
7th Floor, Newgate House, Newgate Street
☏ 091-232 6453

Norwich
Rouen House, Rouen Road ☏ (0603) 660779

Nottingham
Main Road, Watnall ☏ (0602) 384092

Southampton
160 High Street, Below Bar ☏ (0703) 228844

If you require weather information as a guide when planning your holidays, you should contact the national tourist offices of the countries concerned (see *Country sections*). When you are abroad, you should contact the nearest office of the appropriate national motoring club. It is advisable to check on conditions ahead as you go along and hotels and garages are often helpful in this respect.

Winter conditions Motoring in Europe during the winter months is restricted because of the vast mountain ranges — the Alps sweeping in an arc from the French Riviera, through Switzerland, Northern Italy and Austria to the borders of Yugoslavia, the Pyrénées which divide France and Spain — as well as extensive areas of Spain, France and Germany which are at an altitude of well over 1,000ft. However matters have been eased with improved communications and modern snow clearing apparatus.

Reports on the accessibility of mountain passes in Austria, France, Italy and Switzerland are received by the AA from the European Road Information Centre in Geneva. Additionally during the winter months and also under certain weather conditions, the AA Port Agents in Belgium and France collect information regarding the state of approach roads to the continental Channel ports. **To obtain information ring the AA Overseas Routes Unit at Basingstoke during office hours, tel (0256) 20123, or the AA London Operations Centre (24-hr service) ☏ 01-954 7373 or enquire at the AA Port Service Centre before embarking.**

Details of road and rail tunnels which can be used to pass under the mountains are given on pages 34-36 and the periods when the most important mountain passes are usually closed are given on pages 37-48. If you want a conventional seaside holiday between October and March, you will probably have to travel at least as far south as Lisbon, Valencia, or Naples to be reasonably certain of fine weather. See also *Country sections* for *Austria, Belgium, France, Germany, Italy, Norway, Spain, Sweden* and *Switzerland.* Further information on this subject is given in the leaflet entitled *Continental Weather and Motoring in Winter* which is available from the AA.

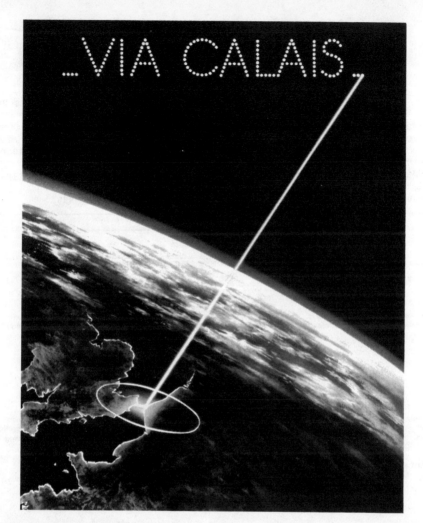

CALAIS—So close you could touch it.
Once the only landfall for Britons bound for the Continent and far and away the best route today.

Seven modern jumbo size car ferries plus giant hovercraft provide a choice of over 100 crossings daily during the Summer and never less than 58 off Peak.

Dover Calais, the shortest sea route—from 75 minutes by car ferry and from 30 minutes by hovercraft.

By far the fastest and the best way to go and come back

Customs Offices

Many Customs offices at the main frontier crossings are open 24 hours daily to deal with touring documents.

Major offices with restricted opening times are listed below. During these hours the Customs handle normal tourist entry into their country.

However, persons with dutiable items to declare or other business to transact should cross the frontier during normal business hours only. For additional information see also **Customs regulations for European countries** page 9.

The table can be read in either direction eg for France-Belgium read from left to right, for Belgium-France read from right to left.

Nearest town	Road No.	Frontier post	Opening times		Frontier post	Road No.	Nearest town
France					**Belgium**		
Dunkirk	D916A	Oost-Cappel	07.00-20.00		Kapelhoek	N9	**Ypres (Ieper)**
Lille	D941	Baisieux	08.00-12.00 14.00-18.00 Mon-Fri	08.00-18.00	Hertain	N8	**Tournai**
Valenciennes	D169	Maulde	06.00-22.00		Bléharies	N71	**Tournai**
Maubeuge	D936	Cousoire	09.00-21.00	08.00-18.00 Mon-Fri 07.00-20.00 Sat, Sun and Public holidays 1Apr-30Sep; 08.00-18.00 Sat, Sun and Public holidays 1Oct-31Mar	Leugnies	N36	**Beaumont**
Avesnes	D962	Hestrud	07.00-22.00	07.00-19.00	Grandrieu	N21	**Beaumont**
Givet	D949	Givet	08.00-18.00		Petit Doische	N46	**Philippeville**
Givet	D949	Givet	08.00-18.00		Dion	N46	**Beauraing**
France					**Germany**		
Metz	D954	Villing	06.00-22.00		Ittersdorf Villinger Strasse	269	**Saarlouis**
France					**Spain**		
Bayonne	D20	Ainhoa	1May-30Sep 07.00-24.00 1Oct-30Apr 07.00-22.00		Dancharinea	N121	**Pampiona**
St-Jean-Pied-de-Port	D933	Arnéguy	as above		Valcarlos	C135	**Pamplona**
Orlon-Ste-Marie	N134	Urdos	16Jun-30Sep Always 1Oct-15Jun 08.00-22.00		Canfranc	N330	**Jaca**
Pau	D934	Eaux-Chaudes	1May-31Oct 07.00-24.00 1Nov-30Nov 08.00-22.00 (Closed in winter)		Sallent-de Gállego	C136	**Huesca**
Bagnères de Luchon	D618	Bagnères de Luchon	08.00-22.00		Bossost	C141	**Viella**
Montréjeau	N125	Fos	1Oct-30Apr 08.00-24.00 1May-30Sept Always		Lés	N230	**Viella**

Nearest town	Road No.	Frontier post	Opening times	Frontier post	Road No.	Nearest town
Amélie-les-Bains	D115	Prats-de-Mollo	08.00-20.00 (Holidays 07.00-24.00)	Camprodón	C151	**Ripoll**
Belgium				**Netherlands**		
Maldegem	N310	Strobrugge	07.00-21.00 1Apr-30Sep 07.00-24.00 1Oct-31Mar 07.00-21.00	Eede	Unclass	**Breskens**
Gent	N56	Watervliet	07.00-19.00	Veldzicht	Unclass	**Breskens**
Turnhout	N20	Weelde	06.00-24.00 Mon-Fri 07.00-17.00 Saturday 09.00-17.00 Sun and Public holidays 07.00-24.00	Baarle-Nassau	Unclass	**Breda**
Netherlands				**Germany**		
Emmen	Unclass	Coevorden	06.00-24.00	Eschebrügge	403	**Nordhom**
Zutphen	Unclass	's-Heerenberg	06.00-22.00 (08.00-22.00 Sundays)	Heerenber-gerbrücke	220	**Emmerich**
Venlo	Unclass	Herungerweg	06.00-22.00	Niederdorf	60	**Moers**
Italy				**Switzerland**		
Domodóssola	SS337	Ponte Ribellasca	07.00-22.00	Cámedo	69	**Locarno**
Luino	SS394	Zenna	05.00-24.00 Mon-Fri 05.00-01.00 Sat-Sun	Dirinella	Unclass	**Locarno**
Luino	Unclass	Fornasette	05.00-01.00 1May-30Sept 06.00-01.00 1Oct-30Apr 06.00-23.00	Fornasette	Unclass	**Lugano**
Chiavenna	SS36	Montespluga	1Jun-30Jun 05.00-22.00 1Jul-30Sept 05.00-24.00 1Oct-Autumn 06.00-22.00	Splügen Pass	64	**Thusis**
Tirano	SS38A	Piattamala	8Jan-21Dec 05.00-00.30 22Dec-7Jan 05.00-14.00	Campo-cologno	29 via Bernina Pass	**Pontresina**
Bórmio	SS38	Giogo di Santa Maria (Stelvio)	1June-30June 06.00-20.00 1Jul-30Sept 06.00-22.00 (Closed in Winter)	Umbrail Pass	66	**Santa Maria**
Glorenza	SS41	Tubre	05.00-24.00 1May-31Oct 04.00-24.00 Mon-Fri 00.00-24.00 Sat-Sun 1Nov-30Apr 05.00-24.00	Müstair	28	**Santa Maria**
Switzerland				**Austria**		
Zernez	27	Martina	05.00-24.00	Nauders (Zollhaus)	185	**Nauders**
Italy				**Austria**		
Merano	SS44b	Passo del Rombo	07.00-20.00 (when pass is open)	Timmelsjoch	186	**Sölden**

Nearest town	Road No.	Frontier post	Opening times		Frontier post	Road No.	Nearest town
Portugal					**Spain**		
Valença do Minho	N301	São Gregório	1Mar-31Oct 07.00-24.00 1Nov-28Feb 07.00-21.00	1Mar-31Oct 08.00-01.00 1Nov-28Feb 08.00-22.00	Ponte Barxas	Unclass	**Orense**
Chaves	N103-5	Vila Verde da Raia	24Mar-6Apr 1Jul-30Sep 18Dec-3Jan 00.00-24.00 at other times 07.00-24.00	12Apr-25Apr 1Jul-30Sep 18Dec-3Jan 00.00-24.00 at other times 08.00-01.00	Feces de Abajo	C532	**Orense**
Bragança	N103-7	Portelo	1Jul-31Oct 07.00-24.00 1Nov-30Jun 07.00-21.00	1Mar-31Oct 08.00-01.00 1Nov-28Feb 08.00-22.00	Calabor	C622	**Puebla de Sanabria**
Bragança	N218-1	Quintanilha	1Mar-31Oct 07.00-24.00 1Nov-28Feb 07.00-21.00	1Mar-31Oct 08.00-01.00 1Nov-28Feb 08.00-22.00	San Martin del Pedroso/Alcañices	N122	**Zamora**
Bragança	N218	Miranda do Douro	1Jul-31Oct 07.00-24.00 1Nov-30Jun 07.00-21.00	1Mar-31Oct 08.00-01.00 1Nov-28Nov 08.00-22.00	Torregamones	Unclass	**Zamora**
Mogadouro	N221-7	Bemposta	1Jul-31Oct 07.00-24.00 1Nov-30Jun 07.00-21.00	1Mar-31Oct 08.00-01.00 1Nov-28Nov 08.00-22.00	Fermoselle	C527	**Zamora**
Castelo Branco	N355	Segura	1Mar-31Oct 07.00-24.00 1Nov-28Feb 07.00-21.00	1Mar-31Oct 08.00-01.00 1Nov-28Feb 08.00-22.00	Piedras Albas	C523	**Cáceres**
Portalegre	N246-1	Galegos Marvão	1Mar-31Oct 07.00-24.00 1Nov-28Feb 07.00-21.00	1Mar-31Oct 08.00-01.00 1Nov-28Feb 08.00-22.00	Valencia de Alcàntara	N521	**Cáceres**
Mourão	N256-1	São Leonardo	1Mar-31Oct 07.00-24.00 1Nov-28Feb 07.00-21.00	1Mar-31Oct 08.00-01.00 1Nov-28Feb 08.00-22.00	Villanueva del Fresno	C436	**Zafra**
Beja	N260	Vila Verde de Ficalho	1Mar-31Oct 07.00-24.00 1Nov-28Feb 07.00-21.00	1Mar-31Oct 08.00-01.00 1Nov-28Feb 08.00-22.00	Rosal de la Frontera	N433	**Seville**
Faro	N125	Vila Real de Santo António	1May-31Oct 08.00-23.00 1Nov-30Apr 08.00-20.00	1May-31Oct 09.00-24.00 1Nov-30Apr 09.00-21.00	Ayamonte	N431	**Huelva**

Denmark				**Germany**		
Åbenrå	Unclass	Padborg	06.00-24.00	Harrislee	Unclass	**Flensburg**

Sweden*				**Norway***		
Hällavadsholm	165	Vassbotten	09.00-16.00 Mon-Fri 09.00-13.00 Sat	Vassbotten	22	**Halden**
Torsby	239	Vittjärn	07.00-21.00 Mon-Fri 09.00-16.00 Sat	Vittjärn	204	**Kongsvinger**
Sälen	Unclass	Østby	07.00-21.00	Østby	25	**Elverum**
Idre	70	Flötningen	08.00-18.00 Mon-Sat	Flötningen	218	**Drevsjø**
Östersund	Unclass	Ådalsvollen	09.00-16.00	Ådalsvollen	72	**Levanger**
Gäddede	342	Gäddede	07.00-21.00	Gäddede	74	**Grong**
Tärnaby	E79	Tärnaby	07.00-21.00	Tärnaby	E79	**Mo-i-Rana**
Arjeplog	95	Junkerdal	08.00-21.00 Mon-Fri 08.00-15.00 Sat	Junkerdal	77	**Storjord**
Kiruna	98	Björkliden	08.00-21.00 Mon-Fri 08.00-15.00 Sat	Björkliden	70	**Narvik**

**Note* All Customs offices on the Swedish/Norwegian frontier may be passed at any time of the day, regardless of whether they are open or not, on condition that the visitor has no goods to declare.

Journey times

As there are several aspects of a journey to consider it will be difficult accurately to estimate how long a journey will take. Customs clearance, traffic and weather conditions, the time of day, the negotiating of mountain passes and other factors will affect calculations. However, an approximate travelling time can be arrived at by considering the kilometre distance as minutes: ie 60km (37½miles) takes about 60 minutes. Thus to travel 300km will take about 300 minutes or 5 hours. Allowance will, of course, have to be made in the light of your experience when travelling along motorways (where an average speed of 55mph is possible) and secondary roads.

The table below is a guide to journey times at average speeds expressed in kilometres.

Distance in kilometres	30		40		50		60		70	
	hrs	*mins*	*hrs*	*mins*	*hrs*	*mins*	*hrs*	*mins*	*hrs*	*mins*
20		25		19		15		13		11
30		37		28		22		19		16
40		50		37		30		25		21
50	1	2		47		37		31		27
60	1	15		56		45		38		32
70	1	25	1	5		52		43		36
80	1	39	1	15	1	0		50		42
90	1	52	1	24	1	7		56		48
100	2	4	1	33	1	15	1	2		53
150	3	6	2	20	1	52	1	33	1	20
200	4	8	3	6	2	30	2	4	1	46
250	5	10	3	53	3	7	2	35	2	13
300	6	12	4	40	3	44	3	6	2	40
350	7	14	5	27	4	21	3	37	3	7
400	8	16	6	12	5	0	4	8	3	32
450	9	18	6	59	5	37	4	39	3	59
500	10	20	7	46	6	14	5	10	4	26

(Column headings 30–70: **Average speed in mph**)

Major road tunnels

See *Lights* page 14. There are also minimum and maximum speed limits in operation in the tunnels. **All charges listed below should be used as a guide only.**

Bielsa France-Spain

The trans-Pyrenean tunnel is 3km (2 miles) long, and runs nearly 6,000ft above sea level between Aragnouet and Bielsa. The tunnel is usually closed from October to Easter.

Cadí Spain

A new road tunnel has been opened in Catalonia (road number C1411), between the villages of Bellver de Cerdanya and Bagá, and to the west of the Toses (Tosas) Pass.

The tunnel is 5km (3 miles) long and runs at about 4,000ft above sea level under the Sierra del Cadí mountain range. 18km (11 miles) of new access roads have also been completed.

Charges (in *Pesetas*)

cars	**410**
cars with caravans	**890**
motorcycles	**330**

Fréjus France-Italy

This tunnel (opened July 1980) is over 4,000ft above sea level; it runs between Modane and Bardonecchia. The tunnel is 12.8km (8 miles) long, 4.5m (14ft 9in) high, and the two-lane carriageway is 9m (29ft 6in) wide. Toll charges as Mont Blanc Tunnel (see below).

Mont Blanc Chamonix (France)-Courmayeur (Italy)

The tunnel is over 4,000ft above sea level. It is 11.6km (7 miles) long. Customs and passport control are at the Italian end. The permitted maximum dimensions of vehicles are: height 4.15m (13ft 7in); length 18m (59ft); width 2.5m (8ft 2in). Total weight 35 metric tons (34tons 9cwt); axle weight 13 metric tons (12tons 16cwt). The minimum speed is 50kph (31mph) and the maximum 80kph (49mph). Do not stop or overtake. There are breakdown bays with telephones. From November to March wheel chains may occasionally be required on the approaches to the tunnel.

Charges (in *French francs*)

The tolls are calculated on the wheelbase.

cars	wheelbase up to 2.30m (7ft 6½in)	**60**
	wheelbase from 2.30m to 2.63m (7ft 6½in to 8ft 7½in)	**95**
	wheelbase from 2.64m to 3.30m (8ft 7½in to 10ft 10in) and cars with caravans	**120**
	wheelbase over 3.30m (10ft 10in)	**305**
vehicles	with three axles	**465**
	with four, or more axles	**610**

Grand St Bernard Switzerland-Italy

The tunnel is over 6,000ft above sea level; although there are covered approaches, wheel chains may be needed to reach it in winter. The Customs, passport control, and toll offices are at the entrance. The tunnel is 5.9km (3½ miles) long. The permitted maximum dimensions of vehicles are: height 4m (13ft 1in), width 2.5m (8ft 2½in). The minimum speed is 40kph (24mph) and the maximum 80kph (49mph). Do not stop or overtake. There are breakdown bays with telephones on either side.

Charges (in *Swiss francs*)

The toll charges are calculated according to the wheelbase.

motorcycles		**5**
cars	wheelbase up to 2.08m (6ft 10in)	**15**
	wheelbase from 2.08m to 3.20m (6ft 10in to 10ft 6in)	**22.50**
	wheelbase over 3.20m (10ft 6in)	**34**
	with caravan	**34**
minibuses		**34**
coaches		**62-103**

St Gotthard Switzerland

The world's longest road tunnel opened in September 1980. The tunnel is about 3,800ft above sea level; it runs under the St Gotthard Pass from Göschenen, on the northern side of the Alps, to Airolo in the Ticino. The tunnel is 16.3km (10 miles) long, 4.5m (14ft 9in) high, and the two-lane carriageway is 7.5m (25ft) wide. Forming part of the Swiss national motorway network, the tunnel is subject to the annual motorway tax, and the tax disc must be displayed (see page 388).

From December to February wheelchains may occasionally be required on the approaches to the tunnel, but they are *NOT* allowed to be used in the tunnel. (Lay-bys are available for the removal and refitting of wheel chains.)

San Bernardino Switzerland

This tunnel is over 5,000ft above sea level. It is 6.6km (4 miles) long, 4.8m (15ft 9in) high, and the carriageway is 7m (23ft) wide. Do not stop or overtake in the tunnel. Keep 100m (110yds) between vehicles. There are breakdown bays with telephones. No tolls. From November to March wheel chains may occasionally be required on the approaches to the tunnel.

Forming part of the Swiss national motorway network, the tunnel is subject to the annual motorway tax, and the tax disc must be displayed (see page 388).

Arlberg Austria

This tunnel is 14km (8¾ miles) long and runs at about 4,000ft above sea level, to the south of and parallel to the Arlberg Pass.

Charges

The toll charges for cars (with or without caravans) are 140 *Austrian Schillings* each way.

Bosruck Austria

This tunnel (opened October 1983) is 2,434ft above sea level. It is 5.5km (3½ miles) long and runs between Spital am Pyhrn and Selzthal, to the east of the Pyhrn Pass. With the Gleinalm Tunnel (see below) it forms an important part of the A9 Pyhrn Autobahn between Linz and Graz, now being built in stages.

Charges

The toll charges for cars (with or without caravans) are 60 *Austrian schillings* for a single journey.

Felbertauern Austria

This tunnel is over 5,000ft above sea level; it runs between Mittersill and Matrei, to the west of and parallel to the Grossglockner Pass. The tunnel is 5.2km (3¼ miles) long, 4.5m (14ft 9in) high, and the two-lane carriageway is 7m (23ft) wide. From November to April wheel chains may be needed on the approach to the tunnel.

Charges (in *Austrian schillings*)

		Single
cars	summer rate	**180**
	winter rate	**100**
caravans		**free**
motorcycles		**100**

Gleinalm Austria

This tunnel is 2,680ft above sea level, it is 8.3km (5 miles) long and runs between St Michael and Friesach, near Graz. The tunnel forms part of the A9 Pyhrn Autobahn which will, in due course, run from Linz via Graz to Yugoslavia.

Charges

The toll charges for cars (with or without caravan) are 120 *Austrian schillings* for a single journey.

Tauern Autobahn (Austria)

Two tunnels, the Katschberg and the Radstädter Tauern, form the key elements of this toll motorway between Salzburg and Carinthia.

The **Katschberg** tunnel is 3,642ft above sea level. It is 5.4km (3½ miles) long, 4.5m (14ft 9in) high, and the two-lane carriageway is 7.5m (25ft) wide.

The **Radstädter Tauern** tunnel is 4,396ft above sea level and runs to the east of and parallel to the Tauern railway tunnel. The tunnel is 6.4km (4 miles) long, 4.5m (14ft 9in) high, and the two-lane carriageway is 7.5m (25ft) wide.

Charges (in *Austrian schillings*) for the whole toll section between Flachau and Rennweg

		Single
cars	summer rate	**180**
	winter rate	**100**
caravans		**free**
motorcycles		**90**

Major rail tunnels

Vehicles are conveyed throughout the year through the **Simplon** Tunnel (Brig-Iselle) and the **Lötschberg** Tunnel (Kandersteg-Goppenstein). It is also possible to travel all the way from Kandersteg to Iselle by rail via both the Lötschberg and Simplon Tunnels. Services are frequent and no advance booking is necessary and although the actual transit time is 15/20 minutes, some time may be taken by the loading and unloading formalities.
The operating company issues a full timetable and tariff list which is available from the AA (Overseas Routes, see page 27 for address), the Swiss National Tourist Office (see page 390 for address) or at most Swiss frontier crossings.

Albula Tunnel

Switzerland

Thusis (2,372ft)
Tiefencastel (2,821ft) –
Samedan (5,650ft)

The railway tunnel is 5.9km (3½ miles) long. Motor vehicles can be conveyed through the tunnel, but you are recommended to give notice. Thusis *tel*(081)811113, Tiefencastel (081)711112, Samedan (082)65404.

Services

9 trains daily going south; 6 trains daily north.

Charges

These are given in *Swiss francs* and are likely to increase.

cars (including driver)	67
additional passengers	8.80
car and caravan	125

Furka Tunnel

Switzerland

Oberwald (4,482ft) – ***Realp*** (5,046ft)

The railway tunnel is 15.3km (9½ miles) long. Journey duration 20 minutes.

Services

Hourly from 06.50-21.00 hrs.

Charges

Cars including passengers 18 *Swiss francs.*

Oberalp Railway

Switzerland

Andermatt (4,737ft) – ***Sedrun*** (4,728ft)

Journey duration 50 minutes.

Booking

Advance booking is necessary, Andermatt *tel* (044) 67220, Sedrun (086) 91137.

Services

2-4 trains daily, winter only.

Charges

Cars including driver 51 *Swiss francs*. Additional passengers 8.40 *Swiss francs.*

Tauern Tunnel Austria

Böckstein (3,711ft) (near Badgastein) –
Mallnitz 8.5km (5½ miles) long.

Maximum dimensions for caravans and trailers are height 8ft 10½in, width 8ft 2½in.

Booking

Advance booking is unnecessary (except for request trains), but motorists must report at least 30 minutes before the train is due to start. The driver must drive his vehicle on and off the wagon.

Services

At summer weekends, trains run approximately every half-hour in both directions, 07.30-18.30hrs; and every hour during the night. During the rest of the year there is an hourly service from 06.30-22.30hrs. *Duration 12 minutes.*

Charges

These are given in *Austrian schillings* and are for a single journey.

cars (including passengers)	160
motorcycles (with or without sidecar)	30
caravans	free

Karawanken Tunnel

Austria-Yugoslavia
Rosenbach-Jesenice

This tunnel is 8.5km (5½ miles) long. Since the opening of the Loibl Tunnel, see page 44, assuring an all-year-round link between Klagenfurt and Ljubljana, the use of the Karawanken Tunnel by motorists is not an economic proposition.

Principal Mountain Passes

It is best not to attempt to cross mountain passes at night, and daily schedules should make allowance for the comparatively slow speeds inevitable in mountainous areas.

Gravel surfaces (such as grit and stone chips) vary considerably; they are dusty when dry, slippery when wet. Where known to exist, this type of surface has been noted. Road repairs can be carried out only during the summer, and may interrupt traffic. Precipitous sides are rarely, if ever, totally unguarded; on the older roads stone pillars are placed at close intervals. Gradient figures take the mean on hairpin bends, and may be steeper on the insides of the curves, particularly on the older roads.

Before attempting late evening or early morning journeys across frontier passes, check the times of opening of the Customs offices. A number of offices close at night, *eg* the Timmelsjoch border crossing is closed between 20.00 and 07.00hrs.

Always engage a low gear before either ascending or descending steep gradients, keep well to the right side of the road and avoid cutting corners. Avoid excessive use of brakes. If the engine overheats, pull off the road, making sure you do not cause an obstruction, leave the engine idling, and put the heater controls, including the fan, into the maximum heat position. Under no circumstances remove the radiator cap until the engine has cooled down. Do not fill the coolant system of a hot engine with cold water.

Always engage a lower gear before taking a hairpin bend, give priority to vehicles ascending and remember that as your altitude increases so your engine power decreases. Priority must always be given to postal coaches travelling in either direction. Their route is usually signposted.

Caravans

Passes *suitable for caravans* are indicated in the table (pages 37-48). Those shown to be *negotiable by caravans* are best used only by experienced drivers driving cars with ample power. The remainder are probably best avoided. A correct power-to-load ratio is always essential.

Conditions in winter

Winter conditions are given in italics in the last column. *UO* means usually open although a severe fall of snow may temporarily obstruct the road for 24-48 hours, and wheel chains are often necessary; *OC* means occasionally closed between the dates stated and *UC* usually closed between the dates stated. Dates for opening and closing the passes are approximate only. Warning notices are usually posted at the foot of a pass if it is closed, or if chains or snow tyres should or must be used.

Wheel chains may be needed early and late in the season, and between short spells (a few hours) of obstruction. At these times conditions are usually more difficult for caravans.

In fair weather, wheel chains or snow tyres are only necessary on the higher passes, but in severe weather you will probably need them (as a rough guide) at altitudes exceeding 2,000ft.

Conversion table gradients

All steep hill signs show the grade in percentage terms. The following conversion table may be used as a guide:

30%	1 in 3	14%	1 in 7
25%	1 in 4	12%	1 in 8
20%	1 in 5	11%	1 in 9
16%	1 in 6	10%	1 in 10

Pass and height	**From To**	**Distances from summit and max gradient**		**Min width of road**	**Conditions (See page 37 for key to abbreviations)**
***Albula** 7,595ft (2315m) Switzerland	Tiefencastel (2,821ft)	30km	1 in 10	12ft	*UC Nov-early Jun.* An inferior alternative to the Julier; tar and gravel; fine scenery. Alternative rail tunnel.
	La Punt (5,546ft)	9km	1 in 10		
Allos 7,382ft (2250m) France	Barcelonnette (3,740ft)	20km	1 in 10	13ft	*UC early Nov-early Jun.* Very winding, narrow, mostly unguarded but not difficult otherwise; passing bays on southern slope, poor surface (maximum width vehicles 5ft 11in).
	Colmars (4,085ft)	24km	1 in 12		
Aprica 3,858ft (1176m) Italy	Tresenda (1,220ft)	14km	1 in 11	13ft	*UO.* Fine scenery; good surface, well graded; *suitable for caravans.*
	Edolo (2,264ft)	15km	1 in 16		
Aravis 4,915ft (1498m) France	La Clusaz (3,412ft)	8km	1 in 11	13ft	*OC Dec-Mar.* Outstanding scenery, and a fairly easy road.
	Flumet (3,008ft)	12km	1 in 11		
Arlberg 5,912ft (1802m) Austria	Bludenz (1,905ft)	33km	1 in 8	20ft	*OC Dec-Apr.* Modern road; short steep stretch from west easing towards the summit; heavy traffic; parallel toll road tunnel available. *Suitable for caravans,* using tunnel. Pass road closed to vehicles towing trailers.
	Landeck (2,677ft)	35km	1 in 7½		
Aubisque 5,610ft (1710m) France	Eaux Bonnes (2,461ft)	11km	1 in 10	11ft	*UC mid Oct-Jun.* A very winding road; continuous but easy ascent; the descent incorporates the Col de Soulor (4,757ft); 8km of very narrow, rough, unguarded road, with a steep drop.
	Argelès-Gazost (1,519ft)	32km	1 in 10		
Ballon d'Alsace 3,865ft (1178m) France	Giromagny (1,830ft)	17km	1 in 9	13ft	*OC Dec-Mar.* A fairly straightforward ascent and descent, but numerous bends; *negotiable by caravans.*
	St-Maurice-sur-Moselle (1,800ft)	9km	1 in 9		
Bayard 4,094ft (1248m) France	Chauffayer (2,988ft)	18km	1 in 12	20ft	*UO.* Part of the Route Napoléon. Fairly easy, steepest on the southern side; *negotiable by caravans* from north to south.
	Gap (2,382ft)	8km	1 in 7		
***Bernina** 7,644ft (2330m) Switzerland	Pontresina (5,915ft)	15.5km	1 in 10	16ft	*OC Dec-Mar.* A good road on both sides; *negotiable by caravans.*
	Poschiavo (3,317ft)	18km	1 in 8		
Bonaigua 6,797ft (2072m) Spain	Viella (3,150ft)	23km	1 in 12	14ft	*UC Nov-Apr.* A sinuous and narrow road with many hairpin bends and some precipitous drops; the alternative route to Lleida (Lérida) through the Viella tunnel is open in winter.
	Esterri d'Aneu (3,140ft)	21km	1 in 12		
Bracco 2,011ft (613m) Italy	Riva Trigoso (141ft)	15km	1 in 7	16ft	*UO.* A two-lane road with continuous bends; passing usually difficult; *negotiable by caravans,* alternative toll motorway available.
	Borghetto di Vara (318ft)	18km	1 in 7		
Brenner 4,508ft (1374m) Austria-Italy	Innsbruck (1,885ft)	39km	1 in 12	20ft	*UO.* Parallel toll motorway open; heavy traffic may delay at Customs; *suitable for caravans* using toll motorway. Pass road closed to vehicles towing trailers.
	Vipiteno (3,115ft)	14.5km	1 in 7		

*Permitted maximum width of vehicles 7ft 6in

Pass and height	From To	Distances from summit and max gradient		Min width of road	Conditions (See page 37 for key to abbreviations)
†**Brünig** 3,304ft (1007m) Switzerland	Brienzwiler Station (1,886ft)	6km	1 in 12	20ft	*UO*. An easy but winding road; heavy traffic at weekends; *suitable for caravans.*
	Giswil (1,601ft)	13km	1 in 12		
Bussang 2,365ft (721m) France	Thann (1,115ft)	22km	1 in 10	13ft	*UO*. A very easy road over the Vósges; beautiful scenery; *suitable for caravans.*
	St-Maurice-sur-Moselle (1,800ft)	8km	1 in 14		
Cabre 3,871ft (1180m) France	Luc-en-Diois (1,870ft)	22km	1 in 11	18ft	*UO*. An easy pleasant road; *suitable for caravans.*
	Aspres-sur-Buëch (2,497ft)	17km	1 in 14		
Campolongo 6,152ft (1875m) Italy	Corvara in Badia (5,145ft)	6km	1 in 8	16ft	*OC. Dec-Mar.* A winding but easy ascent; long level stretch on summit followed by easy descent; good surface; *suitable for caravans.*
	Arabba (5,253ft)	4km	1 in 8		
Cayolle 7,631ft (2326m) France	Barcelonnette (3,740ft)	32km	1 in 10	13ft	*UC early Nov-early Jun.* Narrow and winding road with hairpin bends; poor surface and broken edges, steep drops. Long stretches of single-track road with passing places.
	Guillaumes (2,687ft)	33km	1 in 10		
Costalunga (Karer) 5,751ft (1753m) Italy	Cardano (925ft)	24km	1 in 8	16ft	*OC Dec-Apr.* A good, well-engineered road but mostly winding; *caravans prohibited.*
	Pozza (4,232ft)	10km	1 in 7		
Croix 5,833ft (1778m) Switzerland	Villars-sur-Ollon (4,111ft)	8km	1 in 7½	11ft	*UC Nov-May.* A narrow and winding route but extremely picturesque.
	Les Diablerets (3,789ft)	9km	1 in 11		
Croix-Haute 3,858ft (1176m) France	Monestier-de-Clermont (2,776ft)	36km	1 in 14	18ft	*UO*. Well-engineered; several hairpin bends on the north side; *suitable for caravans.*
	Aspres-sur-Buëch (2,497ft)	28km	1 in 14		
Envalira 7,897ft (2407m) Andorra	Pas de la Casa (6,851ft)	5km	1 in 10	20ft	*OC Nov-Apr.* A good road with wide bends on ascent and descent; fine views; *negotiable by caravans* (max height vehicles 11ft 6in on northern approach near L'Hospitalet).
	Andorra (3,375ft)	29km	1 in 8		
Falzárego 6,945ft (2117m) Italy	Cortina d'Ampezzo (3,983ft)	17km	1 in 12	16ft	*OC Dec-Apr.* Well-engineered bitumen surface; many hairpin bends on both sides; *negotiable by caravans.*
	Andraz (4,622ft)	9km	1 in 12		
Faucille 4,341ft (1323m) France	Gex (1,985ft)	11km	1 in 10	16ft	*UO*. Fairly wide, winding road across the Jura mountains; *negotiable by caravans* but it is probably better to follow La Cure—St-Cerque—Nyon.
	Morez (2,247ft)	28km	1 in 12		
Fern 3,967ft (1209m) Austria	Nassereith (2,742ft)	9km	1 in 10	20ft	*UO*. An easy pass but slippery when wet; *suitable for caravans.*
	Lermoos (3,244ft)	10km	1 in 10		

†Permitted maximum width of vehicles 8ft 2½in

Pass and height	From To	Distances from summit and max gradient		Min width of road	Conditions (See page 37 for key to abbreviations)
Flexen 5,853ft (1784m) Austria	Lech (4,747ft) Rauzalpe (near Arlberg Pass) (5,341ft)	6.5km 2km	1 in 10 1 in 10	18ft	*UO.* The magnificent 'Flexenstrasse', a well-engineered mountain road with tunnels and galleries. The road from Lech to Warth, north of the pass, is usually closed between November and April due to danger of avalanches.
***Flüela** 7,818ft (2383m) Switzerland	Davos-Dorf (5,174ft) Susch (4,659ft)	13km 13km	1 in 10 1 in 8	16ft	*OC Nov-May.* Easy ascent from Davos; some acute hairpin bends on the eastern side; bitumen surface; *negotiable by caravans.*
†Forclaz 5,010ft (1527m) Switzerland France	Martigny (1,562ft) Argentière (4,111ft)	13km 19km	1 in 12 1 in 12	16ft	*UO Forclaz; Montets OC Dec-early Apr.* A good road over the pass and to the frontier; in France narrow and rough over Col des Montets (4,793ft); *negotiable by caravans.*
Foscagno 7,516ft (2291m) Italy	Bormio (4,019ft) Livigno (5,958ft)	24km 14km	1 in 8 1 in 8	11ft	*OC Nov-Apr.* Narrow and winding through lonely mountains, generally poor surface. Long winding ascent with many blind bends; not always well guarded. The descent includes winding rise and fall over the Passo d'Eira (7,218ft).
Fugazze 3,802ft (1159m) Italy	Rovereto (660ft) Valli del Pasubio (1,148ft)	27km 12km	1 in 7 1 in 7	10ft	*UO.* Very winding with some narrow sections, particularly on northern side. The many blind bends and several hairpin bends call for extra care.
***Furka** 7,976ft (2431m) Switzerland	Gletsch (5,777ft) Realp (5,046ft)	10km 13km	1 in 10 1 in 10	13ft	*UC Oct-Jun.* A well-graded road, with narrow sections and several sharp hairpin bends on both ascent and descent. Fine views of the Rhône Glacier. Alternative rail tunnel.
Galibier 8,678ft (2645m) France	Lautaret Pass (6,752ft) St-Michel-de-Maurienne (2,336ft)	7km 34km	1 in 14 1 in 8	10ft	*UC Oct-Jun.* Mainly wide, well-surfaced but unguarded. Ten hairpin bends on descent then 5km narrow and rough. Rise over the Col du Télégraphe (5,249ft), then eleven more hairpin bends. (Tunnel under the Galibier summit is closed).
Gardena (Grödner-Joch) 6,959ft (2121m) Italy	Val Gardena (6,109ft) Corvara in Badia (5,145ft)	6km 10km	1 in 8 1 in 8	16ft	*OC Dec-Jun.* A well-engineered road, very winding on descent.
Gavia 8,599ft (2621m) Italy	Bormio (4,019ft) Ponte di Legno (4,140ft)	25km 16km	1 in 5½ 1 in 5½	10ft	*UC Oct-Jul.* Steep and narrow but with frequent passing bays; many hairpin bends and a gravel surface; not for the faint-hearted; extra care necessary (maximum width vehicles 5ft 11in).
Gerlos 5,341ft (1628m) Austria	Zell am Ziller (1,886ft) Wald (2,890ft)	29km 15km	1 in 12 1 in 11	14ft	*UO.* Hairpin ascent out of Zell to modern toll road; the old, steep narrow, and winding route with passing bays and 1-in-7 gradient is not recommended, but is negotiable with care.

*Permitted maximum width of vehicles 7ft 6in
†Permitted maximum width of vehicles 8ft 2½in

Pass and height	From To	Distances from summit and max gradient		Min width of road	Conditions (See page 37 for key to abbreviations)
†**Grand St Bernard** 8,114ft (2473m) Switzerland Italy	Martigny (1,562ft)	44km	1 in 9	13ft	*UC Oct-Jun.* Modern road to entrance of road tunnel (usually open; see page 34) then narrow but bitumen surface over summit to frontier; also good in Italy; *suitable for caravans,* using tunnel. Pass road closed to vehicles towing trailers.
	Aosta (1,913ft)	33km	1 in 9		
***Grimsel** 7,100ft (2164m) Switzerland	Innertkirchen (2,067ft)	25km	1 in 10	16ft	*UC mid Oct-late Jun.* A fairly easy, modern road, but heavy traffic at weekends. A long, winding ascent, finally hairpin bends; then a terraced descent with six hairpins into the Rhône valley.
	Gletsch (5,777ft)	6km	1 in 10		
Grossglockner 8,212ft (2503m) Austria	Bruck an der Glocknerstrasse (2,480ft)	33km	1 in 8	16ft	*UC late Oct-early May.* Numerous well-engineered hairpin bends; moderate but very long ascents; toll road; very fine scenery; heavy tourist traffic; *negotiable preferably from south to north, by caravans.*
	Heiligenblut (4,268ft)	15km	1 in 8		
Hochtannberg 5,510ft (1680m) Austria	Schröcken (4,163ft)	5.5km	1 in 7	13ft	*OC Jan-Mar.* A reconstructed modern road.
	Warth (near Lech) (4,921ft)	4.5km	1 in 11		
Ibañeta (Roncesvalles) 3,468ft (1057m) France-Spain	St-Jean-Pied-de-Port (584ft)	26km	1 in 10	13ft	*UO.* A slow and winding, scenic route; *negotiable by caravans.*
	Pamplona (1,380ft)	52km	1 in 10		
Iseran 9,088ft (2770m) France	Bourg-St-Maurice (2,756ft)	49km	1 in 12	13ft	*UC mid Oct-late Jun.* The second highest pass in the Alps. Well graded with reasonable bends, average surface; several unlit tunnels on northern approach.
	Lanslebourg (4,587ft)	33km	1 in 9		
Izoard 7,743ft (2360m) France	Guillestre (3,248ft)	32km	1 in 8	16ft	*UC late Oct-mid Jun.* A winding and at times narrow road with many hairpin bends. Care required at several unlit tunnels near Guillestre.
	Briançon (4,396ft)	20km	1 in 10		
***Jaun** 4,951ft (1509m) Switzerland	Broc (2,378ft)	25km	1 in 10	13ft	*UO.* A modernised but generally narrow road; some poor sections on ascent, and several hairpin bends on descent; *negotiable by caravans.*
	Reidenbach (2,769ft)	8km	1 in 10		
†**Julier** 7,493ft (2284m) Switzerland	Tiefencastel (2,821ft)	36km	1 in 10	13ft	*UO.* Well-engineered road approached from Chur by Lenzerheide Pass (5,098ft); *suitable for caravans.*
	Silvaplana (5,958ft)	7km	1 in 7½		
Katschberg 5,384ft (1641m) Austria	Spittal (1,818ft)	35km	1 in 5½	20ft	*UO.* Steep though not particularly difficult; parallel toll motorway, including tunnel available; *negotiable by light caravans,* using tunnel.
	St Michael (3,504ft)	6km	1 in 6		
***Klausen** 6,391ft (1948m) Switzerland	Altdorf (1,512ft)	25km	1 in 11	16ft	*UC late Oct-early Jun.* Narrow and winding in places, but generally easy in spite of a number of sharp bends; *no through route for caravans as they are prohibited from using the road between Unterschächen and Linthal.*
	Linthal (2,126ft)	23km	1 in 11		

*Permitted maximum width of vehicles 7ft 6 in
†Permitted maximum width of vehicles 8ft 2½in

Pass and height	From To	Distances from summit and max gradient		Min width of road	Conditions (See page 37 for key to abbreviations)
Larche (della Maddalena) 6,542ft (1994m) France-Italy	Condamine (4,291ft) Vinadio (2,986ft)	19km 32km	1 in 12 1 in 12	10ft	*OC Dec-Mar*. An easy, well-graded road; narrow and rough on ascent, wider with better surface on descent; *suitable for caravans.*
Lautaret 6,752ft (2058m) France	Le Bourg-d'Oisans (2,359ft) Briançon (4,396ft)	38km 28km	1 in 8 1 in 10	14ft	*OC Dec-Mar*. Modern, evenly graded, but winding, and unguarded in places; very fine scenery; *suitable for caravans.*
Loibl (Ljubelj) 3,500ft (1067m) Austria-Yugoslavia	Unterloibl (1,699ft) Kranj (1,263ft)	10km 29km	1 in 5½ 1 in 8	20ft	*UO*. Steep rise and fall over Little Loibl Pass to tunnel (1.6km long) under summit; from south to north *just negotiable by experienced drivers with light caravans*. The old road over the summit is closed to through traffic.
***Lukmanier (Lucomagno)** 6,286ft (1916m) Switzerland	Olivone (2,945ft) Disentis (3,772ft)	18km 22km	1 in 11 1 in 11	16ft	*UC Nov-late May*. Rebuilt, modern road; *no throughroute for caravans as they are prohibited from using the road between the Lukmanier Pass and Olivone.*
†Maloja 5,955ft (1815m) Switzerland	Silvaplana (5,958ft) Chiavenna (1,083ft)	11km 32km	level 1 in 11	13ft	*UO*. Escarpment facing south; fairly easy but many hairpin bends on descent; *negotiable by caravans,* possibly difficult on ascent.
Mauria 4,258ft (1298m) Italy	Lozzo Cadore (2,470ft) Ampezzo (1,837ft)	14km 31km	1 in 14 1 in 14	16ft	*UO*. A well-designed road with easy, winding ascent and descent; *suitable for caravans.*
Mendola 4,472ft (1363m) Italy	Appiano (Eppan) (1,348ft) Sarnonico (3,208ft)	15km 8km	1 in 8 1 in 10	16ft	*UO*. A fairly straightforward, but winding road; well guarded; *suitable for caravans.*
Mont Cenis 6,834ft (2083m) France-Italy	Lanslebourg (4,587ft) Susa (1,624ft)	11km 28km	1 in 10 1 in 8	16ft	*UC Nov-May*. Approach by industrial valley. An easy broad highway but with poor surface in places; *suitable for caravans.* Alternative Fréjus road tunnel available (see page 34).
Monte Croce di Comélico (Kreuzberg) 5,368ft (1636m) Italy	San Candido (3,847ft) Santo Stefano di Cadore (2,979ft)	15km 21km	1 in 12 1 in 12	16ft	*UO*. A winding road with moderate gradients; beautiful scenery; *suitable for caravans.*
Montgenèvre 6,070ft (1850m) France-Italy	Briançon (4,396ft) Cesana Torinese (4,429ft)	12km 8km	1 in 14 1 in 11	16ft	*UO*. An easy, modern road; *suitable for caravans.*
Monte Giovo (Jaufen) 6,870ft (2094m) Italy	Merano (1,063ft) Vipiteno (3,115ft)	40km 19km	1 in 8 1 in 11	13ft	*UC Nov-May*. Many well-engineered hairpin bends; *caravans prohibited.*
Montets (see Forclaz)					
Morgins 4,491ft (1369m) France-Switzerland	Abondance (3,051ft) Monthey (1,391ft)	14km 15km	1 in 11 1 in 7	13ft	*UO*. A lesser used route through pleasant, forested countryside crossing the French/Swiss border.

*Permitted maximum width of vehicles 7ft 6in
†Permitted maximum width of vehicles 8ft 2½in

Pass and height	From To	Distances from summit and max gradient		Min width of road	Conditions (See page 37 for key to abbreviations)
***Mosses** 4,740ft (1445m) Switzerland	Aigle (1,378ft) Château-d'Oex (3,153ft)	18km 15km	1 in 12 1 in 12	13ft	*UO.* A modern road; suitable for caravans.
Nassfeld (Pramolio) 5,020ft (1530m) Austria-Italy	Tropolach (1,972ft) Pontebba (1,841ft)	10km 12km	1 in 5 1 in 10	13ft	*OC late Nov-Mar.* The Austrian section is mostly narrow and winding, with tight, blind bends; the winding descent in Italy has been improved.
***Nufenen (Novena)** 8,130ft (2478m) Switzerland	Ulrichen (4,416ft) Airolo (3,747ft)	13km 24km	1 in 10 1 in 10	13ft	*UC mid Oct-mid Jun.* The approach roads are narrow, with tight bends, but the road over the pass is good; *negotiable by light caravans* (limit 1.5 tons).
***Oberalp** 6,706ft (2044m) Switzerland	Andermatt (4,737ft) Disentis (3,772ft)	10km 22km	1 in 10 1 in 10	16ft	*UC Nov-late May.* A much improved and widened road with a modern surface; many hairpin bends but long level stretch on summit; *negotiable by caravans.* Alternative rail tunnel during the winter.
***Ofen (Fuorn)** 7,051ft (2149m) Switzerland	Zernez (4,836ft) Santa Maria im Münstertal (4,547ft)	22km 14km	1 in 10 1 in 8	12ft	*UO.* Good, fairly easy road through the Swiss National Park; *suitable for caravans.*
Petit St Bernard 7,178ft (2188m) France-Italy	Bourg-St-Maurice (2,756ft) Pré St-Didier (3,335ft)	31km 23km	1 in 16 1 in 12	16ft	*UC mid Oct-Jun.* Outstanding scenery; a fairly easy approach but poor surface and unguarded broken edges near the summit; good on the descent in Italy; *negotiable by light caravans.*
Peyresourde 5,128ft (1563m) France	Arreau (2,310ft) Luchon (2,067ft)	18km 14km	1 in 10 1 in 10	13ft	*UO.* Somewhat narrow with several hairpin bends, though not difficult.
***Pillon** 5,072ft (1546m) Switzerland	Le Sépey (3,212ft) Gsteig (2,911ft)	14km 7km	1 in 11 1 in 11	13ft	*OC Jan-Feb.* A comparatively easy modern road; *suitable for caravans.*
Plöcken (Monte Croce Carnico) 4,468ft (1362m) Austria-Italy	Kötschach (2,316ft) Paluzza (1,968ft)	14km 16km	1 in 7 1 in 14	16ft	*OC Dec-Apr.* A modern road with long reconstructed sections; heavy traffic at summer weekends; delay likely at the frontier; *negotiable by caravans.*
Pordoi 7,346ft (2239m) Italy	Arabba (5,253ft) Canazei (4,806ft)	9km 12km	1 in 10 1 in 10	16ft	*OC Dec-Apr.* An excellent modern road with numerous hairpin bends; *negotiable by caravans.*
Port 4,098ft (1249m) France	Tarascon (1,555ft) Massat (2,133ft)	18km 13km	1 in 10 1 in 10	14ft	*OC Nov-Mar.* A fairly easy road but narrow on some bends; *negotiable by caravans.*
Portet-d'Aspet 3,507ft (1069m) France	Audressein (1,625ft) Fronsac (1,548ft)	18km 29km	1 in 7 1 in 7	11ft	*UO.* Approached from the west by the easy Col des Ares (2,611ft) and Col de Buret (1,975ft); well-engineered road, but calls for particular care on hairpin bends; rather narrow.

*Permitted maximum width of vehicles 7ft 6 in

Pass and height	From To	Distances from summit and max gradient		Min width of road	Conditions (See page 37 for key to abbreviations)
Pötschen 3,221ft (982m) Austria	Bad Ischl (1,535ft) Bad Aussee (2,133ft)	19km 9km	1 in 11 1 in 11	23ft	*UO.* A modern road; *suitable for caravans.*
Pourtalet 5,879ft (1792m) France-Spain	Eaux-Chaudes (2,152ft) Biescas (2,821ft)	23km 34km	1 in 10 1 in 10	11ft	*UC late Oct-early Jun.* A fairly easy, unguarded road, but narrow in places; poor but *being rebuilt on Spanish side.*
Puymorens 6,283ft (1915m) France	Ax-les-Thermes (2,362ft) Bourg-Madame (3,707ft)	28km 27km	1 in 10 1 in 10	18ft	*OC Nov-Apr.* A generally easy modern tarmac road, but narrow, winding, and with a poor surface in places; not suitable for night driving; *suitable for caravans* (maximum height vehicles 11ft 6in). Alternative rail service available between Ax-les-Thermes and Latour-de-Carol.
Quillane 5,623ft (1714m) France	Quillan (955ft) Mont-Louis (5,135ft)	63km 5km	1 in 12 1 in 12	16ft	*OC Nov-Mar.* An easy, straightforward ascent and descent; *suitable for caravans.*
Radstädter-Tauern 5,702ft (1738m) Austria	Radstadt (2,808ft) Mauterndorf (3,681ft)	21km 17km	1 in 6 1 in 7	16ft	*OC Jan-Mar.* Northern ascent steep but not difficult otherwise; parallel toll motorway including tunnel available; *negotiable by light caravans, using tunnel.*
Résia (Reschen) 4,934ft (1504m) Italy-Austria	Spondigna (2,903ft) Pfunds (3,182ft)	30km 21km	1 in 10 1 in 10	20ft	*UO.* A good straightforward alternative to the Brenner Pass; *suitable for caravans.*
Restefond (La Bonette) 9,193ft (2802m) France	Jausiers (near Barcelonnette) (3,986ft) St-Etienne-de-Tinée (3,766ft)	23km 27km	1 in 9 1 in 9	10ft	*UC Oct-Jun.* The highest pass in the Alps, completed in 1962. Narrow, rough, unguarded ascent with many blind bends, and nine hairpins. Descent easier; winding with twelve hairpin bends.
Rolle 6,463ft (1970m) Italy	Predazzo (3,337ft) Mezzano (2,098ft)	21km 25km	1 in 11 1 in 14	16ft	*OC Dec-Mar.* Very beautiful scenery; bitumen surface; a well-engineered road; *negotiable by caravans.*
Rombo (see Timmelsjoch)					
Route des Crêtes 4,210ft (1283m) France	St-Dié (1,125ft) Cernay (902ft)	— —	1 in 8 1 in 8	13ft	*UC Nov-Apr.* A renowned scenic route crossing seven ridges, with the highest point at Hôtel du Grand Ballon.
†St Gotthard (San Gottardo) 6,916ft (2108m) Switzerland	Göschenen (3,629ft) Airolo (3,747ft)	19km 15km	1 in 10 1 in 10	20ft	*UC mid Oct-early Jun.* Modern, fairly easy two or three lane road. Heavy traffic; *negotiable by caravans* (max height vehicles 11ft 9in). Alternative road tunnel available (see page 34).
***San Bernardino** 6,778ft (2066m) Switzerland	Mesocco (2,549ft) Hinterrhein (5,328ft)	22km 9.5km	1 in 10 1 in 10	13ft	*UC Oct-late Jun.* Easy, modern roads on northern and southern approaches to tunnel (see page 35); narrow and winding over summit; via tunnel *suitable for caravans.*

*Permitted maximum width of vehicles 7ft 6in
†Permitted maximum width of vehicles 8ft 2½in

Pass and height	From To	Distances from summit and max gradient		Min width of road	Conditions (See page 37 for key to abbreviations)
Schlucht 3,737ft (1139m) France	Gérardmer (2,182ft) Munster (1,250ft)	15km 17km	1 in 14 1 in 14	16ft	*UO.* An extremely picturesque route crossing the Vosges mountains, with easy, wide bends on the descent; *suitable for caravans.*
Seeberg (Jezersko) 3,996ft (1218m) Austria-Yugoslavia	Eisenkappel (1,821ft) Kranj (1,263ft)	14km 33km	1 in 8 1 in 10	16ft	*UO.* An alternative to the steeper Loibl and Wurzen passes; moderate climb with winding, hairpin ascent and descent.
Sella 7,349ft (2240m) Italy	Plan (5,269ft) Canazei (4,806ft)	9km 13km	1 in 9 1 in 9	16ft	*OC Dec-Jun.* A finely engineered, winding road; exceptional views of the Dolomites.
Semmering 3,232ft (985m) Austria	Mürzzuschlag im Mürztal (2,205ft) Gloggnitz (1,427ft)	13km 16km	1 in 16 1 in 16	20ft	*UO.* A fine, well-engineered highway; *suitable for caravans.*
Sestriere 6,670ft (2033m) Italy	Cesana Torinese (4,429ft) Pinerolo (1,234ft)	12km 55km	1 in 10 1 in 10	16ft	*UO.* Mostly bitumen surface; *negotiable by caravans.*
Silvretta (Bielerhöhe) 6,666ft (2032m) Austria	Partenen (3,451ft) Galtür (5,195ft)	15km 10km	1 in 9 1 in 9	16ft	*UC late Oct-early Jun.* For the most part reconstructed; thirty-two easy hairpin bends on western ascent; eastern side more straightforward. Toll road; *caravans prohibited.*
†**Simplon** 6,578ft (2005m) Switzerland-Italy	Brig (2,231ft) Domodóssola (919ft)	22km 41km	1 in 9 1 in 11	23ft	*OC Nov-Apr.* An easy reconstructed modern road, but 13 miles long, continuous ascent to summit; *suitable for caravans.* Alternative rail tunnel.
Somport 5,354ft (1632m) France-Spain	Bedous (1,365ft) Jaca (2,687ft)	31km 30km	1 in 10 1 in 10	12ft	*UO.* A favoured, old established route; generally easy, but in parts narrow and unguarded; fairly good-surfaced road; *suitable for caravans.*
***Splügen** 6,932ft (2113m) Switzerland-Italy	Splügen (4,780ft) Chiavenna (1,083ft)	9km 30km	1 in 9 1 in 7½	10ft	*UC Nov-Jun.* Mostly narrow and winding, with many hairpin bends, and not well guarded; care also required at many tunnels and galleries (max height vehicles 9ft 2 in).
††**Stelvio** 9,045ft (2757m) Italy	Bormio (4,019ft) Spondigna (2,903ft)	22km 28km	1 in 8 1 in 8	13ft	*UC Oct-late Jun.* The third highest pass in the Alps; the number of acute hairpin bends, all well-engineered, is exceptional — from forty to fifty on either side; the surface is good, the traffic heavy. Hairpin bends are too acute for long vehicles.
†**Susten** 7,297ft (2224m) Switzerland	Innertkirchen (2,067ft) Wassen (3,005ft)	28km 19km	1 in 11 1 in 11	20ft	*UC Nov-Jun.* A very scenic route and well guarded mountain road; easy gradients and turns; heavy traffic at weekends; *negotiable by caravans.*
Tenda (Tende) 4,334ft (1321m) Italy-France	Borgo S Dalmazzo (2,103ft) La Giandola (1,010ft)	24km 29km	1 in 11 1 in 11	18ft	*UO.* Well guarded, modern road with several hairpin bends; road tunnel at summit; *suitable for caravans, but prohibited during the winter.*

*Permitted maximum width of vehicles 7ft 6in
†Permitted maximum width of vehicles 8ft 2½in
††Maximum length of vehicles 30ft

Pass and height	From To	Distances from summit and max gradient		Min width of road	Conditions (See page 37 for key to abbreviations)
Thurn 4,180ft (1274m) Austria	Kitzbühel (2,500ft)	19km	1 in 12	16ft	*UO*. A good road with narrow stretches; northern approach rebuilt; *suitable for caravans.*
	Mittersill (2,588ft)	11km	1 in 16		
Timmelsjoch (Rombo) 8,232ft (2509m) Austria-Italy	Obergurgl (6,322ft)	14km	1 in 7	12ft	*UC mid Oct-late Jun.* Roadworks on Italian side still in progress. The pass is open to private cars (without trailers) only as some tunnels on the Italian side are too narrow for larger vehicles; toll road.
	Moso (3,304ft)	23km	1 in 8		
Tonale 6,178ft (1883m) Italy	Edolo (2,264ft)	30km	1 in 14	16ft	*UO*. A relatively easy road; *suitable for caravans.*
	Dimaro (2,513ft)	27km	1 in 8		
Toses (Tosas) 5,905ft (1800m) Spain	Puigcerdá (3,708ft)	25km	1 in 10	16ft	*UO*. Now a fairly straightforward, but continuously winding two-lane road with many sharp bends; some unguarded edges; *negotiable by caravans.*
	Ribes de Freser (3,018ft)	25km	1 in 10		
Tourmalet 6,936ft (2114m) France	Luz (2,333ft)	19km	1 in 8	14ft	*UC Oct-mid Jun.* The highest of the French Pyrénées routes; the approaches are good though winding and exacting over summit; sufficiently guarded.
	Ste-Marie-de-Campan (2,811ft)	17km	1 in 8		
Tre Croci 5,935ft (1809m) Italy	Cortina d'Ampezzo (3,983ft)	7km	1 in 9	16ft	*OC Dec-Mar.* An easy pass; very fine scenery; *suitable for caravans.*
	Auronzo di Cadore (2,835ft)	26km	1 in 9		
Turracher Höhe 5,784ft (1763m) Austria	Predlitz (3,024ft)	20km	1 in 5½	13ft	*UO*. Formerly one of the steepest mountain roads in Austria; now much improved; steep, fairly straightforward ascent, followed by a very steep descent; good surface and mainly two lane width; fine scenery.
	Ebene-Reichenau (3,563ft)	8km	1 in 4½		
***Umbrail** 8,205ft (2501m) Switzerland-Italy	Santa Maria im Münstertal (4,547ft)	13km	1 in 11	14ft	*UC early Nov-early Jun.* Highest of the Swiss passes; narrow; mostly gravel surfaced with thirty-four hairpin bends but not too difficult.
	Bormio (4,019ft)	19km	1 in 11		
Vars 6,919ft (2109m) France	St-Paul-sur-Ubaye (4,823ft)	8km	1 in 10	16ft	*OC Dec-Mar.* Easy winding ascent with seven hairpin bends; gradual winding descent with another seven hairpin bends; good surface, *negotiable by caravans.*
	Guillestre (3,248ft)	20km	1 in 10		
Wurzen (Koren) 3,520ft (1073m) Austria-Yugoslavia	Riegersdorf (1,775ft)	7km	1 in 5½	13ft	*UO*. A steep two-lane road which otherwise is not particularly difficult; *caravans prohibited.*
	Kranjska Gora (2,657ft)	6km	1 in 5½		
Zirler Berg 3,310ft (1009m) Austria	Seefeld (3,870ft)	7km	1 in 7	20ft	*UO*. An escarpment facing south, part of the route from Garmisch to Innsbruck; a good modern road but heavy tourist traffic and a long steep descent, with one hairpin bend, into the Inn Valley. Steepest section from the hairpin bend down to Zirl.
	Zirl (2,041ft)	5km	1 in 6		

*Permitted maximum width of vehicles 7ft 6in

About the Gazetteer

AA signs

The AA issues signs on request to hotels listed in this Guide. You are advised, however, not to rely solely on the sign, but to check that the establishment still appears in this edition.

Charges

The gazetteer normally quotes terms minimum and maximum for one and two persons with Continental breakfast price added to the room tariff to give inclusive terms for bed and breakfast with and without private facilities.

DPn indicates *demi-pension* (half-board) terms only available which means that in addition to the charge for rooms, guests are expected to pay for one main meal whether it is taken or not.

Pn indicates *full pension* (full board) terms only available. Both these terms are shown minimum and maximum with and without private facilities for one and two persons.

Hotels are not required by law to exchange travellers cheques for guests, and many small hotels are unable to do so. You must expect to pay a higher rate of commission for this service at a hotel than you would at a bank.

All prices quoted in this guide refer to 1986. They are shown purely to indicate the relative costs of the hotels listed, but cannot reflect any subsequent movement in prices.

Classification

Although the system of classification in Europe is similar to the AA system in this country, the variations in the traditions and customs of hotel-keeping abroad often make identical grading difficult.

Gazetteer entry and example

The gazetteer entries are compiled from information which is supplied by the proprietors of the establishments concerned, and every effort is made to ensure that the information given is up-to-date. Where this has not been possible, *establishment names have been printed in italics to show that particulars have not been confirmed by the management.*

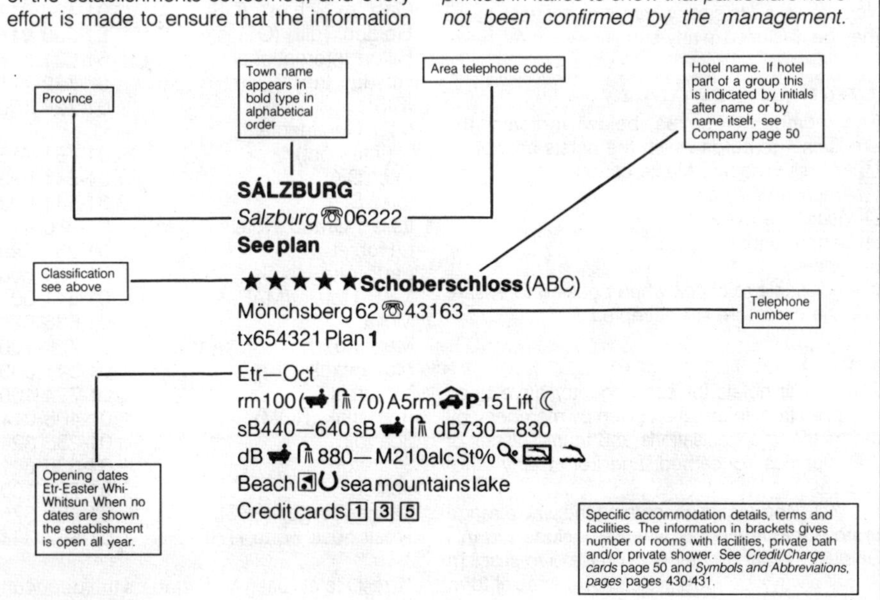

Hotels and motels are classified by stars. The definitions are intended to indicate the type of hotel rather than the degree of merit. Meals, service, and hours of service should be in keeping with the classification, and all establishments with restaurants must serve meals to non-residents and are expected to give good value for money.

★ Hotels simply furnished but clean and well kept; all bedrooms with hot and cold running water; adequate bath and lavatory facilities.
★★ Hotels offering a higher standard of accommodation; adequate bath and lavatory facilities on all main floors and some private bathrooms and/or showers.
★★★ Well-appointed hotels; with a large number of bedrooms with private bathrooms/ showers.
★★★★ Exceptionally well-appointed hotels offering a very high standard of comfort and service with all bedrooms providing private bathrooms/showers.
★★★★★ Luxury hotels offering the highest international standards.

Complaints

You are advised to bring any criticism to the notice of the hotel management immediately. This will enable the matter to be dealt with promptly to the advantage of all concerned. If a personal approach fails, members should inform the AA. You are asked to state whether or not your name may be disclosed in any enquiries we may make.

Credit/Charge cards

The numbered boxes below indicate the credit/charge cards which the hotels accept
[1] Access/Eurocard/Mastercard
[2] American Express
[3] Visa/Carte Bleue
[4] Carte Blanche
[5] Diners
It is advisable to check when booking to ensure that the cards are still accepted.

Hotels

The lists of hotels for each country have been compiled from information given by members, by the motoring organisations and tourist offices of the countries concerned, and from many other sources.

Your comments concerning the whole range of hotel information — whether included in this Guide or not, and whether in praise or in criticism — will always be most welcome; a special form will be found at the back of this book, and all information will be treated in the strictest confidence.

Hotel Groups

Most of the hotel groups shown below have agreements with AA Travel. If you want to reserve accommodation and make payment in advance, any AA Travel Agency will be happy to undertake these arrangements. A full list of AA Travel Agencies is shown in the current AA Members' Handbook. If you would prefer to make your reservations by telephone a special unit is operated at the AA Travel Agency in Brighton, and payment by Access or Visa credit cards is accepted. Please telephone (0273) 24934 Mon-Fri 09.00-17.00hrs and Sat 09.00-12.30.

Key to abbreviations and company reservation telephone numbers:

Company	**tel**
Ambassador (Amb)	01-940 9766
Astir	01-636 0818
Best Western (BW)	01-541 0033
Climat de France	01-630 9161
Crest* (Crest)	01-236 3242
ETAP/PLM/Euromotels (ETAP)	01-621 1962
FAH	0253 594185
Fimotel	01-630 9161
Forum	01-491 7181
Frantel	01-621 1962
Gast im Schloss (GS)	01-408 0111
Golden Tulip (GT)	01-568 9144
Hilton International	01-631 1767
Holiday Inns	01-722 7755
IBIS	01-724 1000
Inter Continental (Intercont)	01-491 7181
Inter DK	01-541 0033
Inter S	01-541 0033
Italian Grand Hotels (CIGA)	01-930 4147
L'Horset	01-951 3990
Ladbroke Hotels	01-734 6000
MAP Hotels (MAP)	01-541 0033
Melia	01-636 5242
Mercure	01-724 1000
Mövenpick	01-541 0033
Novotels	01-724 1000
Romantik (ROM)	01-408 0111
Scandic	01-236 3242
Sheraton	01-636 6411
Sofitel	01-724 1000
Steigenberger (SRS)	01-486 5754
Trusthouse Forte (THF)	01-567 3444

*Crest Hotels offer AA members the opportunity to book a double room at the normal single rate (for double occupancy). For details of terms and conditions please see the special leaflet obtainable from Crest Hotels or the AA.

Location maps

The location maps are at the beginning of each country section except those for Luxembourg, Portugal and Sweden where they are incorporated in the Belgian, Spanish and Norwegian maps respectively. These maps are intended to assist the reader who wishes to stay in a certain area by showing only those towns for which there is an entry in the gazetteer. Thus someone wishing to stay in the Innsbruck area will be able to select suitable towns by looking at the map. The location maps in this book use the symbols below to indicate adjoining countries:

Symbols used for country identification

All location maps in this book use the following symbols to indicate adjoining countries.

AL	Albania	I	Italy
AND	Andorra	FL	Liechtenstein
A	Austria	L	Luxembourg
B	Belgium	NL	Netherlands
BG	Bulgaria	N	Norway
CS	Czechoslovakia	PL	Poland
DK	Denmark	P	Portugal
SF	Finland	RO	Romania
F	France	E	Spain
D	W. Germany	S	Sweden
DDR	Germany (DDR)	CH	Switzerland
GR	Greece	TR	Turkey
H	Hungary	SU	USSR
IRE	Ireland, Rep of	YU	Yugoslavia

It must be emphasised that these maps are not intended to be used to find your way around the country and we recommend readers to buy the AA Big Road Atlas of Europe.

Reservations

The practice is the same on the Continent as it is in this country; rooms are booked subject to their still being available when confirmation is received. It is therefore most important that confirmation should be sent to the hotel as soon as possible after the rooms have been offered. Regrettably, many hotels will not accept bookings for one or two nights only. Sometimes a deposit is required which can be arranged through your bank. Many hotels do not hold reservations after 19.00hrs, and you should advise hotels if you anticipate a late arrival or if you are unable to take up your booking for any reason. Unwanted rooms can then often be relet and you will be saved the expense of paying for them, as a confirmed booking represents a legal contract.

Hotel telephone numbers are given in the gazetteer. In some entries the name of the group operating the hotel is indicated and a key to the abbreviations used may be found on page 50 together with the telephone numbers for reservations. Most of the hotel groups listed have agreements with AA Travel and reservations may also be made at any AA Travel Agency.

The AA regrets that it cannot make reservations on your behalf at other hotels, except in conjunction with a holiday scheme, details of which are available from any AA Travel Agency.

When writing direct to hotels abroad, it is advisable to enclose an international reply coupon; these are available from any post office.

When reservations are made on the spot, it is the custom to inspect the rooms offered and to ask for the price before accepting them. No embarrassment is caused by this practice, and British visitors are urged to adopt it also, as it will be in their own interests.

Double rooms may not be reduced in price when let to one person; however, a double room is generally cheaper than two rooms. Accommodation in an annexe may be of different standard from rooms in the main hotel building; it is advisable to check the exact nature of the accommodation at the time of reservation.

Specimen letters for booking hotels

Please use **block letters** and enclose an **International Reply Coupon,** obtainable from the post office. Be sure to include your own name and address clearly written.

English

Dear Sir

Please send me by return your terms with tax and service included, and confirm availability of accommodation with: Full Board/Half Board/Bed and Breakfast*

I would arrive on ....
and leave on ....
I would need............rooms with single bed with/without* bath/shower*
...........rooms with double bed with/without* bath/shower*
.............rooms with twin beds with/without* bath/shower*
.............cots in parents' room
We are.................................Adults
Our party also includes.......Children;.......
boys aged..........years and..........girls
aged......................................years.

I look forward to receiving your reply and thank you in advance.

German

Sehr geehrte Damen und Herren

Bitte senden Sie mir umgehend Angaben Ihrer Preise, einschl. Steuer-und Bedienungskosten, und bestätigen, ob Sie Zimmer frei haben, für eine Unterbringung mit: Vollpension/Halbpension/Zimmer mit Frühstück*

Ankunftsdatum ....
Abfahrtsdatum ....
Ich möchte............Einzelzimmer mit/ohne* Bad/Dusche*
..........Zimmer mit Doppelbett mit/ohn* Bad/Dusche*
.........Zimmer mit zwei Betten mit/ohne* Bad/Dusche*
..............Kinderbettchen im Elternzimmer
Wir sind..........................Erwachsene
und zusätzlich........Kinder........Jungen
......Jahreund......Mädchen......Jahre.
Iche sehe Ihrer Antwort gern entgegen und danke Ihnen im voraus für Ihre Bemülhungen.

French

Monsieur

Pourriez vous m'indiquer par retour si vous pouvez réserver et à quel tarif, taxe et service compris, pour un séjour en: Pension/Demi-pension/Chambre et petit déjeuner*

J'arriverais le ....
et je repartirais le ....
Il me faudrait.........Chambres à un lit d'une personne avec/sans* bain/douche*
................Chambres à grand lit avec/sans* bain/douche*
...............Chambres à deux lits avec/sans* bain/douche*
..............Lits d'enfants dans la chambre des parents.
Nous sommes.......................Adultes
Accompagnés de.........Enfants;.........
Garçons de............ans et............
Filles de.................................ans.
J'attends vos renseignements et vous remercie par avance.

Italian

Egregio Direttore

Potrebbe indicarmi a ritorno di posta le condizioni d'alloggio con tasse e servizio inclusi, e se é possibile riservare con: Pensione completa/mezza pensione/camera e colazione*

Data d'arrivo ....
dat di partenza ....
Vorrei riservare..............camere con letto singolo e con/senza* bagno/doccia*
.... camere con letto matrimoniale e con/senza* bagno/doccia*
.... camere a due letti e con/senza* bagno/doccia*
.... lettino neela camera dei genitori
Siamo..................................adulti
Accompagnati da.................bambini di
.......anni e.......bambine di.......anni.
Resto in attesa di una sua cortese risposta e la ringrazio.

Spanish

Muy Señor mio

Sirvase comunicarme a vuelta de correo sus condiciones de alojamiento con impuestos y servicio incluidos, y si puedo reservar con: Pensión completa/media pensión/habitación y desayuno*

Fecha de ilegada ....
fecha de salida...............................
Necesitaria..................habitaciones de una sola cama con/sin* baño/ducha*
..............habitaciones con cama de matrimonio con/sin* baño/ducha*
..........habitaciones de dos camas con/sin* baño/ducha*
.................camita en la habitación de los padres
Somos...........................adultos
Acompañados por.........niños de.........
años y...........niñas de...........años.
Quedo a là espera de sus noticias y le doy las gracias.

*delete where inapplicable.

Town plans

Listed below are major towns and cities for which there are town plans, followed by page numbers. A list of hotels showing the plan number can be found adjacent to the relevant plan. In addition, the appropriate plan number will appear following the telephone number in the hotel entry. These numbers correspond to the number on the plan thereby giving the location of the hotel.

Garages

(*See also France page 108 and Spain page 350*)
The garages listed in the gazetteer for each country are those which are most likely to be of help to members on tour, because of their situation and the services they have stated they can provide. Although the AA cannot accept responsibility for difficulties over repairs to members' cars, any unsatisfactory cases will be noted for amendment in future editions of the guide.

It cannot be emphasised too strongly that disputes with garages on the Continent must be settled on the spot. It has been the AA's experience that subsequent negotiations can seldom be brought to a satisfactory conclusion.

In selecting garages, preference has been given to those which provide a breakdown service (see below) and those accepting AIT Credit Vouchers. The number of garages holding each agency reflects, as far as possible, the relative popularity of the various makes of cars. Although firms normally specialise in the makes for which they are accredited agents, they do not necessarily hold stocks of spare parts. Certain garages will repair only the make of car for which they are officially agents as indicated in the text. The symbol 'P' indicates that the establishments undertake the garaging of cars.

A complete list of service agencies for your own make of car is generally available through your own dealer. It has been found on occasions that some garages in Europe make extremely high charges for repairing tourists' cars; always ask for an estimate before authorising a repair.

Breakdown service

The breakdown service of garages listed in the gazetteer is not free and any assistance obtained must be paid for. The AA's free breakdown service for members operates in the United Kingdom and Republic of Ireland only. Therefore motorists travelling in Europe are advised to purchase AA 5-Star Service, see *Breakdown* page 6 for further information.

Hours of opening

In most European countries business hours are 08.00-18.00hrs; these times may be altered on Sundays and public holidays, when repairs, breakdown service, and petrol are often unobtainable.

In many countries, especially France, it may be difficult to get a car repaired during August because many garages close down for annual holidays.

Service Agents

The service agencies held by garages are indicated by the following abbreviations:

ALF	Alfa Romeo	**MAZ**	Mazda
AST	Aston Martin	**MER**	Mercedes-Benz
AUD	Audi	**OPE**	Opel
AR	Austin/Rover	**PEU**	Peugeot
BMW	BMW	**POR**	Porsche
CIT	Citroen	**REN**	Renault
COL	Colt (Mitsubishi)	**RR**	Rolls-Royce Bentley
DAI	Daihatsu		
DAT	Datsun (Nissan)	**SAA**	Saab
DJ	Daimler/Jaguar	**SKO**	Skoda
FIA	Fiat	**TAL**	Talbot
FOR	Ford	**TOY**	Toyota
HON	Honda	**VAU**	Vauxhall
LAN	Lancia	**VW**	Volkswagen
LOT	Lotus	**VOL**	Volvo
LR	Land Rover		

International distinguishing sign

Area *32,374 sq miles*
Population *7,550,000*
Local time *GMT + 1 (Summer GMT + 2)*

National flag
Horizontal tricolour, red, white and red

How to get there

The usual approach from Calais, Oostende and Zeebrugge is via Belgium to Aachen to join the German *Autobahn* network, then onwards via Köln (Cologne) to Frankfurt. Here the routes branch southwards via Karlsruhe and Stuttgart for Innsbruck and the Tirol or eastwards via Nürnberg and München (Munich) to Salzburg for central Austria. The distance to Salzburg is about 700 miles and usually requires two night stops. Wien (Vienna) the capital is a further 200 miles east. Travelling via the Netherlands is a straightforward run joining the German *Autobahn* system near Arnhem. Alternatively, Austria can be reached via northern France to Strasbourg and Stuttgart or via Basel and northern Switzerland. This is also the route if travelling from Dieppe, Le Havre, Caen or Cherbourg. Car-sleeper services operate during the summer from Brussels and 's-Hertogenbosch to Salzburg and Villach.

Motoring regulations and general information

This information should be read in conjunction with the general content of the European ABC (pages 4-26). **Note** As certain regulations and requirements are common to many countries they are covered by one entry in the ABC and the following headings represent some of the subjects dealt with in this way:
AA Agents
Crash or safety helmets
Customs regulations for European countries
Drinking and driving
Fire extinguisher
International distinguishing sign
Medical treatment
Mirrors
Overtaking
Police fines
Radio telephones/Radio transmitters
Road signs
Seat belts
Tyres
Visitors' registration

Accidents

Fire 122 **police** 133 **ambulance** 144.
A driver who is involved in an accident must stop and exchange particulars with the other party. If personal injury is sustained it is obligatory that you obtain medical assistance for the injured persons and immediately report the incident to the police. All persons who arrive at the scene of an accident are obliged to render assistance unless it is obvious that everything necessary has already been done. See also *Accidents* page 5.

Accommodation

The official guide giving details of hotel classifications is available from the Tourist Office in London. Additional information on accommodation at small inns, in private homes and at farmhouses may be obtained from local and regional tourist information offices. Hotels are officially classified from five-star (luxury) to one-star (simple hotels). Room, pension, service and heating charges are exhibited in bedrooms.

Boats

(See also page 6)
Motorboats are not allowed on most of Austria's lakes. It is advisable to check with the Tourist Office before taking boats to Austria.

Breakdown

If your car breaks down, try to move it to the side of the road so that it obstructs the traffic flow as little as possible. The Austrian motoring club Österreichischer Automobil-, Motorrad-und Touring Club (ÖAMTC) maintains a roadside assistance service (Pannenhilfe) and a towing service (Abschleppdienst). A patrol service (Strassenwacht) operates around Wien and on the

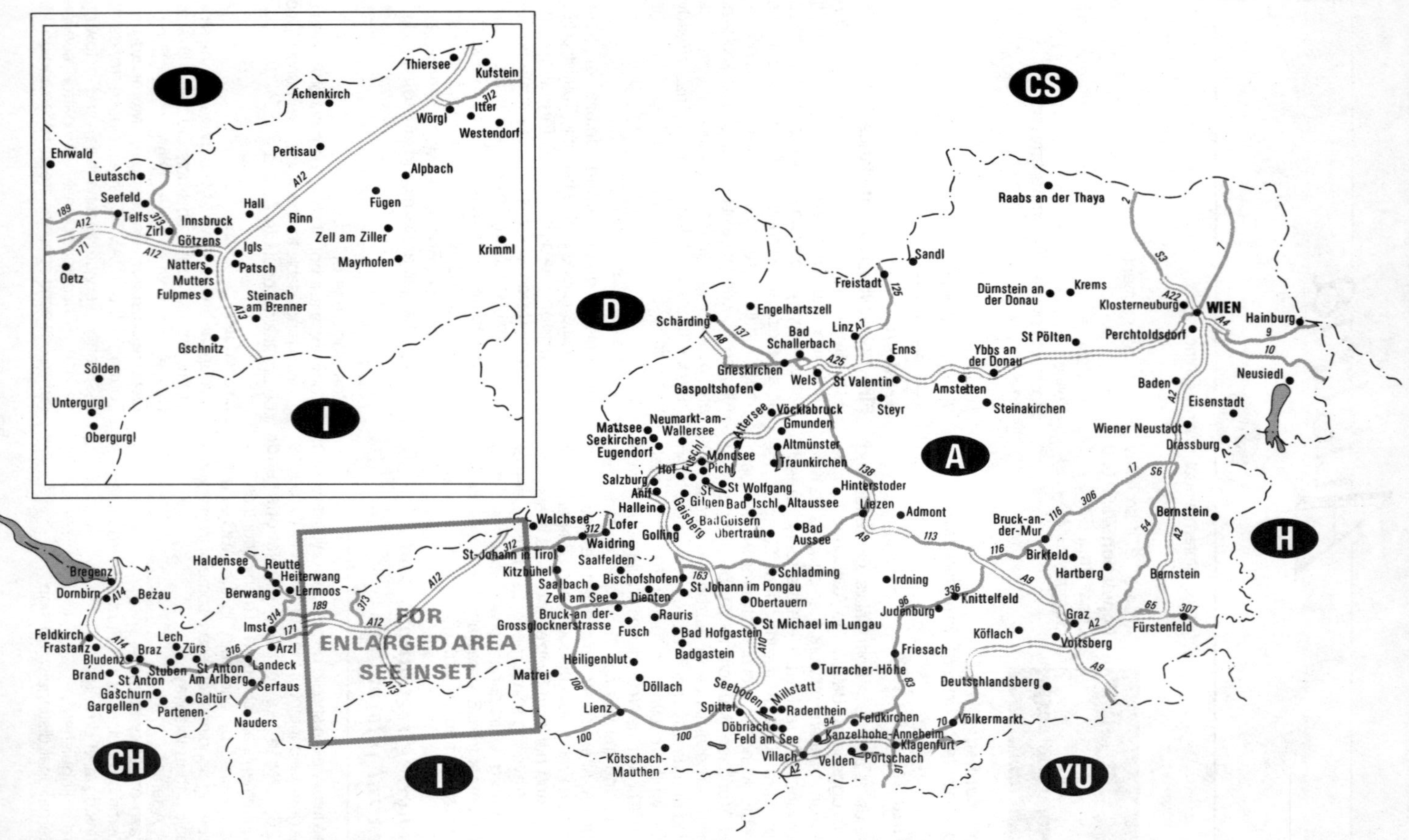

For key to country identification - see page 51

south and west motorways when the volume of traffic demands it. See also *Breakdown* page 6, *Motorways* page 58 and *Warning triangle* page 60.

British Embassy/Consulates

(See also page 6)
The British Embassy together with its consular section is located at *1030 Wien* Reisnerstrasse 40 ☎ (0222) 731575/9; consular section 756117/8. There are British Consulates with Honorary Consuls in Graz, Innsbruck and Salzburg.

Currency including banking hours

(See also page 9)
The unit of currency is the Austrian Schilling (*ASch*) divided into 100 *Groschen*. At the time of going to press £1 = *ASch* 21.30. Denominations of bank notes are *ASch* 20, 50, 100, 500, 1,000; standard coins are *ASch* 1, 5, 10, 20, 25, 50 and *Groschen* 2, 5, 10, 50. There are no restrictions on the amount of foreign or Austrian currency that a bona fide tourist may import into the country. No more than *ASch* 15,000 in local currency may be exported, but there is no restriction on the export of foreign currency.

Banks are open Monday to Friday from 08.00-12.30hrs and 13.30-15.00hrs extended to 17.30hrs on Thursday. The bank counter at the ÖAMTC head office is open during office hours; exchange offices at some main railway stations are open on Saturdays, Sundays and public holidays.

Dimensions and weight restrictions

Private **cars** and towed **trailers** or **caravans** are restricted to the following dimensions — height: 4 metres; width: 2.50 metres; length: 12 metres. The maximum permitted overall length of vehicle/trailer or caravan combination is 18 metres.

Trailers without brakes may weigh up to 750kg and may have a total weight of up to 50% of the towing vehicle.

Driving licence

A valid British licence is acceptable in Austria and although language difficulties may give rise to misunderstanding in a few isolated cases, it is legally valid. The minimum age at which a visitor may drive a temporarily imported car or motorcycle (exceeding 50cc) is 18 years. The Austrian motoring club (ÖAMTC) will supply a free translation of your licence into German, but this is only available from their head office in Vienna and therefore will only be of use if touring in eastern Austria. However, an International Driving Permit is required by the holder of a licence issued in the Republic of Ireland. See under *Driving Licence and International Driving Permit* page 11 for further information.

Emergency messages to tourists

(See also page 11)
Emergency messages to tourists are broadcast daily by Austrian Radio in the *Autofahrer unterwegs* programme. These messages are transmitted in German on short wave between 11.30-12.45hrs Monday to Saturday and 12.00-13.00hrs on Sundays and public holidays.

First-aid kit

(See also page 12)
In Austria all vehicles (including motorcycles) must be equipped with a first-aid kit by law and visitors are expected to comply. This item will not be checked at the frontier, but any motorist can be stopped at the scene of an accident and his first-aid kit demanded; if this is not forthcoming the police may take action.

Hitch-hiking

In Austria, hitch-hiking is generally prohibited on motorways and highways. In Upper Austria, Styria, Burgenland and Vorarlberg hitch-hiking is prohibited for persons under the age of 16.

Horn, use of

The horn must not be used where the relevant sign is displayed (see inside front cover). Generally the use of the horn is prohibited at night in large towns and resort areas; it is prohibited at all times in Wien.

Insurance

(See also page 13)
All temporarily imported trailers must be covered by a separate policy, not the policy covering the towing vehicle.

Lights

(See also page 14)
Although it is prohibited to drive with undipped headlights in built-up areas, motorists may give warning of approach by flashing their lights. It is prohibited to drive on unlit urban motorways and outside built-up areas with sidelights only. In poor visibility motorists may use fog lamps in conjunction with both sidelights and dipped headlights. Parking lights are not required if the vehicle can be seen from 50 metres (55 yds). Lights on lamp-posts which are ringed with red

do not stay on all night and parking lights will be required. It is compulsory for *motorcyclists* to use dipped headlights during the day.

Motoring club

The **Österreichischer Automobil-, Motorrad-und Touring Club** (ÖAMTC) which has its headquarters at *1010 Wien* Schubertring 1-3 ☎ (0222)72990 has offices at the major frontier crossings and is represented in most towns either direct or through provincial motoring clubs. The offices are usually open between 08.30 and 18.00hrs weekdays, 09.00 to 12.00hrs on Saturdays and are closed on Sundays and public holidays. See also page 16 and *Town Plan of Central Wien* pages 72-73.

Motorways

About 805 miles of motorway (Autobahn) are open and more stretches are under construction. A network of just over 1,000 miles is planned. Only three motorways carry a toll; the Brenner Autobahn, the Tauern Autobahn and the Pyhrn Autobahn (Gleinalm and Bosruck Tunnels). The toll for the Brenner Autobahn is *ASch* 120 and return toll tickets *ASch*220.

There are *emergency telephone posts* sited at 2km (1¼m) intervals. Small triangles on the guardrails or limitation posts point towards the nearest emergency telephone. To use the telephone lift the speaking flap and you will be automatically connected to the motorway control. The location of the post is printed inside the speaking flap; read this into the telephone, standing 6 to 8in away from the microphone. If you ask for help and then find you do not need it, you must tell the motorway control. On the Brenner motorway emergency call posts of a different type have been installed. They are coloured red and orange and are furnished with a speaking tube and four levers bearing the symbols for police, Red Cross, repair service and telephone connection. By pressing the appropriate lever, a motorist will be connected with the required emergency service. When one of the first three levers is used, sufficient indication of what type of help is needed is conveyed to the headquarters in Innsbruck; when the telephone connection lever is used a motorist can talk direct to headquarters which will send help if required.

At the top of each telephone post there is an orange/yellow light which flashes if there is danger on that stretch of the motorway.

Orange badge scheme for disabled drivers

(See also page 16)

In Austria badge holders are allowed to park without any time limit in areas where restricted or prohibited parking signs appear (red ring and bars with blue blackground). In some areas the local authority provides special parking places for disabled people's vehicles near hospitals and public service facilities.

Parking

(See also page 17)

Before you leave your vehicle make sure it does not contravene parking regulations; cars must be parked in the direction of the traffic flow. Parking is forbidden on a main road or one carrying fast-moving traffic. In addition, parking is prohibited wherever there is a sign reading *Beschränkung für Halten oder Parken* (restriction for stopping or parking). There is a total ban on stopping on roads which have priority (as a rule Federal roads) in case of fog or any other impediment to visibility. It is forbidden to leave a caravan trailer without its towing vehicle in a public parking place. Spending the night in a vehicle or trailer on the roadside is prohibited.

In *Blue Zones* or short-term parking areas there are no signs other than those on entering the zone, so tourists unfamiliar with the area should be alert to the fact that they will have no reminders. The zones are indicated by the *No Parking* sign bearing the words *Zone* or *Kurzparkzone* and, sometimes, blue road markings. In Wien, Graz, Innsbruck, Klagenfurt, St Veit/Glan, Villach, Völkermarkt and Salzburg a charge is made for all vehicles parked in a *Blue Zone*. Parking tickets must be purchased in advance from the ÖAMTC, banks or tobacconists and the date and time of arrival indicated on the ticket. Parking is allowed for up to 3 hours unless the *Kurzparkzone* sign indicates otherwise. Free parking for up to 90 minutes is allowed in the *Blue Zones* of other towns. However, all vehicles including motorcycles must display a parking disc which is available free of charge from any tobacconist.

In Wien there is no parking in the centre of the city as it is a pedestrian zone. Parking on roads with tram lines is prohibited at night from 15 December to 31 March.

Passengers

(See also page 18)

Children under 12 are not permitted to travel in a vehicle as front-seat passengers unless they are using special seats or safety belts suitable for children.

Petrol
(See also page 18)
Credit cards Petrol stations generally accept recognised credit cards.
Duty-free petrol In addition to the petrol in the vehicle tank up to 10 litres in a can may be imported free of customs duty and tax.
Petrol (leaded) Super benzin (96 Octane) grade.
Petrol (unleaded) is sold in Austria as the Normal benzin (91 octane) grade. Pumps dispensing unleaded petrol may be coloured green, but the octane rating is clearly marked on the individual pumps except for those in a few non-brand garages.

Postal information
Mail Postcards *ASch*4.50; letters up to 20gm *ASch*6.50.
Post offices There are 2,300 post offices in Austria. Opening hours in major towns are from 08.00-17.00hrs Monday to Friday,08.00-10.00hrs Saturday. Elsewhere they are open 08.00-12.00hrs and 14.00-16.00hrs Monday to Friday. Some large offices are open for longer hours.

Postcheques
(See also page 20)
Postcheques may be cashed at all post offices for any amount up to *ASch*1,700 per cheque. Counter positions are identified by the *Postcheque* window sticker. See *Postal information* for post office opening hours.

Priority
Vehicles which continue straight ahead or make a right-hand turn at a crossroads or intersection have priority over oncoming vehicles turning left, providing that there are no signs to the contrary; in this case even trams cede priority. If you wish to turn across the flow of traffic at a junction controlled by a policeman, pass in front of him unless otherwise directed. See also *Priority including Roundabouts* page 21.

Public holidays
Official public holidays in Austria for 1987 are given below. See also *Public holidays* page 21
January 1 (New Year's Day)
January 6 (Epiphany)
April 20 (Easter Monday)
May 1 (Labour Day)
May 28 (Ascension Day)
June 8 (Whit Monday)
June 18 (Corpus Christi)
August 15* (Assumption)
October 26 (National Day)
November 1† (All Saints Day)
December 8 (Immaculate Conception)
December 25 (Christmas Day)
December 26* (St Stephens day)

*Saturday †Sunday

Roads including holiday traffic
The motorist crossing into Austria from any frontier enters a network of well-engineered roads.

The main traffic artery runs from Bregenz in the west to Wien (Vienna) in the east, via the Arlberg Tunnel (Toll: see page 35), Innsbruck, Salzburg, and Linz. Most of the major Alpine roads are excellent, and a comprehensive tour can be made through the Tirol, Salzkammergut and Carinthia without difficulty. Service stations are fairly frequent, even on mountain roads.

In July and August, several roads across the frontier become congested. The main points are on the Lindau-Bregenz road; at the Brenner pass (possible alternative-the Resia Pass); at Kufstien; on the München (Munich)-Salzburg *Autobahn* and on the Villach-Tarvisio road. For details of mountain passes, see page 37. See also *Road conditions* page 22.

Shopping hours
Generally shops are open 08.00-18.00hrs Monday-Friday with a one or two hour break for lunch, except in central Wien where shops do not close for lunch; on Saturday most shops close at midday throughout Austria.

Some shops operate a tax-free service whereby, on leaving the country, visitors are reimbursed for VAT paid. A special form (U34) must be obtained, completed and stamped, from the shop and presented to the Austrian customs when crossing the border. Look for shops displaying the blue 'Tax-free Shopping' sign, or go to the local tourist information or ÖAMTC office for address lists.

Speed limits
(See also page 22)
The beginning of a built-up area is indicated by the sign *Ortsanfang* and the end by a sign bearing the inscription *Ortsende* (end of area) followed by the name of the place. In these areas the maximum speed for all vehicles (except mopeds) is 50 kph (31mph); mopeds 40 kph (24 mph). Outside built-

up areas, private cars are subject to a speed limit of 100kph (62mph) which is increased to 130kph (80 mph) on motorways unless lower speed limits are indicated. Private vehicles towing trailers with a total weight of less than 750kg* (1,650lb) are restricted to 100kph (62mph) on all roads, including motorways, outside built-up areas. If the trailer is over 750kg* then the limit is 100kph on motorways and 80 kph (49 mph) on main roads outside built-up areas. At certain periods during the summer, lower speed restrictions are imposed.

*If the weight of the trailer exceeds that of the towing vehicle or if the total weight of the two vehicles exceeds 3,500kg the limit outside built-up areas is 60kph (37mph) and 70 kph (43mph) on motorways. **Note** When the total weight of the two vehicles exceeds 3,500kg it is not permissible to tow with a motorcar driving licence.

Spiked or studded tyres

Spiked tyres may be used between 15 November and 7 April, although local regulations may extend this period. They may only be used on vehicles with a maximum total authorised weight not exceeding 3,500kg. Spiked tyres must be fitted on all wheels or on two wheels if the drive wheels are fitted with wheel chains. Speed must be restricted to 80kph (49mph) outside built-up areas and 100kph (62mph) on motorways. See also *Cold weather touring* page 8.

Tourist information

(See also page 24)
The Austrian National Tourist Organisation maintains an information office in London at 30 St George Street, W1R 0AL ☎ 01-629 0461 and will be pleased to assist you with any information regarding tourism. In most towns in Austria there will be found a local or regional tourist office which will supply detailed local information.

Traffic lights

(See also page 24)
A flashing green light indicates that the green phase is about to end; a flashing orange light with the red light indicates that the green phase is about to begin.

Using the telephone

(See also page 24)
Insert coin **after** lifting the reciever (instructions in English in many callboxes). Use *ASch*1 coins for local calls and *ASch*10 or *ASch*20 coins for national and international calls.

International callbox identification Boxes with three/four coin slots.

Telephone rates A telephone call to the UK costs *ASch*13.41 for 1 minute.
What to dial for the Irish Republic 00 353.
What to dial for the UK 00 44.

Warning triangle

The use of a warning triangle is compulsory for all vehicles except two-wheelers. The triangle must be placed on the road an adequate distance behind the vehicle or obstacle and must be clearly visible from 200 metres (219yds). See also *Warning triangles/Hazard warning lights* page 25.

Wheel chains

If you plan to motor in areas of high altitude during winter you may find wheel chains are compulsory in certain local conditions. It is probably better to consider hiring or purchasing these at home prior to departure; they can be hired from the AA (allow at least 28 days prior to departure date) or purchased from a multiple car accessory retailer (allow 6-8 weeks for delivery). This will have the advantage of ensuring a proper fit and their availability when you want them. Further, they may be useful at home in certain winter conditions. Alternatively they may be hired from the ÖAMTC for a maximum period of 60 days but a deposit will have to be paid. They are delivered in a packed condition and if they are returned unused then the deposit is returned, less a percentage reduction according to the length of hire. The conditions of hire are fully described in a leaflet issued by the ÖAMTC from any of their offices. See also *Cold weather touring* page 8.

Winter conditions

(See also page 26)
Entry from southern Germany The main approaches to Innsbruck and to Salzburg and Wien (Vienna) are not affected.

Entry from Switzerland The approach to Vorarlberg and Tirol is available at all times through the Arlberg Tunnel (toll).

From Austria into Italy The Resia and Brenner Passes are usually open throughout the year, but snow chains may be necessary in severe weather. The Plöcken Pass is occasionally closed in winter. Roads entering Italy at Dobbiaco and Tarvisco are usually clear, providing an unobstructed throughroute from Wien (Vienna) to Venice.

From Austria to Yugoslavia It is best to travel via Lavamünd and Dravograd, or via Graz and Maribor. Entry via the Wurzen and Seeburg Passes and the Loibl Pass road tunnel is possible but not advised.

Within Austria in the provinces of Upper Austria, lower Austria and Burgenland motoring is unaffected by winter conditions; elsewhere, because of the altitude, it is restricted.

When the Grossglockner Pass is closed, Ost Tirol and Carinthia can be reached by either the Felbertauern road tunnel, the Tauern Autobahn or the Tauern railway tunnel between Böckstein (near Badgastein) and Mallnitz (see page 36).

Winter-sports resorts The main approach roads are swept and are closed only in the most severe weather. Zürs and Lech can be reached via the Arlberg Pass only.

Prices are in Austrian Schillings
Abbreviations
pl platz
str strasse

ACHENKIRCH AM ACHENSEE
Tirol (☎05246)

★**Sporthotel Imhof** ☎6309
15 Dec—20 Oct
🛁🚿30 🚗P40 Lift sB🛁🚿350—410
dB🛁🚿580—700 M100—140 mountains
Credit card [1]

ADMONT
Steiermark (☎03613)

★★***Post*** ☎2416
rm35 (🛁🚿15) 🚗P mountains

AIGEN See **SALZBURG**

ALPBACH
Tirol (☎05336)

★★★★**Böglerhof** (ROM) Dorfpl ☎5227 tx051160
mid Dec—mid Apr & mid May—mid Oct
🛁🚿48 🚗P45 Lift sB🛁🚿580—720
dB🛁🚿800—940 🎾 ▣ ≈ mountains
Credit card [5]

★★**Alpbacher-Hof** ☎5237
Dec—Mar & May—Sep
🛁🚿54 🚗P Lift
sB🛁🚿640—860 dB🛁🚿1280—1520
M180—300 ▣ mountains

ALTAUSSEE
Steiermark (☎06152)

★★★**Tyrol** ☎71636
Apr—Oct
🛁21 🚗P25 Lift ☾ sB🛁445—570
dB🛁890—1140 mountains lake
Credit cards [1] [2] [3] [5]

★★**Hubertushof** Puchen 86 (n. rest) ☎71280
Jun—Sep
🛁🚿8 A1rm 🚗P10 sB🛁🚿380—500
dB🛁🚿760—1160 mountains lake

★★***Kitzer*** Hauptstr 21 ☎71227
rm25 (🛁🚿12) 🚗P80 ☾ mountains lake

ALTMÜNSTER
Oberösterreich (☎07612)

★★**Reiberstorfer** Ebenzweier 27 ☎8105
🛁🚿37 🚗P60 Lift sB🛁🚿335—415
dB🛁🚿590—730 M90—150 mountains lake
Credit cards [1] [2] [3] [5]

AMSTETTEN
Niederösterreich (☎07472)

★★★**Hofmann** Bahnhofstr 2 ☎2517 tx19212
rm60 (🛁🚿39) 🚗P25 Lift ☾ sB230—250
sB🛁🚿260—300 dB430—470
dB🛁🚿490—800
Credit cards [1] [2] [3] [5]

ANIF
Salzburg (☎06246)

★★***Schlosswirt*** (ROM) ☎2175
rm36 (🛁🚿26) A17m 🚗P mountains

ARZL IM PITZTAL
Tirol (☎05412)

★★**Post** ☎3111 tx58240
rm70 (🛁🚿50) A30rm 🚗P30 Lift
sB190—230 sB🛁🚿220—280 dB320—400
dB🛁🚿380—500 M100—130 mountains

ATTERSEE
Oberösterreich (☎07666)

★★**Oberndorfer** ☎364
rm26 (🛁🚿24) 🚗P50 sB280—300
sB🛁🚿420—450 dB🛁🚿740—1360
M150—400 mountains lake
Credit card [2]

AUSSEE (BAD)
Steiermark (☎06152)

★★★**Erzherzog Johann** Kurhausplatz 62 ☎2507 tx03817527
🛁62 P40 Lift ☾ sB🛁630—750
dB🛁1060—1300 mountains
Credit cards [1] [2] [3] [5]

★★**Kristina** Altausseerstr 54 ☎2017
🛁🚿12 🚗P20 sB🛁🚿362—412
dB🛁🚿644—744 M130—150 mountains
Credit cards [1] [2] [5]

★***Stadt Wien*** ☎2068
rm20 (🚿4) P20 mountains
Credit card [2]

BAD Each name preceded by 'Bad' is listed under the name that follows it.

BADEN BEI WEIN
Niederösterreich (☎02252)

★★★**Herzoghof** (BW) Theresiengasse 5 ☎48395 tx14480
🛁🚿86 P8 Lift ☾ sB🛁🚿680—800
dB🛁🚿1080—1200 M100—340 ≈
Credit cards [1] [2] [3] [4] [5]

★★★**Krainerhütte** Helenental ☎44511 tx014303
🛁🚿68 🚗P120 Lift ☾ sB🛁🚿800—900
dB🛁🚿1320—1440 🎾 ▣
Credit cards [1] [2] [5]

★★★**Schloss Wiekersdorf** Schlossgasse 9—11 ☎48301 tx014420
🛁103 P Lift ☾ sB🛁495—650
dB🛁770—1040 Mfr160 🎾 ≈
Credit cards [1] [2] [3] [5]

BADGASTEIN
Salzburg (☎06434)

★★★★***Elisabethpark*** ☎25510 tx67518
Dec—Mar & May—Sep
🛁135 🚗P Lift

★★★★***Habsburgerhof*** Kaiser Wilhelm Prom ☎2561 tx67528
18 Dec—25 Mar & Jun—Sep
🛁45 Lift ☾ ≈ mountains lake

★★★**Eurotel** (BW) ☎25260 tx67556
🛁🚿131 🚗P Lift sB🛁🚿1000
dB🛁🚿1700 🎾 ≈ mountains
Credit cards [1] [2] [3] [5]

★★★**Parkhotel Bellevue** ☎25710 tx67524
15 Dec—15 Oct
rm161 (🛁102) P Lift ☾ sB🛁750—1100
dB🛁1400—2000 M180—300 ≈ ▣ mountains
Credit card [1]

★★★**Savoy (DPn)** ☎2588 tx67668
20 Dec—20 Oct
rm60 (🛁🚿54) 🚗P25 Lift ☾ **DPn** 420—470
M135—270 ≈ mountains
Credit cards [1] [2] [3] [5]

★★**Bristol** ☎2219
Dec—Apr & 15 May—Sep
rm24 (🛁21) P mountains

★★**Grüner Baum** (Relais et Châteaux/ROM) ☎25160 tx67516
17 May—12 Oct & 20 Dec—5 Apr
rm95 (🛁🚿88) 🚗P **Pn**600—900 ≈ mountains

★★***Kurhotel Eden*** ☎2076
rm37 🛁11 P Lift mountains

Austria

BERNSTEIN
Burgenland (☎03354)

★★★**Burg Bernstein**

Etr—Sep
🛁 11 ⌂ **P** sB🛁 470—510 dB🛁 520—560
Mfr130 ≈ mountains
Credit cards [2] [3] [5]

BERWANG
Tirol (☎05674)

★★★**Singer** (Relais et Châteaux) Haus Am Sonnenhang ☎8181 tx5544

13 May—4 Oct & 17 Dec—7 Apr
rm53 (🛁 45) **P**50 Lift sB300—540
sB🛁 360—700 dB540—900
dB🛁 660—1420 M70—300 mountains
Credit card [5]

BEZAU
Vorarlberg (☎05514)

★★**Post** Haupstr ☎2207

20 Dec—20 Oct
🛁 42 **P**45 Lift sB🛁 400—460
dB🛁 900—1100 ▭ mountains

BIRKFELD
Steiermark (☎03174)

🚗 **K & M Friesenbichler** Edelsee 332 ☎4544 **P** For Peu Tal

---

BISCHOFSHOFEN
Salzburg (☎06462)

★**Tirolerwirt** Gasteinerstr 3 ☎2776

🛁🚿 10 A2rm ⌂ **P**10 sB🛁🚿 280—300
dB🛁🚿 540—560 M90—150

BLUDENZ
Vorarlberg (☎05552)

★★**Schlosshotel** ☎63016 tx52175

🛁🚿 36 A6rm ⌂ **P**30 ☾ sB🛁🚿 450—580
dB🛁🚿 660—900 M100—200 mountains
Credit cards [1] [2] [3] [5]

🚗 **W Schmidmayr** Austr 4 ☎62730
P Cit Maz

At **NÜZIDERS** (2.5km NW)

🚗 **S Amann** Walgaustr 83 ☎62387
P Cit Dat Saa

BRAND
Vorarlberg (☎05559)

★★★**Scesaplana** ☎221

May—15 Oct & 15 Dec—15 Apr
🛁 62 **P**100 Lift **DPn**590—1090 M100—250
ﾍ ≈ ▭ mountains
Credit cards [1] [2] [3] [5]

★★**Hämmerle** ☎213

Closed Nov—14 Dec
🛁🚿 35 **P**30 Lift **DPn**250—600 mountains

★***Zimba*** ☎351

Closed Nov
rm21 (🛁🚿 20) A1rm ⌂ **P**30 mountains
Credit cards [1] [2]

BRAZ
Vorarlberg (☎05552)

★**Landhaus Walch** ☎8102

Dec—Sep
🛁🚿 10 ⌂ **P**10 sB🛁🚿 310—335
dB🛁🚿 550—600 mountains
Credit card [2]

BREGENZ
Vorarlberg (☎05574)

★★**Weisses Kreuz** (BW) Römerstr 5 ☎22488 tx57741

🛁🚿 44 **P** Lift ☾ sB🛁🚿 460—720
dB🛁🚿 780—1100 M110—280
Credit cards [1] [2] [3] [5]

BRUCK AN DER GROSS-GLOCKNERSTRASSE
Salzburg (☎06545)

★★**Lukashansl** ☎458

🛁 100 ⌂ **P** Lift sB🛁 330—400
dB🛁 600—750 M100—150 mountains

★***Höllern*** ☎240

15 Dec—Sep
🛁 45 **P** Lift mountains

BRUCK AN DER MUR
Steiermark (☎03862)

★★**Bauer 'Zum Schwarzen Adler'** Mittergasse 23 ☎51331

rm60 (🛁🚿 42) ⌂ **P**13 Lift sB175—215
sB🛁🚿 285—370 dB295—375
dB🛁🚿 475—560 M89—138
Credit cards [1] [2]

★★**Bayer** ☎51218 tx036639

20 Jan—20 Dec
rm33 (🛁🚿 16) **P**40 sB240—260
sB🛁🚿 380—460 dB420 dB🛁🚿 660
M100—200 mountains
Credit cards [1] [2] [3] [5]

🚗 **R Reichl** Grazer Str 17 ☎51633 M/c For

DEUTSCHLANDSBERG
Steiermark (☎03462)

🚗 **Autohaus Hermann** Dr-Verdross-Str 1 ☎3596 M/c **P** Ope

DIENTEN AM HOCHKÖNIG
Salzburg (☎06416)

★***Pesentheiner*** ☎207

Jun—Sep & 18 Dec—20 Apr
rm25 (🛁🚿 18) **P** ≈

DÖBRIACH
Kärnten (☎04246)

🚗 **F Burgstaller** Hauptstr 49 ☎7736 M/c For

DÖLLACH
Kärnten (☎04825)

★★**Schlosswirt** ☎211 tx48180

Closed 11 Jan—4 Apr
rm 58 (🛁🚿 40) **P** sB🛁🚿 395—540 ﾍ U
≈ mountains

DORNBIRN
Vorarlberg (☎05572)

★★★***Park*** Goethestr 6 ☎62691 tx059109

rm35 (🛁🚿 31) **P** Lift ☾

★★**Hirschen** Haselstauderstr 31 ☎66363

🛁🚿 45 A15rm ⌂ **P** ☾ sB🛁🚿 330—350
dB🛁🚿 600—700 mountains

🚗 **E Bohle** Im Schwefel Nr 44 ☎62824
P AR Col

🚗 **Gerster** Schwefel 84 ☎65551 Ope

🚗 **W Luger** Moosmahdstr 10a ☎62602
P Hon

DRASSBURG
Burgenland (☎02686)

★★★***Schloss Drassburg*** ☎2220

Closed 16 Jan—Feb
🛁🚿 35 A19rm ⌂ **P**60 Lift ☾ ﾍ ≈ U
Credit card [5]

DÜRNSTEIN AN DER DONAU
Niederösterreich (☎02711)

★★★**Schloss Dürnstein** (Relais et Châteaux) ☎212 tx71147

20 Mar—10 Nov
🛁🚿 37 **P**35 Lift ☾ sB🛁🚿 650—750
dB🛁🚿 940—1850 M245—320 ≈
Credit cards [1] [2] [3] [5]

★★***Richard Löwenherz*** ☎222 tx071199

Mar—Nov
🛁🚿 46 **P** ☾ ≈

EHRWALD
Tirol (☎05673)

★★★**Schönruh** ☎2322

15 Dec—10 Oct
rm45 (🛁🚿 41) ⌂ **P**35 ☾ sB🛁🚿 540—590
dB🛁🚿 780—880 mountains

★★**Halali** ☎2101

Dec—Oct
🛁🚿 14 ⌂ **P**20 ☾ **DPn**300—480 mountains

★★**Sonnenspitze** Kirchpl 14 ☎2208

Closed Nov
rm32 (🛁🚿 20) ⌂ **P**20 mountains
Credit cards [1] [2] [3]

★★***Spielmann*** Wettersteinstr 24 ☎2225

mid Dec—mid Apr & end May—Sep
rm30 (🛁🚿 28) ⌂ **P**20 sB310—370
sB🛁🚿 390—440 dB520—640
dB🛁🚿 680—780 M130—200 ≈
mountains

EISENSTADT
Burgenland (☎02682)

★★★**Burgenland** Schubertpl 1 ☎5521 tx17527

🛁 88 ⌂ **P** Lift ☾ sB🛁 600—680
dB🛁 840—960 ≈
Credit cards [1] [2] [3] [5]

★**Eisenstadt** Sylvesterstr 5 (n. rest) ☎3350

Apr—15 Nov
rm14 (🛁🚿 5) ⌂ **P**12 sB190—250
sB🛁🚿 320—400 dB290—340
dB🛁🚿 380—500

ENGELHARTSZELL
Oberösterreich (☎07717)

★★**Ronthalerhof** Nibelungenstr ☎8083

🛁🚿 24 ⌂ **P**24 Lift sB🛁🚿 323—370
dB🛁🚿 488—545 M65—120
Credit cards [1] [2] [5]

Austria

ENNS
Oberösterreich (☎07223)

★★***Lauriacum*** Wiener Str 5–7 ☎2315
🛁🚿30 🚗 **P** Lift

EUGENDORF
Salzburg (☎06212)

★★**Wallersee** ☎8675
🛁🚿12 🚗 **P**20 sB🛁🚿290–380
dB🛁🚿460–620 M100–200 mountains
Credit cards 1 2 3

FELD AM SEE
Kärnten (☎04246)

★★**Lindenhof** ☎2274
🛁🚿26 **P**30 **DPn**340–460 🎾 mountains
Credit card 1

FELDKIRCH
Vorarlberg (☎05522)

★★★**Central-Löwen** Neustadt 17
☎22070 tx52311
🛁🚿50 **P** Lift ☾ sB🛁🚿460–500
dB🛁🚿780–840 mountains

★★★***III Park*** ☎24600 tx2119
🛁92 **P** Lift ☾ ≈ mountains

★★**Alpenrose** Rosengasse 6 (n.rest)
☎22175
🛁🚿16 🚗 **P**15 sB🛁🚿350–380
dB🛁🚿550–650
Credit cards 1 2 3 5

🚘 **Stadion** Noflerstr 29 ☎24933
P Hon Saa

FELDKIRCHEN
Kärnten (☎04276)

★★***Dauke*** ☎2413
🛁🚿24 **P** ☾ mountains

🚘 **Pirker** Dr-A-Lemisch-Str 6 ☎2345 M/c
P Ope

🚘 **R Truppe** Ossiacher Bundesstr 14
☎2294 M/c **P** BMW Toy

FRASTANZ
Vorarlberg (☎05522)

★★**Stern** ☎51517 tx52502
Closed 5 Nov–4 Dec
🛁🚿50 A20rm 🚗 **P**100 Lift
sB🛁🚿430–470 dB🛁🚿720–800
M140–180 mountains
Credit cards 1 2 3 4 5

FREISTADT
Oberösterreich (☎07942)

★★**Goldener Hirsch** Böhmerg 8 ☎2258
rm25 (🛁🚿20) **P**5 sB180 sB🛁🚿270
dB340 dB🛁🚿480 M60–130
Credit card 5

FRIESACH
Kärnten (☎04268)

🚘 **M Baier** Neumarkterstr 56 ☎2389 M/c
P Ope

FÜGEN
Tirol (☎05288)

★***Post*** ☎3212
Closed Nov
🛁🚿54 **P**35 Lift sB🛁🚿285–460
dB🛁🚿510–820 M100–250 📺
mountains

FULPMES
Tirol (☎05225)

★★**Alphof** Herrengasse ☎3163
Closed Nov
🛁🚿30 **P**30 Lift sB🛁🚿350–440
M90–120 🎾 mountains
Credit cards 1 2

FÜRSTENFELD
Steiermark (☎03382)

★★***Hitzl*** ☎2144
rm35 (🛁30) **P**

🚘 **M Koller** Fehringer Str 13 ☎2527 M/c **P**
For Mer

FUSCH
Salzburg (☎06546)

★★**Post Hofer** ☎226
20 Dec–15 Oct
🛁🚿45 A14rm 🚗 **P**40 sB🛁🚿180–220
dB🛁🚿360–440 M100–170 🎾 mountains

★**Lamperhäusl** Grossglocknerstr ☎215
8 Dec–Oct
🛁🚿34 🚗 **P**60 sB🛁🚿160–170
dB6🛁🚿270–290 🎾 mountains

FUSCHL AM SEE
Salzburg (☎06226)

★★★***Parkhotel Waldhof*** ☎264
tx632795
Mar 20–Oct
🛁🚿65 **P**50 Lift 📺 mountains lake

★★**Seehotel Schlick** ☎237 tx632795
🛁🚿39 🚗 **P**20 sB🛁🚿330–450
dB🛁🚿660–820 M120–150 ≈
mountains lake
Credit cards 1 2 3 4

GAISBERG
Salzburg (☎0662)

See also **SALZBURG**

★★★**Zistelalm** ☎20104
Closed Nov–14 Dec
rm36 (🛁🚿21) A6rm 🚗 **P** sB215–250
sB🛁🚿315–350 dB450–500
dB🛁🚿670–880 ≈ mountains
Credit cards 1 2 3 5

GALTÜR
Tirol (☎05443)

★★***Berghaus Franz Lorenz*** ☎206
Dec–Apr & 15 Jun–Sep
🛁🚿22 🚗 **P** Lift mountains

★★**Fluchthorn** ☎202 tx58271
Closed Oct–14 Dec
🛁🚿50 🚗 **P**50 Lift ☾ sB🛁🚿430–630
dB🛁🚿720–980 M120–220 mountains

GARGELLEN
Vorarlberg (☎05557)

★★**Alpenrose** ☎6314
Dec–20 Apr & Jun–15 Oct
🛁🚿19 🚗 **P**20 ☾ **DPn**410–760
M150–200 mountains

GASCHURN
Vorarlberg (☎05558)

★★★**Sporthotel Epple** ☎8251 tx52389
Dec–Apr
🛁🚿70 🚗 **P**30 Lift ☾ **DPn**790–1150 🎾
📺 mountains

GASPOLTSHOFEN
Oberösterreich (☎07735)

🚘 **R Danner** Jeding 17 ☎6210 For

GMUNDEN
Oberösterreich (☎07612)

★★★**Parkhotel am See** Schiffslände 17
☎4230
17 May–23 Sep
rm50 (🛁🚿42) 🚗 **P**20 Lift sB455–525
sB🛁🚿530–620 dB780–920
dB🛁🚿930–1110 M95–140 mountains
lake
Credit cards 1 2 3 5

🚘 **L Woffsgruber** Kuferzeile 14–16 ☎4629
P Alf Saa Sko

GOISERN (BAD)
Oberösterreich (☎06135)

★★***Agathawirt*** ☎8341 tx68186
🛁45 🚗 **P**50 ≈ mountains
Credit cards 1 2 3 5

GOLLING
Salzburg (☎06244)

★**Goldener Stern** ☎2200
🛁🚿20 🚗 **P** sB🛁🚿260–395
dB🛁🚿460–670 Mfr85 ≈ 📺 mountains
Credit cards 1 2 3 5

GÖTZENS
Tirol (☎05227)

★***Haus Elisabeth*** ☎8209
rm30 (🛁🚿11) 🚗 **P** mountains

GRAZ
Steiermark (☎0316)

★★★**Daniel** (BW) Europapl 1 ☎911080
tx31182
rm100 (🛁🚿94) 🚗 **P**20 Lift ☾
sB🛁🚿655–820 dB🛁🚿980–1100
M160
Credit cards 1 2 3 4 5

★★★**Park** Leonhardstr 8 ☎33511
tx31498
🛁65 🚗 **P**60 Lift ☾ sB🛁690–740
dB🛁980–1060 M alc
Credit cards 1 2 3 5

★★★**Steirerhof** Jakominipl 12 ☎76356
tx031282
rm94 (🛁🚿89) **P**9 Lift ☾ sB🛁🚿700–1340
dB🛁🚿1006–1700
Credit cards 2 5

★★★Weltzer Goldener Ochs Griesgasse 15 ☎913801 tx31284
rm165 (145) **P**15 Lift sB 655—1010 dB 980—1620 M160
Credit cards 1 2 3 4 5

★★★Alba Wiesler Graz Grieskai 4 ☎913241 tx311130
98 **P** Lift sB 770—948 dB 948—1128 M180
Credit cards 1 2 3 5

★★Mariahilf Mariahilfer Str 9 ☎913163 tx031087
rm44 (36) Lift sB 580—680 dB 850—950 Mfr150
Credit cards 1 2 3 5

E Fior Kärntner Str 69—71 ☎271255
P Dat Ope Peu Tal

A Gaberszik Fabriksgasse 15 ☎911605
P For

J Jacomini Kärtner Str 115 ☎271474
AR DJ Hon

H Krajacic Idlhofgasse 17 ☎912823 **P**
AR Dat

GRIESKIRCHEN
Oberösterreich (☎07248)

R Danner Schlüsslberg ☎32110
P For

GSCHNITZ
Tirol (☎05276)

★★Gschnitzer Hof ☎213
Jun—20 Dec & Sep—20 Apr
rm30 (20) **P**20 sB270—290 sB 310—330 dB480—520 dB 560—600 M80—220 mountains

HAAG See **LINZ**

HAINBURG
Burgenland (☎02165)

G Bauer Hummelstr 1 ☎2366 M/c
P Hon Mer

HALDENSEE
Tirol (☎05675)

★★Rot-Fluh ☎6465 tx05546
78 **P**120 Lift sB 620—770 dB 920—1280 M90—105 mountains lake

HALL IN TIROL
Tirol (☎05223)

★★★Tyrol ☎6621 tx54223
36 **P** sB 390 dB 680 mountains
Credit cards 1 2 3 5

F Autherith Burgfrieden 5 ☎7571 M/c
All makes

Hollaus Burgfrieden 2 ☎6560
P Ope

HALLEIN
Salzburg (☎06245)

★Stern (n.rest) ☎2610
May—Sep

rm35 (12) **P**8 sB220—240 sB 320—340 dB450—460 dB 500—550 mountains

Voith R-Winkler-Str 33a ☎2992
P For

HARTBERG
Steiermark (☎03332)

Kappler Ressavarstr 64 ☎2754 M/c
P Dat

HEILIGENBLUT
Kärnten (☎04824)

★★★★Glocknerhof ☎2244 tx048154
25 May—5 Oct & 15 Dec—15 Apr
rm63 (52) A10rm **P**30 Lift sB 595—745 dB 990—1390 M130—300 mountains
Credit card 1

★★★Kaiser Franz Josef Haus ☎2512 tx48270
15 May—10 Oct
50 **P**50 sB 520—600 dB 1030—1290 M120—250
Credit cards 1 2 3 5

★★★Post ☎2245 tx3476201
Closed Oct—Nov
51 **P**15 Lift sB 350—370 dB 600—640 mountains

M Kramser Pockhorn 29 ☎2122 M/c
P Ope

HEITERWANG
Tirol (☎05674)

★Fischer-Am-See ☎5116
20 Dec—10 Jan, Feb—7 Apr & May—10 Oct
11 **P**50 sB 300—330 alc mountains lake

HINTERSTODER
Oberösterreich (☎07564)

★★★*Berghotel* ☎5421 tx023379
15 Dec—Apr
26 **P** Lift mountains

★Dietigut ☎5248
10 Dec—20 Oct
rm22 (19) A16rm **P DPn**360—390 mountains

HOF BEI SALZBURG
Salzburg (☎06229)

★★★★*Schloss Fusch* (Relais et Châteaux) ☎253 tx0633454
Apr—Oct
86 A40rm **P**100 mountains lake
Credit cards 1 2 3 4 5

HOFGASTEIN (BAD)
Salzburg (☎06432)

★★★Grand Park Kurgarten Str 26 ☎63560 tx 67756
rm92 (87) **P**60 Lift sB 600—1000 dB 1000—2100

M230—260 mountains
Credit card 5

★★Österreichischer Hof Kurgartenstr 9 ☎62160
3 May—11 Oct & 20 Dec—29 Mar
58 **P**16 Lift sB 580—730 dB 1060—1360 M110—130 mountains

IGLS
Tirol (☎05222)

★★★★Sporthotel ☎77241 tx53314
90 **P**50 Lift sB 695—915 Mfr150 mountains
Credit cards 1 2 3 5

★★★Aegidihof Bilgeristr 1 ☎77108 tx54123
Closed Nov
rm29 (27) **P**6 Lift sB430—580 sB 300—400 dB540—680 dB 800—1040 mountains
Credit cards 1 2 3 4 5

★★★Alpenhof (BW) Iglerstr 47 ☎77491 tx054119
15 May—Sep & 15 Dec—30 March
38 **P**25 Lift sB400—450 sB 500—550 dB750—850 dB 950—1050 Mfr120 mountains
Credit cards 1 2 3 4 5

★★★*Park* ☎77035 tx53576
Closed Nov
rm65 (60) **P**30 Lift mountains
Credit cards 1 2 3 4

★★Batzenhäusl ☎77104 tx053495
15 Dec—15 Oct
rm28 (26) **P**25 Lift sB640 sB 590—790 dB630 dB 1080—1380 M120—150 mountains
Credit cards 1 2 3 4

★★Romedihof ☎77141
Jul—Aug
22 **P**14 sB 260 dB 480—600 M90—110 mountains
Credit card 2

★★Waldhotel ☎77272
Dec—Oct
20 **P**18 Lift sB 500—630 dB 840—1000 M140—195 mountains
Credit cards 1 2 3 5

★*Bon-Alpina* Hilberstr 8 ☎77600 tx53509
15 Dec—25 Oct
100 **P**40 Lift lake

★Gothensitz (n.rest) ☎ 77211
rm15 (7) **P**10 sB 260—300 dB340—400 dB 460—500 mountains

IMST
Tirol (☎05412)

★★Post (ROM) Postpl 3 ☎2554
15 Dec—20 Oct
rm42 (30) A2rm **P**30 Lift sB310—360 sB 360—510 dB500—600 dB 640—770 M120—250 mountains
Credit cards 2 3 5

Autohof Imst T-Walch-Str 45 ☎3182
P Ope

INNSBRUCK
Tirol (☎05222)

The area around the Herzog—Friedrich Str is a pedestrian precinct and only open to vehicular traffic at certain times of the day.

★★★★**Europa Tyrol** (SRS) Südtirolerpl 2 ☎35571 tx53424
→⋔131 ⌂P45 Lift ☾ sB→⋔1045—1655 dB→⋔1590—2790 M200 mountains
Credit cards 1 2 3 5

★★★★**Holiday Inn** Salurnerstr 15 ☎365010 tx53484
→⋔194 P Lift ☾ sB→⋔1150—1670 dB→⋔1950—2630 M120—160 ▣ mountains
Credit cards 1 2 3 4 5

★★★**Goldener Adler** Herzog—Friedrich Str 6 ☎26334 tx53415
→⋔37 P Lift ☾ sB→⋔600—800 dB→⋔800—1600 Mfr170 mountains
Credit cards 1 2 3 4 5

★★★**Maria Theresia** (BW) Maria Theresienstr 31 ☎35615 tx053300
→⋔104 P100 Lift ☾ sB→⋔615—945 dB→⋔975—1485 M150
Credit cards 1 2 3 4 5

★★★**Schwarzer Adler** (ROM) Kaiserjagerstr 2 ☎27109
→⋔30 P Lift ☾ sB→⋔600—850 dB→⋔900—1400 M170—180 mountains
Credit cards 1 2 3 5

★★***Binder*** Dr. Glatzstr 20 ☎42236 tx054404
rm36 (→⋔16) ⌂P ☾ mountains

★★**Central** Erlerstr 11 ☎24866 tx53824
→⋔87 P Lift ☾ sB→⋔800—1200 dB→⋔1100—1680 ▣ mountains
Credit cards 1 2 3 5

★★**Grauer Bär** Universitätstr 5—7 ☎34531 tx053387
rm135 (→⋔115) P30 Lift ☾ sB610—650 sB→⋔740—800 dB920—1000 dB→⋔1180—1300 Mfr150 mountains
Credit cards 1 2 3 5

★★**Ibis** Schützenstrasse 43 ☎65544 tx054433
→⋔96 ⌂P45 Lift ☾ sB→⋔450—610 dB→⋔640—870 M130 mountains
Credit cards 1 2 3 5

★**Greif** Leopoldstr 3 ☎27401 tx53111
→⋔66 P15 Lift ☾ sB→⋔520—800 dB→⋔820—1300 mountains

★**Paula** Weiherburggasse 15 (n.rest) ☎37795
rm13 (→⋔6) P10 sB200—220 sB→⋔300—340 dB340—360 dB→⋔440—500 mountains

At **NEURUM**

W Lüftner Austr 10 ☎61204 **P** Dat Peu Tal

At **VÖLS** (5km W on No 1A)

Auto—Meisinger Innsbruckstr 57 ☎(95)34516 **P** AR DJ LR Peu RR

Austria

IRDNING
Steiermark (☎03682)

★★★**Schloss Pichlarn** Gatschen 28 ☎2841 tx38190
Closed Nov—19 Dec
→⋔72 ⌂P70 Lift ☾ **Pn**1200—3000 Mfr250 🎾 ≈ ▣ ▣ ∪ mountains
Credit cards 1 2 3 5

ISCHL (BAD)
Oberösterreich (☎06132)

★★★★**Kurhotel** (BW) Voglhuberstr 10 ☎4271 tx68127
→⋔115 ⌂P50 Lift ☾ sB→⋔780—880 dB→⋔1400—1560 M145—165 ≈ mountains
Credit cards 1 2 3 5

★★**Freischütz** Rottenbach 96 ☎3354
Apr—Oct
rm25 (→8) ⌂P30 sB170—200 sB→300 dB340—400 dB→540—600 M85—100 mountains

ITTER
Tirol (☎05332)

★★**Tirolerhof** ☎2690
20 May—Sep & 20 Dec—Mar
→⋔63 A15rm P30 Lift sB→⋔260—280 dB→⋔450—500 Malc ≈ mountains
Credit cards 2 3

JUDENBURG
Steiermark (☎03572)

Kienzl Burggasse 103 ☎3572 M/c **P** For

JUDENSTEIN See **RINN**

KANZELHOHE—ANNENHEIM
Kärnten (☎04248)

★★★**Sonnenhotel** ☎2713
Jun—Sep & Dec—Mar
→34 P25 Lift **DPn**400—560 Mrfr120 🎾 ▣ ≈ mountains
Credit card 2

KITZBÜHEL
Tirol (☎05356)

★★★★***Hirzingerhof*** Schwarzsee Str 8 ☎3211 tx05117124
Jun—1 Dec
→⋔26 ⌂P30 Lift mountains
Credit cards 1 2 3 5

★★★★**Tennerhof** (ROM) Griesenauweg ☎3181 tx5118426
30 May—6 Oct
→⋔42 ⌂P25 ☾ sB→⋔560—1075 dB→⋔860—1670 M240—360&alc ≈ ▣ mountains
Credit cards 1 3 5

★★★**Goldener Greif** ☎4311 tx5117118
18 May—12 Oct & 13 Dec & 12 Apr
→⋔55 P Lift ☾ mountains
Credit cards 2 3 5

★★★**Schloss Lebenberg** Lebenbergstr 17 ☎4301 tx5118414
Apr—15 Oct & 15 Dec—10 May
→96 ⌂P Lift ☾ ▣ lake mountains
Credit cards 1 2 3 5

★★**Erika** J—Pirchistr 21 ☎4885 tx051264
18 May—5 Oct
→36 ⌂P35 Lift **DPn**480—520 ▣ mountains
Credit cards 2 5

★★***Klausner*** Bahnhofstr ☎2136 tx05118418
mid Dec—Mar & mid May—Oct
rm48 (→⋔44) ⌂P20 Lift ☾ mountains
Credit cards 1 2

★★**Schweizerhof** Hahnenkampstr 4 ☎2735 tx51370
May—Oct & Dec—Apr
rm42 (→⋔41) ⌂P22 sB400—500 sB→⋔450—700 dB→⋔800—1200 M130—200 mountains
Credit cards 2 5

Herz J—Pirchl Str 30 ☎4638 **P** For

KLAGENFURT
Kärnten (☎04222)

★★★**Sandwirt** (BW) Pernhartgasse 9 ☎56209 tx422329
rm55 (→⋔40) ⌂P Lift ☾ sB440—480 sB→⋔540—810 dB740—770 dB→⋔1100—1340 Mfr190 mountains
Credit cards 1 2 3 5

★★**Kurhotel Carinthia** 8 Maistr 41 (n.rest) ☎511645 tx422399
→32 P20 Lift ☾ sB→590—960 dB→820—1520 mountains
Credit cards 1 2 3 4 5

Joweinig Südbahngürtel 14 ☎32307 Dat Saa

Kaposi Pischeldorfer Str219 ☎42200 M/c **P** For

J Sintschnig Südbahngürtel 8 ☎32144 **P** For

A Wiesner Rosentalerstr 205 ☎22206 **P** AR

KLOSTERNEUBURG
Niederösterreich (☎02243)

★★★**Martinschloss** Martinstr 34—36 ☎7426 tx114257
rm32 (→⋔29) A5rm **P**29 ☾ sB→⋔550—1350 dB800—900 dB→⋔1000—1850 Malc ≈ mountains
Credit cards 1 2 3 5

F Nagl Wiener Str 152 ☎2392 M/c **P** Ope

KNITTELFELD
Steiermark (☎03512)

Weidlinger Wienerstr 40 ☎2789 Ren

KÖFLACH
Steiermark (☎03144)

At **PICHLING**

H Mayer Lagerstr 10 ☎2195 **P** Toy

KÖTSCHACH-MAUTHEN
Kärnten (☎04715)

★★**Post** ☎221
15 Dec–1 Nov
27 P30 sB 330–350
dB 560–600 M85–100 mountains
Credit cards 1 2 3

J Schwarzenbacher Nr 181 ☎343 M/c
P Ope

KREMS AN DER DONAU
Niederösterreich (☎02732)

★★★***Park*** E–Hofbauerstr 19 ☎3266
tx071130
72 **P** Lift ☾

Auer Wiener Str 82 ☎3501 M/c Ope Vol

H Kneth Hafenstr 65 ☎3662
P For

K Teuschl Hafenstr 50 ☎3428
P Alf Col AR DJ

KRIMML
Salzburg (☎06564)

★★**Klockerhaus** ☎208 tx66552
40 **P** Lift sB 300–340
dB 520–620 M80–120 mountains

KUFSTEIN
Tirol (☎05372)

A Relbmayr Fischergries 16 ☎2141 **P**
Ope

LANDECK
Tirol (☎05442)

★★***Post*** Maiserstr 19 ☎2383
75 **P** Lift ☾ mountains

At **ZAMS** (2km NE)

Auto-Plaseller Buntweg 8 ☎2304 For

LECH AM ARLBERG
Vorarlberg (☎05583)

★★★**Post** (Relais et Châteaux/ROM)
☎2206 tx5239118
28 Jun–Sep
41 A4rm **P50** Lift ☾ sB 600
dB 800–900 M120–350
mountains

★★★**Tannbergerhof** ☎2202 tx5239117
Jun–Sep & Dec–Apr
30 **P**(summer only) Lift ☾(winter
only) sB 450–1510
dB 800–2840 M230–500 mountains

★★**Arlberg** ☎2134 tx05239122
Jul–Sep & Nov–Apr
46 **P22** Lift ☾ **DPn**540–1370
M250–310 mountains
Credit cards 1 2 5

★★**Schneider** ☎3500 tx5239115
Sep–20 Apr
rm64 (62) **P** Lift ☾ **Pn**1540–2600
mountains

LERMOOS
Tirol (☎05673)

★★★**Drei Mohren** Haupstr 25 ☎2362
tx05558
rm50 (44) **P** Lift sB370–485

sB 570–620 dB310–390
dB 360–580 mountains

★★***Post*** ☎2281
Dec–Oct
rm61(48) **P25** sB309–489
sB 439–589 dB538–838
dB 738–1038 Mfr150 mountains

★***Loisach*** Unterdorf 6 ☎2394
20 Dec–15 Oct
46 **P40** Lift mountains
Credit cards 2 3 5

J Hundertpfund Innsbruckerstr 25
☎2411 M/c Toy

LEUTASCH WEIDACH
Tirol (☎05214)

★***Waldheim*** ☎6288
rm12 (6) **P** mountains

LIENZ
Tirol (☎04852)

★★★**Traube** (Relais et Châteaux/ROM)
Haupt Pl 14 ☎2551 tx46515
50 **P5** Lift ☾ sB 490–800
dB 980–1520 mountains
Credit cards 1 2 3 5

★★**Glocknerhof** Schillerster 4 ☎2167
20 Dec–16 Apr & May–Oct
16 **P20** sB 245–270
dB 490–540 mountains
Credit cards 1 2 3 5

★★**Post** Südtirolerpl 7 ☎2505
rm26 (25) **P** ☾ mountains

★★**Sonne** (BW) Südtirolerpl ☎3311
tx46661
rm57 (50) **P** Lift ☾
sB 490–540 dB 860–940
mountains
Credit cards 1 2 3 4 5

W Rogen Kärntner Str 36 ☎2335 M/c
Ope Vau

G Troger Dr-K-Renner Str 12 ☎3411 For

LIEZEN
Steiermark (☎03612)

★★**Karow** Bahnhofstr 4 ☎22381
rm33 (10) **P30** sB250–280
sB 290–320 dB450–520
dB 580–640 M100–150 mountains

LINZ AN DER DONAU
Oberösterreich (☎0732)

★★★★**Schillerpark** Rainerstr2–4
☎554050 tx022107
107 Lift ☾ sB 1010
dB 1350
Credit cards 1 2 3 4 5

★★★★**Spitz** K-Fiedlerstr 6 ☎236441
tx22784
56 **P** Lift ☾ sB fr830
dB fr1160

★★★★**Tourotel** Untere Donaulände 9
☎275075 tx21962
176 **P40** Lift ☾ sB 920–1070
dB 1120–1370
Credit cards 1 2 3 5

★★★***Ebelsbergerhof*** Wiener Str 485
☎42125 tx022415
40 **P** Lift ☾

★★★**Mercure** Wankmüllerhofstr 39
☎42361 tx21795
rm105 (95) **P100** Lift ☾ sB 865
dB 1100 Mfr140
Credit cards 1 2 3 5

★★★**Novotel** Wankmüllerhofstr 37
☎47281 tx22618
115 **P150** Lift ☾ sB 490
dB 660
Credit cards 1 2 3 5

★★***Wolfinger*** ☎73291
rm22 (9) **P** Lift ☾

Günther Hamerlingstr 13–15
☎(0732)55025

At **HAAG** (6 km SW)

Tarbuk Welserstr 17–19 ☎56461
P AR Dat DJ Saa Sko Tal

At **PASCHING** (10 km SW)

F Mitterbauer Wagram 195 ☎61028 Toy

LOFER
Salzburg (☎06588)

★★★★**St-Hubertus** ☎266 tx66547
Closed Nov
55 **P** Lift sB 320–390
dB 520–780 M100–450 mountains
Credit cards 1 2

★★**Bräu** Hauptstr ☎2070 tx66535
27 **P** Lift sB 520–770
dB 420–670 mountains

★★**Post** Hauptpl ☎3030 tx66535
16 Dec–Mar & 20 May–15 Sep
rm35 (17) **P40** sB320–465
sB 420–670 dB220–385
dB 320–570 mountains
Credit cards 1 2 3 5

★**Lintner** ☎240 tx66533
20 Dec–10 Oct
rm28 (14) **P25** sB265–325
sB 265–325 dB630–690
dB 950–1010 M90–100 mountains
Credit cards 1 2 3 4 5

MATREI
Tirol (☎04875)

J Mayr Lienzer Str 38 ☎6554 M/c
P Ope

MATTSEE
Salzburg (☎06217)

★★**Gasthof Post** ☎207
May–Oct
rm22 (20) A5rm **P50**
sB 265–285 dB470–510
dB 530–570 M80–120

MAYRHOFEN
Tirol (☎05285)

★★★***Krammerwirt*** ☎2615 tx53841
15 Dec—5 Nov
rm70 (⇌ ⋒62) **P** Lift

MILLSTATT
Kärnten (☎04766)

★★***Forelle*** ☎2050
1 May—15 Oct
rm50 (⇌ ⋒47) **P**35 Lift ☾ ✂ ⛱ mountains lake

MONDSEE
Oberösterreich (☎06232)

★★★**Euromotel Mondsee** (ETAP)
Innerschwandt 150 ☎2876 tx633357
⇌46 **P**100 Lift ☾ sB⇌685 dB⇌1130 Mfr140 ⛱ mountains lake
Credit cards [1] [2] [5]

★★★**Mondsee** (n.rest) ☎2154
rm25 (⇌22) ⌂ **P**40 ☾ sB⇌495—550 dB⇌900—990 ⛱ mountains
Credit cards [2] [3] [5]

★**Leitnerbräu** Marktpl 9 ☎2219
rm18 (⇌ ⋒6) A10rm ⌂ **P**20 sB205 dB410 dB⇌ ⋒410—480 M80—180
Credit cards [1] [2] [3]

🚗 **M Stabauer** Herzog-Odilo-Str 82 ☎2476 For

W Widlroither Südtiroler Str 4 ☎2612 M/c AR Toy

At **LOIBICHL** (14 km SE)

★★**Seehof am Mondsee** ☎25500
16 May—22 Sep
⇌22 ⌂ **P**80 sB⇌630—1270 dB⇌1260—2540 M200—320 ✂ ⛱ mountains lake
Credit cards [2] [3] [5]

MUTTERS
Tirol (☎05222)

★★**Muttererhof** ☎27491
20 Dec—10 Apr & May—25 Oct
rm23 (⇌ ⋒17) ⌂ **P**30 sB310 sB⇌ ⋒350 dB560 dB⇌ ⋒640 M105—135 ▭ mountains

NATTERS
Tirol (☎05222)

★**Eichhof** ☎266555
May—Oct
rm20 (⋒5) **P**20 **DPn**fr250 M45—100 mountains

★**Steffi** ☎29402
15 Jun—10 Sep
⋒12 ⌂ **P**4 sB⋒fr220 dB⋒fr400 mountains

NAUDERS
Tirol (☎05473)

★★***Tirolerhof*** ☎255 tx58172
Dec—Sep
⇌ ⋒70 ⌂ **P**40 Lift ☾ mountains ▭
Credit cards [1] [2] [3] [5]

★**Post** ☎202
30 May—Sep
rm60 (⇌ ⋒51) ⌂ **P**30 sB190—230 sB⇌ ⋒230—260 dB320—400 dB⇌ ⋒400—460 mountains

★**Verzasca** (n.rest) ☎237
15 Dec—15 Apr & Jun—Sep
rm18 (⇌ ⋒10) ⌂ **P**14 sB150—250 sB⇌ ⋒250—350 dB200—300 dB⇌ ⋒400—600 mountains

NEUMARKT AM WALLERSEE
Salzburg (☎06216)

★**Lauterbacher** ☎456
⇌ ⋒10 ⌂ **P**20 sB⇌ ⋒220—230 dB⇌ ⋒360—380 mountains lake

NEURUM See **INNSBRUCK**

NEUSIEDL AM SEE
Burgenland (☎02167)

★★★**Wende** (BW) Seestr 40—42 ☎8111 tx18182
⇌ ⋒106 ⌂ **P**200 Lift ☾ sB⇌ ⋒440—490 dB⇌ ⋒790—850 ✂ ⛱
Credit cards [1] [2] [3] [5]

NÜZIDERS See **BLUDENZ**

OBERGURGL
Tirol (☎05256)

★★★**Edelweiss & Gurgl** ☎223 tx54347
Closed mid Oct—mid Nov
⇌ ⋒97 ⌂ **P** Lift **Pn**450—1800 ▭ mountains
Credit cards [1] [2] [5]

OBERTAUERN
Salzburg (☎06456)

★★**Pohl** ☎209
21 Jun—21 Sep & 7 Dec—20 Apr
⇌ ⋒17 **P**30 dB⇌ ⋒380—860 M110—180 mountains
Credit card [5]

OBERTRAUN
Oberösterreich (☎06135)

★★**Berghotel Krippenstein** ☎7129
22 Dec—15 Oct
rm42 (⋒25) **P** Lift sB245 dBfr490 dB⋒fr560 mountains
Credit cards [1] [2] [5]

OETZ
Tirol (☎05252)

★★**Alpenhotel Oetz** Bielefeldstr 4 ☎6232
⇌ ⋒53 **P**30 Lift sB⇌ ⋒280—330 dB⇌ ⋒500—600 M110 mountains
Credit card [2]

★★**Drei Mohren** Haupstr ☎6301
⇌ ⋒24 ⌂ **P**50 Lift sB⇌ ⋒295—365 dB⇌ ⋒590—730 ✂ mountains
Credit cards [1] [2] [3] [4] [5]

PARTENEN
Vorarlberg (☎05558)

★★★**Bielerhohe** ☎246
12 May—6 Oct
rm50 (⇌ ⋒31) ⌂ **P** Lift ⛱ mountains lake

PASCHING See **LINZ**

PATSCH
Tirol (☎05222)

★★***Grünwalderhof*** ☎77304
15 May—Sep & 18 Dec—15 Mar
rm30 (⇌ ⋒22) ⌂ **P** ✂ ⛱ mountains

PERCHTOLDSDORF
Niederösterreich (☎0222)

🚗 **K Skala** Vierbatzstr 3 ☎862345 **P** Ren

PERTISAU AM ACHENSEE
Tirol (☎05243)

★★***Pfandler*** ☎5223 tx54180
15 Dec—15 Oct
⇌ ⋒54 **P** Lift mountains lake

PICHLING See **KÖFLACH**

PÖRTSCHACH AM WÖRTHERSEE
Kärnten (☎04272)

★★★★**Park** Elisabethstr 22 ☎26210 tx422344
May—15 Oct
⇌ ⋒182 ⌂ **P** Lift ☾ sB⇌ ⋒685—1035 dB⇌ ⋒1210—1850 M185 ✂ ▭ lake

★★★***Schloss Leonstein*** ☎28160 tx422019
25 May—Sep
rm37 (⇌ ⋒32) ⌂ **P** ☾ ✂

★★**Sonnengrund** Annastr 9 ☎2343
20 Apr—10 Oct
rm48 (⇌ ⋒44) **P**21 Lift sB410—670 sB⇌ ⋒410—870 dB540—820 dB⇌ ⋒540—1020 M120—180 mountains lake

★★**Schloss Seefels** (Relais et Châteaux)
Töschling 1 ☎2377 tx422153
Closed mid Oct—mid Dec
rm86 (⇌ ⋒73) A40rm **P**70 ☾ sB550—850 sB⇌ ⋒550—1160 dB900—1700 dB⇌ ⋒1100—2960 ✂ ⛱ ▭ lake
Credit cards [1] [2] [3] [5]

★★***Werzer Astoria*** Werzer Promenade 8 ☎2231 tx422940
May—Oct
rm125 (⇌ ⋒109) **P** Lift ☾ ✂ ⛱ lake

RAABS AN DER THAYA
Niederösterreich (☎02846)

🚗 **Steinmetz & Dallamassl**
Karlsteinerstrasse 2 ☎290
P BMW For Vol

RADENTHEIN
Kärnten (☎04246)

★★**Metzgerwirt** ☎2052
rm20 (⋒18) ⌂ **P** sB260 sB⋒360 dB420 dB⋒520 mountains

RAURIS
Salzburg (☎06544)

★★***Rauriserhof*** ☎213
rm94 (⇌ ⋒56) Lift ⛱

REITH See **SEEFELD**

Austria

REUTTE
Tirol (☎05672)

★★**Tirolerhof** Bahnhofstr 16 ☎2557
15 Dec—5 Nov
rm37 (→ ⋒ 25) ⌂ **P** Lift sB220
sB → ⋒ 240—280 dB400 dB → ⋒ 440—520
mountains

⛟ **Auto-Schiaffer** Allgäuer Str 68 ☎2622
M/c Cit Toy

RINN
Tirol (☎05223)

At **JUDENSTEIN** (1km N)

★★***Judenstein*** ☎8168
rm32(→ ⋒ 20) ⌂ **P** Lift ≏

SAALBACH
Salzburg (☎06541)

★★★**Bergers Sporthotel** ☎577 tx66504
Closed Oct & Nov
→ ⋒ 55 ⌂ **P**30 Lift ☾ **DPn**440—1030
M80—180 ▣ mountains
Credit cards [1] [2] [3] [5]

★★★**Kendler** ☎225 tx066508
20 Dec—Mar & 15 May—Sep
→ 52 ⌂ **P**50 Lift sB → 395—480
dB → 610—1040 M150 mountains
Credit cards [1] [2] [3]

★★**Saalbacherhof** ☎7111 tx66502
Dec—15 Nov
→ ⋒ 100 ⌂ **P**60 Lift ☾ sB → ⋒ 980—1300
dB → ⋒ 1560—2200 ⚲ ≏ mountains
Credit cards [2] [5]

SAALFELDEN
Salzburg (☎06582)

★★**Dick** Bahnhofstr 106 ☎2215
15 Dec—Oct
rm30 (→ ⋒ 25) ⌂ **P**20 sB320—370
sB → ⋒ 380—450 dB540—640
dB → ⋒ 660—780 M120—180 ≏
mountains

★★**Schoerhof** ☎2210
→ ⋒ 30 A2rm ⌂ **P60 DPn**335—375
M40—90 ≏ mountains
Credit cards [1] [2] [3]

G Altendorfer Loferer Bundesstr 13 ☎2085
Ope

ST ANTON
Vorarlberg (☎05552)

★★★**Adler** ☎7118
Closed Nov
rm35 (→ ⋒ 23) ⌂ **P60** Lift sB345—495
sB → ⋒ 445—575 dB590—790
dB → ⋒ 790—990 M110—180 ≏
mountains

ST ANTON AM ARLBERG
Tirol (☎05446)

★★★***Post & Alte Post*** ☎2213
Dec—Oct
→ ⋒ 56 **P** Lift ☾ mountains

★★***Montjola*** ☎2302
2 Dec—15 Apr
rm20 (→ ⋒ 18) A9rm **P** mountains

★**Bergheim** (n.rest) ☎2255
Dec—Apr
rm30 (→ ⋒ 27) ⌂ **P** sB270—350
sB → ⋒ 360—460 dB500—700
dB → ⋒ 700—920 mountains

ST GILGEN AM WOLFGANGSEE
Salzburg (☎06227)

★★★**Parkhotel Billroth** ☎217
May—Sep
rm45 (→ ⋒ 43) **P**60 ☾ sB330—550
sB → ⋒ 375—650 dB600—1200
dB → ⋒ 650—1300 M100—170 ⚲ ≏
mountains lake
Credit cards [2] [4] [5]

★★**Alpenland am See** (n.rest) ☎330
Jun—Sep
→ ⋒ 16 ⌂ **P**10 sB → ⋒ 130—190
dB → ⋒ 260—460 ≏ mountains lake

★★**Hollweger** Mondseer Bundesstr 2
☎226
15 Dec—Oct
→ ⋒ 42 A8rm ⌂ **P** sB → ⋒ 380—540
dB → ⋒ 540—1020 mountains lake

★★***Radetzky*** Streicherpl 1 ☎232
Apr—Oct
rm25 (→ ⋒ 14) **P** mountains lake

★**Mozartblick** (n.rest) ☎403
rm27 (→ ⋒ 25) A12rm ⌂ **P**14
sB → ⋒ 150—175 dB260—300
dB → ⋒ 280—350 mountains lake

ST JOHANN IM PONGAU
Salzburg (☎06412)

★★★***Prem*** ☎6320
→ 38 A7rm ⌂ **P** Lift ⚲ mountains
Credit cards [1] [2]

ST JOHANN IN TIROL
Tirol (☎05352)

★★**Kaiserhof** ☎2577
15 Dec—Sep
rm35 (→ ⋒ 26) ⌂ **P**30 Lift
sB → ⋒ 480—710 dB → ⋒ 880—1300
M120—250 mountains
Credit cards [1] [3]

⛟ **E Foidl** Pass Thurn Str 11 ☎2129
AR Dat LR

⛟ **F Reiter** Fieberbranner Str 35 ☎2417 For

⛟ **Auto-Sparer** Innsbrucker Str 21 ☎2385
M/c **P** Ope

ST MICHAEL IM LUNGAU
Salzburg (☎06477)

⛟ **H Neubauer** Höf Nr 39 ☎260
P Ope

ST PÖLTEN
Niederösterreich (☎02742)

⛟ **M Hänfling** Kremser Landstr 67 ☎62838
AR Dai Hon

⛟ **Schirak** Porschestr 19 ☎67531
P Alf Dat Saa

ST VALENTIN
Niederösterreich (☎07435)

★★★**St Valentin** Westautobahn ☎2002
tx19275
rm48 (→ ⋒ 42) ⌂ **P**100 sB → ⋒ 450—480
dB → ⋒ 700—760
Credit cards [1] [2] [3] [5]

ST WOLFGANG AM WOLFGANGSEE
Oberösterreich (☎06138)

★★★**Weisses Rossl** (ROM) ☎2306
tx68148
rm68 (→ 49) ⌂ **P**42 Lift ☾ sB300—450
sB → 500—700 dB → 600—1300
M125—190 ⚲ ≏ ▣ lake
Credit cards [1] [2] [3] [5]

★★***Appesbach*** ☎2209
15 Apr—15 Oct
→ ⋒ 21 A7rm **P** ⚲ mountains lake

★★**Post & Schloss Elbenstein** ☎2346
Apr—Oct
rm130 (→ ⋒ 120) ⌂ **P** Lift sB215—270
sB → ⋒ 375—450 dB430—540
dB → ⋒ 570—820 ▣ ≏ mountains lake
Credit cards [1] [2] [3] [4] [5]

SALZBURG
Salzburg (☎0662)

See also **GAISBERG**

★★★★★**Schloss Mönchstein** (BW) am
Mönchsberg 26 ☎8413630 tx632080
Mar—Oct & Dec—Jan
→ ⋒ 17 ⌂ **P**25 Lift ☾ sB → ⋒ 1200—2000
dB → ⋒ 2000—4800 ⚲
Credit cards [1] [2] [3] [5]

★★★★***Europa*** Rainerstr 31 ☎73391
tx06-33424
→ ⋒ 104 **P**35 Lift ☾ mountains
Credit cards [1] [2] [3] [5]

★★★★**Österreichischer Hof** (SRS)
Schwarzstr 5—7 ☎72541 tx633590
→ ⋒ 124 ⌂ **P**60 Lift ☾ sB → ⋒ 1075—1375
dB → ⋒ 1360—2530 M280—350
Credit cards [1] [2] [3] [5]

★★★★**Winkler** F-Josefstr 7—9 ☎73513
tx633961
→ 103 **P** Lift ☾ sB → 765—940
dB → 1280—1570 mountains
Credit cards [1] [2] [3] [5]

★★★**Auersperg** Auerspergstr 61
☎71721 tx633817
→ ⋒ 55 ⌂ **P**16 Lift ☾ sB → ⋒ 470—840
dB → ⋒ 710—1360
Credit cards [1] [2] [3] [5]

★★★**Gablerbräu** Linzergasse 9 ☎73441
tx631067
rm54 (→ ⋒ 53) Lift ☾ sB → ⋒ 510—630
dB → ⋒ 920—1120 Mfr130
Credit cards [1] [2] [3] [5]

★★★***Goldener Hirsch*** Getreidegasse 37
☎41511 tx632967
→ 56 **P** Lift ☾ mountains
Credit cards [1] [2] [3] [5]

★★★**Kasererhof** (BW) Alpenstr 6
☎21265 tx633477
→ ⋒ 53 **P** Lift ☾ sB → ⋒ 810—1260

dB ➡ ⋔ 1615–2415 M200 mountains
Credit cards [1] [2] [3]

★★★**Schlosshotel St-Rupert** Morzgerstr 31 ☎843231
Apr–Oct
rm30 (➡ ⋔ 23) ⌂ **P**40 ☾ sB800–900 sB ➡ ⋔ 1000–1100 dB1000–1100 dB ➡ ⋔ 1600–2200 M280–440&alc mountains
Credit cards [1] [2] [3] [5]

★★**Carlton** Markus Sittikusstr 3 ☎74343
7 Jan–20 Dec
rm43 (➡ ⋔ 22) ⌂ **P**10 Lift ☾ sB330–400 sB ➡ ⋔ 390–470 dB580–720 dB ➡ ⋔ 840–960 M90–95

★★**Gastein** Ignaz Rieder Kai 25 (n.rest) ☎22565 tx632760
➡ ⋔ 12 ⌂ **P**10 ☾ sB ➡ ⋔ 800–1200 dB ➡ ⋔ 1400–1800 mountains
Credit cards [1] [2] [3] [4] [5]

★★**Markus Sittikus** M-Sittikusstr 20 (n.rest) ☎71121
rm40 (➡ ⋔ 33) **P** Lift ☾ sB360–395 sB ➡ ⋔ 490–630 dB590–690 dB ➡ ⋔ 790–990
Credit cards [1] [2] [3] [5]

★★**Pitter** Rainerstr 6–8 ☎78571 tx633532
➡ ⋔ 220 ☾ sB ➡ ⋔ 570–850 dB ➡ ⋔ 990–1600 M170–190
Credit cards [1] [2] [3] [4] [5]

★★**Schwarzes Rössl** Priesterhausgasse 6 (n.rest) ☎74426
Jul–Sep
rm51 (➡ 4) **P** Lift ☾ sBfr310 sB ➡ fr375 dBfr490 dB ➡ fr620
Credit cards [1] [2] [3]

★★**Stein** Staatsbrücke ☎74346
22 Dec–25 Oct
rm80 (➡ 41) Lift ☾ sB420–500 sB ➡ ⋔ 560–640 dB680–800 dB ➡ ⋔ 900–1100 M150–160

★★***Traube*** Linzergasse 4 (n.rest) ☎74062
Jul–Sep
rm40 (➡ ⋔ 22) Lift ☾
Credit cards [2] [3]

★★**Weisse Taube** Kaigasse 9 (n.rest) ☎842404 tx633065
rm30 (➡ ⋔ 28) **P** Lift sB360–390 sB ➡ ⋔ 580–650 dB580–680 dB ➡ ⋔ 860–1250
Credit cards [1] [2] [3] [4] [5]

★***Elefant*** S-Haffnergasse 4 ☎43397 tx632725
➡ ⋔ 37 **P** Lift ☾ M alc
Credit cards [1] [2] [3] [5]

Auto-Grasser Sterneckstr 28–30 ☎76314 **P** AR DJ Maz RR

M & J J Decker Alpenstr 142 ☎20477 M/c **P** Ope

G Eibl Linzer-Bundesstr 39 ☎78435 Toy

Fieber Wasserfeldstr 15 ☎50515 **P** AR Dat DJ LR Saa

E Scheidinger Schallmoser Hauptstr 24 ☎71176 For

Austria

At **AIGEN** (3km SE)

★★★**Doktorwirt** Glaserstr 9 ☎22973 tx632938
➡ ⋔ 39 ⌂ **P**35 sB ➡ ⋔ 400–520 dB ➡ ⋔ 600–850 M100–150 ≈ mountains
Credit cards [1] [2] [3]

SANDL
Oberösterreich (☎07944)

★★***Braun*** ☎250
Closed Apr & Nov
➡ ⋔ 18 **P**20
Credit card [1]

SCHALLERBACH (BAD)
Oberösterreich (☎07249)

★★**Grünes Türl** ☎8163
➡ 30 ⌂ **P**100 sB ➡ 314–336 dB ➡ 628–672 M70–170 ⚲
Credit cards [1] [2] [3] [5]

SCHÄRDING
Oberösterreich (☎07712)

★★**Schärdinger Hof** Innsbruckstr 8 ☎2651 tx027459
rm31 (➡ ⋔ 26) ⌂ **P** sB240 sB ➡ ⋔ 290 dB400 dB ➡ ⋔ 500 ⚲

F Psotka Haraberg 12 ☎2647 **P** For

F Schachner Haid 21 ☎2845 AR Dat

SCHLADMING
Steiermark (☎03687)

★★★**Alte Post** (ROM) ☎22571 tx38282
Closed 27 Oct–27 Nov
➡ ⋔ 34 **P**25 Lift sB ➡ ⋔ 530–660 dB ➡ ⋔ 880–1140 M100–130 mountains
Credit cards [1] [2] [5]

SCHUTTDORF See ZELL AM SEE

SCHWECHAT See WIEN (VIENNA)

SEEBODEN
Kärnten (☎04762)

★★★★***Royal Hotel Seehof*** ☎81714 tx048122
2 May–2 Oct
➡ ⋔ 75 A29rm ⌂ **P**50 Lift ⚲ ≈ ▭ mountains lake

★★**Seehotel Steiner** ☎81713
May–Oct
➡ ⋔ 50 ⌂ **P**40 ☾ sB ➡ ⋔ 350–470 dB ➡ ⋔ 700–940 ⚲ ≈ ▭ mountains lake

SEEFELD
Tirol (☎05212)

★★★★**Astoria** ☎2272 tx05-385523
Dec–Mar & Jun–Aug
➡ ⋔ 53 ⌂ **P**40 Lift ☾ **Pn**640–970 ▭ mountains

★★★★**Gartenhotel Tümmlerhof** ☎2571 tx232/3522350
Dec–Mar & Jun–Sep
➡ 66 ⌂ **P**50 Lift ☾ **DPn**540–1400 ≈ ▭ mountains

★★★**Philipp** Münchnerstr 68 ☎2301 tx5385526
May–Oct
➡ ⋔ 60 ⌂ **P**10 Lift ☾ sB ➡ ⋔ 350–400 dB ➡ ⋔ 500–800 M150–200 mountains
Credit cards [1] [2] [3] [5]

Auto-Nemeth Münchner Str 75 ☎2407 **P** For

At **REITH** (2km S)

★★★**Alpenkönig Crest** ☎3220 tx054665
➡ 150 ⌂ **P** Lift ☾ sB ➡ 1070–2550 dB ➡ 1540–4500 ⚲ ≈ ▭ mountains
Credit cards [1] [2] [3] [4] [5]

SEEKIRCHEN
Salzburg (☎06212)

I & J Heiss-Hutticher Hauptstr 14 ☎236 **P** Toy

SERFAUS
Tirol (☎05476)

★***Furgler*** ☎6201
Dec–Oct
➡ ⋔ 42 ⌂ **P** Lift ≈ mountains

SÖLDEN
Tirol (☎05254)

★★★***Central*** ☎2260 tx053353
Jul–Apr
➡ 70 **P** Lift ☾ ⚲ ≈ mountains

★★★**Sonne** ☎2203
rm84 (➡ ⋔ 73) A55rm ⌂ **P**15 sB ➡ ⋔ 250–300 dB ➡ ⋔ 500–600 ⚲ mountains

SPITTAL AN DER DRAU
Kärnten (☎04762)

★★★**Salzburg** Tirolerstr 12 ☎3165 tx048111
➡ ⋔ 85 ⌂ **P**20 Lift ☾ **DPn**450 M100&alc ▭
Credit cards [1] [2] [3] [5]

J Buchleitner Neuer Pl 21 ☎3421

STEINACH AM BRENNER
Tirol (☎05272)

★★★***Post*** ☎6239 tx53245
Nov–Sep
rm34 (➡ ⋔ 29) A4rm ⌂ **P** ☾ mountains

★★★**Weisses Rossl** Brennerstr 23 ☎6206
20 Dec–25 Mar
➡ ⋔ 43 A27rm ⌂ **P** Lift sB ➡ ⋔ 400–420 dB ➡ ⋔ 620–700 ▭ mountains

★★***Steinacherhof*** ☎6241 tx54440
Dec–Oct
➡ 60 ⌂ **P**30 Lift ☾ ⚲ ▭ mountains
Credit cards [1] [2] [3] [5]

★★**Wilder Mann** ☎6210 tx53245
20 Dec–6 Apr & May–15 Oct →

🛁🚿51 A3rm 🏠P25 Lift sB🛁🚿455—575 dB🛁🚿830—1110 M70—150 🎾 ▣ mountains
Credit cards [1] [5]

STEINAKIRCHEN AM FORST
Niederösterreich (☎07488)

★★★**Schloss Ernegg** ☎214 tx19289
May—Sep
rm20 (🛁🚿15) **P**35 sB395—544 sB🛁🚿465—698 dB590—868 dB🛁🚿730—1176 ◪ Ω
Credit cards [3] [5]

STEYR
Oberösterreich (☎07252)

★★★**Mader** Stadtpl 36 ☎23358 tx028302
🛁🚿55 🏠**P**5 Lift sB🛁🚿420—480 dB🛁🚿560—680 M80—150
Credit cards [1] [3]

★★**Ibis** Eisenstr 18 ☎22327 tx28319
🛁🚿42 **P** sB🛁🚿fr400 dB🛁🚿fr500

★★**Minichmayr** Haratzmüllerstr 1 ☎23410 tx028134
🛁🚿51 **P**30 Lift ☾ sB🛁🚿250—515 dB🛁🚿430—715 lake
Credit cards [2] [5]

STUBEN
Vorarlberg (☎05582)

★★***Post*** ☎761 tx052459
15 Dec—20 Apr & Jun—Sep
rm47 (🛁🚿33) A19rm **P**5 mountains
Credit cards [1] [3]

TELFS
Tirol (☎05262)

★**Hohe Munde** Untermarkstr 17 ☎2408
rm23 (🛁🚿20) 🏠**P**20 sB🛁🚿285 dB🛁🚿470 ▣ mountains
Credit cards [1] [2] [3] [5]

🚗 **Prantl** Untermarkt 72 ☎4041 Ope

THIERSEE
Tirol (☎05376)

★★**Haus Charlotte** ☎5500
27 Mar—15 Oct & 15 Dec—2 Mar
rm35 (🛁🚿30) A10rm 🏠**P**45 Lift sB350—610 sB🛁🚿450—750 dB700—960 dB🛁🚿960—1140 M60—170 ▣ mountains lake

TRAUNKIRCHEN AM TRAUNSEE
Oberösterreich (☎07617)

★★***Post*** ☎307 tx24555
🛁60 **P**50 Lift ≈ mountains lake
Credit cards [1] [2] [3] [5]

TURRACHER-HÖHE
Kärnten (☎04275)

★★***Hochschober*** ☎8213 tx422152
12 Apr—6 Oct
rm72 (🛁🚿58) A15rm 🏠**P** 🎾 ▣ lake mountains

UNTERGURGL
Tirol (☎05256)

★★**Alpenglühn** (n.rest) ☎301
Oct—May

Austria

🛁🚿12 **P**12 sB🛁🚿310—450 dB🛁🚿520—800 mountains

VELDEN AM WÖRTHERSEE
Kärnten (☎04274)

★★★**Schloss Velden** am Corso 24 ☎2655
15 May—25 Sep
rm105 (🛁101) 🏠**P**100 ☾ 🎾 ≈ lake
Credit card [2]

★★★**Seehotel Europa** (BW) Wrannpark 1—3 ☎2770 tx422608
May—Oct
🛁🚿64 **P** Lift ☾ sB🛁🚿850 dB🛁🚿1700 🎾 mountains lake
Credit cards [1] [2] [3] [5]

★★★**Seehotel Veldnerhof-Mösslacher** am Corso 17 ☎2018
May—Oct
rm107 (🛁🚿81) **P** Lift ☾ 🎾 ≈ lake
Credit card [2]

★★**Alte Post-Wrann** Europapl 4 ☎2141 tx422608
🛁🚿40 🏠**P**30 sB🛁🚿340—500 dB🛁🚿600—900 M120—160 🎾 ≈ mountains
Credit cards [1] [2] [3] [5]

★★**Seehotel Hubertushof** ☎2676
May—20 Oct
🛁🚿35 A15rm **P**30 sB🛁🚿370—780 dB🛁🚿680—1450 M180 🎾 ▣ ≈ mountains lake

VIENNA See **WIEN**

VILLACH
Kärnten (☎04242)

★★★***City*** Bahnhof pl 3 ☎27896 tx45602
🛁🚿61 **P**30 Lift ☾ mountains
Credit cards [1] [2] [3] [4] [5]

★★★**Parkhotel** Moritschstr 2 ☎23300 tx045582
🛁170 🏠**P**100 Lift ☾ sB🛁410—690 dB🛁710—1260 M125—185 mountains
Credit cards [1] [2] [5]

★★**Mosser** Bahnhofstr 9 ☎24115 tx45728
🛁🚿30 **P**50 ☾ sB🛁🚿400—510 dB🛁🚿700—800 M100—150
Credit cards [1] [2] [3] [5]

★★***Post*** (ROM) Hauptpl 26 ☎26101 tx45723
🛁🚿77 **P** Lift ☾ mountains

🚗 **S Papp** Steinwenderstr 15 ☎24826 **P** For

🚗 **R Prohinig** St-Georgen 117 ☎28186 **P** AR Hon

🚗 **R Thalmeiner** Tiroler Str 19 ☎24590 **P** Ope

At **WARMBAD** (5km S)

★★★**Josefinenhof** ☎25531 tx45652
rm61 (🛁🚿50) **P**50 Lift ☾ sB480—660 sB🛁🚿580—930 dB🛁🚿1100—1820 Mfr150 🎾 ≈ ▣ mountains
Credit card [3]

VÖCKLABRUCK
Oberösterreich (☎07672)

🚗 **Autohandels** R-Kunz Str 3 ☎4295 **P** Dat Fia

VOITSBERG
Steiermark (☎03142)

🚗 **Rossmann** Grazer Vorstadt 72 ☎2670 For

VÖLKERMARKT
Kärnten (☎04232)

🚗 **R Pribasnig** Grifferstr 11 ☎2229 M/c **P** Ope

VÖLS See **INNSBRUCK**

VÖSENDORF See **WIEN (VIENNA)**

WAIDRING
Tirol (☎05353)

★★**Tiroler Adler** ☎5311
Closed Nov—14 Dec
🛁🚿35 🏠**P**20 Lift sB🛁🚿420—470 dB🛁🚿840—940 M90—140 mountains
Credit cards [1] [5]

WALCHSEE
Tirol (☎05374)

🚗 **A Greiderer** Dorf 16 ☎5620 M/c **P** For

WARMBAD See **VILLACH**

WELS
Oberösterreich (☎07242)

★★★**Rosenberger** (BW) Adlerstr 1 ☎82236 tx0613732211
🛁106 🏠**P**400 Lift sB🛁730 dB🛁1060
Credit cards [1] [2] [3] [5]

🚗 **Mühlbachler** Eferdingerstr 69 ☎82902 AR Hon

🚗 **Reiter** Salzburgerstr 178 ☎6590 M/c **P** Toy

WESTENDORF
Tirol (☎05334)

★**Jakobwirt** ☎6245
Dec—Mar & May—Sep
🛁🚿60 **P**20 Lift ☾ sB🛁🚿440—470 dB🛁🚿760—820 ▣ mountains
Credit cards [1] [4]

WIEN (VIENNA) (☎0222)

See Plan page 72
Bezirk I

★★★★★**Ambassador** Neuer Markt 5 ☎51466 tx111906 Plan **1**
🛁🚿107 **P** Lift ☾ sB🛁🚿1000—1500 dB🛁🚿1450—2400 Mfr270
Credit cards [2] [3] [4] [5]

★★★★★**Bristol** (SRS) Kärntner Ring 1 ☎529552 tx112474 Plan **2**
🛁152 **P** Lift ☾ sB🛁1820—2520 dB🛁2340—3640
Credit cards [1] [2] [3] [5]

★★★★★**Imperial** Kärntner Ring 16 ☎651765 tx112630 Plan **3**
🛁🚿158 **P** Lift ☾ sB🛁🚿1820—2760

dB 🛁 🚿 2440—4440 Mfr480 🎾 ⛱ 📺 🏊
U
Credit cards 1 2 4 5

★★★★★**Sacher** Philharmonikerstr 4 ☎525575 tx112520 Plan **5**

rm124 (🛁 🚿 118) **P** Lift ☾ sBfr600 sB 🛁 🚿 1100—1600 dB 🛁 🚿 1900—3000 Mfr480

★★★★**Europa** Neuer Markt 3 ☎515940 tx112292 Plan **6**

🛁 102 **P** Lift ☾ sB 🛁 1220 dB 🛁 1770 M280
Credit cards 1 2 3 5

★★★★**Parkring** (BW) Parkring 12 ☎526524 tx113420 Plan **7**

🛁 64 🚗 Lift ☾ sB 🛁 1245—1355 dB 🛁 1730—1810 Mfr270
Credit cards 1 2 3 5

★★★★**Royal** Singerstr 3 ☎524631 tx112870 Plan **9**

🛁 81 **P** Lift ☾ sB 🛁 650—1150 dB 🛁 990—1980
Credit cards 1 2 3 5

★★★★**Stephansplatz** Stephanspl 9 ☎635605 tx114334 Plan **9A**

🛁 🚿 62 Lift ☾ sB 🛁 🚿 1040 dB 🛁 🚿 1540
Credit cards 1 2 3 5

★★★**Amadeus** Wildpretmarkt 5 (n.rest) ☎638738 Plan **10A**

7 Jan—22 Dec
🛁 🚿 30 Lift ☾ sB 🛁 🚿 890—1200 dB 🛁 🚿 1540
Credit cards 2 4

★★★***Astoria*** Kärnterstr ☎526585 tx112856 Plan **11**

rm108 (🛁 103) **P** Lift 🚗

★★★**Kärntnerhof** Grashofgasse 4 (n.rest) ☎521923 tx112535 Plan **16**

rm45 (🛁 🚿 36) **P**10 Lift ☾ sB490 sB 🛁 🚿 730 dB740 dB 🛁 🚿 980—1160
Credit cards 1 2 3 5

★★★**Römischer Kaiser** (BW/ROM) Anngasse 16 (n.rest) ☎527751 tx113696 Plan **19**

🛁 🚿 27 **P** Lift ☾ sB 🛁 🚿 1100 dB 🛁 🚿 1800
Credit cards 1 2 3 5

★★**Austria** Wolfengasse 3 (n.rest) ☎51523 tx112848 Plan **24**

rm51 (🛁 🚿 40) **P**10 Lift ☾ sB480—580 sB 🛁 🚿 690—860 dB710—830 dB 🛁 🚿 1050—1280
Credit cards 1 2 3 5

★★**Graben** Dorotheergasse 3 ☎521531 tx114700 Plan **25**

🛁 46 **P** Lift ☾ sB 🛁 750—1250 dB 🛁 980—1600
Credit cards 1 2 3 4 5

Bezirk II

🚗 **E Glaser** Czerningasse II ☎246465 **P** Alf AR Saa

Bezirk III

★★★★★***Hilton International*** am Stadtpark ☎752652 tx136799 Plan **2A**

Austria

🛁 620 🚗 **P** Lift ☾
Credit cards 1 2 3 4 5

★★★★★***Inter-Continental*** Johannesgasse 28 ☎7505 tx131235 Plan **4**

🛁 498 🚗 **P** Lift ☾ 🎾

★★★**ETAP Vienna** am Heumarkt Ecke Lisztstr ☎752535 tx111822 Plan **13A**

🛁 🚿 211 🚗 **P**39 Lift ☾ sB 🛁 🚿 875—990 dB 🛁 🚿 1150—1380
Credit cards 1 2 3 5

★★★***Palais Schwarzenberg*** (Relais et Châteaux) Schwarzenbergpl 9 ☎784515 tx136124 Plan **17**

🛁 40 🚗 **P**50 Lift ☾ 🎾 ⛱
Credit cards 1 2 3 4 5

Bezirk IV

★★★★**Erzherzog Rainer** (BW) Wiedner Hauptstr 27—29 ☎654646 tx132329 Plan **5A**

🛁 🚿 84 🚗 Lift ☾ sB 🛁 🚿 1050—1200 dB 🛁 🚿 1400—1660
Credit cards 1 2 3 4 5

★★★★**Prinz Eugen** (ETAP) Wiedner Gürtel 14 ☎651741 tx132483 Plan **8**

🛁 🚿 110 **P** Lift ☾ sB 🛁 🚿 690—1100 dB 🛁 🚿 1040—1810 M245
Credit cards 1 2 3 4 5

★★★**Kaiserhof** (BW) Frankenberggasse 10 ☎651701 tx136872 Plan **15**

🛁 🚿 74 **P** Lift ☾ sB 🛁 🚿 680—850 dB 🛁 🚿 880—1300 M140
Credit cards 1 2 3 5

Bezirk V

★★★**Alba** Margarethenstr 53 ☎58800 tx113264 Plan **10**

🛁 48 🚗 **P**8 Lift ☾ sB 🛁 850—1090 dB 🛁 1150—1540 M180
Credit cards 1 2 3 4 5

Bezirk VI

★★★**Tyrol** Mariahilferstr 15 ☎564134 tx111885 Plan **21**

🛁 🚿 40 **P**3 Lift ☾ sB 🛁 🚿 720—750 dB 🛁 🚿 1180—1240 M100—120

★★**Ibis** M-Hilfergürtel 22—24 ☎565626 tx133833 Plan **25A**

🛁 🚿 341 🚗 **P** Lift ☾ sB 🛁 🚿 780—980 dB 🛁 🚿 1070—1270

🚗 **G Wittek** Liniengasse 28—30 ☎564283 For

Bezirk VIII

★★★**Weisser Hahn** Josefstädter Str 22 ☎423648 tx115533 Plan **23**

rm62 (🛁 🚿 54) Lift ☾ sB480—540 sB 🛁 🚿 625—830 dB 🛁 🚿 1120—1650 M180
Credit cards 1 2 3 5

Bezirk IX

★★★**Bellevue** Althanstr 5 ☎3456310 tx114906 Plan **12**

🛁 🚿 160 🚗 **P**15 Lift ☾ sB 🛁 🚿 fr1050 dB 🛁 🚿 fr1450 Mfr190
Credit cards 1 2 3 5

★★★**Regina** Rooseveltpl 15 ☎427681 tx114700 Plan **18A**

rm128 (🛁 🚿 124) **P** Lift ☾ sB 🛁 🚿 680—1130 dB 🛁 🚿 900—1700
Credit cards 1 2 3 5

Bezirk X

🚗 **E Janko** Laxenburgerstr 96 ☎641638 BMW Hon RR

Bezirk XIII

★★★**Parkhotel Schönbrunn** (SRS) Hietzinger Hauptstr 10—14 ☎822676 tx132513 Plan **18**

rm500 (🛁 🚿 431) A92rm 🚗 **P** Lift ☾ sB 🛁 🚿 895—1385 dB 🛁 🚿 1690—2300 Mfr290 📺
Credit cards 1 2 3 4 5

Bezirk XIV

★★★***Novotel Wien West*** Autobahnstation Auhof ☎972542 tx135584 Not on plan

🛁 114 **P**300 Lift ☾ ⛱
Credit cards 1 2 3 5

Bezirk XV

★★***Stieglbräu*** Mariahilferstr 156 (n.rest) ☎833621 tx133636 Plan **28**

rm54 (🛁 🚿 41) Lift ☾

Bezirk XVII

★★**Madeleine** Geblergasse 21 (n.rest) ☎434741 tx115121 Plan **26**

🛁 80 🚗 **P**15 Lift ☾ sB 🛁 590—810 dB 🛁 900—1320 M150
Credit cards 1 2 3 4 5

🚗 **R Moser** Hernalser Hauptstr 220 ☎463190

🚗 **P Reimann** Bergsteiggasse 48 ☎424471 **P** Toy

Bezirk XIX

★★★***Kahlenberg*** Kahlenberg ☎321251 tx74970 Plan **14**

rm32 (🛁 🚿 28) **P** Lift

Bezirk XX

Stahl Heistergasse 4—6 ☎334601 AR Dai Hon

Bezirk XXIII

E Hanzl Draschestr 36 ☎671159 **P** Toy

🚗 **H Hölbl** Dr-H-Wenzelgasse 20 ☎691329 Toy

🚗 **J Holzer** Gregorygasse 8 ☎842561 **P** Toy

🚗 **Wöhrer** R-Strauss-Str 17 ☎612525 M/c **P** Hon Peu Tal

At **SCHWECHAT** (Airport) (10kmSE)

★★★**Novotel** ☎776666 tx111566 Not on plan

🛁 🚿 187 **P**120 Lift ☾ sB 🛁 🚿 fr950 dB 🛁 🚿 fr1280 ⛱
Credit cards 1 2 3 5

WIEN (VIENNA) Bezirk

1	★★★★★	Ambassador	I
2	★★★★★	Bristol	I
2A	★★★★★	Hilton International	III
3	★★★★★	Imperial	I
4	★★★★★	Inter-Continental	III
5	★★★★★	Sacher	I
5A	★★★★	Erzherzog Rainer	IV
6	★★★★	Europa	I
7	★★★★	Parkring	I
8	★★★★	Prinz Eugen	IV
9	★★★★	Royal	I
9A	★★★★	Stephansplatz	I
10	★★★	Alba	V
10a	★★★	Amadeus	I
11	★★★	Astoria	I
12	★★★	Bellevue	IX
13A	★★★	ETAP Vienna	III
14	★★★	Kahlenberg	XIX
15	★★★	Kaiserhof	IV
16	★★★	Kärntnerhof	I
17	★★★	Palais Schwarzenberg	III
18	★★★	Parkhotel Schönbrunn	XIII
18A	★★★	Regina	IX
19	★★★	Römischer Kaiser	I
21	★★★	Tyrol	VI
23	★★★	Weisser Hahn	VIII
24	★★	Austria	I
25	★★	Graben	I
25A	★★	Ibis	VI
26	★★	Madeleine	XVII
28	★★	Stieglbräu	XV

At **VÖSENDORF** (10km S)

★★★**Novotel Wien Süd** ☎692601 tx134793 Not on plan

🛁 102 **P**100 Lift ☾ sB🛁 685–900 dB🛁 905–1180 M80–300 ⛰ mountains
Credit cards 1 2 3 5

WIENER NEUSTADT
Niederösterreich (☎02622)

★★★**Corvinus** Ferdinand Porsche Ring ☎413438 tx16724

🛁 68 **P**50 Lift ☾ sB🛁 580–620 dB🛁 790–860 M130–260
Credit cards 1 2 3 5

WÖRGL
Tirol (☎05332)

★★★**Angath Rosenburger** (BW) ☎4375 tx51135

🛁 45 **P**100 Lift sB🛁 592 dB🛁 879 M125 mountains
Credit cards 1 2 3 5

★★***Central*** Bahnhofstr 27 ☎2459 rm55 (🛁 🚿 28) A7rm **P** Lift ⛰ mountains

F Holzknecht Innsbrucker Str 64 ☎2928 **P** Ope

YBBS AN DER DONAU
Niederösterreich (☎07412)

★***Steiner*** Burgpl 2 ☎2629

🛁 🚿 20 A40rm **P**

ZAMS See **LANDECK**

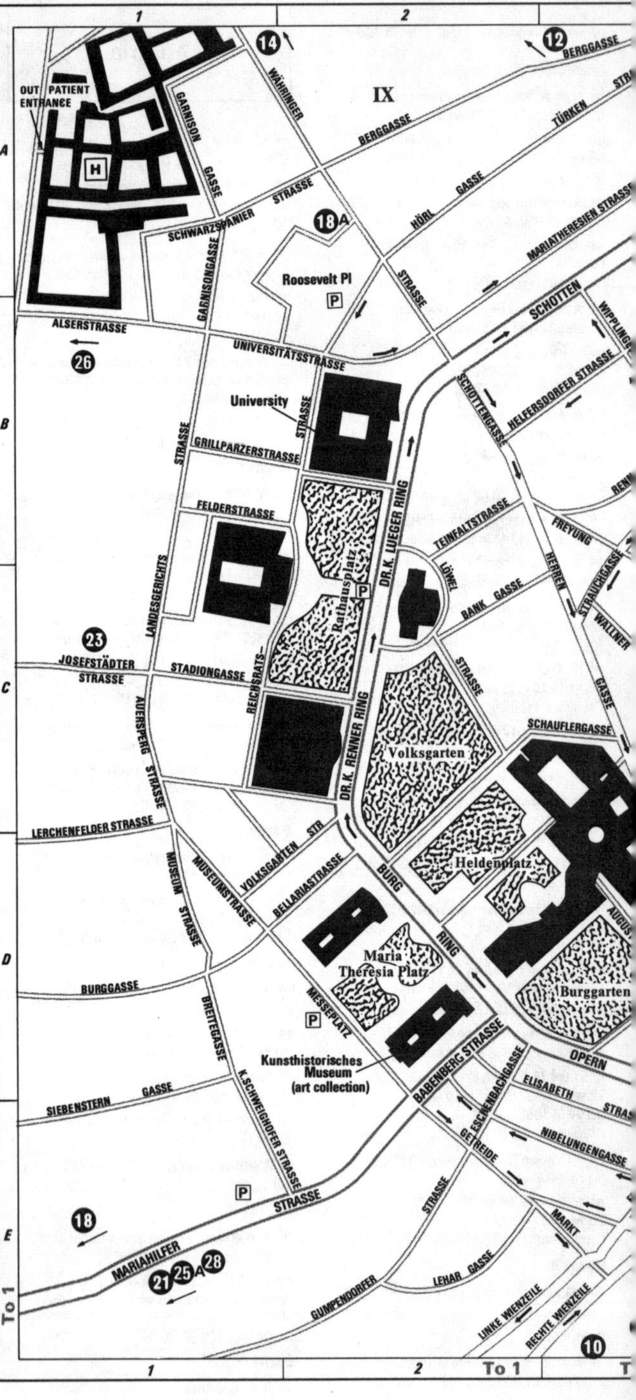

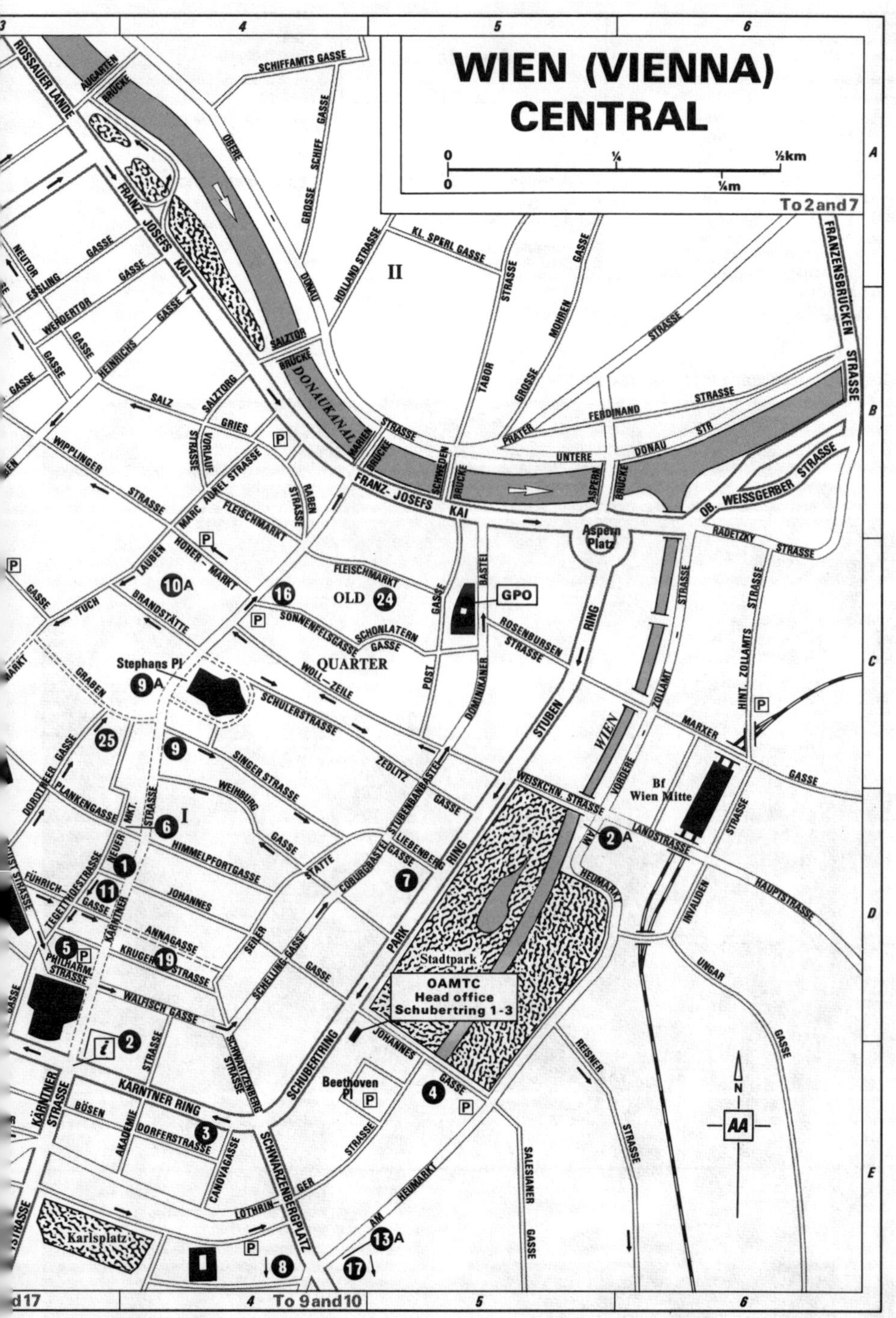
WIEN (VIENNA)
CENTRAL
0
¼
½km
0
¼m
To 2 and 7
To 9 and 10
Donaukanal
Franz-Josefs Kai
Stephans Pl
Old Quarter
GPO
Aspern Platz
Bf Wien Mitte
Stadtpark
OAMTC
Head office
Schubertring 1-3
Beethoven Pl
Karlsplatz
Schwarzenbergplatz
Kärntner Ring
Schubertring
Park Ring
Stuben Ring
Landstrasse
Hauptstrasse

ZELL AM SEE
Salzburg (☎06542)

★★★**St Georg** (BW) Schillerstr ☎3533 tx66706

20 Dec—15 Apr & 30 May—15 Oct
🛁 37 🏠 **P**20 Lift sB 🛁 520—700
dB 🛁 1040—1500 ⛆ mountains
Credit cards [1] [2] [3] [5]

★★**Berner** N-Gassner-Promenade 1 ☎2557 tx66630

Closed Oct & Nov
🛁 30 **P**25 Lift sB 🛁 300—440
dB 🛁 520—800 M80—120 lake mountains
Credit cards [2] [3]

🚗 **K Lederer** Loferer Bundestr 25 ☎2441 Hon Mer

Austria

ZELL AM ZILLER
Tirol (☎05282)

★★★***Tirolerhof*** ☎2227

22 Dec—9 Oct
🚿 40 **P** Lift mountains

🚗 **W Haidacher** An der Umfahrungsstr ☎3112 M/c **P** Fia Hon

ZIRL
Tirol (☎05238)

★★**Goldener Löwe** (BW) Hauptpl ☎2330 tx53350

🛁 12 🏠 **P**50 sB 🛁 470—540
dB 🛁 740—855 mountains
Credit cards [1] [2] [3] [4] [5]

ZÜRS AM ARLBERG
Vorarlberg (☎05583)

★★★***Zürserhof*** ☎513 tx5239114

24 Nov—15 Apr
🛁 120 🏠 **P** Lift ☾

A view of Mirabellgarten and Mirabell Castle, Saltzburg

Belgium

International distinguishing sign

Area *11,775 sq miles*
Population *9,800,000*
Local time *GMT + 1*
(Summer GMT + 2)

National flag
Vertical tricolour of black, yellow and red

How to get there

Many cross-Channel ferries operate direct from Dover to Oostende or from Dover, Felixstowe and Hull to Zeebrugge. Alternatively, it is possible to use the shorter Channel crossings from Dover to France and drive along the coastal road to Belgium. Fast hovercraft services operate from Dover to Calais and Boulogne.

Motoring regulations and general information

This information should be read in conjunction with the general content of the European ABC (pages 4-26). **Note** As certain regulations and requirements are common to many countries they are covered by one entry in the ABC and the following headings represent some of the subjects dealt with in this way:

Crash or safety helmets
Drinking and driving
Fire extinguisher
First-aid kit
Insurance
International distinguishing sign
Medical treatment
Mirrors
Overtaking
Police fines
Radio telephones/Radio transmitters
Road signs
Seat belts
Tyres
Visitors' registration

AA Port agent

8400 Oostende G E Huyghe & Son, Zuidstraat 10 ☎ (059) 702855. See also *AA Agents* page 5 and *Town Plan of Oostende* page 87.

Accidents

Fire and **ambulance** ☎ 900 **police** ☎ 901 (and also 906 in Antwerpen, Bruxelles, Brugge, Charleroi, Gent, Liege and Mechelen). The police must be called if an unoccupied stationary vehicle is damaged or if injuries are caused to persons; in the latter case the car must not be moved, see recommendations under *Accidents* page 5.

Accommodation

The official hotel guide classifies hotels 1-4 according to the *Benelux Classification*. Standards for amenities and comfort are laid down by law for establishments designated as *Hotel, Pension, Hostellerie, Auberge, Gasthof* and *Motel*. Such hotels exhibit the distinctive sign issued by the Belgian Tourist Office.

Room prices are exhibited in hotel reception areas and full details of all charges including service and taxes are shown in each room. They are subject to approval by the Ministry of Economic Affairs.

There is a reservation service operated by Belgium Tourist Reservations (BTR), BP41, 1000 Bruxelles 23 ☎ (02)2305029 or telex 65888 who provide a free hotel booking service throughout the country. Once in Belgium tourist offices in major towns can also arrange hotel bookings for visitors; the service is free but a deposit is payable in advance which will be deducted from the final bill.

Boats

When temporarily importing boats into Belgium documentation, in addition to the *Customs regulations* referred to below, may be required if your route takes you through France. See *Boats* page 6 for further information.

Breakdown

The Belgian motoring club, Touring Club Royal de Belgique (TCB), maintains an efficient breakdown service known as Touring Secours/Touring Wegenhulp. The Touring

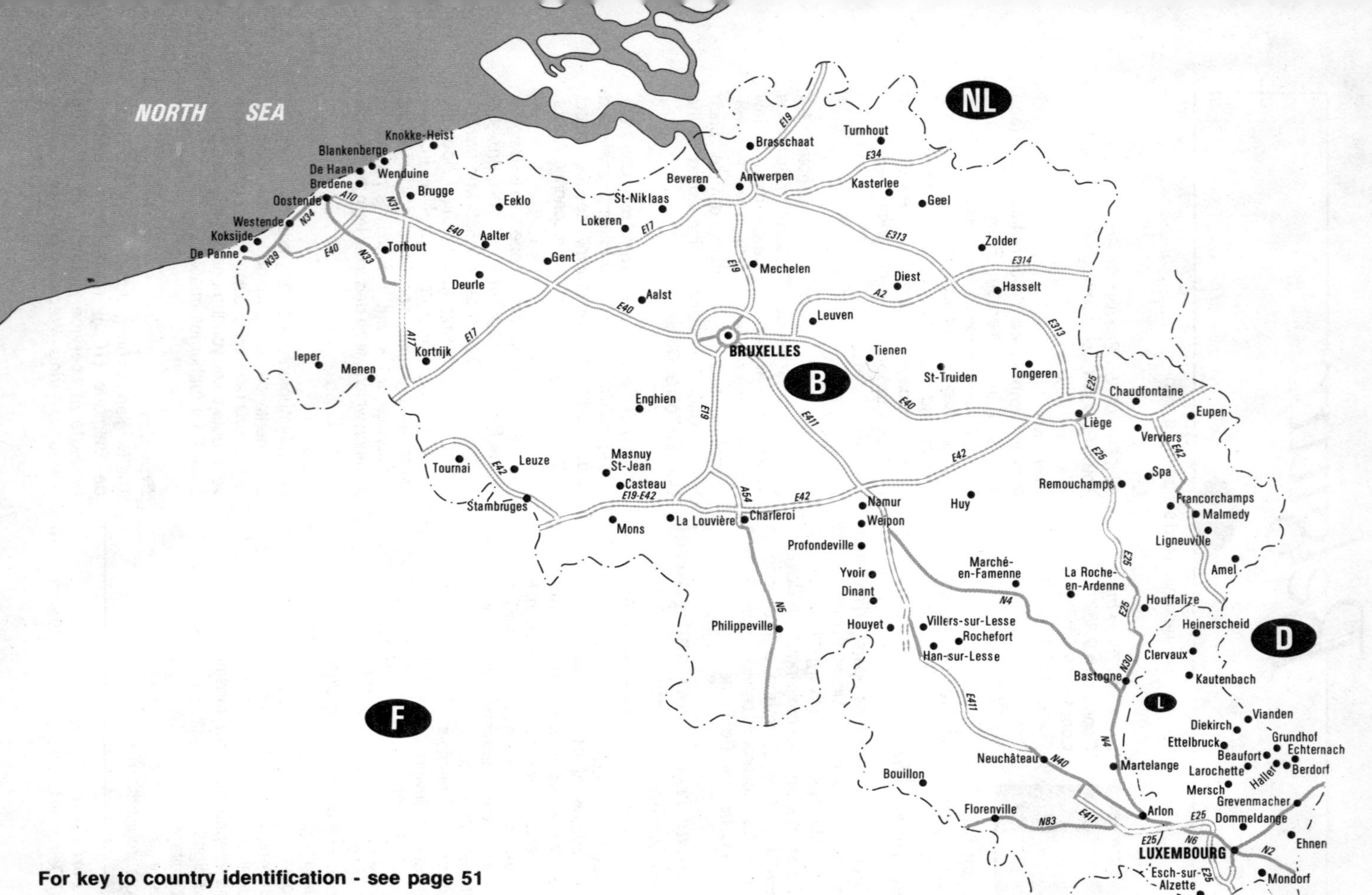

For key to country identification - see page 51

Secours/Touring Wegenhulp operates a 24 hour breakdown service throughout the year.

The Flemish Automobile Club (VAB-VTB operates only in the Flemish area) and the Royal Automobile Club of Belgium (RACB) each have patrol cars displaying the signs 'Wacht op de Weg' or 'RACB'. However, neither is associated with the AA and motorists will have to pay for all services. See also *Breakdown* page 6 and *Warning triangle* page 80.

British Embassy/Consulates

The British Embassy is located at *1040 Bruxelles* Britannia House, 28 rue Joseph II ☏ (02)2179000; consular section 32 rue Joseph II ☏ 2179000. There are British Consulates with Honorary Consuls in Antwerpen, Gent and Liège. See also page 6 and *Town Plan of Central Bruxelles* pages 82-83.

Currency including banking hours

(See also page 9)
The unit of currency is the Belgian Franc (*BFr*) divided into 100 *Centimes.* At the time of going to press £=*BFr*63.45. Denominations of bank notes are *BFr* 50, 100, 500, 1,000, 5000; standard coins are *BFr* 1, 5, 20 and *Centimes* 50. There are no restrictions on the amount of Belgian or foreign currency which may be taken into or out of Belgium.

Banks are open Monday to Friday from 09.00-15.30hrs; some close during the lunch hour and others remain open until 16.00hrs on Friday. Outside banking hours currency can be exchanged in Bruxelles at the Gare du Nord and the Gare du Midi, open 07.00-22.00hrs daily and at Zaventem Airport open 07.30-22.00hrs daily.

Customs regulations

A *Customs Carnet de Passages en Douane* is required for all pleasure craft temporarily imported by road, except craft without motors not exceeding 18ft (5.5 metres) in length, and for trailers not accompanied by the towing vehicle. See also *Customs regulations for European countries* page 9 for further information.

Dimensions and weight restrictions

Private **cars** and towed **trailers** or **caravans** are restricted to the following dimensions — height: 4 metres; width: 2.50 metres; length: (including any coupling device) up to 2,500kg 8 metres, over 2,500kg 10 metres. The maximum permitted overall length of vehicle/trailer or caravan combination is 18 metres.

Trailers without brakes may have a total weight of up to 50% of the weight of the towing vehicle (unladen) with a maximum of 750kg.

Driving licence

(See also page 11)
A valid British driving licence is acceptable in Belgium. The minimum age at which a visitor may drive a temporarily imported car or motorcycle is 18 years.

Emergency messages to tourists

(See also page 11)
Emergency messages to tourists are broadcast daily on Belgian Radio in French and Dutch.

Radio Television Belge transmitting on 483 metres medium wave broadcasts these messages in French during the news at 14.00hrs and after the news at 19.00hrs Monday to Friday and after the news at 13.00 and 19.00hrs on Saturday and Sunday.

Belgische Radio en Televisie (BRT1) transmitting on 323.6 metres medium wave broadcasts the messages daily in Dutch after the news at 07.00, 08.00, 12.00, 17.00, 19.00 and 22.00hrs.

Radio Television Belge (RTBF) transmitting on 16 and 49 metres short wave broadcasts the messages daily in French at 12.45hrs.

Belgische Radio en Televisie (BRT) transmitting on 50.89 metres short wave broadcasts the messages in Dutch after the news at 09.00 hrs Monday to Friday and on 198.4 metres medium wave between 19.00-22.00hrs Monday to Saturday and 19.00hrs on Sunday.

Lights

(See also page 14)
Between dusk and dawn and in all cases where visibility is restricted to 200m, dipped or full headlights must be used. However, headlights must be dipped: where street lighting is continuous permitting clear vision for 100m; at the approach of oncoming traffic (including vehicles on rails); when following another vehicle at a distance of less than 50 metres and, where the road is adjacent to water, at the approach of oncoming craft if the pilot is likely to be dazzled. It is compulsory for *motorcyclists* to use dipped headlights during the day.

Vehicles parked on the public highway must use position lights (parking lights) both day and night if vehicles are not visible from 100 metres.

In built-up areas the position lights may be replaced by a single parking light displayed on the side nearest to the centre of the road providing the vehicle is not more than 6 metres long and 2 metres wide, has no trailer attached to it and its maximum carrying capacity is not more than eight persons excluding the driver.

Motoring club

The **Touring Club Royal de Belgique** (TCB) has its head office at *1040 Bruxelles* 44 rue de la Loi ☎ (02)2332211 and branch offices in most towns. The Bruxelles head office is open weekly 09.00-18.00hrs; Saturday 09.00-12.00hrs. Regional offices are open weekdays 09.00-12.30hrs (Monday from 09.30hrs) and 14.00-18.00hrs; Saturday 09.00-12.00hrs. All offices are closed on Saturday afternoons and Sundays. See also page 16 and *Town Plan of Central Bruxelles* pages 82-83.

Motorways

There is a comprehensive system of toll free motorways linking major towns and adjoining countries. Two numbering systems are in force, a national network (white and black numbers with prefix 'A'), and an international network (green and white signs with the prefix 'E').

Nearly all motorways are part of the European international network, and carry only an 'E' number in preference to the 'A' number, which is used for the remainder of the motorway network. Recently a new numbering system of the European international network was introduced. Below is a list of the old and new 'E' numbers:

Old No	Route	New No
E3	Kortrijk — Gent — Antwerpen	E 17
E3	Antwerpen — Dutch Frontier (Eindhoven)	E 34
E5	Veurne — Brussel — Liège — Aachen (D)	E 40
E9	Maastricht (NL) — Liège — Arlon — Luxembourg	E 25
E10	Valenciennes (F) — Brussel — Dutch Frontier (Breda)	E 19
E39	Antwerpen — Lummen (nr. Hasselt)	E313
E39	Lummen (nr. Hasselt) — Dutch Frontier (Heerlen)	E314
E40	Brussel — Arlon	E411
E41	Mons — Liège	E 42
A13	Lummen (nr. Hasselt) — Liège	E313
A16	Tournai — Mons	E 42
A27	Verviers — St Vith	E 42

Orange badge scheme for disabled drivers

(See also page 16)

In Belgium special parking places are reserved for disabled drivers and are indicated by parking sign (white letter on blue panel) with the international disabled symbol added. Badge holders may also park without time limit by road signs and in *blue zones* where parking time is otherwise restricted. In addition many local authorities do not require badge holders to pay at parking meters. However, badge holders are not allowed to park in places where parking is otherwise prohibited.

Parking

(See also page 17)

Regulations differentiate between *waiting* (long enough to load or unload goods or for passengers to get in or out) and *parking*. Vehicles must be left on the right-hand side of the road, except in one-way streets when they can be left on either side. Where possible the vehicle must be left on the level shoulder inside built-up areas and on the shoulder, level or otherwise, outside these areas. If the shoulder is used by pedestrians, then at least 1 metre must be left for them on the side farthest away from the traffic. Parking restrictions are similar to those in the UK. Before leaving your vehicle make sure it does not restrict the movement of other road users and do not park on major roads outside built-up areas; on a carriageway marked in traffic lanes or where broken yellow lines are painted; opposite another stationary vehicle if this would hamper the crossing of **two** other vehicles and on the central reservation of dual carriageways.

In many towns and cities there are short-term parking areas known as *blue zones* where parking discs must be displayed. Outside these areas a parking disc must be used where the parking sign has an additional panel showing a parking disc. In some areas parking meters may also be found, in which case the parking disc is not valid in the meter bay. Where these are used the instructions for use will be on the meter.

Passengers

(See also page 18)

Children under 12 are not permitted to travel in

a vehicle as front seat passengers when rear seating is available.

Petrol

(See also page 18)
Credit cards Some petrol stations will accept Diners Club International and Visa.
Duty-free petrol In addition to the petrol in the vehicle tank up to 10 litres in a can may be imported free of customs duty and tax.
Petrol (leaded) Normal (92-94 octane) and Super (98-100 octane) grades.
Petrol (unleaded) is sold in Belgium where it is known as *2085*. Distributed mainly by Gulf (Kuwait Petroleum) it has an octane rating of 95 which is clearly indicated on the pumps.

Postal information

Mail Postcards *BFr*14.00, letters up to 20g *BFr*14.00.
Post Offices There are 1,800 post offices in Belgium. The opening hours of larger offices are from 09.00-17.00hrs Monday to Thursday and 09.00-19.00hrs Friday. Some large offices are also open on Saturdays 09.00-12.00hrs. The smaller offices open from 09.00-12.30hrs and 14.00-16.00hrs Monday to Friday.

Postcheques

(See also page 20)
Postcheques may be cashed for any amount up to a maximum of *BFr*5,000 per cheque, but only at main post offices. Counter positions are identified by the words *Chèques Postaux* or *Postchecks*. See *Postal information* for post office opening hours.

Priority

In built-up areas, a driver must give way to bus drivers who have used their direction indicators to show they intend driving away from a bus stop. Trams have priority from both right and left. See also *Priority including Roundabouts* page 21.

Public holidays

Official public holidays in Belgium for 1987 are given below. See also *Public holidays* page 21
January 1 (New Year's Day)
April 20 (Easter Monday)
May 1 (Labour Day)
May 28 (Ascension Day)
June 8 (Whit Monday)
July 21 (National Day)
August 15* (Assumption Day)
November 1† (All Saints Day)
November 11 (Armistice Day)
December 25 (Christmas Day)

*Saturday †Sunday

Religious services

(See also page 22)
The Intercontinental Church Society welcomes visitors from any denomination to English language services in the following centres: *8000 Brugge* The Revd Merry Hart, Niklaas Desparstraat 6 ☏ (050)341194
1050 Bruxelles The Ven John Lewis, 38 Avenue Guillaume Gilbert ☏ (02)5117183

Roads

A good road system is available. However, one international route that has given more cause for complaints than any other is, without doubt, that from Calais (France) through Belgium to Köln (Cologne) (Germany). The problem is aggravated by the fact that there are two official languages in Belgium; in the Flemish part of Belgium all signs are in Flemish only while in Wallonia, the French-speaking half of the country, the signs are all in French. Brussels (Bruxelles-Brussel) seems to be the only neutral ground where the signs show the two alternative spellings of placenames (Antwerpen-Anvers; Gent-Gand; Liège-Luik; Mons-Bergen; Namur-Namen; Oostende-Ostende; Tournai-Doornik). From the Flemish part of the country, Dunkirk (Dunkerque) in France is signposted *Duinkerke* and Lille is referred to as *Rijsel* and even Paris is shown as *Parijs*.

Road number changes A new numbering system, retaining the prefix N, has been introduced for Belgian main roads, with the exception of N1-N5 which retain their original numbers. The change-over took place during 1986, but some irregularities may still occur when the same road may have signs showing two different numbers.

Shopping hours

All shops are usually open 09.00-18.00, 19.00 or 20.00hrs from Monday to Saturday, however, *food shops* may close 1hr later.

Speed limits

(See also page 22)
The following limits apply even if they are not indicated unless there are signs to the contrary. A placename denotes the start of a built-up area:

Car/caravan/trailer
Built-up area 60kph (37mph)
Other roads 90kph (56mph)
Motorways & 4 lane roads 120kph (74mph)

Minimum speed on motorways on straight level stretches is 70kph (43mph). Vehicles being towed after an accident or breakdown are limited to 25kph (15mph) on all roads and, if on a motorway, must leave at the first exit.

Spiked or studded tyres

Spiked tyres are permitted between 1 November and 31 March on vehicles under 3.5 tonnes. They must be fitted to all four wheels and also to a trailer over 500kg. Speed should not exceed 90kph (56mph) on motorways and other roads having four or more lanes and 60kph (37mph) on all other public roads. See also *Cold weather touring* page 8.

Tourist information

(See also page 24)

The Belgian Tourist Organisation maintains an information office in London at 38 Dover Street, W1X 3RB ☏ 01-499 5379 and will be pleased to supply information on all aspects of tourism. In Belgium the national Tourist Organisation is supplemented by the Provincial Tourist Federation, whilst in most towns there are local tourist offices. These organisations will help tourists with information and accommodation.

Traffic lights

(See also page 24)

The three-colour traffic light system operates in Belgium. However, the lights may be replaced by arrows of the individual colours and these have the same meaning as the lights, but only in the direction in which the arrow points.

Using the telephone

(See also page 24)

Insert coin **after** lifting receiver, dialling tone same as UK. When making calls to subscribers within Belgium precede number with relevant area code (shown in parentheses against town entry in gazetteer). Use *BFr*5 coins for local calls and *BFr*5, 10 or 20 coins for national and international calls.

International callbox identification Boxes identified with European flags.

Telephone rates A telephone call to the UK costs *BFr*25 for each minute.

What to dial for the Irish Republic 00 *353.

What to dial for the UK 00 *44.

*Wait for second dialling tone or see instructions in callbox.

Warning triangle

The use of a warning triangle is compulsory for all vehicles except two-wheelers. The triangle must be placed 30 metres (33yds) behind the vehicle on ordinary roads and 100 metres (109yds) on motorways to warn following traffic of any obstruction; it must be visible at a distance of 50 metres (55yds). See also *Warning triangles/Hazard warning lights* page 25.

Winter conditions

(See also page 26)

Motoring is rarely restricted by weather conditions, although in the Ardennes snow and ice may be found when the weather is very severe. From 1 November to 31 March information on road conditions in Belgium and on main routes abroad can be obtained by telephoning (02)2332236 between 07.00-21.00hrs daily; from 1 April to 31 October information may be obtained between 09.00-18.00hrs Monday to Friday and 09.00-12.00hrs on Saturday by telephoning the same number.

Prices are in Belgian Francs

St% Service and tax charge
Supplementary local taxes are payable in addition to the charges shown. These vary from town to town.

Abbreviations:

av	avenue	r	rue
bd	boulevard	rte	route
esp	esplanade	str	straat
pl	place, plein		

Belgium is divided into the Flemish region in the north and the French-speaking Walloon region in the south. Some of the town names in the gazetteer show both languages, and that shown first is the one used locally. Brussels (Bruxelles/Brussel) is officially bi-lingual.

AALST (ALOST)
Oost-Vlaanderen (☎053)

★***Borse van Amsterdam*** Grote Markt 26 ☎211581
Closed 2—14 Jul
rm6(🛁 1)

🚗 ***Van der Haegen*** Kareelstr 2 ☎216011 Ope Vau

AALTER
Oost-Vlaanderen (☎091)

★★**Memling** Markt 11 (n.rest) ☎741013
🛁 🚿 9 sB🛁 🚿 1000 dB🛁 🚿 1500

AARLEN See **ARLON**

ALBERT PLAGE See **KNOKKE-HEIST**

AMEL (AMBLEVE)
Liège (☎080)

★**Oos Heem** Deidenberg 124 ☎349692
rm19 (🚿 2) **P** sB890 sB🚿 955 dB1400 dB🚿 1540 🏊

ANTWERPEN (ANVERS)
Antwerpen (☎03)

★★★★**Crest (See page 50)**
G-Lagrellelaan 10 ☎2372900 tx33843
🛁 253 🏠 **P**250 Lift ☾ sB🛁 3650 dB🛁 4250
Credit cards [1] [2] [3] [4] [5]

★★★**Novotel Antwerpen Nord**
Luihagen-Haven 6 ☎5420320 tx32488
🛁 119 **P** Lift sB🛁 2315 dB🛁 3110 🎾 🏊
Credit cards [2] [3] [5]

★★★**Plaza** Charlottalei 43 (n.rest) ☎2189240 tx31531
🛁 🚿 79 🏠 Lift sB🛁 🚿 2310—3200 dB🛁 🚿 3125—5250 📺

★★★**Switel** (GT) Copernicuslaan 2 ☎2316780 tx33965
🛁 🚿 350 🏠 **P** Lift sB🛁 🚿 2640—3550 dB🛁 🚿 3820—4520 🎾 📺
Credit cards [1] [2] [3] [5]

★★★***Waldorf*** (GT) Belgielei 36 ☎2309950 tx32948
🛁 74 🏠 **P** Lift
Credit cards [1] [2] [3] [5]

Berg Motors NV J van Gentstraat 7—17 ☎2309999 Vau Vol

Belgium

🚗 **J Lins** Tunnelpl 3—7 ☎2339928 **P** Dat LR

🚗 **New Antwerp Car Service** Ijzelaan 52 ☎2329830 **P** Lot Peu Toy

At **BORGERHOUT**

★★★**Holiday Inn** L-Lippenslaan 66 ☎2359191 tx34479
🛁 🚿 176 🏠 **P** Lift ☾ sB🛁 🚿 2650 dB🛁 🚿 3350 📺
Credit cards [1] [2] [3] [5]

ARLON (AARLEN)
Luxembourg (☎063)

★★**Nord** r des Faubourgs 2 ☎220283
rm23 (🛁 🚿 12) **P** sB860 sB🛁 🚿 1106 dB1100 dB🛁 🚿 1600

🚗 **Beau Site** av de Longwy 163—167 ☎220389 For

BALMORAL See **SPA**

BASTOGNE
Luxembourg (☎062)

★★**Lebrun** r de Marché 8 ☎215421
Closed 16 Feb—14 Mar
🛁 🚿 17 🏠 sB🛁 🚿 1550 dB🛁 🚿 1850

🚗 **F Luc-Nadin** r des Scieries 16 ☎211806 **P** AR

BERGEN See **MONS**

BEVEREN-WAAS
Oost-Vlaanderen (☎03)

★★★***Beveren*** Gentseweg 280 ☎7758623
🛁 🚿 29 **P** 🏊

BLANKENBERGE
West-Vlaanderen (☎050)

★★★**Ideal** Zeedijk 244 ☎411691 tx26937
Apr—20 Sep
🛁 50 🏠 Lift sB🛁 1220—1365 dB🛁 2150—2400 📺

★★***Marie-José*** av Maria-José 2 ☎411639
Apr—Aug
rm53 (🛁 🚿 29) Lift

★★***Pacific*** J-de-Troozlaan 48 ☎411542
Closed 16—31 Oct
rm24 (🚿 12) Lift

BOUILLON
Luxembourg (☎061)

★★**Panorama** r au Dessus de la Ville ☎466138
Apr—15 Nov
rm45 (🛁 🚿 32) Lift sB720 sB🛁 🚿 950 dB1100—1200 dB🛁 🚿 1450

★★**Poste** pl St-Arnould 1 ☎466506 tx41678
rm75 (🛁 🚿 40) 🏠 **P** Lift sB900 sB🛁 🚿 1500 dB1400 dB🛁 🚿 2100

★**Semois** r du Collège 46 ☎466027
rm45 (🛁 🚿 27) **P** Lift sB485 sB🛁 🚿 965 dB925 dB🛁 🚿 1485

BOUVIGNES See **DINANT**

BRASSCHAAT-POLYGOON
Antwerpen (☎031)

★★**Dennenhof** Bredabaan 940 ☎6630509
🛁 🚿 64 **P** sB🛁 🚿 1150 dB🛁 🚿 1300 🏊

BREDENE
West-Vlaanderen (☎059)

★***Zomerlust*** P-Benoitlaan 26 ☎320340
rm20

🚗 **Oostende Internationale** Brugsesteenweg 45 ☎322105 **P**

BRUGGE (BRUGES)
West-Vlaanderen (☎050)

★★★★**Holiday Inn** Boeveriestr 2 ☎335341 tx81369
🛁 128 🏠 Lift sB🛁 3300 dB🛁 4200 📺
Credit cards [1] [2] [3] [5]

★★★**Navarra** St-Jacobsstr 41 (n.rest) ☎340561
rm64 (🛁 🚿 55) **P**35 Lift sB1200 sB🛁 🚿 1650—2100 dB2000 dB🛁 🚿 2900
Credit cards [1] [2] [3] [5]

★★★***Novotel*** Chartreuseweg 20 ☎382851 tx81507
🛁 🚿 101 **P** Lift
Credit cards [2] [3] [5]

★★★**Park** t'Zand Vrydagmarkt 5 (n.rest) ☎333364 tx81686
🛁 61 🏠 Lift sB🛁 2200—2500 dB🛁 3000—3500

★★***Duc de Bourgogne*** Huidenvetterspl 12 ☎ 332038
Closed Jan & Jul
🛁 9

★★**Europ** Augustynerei 18 (n.rest) ☎337975
Mar—15 Nov
rm30 (🛁 🚿 27) 🏠 Lift sB1750 sB🛁 🚿 2070—2750 dB1900 dB🛁 🚿 2920

★★**Jacobs** Baliestr 1 (n.rest) ☎339831 tx81693
Closed Jan
rm27 (🛁 🚿 22) Lift sB840 sB🛁 🚿 1270 dB1170 dB🛁 🚿 1700

★★**Sablon** Noordzandstr 21 ☎333902 tx83033
rm46 (🛁 🚿 30) Lift sB1050 sB🛁 🚿 1350 dB1650 dB🛁 🚿 2000

★**Févéry** Collaert Mansionstr 3 (n.rest) ☎331269
🛁 🚿 11 Lift sB🛁 🚿 1200 dB🛁 🚿 1600

★★***Lybeer*** Korte Vuldersstr 31 (n.rest) ☎334355
Mar—Oct
rm24

🚗 **Canada** St-Pieterskaai 15 ☎317370 For

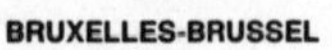

BRUXELLES-BRUSSEL
Brabant (☏02)

See Plan

★★★★★**Brussels Sheraton** pl Rogier 3 ☏2193400 tx26887 Plan **1**
523 **P** Lift ☾ sB 5000 dB 5800

★★★★★**Hilton International** bd de Waterloo 38 ☏5138877 tx22744 Plan **2**
369 **P**120 Lift ☾ sB 5200–5800 dB 6100–6700
Credit cards 1 2 3 4 5

★★★★***Amigo*** r de l'Amigo 1–3 ☏5115910 tx21618 Plan **3**
183 Lift

★★★★**Astoria** (ETAP) r Royale 103 ☏2176290 tx25040 Plan **4**
125 Lift sB 3050–3530 dB 4620
Credit cards 1 2 3 5

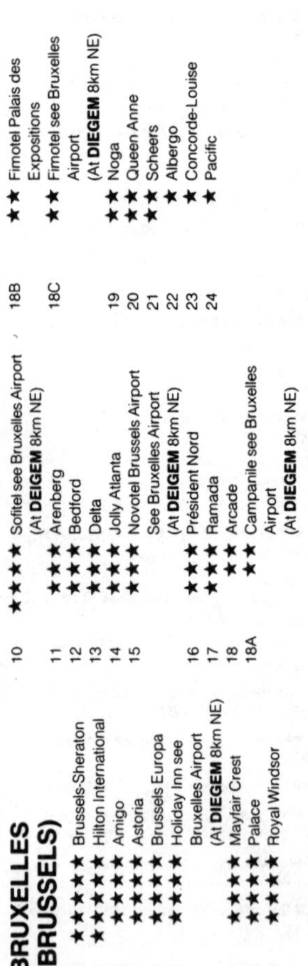

BRUXELLES (BRUSSELS)

1 ★★★★★ Brussels-Sheraton
2 ★★★★★ Hilton International
3 ★★★★ Amigo
4 ★★★★ Astoria
5 ★★★★ Brussels Europa
6 ★★★★ Holiday Inn see Bruxelles Airport (At **DIEGEM** 8km NE)
7 ★★★★ Mayfair Crest
8 ★★★★ Palace
9 ★★★★ Royal Windsor
10 ★★★★ Sofitel see Bruxelles Airport (At **DEIGEM** 8km NE)
11 ★★★ Arenberg
12 ★★★ Bedford
13 ★★★ Delta
14 ★★★ Jolly Atlanta
15 ★★★ Novotel Brussels Airport See Bruxelles Airport (At **DEIGEM** 8km NE)
16 ★★★ Président Nord
17 ★★★ Ramada
18 ★★ Arcade
18A ★★ Campanile see Bruxelles Airport (At **DIEGEM** 8km NE)
18B ★★ Fimotel Palais des Expositions
18C ★★ Fimotel see Bruxelles Airport (At **DIEGEM** 8km NE)
19 ★★ Noga
20 ★★ Queen Anne
21 ★★ Scheers
22 ★ Albergo
23 ★ Concorde-Louise
24 ★ Pacific

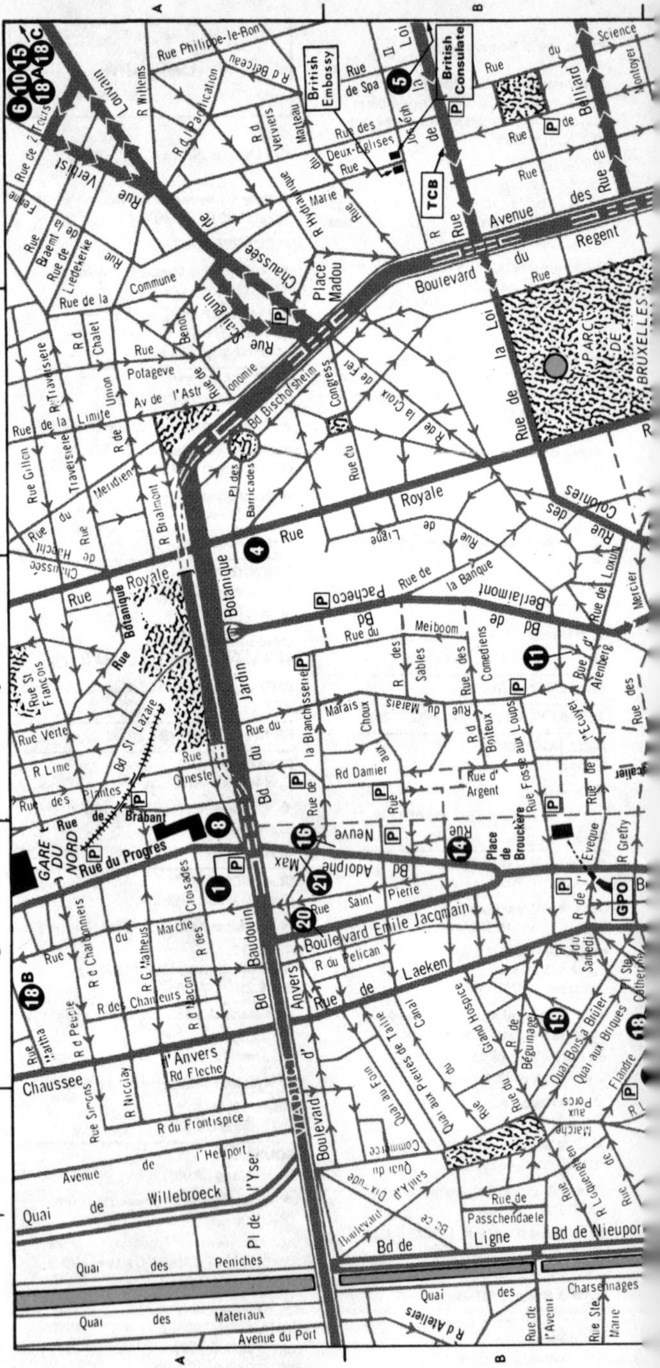

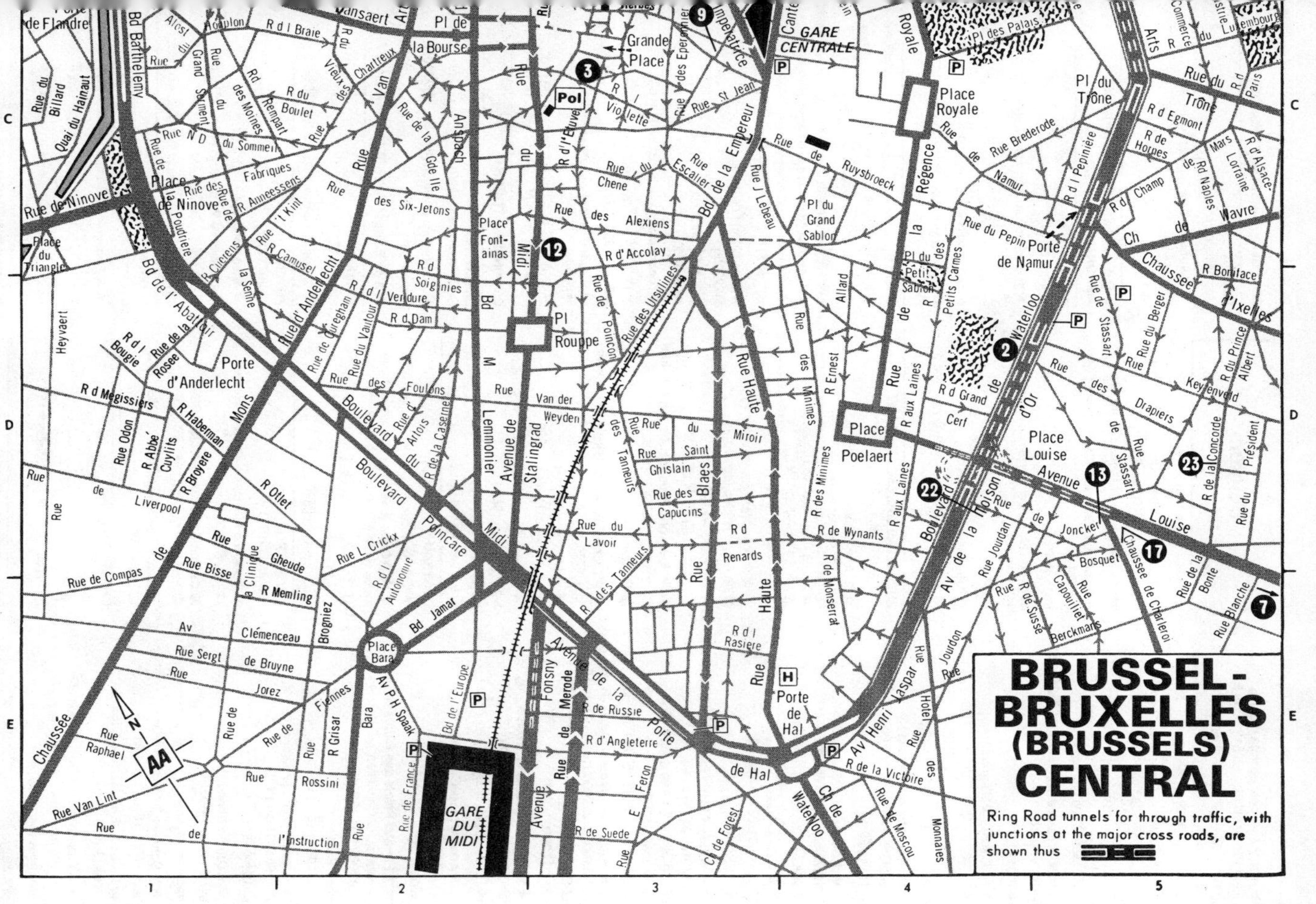
BRUSSEL-
BRUXELLES
(BRUSSELS)
CENTRAL
Ring Road tunnels for through traffic, with junctions at the major cross roads, are shown thus
GARE CENTRALE
GARE DU MIDI
Place Royale
Place Poelaert
Place Louise
Porte de Namur
Porte de Hal
Porte d'Anderlecht
Place Bara
Grande Place
Anspach
Bd M Lemmonier
Avenue de Stalingrad
Rue du Midi
Rue Haute
Rue Blaes
Avenue Louise
Boulevard de Waterloo
Boulevard du Midi
Bd de l'Abattoir
Bd Barthelemy
Chaussée de Mons
Rue de la Régence
Bd de la Empereur
Avenue de la Porte de Hal
Boulevard Poincare

★★★★**Brussels Europa** (Forum)
Wetstr 107 ☎2301333 tx25121 Plan **5**
🛁🚿240 🏠 Lift ☾ sB🛁🚿3465
dB🛁🚿4565
Credit cards 1 2 3 5

★★★★***Mayfair Crest* (See page 50)**
av Louise 381—383 ☎6499800 tx24821
Plan **7**
🛁99 Lift ☾
Credit cards 1 2 3 4 5

★★★★***Palace*** pl C-Rogier 22 ☎2176200
tx65604 Plan **8**
🛁🚿352 Lift

★★★★***Royal Windsor*** (SRS)
Duquesnoystr 5—7 ☎5114215 tx62905
Plan **9**
🛁🚿275 🏠 Lift

★★★***Arenberg*** r d'Assaut 15
(n.rest)☎5110770 tx25660 Plan **11**
🛁🚿158 🏠 Lift

★★★***Bedford*** (MAP) r du Midi 135
☎5127840 tx24059 Plan **12**
🛁250 🏠 Lift

★★★***Delta*** chaussée de Charleroi 17
☎5390160 tx63225 Plan **13**
🛁🚿253 🏠 Lift

★★★**Jolly Atlanta** bd A-Max 7 (n.rest)
☎2170120 tx21475 Plan **14**
🛁242 🏠 Lift ☾ sB🛁3960—4260
dB🛁5060—5360
Credit cards 1 2 3 4 5

★★★**Président Nord** (MAP) bd A-Max
107 (n.rest) ☎2190060 tx61417 Plan **16**
🛁🚿63 Lift sB🛁🚿2460—2660
dB🛁🚿2520—2860

★★★***Ramada*** Charleroisesteenweg 38
☎5393000 tx25539 Plan **17**
🛁🚿201 🏠 Lift

★★***Arcade*** pl Ste-Catherine ☎5137620
tx22476 Plan **18**
🛁234

★★**Fimotel Palais des Expositions**
av Imperatrice Charlotte ☎42615014
tx215269 Plan **18B**
🛁81 **P** Lift
Credit cards 1 2 3 5

★★***Noga*** r de Béguinage 38 (n.rest)
☎2186763 Plan **19**
rm19 (🛁🚿17) Lift

★★***Queen Anne*** bd E-Jacqmain 110
(n.rest) ☎2171600 Plan **20**
rm59 (🛁54) Lift

★★**Scheers** (Inter) bd A-Max 132
☎2177760 tx21675 Plan **21**
🛁🚿62 Lift sB🛁🚿2370—3185
dB🛁🚿2730—3495

★★***Van Belle*** Chaussée de Mons 39
☎5213516 tx63840 Not on plan
rm146 (🛁🚿136) 🏠 Lift

★***Albergo*** av de la Toison d'Or 58
☎5382960 Plan **22**
🛁🚿58 🏠 **P** Lift

Belgium

★**Concorde-Louise** r de la Concorde 59
(n.rest) ☎5128610 Plan **23**
🛁🚿20 🏠 Lift sB🛁🚿1130 dB🛁🚿1480

★***Pacific*** r A-Dansaert 57 ☎5118459
Plan **24**
rm15 🏠 **P** Lift

🚗 **Group Motors** chaussée de Waterloo
1250 ☎375442
Ope Vau

At **KRAAINEM** (14km NE)

🚗 **Arema** av de Kraainem 33 ☎7317140 **P**
Saa

BRUXELLES-BRUSSEL AIRPORT
At **DIEGEM** (8km NE)

★★★★**Holiday Inn** Holidaystr 7
☎7205865 tx24285 Plan **6**
🛁🚿288 **P** Lift ☾ sB🛁🚿3950—4300
dB🛁🚿4775—5600 🎾 ▭
Credit cards 1 2 3 5

★★★★***Sofitel*** Bessenveldstr 15
☎7206050 tx26595 Plan **10**
🛁125 **P**500 ≈ ▭
Credit cards 1 2 3 5

★★★***Novotel Brussels Airport*** Olmenstr
☎7205830 tx26751 Plan **15**
🛁🚿158 **P** Lift ≈

★★**Campanile** 2 av Excelsior ☎7209862
tx20667 Plan **18A**
🛁49 **P** sB🛁1943—2153
dB🛁2101—2311 M483—630

★★**Fimotel** av J-F-Kennedy ☎42615014
tx215269 Plan **18C**
🛁80 **P** Lift
Credit cards 1 2 3 5

CASTEAU
Hainaut (☎065)

★★★**Crest (See page 50)** chausée de
Bruxelles 38 ☎728741 tx57164
🛁🚿71 **P**100 ☾ sB🛁🚿1985
dB🛁🚿2800
Credit cards 1 2 3 4 5

CHARLEROI
Hainaut (☎071)

🚗 ***Colson & Fils*** chaussée de Bruxelles
11—25 ☎320070 For

🚗 ***Colson & Fils*** rte de Bomerié 26a
☎360143 For

J Lescot chaussée de Bruxelles 268—272
☎310145 For

CHAUDFONTAINE
Liège (☎041)

★★**Palace** esp 2 ☎650070
rm24 (🛁20) **P** Lift sB1235 sB🛁1550
dB🛁1900—2250

COQ (LE) See **HAAN (DE)**

COURTRAI See **KORTRIJK**

COXYDE-SUR-MER See **KOKSIJDE**

DEURLE
Oost-Vlaanderen (☎091)

★★***Auberge de Pêcheur*** Pontstr 42
☎824444
🛁11 **P**

DIEGEM See **BRUXELLES-BRUSSEL AIRPORT**

DIEST
Brabant (☎013)

★★**Modern** Leuvensesteenweg 93
☎311066
Closed Jul
🛁🚿13 **P** sB🛁🚿775 dB🛁🚿1320—1455

🚗 **Meelbergs NV** Leuvensesteenweg 108
☎333386 **P** For

DINANT
Namur (☎082)

★★***Couronne*** r A-Sax 1 ☎222441
rm24 (🛁🚿10) **P** Lift

★***Belle Vue*** r de Philippeville 1—3
☎222924
rm7 (🛁5) **P**

★**Gare (DPn)** r de la Station 39—41
☎222056
rm25 (🛁7) 🏠 **P** Lift sB800 dB1000
dB🛁1400

🚗 ***Dinant Motors*** rte de Bouvignes 53
☎223026 **P** Ope

At **BOUVIGNES** (2km NW)

★★**Auberge de Bouvignes** r Fétis 1—12
☎611600
rm6 (🛁3) 🏠 **P** sB1300 sB🛁1500 dB1500
dB🛁1800

DOORNIK See **TOURNAI**

EEKLO
Oost-Vlaanderen (☎091)

★***Rembrandt*** Koningin Astridpl 2 ☎772570
rm8 (🛁2)

🚗 **B de Baets** Markt 85 ☎771285 Aud VW

ENGHIEN
Hainaut (☎02)

🚗 **Chapelle** r d'Hoves 132 ☎3951509 Cit

EUPEN
Liège (☎087)

★★**Bosten** Verviersestr 2 ☎742209
rm14 (🛁6) 🏠 **P** sB610 sB🛁755 dB1160
dB🛁1360

🚗 ***P Ohn*** rte de Herbestal 120 ☎552931 For

FLORENVILLE
Luxembourg (☎061)

★★**France** r des Généraux Cuvelier 26
☎311032
16 Feb—20 Sep & Oct—Dec
rm38(🛁🚿11) 🏠 **P** Lift sB950 sB🛁1150
dB1250 dB🛁1400

🚗 ***Mauxhin & Fils*** r de la Station 32c
☎311055 Cit

Belgium

FRANCORCHAMPS
Liège (☎087)

★★★**Roannay (DPn** at wknds) rte de Spa 155 ☎275311 tx49031

17 Dec—16 Mar & 2 Apr—16 Nov
rm22 (🛁🚿19) 🏠 **P** sB1060
sB🛁🚿1730—2225 dB1345
dB🛁🚿2140—4050 ≋

GEEL
Antwerpen (☎014)

🚗 **Dierckx** Passstr 170 ☎588020 **P** BMW

GENT (GAND)
Oost-Vlaanderen (☎091)

★★★★***Holiday Inn***
Ottergemsesteenweg 600 ☎225885 tx11756

🛁120 **P** Lift 🎾 ≋

★★★**Europa** Gordunakaai 59 ☎226071 tx11547

🛁37 🏠 **P** Lift sB🛁1500 dB🛁2150

★★★**Novotel Gent Centrum** Gouden Leeuwpl 7 ☎242230 tx11400

🛁117 🏠 **P**20 Lift sB🛁3100 dB🛁3900 ≋

Credit cards [1] [2] [3] [5]

★★**St-Jorishof** Botermarkt 1 ☎242424 tx12738

9 Jan—23 Dec
🛁🚿31 🏠 **P** Lift sB1340—1450
sB🛁🚿1650 dB1620 dB🛁🚿3400

PVBA Centralgarage Doornzelestr 21 ☎234567 Aud VW

🚗 **Vernaeve** Doornzelestr 31 ☎230384 AR DJ LR

🚗 ***A Martens*** Kuitenberg 42 ☎530517 **P** Vau

A Vandersmissen Brusselsesteenweg 577 ☎257637 For

HAAN (DE) (LE COQ)
West-Vlaanderen (☎059)

★★★**Dunes** Leopoldpl 5 (n.rest) ☎233146

15 Mar—15 Oct
🛁🚿27 **P** Lift sB🛁🚿1400
dB🛁🚿1500—2100

★★**Auberge des Rois** Zeedijk 1 ☎233018

Closed 11 Nov—22 Dec & 7—24 Jan
rm28 (🛁🚿24) 🏠 **P** Lift
dB🛁🚿1860—2400 sea

★★**Bellevue** Koningspl 5 ☎233439

Etr—15 Oct
rm50 (🛁🚿31) **P** Lift sB650—825
dB1300—1500 dB🛁🚿1600—1800

HAN-SUR-LESSE
Namur (☎084)

★★**Voyageurs** r de C-Ardennais ☎377237 tx42079

rm42 (🛁🚿31) **P** Lift sB700 sB🛁🚿850
dB1000—1150 dB🛁🚿1265—1430

HASSELT
Limburg (☎011)

★**Century** Leopoldpl 1 ☎224799

rm14 (🚿10) sB700 sB🚿850 dB1350
dB🚿1500

🚗 ***Hoffer*** Demerstr 66 ☎224911 Ren

HERSTAL See **LIÈGE (LUIK)**

HOEI See **HUY**

HOUFFALIZE
Luxembourg (☎062)

★**Clé des Champs** rte de Libramont 22 ☎288044

rm13 (🚿8) 🏠 **P** sB650 sB🚿750—950
dB950 dB🛁🚿1150—1500

🚗 **Lambin** rte de Liège 10 ☎288035 AR

HOUYET
Namur (☎082)

★***Marquisette*** rte de Dinant (4km NE) ☎666429

Closed 20 Jun—10 Jul
🛁🚿10 🏠 **P**

HUY (HOEI)
Liège (☎085)

★★***Fort*** Chaussée Napoléon 5—6 ☎212403

rm22 (🛁12)

IEPER (YPRES)
West-Vlaanderen (☎057)

★***St Nicholas*** G-de Stuerstr 6 ☎200622

Closed 18 Jul—8 Aug
rm8 (🛁4)

🚗 ***N V Mottrie*** Meenseweg 214 ☎201666 **P** Ope

JAMBES See **NAMUR**

KASTERLEE
Antwerpen (☎014)

★★***Dennen*** Lichtaarsebaan 79 ☎556107

Closed 1—14 Jan
rm12 (🛁5) **P**

KNOKKE-HEIST
West-Vlaanderen (☎051)

At **ALBERT PLAGE**

★★★***Lido*** Zwalluwenlaan 18 ☎601925

Jun—Sep
🛁🚿40 🏠 **P** Lift

At **KNOKKE**

★★***Cecil*** Elizabethlaan 20 ☎601033

15 Apr—Sep & 22 Dec—4 Jan
🛁🚿12

At **ZOUTE (LE)**

★★★**Majestic** Zeedijk 697 ☎611144

Apr—24 Sep
rm61 (🛁🚿52) 🏠 Lift sB1250 sB🛁🚿1350
dB2500 dB🛁🚿2900

KOKSIJDE (COXYDE-SUR-MER)
West-Vlaanderen (☎058)

★★**Royal Plage** Zeedijk 65 ☎511300

Apr-5 Sep
rm29 (🛁7) Lift sB650—1100 dB900—1250
dB🛁1300—1600

KORTRIJK (COURTRAI)
West-Vlaanderen (☎056)

★★***Damier*** Grote Markt 41 ☎ 221547

rm43 (🛁20) Lift

🚗 **Vanneste & Zonen** Kortrijksteenweg 405, Harelbeke ☎201000 Dat Fia Lan

KRAAINEM See **BRUXELLES-BRUSSEL**

LA Each name preceded by 'La' is listed under the name that follows it.

LAC-DE-WARFAZ See **SPA**

LE Each name preceded by 'Le' is listed under the name that follows it.

LEUVEN (LOUVAIN)
Brabant (☎016)

At **WINKSELE** (3km NW)

🚗 **Hergon** Brusselsesteenweg 57 ☎223506 For

LEUZE
Hainaut (☎069)

★**Couronne** pl de la Gare 18 ☎662166

Closed Aug
rm10 dB800

LIÈGE (LUIK)
Liège (☎041)

★★★★**Holiday Inn** esp de l'Europe 2 (n.rest) ☎426020 tx41156

🛁224 🏠 **P** Lift sB🛁2595—2810
dB🛁3470—3630 ▣
Credit cards [1] [2] [3] [5]

★★★★**Ramada** bd de la Sauvenière 100 ☎224910 tx41896

🛁105 🏠 Lift sB🛁2600 dB🛁3180 ▣

★★**Cygne d'Argent** r Beekman 49 ☎237001 tx42617

🛁🚿27 Lift sB🛁🚿1185—1465
dB🛁🚿1565—1765

★★**Urbis** 41 pl de la République (n.rest) ☎236085 tx42369

🛁78 **P** Lift sB🛁2105 dB🛁2560

🚗 ***Grosses Battes*** quai des Ardennes 117 ☎653990 For

🚗 **Sodia** r L-Boumal 24 ☎526862 AR LR

At **HERSTAL** (8km NE on E5)

★★★**Post House** (THF) r Hurbise (SE5 at exit 34 Hermée-Hauts-Sarts) ☎646400 tx41103

🛁🚿100 **P** Lift sB🛁🚿2580—2800
dB🛁🚿3200—3500 ≋
Credit cards [1] [2] [3] [5]

LIGNEUVILLE
Liège (☎080)

★★**Moulin** r de Centre 91 ☎570081

Closed 21 Nov—21 Dec →

rm19 (➡ 7) 🚘 P sB475 sB ➡ 650 dB900 dB ➡ 1750

LOKEREN
Oost-Vlaanderen (☎091)

★★***Park*** Antwerpsesteenweg 1 ☎482046

18 Jan—14 Jul & 31 Jul—8 Jan
➡ 🚿 9 🚘 **P**

🚗 **Siau** Weverslaan 14 ☎481400 **P** BMW

LOUVAIN See **LEUVAN**

LOUVIÈRE (LA)
Hainaut (☎064)

🚗 **J Dupire** r L-Dupuis 10 ☎224031 **P** AR DJ LR

LUIK See **LIÈGE**

MALINES See **MECHELEN**

MALMÉDY
Liège (☎080)

🚗 **E Nachsem-Lejoly** Baugnez 9a ☎338301 **P** Toy

At **XHOFFRAIX** (5km N on N28)

★★**Trôs Marets (DPn)** (Relais et Châteaux) rte de Mont 1 ☎337917

Closed 16 Nov—21 Dec
➡ 🚿 11 **P** sB ➡ 🚿 2000—3250
dB ➡ 🚿 2250—3800

MARCHE-EN-FAMENNE
Luxembourg (☎084)

★★***Cloche*** r de Luxembourg 2 ☎311579
➡ 6 **P**

Leunen rte de Bastogne 51A ☎311582 **P** Fia

🚗 **Marlair** Chaussée de Liège 19 ☎312084 **P** Ope Vau

🚗 **Verhuist** rte de Liège 50 ☎311673 M/c AR

MARTELANGE
Luxembourg (☎063)

★***Maison Rouge*** rte d'Arlon 5 ☎64006

Closed Oct
rm12 🚘 **P**

MASNUY-ST-JEAN
Hainaut (☎065)

★★★***Amigo*** chaussée Brunehault 4 ☎728721 tx57313

➡ 🚿 56 **P** Lift

MECHELEN (MALINES)
Antwerpen (☎015)

★**Claes** O.L. Vrouwstr 51 (n.rest) ☎412866

rm15 (🚿 9) sB700 sB🚿 920 dB1100
dB🚿 1540

🚗 **Festraets** M-Sabbestr 123 ☎202752 Fia Lnc Vau

MENEN (MENIN)
West-Vlaanderen (☎056)

🚗 **Imecar** Kortrijk Str 269 ☎513535 Ren

MONS (BERGEN)
Hainaut (☎065)

🚗 **Willems** bd Sainctelette 39 ☎346363 Ope Vau

Belgium

NAMUR (NAMEN)
Namur (☎081)

🚗 ***Carco*** chaussée de Louvain 320 ☎212711 **P** AR

At **JAMBES**

🚗 **Jambes** pl-Charlotte 18 ☎301451 **P** For

NEUFCHÂTEAU
Luxembourg (☎061)

🚗 ***Michaux*** av de la Gare 43 ☎277444 For

NIVELLES (NIJVEL)
Brabant (☎067)

★★***Nivelles-Sud*** chaussée de Mons 22 ☎218721 tx57788

➡ 60 **P** Lift ☾

🚗 **Flash Service** Chaussée de Namur 63 ☎212171 **P** All makes

🚗 **Nivelles Motors** faubourg de Mons ☎213023 M/c Ope

OOSTENDE (OSTENDE)
West-Vlaanderen (☎059)

See Plan

★★★***Bellevue-Britannia*** Prom Albert 1 55—56 (n.rest) ☎706373 Plan **1**

16 Dec—14 Nov
rm58 (➡ 🚿 49) **P** Lift

★★★**Imperial** van Iseghemlaan 74—76 ☎705481 tx81167 Plan **2**

➡ 🚿 61 🚘 **P** Lift sB ➡ 🚿 1150—1850
dB ➡ 🚿 2500

★★★**Prado** Leopold II Laan 22 (n.rest) ☎705306 tx82237 Plan **3**

rm31 (➡ 🚿 27) 🚘 Lift dB1200 dB ➡ 🚿 1900

★★★**Ter Streep** Leopold II Laan 14 (n.rest) ☎700912 tx82261 Plan **5**

➡ 35 Lift sB ➡ 1100—2000
dB ➡ 1540—2520

★★★***Westminster*** van Iseghemlaan 22 ☎702411 Plan **6**

➡ 🚿 60 **P** Lift

★★**Ambassadeur** Wapenpl 8A ☎700941 tx81415 Plan **7**

➡ 🚿 23 🚘 **P** Lift sB ➡ 🚿 1600
dB ➡ 🚿 2000

★★**Bero** Hofstr 1A ☎702335 tx82163 Plan **8**

➡ 60 🚘 Lift sB ➡ 1200—1500
dB ➡ 1600—1900

★★**Europe** Kapucijnenstr 52 (n.rest) ☎701012 tx81659 Plan **10**

Mar—15 Oct
rm65 (➡ 🚿 55) **P** Lift sB875
sB ➡ 🚿 1150—1350 dB1350—1500
dB ➡ 🚿 1500—1750

★★***Lido*** L-Spilliaetstr 1 ☎700806 tx81035 Plan **11**

20 Apr—17 Aug
rm69 (🚿 68) Lift

★★**Parc** Marie Josépl 3 (n.rest) ☎706580 Plan **12**

rm47 (➡ 🚿 14) Lift sB900 dB1100
dB ➡ 🚿 1400

★**Glenmore** Hofstr 25 ☎702022 Plan **14**

Mar—Dec
rm42 (➡ 🚿 33) Lift sB800 sB ➡ 🚿 1000
dB1300 dB ➡ 🚿 1700 sea

★***Nieuwe Sportman*** de Smet de Naeyerlaan 9 ☎702384 Plan **15**

rm10

★***Pacific*** Hofstr 11 ☎701507 Plan **16**

Apr—15 Oct
rm51 (🚿 35) 🚘 Lift

★**Strand** Visserksaai 1 ☎703383 tx81357 Plan **18**

Feb—Nov
rm21 (➡ 🚿 20) Lift sB990
sB ➡ 🚿 1800—2300 dB ➡ 🚿 2300

🚗 **Casino Kursaal** Torhoutsesteenweg 684 ☎703240 **P** Peu Tal

🚗 **Delta** Steenweg op Torhout 529 ☎801503 For

🚗 **Royal-Auto** Koninginnelaan 52 ☎707635 M/c Fia Lan

F Stoops chaussée de Torthoutsteenweg 54 ☎702472 Alf Toy

PANNE (DE) (LA PANNE)
West-Vlaanderen (☎508)

★★***Regina Maria*** Bortierlaan 13 ☎411222

Closed 6 Jan—4 Feb
rm72 (➡ 🚿 52) Lift

★★***Strand*** Nieuwpoortlaan 153 ☎411196

Apr—Sep
rm51 (➡ 🚿 43) 🚘 **P** sea

PHILIPPEVILLE
Namur (☎071)

★**Croisée** r de France 45 ☎666231

14 Feb—26 Aug & 15 Sep—Dec
rm12 (➡ 5) 🚘 **P**

PROFONDEVILLE
Namur (☎081)

★**Auberge d'Alsace** av Gl-Garcia 42 ☎412228

➡ 6 **P** sB ➡ 900 dB ➡ 1200

REMOUCHAMPS
Liège (☎041)

★★**Royal Étrangers** r de la Reffe 26 ☎844006

Closed 16 Nov—9 Dec
rm15 (➡ 5) 🚘 **P** sB675 sB ➡ 750 dB1350
dB ➡ 1500

ROCHE-EN-ARDENNE (LA)
Luxembourg (☎084)

★★★***Air Pur* (DPn)** rte d'Houffalize 11, Villez ☎411223

Apr—15 Nov & 15—31 Dec
rm11 (➡ 10) 🚘 **P**

★★★**Ardennes (DPn)** r de Beausaint 2 ☎411112

15 Mar—20 Nov & 20 Dec—2 Jan
➡ 12 🚘 **P** sB ➡ 1200—1600 dB ➡ 1700

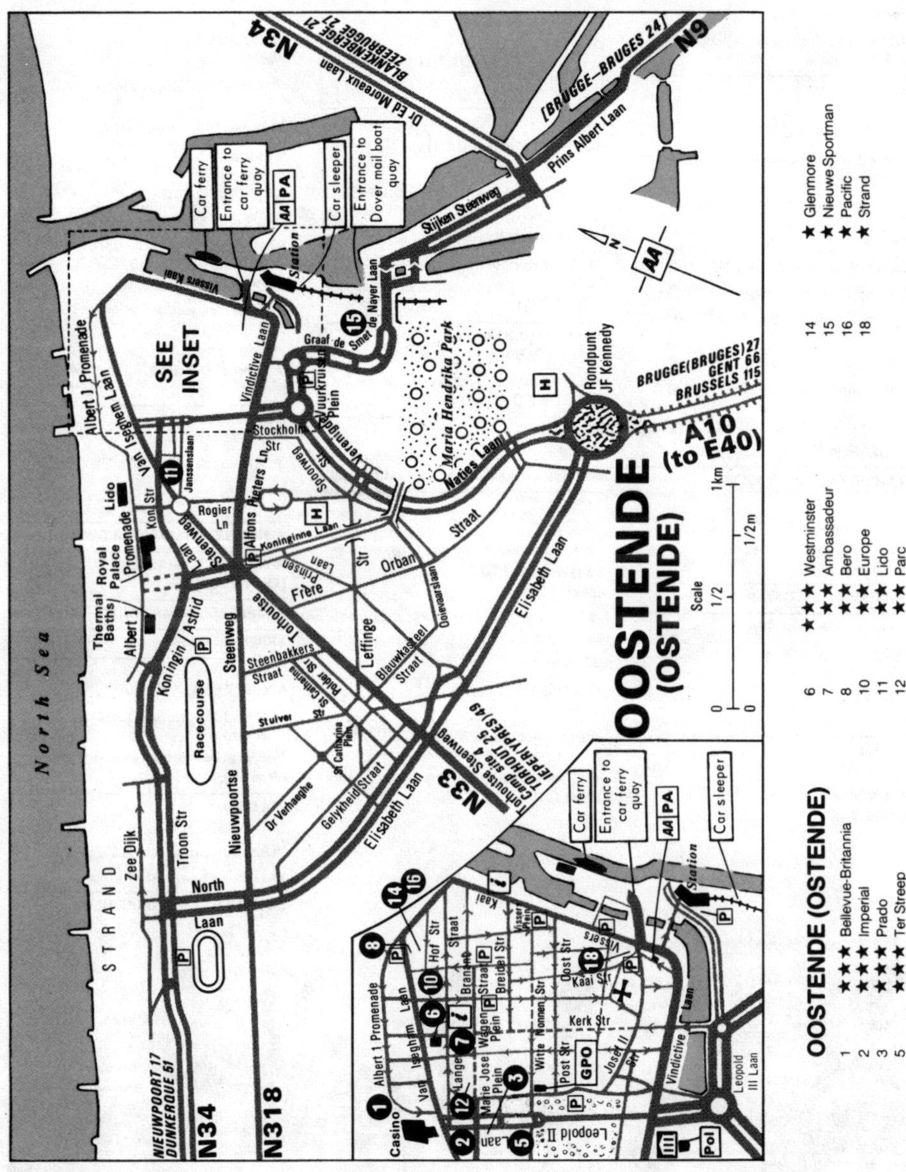

★★**Belle Vue** av de la Gare 10 ☎411187

Closed Jun
rm13 (🛁 🚿 6) **P** sB950 sB 🛁 🚿 1150
dB1220 dB 🛁 🚿 1520

ROCHEFORT
Namur (☎084)

★***Central*** pl Albert 1er 30 (n.rest) ☎211044

Closed Oct
rm7 (🛁 2) **P**

★***Fayette*** r Jaquet 87 ☎211024

Closed 16 Sep—5 Oct
rm21 (🛁 🚿 12) **P**

🚗 ***Pigeon & Jacquemin*** r de la Libération 71—73 ☎211523 **P** Ope

SINT NIKLAAS (ST-NICOLAS)
Oost-Vlaanderen (☎03)

★★**Serwir** Koningen Astridlaan 49
☎7765311 tx32422

Closed 8—27 Jul

🛁 🚿 28 **P** Lift sB 🛁 🚿 1320—1680
dB 🛁 🚿 2150

🚗 **Central** Dalstr 28 ☎7763830 For

🚗 **Sint-Christoffel** Wegvoeringstr 88
☎7761338 AR LR

SINT TRUIDEN (ST-TROND)
Limburg (☎011)

🚗 **Cells** Naamsestweg 239 ☎689951 Vol

🚗 **Milou** Tiensesteenweg 109 ☎683941 **P** Fia Ren

🚗 ***C Morren*** Industriezone St-Jorisstr 13 ☎681526 Vau

SPA
Liège (☎087)

At **BALMORAL** (3km N)

★★★**Dorint Ardennes** rte de Balmoral 33 ☎772581 tx49209

🛁96 **P**40 Lift ☾ sB🛁1500—1850 dB🛁2400—3000 Credit cards [1] [2] [3] [5]

At **LAC-DE-WARFAZ** (2.5km NE)

★★**Lac (DPn)** av A-Hesse 45 ☎771074

rm12 (🛁🚿8) ⌂ **P** sB900 sB🛁🚿950 dB1000 dB🛁🚿1250

At **TIÈGE-LEZ-SPA** (5km NE)

★★★**Charmille** r de Tiège ☎474313

Apr—15 Nov
rm33 (🛁🚿23) ⌂ **P** Lift sB900 sB🛁🚿1000 dB1200 dB🛁🚿1330

STAMBRUGES-GRANDGLISE
Hainaut (☎069)

★★***Vert Gazon*** rte de Mons 1 ☎575984

15 Jan—15 Jun & Jul—Dec
🛁🚿6 ⌂ **P**

THOUROUT See **TORHOUT**

TIÈGE-LEZ-SPA See **SPA**

TIENEN (TIRLEMONT)
Brabant (☎016)

Dalaisse Leuvensestr 115—117 ☎811077 **P** Toy

TONGEREN
Limburg (☎012)

★***Lido*** Grote Markt 19 ☎231948

rm9 (🛁🚿5)

Belgium

TORHOUT (THROUROUT)
West-Vlaanderen (☎050)

🚗 **Deketelaere** Vredelaan 69 ☎212623 Hon Vau

At **WYNENDALE** (3km)

★★***t'Gravenhof*** Oostendestr 343 ☎212314

rm8 (🛁🚿4) **P**

TOURNAI (DOORNIK)
Hainaut (☎069)

🚗 ***Lintermans*** quai Staline 14—16 ☎222116 **P** Ope Vau

TURNHOUT
Antwerpen (☎014)

🚗 **Perfect** Nieuwekaai 9—11 ☎413588 M/c

VERVIERS
Liège (☎087)

★★★**Amigo** r Herla 1 ☎316767 tx49128

🛁🚿54 **P** Lift sB🛁🚿1600—2300 dB🛁🚿2750—4300 ▭

★★**Grand** r du Palais 145 ☎223177

rm28 (🛁🚿13) Lift sB800 sB🛁🚿1650 dB1025 dB🛁🚿1800

VILLERS-SUR-LESSE
Namur (☎084)

★**Beau Séjour** r du Village 15 ☎377115

Mar—15 Jan
rm22 (🛁9) ⌂ **P** sB🛁1200—1315 dB🛁1475—1870 ≈

WENDUINE
West-Vlaanderen (☎050)

★★***Mouettes*** Zeedijk ☎411514

15 Apr—Sep
rm30 (🛁🚿18) Lift sea

WEPION
Namur (☎081)

★★★★**Sofitel Namur** chaussée de Dinant 1149 ☎460811 tx59031

🛁118 **P**250 sB🛁2075—2375 dB🛁2650—3150 Mfr500 ▭ ≈ Credit cards [1] [2] [3] [4] [5]

★**Frisla** chaussée de Dinant 1455 ☎411106

15 Mar—Oct
rm10 (🛁🚿7) **P** sB🛁🚿850 dB🛁🚿1200 sea

WESTENDE
West-Vlaanderen (☎059)

★★***Rotonda*** Zeedijk 300 ☎300495

Mar—Dec
rm18 (🛁10) ⌂ **P**

WINKSELE See **LEUVEN (LOUVAIN)**

WYNENDALE See **TORHOUT (THOUROUT)**

XHOFFRAIX See **MALMÉDY**

YPRES See **IEPER**

YVOIR
Namur (☎082)

★★**Vachter** chaussée de Namur 140 ☎611314

rm9 (🛁8) ⌂ **P** sB1075 sB🛁1375 dB1525 dB🛁1925

ZOLDER
Limburg (☎011)

★**Pits** Omloop Terlaemen ☎251899

🛁12 **P** sB🛁1215 dB🛁1770 ≈

ZOUTE (LE) See **KNOKKE-HEIST**

Houffalize, a well-known summer resort

Denmark

International distinguishing sign

Area *16,631 sq miles*
Population *5,119,155*
Local time *GMT + 1 (Summer GMT + 2)*

National flag *White upright cross on a red field*

How to get there

The two main ways of reaching Denmark are either by using the direct ferry services from Newcastle or Harwich to Esbjerg in western Jutland, Harwich to Hirtshals in northern Jutland, or by using one of the short Channel crossings to France or Belgium and driving through the Netherlands and northern Germany to Denmark. The distance from the Channel ports to København (Copenhagen) is roughly 660 miles and the journey would require one or two night stops.

Another possibility is to use the ferry operating between Harwich and Hamburg and drive the short distance to southern Denmark.

Inter-island travel is made easy by either bridge links or frequent vehicle ferries.

Motoring regulations and general information

This information should be read in conjunction with the general content of the European ABC (pages 4-26). **Note** As certain regulations and requirements are common to many countries they are covered by one entry in the ABC and the following headings represent some of the subjects dealt with in this way:

AA Agents
Crash or safety helmets
Customs regulations for European countries
Drinking and driving
Fire extinguisher
First-aid kit
Insurance
International distinguishing sign
Medical treatment
Mirrors
Overtaking
Passengers
Police fines
Radio telephones/Radio transmitters
Road signs
Seat belts
Traffic lights
Tyres
Visitors' registration

Accidents

Fire, police, ambulance ☏ 000. If you are involved in a collision or other traffic accident you must stop and exchange particulars with any other person concerned. If personal injury is sustained, it is obligatory to obtain medical assistance for the injured persons. The incident should then be reported to the police. See also *Accidents* page 5.

Accommodation

A list of hotels, pensions, inns and motels is available from the Tourist Office in London with full details of charges, but there is no official classification. Prices generally include VAT (22%) and service (15%).

Visitors arriving in København without accommodation are advised to make personal application to the Accommodation Service, Kiosk P, Central Railway Station, where assistance will be given in finding accommodation in an hotel or, failing that, a private home.

Provincial tourist associations will also provide information on accommodation in their area and will effect reservations in response to written applications. Accommodation is also available at farmhouses and the renting of summer cottages can be arranged through tourist associations on written application.

Hotel cheques are generally available in Denmark from Tourist Offices (see page 93) and FDM Travel Agencies and, if purchased by AA members from the FDM (see page 91) a discount of 5% is given on production of a valid membership card. The cheques cover accommodation for one person,

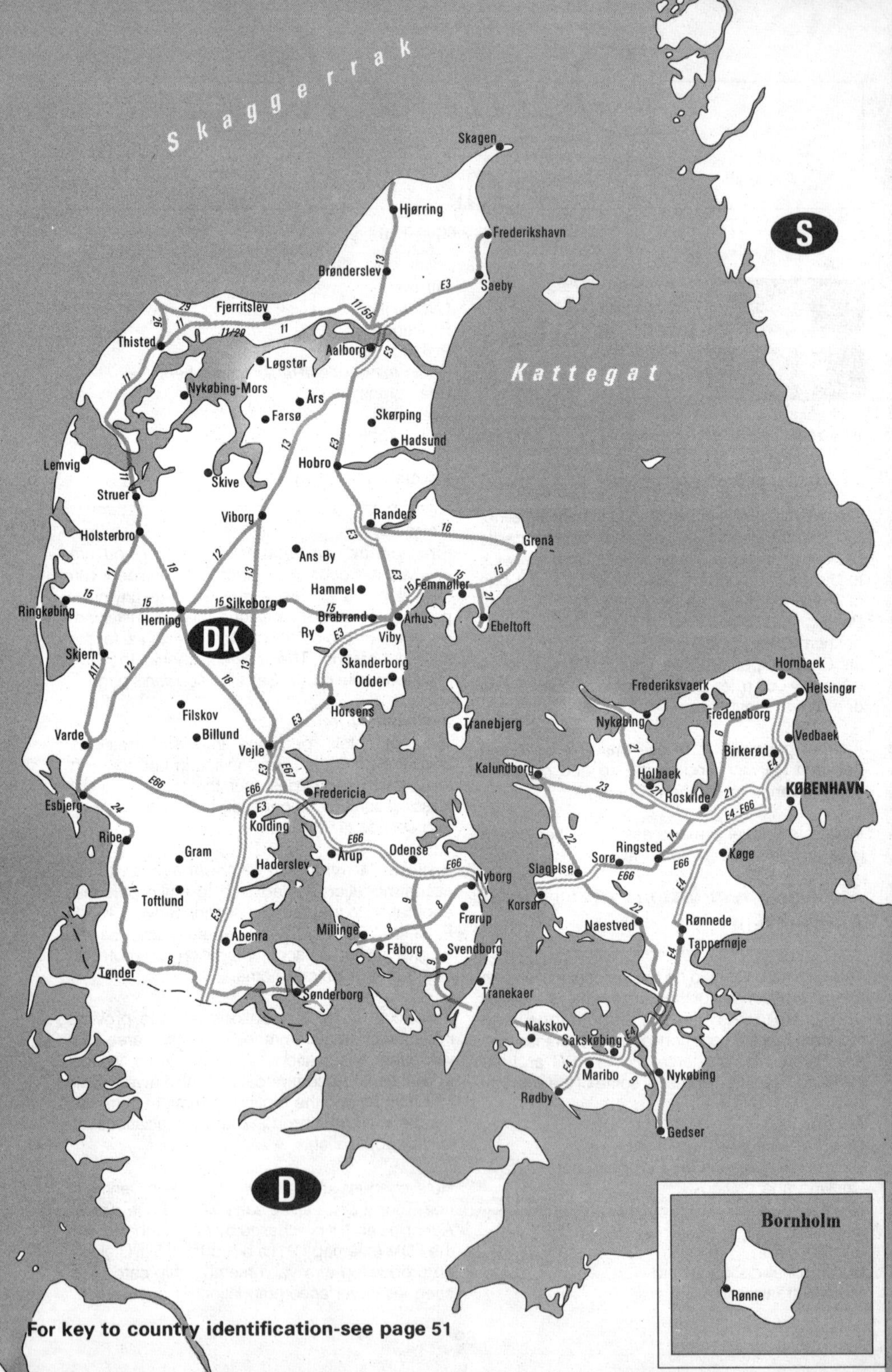

For key to country identification-see page 51

breakfast, service and taxes and charges are as follows:
Kro (Inn) check *Dkr*175.

Breakdown

If your car breaks down, try to move it to the verge of the road so that it obstructs the traffic flow as little as possible. The Danish Motoring Club, (FDM) is unable to provide roadside assistance. In the event of a breakdown assistance may be obtained from either the *Falck Organisation* or *Dansk Autohjaelp* (Danish Automobile Association) both of which operate a 24-hour service. See local telephone directory for number of nearest station. If you break down on a motorway and call for assistance from an emergency telephone you must specify whether help is required from Falck or Dansk Autohjaelp. Any service received must be paid for. See also *Breakdown* page 6 and *Warning triangle* page 93.

British Embassy/Consulates

The British Embassy together with its consular section is located at *DK-2100 Kǿbenhavn* 36-40 Kastelsvej ☎ (01)264600. There are British Consulates with Honorary Consuls in Åbenrå, Ålborg, Århus, Esbjerg, Fredericia and Odense. See also page 6 and *Town Plan of Kǿbenhavn* pages 96-97.

Currency including banking hours

(See also page 9)
The unit of currency is the Danish Krone (*Dkr*) divided into 100 ǿre. At the time of going to press £=*Dkr*11.49. Denominations of bank notes are *Dkr* 20, 50, 100, 500, 1,000; standard coins are *Dkr* 1, 5, 10 and ǿre 5, 10, 25. There are no restrictions on the amount of foreign or Danish currency that may be imported. Visitors may export any amount of foreign or Danish currency provided:
a the foreign currency exported was declared on entry;
b the Danish currency exported was imported or obtained by conversion of imported foreign securities.
In Kǿbenhavn banking hours are 09.30-16.00hrs Monday, Tuesday, Wednesday and Friday and Thursday 09.30-18.00hrs. At the Central Railway Station and the Air Terminal banks are open until 22.00hrs. Outside Kǿbenhavn banking hours are generally 09.30-12.00hrs and 14.00-16.00hrs. All banks are closed on Saturday, except Exchange offices on the Danish/German border which close between 13.00 and 15.00hrs. These offices may also open on Sundays during the summer.

Dimensions and weight restrictions

Private **cars** and towed **trailers** or **caravans** are restricted to the following dimensions — height: 4 metres; width: 2.50 metres; length: 12 metres. The maximum permitted overall length of vehicle/trailer or caravan combination is 18 metres.

Trailers without brakes may have a total weight of up to 50% of the weight of the towing vehicle; trailers with brakes may have a total weight up to 90% of the weight of the towing vehicle.

Driving licence

(See also page 11)
A valid British driving licence is acceptable in Denmark. The minimum age at which a visitor may drive a temporarily imported car or motorcycle is 17 years.

Emergency messages to tourists

(See also page 11)
Emergency messages to tourists are broadcast Monday to Saturday on *Radio Denmark* in English from May to August. The messages are transmitted on 282 metres medium wave and 1224 metres long wave at 08.30hrs.

Lights

(See also page 14)
Headlights should be dipped early when meeting another vehicle as the lighting of Danish-registered vehicles is of lower density than that of UK-registered vehicles. Driving with only one headlight or spotlight is not allowed. Fog lamps may be used in pairs in conjunction with sidelights (but not headlights). It is compulsory for *motorcyclists* to use dipped headlights during the day.

Motoring club

The **Forenede Danske Motorejere** (FDM) has its headquarters at *2100 Kǿbenhavn* Ⓞ Blegdamsvej 124 ☎ (01)382112 and branch offices are maintained in major towns throughout the country. The offices are usually open between 09.00 and 17.00hrs from Monday to Friday. During the summer the headquarters and many branch offices are open on Saturday to personal callers between 09.00-12.00hrs. See also page 16 and *Town Plan of Kǿbenhavn* pages 96-97.

Motorways

Approximately 380 miles of toll-free motorways (motorvej) are at present open and more stretches of the planned 560 mile network are under construction. Nearly all motorways are part of the

European international network of E-roads, which are marked with green and white signs with the prefix 'E'.

Orange badge scheme for disabled drivers

(See also page 16)
Concessions are extended to badge holders who are allowed to park for up to 1 hour where a shorter time limit applies to other motorists. Unlimited parking is permitted where a time limit of 1 hour or longer would otherwise apply.

Parking

(See also page 17)
Regulations are similar to those in the UK but it is advisable to use public car parks. In central København, kerbside parking is restricted to one hour; three hours where there are parking meters. Vehicles illegally parked will be removed by the police at the owner's expense and a fine will be imposed. Parking discs which are obtained from the police, FDM offices or service stations are obligatory. These discs are set at the time of parking and show when the parking time expires according to the time limit allowed in the district. Failure to observe zonal regulations could result in a fine or the vehicle being towed away. Parking lights must be used in badly lit areas and when visibility is poor.

Petrol

(See also page 18)
Credit cards Some recognised credit cards accepted at petrol stations.
Duty-free petrol In addition to the petrol in the vehicle tank up to 10 litres in a can may be imported free of customs duty and tax.
Petrol (leaded) Normal Benzin (92 octane) and Super Benzin (96-98 octane) grades.
Petrol (unleaded) is sold in Denmark. It has an octane rating of 95 which is indicated on the pump, together with the word *ublyet* (lead free).

Postal information

Mail Postcards *Dkr* 2.80, letters up to 20gm *Dkr* 2.80.
Post offices There are 300 post offices in Denmark. Large offices are open 09.00-17.00hrs or 10.00-17.00hrs Monday to Friday and 09.00-12.00hrs or 10.00-12.00hrs Saturday. Opening hours for small offices vary. In København the Head Post Office is open 09.00-19.00hrs Monday to Friday and 09.00-13.00hrs Saturday. The post office at the Central Station is open 09.00-21.00hrs Monday to Friday, 09.00-18.00hrs Saturday and 10.00-16.00hrs Sundays and Public holidays.

Postcheques

(See also page 20)
All post offices except the smallest will encash postcheques for any amount up to a maximum of *Dkr* 900 per cheque. Counter positions are identified by a sign bearing the flags of the issuing countries and the words *Postcheques* and *Postsparebank*. See *Postal information* for post office opening hours.

Priority

A line of white triangles painted across the road indicates that you must give way to traffic on the road you are entering. See also *Priority including Roundabouts* page 21.

Public holidays

Official public holidays in Denmark for 1987 are given below. See also *Public holidays* page 00
January 1 (New Year's Day)
April 16 (Maundy Thursday)
April 17 (Good Friday)
April 20 (Easter Monday)
May 15 (Store Bededag or Great Prayer Day)
May 28 (Ascension Day)
June 5 (Constitution Day)†
June 8 (Whit Monday)
December 24 (Christmas Eve)
December 25 (Christmas Day)
December 26* (Boxing Day)
December 31 (New Year's Eve)†

*Saturday
†Officially a public holiday from noon

Roads

The roads in Denmark are generally of a very high standard and well signposted. They are classified into three categories, showing E-roads (green and white signs with prefix 'E'), primary roads (one or two digit black numbers on yellow boards) and secondary roads (three digit black numbers on white boards). See also *Road conditions* page 22.

Shopping hours

Shops are usually open between 09.00hrs and 17.30hrs (19.00 or 20.00hrs on Friday). Most shops are closed on Saturday afternoons.

Speed limits

(See also page 22)
Unless indicated by signs the following limits apply:

	Built-up area (indicated by the placename)
Car	50 kph (31 mph)
Car/caravan/trailer	50kph (31 mph)
	Other roads.
Car	80 kph (49 mph)
Car/caravan/trailer	70kph (43 mph)
	Motorways
Car	100 kph (62 mph)
Car/caravan/trailer	70 kph (43 mph)

Even minor infringement of these limits can result in a fine.

Spiked or studded tyres

Spiked or studded tyres may be used between 1 October and 30 April. When spiked tyres are used no special speed limits apply but the spiked tyres must be fitted to all wheels. Generally, motoring in Denmark is rarely restricted by bad weather. See also *Cold weather touring* page 8.

Tourist information

(See also page 24)
The Danish Tourist Board maintains an information office in London at Sceptre House, 169/173 Regent Street, (entrance New Burlington Street), W1R 8PY ☎ 01-734 2637/8. In Denmark the Danish Tourist Board has offices in all the main towns.

Using the telephone

(See also page 24)
Insert coin **after** lifting receiver, dialling tone continuous tone. When making calls to subscribers within Denmark precede number with relevant area code (shown in parentheses against town entry in gazetteer). Use *Dkr*1 coin or two 25øre coins for local calls and *Dkr*1 or 5 coins for national and international calls. Coins inserted in a callbox are not returned even if the number is engaged, but repeat attempts may be made until the time runs out.
International callbox identification All callboxes.
Telephone rates A telephone call to the UK costs *Dkr* 3.60 for each minute.
What to dial for the Irish Republic 009 353.
What to dial for the UK 009 44.

Warning triangle

The use of a warning triangle is compulsory for all vehicles except two-wheelers. The triangle must be placed at least 50 metres (55yds) behind the vehicle on ordinary roads and 100 metres (109yds) on motorways to warn following traffic of any obstruction. See also *Warning triangles/Hazard warning lights* page 25.

Prices are in Danish Kroner
The Danish alphabet differs from the English one in that the last letters after **Z** are Æ, Ø, Å; this must be borne in mind when using Danish reference books.

Abbreviations:
bd boulevard
pl plads

AALBORG
Jylland (☎08)

★★★★***Hvide Hus*** Vesterbro 2 ☎138400 tx69690
200 **P** Lift ☾ sea
Credit cards 1 2 3 5

★★★***Limfjordshotellet*** Ved Stranden 14—16 (n.rest) ☎164333
85 **P** Lift ☾

★★★**Phønix** Vesterbro 77 ☎120011 tx69782
160 **P**100 Lift ☾ sB 510 dB 730 M140—170
Credit card 3

★★★***Scheelsminde*** (Inter DK) Scheelsmindevej 35 ☎183233
60 **P** ☾
Credit cards 1 2 3 5

★★**Central** Vesterbro 38 ☎126933
rm73 (44) **P** Lift ☾ sB220—290 sB 350—380 dB440 dB 570
Credit cards 1 2 3

Vilh Nellemann Jyllandsgade 28 ☎126377 **P** AR DJ

ÅBENRA
Jylland (☎04)

★★★***Hvide Hus*** Flensborgvej 50 ☎624700 tx52182
51 A17rm **P**50 ☾ sea
Credit cards 1 2 3 5

E Grodt Vestermarksvej 7—9 ☎622028 Peu Tal

M Jensen Flensborgvej 2 ☎621355 Cit Ope

Skifter Andersen Langrode, Vestvejen ☎621333 Vol

ALBERTSLUND See **KØBENHAVN (COPENHAGEN)**

ANS BY
Jylland (☎06)
At **KONGENSBRO** (5km SE)

★★**Kongensbro Kro** Gl-Kongevej 70 ☎870177
rm16 (14) **P**50 sB 340—375 dB 455—495
Credit cards 1 3 5

ÅRHUS
Jylland (☎06)

★★★★**Atlantic** Europapl ☎131111 tx64301
101 **P**50 Lift ☾ sB 515—625 dB 690—790 sea
Credit cards 1 2 3 4 5

★★★**Marselis** Strandvejen 25 ☎144411 tx68751
100 **P**150 Lift ☾ sB 500 dB 675 M150—180 Beach sea
Credit cards 1 2 5

★★★**Ritz** (Inter DK) Banegaardsplads 12 ☎134444
Closed 24—31 Dec
63 **P**8 Lift ☾ sB 385—400 dB 500—525
Credit cards 1 2 3 5

★★***Ansgar*** Banegaardspl 14 ☎124122
rm184 (154) **P**60 Lift ☾

★★**Royal** Store Torv 4 ☎120011 tx64500
Closed 23 Dec—1 Jan
124 Lift ☾ sB 600—1100 dB 800—1300 M125—175
Credit cards 1 2 3 4 5

At **HØJBJERG** (3km SE)

★★★★**Scanticon** Ny Maesgardvej ☎273233 tx68715

🛁 110 **P**250 sB 🛁 487 dB 🛁 599 M120—140 ▭ sea
Credit cards [1] [2] [5]

ÅRS
Jylland (☎08)

L Rold Vestre Boulevard 21 ☎621511 **P** For

ÅRUP
Fyn (☎09)

H Obelitz ☎431005 **P** Ren Vol

BILLUND
Jylland (☎05)

★★**Vis-a-Vis** ☎331244 tx60717

🛁 60 **P**100 ☾ sB 🛁 418 dB 🛁 586
Credit cards [1] [2] [5]

BIRKERØD
Sjælland (☎02)

M Klingsholm Kongevejen 74-76 ☎810080 Ope Vau

BLOMMENSLYST See **ODENSE**

BORNHOLM (ISLE OF) See **RØNNE**

BRABRAND
Jylland (☎06)

★★**Aarslev Kro** Silkeborgvej 900 ☎260577

🚿 32 **P** sB🚿 320 dB🚿 550 M60—180

BRØNDERSLEV
Jylland (☎08)

J Andersen Østergade ☎820588 Ope

COPENHAGEN See **KØBENHAVN**

EBELTOFT
Jylland (☎06)

★★★★**Ebeltoft Strand** Nordre Strandvej 3 ☎343300 tx60967

🛁 68 **P**250 Lift ☾ sB 🛁 365—395 dB 🛁 555—595 M145—165 ▭ sea mountains
Credit cards [1] [2] [3] [4] [5]

★★★★***Hvide Hus*** Strandgaardshøj ☎341466 tx60872

🛁 53 **P** A10rm Lift ☾ ▣ sea ▭
Credit cards [1] [2] [3] [5]

★★***Vigen*** Adelgade 5 ☎341433

rm30 (🛁 🚿 9)

ELSINORE See **HELSINGØR**

ESBJERG
Jylland (☎05)

★★★**Britannia** Torvet ☎130111

🛁 79 **P**100 Lift ☾ sB 🛁 420 dB 🛁 550
Credit cards [1] [2] [3] [4] [5]

★★***Bangs*** Torvet 21 ☎126933 tx54388

rm75 (🚿 15) **P**20 Lift ☾
Credit cards [1] [2] [3] [4] [5]

★★**Missionshotellet Ansgar** Skolegaade 36 ☎128244

rm63 (🛁 51) **P**45 Lift ☾ sB247 sB 🛁 292—332 dB384 dB 🛁 454—474

Denmark

M40—85
Credit cards [1] [2] [3] [5]

★★***Palads*** Skolegaade 14 ☎123000

rm48 (🚿 30) **P** Lift ☾
Credit cards [1] [2] [3] [5]

K S Kristensen Hovedvej 1 ☎142111 For

FÅBORG
Fyn (☎09)

★★**Faaborg Fjord** ☎611010 tx50312

Closed 23 Dec—5 Jan
rm45 (🛁 41) A5rm **P**50 sB255 sB 🛁 335 dB385 dB 🛁 495 M95 ▭ Beach

FARSØ
Jylland (☎08)

M Nielsen Norregade 18—20 ☎631600 M/c Ope Vau

FEMMØLLER
Jylland (☎06)

★★***Molskroen*** Femmøller Strand ☎362200

🛁 🚿 26 **P** ☾ sea

★★***Vaegtergarden*** ☎362211

rm26 (🛁 13) **P**

FILSKOV
Jylland (☎05)

★**Filskov Kro** ☎348111

Closed 24—25 Dec & New Year
rm45 (🛁 42) A3rm ⌂ **P**30 sB250 sB 🛁 395 dB400 dB 🛁 480 M70—130 🔑 ⛴
Credit cards [1] [2] [3] [5]

FJERRITSLEV
Jylland (☎08)

Auto-Ċentralen Sondergrade 15 ☎211666 Ope

FREDENSBORG
Sjælland (☎02)

★★★★***Store Kro*** Slotsgade 6 ☎280047

🛁 33 A16rm **P**75 Lift ☾
Credit cards [1] [2] [3] [5]

FREDERICIA
Jylland (☎05)

★★★**Landsoldaten** Norgesgade 1 ☎921555 tx51100

2 Jan—23 Dec
🛁 49 **P**12 Lift ☾ sB 🛁 295—325 dB 🛁 395—425
Credit cards [1] [2] [3] [5]

★★★**Postgaarden** Oldenborggade 4 ☎921855 tx51100

🚿 24 **P**24 ☾ sB🚿 350 dB🚿 450
Credit cards [1] [3] [5]

Fredericia Automobilhandel Vejlevej 30 ☎920211 For

FREDERIKSHAVN
Jylland (☎08)

★★★**Jutlandia** Havnepladsen 1 ☎424200 tx67142

Closed 23 Dec—5 Jan
🛁 105 ⌂ **P**60 Lift ☾ sB 🛁 405—595 dB 🛁 735—1040 M100—120 sea
Credit cards [1] [2] [3] [5]

★★**Hoffmans** Tordenslejoldsq 3 ☎422166

Closed Xmas
rm74 (🚿 36) **P**28 Lift sB245 sB🚿 305 dB430 dB🚿 490
Credit cards [1] [2] [3] [5]

A Precht-Jensen Hjørringvej 12—14 ☎423366 Saa

B Sørensen Grønlandsvej 10 ☎422877 **P** AR Ren

FREDERIKSVÆRK
Sjælland (☎02)

Thorkild Sørensen Hillerødvej 103, Kregme ☎121800 AR

FRØRUP
Fyn (☎09)

★★**Øksendrup Kro** Svendborg Landevej 30, Øksendrup ☎371057

🛁 🚿 15 **P**15 sB 🛁 🚿 fr240 dB 🛁 🚿 fr385

GAMMEL SKAGEN See **SKAGEN**

GEDSER
Falster (☎03)

★***Gedser*** Langgade 59 ☎879302

rm15 (🛁 🚿 12) **P**10
Credit cards [1] [2] [3]

GENTOFTE See **KØBENHAVN (COPENHAGEN)**

GLOSTRUP See **KØBENHAVN (COPENHAGEN)**

GRAM
Jylland (☎04)

★★***Gamle Kro*** Slotsvej 47 (n.rest) ☎821620

rm24 (🛁 18) **P**50
Credit cards [1] [2] [3] [5]

GRENÅ
Jylland (☎06)

★★★***Nord*** (Inter DK) Kystvej 25 ☎322500 tx63480

🛁 100 **P** Lift ☾ ⛴ sea
Credit cards [1] [2] [3] [5]

HADERSLEV
Jylland (☎04)

★★★**Norden** (Inter DK) Storegade 55 ☎524030

🛁 46 ⌂ **P**100 sB 🛁 275—375 dB 🛁 420—495 M90 lake
Credit cards [1] [2] [3] [4] [5]

★★**Haderslev** Damparken ☎526010 tx51599

🛁 🚿 70 **P**100 Lift sB 🛁 🚿 375—425 dB 🛁 🚿 545—605 M98—140 lake
Credit cards [1] [2] [3] [4] [5]

🚗 ***E Grodt*** Sønderbro 10 ☎521750 M/c Cit

Skifter Andersen Bil Norgesvej 9 ☎520353 Ren Vol

HADSUND
Jylland (☎08)

★***Øster Hurup*** Kystvegen 57, Øster, Hurup ☎588014
rm13 🚗 **P**

🚗 ***Autogarden*** Østergade 14 ☎571677 M/c **P** Ope Vau

HAMMEL
Jylland (☎06)

🚗 **J B Winter** Anbaekvej 36 ☎933855 Ren Vol

HELSINGØR (ELSINORE)
Sjælland (☎02)

★★★★**Marienlyst** (SRS) Nordre Strandvej 2 ☎211801 tx41116
🛁 213 A53rm **P** Lift ☾ sB 🛁 fr605
dB 🛁 810—1160 M125—165 ⛱ Beach sea
Credit cards [1] [2] [3] [4] [5]

★***Missions*** (Temperance) Bramsstraede 5 ☎210591
rm46 (🛁 🚿 28) **P** Lift ☾

🚗 ***Sommer Automobiler Helsingør*** Kongevej 101 ☎213111 Ren Vol

HERNING
Jylland (☎07)

★★★***Eyde*** (Inter DK) Torvet 1 ☎221800 tx62195
🛁 98 **P** Lift ☾
Credit cards [1] [2] [5]

HIMMELEV See **ROSKILDE**

HJØRRING
Jylland (☎08)

🚗 **L Karlborg** Frederikshavnsvej 76 ☎923011 Ren Vol

HOBRO
Jylland (☎08)

E Nielsen ☎523111 BMW Hon

HØJBJERG See **ÅRHUS**

HOLBÆK
Sjælland (☎03)

★★**Strandparken** Kalundborvej 58 ☎430616
🛁 31 **P**95 ☾ sB 🛁 310—425
dB 🛁 450—700 Beach sea
Credit cards [1] [3] [5]

🚗 **'Trekanten'** Taastrup Møllevej 6 ☎431313 Cit Col Ren

HOLSTEBRO
Jylland (☎07)

★★★**Bel Air** ☎426666
🛁 57 🚗 **P**600 Lift ☾ sB 🛁 340 dB 🛁 495
Credit cards [1] [2] [3] [5]

★★**Schaumburg** Norregade 26 ☎423111
rm34 (🛁 🚿 20) **P**30 sB250 sB 🛁 🚿 350
dB350 dB 🛁 🚿 450

Denmark

HORNBÆK
Sjælland (☎02)

★★★**Trouville** Kystvej 20 ☎202200 tx41241
rm50(🛁 49) A3rm **P**100 Lift ☾
sB 🛁 470—535 dB740—840
dB 🛁 790—890 M125—195 ⛱ Beach
Credit cards [1] [2] [3] [5]

HORNDRUP See **SKANDERBORG**

HORSENS
Jylland (☎05)

★★★**Bygholm Park** Schuttesvej 6 ☎622333
rm70 (🛁 50) **P**150 ☾ sB200—300
sB 🛁 375—450 dB375—450
dB 🛁 550—650 M120—150
Credit cards [1] [2] [3] [5]

★★***Postgarden*** Gl-Jernbanegade 6 ☎621800
rm50 🚗 **P**

🚗 ***Bilforum*** Silkeborgvej 2 ☎626000 Ope Vau

HVIDOVRE See **KØBENHAVN (COPENHAGEN)**

KALUNDBORG
Sjælland (☎03)

🚗 ***Autohallen*** Slagelsevej 242 ☎510982 AR Dat

KASTRUP See **KØBENHAVN (COPENHAGEN)**

KØBENHAVN (COPENHAGEN) (☎01)
See Plan page 96

★★★★★**Angleterre** (Intercont) Kongens Nytorv 34 ☎120095 tx15877 Plan **1**
🛁 🚿 139 🚗 Lift ☾ sB 🛁 🚿 1180—1380
dB 🛁 🚿 1585—1910 M200—300
Credit cards [1] [2] [3] [4] [5]

★★★★★**SAS Royal** (SRS) Hammerichsgade 1 ☎141412 tx27155 Plan **2**
🛁 273 🚗 **P** Lift ☾ sB 🛁 1125—1550
dB 🛁 1395—1850
Credit cards [1] [2] [3] [5]

★★★★★**Sheraton** Vester Søgade 6 ☎143535 tx27450 Plan **2A**
🛁 471 **P**1200 Lift ☾ sB 🛁 1220—1970
dB 🛁 1490—2040 Malc
Credit cards [1] [2] [3] [4] [5]

★★★★**Codan** St Annæ Pl 21 ☎133400 tx15815 Plan **3**
🛁 134 **P**6 Lift ☾ sB 🛁 526—741
dB 🛁 797—1002 M119—150

★★★★**Copenhagen Admiral** Toldbodgade 24 ☎118282 tx15941 Plan **3A**
🛁 366 **P**80 Lift sB 🛁 526—666
dB 🛁 792—897 Malc
Credit cards [1] [3] [5]

★★★★**Imperial** (THF) Vester Farimagsgade 9 ☎128000 tx15556 Plan **6**
🛁 163 **P** Lift ☾ sB 🛁 770—1075
dB 🛁 990—1350 M110—220
Credit cards [1] [2] [3] [4] [5]

★★★★***Ladbroke Palace*** Raadhuspl 57 ☎144050 tx19693 Plan **6A**
🛁 170 **P** Lift ☾
Credit cards [1] [2] [3] [4] [5]

★★★★**Mercur** Vester Farimagsgade 17 ☎125711 tx19767 Plan **7**
🛁 108 **P** Lift ☾ sB 🛁 740 dB 🛁 920—1100 M165 ✂
Credit cards [1] [2] [5]

★★★★**Richmond** Vester Farimagsgade 33 ☎123366 tx19767 Plan **9**
Closed 23 Dec—1 Jan
🛁 🚿 132 **P** Lift ☾ sB 🛁 🚿 740
dB 🛁 🚿 920—1100 M165—330 ✂
Credit cards [1] [2] [5]

★★★***Alexandra*** H-C-Andersens bd 8 (n.rest) ☎142200 Plan **10**
🛁 65 A1rm 🚗 Lift

★★★**Astoria** Banegaardspladsen 4 ☎141419 tx16319 Plan **11**
🛁 91 **P**5 Lift ☾ sB 🛁 797—997
dB 🛁 1096—1346 Malc
Credit cards [1] [2] [3] [5]

★★★**Grand** Vesterbrogade 9 ☎313600 tx15343 Plan **15**
rm113 (🛁 🚿 90) **P** Lift ☾ sB325
sB 🛁 🚿 680—720 dB450—480 dB 🛁 🚿 960
Credit cards [2] [5]

★★★***Ladbroke*** Løngangstrade 27 ☎126570 tx16488 Plan **15A**
🛁 200 🚗 **P**25 Lift
Credit cards [1] [2] [3] [5]

★★★**71 Nyhavn** Nyhavn 71 ☎118585 tx27558 Plan **16**
🛁 🚿 82 **P**8 Lift ☾ sB 🛁 🚿 768—1088
dB 🛁 🚿 998—1318 M140—245
Credit cards [1] [2] [3] [4] [5]

★★★**SAS Globetrotter** 171 Engvej ☎551433 tx31222 Plan **17**
🛁 154 **P**250 Lift ☾ sB 🛁 fr625 dB 🛁 fr815 M155
Credit cards [1] [2] [3] [4] [5]

★★★***Tre Falke*** (Inter DK) Falkoner Alle 9 ☎198001 tx15550 Plan **19**
🛁 162 **P** Lift ☾
Credit cards [2] [5]

★★**Missionhotellet Hebron** Helgolandsgade 4 (n.rest) ☎316906 tx27416 Plan **20**
rm119 (🚿 78) Lift sB245—270
sB🚿 360—500 dB390—450 dB🚿 530—610
Credit cards [1] [2] [3] [5]

★★***Viking*** Bregade 65 (n.rest) ☎124550 tx19590 Plan **21**
rm91 (🛁 19) **P**4 Lift ☾
Credit cards [1] [2] [3] [4] [5]

★***Vestersøhus*** Vesterøgade 58 (n.rest) ☎113870 Plan **22**
rm53 (🛁 22🚿 5) A9rm **P**30 Lift ☾ lake
Credit cards [1] [2] [3] [5]

Baunsoe Biler Middelfartgade 15 ☎297711 Cit Dat Peu

🚗 ***BMW City*** Lautrupsgade 2—4 ☎209560 M/c BMW

🚗 ***V Nelleman*** Vodroffsvej 55—57 ☎353333 AR

B P Parkeringshuset Nyropsgade 6 ☎126765 **P** BMW

At **ALBERTSLUND** (15km W on N1)

★**Wittrup** Roskidevej 251 ☎(02)649551 Plan **23**

Closed Xmas & New Year
rm56 (⋒48) **P**75 ☾ sB230 sB⋒275 dB⋒375
Credit cards 1 2 3 5

At **GENTOFTE** (5km N)

★★★**Gentofte** Gentoftegade 29 ☎680911 tx15610 Plan **14**

🍴⋒70 **P**50 Lift ☾ sB🍴⋒540—560 dB🍴⋒715—745 M120—150
Credit cards 1 2 3 5

At **GLOSTRUP** (11km W on N1)

🚗 ***Monk's Automobiler*** Vibeholmsvej 26—28 ☎(02)459000 Toy

At **HVIDOVRE** (6km SW)

★★★***Scandic*** Kettevej 4 ☎498222 tx15517 Plan **18**

🍴220 **P**150 Lift ☾

At **KASTRUP**/Airport (9km SE)

★★★★***Dan*** Kastruplundgade 15 ☎511400 tx31111 Plan **4**

🍴⋒271 **P** Lift ☾ Beach sea

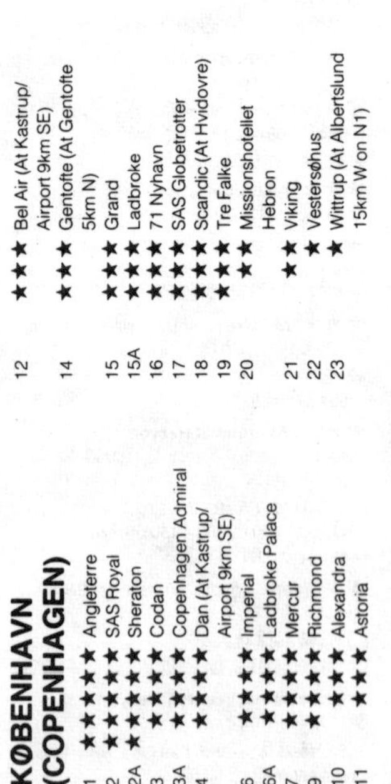

KØBENHAVN (COPENHAGEN)

1 ★★★★★ Angleterre
2 ★★★★★ SAS Royal
2A ★★★★★ Sheraton
3 ★★★★ Codan
3A ★★★★ Copenhagen Admiral
4 ★★★★ Dan (At Kastrup/ Airport 9km SE)
6 ★★★★ Imperial
6A ★★★★ Ladbroke Palace
7 ★★★★ Mercur
9 ★★★★ Richmond
10 ★★★ Alexandra
11 ★★★ Astoria
12 ★★★ Bel Air (At Kastrup/ Airport 9km SE)
14 ★★★ Gentofte (At Gentofte 5km N)
15 ★★★ Grand
15A ★★★ Ladbroke
16 ★★★ 71 Nyhavn
17 ★★★ SAS Globetrotter
18 ★★★ Scandic (At Hvidovre)
19 ★★★ Tre Falke
20 ★★ Missionshotellet Hebron
21 ★★ Viking
22 ★ Vestersøhus
23 ★ Wittrup (At Albertslund 15km W on N1)

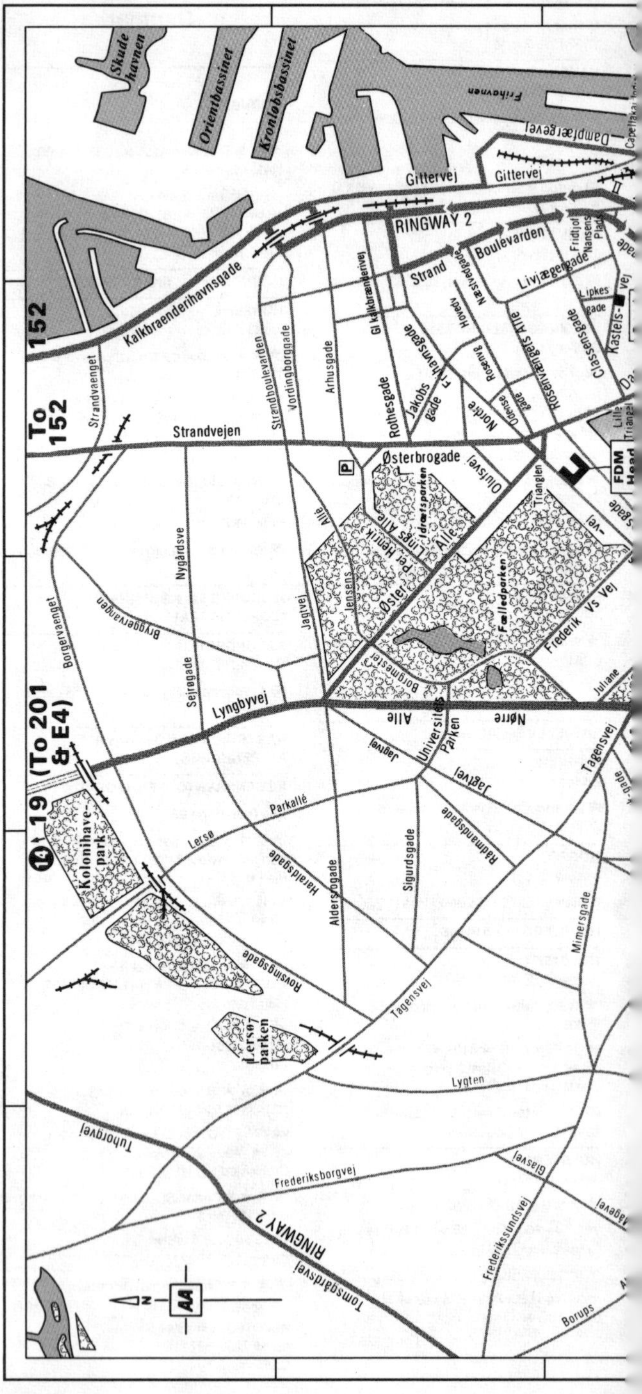

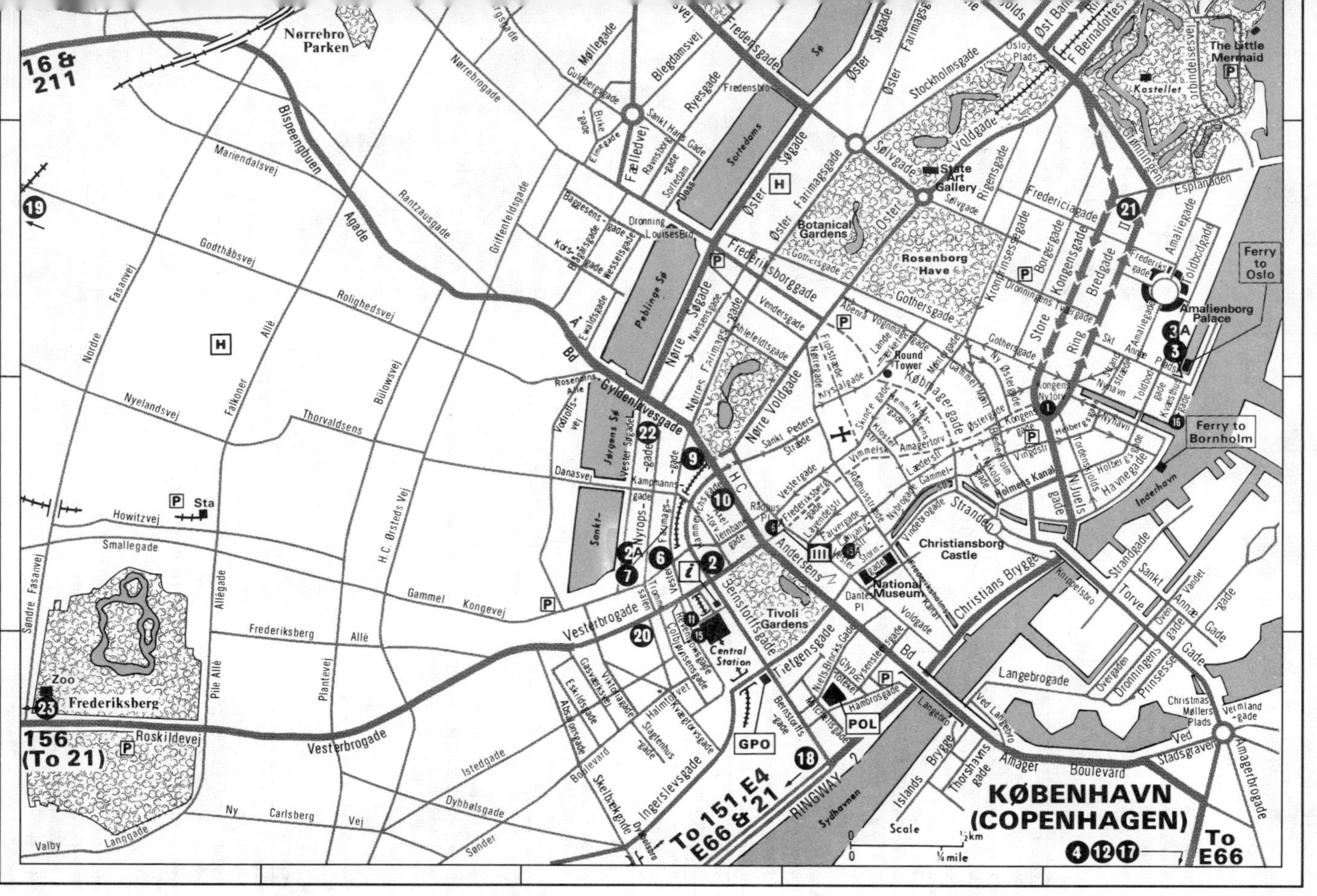
KØBENHAVN
(COPENHAGEN)
To E66
Scale
½ km
¼ mile
The Little Mermaid
Kastellet
Amalienborg Palace
Ferry to Oslo
Ferry to Bornholm
State Art Gallery
Rosenborg Have
Botanical Gardens
Round Tower
Christiansborg Castle
National Museum
Tivoli Gardens
Central Station
GPO
POL
Pebling Sø
Sortedams Sø
Jørgens Sø
Nørrebro Parken
Frederiksberg
Zoo
Sta
To 151, E4
E66 & 21
156
(To 21)
16 &
211
Amaliegade
Bredgade
Store Kongensgade
Kronprinsessegade
Gothersgade
Øster Voldgade
Øster Søgade
Nørre Søgade
Nørre Voldgade
Frederiksborggade
Købmager gade
Strandgade
Christians Brygge
Vesterbrogade
Gyldenløvesgade
H.C. Andersens Bd
Bernstorffsgade
Istedgade
Ingerslevsgade
Gammel Kongevej
H.C. Ørsteds Vej
Bülowsvej
Rolighedsvej
Thorvaldsens
Falkoner Allé
Godthåbsvej
Nyelandsvej
Nordre Fasanvej
Søndre Fasanvej
Bispeengbuen
Nørrebrogade
Rantzausgade
Griffenfeldsgade
Fælledvej
Blegdamsvej
Frederiksberg Allè
Pile Allè
Roskildevej
Ny Carlsberg Vej
Smallegade
Howitzvej
Amager Boulevard
Langebrogade
Islands Brygge
Ringway
Amagerbrogade
Valby Langgade

★★★Bel Air Løjtegårdsvej 99 ☎513033 tx31240 Plan **12**

➡ 55 A160rm **P**150 ☾ sB➡ 500—550 dB➡ 600—650 M105—115
Credit cards 1 2 3 5

KØGE
Sjælland (☎03)

★★★*Hvide Hus* Strandvejen 111 ☎653690 tx43501

➡ 118 A13rm ⌂ **P**250 ☾
Credit cards 1 2 3 4 5

🚗 *G Due* Tangmosevej 105 ☎653400 Maz Ope

KOLDING
Jylland (☎05)

★★★Saxildhus (Inter DK) Banegaardspl ☎521200 tx51446

Closed 21 Dec—1 Jan
➡ 82 **P**200 Lift ☾ sB➡ 320—650 dB➡ 450—800
Credit cards 1 2 3 4 5

★★★Tre Roser Grønningen 2, Byparken ☎532122

➡ 83 **P**65 sB➡ 390—535 dB➡ 535—680 Malc ▭
Credit cards 1 2 3 5

🚗 H G Nielsen Vejlevej 108 ☎522555 For

KONGENSBRO
See **ANS BY**

KORSØR
Sjælland (☎03)

🚗 *Bilhuset T Nielsen* Tårnborgvej 170 ☎572900 AR Sko Vol

LEMVIG
Jylland (☎07)

★★★*Niørre Vinkel* Søgårdevejen 6, Vinkelhage ☎822211

➡ 26 **P** Lift ☾ lake

LØGSTØR
Jylland (☎08)

★★Nord Havnevej 38 ☎671711

rm22 (➡ 7) **P**75 sB236 sB➡ 266 dB387 dB➡ 447 M68 sea
Credit cards 1 3 5

MARIBO
Lolland (☎03)

★★★*Hvide Hus* Vestergade 57 ☎881011

➡ 69 ⌂ **P**20 Lift ☾ ⩩ lake
Credit cards 1 2 3 5

MILLINGE
Fyn (☎09)

★★Falsled Kro Assensvej 513, Falsled ☎681111 tx50404

Closed Jan & Feb
➡ 14 **P**64 sB➡ 480 dB➡ 1680 M110—410 sea
Credit cards 1 2 5

NÆSTVED
Sjælland (☎03)

★★★Mogenstrup Kro Praestø Landevej, Mogenstrup ☎761130 tx46201

➡ 38 A9rm **P**120 ☾ sB➡ 438—498 dB➡ 586—636 M110—195 ▭
Credit cards 1 2 3 4 5

★★★Vinhuset St-Peders Kirkepl 4 ☎720807 tx46279

➡ 58 **P**30 ☾ sB➡ 360—395 dB➡ 565—675 M105—160
Credit cards 1 2 3 5

NAKSKOV
Lolland (☎03)

★★*Harmonien* Nybrogade 2 ☎922100 rm39 (➡ ⫪ 33)

★★Skovrider Gaarden Svingelen ☎ 920355

➡ 10 A5rm **P** sB➡ 240—260 dB➡ 370—399 lake
Credit cards 1 2 5

NYBORG
Fyn (☎09)

★★★★Hesselet Christianslundsvej 119 ☎313340 tx9297122

5 Jan—20 Dec
➡ 46 **P**80 Lift ☾ sB➡ 545—600 dB➡ 870—1020 M155—265 ▭ Beach sea
Credit cards 1 2 3 5

★★*Nyborg Strand* (Inter DK) Osterovej 2 ☎313131 tx50371

➡ 260 **P** Lift ☾ sea
Credit cards 1 2 3 5

NYKØBING
Falster (☎03)

★★★Baltic Jernbangegade 45 (n.rest) ☎853066

➡ ⫪ 70 **P**200 Lift ☾ sB➡ ⫪ 240 dB➡ ⫪ 400 M80
Credit cards 1 2 3 4 5

🚗 Auto Co Frisegade 31 ☎853155

🚗 Breitenstein Randersvej 4 ☎852266 Saa

🚗 A Hansen Randersvej 8 ☎850600 For

At **SUNDBY** (2km N)

★Liselund Lundevej 22 ☎851566

➡ 25 **P**35 ☾ sB➡ 260 dB➡ 375 sea
Credit card 2

NYKØBING-MORS
Jylland (☎07)

🚗 H D Pedersen Limfjordvej 44 ☎723044 Ren Vol

NYKØBING-SJÆLLAND
Sjælland (☎03)

P Tamstorf Kirkestraede 5 ☎411400 For

ODDER
Jylland (☎06)

🚗 A Rasmussen Ballevej 14 ☎543000 Toy

ODENSE
Fyn (☎09)

★★★Grand Jernbanegade 18 ☎117171 tx59972

➡ 139 ⌂ **P** ☾ sB➡ 480—1050 dB➡ 625—1500 M140—170
Credit cards 1 2 3 4 5

★★★H C Andersen C-Bergsgade 7 ☎147800 tx59694

➡ 148 **P** Lift sB➡ 595 dB➡ 790
Credit cards 1 2 3 5

★★Golf Plaza Østre Stationsvej 24 ☎117745

➡ 70 **P**25 Lift ☾ sB➡ 568—978 dB➡ 846—1216 M85—240
Credit cards 1 2 3 5

★★*Odense* (Inter DK) Hunderupgade 2 ☎114213

➡ 46 **P** ☾
Credit cards 1 2 3 5

★★Windsor Vindegade 45 ☎120652 tx59662

➡ 62 **P**30 Lift ☾ sB➡ 475—775 dB➡ 650—775 M100—150
Credit cards 1 2 3 4 5

★*Ansgarhus* Kirkegårds allé 17—19 ☎128800

Closed Oct
rm17 (➡ 4) ⌂

🚗 V Hansen Odensevej 121 ☎117255 Ren Vol

🚗 EM Jensen Odensevej 101 ☎115810 AR Dai LR DJ Saa Sko

Odense Dalumvej 67 ☎140400 BMW Hon

At **BLOMMENSLYST** (10km W on A1 [E66])

★★*Brasillia* (Inter DK) Middelfartvej 420 ☎967012 tx27459
➡ 52 **P** ☾

RANDERS
Jylland (☎06)

★★★★Randers Torvegade 11 ☎423422

Closed Xmas & New Year
➡ 85 ⌂ **P**35 Lift ☾ sB➡ 375—440 dB➡ 560—700 M120—140
Credit cards 1 2 3 4 5

★★★Kogens Ege Hadsundvej 2 ☎430300 tx65130

Closed 23 Dec—1 Jan
➡ 88 ⌂ **P**250 Lift ☾ sB➡ 380—530 dB➡ 590—720 Mfr138 lake
Credit cards 1 2 3 4 5

🚗 *Bohnstedt-Petersen* Ny Grenåvej ☎425399 Mer

🚗 J Madson Århusvej 108 ☎427800 Ope

🚗 *R Nellemann* Strømmen 27, Grenåvej ☎423233 For

RIBE
Jylland (☎05)

★★*Dagmar* (Inter DK) Torvet 1 ☎420033

➡ 42 **P** ☾
Credit cards 1 2 3 5

🚗 V Vejrup Industrivej 1 ☎420600 **P** Aud VW

RINGKØBING
Jylland (☎07)

★★★***Fjordgaarden*** (Inter DK) Vesterkaer 28 ☎321400
🛁60 **P** ☾ lake
Credit cards [1] [2] [5]

🚗 **N Hansens** Enghavevej 11 ☎321133 For

RINGSTED
Sjælland (☎03)

🚗 **H Larsen** Nørregade 90—92 ☎612518 For

RØDBY
Lolland (☎03)

★★★**Danhotel** Havnegade 2 ☎905366 tx40890
🛁🚿39 **P**150 Lift ☾ sB🛁🚿325—380 dB🛁🚿450—550 Malc sea
Credit cards [1] [2] [3] [5]

RØNNE
Isle of Bornholm (☎03)

🚗 ***F Jorgensen*** Ringvejen ☎950250 Ope Vau

🚗 ***G Larsen*** Åkirkebyvej 51 ☎950804 **P** For

RØNNEDE
Sjælland (☎03)

★***Axelved*** Ronnedevej 1, Axelved ☎711401
rm8

ROSKILDE
Sjælland (☎02)

★★**Prindsen** Algade 13 ☎358010
rm41 (🛁🚿36) **P** sB295 sB🛁🚿390—440 dB395 dB🛁🚿530—580 M115—195

🚗 ***Bekkers Autoservice*** Praestemarksvej 16 ☎757702 M/c Dat

At **HIMMELEV** (3km N on N6)

★★**B P Motel** Hovedvej A1 ☎354385
🚿16 A13rm **P**10 sB235 sB🚿355 dB330 dB🚿500
Credit cards [1] [2] [3] [5]

RY
Jylland (☎06)

★★**Ry** Kyhnsvej 2 ☎891911
🛁60 A17rm **P**80 **DPn**228—348 M95 lake
Credit cards [1] [2] [3] [5]

SAEBY
Jylland (☎08)

🚗 ***O Christensen*** Ålborgvej 32—34 ☎462255 **P** Peu

SAKSKØBING
Lolland (☎03)

🚗 **M Skotte** Nykøbingvej 8 ☎894285 Ope Vau

SILKEBORG
Jylland (☎06)

★★★***Dania*** Torvet 5 ☎820111 tx63269
rm48 (🛁35) **P** ☾ lake

★★★***Impala*** (Inter DK) Vester Ringvej ☎820300
🛁41 **P** ☾ 🏊 lake
Credit cards [1] [2]

SKAGEN
Jylland (☎08)

★★★**Skagen** Gammel Landevej ☎442233
🛁63 **P**180 sB🛁455 dB🛁655—755 M95—185 🏊

🚗 **G A Hylander** Øresundsvej 8 ☎445200 Fia

At **GAMMEL SKAGEN** (2km W)

★***Ruth's*** H-Ruthsvej 1 ☎441124
Jun—Aug
rm110 A20rm ⛍ sea

SKANDERBORG
Jylland (☎06)

★★★**Skanderborghus** Dyre Haven ☎520955
rm51 (🛁45) ⛍ **P**60 ☾ sB250—290 sB🛁350—400 dB350—400 dB🛁510—600 M96—148
Credit cards [1] [2] [3] [5]

★***Slotskroen*** Adelgade 23 ☎520012
🛁🚿14 A2rm ⛍ **P**15 lake
Credit cards [1] [2] [3] [5]

🚗 ***Skanderborg Motor*** Nørregade 1 ☎520566 AR

At **HORNDRUP** (10km S)

★★***Oasen*** ☎579228
🛁12 ⛍ lake

SKIVE
Jylland (☎07)

★★***Gl Skivehus*** (Inter DK) Sdr 1, Østertorv ☎521144
🛁60 **P** Lift ☾ lake
Credit cards [1] [2] [3] [5]

★★**Hilltop** Sondre-Boulevard ☎523711
Closed 23—30 Dec
🛁68 **P**100 ☾ sB🛁320 dB🛁490
Credit cards [1] [2] [3] [5]

🚗 **J Fogh** Sdr Boulevard 9 ☎522100 **P** For

SKJERN
Jylland (☎07)

🚗 ***Moller*** Vardevej 87 ☎350911 Mer

SKØRPING
Jylland (☎08)

★★★***Rold Stor-Kro*** (Inter DK) Storegade 27 ☎375100
🛁53 **P** ☾ 🎾 🏊
Credit cards [1] [2] [3] [5]

SLAGELSE
Sjælland (☎03)

G Kjeruiff Sverigesvej 12 ☎520815 Ope

SØNDERBORG
Jylland (☎04)

★★***City*** Kongevej 64 ☎421626 tx16600
rm13 (🛁11) **P** ☾

SORØ
Jylland (☎03)

★★***Postgården*** Storgade 27 ☎632222
8 Jan—22 Dec
rm26 (🛁9) **P**

STRUER
Jylland (☎07)

★★***Grand*** Østergade 24 ☎850400
rm39 (🛁14) **P**50
Credit cards [1] [2] [3] [5]

SUNDBY See **NYKØBING**

SVENDBORG
Fyn (☎09)

★★★***Svendborg*** (Inter DK) Voldgade 10 ☎211700
🛁60 **P** Lift ☾
Credit card [2]

🚗 **Bilhuset** Grønnemosevej 6 ☎221111 AR Dai Fia LR Saa

🚗 ***C Bukkehave*** Lerchesvej 11 ☎211313 M/c **P** All makes

🚗 ***N Kjær Bilcentret*** Odensvej 94 ☎212323 **P** For

🚗 ***S Nauerby*** Odensevej 42 ☎213811 Ren Vol

TAPPERNØJE
Sjælland (☎03)

🚗 **Tappernøje Autoservice** Hovedvejen 67 ☎765099 AR Dai

THISTED
Jylland (☎07)

★★★**Ålborg** Storegade 29 ☎923566
rm32 (🛁23) ⛍ **P**40 ☾ sB190 sB🛁310 dB400 dB🛁475 M65—70 sea
Credit cards [1] [2] [3] [5]

🚗 **A P Anderson** Rosenkrantzgade 1 ☎921600 **P** Ope Vau

TOFTLUND
Jylland (☎04)

P Henriksen Østergade 23 ☎831122 Ope Vau

TØNDER
Jylland (☎04)

★★★***Tønderhus*** Jomflustien 1 ☎722222
rm31 (🛁17) A18rm ⛍ **P**15 ☾
Credit cards [1] [2] [5]

★★***Hostrups*** Søndergade 30 ☎722129
3 Jan—22 Dec
rm27 (🛁🚿26) A5rm ⛍ **P**

TRANEBJERG
Samsø (☎06)

🚗 **Ole's Autoservice** Langgade 2 ☎590265 VW

TRANEKAER
(Island of Langeland) (☎09)

★**Gjaestgivergaarden** Slotsgade 74 ☎591204

Closed 16 Feb—28 Feb
🚿12 **P**20 sB🚿275 dB🚿390—450

VARDE
Jylland (☎05)

★★**Varde** Hj Ribevej/Tømrervej ☎221500

🛁24 **P**50 sB🛁275 dB🛁430 M68
Credit cards [1] [3] [5]

🚗 **Varde Motor Compagni** V Landevej 78 ☎220499 **P** For

VEDÆK
Sjælland (☎02)

★★★**Marina** Vedbaek Strandvej 391 ☎891711 tx37217

🛁🚿106 🏠**P**200 Lift ☾ sB🛁🚿425—480 dB🛁🚿555—625 M135—185 Beach sea
Credit cards [1] [2] [5]

VEJLE
Jylland (☎05)

★★★★★**Australia** Daemningen 6 ☎824311 tx61104

6 Jan—22 Dec
🛁85 🏠**P**250 Lift ☾ sB🛁495 dB🛁700 M80—95 lake
Credit cards [1] [2] [3] [5]

★★★★**Munkebjerg** Munkebjergvej 125 ☎827500 tx61103

2 Jan—23 Dec
🛁125 A23rm **P**300 Lift ☾ sB🛁440 dB🛁640—690
Credit cards [1] [2] [3] [4] [5]

★★***Missionshotellet 'Caleb'*** Daemningen 52 (n.rest) ☎823211

Closed Jan
rm40 (🛁20) **P**25 Lift ☾
Credit cards [1] [2] [3] [5]

🚗 **Bøje & Brøchner** Boulevarden ☎826000 For

🚗 **M Kjae** Boulevarden 54 ☎828255 Ope Vau

Neergaard Vestre Engvej 7 ☎823366 M/c BMW Hon

VIBORG
Jylland (☎06)

★★★**Golf** Randersvej 2 ☎610222 tx66243

🛁110 **P**100 Lift ☾ sB🛁495—745 dB🛁685—935 M98—145 lake
Credit cards [1] [2] [3] [5]

★★***Missionshottellet*** St-Matthiasgade 5 ☎623700

rm49 (🛁44) A5rm 🏠**P**60 Lift ☾
Credit cards [1] [2] [3] [5]

🚗 ***Citröen Viborg*** Randersvej 51—53 ☎626000 Cit

🚗 ***F Jøorgensen*** Skivevej ☎623511 For

🚗 **V Sølvsten** Marsk Stigsvej 9 ☎610066 Mer

🚗 **P Wraa** Falkevej 23 ☎624600 Aud VW

VIBY
Jylland (☎06)

★★★**Mercur** Viby Torv ☎141411 tx68746

Closed 22 Dec—1 Jan
🛁125 🏠**P** Lift ☾ sB🛁465—515 dB🛁600—650 M95—135 lake
Credit cards [1] [2] [3] [4] [5]

Looking over Himmelbjerget towards Sky Mountain

International distinguishing sign

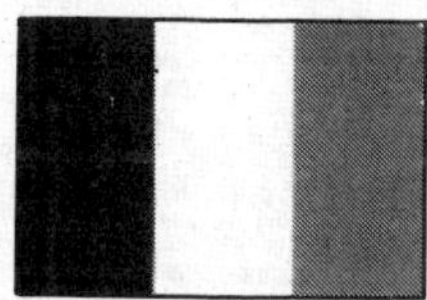

Monaco *See page 112*
Area *213,000 sq miles*
Population
54,300,000
Local time *GMT + 1*
(Summer GMT + 2)

National flag
Vertical tricolour of blue, white and red

A leaflet entitled *Motoring in Corsica* is available to AA members.

How to get there

Motorists can cross the Channel by ship or hovercraft services. Short sea crossings operate from Dover to Boulogne and Calais (1¼-1¾hrs), and Folkestone to Boulogne (1¾hrs). Longer Channel crossings operate from Ramsgate to Dunkerque (2½hrs), Newhaven to Dieppe (4hrs), Portsmouth to Le Havre (5½hrs) or Caen (5½-6½hrs) or Cherbourg (4-6½hrs) or St-Malo (9hrs), Poole to Cherbourg (4½hrs), Plymouth to Roscoff (6hrs) and Weymouth to Cherbourg (4 hrs). Fast hovercraft services operate between Dover and Boulogne or Calais (30-35 mins).

Motoring regulations and general information

This information should be read in conjunction with the general content of the European ABC (pages 4-26). **Note** As certain regulations and requirements are common to many countries they are covered by one entry in the ABC and the following headings represent some of the subjects dealt with in this way:
Crash or safety helmets
Drinking and driving
Fire extinguisher
First-aid kit
Insurance
International distinguishing sign
Medical treatment
Mirrors
Overtaking
Police fines
Radio telephones/Radio transmitters
Road signs
Seat belts
Tyres
Visitors' registration

AA Port agents

62201 Boulogne-sur-Mer G A Gregson & Sons, The Automobile Association, Tour Damremont (18 eme), Boulevard Chanzy BP No. 21 ☎ 21872121.

62100 Calais G A Gregson & Sons, The Automobile Association, Terminal Est ☎ 21964720

50100 Cherbourg Agence Maritime Tellier, Gare Maritime ☎ 33204338; Port office (when ferries operating), car ferry terminal ☎ 33204274.

76200 Dieppe G A Gregson & Sons, The Automobile Association, Car Ferry Terminal, Esplanade ☎ 35841941.

76600 Le Havre G A Gregson & Sons, The Automobile Association, 47 Boulevard John Kennedy ☎ 35420566. See also *AA Agents* page 5 and *Town Plans of Boulogne-sur-Mer* page 126, *Calais* pages 130-131, *Cherbourg* page 137, *Dieppe* page 142 and *Le Havre* page 150.

Accidents

Fire ☎ 18 **police** and **ambulance** ☎ 17. Contact the police (*brigade de gendarmerie*), particularly in cases of injury. Emergency telephone boxes are stationed every 20km on some roadways and are connected direct to the local police station. In the larger towns emergency help can be obtained from the *police secours* (emergency assistance department).

Motorists involved in a traffic accident must complete a *constat à l'amiable* before the vehicle is moved. If the vehicle has been seriously damaged an expert's examination is advised prior

ENGLISH CHANNEL

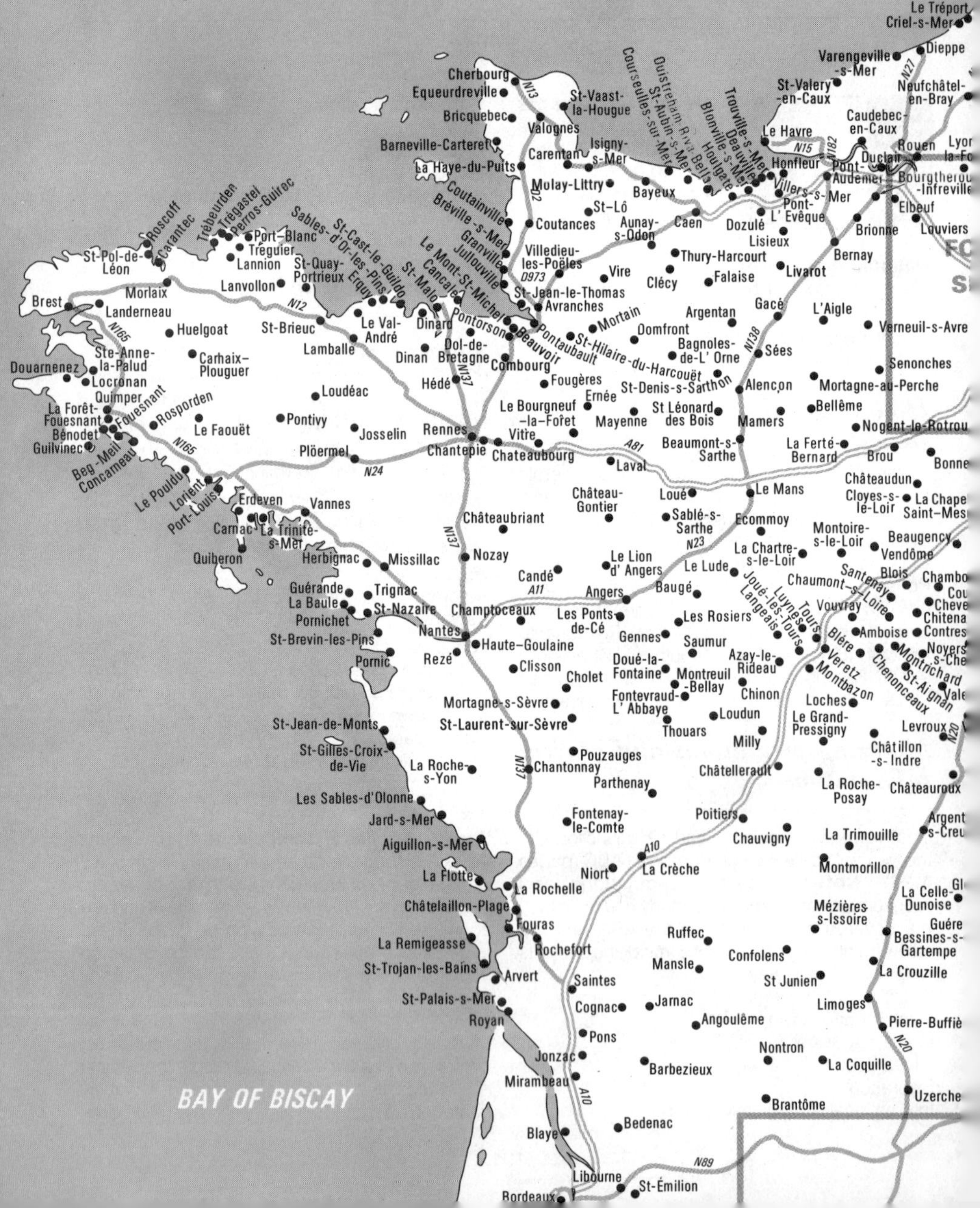

For key to country identification - see page 51

B

D

L

F

CH

I

ENLARGED AREA
EAST MAP PAGE
THIS SECTION

Dunkerque
Blériot-Plage
Calais
N1
Bergues
Wimereux
Ardres
Le Wast
N43
St-Omer
Boulogne-s-Mer
A22
Tourcoing
Le Portel
Aire-s-la-Lys
Lille
Roubaix
Le Touquet
Beaurainville
Béthune
Noeux-les-Mines
Bully-les-Mines
Berck-Plage
Hesdin
St-Pol-s-Ternoise
Lens
Douai
Valenciennes
Frévent
Arras
A2
Henin-Beaumont
A26
Cambrai
Cousolre
Abbeville
Louvroil
Bapaume
Le Nouvion-en-Thiérache
Fourmies
Blangy-s-Bresle
Albert
Hermies
Rancourt
Amiens
Fumay
Péronne
Rocroi
Aumale
St-Quentin
N43
Poix-de-Picardie
Vervins
Auvillers-les-Forges
Charleville-Mézières
Roye
La Fère
A203
A1
N44
Noyon
Laon
Inor
Longwy
Rethel
Longuyon
N1
Soissons
A31
Thionville
Reims
Fère-en-Tardenois
Beaumont-s-Vesle
Étain
A32
Château-Thierry
Ste-Menehould
Verdun
Forbach
Épernay
Sept-Saulx
Jarny
St-Avold
Sarreguemines
A4
Bonneil-s-Marne
Montmort
Metz
Châlons-s-Marne
A31
Montmirail
Pont-a-Mousson
La Petite-Pierre
A10
N44
A4
Sézanne
Commercy
Saverne
Vitry-le-François
N4
Stainville
Nancy
Marlenheim
Romilly-s-Seine
St-Dizier
Méréville
Obersteigen
Lunéville
N67
Lingolsheim
Strasbourg
Arcis-s-Aube
Obernai
N19
Domrémy-la-Pucelle
N83
Pont-s-Yonne
Joinville
Andlau
Nemours
Charmes
Sens
Troyes
Neufchâteau
Souppes-s-Loing
Savigny-s-Clairis
Villeneuve-s-Yonne
Dolancourt
Dompaire
N57
Pithiviers
A35
Dordives
Joigny
Migennes
Auxon
Bar-s-Aube
Colombey-les-Deux-Eglises
Epinal
Les Trois-Epis
Orléans
Courtenay
St-Florentin
Bar-s-Seine
Contrexéville
Gérardmer
Colmar
Olivet
Châteauneuf-s-Loire
Montargis
Polisot
Chaumont
Montigny-le-Roi
Remiremont
Neuf-Brisach
La Ferté-St Aubin
Montigny-la-Resle
Foulain
N19
N66
A6
Châtillon-s-Seine
Plombières-les-Bains
Rouffach
Sully-s-Loire
Aillant-s-Tholon
Tonnerre
A26
St-Maurice-s-Moselle
Le Rabot
Gien
Auxerre
Chablis
A31
Langres
Luxeuil-les-Bains
Lutterbach
Aisey-s-Seine
Mulhouse
L'Isle-s-Serein
N19
A36
Nouan-le-Fuzelier
Briare
Montbard
Combeaufontaine
Belfort
Altkirch
A35
Bonny-s-Loire
Semur-en-Auxois
Les Laumes
Vesoul
St-Louis
Salbris
St-Satur
Cosne-s-Loire
Avallon
L'Isle-s-le-Doubs
Lamotte-Beuvron
Gray
D67
Montbéliard
Rouvray
Val-Suzon
Pouilly-en-Auxois
Mehun-s-Yevre
Sancerre
Pouilly-s-Loire
Quarré-les-Tombes
Marsannay-la-Côte
Pesmes
Baume-les-Dames
Dijon
Recologne
Saulieu
Fixin
N5
A36
Goumois
N7
Chenôve
Besançon
Bourges
Arnay-le-Duc
Nuits-St-Georges
Auxonne
Valdahon
A6
Château-Chinon
Beaune
Dole
Issoudun
Nevers
Châtillon-en-Bazois
Meursault
Mouthier-Haute-Pierre
St-Gervais-en-Vallière
Autun
Nolay
Chagny
Verdun-s-le-Doubs
Arbois
Pontarlier
Le Veurdre
Chalon-s-Saône
Sellières
Le Creusot
Poligny
Malbuisson
Bourbon-Lancy
St-Martin-en-Bresse
Champagnole
Jougne
Trévol
Sennecey-le-Grand
Beaurepaire-en-Bresse
Lons-le-Saunier
Moulins
Tournus
Paray-le-Monial
Clairvaux-les-Lacs
Morez
Montluçon
Digoin
Cluny
St-Amour
Oyonnax
Evian-les-Bains
Charolles
Igé
Gex
St-Pourcain-s-Sioule
Chambon-sur-Voueize
Mâcon
Bourg-en-Bresse
St-Genis-Pouilly
Morzine
N9
Nantua
St-Germain-de-Joux
Gaillard
Les Gets
St-Éloy-les-Mines
Thoissey
Annemasse
Belegarde-s-Valserine
Vichy
N7
Roanne
Anse
St-Julien-en-Genevois
Sallanches
Aubusson
Combronde
Renaison
Villefranche-s-Saône
Pont-d'Ain
Seyssel
Passy
Les Houches
Châtelguyon
Tarare
Pérouges
St-Martin-Bellevue
Bonneville
Chamonix-Mont-Blanc
Clermont-Ferrand
Thiers
Civrieux-d'Azergues
Vaulx-en-Velin
Ambérieu-en-Bugey
Annecy
Veyrier-du-Lac
St-Gervais-les-Bains
N89
A72
Artemare
Sevrier
Talloires
Royat
Lyon
Faverges
Megève
Le Mont-Dore
Lac Chambon
N89
Bourgoin-Jallieu
Belley
Yenne
Aix-les-Bains
Albertville
Bourg-St-Maurice
St-Etienne Airport
Chasse-s-Rhône
Chambéry
Besse-en-Chandresse
Issoire
Ambert
Givors
La Tour du Pin
Moûtiers
Villars
Les Abrets
Pontcharra
St-Jean-de-Maurienne
St-Etienne
Vienne
Charavines
St-Michael-de-Maurienne
Val d' Isère
La Chaise Dieu
Firminy
Rive-de-Gier
Condrieu
Roussillon
Massiac
Les Roches-de-Condrieu
St-Pierre-de-Chartreuse
Lanslevillard
Brioude
St-Rambert-d'Albon
Salers
N9
Fontaine
Lanslebourg-Mont-Cenis
St-Vallier
Grenoble
Tain L'Hermitage
Romans-s-Isère
Eybens
Valloire
Modane
Vic-s-Cère
St-Flour
Vizille

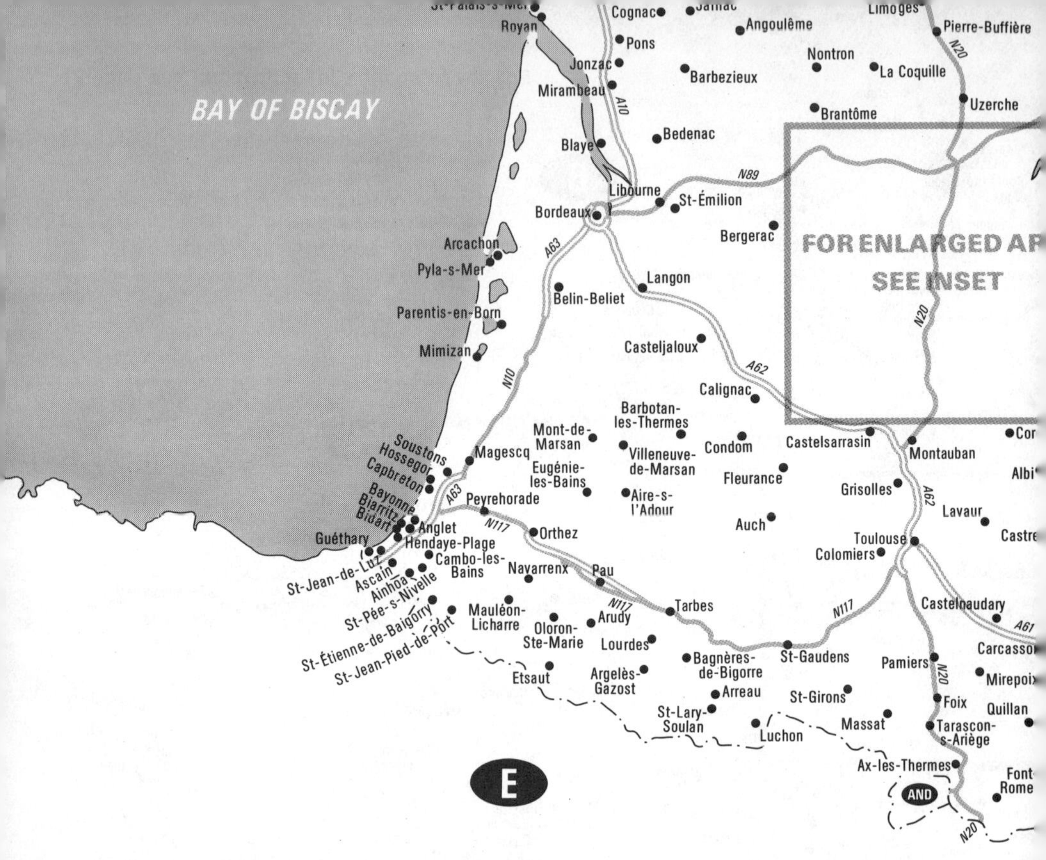

BAY OF BISCAY
Royan
Cognac
Angoulême
Limoges
Pierre-Buffière
Pons
Jonzac
Barbezieux
Nontron
La Coquille
Mirambeau
A10
Brantôme
Uzerche
Blaye
Bedenac
N89
Libourne
St-Émilion
Bordeaux
Bergerac
FOR ENLARGED AR
SEE INSET
Arcachon
A63
Pyla-s-Mer
Langon
Belin-Beliet
N20
Parentis-en-Born
Casteljaloux
Mimizan
A62
N10
Calignac
Barbotan-
les-Thermes
Mont-de-
Marsan
Soustons
Hossegor
Magescq
Villeneuve-
de-Marsan
Condom
Castelsarrasin
Montauban
Capbreton
Eugénie-
les-Bains
Fleurance
Albi
Bayonne
Biarritz
Bidart
A63
Peyrehorade
Aire-s-
l'Adour
Grisolles
A62
Anglet
N117
Orthez
Auch
Lavaur
Guéthary
Hendaye-Plage
Toulouse
Castre
St-Jean-de-Luz
Ascain
Ainhoa
Cambo-les-
Bains
Navarrenx
Pau
Colomiers
St-Pée-s-Nivelle
Mauléon-
Licharre
N117
Arudy
Tarbes
N117
Castelnaudary
St-Étienne-de-Baigorry
Oloron-
Ste-Marie
A61
St-Jean-Pied-de-Port
Lourdes
Bagnères-
de-Bigorre
St-Gaudens
Carcasso
Pamiers
N20
Etsaut
Argelès-
Gazost
Mirepoix
Arreau
St-Girons
Foix
Quillan
St-Lary-
Soulan
Massat
Tarascon-
s-Ariège
Luchon
Ax-les-Thermes
E
Font
Rome
AND
N20

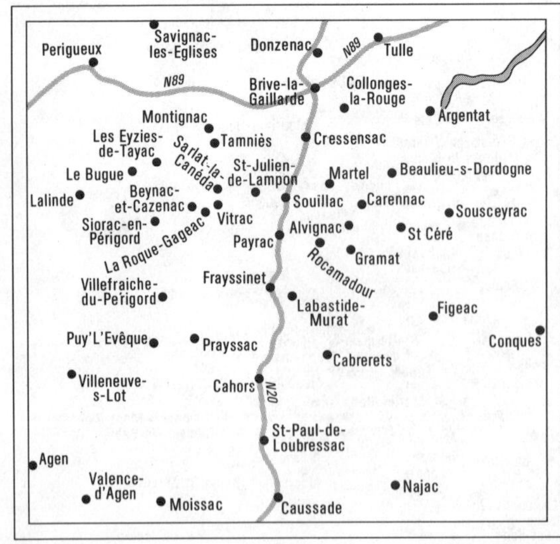

For key to country identification-see page 51

Gournay-en-Bray
Beauvais
Ressons-s-Matz
Compiègne
N1
A1
Nogent-s-Oise
Les Andelys
Creil
A13
Gaillon
Chantilly
Senlis
Villers Cotterêts
Fontaine-Chaalis
Ermenonville
Survilliers-St-Witz
Charles-de-Gaulle Airport
Évreux
Pacy-s-Eure
Rolleboise
Pontoise
Montsoult
Ecoven
Gonesse
A4
Mantes-la-Jolie
Les Mureaux
Meulan
Conflans-Ste-Honorine
Le Bourget Airport
Argenteuil
Sannois
Montmorency
Sevran
A13
Maisons-Laffitte
St-Denis
Montesson
Épinay-sur-Seine
Aulnay-sous-Bois
Meaux
Ivry-la-Bataille
Orgeval
Epone
Gennevilliers
St-Germain-en-Laye
Courbevoie
Bobingy
La Ferté-sous-Jouarre
Suresnes
PARIS
Fontenay-sous-Bois
Vaires-s-Marne
Noisiel
Plaisir
Quincy-Voisins
Champs-s-Marne
Houdan
Versailles
Nonancourt
Verrières-le-Buisson
La Queue-en-Brie
Buc
St-Quentin-en-Yvelines
Dreux
Palaiseau
Pontault-Combault
Rungis
Orsay
Longjumeau
Les Ulis
Orly Airport
Rambouillet
Viry-Châtillon
Épinay-sur-Orge
Evry
St Michel-sur-Orge
A10
Corbeil-Essonnes
A6
Brétigny-sur-Orge
N19
Melun
A11
Dourdan
Ponthierry
Chartres
A10
Barbizon
Fontainebleau

to the return to the UK. The *constat à l'amiable* was introduced by the French insurance companies and represents the 'European Accident Statement Form'. It must be signed by the other party, but if a dispute arises and one of the parties involved should refuse to complete the *constat à l'amiable* then the other party should immediately obtain a written report from a bailiff (*huissier*), which is known as a *constat d'huissier*. A bailiff can usually be found in any large town and charges a fee of Fr400 for preparing the report. Normally the police are only called out to accidents where persons are injured, a driver is under the influence of alcohol or the accident impedes traffic flow. When attending an accident the police prepare a report known as a *procès verbal*.

After an accident the French authorities, at their discretion, may request a surety payment to cover the court costs or fines. See also *Accidents* page 5.

Accommodation

There is a large selection of hotels of all categories. The French Ministry of Tourism classifies hotels in five categories: one-star to four-star and four-star *luxe*. Local tourist information offices (see page 111) can provide details of hotels and restaurants in the area.

Rates for rooms are usually officially controlled and must be displayed in each room but this does not apply to the cost of meals always displayed outside restaurants. Many hotels offer half-board terms only, as indicated in the gazetteer (**DPn**).

Accueil de France Tourist offices showing this sign will make hotel bookings **only for personal callers** and only for up to a week ahead. Bookings are made in the same town or at one of some 35 major towns and cities, including Calais, Le Havre and Rouen (open to 18.30hrs weekdays, sometimes later in season). The head office in Paris is the Office de Tourisme, 127 avenue des Champs-Elysées, Paris 8, open every day from 09.00-20.00hrs, Sundays and Bank Holidays from 09.00-18.00hrs.

Gites de France. This is furnished accommodation in rural France, often at farms, for those who prefer to cater for themselves. There are some 23,000 Gites in 4,000 villages, created with the financial support of the French Government and governed by a charter laid down by the Fédération Nationale des Gîtes de France. For information on membership write to Gites de France Ltd, 178 Piccadilly, London W1V 0PQ enclosing details of preferred regions, choice of dates and a stamped addressed envelope.

Logis de France These are privately owned, mostly family run hotels equivalent to the one-star or two-star and some three-star categories. They are generally located off the beaten track and offer a high standard for their type and good value for money. There are more than 4,000 Logis, some of which are listed in the gazetteer, and they are marked by the symbol LF. There are none in Paris. A copy of the Logis Hotel Guide may be obtained from the French Government Tourist Office, 178 Piccadilly, London W1V 0AL (against payment of 50p in stamps to cover postage and packing).

Relais Routiers These are restaurants situated on main roads offering simple accommodation and providing a good meal at a reasonable price. The *Relais Routiers Guide* issued each year can be purchased through bookshops and AA Centres.

Boats

Boat registration documentation is compulsory for all craft over approximately 10ft in length. See page 6 for further information.

Breakdown

If your car breaks down, try to move it to the verge of the road so that it obstructs the traffic flow as little as possible. Place a warning triangle to the rear of the vehicle to warn following traffic.

You are advised to seek local assistance as, at the time of going to press, there is no nationwide road assistance service in France. See also *Breakdown* page 6 and *Warning triangle/Hazard warning lights* page 112.

British Embassy/Consulates

The British Embassy is located at *75383 Paris Cédex 08* 35 rue du Faubourg St-Honoré ☎ 42669142; consular section *75008 Paris* 2 Cité du Retiro (third floor) ☎ 42669142. There are British Consulates in Bordeaux, Lille, Lyons and Marseilles; there are British Consulates with Honorary Consuls in Boulogne-sur-Mer, Calais, Cherbourg, Dunkerque, Le Havre, Nantes, Nice, Perpignan, St Malo-Dinard and Toulouse. See also page 6 and *Town Plan of Paris* pages 170-171.

Currency including banking hours
(See also page 9)
The unit of currency is the Franc (*Fr*) divided into 100 *Centimes*. At the time of going to press £=*Fr*9.93. Denominations of bank notes are *Fr* 10, 20, 50, 100, 200, 500; standard coins are *Fr* 1, 2, 10, 50 and *Centimes* 5, 10, 20, 50.

There is no restriction on the amount of foreign currency that may be taken into France. Travellers are, however, restricted to taking *Fr*5,000 with them when leaving the country, unless, of course, they imported more currency on entry and completed the appropriate form at the time.

In most large towns banks are open from Monday to Friday 09.00-12.00hrs and 14.00-16.00hrs and closed on Saturday and Sunday; in the provinces they are open from Tuesday to Saturday as above and closed on Sunday and Monday. Banks close at midday on the day prior to a national holiday and all day on Monday if the holiday falls on a Tuesday.

The *Crédit Lyonnais* has offices at the Invalides air terminal in Paris for cashing travellers' cheques and the *Société Générale* has two offices at Orly airport whilst at the Charles de Gaulle airport exchange facilities are available.

Customs regulations
A *Customs Carnet de Passages en Douane* is required for temporarily imported outboard engines, exceeding 92cc (5cv as applied to marine engines), imported without the boats with which they are to be used, and for cycles with auxiliary motors up to 50cc which are new or show no signs of use. See also *Customs regulations for European countries* page 9 for further information.

Dimensions and weight restrictions
Private **cars** and towed **trailers** or **caravans** are restricted to the following dimensions — height: no restriction, but 4 metres is a recommended maximum; width: 2.50 metres; length: 11 metres (excluding towing device). The maximum permitted overall length of vehicle/trailer or caravan combination is 18 metres.

If the weight of the trailer exceeds that of the towing vehicle, see also *Speed limits* page 111.

Driving licence
A valid British driving licence is acceptable in France. The minimum age at which a visitor may drive a temporarily imported car or motorcycle (exceeding 80cc) is 18 years. See also page 11 and *Speed limits* page 111.

Emergency messages to tourists
(See also page 11)
Emergency messages to tourists are broadcast Monday to Friday on *Radio Monte Carlo*. These messages are transmitted in French on 1400 metres long wave between 21.00 and 22.30hrs.

Garages
(See also page 53)
All prices must be displayed on the premises so that they are clearly visible and legible. When you have had a repair carried out you should receive an invoice stating the labour charge, *ie* the hourly rate (displayed) multiplied by the time spent or the time shown on the time schedule for each operation and not just a lump sum. The price of supplies and spares should be shown separately. Parts which have been replaced must be returned to you unless it is a routine replacement or the repair is carried out free during the guarantee period.

Lights
(See also page 14)
It is obligatory to use headlights as driving on sidelights only is not permitted. In fog, mist or poor visibility during the day either two fog lamps or two dipped headlights must be switched on in addition to two sidelights. It is also compulsory for *motorcyclists* riding machines exceeding 125cc to use dipped headlights during the day. Failure to comply with these regulations will lead to an *on the spot* fine (see *Police fines* page 20).

It is recommended that visiting motorists equip their vehicle with a set of replacement bulbs; drivers unable to replace a faulty bulb when requested to do so by the police may be fined. In France a regulation requires all locally registered vehicles to be equipped with headlights which show a yellow beam and, in the interests of safety and courtesy, visiting motorists are advised to comply. If you are able to use beam deflectors to adjust your headlights for driving abroad you can purchase deflectors with yellow lens. However, with headlamp converters it is necessary to coat the outer surface of the headlamp glass with a yellow plastic paint which is removable with a solvent. The yellow plastic paint can be purchased from your nearest AA Centre.

Motoring club

(See also page 16)

The AA is affiliated to the *Association Française des Automobilistes* (AFA) whose office is at *F-75017 Paris* 9 rue Anatole-de-la-Forge ☎ 42278200.

Motorways

There are about 4,022 miles of motorway (Autoroute) open, and more are under construction or in preparation. To join a motorway follow signs with the international motorway symbol, or signs with the words 'par Autoroute' added. Signs with the added words 'Péage' or 'par péage' lead to toll roads. With the exception of a few sections into or around large cities, all motorways (autoroutes) have a toll charged according to the distance travelled; *eg* toll charges for a single journey from Calais to Nice cost about £29 for a car and about £44 for a car with caravan.

On the majority of the toll motorways a travel ticket is issued on entry and the toll is paid on leaving the motorway. The travel ticket gives all relevant information about the toll charges including the toll category of your vehicle. At the exit point the ticket is handed in and the amount due shows up on an illuminated sign at the toll booth. On some motorways the toll collection is automatic; have the correct amount ready to throw into the collecting basket. If change is required use the marked separate lane.

For assistance on a motorway, use one of the *telephone boxes* sited at 2.4km (1½ mile) intervals; they are connected to police stations. A leaflet entitled *Motorways in France* is available to AA members.

Orange badge scheme for disabled drivers

(See also page 16)

There is no formal system of concessions in operation and responsibility for parking in built-up areas rests with the local authorities. Any parking places reserved for the disabled are indicated by the international symbol. However, the police are instructed to show consideration where parking by the disabled is concerned. In some towns and cities including Paris, badge holders may be allowed to park at meter bays and pay only the initial charge.

Parking

(See also page 17)

Regulations are similar to those in the UK. As a general rule all prohibitions are indicated by road signs or by yellow markings on the kerb. It is prohibited to leave a vehicle parked in the same place for more than 24 consecutive hours in Paris and surrounding departments.

On some roads in built-up areas, parking is allowed from the 1st to the 15th day of each month on the side of the road where the numbers of the buildings are odd and from the 16th to the last day of the month on the side with even numbers. This is called alternate unilateral parking.

There are short-term parking areas known as *blue zones* in most principal towns; in these areas discs must be used (placed against the windscreen) every day, except Sundays and public holidays, between 09.00 and 12.30hrs and 14.30 and 19.00hrs. They permit parking for up to one hour. Discs are sold at police stations, but at tourist offices and some clubs and commercial firms they are available free of charge. There are *grey zones* where parking meters are in use; in these zones a fee must be paid between 09.00 and 19.00hrs. Motorists using a ticket issued by an automatic machine must display the ticket behind the windscreen or nearside front window of their car.

In *Paris* cars towing caravans are prohibited from the *blue zone* between 14.00 and 20.30hrs. Cars towing trailers with an overall surface of 10 square metres or more may neither circulate nor park in the central *green zone* between 14.00-20.30hrs, except on Sundays and public holidays. Vehicle combinations with an overall surface exceeding 16 square metres may neither circulate nor park in the *green zone* between 08.00-20.30hrs. Those wishing to cross Paris during these hours with vehicle/ trailer combinations can use the boulevard Périphérique, although the route is heavily congested, except during public holiday periods. In some parts of the *green zone* parking is completely forbidden. It is prohibited to park caravans, even for a limited period, not only in the *green zone* but in almost all areas of Paris.

Vehicles which are parked contrary to regulations are liable to be removed by the police at the owner's risk and the driver will be liable for any costs incurred including a heavy fine.

Passengers

(See also page 18)

Children under 10 are not permitted to travel in a vehicle as front seat passengers.

Petrol

(See also page 18)

Credit cards The most widely accepted credit cards at petrol stations in France are Eurocard/Mastercard and Visa which can be used for purchases of petrol at many main garages.

Duty-free petrol The petrol in the vehicle tank may be imported free of customs duty and tax.

Petrol (leaded) Essence Normale (90 octane) and Essence Super (98 octane) grades.

Petrol (unleaded) is sold in France as Essence Super (95 octane). Pumps dispensing unleaded petrol are clearly marked with a sticker *super sans plomb* (super grade unleaded).

Postal information

Mail Postcards *Fr*1.80; letters up to 20gm *Fr*2.40.

Post offices There are 17,500 post offices in France. They are open 09.00-12.00hrs and 14.00-17.00hrs Monday to Friday and 09.00-12.00hrs Saturday. Opening hours of small offices in rural areas may vary. In Paris the office at 52 rue de Louvre is open 24 hours a day.

Postcheques

(See also page 20)

Postcheques may be cashed at all post offices for any amount up to a maximum of *Fr*750 per cheque. Counter positions are identified by the words *Paiement des mandats* or *Chèques postaux*. See *Postal information* for post office opening hours.

Priority including Roundabouts

In built-up areas drivers must slow down and be prepared to stop at all road junctions. If there are no priority signs give way to traffic from the right, but you have priority on roads bearing the sign *Passage Protégé*. New signs are being introduced (inverted triangle with red border) some of which bear an additional panel with the word 'STOP' and distance in metres to the stop sign or the words *Cédez le passage*. A major road which has priority over side turnings will generally display signs to indicate this, usually a yellow square within white square with points vertical; a thick black band through the sign indicates end of priority. At roundabouts with signs bearing the words *Vous n'avez pas la priorité* traffic on the roundabout has priority; where no such sign exists traffic entering the roundabout has priority. See also page 21 and *Inside front cover* for road signs referred to above.

Public holidays

Official public holidays in France for 1987 are given below. See also *Public holidays* page 21

January 1 (New Year's Day)
April 19 (Easter Sunday)
April 20 (Easter Monday)
May 1 (Labour Day)
May 8 (VE Day)
May 28 (Ascension Day)
June 7 (Whit Sunday)
June 8 (Whit Monday)
July 14 (National Holiday)
August 15* (Assumption)
November 1† (All Saints' Day)
November 11 (Armistice Day)
December 25 (Christmas Day)

*Saturday †Sunday

Religious services

(See also page 22)

The Intercontinental Church Society welcomes visitors from any denomination to English language services in the following centres:

06400 Cannes The Revd Ian Watts, Chaplain's Apartment, 'Residence Kent', rue General Ferrie ☎ 93945461

60500 Chantilly The Revd Anthony Creery-Hill, 5 Residence Sylvie ☎ 44582012

59140 Dunkerque The Revd David Dicker, 130 rue de l'Ecole Maternelle ☎ 28633947

78600 Maisons-Laffitte The Revd Russel Avery, 15 avenue Carnot (Paris area) ☎ 39623497

75008 Paris The Ven Brian Lea, 5 rue d'Aguesseau ☎ 47427088

64000 Pau The Revd Kenneth Forrester, Apartment 11, 43 rue Montpensier ☎ 59625645

69110 Sainte Foy-Les-Lyon The Revd Gerald Hovenden, Le Coteau, 38 Chemin de Taffignon (serving Lyon and Grenoble) ☎ 78596706

31500 Toulouse The Revd Arthur Harvey, 5 Impasse Joseph Anglade ☎ 61543005

78140 Vélizy-Villacoublay The Revd Jonathan Wilmot, 126 rue Lavoisier (Nr Versailles) ☎ 39461386

Roads including holiday traffic

France has a very comprehensive network of roads; the surfaces of which are normally good; exceptions are usually signposted *Chaussée déformée*. The camber is often severe and the edges rough. See also *Road conditions* page 22.

During July and August and especially at weekends traffic on main roads is likely to be very heavy. Special signs are erected to indicate alternative routes with the least traffic congestion. Wherever they appear it is usually advantageous to follow them although you cannot be absolutely sure of gaining time. The alternative routes are quiet but they are not as wide as the main roads. They are **not** suitable for caravans.

A free road map showing the marked alternative routes, plus information centres and petrol stations open for 24hrs, is available from service stations displaying the *Bison Futé* poster (a Red Indian chief in full war bonnet). These maps are also available from *Syndicats d'Initiative* and Information offices.

Road number changes Following the 1974-78 decentralisation, when many secondary National highways were transferred to the Departments ('N' — to 'D' roads; when N315 became D915, and N16 became D916 etc), further modifications to the road system are taking place. These latest changes involve about 4,000-5,000km on N-roads throughout France, and some irregularities may occur during the changeover period when the same road may have signs showing two different numbers.

Traffic lanes (Paris) There are special lanes for buses and taxis only in some streets; they are marked by a continuous yellow line painted one vehicle width from the kerb. Usually, buses and taxis in the special lane travel in the opposite direction to other traffic.

Shopping hours

Department stores are usually open from Monday to Saturday 09.00-18.30/19.00hrs closing for lunch only in the provinces; *food shops* open at 07.00hrs and may also open on Sunday mornings.

Speed limits

(See also page 22)

The beginning of a built-up area is indicated by a sign bearing the placename in blue letters on a light background; the end by the placename sign with a thin red line diagonally across it. Unless otherwise signposted speed limits are:

Built-up areas 60 kph (37 mph).

Outside built-up areas on normal roads 90 kph (56 mph); on dual carriageways separated by a central reservation 110 kph (68 mph).

On Motorways 130 kph (80 mph) (*Note* The minimum speed in fast lane on level stretch of motorway during good daytime visibility is 80 kph (49 mph) and drivers travelling below this speed are liable to be fined. The maximum speed on urban stretches of motorway is 110 kph (68 mph). In wet weather speed limits outside built-up areas are reduced to 80 kph (49 mph), 100 kph (62 mph) and 110 kph (68 mph) on motorways.

These limits also apply to private cars towing a trailer or caravan, if the latter's weight does not exceed that of the car. However, if the weight of the trailer exceeds that of the car by less than 30% the speed limit is 65kph (39mph), if more than 30% the speed limit is 45kph (28mph). Additionally these combinations must:

i Display a disc at the rear of the caravan/trailer showing the maximum speed.

ii Not be driven in the fast lane of a 3-lane motorway.

Both French residents and visitors to France, who have held a driving licence for less than one year, must not exceed 90 kph (56 mph) or any lower signposted limit when driving in France.

Spiked or studded tyres

Spiked or studded tyres may be used from 9 November to 30 March by vehicles with a total authorised laden weight not exceeding 3,500kg, provided that a speed of 90 kph (56 mph) is not exceeded. The speed limitation disc bearing the figure 90 is only obligatory for French registered vehicles. See also *Cold weather touring* page 8.

Tourist information

(See also page 24)

The French Government Tourist Office maintains a full information service in London at 178 Piccadilly, London W1V 0AL (Mon-Fri) and will be pleased to answer any enquiries on touring in France. The telephone number is 01-491 7622 for general enquiries and 01-499 6911 for the 24hr recorded information service.

Once in France you should contact the local tourist office, *Syndicat d'Initiative* which will be found in all larger towns and resorts. They are pleased to give advice on local events, amenities and excursions and can also answer specific local queries such as bus timetables and local religious services (all denominations) not available in the UK.

A further source of information within the country, is the *Accueil de France* (welcome office) who will also book hotel reservations within their area for the same night, or up to seven days in advance **for personal callers only.** There are not so many of these offices and mainly they are located at important stations and airports.

The hours of opening vary considerably depending upon the district and the time of year. Generally the offices are open between 09.00-12.00hrs and 14.00-18.00hrs from Monday to Saturday but in popular resort areas *Syndicats d'Initiative* are sometimes open later and on Sunday mornings.

Traffic lights

(See also page 24)
The three-colour system, as in the United Kingdom, is in operation, with the addition of miniatures set at eye-level and with the posts placed in irregular positions, sometimes overhead and possibly without a set on the opposite side of the junction. It must be stressed that the lights themselves are extremely dim, and easily missed.

A flashing amber light is a warning that the intersection or junction is particularly dangerous. A flashing red light indicates no entry, or may be used to mark obstacles.

Using the telephone

(See also page 24)
Insert coin **after** lifting receiver, dialling tone is a continuous tone. Generally to make a local call use *Fr*1 coin or *jeton* (special telephone coin) bought from the point where the call is made, but 2 x 50 centimes are required in some callboxes. For toll or trunk calls you will need to go to a post office. Highest value coin accepted is *Fr*5.

Within France to call one provincial number from another or one Paris area number (Paris, Seine St Denis, Hauts de Seine and Val de Marne) from another simply dial the 8 digit number. To call a Paris area number from the provinces precede the 8 digit number with 161 and to call a provincial number from the Paris area precede the 8 digit number with 16.
International callbox identification Metallic grey.
Telephone rates The charge for a call to the UK is *Fr*0.5 for 11 seconds with a surcharge if the call is made from an hotel. A reduced rate is available for calls made between 21.00-08.00hrs.
What to dial for the Irish Republic 19 *353.
What to dial for the UK 19 *44.
*Wait for second dialling tone

Warning triangle/Hazard warning lights

The use of a warning triangle or hazard warning lights is compulsory for all vehicles except two-wheelers. As hazard warning lights may be damaged or inoperative it is recommended that a warning triangle be carried. The triangle must be placed on the road 30 metres (33yds) behind the vehicle and clearly visible from 100 metres (109yds). For vehicles over 3,500kg warning must be given by at least a warning triangle. See also *Warning triangles/Hazard warning lights* page 25.

Wheel chains

These can be purchased from vehicle accessory shops in large towns. Wheel chains can be hired from some garages; however, they have only small supplies. See also *Cold weather touring* page 8.

Winter conditions

Although there are five mountain regions — the Vosges, Jura, Massif Central, Alps and Pyrénées — motoring in winter is not severely restricted. The main channels for south-bound traffic wanting to avoid the Alps and Massif Central are the A7 and N7 route along the Rhône Valley, the N20 from Limoges to Toulouse, and the highways farther west. Roads into Belgium, Luxembourg and Germany are generally not affected by road closures in winter.

All-the-year-round approaches to Strasbourg and Basle avoiding the Vosges and Jura are the Paris-Strasbourg Motorway A4, and the Paris-Beaune-Belfort motorway A6-A36 respectively. The approach to Switzerland via Pontarlier is very seldom obstructed, and during very severe weather is a better route to Geneva than over the Faucille Pass; alternatively the road via Bourg to Geneva is always open. Italy can be entered via the Mont Blanc road tunnel, the Fréjus road tunnel, or along the French Riviera via Menton. The main routes to Spain via Biarritz and Perpignan avoid the Pyrénées.

Whenever possible roads are swept and kept clear. However, during periods of thaw some barred roads may be used by certain classes of traffic at the driver's risk; passenger vehicles without trailers being used privately may proceed provided they do not exceed 80 kph (49 mph).

Monaco

National flag *Red over white in two strips of equal breadth.*

The Principality of Monaco has a population of 24,000 and an area of 8 sq miles. The official Monaco information centre in the UK is the Monaco Government Tourist and Convention Office, 25 Whitehall, London SW1A 2BS ☎ 01-930 4699. Although a sovereign state, it is very much under the influence of France and its laws are similar to those of the major country.

Monaco is one large city/state but Monaco Town and Monte Carlo are the two towns of the State.

Motoring regulations are the same as in France but it should be stated that whilst caravans are permitted to pass through the Principality they are not allowed to stop or park.

Prices are in French Francs (F Frs)
For additional information on French hotels, see page 107.
The department name follows the town name.
For information on making internal local telephone calls see page 112.

Abbreviations:

av	avenue
bd	boulevard
cpt	Capitaine
Cdt	Commandant
espl	esplanade
fbg	faubourg
Gl	Général
Ml	Marshal, Maréchal
Mon	Monseigneur
pl	place
Prés	Président
Prof	Professeur
prom	promenade
r	rue
rte	route
sq	square

ABBEVILLE
Somme

★★**Ibis** 234 rte d'Amiens ☎22248080 tx145045
🛁45 **P**50 ☾ sB🛁208—215 dB🛁247—255 M42—120 ✂ ▭
Credit card [1]

★**Conde (DPn)** 14 pl de la Libération ☎22240633
Closed Xmas—New Year & 7 Aug—9 Sep
rm7 sB79 dB93—125 M50—85

★**Jean Bart** 5—7 r Ste-Catherine ☎22242171
rm16 (🚿5) **P**10 sB78—102 sB🚿fr128 dB115—171 dB🚿141—171 Malc
Credit cards [2] [3]

🚗 **SADRA** 53 av R-Schumann ☎22243481 Closed Sat Aud VW

ABRETS (LES)
Isère

★***Belle Etoile*** LF 4 r V-Hugo ☎76320497
rm15 (🛁🚿4) ⌂ **P** mountains

★***Hostellerie Abrésienne*** 75 rte de Grenoble (N75) ☎76320428
rm22 (🛁🚿6) ⌂ **P**25 lake mountains

🚗 **Gadou** (N6) ☎76320155 Closed Sun Ren

AGAY
Var

🚗 **Agay** av du Gratadis ☎94820616 M/c AR

At **DRAMONT (LE)** (2km SW)

★★★**Sol et Mar** ☎94952560
Apr—15 Oct
🛁47 **P**40 Lift ☾ sB🛁325—425 dB🛁350—450 M95—150 Beach sea mountains

AGDE
Hérault

★★**Tamarissière** (Inter) 21 quai Théophile Cornu ☎67942087 tx490225
15 Mar—15 Dec
🛁🚿35 sB🛁🚿215—372 dB🛁🚿241—398 M79—180 sea
Credit cards [1] [2] [3] [5]

🚗 **Four** 12 av Gl-de Gaulle ☎67941141 & 67941783 Closed Sat & Sun Aud VW

🚗 **Gare** 1 av V-Hugo ☎67942268 Closed Sun Ope Peu

🚗 **Midi** 46 r de République ☎67941354 Closed Sun All makes

At **CAP D'AGDE** (7km SE)

★★★★***Matago*** Trésor Royal ☎67260005 tx480978
🛁90 **P**60 Lift ⩳ sea
Credit cards [1] [2] [3] [5]

★★★***Sablotel*** Plage du Môle ☎67260004 tx480980
Apr—Oct
🛁131 **P** Lift ⩳ sea

AGEN
Lot-et-Garonne

★★**Ibis** Ilot 5, bd Carnot ☎53473123
🛁39 **P** Lift sB🛁187—193 dB🛁227—232 Mfr55 S%
Credit cards [1] [3]

★★***Périgord*** LF 42 pl XIV Juillet ☎53661001
rm23 (🛁20) **P** Lift

★★**Résidence Jacobins** LF 1 pl Jacobins (n.rest) ☎53470331 tx560800
🛁🚿15 **P**20 ☾ sB🛁🚿180 dB🛁🚿350—420

F Tastets 182 bd de la Liberté ☎53471063 Closed Sat & Sun pm AR

AIGLE (L')
Orne

★★★**Dauphin** (BW/MAP) (**DPn**) pl de la Halle ☎33244312 tx170979
rm24 (🛁18) **P**8 ☾ sB204 sB🛁307—337 dB231—258 dB🛁334—444 M98—280
Credit cards [1] [2] [3] [5]

AIGUEBELLE
Var

★★★★***Roches Fleuries*** (4km on N599 to Le Lavandu) ☎94710507 tx403997
Apr—15 Oct
🛁48 ⌂ **P**35 ☾ ⩳ Beach sea
Credit cards [2] [3] [5]

★★***Plage*** ☎94058074
25 May—24 Sep
rm52 (🛁🚿48) A29rm sea

AIGUILLON-SUR-MER
Vendée

★★**Port** 2 r Belle Vue ☎51564008
Mar—Oct
rm33 (🛁🚿23) **P** dB85—220 ✂ ⩳

AILLANT-SUR-THOLON
Yonne

🚗 **St-Antoine** 10 Grande r, St-Antoine ☎86634681 M/c Closed Sun Fia

AINHOA
Pyrénées-Atlantiques

★★★***Argi-Eder*** (BW/MAP) rte de la Chapelle ☎59299104 tx570067
Apr—15 Nov
🛁🚿36 A4rm **P**80 ✂ ⩳ mountains
Credit cards [1] [2] [3] [5]

AIRE-SUR-L'ADOUR
Landes

🚗 **Saema** rte de Bordeaux ☎58766001 Closed Sat pm, Sun & Mon am Ren

🚗 **Tolerie** 65 av de Bordeaux ☎5876621 M/c Cit Mer Ope

AIRE-SUR-LA-LYS
Pas-de-Calais

★**Europ** 14 Grand Pl (n.rest) ☎21390432
rm16 (🚿9) ⌂ **P**16 sB69 sB🚿94 dB98 dB🚿188
Credit cards [1] [2] [3]

🚗 **H Delgery** 5 pl J-d'Aire ☎21390298 Closed Sat pm Ren

AISEY-SUR-SEINE
Côte-d'Or

★★**Roy (Pn)** LF ☎80932163
rm10 (🛁🚿8) **P**10 Lift sB106 sB🛁🚿106 dB152 dB🛁🚿192 M42—84

France

AIX-EN-PROVENCE
Bouches-du-Rhône

★★★★**PLM le Pigonnet** 5 av Pigonnet (off rd N8 towards Marseille) ☎42590290 tx410629
→ 50 A14rm P50 Lift ☾
sB 388—478 dB 526—646 M145
Credit cards 1 2 3 5

★★★**Manoir** r d'Entrecasteaux 8 (n.rest) ☎42262720
15 Feb—15 Jan
43 P25 Lift ☾ sB 178—399
dB 276—428
Credit cards 1 2 3 4 5

★★★***Novotel Beaumanoir*** Résidence Beaumanoir (A8) ☎42274750 tx400244
102 **P** Lift
Credit cards 1 2 3 5

★★★***Novotel Sud*** Périphérique Sud, Arc de Meyran ☎42279049 tx420517
80 **P** Lift

★★★**Paul Cézanne** 40 av V-Hugo (n.rest) ☎42263473
rm44 (42) **P** Lift ☾ sB fr447
dB fr694

★★★**Résidence Rotonde** 15 av des Belges (n.rest) ☎42262988
Closed 21 Dec—9 Jan
42 P20 Lift ☾ sB 159—215
dB 228—290
Credit cards 1 2 3 4 5

★★**Campanile** ZAC du Jas de Bouffan ☎42594073 tx441273
50 **P** sB 217—238 dB 239—260
M61—82
Credit card 3

★★**Ibis** Chemin des Infirmeries ☎42279820 tx420519
83 **P**80 sB 222—250 dB 261—289
M alc
Credit cards 1 3

★★***Renaissance*** 4 bd de la République (n.rest) ☎42262422
rm36 (21) **P**
Credit card 3

J Mavel R N Luynes ☎42240580
Closed Sun & Jul AR

Michelon r des Milles ☎42277598
Closed Sat & Sun Cit

Monjo Montée d'Avignon ☎42234908
Closed Sat & Sun Maz

At **EGUILLES** (11km NW)

★★**Belvedere (DPn)** quartier des Landons ☎42925292
38 A32rm **P** sB 202—312
dB 224—334 M81
Credit cards 1 3 5

At **MILLES (LES)** (5km S off D9)

★★***Climat*** r Ampère, ZI ☎42203077 tx612241
38 **P**

AIX-LES-BAINS
Savoie

★★★***Iles Britanniques*** pl de l'Etablissement Thermal ☎79610377
May—Sep
rm90 (65) A10rm **P** Lift ☾ mountains lake

★★★**International Rivollier** 18 av C-de-Gaulle ☎79352100 tx320410
rm62 (54) **P**10 Lift ☾ sB191—234
sB 215—234 dB292—365
dB 354—365 M95—185 mountains
Credit cards 1 2 3 5

★★★**Manoir** (Inter) 37 r Georges Ier ☎79614400 tx980793
24 Jan—24 Dec
rm72 (66) **P**10 Lift
sB 198—350 dB 220—350
M100—165
Credit cards 1 3 5

★★**Campanile** av du Golf de Marlioz ☎79613066 tx980090
43 **P** sB 204—225 dB 226—247
M61—82
Credit card 3

★★***Cecil*** 20 av Victoria (n.rest) ☎79350412
rm18 (11) Lift mountains

★★**Paix** 11 rue Lamartine ☎79350210
10 Mar—Nov
rm77 (39) **P**30 Lift ☾ sB125—145
sB 145—200 dB 215 M65—76
mountains lake
Credit cards 3 5

★★**Parc** 28 r de Chambéry ☎79612911
20 Apr—25 Oct
rm50 (13) A10rm Lift ☾
Pn195—240 M75—85 mountains

★★**Pavillion Rivollier** pl Gare ☎79351904
May—Oct
rm40 (30) A1rm Lift ☾ sB191—234
sB 215—234 dB292—365
dB 354—365 M67 mountains
Credit cards 1 2 3 4 5

ALBERT
Somme

★**Basilique** (**DPn** in season) 3—5 r Gambetta ☎22750471
rm10 (8) sB64—154 sB 102—154
dB 116—168 M45—120 & alc
Credit cards 1 3

★**Paix** 43 r V-Hugo ☎22750164
rm15 (6) A3rm **P**6 sB72—85
sB 87—151 dB90—109
dB 112—198 M48—120
Credit cards 1 3

ALBERTVILLE
Savoir

★★★**Million** 8 pl de la Liberté ☎79322515
rm29 (26) **P** Lift sB131—223
sB 175—243 dB250—366
dB 315—366 M120—380 mountains
Credit cards 2 3 5

★★**Costaroche** 1 chemin P-du-Roy ☎79320202
20 **P**20 sB 130—168 dB 187
M64—113 mountains

ALBI
Tarn

★★★**Chiffre** (Inter) 50 r Séré de Rivières ☎63540460 tx51794
39 **P**25 Lift sB 184
dB 268—378 M70—110&alc
Credit cards 1 2 5

★★★**Grand St-Antoine** (BW/MAP) 17 r St-Antoine ☎63540404 tx520850
56 **P**25 Lift ☾ sB 320—430
dB 410—630 M100—250
Credit cards 1 2 3 5

★★**Orléans** (FAH) pl Stalingrad ☎63541656 tx521605
Closed 21 Dec—6 Jan
64 Lift ☾ sB 120 dB 260
M72—115
Credit cards 1 2 3 5

★**Viell Alby (Pn)** 25 r Toulouse-Lautrec ☎63541469
rm9 (5) sB87—92 sB 106—112
dB106—133 M42
Credit cards 1 3

Albi Auto 22 av A-Thomas ☎63607903
Closed Aug, Sat & Sun For

At **FONVIALANE** (3km N on N606)

★★★**Réserve (Pn)** (Relais et Châteaux) rte de Cordes ☎63607979 tx520850
Apr—Oct
20 **P** ☾ sB 395—445
dB 435—675 M130—250 lake
Credit cards 1 2 3 5

ALENÇON
Orne

See also **ST-LÉONARD-DES-BOIS**

★★★***Grand Cerf*** 21 r St-Blaise ☎33260051 tx170296
15 Jan—15 Dec
rm33 (25) **P** Lift
Credit cards 1 2 3 5

★★**Campanile** rte de Paris ☎33295385 tx171908
35 **P** sB 191—212 dB 213—234
M61—82
Credit card 3

★★**France** 3 r St-Blaise (n.rest) ☎33262636
rm31 (18) **P** sB110 sB 170
dB125—145 dB 185—245
Credit card 3

★★**Gare** 50 av Wilson ☎33290393
rm22 (16) **P** sB113—118
sB 168—198 dB131—146
dB 211—236 M44—95

★Industrie LE 20—22 pl du Gl-de-Gaulle ☎33290651

rm9 (🛁 🚿 4) **P**10 sB75—117
sB 🛁 🚿 100—117 dB115—178
dB 🛁 🚿 140—178 M150—110
Credit cards [1] [3]

★Paris 26 r D-Papin (opposite station) (n.rest) ☎33290164

6 Jan—10 Aug & 25 Aug-21 Dec
rm16 (🛁 🚿 9) 🚘 sB104 sB 🛁 🚿 133 dB122
dB 🛁 🚿 156
Credit cards [1] [3]

ALÈS
Gard

★★★*Mercure* 18 r E-Quinet ☎66522707 tx480830

🛁 75 **P**45 Lift
Credit cards [1] [2] [3] [5]

🔧 **Auto Service** 914 rte d'Uzès ☎66302569 M/c Closed Sat & Sun AR Hon

ALPE-D'HUEZ(L')
Isère

★★★Chamois d'Or (Pn) r de Fontbelle ☎76803132

15 Dec—15 Apr
rm41 (🛁 🚿 36) **P**30 Lift **Pn**325—475 M109
mountains

★★★*Ours Blanc* (DPn) (MAP) av des Jeux ☎76803111 tx320807

20 Dec—20 Apr
🚿 37 🚘 **P**40 mountains
Credit cards [1] [2] [3] [5]

ALTKIRCH
Haut-Rhin

★★Terrasse LE 44—46 r du 3e-Zouave ☎89409802

rm20 (🛁 15) 🚘 **P** sB110—120
sB 🛁 160—180 dB200 dB 🛁 200—225
M40—80
Credit cards [3] [5]

★*Sundgovienne* LE (3.5km W on N19) rte de Belfort ☎89409718

Feb—23 Dec
rm31 (🛁 🚿 24) 🚘 **P**50 Lift
Credit cards [1] [2] [3] [5]

At **WALHEIM** (3.5km NE off D432)

🔧 **Schmitt** ☎89409162 M/c All makes

ALVIGNAC
Lot

★★★Palladium ☎65336023

15 Jun—15 Sep
🛁 🚿 19 A6rm **P**20 sB170 sB 🛁 🚿 230—280
dB190—205 dB 🛁 🚿 250—300 M55—150
🎾 🏊
Credit cards [2] [3]

AMBÉRIEU-EN-BUGEY
Ain

★★★*Savoie* (Inter) (2km N on D36) ☎74380690

Feb—23 Dec
🛁 45 **P** Lift

France

AMBERT
Puy-de-Dôme

★★Livradois (DPn) 1 pl du Livradois ☎73821001

rm14 (🛁 🚿 7) 🚘 **P** sB88—168
sB 🛁 🚿 168—205 dB106—223
dB 🛁 🚿 186—223 M91—210
Credit cards [1] [2] [5]

★*Gare* 17 av de la Gare ☎73820027

15 Nov—15 Oct
rm22 (🛁 🚿 7) 🚘 **P**12

AMBOISE
Indre-et-Loire

★★★Novotel 17 r des Sablonnières ☎47574207 tx751203

🛁 82 **P**90 Lift sB 🛁 313—328
dB 🛁 386—401 Malc 🎾 🏊 mountains
Credit cards [1] [2] [3] [5]

★★Château de Pray (Pn) (2km NE on N751) ☎47572367

10 Feb—Dec
rm16 (🛁 🚿 14) 🚘 **P**30 sB 🛁 🚿 270
dB 🛁 🚿 412 M162
Credit cards [1] [2] [3] [5]

★★*Lion d'Or* LE 17 quai C-Guinot ☎47570023

Apr—1 Nov
rm23 (🛁 🚿 16) 🚘 ☾
Credit card [3]

★★Parc LE **(DPn)** 8 r L-de-Vinci ☎47570693

Mar—3 Nov
🛁 🚿 19 A1rm **P**25 sB 🛁 🚿 177—327
dB 🛁 🚿 204—404 M85—220
Credit cards [1] [3]

★Bréche (DPn) 26 r J-Ferry ☎47570079

Mar—Oct
rm15 (🛁 🚿 6) 🚘 **P**10 Lift sB99—111
sB 🛁 🚿 159—179 dB148—164
dB 🛁 🚿 203—228 M59—92
Credit cards [1] [2] [3] [5]

★*France et Cheval Blanc* (DPn) 6—7 quai C-de-Gaulle ☎47570244

Mar—mid Nov
rm26 (🛁 🚿 21) 🚘 **P**
Credit cards [3] [4]

AMIENS
Somme

★★★Grand Hotel de l'Universe
2 r Noyon (n.rest) ☎22915251 tx145070

🛁 🚿 41 Lift ☾ sB 🛁 🚿 286—326
dB 🛁 🚿 312—352
Credit cards [1] [2] [3] [5]

★★Carlton-Belfort 42 r de Noyon ☎22922644 tx140754

🛁 🚿 36 Lift ☾ sB 🛁 🚿 270—345
dB 🛁 🚿 380—450 M110—130
Credit cards [1] [2] [3] [4] [5]

★★*Gritti* (Inter) 8 pl A-Fiquet ☎22913632 tx14075

rm23 (🛁 🚿 19) 🚘 **P**

★★*Ibis* 'Le Centrum', r Ml-de-Lattre-de-Tassigny ☎22925733 tx140765

🛁 94 Lift
Credit cards [1] [3]

★★Nord-Sud 11 r Gresset ☎22915903

rm26 (🛁 20) sB100 sB 🛁 150 dB113
dB 🛁 180—200

★★Paix 8 r de la République (n.rest) ☎22913921

25 Jan—15 Dec
rm26 (🛁 11) **P**17 sB106 sB 🛁 153 dB168
dB 🛁 175

★Normandie 1 bis r Lamartine (n.rest) ☎22917499

rm26 (🛁 🚿 13) 🚘 sBfr109 sB 🛁 🚿 197
dBfr218 dB 🛁 🚿 294

🔧 **Auto-Picardie** 1 bis chemin des Vignes ☎22460417 Fia Lan

At **BOVES** (7km SE of D934)

★★★Novotel Amiens Est (CD 934) ☎22462222 tx140731

🛁 91 **P**200 sB 🛁 285 dB 🛁 340 Malc 🏊
Credit cards [1] [2] [3] [5]

AMMERSCHWIRH See **COLMAR**

ANDELYS (LES)
Eure

★★*Chaine d'Or* LE 27 r Grande, pl St-Sauveur ☎32540031

Closed Jan
rm12 (🛁 🚿 8) A1rm
Credit card [3]

★Normandie (Pn) 1 r Grande ☎32541052

Closed Dec
rm11 (🛁 🚿 3) **P**15 sB84—98 sB 🛁 🚿 133
dB168—196 dB 🛁 🚿 236—288 M55—160

ANDLAU
Bas-Rhin

★★*Kastelberg* r du Gl-Koenig ☎88089783

🛁 🚿 28 **P**28 mountains

ANDRÉZIEUX-BOUTHÉON
See **ST-ETIENNE AIRPORT**

ANGERS
Maine-et-Loire

★★★Anjou (BW/MAP) 1 bd Ml-Foch ☎41882482 tx720521

🛁 🚿 51 🚘 Lift sB 🛁 🚿 210—320
dB 🛁 🚿 285—420 M90
Credit cards [1] [2] [3] [5]

★★★Mercure bd Carnot ☎41603481 tx722139

🛁 86 **P**50 sB 🛁 374—387 dB 🛁 435—447
Mfr120
Credit cards [1] [2] [5]

★★Boule d'Or 27 bd Carnot ☎41437656

🛁 🚿 33 🚘 **P**18 sB 🛁 🚿 107
dB 🛁 🚿 160—193 M70—110
Credit card [1]

★★**Climat** r du Château-d'Orgemont ☎41663045
🛁 42 **P**50 sB🛁 219—239 dB🛁 238—258 M51&alc
Credit cards [1] [2] [3]

★★**Croix de Guerre** 23 r Château Gontier ☎41886659 tx720930
rm29 (🛁🚿 14) ⌂ **P**35 sB99 sB🛁🚿 158—196 dB🛁🚿 176—214 M68—148
Credit cards [1] [2] [3] [4]

★★**Fimotel** 23 r P-Bert ☎41881010 tx215269
🛁 57 **P** Lift
Credit cards [1] [2] [3] [5]

★★**France** (FAH) 8 pl de la Gare ☎41884942 tx720895
🛁🚿 56 Lift ☾ sB🛁🚿 225—275 dB🛁🚿 300—390 Mfr75
Credit cards [1] [2] [3] [5]

★★**Ibis** r de la Poissonnerie ☎41861515 tx720916
🛁 95 **P** Lift sB🛁 220—240 dB🛁 265—285 M60—70

★★***Progrès*** (Inter) 26 r D-Papin (n.rest) ☎41881014 tx720982
🛁 41 Lift ☾

★★**Univers** 2 r de la Gare (n.rest) ☎41884358 tx720930
rm45 (🛁🚿 42) Lift ☾ sB104 sB🛁🚿 142 dB167—181 dB🛁🚿 198—231
Credit cards [1] [2] [3] [5]

🚗 **Clogenson** 30 r Coste et Bellonte ☎41668266 All makes

ANGLET
Pyrénées-Atlantiques

★★★**Chiberta & Golf** (Inter) (**DPn** in high season) 104 bd Plage ☎59638830 tx550637
🛁🚿 80 **P**80 Lift sB🛁🚿 273—583 dB🛁🚿 326—666 M98— t% 🏊 ⊡ sea lake
Credit cards [1] [2] [3] [5]

★★***Biarritz Golf*** 20 av Guynemer à la Chambre d'Amour ☎59038302
Apr—Sep
rm25 (🛁🚿 11) **P**

★★**Ibis** 64 av d'Espagne (N10) ☎59034545 tx560121
🛁 59 **P** Lift sB🛁 225—250 dB🛁 271—298 M70—80&alc

★***Fauvettes*** 69 r Moulin Barbot à la Chambre d'Amour (rest for guests only) ☎59037558
Apr—Sep
rm11 (🚿 5) ⌂ sea

Auto-Durruty des Pontots ☎59630968 Closed Sat & Sun For

🚗 **J-Iribarren** quartier Sutar, av de Cambo ☎59636056 Cit

ANGOULÊME
Charente

★★★**Grand France** (Inter) 1 pl des Halles ☎45954795 tx791020
rm60 (🛁🚿 47) ⌂ **P**20 Lift ☾ sB141

France

sB🛁🚿 231—251 dB212 dB🛁🚿 302—342 M110
Credit cards [1] [2] [3] [5]

★★***Epl d'Or*** (Inter) 66 bd R-Chabasse (n.rest) ☎45956764
🛁🚿 32 **P**25 Lift ☾
Credit cards [1] [2] [3] [5]

★**Flore** 414 rte de Bordeaux ☎45919946 tx791573
rm40 (🚿 14) A2rm ⌂ **P**20 ☾ sB126 sB🚿 158 dB209 M43—165&alc
Credit cards [1] [2] [3] [4] [5]

🚗 **Boutlin** 74 r de Paris ☎45950493 All makes

At **CHAMPNIERS** (7km NE)

★★★**Novotel Angoulême Nord** (N10) ☎45685322 tx790153
🛁 100 **P**100 Lift sB🛁 285—300 dB🛁 330—355 Malc 🏊
Credit cards [1] [2] [3] [4] [5]

★★**PM16** rte de Poitiers ☎45680322 tx790345
🛁🚿 41 **P**60 ☾ sB🛁🚿 199—239 dB🛁🚿 238—268 Mfr60
Credit cards [1] [2] [3] [5]

ANNECY
Haute-Savoie

See also: **TALLOIRES; VEYRIER-DU-LAC**

★★★**Mercure Annecy Sud** rte d'Aix (N201) Seynod ☎50510347 tx385303
🛁 69 **P**100 sB🛁 324—336 dB🛁 388—400 M75—80 🏊
Credit cards [1] [2] [3] [5]

★★★**Splendid** 4 quai E-Chappuis (n.rest) ☎50452000 tx385233
🛁🚿 51 Lift sB🛁🚿 185—285 dB🛁🚿 300—360 lake mountains
Credit cards [1] [3]

★★**Campanile** Impasse de Crêts ☎50677466 tx385565
🛁 40 **P** sB🛁 217—238 dB🛁 239—260 M61—82
Credit card [3]

★★**Faisan Doré** LE (**Pn** in season) 34 av d'Albigny ☎50230246
rm41 (🛁🚿 32) ⌂ Lift sBfr135 sB🛁🚿 fr225 dBfr180 dB🛁🚿 fr300 M75—140

★★ **Ibis** quartier de la Manufacture, r de la Gare ☎50454321 tx385585
🛁 83 Lift sB🛁 204—227 dB🛁 256—283 Malc
Credit cards [1] [3]

🚗 **Parmelan** av du Petit Port, Annecy-le-Vieux ☎50231285 Closed Sat & Sun Ope Vau

ANNEMASSE
Haute-Savoie

See also **GAILLARD**

★★★***Parc*** (MAP/BW) 19 r de Genève ☎50384460 tx309034
🛁🚿 30 ⌂ **P** Lift ☾
Credit cards [1] [2] [3] [5]

★★**National** (Inter) 10 pl J-Deffault (n. rest) ☎50920644
rm45 (🛁🚿 42) ⌂ **P**17 Lift sB🛁🚿 180—198 dB🛁🚿 220—248 mountains
Credit cards [1] [2] [3] [5]

🚗 **Mont-Blanc** chemin de la Chamarette ☎50920632 All makes

ANSE
Rhône

🚗 **Aux Pierres Dorées** 29 av de la Gare ☎74670335 Closed Aug 1—10 & Sun Ope

🚗 **Centre** 18 r des Marronniers ☎74670196 Closed Sat pm & Sun Cit

🚗 **M Salel** 59 r Nationale ☎74670368 Closed Sep 1—10 All makes

ANTHÉOR
Var

★★**Réserve d'Anthéor** (N98) ☎94448005
Feb—Oct
🛁🚿 13 **P**25 sB🛁🚿 154—194 dB🛁🚿 210—262 M75—130 Beach sea
Credit cards [1] [2] [3] [5]

ANTIBES
Alpes-Maritimes

★★★★**Tananarive** rte de Nice (N7) (n.rest) ☎93333000 tx470851
🛁🚿 50 ⌂ **P**20 Lift sB🛁🚿 225—341 dB🛁🚿 310—415 🎾 🏊 sea
Credit cards [1] [2] [3] [5]

★★★**First** 21 av des Chêne ☎93618737 tx470673
🛁🚿 17 **P** ☾ sB🛁🚿 267—377 dB🛁🚿 439—504 Mfr100 t% sea
Credit cards [1] [2] [3] [4] [5]

★★★**Mercator** chemin des Groules, quartier de la Brague (4km N via N7) (n.rest) ☎93335075
15 Dec—15 Nov
🛁 18 A2rm **P**20 dB🛁 249—274 🎾
Credit cards [1] [2] [3] [5]

★★***Fimotel*** rte de Grasse ☎93744636 tx461181
🛁 75 **P** Lift 🎾 🏊
Credit cards [2] [3] [5]

🚗 **Dugommier** 16bd Dugommier ☎93745999 Closed Sat pm & Sun Ope

🚗 **Molineri** chemin de St-Maymes ☎93616203 Closed Sat pm & Sun All makes

At **CAP D'ANTIBES**

★★★**Gardiole** chemin de la Garoupe ☎93613503
Feb—3 Nov
🛁🚿 21 sB🛁🚿 175—205 dB🛁🚿 300—400 M86—89 mountains
Credit cards [1] [2] [3] [5]

★★**Beau Site** 141 bd Kennedy (n.rest) ☎93615343

Etr—Oct
🛁 ⛆26 A6rm **P**30 dB 🛁 ⛆330—350 sea

APPOIGNY See **AUXERRE**

APT
Vaucluse

★★★**Ventoux** LF 67 a V-Hugo ☎90740758

Feb—Dec
🛁 ⛆13 Lift sB 🛁 ⛆119—194
dB 🛁 ⛆238—388 M57—149
Credit cards 1 2 3 4 5

ARBOIS
Jura

★★***Messageries*** LF 2 r Courcelles (n.rest) ☎84661545

Mar—Nov
rm27 (🛁 ⛆12) 🚗
Credit card 3

★**Paris** LF (FAH) (**Pn**) 9 r de l'Hôtel-de-Ville ☎84660567

15 Mar—15 Nov
🛁 ⛆18 A6rm 🚗 **P**4 sB 🛁 ⛆137—210
dB 🛁 ⛆239—335 M90—290
Credit cards 1 2 3 5

ARCACHON
Gironde

See also **PYLA-SUR-MER**

★★★**Arc** 89 bd Plage (n.rest) ☎56830685

🛁 30 **P**30 Lift ☾ sB 🛁 230—690
dB 🛁 320—810 ⛱ sea
Credit cards 1 2 3 5

★★★**Tamarins** 253 bd Côte d'Argent (n.rest) ☎56225096

🛁 ⛆28 A4rm Lift sB 🛁 ⛆141—231
dB 🛁 ⛆192—282 St%
Credit cards 1 3

ARCIS-SUR-AUBE
Aube

🚘 **S A Allais** r de Troyes ☎25378482
Closed Aug, Sat pm & Sun Cit

🚘 **Leroy** 17 rte de Chalons ☎25378452
Closed Aug 5—25 & Sun Tal

ARDRES
Pas-de-Calais

★★★**Grand Clément** (**Pn**) pl du Gl-Leclerc ☎21822525 tx130886

15 Feb—15 Jan
rm17(🛁 ⛆16) 🚗 **P**15 sB175—265
sB 🛁 ⛆175—265 dB 🛁 ⛆200—290
M100—280
Credit cards 1 2 3 4 5

★★**Relais** LF (**Pn** in high season) bd C-Senlecq ☎21354200

6 Feb—1 Jan
🛁 ⛆10 A1rm **P**20 dB 🛁 ⛆180—245
M59—170
Credit cards 1 2 3

★**Chaumière** 67 av de Rouville (n.rest) ☎21354124

🛁 ⛆12 **P**5 sB 🛁 ⛆132—196
dB 🛁 ⛆264—392

France

ARGELÈS-GAZOST
Hautes-Pyrénées

★**Bernède** LF (FAH) 51 r Ml-Foch ☎62970664 tx531040

rm41 (🛁 25) **P**32 Lift mountains
Credit cards 1 2 3 5

★**Mon Cottage** (**DPn**) 3 r Yser ☎62970792

Apr—Oct
rm24 (🛁 18) A8rm **P**25 Lift sB135 sB 🛁 195
dB290 dB 🛁 290 M40 mountains

ARGELÈS-SUR-MER
Pyrénées-Orientales

★★★**Plage des Pins** allée des Pins, à la Plage ☎68810905

Jun—Sep
🛁 49 **P**49 Lift ☾ sB 🛁 284—329
dB 🛁 308—353 M86—108 🎾 ⛱ sea

★**Grand Commerce** (**DPn** in season) 14 rte de Collioure (N22) ☎68810033

Closed Jan
rm63 (🛁 ⛆46) A23rm **P**63 Lift sB107
sB 🛁 ⛆157 dB134 dB 🛁 ⛆232 M48—121
⛱
Credit cards 2 3 5

ARGENTAN
Orne

★★***Renaissance*** LF av de la 2E D-B ☎33671611

rm15 (🛁 ⛆12) 🚗 **P**50
Credit cards 2 3 5

ARGENTAT
Corrèze

★★**Gilbert** LF (**DPn**) av J-Vachal ☎55280162

Mar—Nov
rm30 (🛁 ⛆19) 🚗 **P**8 Lift sB100—110
sB 🛁 ⛆150—200 dB130—150
dB 🛁 ⛆190—260 M60—160 mountains
Credit cards 1 2 3 5

🚘 **Manaux** 1 rte de Tulle ☎55280332
Closed Sun Peu

ARGENTEUIL
Val-d'Oise

★★**Climat** bd Lénine angle du Perreux ☎39619805 tx692844

🛁 43 **P**50 dB 🛁 233—258 M52—67
Credit cards 1 3

★★**Fimotel** 148 rte de Pontoise (N192) ☎34105200 tx699681

🛁 40 🚗 **P**80 Lift sB 🛁 205—219
dB 🛁 237—248 M50—90
Credit cards 1 2 3 5

ARGENTON-SUR-CREUSE
Indre

★★**Manoir de Boisvillers** 11 r Moulin de Bord (n.rest) ☎54241388

rm15 (🛁 ⛆11) A5rm **P**10 sBfr99
sB 🛁 ⛆170—207 dB145—156
dB 🛁 ⛆240—277
Credit cards 1 3

★**France** LF 8 r J-J-Rousseau ☎54240331

rm24 (🛁 ⛆13) A8rm 🚗 **P**6 sB77
sB 🛁 ⛆95—140 dB110—193 dB 🛁 ⛆193
M51—96
Credit cards 1 2 3 5

🚘 **Chavegrand** rte de Limoges ☎54240432 Peu

ARLEMPDES
Haute-Loire

★★***Manoir*** LF ☎71571714

rm16 (⛆11) mountains

ARLES
Bouches-du-Rhône

★★★★**Jules César** (Relais et Châteaux) bd des Lices ☎90934320 tx400239

23 Dec—3 Nov
🛁 ⛆60 🚗 **P**7 ☾ sB 🛁 ⛆446—646
dB 🛁 ⛆642—842 M150—250
Credit cards 1 2 3 4 5

★★★**Cantarelles** Ville Vieille ☎90964410 tx401582

15 Mar—15 Nov
🛁 35 🚗 **P**20 dB 🛁 266—300 ⛱
Credit cards 1 2 3 5

★★★**Forum** 10 pl Forum (n.rest) ☎90934895

15 Feb—30 Oct
rm45 (🛁 ⛆41) **P**30 Lift ☾ sB96—126
sB 🛁 ⛆221—271 dBfr147
dB 🛁 ⛆242—342 ⛱

★★★**Primotel** av de la 1er Division Français Libre (opposite Palais du Congrés) ☎90939880 tx401001

🛁 148 **P**150 Lift sB 🛁 fr279 dB 🛁 fr347 M alc 🎾 ⛱
Credit cards 1 2 3 5

★★★***Select*** 35 bd G-Clemenceau ☎90960831

🛁 ⛆24 🚗 Lift
Credit cards 1 2 3 5

★★**Arlatan** 26 r Sauvage (n.rest) ☎90935666 tx441203

🛁 ⛆46 🚗 ☾ sB 🛁 ⛆266
dB 🛁 ⛆355—455
Credit cards 2 3 5

★★**Cloître** 18 r du Cloître (n.rest) ☎90962950 tx440096

15 Mar—15 Nov
🛁 ⛆33 A10rm sB 🛁 ⛆210 dB 🛁 ⛆250
Credit card 3

★★**Ibis** quartier de Fourchon ☎90931674 tx440201

🛁 64 **P**80 sB205—236 dB 🛁 253—284 M85 & alc ⛱
Credit cards 1 3

★★**Mireille** (Inter) (**DPn**) 2 pl St-Pierre ☎90937074 tx440308

Mar—15 Nov
rm35 (🛁 ⛆33) A16rm 🚗 **P**40 ☾ sB136
sB 🛁 ⛆225 dB182 dB 🛁 ⛆307—362
M79—140&alc ⛱
Credit cards 1 2 3 5

★★**Montmajour et Le Rodin** (FAH/Inter) 84 rte de Tarasçon ☎90939833 tx420776
🛁🚿30 A20rm **P**50 sB🛁🚿176—233 dB🛁🚿225—308 M63&alc 🏊
Credit cards [1] [2] [3] [4] [5]

★**Mirador** 3 r Voltaire (n.rest) ☎90962805
Closed Feb
🛁🚿15 dB🛁🚿177

🚗 **Sovra** 69 rte de Crau ☎90961075 Closed Sat pm & Sun Alf Fia Hon Mer Por Toy

At **RAPHÈLE-LES-ARLES** (8km SE on N453)

★★★**Auberge la Fenière** ☎90984744 tx441237
🛁🚿25 🏠**P**25 sB🛁🚿231—279 dB🛁🚿262—507 M118—165
Credit cards [1] [2] [3] [5]

ARMBOUTS CAPPEL See **DUNKERQUE**

ARNAGE See **MANS (LE)**

ARNAY-LE-DUC
Côte-d'Or

★**Terminus** LF r Arquebuse ☎80900033
rm12 (🚿6) 🏠**P**20 sB72—132 sB🚿92—192 dB144—264 dB🚿184—384 M60—160
Credit cards [1] [3] [4]

🚗 **Binet** (N6) ☎80901007 Cit

ARRAS
Pas-de-Calais

★★★**Univers** (Inter) 3 pl Croix Rouge ☎21713401
rm36 (🛁🚿30) A1rm 🏠**P**40 ☾ sB178—288 sB🛁🚿288 dB356—576 dB🛁🚿576—636
Credit cards [1] [2] [3]

★★**Astoria** 12 pl MI-Foch ☎21710814 tx160768
rm33 (🛁🚿14) ☾
Credit cards [1] [2] [3] [5]

★★**Commerce** 24 r Gambetta (n.rest) ☎2171107
rm40 (🛁🚿17) 🏠**P**25 Lift ☾ sB120—132 sB🛁🚿168—206 dB140—177 dB🛁🚿226—250

★★**Moderne** (Inter) 1 bd Faidherbe (n.rest) ☎21233957
Closed Xmas & New Year
rm54 (🛁50) Lift sB🛁205—235 dB🛁250—290
Credit cards [1] [2] [3] [5]

★**Chánzy** LF 8 r Chánzy ☎21710202
rm23 (🛁🚿13) A11rm **P**2 sB110—200 sB🛁🚿160—200 dB140—250 dB🛁🚿190—250 M80—150
Credit cards [1] [2] [3] [4] [5]

🚗 **Artois Polds Lourds** rte Nationale Ste-Catherine (N113) ☎21236822 Closed Sat & Sun All makes

🚗 **Cyr Leroy** 75 r de Cambrai ☎21732626 Closed Sun Tal

🚗 **Llevinolse Auto** 16 av P-Michonneau ☎21554242 Closed Sat & Sun For

Michonneau 6 av P-Michonneau ☎21553751 Closed Aug 11—25, Sat & Sun Fia

France

At **ST-NICOLAS** (N off N17)

★★**Campanile** Zone d'Emploi des Alouettes ☎21555630 tx133616
🛁42 **P** sB🛁217—238 dB🛁239—260 M61—82

ARREAU
Hautes-Pyrénées

At **CADÉAC** (2km S)

★★**Val d'Aure** rte de St-Lary ☎62986063
Jun—Oct
🛁🚿23 A8rm 🏠**P**20 sB🛁🚿158—233 dB🛁🚿202—256 Mfr55 ⚲ mountains

ARTEMARE
Ain

★***Valromey*** (Inter) ☎79873010
rm25 (🛁🚿19) A16rm 🏠**P** mountains

ARTIGUES See **BORDEAUX**

ARUDY
Pyrénées-Atlantiques

🚗 **M-Versavaud** rte de Pau ☎59056070 Closed Sun Tal

ARVERT
Charente-Maritime

★★**Villa Fantaisie** LF **(DPn)** ☎46364009
Closed Mar—Jan
rm23 (🛁🚿16) A10rm **P**100 sB270—390 sB🛁🚿370—390 dB260—360 dB🛁🚿340—360 M90—180
Credit cards [1] [2] [3]

ASCAIN
Pyrénées-Atlantiques

★★***Rhune*** pl d'Ascain ☎59540004
Mar—15 Nov
🛁🚿42 A15rm **P**30 🏊 mountains

ASSEVILLIERS See **PÉRONNE**

ATHIS-MONS See **PARIS AIRPORTS** under **ORLY AIRPORT**

AUBENAS
Ardèche

★★**La Pinede** LF rte du Camping des Pins ☎75352588
Closed 15 Dec—20 Jan
rm32 (🛁30) **P** sB125—165 sB🛁125—165 dB175—215 dB🛁175—215 M61—110
Credit card [3]

🚗 **Gounon** 22 St-Didier ☎75350821 Closed 25 Aug—15 Sep, Sat pm & Sun Fia

AUBUSSON
Creuse

★★**France** LF (FAH) **(DPn)** 6 r de Portes-Politiques ☎55661022
rm24 (🛁🚿17) 🏠 sB88 sB🛁🚿108—213 dB176—232 dB🛁🚿216—281 M60—210
Credit cards [1] [2] [3] [5]

★***Lion d'Or*** pl d'Espagne ☎55661388
rm15 (🛁🚿9) **P** mountains
Credit cards [2] [3] [5]

At **FOURNEAUX** (11km NW of D942)

★★***Tuilerie*** (Inter) ☎556624809
🛁24 **P**40 ⛴
Credit cards [1] [2] [5]

AUCH
Gers

★★★***France*** (BW/MAP) pl de la Libération ☎62050044 tx520474
🛁🚿30 🏠**P** Lift ☾
Credit cards [1] [2] [3] [4] [5]

★★**Poste** (Inter) 5 r-C-Desmoulins ☎62050236
rm27 (🛁🚿24) 🏠**P** sB135—200 sB🛁🚿200 dB170—250 dB🛁🚿250 Mfr60
Credit cards [1] [2] [5]

AULNAT AÉROPORT See **CLERMONT FERRAND**

AULNAY-SOUS-BOIS
Seine

★★★***Novotel Paris Aulnay-sous-Bois*** (N370) ☎48662297 tx230121
🛁🚿138 **P**100 Lift 🏊
Credit cards [1] [2] [3] [5]

AUMALE
Seine-Maritime

★***Dauphin*** r St-Lazare ☎35934192
rm11 (🛁🚿10) **P**6
Credit cards [2] [4]

🚗 **Fertun** 3 av Foch ☎934121 Closed Sun Peu

AUNAY-SUR-ODON
Calvados

★**Place** LF ☎31776073
rm18 🏠**P**20 Lift sBfr73 dBfr104 M38—75

★**St-Michel** LF **(Pn)** 6 & 8 r Caen ☎31776316
rm7 **P**12 dB102 M58—147
Credit cards [1] [3]

AURILLAC
Cantal

★★**Grand Bordeaux** LF (BW/MAP) 2 av de la République (n.rest) ☎71480184 tx990316
rm37 (🛁🚿30) 🏠 Lift sB165—245 sB🛁🚿195—245 dB230—330
Credit cards [1] [2] [3] [4] [5]

AURON
Alpes-Maritimes

★★★***Pilon*** ☎93230015 tx470300
15 Dec—20 Apr & Jul—Aug
🛁🚿30 **P** Lift 🏊 mountains

AUTUN
Saône-et-Loire

★★**Tête Noir** LF **(DPn)** 1—3 de l'Arquebuse ☎85522539
Closed Mar
rm20 (🛁🚿14) 🏠 sBfr93 sB🛁🚿125—181 dBfr110 dB🛁🚿140—210 M55—105
Credit cards [1] [3]

France

AUVILLERS-LES-FORGES
Ardennes

★★**Lenoir** LE ☎24543011
Mar—Dec
rm21 (🛁 🚿 18) A21rm **P**30 Lift dB175
dB 🛁 🚿 292 M195—274
Credit cards 1 2 3 4 5

AUXERRE
Yonne

★★★***Clairions*** LE av Worms ☎86468564 tx800039
🛁 44 **P** Lift

★★★**Maxime** 2 quai de la Marine ☎86521419
🛁 🚿 25 🏠 **P** Lift ☾ sB 🛁 🚿 250—295
dB 🛁 🚿 242—246 M90—163
Credit cards 1 2 3 5

★★**Cygne** 14 r du 24 Août (n.rest) ☎86522651
🛁 🚿 24 **P**10 dB 🛁 🚿 162—262
Credit cards 1 3

★★**Normandie** (Inter) 41 bd Vauban (n.rest) ☎86525780
🛁 🚿 48 🏠 **P**100 ☾ sB 🛁 🚿 176
dB 🛁 🚿 222
Credit cards 1 2 3 4 5

★★**Seignelay** LE **(DPn)** 2 r Pont ☎86520348
10 Feb—10 Jan
rm24 (🛁 🚿 12) 🏠 sB90—128 sB 🛁 🚿 148
dB146—166 dB 🛁 🚿 217—226 M55—75
Credit cards 1 3

🚗 **Carette** 34—36 av C-de-Gaulle ☎86469638 Closed Sat pm & Sun Dat Vol

🚗 **Casimir** rte de Chablis ☎86469876 Closed Sun & Mon am All makes

🚗 **Grand Garage Gambetta** 8 av Gambetta ☎86469718 For

🚗 **B Jeannin** 40 av C-de-Gaulle ☎86523383 Closed Sat pm Aud VW

🚗 **Route de Lyon** 15 av MI-Juin ☎86469805 Closed Sun Peu

🚗 **Sodiva** 2 av J-Mermoz ☎86467575 Closed Sat pm & Sun Ren

At **APPOIGNY** (9.5km NW via N6)

★★★**Mercure** C D 319 Lieu-dit-Le Chaumois ☎86532500 tx800095
🛁 82 **P**100 sB 🛁 288—303
dB 🛁 🚿 366—381 M120—250 ⛱
Credit cards 1 2 3 5

★★***Climat*** chemin des Ruelles ☎86539711
🛁 24 **P**24

AUXON
Aube

🚗 **Domagala** Le Péage (N7) ☎25457012 M/c Closed Sun Peu

AUXONNE
Côte-d'Or

★**Corbeau** LE **(Pn)** 1 r de Berbis ☎80381188
28 Jan—22 Dec
🛁 10 **P**10 sB 🛁 126—170 dB 🛁 182—230
M54—130 S10%
Credit cards 1 2 3 5

At **VILLERS-LES-POTS** (5km NW)

★★***Auberge de Cheval Rouge*** ☎80373411
🛁 🚿 10 **P**20
Credit cards 3 5

AVALLON
Yonne

★★★★***Poste*** (Relais et Châteaux) 13 pl Vauban ☎86340612
Feb—Nov
🛁 23 🏠 **P**20 ☾
Credit cards 2 3 5

★★★***Moulin des Ruats*** (4.5km W via D957 & D427) Vallée du Cousin ☎86340714
Mar—Oct
rm21 (🛁 🚿 15) **P**20
Credit cards 1 2 3 5

★★**Relais Fleuri** LE (5km E on N6) ☎86340285 tx800084
🛁 48 **P**48 sB 🛁 243—263 dB 🛁 286—336
M84—130 ⛱
Credit cards 1 2 3 5

🚗 **Avallon-Autos** 15 r Carnot ☎86340647 Closed Sun & Mon For

🚗 **Gallmard** 2 rte de Paris ☎86341303 Closed Xmas & New Year Toy

🚗 **Gueneau** 30 r de Paris ☎86341927 Closed Sun Ren

AVIGNON
Vaucluse

See also **VILLENEUVE-LES-AVIGNON**

★★★**Mercure Avignon-Sud** rte Marseille-La Barbière ☎90889110 tx431994
🛁 105 **P**190 Lift sB 🛁 296—305
dB 🛁 382—394 Malc t4% ⛱
Credit cards 1 2 3 5

★★★***Novotel Avignon Sud*** rte de Marseille (N7) ☎90876236 tx432878
🛁 79 🏠 **P** M alc ⛱
Credit cards 1 2 3 5

★★**Angleterre** LE 29 bd de Raspail (n.rest) ☎90863431
16 Jan—14 Dec
rm40 (🛁 🚿 37) **P**14 Lift sB106—149
sB 🛁 🚿 162—244 dB120—163
dB 🛁 🚿 176—258 t3%

★★**Midi** (Inter) 53 r de la République (n.rest) ☎90821556 tx431074
26 Jan—14 Dec
🛁 🚿 57 Lift sB 🛁 🚿 240—250
dB 🛁 🚿 260—280
Credit cards 1 2 3 5

★***Jaquemart*** 3 r F-David (n.rest) ☎90863471
rm20 (🛁 🚿 9)

🚗 **C Delage** 14 bd de la Liberté ☎90851320 Closed Sat pm & Sun Vol

🚗 **EGSA** Centre des affaires Cap Sud — rte de Marseille ☎90876322 Closed Sat pm & Sun Aud VW

🚗 **Parking** 77 av de Marseille ☎90885594 Closed Sat pm & Sun BMW

🚗 **Scandolera** 1 bis rte de Morieres (N7) ☎90821676 Closed Sat pm & Sun For

At **AVIGNON NORD AUTOROUTE JUNCTION** (A7) (8km E by D942)

★★★★**Sofitel** ☎90311643 tx432869
🛁 100 **P**150 Lift sB 🛁 357 dB 🛁 424 🎾 ⛱
Credit cards 1 2 3 5

At **MONTFAVET** (5.5km E)

★★**Campanile** Za du Clos de la Cristole ☎90899977 tx432060
🛁 42 **P** sB 🛁 217—238 dB 🛁 239—260
M61—82
Credit card 3

★★***Climat de l'Amandier*** allée des Fenaisons ☎90881300
🛁 🚿 30 🏠 **P**40 Lift

★★***Ibis*** rte de Marseille (RN7), Zone de la Cristole ☎90871100 tx432811
🛁 65 **P**65 ⛱
Credit cards 1 2 3 4 5

Daures Shell Service Station, Cantarel (N7) ☎90880295 Closed 1—15 Sep & Sun Ren

AVRANCHES
Manche

★★**Croix d'Or** **(DPn)** 83 r de la Constitution ☎33580488
mid Mar—mid Nov
rm30 (🛁 🚿 25) A4rm 🏠 **P**30 sBfr75
dB110—130 dB 🛁 🚿 210—400 M75—200
Credit card 3

★★**St-Michel** **(DPn)** 5 pl Gl-Patton ☎33580191
20 Mar—Nov
rm24 (🛁 🚿 17) 🏠 **P**18 sB98—187
sB 🛁 🚿 98—187 dB 🛁 🚿 114—203
M59—87
Credit cards 1 3

🚗 **Total Station Loisirs** 182 av de la Liberté ☎33581475 All makes

AX-LES-THERMES
Ariège

★★★***Royal Thermal*** (BW/MAP) espl de Couloubret ☎61642251 tx530955
rm68 (🛁 54) ☾ Lift mountains
Credit cards 1 2 3 5

★★**Modern** LE **(DPn)** 20 av du Dr-Gomma ☎61642024
10 Feb—Oct
rm22 (🛁 🚿 11) 🏠 Lift sB85—142
sB 🛁 🚿 142 dB115—129 dB 🛁 🚿 171—199
M45—70 mountains

★★**Roy René** LE **(DPn)** 11 av du Dr-Gomma ☎61642228
Jan—Oct
rm29 (🛁 🚿 26) 🏠 **P**18 sB95 dB150—160
dB 🛁 🚿 200—220 M60—150 Lift mountains
Credit cards 1 2 3

★**Lauzeraie** prom due Couloubert
☎61642070 tx530806
Feb—Nov
rm28 (🛁🚿12) A2rm **P**7 sB89—93 dBfr115
dB🛁🚿155—173 M39—120 mountains

AZAY-LE-RIDEAU
Indre-et-Loire
★★**Grand Monarque** (LE) (**DPn**)
☎47454008
rm30 (🛁🚿15) A12rm 🚗 **P**12 sBfr115
sB🛁🚿275 dB175—230 dB🛁🚿300—350
M80—190&alc
Credit cards [1] [2] [3]

BAGNÈRES-DE-BIGORRE
Hautes-Pyrénées
★★**Résidence** Parc Thermal de Salut
☎62950397
Apr—15 Oct
🛁🚿41 A10rm sB🛁🚿fr225 dB🛁🚿fr235
🏊 mountains
★★***Vignaux*** (LE) 16 r de la République
☎62950341
rm15 (🛁2)

BAGNEAUX See **SAUMUR**

BAGNOLES-DE-L'ORNE
Orne
★★★***Lutetia-Reine Astrid*** bd P-Chalvet, pl du Gl-de-Gaulle ☎33379477
Apr—Oct
rm30 (🛁19) **P**
★★**Bois Joli** (**Pn**) av P-du Rosier
☎33379277 tx171782
Apr—Oct
rm20 (🛁🚿17) **P**15 Lift sB202—317
sB🛁🚿272—317 dB304—354
dB🛁🚿304—354 M100
Credit cards [1] [2] [3] [5]
★★***Ermitage*** (Inter) 24 bd P-Chalvet (n.rest) ☎33379622
15 Apr—15 Oct
rm39 (🛁🚿25) 🚗 **P**12
Credit card [3]

BAGNOLS-EN-FORÊT
Var
★★***Auberge Bagnolaise*** (LE) rte Fayence
☎94406024
Mar—Sep
🛁8 **P** mountains

BAGNOLET See **PARIS**

BAIX
Ardèche
★★★**Cardinale** (Relais et Châteaux) (**DPn**) quai du Rhône ☎75858040
15 Feb—2 Jan
🛁15 A10rm **P**20 dB🛁fr685 M160—250 🎾
🏊 mountains
Credit cards [1] [2] [3] [5]

BANDOL
Var
★★★★**PLM Ile Rousse** (**Pn** Jul & Aug) bd L-Lumière ☎94294686 tx400372
🛁55 🚗 **P** Lift sB🛁370—910
dB🛁470—1050 M160&alc 🏊 Beach sea
Credit cards [1] [2] [3] [5]

France

★★**Bale** 62 r Marçon (n.rest) ☎94294082
tx400479
Closed Jan
🛁🚿14 ☾ sB🛁🚿220 dB🛁🚿440 sea
Credit cards [1] [3]
★★**Golf** Plage de Renécros (n.rest)
☎94294583
Etr—Oct
rm24 (🛁🚿22) **P**20 ☾ sB🛁🚿fr213
dB232—321 dB🛁🚿232—321 Beach sea
★★**Provençal** r des Écoles ☎94295211
tx400308
🛁22 🚗 sB🛁229 dB🛁248—268
M110—130
Credit cards [1] [2] [3] [5]
★★**Réserve** rte de Sanary ☎94294271
15 Jan—Nov
rm16 (🛁🚿15) **P**13 dBfr147 dB🛁🚿256
Mfr100 sea
Credit cards [3] [5]

BANYULS-SUR-MER
Pyrénées-Orientales
★★★**Catalan** ☎68383244
Apr—Oct
🛁🚿36 🚗 **P** Lift 🎾 🏊 sea mountains
Credit card [5]

BAPAUME
Pas-de-Calais
★**Paix** 11 av A-Guidet ☎21071103
4 Jan—Jul & 15 Aug—20 Dec
rm16 (🛁9) 🚗 **P**35 sB86—166 sB🛁166
dB112—182 dB🛁112—202 M54-140
Credit cards [1] [2] [3]
🔧 **Greselle** 38 r de Péronne ☎21071413
Closed Sat & Sun Peu
🔧 **Piscine** av A-Guidet ☎21071304 Closed Sat pm & Sun Cit
Sellier 22 fbg d'Arras ☎21071279 Tal

BARBEN (LA) See **SALON-DE-PROVENCE**

BARBEREY See **TROYES AIRPORT**

BARBEZIEUX
Charente
★★***Boule d'Or*** (LE) (Inter) (**DPn**) 11 bd Gambetta ☎45782272
rm28 (🛁14) **P**16 🏊
Credit cards [1] [2] [3]
🔧 **Cholet** av Vergne ☎45781166 M/c
Closed Sun Peu
🔧 **Gaborlaud** 13 bd Gambetta ☎45781213
Closed Sun & Mon am VW
At **BOIS VERT** (11km S on N10)
★★★**Venta** ☎45784095
🛁23 **P**100 sB🛁92—132 dB🛁184—264
M44—115 🎾 🏊
Credit cards [1] [3] [4]

BARBIZON
Seine-et-Marne
★★★★★**Bas-Breau** (Relais et Châteaux) (**Pn**) Grand Rue ☎60664005 tx690953
mid Feb—mid Jan
🛁19 🚗 **P** ☾ sB🛁760 dB🛁1070 M alc
🏊 S15% 🎾
Credit cards [1] [2]
★★**Charmettes** (**Pn**) Grand Rue
☎60664021
🛁🚿39 A3rm 🚗 **P**25 sB🛁🚿130—240
dB🛁🚿260—480 S15%

BARBOTAN-LES-THERMES
Gers
★★**Château-de-Bégue** (2km SW on N656) ☎62695008 tx531918
2 May—Sep
rm14 (🛁🚿11) 🚗 **P**50 Lift sB165
sB🛁🚿265—295 dB315—345
dB🛁🚿315—345 M alc 🏊
Credit card [3]

BARENTIN See **ROUEN**

BARNEVILLE-CARTERET
Manche
At **BARNEVILLE PLAGE**
★★**Isles** (LE) bd Maritime ☎33649076
15 Jan—15 Nov
rm35 (🛁🚿30) sB123—243 sB🛁🚿253
dB241—271 dB🛁🚿271 M95 sea
At **CARTERET**
★★**Angleterre** (LE) 4 r de Paris
☎33538604
15 Mar—5 Nov
rm43 (🛁23) **P**20 sB125—155
sB🛁185—305 dB250—310
dB🛁370—550 M90—172 sea
Credit cards [1] [2] [3] [5]
★★**Marine** (LE) 2 r de Paris ☎33543331
Mar—5 Nov
rm31 (🛁🚿26) **P**12
Credit card [5]

BAR-SUR-AUBE
Aube
★***Commerce*** 38 r Nationale ☎25270876
Closed Jan
rm15 (🛁🚿12) 🚗 **P**15
Credit cards [1] [2] [3] [5]

BAR-SUR-SEINE
Aube
★★**Barséquanais** 7 av Gl-Leclerc
☎25298275
Feb—Dec
rm24 (🛁🚿14) A14rm **P**24 sB84—90
sB🛁🚿124—155 dB108—115
dB🛁🚿158—190 M45—80

BASTIDE-PUYLAURENT (LA)
Lozère
★★***Pins*** ☎66460007
🚿25

BAUGÉ
Maine-et-Loire
★**Boule d'Or** (LE) (**Pn**) 4 r du Cygne
☎41898212

15 Feb—15 Jan
rm12 (🛁 🚿6) 🚗 sB 🛁 🚿 105—155
dB 🛁 🚿 180—210 M50—140

BAULE (LA)
Loire-Atlantique

★★★**Bellevue Plage** (**Pn**) 27 bd Océan
☎40602855 tx710459
Mar—Oct
🛁 34 **P**28 Lift ☾ sB 🛁 273—398
dB 🛁 341—441 Mfr120 sea
Credit cards 1 2 3 5

★★★**Majestic** espl F-André (n.rest)
☎40602486
14 Apr—Sep
🛁 67 **P**30 Lift ☾ sB 🛁 375—415
dB 🛁 395—440 sea
Credit cards 2 3 5

★★**Concorde** 1 av de la Concorde (n.rest)
☎40602309
Apr—Sep
🛁 🚿 47 🚗 **P**8 Lift sB 🛁 🚿 210—315
dB 🛁 🚿 240—335 sea
Credit card 1

★★**Palmeraie** LF (Inter) (**Pn** in season)
7 allée Cormorans ☎40602441
25 Mar—Sep
🛁 🚿 23 dB 🛁 🚿 234—284 M85—100
Credit cards 1 2 3 5

★★**Riviera** 16 av des Lilas (n.rest)
☎40602897
May—Sep
rm20 (🛁 🚿 16) dBfr100 dB 🛁 🚿 170—240

★★**Welcome** 7 av des Impairs (n.rest)
☎40603025
Mar—Sep
🛁 🚿 18 dB 🛁 🚿 242—282 sea
Credit cards 1 3

🚘 **Sté-Atlantic** 33 av-G-Clemenceau
☎40602375 Closed Sep 26—Oct 20, Sat pm & Sun Alf AR Mer

BAUME-LES-DAMES
Doubs

🚘 **Duffing** av du Gl-Leclerc ☎81840995
For

At **HYÈVRE PAROISSE** (7km E)

★★**Ziss** (N83) ☎81840788
🛁 21 🚗 **P** Lift sB 🛁 200 dB 🛁 220—240
M45—130 mountains
Credit cards 2 3

BAVANS See **MONTBÉLIARD**

BAYEUX
Calvados

★★★**Lion d'Or** LF (**Pn**) 71 r St-Jean
☎31920690
22 Jan—19 Dec
rm29 (🛁 🚿 25) 🚗 **P**22 Lift ☾ sB144—218
sB 🛁 🚿 204—288 dB218—356
dB 🛁 🚿 218—356 M75—195
Credit cards 2 3 5

★★***Bayeux*** 9 r de Tardif (n.rest)
☎31927008
15 Mar—15 Nov
🛁 🚿 31 🚗 **P**14

France

★★**Mogador** 20 r A-Chartier (n. rest)
☎31922458
🛁 🚿 14 **P** sB 🛁 🚿 154—159
dB 🛁 🚿 208—238
Credit cards 1 3

BAYONNE
Pyrénées-Atlantiques

★★★***Agora*** av J-Rostand ☎59633090
tx550621
🛁 🚿 110 **P** Lift
Credit cards 1 2 3 4 5

★★**Basses-Pyrénées** 12 r Tour de Sault
☎59590029 tx541535
rm48 (🛁 🚿 25) A10rm 🚗 Lift ☾ sB99—114
sB 🛁 🚿 134—168 dB133—153
dB 🛁 🚿 187—212 M49—120 t% mountains
Credit cards 1 2 3 5

★★***Capagorry*** (BW/MAP) 14r Thiers
(n.rest) ☎59254822
rm48 (🛁 🚿 35) Lift 🚗 **P**3 ☾
Credit cards 1 2 3 5

🚘 **Marmande** rte de Pau ☎59550561
Closed Sat & Sun AR

🚘 **Sajons** 36 allée Marines ☎59254579
All makes

BEAUCAIRE
Gard

★★★**Vignes Blanches** (Inter) rte de
Nîmes ☎66591312 tx480690
Apr—15 Oct
🛁 🚿 62 **P**30 Lift sB 🛁 🚿 215—255
dB 🛁 🚿 262—302 M80—92 ⛱
Credit card 3

★★***Robinson*** LF r de Pont du Gard
☎66692132
rm30 (🛁 🚿 25) **P** 🎾 ⛱

BEAUGENCY
Loiret

★★**Ecu de Bretagne** LF pl du Martroi
☎38446760
Mar—25 Jan
rm26 (🛁 🚿 17) A11rm 🚗 **P**30 sB91—156
sB 🛁 🚿 146—156 dB107 dB 🛁 🚿 172—262
M70—200
Credit cards 1 2 3 5

BEAULIEU-SUR-DORDOGNE
Corrèze

★★**Central** LF (**DPn**) ☎55910134
Mar—Nov
rm33 (🛁 🚿 20) **P**20 sB85—105 sB 🛁 🚿 155
dB120—140 dB 🛁 🚿 170—230 M65—120

★★**Chasseing Farges** LF (**Pn**) pl du
Champ de Mars ☎55911104
15 Mar—Sep
rm20 (🛁 🚿 10) A6rm sB71—135
sB 🛁 🚿 116 dB 🛁 🚿 142—270 M48—130
mountains

BEAULIEU-SUR-MER
Alpes-Maritimes

★★★★★**Réserve de Beaulieu** (**DPn**
Jul—Sep) 5 bd Gl-Leclerc ☎93010001
tx470301
10 Jan—Nov
🛁 50 🚗 **P**10 Lift ☾ sB 🛁 455—1035
dB 🛁 710—1660 M alc S15% 🏊 sea

★★★★**Métropole** (Relais et Châteaux)
(**Pn**) bd Gl-Leclerc ☎93010008 tx470304
20 Dec—20 Oct
🛁 50 **P** Lift ☾ **DPn**670—1490 M320—390
🎾 ⛱ Beach sea

★★★***Victoria*** 47 bd Marinoni
☎93010220 tx470303
20 Dec—Sep
rm80 (🛁 🚿 60) Lift ☾ sea mountains

BEAUMONT-SUR-SARTHE
Sarthe

★**Barque** 11 pl de la Libération
☎43970016
10 Jan-20 Dec
rm25 (🛁 🚿 16) **P**12 sB 🛁 🚿 fr112
dB 🛁 🚿 fr135 M61—96
Credit cards 1 2 3

★**Chemin de Fer** LF La Gare (1.5km E on
D26) ☎43970005
4 Mar—15 Oct & Nov—9 Feb
rm16 (🛁 🚿 8) 🚗 sBfr85 sB 🛁 🚿 161
dBfr170 dB 🛁 🚿 322 M52—140
Credit cards 1 3

🚘 **Thureau** rte Nationale 138 ☎43970033
Closed last 3 weeks Aug, Sat pm & Sun Tal

BEAUMONT-SUR-VESLE
Marne

★**Maison du Champagne** LF (**DPn**)
☎26616245 tx51400
rm10 (🛁 6) 🚗 sB70—115 sB 🛁 fr117
dBfr100 dB 🛁 fr155 M46—125
Credit cards 1 2 3 5

BEAUNE
Côte-d'Or

★★★**Cep** 27 r Maufoux (n.rest)
☎80223548 tx351256
15 Mar—20 Nov
🛁 🚿 21 🚗 ☾ sB 🛁 🚿 335—485
dB 🛁 🚿 570—700
Credit cards 1 2 3 5

★★★**PLM** (A6) ☎80214612 tx350627
🛁 150 sB 🛁 272 dB 🛁 304
Credit cards 1 2 3 5

★★★**Poste** 5 bd Clemenceau
☎80220811 tx350982
26 Mar—16 Nov
rm25 (🛁 🚿 24) 🚗 **P** Lift ☾ sB620
sB 🛁 🚿 665 dB665 dB 🛁 🚿 755 mountains

★★**Bourgogne** LF av C-de-Gaulle
☎80222200 tx350666
🛁 120 **P**150 Lift sB 🛁 fr225 dB 🛁 fr287
Mfr85 ⛱
Credit cards 1 2 3 5

★★**Central** LF (**DPn**) 2 r V-Millot
☎80247724
Jan—20 Nov →

rm22 (→ ⋔ 17) dBfr150 dB → ⋔ 200—260 M110—150
Credit card [3]

★★**Climat** ZA de la Chartreuse ☎80227410 tx305551

→ 38 **P**30 sB → 212—226 dB → 231—245 M52—75 S6%
Credit cards [1] [3]

★★***Samotel*** rte de Pommard (N74) ☎80223555 tx350596

→ 66 **P** ≈ mountains

🚗 **Bolatre** 40 fbg Bretonnière ☎80222803 Closed Sat & Sun Fia

🚗 **M Marinho** rte de Seurre ☎80224500 Closed Sat & Sun Ren

🚗 **M Monnot** 146 rte de Dijon ☎80221102 Closed Aug 8—18, Sat pm & Sun For

At **BROUZE-LES-BEAUNE** (6.5km NW on D970)

🚗 **Niquet Frères** ☎80224059 Closed Sat pm & Sun Tal

At **LADOIX-SERRIGNY** (5km NE)

★★**Paulands** ☎80264105 tx350293

→ ⋔ 21 A12rm **P**20 dB → ⋔ 193—248 M alc
Credit card [3]

At **LEVERNOIS** (5km SE)

★★**Campanile** rte de Verdun ☎802226550 tx350156

→ 42 **P** sB → 217—238 dB → 239—260 M61—82
Credit card [3]

BEAURAINVILLE
Pas-de-Calais

★**Val de Canche** LE **(Pn)** ☎21903222

rm10 (→ ⋔ 4) ⌂ **P**10 sB110—182 sB → ⋔ 182 dB127—154 dB → ⋔ 154—199 M45—110
Credit cards [1] [3]

BEAUREPAIRE
Isère

★★**Fiard** 25 r de la République ☎74846202

Closed Jan—20 Feb
rm21 (→ ⋔ 20) sB133—193 sB → ⋔ 163—193 dB → ⋔ 216 M90—300
Credit cards [1] [2] [3] [4] [5]

BEAUSSET (LE)
Var

★★**Auberge de la Gruppi** LE 46 rte Nationale 8 ☎94987018

Etr—20 Sep
rm12 (→ ⋔ 7) sB125 sB → ⋔ 135—160 dB145 dB → ⋔ 192—230 M61—120 mountains
Credit cards [1] [2] [3] [5]

BEAUVAIS
Oise

★★★***Mercure*** ZAC St-Lazare, av Montaigne ☎44020336 tx150210

→ 60 **P**120 ≈
Credit cards [1] [2] [3] [5]

★★**Campanile** av Descartes ☎44052700 tx150992

→ 47 **P** sB → 217—238 dB → 239—260 M61—82
Credit card [3]

★**Commerce** LE 11 & 13 r Chambiges (n.rest) ☎44481784

rm14 (⋔ 6) ⌂ **P**6 sB82—122 sB⋔ 114—122 dB134 dB⋔ 144

★**Palais** 9 r St-Nicholas (n.rest) ☎44451258

→ ⋔ 14 **P**5 sB → ⋔ 124—187 dB → ⋔ 149—217
Credit card [1]

🚗 **Beauvais** 5 r du Pont Laverdure ☎44450413 All makes

🚗 **Boullanger** 124 r de Clemont ☎44480522 All makes

BEAUVALLON
Var

See also **STE-MAXIME**

★**Marie Louise (DPn)** Guerrevieile (1km NE) ☎94960605

15 Feb—15 Oct
⋔ 14 **P**9 sB⋔ fr132 dB⋔ fr264 M75—100 sea

BEAUVOIR
Manche

★★**Gué de Beauvoir** Château de Beauvoir (n.rest) ☎33600923

Etr—10 Nov
rm21 (→ ⋔ 10) **P**30 sB109—119 sB → ⋔ 134—204 dB113—133 dB → ⋔ 148—218

BEDENAC
Charente-Maritime

🚗 **Pacha** rte Nationale 10, le Jarculet ☎46044548 Closed Sun pm For

BEG-MEIL
Finistère

★★**Bretagne** ☎98949804

Apr—Sep
rm39 (→ ⋔ 20) A18rm **P**70 sB89—91 sB → ⋔ 114—139 dB178—182 dB → ⋔ 228—278 M50—120
Credit cards [1] [3]

★★**Thalamot** LE Le Chemin Creux Fouesnant ☎98949738

May—Sep
rm35 (→ ⋔ 23) A4rm sB124 dB144 dB → ⋔ 191—271 sea
Credit cards [1] [2] [3]

BELFORT
Territoire-de-Belfort

★★★**Grand Lion** (ETAP) 2 r G-Clemenceau ☎84211700 tx360914

→ ⋔ 82 **P**100 Lift sB → ⋔ 253—310 dB → ⋔ 320—375
Credit cards [1] [2] [3] [5]

★★***Climat*** de l'As de Carrea ☎84220984

→ 46 **P** Lift mountains

🚗 **M Dartier** 86 fbg de Montbeliard ☎84281970 Closed Sun All makes

🚗 **J Wittlinger** 10—15 r de Turenne ☎84216399 Closed Aug 1—22, Sat & Sun For

At **BESSONCOURT** (7km NE)

★★**Campanile** Exchangeur Belfort Nord ☎84299442 tx360977

→ 46 **P** sB → 204—225 dB → 226—247 M61—82
Credit card [3]

At **DANJOUTIN** (3km S)

★★★**Mercure** r de Dr-Jacquot ☎84215501 tx360801

→ 80 **P**150 Lift ☾ sB → 293 dB → 341 M95—105&alc ≈
Credit cards [1] [2] [3] [5]

🚗 **L Maldiney** 25 r du Gl-de-Gaulle ☎84282415 All makes

BELIN-BELIET
Gironde

★***Allenor d'Aquitaine*** LE ☎56880123

→ ⋔ 12 ⌂ **P**20

BELLEGARDE-SUR-VALSERINE
Ain

★★**Campanile** av de Lattre de Tassigny ☎50481410

→ 42 **P** sB → 191—212 dB → 213—234 M61—82
Credit card [3]

BELLÈME
Orne

★**Relais St-Louis** 1 bd Bansart-des-Bois ☎33731221

3 Mar—15 Dec
rm8 (→ ⋔ 6) ⌂ **P**8 sBfr75 sB → ⋔ fr116 dB → ⋔ 156—186 M49—114
Credit card [2]

BELLEY
Ain

★★***Pernollet*** 9 pl de la Victoire ☎79810618

15 Dec—15 Nov
rm20 (→ 19) ⌂ mountains

BÉNODET
Finistère

★★**Ancre de Marine** 6 av l'Odet ☎98570529

Mar—Nov
rm25 (→ ⋔ 14) A15rm sB135—165 sB → ⋔ 195—275 dB160—190 dB → ⋔ 280—300 M75—160 sea
Credit cards [1] [3]

★★**Poste** r Église ☎98570109

rm38 (→ ⋔ 26) A16rm ⌂ **P**10 sBfr156 sB → ⋔ 220—286 dBfr187 dB → ⋔ 272—307 Mfr80
Credit cards [2] [5]

BERCK-PLAGE
Pas-de-Calais

★★**Homard Bleu** 44—48 pl de l'Entonnoir ☎21090465

rm18 (🛁🚿15) sBfr100 sB🛁🚿161—185 dB🛁🚿175—282 M60—95 S15% sea
Credit cards [1] [3]

BERGERAC
Dordogne

★★**Bordeaux** LF (Inter) 38 pl Gambetta ☎53571283 tx550412

Feb—Dec
rm42 (🛁15) 🏠P10 Lift ☾ sB169—209 sB🛁169—209 dB🛁218—248 M68—200 ≈
Credit cards [1] [2] [3] [5]

★★**Commerce** 36 pl Gambetta ☎53273050 tx541888

24 Jan—15 Nov
🛁🚿30 Lift sB🛁🚿136—210 dB🛁🚿180—230 Mfr70
Credit cards [1] [2] [3] [5]

BERGUES
Nord

See also **DUNKERQUE**

★★**Motel 25** (2km S at interchange Autoroute Lille-Dunkerque) ☎28687900

🛁42 🏠P200 sB🛁220 dB🛁290 M50—150 🎾
Credit cards [1] [2] [3] [5]

★**Tonnelier** 4 r de Mont de Piété ☎28687005

Closed 18 Aug—10 Sep
rm12 (🚿4) 🏠P6 sB91—106 sB🚿161—171 dB127—172 dB🚿212—222 M50—95

BERNAY
Eure

★**Angleterre et Cheval Blanc** (**DPn**) LF 10 r Gl-de-Gaulle ☎32431259

rm22 (🛁1🚿2) 🏠P30 sBfr112 sB🛁🚿fr152 dB139—174 dB🛁🚿fr174 Mfr80
Credit cards [1] [2] [3] [5]

BESANÇON
Doubs

★★★★**Frantel** av E-Droz ☎81801444 tx360268

🛁🚿95 P100 Lift sB🛁🚿293—363 dB🛁🚿376—456 M130
Credit cards [1] [2] [3] [4] [5]

★★★**Novotel** 22 bis r de Trey ☎81501466 tx360009

🚿107 Lift sB🚿275—305 dB🚿335—365 M alc ≈
Credit cards [1] [2] [3] [4] [5]

★★**Balladins** r B-Russell ☎81515251 tx649394

🛁🚿28 🏠P28 sB🛁🚿166 dB🛁🚿182 M56—77
Credit cards [1] [2] [3]

★★**Ibis** 4 av Carnot ☎81803311 tx361276

🛁66 P15 Lift sB🛁235—240 dB🛁275—280 M50—80
Credit cards [1] [3]

France

★**Granvelle** 13 ru du Gl-Lecourbe (n.rest) ☎81813392

rm23 (🛁13) P12 ☾ sB92—190 sB🛁147—190 dB129—210 dB🛁190—210
Credit cards [1] [3] [5]

★**Gambetta** 13 r Gambetta (n.rest) ☎81820233

rm28 (🛁🚿19) ☾ sB106—186 sB🛁🚿169—186 dB122—202 dB🛁🚿185—242
Credit cards [1] [2] [3] [5]

🚗 **Auto Dépannage** 9 r A-Fanart ☎81501332 Closed Sat pm & Sun Cit

🚗 **G Bever** 4 r Pergaud ☎81812801 Closed Sun Aud BMW Ope VW

🚗 **J Petetin** 7 r Demangel ☎81501202 Closed Sat pm & Sun Ope Vau

At **CHÂTEAU-FARINE** (6km SW)

★★★**Mercure** 159 r de Dôle ☎81520400 tx360167

🛁59 P60 Lift sB🛁298—314 dB🛁357—376 M65—128 ≈
Credit cards [1] [2] [5]

At **ÉCOLE VALENTIN** (4.5km NW)

★★**Campanile** ZAC de Valentin ☎81535222 tx361172

🛁55 P sB🛁204—225 dB🛁226—247 M61—82
Credit card [3]

★★**Climat** la Combe Oudotte ☎81880411

🛁43 P40 dB🛁240—260 M54—70 🎾
Credit cards [1] [3]

BESSE-EN-CHANDESSE
Puy-de-Dôme

★★**Beffroy** ☎73795008

School hols
rm17 (🛁🚿12) 🏠P sBfr100 dB🛁🚿228 M65—210 St%

BESSINES-SUR-GARTEMPE
Haute-Vienne

★★★**Toit de Chaume** (5km S on Limoges rd) ☎55760102

🛁20 🏠P30 ≈
Credit cards [2] [3] [5]

★★**Vallée** (**DPn**) (N20) ☎55760166

Closed Feb
rm20 (🛁🚿16) 🏠P20 sBfr84 sB🛁🚿fr143 dBfr98 dB🛁🚿157—175 M39—137 St%
Credit cards [1] [3]

BESSONCOURT See **BELFORT**

BÉTHUNE
Pas-de-Calais

★★***Vieux Beffrol*** 48 Grand Pl ☎21681500

rm65 (🚿33) A23 P200 Lift ☾
Credit cards [1] [2] [3] [5]

★***Bernard et Gare*** LF 3 pl de la Gare ☎21572002

rm30 (🛁🚿21)
Credit cards [1] [5]

🚗 **Auto-Béthunoise** 225 bd Thiers ☎21572430 Closed Sun All makes

At **BEUVRY** (4km SE)

★★★**France** (Inter) 11 r du Gl-Leclerc ☎21573434 tx110691

🛁156 🏠P100 Lift ☾ sB🛁263—286 dB🛁308—328 M80—180
Credit cards [1] [2] [3] [4] [5]

BEYNAC-ET-CAZENAC
Dordogne

★★**Bonnet** LF (**DPn**) ☎53295001

Etr—15 Oct
rm22 (🛁🚿21) 🏠P50 sB🛁🚿108—152 dB🛁🚿174—244 M78—160 🎾 mountains

BÉZIERS
Hérault

★★★**Imperator** (Inter) 28 allées P-Riquet (n.rest) ☎67490225

🛁🚿45 A3rm P Lift ☾ sB🛁🚿180 dB🛁🚿227—260
Credit cards [1] [2] [5]

★★**Ibis** (5km S—exit Bèziers Est from A9) ☎67625514 tx480938

🛁50 P100 Lift sB🛁209—240 dB🛁266—300 M65&alc
Credit cards [1] [2] [3] [5]

🚗 **Grand Garage Foch** 117 av Ml-Foch ☎67312742 Closed Sat & Sun AR

🚗 **Grand Garage Rech** rte de Bessan ☎67622269 Closed Sat & Sun Tal

🚗 **St-Säens Auto's** 12 av St-Säens ☎67763568 Closed Sat pm & Sun Aud VW

🚗 **Socra** 6 r Amiral Courbet ☎67765754 Closed Sat pm & Sun Maz Vol

BIARD See **POITIERS**

BIARRITZ
Pyrénées-Atlantiques

★★★★★**Palais** 1 av de l'Impératrice ☎59240940 tx570000

Apr—Nov
🛁140 P Lift ☾ sB🛁710—1100 dB🛁1020—1620 Mfr165 🎾 ≈ sea
Credit cards [1] [2] [3] [5]

★★★★**Eurotel** 19 av Perspective ☎59243233 tx570014

Mar—Oct
🛁🚿60 🏠P20 Lift sB🛁🚿345—725 dB🛁🚿640—770 Malc t4% sea
Credit cards [2] [3] [5]

★★★★**Miramar** av de l'Impératrice ☎59248520 tx540831

🛁122 P35 Lift ☾ sB🛁470—1440 dB🛁690—1680 M220 ≈ sea
Credit cards [1] [2] [3] [4] [5]

★★★***Regina & Golf*** 52 av de l'Impératrice ☎59240960 tx541330

🛁50 P Lift sea
Credit cards [2] [3] [4] [5]

★★★**Windsor** (Inter) Grande Plage ☎59240852
15 Mar—15 Oct
⇌ 37 Lift ☾ sB 221—371 dB 262—412 Mfr85 sea
Credit cards 1 2 3 4

★★**Beau-Lieu** 3 espl du Port-Vieux ☎59242359
15 Mar—Oct
rm28 (16) **P** dB160 dB 204—231 sea

★***Palacito*** r Gambetta (n.rest) ☎59240689
rm26 (21)
Credit cards 1 2

Biarritz Assistance Auto 109 av de la Marne ☎59410562 Closed Sat & Sun All makes

Paris Biarritz Auto 48 av du Ml-Foch ☎59230583 Closed Sat & Sun Aud Por VW

BIDART
Pyrénées-Atlantiques

★★★**Bidartea** (BW/MAP) rte d'Espagne (N10) ☎59549468 tx549480
Mar—Oct
30 A6rm **P**60 Lift sB 205—264 dB 288—368 M68—108 sea mountains
Credit cards 1 2 3 5

BLAGNAC See **TOULOUSE AIRPORT**

BLAGNY-SUR-BRESLE
Seine-Maritime

★**Poste** 44 Grande Rue ☎35935020
rm12 **P**10 sB100 dB130 M48—82

★**Ville** (**DPn**) 2 r Notre Dame ☎35935157
Closed 4—24 Aug
rm9 (4) A3rm sB108—125 sB 148—170 dB141—155 dB 186—220 M50—140
Credit cards 1 3

St-Denis 6 r St-Denis ☎935042 Ren

BLAYE
Gironde

★★**Citadelle** pl d'Armes ☎57421710 tx540127
21 sB 199 dB 254 Mfr70
Credit cards 2 3 5

BLÉRE
Indre-et-Loire

★**Cher** 9 r Pont ☎47579515
19 A8rm **P**11 sB fr173 dB fr191 M50—105
Credit card 3

BLÉRIOT-PLAGE
Pas-de-Calais

★**Dunes** (N48) ☎21345430
Closed Oct—Feb
rm13 (7) **P**20 sB96—196 sB 156—196 dB122—212 dB 172—212 M70—180
Credit cards 2 3

France

BLOIS
Loir-et-Cher

★★**Campanile** 15 r de la Vallée Maillard ☎54744466 tx751628
42 **P** sB 204—225 dB 226—247 M61—82
Credit card 3

★★***Ibis*** r de la Vallée Maillard ☎746060
40

★**Bellay** LE 12 r Minimes (n.rest) ☎54782363 tx750135
rm12 (6) A2rm **P** dB138 dB 230
Credit cards 2 4

★***Gerbe d'Or*** 1 r Bourg-Neuf ☎54742645
rm28 (18) A10rm **P**8
Credit cards 1 3

★**St-Jacques** LE pl Gare (n.rest) ☎54780415
rm33 (17) ☾ sB105 sB 140 dB135 dB 190
Credit cards 1 3

★***Viennols*** LE 5 quai A-Coutant ☎54741280
15 Jan—15 Dec
rm26 (10) A15rm lake

M Gueniot 74 Leveé des Tuileries ☎54789463 All makes

Peigné 20 av Maunoury ☎54740634 Closed Sat pm, Sun & Mon am For

At **CHAUSSÉE ST-VICTOR (LA)** (4km N)

★★★**Novotel Blois l'Hermitage** 20 r des Pontières ☎54783357 tx750232
116 **P**110 Lift sB fr322 dB fr377 M100&alc
Credit cards 1 2 3 5

At **ST-GERVAIS-LA-FORÊT** (3km SE)

★★**Balladins** r G-Melies ☎54426990 tx649394
36 **P**36 sB 166 dB 182 M56—77
Credit cards 1 2 3

At **VINEUIL** (4km SE)

★★**Climat** 48 r des Quatre-Vents ☎54427022
38 **P**30 sB 212 dB 230 M53—92
Credit cards 1 3

BLONVILLE-SUR-MERE
Calvados

★***Mer*** LE 93 av de la République (n.rest) ☎31879323
Apr—Sep
rm20 (13) **P**20 sea

BOBIGNY
Seine-St-Denis

★★**Ibis** 15 rue H-Berlioz ☎48960730
80 **P**50 Lift

BOIS GUILLAUME See **ROUEN**

BOLLENBERG See **ROUFFACH**

BOLLÈNE
Vaucluse

★★**Campanile** av T-Aubanel ☎90300042 tx432017
30 **P** sB 204—225 dB 226—247 M61—82
Credit cards 3

Carrosserie des Grès les Grès du Fourmillier ☎90301704 All makes

R David 1 r du Souvenir ☎90301223 Closed Sun VW

Portes de Provence ☎90301046 Peu

BONDY See **PARIS**

BONNEIL-SUR-MARNE
Val-de-Marne

★★**Campanile** ZA des Petits Carreaux, 1 av des Bleuets ☎43777029 tx211251
50 **P** sB 217—238 dB 239—260 M61—82
Credit card 3

BONNEVAL
Eure-et-Loire

★★***Bois Gulbert*** (N10) ☎37472233
rm14 (8) **P**40
Credit cards 3 5

BONNEVILLE
Haute-Savoie

At **CONTAMINE-SUR-ARVE** (8km NW)

★**Tourne-Bride** (**DPn**) ☎50036218
rm7 **P** sBfr89 dB104—127 M48—110

BONNY-SUR-LOIRE
Loiret

★★***Fimotel-Val de Loire*** (N7) ☎38316462
46 **P**70
Credit cards 2 3 5

Parot 139 Grande Rue ☎38316332 Closed Sun Ren

BORDEAUX
Gironde

★★★★***Aquitania Sofitel*** Parc des Expositions ☎56508380 tx570557
210 **P** Lift lake
Credit cards 1 2 3 5

★★★★**Frantel** 5 r R-Lateulade ☎56909237 tx540565
196 Lift
Credit cards 1 2 3 5

★★★★***Mercure Bordeaux le Lac*** quartier du Lac ☎56509030 tx540077
108 **P**115 Lift lake
Credit cards 1 2 3 5

★★★**Normandie** 7 cours 30 Juillet (n.rest) ☎56521680 tx570481
100 Lift sB 175—195 dB 250—330
Credit cards 1 2 3 5

★★★***Novotel Bordeaux-le-Lac*** quartier du Lac ☎56509970 tx570274
173 **P** Lift Pool

★★★*Sofitel* Centre Hôtelier ☎56509014 tx540097

🛁100 **P** Lift 🎾 ≈

Credit cards [1] [2] [3] [5]

★★*Arcade* 60 r E-le-Roy ☎56909240 tx550952

🚿140 Lift sB🚿182—186 dB🚿211—216 M55—90

Credit card [3]

★★**Bayonne** (Inter) 15 cours de l'Intendance (n.rest) ☎56480088

rm37 (🛁🚿26) Lift sB127 sB🛁🚿167—231 dB148 dB🛁🚿188—252

Credit card [3]

★★**Campanile** quartier du Lac ☎56395454 tx560425

🛁40 **P** sB🛁204—225 dB🛁226—247 M61—82

Credit card [3]

★★**Campaville** quartier du Lac (n.rest) ☎399540 tx572877

🛁41 sB🛁211—228 dB🛁255—271

Credit card [3]

★★**Campaville** angle cours Clemenceau (n.rest) ☎529898 tx541079

🛁45 sB🛁fr265

Credit card [3]

★★*Ibis* quartier du Lac ☎56509650 tx550346

🛁119 **P** Lift

★★**Sèze** 23 allées Tourny (n.rest) ☎56526554

rm25 (🛁🚿21) Lift sB146—316 sB🛁🚿286—336 dB172—342 dB🛁🚿312—362

Credit cards [2] [3] [5]

★**Etche-Ona** (Inter) 11 r Mautrec (n.rest) ☎56443649 tx570362

rm33 (🛁🚿20) A12rm Lift sB🛁🚿193—223 dB🛁🚿169—256

P Mercier 162—166 r de la Benauge ☎56862133 Closed Sat pm AR DJ RR

At **ARTIGUES** (7km NE)

★★**Campanile** av de la Prairie ☎56327332 tx541745

🛁50 **P** sB🛁204—225 dB🛁226—247 M61—82

Credit card [3]

At **BRUGES** (5km NW)

🚗 **A Pigeon** 469 rte due Médoc ☎56288428 Closed Sat pm & Sun Ope

At **CESTAS** (15km SW)

★★**Campanile** Aire de Service de Bordeaux Cestas, A63 ☎56218068 tx540408

🛁39 **P** sB🛁204—225 dB🛁226—247 M61—82

Credit card [3]

At **LORMONT** (5km NE)

★★*Climat* Carrefour des 4 Pavillions, N10 ☎56329610 tx612241

🛁38 **P**

At **MÉRIGNAC** (5km W on D106)

★★★*Novotel Bordeaux Aéroport* av du Prés-Kennedy ☎56341025 tx540320

🛁100 ≈

★★**Campanile** av J-F-Kennedy ☎56344362 tx550496

🛁47 **P** sB🛁217—228 dB🛁239—260 M61—82

Credit cards [3]

★★**Ibis Bordeaux Aéroport** av du Prés-Kennedy ☎56341019 tx541430

🛁64 **P**60 sB🛁202—225 dB🛁242—265 M65

Credit cards [1] [3]

BORMES-LES-MIMOSAS
Var

★★**Safari** rte Stade ☎94710983 tx404603

25 Mar—15 Oct

rm33 (🛁31) **P** sB172 dB🛁382 ≈ 🎾 sea

★**Belle Vue** LF pl Gambetta ☎94711515

Feb—Sep

rm14 (🚿13) sB118—128 sB🚿118—138 dB🚿153—187 M75—90 sea

Credit card [1]

🚗 **Pin** ☎94711177 Closed Nov 1—20, Sat pm & Sun All makes

BOSSONS (LES) See **CHAMONIX-MONT-BLANC**

BOULOGNE-BILLANCOURT See **PARIS**

BOULOGNE-SUR-MER
Pas-de-Calais

See Plan page 126

[AA] **Agent: see page 101**

See also **PORTEL (LE)**

★★**Alexandra** 93 r Thiers ☎21305222 Plan **1**

Feb—Dec

rm20 (🛁🚿14) sB70—205 sB🛁🚿135—205 dB108—221 dB🛁🚿151—221 t3%

Credit cards [1] [2] [3]

★★**Climat** pl Rouget de Lisle ☎21801450 tx135570 Plan **1A**

🛁46 Lift sB🛁fr215 dB🛁fr234

Credit cards [1] [2] [3] [5]

★★**Faidherbe** 12 Faidherbe (n.rest) ☎21316093 Plan **2**

rm35 (🛁🚿30) **P**10 Lift sB122—252 sB🛁🚿216—272 dB194—294 dB🛁🚿238—314 Mfr19 sea

★★**Ibis** (Inter) quartier L-Danremont, bd Diderot ☎21301240 tx160485 Plan **3**

🛁79 **P**160 Lift sB🛁189—213 dB🛁240—261 M53—68 sea

Credit cards [1] [3]

★★**Lorraine** 7 pl de Lorraine (n.rest) ☎21313478 Plan **4**

rm21 (🛁🚿14) sB111—176 dB137—192

Credit cards [1] [3]

★★**Métropole** (Inter) 51 r Thiers (n.rest) ☎21315430 Plan **6**

rm27 (🛁🚿21) Lift sBfr125 sB🛁🚿fr212 dBfr154 dB🛁🚿fr249 t3%

Credit cards [1] [3]

★*Hamoit* 1 r Faidherbe ☎21314420 Plan **7**

rm23 Lift

★*Londres* 22 pl de France (n.rest) ☎21313563 Plan **8**

rm20 (🛁🚿16) **P**8 Lift

Credit cards [1] [3]

🚗 **Paris** 33 av Kennedy ☎21920522 Closed Sat & Sun For

🚗 **St-Christophe** 128 bd de la Liane, ZI ☎21920911 Closed Sun Alf Ope Vau

At **ST-LÉONARD** (4km S off N1)

🚗 **Citroën** bd de la Liane, ZI ☎21922111 Closed Sat & Sun Cit

BOULOU (LE)
Pyrénées-Orientales

🚗 **M Borg** 1 r E-Zola ☎68833057 All makes

🚗 **Perrin** 5 av J-Moulin ☎68831321 Ren

BOURBON-LANCY
Seine-et-Loire

★★**Raymond** (**DPn**) LF 8 r d'Autun ☎85891739

rm20 (🛁🚿12) ⌂ **P**15 sB95—165 sB🛁🚿160—165 dB125—205 dB🛁🚿185—205

Credit cards [1] [3] [5]

BOURDEILLES See **BRANTÔME**

BOURG See **LANGRES**

BOURG-EN-BRESSE
Ain

★★★*Logis de Brou* 132 bd Brou (n.rest) ☎74221155

🛁🚿30 ⌂ **P**10 Lift ☾

Credit cards [2] [3] [5]

★★★**Prieuré** 49 bd de Brou (n.rest) ☎74224460

🛁14 ⌂ **P** Lift ☾ sB🛁282—384 dB🛁364—488

★★**Chantecler** (BW/MAP) 10 av Bad Kreuznach ☎74224488 tx380468

🛁28 **P**30 sB🛁197—207 dB🛁249—264 M80—140

Credit cards [1] [2] [3] [4] [5]

★★**Ibis** ZAC de la Croix Blanche, bd Ch-de-Gaulle ☎74225266 tx900471

🛁42 **P**50 sB🛁196—218 dB🛁242—266 Mfr68

Credit cards [1] [2] [3]

BOURGES
Cher

★★*D'Artagnan* 19 pl Séraucourt ☎48246751

🛁🚿71 ⌂ **P** Lift

★★**Christina** 5 r Halle (n.rest) ☎48705650

rm77 (🛁🚿72) ⌂ **P** Lift ☾ sB117—177 sB🛁🚿162—177 dB133 dB🛁🚿174—199

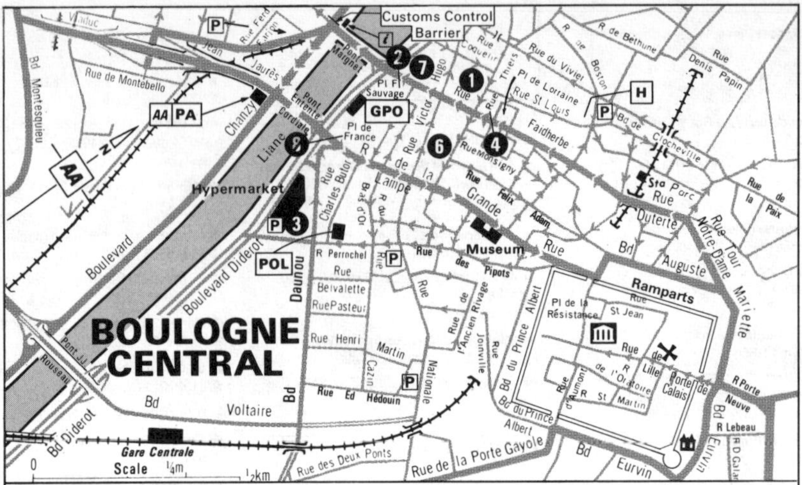

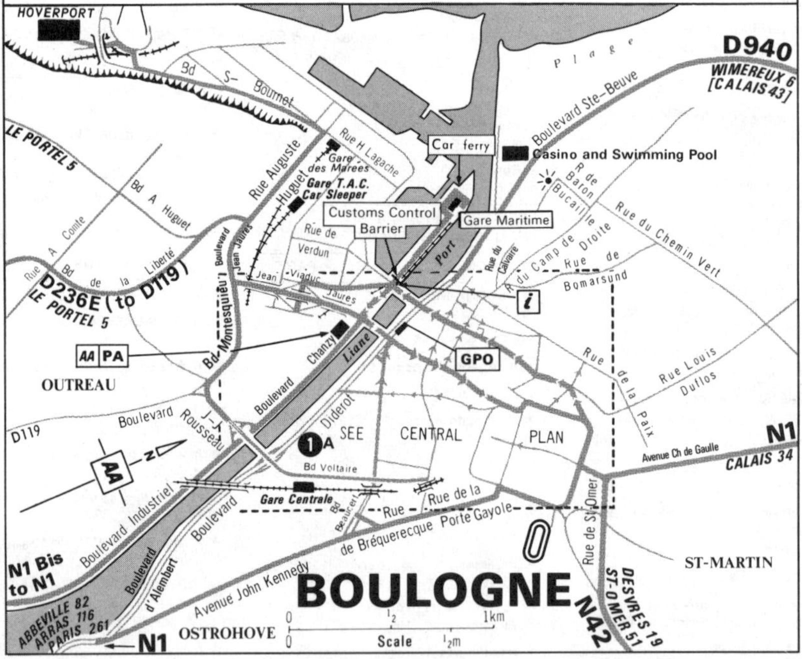

BOULOGNE CENTRAL

BOULOGNE

1	★★	Alexandra
1A	★★	Climat
2	★★	Faidherbe
3	★★	Ibis
4	★★	Lorraine
6	★★	Métropole
7	★	Hamiot
8	★	Londres

BOURGES (Cont)

★★**Monitel** 73 r Babes ☎48502362 tx783397

🛁 🚿 48 🚗 **P**12 Lift sB 🛁 🚿 160—206 dB 🛁 🚿 180—260 M80

Credit cards [1] [2] [3] [5]

★★***Poste*** 22 r Moyenne (n.rest) ☎48700806

rm34 (🛁 🚿 22) A5rm 🚗 **P**12 Lift ☾

★★**St-Jean** 23 av M-Dormoy (n.rest) ☎48241348

Closed Feb

rm24 (🛁 🚿 20) 🚗 **P**10 Lift sB79—100 sB 🛁 🚿 142 dB79—92 dB 🛁 🚿 142

Credit cards [1] [3]

★★***Tilleuls*** (Inter) 7 pl de la Pyrotechnic (n.rest) ☎48204904 tx782026

🛁 🚿 29 A9rm 🚗 **P**

🚗 **Guerenne** rte de la Chapelle St Ursin, ZI ☎48505343 Ren

At **ST DOULCHARD** (2km S)

★ ★**Campanile** rte de Vierzon ☎48702053 tx780400
🛁 42 **P** sB 🛁 217—238 dB 🛁 239—260 M61—82
Credit card [3]

BOURGET AIRPORT (LE)
See **PARIS AIRPORTS**

BOURG-LÈS-VALENCE See **VALENCE**

BOURGNEUF-LA-FORÊT (LE)
Mayenne

★***Vieille Auberge*** pl de l'Église ☎43015112
rm8 (🚿 2) 🚗 **P**8
Credit cards [1] [3]

BOURGOIN-JALLIEU
Isère

★ ★**Campanile** Zac de St-Hubert l'Isle d'Abeau Est ☎74270122 tx340396
🛁 50 **P** sB 🛁 204—225 dB 🛁 226—247 M61—82
Credit card [3]

★ ★**Climat** 15 r E-Branly, ZAC de la Maladière ☎74285229
🛁 42 **P**45 sB 🛁 210—221 dB 🛁 229—240
Credit cards [1] [3]

BOURG-ST-MAURICE
Savoie

★ ★**Petit St-Bernard** 2 av Stade ☎79070432
20 Dec—15 Apr & 28 Jun—15 Sep
rm24 (🛁 🚿 18) 🚗 **P**20 sB125 sB 🛁 🚿 190 dB145—240 dB 🛁 🚿 205—240 M60—80 mountains
Credit cards [2] [3] [5]

BOURGTHEROULDE-INFREVILLE
Eure

★***Corne d'Abondance*** **LF** pl de la Mairie ☎35876008
rm9 (🛁 1) 🚗 **P**

🚗 **J Noyelle** rte d'Elbeuf ☎35776009 Closed Aug, Sat pm & Sun Ren

BOUZE-LES-BEAUNE See **BEAUNE**

BOVES See **AMIENS**

BRANTÔME
Dordogne

★ ★ ★**Chabrol** (**DPn**) 59 r Gambetta ☎53057015
🛁 🚿 12 A8rm sB 🛁 🚿 230 dB 🛁 🚿 360 Mfr100
Credit cards [2] [3] [5]

At **BOURDEILLES** (10km SW)

★ ★ ★**Griffons** (**DPn**) ☎53057561
Apr—15 Oct
🛁 10 🚗 **P**10 Lift dB 🛁 310—340 Mfr90 🎾 🏊
Credit cards [1] [3] [5]

France

BREST
Finistère

★ ★ ★**Novotel de Brest** ZAC de Kergaradec, rte du Gouesnou ☎98023283 tx940470
🛁 85 sB 🛁 303—323 dB 🛁 374—394 M50—80 S15% 🏊
Credit cards [1] [2] [3] [5]

★ ★ ★**Sofitel Océania** 82 r de Siam ☎98806666 tx940951
🛁 82 Lift sB 🛁 330—430 dB 🛁 402—512 Mfr65 S%
Credit cards [1] [2] [3] [5]

Sébastopol Autos 56 r Sébastopol & 231 r J-Jaurès ☎98441979 Closed Sat & Sun AR

At **GOUESNOU** (6km N)

★ ★**Campanile** Za d'Activities de Kergaradec ☎98416341 tx941413
🛁 42 **P** sB 🛁 217—238 dB 🛁 239—260 M61—82
Credit card [3]

At **PLOUGASTEL-DAOULAS** (9.5km SE)

★ ★**Ibis Brest** rte de Quimper, quartier de Ty-Menez ☎98405028 tx940731
🛁 45 **P**50 sB 🛁 180—195 dB 🛁 225 Mfr67
Credit cards [1] [3] [5]

BRÉTIGNY-SUR-ORGE
Essone

★ ★**Climat** ☎69019760
🛁 43 **P** sB 🛁 219 dB 🛁 242 M67—88 🎾
Credit cards [1] [3]

BRÉVILLE-SUR-MER
Manche

★ ★**Mougine des Moulins à Vent** Les Moulins à Vent (D971) (n.rest) ☎33502241
🛁 7 **P**15 sB 🛁 213—252 dB 🛁 235—274 sea
Credit cards [1] [2] [3] [5]

BRIANÇON
Hautes-Alpes

★ ★**Cristol** **LF** 6 rte d'Italie ☎92202011
Closed Nov—24 Dec
🛁 🚿 16 dB 🛁 🚿 fr236 Mfr80 mountains

🚗 **R Rignon** 3 rte d'Italie ☎92211073 Closed Sep 8—21, Sat pm & Sun BMW Fia

At **STE-CATHÉRINE**

★ ★ ★***Mont Brison*** 1 av Gl-de-Gaulle (n.rest) ☎92211455
15 Dec—Oct
rm44 (🛁 🚿 36) **P**20 Lift mountains

★ ★ ★**Vauban** (**Pn**) 13 av Gl-de-Gaulle ☎9221211
20 Dec—12 Nov
rm44 (🛁 🚿 38) 🚗 **P**25 Lift sBfr143 sB 🛁 🚿 fr223 dB176 dB 🛁 🚿 296—306 M78—95 mountains
Credit card [3]

BRIARE
Loiret

★**Cerf** 22 bd Buyser ☎38370080
Mar—15 Feb
rm20 (🛁 🚿 8) A8rm 🚗 **P**20 sBfr81 sB 🛁 🚿 108—137 dBfr162 dB 🛁 🚿 216—274 M47—122
Credit cards [1] [3]

🚗 **SARL Relais Briarois Autos** 17 av de Lattre de Tassigny ☎38370161 Closed Sat pm & alternate Sun Tal

BRICQUEBEC
Manche

★**Vieux Château** **LF** 4 cour du Château ☎33522449
rm22 (🛁 🚿 19) A5rm 🚗 **P**50 Lift sB113—118 sB 🛁 🚿 148—228 dB166—246 dB 🛁 🚿 216—246 M45—150
Credit cards [1] [3]

BRIDORÉ See **LOCHES**

BRIGNOLES
Var

🚗 **A Mangini** ☎94690575 M/c All makes

🚗 **Marcel** rte de Nice ☎94694208 M/c Closed Sun Aud VW

BRIONNE
Eure

★**Logis de Brionne** **LF** (**Pn**) 1 pl St-Denis ☎32448173
rm16 (🛁 🚿 8) 🚗 **P** sB94—139 sB 🛁 🚿 fr139 dB128—143 dB 🛁 🚿 158—203
Credit cards [1] [3]

★**Vieux Donjon** (**Pn**) 19 r de la Soie ☎32448062
Closed Dec—15 Feb & Mar—15 Sep
rm9 (🛁 🚿 3) 🚗 **P**20 sB98—138 sB 🛁 🚿 138 dB116 dB 🛁 🚿 156 M80
Credit cards [1] [3]

BRIOUDE
Haute-Loire

★ ★**Brivas** **LF** (Inter) rte Puy ☎71501049 tx392817
🛁 🚿 30 **P**300 Lift sB 🛁 🚿 157—407 dB 🛁 🚿 206—259 M58—125 mountains
Credit cards [1] [2] [3] [4] [5]

★ ★***Moderne*** **LF** (FAH) 12 av V-Hugo ☎71500730
🛁 🚿 17 **P**17

BRIVE-LA-GAILLARD
Corrèze

★ ★ ★ ★***Mercure*** rte Objat ☎55871503 tx590096
🛁 57 **P**80 Lift 🏊
Credit cards [1] [2] [3] [5]

★ ★**Campanile** av Gl-Pouyade ☎55881355 tx590838
🛁 42 **P** sB 🛁 217—238 dB 🛁 🚿 239—260 M61—82

★ ★**Crémaillère** **LF** 53 av de Paris ☎55743247
Mar—Dec
rm12 (🛁 8) sB 🛁 138 dB186 dB 🛁 186 M60—150
Credit card [2]

★★**Truffe Noir** 22 bd A-France
☎55743532
🛁 🚿35 Lift ☾ sB🛁 🚿175—275
dB🛁 🚿230—370 Mfr120
Credit cards 1 2 3 5

★**Montauban** LF (**DPn** in season)
6 av E-Herriot ☎55240038
Closed Jan
rm21 (🛁 🚿13)
Credit card 3

🚗 **G Cremoux** 20 av du Ml-Bugeaud
☎55236922 Closed Sat pm & Sun AR

🚗 **Socoda** av du Prés Kennedy
☎55740731 Closed Sat & Sun Aud VW

🚗 **M Taurisson** 21—23 av de Toulouse
☎55742542 Closed Sun BMW

At **VARETZ** (14km NW)

★★★**Château de Castel Novel** (Relais et Châteaux) LF ☎55850001 tx590065
May—Oct
🛁28 A10rm **P**50 Lift ☾ sB🛁298—508
dB🛁446—1326 🎾 ≈
Credit cards 2 3 5

BRON See **LYON**

BROU
Eure-et-Loir

★**Plat d'Etain** LF pl des Halles ☎37470398
tx782187
6 Feb—5 Jan
rm20 (🛁 🚿9) 🏠 **P**20 sB103—127
sB🛁 🚿127—218 dB151—236
dB🛁 🚿196—236

BRUGES See **BORDEAUX**

BUC
Yvelines

★★**Climat** r L-Pasteur ☎39564811
tx699220
🛁35 **P**60 sB🛁204—230 dB🛁222—248
M67—131 🎾
Credit cards 1 3

BUCHÈRES See **TROYES**

BUGUE (LE)
Dordogne

★★★**Royal Vezère** (BW/MAP) pl H-de-Ville ☎53072001 tx540710
29 Apr—Sep
🛁 🚿53 🏠 Lift ☾ sB🛁 🚿264—348
dB🛁 🚿292—402 ≈

BULLY-LES-MINES
Pas-de-Calais

★**Moderne** 144 r de la Gare ☎21291422
rm36 (🛁 🚿10) 🏠 **P**200 sB94 sB🛁 🚿124
dB128—168 dB🛁 🚿148—168 M50—120
Credit card 1

🚗 **Derache** 59 r R-Salengro ☎21291799
Closed Sat pm & Sun Ren

CABRERETS
Lot

★**Grottes** LF (**DPn**) ☎65312702
23 Mar—12 Oct
rm17 (🛁 🚿8) A5rm **P**20 sB103—117
sB🛁 🚿130—169 dB120—134
dB🛁 🚿147—186 M51—97 ≈

France

CADÉAC See **ARREAU**

CAEN
Calvados

★★★★**Relais des Gourmets** 15 r Geôle
☎31860601 tx171657
🛁 🚿32 **P** Lift ☾ sB🛁 🚿215—355
dB🛁 🚿250—390 M100—220 S15%
Credit cards 1 2 3 4 5

★★★**Malherbe** pl Ml-Foch (n.rest)
☎31844006 tx170555
🛁 🚿44 **P**100 Lift ☾ sB🛁 🚿235—314
dB🛁 🚿315—465
Credit cards 1 2 3 4 5

★★★**Moderne** (BW/MAP) 116 bd Gl-Leclerc ☎31860216 tx171106
rm56 (🛁 🚿54) 🏠 Lift sB🛁 🚿265—360
dB🛁 🚿325—420 M80—130
Credit cards 1 2 5

★★ ★**Novotel** av de la Côte de Nacre
☎31930588 tx170563
🛁126 **P**250 Lift sB🛁fr313 dB🛁fr356
Mfr95&alc ≈
Credit cards 1 2 3 5

★★**Bristol** (Inter) 31 r du XI Novembre
(n.rest) ☎31845976 tx170353
rm25 (🛁 🚿16) **P**20 Lift dB126—226
dB🛁 🚿226
Credit cards 1 2 3

★★**Château** 5 av du 6-Juin (n.rest)
☎31861537
rm21 (🛁 🚿19) Lift sB108 sB🛁 🚿158
dB196 dB🛁 🚿206—236
Credit card 1

★★**Climat** av Montgomery, quai de la Folie
Couvrechef ☎31443636 tx692844
🛁43 sB🛁214—235 dB🛁233—254
M51—72
Credit card 1

★★**Métropole** (Inter) 16 pl de la Gare
(n.rest) ☎31822676 tx170165
rm71 (🛁 🚿64) **P** Lift

★**Bernières** 50 r Bernières (n.rest)
☎31860126
rm15 (🛁 🚿12) ☾ sBfr96 sB🛁 🚿113—156
dB🛁 🚿129—172
Credit cards 1 3

★**St-Jean** 20 r des Martyrs (n.rest)
☎31862335
🛁15 **P**6 sB🛁95—106 dB🛁190—212

🚗 **Auto Secours** 7 bis r Marchaud
☎31824555 All makes

At **HÉROUVILLE-ST-CLAIR**

★★**Campanile** Parc Tertaire, bd du Bois
☎31952924 tx170618
🛁43 **P** sB🛁204—225 dB🛁226—247
M61—82
Credit card 3

★★**Ibis Caen** 4 quartier Savary
☎31935446 tx170755
🛁89 **P**50 Lift sB🛁192—210
dB🛁234—250 M62&alc
Credit cards 1 3

At **MONDEVILLE** (3.5km SE)

★★**Fimotel** rte de Paris (RNI) ☎31343700
tx171514
🛁42 **P** Lift
Credit cards 1 2 3 5

CAGNES-SUR-MER
Alpes-Maritimes

★★★**Cagnard** (Relais et Châteaux)
r Pontis Long ☎93207321 tx462223
Closed 1—4 Nov
🛁19 A8rm **P**10 Lift sB🛁304—454
dB🛁328—858 Mfr275 sea mountains
Credit cards 1 2 3 5

★★★***Tierce*** bd de la Plage/bd Kennedy
☎93200209
6 Dec—25 Oct
🛁 🚿23 🏠 **P**23 Lift ☾ sea mountains

At **CROS-DE-CAGNES** (2km SE)

★★**Horizon** 111 bd de la Plage (n.rest)
☎93310995
15 Dec—5 Nov
rm44 (🛁 🚿35) **P**30 Lift sB120—180
sB🛁 🚿180—290 dB160—220
dB🛁 🚿240—370 t4% sea mountains
Credit cards 1 2 3 5

🚗 **Grand Garage Modern** 90 av de Nice
☎93310081 Closed Sun All makes

At **VILLENEUVE-LOUBET PLAGE**

★★**Méditerranée** (N98) (n.rest)
☎93200007
Closed 1 Nov—23 Dec
🛁16 **P**16 dB🛁138—187 t%

CAHORS
Lot

★★★**Wilson** 72 r Prés-Wilson (n.rest)
☎65354180 tx521455
🛁 🚿35 **P**12 Lift sB🛁 🚿233—261
dB🛁 🚿316—353
Credit cards 1 3

★★**France** LF (Inter) 252 av-J-Jaurès
(n.rest) ☎65351676 tx520394
🛁 🚿79 🏠 **P**40 Lift sB🛁 🚿164—237
dB🛁 🚿183—264
Credit cards 1 2 3 5

★**Terminus** LF 5 av C-de-Freycinet
☎65352450
🛁 🚿31 🏠 **P**7 Lift ☾ sB🛁 🚿236—251
dB🛁 🚿262—282
Credit cards 1 3

🚗 **Grandes Garages** rte de Toulouse
☎65356725 Closed Sat & Sun Tal

🚗 **Lacassange** av A-de-Monsie
☎65354510 Closed 19 Aug—9 Sep & Sun
All makes

🚗 **E Marcou** Rivière de Regourd
☎65351880 Closed Sat & Sun AR Vol

Recuper-Autos rte de Villefranche
☎65351516 Closed Mon AR Dat Maz Toy

At **LAROQUE-DES-ARC** (5km N)

★**Beau Rivage** ☎65353058
15 Mar—15 Oct
🛁 ⌂ 16 **P**50 dB 🛁 ⌂ 125—225
Credit cards 1 2 3

CAISSARGUES BOUILLARGUES
See **NÎMES**

CALAIS
Pas-de-Calais

See Plan page 130

AA **agent; see page 101**

★★★**Meurice** 5 r E-Roche ☎21345703
Plan **1**
🛁 ⌂ 30 A15rm 🚗 **P**25 Lift ☾
sB 🛁 ⌂ 201—211 dB 🛁 ⌂ 237—277
Credit cards 2 3 5

★★**Bellevue** 25 pl d'Armes (n.rest)
☎21361873 tx136702 Plan **2**
rm42 (🛁 ⌂ 33) 🚗 **P**30 Lift sB84—150
sB 🛁 ⌂ 181—206 dB117—182
dB 🛁 ⌂ 213—257
Credit cards 1 2 3 4 5

★★**Campanile** r de Maubeuge
☎21343070 tx135229 Plan **2A**
🛁 42 **P** sB 🛁 217—238 dB 🛁 239—260
M61—82

★★***CAP*** quai du Danube ☎21961010
Plan **2B**
⌂ 48 **P**30
Credit card 3

★★**George V** (Inter) 36 r Royale
☎21976800 tx135159 Plan **3**
rm45 (🛁 40) **P**15 sB124 sB 🛁 204 dB178
dB 🛁 258—298 M60—150 St%
Credit cards 1 2 3 5

★★**Ibis** r Greuze, ZUP de Beau-Marais
☎21966969 tx135004 Plan **4**
🛁 52 **P**60 sB 🛁 194—208 dB 🛁 240—245
M38—120
Credit cards 1 3

★★**Pacific** 40 r de Duc de Guise
☎21345024 Plan **5**
rm30 (🛁 ⌂ 17) A10rm 🚗 **P** sB153
sB 🛁 ⌂ 268 dB236 dB 🛁 ⌂ 286
M33—85&alc

★***Beffroi*** 10 r A-Gerschel (n.rest)
☎21344751 Plan **7**
rm20 (🛁 ⌂ 12)
Credit cards 2 4

★**Richelieu** 17 r Richelieu (n.rest)
☎21346160 Plan **8**
rm15 (🛁 ⌂ 10) 🚗 **P**6 sB115—118
sB 🛁 ⌂ 172—210 dB163—184
dB 🛁 ⌂ 200—227
Credit cards 1 2 3

★**Sole Meunière** 53 r de la Mer (n.rest)
☎21343608 Plan **9**
🛁 ⌂ 15 **P**30 sB 🛁 ⌂ 180—218
dB 🛁 ⌂ 240—270 sea
Credit card 3

🚗 **Calaislenne d'Autos** 36 1 av de St-Exupéry ☎21967242 Peu

France

CALIGNAC
Lot-et-Garonne

★**Palmiers** ☎58971102
🛁 ⌂ 25 **P** dB 🛁 ⌂ 260 M73 ≈

CAMBO-LES-BAINS
Pyrénés-Atlantiques

★**Bellevue** r des Terrasses ☎59297322
rm28 A3rm **P**30 sB110—166 dB126—222
M52—140 mountains
Credit card 3

CAMBRAI
Nord

★★★**Beatus** 718 av de Paris (n.rest)
☎27814570 tx820211
🛁 ⌂ 26 🚗 **P**26 sB 🛁 ⌂ 206—245
dB 🛁 ⌂ 270—304
Credit cards 1 2 3 5

★★★**Château de la Motte Fenelon**
sq du Château ☎27836138 tx120285
rm33 (🛁 27) A26rm sB130—215
sB 🛁 170—215 dB210—270
dB 🛁 210—270 🎾 ▭
Credit cards 2 3 5

★★**Ibis** rte de Bapaume, Fontaine Notre Dame ☎27835454 tx135074
🛁 27 sB 🛁 202—226 dB 🛁 249—272
Mfr85
Credit cards 1 3

★★***Mounton Blanc*** 33 r Alsace-Lorraine
☎27813016 tx133365
rm32 A4rm 🚗 **P**4 Lift
Credit cards 1 2 3 4 5

★★**Poste** 58—60 av de la Victoire (n.rest)
☎27813469
rm33 (🛁 ⌂ 31) 🚗 **P**12 Lift sB127—227
sB 🛁 ⌂ 177—227 dB194—244
dB 🛁 ⌂ 204—244
Credit card 3

★**France** 37 r Lille (n.rest) ☎27813880
Closed Aug
rm24(🛁 ⌂ 8) sB90—105 sB 🛁 ⌂ 131—174
dB121—194 dB 🛁 ⌂ 147—194

🚗 **P Decamps** Fontaine-Notre Dame (N30)
☎27815583 All makes

CAMP ST-LAURENT See **TOULON**

CANCALE
Ille-et-Vilaine

★★**Continental** LF (**Pn**) quai au Thomas
☎99896016
20 Mar—14 Nov
rm20 (🛁 ⌂ 19) sB106—300
sB 🛁 ⌂ 200—300 dB212—320
dB 🛁 ⌂ 220—320 M85—160 sea
Credit cards 1 3

CANDÉ
Maine-et-Loire

★***Tonnelles*** LF 6 pl des Halles ☎41927112
rm10 (🛁 2)

CANET-PLAGE
Pyrénées-Orientales

★★★**Sables** (Inter) r Vallée du Rhône
☎68802363 tx505213
🛁 ⌂ 41 A12rm **P**15 Lift sB 🛁 ⌂ 170—240
dB 🛁 ⌂ 190—300 t3% ≈ ▭ sea
Credit cards 1 2 3 5

★★***Mar-I-Cel*** pl Centrale ☎68803216
tx500997
Apr—Oct
🛁 ⌂ 60 **P** Lift sea mountains
Credit cards 1 2

CANNES
Alpes-Maritimes

★★★★★**Carlton** (Intercont)
58 La Croisette ☎93689168 tx470720
🛁 355 🚗 **P**8 Lift ☾ sB 🛁 806—1416
dB 🛁 1087—1682 st% Beach
Credit cards 1 2 3 4 5

★★★★★**Majestic** (SRS)
163 bd Croisette ☎93689100 tx470787
Closed Nov—14 Dec
🛁 262 🚗 Lift ☾ sB 🛁 650—1500
dB 🛁 800—1700 M alc S15% ≈ Beach
sea
Credit cards 1 2 3 4 5

★★★★★**Martinez-Concorde**
73 bd Croisette ☎93689191 tx470708
15 Jan—15 Dec
🛁 420 🚗 **P**70 Lift ☾ sB 🛁 415—1780
dB 🛁 490—2000 M180&alc ≈ Beach sea
Credit cards 1 2 3 5

★★★★***Frantel Beach*** 13 r du Canada
☎93382232 tx470034
Jan—Oct
🛁 95 🚗 Lift ▭

★★★★**Grand** 45 bd Croisette
☎93381545 tx470727
🛁 76 **P**43 Lift ☾ sB 🛁 715—1065
dB 🛁 940—1430 Mfr150 Beach sea
Credit cards 2 3

★★★★**Sofitel Méditerranée**
1 bd J-Hibert ☎93388787 tx470728
Closed 22—30 Nov
🛁 150 🚗 Lift ☾ sB 🛁 355—885
dB 🛁 450—1100 M150 ≈ sea
Credit cards 1 2 3 5

★★★**Embassy** 6 r de Bone ☎93387902
tx470081
🛁 60 🚗 **P**15 Lift sB 🛁 270—510
dB 🛁 300—550 M85—120 Beach sea
Credit cards 1 2 3 5

★★★***Savoy*** 5 r F-Einsey ☎93381774
20 Dec—Oct
rm55 (🛁 48) Lift ☾
Credit cards 2 5

★★**Campanile** Aérodrome de Cannes-Mandelieu ☎93486941 tx461570
🛁 49 **P** sB 🛁 217—238 dB 🛁 239—260
M61—82
Credit card 3

★★**France** 85 r d'Antibes (n.rest)
☎93392334 tx470673
🛁 ⌂ 34 Lift sB 🛁 237—297
dB 🛁 ⌂ 274—329 mountains
Credit cards 2 3

CALAIS

1	★★★	Meurice
2	★★	Bellevue
2A	★★	Campanile
2B	★★	CAP
3	★★	George V
4	★★	Ibis
5	★★	Pacific
7	★	Beffroi
8	★	Richelieu
9	★	Sole Meunière

★★Roches Fleuries
92 r G-Clemenceau (n.rest) ☎93392878
27 Dec—15 Oct
rm24 ⌂ **P**14 Lift sB80—100 dBfr110 sea mountains

🚗 **Carlton et du Canada** r F-Einsey ☎93380451 Closed Nov—Dec 15 & Sun All makes

Carnot Autos 48 bd Carnot ☎93682025 Cit

Europa Bretelle Autoroute au Cannet ☎93451700 Alf

At **LA BOCCA**

★★*Climat* 232 av Francis Tonner ☎93902222 tx970257
🛁 44 **P** Lift ♨

CANNET (LE)
Alpes-Maritimes

★★*Ibis* 87 bd Carnot ☎93457976 tx470095
🛁 40 **P**

🚗 ***Europe*** Bretelle Autoroute ☎93468646 Closed Sat & Sun Hon RR

CAPBRETON
Landes

★★Océan 🏨 av de la Plage ☎58721022
May—Oct
rm45 (🛁 🚿 41) A20rm **P**40 Lift sB100—104 sB 🛁 🚿 113—118 dB148—153 dB 🛁 🚿 190—229 M55—168&alc sea
Credit cards 1 5

CAP D'AGDE See **AGDE**

CAP D'AIL
Alpes-Maritimes

★★Cigogne 🏨 r de la Gare ☎93782960
20 May—2 Nov
🛁 15 dB 🛁 270—300 M100—120 sea
Credit card 3

★★Miramer 126 av du 3 Septembre ☎93780660
15 Jan—Nov
rm27 (🚿 21) **P**12 dB141 dB🚿 191—221 M60&alc sea
Credit card 3

CAP D'ANTIBES See **ANTIBES**

CAP FERRAT See **ST-JEAN-CAP-FERRAT**

CAP-MARTIN See **ROQUEBRUNE-CAP-MARTIN**

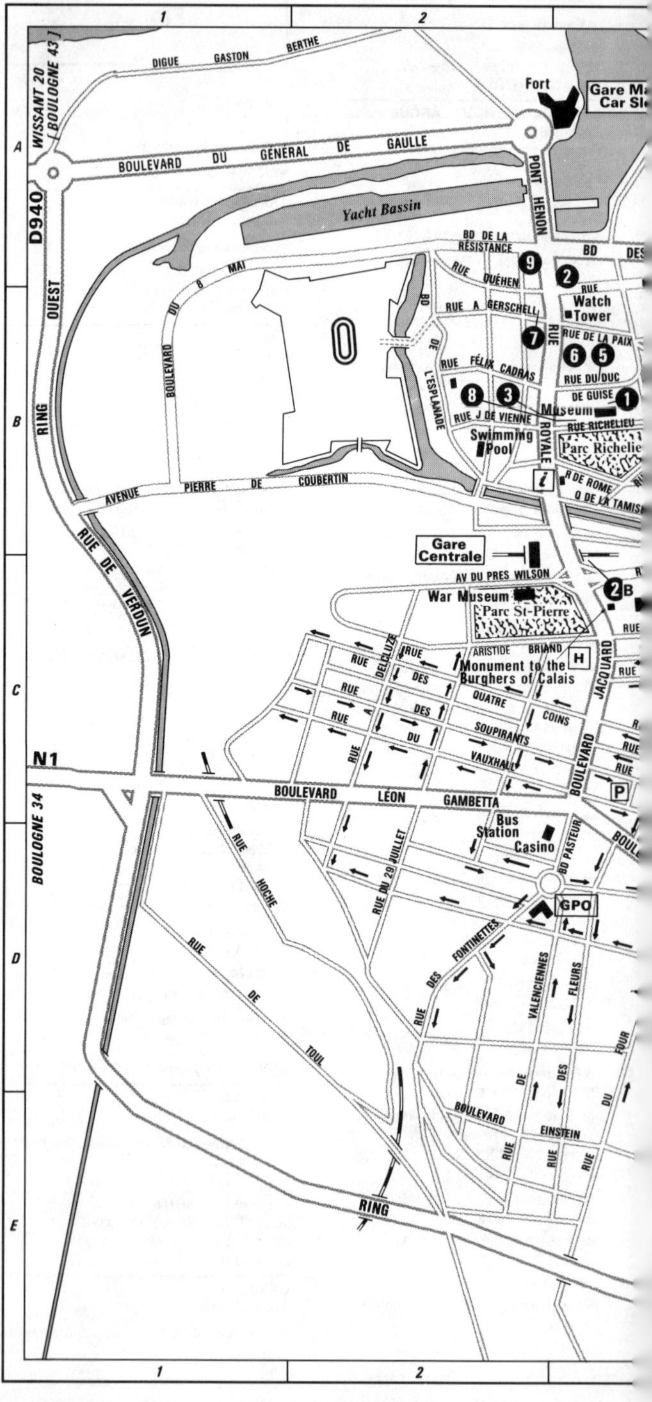

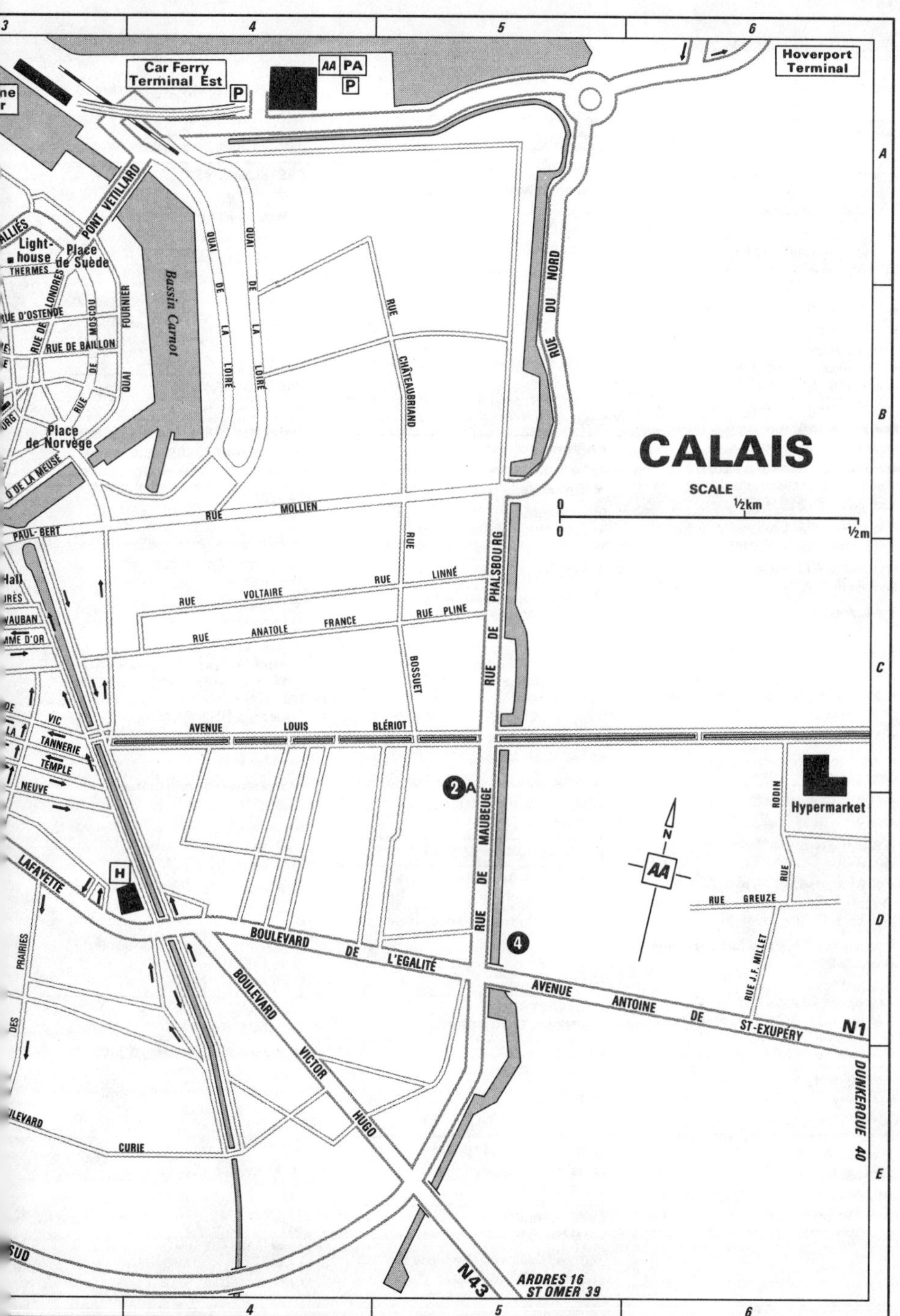

Car Ferry Terminal Est
AA
PA
P
Hoverport Terminal
Light-house
Place de Suède
Bassin Carnot
QUAI DE LA LOIRE
RUE DU NORD
RUE CHÂTEAUBRIAND
PONT VETILLARD
RUE D'OSTENDE
RUE DE LONDRES
RUE DE MOSCOU
RUE DE BAILLON
QUAI FOURNIER
Place de Norvège
CALAIS
SCALE
½km
½m
RUE MOLLIEN
PAUL-BERT
RUE LINNÉ
RUE VOLTAIRE
RUE ANATOLE FRANCE
RUE PLINE
RUE BOSSUET
RUE DE PHALSBOURG
AVENUE LOUIS BLÉRIOT
VIC
TANNERIE
TEMPLE
NEUVE
LAFAYETTE
H
RUE DE MAUBEUGE
Hypermarket
RODIN
RUE GREUZE
RUE J.F. MILLET
BOULEVARD DE L'EGALITÉ
AVENUE ANTOINE DE ST-EXUPERY
N1
BOULEVARD VICTOR HUGO
DUNKERQUE 40
CURIE
N43
ARDRES 16
ST OMER 39

CARANTEC
Finistère

★**Falaise** pl du Kelenn ☎98670053

Etr—20 Sep
rm26 (🛁 13) **P**35 sB72 sB🛁 98
dB105—116 dB🛁 146—163 M56—101 sea

CARCASSONNE
Aude

★★★★**Domaine d'Auriac** (Relais et Châteaux) **(DPn)** (4km SE via D104, D42, D342) rte St-Hilaire ☎68257222 tx500385

Closed 16 Jan—Feb
🛁 23 🚗 **P**100 Lift ☾ sB🛁 476—616
dB🛁 582—652 🎾 ≈ mountains
Credit cards [1] [2] [3] [5]

★★★**Cité** pl St-Nazaire ☎68250334 tx500829

17 Apr—20 Oct
🛁🚿 54 🚗 Lift ☾ sB🛁🚿 590
dB🛁🚿 710—810 M150—280 mountains
Credit cards [1] [2] [3] [5]

★★★**Donjon** LF (BW/MAP) 2 r Comte Roger ☎68710880 tx505012

🛁 36 **P**40 Lift ☾ sB🛁 208—318
dB🛁 246—376 Malc
Credit cards [1] [2] [3] [4] [5]

★★★***Terminus*** (Inter) 2 av MI-Joffre (n.rest) ☎68252500 tx500198

rm110 (🛁 92) 🚗 **P**30 Lift
Credit cards [2] [3] [5]

★★**Aragon** (FAH/Inter) 15 Montée Combéléran (n.rest) ☎68471631

🛁 19 **P**22 sB🛁 217—257 dB🛁 244—324
Credit cards [1] [2] [3] [5]

★★***Climat*** 8 r des Côteaux de Pech-Mary ☎68711620

🛁 26 **P** mountains

★★**Croque Sel** rte Narbonne (N113) ☎68251415

🛁 11 **P**50 dB🛁 206 M45—59&alc
Credit cards [1] [2] [3] [5]

★★**Ibis** rte de Barriec ☎68479835 tx500554

🛁 60 **P**100 sB🛁 197 dB🛁 247—250 mountains
Credit cards [1] [3]

★★**Logis de Trencavel** LF 286 av du Gl-Leclerc ☎68710953

10 Feb—10 Jan
rm12 (🛁🚿 9) 🚗 **P**50 sB125—215
sB🛁🚿 215 dB150—270 dB🛁🚿 240—270
M90—195
Credit cards [1] [2] [3] [5]

★★**Monteségur** 27 allée d'Iéna ☎68253141

Closed 15 Dec—15 Jan
🛁🚿 21 **P**16 Lift ☾ sB🛁🚿 194—304
dB🛁🚿 288—368
Credit cards [1] [2] [3] [5]

🚘 **Laporta** 47 av H-Gout ☎68251150
Closed Sat pm & Sun AR

CARENNAC
Lot

★**Fenelon** LF ☎65386767

rm21 (🛁🚿 17) **P**20 sB🛁🚿 107—116
dB🛁🚿 143—178 M53—176
Credit card [3]

CARENTAN
Manche

★***Auberge Normande*** LF bd Verdun ☎33420299

rm8 (🛁🚿 3) **P**12
Credit cards [1] [3] [5]

🚘 **J Santini** 7 bd de Verdun ☎33420266
Closed Sat Fia For

CARHAIX-PLOUGUER
Finistère

★★**Gradlon** (Inter) 12 bd de la République ☎98931522

🛁 43 **P**20 Lift sB🛁 fr200 dB🛁 fr260 Mfr60
Credit cards [1] [2] [3] [5]

CARNAC
Morbihan

★★**Armoric** 53 av de la Poste ☎97521347

Etr—15 Sep
🛁🚿 25 **P**50 sB🛁🚿 230 dB🛁🚿 248 M82 🎾

At **CARNAC-PLAGE**

★★★***Novotel Tal-Ar-Mor*** av de l'Atlantique ☎97521666 tx950324

3 Jan—18 Nov
🛁 106 **P** Lift ≈

★★★**Celtique** 17 av Kermario ☎97521149

Whit—Sep
rm35 (🛁🚿 27) **P**15 sBfr152 sB🛁🚿 fr179
dB189 dB🛁🚿 258—296

★★***Genêts*** 45 av Kermario ☎97521101

29 Mar—15 Apr & 25 May—28 Sep
rm33 (🛁🚿 24) A4rm **P**12

CARQUEFOUR See **NANTES**

CARQUEIRANNE
Var

★★**Plein Sud** av du Gl-de-Gaulle/rte des Salettes ☎94585286

16 Dec—Oct
🛁🚿 17 **P**20

CARTERET See **BARNEVILLE-CARTERET**

CASSIS
Bouches-du-Rhône

★★★**Plage** pl Bestouan ☎42010570 tx441287

Apr—Oct
🛁🚿 29 Lift ☾ sB🛁🚿 123—273
dB🛁🚿 206—376 sea
Credit card [2]

CASTELJALOUX
Lot-et-Garonne

★***Grand Cadets de Gascogne*** LF pl Gambetta ☎53930059

rm15 (🛁 10) 🚗 **P**10 Lift
Credit cards [1] [2] [3] [5]

CASTELLANE
Alpes-de-Hautes-Provence

★***Ma Petit Auberge*** pl M-Sauvaire ☎92836206

Mar—Nov
rm18 (🛁🚿 16) **P**6 mountains

CASTELNAUDARY
Aude

★★***Palmes*** (BW/MAP) 10 MI-Foch ☎231710 tx500372

rm20 (🛁🚿 15) 🚗 Lift
Credit cards [1] [2] [3] [5]

★**Fourcade** 14 r des Carmes ☎68230208

rm14 (🛁🚿 10) sB84—119 sB🛁 106
dB138—168 dB🛁🚿 168—188 M52—170
Credit cards [1] [2] [3] [4] [5]

CASTELSARRASIN
Tarn-et-Garonne

★**Moderne** 54 r de l'Egalité ☎63323010

rm12 (🚿 3) 🚗 **P** ☾ sB59 sB🚿 73 dB96
dB🚿 118—145 🎾 ≈

CASTRES
Tarn

★★**Fimotel** ZI de la Chartreuse (N622) ☎63598999 tx215969

🛁 60 **P**20

★★**Grand** (Inter) 11 r de la Libération ☎63590030

15 Jan—15 Dec
rm40 (🛁🚿 37) 🚗 Lift ☾ sB129—159
sB🛁🚿 164—185 dB🛁🚿 213—276
M55—135
Credit cards [1] [2] [3] [5]

CAUDEBEC-EN-CAUX
Seine-Maritime

★★★**Marine** 18 quai Guilbaud ☎35962011 tx770404

20 Jan—Dec
rm33 (🛁🚿 28) **P**12 Lift lake
Credit cards [1] [2] [3] [5]

★★**Normandie** LF **(Pn)** quai Guilbaud ☎35962511

Closed Feb
🛁🚿 16 **P**16 sBfr138 sB🚿 fr138 dBfr187
dB🛁 fr196 M49—127
Credit cards [1] [2] [3]

CAUSSADE
Tarn-et-Garonne

★★**Dupont** 25 r Recollets ☎63650500

Closed Dec & Jan
rm31 (🛁🚿 23) A8rm 🚗 **P**30 sB92—166
sB🛁🚿 131—166 dB109—182
dB🛁🚿 147—182 M58—98
Credit cards [1] [3]

★★**Larroque** LF av de la Gare ☎63931014

15 Jan—25 Dec
🛁🚿 27 A12rm 🚗 **P**12 sB128—155
sB🛁🚿 138—165 dB156—190
dB🛁🚿 171—220 M65—150
Credit cards [1] [2] [3] [5]

CAVAILLON
Vaucluse

★★★***Christel*** Digue de Gd. Jardin ☎90710779 tx431547

🛁 109 **P** Lift ♒

★★**Toppin** 70 cours Gambetta ☎90713042

🛁🚿 32 🚗 **P**20 sB🛁🚿 148—198 dB🛁🚿 186—236 M65—150 Credit cards [1] [2] [3] [5]

CAVALAIRE-SUR-MER
Var

★★**Bonne Auberge (Pn)** 400 av des Alliés, rte Nationale ☎94640296

Mar—Oct
rm31 (🛁🚿 12) **P**24 dB128—226 dB🛁🚿 142—226 Mfr56

CAVALIÈRE
Var

★★★***Surplage*** **(DPn)** ☎94058019

Apr—Oct
🛁🚿 63 **P**36 Lift ☾ 📺 Beach sea

★★***Cap Nègre*** ☎94058046

May—Sep
rm32 **P**30 Lift sea
Credit cards [1] [3]

CELLE-DUNOISE (LA)
Creuse

★**Pascaud** LF ☎55891066

Closed Oct
rm10 (🚿 4) 🚗 **P**6 sB64 dB98 dB🚿 113 M45—135

CERGY See **PONTOISE**

CESSON-SÉVIGNÉ See **RENNES**

CESTAS See **BORDEAUX**

CHABLIS
Yonne

★**Étoile (Pn)** 4 r Moulins ☎86421050

Feb—15 Dec
rm15 (🛁🚿 9) 🚗 sB88—118 sB🛁🚿 168 dB126—146 dB🛁🚿 196—236 M65—120

CHAGNY
Saône-et-Loire

★★★***Lameloise*** 36 pl d'Armes ☎85870885

Closed 18—26 Jul & 5 Dec—3 Jan
🛁🚿 25 🚗

★★**Capucines** LF **(DPn)** 30 rte de Châlon ☎85870817

rm15 (🛁🚿 12) A4rm **P**50 dB🛁🚿 211—272 M60—200
Credit cards [1] [3]

★**Paris** 6 r de Beaune ☎85870838

15 Feb—15 Nov
rm11 (🛁🚿 3) **P**12 dBfr107 dB🛁🚿 fr125 M45—95

🔧 **G Guyot** les Creusottes (N6) ☎85872228 Ren

🔧 **Thevenaut** pl du Creux des Nazoires ☎85871787 Closed Sat & Sun All makes

France

At **CHASSEY-LE-CAMP** (6km W)

★★**Auberge du Camp Romain** LF ☎85870991

Closed Jan
rm25 (🛁🚿 22) 🚗 **P** sB108—271 sB🛁🚿 108—271 dB125—288 dB🛁🚿 125—288 M72—112 🎾 mountains
Credit card [3]

CHAIGNES See **PACY-SUR-EURE**

CHAINTRÉ-LA-CHAPELLE-DE-GUINCHAY See **MÂCON**

CHAISE DIEU (LA)
Haute-Loire

★★**Tremblant** LF (D906) ☎71000185

Apr—15 Nov
rm28 (🛁🚿 17) 🚗 **P**15 sB102—107 sB🛁🚿 167—182 dB119—124 dB🛁🚿 184—199 M55—100 mountains
Credit card [3]

CHALLES-LES-EAUX
Savoie

★★★**Château** Montée du Château ☎79852145

Feb—Oct
rm72 (🛁🚿 49) A51rm **P**50 sB110—130 dB110—130 dB🛁🚿 210—345 M80—170 🎾 ♒ mountains
Credit cards [1] [2] [3] [5]

★★**Château de Trivier** ☎79850727

rm30 (🛁🚿 22) A16rm 🚗 **P**150 sB🛁🚿 315—362 dB201—252 dB🛁🚿 333—380 M55—140 mountains
Credit cards [1] [2] [3] [4] [5]

★★**Climat** r J Denarie ☎79703036

🛁 29 **P** sB🛁 213 M51—66 mountains
Credit cards [1] [3]

CHÂLONS-SUR-MARNE
Marne

★★**Angleterre (Pn)** 19 pl Mgr-Tissier ☎26682151

6 Jan—28 Jun & 21 Jul—19 Dec
rm18 (🛁🚿 14) **P**10 ☾ sB149—305 sB🛁🚿 278—305 dB306—345 dB🛁🚿 306—345 M135—280
Credit cards [1] [2] [3] [5]

★★**Bristol** 77 av P-Sémard (n.rest) ☎26682463

🛁🚿 24 🚗 **P**25 sB🛁🚿 134—186 dB🛁🚿 148—202

★★***Ibis*** rte de Sedan, Complexe Agricole ☎26651665 tx830595

🛁 40 **P**70
Credit cards [1] [3]

★★***Mont des Logès*** r de Champagne ☎26673343

rm19 (🛁🚿 19) **P**

★★**Pasteur** 46 r Pasteur (n.rest) ☎26681000

rm28 (🛁🚿 24) 🚗 **P**15 sB106—182 sB🛁🚿 106—182 dB149—214
Credit cards [1] [3]

🔧 **Raige** 17 r C-Jacquiert ☎26681431 Closed Sun

At **COURTISOLS** (10.5km NE off N3)

🔧 **Montel** 63 rte Nationale ☎26696004 M/c Ren

At **ÉPINE (L')** (8.5km E on N3)

★★**Armes de Champagne** (N3) ☎26681043 tx830998

11 Feb—6 Jan
rm40 (🛁🚿 38) A16rm 🚗 **P** sB🛁🚿 176—366 dB🛁🚿 252—392 M75—250 ⛳
Credit cards [1] [2] [3]

CHALON-SUR-SAÔNE
Saône-et-Loire

★★★***Mercure*** Centre Commercial de la Thalie, av de l'Europe ☎85465189 tx800132

🛁 85 **P**100 Lift ♒
Credit cards [1] [2] [3] [4] [5]

★★★**Royal** (BW/MAP) 8 r du Port Villiers ☎85481586

🛁🚿 51 🚗 **P**20 Lift ☾ sB🛁🚿 203—293 dB🛁🚿 281—406 M75—190
Credit cards [1] [2] [3] [4] [5]

★★★**St-Georges et Terminus** (Inter) 32 av J-Jaurès ☎85482705 tx800330

🛁🚿 48 🚗 **P** Lift ☾
Credit cards [1] [2] [3] [5]

★★★**St-Regis** (BW/MAP) 22 bd de la République ☎85480728 tx801624

rm40 (🛁🚿 36) 🚗 Lift ☾ sB🛁🚿 290—330 dB🛁🚿 360—420 M85
Credit cards [1] [2] [3] [5]

★★**Ibis** Carrefour des Moirots (n.rest) ☎85466462 tx800132

🛁 41 **P** sB🛁 210—220 dB🛁 280—290
Credit cards [1] [3]

★★**Rotonde** ☎85483593

rm32 (🚿 10) 🚗 sB91 sB🚿 116—136 dB122 dB🚿 152—172
Credit cards [1] [3]

★★**St-Jean** 24 quai Gambetta (n.rest) ☎85484565

rm25 (🛁🚿 18) sBfr94 sB🛁🚿 fr197 dBfr214 dB🛁🚿 fr214

★★**St-Rémy** LF 89 r A-Martin, St-Rémy (n.rest) ☎85483804 tx800175

🛁🚿 40 **P**30 sB🛁🚿 98—176 dB🛁🚿 147—222
Credit cards [1] [3] [5]

🔧 **Bourgogne Véhicules Industriels** (N6 Lux-Chalon Sud) ☎85488857 Closed Sun Mer

🔧 **Duval** 10 rte de Lyon ☎85487663 Closed Sun Fia

Moderne r des P-d'Orient ☎85465212 Closed Sat & Sun Cit

🔧 **Soreva** 4 av J-F-Kennedy ☎85464945 Closed Sun For

At **CHAMPFORGEUIL** (4km NW)

★★***Climat*** ZAC des Blettrys
☎8564460123 tx692844

➡ 42

CHAMBÉRY
Savoie

★★★★**Grand** 6 pl de la Gare
☎79695454 tx320910

➡ ⋔ 50 ⌂ Lift ☾ sB ➡ ⋔ 270—480
dB ➡ ⋔ 340—590 M100—190 mountains
Credit cards [2] [3] [5]

★★★**France** 22 fbg Reclus (n.rest)
☎79335118 tx320410

➡ ⋔ 48 ⌂ ☾ sB ➡ ⋔ 217—277
dB ➡ ⋔ 304—329
Credit cards [1] [2] [3] [4] [5]

★★★***Novotel*** Le Cheminet ☎79692127
tx320446

➡ 103 **P**120 Lift ⛱ mountains
Credit cards [1] [2] [3] [5]

★★★**Touring** 12 r Sommeiller (n.rest)
☎79623726

rm35 (➡ ⋔ 28) ⌂ Lift sBfr134 sB ➡ ⋔ fr173
dB153 dB ➡ ⋔ 192—244
Credit cards [1] [2] [3] [5]

🚗 **Gare** 29 av de la Baisse ☎79623637 M/c
Closed Sat & Sun Fia

At **CHAMNORD**

★★***Ibis Chambéry*** av E-Ducretet
☎79692836 tx320457

➡ 88 **P**100 Lift mountains
Credit cards [1] [3]

CHAMBON (LAC)
Puy-de-Dôme

★★**Bellevue** LE ☎73886106

Apr—Sep
rm25 (➡ ⋔ 23) A8rm **P**20 dB95
dB ➡ ⋔ 174—189 lake

★★**Grillon** LE (**Pn**) ☎73886066

Etr—Oct
rm20 (➡ ⋔ 18) **P**15 sB90—174
sB ➡ ⋔ 164—174 dB94—188
dB ➡ ⋔ 178—188 Mfr65 mountains
Credit card [1]

CHAMBON-SUR-VOUEIZE
Creuse

★★**Etonneries** LE (**Pn**)
41 av G-Clemenceau ☎55821466

Mar—22 Dec
rm10 (➡ ⋔ 6) **P**20 sB82 dB111
dB ➡ ⋔ 178—268 mountains
Credit card [5]

CHAMBORD
Loir-et-Cher

★★**St-Michel** LE Face au Château
☎54203131

Closed 14 Nov—21 Dec
rm38 (➡ ⋔ 11) ⌂ **P**23 ♈
Credit card [3]

CHAMBOURCY See
ST-GERMAIN-EN-LAYE

CHAMBRAY-LES-TOURS See **TOURS**

CHAMNORD See **CHAMBÉRY**

France

CHAMONIX-MONT-BLANC
Haute-Savoie

★★★★**Croix Blanche** 7 r Vallot
☎50530011 tx385614

Closed Jun
➡ ⋔ 35 ⌂ **P**7 ☾ sB ➡ ⋔ 167—237
dB ➡ ⋔ 198—290 ♈ ⛱ ▣ mountains
Credit cards [1] [2] [3] [5]

★★★**Mont Blanc** pl d'Église ☎50530564
tx385614

➡ 50 ⌂ **P**20 Lift **Pn**383—471 ♈ ⛱
mountains
Credit cards [1] [2] [3] [4] [5]

★★★**Richemond** 228 r Dr-Paccard
☎50530885 tx385417

20 Dec—14 Apr & 15 Jun—14 Sep
rm52 (➡ 40) **P**25 Lift ☾ sB95—107
sB ➡ 184—199 dB170—190
dB ➡ 270—306 M66—76 mountains
Credit cards [1] [2] [3] [4] [5]

★★★**Sapinière-Montana** (**DPn** in season) 102 r Mummery ☎50530763
tx385831

15 Dec—Sep
rm34 (➡ ⋔ 30) A6rm ⌂ **P**25 Lift ☾
mountains
Credit cards [1] [2] [3] [5]

At **BOSSONS (LES)** (3.5km S)

★★**Aiguille du Midi** LE (**Pn**) ☎50530065

Seasonal
rm50 (➡ ⋔ 42) A12rm **P**100 Lift
dB200—208 dB ➡ ⋔ 262—270 M90 ♈ ⛱
mountains

CHAMPAGNOLE
Jura

★★★**Ripotot** 54 r Ml-Foch ☎84521545

Apr—Oct
rm60 (➡ ⋔ 26) ⌂ **P**30 sB113 sB ➡ ⋔ 188
dB139 dB ➡ ⋔ 231—241 Mfr75 ♈
Credit cards [1] [2] [3] [5]

CHAMPFORGEUIL See
CHALON-SUR-SAÔNE

CHAMPILLON See **ÉPERNAY**

CHAMPNIERS See **ANGOULÊME**

CHAMPS-SUR-MARNE
Seine-et-Marne

At **ÉMERAINVILLE**

★★***Climat*** Le Pavé Neuf (CD51)
☎60063834 tx612241

➡ 38 **P**

CHAMPTOCEAUX
Marne-et-Loire

★★***Côte*** LE (**DPn**) 2 r du Dr-Giffard
☎40835039 tx711592

rm28 (➡ ⋔ 19) ⌂ **P**

CHANAS See **ROUSSILLON**

CHANTEPIE
Ille-et-Vilaine

★★**Campanile** ZAC des deux Ruisseaux,
r de la Chalotais ☎99537676 tx740436

➡ 39 **P** sB ➡ 217—238 dB ➡ 240—261
M61—82
Credit card [3]

CHANTILLY
Oise

★★**Campanile** rte de Creil (N16)
☎44573924 tx140065

➡ 50 **P** sB ➡ 204—225 dB ➡ 227—248
M61—82
Credit card [3]

★**Petit Vatel** ☎44570166

Closed 2 wks Xmas, Feb, 1 Nov
rm15 (⋔ 3) sB67—101 dB81 dB⋔ 129
M39—65
Credit cards [3] [4]

SADELL 33 av du Ml-Joffre ☎44570509
Closed Sat pm & Sun Ope

At **LAMORLAYE** (5km S)

★★★**Hostellerie du Lys** 7th Avenue
☎44212619 tx150298

➡ ⋔ 35 A20rm **P**80 ☾ sB ➡ ⋔ 215—285
dB ➡ ⋔ 240—310 M115—130
Credit cards [1] [2] [3] [5]

CHANTONNAY
Vendée

★★**Moulin Neuf** LE (**DPn**) ☎51943027

➡ ⋔ 49 **P**50 sB ➡ ⋔ 123—137
dB ➡ ⋔ 163—234 M43—95 ♈ ⛱ ▣ lake
Credit card [3]

★**Mouton** LE (**DPn**) 31 r Nationale
☎51943022

Seasonal Closed Mon
➡ ⋔ 11 ⌂ **P**11 sB ➡ ⋔ fr160
dB ➡ ⋔ 208—232 M50—125
Credit cards [1] [2] [3]

CHAPELLE-EN-VERCORS (LA)
Drôme

★**Bellier** ☎75482003

20 Jun—20 Sep
rm12 (➡ ⋔ 8) **P**15 sBfr90 sB ➡ ⋔ 220
dB160—320 dB ➡ ⋔ 270—340 M120—190
mountains
Credit cards [2] [3] [5]

CHAPELLE-SAINT-MESMIN (LA)
Loiret

★★**Fimotel** 7 r d'Aquitaine ☎38437144
tx781265

➡ 42 **P**40 Lift sB ➡ 209—218
dB ➡ 241—250 M54—94&alc
Credit cards [1] [2] [3] [5]

CHARAVINES
Isère

★★**Hostellerie Lac Bleu** LE (1.5km N on D50) ☎76066048

15 Mar—Oct
rm13 (➡ ⋔ 10) ⌂ **P**20 sB ➡ ⋔ 168—188
dB201 dB ➡ ⋔ 226 M68—170 mountains
lake

CHARBONNIÈRES-LES-BAINS See **LYON**

CHARLES DE GAULLE AIRPORT See **PARIS AIRPORTS**

CHARLEVILLE-MÉZIÈRES
Ardennes

★★★**Cleves** 43 r de l'Arquebuse ☎24331075 tx841164
49 P Lift sB 223—288 dB 351 M60—110 S15%

At **VILLERS-SEMEUSE** (5km E)

★★★***Mercure*** r L-Michel ☎24375529 tx840076
67 P

CHARMES
Vosges

★**Central** (**DPn**) 4 r des Capucins ☎29380240
Jan—15 Feb & 28 Feb—31 Dec
10 P sB 95—187 dB 121—204 M80—160
Credit cards 1 5

CHAROLLES
Saône-et-Loire

★★**Moderne** 10 av de la Gare ☎85240702
Feb—28 Dec
rm18 (16) A7rm P10 dB135 dB 200—270 M100—220 mountains
Credit cards 2 3 5

CHARTRES
Eure-et-Loir

★★★***Grand Monarque*** (BW/MAP) 22 pl des Epars ☎37210072 tx760777
Closed Feb
rm42 (38) P

★★★***Novotel*** av M-Proust, le Madeleine ☎37348030 tx781298
78 P100
Credit cards 1 2 3 5

★★**Cap** 5 av M-Proust ☎37359111 tx781284
47 P sB 169—200 dB 188—220 M60—80
Credit cards 1 3

★★**Poste** 3 r du Gl-König ☎37210427 tx760533
rm60 (57) P18 Lift sB106 sB 171—184 dB192—205 dB 205—257 M49—98
Credit cards 1 2 3 5

★***Ouest*** (**DPn**) 3 pl Sémard (n.rest) ☎37214327
rm29 (14)
Credit card 2

GARD 28 55 r des V-Capucins ☎37219439 All makes

At **LUCÉ** (3km SW on N23)

★★***Ibis*** Impasse du Perigord (N23) ☎3735700 tx780348
54 P

Chartres Auto Sport rte d'Illiers ☎37352479 Closed Mon AR

France

CHARTRE-SUR-LE-LOIR (LA)
Sarthe

★★**France** (**DPn**) 20 pl de la République ☎43444016
15 Dec—15 Nov
rm30 (27) A14rm P12 sB85—95 sB 195 dB120 dB 210 M55—165
Credit card 3

CHASSENEUIL-DU-POITOU See **POITIERS**

CHASSE-SUR-RHÔNE
Isère

★★★***Mercure Lyon Sud*** CD4-Les Roues ☎78731394 tx300625
115 P Lift
Credit cards 1 2 3 5

CHASSEY-LE-CAMP See **CHAGNY**

CHÂTEAU-ARNOUX
Alpes-de-Haute-Provence

★★★**Bonne Étape** (Relais et Châteaux) (**DPn**) (N85) ☎92640009 tx430605
12 Feb—5 Jan
18 P18 dB 454—754 M180—320 mountains lake
Credit cards 1 2 3 5

CHÂTEAUBOURG
Ille-et-Vilaine

★★★***Ar Milin*** (FAH) ☎003091 tx99740083
15 Jan—15 Dec
33 A20rm P Lift

CHÂTEAUBRIANT
Loire-Atlantique

★★★**Hostellerie de la Ferrière** (FAH/Inter) rte de Nantes ☎40280028
rm25 (24) A14rm P250 dB 250—300 M78—125
Credit cards 1 2 3 5

★***Armour*** 19 pl Motte (n.rest) ☎40811119
rm20 (13) Lift
Credit cards 2 5

CHÂTEAU-CHINON
Nièvre

★★**Vieux Morvan** (**DPn**) 6 pl Gudin ☎86850501
15 Jan—15 Nov
rm24 (11) sB70—106 sB 169 dB98—159 dB 185—204 M53—90
Credit card 1

CHÂTEAU D'OLONNE See **SABLES D'OLONNE (LES)**

CHÂTEAUDUN
Eure-et-Loir

★★**Armorial** 59 r Gambetta (n.rest) ☎37451957
rm15 (12) sBfr84 sB 101—149 dBfr117 dB 122—192
Credit cards 1 3

★★**Beauce** (Inter) 50 r de Jallans (n.rest) ☎37451475
Closed 15 Dec—15 Jan
rm24 (18) sB111 sB 185—196 dB 187—193

★***Rose*** (**DPn**) 12 r L-Licors ☎37452182
rm8 (7)

★**Trois Pastoureaux** (**Pn**) 31 r A-Gillet ☎37450162
rm12 (2) P3 sB91 sB 118 dB182 dB 236 M55—101
Credit cards 1 2 3 4

CHÂTEAU-FARINE See **BESANÇON**

CHÂTEAU-GONTIER
Mayenne

★★***Mirwault*** ☎43071317
Feb—23 Dec
rm12 (10) P30
Credit cards 1 2 3 5

CHÂTEAUNEUF (Côte-d'Or)
See **POUILLY-EN-AUXOIS**

CHÂTEAUNEUF-DE-GRASSE
Alpes-Maritimes

★★**Campanile** Le Pré du Lac ☎93425555 tx470092
41 P dB 194—215
Credit card 3

CHÂTEAUNEUF-SUR-LOIRE
Loiret

★**Novotel du Loiret** 4 pl A-Briand ☎38584228
20 Jan—20 Dec
rm21 (11) sB100—131 sB 144—184 M69—135
Credit cards 1 2 3 5

CHÂTEAUROUX
Indre

★★★***France*** (Inter) 16 r V-Hugo ☎54270080 tx751676
48 Lift
Credit cards 2 3 5

★**Central** 19 av de la Gare ☎54220100
Closed 22 Dec—2 Jan
11 sB 147—173 dB 188—195

Aubert & Chatein 24 r des Fontaines ☎54324672 Closed Sun Ren

CHÂTEAU-THIERRY
Aisne

★★**Ile de France** (Inter) (3km N on N37) ☎23691012 tx150666
rm56 (47) P Lift sB111 sB 201—206 dB162—202 dB 258—297 M52—152 S15%
Credit cards 1 2 3 5

★**Girafe** pl A-Briand (n.rest) ☎23830206
rm30 (12) A10rm P20 sB96—158 sB 156—158 dB152—206 dB 202—206
Credit card 3

SA Aisne Auto 8 av de Montmirail ☎23832380 Closed Sat pm & Sun Cit

🚘 **Verdel** 18 av d'Essonnes ☎23832025 Closed Sat pm, Sun & Mon am Peu

At **NOGENTEL** (3.5km S on D15)

🚘 **Tourisport** Carrefour Luxembourg ☎23811128 Closed Sat pm & Mon am AR

CHÂTELAILLON-PLAGE
Charente-Maritime

★★***L'Hermitage*** 13 av Gl-Leclerc ☎46562097
rm27 (🛁🚿17) 🚗 **P**20
Credit cards [1] [2] [3]

★★***Hostellerie Select*** 1 r G-Musset ☎46562431
rm21 (🛁🚿18) **P**

★★**Majestic** LE pl de St-Marsault ☎46562053
10 Jan—15 Dec
rm30 (🛁🚿26) 🚗 **P**20 sB102—137 sB🛁🚿187—207 dB209—239 dB🛁🚿209—239 M80—100
Credit cards [1] [2] [4] [5]

CHÂTELGUYON
Puy-de-Dôme

★★★★***Splendid*** (BW/MAP) 5—7 r d'Angleterre ☎73860480 tx990585
25 Apr—15 Oct
🛁🚿93 **P**100 Lift ☾ ≈ sea lake
Credit cards [1] [2] [3] [5]

★★★**International** r A-Punnet ☎73860672
2 May—Sep
rm68 (🛁🚿55) Lift ☾ sB155—185 sB🛁🚿215—250 dB240 dB🛁🚿275—330 M90—125 mountains
Credit card [3]

CHÂTELLERAULT
Vienne

★★★***Moderne*** (BW/MAP) 74 bd Blossac ☎49213011 tx791801
rm37 🚗 **P** Lift
Credit cards [1] [2] [3] [4] [5]

★★**Croissant** 19 av Kennedy ☎49210177 tx86100
rm20 (🛁🚿11) **P** sBfr102 sB🛁🚿fr120 dBfr204 dB🛁🚿fr240 M36—158
Credit cards [1] [2] [3]

★★**Ibis** av Camille Plage, quartier de la Forêt ☎49217577 tx791488
🛁72 Lift sB🛁202 dB🛁256 M alc
Credit cards [1] [3]

★★**Univers** 4 av G-Clemenceau ☎49212353 tx791344
15 Jan—15 Dec
rm30 (🛁🚿18) 🚗 Lift
Credit cards [1] [2] [3]

🚘 **Rousseau** 91 av L-Ripault ☎49210613 Closed Aug 15—Sep 9, 1 wk Feb & Sat pm Pau

CHÂTILLON-EN-BAZIOS
Nièvre

★**Poste** LE (**Pn** in season) Grande Rue ☎86841468
20 Jan—20 Dec
rm12 (🚿4) 🚗 **P**30 dBfr100 dB🚿129—135 M44—94

CHÂTILLON-SUR-INDRE
Indre

★**Auberge de la Tour** LE (**DPn**) ☎54387217
rm11 (🛁🚿5) 🚗 **P**6 sBfr114 sB🛁🚿157—193 dBfr131 dB🛁🚿174—240 M49—110

CHÂTILLON-SUR-SEINE
Côte-d'Or

★★**Côte d'Or** (**Pn**) r C-Ronot ☎80911329
15 Jan—15 Dec
rm11 (🛁🚿9) 🚗 **P**10 sB153—163 sB🛁🚿215—278 dB191 dB🛁🚿246—336 M101
Credit cards [1] [2] [3] [5]

★★**Sylvia** 9 av de la Gare (n.rest) ☎80910244
rm21 (🛁🚿14) A8rm 🚗 **P**21 sB82—102 sB🛁🚿127—177 dB99—129 dB🛁🚿144—204
Credit cards [1] [3]

★**Jura** 19 r Dr-Robert (n.rest) ☎80912696
rm10 (🛁🚿6) **P**6 sB75—85 sB🛁🚿105—135 dB100—130 dB🛁🚿120—170
Credit cards [1] [3]

🚘 **Berthier** rte de Troyes ☎80910560 Closed Sat pm & Sun Peu

CHATTANCOURT See **VERDUN**

CHAUMONT
Haute-Marne

★★★**Terminus Reine** (BW/MAP) pl du Gl-de-Gaulle ☎25030408 tx840920
rm69 (🛁🚿63) 🚗 **P**20 Lift ☾ sB120—275 sB🛁🚿200—305 dB140—300 dB🛁🚿220—330 M60—200
Credit cards [1] [2] [3] [4] [5]

★★***Étoile d'Or*** LE 103 av de la République ☎25030223
rm16 (🛁🚿10) A4rm **P**

★★**Grand Val** (Inter) rte de Langres (N19) ☎25039035
rm64 (🛁🚿32) 🚗 **P**15 Lift sB102 sB🛁🚿162 dB134 dB🛁🚿190 M45—90
Credit cards [1] [2] [5]

★***France*** 25 r Toupot de Beveaux ☎25030111
rm37 (🛁🚿20)
Credit cards [1] [2] [5]

🚘 **François** rte de Langres ☎25030888 M/c Closed Sat pm & Sun AR

CHAUMONT-SUR-LOIRE
Loir-et-Cher

★★★**Château** LE (**DPn**) r du M-de-L-de-Tassigny ☎54209804
15 Mar—15 Nov
🛁15 **P**15 sB🛁230—330 dB🛁345—549 ≈
Credit cards [1] [2] [3] [5]

CHAUSSÉE-ST-VICTOR See **BLOIS**

CHAUVIGNY
Vienne

★★**Balladins** ZI les Clairs Chênes D974 ☎83576363 tx649394
🛁🚿28 🚗 **P**28 sB🛁🚿166 dB🛁🚿182 M56—77
Credit cards [1] [2] [3]

★**Lion d'Or** LE 8 r Marché ☎49463028
Closed 16 Dec—14 Jan
rm27 (🛁🚿21) A16rm **P**10 sB🛁🚿163 dB134 dB🛁🚿221 Mfr60&alc
Credit card [3]

CHAVAGNÉ See **CRÉCHE (LA)**

CHÊNEHUTTE-LES-TUFFEAUX See **SAUMUR**

CHENONCEAUX
Indre-et-Loire

★★**Bon Laboureur et Château** (N75) ☎47239002
15 Feb—15 Dec
🛁30 🚗 **P**25 sB🛁297—317 dB🛁344—414 M100—200
Credit cards [1] [2] [3] [5]

★**Roy** 9 r Dr-Bretonneau ☎47239017
Feb—Nov
rm42 (🛁🚿24) A12rm **P**30 sB77—106 sB🛁🚿168—196 dB100—122 dB🛁🚿183—258 M45—108
Credit cards [1] [3] [4]

CHENÔVE
Côte-d'Or

★★**Balladins** 18 r J-Moulin ☎80521511 tx649394
🛁🚿36 🚗 **P**36 sB🛁🚿166 dB🛁🚿182 M56—77
Credit cards [1] [2] [3]

CHERBOURG
Manche

See Plan

AA agent; see page 101

★★★**Mercure** Gare Maritime ☎33440111 tx170613 Plan **1**
🛁🚿81 **P**50 Lift sB🛁🚿281—366 dB🛁🚿337—422 sea
Credit cards [1] [2] [3] [5]

★★**Beauséjour** 26 r Grande Vallée (n.rest) ☎33531030 Plan **1A**
rm27 (🛁18) 🚗 ☾ sB71—86 sB🛁133—186 dB98—151 dB🛁147—256
Credit card [3]

★★**Chantereyne** Port de Plaisance (n.rest) ☎33930220 tx171137 Plan **1B**
🛁50 **P**50 ☾ sB🛁270—300 dB🛁290—320 sea
Credit cards [1] [2] [3] [5]

★★***France*** LE 41 r Ml-Foch ☎33531024 tx170764 Plan **2**
8 Jan—20 Dec
rm50 (🛁🚿30) A9rm Lift
Credit card [3]

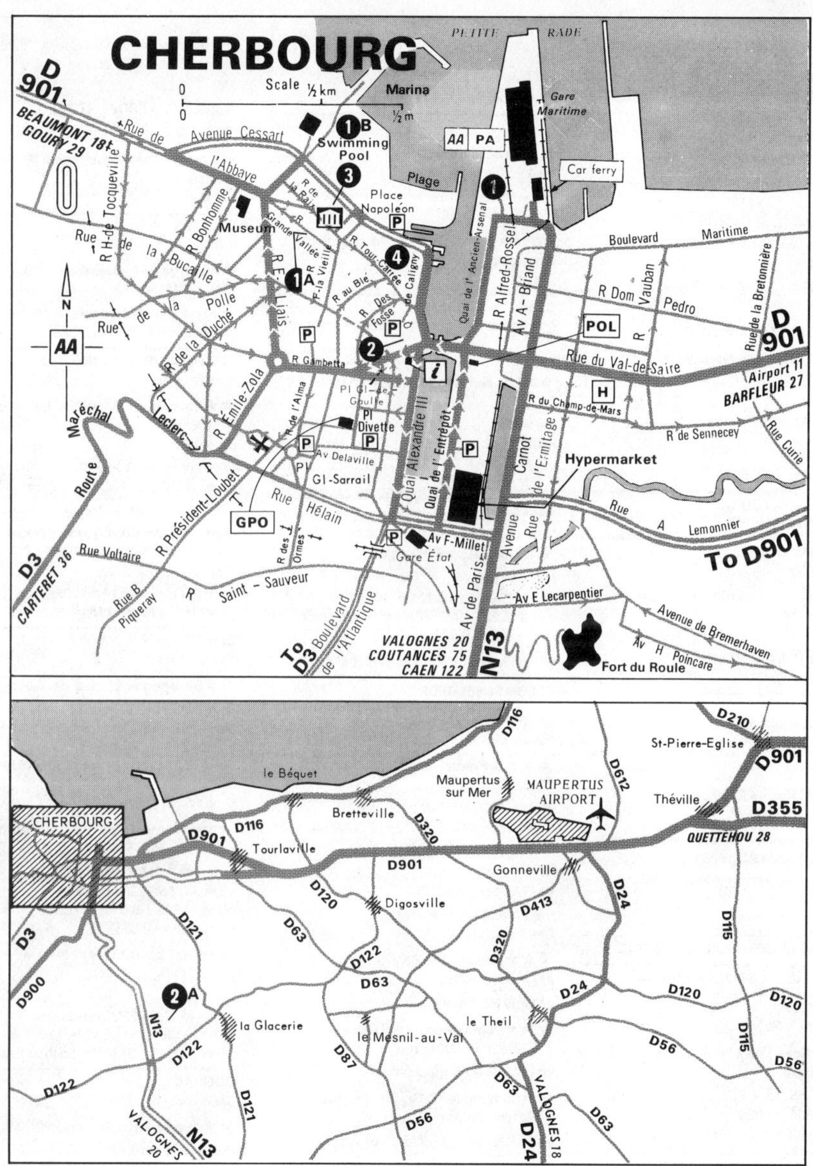

★★**Louvre** 28 r de la Paix (n.rest) ☎33530228 tx171132 Plan **3**

Closed 25 Dec—1Jan
rm42 (🛁 🚿32) 🏠 Lift sB113
sB 🛁 🚿 151—269 dB130 dB 🛁 🚿 168—286
Credit cards [1] [3]

★**Renaissance** 4 r de l'Église ☎33432390 Plan **4**

rm12 (🛁 🚿11) **P**20 ☾ sB109—115
sB 🛁 🚿 139—245 dB 🛁 🚿 158—270 sea

🚗 **Accessoirauto** 124 r du Val de Saire ☎33442591 All makes

🚗 **Rond Point** 5 av A-Briand ☎33536924 Closed Sat pm & Sun AR

At **GLACERIE (LA)** (6km SE via N13)

★★**Campanile** r Montmartre ☎33434343 Plan **2A**

🛁 43 **P** sB 🛁 217—238 dB 🛁 239—260
M61—82
Credit card [3]

CHERBOURG

1	★★★	Mercure
1A	★★	Beauséjour
1B	★★	Chantereyne
2	★★	France
2A	★★	Campanile (At La Glacerie)
3	★★	Louvre
4	★	Renaissance

France

CHILLY-MAZARIN See **PARIS**

CHINON
Indre-et-Loire

★**Boule d'Or** LF 66 quai J-d'Arc ☎47930313
Feb—Nov
rm21 (➡ ⋒ 12) sB85—218 sB ➡ ⋒ fr218 dB113—266 dB ➡ ⋒ fr266 M51—160
Credit cards [1] [2] [3] [4] [5]

★***Gargantua*** 73 r Voltaire ☎47930471
Mar—Jan
rm8 (➡ ⋒ 4) A3rm ⌂ **P**4
Credit cards [2] [3]

At **MARCAY** (7km S on D116)

★★★**Château de Marcay** (Relais et Châteaux) ☎47930347 tx751475
Mar—Jan
➡ ⋒ 38 A11rm **P**60 Lift ☾
sB ➡ ⋒ 450—605 dB ➡ ⋒ 750—1085 M alc
Credit cards [1] [2] [3]

CHISSAY-EN-TOURAINE
See **MONTRICHARD**

CHITENAY
Loir-et-Cher

★***Clé des Champs*** rte de Fougères ☎54704203
Mar—Dec
rm10 (➡ ⋒ 3) **P**40
Credit cards [1] [3]

CHOLET
Maine-et-Loire

★★★***Fimotel*** av Sables d'Olonne (2km S) ☎41624545
rm42 (➡ ⋒ 36) ⌂ **P**100 Lift
Credit cards [2] [3] [5]

★★**Campanile** Parc de Carteron, sq de la Nouvelle France ☎41628679
➡ 43 **P** sB ➡ 217—238 dB ➡ 239—260 M61—82
Credit card [3]

CHONAS-L'AMBALLAN See **VIENNE**

CIBOURNE See **ST-JEAN-DE-LUZ**

CIOTAT (LA)
Bouches-du-Rhône

★★★**Rose Thé** 4 bd Beau Rivage ☎42830923
20 Apr—15 Oct
rm22 (➡ ⋒ 15) **P**25 ☾ sB136—175 sB ➡ ⋒ 166—225 dB162—210 dB ➡ ⋒ 182—290 sea
Credit cards [1] [2] [5]

★★**Rotonde** 44 bd de la République (n.rest) ☎42086750
rm32 (➡ ⋒ 26) **P**8 Lift dB144—174 dB ➡ ⋒ fr224
Credit card [3]

Coussy quartier St-Estève ☎42831809

CIVRIEUX-D'AZERGUES
Rhône

★★***Roseraie*** LF (**DPn**) ☎78430178
rm10 (➡ ⋒ 9) ⌂
Credit card [1]

CLAIRVAUX-LES-LACS
Jura

★**Lac** ☎84255711
Dec—Oct
rm38 (➡ 6) **P**40 dB110 dB ➡ 160 Mfr45 mountains lake
Credit cards [1] [2] [5]

CLAIX See **GRENOBLE**

CLÉCY
Calvados

★★**Site Normand** LF (**DPn**) ☎31697105 tx170234
Mar—Oct
rm12 (➡ ⋒ 10) A5rm **P**30 ☾ dBfr154 dB ➡ ⋒ 216 M73—102
Credit cards [2] [5]

CLELLES
Isère

★★**Ferrat** LF (**Pn**) ☎ 76344270
Feb—11 Nov
➡ ⋒ 17 A10rm ⌂ **P**20 sB ➡ ⋒ 170 dB ➡ ⋒ 220—310 M62—150 mountains
Credit cards [1] [2]

Trieves (N75) ☎76344035 Ren

CLÉON See **ELBEUF**

CLERMONT-FERRAND
Puy-de-Dôme

★★★★**Frantel** 82 bd Gergovia ☎73930575
➡ 124 ⌂ **P** Lift sB ➡ 352—378 dB ➡ 426—474 M117
Credit cards [1] [2] [3] [5]

★★★***Colbert*** (MAP) 19 r Colbert (n.rest) ☎73932566 tx990125
rm62 (➡ ⋒ 46) ⌂ **P**30 Lift
Credit cards [1] [2] [3] [5]

★★★***Gallieni*** 51 r Bonnabaud ☎73935969 tx392779
➡ ⋒ 80 **P** Lift mountains

★★★***PLM Arverne*** 16 pl Delille ☎73919206 tx392741
➡ ⋒ 57 ⌂ **P** Lift mountains

★★**Campanile** r C-Guichard ☎73918891 tx394166
➡ 43 **P** sB ➡ 204—225 dB ➡ 226—247 M61—82
Credit card [3]

★★***Minimes*** (Inter) 10 r des Minimes (n.rest) ☎73933149
rm28 (➡ 13) ☾ mountains
Credit cards [1] [2] [3] [5]

★**Foch** 22 r Ml-Foch (n.rest) ☎73934840
rm19 (⋒ 15) **P** dB85 dB⋒ 105—119
Credit cards [1] [2]

★**Ravel** (FAH) 8 r de Maringues (n.rest) ☎73915133
rm20 (➡ ⋒ 11) dB122 dB ➡ ⋒ 142—192

Auvergne Auto 4 r B-Palissy, Zi du Brézet ☎73917656 Closed Sat & Sun Ope Vau

At **AULNAT AÉROPORT** (5km E)

★★**Climat** ☎73927202 tx392724
➡ 42 **P**15 sB ➡ 208 dB ➡ 237 M51—89 mountains
Credit cards [1] [3]

CLISSON
Loire-Atlantique

★**Auberge de la Cascade** Gervaux ☎40780241
rm10 (➡ ⋒ 6) **P**50 Lift dB87—103 dB ➡ ⋒ 156—181 Mfr45 lake

CLOYES-SUR-LE-LOIR
Eure-et-Loire

★★**St-Jacques** (FAH) 35 r Nationale ☎37985008
Feb—Nov
rm20 (➡ ⋒ 18) ⌂ **P**25 dB224—254 dB ➡ ⋒ 299—314 M135—250
Credit cards [1] [2] [3] [5]

★**St-Georges** (**DPn**) 13 r du Temple ☎37985436
3 Jan—Nov
rm10 (➡ ⋒ 6) ⌂ **P**14 dB128—139 dB ➡ ⋒ 171 M50—115

CLUNY
Saône-et-Loire

★★**Bourgogne** (**DPn**) pl de l'Abbaye ☎85590058
Mar—15 Nov
rm18 (➡ ⋒ 16) ⌂ **P**15 sBfr179 sB ➡ ⋒ 274—317 dB ➡ ⋒ 306—379 M160—280
Credit cards [1] [2] [3] [5]

★★**Moderne** (**DPn** in season) Pont de l'Étang ☎85590565
rm15 (➡ ⋒ 9) **P**6 sB102—123 sB ➡ ⋒ 165—220 dB131—143 dB ➡ ⋒ 205—240 M80—150
Credit cards [1] [2] [3] [5]

★**Abbaye** LF (**DPn**) av de la Gare ☎85591114
Mar—Nov
rm18 (➡ ⋒ 9) ⌂ **P**20 sB91—181 sB ➡ ⋒ 136—181 dB112—132 dB ➡ ⋒ 152—197 M75—95 mountains

COGNAC
Charente

★★***Auberge*** 13 r Plumejeau ☎45320870
rm25 (➡ ⋒ 20)
Credit cards [1] [3]

★★**Moderne** LF 24 r E-Mousnier, pl de la S-Préfecture (n.rest) ☎45821953
10 Jan—20 Dec
➡ 40 ⌂ **P**15 Lift sB ➡ 158—208 dB ➡ 176—246
Credit cards [1] [3] [5]

At **ST-LAURENT-DE-COGNAC** (6km W)

★★**Logis de Beaulieu** LF (**DPn**) (N141) ☎45823050 tx791020
Jan—23 Dec
rm21 (➡ ⋒ 16) ⌂ **P** ☾ sB129—320

sB🛁🚿160—320 dB159—466
dB🛁🚿190—466 M94—150&alc
Credit cards [1] [2] [3] [5]

COGOLIN
Var

🚚 **Finet** quartier Font-Mourier ☎94560412
Closed Dec & Sun For

COL DE CUREBOURSE See **VIC-SUR-CÊRE**

COLLIOURE
Pyrénées-Orientales

★★**Madeloc** (Inter) av R-Rolland (n.rest)
☎68820756

May—15 Oct
🛁🚿22 **P**18 sB🛁🚿224—310
dB🛁🚿248—335 mountains
Credit cards [2] [3] [5]

COLLONGES-LA-ROUGE
Corrèze

★***Relais St-Jacques de Compostelle***
☎55254102

rm17 (🛁🚿7) **P**3
Credit cards [3]

COLMAR
Haut-Rhin

★★★**Champs de Mars** (ETAP) 2 av de la Marne (n.rest) ☎89415454 tx880928

🛁75 🏠**P**20 Lift sB🛁290 dB🛁310
Credit cards [1] [2] [3] [5]

★★★**Novotel** 49 rte de Strasbourg
☎89414914 tx880915

🛁66 **P** sB🛁310 dB🛁369 〰 mountains
Credit cards [1] [2] [3] [5]

★★★**Terminus Bristol** (BW/MAP) 7 pl de la Gare ☎89235959

🛁🚿70 **P**50 Lift ☾ sB🛁🚿385—390
dB🛁🚿470—740 M180—315
Credit cards [1] [2] [3] [5]

★★**Campanile** r des Frères Lumière, ZI Nord ☎89241818 tx880867

🛁42 **P** sB🛁207—238 dB🛁230—261
M61—82
Credit card [3]

★★**Climat** r de la 1ère Armée Francaise
☎89411110

🛁42 **P**15 sB🛁205—230 dB🛁225—250
M51—67
Credit cards [1] [3]

★★**Turenne** 10 rte Bâle (n.rest)
☎89411226 tx880959

🛁🚿72 🏠**P**25 Lift sB🛁🚿fr120
dB🛁🚿154—189
Credit cards [1] [2] [3] [4]

At **AMMERSCHWIHR** (7km NW)

★**Arbre Vert** LF (**DPn**) r des Cigognes
☎89471223

Apr—Jan
rm13 (🛁🚿10) sB76 sB🛁🚿146
dB🛁🚿202 M60—190

At **KAYSERSBERG** (1km NW)

★★**Remparts** LF r de la Flieh (n.rest)
☎89471212

🛁24 A6🛁 🏠**P**20 sB🛁140—180
dB🛁220—230 mountains

France

COLOMBEY-LES-DEUX-ÉGLISES
Haute-Marne

★★★**Dhuits** LF (BW/MAP) N19
☎25015010 tx840920

10 Jan—20 Dec
🛁30 🏠**P**60 sB🛁fr180 dB🛁fr200 Mfr80
Credit cards [1] [2] [3] [5]

COLOMBIER See **FRÉJUS**

COLOMIERS
Haute-Garonne

★★**Fimotel** pl de la Gare, rte d'Auch
☎61789292 tx531782

🛁42 **P**50 Lift sB🛁226—243
dB🛁260—277 M52—85
Credit cards [1] [2] [3] [5]

COMBEAUFONTAINE
Haute-Saône

★**Balcon** LF rte de Paris ☎84921113

rm26 (🛁🚿15) 🏠**P**10 sBfr100 dB120—170
dB🛁🚿140—190 M65—240
Credit cards [1] [2] [3] [5]

COMBOURG
Ille-et-Vilaine

★★**Châteaux et Voyageurs** LF (FAH) (**DPn**) 1 pl Châteaubriand ☎99730038

25 Jan—15 Dec
rm33 (🛁🚿19) A9rm 🏠**P**12 sB90—290
sB🛁🚿131—320 dB110—340 M55—250
lake
Credit cards [1] [2] [3] [5]

COMBRONDE
Puy-de-Dôme

★***Family*** ☎73971001

15 Nov—15 Oct
rm18 (🚿4) **P**

COMMERCY
Meuse

★★***Stanislas*** LF 13 r R-Grosdidier
☎299911236

🛁32 A5rm Lift

COMPIÈGNE
Oise

★★**Campanile** av de Huy ☎44204235
tx150088

🛁43 **P** sB🛁157—238 dB🛁239—260
M61—82
Credit card [3]

★★**Harlay** 3 r Harlay (n.rest) ☎44230150

6 Jan—23 Dec
🛁🚿20 **P** Lift sB🛁🚿205
dB🛁🚿290—320
Credit cards [1] [2] [3] [5]

★★**Ibis** 18 r E-Branly, quartier de l'Université ☎44231627 tx145991

🛁40 sB🛁117 dB🛁180
Credit cards [1] [3]

Sova Autos 23 r du Bataillion de France
☎44403307 Closed Sat pm & Sum AR Toy Vol

Thiry Centre C-de-Venette ☎44400992
Closed Sat pm & Sun Aud VW

At **MARGNY** (2km W on D935)

🚚 **Sarl Depan'Nord** 2 r d'A-Lorraine
☎44832884 All makes

CONCARNEAU
Finistère

★★**Grand** 1 av P-Guéguen (n.rest)
☎98970028

Etr—Oct
rm33 (🛁🚿22) **P**10 ☾ sB116—126
sB🛁🚿156—226 dB147—170
dB🛁🚿176—277 sea

★★**Sables Blancs** LF Plage des Sables
☎98970139

20 Mar—7 Nov
rm48 (🛁🚿42) A10rm sB127—277
sB🛁🚿177—197 dB199—220
dB🛁🚿224—294 M65—160 sea
Credit cards [1] [2] [3] [5]

CONCHE-DE-NAUZAN See **ROYAN**

CONDOM
Gers

🚚 **C Durrieu** 20 bd St-Jacques ☎62280053
Closed Sat pm, Sun & Mon am Tal

CONDRIEU
Rhône

★★★**Beau Rivage** (Relais et Châteaux) quai St-Abdon ☎74595224 tx308946

15 Feb—5 Jan
🛁🚿26 A18rm 🏠**P** sB🛁🚿266
dB🛁🚿452—672 M207—297
Credit cards [1] [2] [3] [5]

CONFLANS-STE-HONORINE
Yvelines

★★**Campanile** r des Frères Dammes
☎39192100 tx699149

🛁50 **P** sB🛁217—238 dB🛁240—261
M61—82
Credit card [3]

CONFOLENS
Charente

★**Auberge Belle Etoile** LF (**DPn**) 151 bis rte Angoulême ☎45840235

rm14 (🛁🚿6) 🏠**P**

CONQUES
Aveyron

★**Ste-Foy** ☎65698403

Apr—15 Oct
🛁🚿20 🏠**P**10 sB🛁🚿128—278
dB🛁🚿176—356 M85—150

CONTAMINE-SUR-ARVE See **BONNEVILLE**

CONTRES
Loir-et-Cher

★★**France** LF 33 r P-H-Mauger
☎54795014

Closed Feb
rm42 (🛁🚿30) **P** dB88—107
dB🛁🚿122—227 M61 🔑

CONTREXEVILLE
Vosges

★★**Douze Apôtres** 25 r G-Thomson ☎29080412

Apr—15 Oct
rm38 (25) A12rm P7 sBfr120 sB fr200 dBfr140 dB fr220 M70—100

COQUILLE (LA)
Dordogne

★★**Voyageurs** r de la République (N21) ☎53528013

Apr—Oct
rm10 (7) **P**10 sBfr121 sB 151—171 dBfr152 dB 172—227 M57—175
Credit cards 1 2 3 5

CORBEIL-ESSONNES
Essonne

See also **EVRY**

★★**Campanile** av P-Mantenant ☎60894145 tx600934

50 **P** sB 217—238 dB 240—261 M61—82
Credit card 3

Diffusion-Auto-Européenne 27 bd de Fontainebleau ☎60891414 Closed Sat pm & Sun Aud VW

Grand Garage Feray 46 av du Mai 1945 ☎60889200 Closed Sat pm & Sun Ren

At **PLESSIS-CHENET (LE)** (4km S)

★★**Climat** 2 r Panhard ☎64938536 tx692844

50 **P**200 dB 226—238 M51—85
Credit cards 1 3 4

CORDES
Tarn

★★★***Grand-Ecuyer*** Voltaire ☎63560103

Apr—15 Oct
Credit cards 2 3 5

CORPS
Isère

★★**Poste** (**DPn**) pl de la Mairie ☎76300003

15 A5rm sB 154—189 dB178—254 dB 178—254 M63—160 mountains

R Rivière pl Napoléon ☎76300113 M/c Peu Ren

CORSE (CORSICA)

PORTICCIO *Corse du Sud*

★★★★**Sofitel Porticcio** Pointe de Porticcio ☎95250034 tx460708

100 **P**100 Lift sB 470—1180 dB 660—1780 M195—215 Beach sea
Credit cards 1 2 3 5

PORTO-VECCHIO *Corse du Sud*

★★★**Ziglione** (5km E on N198) ☎95700983

15 May—15 Sep
32 **P DPn**400—475 Beach sea

France

COSNE-SUR-LOIRE
Nièvre

★★***Grand Cerf*** 43 r St-Jaques ☎86280446

10 Jan—10 Dec
rm20 (12)
Credit cards 1 3

★***Vieux Relais*** (**DPn**) 11 r St-Agnan ☎86282021

Feb—24 Dec
rm11 (10)

COULANDON See **MOULINS**

COURBEVOIE
Hauts-de-Seine

★★★**Novotel Paris La Défense** 2 bd de Neuilly, Défensei ☎47781668 tx630288

276 **P** Lift sB 563 dB 636

★★★**Paris Penta** 18 r Baudin ☎47885051 tx610470

494 **P**40 Lift sB 434—445 dB 477—499 M35—55
Credit cards 1 2 3 4 5

COUR-CHEVERNY
Loir-et-Cher

★★***St-Hubert*** (Inter) (**DPn**) ☎54799660

20 **P**

★★***Trois Marchands*** (FAH) (**DPn**) 3 pl Église ☎54799644

rm44 (23) **P**

COURSEULLES-SUR-MER
Calvados

★★**Cremaillere** bd de la Plage ☎31374673 tx171952

34 A25rm **DPn**205
Credit cards 1 2 3 5

COURTABOEUF See **ORSAY**

COURTENAY
Loiret

ACA rte de Sens ☎38974371 Closed Mon Peu

Chenardière rte de Sens ☎38974185 Tal

P Vinot Esso Station, rte de Sens ☎38973003 Closed Sun Fia Lan

COURTISOLS See **CHÂLONS-SUR-MARNE**

COUSOLRE
Nord

★★***Viennois*** (N49) ☎20632173

10 **P**

COUTAINVILLE
Manche

★**Hardy** (**DPn**) pl 28 Juillet ☎33470411

10 Feb—10 Jan
13 sB 172 dB 164—191

M64—200
Credit cards 1 2 3 4 5

COUTANCES
Manche

★**Moderne** (Inter) 25 bd Alsace-Lorraine ☎33451377

15 Jan—15 Dec
rm17 (2) **P**10 dB100—113 dB 152 M54—79
Credit cards 1 3

CRÉCHE (LA)
Deux-Sèvres

★★**Campanile** rte de Paris ☎49255622 tx791216

47 sB 198—219 dB 221—242 M61—82
Credit card 3

At **CHAVAGNE** (4km SW)

★★★***Rocs*** ☎49255038 tx790632

51 **P**

CRÈCHES-SUR-SAÔNE See **MÂCON**

CREIL
Oise

★★**Climat** r H-Bessemer ☎44244692 tx692844

42 **P**30 sB 213—235 dB 233—255 M51—67
Credit cards 1 3

Central 90 r J-Jaurès ☎44554197 Closed Sat & Sun AR

CRESSENSAC
Lot

★**Chez Gilles** (N20) ☎65377006

rm25 (12) A19rm sB130—212 sB 190—222 dB160—269 dB 210—269 M72—165

CRÉTEIL See **PARIS**

CREUSOT (LE)
Saône-et-Loire

At **MONTCHANIN** (8km E off D28)

★★★***Novotel*** r du Pont J-Rose ☎85557211 tx800588

87 Lift
Credit cards 1 2 3 5

At **TORCY** (4km SE)

★★**Fimotel** bd de Beaubourg ☎42615014 tx215269

42 **P** Lift
Credit cards 1 2 3 5

CRIEL-SUR-MER
Seine-Maritime

★★**Hostellerie de la Vielle Ferme** (**DPn**) 23 r de la Mer ☎35867218

Feb—2 Jan
rm36 (31) **P** sB185—215 sB 185—215 dB240—325 dB 240—325 M100—200

CROIX-VALMER
Var

★★***Mer*** (2.5km SE on N559) ☎94796961

Apr—Sep
rm31 (🛁 🚿 27) **P** ≈ Beach mountains

CROS-DE-CAGNES See **CAGNES-SUR-MER**

CROUZILLE (LA)
Haute-Vienne

At **NANTIAT**

★★***Relais St-Europe*** ☎55399121
rm25 (🛁 20) **P**50 mountains

CUVILLY See **RESSONS-SUR-MATZ**

DAMMARIE-LES-LYS See **MELUN**

DANJOUTIN See **BELFORT**

DARDILLY See **LYON**

DEAUVILLE
Calvados

★★★★★**Normandy** r J-Mermoz ☎31880921 tx170617
🛁 300 Lift ☾ sB 🛁 690—1350 dB 🛁 790—1350 M175 ⊡ Beach sea
Credit cards [1] [2] [3] [5]

★★★★★**Royal** ☎31881641 tx170549
Etr—Oct
rm314 (🛁 🚿 285) **P**180 Lift ☾ sB 🛁 🚿 540—1400 dB 🛁 🚿 640—1400 M175 s15% t5% ≈ ⊡ Beach sea
Credit cards [1] [2] [3] [5]

★★★**Golf** Centre du New Golf ☎31881901 tx170448
May—Sep
🛁 170 **P**150 Lift ☾ sB 🛁 🚿 475—725 dB 🛁 🚿 530—790 M155—170 🎾 ≈ ⊡
Credit cards [1] [2] [3] [4] [5]

★★★**PLM Port Deauville** bd Cornuché ☎31886262 tx170364
🛁 73 **P**50 Lift sB 🛁 262—362 dB 🛁 374—524 sea
Credit cards [1] [2] [3] [5]

★★**Ibis** 9 quai de la Marine ☎31983090 tx171295
🛁 94 **P** Lift sB 🛁 278—300 dB 🛁 326—350 M70—105 t% sea

At **TOUQUES** (2.5km S)

★★★**Amirauté** (N834) ☎31889062 tx171665
🛁 121 **P**300 Lift dB 🛁 504—559 🎾 ≈
Credit cards [1] [2] [3] [5]

DIEPPE
Seine-Maritime

See Plan page 142

[AA] agent; see page 101

★★★★**Présidence** 1 bd de Verdun ☎35843131 tx180865 Plan **1**
rm89 (🛁 🚿 80) 🚗 **P**52 Lift ☾ sBfr228 sB 🛁 🚿 300—377 dBfr291 dB 🛁 🚿 357—451 M alc sea
Credit cards [1] [2] [3] [5]

★★★**Aguado** 30 bd de Verdun (n.rest) ☎35842700 Plan **2**
🛁 🚿 56 Lift ☾ sB 🛁 🚿 217—292 dB 🛁 🚿 318—368 sea

France

★★**Ibis Dieppe** le Val Druel ☎35826530 tx180067 Not on plan
🛁 43 **P**60 sB 🛁 179—199 dB 🛁 218—249
Credit cards [1] [3]

★★**Select** 1 r Toustain, pl de la Barre (n.rest) ☎35841466 Plan **4**
rm25 (🛁 23) A3rm **P** Lift
Credit cards [2] [3]

★★**Windsor** LF (**Pn** in season) 18 bd de Verdun ☎35841523 tx770741 Plan **6**
17 Dec—11 Nov
rm47 (🛁 41) **P**10 Lift ☾ sB111—142 sB 🛁 209—254 dB129—160 dB 🛁 227—272 M79—95 sea
Credit cards [1] [2] [3] [4] [5]

DIGNE
Alpes-de-Haute-Provence

★★**Algion** LF (**Pn**) 1 r de Provence ☎92310270 tx430605
Feb—Nov
rm33 (🛁 🚿 15) A9rm **P**10 sB106—116 sB 🛁 🚿 141—156 dB139—152 dB 🛁 🚿 204—215 M53—140 mountains
Credit cards [1] [2] [3] [4]

★★**Mistre** 65 bd Gassendi ☎92310016
Closed Dec
🛁 🚿 19 🚗 Lift sB 🛁 🚿 238—298 dB 🛁 🚿 266—386 M120—220 mountains
Credit cards [1] [2] [3]

🚘 **P Touret** pl du Gl-de-Gaulle ☎310423 Closed Sun Ope

DIGOIN
Saône-et-Loire

★***Gare*** 79 av Gl-de-Gaulle ☎85530304
Feb—Dec
🛁 🚿 13 A4rm **P**18
Credit cards [2] [3] [5]

★***Terminus*** (**DPn**) 76 av de Gl-de-Gaulle ☎85531726
Closed 7 Jan—7 Feb
rm17 (🛁 🚿 6) 🚗 **P**20
Credit cards [1] [2] [3]

DIJON
Côte-d'Or

★★★★**Cloche** 14 pl Darcy ☎80301232 tx350498
🛁 80 🚗 **P** Lift sB 🛁 335—415 dB 🛁 435—480

★★★★***Frantel*** 22 bd de la Marne ☎80723113 tx350293
🛁 124 🚗 Lift ≈
Credit cards [1] [2] [3] [5]

★★★**Chapeau Rouge** (BW/MAP) 5 r Michelet ☎80302810 tx350535
🛁 🚿 33 Lift ☾ sB 🛁 🚿 310—425 dB 🛁 🚿 425—495 Mfr150
Credit cards [1] [2] [3] [5]

★★★***Ibis Central*** 3 pl Grangier ☎80304400 tx350606
🛁 🚿 90 Lift ☾
Credit cards [1] [3] [5]

★★**Hostellerie du Sauvage** 64 r Monge ☎80413121
rm22 (🛁 🚿 15) 🚗 **P**14 sB85—178 sB 🛁 🚿 178 dBfr98 dB 🛁 🚿 191—256
Credit card [3]

★★***Jura*** (Inter) 14 av Ml-Foch (n.rest) ☎80416112 tx350485
rm65 (🛁 🚿 64) A10rm 🚗 **P**40 Lift ☾
Credit cards [1] [2] [3] [5]

★**Nord** 2 r Liberté ☎80305858 tx351554
14 Jan—23 Dec
rm24 (🛁 🚿 16) sB105—120 sB 🛁 🚿 151—252 dBfr136 dB 🛁 🚿 268—440
Credit cards [1] [2] [3] [5]

🚘 **Depan-Auto** 22 r de l'Égalité ☎80415727 All makes

🚘 **J Faisca** 5 bis av Garibaldi ☎80734690 Closed Aug 15—30 & Sun Ope

🚘 **Lignier** 3 r des G-Champs ☎80663905 All makes

At **HAUTEVILLE-LÈS-DIJON** (7km NE on D107)

★**Musarde** (**DPn** in season) LF ☎80562282
rm11 (🛁 🚿 8) **P**10 sB 🛁 🚿 129—150 dB 🛁 🚿 165—200 M60—100
Credit cards [1] [3] [5]

At **PERRIGNY-LÈS-DIJON** (9km S on N74)

★★★***Novotel Dijon Sud*** rte de Beaune (N74) ☎80521422 tx350728
🛁 124 **P**200
Credit cards [1] [2] [3] [5]

★★**Ibis** rte de Lyon-Beaune ☎80528645 tx351510
🛁 48 **P**70 sB 🛁 195—215 dB 🛁 243—263 Mfr70
Credit cards [1] [3]

At **QUÉTIGNY** (5km E via CD 107b)

★★***Climat*** 14 av de Bourgogne ☎80460446 tx692844
🛁 42 **P**
Credit cards [1] [3]

At **ST-APOLLINAIRE** (3km E)

★★**Campanile** rte de Gray ☎80724538 tx350566
🛁 50 **P** sB 🛁 204—225 dB 🛁 226—247 M61—82
Credit card [3]

At **SENNECEY-LE-DIJON** (3km SW)

★★★***Flambée*** (BW/MAP) rte de Genève ☎80473535 tx350273
🛁 🚿 23 **P**40 Lift
Credit cards [1] [2] [5]

DINAN
Côtes-du-Nord

★★**Avaugour** LF 1 pl du Champs Clos ☎99390749
🛁 🚿 27 Lift sB 🛁 🚿 240—285 dB 🛁 🚿 305—370

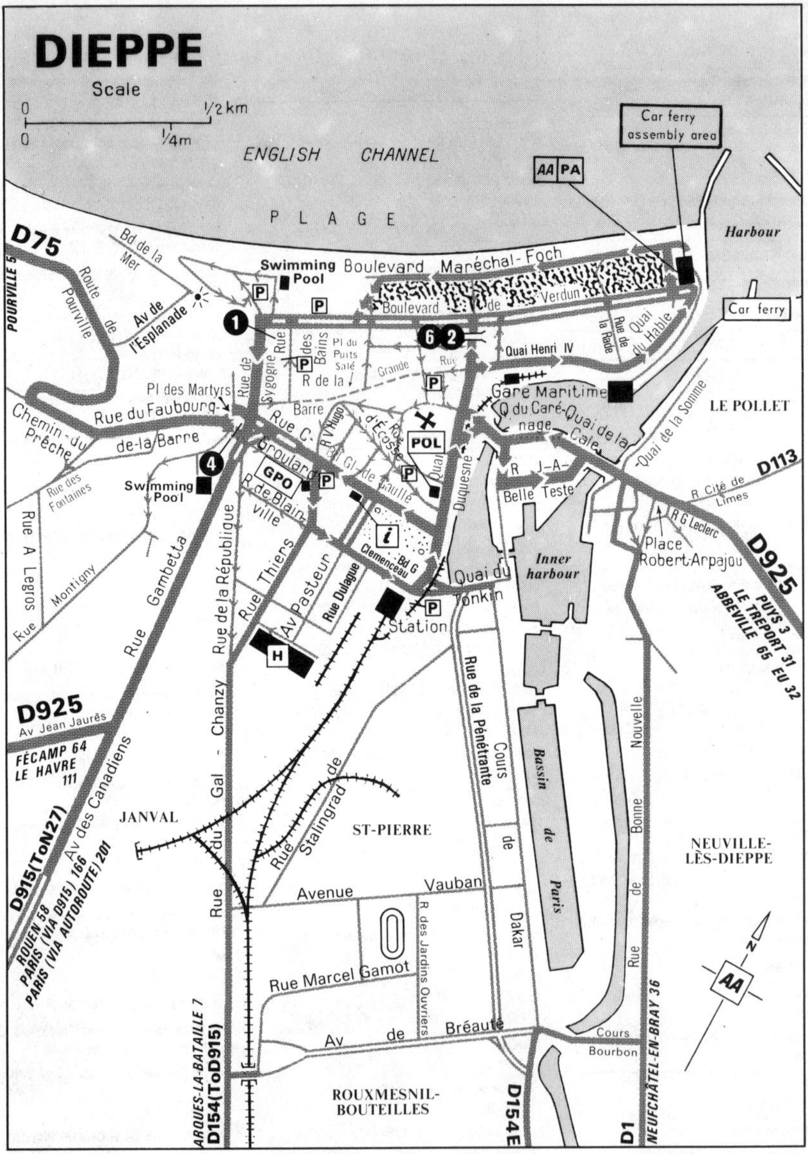

DIEPPE

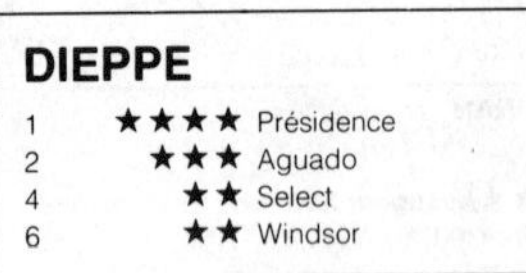

DIEPPE

1	★★★★	Présidence
2	★★★	Aguado
4	★★	Select
6	★★	Windsor

DINARD
Ille-et-Vilaine

★★★★***Grand*** 46 av George-V ☏99461028 tx740522
Apr—Oct
🛁 🚿100 **P**80 Lift ☾ sea
Credit cards [1] [2] [3] [5]

★★**Bains** 38 av George-V ☏99461371 tx740802
15 Mar—Oct
rm39 (🛁 🚿35) Lift sB108—138 sB🛁 🚿178 dB156 dB🛁 🚿236—296 M90 sea
Credit cards [2] [3]

★★**Climat** la Millière ☏99466955 tx740300
🛁26 **P**30 sB🛁225—240 dB🛁245—260 M51—120 sea
Credit cards [1] [3]

★★**Dunes** LF 5 r G-Clemenceau ☏99461272
Mar—Oct
rm32 (🛁 🚿20) sB92—94 dB154—157

dB ⛽ 230—289 M50—102
Credit cards 1 2 3 5

★★**Emeraude Plage** 1 bd Albert Ier ☎99461579 tx740802
Apr—Sep
rm59 (46) A5rm P5 Lift ☾ sB106—116 sB 216—266 dB192—232 dB 262—412 M100—120

★★***Printania*** **(DPn)** 5 av George-V ☎99461307
Etr—Sep
77 A30rm sea
Credit cards 2 3

Parc 10 r Y-Verney ☎99461338 Closed Oct 1—15, Sat pm & Sun AR

DOLANCOURT
Aube

★★**Moulin du Landion** LE **(DPn)** ☎25261217
4 Jan—20 Nov
16 **P**30 sB 215 dB 245 M90—170
Credit cards 1 3 5

DOL-DE-BRETAGNE
Ille-et-Vilaine

★★**Bresche Arthur** LE **(Pn** in season) (Inter) bd Deminiac ☎99480144 tx730808
rm25 (23) **P**12 sB135 sB 205 dB230 dB 250 M65—200
Credit cards 1 2 3 4 5

★★**Bretagne** LE 17 pl Châteaubriand ☎99480203
rm29 (12) sB73—85 sB 104—150 dB91—104 dB 129—184 M48—85
Credit card 3

DOLE
Jura

★★★***Chandioux*** (BW/MAP) pl Grévy ☎84790066 tx360498
33 **P**23 ☾
Credit cards 1 2 3 4 5

G Cuynet 8 r Sombardier ☎84822111 Closed Aug 8—15, Sep & Sun Aud VW

DOMFRONT
Orne

★★**Poste** LE **(DPn)** 15 r Ml-Foch ☎33385100
Closed 16 Jan—24 Feb
rm29 (14) **P**22 sB82 sB 162 dB109 dB 199 Mfr58
Credit cards 1 2 5

★**France** LE r Mont-St-Michel ☎33385144
Closed 5 Jan—9 Feb
rm22 (7) **P**25 sB98 sB 128—186 dB114 dB 144—202 M45—90
Credit cards 1 3

DOMPAIRE
Vosges

★★**Commerce** LE pl Ml-Leclerc ☎29365028
11 sB 125—157 dB 150—183 Mfr45
Credit cards 1 2 3 4 5

France

DOMRÉMY-LA-PUCELLE
Vosges

★***Basilique*** **(DPn)** le Bois Chenu (1.5km S by D53) ☎29940781 tx88300
Closed Jan
rm28 (7) **P**

DONZENAC
Corrèze

A Chamournie av de Paris ☎55857237 Closed Sat pm & Sun Cit Tal

At **ST-PARDOUX L'ORTIGLER** (9km N off N20)

M Dely (N20) ☎55857341 Closed Oct, Sun pm & Mon Peu

DONZÈRE
Drôme

Porte Provence quartier Greo (N7) ☎75986052 Closed Sat & Sun All makes

Renault 55 B-Bourgade ☎75516109 Closed Sun pm Ren

Sud (N7) ☎75986074 All makes

R Thomas 36 B-Bourgade ☎75986160 Peu

DORDIVES
Loiret

★★**César** LE 8 r de la République (n.rest) ☎38927320
rm24 (16) **P**24 ☾ sB68—212 dB 97—274

DOUAI
Nord

★★**Climat** pl P-Brossolette ☎27882997 tx692844
42 **P** sB 227—246 dB 247—266 M52—90
Credit cards 1 3

★★**Grand Cerf** 46 r St-Jacques ☎27887960
rm36 (26) **P**12 ☾ sB103 sB fr167 dBfr184 dB fr172 Mfr74
Credit cards 1 2

DOUARENEZ
Finistère

★★**Bretagne** LE 23 r Duguay-Trouin (n.rest) ☎98923044 tx29100
rm27 (23) Lift sB111—179 sB 166—179 dB127—207 dB 189—207

DOUÉ-LA-FONTAINE
Maine-et-Loire

★**Dagobert** LE **(DPn)** 14 pl Champ-de-Foire ☎41591444
Closed Dec & Jan
rm20 (8) **P** sBfr74 sB 95—126 dB86—107 dB 107—191 M43—125
Credit card 3

DOURDAN
Essonne

★★★**Blanche de Castille** pl des Halles ☎64596892 tx690902
40 **P**40 Lift sB 230—285 dB 310—370 Mfr250
Credit cards 1 2 3 5

DOUSSARD See **FAVERGES**

DOZULÉ
Calvados

R Marci fbg du Pont Mousse ☎31792041 Closed Sep, Sat pm & Sun Peu

St-Christophe 102 Grande Rue ☎31792036 Closed 1—15 Sep & Sun Ren

DRAGUIGNAN
Var

★★**Col de l'Ange** (Inter) rte de Lorgues ☎94682301 tx970423
30 A2rm **P**50 dB 300—450 mountains
Credit cards 1 2 3 5

Sodra ZI rte de Lorgues ☎94688244 Closed Sat & Sun Aud VW

DRAMONT (LE) See **AGAY**

DREUX
Eure-et-Loire

★★**Aub Normande** LE 12 pl Metezeau ☎37500203
16 **P** ☾ sB 169—179 dB 187—197 M70
Credit cards 1 2 3 4 5

★★**Climat** r du Nuisement ☎37467541 tx692844
26 **P** sB 212—238 dB 234—260 M51—90
Credit cards 1 3

Ouest 51 av des Fenots ☎37461145 Closed Aug AR

At **MONTREUIL** (8km NE)

★★***Auberge Gué des Grues*** ☎37435025
3 2 **P** Lift

DUCLAIR
Seine-Maritime

★★**Poste (DPn)** LE 286 quai de la Liberation ☎35375004
20 sB 109—149 dB 138—168 M50—130
Credit cards 1 2 3

DUNKERQUE (DUNKIRK)
Nord

★★★★**Frantel** r J-Jaurès (n.rest) ☎28591111 tx110587
126 **P**5 sB 273—330 dB 331—396 sea
Credit cards 1 2 3 4 5

★★★**Borel** (Inter) 6 r l'Hermitte (n.rest) ☎28665180 tx820050
40 Lift sB 240 dB 290
Credit cards 1 2 3 5

★★★**Europ** (BW/MAP) 13 r de Leughenaer ☎28662907 tx120084 →

🛁 🚿 130 🚗 P30 Lift sB 🛁 🚿 fr268
dB 🛁 🚿 fr336 M86—120
Credit cards 1 2 3 4 5

🚙 **Patfoort** 9 r du Leughenaer ☎28665112
Closed Sat & Sun Fia

At **ARMBOUTS CAPPEL** (6km S)

★★★**Mercure** Voie Express-Bodure du Lac ☎28607060 tx820916

🛁 🚿 64 sB 🛁 🚿 234—315
dB 🛁 🚿 374—388 M70—120 lake
Credit cards 1 2 3 5

ÉCOLE VALENTIN See **BESANÇON**

ÉCOMMOY
Sarthe

★**Commerce** LF (**DPn**) 19 pl République ☎43471034

Closed 16 Sep—14 Oct
rm13 (🚿 6) 🚗 **P**10 sB109 dB148 dB🚿 183 M50—65&alc

ECOUEN
Val d'Oise

★★**Campanile** la Redoute du Moulin (N16) ☎439944600

🛁 50 **P** sB 🛁 217—238 dB 🛁 239—260 M61—82
Credit card 3

ECULLY See **LYON**

EGUILLES See **AIX-EN-PROVENCE**

ELBEUF
Seine-Maritime

At **CLÉON** (5km N over river)

★★***Campanile*** r de l'Église ☎35813800 tx172691
🛁 42
Credit card 3

At **LONDE (LA)** (5km NW on unclass rd off D913)

🚙 **Maison Brulée** ☎35923055 M/c Closed 2 wks Jun & 2nd Tue per month Fia

ELNE
Pyrénées-Orientales

🚙 **R Jammet** 9 bd Voltaire ☎68220858
Closed Sat pm & Sun Peu

🚙 **Mary** 10 av de Perpignan ☎68220101
Closed Sep 8—29, Sat & Sun Cit

ÉMERAINVILLE See **CHAMPS-SUR-MARNE**

ENGLOS See **LILLE**

ÉNTRAYGUES-SUR-TRUYÈRE
Aveyron

★★**Truyère** LF ☎65445110 tx530366

🛁 🚿 26 🚗 P20 Lift sB 🛁 🚿 143—178
dB 🛁 🚿 190—235 M56—130 mountains
Credit cards 1 3

ÉPERNAY
Marne

★★★**Berceaux** 13 r Berceaux ☎26552884

🛁 🚿 29 **P** Lift sB 🛁 🚿 249—329
dB 🛁 🚿 262—354
Credit cards 1 2 3 4 5

France

★★***Pomme d'Or*** 12 r E-Mercier (n.rest) ☎26531144 tx841150

🛁 🚿 26 Lift

★***Europe*** 18 r Porte-Lucas ☎26518028
rm26 (🚿 5) 🚗
Credit cards 1 2 3 5

At **CHAMPILLON** (6km N on N51)

★★★***Royal Champagne*** (Relais et Châteaux) Bellevue ☎26511151 tx830111

🛁 23 **P** ☾
Credit cards 1 2 3 5

At **VINAY** (6km S on N51)

★★★**Briqueterie** rte de Sézanne ☎26541122 tx842007

🛁 🚿 42 **P60** sB 🛁 🚿 260—374
dB 🛁 🚿 314—464
Credit cards 1 2 3 5

ÉPINAL
Vosges

★★★**Mercure** 13 pl Stein ☎29351868 tx960277

🛁 🚿 22 A20(🛁 🚿)rm 🚗 **P** Lift ☾
sB 🛁 🚿 250—365 dB 🛁 🚿 320—460

★★***Résidence*** 39 av des Templiers (n.rest) ☎29824564

Closed Xmas & New Year
🛁 🚿 18 **P**

★***Azur*** 54 quai des Bons Enfants (n.rest) ☎29822915

rm21 (🛁 🚿 7)

At **CHAVELOT** (8km N)

★★***Climat*** ☎29313940

🛁 26

ÉPINAY-SUR-ORGE
Essonne

★★**Campanile** r du Grand Vaux ☎64486020 tx600148

🛁 50 **P** sB 🛁 217—238 dB 🛁 239—260 M61—82
Credit card 3

ÉPINAY-SUR-SEINE
Seine-et-Denis

★★***Ibis*** av du 18 Juin 1940 ☎48298341 tx614354

🛁 64 **P** Lift M alc

ÉPINE (L) See **CHÂLONS-SUR-MARNE**

EPONE
Yvelines

★★***Routel*** (D113) ☎30956870 tx801059

🛁 49 **P** 🎾

EQUEUDREVILLE
Marche

★★**Climat** de la Paix ☎33934294 tx692844

🛁 42 **P50** sB 🛁 fr238 dB 🛁 258 M50—80
Credit cards 1 3

ERDEVEN
Morbihan

★★**Auberge du Sous Bois** LF (**DPn**) (FAH) rte de Pont Lorois ☎97556610 tx950581

15 Apr—15 Oct
🛁 🚿 22 **P50** sB 🛁 🚿 195—217
dB 🛁 🚿 213—235 M56—94
Credit cards 1 2 3 5

ERMENONVILLE
Oise

★★**Aub de la Croix d'Or** LF (**DPn**) 2 r P-Radziwil ☎44540004

8 Feb—15 Dec
rm11 (🛁 9) **P**18 sBfr118 sB 🛁 fr118 dBfr142
dB 🛁 142—195 Mfr84

ERNÉE
Mayenne

★★★**Relais de Poste** LF 1 pl de l'Église ☎43052033 tx730956

🛁 🚿 35 🚗 **P** Lift sB 🛁 🚿 fr191
dB 🛁 🚿 fr237
Credit cards 1 3

ERQUY
Côtes-du-Nord

★***Beauregard*** LF bd de la Mer ☎96723003

rm17 A8rm **P**5 sea
Credit cards 1 3 5

🚙 **P Thomas** 11 de la Corniche ☎96723037 Ren

ÉTAIN
Meuse

🚙 **Beauguitte** 87 r-Poincaré ☎29781290 Ren

🚙 **Boulard** 6 av du Gl-de-Gaulle ☎29871002 M/c Closed Sun Cit

🚙 **R Thevenin** av du Gl-de-Gaulle ☎29871214 Peu

ETSAUT
Pyrénées-Atlantiques

★**Pyrénées** LF (**Pn**) ☎59348862

Closed 21 Nov—21 Dec
rm22 (🛁 🚿 17) 🚗 **P**15 sB78 sB 🛁 🚿 127
dB108 dB 🛁 🚿 141 Mfr55 mountains

EUGÉNIE-LES-BAINS
Landes

★★***Climat*** 4 chemin Communal ☎58511414

🛁 🚿 35 **P40**
Credit cards 1 3

EVIAN-LES-BAINS
Haute-Savoie

★★★★★**Royal** ☎50751400 tx385759

6 Feb—15 Dec
🛁 200 🚗 **P** Lift ☾ sB 🛁 310—1440
dB 🛁 520—1780 M260 🎾 mountains lake
Credit cards 1 2 3 4 5

★★★***Bellevue*** 6 r B-Moutardier ☎50750113

20 May—20 Sep
rm50 (🛁 🚿 49) **P**10 Lift lake
Credit card 2

★★**Mateirons** (Inter) ☎50750416
15 Mar—15 Oct
rm22 (🛁 18) **P** sB🛁 167—177 dB134—144
dB🛁 214—244 Mfr65 mountains lake
Credit card [2]

ÉVREUX
Eure

★★**Climat** Zone tertiaire de la Madelèine ☎32311047
🛁 50 **P**50 sB🛁 216—236 dB🛁 236—256
M52—80
Credit cards [1] [3]

★★***France*** LF 29 r St-Thomas ☎32391337
rm15 (🛁 🚿 11) **P**8
Credit cards [2] [3]

★★**Grenoble** 17 r St-Pierre (n.rest) ☎32330731
Seasonal
rm19 (🛁 🚿 8) 🚗 sB109—129
sB🛁 🚿 149—164 dB🛁 🚿 193—225
Credit card [3]

★★**Ibis** av W-Churchill ☎32381636 tx172748
🛁 60 **P**50 sB🛁 198 dB🛁 245
Credit cards [1] [3]

★★**Normandy** 37 r E-Féray ☎32331440
rm27 (🛁 🚿 28) 🚗 **P**20 sB🛁 🚿 201
dB🛁 🚿 292 M60—200
Credit cards [1] [2] [3] [5]

★★**Orme** LF 13 r Lombards (n.rest) ☎32393412
rm27 (🛁 🚿 18) **P**3 sB103—118 sB🛁 🚿 228
dB125—140 dB🛁 🚿 250
Credit cards [1] [2]

🚗 **Lemoine** 1 r de Cocherel ZI ☎32394073
Closed Sat AR

ÉVRY
Essonne

See also **CORBEIL-ESSONNES**

★★**Balladins** pl G-Crémieux ☎64972121 tx649394
🛁 🚿 28 🚗 **P**28 sB🛁 🚿 166 dB🛁 🚿 182
M56—77
Credit cards [1] [2] [3]

★★**Novotel Paris Évry** (A6) ☎60778270 tx600685
🛁 174 Lift sB🛁 fr347 dB🛁 fr404 ⛱
Credit cards [1] [2] [3] [5]

★★**Arcade** cours B-Pascal, Butte Creuse ☎60782990 tx691249
🚿 100 **P**200 Lift sB🚿 192—198
dB🚿 208—214 Mfr57
Credit cards [1] [3]

★★***Ibis*** 1 av du Lac (n.rest) ☎60777475 tx691728
🛁 82 **P** Lift

EYBENS
Isère

★★**Fimotel** 20 av J-Jaurès ☎76242312 tx980371
🛁 42 **P**39 Lift sB🛁 218—226
dB🛁 247—255 Mfr49 mountains
Credit cards [1] [2] [3] [5]

France

EYZIES-DE-TAYAC (LES)
Dordogne

★★★**Cro-Magnon** (BW/MAP) ☎53069706 tx570637
May—12 Oct
🛁 🚿 27 A12rm **P**30 dB🛁 🚿 252—382
M100—280 ⛱
Credit cards [1] [2] [3] [5]

★★**Centenaire** (Relais et Châteaux) LF ☎53069718
Apr—4 Nov
🛁 🚿 30 A10rm 🚗 **P**22 sB🛁 🚿 240
dB🛁 🚿 330—480 M135—350 ⛱
Credit cards [1] [2] [3] [4] [5]

★★***Centre*** LF les Sireuils ☎53069713
Mar—15 Nov
🛁 18
Credit card [3]

★★**Glycines** ☎53069707
Apr—6 Nov
🛁 25 🚗 **P**60 sB🛁 266—271
dB🛁 302—307 M88—225
Credit cards [2] [3]

★**France — Auberge de Musée** LF **(DPn)** ☎53069723
23 Mar—4 Nov
rm16 (🛁 🚿 9) **P**16 sB84—156
sB🛁 🚿 128—156 dB103—198
dB🛁 🚿 175—198 M62—198 mountains

🚗 **J C Dupuy** pl de la Porte ☎53069732
Ren

ÉZE-BORD-DE-MER
Alpes-Maritimes

★★★★***Cap Estel*** ☎93015044 tx470305
Feb—Oct
🛁 43 **P** Lift ☾ ⛱ Beach sea

★★***Cap Roux*** Basse Corniche (n.rest) ☎93015123
15 Mar—Sep
🛁 🚿 30 **P**25 Lift sea

FALAISE
Calvados

★★**Normandie** 4 r Al-Courbet ☎31901826
rm28 (🛁 🚿 15) 🚗 sB101—116 sB🛁 🚿 141
dB132 dB🛁 🚿 212 M50—70

★★**Poste** LF 38 r G-Clemenceau ☎31901314
rm19 (🛁 🚿 12) 🚗 **P**12 sB108—188
sB🛁 🚿 188 dB125 dB🛁 🚿 205 M50—130

FAOUËT (LE)
Morbihan

★**Croix d'Or (DPn)** 9 pl Bellanger ☎97230733
rm16 (🛁 🚿 4) 🚗 **P** sB67—77
sB🛁 🚿 123—143 dBfr128 dB🛁 🚿 fr147
M38—72&alc

FARLÈDE (LA) See **TOULON**

FAVERGES
Haute-Savoie

★**Parc** rte d'Albertville ☎50445025
🛁 🚿 12 **P**20 sB🛁 🚿 210—250
dB🛁 🚿 240—290 M70—200 mountains
Credit cards [1] [3]

At **DOUSSARD** (7km NW)

★★**Marceau (DPn)** Marceau Dessus (2km W) ☎50443011 tx309346
Feb—Oct
🛁 🚿 18 A3rm 🚗 **P** sB155 dB370—550
dB🛁 🚿 370—550 M92—230 🎾 mountains lake
Credit cards [2] [3]

FAYENCE
Var

🚗 **Difant Georges** quartier Pré-Gaudin ☎94760740 All makes

🚗 **St-Eloy** quartier de la Gare ☎94760072
M/c Fia Mer Por

At **TOURRETTES** (1km W)

★**Grillon** (N562) ☎94760296
🚿 28 **P**30 ☾ sB🚿 fr167 dB🚿 fr220 ⛱
mountains
Credit cards [1] [3]

FÈRE (LA)
Aisne

★**Tourelles** (n.rest) 51 r de la République ☎23563166
rm16 (🛁 🚿 8) 🚗 **P**13 sB67—70 dB94—105
dB🛁 🚿 137—155
Credit cards [1] [2] [3]

FÈRE-EN-TARDENOIS
Aisne

★★★★**Château (DPn)** (Relais et Châteaux) ☎23822113 tx145526
Closed Feb
🛁 23 **P**100 sB🛁 fr452 dB🛁 fr564
M240—360 🎾 ⛱
Credit cards [1] [2]

FERNEY VOLTAIRE See **GENEVA AIRPORT** Switzerland

FERTÉ-BERNARD (LA)
Sarthe

★★***Climat*** 43 bd Gl-de-Gaulle ☎43938470
🛁 26 **P**

FERTÉ-ST-AUBIN (LA)
Loiret

★★**Perron** (FAH) 9 r du Gl-Leclerc ☎38765336
Closed 15—30 Jan
rm30 (🛁 🚿 13) A12rm **P**40 sB98—192
sB🛁 🚿 206—230 dB143—248
dB🛁 🚿 224—248 M70—149
Credit cards [1] [2] [5]

FERTÉ-SOUS-JOUARRE (LA)
Seine-et-Marne

🚗 **Condé** 48 r de Condé ☎71020810
Closed Sep For

🚗 **Parc** 10 av de Montmirail ☎71020136
Closed Aug, Sat pm, Sun am Cit

FIGEAC
Lot

★★**Carmes** LF (FAH) enclos des Carmes ☎65342070 tx520794
15 Jan—15 Dec
➡⋒32 **P**35 Lift sB➡⋒236—266 dB➡⋒292—312 M85—170 ≈
Credit cards [1] [2] [3] [5]

FIRMINY
Loire

★★***Firm*** 37 r J-Jaurès ☎77560899
rm20 (➡⋒18) **P** ☾
Credit cards [1] [2] [3] [5]

★★**Table du Pavilion** (FAH) 4 av de la Gare ☎77560045
➡22 🚗 **P**20 Lift sB➡⋒170—190 dB➡⋒220—250 M55—180
Credit cards [1] [2] [3] [5]

FIXIN
Côte-d'Or

★★**Chez Jeannette** LF (**DPn**) ☎80524549
Closed Jan
rm11 (⋒9) sB80 sB⋒128 dB141 dB⋒168 M95—135
Credit cards [1] [2] [3] [5]

FLEURAC See **JARNAC**

FLEURANCE
Gers

★★***Fleurance*** rte d'Agen ☎62061485
rm25 (➡⋒17) **P**80
Credit cards [1] [2] [3] [4] [5]

FLORAC
Lozère

★★**Parc** 47 av J-Monestier ☎66450305
15 Mar—1 Dec
rm58 (➡⋒44) A26rm 🚗 **P**45 sB87—187 dB114—124 dB➡⋒244 M60—145 mountains
Credit cards [2] [3] [5]

★**Gorges du Tarn** 48 r du Pecher (n.rest) ☎66450063
May—Sep
rm31 (➡⋒17) A12rm 🚗 **P** sB100—122 sB➡⋒135—167 dB150—174 dB➡⋒190—214

FLORENSAC
Hérault

★★**Leonce** LF 2 pl de la République ☎67770305
Mar—Sep (Closed Sun & Mon Jul—Aug)
rm18 (➡⋒10) Lift sB108—168 sB➡⋒168 dB126—156 dB➡⋒186—221 M105—210
Credit cards [2] [3] [5]

FLOTTE (LA) See **RÉ (ILE DE)**

FOIX
Ariège

★★★***Barbacane*** 1 av de Lérida ☎61655044
Mar—Nov
➡⋒22 🚗 **P**18 mountains
Credit card [3]

France

★★★**Tourisme** 2 cours I-Cros ☎616549121 tx530955
➡⋒29 sB➡⋒120—123 dB➡⋒165—196 M48—150 mountains
Credit cards [1] [2] [3]

FONTAINE
Isère

⛏ **MA Mignot** 2 r Baptiste Harcet, ZI de L'Argentière ☎76266946 All makes

FONTAINEBLEAU
Seine-et-Marne

★★★**Aigle Noir** (BW/MAP) 27 pl N-Bonaparte ☎64223265 tx600080
➡⋒30 A4rm **P** Lift ☾ sB➡⋒715 dB➡⋒845
Credit cards [1] [2] [3] [5]

★★**Ile de France** LF (Inter) 128 r de France ☎64228515 tx692131
➡⋒25 **P**25 ☾ sB➡⋒220—240 dB➡⋒260—285 M70—100
Credit cards [1] [2] [3] [4] [5]

★★**Londres** (**DPn**) 1 pl du Gl-de-Gaulle ☎64222021
Feb—Dec
rm22 (➡⋒7) 🚗 **P**20 ☾ sB170—185 sB➡⋒295—305 dB195—210 dB➡⋒330
Credit card [2]

★★**Toulouse** 183 r Grande (n.rest) ☎64222273
Closed 21 Dec—19 Jan
rm18 (➡⋒15) 🚗 sB80 sB➡⋒146—176 dB94 dB➡⋒181—221
Credit card [3]

★**Forêt** 79 av Prés-Roosevelt (n.rest) ☎64223926
rm24 (➡⋒19) A7rm 🚗 **P**18 sBfr89 sB➡⋒fr125 dB123—133 dB➡⋒168—213 M55—140 ≈
Credit cards [1] [3]

★***Neuville*** (**DPn**) 196 r Grande ☎64222339
Closed Feb
rm20 (➡⋒10) A4rm 🚗 **P**6

⛏ **Ile de France Autos** 86 r de France ☎64223159 Closed Sat pm & Sun Alf

At **URY** (6km SW on N51)

★★★***Novotel*** ☎64224825 tx600153
➡127 **P**250 ✂ ≈
Credit cards [1] [2] [4] [5]

FONTAINE-CHAALIS
Oise

★**Auberge de Fontaine** (**Pn**) Grande Rue ☎44542022
➡⋒7 sB➡⋒185—196 dB➡⋒210—236 M85—200

FONTENAY-AUX-ROSES See **PARIS**

FONTENAY-LE-COMTE
Vendée

★★**Rabelais** (Inter) rte Parthenay ☎51698620 tx710703
➡⋒35 🚗 **P**40 Lift sB➡⋒192—205 dB➡⋒249—270 M50—100 ≈
Credit cards [1] [2] [3] [5]

FONTENAY-SOUS-BOIS
Val-de-Marne

★★***Climat*** Rabelais ☎48762198 tx629844
➡42 **P**30

★★**Fimotel** pl du Gl-de-Gaulle, av du Val de Fontenay ☎48766771 tx232748
➡80 **P** Lift
Credit cards [1] [2] [3] [5]

FONTEVRAUD-L'ABBAYE
Maine-et-Loire

★★**Croix Blanche** (**DPn**) LF 7 pl Plantagenets ☎41517111
rm19 (➡⋒16) 🚗 **P**20

FONT-ROMEU
Pyrénées-Orientales

★★★***Bellevue*** av du Dr-Capelle ☎68300016
Rest closed 15 Sep—15 Dec
rm65 (➡30) **P** ☾ mountains

★★★**Carlit** ☎68300745 tx500802
15 Dec—10 Apr & Jun—Sep
➡⋒60 A23rm Lift dB➡⋒295—349 M60—75 mountains
Credit cards [1] [3]

★★**Pyrénées** pl des Pyrénées ☎68300149
20 Dec—15 Apr & May—10 Nov
➡37 Lift sB➡178—218 dB➡196—236 M65 mountains
Credit card [2]

FONVIALANE See **ALBI**

FORBACH
Moselle

★★***Fimotel*** r Felix Barth ☎87870606 tx215269
➡42 **P**20 Lift
Credit cards [2] [3] [5]

FORÊT-FOUESNANT (LA)
Finistère

★★**Baie** LF ☎98569735
rm20 (➡12) **P**100 sB96—116 sB➡136—196 dB137—157 dB➡182—222 M65 sea
Credit cards [1] [3]

★★**Esperance** ☎98569658
Apr—Sep
rm30 (➡⋒18) A19rm **P**10 sB89—103 sB➡⋒113—178 dB123—141 dB➡⋒154—235 M50—150 sea

★**Beauséjour** 47 r de la Baie ☎98569718
22 Mar—Sep
rm30 (⋒12) **P**20 sB99—104 sB⋒114—144 dB113—118 dB⋒128—158 M47—180 sea
Credit cards [1] [3]

FOS-SUR-MER
Bouches-du-Rhône

★★★★**Frantel Camargue** La Bastidonne, rte d'Istres ☏42050057 tx410812

⇌ 130 sB⇌ 303—358 dB⇌ 366—426 M67—129 ⩯
Credit cards 1 2 3 4 5

FOUESNANT
Finistère

★★**Pointe du Mousterlin** Pointe de Mousterlin ☏98560412

17 May—20 Sep
rm47 (⇌ ⋒ 35) ⌂ **P**40 sB93 dB133—146 dB⇌ ⋒ 159—301 M60—160 ✎ sea

★**Armorique** **LF** (**DPn**) ☏98560019

Apr—Sep
rm25 (⇌ ⋒ 14) A12rm **P**15 sB98 dBfr120 dB⇌ ⋒ 240—245 M60—155 t%
Credit card 1

J L Bourhis rte de Quimper ☏98560265 Closed Sep 15—30 Ren

FOUGÈRES
Ille-et-Vilaine

★★**Mainhotel** (N12) ☏99998155 tx730956

⇌ 50 **P** sB⇌ fr191 dB⇌ fr237

★★**Voyageurs** 10 pl Gambetta ☏99990820

8 Jan—22 Dec
rm36 (⇌ ⋒ 35) A10rm ⌂ **P**10 Lift sB⇌ ⋒ 132—178 dB⇌ ⋒ 158—196 M70—90
Credit cards 1 2 3 4 5

★**Modern** **LF** 15 r Tribunal ☏99990024

rm27 (⇌ ⋒ 23) ⌂ **P** sB86 sB⇌ ⋒ 136 dB167 dB⇌ ⋒ 182 M60
Credit cards 1 2 3 4 5

FOULAIN
Haute-Marne

★**Chalet** (N19) ☏25311111

rm12 (⇌ 5) **P**10 sB76—116 sB⇌ 101—116 dB91—200 dB⇌ 127—200 M50—140
Credit cards 2 3 5

FOURAS
Charente-Maritime

★★**Grand Hotel des Bains** (**Pn**) 15 r Gl-Bruncher ☏46840344

May—22 Sep
rm36 (⇌ ⋒ 35) ⌂ dB101—139 dB⇌ ⋒ 190—210 M67—124

FOURMETOT See **PONT-AUDEMER**

FOURMIES
Nord

★★**Ibis** Etangs des Moines (n.rest) ☏27602154 tx810172

⇌ 31 **P**50 sB⇌ 221 dB⇌ 270 lake
Credit cards 1 3

FOURNEAUX (Creuse) See **AUBUSSON**

FOURNEAUX (Savoie) See **MODANE**

France

FRAYSINET
Lot

★***Bonne Auberge*** (**DPn**) ☏65310002

Mar—Nov
⋒ 10 A2rm ⌂ **P**40

★**Escale** **LF** (**Pn**) ☏65310001

15 Feb—Dec
⋒ 8 **P**20 dB⋒ 165—195 M55—120
Credit cards 1 3

Societe Drianne Campana (N20) ☏65310017

At **PONT-DE-RHODES** (1km N on N20)

★**Relais** ☏65310016

15 Mar—15 Nov
rm26 (⇌ ⋒ 24) ⌂ **P**20 sB80—118 dB⇌ ⋒ 116—183 Mfr55 ✎ ⩯

FRÉJUS
Var

★★★**St-Aygulf** 214 rte Nationale 98 ☏94810123

⇌ 83 **P** Lift dB⇌ 250—350 sea mountains

Auge Christian 280 av de Verdun ☏94510299 Closed Oct 1—5, Sat pm & Sun AR

Daniel Depannages 25 r d'Aubenas ☏94510356

Grand Garage de Fréjus Plage 137 bd de la Libération ☏94512319 Closed Sat pm & Sun Tal

Satac (N7) ☏94514061 Ren

At **COLOMBIER** (3km W)

★★★**Residences du Colombier** (MAP) rte de Bagnols ☏94514592 tx470328

Apr—Oct
⇌ ⋒ 60 **P**200 ✎ ⩯
Credit cards 1 2 3 5

FRÉVENT
Pas-de-Calais

★***Amiens*** **LF** 7 r Doullens ☏21042543

rm10 (⇌ ⋒ 4) ⌂ **P**5
Credit cards 1 3

FRONTIGNAN
Hérault

★★**Balajan** (Inter) (4km NE on N112) ☏67481399

rm21 (⇌ ⋒ 16) ⌂ **P** sB134—159 sB⇌ ⋒ 177—325 dB184—226 dB⇌ ⋒ 226—350 M55—147 (**DPn**fr152 Jul & Aug) mountains
Credit card 3

Peugeot Frontignan rte de Montpellier ☏67481368 Closed Sat & Sun Peu

FUMAY
Ardennes

★★**Roches** 82 av J-Jaurès ☏24411012

Apr—Nov
rm31 (⇌ ⋒ 14) **P**30 sB108—181

sB⇌ ⋒ 123—181 dB139—225 dB⇌ ⋒ 171—225 Mfr50 mountains
Credit cards 1 3 5

GACÉ
Orne

★★★**Champs** **LF** (**DPn**) rte d'Alençon-Rouen ☏33355145

15 Feb—15 Nov
rm13 (⇌ 11) **P**30 sB⇌ 198—323 dB161 dB⇌ 221—343 M88—200 ✎ ⩯
Credit cards 1 3 4 5

★★**Morphée** 2 r de Lisieux (n.rest) ☏33355101

Closed Jan
⇌ ⋒ 10 A4rm dB⇌ ⋒ 211—284
Credit cards 2 3

★**Etoile d'Or** (**DPn**) 60 Grande Rue ☏33355003

Closed 9—14 Mar
rm12 (⇌ 2) ⌂ **P**8 sB61—115 dB97—165 dB⇌ ⋒ 127—165 M39—120

P Agerue l (N138) ☏33356247 Closed Sep 1—15 Cit

GAILLARD
Haute-Savoie

See also **ANNEMASSE**

★★★***Mercure*** (exit Annemasse — B41) r des Jardins ☏50920525 tx385815

⇌ ⋒ 78 **P**250 Lift ⩯ mountains
Credit cards 1 2 3 5

GAILLON
Eure

Orienne 21 av du Ml-Leclerc ☏32530502 Closed Jul, Sun pm & Mon Cit Peu

Poupardin Côte des Sables ☏32530337 All makes

GAP
Hautes-Alpes

★★**Fons Régina** **LF** (2km S on N85) quartier de Fontreyme ☏92510253

Dec—15 Oct
rm20 (⇌ ⋒ 14) **P** mountains

★★**Grille** 2 pl F-Euzière ☏92538484

Closed 6 Dec—4 Jan
⇌ ⋒ 30 Lift **DPn**217—237 Mfr80
Credit cards 1 2 3 5

★★**Mokotel** (3km S) quartier Graffinel, rte de Marseille (n.rest) ☏92515782

⇌ ⋒ 27 **P**27 Lift sB⇌ ⋒ 144—190 dB⇌ ⋒ 172—238 mountains
Credit cards 1 2 3

Gap Auto av d'Embrun ☏92520561 Closed Sat & Sun Ren

Verdun 4 r P-Bert ☏92512618 Closed Sat & Sun AR

At **PONT-SARRAZIN** (4km NE on N94)

Bernard ☏92512861 Closed Sun

Berta ☏92511376 Closed Sat pm & Sun, Feb—May & Oct—Nov VW

GARDE-ST-CAST (LA) See **ST-CAST-LE-GUILDO**

GEISPOLSHEIM See **STRASBOURG**

GÉMENOS
Bouches-du-Rhône

★★★★**Relais de la Magdeleine** rte d'Aix-en-Provence ☎42822005
15 Mar—Oct
🛁 🚿 20 **P**40 sB 🛁 🚿 318—438 dB 🛁 🚿 396—536 Mfr155&alc ≈ mountains
Credit card [3]

GENNES
Maine-et-Loire

★★**Loire** LE (**DPn**) ☎41518103
10 Feb—27 Dec
rm11 (🛁 🚿 7) 🏠 **P**16 sB93—143 sB 🛁 🚿 143—218 dB121—161 dB 🛁 🚿 171—256 M54—124

★★**Naulets d'Anjou** (**DPn**) r Croix de Mission ☎41518188
Etr—Oct
🛁 20 **P**20 sB 🛁 192—232 dB 🛁 214—254 Mfr120 ≈

GENNEVILLIERS
Hauts-de-Seine

★★**Fimotel** Ilot des Chevrins ☎42615014 tx215269
🛁 60 **P** Lift
Credit cards [1] [2] [3] [5]

GENTILLY See **PARIS**

GÉRARDMER
Vosges

★★★★**Grand Bragard** pl du Tilleul ☎29630631 tx960964
🛁 50 🏠 **P**40 Lift ☾ sB 🛁 230—410 dB 🛁 320—500 M85—200 ≈ mountains lake
Credit cards [1] [2] [3] [5]

★★**Parc** LE 12—14 av de Ville-de-Vichy ☎29633243 tx961408
Apr—Sep & Feb
rm38 (🛁 🚿 24) A14rm 🏠 **P**20 sBfr92 sB 🛁 🚿 217 dB89 dB 🛁 🚿 254 M53—170 mountains lake
Credit cards [1] [3]

★**Echo de Ramberchamp** (n.rest) ☎29630227
20 Dec—15 Nov
rm16 (🛁 11) **P**40 sB87—95 sB 🛁 115—119 dB111—113 dB 🛁 131—138 mountains lake

At **SAUT-DES-CUVES** (3km NE on N417)

★★★**Saut-des-Cuves** ☎29633046 tx961408
🛁 🚿 27 🏠 **P**30 Lift sB 🛁 🚿 182—257 dB 🛁 🚿 223—278 M85 mountains
Credit cards [1] [2] [3] [5]

GETS (LES)
Haute-Savoie

★★★**Marmotte** LE (**Pn**) ☎50797539 tx385026
22 Dec—10 Apr & Jul—Aug
🛁 🚿 45 🏠 **P** Lift dB 🛁 🚿 350—450 M90—100 ≈ 📺 mountains
Credit cards [1] [3] [5]

GEX
Ain

★**Bellevue** (**DPn** in season) av de la Gare ☎50415540
Feb—15 Dec
rm22 (🛁 🚿 11) 🏠 **P**4 sB138 dB 🛁 🚿 166 mountains lake

GIEN
Loiret

★★**Rivage** LE (**DPn**) 1 quai de Nice ☎38672053
rm29 (🛁 19) **P**15 sB115 sB 🛁 216—227 dB143 dB 🛁 181—276 M70—230
Credit cards [1] [2] [3] [4] [5]

🚗 **Reverdy** rte de Bourges ☎38672898
Closed Sat pm, Sun & Mon am Ren

GIVORS
Rhône

★★**Balladins** Centre commercial de la vallée du Gier ☎72241556 tx649394
🛁 🚿 28 🏠 **P**28 sB 🛁 🚿 166 dB 🛁 🚿 182 M56—77
Credit cards [1] [2] [3]

GLACERIE (LA) See **CHERBOURG**

GLÉNIC
Creuse

★★**Moulin Noyé** ☎55520911
rm32 (🛁 12) 🏠 **P**

GLUGES See **MARTEL**

GONESSE
Val-d'Oise

★★**Campanile** ZA Economiques de la Grande Couture ☎39857999 tx609021
🛁 50 **P** sB 🛁 217—238 dB 🛁 239—260 M61—82
Credit card [3]

★★***Climat*** la Croix St Benoît, r d'Aulnay (off N370) ☎39874244
🛁 🚿 66 **P**
Credit card [1]

★★**Ibis** (N2) Patte d'Oie de Gonesse ☎39872222 tx609078
🛁 41 **P** Lift dB 🛁 238

GONFREVILLE L'ORCHER
See **HAVRE (LE)**

GOUESNIÈRE (LA) See **ST-MALO**

GOUMOIS
Doubs

★★**Taillard** LE (**DPn**) ☎81442075
Mar—Oct
rm17 (🛁 🚿 16) 🏠 **P**25 dB166—186 dB 🛁 🚿 191—276 M85—200 mountains
Credit cards [1] [2] [3] [5]

GOURNAY-EN-BRAY
Seine-Maritime

🚗 **Central** F-Faure ☎35900075 Closed Aug 15—31 also Sun & Mon Cit

GRAMAT
Lot

★★**Centre** LE pl République ☎65387337
🛁 🚿 14 🏠 **P**6 sB 🛁 🚿 128—168 dB 🛁 🚿 176—236 M60—180
Credit cards [1] [3]

★**Lion d'Or** LE (**DPn** in season) pl République ☎65387318
13 Jan—13 Dec
🛁 🚿 15 🏠 **P**10 sB 🛁 186—266 dB 🛁 252—312 M70—200
Credit card [1]

At **RIGNAC** (4.5km NW)

★★★**Château de Roumégouse** (Relais et Châteaux) (**DPn**) (4.5km NW on N140) ☎65336381
May—2 Nov
🛁 14 **P**50 sB 🛁 270—310 dB 🛁 350—680 M85—230
Credit cards [1] [2] [3] [5]

GRANDE-MOTTE (LA)
Hérault

★★★★***Frantel*** r du Port ☎6756981 tx480241
May—Oct
🛁 135 **P** Lift ≈ sea
Credit cards [1] [2] [3] [5]

GRAND-PRESSIGNY (LE)
Indre-et-Loire

★***Espérance*** (**DPn**) ☎47949012
Closed 6 Jan—6 Feb
rm10 **P**

GRANVILLE
Manche

★★**Bains** 19 r G-Clemenceau ☎33501731 tx214235
🛁 🚿 56 Lift sB 🛁 🚿 139—235 dB 🛁 🚿 167—313 Mfr72 sea

🚗 **A Harel** 5 r C-Desmaisons ☎33510104
Closed Sep 8—30, Sat pm & Sun Tal

🚗 **C Poulain** av des Vendéens ☎33500214 Ren

GRASSE
Alpes-Maritimes

See also **CHÂTEAUNEUF-DE-GRASSE**

★★**Aromes** LE (N85) ☎9304201
Feb—1 Nov
rm7 (🛁 6) sB 🛁 150—178 dB160—196 dB 🛁 160—196 M68—148 mountains

GRAVESON
Bouches-du-Rhône

★★**Mas des Amandiers** LE r d'Avignon (n.rest) ☎90958176
Feb—Oct
🛁 21 **P**40 sB 🛁 203—218 dB 🛁 241—296 🎾 ≈
Credit cards [1] [2] [3] [5]

GRAY
Haute-Saône

★★★**Château de Rigny** (**DPn**) ☎84652501 tx362926
🛁 24 A10rm 🏠 **P**80 sB 🛁 268

dB 🛁 346—456 M150—200 〰 🎾 lake
Credit cards [1] [2] [3] [5]

★ ★**Bellevue** LF av Carnot 1 ☎84654776
Jan—Nov
rm15 (🛁 🚿 9) **P**8 sB69 sB 🛁 🚿 89
dB84—95 dB 🛁 🚿 119—137
Credit cards [1] [2] [3] [5]

★ ★**Fer-a-Cheval** LF 4 av Carnot (n.rest)
☎84653255
5 Jan—3 Aug & 19 Aug—24 Dec
rm44 (🛁 43) 🏠 **P**35 sB 🛁 122
dB 🛁 173—207
Credit cards [1] [2] [3] [5]

GRENOBLE
Isère

★ ★ ★ ★***Mercure*** 1 av d'Innsbruck
☎76095427 tx980470
🛁 100 🏠 **P**35 Lift 〰 mountains
Credit cards [1] [2] [5]

★ ★ ★ ★**Park** 10 pl P-Mistral ☎76872911
tx320767
Closed Xmas & New Year & 9—24 Aug
🛁 🚿 59 🏠 Lift ☾ sB 🛁 🚿 533—688
dB 🛁 🚿 626—866 M140 mountains
Credit cards [1] [2] [3] [5]

★ ★ ★**Angleterre** 5 pl V-Hugo (n.rest)
☎76873721 tx320297
🛁 🚿 70 Lift sB 🛁 🚿 285—355
dB 🛁 🚿 330—410 mountains
Credit cards [1] [2] [3] [5]

★ ★ ★**Grand** (Inter) 5 r de la République
☎76444936 tx980918
🛁 🚿 72 Lift sB 🛁 🚿 210—230
dB 🛁 🚿 265—300 mountains
Credit cards [1] [2] [3] [5]

★ ★ ★***Terminus*** 10 pl Gare (n.rest)
☎76872433 tx320245
Closed Aug
rm50 (🛁 🚿 44) Lift

★ ★**Alpazur** 59 av Alsace-Lorraine (n.rest)
☎76464280
rm30 (🛁 🚿 20) **P** sB98—152 sB 🛁 🚿 fr152
dBfr133 dB 🛁 🚿 195
Credit cards [1] [2]

★ ★**Dauphiné** 15 r du Dr-Schweitzer,
Seyssins ☎76217612 tx305551
🛁 45 sB 🛁 fr220 dB 🛁 fr241 M50—92 🎾
mountains
Credit card [1]

★ ★***Fimotel*** 20 av J-Jaurès ☎76242312
🛁 42 **P** Lift mountains

★ ★**Gallia** 7 bd Ml—Joffre (n.rest)
☎76873921 tx980882
Closed Aug
rm35 (🛁 🚿 27) 🏠 Lift sB119—204
sB 🛁 🚿 204 dBfr158 dB 🛁 🚿 268
Credit cards [1] [2] [3] [5]

★ ★***Ibis*** Centre Commerciale des Trois
Dauphins, r F-Poulat ☎76474849 tx320890
🛁 71 **P** Lift

★ ★**Paris Nice** 61 bd J-Vallier (n.rest)
☎76963618
rm29 (🛁 🚿 23) 🏠 **P**30 ☾ sB119—204
sB 🛁 🚿 171—204 dB135—220

dB 🛁 🚿 187—220 mountains
Credit cards [1] [2] [5]

🚗 **Albertiny** 38 av F-Viallet ☎76090087
Closed Sat pm AR

At **CLAIX** (10.5km S on N75 & D269)

★ ★ ★**Oiseaux** ☎76980774
rm20 (🛁 🚿 15) 🏠 **P**20 sB135—138
sB 🛁 🚿 175—208 dB 🛁 🚿 225—296
Mfr70&alc 〰 mountains

At **MEYLAN** (3km NE on N90)

★ ★**Climat** chemin du Vieux Chêne
☎76907690 tx305551
🛁 38 **P**50 sB 🛁 fr225 dB 🛁 243—248
M51—90 mountains
Credit cards [1] [3]

At **PONT-DE-CLAIX** (8km S on N75)

★ ★***Villancourt*** cours St-André
☎76981854
🛁 🚿 30 🏠 **P**50 Lift mountains

At **ST-ÉGRÈVE** (10km NW)

★ ★**Campanile** ☎76755788 tx980424
🛁 42 **P** sB 🛁 217—238 dB 🛁 239—260
M61—82
Credit card [3]

At **VOREPPE** (12km NW by A48)

★ ★ ★***Novotel*** Autoroute de Lyon
☎76508144 tx320273
🛁 114 **P** Lift 〰 mountains
Credit cards [1] [2] [3] [5]

🚗 **Echallion** ☎76502385 Closed Sat & Sun
Tal

GRÉOUX-LES-BAINS
Alpes-de-Hautes-Provence

★ ★ ★***Villa Borghèse*** (BW/MAP) av des
Thermes ☎92780091 tx401513
Mar—Nov
🛁 70 🏠 **P** Lift ☾ 🎾 〰 mountains

GRIMAUD
Var

Cheillan rte Nationale ☎94432060 All
makes

At **PORT-GRIMAUD** (5.5km E)

★ ★ ★**Port** pl du Marché (n.rest)
☎94563618
🛁 35 **P**35 Lift ☾ sB 🛁 278—428
dB 🛁 376—476 🎾 Beach sea
Credit cards [1] [3] [4]

GRISOLLES
Tarn-et-Garonne

★ ★***Relais des Garrigues*** (N20)
☎63303159
Closed 4 Jan—10 Feb
rm27 (🚿 20) 🏠 **P**40 ☾
Credit card [2]

GUÉRANDE
Loire-Atlantique

🚗 **Cottais** rte de la Turballe ☎40249039
Peu

GUÉRET
Creuse

★**Auclair** LF 19 av de la Sénatorerie
☎55520126
rm33 (🛁 🚿 21) A5rm 🏠 **P** sB100
sB 🛁 🚿 148—193 dB118 dB 🛁 🚿 210—234
mountains

GUÉTHARY
Pyrénées-Atlantiques

★ ★**Mariéna** av Mon-Mugabure (n.rest)
☎59265104
Jun—Sep
rm14 (🛁 🚿 5) **P**6 sB75 sB 🛁 🚿 135
dB106—113 dB 🛁 🚿 150—183 sea
Credit cards [1] [2]

GUILVINEC
Finistère

At **LECHIAGAT** (1km E)

★ ★**Port** (FAH) (**DPn**) ☎98581010
6 Jan—22 Dec
🛁 🚿 40

HAUCONCOURT See **METZ**

HAUTE-GOULAINE
Loire-Atlantique

★ ★ ★**Lande St-Martin** rte de Poitiers
(N149) ☎40800080 tx 700520
🛁 🚿 40 🏠 **P** Lift ☾ sB 🛁 🚿 160—233
dB 🛁 🚿 200—293 M60—200
Credit cards [1] [2] [3] [5]

HAUTEVILLE-LÈS-DIJON See **DIJON**

HAVRE (LE)
Seine-Maritime
See Plan page 150

[*AA*] **agent; See page 101**

★ ★ ★**Bordeaux** (Inter) 147 r L-Brindeau
(n.rest) ☎35226944 tx190428 Plan **1**
🛁 🚿 31 Lift ☾ sB 🛁 🚿 285—320
dB 🛁 🚿 370—475 sea
Credit cards [1] [2] [3] [5]

★ ★ ★**Marley** (Inter) 121 r de Paris (n.rest)
☎35417248 tx190369 Plan **1A**
rm36 (🛁 🚿 32) Lift sB140—280 sB 🛁 🚿 280
dB160—300 dB 🛁 🚿 300
Credit cards [1] [2] [3] [5]

★ ★ ★**Mercure** chaussée d'Angoulême
☎35212345 tx190749 Not on plan
🛁 96 **P**100 Lift sB 🛁 377 dB 🛁 419—504
Credit cards [1] [2] [3] [5]

★ ★**Foch** 4 r Caligny (n.rest) ☎35425069
tx190369 Plan **3**
rm33 (🛁 🚿 23) Lift dB107—139
dB 🛁 🚿 172—230
Credit cards [1] [2] [3]

★ ★**Grand Parisien** (Inter) 1 cours de la
République (n.rest) ☎35252383 tx190369
Plan **7**
rm22 (🛁 🚿 18) **P**12 Lift ☾ sBfr110 →

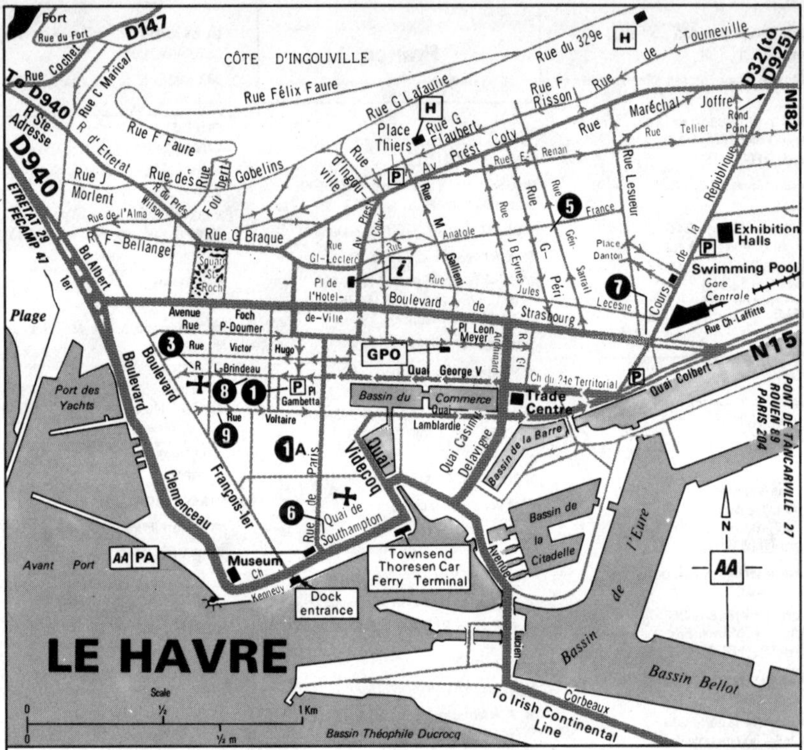

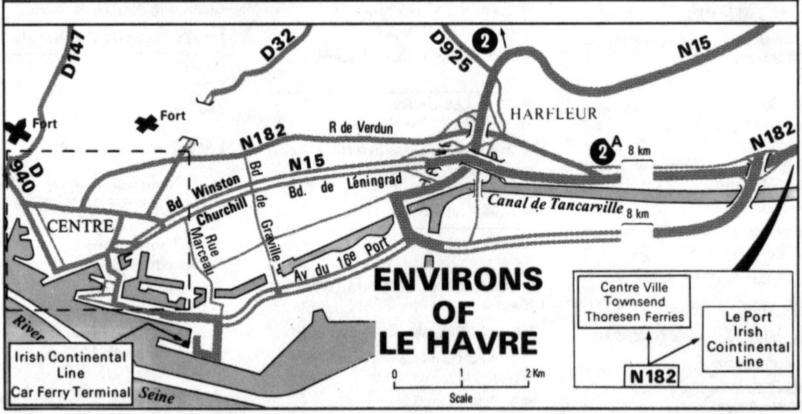

LE HAVRE

ENVIRONS OF LE HAVRE

HAVRE (LE)

1	★★★	Bordeaux
1A	★★★	Marly
2A	★★	Campanile (At Gonfreville l'Orcher)
2	★★	Climat (At Montivilliers)
3	★★	Foch
5	★★	Ile de France
6	★★	Moncaco
7	★★	Grand Parisien
8	★★	Petit Vatel
9	★	Voltaire

sB ⇌ ⋒ 165—220 dB155—260
dB ⇌ ⋒ 205—305 sea
Credit cards 1 2 3 4 5

★★**Ile de France** 104 r A-France (n.rest) ☏35424929 Plan **5**

rm16 (⇌ ⋒ 10) dB107—190
dB ⇌ ⋒ 118—190
Credit cards 1 3

★★**Monaco** 16 r de Paris ☏35422101 Plane **6**

3 Mar—Aug & 16 Sep—14 Feb

rm11 (⇌ ⋒ 8) **P**4 sB104—121
sB ⇌ ⋒ 159—181 dB137—162
dB ⇌ ⋒ 227—282 M70—180&alc S15% sea
Credit cards 1 2 3 5

★★**Petit Vatel** 86 r L-Brindeau (n.rest) ☏35417207 Plan **8**

rm29 (⇌ ⋒ 25) sB101 sB ⇌ ⋒ 116—166
dB122 dB ⇌ ⋒ 147—212
Credit card 3

★**Voltaire** 14 r Voltaire (n.rest) ☏35413091 Plan **9**

rm24 (🚿15) **P** sB97—102 sB🚿118—138
dB124—129 dB🚿147—174
Credit card [1]

Auto 91 r J-Lecesne ☎35226969 Closed Aug 15—Sep 1 & Sun BMW

At **GONFREVILLE L'ORCHER** (10km E)

★★**Campanile** Zone d'Activities du Camp Dolent ☎35514300 tx771609 Plan **2A**

🛁49 ⌂ **P** dB🛁240—261 M61—82
Credit card [3]

At **MONTIVILLIERS** (7km NE)

★★***Climat*** ZAC de la Lézarde ☎35304139 tx612441 Plan **2**

🛁38 **P**

At **STE-ADRESSE** (4km NW)

★★**Phares** 29 r Gl-de-Gaulle ☎35463186 Not on Plan

rm26 (🛁🚿18) ⌂ **P**9 dB113
dB🛁🚿159—168

HAYE-DU-PUITS (LA)
Manche

★**Gare** **LF** **(Pn)** ☎33460422

15 Jan—15 Dec
rm12 (🛁1) **P**40 sB88—124 sB🛁🚿124
dB105—141 dB🛁🚿141 M44—97
Credit cards [1] [3] [5]

HÉDÉ
Ille-et-Vilaine

★★★**Hostellerie du Vieux Moulin** **LF** **(DPn)** (N137) ☎99454570

Closed 16 Dec—Jan
rm14 (🛁🚿11) ⌂ **P**12 sB116
sB🛁🚿156—160 dB132 dB🛁🚿172—205
M65—180
Credit cards [3] [5]

HENDAYE-PLAGE
Pyrénées-Atlantiques

★★★**Liliac** 2 r des Clematites (n.rest)
☎59200245

🛁🚿23 Lift sB🛁🚿187—257
dB🛁🚿209—279
Credit cards [1] [2] [3] [5]

★★★***Paris*** Rond-Point (n.rest)
☎59200506

15 May—Sep
rm39 (🛁🚿29) Lift
Credit cards [3] [5]

HENIN-BEAUMONT
Pas-de-Calais

At **NOYELLES-GODAULT** (3km NE)

★★★**Novotel Henin Douai** (A1)
☎21751601 tx110352

🛁79 **P**79 sB🛁fr308 dB🛁fr368 ≈
Credit cards [1] [2] [3] [5]

★★**Campanile Henin Beaumont** Zone Artisanale et Commerciale, rte de Beaumont ☎21762626 tx134109

🛁42 **P** sB🛁217—238 dB🛁239—260
M61—82
Credit card [3]

France

HERBIGNAC
Loire-Atlantique

🚗 **Thudot** ☎40889174 Closed Sep Sat pm, Sun & Mon am ex Jul & Aug Cit

HERMIES
Pas-de-Calais

🚗 **Bachelet** 62 r d'Havrincourt ☎21074184 Closed Sun Peu

🚗 **Gustin** 12—13 Grand Place ☎210704010 Closed Sat pm & Sun Tal

HÉROUVILLE-ST-CLAIR See **CAEN**

HESDIN
Pas-de-Calais

★★**Flandres** **LF** **(DPn)** 22 r d'Arras
☎21868021

7 Jan—15 Dec
rm14 (🛁🚿12) ⌂ **P**15 sB86—229
sB🛁🚿109—229 dB101—308
dB🛁🚿124—308 M50—140
Credit card [3]

HONFLEUR
Calvados

★★★***Ferme St-Siméon et Son Manoir*** (Relais et Châteaux) r A-Marais ☎31892361

Feb—2 Dec
🛁🚿21 A11rm **P**50 ☾ sea

★★**Dauphin** 10 pl P-Berthelot (n.rest)
☎31891553

Feb-Dec
🛁🚿15 A15rm dB🛁🚿182—260
Credit card [3]

🚗 **Nicolle** 55 r de la République ☎31890164 Closed 15—30 Sep, Sat pm & Sun Aud AR VW

🚗 **Port** 15 pl A-Normand ☎31891613 Closed Sat pm & Sun Peu

HOSSEGOR
Landes

★★**Beauséjour** av Genets par av Tour du Lac ☎58435107
4 Jun—17 Sep
🛁🚿45 ⌂ **P**10 Lift ☾
sB🛁🚿170—246 dB🛁🚿257—392
M115—130 ≈

★★**Ermitage** **LF** **(DPn)** allées des Pins Tranquilles ☎58435222

Jun—Sep
🛁🚿14 **P** **DPn** 186 🔑

HOUCHES (LES)
Haute-Savoie

★★**Piste Bleue** rte les Chavants
☎50544066

20 Dec—Etr & Jul—Aug
rm25 (🛁16) **P**8 sB80—87 dB159—179
dB🛁190—208 M52—62 mountains

HOUDAN
Yvelines

★**St-Christophe** **LF** 6 pl du Gl-de-Gaulle
☎ 30596161 tx78550

🛁🚿9 dB🛁🚿186—236 M55—120
Credit card [3]

HOUDEMONT See **NANCY**

HOULGATE
Calvados

★★***Centre*** 31 r des Bains (n.rest)
☎31911815

15 May—18 Sep
rm24 (🛁🚿16)

HUELGOAT
Finistère

★★**Triskel** 72 r des Cieux (n.rest)
☎98997185

Closed 15 Nov—15 Dec
🛁🚿11 **P**12 sB🛁🚿119—139
dB🛁🚿138—168

HYÈRES
Var

Fleschl 7 rte de Toulon ☎94650283 Fia

🚗 **M Pique** quartier de la Vilette ☎94577525 Closed Sat & Sun Aud Tal VW

HYÈVRE-PAROISSE See **BAUME-LES-DAMES**

IGÉ
Saône-et-Loire

★★★***Château d'Ige*** (Relais et Châteaux)
☎85333399

15 Mar—5 Nov
🛁12 A1rm ⌂ **P**16
Credit cards [1] [2] [3] [5]

ILLKIRCH-GRAFFENSTADEN See **STRASBOURG**

INOR
Meuse

★**Falsan Doré** **LF** **(DPn)** r de l'Ecluse
☎29803545

🛁13 **P**25 sB🛁173—178 dB🛁215
M38—150
Credit cards [1] [3]

ISIGNY-SUR-MER
Calvados

★★**France** **LF** 17 r Demagny ☎31220033 tx170234

Feb—15 Nov
rm20 (🛁15) **P**25 ☾ dBfr132
dB🛁238—252 M68—85&alc ≈
Credit card [3]

ISLE-SUR-LE-DOUBS (L')
Doubs

🚗 **A Bouraly** 23 r du Moulin ☎81927086 For Tal

🚗 **C Marcoux** 64 r du Magny ☎81963154 Closed Sat pm & Sun Ren

ISLE-SUR-SEREIN (L')
Yonne

🚗 **A Gentil** rte de Tonnerre ☎86338414 M/c Closed Sun pm Cit

ISSOIRE
Puy-de-Dôme

★★**Pariou** **LF** 18 av Kennedy ☎73892211
rm29 (🛁🚿23) **P** sB94 sB🛁🚿119—171 →

dB110—122 dB 🛁 🚿 135—187 M47—91
Credit cards 1 3

🚗 **SA Arverne Auto** rte de Clermont ☎73891631 Cit

ISSOUDUN
Indre

★★**France & Commerce** LF (FAH) 3 r P-Brossolette ☎54210065 tx751422
Mar—14 Jan
🛁 🚿 28 ⌂ P ☾ sB 🛁 🚿 180 dB 🛁 🚿 200

IVRY-LA-BATAILLE
Eure

★★**Grand St-Martin** LF **(DPn)** 9 r Ezy ☎32364139
Feb—16 Dec
rm10 (🛁 🚿 8) sB142 sB 🛁 🚿 182 dB224
dB 🛁 🚿 304 M120—220
Credit card 3

JANVILLE
Eure-et-Loire

J Godart 8 r du Moulin à Vent ☎37900024
Closed 20 Dec—3 Jan Peu

JARD-SUR-MER
Vendée

★★**Parc de la Grange** LF (FAH) rte du Payré ☎51334488
Apr—Sep
🛁 🚿 55 A7rm **P**45 dB 🛁 🚿 204—321
M55—120 🎾 ≋
Credit cards 1 3 5

JARNAC
Charente

At **FLEURAC** (10km NE via D66 and D157)

★★**Domaine de Fleurac** (Inter) ☎45817822
Closed Nov
🛁 🚿 6 **P**40 sB 🛁 🚿 165—175
dB 🛁 🚿 290—450 M120
Credit cards 1 3 5

JARNY
Meurthe-et-Moselle

🚗 **R Rilliard** 53 av Lafayette ☎82330486 Peu

🚗 **Rouy** r Gambetta et av Lafayette ☎82330221 Closed Aug 4—25, Sat & Sun Cit

JOIGNY
Yonne

★★★**Côte St-Jacques** (Relais et Châteaux) 14 fbg de Paris ☎86620970 tx801458
12 Feb—4 Jan
🛁 🚿 33 ⌂ **P**15 Lift sB 🛁 🚿 305—405
dB 🛁 🚿 460—2110 M280—380 ▭
Credit cards 2 3 5

★★**Modern** LF (BW/MAP) **(DPN)** 17 av R-Petit ☎86621628 tx801693
rm21 (🛁 🚿 18) ⌂ **P**30 sB225—291
sB 🛁 🚿 255—291 dB240—317
dB 🛁 🚿 270—317 M135—260 🎾 ≋
Credit cards 1 2 3 5

🚗 **R Blondeau** 6 fbg de Paris ☎86620502
Closed Sun Ope

JOINVILLE
Haute-Marne

★**Poste** LF **(DPn)** (FAH) pl Grève ☎25961263
10 Feb—10 Jan
rm11 (🛁 🚿 8) ⌂ **P**20 sB75—95
sB 🛁 🚿 105—135 dB100—120
dB 🛁 🚿 120—170 M65—140
Credit cards 2 3 4 5

★**Soleil d'Or** LF 7 r des Capucins ☎25961566
Mar—10 Feb
🛁 🚿 11 ⌂ sB 🛁 🚿 156—176
dB 🛁 🚿 172—212 M75—120
Credit cards 1 2 3 4 5

JONZAC
Charente-Maritime

★★***Club*** 8 pl Église (n.rest) ☎46480227
rm16 (🛁 🚿 12) A3rm

JOSSELIN
Morbihan

★★**Château** LF (Inter) 1 r Gl-de-Gaulle ☎ 97222011
Closed 11 Dec—14 Jan
rm36 (🛁 🚿 27) ⌂ **P**30 dBfr95
dB 🛁 🚿 158—205
Credit cards 1 3

JOUÉ-LÉS-TOURS
Indre-et-Loitre

See also **TOURS**

★★**Campanile** av du Lac, les Bretonnières ☎47672489 tx751683
🛁 50 **P** sB 🛁 217—238 dB 🛁 239—260
M61—82
Credit card 3

★★**Château de Beaulieu (DPn)** ☎47532026
🛁 🚿 19 A10rm **P** dB 🛁 🚿 310—540
M140—180
Credit card 3

★★***Parc*** (Inter) 17 bd Chinon (n.rest) ☎47251538
🛁 🚿 30 ⌂ **P**30 Lift
Credit cards 1 2 3

JOUGNE
Doubs

★**Deux Saisons (DPn)** ☎81490004
18 Dec—20 Apr & Jun—Sep
rm21 (🛁 🚿 19) ⌂ **P**15 sB 🛁 🚿 109—114
dB123—128 dB 🛁 🚿 163—178 M50—150
mountains
Credit card 3

JUAN-LES-PINS
Alpes-Maritimes

★★★★***Belles Rives*** **(DPn)** bd Littoral ☎93610279 tx470984
Apr—10 Sep
🛁 🚿 44 Lift ☾ Beach sea
Credit card 2

★★★★**Juana** av G-Gallice, la Pinède ☎93610870 tx470778
20 Apr—Oct
🛁 45 ⌂ **P**25 Lift ☾ sB 🛁 695—1005
dB 🛁 1260—2020 M225&alc ≋ Beach sea

★★★***Apparthotel Astor*** 61 Chemin Fournel Badine ☎93610738
🛁 🚿 37 ⌂ **P**15
Credit cards 1 2 3 4 5

★★★**Helios (DPn** in summer) 3 av Dauchevile ☎93615525 tx970906
18 Apr—19 Oct
🛁 70 ⌂ **P**20 Lift ☾ sB465—845
dB 🛁 750—1590 M260
Credit cards 2 3 5

★★**Alexandra** r Pauline ☎93610136
26 Mar—15 Oct
rm20 (🛁 🚿 15) sB92—125
sB 🛁 🚿 130—152 dB173—222
dB 🛁 🚿 267—328 M77 Beach
Credit card 1

★★**Cyrano** (Inter) av L-Gallet (n.rest) ☎93610483
Feb—15 Oct
rm40 (🛁 🚿 32) Lift ☾ sB150—180
sB 🛁 🚿 220—260 dB180—220
dB 🛁 🚿 280—380 Beach sea

★★**Emeraude (DPn** in season) 11 av Saramartel ☎93610967 tx470673
Feb—Nov
🛁 🚿 22 ⌂ **P**10 Lift sB 🛁 🚿 220
dB 🛁 🚿 260—380 M80 Beach mountains
Credit cards 1 2 3 5

★★***Noailles*** av Gallice ☎93611170
Jun—Sep
rm22 (🛁 🚿 8) ⌂ **P** sea

★**Midi** 93 bd Poincaré ☎93613516
3 Jan—20 Oct
rm23 (🛁 🚿 20) A10rm **P**10 sB107—110
sB 🛁 🚿 127—130 dB146—153
dB 🛁 🚿 203—208 M70—90
Credit card 3

Wilson 122 bd Wilson ☎93612515
Closed Sat & Sun All makes

JULLOUVILLE
Manche

★★***Casino*** LF r de la mer ☎33618282
10 May—15 Sep
rm57 (🛁 🚿 34) **P**50 Beach sea
Credit card 3

KAYSERSBERG See **COLMAR**

KREMLIN-BICÊTRE See **PARIS**

LA each name preceded by 'La' is listed under the name that follows it.

LABASTIDE-MURAT
Lot

★★**Climat** ☎65211880
🛁 20 **P** sB 🛁 199—220 dB 🛁 199—220
M52—68
Credit cards 1 3 5

LABÈGE See **TOULOUSE**

LADOIX-SERRIGNY See **BEAUNE**

LAFFREY
Isère

★★**Grand Lac** LF ☎76731290
May—Sep
🛁🚿19 A19rm sB🛁🚿89—109
dB🛁🚿127—167 M80—125 lake mountains

LALINDE
Dordogne

★★**Château LF(Pn)** r Verdun ☎53610182
Mar—15 Nov
rm9 (🛁🚿4) sB83—198 sB🛁🚿163—198
dB91—117 dB🛁🚿181—216 Mfr55
Credit cards 1 2 3 5

★★***Résidence*** 3 r Prof-Testut (n.rest)
☎53610181
May—Sep
rm11 (🛁🚿11)

LAMASTRE
Ardèche

★★★**Midi (DPn)** pl Seignobos
☎75064150
Mar—15 Dec
rm20(🛁🚿15) 🚗P10 sB150—230
sB🛁🚿190—230 dB🛁🚿260—310
M130—300 mountains
Credit cards 1 2 3

LAMBALLE
Côtes-du-Nord

★★**Angleterre** LF (FAH/Inter) 29 bd Jobert
☎96310016
🛁🚿22 A13rm 🚗P10 Lift sBfr92
sB🛁🚿162—187 dBfr134
dB🛁🚿239—244 M65—130
Credit cards 1 2 3 5

★★**Auberge du Manoir des Portes**
La Poterie ☎96311362
🛁15 P20 sB🛁250—345 dB🛁250—345
Mfr80

★★**Tour d'Argent** LF 2 r du Dr-Lavergne
☎96310137 tx22400
rm30 (🛁🚿22) A16rm 🚗P6 sB86—148
sB🛁🚿111—178 dB114—226
dB🛁🚿216—236 Mfr60
Credit cards 1 2 3 5

🔧 **Clemenceau** 12 bd Clemenceau
☎96310593 Closed Sep 1—20 & Sun pm
For

LAMORLAYE See **CHANTILLY**

LANÇON-PROVENCE See
SALON-DE-PROVENCE

LANDERNEAU
Finistère

★★**Clos Du Pontic** LF r du Pontic
☎98215091
🛁🚿32 P50 sB🛁🚿173—203
dB🛁🚿232—271 M80—230
Credit cards 1 3

★★**Ibis** ☎98213132 tx940878
🛁42 ☾ sB🛁207 dB🛁252 Mfr64
Credit card 1

LANESTER See **LORIENT**

LANGEAIS
Indre-et-Loire

★★**Hosten** LF 2 r Gambetta ☎47968212
Closed 11—31 Jan, 21 Jun—9 Jul
🛁12 P10 sB🛁212—242 dB🛁274—314
M150—180
Credit cards 2 5

LANGON
Gironde

🔧 **Doux & Trouillot** 50 r J-Ferry
☎56630047 M/c Closed Sun Peu

LANGRES
Haute-Marne

★★**Europe** LF **(Pn)** 23 r Diderot
☎25851088
Closed 29 Sep—20 Oct & 21 Apr—5 May
rm28 (🛁🚿24) A8rm 🚗P20 sB86—98
sB🛁🚿153—163 dB104—151
dB🛁🚿181—204 M50—125
Credit cards 1 2 3 5

★★**Lion d'Or** rte de Vesoul ☎25850330
Closed Jan
rm14 (🛁🚿10) 🚗P20 dB143—151
dB🛁🚿162—196 M50—150 lake
Credit cards 1 3

★**Cheval Blanc** 4 r de l'Estres ☎25850700
Closed Jan
rm23 (🛁🚿22) A8rm 🚗P12 sB87—207
sB🛁🚿107—207 dB104—224
dB🛁🚿154—224
Credit cards 1 3

🔧 **Blosch** 2 av C-Baudoin ☎25852238 M/c
For

🔧 **Europe** rte de Charmont ☎25850378
Closed Aug, Sat & Sun Aud BMW VW

At **BOURG** (9km S on N74)

🔧 **Vallet** (N67) ☎25852515

At **ST-GEOSMES** (4km S on N74)

🔧 **Sabinus** ☎25850433 Ope

LANNION
Côtes-du-Nord

★★**Climat** rte de Perros-Guirec
☎96487018
🛁47 P50 sB🛁208—216 dB🛁229—237
🎾
Credit cards 1 3

LANSLEBOURG-MONT-CENIS
Savoie

★★★***Alpazur*** LF (Inter) ☎79059369
20 Dec—20 Apr & Jun—20 Sep
🛁🚿24 🚗P16 🎾 mountains
Credit cards 1 2 3

★**Relais des Deux Cols** LF 73 Val Cenis
☎79059283
May—Oct & Winter
rm30 (🚿17) A10rm 🚗P5 sB87 sB🚿127
dB122 dB🚿161—219 M60—82 🏊
mountains
Credit cards 3 5

LANSLEVILLARD
Savoie

★★**Étoile des Neiges** ☎79059041
14 Jun—15 Sep & 15 Dec—Apr
🛁🚿23 A5rm 🚗P20 sB🛁🚿123—165
dB🛁🚿166—220 M64—103 🎾 mountains
Credit cards 1 3 5

LANVOLLON
Côtes-du-Nord

At **PLEHEDEL**

★★★**Château de Coatguelen** (Relais et Châteaux) Plehedel ☎96223124
Mar—Nov
🛁🚿16 P40 Lift sB🛁🚿450—535
dB🛁🚿515—1020 M120—200 🎾 🏊 ⛳ U
Credit cards 1 2 3 5

LAON
Aisne

★★**Angleterre** (Inter) 10 bd de Lyon
☎23230462 tx145580
rm30 (🛁🚿22) 🚗P8 Lift ☾ sBfr147
sB🛁🚿fr202 dBfr169 dB🛁🚿fr254
M70—110
Credit cards 1 2 3 5

★★**Bannière de France (DPn)**
11 r de F-Roosevelt ☎23232144
20 Jan—20 Dec
rm19 (🛁🚿13) 🚗 sB100—145
sB🛁🚿215—245 dB130—175
dB🛁🚿235—320 M65—185
Credit cards 1 2 3 5

★★***Fimotel*** ZAC Ile de France (N2)
☎23201811
🛁40 P60 Lift
Credit cards 1 2 3 5

★**Chevaliers** 3 r Serurier ☎23234378
Closed 5 Feb—1 Mar
rm15 (🛁🚿10) 🚗 sB33—210 sB🛁🚿210
dB156—228 dB🛁🚿228 M40—80
Credit cards 1 2 3 5

🔧 **R Leroy** 16 pl V-Hugo ☎23235212 M/c
Closed Aug, Sun & Mon BMW Hon

LARAGNE-MONTEGLIN
Hautes-Alpes

★**Terrasses** LF av Provence ☎92650854
May—Oct
rm17 (🛁🚿8) 🚗P12 sB76—136
sB🛁🚿136 dB118 dB🛁🚿152 M52—100
mountains
Credit cards 1 2 3

LAROQUE-DES-ARCS See **CAHORS**

LAUMES (LES)
Côte-d'Or

★★**Lesprit** LF ☎80960046
rm24 (🛁🚿14) 🚗P15 sB86—176
sB🛁🚿154—176 dB103—193
dB🛁🚿171—193 M62—142&alc
Credit card 3

LAURIS
Vaucluse

★★**Chaumière** LF pl du Portail
☎90680129
15 Feb—Dec
🛁🚿10 sB🛁🚿181—201 →

dB ⇌ ⋒ 222—282 M100—140
Credit cards 1 2 3 5

LAVAL
Mayenne

★★**Climat** bd des Trappistines ☎43490859

⇌ 43 **P**50 sB ⇌ 186—212 dB ⇌ 186—212 M52—66
Credit cards 1 3 4 5

★★**Ibis** rte de Mayenne ☎43538182 tx721094

⇌ 51 **P**70 sB ⇌ 205 dB ⇌ 255 Mfr70 St%
Credit cards 1 3

LAVANDOU (LE)
Var

★★★***Calanque*** 62 av Gl-de-Gaulle ☎94710596

Feb—Oct
⇌ 39 **P**10 Lift ☾ sea
Credit cards 1 2 3 5

★★★***Résidence-Beach*** (**Pn** in season) bd Front-de-Mer ☎94710066

20 May—20 Sep
⇌ 55 **P** Lift ☾ ⚲ Beach sea

★**Petite Bohème** av F-Roosevelt ☎94711030

May—13 Oct
rm20 (⇌ ⋒ 8) A4rm ⌂ sB105—115 dB ⇌ ⋒ 200—290 Mfr85 t2% sea

Central av des Prés ☎94711068
Closed Xmas, New Year, Sat & Sun Peu

LAVAUR
Tarn

At **ST-LIEUX-LES-LAVAUR** (11km NW by D87 & D631)

★★**Château** ☎63337619

⇌ 12 **P** sB ⇌ 137—186 dB ⇌ 153—202 M70—140 S12%

LAVERNAY See **RECOLOGNE**

LAXOU See **NANCY**

LE Each name preceded by 'Le' is listed under the name that follows it.

LECHIAGAT See **GUILVINEC**

LECQUES (LES)
Var

★★★**Grand** ☎94262301 tx400165

Apr—Oct
rm58 (⇌ ⋒ 56) **P** Lift dB ⇌ ⋒ 340—590 Mfr110 ⚲ sea
Credit cards 1 2 3 5

LENS
Pas-de-Calais

At **LIEVEN** (4km W)

★★**Climat** r Silas Goliiet ☎21282222

⇌ 26 **P**26 sB ⇌ 222—237 dB ⇌ 242—257 M51—67&alc
Credit cards 1 3

At **VENDIN-LE-VIEL** (6km NE)

★★**Lensotel** Centre Commercial Lens II ☎21786453 tx120324

⇌ 70 **P**100 sB ⇌ 240—275 dB ⇌ 290—325
Mfr60 ⛆
Credit cards 1 2 3 5

LES Each name preceded by 'Les' is listed under the name that follows it.

LESCAR See **PAU**

LESQUIN See **LILLE AIRPORT**

LEVERNOIS See **BEAUNE**

LEVROUX
Indre

★★***Cloche et St-Jacques*** LF r Nationale ☎54357043

rm30 (⇌ ⋒ 20) A14rm ⌂ **P**5

LÉZIGNAN-CORBIÈRES
Aude

★***Tassigny*** Rond Point de Lattre ☎68271151

Oct—Sep
⇌ 16 ⌂ **P** ⚲ ⛆

Central 12 av de Gaulle ☎68270242
Closed Sat pm & Sun For

LIBOURNE
Gironde

★★**Climat** ☎57514141 tx541707

⇌ 42 **P** sB ⇌ 219—230 dB ⇌ 238—250 M55—90

★★***Loubat*** 32 r Chanzy ☎56511758

rm45 (⇌ ⋒ 35) ⌂ ☾
Credit cards 2 3

LIEVIN See **LENS**

LILLE
Nord

★★★**Bellevue** 5 r J-Roisin (n.rest) ☎20574586 tx120790

⇌ ⋒ 80 **P** Lift ☾ sB ⇌ ⋒ 303—370 dB ⇌ ⋒ 361—416
Credit cards 2 3

★★★**Carlton** (BW/Inter/MAP) 3 r de Paris (n.rest) ☎20552411 tx110400

rm65 (⇌ 61) Lift ☾ sBfr200 sB ⇌ 290—370 dB349—440 dB ⇌ 349—440
Credit cards 1 2 3 5

★★★**Royal** (Inter) 2 bd Carnot (n.rest) ☎20510511 tx820575

rm102 (⇌ ⋒ 98) **P** Lift sB ⇌ ⋒ 273—361 dB ⇌ ⋒ 341—454
Credit cards 1 2 3 5

★★**Campanile** r J-C-Borda ☎20533055 tx136203

⇌ 49 **P** sB ⇌ 217—238 dB ⇌ 239—260 M61—82

Delannoy 208 r du fbg d'Arras ☎20535513 M/c Closed Sat & Sun AR

Vambre 17 r de Seclin ☎20520785
Closed Sat & Sun All makes

At **ENGLOS** (7.5km W on D63)

★★★**Mercure** Autoroute Lille-Dunkerque exit Lomme ☎20923015 tx820302

⇌ ⋒ 95 A25rm **P**450 sB ⇌ ⋒ 239—300 dB ⇌ ⋒ fr359 M95&alc ⚲ ▭
Credit cards 1 2 3 4 5

★★★**Novotel Lille Lomme** Autoroute A25-exit Lomme ☎20070999 tx132120

⇌ 115 **P**200 sB ⇌ 435—450 dB ⇌ 620—650 ⛆
Credit cards 1 2 3 5

At **MARQ-EN-BAROEUL** (4.5km N on N350)

★★★★**Holiday Inn** bd de la Marne ☎20721730 tx132785

⇌ 125 **P**400 Lift sB ⇌ fr364 dB ⇌ fr394 ▭
Credit cards 1 2 3 5

LILLE AIRPORT

At **LESQUIN** (8km SE)

★★★★**Holiday Inn** 110 r J-Jaurès ☎20979202 tx132051

⇌ 212 **P**500 Lift sB ⇌ 364 dB ⇌ 434 M50—85 ▭
Credit cards 1 2 3 5

★★★**Novotel Lille Aéroport** (A1) ☎20979225 tx820519

⇌ 92 **P**75 sB ⇌ fr351 dB ⇌ fr402 ⛆
Credit cards 1 2 3 5

Gallou 46 r Pasteur ☎961359 Closed Sat pm & Sun All makes

LIMOGES
Haute-Vienne

★★★★**Frantel** pl de la République ☎55346530 tx580771

⇌ ⋒ 75 **P** Lift sB ⇌ ⋒ 260—330 dB ⇌ ⋒ 300—380
Credit cards 1 2 3 5

★★★**Luk** 29 pl Jourdan ☎55334400 tx580704

⇌ ⋒ 53 **P** Lift sB ⇌ ⋒ 245—265 dB ⇌ ⋒ 310—330 M90—120

★★**Campanile** Le Moulin Pinard r H-Giffard ☎55373562 tx590909

⇌ 42 **P** sB ⇌ 217—238 dB ⇌ 239—260 M61—82
Credit card 3

★★***Caravelle*** 21 r A-Barbès (n.rest) ☎55777529

⇌ ⋒ 31 ⌂ **P** Lift ☾

★★***Ibis*** r F-Bastiat, ZAC Industrielle Nord 2 ☎55375014 tx580009

⇌ 76 **P**150 Lift
Credit cards 1 3

★★***Jourdan*** (Inter) 2 av du Gl-de-Gaulle ☎55774962

rm45 (⇌ ⋒ 40) Lift

★**Relais Lamartine** 10 r des Coopérateurs (n.rest) ☎55775339

rm20 (⇌ ⋒ 10) ⌂

Auto Sport 14 r Dupuytren ☎55371780 Closed Sat & Sun Aud VW

Bastide 229 av du Gl-Leclerc ☎55371771 Closed Sat pm & Sun Maz Vol

LINGLOSHEIM
Basse-Rhin

★★**Campanile** Parc des Tonneries, 305 rte de Schirmelic ☎781010 tx880454

🛁 50 **P** sB 🛁 217—238 dB 🛁 239—260 M61—82
Credit card [3]

LION D'ANGERS (LE)
Maine-et-Loire

★**Voyageurs** 2 r Gl-Leclerc ☎41953008

10 Feb—Sep & 25 Oct—20 Jan
rm13 (🛁 🚿 6) ⌂ **P**10 sB 🛁 🚿 160—165
dB 🛁 🚿 175—180 M50—120

LISIEUX
Calvados

★★★***Grand Normandie*** LE (Inter) 11 bis r av Char ☎31621605 tx170269

May—Sep
rm80 (🛁 🚿 62) ⌂ Lift ☾
Credit cards [1] [2] [3] [5]

★★★**Place** (BW/MAP) 67 r H-Chéron (n.rest) ☎31311744 tx171862

🛁 🚿 32 ⌂ **P**20 Lift ☾ sB 🛁 🚿 255—330
dB 🛁 🚿 300—400
Credit cards [1] [2] [3] [5]

★★**Lourdes** 4 r av Char (n.rest) ☎31311948

Apr—Oct
rm35 (🛁 🚿 32) ⌂ Lift sBfr120 sB 🛁 🚿 fr204
dBfr147 dB 🛁 🚿 fr232
Credit card [3]

★**Coupe d'Or** LE (FAH) (**DPn**) 49 r Pont-Mortain ☎31311684

rm18 (🛁 🚿 14) sBfr135 sB 🛁 🚿 270—290
dBfr185 dB 🛁 🚿 290—320 M80—175
Credit cards [1] [2] [3] [5]

🔧 **Bouley** 62 r du Gl-Leclerc ☎31311614 Closed Sat pm & Sun AR BMW

🔧 **Samo** 34 r du Gl-Leclerc ☎31620446 Closed Sat & Sun Ope

LIVAROT
Calvados

★**Vivier** LE (**DPn**) pl de la Mairie ☎31635029

Closed 20 Dec—25 Jan
rm11 (🛁 🚿 7) ⌂ **P**20 sB108—198
sB 🛁 🚿 198—218 dBfr227 dB 🛁 🚿 269
M53—100
Credit card [3]

LIVRON-SUR-DRÔME
Drôme

🔧 **Gemenez** Elf Station (N7) ☎75616778 Closed Sun Sep—Mar All makes

LOCHES
Indre-et-Loire

★**France** (**Pn**) 6 r Picois ☎47590032

Closed Jan
rm21 (🛁 🚿 11) ⌂ **P**22 sB84—197
sB 🛁 🚿 117—197 dB101—214
dB 🛁 🚿 134—214 M45—150
Credit card [3]

At **BRIDORÉ** (14km S via N143)

★★★**Barbe Bleue** (**Pn** in season) Oizay ☎47947269

Mar—Dec
🛁 🚿 10 **P**30 sB 🛁 🚿 160—170
dB 🛁 🚿 185—195 M45—150 🔧

LOCRONAN
Finistère

★★***Prieure*** LE 11 r de Prieure ☎98917089

Closed Oct
rm15 (🛁 🚿 10) A5rm **P**

LODÈVE
Hérault

★★**Croix Blanche** (**DPn**) 6 av de Fumel (N9) ☎67441087

Apr—Nov
rm32 (🛁 🚿 27) A13rm ⌂ **P**25 sB69—80
sB 🛁 🚿 115—165 dB95—120
dB 🛁 🚿 130—180 M40—90

LONDE (LA) See **ELBEUF**

LONGJUMEAU
Essonne

At **SAULX-LES-CHARTREUX**

★★**Climat** Le Pont Neuf ☎64480900

🛁 44 sB 🛁 264—284 dB 🛁 288—308
M42—159
Credit cards [1] [3]

LONGUYON
Meurthe-et-Moselle

★★**Lorraine** LE (Inter) face Gare ☎82395007

Closed Jan
rm15 (🛁 12) sB96 sB 🛁 142—199 dB115
dB 🛁 161—244 M80—215
Credit cards [1] [2] [3] [4] [5]

LONGWY
Meurthe-et-Moselle

★★**Fimotel** (N52) ☎82231419 tx861270

🛁 42 **P**48 Lift sB 🛁 218—228
dB 🛁 248—258 M51—89
Credit cards [1] [2] [3] [4] [5]

LONS-LE-SAUNIER
Jura

★★**Genève** 19 pl XI Novembre ☎84241911

rm42 (🛁 🚿 36) ⌂ **P**12 sB130—195
sB 🛁 🚿 230—295 dB175—235
dB 🛁 🚿 260—360 M75—120
Credit cards [1] [2] [3] [5]

Thevenod rte de Champagnole-Perrigny ☎84244185 Closed Sat & Sun Aud VW

LORIENT
Morbihan

★★★***Richelieu*** (BW/MAP) 31 pl J-Ferry ☎97213575 tx950810

🛁 58 Lift
Credit cards [1] [2] [3] [5]

🔧 **Auto du Morbihan** 20 r de Kerolay ☎97370333

🔧 **Olda** 39 r C-Lefort ☎97212315 Closed Sun AR

At **LANESTER** (5km NE)

★★★**Novotel** Zone Commerciale de Bellevue ☎97760216 tx950026

🛁 88 **P**80 sB 🛁 318 dB 🛁 380—390
M78—120 S15% ♨
Credit cards [1] [2] [3] [5]

★★**Climat** Za-Lann Sevelin ☎97764641

🛁 🚿 39 **P**50 sB 🛁 🚿 220—250
dB 🛁 🚿 240—290 M51—88
Credit cards [1] [3] [4]

★★**Ibis** Zone Commerciale de Bellevue (n.rest) ☎97764022 tx950026

🛁 40 **P**50 sB 🛁 210—220 dB 🛁 260—270
Credit cards [1] [3]

LORMONT See **BORDEAUX**

LOUDÉAC
Côtes-du-Nord

★***Voyageurs*** LE 10 r Cadélac ☎96280047

rm32 (🛁 🚿 15) ⌂ **P** Lift

LOUDUN
Vienne

★★★***Mercure*** 40 av Leuze (n.rest) ☎49981922

🛁 29 Lift
Credit cards [1] [2] [3] [5]

LOUÉ
Sarthe

★★★**Ricordeau** (**Pn**) (Relais et Châteaux) 11 r Libération ☎43884003 tx722013

🛁 🚿 13 A8rm ⌂ **P**5 sB 🛁 🚿 498—648
dB 🛁 🚿 796 Mfr160 S15%
Credit cards [1] [2] [3] [5]

LOURDES
Hautes-Pyrénées

★★★***Grotte*** (BW/MAP) 66 r de la Grotte ☎62945887 tx531937

Etr—Oct
🛁 🚿 86 ⌂ Lift ☾ mountains
Credit cards [1] [2] [3] [4] [5]

★★**Ibis** chaussée Marensin ☎62943838 tx521409

🛁 88 **P** Lift sB 🛁 204—253 dB 🛁 268—319
Mfr65 St% mountains

★★**Provençale** (Inter) 4 r Baron Duprat ☎62943134 tx520257

🛁 62 Lift ☾ sB 🛁 275—310
dB 🛁 310—335 Mfr80 mountains
Credit cards [1] [2] [3] [4] [5]

★★***St-Roche*** (**DPn**) 6 pl J-d'Arc ☎62940214

Etr—8 Dec
rm33 (🚿 22) Lift

LOUVIERS
Eure

🔧 **L Parsy** 28 r du 11 Novembre ☎32403394 For

At **ST-PIERRE-DU-VAUVRAY** (8km E)

★★★**Hostellerie de St-Pierre** (**Pn**) ☎32599329

Mar—Dec →

➡ 15 **P**40 Lift dB ➡ 310—440 M130—195 lake
Credit card [3]

At **VAUDREUIL** (4km N A13)

★★★**PLM Le Vaudreuil** ☎32590909 tx180540
➡ 58 **P** Lift sB ➡ 290 dB ➡ 355 M alc ɋ ≋

At **VIRONVAY** (4km SE on N182A)

★★**Saisons** ☎32400256
Closed Feb & 16—24 Aug
➡ 15 ⌂ **P**15 sB ➡ 288—313 dB ➡ 356—481 Mfr135 ɋ
Credit cards [1] [3] [5]

LOUVROIL
Nord

★★★**Mercure** rte d'Avesnes (N2) ☎27649373 tx110696
➡ 59 **P**100 sB ➡ fr288 dB ➡ 331 ≋
Credit cards [1] [2] [3] [5]

LUC (LE)
Var

★**Hostellerie du Parc** (**DPn**) 1 r J-Haurès ☎94607001
➡ ⋒ 12 ⌂ **P**20 sB ➡ ⋒ 155—295 dB ➡ ⋒ 300—350 M130—200
Credit cards [1] [2] [3] [5]

🚗 **M Lacoste** 14 av Barbaraux ☎94735011 Closed Sat pm & Sun Ren

LUCÉ See **CHARTRES**

LUCHON
Haute-Garonne

★★★**Poste & Golf** 29 allées d'Etigny ☎61790040 tx520018
Closed 21 Oct—19 Dec
rm63 (➡ ⋒ 59) ⌂ **P** Lift mountains

★★**Bains** (Inter) 75 allées d'Etigny ☎61790058 tx521437
20 Dec—20 Oct
rm53 (➡ ⋒ 48) **P**15 Lift sBfr131 sB ➡ ⋒ fr186 dB182 dB ➡ ⋒ 242—272 Mfr78 mountains
Credit card [2]

LUDE (LE)
Sarthe

★★***Maine*** **LF** (**DPn**) 23 rte Saumur ☎43946054
Closed 22 Dec—1 Jan
rm24 (➡ ⋒ 17) A6rm **P**20
Credit cards [1] [3]

LUDRES See **NANCY**

LUNEL
Hérault

🚗 **Auto Service 113** 21 rte de Nîmes ☎ 67713495 Dat Vol

🚗 **M Pons** ZI des Fournels, rte de Montpellier ☎67711059 Closed Sat & Sun Aud VW

LUNÉVILLE
Meurthe-et-Moselle

★★**Europe** 56 r d'Alsace (n.rest) ☎83741234

rm30 (➡ ⋒ 20) **P**15 ☾ sB97—136 sB ➡ ⋒ 112—136 dB ➡ ⋒ 124—152

LUS-LA-CROIX-HAUTE
Drôme

★**Chamousset** **LF** (**Pn** in season) ☎92585112
Closed 15 Nov—25 Dec
rm20 (➡ ⋒ 15) A5rm ⌂ **P**15 dB146—186 dB ➡ ⋒ 146—186 M55—75 mountains
Credit cards [1] [2] [3]

★**Touring** 75 rte Nationale ☎92585001
rm17 (⋒ 4) **P** sBfr87 sB⋒ fr99 dBfr118 dB⋒ fr152 Mfr52 mountains

LUTTERBACH
Haute-Rhin

★★**Campanile** 10 r de Pfastatt ☎89536655 tx881432
➡ 43 **P** sB ➡ 217—238 dB ➡ 239—260 M61—82
Credit card [3]

LUXEUIL-LES-BAINS
Haute-Saône

★★**Beau Site** **LF** 18 r Moulimard ☎84401467
rm44 (➡ ⋒ 38) A15rm ⌂ **P** Lift sB76—158 sB ➡ ⋒ 180—200 dB150—170 dB ➡ ⋒ 240—250
Credit card [3]

LUYNES
Indre-et-Loire

★★★★**Domaine de Beauvois** (**DPn**) ☎47555011 tx750204
Mar—Jan
➡ 38 A1rm **P**70 Lift ☾ sB ➡ 328—758 dB ➡ 811—1336 M120—295 ɋ ≋ lake
Credit cards [1] [3] [5]

LYON
Rhône

See also **CHASSE-SUR-RHÔNE**

★★★★**Frantel Lyon** 129 r Servient, Part Dieu Nord ☎78629412
➡ 245 ⌂ **P**70 Lift ☾ sB ➡ 526—571 dB ➡ 617—692 M62—150
Credit cards [1] [2] [3] [4] [5]

★★★★**Grand Concorde** 11 r Grôlée ☎78425621 tx330244
➡ ⋒ 140 ⌂ Lift ☾ sB ➡ ⋒ 348—588 dB ➡ ⋒ 386—706 M90—110&alc
Credit cards [1] [2] [3] [5]

★★★★**Royal** (BW/MAP) 20 pl Bellecour ☎78375731 tx310785
➡ ⋒ 90 ⌂ Lift sB ➡ ⋒ 274—614 dB ➡ ⋒ 413—648 M alc
Credit cards [1] [2] [3] [5]

★★★★**Sofitel** 20 quai Gailleton ☎78427250 tx330225
➡ 200 ⌂ **P**100 Lift ☾ sB ➡ 717—777 dB ➡ 954—1054 M alc t4%
Credit cards [1] [2] [3] [4] [5]

★★★**Beaux Arts** (BW/MAP) 75 r Prés-Herriot (n.rest) ☎78380950 tx330442
➡ ⋒ 79 sB ➡ ⋒ 271—401 dB ➡ ⋒ 345—477 t3%
Credit cards [1] [2] [3] [5]

★★★***Bordeaux et du Parc*** (Inter) 1 r du Bèlier (n.rest) ☎78375873 tx330355
rm83 (➡ ⋒ 75) Lift

★★★**Carlton** (BW/MAP) 4 r Jussieu (n.rest) ☎78425651 tx310787
rm87 (➡ ⋒ 83) ⌂ Lift sB158—378 sB ➡ ⋒ 258—378 dB226—446 dB ➡ ⋒ 326—446
Credit cards [1] [2] [3] [5]

★★★**Terminus Lyon Perrache** 12 cours de Verdun ☎78375811 tx330500
rm140 (➡ ⋒ 125) **P**25 Lift sBfr228 sB ➡ ⋒ 488 dB336 dB ➡ ⋒ 596 Malc
Credit cards [1] [2] [4] [5]

★★**Campaville** (**Pn**) 17 pl Carnot ☎78374847 tx305660
➡ 108 Lift sB ➡ 254—275 dB ➡ 297—318 Mfr59
Credit card [3]

★★**Globe & Cecil** (Inter) 21 r Gasparin (n.rest) ☎78425895 tx305184
rm65 (➡ ⋒ 59) Lift sB ➡ ⋒ 202—257 dB ➡ ⋒ 224—294
Credit cards [1] [2] [3] [5]

★★***Ibis Lyon la Part Dieu Sud*** pl Renaudel ☎78954211 tx310847
➡ 144 ⌂ **P**60 Lift
Credit cards [1] [3]

★★**Moderne** 15 r Dubois (n.rest) ☎78422183
rm31 (➡ ⋒ 26) **P**2 Lift sB98—153 sB ➡ ⋒ 183—236 dB181 dB ➡ ⋒ 199—274

○**Holiday Inn** 29 r de Bonnel ☎78611429
Opening early 1987
➡ 159 **P**159 Lift ☾ sB ➡ 705 dB ➡ 890 M100—200
Credit cards [1] [2] [3] [5]

At **BRON** (10km SE)

★★★***Novotel Lyon Aéroport*** r L-Terray ☎7826748 tx340781
➡ 196 **P** Lift

★★**Campanile** quartier Rebufer, r Maryse-Bastie ☎78264540 tx305160
➡ 50 **P** sB ➡ 217—238 dB ➡ 239—260 M61—82
Credit card [3]

★★**Climat** ☎78265076 tx375941
➡ 39 **P**30 sB ➡ 207—227 dB ➡ 226—246 M51—77
Credit cards [1] [3]

★★**Hostel** 36 av du Doyen J-Lepine ☎78543134 tx380694
➡ 140 **P**200 Lift sB ➡ 173 dB ➡ 230
Credit cards [1] [3]

At **CHARBONNIÈRES-LES-BAINS** (8km NW on N7)

★★★**Mercure** 78 bis rte de Paris (N7) ☎78347279 tx900972
➡ 60 ⌂ **P**50 sB ➡ 245—263

dB 297—315 Malc t2%
Credit cards 1 2 3 5

At **DARDILLY** (10km on N6)

★★★★**Lyon Nord** (BW/MAP) Porte de Lyon ☎78357020 tx900006

204 **P**400 Lift sB 359—459
dB 428—528 M80—200
Credit cards 1 2 3 5

★★★**Mercure Lyon La Part — Dieu** 47 bd Vivier-Merle ☎72341812 tx306469

124 **P** Lift sB 362—382
dB 414—444 Malc

★★★**Mercure Lyon Nord** Autoroute A6, Porte de Lyon ☎78352805 tx330045

175 **P**150 sB 209—265
dB 245—280
Credit cards 1 2 3 5

★★★**Novotel Lyon Nord** Porte de Lyon (A6) ☎78351341 tx330962

107 **P**110 Lift sB 339—349
dB 383—393 M alc
Credit cards 1 2 3 5

★★**Campanile** Porte de Lyon Nord ☎78354844 tx310155

43 **P** sB 217—238 dB 239—260
M61—82
Credit card 3

★★**Climat** Porte de Lyon Nord ☎78359847

38 **P** sB 219 dB 248 M51—87
Credit card 1

★★**Ibis Lyon Nord** Porte de Lyon (A6) ☎78660220 tx305250

47 **P**100 sB 232—258
dB 285—310 M59—75
Credit cards 1 2 3

Technic-Auto Service (N6) ☎78355380 Ren

At **ECULLY** (7.5km NW)

★★**Campanile** av Guy de Collongue ☎78331693 tx310154

50 **P** sB 217—238 dB 260 M61—82
Credit card 3

At **ST-GENIS-LAVAL** (10km SW)

★★**Climat** chemin de Chazelle ☎78566434 tx692844

42 **P**40 sB 203—221
dB 221—239 M51—67
Credit cards 1 3

At **ST-PRIEST** (11km SE by D518)

Kenning's 190 rte de Grenoble ☎78908200 Closed Sat & Sun AR

At **STE-FOY-LES-LYONS** (6km SW)

★★**Campanile** chemin de la Croix-Pivort ☎78593223 tx305850

50 **P** sB 217—238 dB 239—260
M61—82
Credit card 3

★★***Provences*** 10 pl de Saint Luc (n.rest) ☎78250155

14 **P**

France

At **SATOLAS AIRPORT** (18km SW)

★★***Climat*** Zone de Frêt ☎78409644 tx612241

36 **P**

LYONS-LA-FORÊT
Eure

★★***Licorn*** (**DPn**) pl Benserade ☎32496202

rm22 (17) **P**20 sB175—205
sB fr215 dB200—230
dB 300—450 M110—190
Credit cards 1 2 3 5

MÂCON
Saône-et-Loire

★★★★**Frantel** 26 r de Coubertin ☎85382806 tx800830

63 **P** Lift sB 298—363
dB 335—423
Credit cards 1 2 3 5

★★★**Novotel Mâcon Nord** (7km N on A6) ☎85360080 tx800869

106 **P** sB 283—296 dB 344—372
M50—150
Credit cards 1 2 3 5

★★**Bellevue** (BW/MAP) 416—420 quai Lammartine ☎85380507 tx800837

rm28 (26) **P**23 Lift
sB 350—360 dB 440—540
Credit cards 1 2 3 5

★★**Champs Elysées** (Inter) 6 r V-Hugo/2 pl de la Barre ☎85383657 tx351940

rm50 (37) Lift sB94—146
sB 173—184 dB135—192
dB 232—262 M60—102&alc
Credit cards 1 2 3 5

★★**Europe et d'Angleterre** 92—109 quai J-Jaurès (n.rest) ☎85382794 tx800762

Feb—Oct
rm32 (21) **P**20 sB99—217
sB 183—217 dB137—242
dB 210—242
Credit cards 1 2 3 5

★★***Genève*** (Inter) (**DPn** in summer) 1 r Bigonnet ☎85381810 tx351934

rm63 (48) Lift

★★**Terminus** (FAH) 91 r V-Hugo ☎85391711 tx351938

48 **P**14 Lift sB fr248
dB fr340 M60—98
Credit card 1

Bols 39 r Lacretelle ☎85386431 Closed 3 wks Aug, Sat & Sun AR

Chauvot r J-Mermox 'Les Bruyères' ☎85349898 Closed Sat pm & Sun Ope Vol

Corsin 25 r de Lyon ☎85387333 Closed 3 wks Jul—Aug, Sat & Sun For

Duval 53 rte de Lyon ☎85348000 Closed Sun Fia Mer

Favède 18—20 4 Lacretelle ☎85384605 Closed 2 wks Aug, Sat pm & Sun BMW Lan

Ferret 89 rte de Lyon ☎85388355 M/c Closed Sat & Sun Cit

Mâcon Auto 5 r du Concours ☎85389320 Closed Aug 9—18, Sat pm & Sun Ope

Quagliozzi 72 rte de Lyon ☎85385442 Closed Aug, Sat pm & Sun Hon

At **CHAINTRÉ-LA-CHAPELLE-DE-GUINCHAY** (14km SW)

★★**Ibis Mâcon Sud** les Bouchardes ☎85365160 tx351926

45 **P**60 sB 219—241 dB 275—325
M40—100&alc
Credit cards 1 2 3 4

At **CRÈCHES-SUR-SAÔNE** (0.5km NW on D89)

★★**Château de la Barge** (**DPn**) ☎85371204

10 Jan—20 Dec
rm24 (22) **P**30 Lift sB 159—203
dB 190—242 M66—150
Credit cards 1 2 3 4

Perrin (N6) ☎85371261 Closed Jun 23—Jul 14, Sat pm & Sun Ren

Romand (N6) ☎371137 Closed Sun & Mon pm Peu

At **ST-ALBAIN** (10km N)

★★★★***Sofitel*** (A6) ☎85381617 tx800881

100 Lift

At **SANCÉ-LES-MÂCON** (4km N)

★★★***Vielle Ferme*** (FAH) (N6) ☎85384693

32
Credit cards 3 5

★★***Climat*** ZAC des Platières, r du 19 Mars 1962 ☎85392133 tx692844

42 **P**
Credit cards 1 3

MAGESCQ
Landes

★★***Relais de la Poste*** ☎58477025

Closed 11 Nov—24 Dec
16 **P**80

MAISONS-LAFFITTE
Yvelines

★★***Climat*** r de Paris ☎34460123 tx692844

42 **P**

MALBUISSON
Doubs

★★★**Lac** ☎81693480 tx360713

rm54 (48) **P** Lift sB123 sB 176
dB 240 mountains lake

MALÈNE (LA)
Lozère

★★★**Manoir de Montesquiou** ☎66485112

Apr—15 Oct →

🛁🚿12 **P**10 dB🛁🚿241—346 M86—145 mountains
Credit card [5]

MAMERS
Sarthe

★***Croix Blanche*** 79 r P-Bert ☎43976263
Mar—20 Jan
rm10 (🛁🚿4)

MANDELIEU
Alpes-Maritimes

★**Esterel** 1625 av de Fréjus (n.rest) ☎93499220
🚿22 **P**25 sB🚿205—265 dB🚿250—320 mountains

★**Pavillon des Sports** rte de Fréjus ☎93495086
rm11 (🚿8) A3rm **P**30 dBfr45 dB🚿fr185 Mfr55 t2% mountains
Credit cards [1] [2] [3] [5]

MANOSQUE
Alpes-de-Haute-Provence

★★**Campanile** rte de Voix (N96) ☎92875900
🛁30 **P** sB🛁204—225 dB🛁226—247 M61—82
Credit card [3]

MANS (LE)
Sarthe

★★★★***Concorde*** 16 av Gl-Leclerc ☎43241230 tx720487
rm64 (🛁🚿55) **P**12 Lift ☾
Credit cards [1] [2] [3] [5]

★★★**Moderne** 14 r Bourg-Belé ☎43247920
🛁🚿32 A18rm 🚗 **P**20 ☾ sB🛁🚿fr209 dB🛁🚿308—318 M115—207 S15%
Credit cards [1] [2] [3] [5]

★★★**Novotel le Mans Est** ZAC les Sabions, bd R-Schumann ☎43852680 tx720706
🛁94 **P**150 Lift sB🛁fr308 dB🛁fr361 ≈
Credit cards [1] [2] [3] [5]

★★***Central*** (FAH) 5 bd R-Levasseur (n.rest) ☎43240893
rm50 (🛁🚿36) 🚗 **P** Lift

★★**Chantecler** 50 r Pelouse ☎43245853
rm36 (🛁🚿33) **P**20 Lift sBfr103 sB🛁🚿198—253 dB156 dB🛁🚿216—271 M65—115

★★**Climat** Les Grues Rouges ☎43213121
🛁26 **P**40 sB🛁210—233 dB🛁230—253 M51—90
Credit cards [1] [3]

★★**Fimotel** 17 r de la Pointe, Rocade Sud ☎43722780 tx722092
🛁42 **P** Lift sB🛁229—239 dB🛁261—271 M54—90
Credit cards [1] [2] [3] [5]

★★***Ibis*** Angle Quai Ledru-Rollin, 4 r des Ah Ah ☎43231823 tx722035
🛁83 🚗 **P**18 Lift sB🛁226—242 dB🛁274—288 M72
Credit cards [1] [3]

France

★★***Ibis*** r C-Marot ☎43861414 tx720651
🛁49 **P**60
Credit cards [2] [5]

Lessul bd P-le-Faucheux, ZI ☎43846170 Closed Sat & Sun For

At **ARNAGE** (9km S via N23)

★★**Campanile** La Gêmerie bd P-le-Faucheux ☎43218121 tx722803
🛁42 **P** sB🛁204—225 dB🛁226—247 M61—82
Credit card [3]

MANSLE
Charente

🚘 **J Gullment** rte Nationale ☎45203031 All makes

MANTES-LA-JOLIE
Yvelines

★★**Climat** r M-Tabu ☎30330370
🛁41 **P**41 sB🛁213—233 dB🛁233—253 M51—110 lake

★★***Ibis*** allée des Martinets, ZAC des Brosses, Magnanville ☎30926565 tx695358
🛁52 M alc
Credit cards [1] [3]

MARCAY See **CHINON**

MARGNY See **COMPIÉGNE**

MARGUERITTES See **NÎMES**

MARIGNANE See **MARSEILLE AIRPORT**

MARLENHEIM
Bas-Rhin

★★**Cerf** 30 r du Gl-de-Gaulle ☎ 88877373
Open except early Jan
rm19 **P** sBfr150 dB210—310 M150—310
Credit cards [2] [3]

★★***Hostellerie Reeb*** (N4) ☎88875270
🛁🚿35 🚗 **P**100
Credit cards [1] [2] [3] [5]

MARQ-EN-BAROEUL See **LILLE**

MARSANNAY-LA-CÔTE
Côte-d'Or

★★***Bimotel*** Dijon Sud (RN74) Couchey ☎80521266 tx350121
🛁58 **P**80 ≈
Credit cards [1] [2] [5]

MARSEILLE
Bouches-du-Rhône

★★★★**Frantel** Centre Bourse, r Neuve St-Martin ☎ 91919129 tx401886
🛁200 Lift sB🛁462—507 dB🛁559—604 M70—228&alc
Credit cards [1] [2] [3] [5]

★★★★***Grand & Noailles*** (BW/MAP) 66 Canebière ☎91549148 tx430609
🛁70 **P** Lift ☾

★★★★**Sofitel Vieux Port** 36 bd C-Livon ☎91529019 tx401270
🛁222 🚗 **P**160 Lift ☾ ≈ sea
Credit cards [1] [2] [3] [5]

★★★**St-Georges** 10 r du Cpt-Dessemond (n.rest) ☎91525692
🛁🚿27 Lift ☾ sB🛁🚿160—221 dB🛁🚿210—271 t4% sea
Credit cards [1] [2] [3] [5]

★★**Fimotel** 25 bd Rabatau ☎91257300 tx21269
🛁90 **P** Lift
Credit cards [1] [2] [3] [5]

★★**Ibis** 6 r de Cassis ☎91785925 tx400362
🛁119 **P**25 Lift sB🛁207—235 dB🛁245—275 M alc t3%

Auto Diffusion 36 bd National ☎91620805 Closed Sun For

🚘 **Bonneveine** 2 av J-Vidal ☎91733119 Closed Sun All makes

🚘 **Clotti** 11 r J-B-Astier ☎91497534 Closed Sat & Sun
All makes

🚘 **Steg-Ponteves** 20 r de Ponteves ☎91904663 Closed Sat & Sun Ren

🚘 **Touchard** 151 av Montolivet ☎91661239 M/c All makes

At **PENNE-ST-MENET (LA)** (10km E of A52)

★★★***Novotel Marseille Est*** (A52) ☎91439060 tx400667
🛁131 **P** Lift 🎾 ≈

MARSEILLE AIRPORT

At **MARIGNANE** (8km NW)

★★★★***Sofitel*** ☎42899102 tx401980
🛁180 **P**140 ☾ Lift M alc 🎾 ≈
Credit cards [1] [2] [3] [5]

★★***Ibis*** av du 8 Mai 1945 ☎42883535 tx440052
🛁36

At **VITROLLES** (8km N)

★★★**Novotel Marseille Aéroport** (A7) ☎42899044 tx420670
🛁150 **P**500 Lift sB🛁285—305 dB🛁335—355 ≈
Credit cards [1] [2] [3] [5]

★★**Campanile** Le Griffon, rte d'Aix-en-Provence ☎42892511 tx402722
🛁44 **P** sB🛁204—225 dB🛁226—247 M61—82
Credit card [3]

★★***Climat*** ZI de Couperigne (CD20) ☎42752300
🛁41 **P**45 Lift

MARTEL
Lot

At **GLUGES** (5km SE on N681)

★★**Falaises (DPn)** ☎65373359
Mar—Nov
rm15 (🛁🚿13) **P**35 sB95 dB🛁🚿186—206 M63—150
Credit card [3]

MARTIGUES
Bouches-du-Rhône

★★**Campanile** ZAC de Canto-Perdrix, bd de Tholon ☎42801400 tx401378
🛁 42 **P** sB🛁 217—238 dB🛁 239—260 M61—82
Credit card [3]

★★**Fimotel** ZI de Caronte, av Nobre ☎42818494 tx441405
🛁 42 **P** Lift
Credit cards [1] [2] [3] [5]

MARVEJOLS
Lozère

★***Paix*** LE 2 av de Brazza ☎66321017
rm19 (🛁🚿12) 🏠 **P**

MASSAT
Ariège

★★***Trois Seigneurs*** av de St-Girons ☎61969589
Mar—Oct
🛁 20 A10rm **P**40 mountains

MASSIAC
Cantal

★★**Poste** (FAH) av de C-Ferrand (N9) ☎71230201 tx990989
20 Dec—6 Nov
rm36 (🛁🚿26) **P**30 Lift sBfr98 sB🛁🚿150 dB129—148 dB🛁🚿194—221 M47—130 mountains
Credit cards [1] [2] [3]

🚗 **Richard** av de Clermont ☎71230225
Closed Mon Peu

MAULÉON-LICHARRE
Pyrénées-Atlantiques

★★**Bidegain** 13 r de la Navarre ☎59281605
15 Jan—15 Dec
rm30 (🛁🚿15) 🏠 **P**15 sB93—105 sB🛁🚿157—168 dB115—127 dB🛁🚿178—211 M60—120 mountains
Credit cards [1] [2] [3] [5]

MAYENNE
Mayenne

★★***Grand*** LE (FAH) 2 r Ambroise-de-Loré ☎43043735
8 Jan—24 Dec
rm24 (🛁🚿21) 🏠 **P**40 ☾
Credit card [1]

★***Croix Couverte*** LE rte de Paris ☎43043248
🛁🚿11 🏠 **P**70
Credit cards [1] [2] [3]

🚗 **P Legros** 15 r Du Guesclin ☎43041627
Closed Sat pm For

MAZAMET
Tarn

★★★***Grand Balcon*** sq G-Tournier ☎63610115
🛁🚿25 Lift mountains

MEAUX
Seine-et-Marne

★★***Sirène*** 33 r Gl-Leclerc ☎64340780
rm19 (🛁🚿14) **P**20
Credit cards [2] [3] [5]

🚗 **Cornillon** 45 r Cornillon ☎64340558
All makes

🚗 **Vance** 37 av F-Roosevelt ☎64332976
Closed Sat pm & Sun Ren

MEGÈVE
Haute-Savoie

★★★★**Mont Blanc** (Inter) pl de l'Église ☎50212002 tx385854
15 Jun—15 Apr
🛁 54 A10rm 🏠 **P**250 Lift ☾
sB🛁 1035—1905 dB🛁 1090—1960 M180—225 S15% t4% ≈ ⛶ U mountains
Credit cards [1] [2] [3] [5]

★★★***Parc*** r d'Arly (n.rest) ☎50210574
Xmas, Etr & end Jun—mid Sep
🛁 48 **P**40 Lift ☾ mountains

MEHUN-SUR-YEVRE
Cher

★***Croix Blanche*** (**DPn**) 164 r J-d'Arc ☎48573001
20 Jan—20 Dec
rm20 (🛁🚿3) 🏠 **P** ☾

MEILLY-SUR-ROUVRES See **POUILLY-EN-AUXOIS**

MELUN
Seine-et-Marne

See also **PONTHIERRY**

★★★**Grand Monarque Concorde** rte Fontainebleau ☎64390440 tx690140
🛁🚿50 **P** Lift ☾ sB🛁🚿337—357 dB🛁🚿415—458 M145 S15% t19% ≈

★★**Climat** 338 r R-Hervillard, Vaux-le-Pénil ☎64527181 tx693140
🛁 42 **P**50 sB🛁 233—239 dB🛁 242—258 M51—98
Credit cards [1] [3]

★★***Ibis*** av de Meaux ☎60684245 tx691779
🛁 74 **P**

🚗 **Avenue** 58 av Thiers ☎64390754
Closed Sat pm & Sun Alf

At **DAMMARIE-LES-LYS** (5km SW)

★★**Campanile** 346 r C-de-Gaulle ☎64375151 tx691621
🛁 50 **P** sB🛁 204—225 dB🛁 226—247 M61—82
Credit card [3]

At **VERT-ST-DENIS** (NW on N6)

★★**Balladins** av du Bois Vert ☎64416666 tx649394
🛁 38 🏠 **P**38 sB🛁 166 dB🛁 182 M56—77
Credit cards [1] [2] [3]

MENDE
Lozère

★★***Lion d'Or*** (BW/MAP) (**DPn**) 12 bd Britexte ☎66650646 tx480302
Mar—Dec
🛁🚿41 **P** Lift ☾ 🔑 ≈ mountains

★★**Paris** 2 bd du Soubeyran (n.rest) ☎66650003
25 Mar—15 Nov
rm45 🏠 **P**15 Lift sB82—104 dB133 mountains

Carrosserie Crespin SARL av du 11 Novembre ☎66651828 Closed Sat
All makes

MENTON
Alpes-Maritimes

★★★**Europa** 35 bd Verdun (n.rest) ☎93355992 tx470673
🛁 33 🏠 Lift ☾ sB🛁 218—250 dB🛁 300—316

★★★**Méditerranée** 5 r de la République ☎93282525 tx461361
🛁 90 🏠 Lift sB🛁 264—314 dB🛁 318—368 M76 t4%
Credit cards [1] [2] [3] [5]

★★★**Napoléon** 29 Porte de France ☎93358950 tx470312
Closed Nov—15 Dec
🛁 40 🏠 **P**30 Lift ☾ sB🛁 310—430 dB🛁 330—450 M128&alc ⛶ ≈ sea mountains
Credit cards [1] [2] [3] [5]

★★★**Parc** 11 av de Verdun ☎93576666 tx470673
20 Dec—Sep
🛁🚿72 **P**30 Lift ☾ sB🛁🚿268—288 dB🛁🚿376—426 M140 t4% mountains
Credit card [3]

★★★**Princess et Richmond** 32 av Gl-de-Gaulle (n.rest) ☎93358020 tx470673
20 Dec—3 Nov
🛁🚿45 🏠 **P** Lift ☾ sB🛁🚿249—319 dB🛁🚿298—378 sea mountains
Credit cards [1] [2] [3] [5]

★★**Algion** 7 av de la Madone (n.rest) ☎93575555
20 Dec—4 Nov
rm32 (🛁🚿27) **P**20 Lift ☾ sBfr150 sB🛁🚿fr190 dBfr250 dB🛁🚿370 t4% ≈ sea mountains
Credit cards [1] [2] [3]

★★**El Paradiso** (Inter) (**DPn**) 71 Porte de France ☎93357402
Jan—Oct
🛁🚿42 **P** Lift ☾

★★**Floréal** (**DPn**) cours de Centenaire ☎93357581
11 Dec—10 Oct
rm60 **P**18 Lift M60 t3% sea mountains

★★**Londres** 15 av Carnot ☎93357462
10 Jan—8 Oct
rm26 (🛁🚿20) Lift sB163—171 sB🛁🚿194—199 dB187—192 dB🛁🚿215—219 M80—85 t3%

★★**Prince de Galles** 4 av Gl-de-Gaulle ☎93282121 tx470673
⇌ ⋒68 **P**12 Lift ☾ sB⇌ ⋒208—293 dB⇌ ⋒268—314 Mfr60 t4% sea mountains
Credit cards 1 2 3 5

★★**Rives d'Azur** prom Ml-Joffre ☎93576760
15 Dec—Oct
rm36 (⇌ ⋒27) **P**6 Lift sB102—147 sB⇌ ⋒197—267 dB179 dB⇌ ⋒224—304 M60—80 sea

⛟ **Fossan** 1 bd du Fossan ☎93570307 Closed Sep—Oct, Sat pm & Sun All makes

MÉRÉVILLE
Meurthe-et-Moselle

★★***Maison Carrée*** LE ☎83470923
rm23 (⇌ ⋒22) ⛟ **P**50 ☾ beach
Credit cards 1 2 3 5

MÉRIGNAC See **BORDEAUX**

METZ
Moselle

★★★★**Frantel** 29 pl St-Thiébault ☎87361769 tx930417
⇌ 112 **P**50 Lift Malc
Credit cards 1 2 3 5

★★★***Royal Concorde*** 23 av Foch (n.rest) ☎87668111 tx860425
rm75 (⇌ ⋒55) Lift ☾

★★★**Sofitel** Centre St-Jacques, pl des Paraîges ☎87745727 tx930328
⇌ 97 **P**40 Lift sB⇌ 370—395 dB⇌ 472—497 M55—110 ⛱
Credit cards 1 2 3 5

★★***Central*** (Inter) 3 bis r Vauban (n.rest) ☎87755343 tx930281
⇌ ⋒54 ⛟ **P**15
Credit cards 1 2 4

★★**Ibis** quartier du Pontiffroy, r Chambière ☎8731073 tx930278
⇌ 79 Lift sB⇌ 194—215 dB⇌ 238—261 M70&alc
Credit cards 1 3

★★**Urbis Central** 3 bis r Vauban (n.rest) ☎87755343 tx930281
⇌ 72 ⛟ **P**5 Lift sB⇌ 192—229 dB⇌ 236—243
Credit cards 1 3

★***Lutéce*** LE 11 r de Paris ☎87302725
rm21 (⇌ ⋒12) ⛟ **P**5
Credit cards 1 3

⛟ **Jacquot** 2 r P-Boileau ☎8302440 Closed Sat & Sun Peu

At **HAUCONCOURT** (9.5km N on A31)

★★★**Novotel** (A31) ☎87804111 tx860191
⇌ 130 **P**150 Lift sB⇌ 303—360 dB⇌ 361—420 ⛱
Credit cards 1 2 3 5

At **TALANGÉ** (5km N)

★★***Climat*** la Ponte, r des Alliés ☎87721311 tx612241
⇌ 42 **P**50 mountains

France

At **WOIPPY** (5km NW)

★★★**Mercure Metz Nord** r du Fort Gambetta ☎87325279 tx860891
⇌ 83 **P** Lift sB⇌ 305—315 dB⇌ 370—380 M105&alc
Credit cards 1 2 3 4 5

MEULAN
Yvelines

★★★**Mercure** Lieu dit Ile Belle ☎34746363 tx695295
⇌ 69 **P**100 Lift sB⇌ 388—698 dB⇌ 446—736 ⛱
Credit cards 1 2 3 5

MEURSAULT
Côte-d'Or

⛟ **J Hemart** 14 r C-Giraud ☎80212084 Closed Sun All makes

⛟ **Meyrieux** rte Forges ☎80212060 M/c Closed Aug, Sat & Sun BMW Peu

MEYLAN See **GRENOBLE**

MEYRUEIS
Lozère

★★★**Château d'Ayres** ☎66456010
30 Mar—15 Oct
⇌ ⋒24 **P**30 ☾ sB⇌ ⋒fr258 dB⇌ ⋒331—451 Mfr95 mountains
Credit cards 1 2 3 5

★★**Renaissance** (Inter) **(DPn)** ☎66456019
Mar—2 Jan
⇌ 20 sB⇌ 202—252 dB⇌ 224—344 Mfr70 mountains
Credit cards 1 2 3 5

MÉZIÉRE-SUR-ISSOIRE
Haute-Vienne

⛟ **A Boos** rte de Bellac ☎55683028 Closed Sun For

MIGENNES
Yonne

★★**Paris** LE **(Pn)** 57 av J-Jaurès ☎86802322
20 Jan—25 Jul & 25 Aug—2 Jan
rm9 (⇌ ⋒3) ⛟ **P**4 sB108—166 sB⇌ ⋒123—166 dB123—181 dB⇌ ⋒138—181 Mfr65alc
Credit cards 1 3 5

★**Gare et l'Escale** ☎86802099
12rm (⇌ ⋒7) ⛟ **P** sB⇌ ⋒92—166 M55—150
Credit cards 1 2 3 5

⛟ **Migennes Autos** 148 av J-Jaurès ☎86800478 Closed Sat pm & Sun Cit

MIGNE-AUXANCES See **POITIERS**

MILLAU
Aveyron

★★★**International** 1 pl de la Tine ☎65602066 tx520629
rm110 (⇌ 104) ⛟ **P** Lift ☾ sBfr135 dB⇌ 415 M95—250 mountains
Credit cards 1 2 3 5

★★**Moderne** 11 av J-Jaurès ☎65605923 tx520629
Apr—Sep
rm45 (⇌ 40) ⛟ **P** Lift sBfr108 dB⇌ 181 M95—250
Credit cards 1 2 3 5

★**Causses** LE 56 av J-Jaurès ☎65600319
rm22 (⇌ ⋒7) ⛟ sB85 sB⇌ ⋒125 dBfr100 dB⇌ ⋒fr140 M50—85

★**Paris & Poste** 10 av A-Merle ☎65600052
3 Jan—15 Nov
rm22 (⇌ ⋒15) **P**14 Lift sB91—101 sB⇌ ⋒136—156 dB106—116 dB⇌ ⋒156—181 M50—120 t%
Credit cards 3 5

⛟ **J Pineau** 161 av de Calès ☎65600855 M/c All makes

⛟ **J Vaissiére** 6 r L-Blanc ☎65600016 Closed Sun & Mon am Vol

MILLES (LES) See **AIX-EN-PROVENCE**

MILLY
Indre-et-Loire

★**Château de Milly (DPn)** rte de Richelieu et Châtellerault ☎47581456
Etr—15 Oct
rm15 (⇌ ⋒13) ⛟ **P** sB207—351 sB⇌ ⋒301—351 dB292—472 dB⇌ ⋒382—472 M145—185 ⛱
Credit cards 1 2 3 5

MIMIZAN
Landes

⛟ **J Poisson** 48 av de Bordeaux ☎58090873 Closed Sun pm Ren

At **MIMIZAN-PLAGE**

★★**Côte d'Argent (Pn)** 4 av M-Martin ☎58091522
20 May—Sep
⇌ 40 **P** Lift ☾ dB⇌ 348—388 Mfr110 sea
Credit cards 1 2 3 5

⛟ **W Kunz** ☎58090501 Closed Oct 1—15 Ope Vau

MIRAIL (LE) See **TOULOUSE**

MIRAMBEAU
Charente-Maritime

★**Union** r Principale ☎46496164
rm9 (⋒1) A2rm ⛟ **P**10 sB58—81 sB⋒92 dB192 M46—60
Credit cards 1 3

⛟ **Gauvin** 1 a C-Jourdain ☎46496185 All makes

MIREPOIX
Airège

★**Commerce** LE **(DPn)** cours du Dr-Chabaud ☎61681029
Feb—Sep & 15 Oct—Dec
rm31 (⇌ ⋒25) A11rm ⛟ **P**15 sB77—105 sB⇌ ⋒139 dB89—119 dB⇌ ⋒149—183 M45—155
Credit cards 1 3

France

MISSILLAC
Loire-Atlantique

★★★**Golf de la Bretesche** ☎40883005
Closed Feb
rm27 (🛁🚿26) **P**30 🎾 ⛵ lake
Credit card [3]

MODANE
Savoie

At **FOURNEAUX** (3km SW)

M Bellussi 36 av de la Liberté ☎79050774
Closed Sat & Sun Fia

MOISSAC
Tarn-et-Garonne

★★★**Moulin** (MAP) 1 pl du Moulin
☎63040355 tx521615
🛁🚿45 **P** Lift sB🛁🚿200—400
dB🛁🚿300—500
Credit cards [1] [2] [3] [5]

★**Pont Napoléon** 2 allées Montebello
☎63040155
15 Jan—5 Jun & 15 Jun—15 Dec & closed Tue
rm15 (🛁🚿11) ⌂ dB92 dB🛁🚿152—212
M60—180 S15% lake
Credit card [3]

MOLAY LITTRY (LE)
Calvados

★★★**Château de Molay** (BW/MAP)
☎31229082 tx171912
Mar—Nov
🛁38 A5rm **P**100 Lift sB🛁313—333
dB🛁386—646 M140—250 🎾 ⛵
Credit cards [1] [2] [3] [5]

MONDEVILLE See **CAEN**

MONTARGIS
Loiret

★**Tour d'Auvergne** LE 20 r J-Jaurès
☎38850116
Closed Feb
rm14 (🛁🚿12) ⌂ **P**12 sB101—161
dB🛁🚿142—177 M70—124
Credit cards [1] [2] [3] [4] [5]

M Schnaldt 38 r J-Jaurès ☎38932810
Closed Sat pm, Sun & Mon am Mer Vol

At **AMILLY** (5km S)

★★**Climat** av d'Antibes ☎38982021
🛁26 **P**40 sB🛁fr211 dB🛁fr232 Mfr67
Credit cards [1] [3]

MONTAUBAN
Tarn-et-Garonne

★★**Midi** LE (Inter) 12r Notre-Dame
☎63631723 tx531705
rm62 (🛁🚿59) A14rm ⌂ **P**60 Lift ☾
sB111—121 sB🛁🚿141—261 dB137—147
dB🛁🚿172—302 M65—100
Credit cards [1] [2] [3] [4] [5]

★**Orsay** (FAH) (opposite station)
☎63630057 tx520362
🛁20 A34rm ⌂ **P** Lift sB🛁175—210
dB🛁230—260 Mfr100
Credit cards [1] [2] [3] [5]

🔧 **Ateller Auto Speed** 23 r Lassus
☎63030330 M/c **P** All makes

At **MONTBETON** (3km W)

★★★**Coulandrières** (**Pn** in season)
rte Castelsarrasin ☎63674747 tx520200
Feb—Dec
🛁🚿21 A21rm **P** sB🛁🚿297—327
dB🛁🚿324—354 ⛵
Credit cards [1] [2] [3] [5]

MONTBARD
Côte-d'Or

★★**Gare** 10 r MI-Foch, pl de la Gare (n.rest)
☎80920212
rm20 (🛁🚿14) ⌂ **P**15 sBfr75 sB🛁🚿fr175
dBfr113 dB🛁🚿fr205
Credit cards [1] [3]

★***Ecu*** LE (**DPn**) 7 r A-Carré ☎80921166
rm24 (🛁🚿22) ⌂ **P**
Credit cards [1] [3] [5]

MONTBAZON
Indre-et-Loire

★★★★★**Château d'Artigny** (Relais et Châteaux) ☎47262424 tx750900
11 Jan—Nov
🛁🚿53 A22rm **P** Lift ☾ dB🛁🚿516—1066
M200—350&alc 🎾 ⛵ ⛵
Credit card [3]

★★★★**Tortinière** (1.5km N)
☎47260019 tx750806
Mar—15 Nov
🛁🚿21 A10rm **P**50 sB🛁🚿339
dB🛁🚿309—617 🎾 ⛵
Credit cards [1] [3]

At **MONTS** (8km W)

★**Sporting** LE ☎47267015
Closed 15—30 Sep & 14 Feb—7 Mar
rm13 (🛁🚿4) A5rm **P**25 sB83—118
sB🛁🚿118 dB101—136 dB🛁🚿136
M61—158

MONTBÉLIARD
Doubs

★★**Ibis** r J-Foillet, ZAC du Pied d'Egouttes
☎81902158 tx381555
🛁62 sB🛁195 dB🛁240 M60—100
Credit cards [1] [3]

At **BAVANS** (2.5km SW)

🔧 **Esso** 85 Grande Rue ☎81962659 Peu

MONTBETON See **MONTAUBAN**

MONTCABRIER See **PUY L'ÉVÊQUE**

MONTCHANIN See **CREUSOT (LE)**

MONT-DE-MARSAN
Landes

★★★**Richelleu** 3 r Wlerick ☎58061020
tx550238
rm75 (🛁🚿50) ⌂ **P** Lift ☾ sB81—98
sB🛁🚿161—180 dB123—144
dB🛁🚿188—214 M65—180
Credit cards [1] [2] [3] [5]

MONT-DORE (LE)
Puy-de-Dôme

★★★***Carlina*** les Pradets ☎73650422
🛁🚿50 ⌂ **P**50 mountains
Credit card [3]

At **PIED-DU-SANCY** (4km S on N683)

★★**Puy-Ferand** LE (**Pn**) ☎73651899
15 May—20 Sep & 20 Dec—20 Apr
rm42 (🛁🚿34) Lift sB152—168
sB🛁🚿fr193 dBfr187 dB🛁🚿221 M89
t2% mountains
Credit cards [1] [2] [3] [5]

MONTÉLIMAR
Drôme

★★★***Relais de l'Empereur*** (BW/MAP)
(**DPn**) pl M-Dormoy ☎75012900 tx345537
Closed 11 Nov—21 Dec
🛁🚿40 ⌂ **P** ☾ mountains

★★***Climat*** 8 bd du Pêcher ☎75530770
🛁44 **P** Lift

★★**Sphinx** 19 bd Desmarais (n.rest)
☎75018664
🛁🚿25 ⌂ **P**22 sB🛁🚿174—209
dB🛁🚿192—227
Credit card [3]

★**Beausoleil** LE 14 bd Pêcher, pl d'Armes
(n.rest) ☎75011980
rm16 (🛁🚿14) **P**16 sBfr118
sB🛁🚿188—198 dB🛁🚿166—236

🔧 **P Amardell** 115 av J-Jaurès ☎75015821
Closed 24 Feb—2 Mar, Sat pm & Sun
All makes

🔧 **J Brusut** (N7) ☎75510658 Closed Sun
All makes

🔧 **Faure** Q-Blaches, rte de Marseille
☎75012767 Closed Sun Dat

🔧 **G Froux** 130 av du Teil ☎75015704 M/c
Closed Etr All makes

🔧 **Gillet** ZI ☎75011242 Closed Sat pm &
Sun Mer Toy

🔧 **Pélican** (N7) ☎75013607 Closed Sat pm
& Sun Vol

🔧 **Peyrouse** ZI du Sud, rte de Châteauneuf
☎75013916 Closed Sat & Sun For

Sud Auto rte de Marseille ☎75013344
Closed 11—17 Aug, Sat & Sun Tal

At **SAUZET** (9km NE on D6)

🔧 **M Chaix** ☎75467170 Closed Sat pm &
Sun Ren

MONTESSON
Yvelines

★★**Campanile** 9 r du Chant des Oiseaux
☎30716334 tx698906
🛁41 **P** sB🛁217—238 dB🛁239—260
M61—82
Credit card [3]

MONTFAVET See **AVIGNON**

MONTIGNAC
Dordogne

★**Soleil d'Or** 16 r IV Septembre
☎53518022
Mar—Nov →

➡38 A4rm **P** sB➡175—275 dB➡210—300 M75—230 ≈

MONTIGNY-LA-RESLE
Yonne

★★***Soleil d'Or*** LF ☎86418121
Jan—Nov
rm11 (➡⋒) A4rm **P**

MONTIGNY-LE-ROI
Haute-Marne

★★**Moderne** (Inter) av de Neufchâteau ☎25861018 tx840349
rm25 (➡⋒14) ⌂ **P** sB121 dB➡⋒202—227 Mfr60
Credit cards [1] [2] [3] [5]

⌂ **Flagex** (N74) ☎25861034 Closed Sun

MONTIVILLIERS See **HAVRE (LE)**

MONTLUCON
Allier

★★★**Terminus** 47 av M-Dormoy ☎70052893
rm48 (➡⋒33) ⌂ **P** Lift sB95 dB106 dB➡⋒199
Credit cards [1] [2] [3] [5]

★★**Château St-Jean** Parc St-Jean ☎70050465
rm8 (➡⋒5) ⌂ **P** sB➡⋒300—500

MONTMIRAIL
Marne

★**Vert Galant** (**Pn**) 2 pl Vert Galant ☎26812017
rm12 (⋒3) ⌂ **P**10 sB71—73 sB⋒94 dB101—106 dB⋒112—132 M52—95
Credit card [1]

MONTMORENCY
Val-d'Oise

★★**Boscotel Montmorency** 42 rte de Domont ☎34170002 tx699886
➡42 **P**48 Lift sB➡253—288 dB➡316—356 M60—130
Credit cards [1] [3] [4]

MONTMORILLON
Vienne

★★**France Mercier** (**DPn**) 2 bd de Strasbourg ☎49910051
Closed Jan
rm25 (➡⋒16) sB120—170 sB➡⋒160—190 dB160—190 dB➡⋒190—220 M100—280
Credit cards [1] [2] [3] [4] [5]

MONTMORT
Marne

★★**Place** LF 3 pl Berthelot ☎26591038
Closed 25 Jan—20 Feb
rm33 (➡25) A9rm ⌂ **P**20 sB92—144 sB➡92—144 dB109—188 dB➡109—188 M60—120
Credit cards [1] [3]

MONTOIRE-SUR-LE-LOIR
Loire-et-Cher

★★**Cheval Rouge** LF (**DPn**) pl Ml-Foch ☎54850705
Closed Feb
rm17 (➡⋒16) ⌂ **P**12 sB84—125 sB➡⋒124—170 dB103—185 dB➡⋒143—205 M85—205
Credit cards [1] [3]

MONTPELLIER
Hérault

★★★★**Frantel** 218 r de Bastion-Ventadour, quartier le Polygone ☎67646566 tx480362
➡116 ⌂ **P** Lift sB➡308 dB➡383
Credit cards [1] [2] [3] [5]

★★★★**Métropole** (BW/MAP) 3 r C-René ☎67581122 tx480410
➡⋒92 ⌂ Lift ☾ sB➡⋒402—902 dB➡⋒474—974 Malc
Credit cards [1] [2] [3] [5]

★★★★***Sofitel*** le Triangle ☎67540404 tx480140
➡125 **P** Lift ☾

★★★**Mercure Montpellier Est** 662 av de Pompignane ☎67655024 tx480656
➡⋒122 **P** Lift ≈

★★★***Novotel*** 125 bis av de Palavas ☎67640404 tx490433
➡97 **P**100 Lift M alc ≈
Credit cards [1] [2] [3] [5]

★★**Climat** r de Caducée ☎67524333 tx490206
➡42 **P**45 sB➡206 dB➡224 M51—63
Credit cards [1] [3]

★★***Ibis*** rte de Palavas ☎67588230 tx480578
➡102 **P**100 Lift M alc
Credit cards [1] [3]

⌂ **Attard** 33 av de Pontjuvenol ☎67659417 Tal

⌂ **Auto Méditérranée** 26 r E-Michel ☎67929729 Closed Sat pm & Sun BMW

Croix d'Argent 91 rte de Toulouse ☎67428174 Closed Sun Aud VW

⌂ **France Auto** av du M-Gare ☎67926374 Closed Sat & Sun Ope Vau

⌂ **RNU Renault** 700 r de l'Industrie ☎67420075 Closed Sat pm & Sun Ren

MONTREUIL (Eure-et-Loire) See **DREUX**

MONTREUIL
Pas-de-Calais

★★★**Château de Montreuil** (Relais et Châteaux) (**Pn**) 4 chaussée des Capucins ☎21815304 tx135205
Feb—15 Dec
➡⋒14 A3rm ⌂ **P**7 ☾ sB➡⋒335—370 dB➡⋒475—560 M120—280&alc
Credit cards [1] [2] [3] [5]

★**Central** (**DPn**) 7—9 r du Change ☎21861604
24 Jan—23 Dec
rm11 (➡⋒5) A3rm ⌂ sB87—97 sB➡⋒167 dB128—143 dB➡⋒283—333 M59—135
Credit cards [1] [2] [3]

⌂ **Lavogez** 3 r St-Gengoult ☎21061143 Closed Sat pm & Sun Ren

MONTREUIL-BELLAY
Maine-et-Loire

★**Splendid** LF (**Pn**) r Dr-Gaudrez ☎41523021
Closed 10—25 Jan
rm40 (➡⋒38) A22rm **P**20 sB85—130 sB➡⋒100—245 dB105—150 dB➡⋒120—265 M55—160 ≈
Credit cards [1] [3]

MONTRICHARD
Loir-et-Cher

★★**Bellevue** LF (**Pn**) (Inter) quai du Cher ☎54320617
21 Dec—15 Nov
➡⋒29 **P** Lift dB➡⋒285—297 M79—200
Credit cards [1] [2] [3] [5]

★★**Tête-Noire** LF (**DPn**) rte de Tours ☎54320555
Closed 2 Jan—7 Feb
rm39 (➡⋒28) A9rm **P**10 sB123 sB➡⋒161—189 dB146 dB➡⋒144—267 M65—200
Credit card [3]

At **CHISSAY-EN-TOURAINE** (6km W)

★★★**Château Menaudière** ☎54320244 tx751246
15 Mar—Nov
➡⋒25 ⌂ **P** sB➡⋒240 dB➡⋒460—530 M190—250

MONTROUGE See **PARIS**

MONTS See **MONTBAZON**

MONT-ST-MICHEL (LE)
Manche

★★**Digue** LF La Digue (2km S) ☎33601402 tx170157
15 Mar—15 Nov
➡⋒35 **P**40 sB➡⋒190—240 dB➡⋒225—290 M60—170 sea
Credit cards [2] [3] [5]

★★***K*** LF (FAH) La Digue (2km S on D976) ☎33601418 tx170537
Etr—Nov
➡60
Credit card [2]

★★**Mère Poulard** (**DPn**) ☎33601401
28 Mar—Sep
rm27 (➡⋒22) A14rm **DPn** 283—671 M175—450
Credit cards [2] [5]

MONTSALVY
Cantal

★★**Nord** LF (Inter) pl du Barry ☎71492003
Seasonal
rm30 (➡⋒24) **P**15 sBfr102 sB➡⋒127—167 dB➡⋒164—214 M50—160
Credit cards [1] [2] [3] [5]

MONTSOULT
Val d'Oise

★★★**Novotel Château de Mafflers**
☎34739305 tx695701

🛁 80 **P**150 sB🛁 fr448 dB🛁 fr486 Mfr170
🎾 ≈
Credit cards 1 2 3 5

MORANGIS See **ORLY AIRPORT** under **PARIS AIRPORTS**

MOREZ
Jura

★★**Central Modern** (**Pn** in season)
106 r de la République ☎84330307

Closed 14 Jul—15 Aug
rm47 (🛁 🚿 18) A26rm ⌂ **P**35 sB85 dB114
dB🛁 🚿 145—190 M62—130 mountains
Credit card 3

MORLAIX
Finistère

★★★***Grand Hotel d'Europe*** (FAH)
1 r d'Aiguillon ☎98621199 tx940696

15 Jan—15 Dec
rm68 (🛁 🚿 58) Lift
Credit cards 1 2 3 5

★★**Fontaine** rte de Lannion ☎98620955

Closed Feb
🛁 35 **P** dB🛁 243 Mfr50 St% ≈

MORTAGNE-AU-PERCHE
Orne

★**Tribunal** LF 4 pl du Palais ☎33250477

rm19 (🛁 🚿 6) ⌂ **P**4 sBfr52 sB🛁 🚿 129
dBfr168 dB🛁 🚿 fr168 M54—113
Credit cards 1 3

MORTAGNE-SUR-SÈVRE
Vendée

★★★**France** LF (**Pn**) (FAH) 4 pl du Dr-Pichat ☎51676337 tx711403

rm26 (🛁 🚿 23) **P**40 Lift sB125—264
sB🛁 🚿 216—234 dB🛁 🚿 310—351
M62—260 🎾 ≈
Credit cards 1 2 3 5

MORTAIN
Manche

★***Cascades*** LF (**DPn**) 6 r Bassin
☎33590003

rm14 (🛁 🚿 5)
Credit card 3

MORZINE
Haute-Savoie

★★★**Carlina** (**Pn** in season) av J-Plane
☎50790103 tx365596

15 Dec—15 Apr & Jul—Aug
🛁 🚿 22 ⌂ **P**10 sB🛁 🚿 300—370
dB🛁 🚿 380—410 M110—170 mountains
Credit cards 1 2 3 5

★★**Dahu** (**Pn**) ☎50791112 tx309514

20 Dec—15 Apr & Jul—Aug
rm28 (🛁 🚿 22) Lift sB145—170
sB🛁 🚿 210—230 dB260—280
dB🛁 🚿 375—410 M120—140 mountains
Credit card 3

France

MOUGINS
Alpes-Maritimes

🚗 **Central** 723 chemin de Ferrandou
☎93454646 All makes

🚗 **Olympique** chemin de l'Oratoire
☎93454646 All makes

Riviera Technil Bretelle Autoroute
☎93455419 Closed Sat & Sun Aud Por VW

MOULINS
Allier

★★★**Paris** (Relais et Châteaux) (**DPn**)
21 r de Paris ☎70440058 tx394853

🛁 🚿 27 ⌂ **P**20 Lift ☾ sB259—509
sB🛁 🚿 279—509 dB308—538
dB🛁 🚿 308—538 Mfr250
Credit cards 1 2 3 4 5

★★***Dauphin*** 59 pl Allier ☎70443305
tx394860

Closed Jan
rm65 (🛁 🚿 33) **P** Lift ☾

★★***Ibis*** Angle de la rte de Lyon (N7)/bd Primaire ☎70467112

🛁 42 **P**

★★**Moderne** (Inter) 9 pl J-Moulin
☎70440506

🛁 🚿 43 ⌂ **P**25 Lift ☾ sB🛁 🚿 229—249
dB🛁 🚿 248—268 M65—80

★★**Parc** LF 31 av Gl-Leclerc ☎70441225

🛁 🚿 28 A5rm ⌂ **P**25 ☾ dB🛁 🚿 150—290
M70—150&alc

🚗 **M Robin** 8 C-de-Bercy ☎70463282 Ren

At **COULANDON** (7km W)

★★**Chalet** ☎70445008

Feb—15 Nov
🛁 🚿 21 A12rm **P**25 sB🛁 🚿 152—197
dB🛁 🚿 200—254 M56—90
Credit cards 1 3 5

MOUTHIER-HAUTE-PIERRE
Doubs

★**Cascade** LF (**DPn**) ☎81609530

3 Feb—Nov
rm23 (🛁 🚿 22) ⌂ **P**20 sB🛁 🚿 148—198
dB🛁 🚿 166—236 M55—230 mountains

MOÛTIERS
Savoie

★★**Ibis** Colline de Champoulet
☎79242711 tx980611

🛁 🚿 62 **P**70 Lift sB🛁 🚿 179—200
dB🛁 🚿 235—256 M70—90 mountains
Credit cards 1 3

MULHOUSE
Haut-Rhin

★★★★**Frantel** 4 pl Gl-Gaulle
☎89460123 tx881807

🛁 96 ⌂ **P**40 Lift sB🛁 310—360
dB🛁 420—450
Credit cards 1 2 3 4 5

🚗 **Parisl** 38 av de Riedisheim ☎89443322
Closed Aug & Sun All makes

At **SAUSHEIM** (6km NE on D422)

★★★★***Sofitel*** (**DPn**) (N422A)
☎89447575 tx881311

🛁 100 Lift 🎾 ≈
Credit cards 1 2 3 5

★★★**Mercure** l'Ille Napoléon
☎89618787 tx881757

🛁 97 **P**150 Lift sB🛁 267—287
dB🛁 324—344 Malc 🎾 ≈
Credit cards 1 2 3 5

★★★**Novotel** r de l'Ile Napoléon
☎89618484 tx881673

🛁 🚿 77 **P**100 sB🛁 🚿 fr312 dB🛁 🚿 fr374
Malc 🎾 ≈
Credit cards 1 2 3 4 5

★★**Ibis** rte de Sausheim est Ille Napoléon
☎89618383 tx881970

🛁 76 **P**80 Lift sB🛁 204—222
dB🛁 239—257 Malc
Credit cards 1 3

At **WITTENHEIM** (6km NW)

★★**Climat** r des Milleportuis ☎89535331
tx881775

🛁 43 sB🛁 212—232 dB🛁 230—250
M50—120 mountains
Credit cards 1 3

MUREAUX (LES)
Yvelines

★★***Climat*** ZAC du Grand Quest CD43, r des Pléiades ☎34747250 tx692844

🛁 42 **P**40
Credit cards 1 3

MUY (LE)
Var

🚗 **St-Roch** rte National ☎94451067 BMW Cit Fia

NAJAC
Aveyron

★★**Belle Rive** LF (**Pn**) (2km NW on D39)
☎65657420

Apr—15 Oct
rm40 (🛁 🚿 35) A10rm ⌂ sB🛁 🚿 191
M50—150&alc ≈

★★**Oustal del Barry** LF (**Pn**) pl du Bourg
☎65657080

23 Mar—3 Nov
rm28 (🛁 🚿 17) A7rm ⌂ **P**20 Lift sB90
sB🛁 🚿 138—174 dB124—135
dB🛁 🚿 183—207 M54—180 mountains
Credit card 3

NANCY
Meurthe-et-Moselle

★★★**Agora** (ETAP) 6 r Piroux (n.rest)
☎83355805 tx960034

🛁 78 Lift sB🛁 219—239 dB🛁 268—297
Credit cards 1 2 3 5

★★★**Frantel** 11 r R-Poincaré
☎83356101 tx960034

🛁 🚿 112 ⌂ **P**40 Lift sB🛁 🚿 313—428
dB🛁 🚿 376—516 M56—205
Credit cards 1 2 3 4 5

★★★**Grand de la Reine** (Relais et Châteaux) 2 pl Stanislas ☎83350301 tx960367

🛁🚿54 Lift ☾ sB🛁🚿535—1105 dB🛁🚿590—1160 M155—215&alc
Credit cards 1 2 3 5

★★**Albert 1er/Astoria** 3 r Armée-Patton (n.rest) ☎83403124 tx850895

rm136 (🛁🚿114) **P**35 Lift sB142 sB🛁🚿187—282 dB164 dB🛁🚿209—304
Credit cards 1 2 3 4 5

★**Américain** 3 pl A-Maginot (n.rest) ☎8322853 tx961052

🛁🚿51 Lift ☾ sB🛁🚿165—250 dB🛁🚿175—265
Credit cards 1 2 3 5

★**Poincaré** 81 r R-Poincaré (n.rest) ☎83402599

rm25 (🚿7) **P** sB86—137 sB🚿137 dB112—152 dB🚿152

At **HOUDEMONT** (6km S)

★★★***Novotel Nancy Sud*** rte d'Épinal (N57) ☎83561025 tx961124

🛁86 **P**200 ≈
Credit cards 1 2 3 5

At **LAXOU** (3km SW)

★★★***Mercure*** 2 r de la Saône ☎83964221 tx850036

🛁99 **P** Lift ≈

★★★**Novotel Nancy Ouest** (N4) ☎83966746 tx850988

🛁🚿119 **P**180 Lift sB🛁🚿239—299 dB🛁🚿329—359 M80&alc S15% ≈
Credit cards 1 2 3 5

At **LUDRES** (8km S)

★★**Climat** ZI de Ludres ☎83542113

🛁38 **P** sB🛁219—236 dB🛁238—255
Credit cards 1 3

At **VANDOEUVRE LES NANCY** (4km S)

★★**Campanile** ZAC de Brabois, 1 av de la Forêt de Haye ☎83514151 tx960604

🛁42 **P** sB🛁217—238 dB🛁239—260 M61—82
Credit card 3

NANS-LE-PINS
Var

★★★**Châteauneuf** (Relais et Châteaux) (**Pn**) (N560) ☎94789006 tx400747

21 Mar—Oct
🛁🚿34 **P** sB🛁🚿395—505 dB🛁🚿480—650 M165—200 🎾 ≈
Credit cards 1 2 3 5

NANTES
Loire-Atlantique

★★★★**Frantel** 3 r Dr-Zamenhof ☎40471058 tx711440

🛁150 ⌂ **P**40 Lift sB🛁320—380 dB🛁410—480 M130
Credit cards 1 2 3 5

★★★★**Sofitel** r A-Millerand ☎40476103 tx710990

🛁100 **P**100 Lift sB🛁410—470 dB🛁510—570 Malc 🎾 ≈
Credit cards 1 2 3 5

France

★★★**Central** (MAP) 4 r du Couédic ☎40200935 tx700666

🛁🚿121 Lift ☾ sB🛁🚿197—336 dB🛁🚿308—361 M80

★★★**Mercure** (N165) ☎40852317 tx711823

🛁54 **P** sB🛁294 dB🛁343 Mfr80 🎾 ≈

★★★***Vendée*** (Inter) 8 allée Cdt-Charcot (n.rest) ☎40741454 tx700610

🛁🚿89 ⌂ **P** Lift

★★**Astoria** 11 r Richebourg (n.rest) ☎40743990

Closed Aug
🛁🚿45 ⌂ **P** Lift ☾ sB🛁🚿210—280 dB🛁🚿235—325

★★**Bourgogne** 9 allée du Cdt-Charcot (n.rest) ☎40740334 tx700610

5 Jan—20 Dec
rm43 (🛁🚿42) Lift ☾ sB🛁🚿137—242 dB🛁🚿175—338
Credit cards 2 3 5

★★**Graslin** 1 r Piron (off pl Graslin) (n.rest) ☎40891609

🛁🚿47 Lift sB🛁🚿255 dB🛁🚿280
Credit cards 1 3

🚗 **SARL Dao** 14 r G-Clemenceau ☎40746666 All makes

At **CARQUEFOU** (4km NE on D337, of N23)

★★★**Novotel Nantes Carquefou** allée des Sapins ☎40526464 tx711175

🛁98 **P**250 sB🛁318 dB🛁360 Malc St% ≈
Credit cards 1 2 3 5

★★★***PLM Carquefou*** rte de Paris, le Petit Bel Air (N23 exit A11) ☎40302924 tx710962

🛁79 **P** Lift ☾ M alc ≈

★★**Campanile** bd des Pastureaux ☎40300182

🛁77 **P** sB🛁204—225 dB🛁226—247 M61—82
Credit card 3

★★**Climat** CD337, Petit Bel Air ☎40303336

🛁42 **P**40 sB🛁210—262 dB🛁232—284 M51—70
Credit cards 1 3

At **ST-HERBLAIN** (8km W)

★★**Campanile** rte de St Etienne de Montluc ☎40433466 tx711063

🛁50 **P** sB🛁204—225 dB🛁226—247 M61—82
Credit card 3

NANTIAT See CROUZILLE (LA)

NANTUA
Ain

★★★**France** 44 r Dr-Mercier ☎74750055

20 Dec—Oct
🛁19 ⌂ **P**18 sB🛁200—250 dB🛁295—345 M125—215 mountains
Credit cards 1 2 3 5

NAPOULE-PLAGE (LA)
Alpes-Maritimes

★★★★**Ermitage du Riou** (BW/MAP) bd de Mer ☎93499556 tx470072

🛁🚿42 A5rm **P**25 Lift ☾ sB🛁🚿500—845 dB🛁🚿695—1210 Mfr160 ≈ sea mountains
Credit cards 1 2 3 5

NARBONNE
Aude

★★★**Mid** LF av de Toulouse ☎68410462 tx500401

3 Jan—Nov
rm47 (🛁🚿36) ⌂ **P**30 Lift ☾ sB60—120 sB🛁🚿120—150 dB120—170 dB🛁🚿150—180
Credit cards 1 2 3 5

★★★**Novotel Narbonne Sud** quartier Plaisance, rte d'Espagne ☎68415952 tx500480

🛁🚿96 **P**180 Lift sB🛁🚿300 dB🛁🚿355 ≈
Credit cards 1 2 3 5

★★***Ibis*** quartier Plaisance (N9) ☎68411441 tx500480

🛁42 ⌂ Lift ☾

★★**Languedoc** (BW/MAP) 22 bd Gambetta ☎68651474 tx505167

rm45 (🛁🚿34) Lift ☾ sB132—155 sB🛁🚿167—225 dB154—190 dB🛁🚿189—330 M57—105
Credit cards 1 2 3 5

★★**Résidence** 6 r Premier-Mai (n.rest) ☎68321941 tx500441

Closed Jan
🛁🚿26 ⌂ ☾ sB🛁🚿198—236 dB🛁🚿302—342 t3%
Credit cards 1 2 3

★**Lion d'Or** LF 39 av P-Sémard ☎68320692

🛁21 ⌂ **P**10 sB🛁175 dB🛁225 M70—120&alc
Credit cards 2 3 5

🚗 **R Deirleu** 43 r P-L-Courier ☎68320838 Closed Sat pm & Sun Cit

🚗 **Lopez** 180 av de Bordeaux ☎68421631 Closed Sat pm & Sun Peu

🚗 **Marty** 87 av du Gl-Leclerc ☎68411610 Closed Sat pm & Sun Tal

At **NARBONNE-PLAGE** (1.5km E on D168)

★★**Caravelle** LF bd du Front de Mer ☎68498038

May—Sep
🚿24 **P**24 dB🚿152—195 M73—150 t2% sea
Credit card 3

NAVARRENX
Pyrénées-Atlantiques

★★***Commerce*** (Inter) r Principale ☎59665016

Feb—Dec
rm35 (🛁🚿30)
Credit card 1

NEMOURS
Seine-et-Marne

★★★**Euromotel** (ETAP) l'Aire de Service (2km SE on A6) (n.rest) ☎64281032 tx690243

→ 102 **P**102 sB→ 250—262 dB→ 320—335 Credit cards [1] [2] [3] [5]

★★★**Ecu de France** (**DPn**) 3 r de Paris ☎64281154

rm28 (→ ⋔ 20) ⌂ **P**12 ☾ sB125—139 sB→ ⋔ 188—194 dB238—274 dB→ ⋔ 238—274 M85—130 S15% Credit cards [1] [2] [3] [4] [5]

★★**Ibis** r des Moires, ZI de Nemours ☎64288800 tx600212

→ 42 sB→ 176 dB→ 226 Malc Credit cards [1] [3]

★**Roches** (**Pn**) av d'Ormesson, St Pierre ☎64280143

rm16 (→ ⋔ 12) A6rm ⌂ **P**9 sB124—204 sB→ ⋔ 124—204 dB190—222 dB→ ⋔ 190—246 M70—200 Credit cards [1] [2] [3] [5]

★**St-Pierre** 12 av Carnot (opp. station) (n.rest) ☎64280157

15 Mar—Feb
rm25 (→ ⋔ 13) ⌂ **P**30 sB82—192 sB→ ⋔ 152—192 dB108—208 dB→ ⋔ 168—208 Credit cards [1] [3]

⛐ **Gambetta** 70 av Gambetta ☎64280546 Closed Sun VW

⛐ **Royal-Nemours** 95 r de Paris ☎64280047 M/c AR

⛐ **TMA** rte de Montargis ☎64280845 Closed Suns All makes

NEUF-BRISACH
Haut-Rhin

At **VOGELGRUN** (5km E on N415)

★★**Européan** ☎89725157

→ ⋔ 23 ⌂ **P**50 Lift sB→ ⋔ 160—178 dB→ ⋔ 160—200 M84—138 Credit cards [1] [2] [3] [5]

NEUFCHÂTEAU
Vosges

⛐ **Mourot Auto** rte de Langres ☎29943119 Closed Sun & Mon am Aud VW

NEUFCHÂTEL-EN-BRAY
Seine-Maritime

★★**Grand Cerf** (**Pn**) 9 Grande Rue ☎35930002

Jan—Jun & 15 Jul—Dec
rm11 **P**4 M55—148 Credit card [3]

⛐ **Lechopler** 31, Grande Rue, St-Pierre ☎35930082 Closed Sat pm & Sun Ren

⛐ **Lemarchand** 9 rte de Foucamont ☎35930266 Closed Mon Aud VW

NEUILLY-SUR-SEINE See **PARIS**

NEUVÉGLISE
Cantal

⛐ **Sauret** ☎71238090 Closed Sun Oct—Apr, Sun pm May—Sep All makes

NEVERS
Nièvre

★★★**Diane** (BW/MAP) 38 r du Midi ☎86572810 tx801021

20 Jan—20 Dec
→ ⋔ 30 ⌂ Lift sB→ ⋔ 235—325 dB→ ⋔ 320—350 M alc Credit cards [1] [2] [3] [4] [5]

★★★**PLM Loire** quai Medine ☎86615092 tx801112

Rest closed 10 Dec—15 Jan
→ 60 **P** Lift sB→ 264—274 dB→ 340—368 M90—146

★★**Folie** LE rte des Saulaies ☎86570531

7 Jan—20 Dec
→ ⋔ 27 **P**100 sB→ ⋔ 175—218 dB→ ⋔ 193—236 M54—149 Credit cards [1] [3]

★★**Molière** 25 r Molière (n.rest) ☎86572986

15 Jan—15 Dec
→ ⋔ 18 **P**10 sB→ ⋔ 126—178 dB→ ⋔ 157—206

★**Morvan** LE 28 r Mouësse ☎86611416

Closed 3 wks in Jan & Jul
rm11 (⋔ 7) **P**12 sB75—85 sB⋔ 110 dB125 dB⋔ 140 M90—120

★**Ste-Marie** 25 r Petit-Mouësse ☎86611002

Mar—20 Jan
rm17 (→ ⋔ 8) A9rm ⌂ **P**30 sB79—94 sB→ ⋔ 104—119 dB92—107 dB→ ⋔ 117—132 M45—120 Credit cards [1] [2]

At **VARENNES-VAUZELLES** (5km N)

★★***Routel*** (N7) ☎86576944 tx801059

→ 30 **P** ⚲

NICE
Alpes-Maritimes

★★★★★**Négresco** (SRS) 37 prom des Anglais ☎93883951 tx460040

→ ⋔ 155 ⌂ Lift ☾ dB→ ⋔ 1150—1800 sea Credit cards [1] [2] [3] [4] [5]

★★★★**Atlantic** 12 bd V-Hugo ☎93884015 tx460840

→ 123 **P**14 Lift ☾ sB→ fr420 dB→ fr560 Mfr95 Credit cards [1] [2] [3] [5]

★★★★***Frantel*** 28 av Notre-Dame (n.rest) ☎93803024 tx470662

→ 200 **P** Lift ≈ Credit cards [1] [2] [3] [5]

★★★★**Holiday Inn** 179 bd R-Cassin ☎93839192 tx970202

→ 154 ⌂ **P** Lift sB→ 390—730 dB→ 540—850 ≈ Credit cards [1] [2] [3] [5]

★★★★**Sofitel Splendid** 50 bd V-Hugo ☎93886954 tx460938

→ 130 ⌂ **P**25 Lift ☾ sB→ 400—500 dB→ 580—800 M100 ≈ mountains Credit cards [1] [2] [3] [4] [5]

★★★★**Westminster Concorde** 27 prom des Anglais ☎93882944 tx460872

→ ⋔ 110 Lift ☾ sB→ ⋔ 550—750 dB→ ⋔ 800—1000 M alc sea Credit cards [1] [2] [3] [5]

★★★**Bedford** (Inter) 45 r du Ml-Joffre (n.rest) ☎93822839 tx970086

→ ⋔ 50 Lift sB→ ⋔ 230—330 dB→ ⋔ 260—390 M90—100

★★★**Brice** 44 r Ml-Joffre ☎93881444 tx470658

→ ⋔ 60 Lift ☾ sB→ ⋔ 260—300 dB→ ⋔ 360—400 M95 Credit cards [1] [3] [5]

★★★**Continental Massena** 58 r Giofreddo (n.rest) ☎93854925 tx470192

→ ⋔ 116 **P**15 Lift sB→ ⋔ 315—400 dB→ ⋔ 385—535 Credit cards [1] [3] [5]

★★★**Gounod** 3 r Gounod (n.rest) ☎93882620 tx461705

→ ⋔ 50 ⌂ **P** Lift ☾ sB→ ⋔ 290—320 dB→ ⋔ 390—410 ≈ Credit cards [1] [2] [3] [4] [5]

★★★**Locarno** 4 av des Baumettes (n.rest) ☎93962800 tx970015

→ ⋔ 48 ⌂ **P** Lift sB→ ⋔ 210—220 dB→ ⋔ 260—290

★★★**Malmaison** (BW/MAP) 48 bd V-Hugo ☎93876256 tx470410

→ 50 Lift sB→ 275—315 dB→ 370—440 M85—95 Credit cards [1] [2] [3] [4] [5]

★★★***Massenet*** 11 r Massenet ☎93871131

→ 46 ⌂ Lift

★★★**Mercure** 2 r Halevy (n.rest) ☎93823088 tx970656

→ 124 Lift sB→ 380—510 dB→ 460—660 sea Credit cards [1] [2] [3] [5]

★★★**Napoléon** 6 r Grimaldi (n.rest) ☎93877007 tx460949

→ ⋔ 80 **P** Lift ☾ sB→ ⋔ 254—274 dB→ ⋔ 342—367

★★★**Windsor** 11 r Dalpozzo (n.rest) ☎93885935 tx970072

→ ⋔ 60 **P**3 Lift ☾ sB→ ⋔ 230—380 dB→ ⋔ 290—440 ≈ Credit cards [1] [2] [3] [5]

★★***Climat*** 232 rte de Grenoble ☎93718080 tx470673

→ 72 **P** Lift

★★**Fimotel** bd Pasteur ☎42615014 tx215269

→ 81 **P** Lift ≈ Credit cards [1] [2] [3] [5]

Albert-1er 5 r de Cronstadt ☎93883935
Closed Sat & Sun Lot Toy Vol

🚗 **Côte d'Azur** 3 r Trachel ☎93886717
All makes

RMCP 297 rte de Grenoble ☎93298489
Closed Sat & Sun All makes

At **ST-LAURENT-DU-VAR** (7km SW off N7)

★★★***Novotel Nice Cap 3000*** av de Verdun ☎93316115 tx470643
🛁 103 Lift 🏊
Credit cards [1] [2] [3] [5]

NÎMES
Gard

★★★★**Imperator** (BW/MAP) quai de la Fontaine ☎66219030 tx490635
15 Feb—15 Jan
🛁🚿 59 A3rm ⛟ Lift ☾ sB🛁🚿 305—350
dB🛁🚿 430—570 M160—180
Credit cards [1] [2] [3] [4] [5]

★★★***Cheval Blanc et des Arènes*** 1 pl des Arènes ☎66672003 tx480860
🛁🚿 47 Lift ☾
Credit cards [1] [2] [3] [5]

★★★**Mercure Nîmes Ouest** chemin de l'Hostellerie ☎66841455 tx490746
🛁 100 **P**100 Lift sB🛁 290—315
dB🛁 367—390 Malc 🎾 🏊
Credit cards [1] [2] [3] [5]

★★★**Novotel Nîmes Ouest** 124 chemin de l'Hostellerie ☎66846020 tx480675
🛁 96 **P**120 sB🛁 324 dB🛁 382 🏊
Credit cards [1] [2] [3] [5]

★★**Carrière** (Inter) (**DPn**) 6 r Grizot ☎66672489 tx490580
rm55 (🛁🚿 42) ⛟ Lift sB149—199
sB🛁🚿 199—223 dB🛁🚿 fr262 Mfr65
Credit cards [2] [3] [4]

★★**Climat** chemin de la Careizasse ☎66842152 tx485201
🛁 44 **P**50 dB🛁 255—270
Credit cards [1] [3]

★★***Ibis*** chemin de l'Hostellerie ☎66380065 tx490180
🛁 180 **P** Lift

★★***Louvre*** 2 sq de la Couronne ☎66672275 tx480218
🛁🚿 35 ⛟ **P**15 Lift ☾
Credit cards [1] [2] [3] [5]

🚗 **Europe** 186 rte de Montpellier ☎66840440 Closed Sat pm & Sun Fia

🚗 **Fricon** 175 rte d'Alès ☎66231911 All makes

🚗 **SNDA** 2543 rte de Montpellier ☎66849509 Closed Sat pm & Sun Aud VW

At **CAISSARGUES BOUILLARGUES** (4km S)

★★**Campanile** chemin de la Carrèras ☎66842705 tx480510
🛁 50 **P** sB🛁 217—238 dB🛁 239—260
M61—82
Credit card [3]

France

At **MARGUERITTES** (7km NE via N86)

★★***Marguerittes*** rte d'Avignon ☎66260123
🚿 48 **P**

NIORT
Deux-Sèvres

★★★***Brèche*** 8 av Bujault ☎49244178 tx792343
4 Jan—23 Dec
rm49 (🛁🚿 36) Lift ☾
Credit cards [1] [2] [3] [5]

★★***Grand*** 32 av Paris (n.rest) ☎49242221 tx790624
🛁🚿 40 ⛟ **P** Lift ☾

★★***Ibis*** av de la Rochelle ☎49735454 tx791635
🛁 40 **P**30 M alc
Credit cards [1] [3]

★★***Terminus*** LF (FAH) 82 r de la Gare ☎49240038
rm43 (🛁🚿 37) Lift ☾
Credit cards [1] [2] [3] [4] [5]

NOEUX-LES-MINES
Pas-de-Calais

★★**Tourterelles** LF 374 rte Nationale ☎21669075 tx134338
rm18 (🛁🚿 15) **P**25 sB120—220
sB🛁🚿 220—240 dB🛁🚿 240—290
M65—120
Credit cards [1] [2] [3]

NOGENTEL See **CHÂTEAU-THIERRY**

NOGENT-LE-ROTROU
Eure-et-Loir

★★**Dauphin** 39 r Villette-Gate ☎37521730
Mar—Nov
rm26 (🛁🚿 11) ⛟ **P**15 sB105—140
sB🛁🚿 190—240 dB140—180
dB🛁🚿 220—260 M80—140

NOGENT-SUR-OISE
Oise

★★★***Sarcus*** (Inter) 7 r Châteaubriand ☎44740131 tx150047
🛁🚿 62 Lift

NOISIEL
Seine-et-Marne

★★**Climat** 50 cours des Roches, quai du Luzard ☎60061540 tx305551
🛁 56 **P** Lift sB🛁 232—252 dB🛁 254—274
M52—94
Credit cards [1] [3]

NOISY-LE-GRAND See **PARIS**

NOLAY
Côte-d'Or

★***Ste Marie*** LF (**DPn**) 36 r de la République ☎80217319
rm12 (🚿 4) A5rm ⛟ **P**12 M&alc
Credit cards [2] [3] [5]

NONANCOURT
Eure

★***Grand Cert*** LF 17 Grand Rue ☎32581527
🚿 6 ⛟ **P**
Credit cards [1] [2] [3] [5]

NONTRON
Dordogne

★★***Grand*** LF 3 pl A-Agard ☎53561122
rm26 (🛁🚿 17) ⛟ **P** Lift
Credit card [3]

NOUAN-LE-FUZELIER
Loir-et-Cher

★**Moulin de Villiers** LF (**DPn**) (3km N by D44) rte Chaon ☎54887227
20 Mar—Aug & 15 Sep—Dec
rm20 (🛁🚿 16) **P**20 sBfr108
sB🛁🚿 166—211 dB🛁🚿 182—227
M75—130 St%

NOUVION-EN-THIÉRACHE (LE)
Aisne

★**Paix** 37 r V-Vicary ☎23970455
14 Jan—20 Dec
rm25 (🛁🚿 13) **P**10 sB79—180
sB🛁🚿 114—180 dB112—219
dB🛁🚿 145—219 M58—200
Credit cards [1] [3]

NOVES
Bouches-du-Rhône

★★★***Auberge de Noves*** (**DPn**) (2km NW on D28) ☎90941921 tx431312
Mar—Dec
🛁 22 ⛟ **P**50 ☾ 🎾 🏊
Credit cards [1] [2] [3] [5]

NOYELLES-GODAULT See **HENIN-BEAUMONT**

NOYERS-SUR-CHER
Loir-et-Cher

★**Touraine et Sologne** LF (**DPn**) (N76 & N675) ☎54751523
20 Feb—4 Jan
rm14 (🛁🚿 11) **P**35 sB81 sB🛁🚿 101—121
dB🛁🚿 137—202
Credit cards [3] [5]

NOYON
Oise

★***St-Eloi*** 81 bd Carnot ☎44440149
rm31 (🛁🚿 27) **P**28
Credit cards [2] [3]

NOZAY
Loire-Atlantique

★***Gergaud*** LF (**Pn**) 12 rte Nantes ☎40794754
rm8 (🛁🚿 3) **P**20

NUITS-ST-GEORGES
Côtes-d'Or

★★***Ibis*** 1 av Chambolland ☎80611717 tx350954
🛁 52 **P**40
Credit cards [1] [3]

Aubin rte Dijon ☎80610385 Closed Aug, Sat & Sun Mer

⛟ **Grands Crus** rte de Dijon ☎80610223 Closed Aug, Sat pm & Sun Peu

NYONS
Drôme

★★**Colombet** pl de la Libération ☎75260366

5 Jan—5 Nov
rm30 (🛁 🚿20) ⌂ **P**12 Lift ☾ sB122—138 sB 🛁 🚿210—248 dB158—186 dB 🛁 🚿258—336 M68—154 mountains

OBERNAI
Bas-Rhin

★★**Duc d'Alsace** LF 6 pl de la Gare ☎88955534

rm18 (🛁 15) ⌂ **P**5 sB185—197 sB 🛁 185—197 dB202—259 dB 🛁 202—259 t2%
Credit cards 2 3 5

OBERSTEIGEN
Bas-Rhin

★★**Belle Vue (DPn)** (Inter) 16 rte de Dabo ☎88873239

15 Feb—10 Jan
rm40 (🛁 🚿39) A4rm ⌂ **P**70 sB169—245 sB 🛁 🚿169—245 dB188—264 dB 🛁 🚿223—264 M55—180 ≈ mountains
Credit cards 1 2 3 5

OLÉRON (ILE D')
Charente-Maritime

REMIGEASSE (LA)

★★★**Grand Large** (Relais et Châteaux) (**Pn** in high season) la pl de la Remigeasse ☎46753789 tx790395

Apr—Oct
🛁 31 **P**31 sB 🛁 385—765 dB 🛁 460—1220 M170—260&alc 🎾 🏖 sea

ST-TROJAN-LES-BAINS

★★★**Novotel** Plage du Gatseau (2.5km S) ☎46760246 tx790910

🛁 80 **P**100 Lift ☾ sB 🛁 322—498 dB 🛁 374—556 M100—110 🎾 🏖 sea
Credit cards 1 2 3 4 5

OLIVET
Loire

★★★★**Frantel la Reine Blanche** r de la Reine Blanche ☎38664051 tx760926

🛁 65 **P**200 Lift sB 🛁 280—305 dB 🛁 340—365 M72—135&alc 🎾
Credit cards 1 2 3 5

★★***Climat*** ZAC de la rte de Bourges ☎38692055 tx692844

🛁 42 **P**

★★**Rivage (Pn)** 635 r de la Reine Blanche ☎38660293 tx760926

rm20 (🛁 🚿10) **P**40 dB160—260 dB 🛁 🚿180—260 M120—250 🎾
Credit cards 1 2 3 5

OLORON-STE-MARIE
Pyrénées-Atlantiques

★★**Béarn** 4 pl de la Mairie ☎59390099

rm26 (🛁 16) ⌂ Lift sB115 sB 🛁 183 dB142 dB 🛁 255 Malc mountains
Credit cards 1 2 3 5

ORANGE
Vaucluse

★★★**Euromotel Orange** (ETAP) rte de Caderousse ☎96342410 tx431550

🛁 98 **P** ≈

★★***Boscotel*** (Inter) rte de Caderousse ☎9034470 tx431405

🛁 57 **P**
Credit cards 1 2 3 5

★★***Lourvre & Terminus*** 89 av F-Mistral (n.rest) ☎90341008 tx431195

15 Jan—14 Dec
🛁 🚿34 ⌂ **P** Lift ☾

G Ameller 43 av Ml-Foch ☎90341234 Ope Vau VW

⛟ **Auto Service** 78 av Ml-Foch ☎90342435 Closed Sat & Sun For

⛟ **H Castagne** rte de Roquemaure ☎90340825 Closed Sat pm & Sun Cit

⛟ **Cretalles** quartier de Condoulet ☎90345305 Mer

⛟ **H Marquion** av C-de-Gaulle ☎90346844 Closed 7—30 Jun, Sat pm & Sun Ren

ORGEVAL
Yvelines

★★★**Novotel** (N13) ☎39759760 tx697174

🛁 119 **P** Lift sB 🛁 342—362 dB 🛁 394—414 🎾 ≈
Credit cards 1 2 3 5

★★**Moulin d'Orgeval** ☎39759574

8 Feb—20 Dec
rm12 (🛁 5) ⌂ **P**23 sB121-242 sB 🛁 159—242 dB140—261 dB 🛁 261 M alc 🎾

ORLÉANS
Loiret

See also **CHAPELLE-SAINT-MESMIN (LA)**

★★★★***Sofitel*** 44—46 quai Barentin ☎38621739 tx780073

🛁 110 **P** Lift ☾ ≈

★★★**Cedres** (Inter) 17 r du Ml-Foch (n.rest) ☎38622292 tx782314

rm36 (🛁 🚿32) Lift ☾ sB155 sB 🛁 🚿240—270 dB175 dB 🛁 🚿285—340
Credit cards 1 2 3

★★***Arcade*** 4 r Ml-Foch ☎38542311 tx780629

🚿125 ⌂ **P**25
Credit card 1

★★**Marquerite** LF 14 pl Vieux-Marché (n.rest) ☎38537432

rm25 (🛁 🚿14) **P** Lift sB93 dB109 dB 🛁 🚿134—149

★★**Terminus** (FAH) 40 r de la République ☎38532464 tx782230

rm47 (🛁 🚿44) ⌂ **P** Lift sB 🛁 🚿182—192 dB 🛁 🚿264—314 M65
Credit cards 1 2 3

⛟ **Lion Fort** 51 r Porte St-Jean ☎386252829 Closed Sat & Sun AR

At **SARAN** (2km NW on A10)

★★**Ibis** ☎38733993 tx760902

🛁 104 **P**120 Lift sB 🛁 184—218 dB 🛁 224—259 M alc
Credit cards 1 3

⛟ **DAC** 1173 r de Montaran ☎38884736

At **SOURCE (LA)** (10km S off N20)

★★★***Novotel*** 2 r H-de-Balzac ☎38630428 tx760619

🛁 🚿121 **P** Lift 🎾 ≈
Credit cards 1 2 3 5

★★**Campanile** 326 r Châteaubriand ☎38635820 tx781228

🛁 42 **P** sB 🛁 217—238 dB 🛁 239—260 M61—82
Credit card 3

ORLY AIRPORT See **PARIS AIRPORTS**

ORSAY
Essonne

At **COURTABŒUF** (3km S on D35)

★★★***Mercure Paris Orsay*** av du Parana, ZA ☎69076396 tx691247

🛁 108 Lift ≈
Credit cards 1 2 3 5

★★**Climat** av du Cap Horn, ZA ☎69281420 tx692844

🛁 26 sB 🛁 226—243 dB 🛁 245—262 M51—66&alc
Credit cards 1 3

At **SACLAY** (6km N)

★★★***Novotel*** r C-Thomassin, Christ de Saclay ☎69418140 tx691856

🛁 136 **P** Lift 🎾 ≈

ORTHEZ
Pyrénées-Atlantiques

★★***Climat*** r du Soulor ☎(6)594460123 tx692844

🛁 24

⛟ **Laglère** av d'Aquitaine ☎599690212 Closed Sun AR Ope

⛟ **Minjou** 5 r Gl-Foch ☎59690937 For

⛟ **Mousques** av F-Jammes ☎59690978 Closed 28 Jul—2 Aug, Sat pm & Sun Ren

OUISTREHAM-RIVA-BELLA
Calvados

★★***Univers*** LF pl du Gl de Gaulle ☎31971216

🛁 🚿18 A9rm ⌂ **P**30 sea
Credit cards 2 3 5

OYONNAX
Ain

★**Nouvel** 31 r R-Nicod (n.rest) ☎74772811

rm37 (🛁 🚿14) ⌂ Lift sB67 dB 🛁 🚿140

PACY-SUR-EURE
Eure

★★**Etape** 1 r Isambard ☎32361277
Closed 16—29 Jan
rm9 (➡5) **P**

⛟ **Lepée** 98—102 r Isambard ☎32360673 Closed Sat, Sun & Mon For

At **CHAIGNES** (5km E on N13)

⛟ **Lion d'Or** (N13) ☎32369404 All makes

PALAISEAU
Essonne

★★★***Novotel*** 18—20 r E-Baudot, Zone d'Activité de Massy ☎69208491 tx691595
➡⋔ 151 **P**300 Lift ⛱
Credit cards [1] [2] [3] [5]

PAMIERS
Ariège

★★***Parc*** **(DPn)** 12 r Piconnières ☎61670258
rm12 (➡⋔9) ⌂

PANTIN See **PARIS**

PARAMÉ See **ST-MALO**

PARAY-LE-MONIAL
Saône-et-Loire

★★***Trois Pigeons*** 2 r d'Argaud ☎85810377
Closed 3 Jan—7 Feb
rm33 (➡⋔22) A15rm ⌂
Credit cards [1] [3]

★★**Vendanges de Bourgogne** LE 5 r D-Papin ☎85811343
Closed Mar—Nov
rm14 (➡⋔13) ⌂ **P**20 sB109—193
sB➡⋔166—193 dB184—211
dB➡⋔184—211 M80—180
Credit cards [1] [2]

PARENTIS-EN-BORN
Landes

⛟ **Larrieu** r du Stade ☎85784350 Closed Feb & Sun Ren

PARIS

See plan pages 170 and 171

See also **AULNAY-SOUS-BOIS, BOBIGNY, BRETIGNY-SUR-ORGÉ, BUC, CHAMPS-SUR-MARNE, CONFLANS-STE-HONORINE, ECOUEN, ÉPINAY-SUR-ORGÉ, ERMENONVILLE, EVRY, GONESSE, LONGJUMEAU, MONTESSON, MONTSOULT, NOISIEL, ORGEVAL, ORSAY, PALAISEAU, PLAISIR, PONTOISE, QUEUE-EN-BRIE (LA), RAMBOUILLET, ST-GERMAIN-EN-LAYE, SANNOIS, SEVRAN, SURVILLIERS-ST-WITZ, ULIS (LES), VERRIÈRES-LE-BUISSON & VIRY-CHÂTILLON**

1st Arrondissement Opéra, Palais-Royal, Halles, Bourse

★★★★★***Meurice*** (Intercont) 228 r de Rivoli ☎42603860 Plan **45**
➡192 **P** Lift ☾
Credit cards [1] [2] [3] [4] [5]

★★★★★**Ritz** 15 pl Vendôme ☎42603830 tx220262 Plan **54**
➡164 **P** Lift ☾ sB➡fr2047 dB➡fr2599 M230&alc S15%

★★★★**Lotti** (Jolly) 7 r Castiglione ☎42603734 tx240066 Plan **40**
➡130 Lift ☾ sB➡1171—1386
dB➡1527—1862 M alc
Credit cards [1] [2] [3] [4] [5]

★★★★**Mayfair** 3 r R-de-l'Isle (n.rest) ☎42603814 tx240037 Plan **103**
➡53 Lift sB➡615 dB➡880

★★★**Cambon** 3 r Cambon (n.rest) ☎42603809 tx240814 Plan **16**
➡⋔44 Lift ☾ sB➡⋔650—780
dB➡⋔880—940
Credit cards [1] [2] [3] [5]

★★★**Castille** 37 r Cambon ☎42615520 tx213505 Plan **18**
➡76 Lift ☾ sB➡965 dB➡1180
M120—150&alc
Credit cards [1] [2] [3] [5]

★★★**Duminy-Vendôme** 3 r Mont-Thabor (n.rest) ☎42603280 Plan **21**
➡79 **P**50 Lift ☾ sB➡410—450
dB➡540—715
Credit cards [1] [2] [3] [5]

★★★***Ladbroke France et Choiseul*** 239 r St-Honoré, pl Vendôme ☎42615460 tx680959 Plan **69**
➡150 Lift ☾

★★★**Louvre** pl A-Malraux ☎42615601 tx220412 Plan **41**
➡⋔220 **P**150 Lift ☾ sB➡⋔935—1885
dB➡⋔1060—2010 M125
Credit cards [1] [2] [3] [4] [5]

★★★**Montana-Tulleries** 21 r St-Roch (n.rest) ☎42603510 tx214404 Plan **47**
➡⋔25 Lift ☾ sB➡⋔305—375
dB➡⋔400—545
Credit cards [1] [3]

★★***Family*** 35 r Cambon (n.rest) ☎42615484 Plan **24**
rm25 (➡⋔22) Lift ☾

2nd Arrondissement Opéra, Palais-Royal, Halles, Bourse

★★★★**Westminster** 13 r de la Paix ☎42615746 tx680035 Plan **68**
➡102 **P** Lift sB➡1130—1330
dB➡1610—1760
Credit cards [1] [2] [3] [5]

★★★**Horset Opéra d'Antin** 18 r d'Antin (n.rest) ☎47421301 tx680564 Plan **79**
➡⋔60 **P** Lift sB➡⋔400 dB➡⋔515
Credit cards [1] [2] [3] [4] [5]

★★***France*** 4 r du Caire (n.rest) ☎42333098 Plan **27**
rm50 (➡⋔20) Lift ☾

⛟ **Permanence 'Renault'** 19 bd St-Denis ☎42361000

5th Arrondissement Quartier Latin, Luxembourg, Jardin des Plantes

★★**Acacias Gobelins** 18 av des Gobelins ☎45358012 tx206856 Plan **97**
➡⋔23 **P** Lift sB➡⋔263—327
dB➡⋔280—344
Credit cards [1] [2] [3] [5]

★★***Collège de France*** 7 r Thénard (n.rest) ☎43267836 Plan **76**
➡⋔29 Lift
Credit card [2]

6th Arrondissement Quartier Latin, Luxembourg, Jardin des Plantes

★★★★**Lutetia Concorde** 45 bd Raspail ☎45443810 tx270424 Plan **42**
➡⋔293 **P** Lift ☾ sB➡⋔705—1255
dB➡⋔860—1410 M175—350
Credit cards [1] [2] [3] [4] [5]

★★★***Madison*** 143 bd St-Germain (n.rest) ☎43297250 Plan **43**
➡⋔57 Lift ☾

★★★**Senat** 22 r St-Sulpice (n.rest) ☎4325430 tx206367
rm32 (➡26) Lift ☾ sB➡350 dB390
dB➡390 Plan **59**
Credit cards [1] [2] [3] [5]

★★★**Victoria Palace** 6 r Blaise-Desgoffe ☎45443816 tx270557 Plan **67**
➡⋔110 ⌂ **P**16 Lift ☾ sB➡⋔530—683
dB➡⋔605—710
Credit cards [2] [3]

★★***Angleterre*** 44 r Jacob (n.rest) ☎42603472 Plan **4**
rm31 (➡26) Lift

7th Arrondissement Fauborg-St-Germain, Invalides, École Militaire

★★★★***Pont Royal*** (BW/MAP) 7 r Montalembert ☎45443827 tx270113 Plan **72**
➡⋔80 **P**50 Lift ☾
Credit cards [1] [2] [3] [4] [5]

★★★★**Sofitel Bourbon** 32 r St-Dominque ☎45559180 tx250019 Not on plan
➡112 **P**15 Lift ☾ sB➡1090—1770
dB➡1310—1390 M alc
Credit cards [1] [2] [3] [5]

★★★**Bourdonnais** 111—113 av Bourdonnais ☎47054542 tx201416 Plan **80**
➡60 Lift sB➡360
Credit cards [1] [3] [5]

★★★**Bourgogne & Montana** 3 r de Bourgogne ☎45512022 tx270854 Plan **12**
➡⋔35 Lift ☾ sB➡⋔455—520
dB➡⋔480—550 Mfr150
Credit cards [1] [2] [3]

★★★**Cayré** 4 bd Raspail (n.rest) ☎45443888 tx270577 Plan **19**
➡130 **P**15 Lift ☾ sB➡750 dB➡790 M120
Credit cards [1] [2] [3]

★★**Splendid** 29 av de Tourville (n.rest) ☎45592477 tx201204 Plan **62**
rm45 (🛁 🚿 24) Lift sB87—116
sB🛁 🚿 127—167 dB151—185
dB🛁 🚿 191—306

8th Arrondissement Champs-Élysées, St-Lazare, Madeleine

★★★★★**Bristol** (SRS) 112 fbg St-Honoré ☎42669145 tx280961 Plan **15**
🛁 200 **P**200 Lift ☾ sB🛁 1230—1680
dB🛁 1760—2760 Mfr400 t19% 📺
Credit cards [1] [2] [3] [5]

★★★★★***George V* (DPn)** (THF) 31 av George V ☎47235400 tx650082 Plan **30**
🛁 300 **P** Lift ☾ M alc
Credit cards [1] [2] [3] [4] [5]

★★★★★***Plaza-Athénée*** (THF) 25 av Montaigne ☎47237833 tx650092 Plan **51**
🛁 218 Lift ☾ M alc
Credit cards [1] [2] [3] [4] [5]

★★★★★***Prince de Galles*** 33 av George V ☎47235511 tx280627 Plan **52**
🛁 153 ⌂ Lift ☾ M &alc
Credit cards [1] [2] [3] [5]

★★★★★**Royal Monceau** (CIGA) 35 av Hoche ☎45619800 tx650361 Plan **57**
🛁 220 Lift ☾ sB🛁 1390—1790
dB🛁 1780—2080 M300—400 t19% 📺
Credit cards [1] [2] [3] [4] [5]

★★★★**Bedford** 17 r de l'Arcade ☎42662232 tx290506 Plan **10**
🛁 147 Lift ☾ sB🛁 460—580
dB🛁 615—645 M alc
Credit cards [1] [3]

★★★★**Castiglione** 40 r du fbg St Honoré ☎42650750 tx240362 Plan **17**
🛁 114 Lift sB🛁 830—1030
dB🛁 890—1090 M alc
Credit cards [1] [2] [3] [5]

★★★★***Frantel Windsor*** 14 r Beaujon ☎45630404 tx650902 Plan **29**
🛁 135 Lift ☾
Credit cards [1] [2] [3] [5]

★★★★**Horset Astor** 11 r d'Astorg ☎42665656 tx642737 Plan **6**
🛁 128 Lift sB🛁 690 dB🛁 770
Credit cards [1] [2] [3] [4] [5]

★★★★**Horset Royal Malesherbes** 24 bd Malesherbes ☎42655330 tx660190 Plan **81**
🛁 102 Lift sB🛁 690 dB🛁 770

★★★★**Lancaster** 7 r de Berri ☎43599043 tx640991 Plan **38**
🛁 60 ⌂ **P**6 Lift ☾ sB🛁 🚿 1180—1380
dB🛁 🚿 1660—1910
Credit cards [1] [2] [3] [5]

★★★★**Trémoille** (THF) 14 r Trémoille ☎47233420 tx640344 Plan **64**
🛁 111 **P** Lift ☾ sB🛁 1020—1170
dB🛁 1215—1740 M alc S13%
Credit cards [1] [2] [3] [4] [5]

★★★**Atala** 10 r Châteaubriand ☎45620162 tx640576 Plan **7**
🛁 🚿 50 Lift sB🛁 🚿 660—760
dB🛁 🚿 730—850 Mfr170
Credit cards [2] [5]

France

★★★***Elysées Marignan*** (BW/MAP) 12 r de Marignan (n.rest) ☎43595861 tx6600018 Plan **82**
🛁 71 Lift

★★★***Elysées Ponthieu*** 24 r de Ponthieu (n.rest) ☎42256870 tx640053 Plan **83**
🛁 62 Lift

★★★**Royal** 33 av de Friedland ☎43590814 tx280965 Plan **56**
🛁 🚿 57 Lift ☾ sB🛁 🚿 676—759
dB🛁 🚿 795—895 M alc
Credit cards [1] [2] [3] [5]

★★***Brescia*** 16 r d'Edimbourg (n.rest) ☎45221431 tx660714 Plan **14**
🛁 🚿 38 Lift
Credit cards [1] [2] [3] [5]

★★**Élysée** 12 r Saussales (n.rest) ☎42652925 Plan **22**
rm30 (🛁 🚿 24) Lift sBfr131
sB🛁 🚿 246—266 dBfr187
dB🛁 🚿 292—322

★★***Europe*** 15 r Constantinople (n.rest) ☎45228080 Plan **23**
Sep—Jul
rm47 (🛁 🚿 25) Lift
Credit card [3]

★★**Ministère** 31 r de Surène (n.rest) ☎42662143 Plan **46**
rm32 (🛁 22) Lift ☾ sBfr200 sB🛁 220—310
dBfr200 dB🛁 240—380

9th Arrondissement Opéra, Gare du Nord, Gare de l'Est, Grands Boulevards

★★★★***Ambassador Concorde*** (GT) 16 bd Haussmann ☎42469263 tx650912 Plan **3**
🛁 300 **P** Lift ☾

★★★★***Grand*** (Intercont) 2 r Scribe ☎42681213 tx220875 Plan **32**
🛁 588 Lift ☾
Credit cards [1] [2] [3] [5]

★★★**Blanche Fontaine** 34 r Fontaine (n.rest) ☎45267232 tx660311 Plan **11**
🛁 🚿 49 ⌂ **P**13 Lift sB🛁 🚿 310—325
dB🛁 🚿 350—370
Credit cards [2] [3]

★★★***Caumartin*** 27 r Caumartin (n.rest) ☎47429595 tx680702 Plan **84**
🛁 40 Lift

★★★**Excelsior Opéra** 5 r Lafayette (n.rest) ☎48749930 tx641312 Not on plan
🛁 🚿 53 Lift ☾ sB🛁 🚿 410 dB🛁 🚿 430
Credit cards [1] [2] [3] [4] [5]

★★★**Franklin** (BW/MAP) 19 r Buffault ☎42802727 tx64988 Plan **28**
🛁 🚿 64 ⌂ Lift sB🛁 🚿 426—540
dB🛁 🚿 505—599 M alc
Credit cards [1] [2] [3] [5]

★★★**Havane** 44 r de Trévise (n.rest) ☎47707912 tx6411462 Plan **77**
🛁 53 Lift sB🛁 311—335 dB🛁 345—380

★★★**Hélios** 75 r de la Victoire (n.rest) ☎48742864 tx641255 Plan **33**
🛁 🚿 50 Lift ☾ sB🛁 🚿 313 dB🛁 🚿 390
Credit cards [1] [2] [3] [5]

★★**Campaville** 21 bd de Clichy (n.rest) ☎48740112 tx643572 Plan **100**
🛁 84 ☾ sB🛁 fr240 dB🛁 fr309
Credit card [3]

★★**Campaville** II bis r P Semard (n.rest) ☎48782894 tx643861 Plan **94**
🛁 47 Lift sB🛁 249—283 dB🛁 320—356
Credit card [3]

★★**Lorette** 36 r Notre-Dame de Lorette ☎42851881 tx641877 Plan **78**
🛁 83 **P** Lift sB🛁 225—320 dB🛁 290—350
Credit cards [1] [2] [3] [5]

★★**Palmon** 30 r Maubeuge (n.rest) ☎42850761 tx641498 Plan **71**
🛁 🚿 38 Lift sB🛁 🚿 193—272
dB🛁 🚿 205—284
Credit cards [1] [2] [3] [5]

★**Laffon** 25 r Buffault ☎48784991 Plan **37**
Closed 26 Jul—25 Aug
rm46 (🛁 🚿 30) Lift sBfr107
sB🛁 🚿 190—266 dB141—191
dB🛁 🚿 232—282
Credit cards [1] [3]

10th Arrondissement Opéra, Gare du Nord, Gare de l'Est, Grands Boulevards

★★★**Horset Pavillon** 38 r de l'Echiquier (n.rest) ☎42469275 tx641905 Plan **89**
🛁 🚿 91 Lift sB🛁 🚿 395 dB🛁 🚿 450
Credit cards [1] [2] [3] [4] [5]

★★★**Terminus Nord** 12 bd Denain (n.rest) ☎42802000 tx660615 Plan **63**
🛁 🚿 220 Lift sB🛁 🚿 315—450
dB🛁 🚿 420—550

★★**Altona** 166 r du fbg Poissonière (n.rest) ☎48786824 tx260717 Plan **2**
🛁 🚿 55 Lift sB🛁 🚿 196—228
dB🛁 🚿 261—306

★★**Campaville** 26 r de l'Aqueduc (n.rest) ☎42392626 tx216200 Plan **95**
🛁 59 Lift sB🛁 249—283 dB🛁 320—356
Credit card [3]

★★**Modern 'Est** 91 bd de Strasbourg (n.rest) ☎46072472 Plan **86**
🛁 🚿 30 **P** Lift sB🛁 🚿 264—297
dB🛁 🚿 318—354

SE St-Denis 76 r du fbg St-Denis ☎42469998 Ren

11th Arrondissement Bastille, République, Hôtel de Ville

★★★★**Holiday Inn** 10 pl de la République ☎43554434 tx210651 Plan **90**
🛁 333 **P** Lift ☾ sB🛁 820—1070
dB🛁 1070—1180
Credit cards [1] [2] [3] [4] [5]

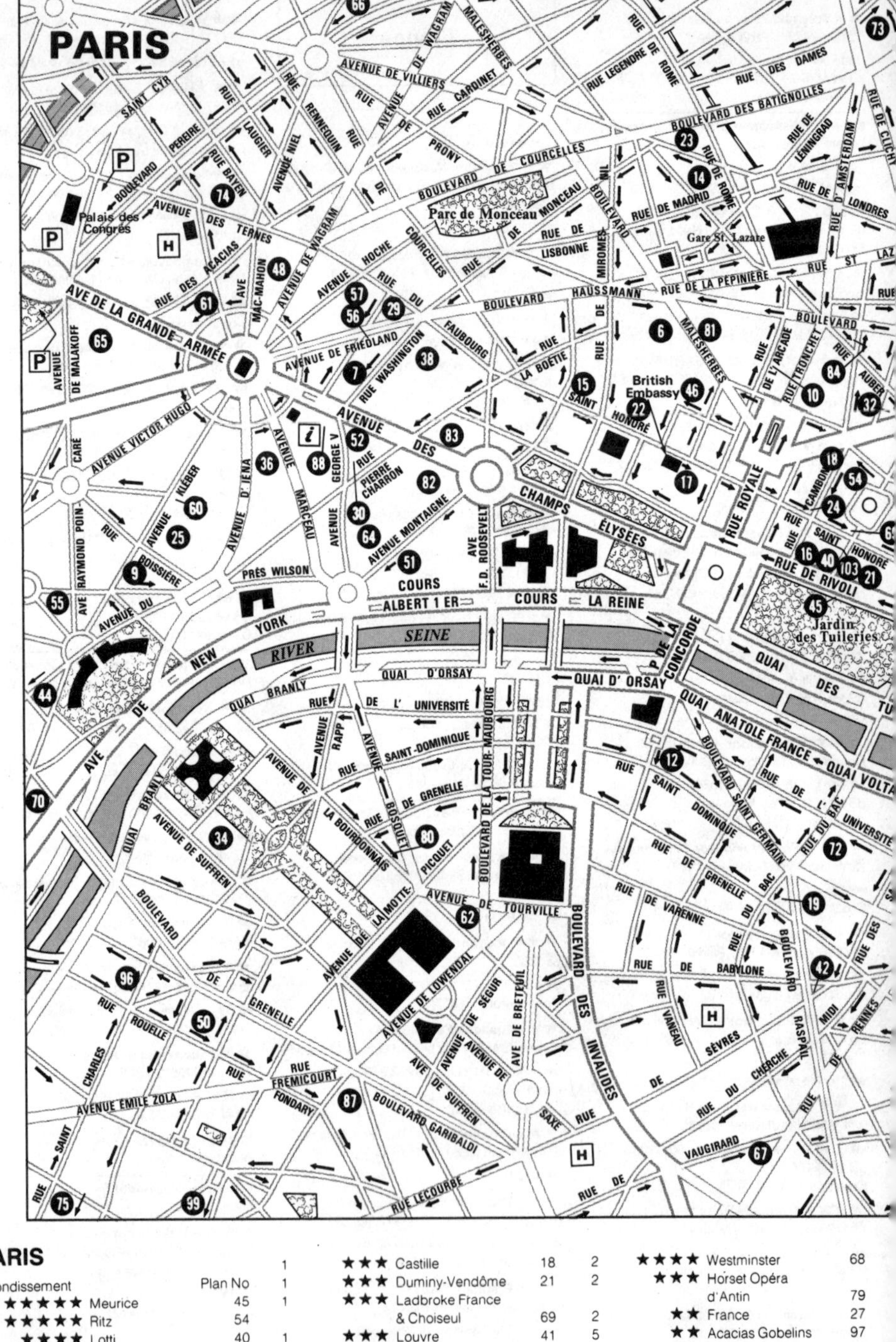

PARIS

Arrondissement			Plan No
1	★★★★★	Meurice	45
1	★★★★★	Ritz	54
1	★★★★	Lotti	40
1	★★★★	Mayfair	103
1	★★★	Cambon	16
1	★★★	Castille	18
1	★★★	Duminy-Vendôme	21
1	★★★	Ladbroke France & Choiseul	69
1	★★★	Louvre	41
1	★★★	Montana-Tuileries	47
1	★★	Family	24
2	★★★★	Westminster	68
2	★★★	Horset Opéra d'Antin	79
2	★★	France	27
5	★★	Acacias Gobelins	97
5	★★	Collège de France	76
6	★★★★	Lutetia Concorde	42

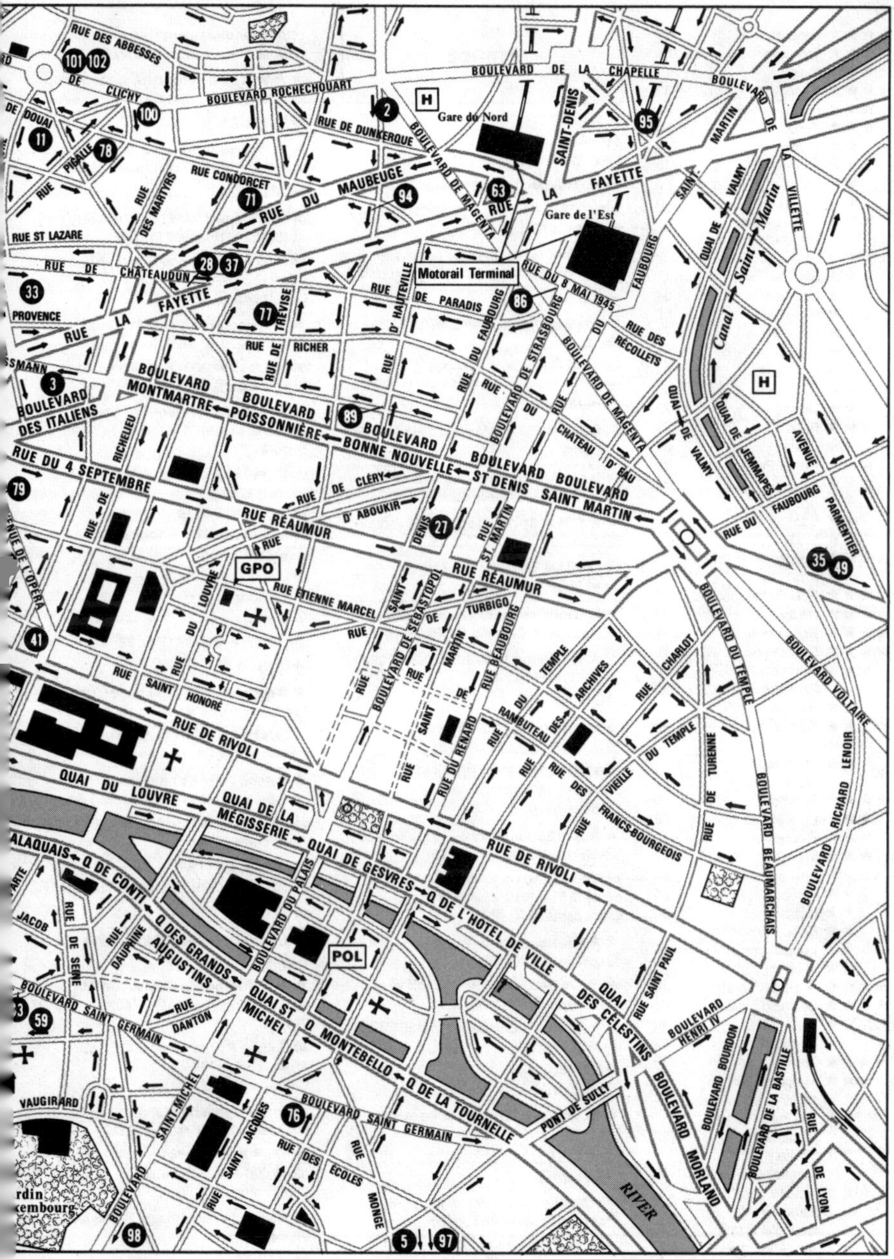

6	★★★	Madison	43
6	★★★	Senat	59
6	★★★	Victoria Palace	67
6	★★	Angleterre	4
7	★★★★	Pont Royal	72
7	★★★	Bourdonnais	80
7	★★★	Bourgogne & Montana	12
7	★★★	Cayré	19
7	★★	Splendid	62
8	★★★★★	Bristol	15
8	★★★★★	George-V	30
8	★★★★★	Plaza-Athénée	51
8	★★★★★	Prince de Galles	52
8	★★★★★	Royal Monceau	57
8	★★★★	Bedford	10
8	★★★★	Castiglione	17
8	★★★★	Frantel Windsor	29
8	★★★★	Horset Astor	6
8	★★★★	Horset Royal Malesherbes	81

→

8	★★★★	Lancaster	38
8	★★★★	Trémoille	64
8	★★★	Atala	7
8	★★★	Élysées Marignan	82
8	★★★	Élysées Ponthieu	83
8	★★★	Royal	56
8	★★	Brescia	14
8	★★	Élysée	22
8	★★	Europe	23
8	★★	Ministère	46
9	★★★★	Ambassador-Concorde	3
9	★★★★	Grand	32
9	★★★	Blanche Fontaine	11
9	★★★	Caumartin	84
9	★★★	Franklin	28
9	★★★	Havane	77
9	★★★	Hélios	33
9	★★	Campaville	94
9	★★	Campaville	100
9	★★	Lorette	78
9	★★	Palmon	71
9	★	Laffon	37
10	★★★	Horset Pavillon	89
10	★★★	Terminus Nord	63
10	★★	Altona	2
10	★★	Campaville	95
10	★★	Modern'Est	86
11	★★★★	Holiday Inn	90
13	★	Arts	5
14	★★★	PLM St-Jacques	98
15	★★★★	Hilton	34
15	★★★★	Holiday Inn	91
15	★★★★	Sofitel Paris	75
15	★★★	Mercure Paris-Vanves	99
15	★★	Arcade	87
15	★★	Campaville	96
15	★★	Pacific	50
15	★★	Timhotel Montparnasse	92
16	★★★★	Baltimore	9
16	★★★	Élysées Bassano	88
16	★★★	Frémiet	70
16	★★★	Massenet	44
16	★★★	Sevigné	60
16	★★	Farnese	25
16	★★	Keppler	36
16	★★	Rond Point de Longchamp	55
16	★★	Vermont	65
17	★★★★	Regents' Garden	74
17	★★★★	Splendid Étoile	61
17	★★	Neva	48
17	★	Verniquet	66
18	★★★★	Terrass	73
18	★★★	Mercure Paris Montmartre	101
18	★★	Ibis Paris Montmartre	102
18	★★	Timhotel Montmartre	93
	★★★	Novotel Paris Bagnolet (At Bagnolet 7km E)	49
	★★	Ibis (At Bagnolet 7km E)	35

12th Arrondissement Bastille, Gare de Lyon, Place d'Italie, Bois de Vincennes

Poniatowski SARL 57 bd Poniatowski ☎43443732 Closed Sat & Sun Ren

13th Arrondissement Bastille, Gare de Lyon, Place d'Italie, Bois de Vincennes

★★***Timhotel Italie*** 22 r Barrault ☎45806767 tx205461 Not on plan
rm73 (➡ ⋒68) Lift

★★***Timhotel Tolbiac*** 35 r de Tolbiac (n.rest) ☎45837494 tx201309 Not on plan
➡ ⋒54 Lift

★**Arts** 8 r Coypel (n.rest) ☎47077632 Plan **5**
rm40 (➡ ⋒27) Lift sB107—127 sB➡ ⋒167—187 dB144—184 dB➡ ⋒204—254

SOS Service 82 bd Massena ☎45846969 All makes

14th Arrondissement Vaugirard, Gare Montparnasse, Grenelle, Denfert-Rochereau

★★★**PLM St-Jacques** 17 bd St-Jacques ☎45898980 tx270740 Plan **98**
➡797 **P** Lift ☾ sB➡850—876 dB➡988—1019 M alc

15th Arrondissement Vaugirard, Gare Montparnasse, Grenelle, Denfert-Rochereau

★★★★***Hilton*** 18 av Suffren ☎42739200 tx200955 Plan **34**
➡489 ⌂ Lift ☾

★★★★**Holiday Inn** 69 bd Victor ☎45337463 tx260844 Plan **91**
➡90 ⌂ **P**50 Lift sB➡615—717 dB➡810—974 Mfr150
Credit cards [1] [2] [3] [5]

★★★★**Sofitel Paris** 8—12 r L-Armand ☎45549550 tx200432 Plan **75**
➡635 ⌂ **P**350 Lift ☾ sB➡ ⋒590—750 dB➡ ⋒680—840 M&alc
Credit cards [1] [2] [3] [5]

★★★**Mercure Paris-Vanves** r du Moulin ☎46429322 tx202195 Plan **99**
➡395 ⌂ **P**400 Lift sB➡fr539 dB➡fr608
Credit cards [1] [2] [3] [5]

★★***Arcade*** 2 r Cambronne ☎45673520 tx203842 Plan **87**
➡530 **P**80 Lift
Credit card [3]

★★**Campaville** 30 r St Charles (n.rest) ☎45786133 tx203086 Plan **96**
➡75 sB➡249—283 dB➡320—356
Credit card [3]

★★**Pacific** (Inter) 11 r Fondary (n.rest) ☎45752049 tx201346 Plan **50**
rm66 (➡ ⋒49) Lift sB129 sB➡ ⋒197 dB182—192 dB➡ ⋒260
Credit card [1]

★★**Timhotel Montparnasse** 22 r de l'Arrivée (n.rest) ☎45489662 tx270625 Plan **92**
➡ ⋒33 Lift sB➡ ⋒266 dB➡ ⋒326—373
Credit cards [1] [2] [3] [5]

16th Arrondissement Passy, Auteuil, Bois de Boulogne, Chaillot, Porte Maillot

★★★★***Baltimore*** 88 bis av Kléber ☎45538333 tx611591 Plan **9**
➡119 Lift ☾

★★★***Élysées Bassano*** 24 r de Bassano (n.rest) ☎47204903 tx611559 Plan **88**
➡40 Lift

★★★**Frémiet** (MAP) 6 av Frémiet (n.rest) ☎45245206 tx630329 Plan **70**
➡ ⋒36 ⌂ Lift ☾ sB➡ ⋒460—530 dB➡ ⋒515—630
Credit cards [1] [2] [3] [4]

★★★**Horset St-Cloud** 21 r Gudin (n.rest) ☎46519922 tx610929 Not on plan
➡47 Lift sB➡360 dB➡405
Credit cards [1] [2] [3] [4] [5]

★★★**Massenet** (BW/MAP) 5 bis r Massenet (n.rest) ☎45244303 tx620682 Plan **44**
rm41 (➡ ⋒39) Lift ☾ sB230 sB➡ ⋒530 dB➡ ⋒630
Credit cards [1] [2] [3] [5]

★★★***Sevigné*** 6 r de Belloy ☎47208890 tx610219 Plan **60**
➡ ⋒30 **P**3 Lift
Credit cards [1] [2] [5]

★★***Farnese*** 32 r Hamelin (n.rest) ☎47205666 tx611732 Plan **25**
➡ ⋒40 Lift ☾

★★**Keppler** (Inter) 12 r Keppler (n.rest) ☎47206505 tx620440 Plan **36**
rm49 (➡44) sB➡fr248 dB➡fr310
Credit cards [2] [3]

★★**Rond Point de Longchamp** 86 r de Longchamp ☎45051363 tx620653 Plan **55**
➡ ⋒59 Lift sB➡ ⋒542 dB➡ ⋒604 M120
Credit cards [2] [5]

★★***Vermont*** 11 bis r Bois-de-Boulogne (n.rest) ☎45000497 tx612208 Plan **65**
➡30 Lift ☾

17th Arrondissement Clichy, Ternes, Wagram

★★★★**Regent's Garden** (BW/MAP) 6 r P-Demours (n.rest) ☎45740730 tx640127 Plan **74**
➡ ⋒40 ⌂ **P**10 Lift sB➡ ⋒425—687 dB➡ ⋒550—774
Credit cards [1] [2] [3] [5]

★★★★**Splendid Étoile** 1 bis av Carnot ☎47664141 tx280773 Plan **61**
➡57 Lift ☾ sB➡588—648 dB➡696—986 M250&alc
Credit cards [1] [2] [3] [5]

★★***Neva*** 14 r Brey (n.rest) ☎43802826 Plan **48**
➡ ⋒35 Lift
Credit card [3]

★***Verniquet*** 3 r Verniquet (n.rest) ☎43802630 Plan **66**
➡ ⋒26 Lift

Boursault 11 r Boursault ☎42936565 Closed Sat pm & Sun AR

18th Arrondissement Montmartre, La Villette, Belleville

★★★★**Terrass** (BW/MAP) 12 r J-de-Maistre ☎46067285 tx280830 Plan **73**

🛁 🚿 108 Lift ☾ sB 🛁 🚿 510—690 dB 🛁 🚿 620—930
Credit cards 1 2 3 5

★★★**Mercure Paris-Montmartre** 1—3 Coulaincourt (n.rest) ☎42941717 tx640605 Plan **101**

🛁 308 Lift sB 🛁 510 dB 🛁 540
Credit cards 1 2 3 5

★★***Ibis Paris Montmartre*** 5 r Caulaincourt ☎42941818 tx640428 Plan **102**

🛁 326 Lift M alc
Credit cards 1 3

★★**Pigalle Urbis Paris** 100 bd Rochechouart (n.rest) ☎46069917 tx290416 Not on plan

🛁 67 Lift sB 🛁 244—271 dB 🛁 313—331
Credit cards 1 2 3

★★**Timhotel Montmartre** 11 pl E-Goudeau (n.rest) ☎42557479 tx650508 Plan **93**

rm63 (🛁 🚿 52) Lift sBfr175 sB 🛁 🚿 fr311 dB 🛁 🚿 337—370
Credit cards 1 2 3 5

The distances shown after the following locations are measured from the Place de la Concorde.

At **BAGNOLET** (7km E adj to Boulevard Périphérique)

★★★**Novotel Paris Bagnolet** 1 av de la République ☎43600210 tx670216 Plan **49**

🛁 611 **P** Lift sB 🛁 490—520 dB 🛁 🚿 525—555 M alc ⛱
Credit cards 1 2 3 5

★★**Ibis** r J-Jaurès ☎43600276 tx240830 Plan **35**

🛁 414 Lift sB 🛁 293
Credit cards 1 3

At **BONDY** (10km NE)

🚗 **B Greuet** 176—180 av Galliéni (N3) ☎48471659 Closed Sat pm, Sun & Mon am For

At **BOULOGNE-BILLANCOURT** (7km W adj to Boulevard Périphérique)

★★**Campaville** 5 r Carnot (n.rest) ☎48252251 tx631863 Not on plan

🛁 57 sB 🛁 249—283 dB 🛁 321—357

🚗 **Parc Auto** 69 r de Billancourt ☎46059100 AR Hon

At **CACHAN** (11km S)

★★**Climat** 2 r Mirabeau ☎45471800 Not on plan

🛁 46 **P**50 Lift sB 🛁 232—262 dB 🛁 254—284
Credit cards 1 3

At **CHILLY-MAZARIN** (20km S)

🚗 **Auto Relais** 3 r du chemin de Fer ☎49344626 Closed 15 Aug—15 Sep & Sun AR Mer

France

🚗 **Mobil Station** 10—14 av P-Brossolette ☎49095427 Closed Sun All makes

At **CRÉTEIL** (12km SE off N5)

★★★**Novotel** rte de Choissy (N186) ☎42079102 tx670396 Not on plan

🛁 110 Lift sB 🛁 fr342 dB 🛁 fr394 ⛱
Credit cards 1 2 3 5

★★***Climat*** quarter de la Brèche, r des Archives ☎48992323 tx692844 Not on plan

🛁 48 **P**
Credit cards 1 3

At **FONTENAY-AUX-ROSES** (9.5km SE)

🚗 **Marchand** 68 r Boucicaut ☎46611088 Closed Sat pm & Sun For

At **GENTILLY** (6km S adj to Boulevard Périphérique)

★★**Ibis** 13 r du Val de Marne ☎46641925 tx250733 Not on plan

🛁 296 Lift sB 🛁 233—257 dB 🛁 277—301
Credit cards 1 3 4

At **KREMLIN-BICÊTRE** (6km SE)

★★**Campanile** bd du Gl-de-Gaulle ☎46701186 tx205026 Not on plan

🛁 155 🏠 **P** Lift sB 🛁 283—305 dB 🛁 307—329 M70—98
Credit card 3

At **LIVRY-GARGAN** (17km NE)

★★**Climat** 119 bd R Schuman (RN3) ☎43854141 Not on plan

🛁 🚿 46 **P**50 Lift sB 🛁 🚿 214—235 dB 🛁 🚿 233—254 M51—110
Credit cards 1 3

At **MONTROUGE** (6km S adj to Boulevard Périphérique)

★★★**Mercure Porte d'Orléans** 13 r F-Ory ☎46571126 tx202528 Not on plan

🛁 192 🏠 **P** Lift sB 🛁 509—541 dB 🛁 578—612 M alc
Credit cards 1 2 3 5

★★**Ibis** 33 r Barbès ☎47469595 tx202527 Not on plan

🛁 402 **P** Lift sB 🛁 267 dB 🛁 348 M100

At **NEUILLY-SUR-SEINE** (8km W)

🚗 **Atelier** 18 bd Vital Bouhot ☎47471919 Closed Sat & Sun DJ

At **NOISY-LE-GRAND** (30km E)

★★**Campanile** r du Ballon ☎43052299 Not on plan

🛁 50 **P** sB 🛁 217—238 dB 🛁 239—260 M61—82
Credit card 3

At **PANTIN** (7km NE)

★★★**Mercure Paris** Porte de Pantin ☎48467066 tx230742 Not on plan

🛁 138 **P**60 Lift sB 🛁 fr482 dB 🛁 fr549 Malc
Credit cards 1 2 3 5

At **VILLENEUVE-LA-GARENNE** (16km N)

★★**Climat** bd C-de-Gaulle ☎7995600 tx692844 Not on plan

🛁 37 sB 🛁 209—226 dB 🛁 227—244 Mfr67
Credit cards 1 3 4 5

At **VINCENNES** (11km E off N34)

🚗 **Wuplan** 7 av de Paris ☎48084428 Closed 4 Aug—1 Sep, Sat & Sun Aud VW

PARIS AIRPORTS BOURGET AIRPORT (LE)

★★★**Novotel** r le Pont Yblon (N2) ☎48674888 tx230115 Not on plan

🛁 143 **P**200 Lift sB 🛁 337 dB 🛁 389 M140 & alc ⛱
Credit cards 1 2 3 5

CHARLES-DE-GAULLE AIRPORT

At **ROISSY-EN-FRANCE** (2km E)

★★★★**Holiday Inn** 1 allée du Verger ☎39880022 tx695143 Not on plan

🛁 240 **P**100 Lift sB 🛁 638 dB 🛁 726
Credit cards 1 2 3 5

★★★★**Sofitel** ☎48622323 tx230166 Not on plan

🛁 352 🏠 **P** Lift ☾ sB 🛁 610—650 dB 🛁 720—760 M100—200
Credit cards 1 2 3 4 5

★★**Arcade** 10 r du Verseau ☎48624949 tx212989 Not on plan

🚿 356 **P**150 Lift sB🚿 203—208 dB🚿 241—247 M alc

★★**Ibis** av de la Raperie ☎39880040 tx699083 Not on plan

🛁 200 **P** Lift sB 🛁 340—350 dB 🛁 410—421 Mfr70

ORLY AIRPORT

See also **RUNGIS**

★★★★**Hilton International** 267 Orly Sud ☎46873388 tx250621 Not on plan

🛁 380 **P**350 Lift ☾ sB 🛁 553—683 dB 🛁 716—876 Mfr110
Credit cards 1 2 3 4 5

★★**Arcade** espl Aérogare Sud ☎46873350 tx203121 Not on plan

🚿 203 **P** Lift sB🚿 219 dB🚿 261 M80
Credit card 3

At **ATHIS-MONS** (2.5km SE)

🚗 **Bidaud** 59 rte de Fontainebleau ☎49388181 Peu

At **MORANGIS** (2.5km SW)

★★**Campanile** 34 av F-de-Lesseps ☎(6)44486130 tx600832 Not on plan

🛁 50 **P** sB 🛁 217—238 dB 🛁 239—260 M61—82
Credit card 3

★★***Climat*** ZI des Sables, r Lavoisier ☎44483155 tx612241 Not on plan

🛁 38 **P**

🚗 **Orly Autos** av C-de-Gaulle, ZI Nord ☎49090897 Closed 10—25 Aug, Sun & Mon For

PARTHENAY
Deux-Sèvres

★★**Grand** 85 bd de la Meilleraie ☎49640016
rm26 (🛁 🚿 10) ⌂ **P**15 sB65—143
sB 🛁 🚿 88—143 dB88—180
dB 🛁 🚿 101—180 M39—120
Credit cards [1] [2] [3] [4] [5]

PASSENANS See **SELLIÈRES**

PASSY
Haute-Savoie

🚗 **Savoie-Arnaud** les Ruttets ☎50581189 All makes

PAU
Pyrénées-Atlantiques

★★★**Continental** (BW/MAP) 2 r Ml-Foch ☎59276931 tx570906
🛁 🚿 100 ⌂ Lift ☾ sB 🛁 🚿 224—278
dB 🛁 🚿 304—380 M85

★★★**Roncevaux** (FAH) 25 r L-Barthou (n.rest) ☎59270844 tx570849
🛁 🚿 44 **P** Lift ☾ dB 🛁 🚿 199—250
Credit cards [1] [2] [3] [5]

★★**Bristol** (Inter) 3 r Gambetta (n.rest) ☎59277298 tx570929
rm26 (🛁 🚿 22) **P**14 Lift sB139—231
sB 🛁 🚿 197—231 dB 🛁 🚿 246—291
Credit cards [1] [2] [3] [5]

★★**Campanile** bd de l'Aviation ☎59803233 tx540208
🛁 43 **P** sB 🛁 204—225 dB 🛁 226—260
M61—82
Credit card [3]

★★**Ibis** 45 r F-Garcia-Lorca ☎59306655 tx550909
🛁 83 ⌂ **P**20 Lift sB 🛁 191—210
dB 🛁 239—255

★***Central*** 15 r L-Daran (n.rest) ☎59277275
rm28 (🛁 🚿 18) ☾

At **LESCAR** (7.5km NW on D945)

★★★***Novotel*** (N117) ☎59321732 tx570939
🛁 61 **P** 🏊 mountains

PAYRAC
Lot

★★**Hostellerie de la Paix** LF ☎65379515 tx521291
Feb—Dec
🛁 50 **P**40 sB 🛁 190—210 dB 🛁 235—265
M64—150 St% 🏊
Credit cards [2] [3]

PENNE-ST-MENET (LA) See **MARSEILLE**

PÉRIGUEUX
Dordogne

★★★**Domino** (Inter) 21 pl Francheville ☎53082580 tx570230
rm37 (🛁 🚿 31) ⌂ Lift ☾ sB115
sB 🛁 🚿 180—237 dB115 dB 🛁 🚿 180—310
M71—200
Credit cards [1] [2] [3] [5]

★★**Ibis** 8 bd Saumande (**Pn**) ☎53536458 tx550159

France

🛁 89 **P**10 Lift sB 🛁 180—205
dB 🛁 234—265 M45—150
Credit cards [1] [3]

🚗 **Zizard-Laroumedie** 182 rte de Bordeaux ☎53080827 Closed 1—15 Aug, Sat pm & Sun AR

PÉRONNE
Somme

★★**St-Claude** LF (**DPn**) 42 pl L-Daudré ☎22844600
rm37 (🛁 🚿 23) ⌂ **P**20 sB103—120
sB 🛁 🚿 143—250 dB136—160
dB 🛁 🚿 176—310 M58—140
Credit cards [1] [2] [3] [5]

★**Remparts** LF (**Pn**) 21 r Beaubois ☎22840122
rm16 (🛁 🚿 12) ⌂ **P**7 sB118
sB 🛁 🚿 166—193 dB184—211 dB 🛁 🚿 211
M55—150
Credit cards [2] [3] [5]

At **ASSEVILLERS** (adj to autoroute A1)

★★★**Mercure** (A1) ☎22841276 tx140943
🛁 🚿 98 **P** Lift sB 🛁 🚿 311—326
dB 🛁 🚿 392—422 M78 🏊
Credit cards [1] [2] [3] [5]

PÉROUGES
Ain

★★★**Vieux Pérouges** pl du Tilleul ☎74610088
Feb—Dec
🛁 28 A10rm ⌂ sB 🛁 430—590
dB 🛁 530—770 M135—250 S15%
Credit card [3]

PERPIGNAN
Pyrénées-Orientales

★★★**Mondial** (MAP) 40 bd Clemenceau (n.rest) ☎68342345 tx500920
🛁 40 **P**8 Lift ☾ sB 🛁 195—240
dB 🛁 215—260
Credit cards [1] [3]

★★★**Windsor** (Inter) 8 bd Wilson (n.rest) ☎68511865 tx500701
Closed Feb
🛁 🚿 57 **P** Lift ☾ sB 🛁 🚿 217—297
dB 🛁 🚿 274—349
Credit card [3]

★★**Campanile** Lotissement Porte d'Espagne, r A-Leverman, rte du Perthus ☎68567575 tx505046
🛁 43 **P** sB 🛁 204—225 dB 🛁 226—260
M61—82
Credit card [3]

★★**Christina** 50 cours de Lassus (n.rest) ☎68352461
rm35 (🛁 🚿 30) ⌂ **P**15 Lift sB123—128
sB 🛁 🚿 158—183 dB146—201
dB 🛁 🚿 201—216
Credit cards [1] [3]

🚗 **Aguilar** 46 av d l'Ancien C-de-Mars ☎68521864 Closed Sun All makes

🚗 **Auto-Service** 14 bd St-Assiscle ☎68540998 Closed Sat pm & Sun Maz Saa

🚗 **Peruchet** 93 av Ml-Joffre ☎68611564 All makes

🚗 **Ribert** 3 r de Thues ☎68344579 M/c All makes

SA-Europe Auto bd P-Langevin ☎68850192 Closed Sat & Sun Aud VW

At **RIVESALTES** (5km NW by N9)

★★★**Novotel** (N9) ☎68640222 tx500851
🛁 86 ⌂ **P**60 M alc S15% 🏊
Credit cards [1] [2] [3] [5]

🚗 **Guillouf** r E-Parés ☎68641350 All makes

PERRIGNY-LÉS-DIJON See **DIJON**

PERROS-GUIREC
Côtes-du-Nord

★★★**Trestraou** bd J-le-Bihan, Trestraou ☎96232405
rm72 (🛁 🚿 68) A3rm **P**50 Lift
sB 🛁 🚿 239—306 dB222—262
dB 🛁 🚿 286—329 M75—85 sea
Credit cards [1] [2] [3] [5]

★★**Morgane** LF 46 av Casino, Plage de Trestraou ☎96232280
15 Mar—Oct
🛁 🚿 25 A5rm **P**30 Lift sB118—202
sB 🛁 🚿 202 dB 🛁 🚿 282—309 M70—150
🏊 sea
Credit cards [1] [2] [5]

At **PLOUMANACH** (6km NW)

★★★**Rochers** (FAH) ☎96232302
Etr—Sep
🛁 🚿 16 **P** sB🚿 204—225 dB 🛁 273—311
M105—176 sea

PESMES
Haute-Saône

★★**France** LF ☎84312005
🛁 🚿 10 A10rm **P**12 ☾ sB 🛁 🚿 119
dB 🛁 🚿 141 M65—95
Credit cards [1] [3]

PETITE-PIERRE (LA)
Bas-Rhin

★★**Vosges** LF 30 r Principale ☎88704505
rm33 (🛁 🚿 32) **P**20 Lift sB 🛁 🚿 150—190
dB 🛁 🚿 202—280 M60—200 mountains
Credit cards [1] [3]

PETIT-QUEVILLY (LE) See **ROUEN**

PEYREHORADE
Landes

★★**Central** LF (**DPn** in season) pl A-Briand ☎58730322
rm8 (🛁 🚿 5) ⌂ sB75 sB 🛁 🚿 105 dB90
dB 🛁 🚿 120—150 M60—250
Credit cards [2] [3]

PIED-DU-SANCY See **MONT DORE (LE)**

PIERRE-BUFFIÉRE
Haute-Vienne

★**Providence** 20 r Nationale ☎55006016
Apr—15 Nov
rm11 (🛁 🚿 8) ⌂ **P**8 sB92—112
sB 🛁 🚿 152—182 dB134—164

dB 🛁 🚿 174—229 M60—160
Credit card [2]

🚗 **R Gauthier** 17 av de Toulouse
☎55006024 Closed Sun pm Cit

PIERRELATTE
Drôme

★★***Hostellerie Tom II*** LE (**DPn** in season) 5 av Gl-de-Gaulle (N7) ☎75040035
rm15 (🚿 12) ⌂ **P**5
Credit cards [1] [2] [3]

🚗 **Atomic** ZI ☎75041286 Ope

🚗 **Mistral** ZI, rte de St-Paul ☎75040158 M/c Closed Sat pm & Sun For

🚗 **Notre-Dame** r N-Dame ☎75040237 Closed Aug, Sat pm & Sun Aud VW

PITHIVIERS
Loiret

★★**Climat** av du 8 Mai ☎38304025
🛁 26 **P**40 sB 🛁 209—229 dB 🛁 228—248 M65
Credit cards [1] [3]

★**Relais de la Poste** 10 Mail Ouest ☎38304030 tx212011
🛁 🚿 14 **P**5 sB 🛁 🚿 145—182
dB 🛁 🚿 181—218 M53—127&alc
Credit cards [1] [2] [3]

PLAISIR
Yvelines

★★**Campanile** ZI des Gâtines ☎30558150 tx697578
🛁 50 **P** sB 🛁 217—238 dB 🛁 239—260 M61—82
Credit card [3]

★★***Climat*** Lieudit le Hameau de la Chaine ☎30557737
🛁 38 **P**70
Credit card [3]

PLEHEDEL See **LANVOLLON**

PLÉRIN See **ST BRIEUC**

PLESSIS-CHENNET (LE) See **CORBEIL-ESSONNES**

PLOËRMEL
Morbihan

★**Commerce-Reberminard** LE 70 r de la Gare ☎97740532
rm20 (🛁 🚿 15) A13rm ⌂ **P**10 sB85—160
sB 🛁 🚿 125—170 dB115—190
dB 🛁 🚿 140—236 M45—150
Credit cards [1] [3]

PLOMBIÉRES-LES-BAINS
Vosges

★**Abbesses** 6 pl de l'Église ☎29660040 tx88370
May—Sep
rm44 (🛁 🚿 24) Lift sB100 sB 🛁 🚿 101
dB216 dB 🛁 🚿 216 Mfr70 mountains

PLOUGASTEL-DAOULAS See **BREST**

PLOUMANACH See **PERROS-GUIREC**

France

POITIERS
Vienne

★★★**France** (MAP) 28 r Carnot ☎49413201 tx790526
rm86 (🛁 🚿 70) ⌂ **P**25 Lift ☾
sB 🛁 🚿 330—430 dB 🛁 🚿 420—660 Mfr110
Credit cards [1] [2] [3] [5]

★★★**Royal Poitou** (3km N on N10) rte de Paris ☎49017286
🛁 🚿 32 **P** ☾ sB 🛁 🚿 289 dB 🛁 🚿 338 M69
Credit cards [1] [2] [3] [5]

★★**Balladins** r A-Haller ☎49415500 tx649394
🛁 🚿 28 ⌂ **P**28 sB 🛁 🚿 166 dB 🛁 🚿 182 M56—77
Credit cards [1] [2] [3]

★★**Climat** 3 r des Frères-Lumière ☎49613875 tx792022
🛁 40 dB 🛁 fr188 Mfr65
Credit cards [1] [3]

★★**Europe** 39 r Carnot (n.rest) ☎49881200
rm50 (🛁 🚿 41) ⌂ **P**35 ☾ sB109—138
sB 🛁 🚿 155—247 dB125—194
dB 🛁 🚿 171—283
Credit card [3]

★★***Ibis Poitiers Sud*** av du 8 Mai 1945 ☎49531313 tx791556
🛁 83 **P** Lift

★★**Ibis** ZAC de Beaulieu 'Les Mâches' ☎49611102 tx790354
🛁 33 **P**30 sB 🛁 202—208 dB 🛁 250—256 Mfr70
Credit cards [1] [3]

★★***Relais du Stade*** 84—86 r J-Coeur (n.rest) ☎49462512
rm25 (🛁 🚿 22) A4rm ⌂ **P**20 Lift

At **BIARD** (2km W)

🚗 **J P Barrault** ZI de Larnay ☎49583543 Vol

At **CHASSENEUIL-DU-POLTOU** (8km N by N10)

★★★**Novotel Poitiers Nord** (N10) ☎49527878 tx791944
🛁 89 **P**300 Lift sB 🛁 306—328
dB 🛁 372—382 M alc 🎾 ≋
Credit cards [1] [2] [3] [5]

★★★**Relais de Poitiers** (N10) ☎49529041 tx790502
rm97 (🛁 🚿 92) **P**500 Lift sB187—387
dB239—414 dB 🛁 🚿 239—414 M60—90 🎾 ≋
Credit cards [1] [2] [3] [5]

★★**Campanile** ZI de Chasseneuil-du-Poitou, Voie Ouest ☎49528540 tx791534
🛁 42 **P** sB 🛁 204—225 dB 🛁 226—247 M61—82
Credit card [3]

At **MIGNE-AUXANCES** (9km NE on N147)

🚗 **Auto Sport** (N147) ☎49582418 Closed Sat Alf AR

POIX-DE-PICARDIE
Somme

★**Poste** 13 pl de la République ☎22900033
rm18 (🛁 🚿 5) **P**12 sB96 sB 🛁 🚿 185 dB125
dB 🛁 🚿 157—200 M60—120
Credit cards [1] [3]

POLIGNY
Jura

★★**Hostellerie des Monts de Vaux** (Relais et Châteaux) Monts de Vaux (4.5km SE) ☎84371250 tx361493
Jan—Oct
🛁 10 ⌂ **P**20 **DPn**460—600 Mfr210
Credit card [2]

★★**Paris** LE 7 r Travot ☎84371387
Feb—4 Nov
🛁 🚿 25 ⌂ **P**12 sB 🛁 🚿 113—168
dB 🛁 🚿 156—236 M75—95 ▭ mountains

★★**Vallée Heureuse** LE rte de Genève ☎84371213
rm10 (🛁 🚿 6) ⌂ **P**10 sB162 sB 🛁 🚿 202
dB184 dB 🛁 🚿 234 M77 mountains
Credit cards [2] [3] [5]

🚗 **Poix** 10 av W-Gagneur ☎84371609 Closed Sun For

POLISOT
Aube

★**Seine** LE (**Pn**) ☎25385441
rm20 (🛁 🚿 8) ⌂ **P**10 sBfr102
sB 🛁 🚿 140—165 dBfr117
dB 🛁 🚿 155—180 M60—148
Credit cards [1] [3] [4]

PONS
Charente-Maritime

★★**Auberge Pontoise** (**DPn**) r Gambetta ☎46940099
Feb—20 Dec
🛁 🚿 22 ⌂ **P**20 sB 🛁 🚿 176—231
dB 🛁 🚿 202—292 M85—195

PONT-A-MOUSSON
Meurthe-et-Moselle

★**Européen** 156 av Metz ☎83810757
Closed 4—27 Aug
rm24 (🛁 🚿 9) A6rm ⌂ **P**40 sB101—193
sB 🛁 🚿 123—193 dB118 dB 🛁 🚿 211 M65
Credit card [3]

★**Poste** (**Pn**) 42 bis r V-Hugo ☎83810116
10 Jan—15 Dec
rm24 (🛁 🚿 14) A8rm ⌂ **P**10 sB119—199
sB 🛁 🚿 174—249 dB193—268
dB 🛁 🚿 248—268 M60—200
Credit cards [1] [3]

PONTARLIER
Doubs

★★***Poste*** LE 55 r de la République ☎81391812
15 Dec—10 Oct
rm52 (🛁 🚿 23) ⌂ **P**25
Credit cards [1] [2] [3] [5]

Beau Site 29 av de l'Armée de l'Est ☎81392395 Closed Sat pm & Sun Peu

PONTAUBAULT
Manche

★★★**13 Assiettes** (DPn) (1km N on N175) ☎33581403 tx170537
15 Mar—15 Nov
rm36 (27) **P**50 sB102—109 sB 112—162 dB119—126 dB 129—179 M47—165
Credit card 3

PONT-AUDEMER
Eure

★★★**Vieux Puits** (**DPn**) 6 r Notre-Dame du Pré ☎32410148
17 Jan—Jun & 10 Jul—15 Dec
rm14 (11) **P** sB116—151 dB188—243 dB 318—358 M alc
Credit card 3

★***Palais & Poste*** (**DPn**) 8 r Stanislas ☎32415074
rm12 (4)

★**Risle** (**Pn**) 16 quai R-Leblanc ☎32411457
rm18 sB69—89 dB103—138 Mfr51

Vittecoq 9 bd Pasteur ☎32410335 Closed Sat pm & Sun All makes

At **FOURMETOT** (6km NE on D139)

Bacheley ☎32574069 Closed Mon All makes

PONTAULT-COMBAULT
Seine-et-Marne

Audebert 84 rte de la Libération ☎60280464 Closed Sat pm & Sun Cit

PONTCHARRA
Rhône

★★**Climat** Lieu dit 'Le Gabion' (N90) ☎76719184 tx305551
24 **P**30 dB 182—197 M52—66 St% mountains
Credit cards 1 3

PONT-D'AIN
Ain

★★**Alliés** ☎74390009
20 Jan—25 May & 2 Jun—21 Dec
rm18 (12) sB121 sB 169—207 dB142—190 dB 190—274 M82—170
Credit card 3

★★**Paris-Nice** 2 r du 1er Septembre 1944 (n.rest) ☎74390380
Closed Nov & Tue
rm20 (6) **P**25 sBfr98 sB fr162 dBfr150 dB fr223

PONT-DE-CLAIX See **GRENOBLE**

PONT-DE-L'ISÈRE
Drôme

★**Portes du Midi** (N7) ☎75846026
Mar—Oct
rm18 (11) **P**50 dB104—134 dB 134 Mfr50 mountains
Credit cards 1 2 3 5

PONT-DE-RHODES See **FRAYSSINET**

France

PONT-DU-GARD
Gard

★★***Vieux Moulin*** ☎66371435
Mar—Nov
rm16 (14)
Credit cards 1 2 5

At **REMOULINS** (4km E)

★★**Moderne** (**DPn**) pl des Grands-Jours ☎66372013
Closed 19 Oct—18 Nov
rm25 (17) sB85—104 sB 104—124 dB123—137 dB 137—158 M42—79
Credit cards 1 2 3 5

PONTHIERRY
Seine-et-Marne

Tractaubat 76 av de Fontainebleau ☎60657039 Closed 1—26 Aug, Sat pm & Sun Ren

Trois Sept 62 av de Fontainebleau ☎60657052 Cit

At **PRINGY** (2km SE)

★★***Ibis*** 4 rte de Melun ☎60655928 tx690723
32 **P**

PONTIVY
Morbihan

★★***Porhoët*** (Inter) 41 av Gl-de-Gaulle (n.rest) ☎97253488
28 **P** Lift

PONT-LÉVÊQUE
Calvados

★★***Lion d'Or*** pl Calvaire ☎31640038
rm16 (10) **P**30
Credit cards 1 2 3 5

Dupults 5 r Melaine ☎31640186 Closed Sat pm & Sun Cit

Garez 37 r de Vaucelles ☎31640211 Closed Sat & Sun Tal

Société van Houtte ZI de Lisieux ☎31641105 Ren

PONTOISE
Val-d'Oise

★★**Campanile** r P-de Coubertin ☎30385544 tx698515
50 **P** sB 217—238 dB 239—260 M61—82
Credit card 3

At **CERGY** (4km SW)

★★★***Novotel*** av du Parc, Ville Nouvelle ☎30303947 tx697264
195 **P**200 Lift

Credit cards 1 2 3 5

★★**Arcade** près Préfecture ☎30309393 tx690470
rm140 **P** Lift sB185—190 dB208—213 Mfr75

★★**Balladins** 17 chaussée J-César ☎30321111 tx649394
28 **P**28 sB 166 dB 182 M56—77
Credit cards 1 2 3

★★***Climat*** ZAC d'Eragny, r des Pinsons ☎30378600 tx696149
41 **P**50

At **ST-OUEN-L'AUMÔNE** (5km SE)

★★★***Grand Cerf*** 59 r Gl-Leclerc ☎34640313
10
Credit cards 2 3

PONTORSON
Manche

★★**Montgomery** (FAH) (**Pn**) 13 r Couesnon ☎33600009 tx171332
Mar—Oct
32 **P**50 sB 167—192 dB 184—274 M60—180
Credit cards 1 2 3 5

Galle Vettori rte d'Avranches ☎83600037 Closed Sat pm & Sun Peu

PONT-SARRAZIN See **GAP**

PONTS-DE-CÉ (LES)
Maine-et-Loire

★★**Campanile** chemin du Moulin-Marcille ☎41683459 tx720959
41 **P** sB 204—225 dB 226—247 M61—82
Credit card 3

PONT-SUR-YONNE
Yonne

★★**Ecu** (**Pn**) 3 r Carnot ☎86670100
Mar—20 Jan
rm8 (6) **P**5 sB81—122 sB 122—165 dB102—175 dB 132—175 M57—94
Credit cards 1 2 3 5

PORNIC
Loire-Atlantique

SARL Gaudin rte Bleue ☎40820026 Closed 15 days Oct, Sun & Mon in low season only Peu

PORNICHET
Loire-Atlantique

★★★**Sud-Bretagne** (**DPn** in Jul & Aug) 42 bd de la République ☎40610268
15 Mar—15 Oct
34 **P**10 Lift dB 330—550 M50—150
Credit cards 1 2 3 5

PORT-BLANC
Côtes-du-Nord

★**Grand** ☎96926652
Etr—Sep
30 **P**10 dB 123—158 M50—115 sea
Credit card 1

PORTEL (LE)
Pas-de-Calais

See also **BOULOGNE-SUR-MER**

★***Beau Rivage et Armada*** **(DPn)** pl Mon-Bourgain ☎21315982
Mar–Oct
rm12 (🛁 🚿 7) **P**10 sea
Credit cards [1] [2] [3] [5]

PORTES-LÉS-VALENCE See **VALENCE**

PORT-GRIMAUD See **GRIMAUD**

PORT-LA-NOUVELLE
Aude

🚗 **Marill** ZI ☎68480486 Closed Xmas, New Year & Sun Fia Lan

🚗 **L Pertil** r J-Jaurès ☎6848006 Closed Sun All makes

PORT-LOUIS
Morbihan

★★**Avel Vor** LF (FAH/Inter) **(DPn)** 25 r de Locmalo ☎97824759 tx950826
🛁 20 Lift sB🛁 203–233 dB🛁 276–330 M55–200 sea
Credit cards [1] [2] [3] [5]

PORTO-VECCHIO See **CORSE (CORSICA)**

POUILLY-EN-AUXOIS
Côte-d'Or

🚗 **S Clair** r de la Gare ☎80908105 Closed Sat pm & Sun Tal

🚗 **J J Jeannin** pl des Alliés ☎80908211 M/c Peu

🚗 **P Orset** ☎80908045 Closed Sun Ren

At **CHÂTEAUNEUF** (10km SE D18)

★★**Hostellerí du Château** LF **(DPn)** ☎80330023
Mar–15 Nov
🛁 🚿 11 dB🛁 🚿 140–290 M100–200
Credit cards [1] [2] [3]

At **MEILLY-SUR-ROUVRES** (6km S on N81)

🚗 **R Perrot** ☎80908660 Closed 15 days Sep, Sat pm & Sun Cit

POUILLY-SUR-LOIRE
Nièvre

★★**Boutelle d'Or** LF **(DPn)** 13 bis rte de Paris ☎86391384
Closed 16 Jan–14 Feb
rm30 (🛁 🚿 27) A8rm sB🛁 🚿 fr130 dBfr146 dB🛁 🚿 196 M60–200&alc

★**Relais Fleuri** LF (0.5km SE on N7) ☎86391299
15 Feb–15 Jan
🛁 🚿 9 🏠 **P**15 dB🛁 🚿 170–194 M50–120
Credit cards [1] [3]

POULDU (LE)
Finistère

★★**Castel Treaz** (n.rest) ☎98399111
10 Jun–10 Sep
rm25 (🛁 🚿 18) **P**19 Lift sB111–116 sB🛁 🚿 251–265 dB132–137 dB🛁 🚿 272–286 sea

★★**Quatre Chemins** LF **(DPn)** ☎98399044
Jun–21 Sep
rm38 (🛁 🚿 25) **P** sB101 sBfr108 sB🛁 🚿 138–220 dBfr156

France

dB🛁 🚿 196–260 M55–160
Credit cards [1] [3] [5]

POUZAUGES
Vendée

★★**Auberge de la Bruyère** LF (FAH) r Dr-Barbanneau ☎51919346
🛁 🚿 30 **P**60 Lift sB🛁 🚿 184–235 dB🛁 🚿 250–330 M42–89 ≈ Beach
Credit cards [1] [2] [3] [5]

POUZIN (LE)
Ardèche

🚗 **M Pheby** (S on N86) ☎75628016 Closed Sat & Sun Cit

🚗 **Renault** rte de Loriol ☎75628022 Ren

PRAYSSAC
Lot

★★***Vidal*** LF (Inter) 3 r des Garabels ☎65224178
Closed Nov–14 Dec
rm11 (🛁 8) 🏠 **P**

PRINGY See **PONTHIERRY**

PUILBOREAU See **ROCHELLE (LA)**

PUY (LE)
Haute-Loire

★★★**Christel** 15 bd A-Clair ☎71022444
🛁 30 **P**25 Lift ☾ sB🛁 205 dB🛁 270 M50–90&alc
Credit cards [1] [2] [3]

PUY-L'ÉVÊQUE
Lot

At **MONTCABRIER** (7km NW)

★★★**Relais de la Dolce** **(DPn)** rte de Villefranche de Périgord (D28) ☎65365342 tx531427
🛁 12 **P** dB🛁 356 M80–220 ≈ mountains
Credit cards [2] [3] [5]

PYLA-SUR-MER
Gironde

★★★***Guitoune*** 95 bd de l'Océan ☎56227010
🛁 🚿 22 **P**30 ☾ sea
Credit cards [1] [2] [3] [4] [5]

★★**Beau Rivage** 10 bd de l'Océan ☎56220182
Apr–Sep
🛁 🚿 17 A5rm sB161–271 sB🛁 🚿 180 dB192–221 dB🛁 🚿 262–342

QUARRÉ-LES-TOMBES
Yonne

★**Nord et Poste** LF **(Pn)** pl de l'Église ☎86322455
rm35 (10 🛁 🚿) A24rm

QUÉTIGNY See **DIJON**

QUEUE-EN-BRIE (LA)
Val-de-Marne

★★**Climat** (D185) ☎45946161 tx262209
🛁 55 **P**60 sB🛁 202–248 dB🛁 220–266 M51–150
Credit cards [1] [3]

QUIBERON
Morbihan

★★★**Sofitel Thalassa** Pointe de Goulvas ☎97502000 tx730712
🛁 113 **P**150 Lift ☾ 📺 sea
Credit cards [1] [2] [3] [5]

★★***Beau Rivage*** 11 r de Port Maria ☎97500839 tx950538
Apr–Sep
rm48 (🛁 🚿 35) Lift sea

★***Ty Breiz*** LF 23 bd Chanard ☎97500990
mid Apr-Sep
rm32 (🛁 🚿 25) A4rm **P** sea

At **ST PIERRE-QUIBERON** (4.5km N on D786)

★★**Plage** LF ☎97309210
25 Mar–Oct
🛁 🚿 46 A4rm **P** Lift **DPn**150–260 sea
Credit card [2]

QUILLAN
Aude

★★**Chaumière** LF (Inter) **(DPn)** bd C-de-Gaulle ☎68201790
rm39 🛁 🚿 30 A21rm 🏠 **P**40 Lift sB90–220 sB🛁 🚿 220–240 dB110–262 dB🛁 🚿 260–280 M50–160 mountains
Credit cards [2] [3]

★**Cartier** (FAH) 31 bd C-de-Gaulle ☎68200514
15 Mar–15 Dec
rm33 (🛁 🚿 26) 🏠 Lift sB106–125 sB🛁 🚿 150–205 dB140–170 dB🛁 🚿 200–270 M55–120 mountains
Credit cards [1] [3]

🚗 **J Escur** av de Marides ☎68200666 Closed Sat pm & Sun Ren

QUIMPER
Finistère

★★★***Griffon*** (Inter) 131 rte de Bénodet ☎98903333 tx940063
🛁 🚿 50 **P**50 📺
Credit cards [1] [2] [3] [5]

★★***Gradion*** LF 30 r Brest (n.rest) ☎98950439
rm25 (🛁 🚿 20) 🏠

★★**Ibis Quimper** r G-Eiffel, ZI de l'Hippodrôme Secteur Ouest ☎98905380 tx940007
🛁 70 A27rm **P**70 sB🛁 198 dB🛁 255 M &alc

★★**Ibis Quimper Nord** le Gourvily, rte de Brest ☎98957764 tx940749
🛁 36 **P**50 ☾ sB🛁 195 dB🛁 243 M &alc

★★**Tour d'Auvergne** LF (FAH) 11–13 r des Règuaires ☎98950870 tx941100
Closed 20 Dec–12 Jan
rm45 (🛁 🚿 40) A2rm 🏠 **P**30 Lift sBfr142 sB🛁 🚿 242–272 dB🛁 🚿 274–304 M70–125
Credit cards [1] [2] [3]

🚗 **Auto Secours** 28 av A-de-Bretagne ☎98531226 All makes

🚗 **Belleguic** 21 rte de Ceray ☎98900369 Closed Sat pm Mer

🚗 **Kemper** 13 av de la Libération ☎98901849

🚗 **Ste des Garages de l'Odet** rte de Douarnenez, ZI de Kernevez ☎98956314 Closed Sat & Sun Ren

QUINCY-VOISINS
Seine-et-Marne

★★**Auberge Demi Lune** (**DPn**) (N36) ☎60041109

rm5 dBfr125 Mfr61

RABOT (LE)
Loir-et-Cher

★★★**Bruyères** (N20) ☎54880570

🛁🚿50 **P**100 sB🛁🚿102—242 dB🛁🚿118—264 M63—120 ≈ 🎾
Credit cards 1 3 5

RAMBOUILLET
Yvelines

★★**Climat** Lieu dit 'la louvière' ☎34856262

🛁43 sB🛁229—256 dB🛁252—277 M51—120 🎾
Credit cards 1 3

★★**Ibis** le Bel Air (N10) ☎30417850 tx698429

🛁63 **P** 🎾

★**St-Charles** 15 r de Groussay (n.rest) ☎34830634 tx696084

6 Jan—20 Dec
🛁🚿12 A2rm ⌂ **P**20 sB🛁🚿fr166 dB🛁🚿177—252

🚗 **Central** 15 r G-Clemenceau ☎34830187 Closed Aug, Sat pm & Sun Alf Dat

RANCOURT
Somme

★★***Prieuré*** (**DPn**) (N17) ☎22850443

Feb—25 Dec
🛁🚿25 ⌂ **P**25
Credit cards 1 2 3

RAPHÈLE-LES-ARLES See **ARLES**

RAYOL (LE)
Var

★★★★**Bailli de Suffren** (**DPn**) ☎94713577 tx420535

mid Jun—mid Sep
🛁🚿47 **P** Lift

RÉ (ILE DE)
Charente-Maritime

FLOTTE (LA)

★★***Richelieu*** (**DPn**) 44 av de la Plage ☎46096070 tx791492

Closed Jan
🛁30 **P** sea

RECOLOGNE
Doubs

★**Escale** LF ☎81863213

Nov—Sep
🛁🚿11 sB82 sB🛁🚿93 dB95 dB🛁🚿144 M40—120

🚗 **Muneret** rte de Noirnote ☎81863181 Ren

At **LAVERNAY** (3.5km S on D13)

🚗 **Pelot** ☎81863362 Closed Sun Tal

REIMS
Marne

★★★★***Frantel*** 31 bd P-Doumer ☎26885354 tx830689

🛁125 ⌂ Lift
Credit cards 1 2 3 5

★★★**Mercure Reims Est** Zise Les Essillards, rte de Châlons ☎26050008 tx830782

🛁98 **P**65 Lift sB🛁288—298 dB🛁326—336 M alc ≈
Credit cards 1 2 3 5

★★★**Paix** (Inter) 9 r Buirette ☎26400408 tx830974

🛁105 ⌂ **P**30 Lift sB🛁259—309 dB🛁298—363 ≈
Credit cards 1 2 3 5

★★**Balladins** r M-Hollande ☎26827210 tx649394

🛁🚿34 ⌂ **P**34 sB🛁🚿166 dB🛁🚿182 M56—77
Credit cards 1 2 3

★★**Campanile** av G-Pompidou ☎26366694 tx830262

🛁41 **P** sB🛁217—238 dB🛁240—261 M61—82
Credit cards 2 3

★★**Climat** (Inter) r B-Russel, ZAC de la Neuvillette ☎26096273

🛁40 **P**50 sB🛁203—218 dB🛁221—236 M51—85
Credit cards 1 3

★★**Continental** 93 pl Drouet d'Erlon (n.rest) ☎26403935 tx830585

5 Jan—20 Dec
🛁🚿60 Lift sB🛁🚿140—260 dB🛁🚿180—290
Credit cards 1 3

★★***Europa*** 8 bd Joffre (n.rest) ☎26403620 tx830600

6 Jan—22 Dec
rm32 (🛁🚿23) **P**15 Lift
Credit cards 1 2 3 5

★★**Grand du Nord** 75 pl Drouet-d'Erlon (n.rest) ☎26473903

6 Jan—20 Dec
🛁🚿50 Lift ☾ sB🛁🚿160—241 dB🛁🚿185—282
Credit cards 1 2 3 5

★★**Touring** 17 ter bd Leclerc (n.rest) ☎26473815

rm14 (🛁🚿11) sB97—147 sB🛁🚿147 dB119—184 dB🛁🚿184
Credit cards 1 3

★★**Univers** (Inter) 41 bd Foch ☎26886808

rm40 (🛁37) Lift sBfr145 sB🛁🚿fr182 dBfr177 dB🛁222
Credit cards 1 2 3

★★**Welcome** 29 r Buirette (n.rest) ☎26473939 tx842145

5 Jan—20 Nov
rm70 (🛁🚿50) sB94—100 sB🛁🚿125—190 dB107—141 dB🛁🚿141—262
Credit cards 1 3

🚗 **Dauphinot** 124 bd Dauphinot ☎26070378 Closed Sun pm All makes

🚗 **Prott** 40 av d'Epernay ☎26080108 Closed Sun All makes

At **TINQUEUX** (4km W off N31)

★★★***Novotel*** rte de Soisson (N31) ☎26081161 tx830034

🛁125 **P** M alc ≈

★★**Ibis** Autoroute A4 (n.rest) ☎26046070 tx842116

🛁51 **P** sB🛁223—234 dB🛁257—267 M alc

REMIGEASSE (LA) See **OLÉRON (ILE D')**

REMIREMONT
Vosges

At **ST-NABORD** (5km N on N57)

★★★**Montiroche** (N57) (n.rest) ☎29620659

Apr—Sep
rm14 (🛁🚿13) **P**30 sB125—165 dB🛁🚿190—210 mountains

REMOULINS See **PONT-DU-GARD**

RENAISON
Loire

★**Jacques Coeur** LF rte Vichy ☎77642534

Mar—Jan
rm10 (🚿6) **P** sB83—91 sB🚿96—106 dB83—91 dB🚿106—112
Credit cards 2 3 5

RENNES
Ille-et-Vilaine

★★★**Frantel** pl du Colombier, r du Capitaine-Maignan ☎99315454 tx730905

🛁140 **P**100 Lift sB🛁293—363 dB🛁436
Credit cards 1 2 3 4 5

★★★**Guesclin** 5 pl de la Gare ☎99314747 tx740748

🛁68 Lift sB🛁fr266 dB🛁fr327 Mfr57&alc
Credit cards 1 2 3 5

★★★***Novotel Rennes Alma*** av du Canada ☎99506132 tx740144

🛁98 **P** ≈
Credit cards 1 2 3 5

★★★**Président** 27 av Janvier (n.rest) ☎99654222 tx730004

🛁🚿34 ⌂ **P**15 Lift sB🛁🚿230—270 dB🛁🚿230—290
Credit cards 1 2 3 5

★★***Climat*** ZAC de Beauregard Sud ☎99541203 tx692844

🛁42 **P**

★★**Urbis** 1–3 bd Solferino (n.rest) ☎99673112 tx730625
⇌60 Lift sB⇌202 dB⇌281
Credit cards 1 3

At **CESSON-SÉVIGNÉ** (6km E)

★★**Ibis Rennes** (N157) La Perrière ☎99839393 tx740321
⇌76 **P**80 Lift sB⇌193–208 dB⇌241–257 M50–78
Credit cards 1 3

★★**Ibis Rennes Beaulieu** rte de Paris ☎99833172 tx740378
⇌35 **P**60 sB⇌194–208 dB⇌240–256 M50–70
Credit cards 1 3

RESSONS-SUR-MATZ
Oise

Blanchard ☎44425031 Closed Mon am Ren

At **CUVILLY** (3km NW on N17)

Brecqueville r Planché ☎44420016 Closed Sun All makes

RETHEL
Ardennes

★★**Moderne** (Inter) pl de la Gare ☎24384454
rm25 (⇌ 20) **P**8 sB155 sB⇌ 153–208 dB176 dB⇌ 196–261 M70–180
Credit cards 1 2 3 4 5

REZÉ DE NANTES
Loire-Atlantique

★★**Fimotel** Impasse Ordronneau ☎40042030 tx700429
⇌42 **P** Lift sB⇌221–241 dB⇌253–274 M54–90&alc
Credit cards 2 3 5

RIGNAC See **GRAMAT**

RIVE-DE-GIER
Loire

★★**Hostellerie de la Renaissance** 41 r Marrel ☎77750431
rm10 (⇌ 8) **P**20 sB235–325 sB⇌ 350–380 dB⇌ 290 M105–400
Credit cards 1 2 3 5

RIVESALTES See **PERPIGNAN**

ROANNE
Loire

★★**France** 19 r A-Roche ☎77712117
rm42 (⇌ 23) **P** sB88–128 sB⇌ 128–168 dB126–146 dB⇌ 186–286
Credit card 1

★★**Ibis** ZI du Côteau, le Côteau (E of River Loire) ☎77683622 tx300610
⇌51 **P**65 sB⇌201–231 dB⇌252–287
Credit cards 1 2 3

★★**Troisgros** (Relais et Châteaux) 22 cours de la République ☎77716697 tx307507
Feb–4 Aug & 20 Aug–Dec
⇌24 **P**30 Lift sB⇌355–575

France

dB⇌555–1010 M200–380
Credit cards 1 2 3 5

Poste 56 r R-Salengro ☎77683199 M/c Closed 27 July–17 Aug, Sat pm, Sun & Mon am For

At **ST-GERMAIN-LESPINASSE** (10km NW on N7)

★★★**Relais de Roanne** (N7) (Inter) ☎77719735 tx307554
⇌ 30 **P**60 sB⇌ 165–215 dB⇌ 225–260 mountains
Credit cards 1 2 3 4 5

ROCAMADOUR
Lot

★★★**Beau Site & Notre Dame** (BW/MAP) r R-le-Preux ☎65336308 tx520421
Apr–Oct
rm55 (⇌ 51) **P** Lift sB170–225 sB⇌ 290 dB255 dB⇌ 320–365 M68–150
Credit cards 1 2 3 5

★★★**Château** (**DPn**) (FAH) rte de Château ☎65336222 tx521871
25 Mar–12 Nov
⇌ 58 A24rm **P**100 sB⇌ 170–190 dB⇌ 220–240 M48–150

★★**Ste-Marie** (**DPn** Jul & Aug) r Grand Escalier, pl des Sehnal ☎65336307
Apr–Oct
⇌22 A5rm **P** sB⇌140–185 dB⇌158–220 M46–150 mountains
Credit card 3

★**Lion d'Or** Porte Figuier ☎65336204
Etr–Oct
rm32 (⇌ 18) A6rm Lift sB78–138 sB⇌ 138 dBfr111 dB⇌ 201 M48–150 t% mountains
Credit card 3

ROCHEFORT
Charente-Maritime

★★★**Remparts Fimotel** 43 r C-Pelletan ☎46871244
⇌63 **P** Lift
Credit cards 1 2 3 5

ROCHELLE (LA)
Charente-Maritime

★★★**Brises** chemin Digue Richeilieu (n.rest) ☎46438937 tx790754
15 Jan–15 Dec
⇌ 46 **P** Lift sB⇌ 230–365 dB⇌ 340–460 sea
Credit cards 1 3

★★★**France et d'Angleterre** (BW/MAP) 22 r Gargoulleau ☎46413466 tx790717
rm76 ⇌ 67 **P**20 sB161–173 sB⇌ 313–341 dB206 dB⇌ 346–374 M110–155 & alc
Credit cards 1 2 3 5

★★★***Yachtman*** 23 quai Valin ☎46413442 tx790762
⇌ 40 Lift
Credit cards 1 2 3 5

★★**Campanile** rte de Paris ☎46340729
⇌30 sB⇌204–225 dB⇌227–248 M61–82
Credit card 3

★★**Ibis** pl du Cdt-de-la-Motte-Rouge ☎46416022 tx791431
⇌76 Lift sB⇌216 dB⇌258 M75
Credit cards 1 3

★★**St-Nicolas** (Inter) 13r Sardinerie (n.rest) ☎46417155
⇌29 **P**10 Lift sB⇌209 dB⇌264
Credit cards 1 2 3 5

★**Trianon et Plage** (FAH) (**DPn**) 6 r de la Monnaie ☎46412135
Feb–Dec
rm25 (⇌ 15) **P**20 dB⇌ 220–300 M80–115
Credit cards 2 3 5

Auto Charente Maritime 47 r du Lignon ☎46345626 M/c All makes

At **PUILBOREAU** (4km NE)

★★**Climat** Zone Commerciale de Beaulieu (N11) ☎46673737
⇌49 **P**80 sB⇌206–224 dB⇌225–243 M50–68 & alc
Credit cards 1 3

Depan Auto ZAC de Beaulieu ☎46671616 Closed Sat & Sun For

ROCHE-POSAY (LA)
Vienne

★**Parc** av Fontaines ☎49862002
May–Sep
rm80 (⇌ 29) **P**50 Lift sB76 sB⇌ 136–173 dB177–199 dB⇌ 199–223 Mfr55 t%

ROCHES-DE-CONDRIEU (LES)
Isère

★★**Bellevue** (**DPn**) 1 quai du Rhône ☎74564142
Closed 4-14 Aug & 16 Feb–10 Mar
rm18 (⇌ 17) A5rm **P**15 sB150–190 sB⇌ 190 dB260 dB⇌ 260 M80–220 lake
Credit card 3

ROCHE-SUR-YON (LA)
Vendée

★★**Campanile** les Bazinères, rte de Nantes ☎51372786
⇌42 **P** sB⇌204–225 dB⇌225–248 M61–82
Credit card 3

★★**Ibis** bd Arago ☎51362600 tx700601
⇌65 **P** sB⇌217 dB⇌254 M53–100

Aillery Ridier 3-13 rte d'Aizenay ☎51362206 Closed Sat & Sun AR

Baudry bd Lavoisier ☎51372235 Closed Sat & Sun For

ROCROI
Ardennes

★★**Commerce** LF pl A-Briand ☎24541115
10 Feb—5 Jan
rm12 (⇌ ⋒ 10) ⌂ sB95—168
sB ⇌ ⋒ 134—168 dB114—187
dB ⇌ ⋒ 153—207 M55—100

RODEZ
Aveyron

★★★**Broussy** (BW/MAP) 1 av V-Hugo (n.rest) ☎65681871
rm70 (⇌ ⋒ 45) ⌂ **P**10 Lift ☾ sB105
sB ⇌ ⋒ 150—195 dB140—180
dB ⇌ ⋒ 180—240
Credit cards 1 2 3 5

★★★**Tour Maje** (Inter) bd Gally (n.rest) ☎65683468
rm48 (⇌ ⋒ 45) Lift ☾ sB ⇌ ⋒ 176—238
dB ⇌ ⋒ 196—280
Credit cards 1 2 3 5

ROISSY-EN-FRANCE See **CHARLES-DE-GAULLE AIRPORT** under **PARIS AIRPORTS**

ROLLEBOISE
Yvelines

⛟ **A Terminarias** (N63) ☎30932128 M/c Closed Aug & Sun Lan Ren

ROMANS-SUR-ISÈRE
Drôme

★★***Terminus*** (Inter) 48 av P-Sémard (n.rest) ☎75024688
rm32 (⇌ ⋒ 18) Lift

ROMILLY-SUR-SEINE
Aube

★★**Climat** av Diderot (angle N19) ☎25249240 tx692844
⇌ 35 **P**

ROMORANTIN-LANTHENAY
Loir-et-Cher

★★**Colombier** LF 10 pl Vieux Marché ☎54761276
15 Feb—15 Sep & 22 Sep—15 Jan
⇌ ⋒ 11 ⌂ **P**10 Lift sB ⇌ ⋒ 162—173
dB ⇌ ⋒ 211—256 M75—145
Credit cards 1 2 3 5

★★**Lion d'Or** LF (Relais et Châteaux) (**DPn**) 69 r G-Clemenceau ☎54760028
Mid Feb—Jan
⇌ 10 ⌂ **P**10 Lift sB ⇌ fr415
dB ⇌ 520—680 M220—365
Credit cards 1 2 3 5

ROQUEBRUNE-CAP-MARTIN
Alpes-Maritimes

★★★**Victoria & Plage** 7 prom du Cap (n.rest) ☎93356590
Feb—2 Nov
⇌ ⋒ 30 ⌂ **P**7 ☾ sB ⇌ ⋒ 320—390
dB ⇌ ⋒ 350—420 sea mountains
Credit cards 1 2 3 5

★★**Westminster** LF (**DPn** 15 Jan—15 Sep) 14 av L-Laurens ☎93350068
Feb—15 Oct
⇌ ⋒ 31 A4rm ⌂ **P**8 sB ⇌ ⋒ 115—135
dB ⇌ ⋒ 170—230 M50—90 sea

ROQUE-GAGEAC (LA)
Dordogne

★***Belle Étoile*** LF ☎53295144
31 Mar—15 Oct
rm16 (⇌ ⋒ 15) ⌂ **P**6

ROQUES-SUR-GARONNE See **TOULOUSE**

ROSCOFF
Finistère

★★★***Gulf Stream*** (**Pn**) r Marquise de Kergariou ☎98697319
Apr—Sep
⇌ ⋒ 32 **P**100 Lift ⚲ sea
Credit cards 1 3

★★**Tallabardon** pl Église ☎98612495 tx29211
Apr—Oct
rm41 (⇌ ⋒ 27) ⌂ Lift sB130—145
sB ⇌ ⋒ 185—240 dB150—165
dB ⇌ ⋒ 205—260 M87 sea

★**Bains** pl Église ☎98612065
May—Oct
rm50 (⇌ ⋒ 15) A25rm Lift sBfr98 dBfr123
dB ⇌ ⋒ 198 M60—65 sea
Credit cards 1 3

ROSIERS (LES)
Maine-et-Loire

★★**Jeanne de Laval** (**DPn**) (N152) ☎41518017
28 Dec—15 Nov
rm14 (⇌ ⋒ 13) A8rm **P**40 sB253—283
sB ⇌ ⋒ 253—283 dB ⇌ ⋒ 266—386
M150—260 & alc

ROSPORDEN
Finistère

★★★**Bourhis** LF (FAH) pl Gare ☎98592389
⇌ 27 **P**4 Lift sB ⇌ fr227 dB ⇌ 284—304
M70—175
Credit cards 1 2 3 5

ROUBAIX
Nord

★★★**PLM Grand** 22 av J-Lebas (n.rest) ☎20734000 tx132301
⇌ ⋒ 92 **P** Lift sB ⇌ ⋒ 230—270
dB ⇌ ⋒ 290—345
Credit cards 1 2 3 5

AT **VILLENEUVE D'ASCQ** (6km S on rte de Lille)

★★**Campanile** La Cousinerie, av de Canteleu ☎20918310 tx133335
⇌ 50 **P** sB ⇌ 204—225 dB ⇌ 227—248
M61—82
Credit cards 2 3

★★**Climat** quartier du Triolo, r Trudaine ☎20050403 tx692844
⇌ ⋒ 37 sB ⇌ ⋒ 207—231
dB ⇌ ⋒ 225—239 Mfr51
Credit cards 1 3

★★**Ibis Lille** quartier de l'Hôtel-de-Ville, Rocade Est ☎20918150 tx160626
⇌ 80 **P**100 Lift sB ⇌ 209—234
dB ⇌ 239—267 M72—100
Credit cards 1 3

⛟ **Renault Lille-Est** Pont de Bois ☎20912035 Closed Sat & Sun Ren

ROUEN
Seine-Maritime

★★★★**Frantel** r de la Croix de Fer ☎35980698 tx180949
⇌ ⋒ 125 ⌂ **P**60 Lift sB ⇌ 372—432
dB ⇌ 524—544 M160
Credit cards 1 2 3 5

★★★**Dieppe** (BW/MAP) pl B-Tissot ☎35719600 tx180413
⇌ ⋒ 44 Lift ☾ sB ⇌ ⋒ 291
dB ⇌ ⋒ 316—353 M100

★★***Arcade*** 20 pl de l'Église St-Sever ☎35628182 tx770675
⋒ 144 **P**Lift

★★**Cardinal** pl de la Cathédrale (n.rest) ☎35702442
Jan—15 Dec
rm22 (⇌ ⋒ 21) Lift sB86—173
sB ⇌ ⋒ 163—173 dB147—209
dB ⇌ ⋒ 198—209

★★**Cathédrale** 12 r St-Romaine (n.rest) ☎35715795
rm24 (⇌ ⋒ 22) Lift sB120—198
sB ⇌ ⋒ fr192 dB171—208 dB ⇌ ⋒ fr247

★★**Europe** 87 r aux Ours (n.rest) ☎35708330
rm27 (⇌ ⋒ 22) **P**27 Lift sB86—186
dB102—202 dB ⇌ ⋒ 202—252
Credit cards 1 2 3

★★**Nord** (Inter) 91 r Gros — Horloge (n.rest) ☎35704141 tx771938
⇌ ⋒ 62 **P**100 Lift sB ⇌ ⋒ 158—206
dB ⇌ ⋒ 197—242

★★**Normandie** (Inter) 19 & 21 r de Bec (off r Aux Juis) (n.rest) ☎35715577 tx771350
⇌ ⋒ 23 Lift sB ⇌ ⋒ 166—206
dB ⇌ ⋒ 202—242
Credit cards 1 2 3 5

★★**Paris** (Inter) 12-14 r de la Champmeslé (off quai de al Bourse) (n.rest) ☎35700926
rm23 (⇌ ⋒ 21) ⌂ **P**10 Lift sB106—192
sB ⇌ ⋒ 135—192 dB142—239
dB ⇌ ⋒ 209—239
Credit cards 1 2 3 5

★★***Québec*** 18-24 r Québec (off r de la République) (n.rest) ☎35700938
rm38 (⇌ ⋒ 21) **P**4 Lift ☾
Credit cards 2 3

★★**Viking** (Inter) 21 quai du Havre (n.rest) ☎35703495 tx180503
⇌ ⋒ 37 ⌂ **P**6 Lift sB ⇌ ⋒ 126—206
dB ⇌ ⋒ 157—242
Credit cards 1 2 3

★***Arcades*** r des Carmes (n.rest)
☎35701030
rm16 (🚿5)

★**Vieille Tour** 42 pl Haute Vieille Tour (n.rest) ☎35700327
rm23 (🛁🚿14) Lift ☾ sB80-99
sB🛁🚿131–181 dB121–128
dB🛁🚿166–217
Credit card ③

At **BARENTIN** (17km NW)

★★***Ibis*** (N15) ☎35910123
🛁40 **P**55
Credit cards ① ③

At **BOIS-GUILLAUME** (5km NE)

★★**Climat** av de l'Europe ☎35616110
🛁🚿42 🏠 **P**45 sB🛁🚿218–238
dB🛁🚿238–258 M52–88
Credit cards ① ③

At **PETIT-QUEVILLY (LE)**

★★**Fimotel** 112 av J-Jaurès ☎35623850 tx770132
🛁42 **P**13 Lift sB🛁216–233
dB🛁241–264 M52–98
Credit cards ① ② ③ ⑤

At **ST-ÉTIENNE-DU-ROUVRAY** (2km S off N138)

★★★***Novotel Rouen Sud*** Le Madrillet ☎35665850 tx180215
🛁131 **P** Lift ⛱

★★**Ibis Rouen Sud** av M-Bastie ☎35660363 tx771014
🛁69 **P**70 sB🛁195–246 dB🛁239–266
M40 & alc
Credit cards ① ③

ROUFFACH
Haut-Rhin

★★***Campanile*** (N83) ☎89496632 tx880214
🛁32
Credit card ③

At **BOLLENBERG** (6km SW)

★★**Bollenberg** LF ☎89496247 tx880896
🛁50 **P**100 sB🛁270 dB🛁320 mountains
Credit cards ① ② ③ ⑤

ROUFFILLAC See **ST-JULIEN-DE-LAMPON**

ROUSSILLON
Isère

★**Garrigon** rte St-Saturnin d'Apt ☎90756322
🛁8 **P** sB🛁486–510 dB🛁550–700
Mfr145 ⛱ U mountains

🚗**R Clemençon** 61 av G-Péri ☎76862224 Closed Sat pm & Sun All makes

🚗**Guillon** 133 rte de la Chapelle ☎76862436 All makes

🚗**Rivoliet** 1 av G-Péri ☎76862303 Closed 1-20 Aug, Sat pm & Sun Cit

At **CHANAS** (6km S on N7, Chanas exit A1)

🚗**Modern** (N7) ☎76842191 Closed Sat pm & Sun Dat

France

ROUVRAY
Côte-d'Or

🚗**J Pernot** ☎80647322 Closed Sun am & Mon am Ren

ROYAN
Charente-Maritime

★★**Grand de Pontaillac** 195 av de Pontaillac (n.rest) ☎46390044
Etr–15 Sep
🛁🚿60 A12rm 🏠 **P**15 Lift ☾ sB🛁🚿fr95
dB🛁🚿250–320 sea
Credit card ①

🚗**E Marche** 75 av de Pontaillac ☎46384888 Closed Sat pm & Sun Ren

At **CONCHE-DE-NAUZAN** (2.5km NW)

★★★**Résidence de Rohan** (n.rest) ☎46390075
Apr–15 Nov
🛁🚿22 **P**20 ☾ dB🛁🚿356–486 sea
Credit cards ② ③

ROYAT
Puy-de-Dôme

★★★***Métropole*** 4 bd Vaquez ☎73358018
May–Sep
rm76 (🛁🚿62) Lift ☾ mountains
Credit card ①

ROYE
Somme

🚗**L Boitel** 16 r St-Médard ☎22871021 Closed Sat pm & Sun Aud VW

🚗**Dallet** 5 pl de la République ☎22871089 Closed 14 Jul–8 Aug, Sat pm & Sun Peu

🚗**Pace & Dequen** 1 r St-Médard/29 r B-Ville ☎22870178 Closed Sat pm, Sun & Mon am For

🚗**Peilieux** 1 rte de Paris ☎22871139 Closed Sun Fia

🚗**Sueur** 36 r de Paris ☎22870112 Closed Aug, Sat pm & Sun Ope Vau

---

RUFFEC
Charente

★***Toque Blanche*** 16 r du Gl-Leclerc ☎45310016
Closed Xmas & New Year
rm22 (🛁🚿5) A9rm **P**

RUNGIS
Val-de-Marne

See also **ORLY AIRPORT** under **PARIS AIRPORTS**

★★★★***Frantel Paris-Orly*** 20 av C-Lindbergh ☎46873636 tx260738
🛁206 🏠 Lift ⛱
Credit cards ① ② ③ ⑤

★★★★**Holiday Inn** 4 av C-Lindbergh ☎46872666 tx204679
🛁170 **P**200 Lift sB🛁fr470 dB🛁fr540
Mfr100 ⛱
Credit cards ① ② ③ ④ ⑤

★★**Campanile** angle r du Pont des Halles et du Mondetours ☎46873529 tx261163
🛁49 **P** sB🛁217–238 dB🛁240–261
M61–82

★★**Ibis** r Baltard bis zone de Delta ☎46872245 tx261173
🛁119 **P** Lift sB🛁269–284
dB🛁303–318 Mfr100

SABLES-D'OLONNE (LES)
Vendée

★★***Résidence*** 36 prom Clemenceau (n.rest) ☎51320666
Mar–Nov
rm35 (🛁🚿27) 🏠 sea
Credit cards ① ② ③ ⑤

At **CHÂTEAU D'OLONNE** (4km E on D36)

🚗**Tixier** la Mouzinère ☎51324104 Closed Sat & Sun Aud VW

SABLES-D'OR-LES-PINS
Côtes-du-Nord

★★★***Bon Accueil*** **(DPn)** LF allée des Acacias ☎96414219
1–15 Apr & 15 May–23 Sep
rm40 (🛁🚿31) **P**30 Lift lake sea
Credit cards ① ③ ⑤

★★**Ajoncs d'Or** allée des Acacias ☎96414212
May–Sep
rm75 (🛁🚿44) A45rm **P**25 sB87–117
sB🛁🚿112–142 dB124–169
dB🛁🚿179–284 M80

★★**Diane** LF av Brouard (n.rest) ☎96414207
22 Mar–Sep
rm40 (🛁🚿35) A10rm **P**60 sB86–113
sB🛁🚿100–143 dB115–181
dB🛁🚿175–310 sea lake

★★**Dunes d'Armor & Mouettes** (n.rest) ☎96414206
May–Oct
rm54 (🛁🚿28) **P**30 sB81–111
sB🛁🚿101–121 dB132–164
dB🛁🚿227–282 sea

★★**Volle d'Or** r de Acacias ☎96414249
15 Mar–15 Nov
rm18 (🛁🚿16) A4rm **P**15 dB141–236
dB🛁🚿201–236 M60–140 sea

SABLÉ-SUR-SARTHE
Sarthe

★★**Campanile** 9 av C-de-Gaulle ☎43953053
🛁31 sB🛁191–212 dB🛁214–235
M61–82
Credit card ③

★**St-Martin** **(DPn)** 3 r Haute St-Martin ☎43950003
Closed Mar
rm10 (🛁🚿5) sB90 sB🛁🚿fr107 dBfr104
dB🛁🚿135–173 M47–80

At **SOLESMES** (3km NE on D22)

★★★**Grand** (FAH) 16 pl Dom Gueranger ☎43954510 tx722903 →

🛁 30 sB 🛁 235—325 dB 🛁 280—400
Mfr83
Credit cards 1 2 3 5

SACLAY See **ORSAY**

ST-AFFRIQUE
Aveyron

★★**Modern** LE 43 av A-Pezet ☎65492044
15 Jan—15 Dec
rm39 (🛁 🚿 27) A11rm 🚗 sB100
sB 🛁 🚿 125—200 dB120—145
dB 🛁 🚿 145—260 M58—220 mountains
Credit cards 1 3

ST-AIGNAN
Loir-et-Cher

★★**St-Aignan (DPn** in season) LE 7—9 quai J—J Delorme ☎54751804
Feb—Dec
rm23 (🛁 🚿 16) 🚗 sB83—109
sB 🛁 🚿 150—158 dB 🛁 🚿 fr306 M60—180

ST-ALBAN See **MÂCON**

ST-AMOUR
Jura

★★**Alliance** rte Ste-Marie ☎84487494
rm16 (🛁 🚿 8) 🚗 **P**10 sB80
sB 🛁 🚿 105—135 dB115 dB 🛁 🚿 140—170
Mfr41
Credit cards 3 5

★**Commerce** LE pl Chevalerie ☎84487305
15 Feb—15 Dec
rm15 (🛁 🚿 7) 🚗 Lift sB79—94
sB 🛁 🚿 117—136 dB143 dB 🛁 🚿 152
M70—160 ⛱
Credit card 3

ST-ANDRÉ-LES-ALPES
Alpes-de-Haute-Provence

🚘 **Chabot** rte de Nice ☎92890001 Cit

ST-ANDRÉ-LES-VERGERS See **TROYES**

ST-APOLLINAIRE See **DIJON**

ST-AUBIN-SUR-MER
Calvados

★★**St-Aubin** LE **(DPn)** r de Verdun ☎31973039
Mar—mid Nov
rm26 (🛁 🚿 20) dB105—115
dB 🛁 🚿 190—220 M55—220 sea
Credit cards 1 2 3

ST-AVOLD
Moselle

★★★**Novotel** (N3A) ☎87922593 tx860966
🛁 61 **P** sB 🛁 308 dB 🛁 371 Malc ⛱
Credit cards 1 2 3 5

ST-BREVIN-LES-PINS
Loire-Atlantique

🚘 **Charriau-Evain** 3 av de la Saulzaie ☎40274483 Closed Mon For

ST-BRIEUC
Côtes-du-Nord

★★★***Alexandre 1'er*** 19 pl du Guesclin ☎96337945
🛁 43 **P** Lift
Credit cards 1 2 3 5

France

★★★**Griffon** (Inter) r de Guernsey ☎96945762 tx950701
🛁 🚿 43 🚗 **P** Lift sB 🛁 🚿 190—200
dB 🛁 🚿 230—265 🎾
Credit cards 2 3 5

At **PLÉRIN** (2km N via N12)

★★**Chêne Vert** LE (FAH/Inter) ☎96746320
🛁 52 🚗 **P**50 sB 🛁 195 dB 🛁 250 Mfr55
Credit cards 1 2 3 5

At **YFFINIAC** (5km W)

★★**Fimotel de la Baie** Aire de Repos (N12) ☎96726410
🛁 42 Lift sB 🛁 178—201 dB 🛁 206—240
Mfr64 sea
Credit card 1

ST-CAST-LE-GUILDO
Côtes-du-Nord

★**Angleterre & Panorama** LE r Fosserole (n.rest) ☎96419144
Jul—7 Sep
rm40 🚗 **P**45 🎾 sea

At **GARDE-ST-CAST (LA)** (2km SE)

★★★***Ar Vro*** **(DPn)** LE 10 bd de la Plage ☎96418501
5 Jun—8 Sep
rm47 (🛁 42) 🚗 **P** Lift sea
Credit cards 1 2 3 5

ST-CÉRÉ
Lot

★★**Coq Arlequin** LE **(DPn** in season) 1 bd du Dr-Roux ☎65380213
🛁 🚿 32 🚗 **P**12 sB 🛁 🚿 163—223
dB 🛁 🚿 226—306 M70—150 🎾 ⛱
Credit card 3

ST-CHÉLY-D'APCHER
Lozère

★***Lion d'Or*** 132 r T-Roussel ☎66310014
Closed 1 Jan—20 Jan
rm30 (🛁 🚿 5) 🚗

ST-CYPRIEN
Pyrénées-Orientales

★★**Ibis** Bassin Nord du Port (n.rest) ☎68213030 tx500459
🛁 🚿 34 **P** Lift sB 🛁 🚿 202—239
dB 🛁 🚿 241—296 sea mountains
Credit cards 1 3

ST-DÉNIS
Seine-St-Denis

★★**Fimotel** Parc du Colombier ☎48094810 tx215269
🛁 60 **P** Lift
Credit cards 1 2 3 5

ST-DENIS-SUR-SARTHON
Orne

★★**Faiencerie** rte Paris—Brest ☎33273016
15 Mar—15 Nov
rm18 (🛁 🚿 14) 🚗 **P**50 mountains

ST-DIZIER
Haute-Marne

★★★**Gambetta** (Inter) 62 r Gambetta ☎25565210
🛁 🚿 63 🚗 **P**40 Lift ☾ sB 🛁 🚿 158—213
dB 🛁 🚿 206—286 M59—89
Credit cards 1 2 3 5

★★★***Soleil d'Or*** (MAP) 64 r Gambetta ☎25056822 tx840946
🛁 60 **P** Lift ⛱

★★**Champagne** 19 r P-Timbaud ☎25056754
🛁 🚿 30 **P** sB 🛁 🚿 167—204
dB 🛁 🚿 188—225 M62—180

★***Auberge la Bobotte*** (3km W on N4) ☎25562003
Etr—Dec
🚿 10 🚗 **P**6 ☾

ST-DOULCHARD See **BOURGES**

ST-ÉGRÉVE See **GRENOBLE**

ST-ÉLOY-LES-MINES
Puy-de-Dôme

★★**Ibis** r J-Jaurés ☎73852150 tx392009
🛁 29 **P** sB 🛁 fr209 dB 🛁 🚿 fr248
M44—130

ST-ÉMILION
Gironde

★★★**Hostellerie de la Plaisance (DPn)** pl Clocher ☎57247232
🛁 12 sB 🛁 257—532 dB 🛁 339—614
M84—178
Credit cards 1 2 3 5

ST-ÉTIENNE
Loire

★★★★**Frantel** r de Wuppertal ☎77252275 tx300050
🛁 120 🚗 **P**12 Lift sB 🛁 298—358
dB 🛁 366—421 M115—190
Credit cards 1 2 3 5

★★★***Grand*** 10 av Libération ☎77329977 tx300811
🛁 🚿 66 Lift ☾

★★★**Terminus du Forez** (FAH) 31 av Denfert-Rochereau ☎77324847 tx330683
rm66 (🛁 🚿 63) A1rm 🚗 **P** Lift sB138—280
sB 🛁 🚿 208—280 dB156—305
dB 🛁 🚿 226—305
Credit cards 1 2 3 5

★★**Ibis** 35 pl Massenet ☎77933187 tx307340
🛁 85 **P**85 🚗 Lift sB 🛁 234—256
dB 🛁 288—310 M58—80
Credit cards 1 3

ST-ÉTIENNE AIRPORT
Loire

At **ANDRÉZIEUX-BOUTHÉON** (2km W of N82)

★★★***Novotel*** Centre de Ville (N82) ☎77365563 tx900722
🛁 98 **P** Lift ⛱

ST-ÉTIENNE-DE-BAIGORRY
Pyrénées-Atlantiques

★★**Arcé** ☎59374014
Mar—Oct
🛁 🚿 27 🚗 **P**30 sB 🛁 🚿 245—265 dB 🛁 🚿 340—370 M120—170 mountains lake
Credit cards [2] [3]

ST-ÉTIENNE-DU-ROUVRÁY See **ROUEN**

ST-FLORENTIN
Yonne

★***Est*** **(DPn)** 7 r fbg St-Martin ☎86351035
Closed Feb
rm30 (🛁 🚿 17) A7rm 🚗 **P**20
Credit cards [1] [2] [3] [5]

At **VENIZY** (5.5km N)

★★**Moulin des Pommerats** **LF** **(DPn)** ☎86350804
🛁 🚿 16 A14rm **P** dB 🛁 🚿 260—440 Mfr120
Credit cards [1] [3] [5]

ST-FLOUR
Cantal

★★★**Étape** **(DPn)** 18 av de la République ☎71601303
🛁 🚿 34 A11rm 🚗 **P**20 Lift sB 🛁 🚿 166—247 dB 🛁 🚿 197—257 M64—220 mountains
Credit cards [1] [2] [3] [5]

★★★**Europe** **(DPn)** 12-13 cours Spydes-Ternes ☎71600364
Mar—Nov
rm45 (🛁 🚿 30) **P** Lift sB87—197 sB 🛁 🚿 87—197 dB104—234 dB 🛁 🚿 104—234 M50—150 mountains
Credit cards [1] [3]

★★**Nouvel Bonne Table** **LF** **(DPn)** (MAP) 16 av de la République ☎71600586 tx393160
Apr—Oct
🛁 🚿 48 🚗 **P**40 Lift sB 🛁 🚿 98—218 dB 🛁 🚿 216—236 M55—140 mountains
Credit cards [1] [2] [3] [4] [5]

★★**St-Jacques** **(DPn)** (FAH) 8 pl Liberté ☎71600920
16 Jan—10 Nov
rm30 (🛁 🚿 25) 🚗 **P** sB95—100 sB 🛁 🚿 fr150 dBfr110 dB 🛁 🚿 150—200 mountains
Credit cards [1] [3]

★★***Voyageurs*** 25 r Collège ☎71603444
Apr—10 Oct
rm39 (🛁 🚿 20) 🚗 **P**25 Lift
Credit cards [1] [2] [3] [5]

ST-GAUDENS
Haute-Garonne

★★***Ferrière & France*** 1 r Gl-Leclerc ☎61891457
rm17 (🛁 🚿 15) **P** ☾

At **VILLENEUVE-DE-RIVIÈRE** (6km W on D117)

★★***Cèdres*** ☎61893600
🛁 🚿 20 **P** 🎾 mountains

France

ST-GENIS-POUILLY
Ain

★★**Climat** Lieudit le Marais ☎50420520
🛁 42 **P**50 dB 🛁 191—212 M51—98 mountains
Credit cards [1] [3]

ST-GENIS-LAVAL See **LYON**

ST-GEOSMES See **LANGRES**

ST-GERMAIN-DE-JOUX
Ain

★**Reygropbellet** **LF** (N84) ☎50598113
Closed Oct—11 Nov
🛁 🚿 10 🚗 **P**10 dB 🛁 🚿 184—219 M70—150 mountains
Credit cards [1] [3] [5]

ST-GERMAIN-EN-LAYE
Yvelines

★★★**Ermitage des Loges** (MAP) 11 av des Loges ☎34518886 tx697112
🛁 34 **P**25 Lift sB 🛁 368 dB 🛁 441—731
Credit cards [1] [2] [3] [5]

★★**Campanile** rte de Mantes, Maison Forestière ☎34515959 tx697547
🛁 49 **P** sB 🛁 217—238 dB 🛁 240—261 M61—82
Credit card [3]

At **CHAMBOURCY** (4km NW)

★★**Climat** r du Mur du Parc ☎30744261
🛁 46 **P**100 sB 🛁 217—229 dB 🛁 236—248 M50—100 🏊
Credit cards [1] [3]

ST-GERMAIN LESPINASSE See **ROANNE**

ST-GERVAIS-EN-VALLIÈRE
Saône-et-Loire

★★**Moulin d'Hauterive** **(DPn)** ☎85915556 tx801391
Feb—20 Dec
🛁 🚿 21 **P**30 sB 🛁 🚿 230 dB 🛁 🚿 350—500 M120—190
Credit cards [1] [2] [3] [5]

ST-GERVAIS-LA-FORÊT See **BLOIS**

ST-GERVAIS-LES-BAINS
Haute-Savoie

★★★***Splendid*** (n.rest) ☎50782133
🛁 🚿 20 Lift mountains

ST-GILLES
Gard

At **SALIERS** (4km E on N572)

★★★**Cabanettes en Camargue** **(DPn)** (MAP) ☎66873153 tx480451
Mid Jan—mid Feb
🛁 29 🚗 **P**50 sB 🛁 330—360 dB 🛁 390 M120 🏊
Credit cards [1] [2] [3] [5]

ST-GILLES-CROIX-DE-VIE
Vendée

★★**Embruns** **(DPn)** 16 bd de la mer ☎51551140
🛁 17 🚗 sB 🛁 134—153 dB 🛁 158—318 M65—110 sea
Credit cards [1] [3]

ST-GIRONS
Ariège

★★★**Eychenne** (BW/MAP) 8 av P-Laffont ☎61662055 tx521273
Feb—20 Dec
rm48 (🛁 🚿 42) 🚗 **P**35 sB138 sB 🛁 🚿 203—278 dBfr166 dB 🛁 🚿 286—406 M80—200 mountains
Credit cards [1] [2] [3] [5]

★★★**Hostellerie la Truite Dorê** **LF** **(DPn)** (1km S) 28 av de la Résistance ☎61661689
15 Dec—Oct
🛁 🚿 15 🚗 **P**20 ☾ sB 🛁 🚿 176 dB 🛁 🚿 232—312 M70—102 mountains
Credit cards [1] [2] [3] [5]

ST-HERBLAIN See **NANTES**

ST-HILAIRE-DU-HARCOUËT
Manche

★★**Cygne** **LF** (FAH) 67 r Waldeck-Rousseau ☎33491184 tx171445
🛁 🚿 45 A25rm 🚗 Lift sB 🛁 🚿 164—201 dB 🛁 🚿 191—239 M57—88
Credit cards [1] [2] [3] [5]

★**Lion d'Or** **LF** 120 r Avranches ☎33491082
Closed Feb & 16-31 Oct
rm17 (🛁 14) **P**40 dBfr114 dB 🛁 159—204 M55—85

★**Relais de la Poste** **(DPn)** 11 r de Mortain ☎33491031
rm12 (🛁 🚿 8) sB78—154 sB 🛁 🚿 108—154 dB91—168 dB 🛁 🚿 121—166 M38—85
Credit card [1]

ST-JEAN-CAP-FERRAT
Alpes-Maritimes

★★★★**Grand Cap Ferrat** bd Gl-de-Gaulle ☎93010454 tx470184
3 May—29 Sep
🛁 🚿 66 🚗 **P**100 Lift ☾ sB 🛁 🚿 615—1180 dB 🛁 🚿 820—2300 M alc 🎾 🏊 Beach sea mountains
Credit cards [1] [2] [3] [5]

ST-JEAN-DE-LUZ
Pyrénées-Atlantiques

★★★★***Chantaco*** rte d'Ascain ☎59261476
Apr—Oct
🛁 24 🚗 **P**30 ☾ 🎾 ▣ mountains lake
Credit cards [2] [5]

★★★**Poste** 83 r Gambetta (n.rest) ☎59260453
rm34 (🛁 🚿 30) sB130—135 dB 🛁 🚿 180—284
Credit cards [1] [2] [3] [5]

★★***Paris*** 1 bd Passicot (n.rest) ☎59260062
15 Mar—15 Dec
rm29 (🛁 🚿 11) mountains

★**Continental** 15 av Verdun ☎59260123
🛁🚿22 Lift sB🛁🚿170—220
dB🛁🚿200—270 M75 mountains
Credit cards [1] [2] [3] [5]

🚗 **Lamerain** bd V-Hugo, Zone de Layas (N10) ☎59269480 Closed Sat pm & Sun Ren

At **CIBOURE** (1km SW off N10)

★***Hostellerie de Ciboure*** 10 av J-Jaurés ☎59470057
rm22 (🛁🚿16) **P** ≈

ST-JEAN-DE-MAURIENNE
Savoie

★★**St-Georges** 334 r République (n.rest) ☎79640106
rm24 (🛁🚿21) **P**8 sB87—186 dB110-202 mountains
Credit card [2]

🚗 **Durleux** ZI ☎79640011 Closed Sun For Lan

ST-JEAN-DE-MONTS
Vendée

★★***Plage*** espl de la Mer ☎51580035
May—Sep
rm52 (🛁🚿31) **P**10 Lift sea
Credit card [2]

🚗 **G Vrignaud** rte de Challans ☎51582674 Closed Sun out of season Ren

ST-JEAN-LE-THOMAS
Manche

★★**Bains (DPn)** (opp Post Office) ☎33488420 tx170380
20 Mar—13 Oct
rm31 (🛁🚿24) A8rm **P**50 sB🛁🚿174—207
dB🛁🚿174—209 M48—141 ≈
Credit cards [1] [2] [3] [4] [5]

ST-JEAN-PIED-DE-PORT
Pyrénées-Atlantiques

★★★**Continental** 3 av Renaud (n.rest) ☎59370025
15 Mar—15 Nov
🛁22 **P**20 Lift sB🛁170—218
dB🛁210—306 mountains
Credit cards [2] [5]

★★**Central** (FAH) 1 pl C-de-Gaulle ☎59370022
5 Feb—28 Dec
🛁🚿14 Lift sB🛁🚿118—172
dB🛁🚿186—282 M68—130 mountains
Credit cards [2] [5]

★★**Pyrénées** pl Marché ☎59370101
22 Dec—3 Jan & 20 Jan—20 Nov
🛁🚿28 ⌂ **P** Lift sB🛁🚿215—250
dB🛁🚿235—270 M100—250 mountains
Credit cards [2] [3]

ST-JULIEN-DE-LAMPON
Dordogne

At **ROUFFILLAC** (N of R Dordogne)

★★**Cayre (DPn)** ☎53297024
Closed Oct
🛁🚿19 A10rm ⌂ **P**80 sB🛁🚿138—168
dB🛁🚿156—186 M80—120 🎾 ≈ mountains

ST-JULIEN-EN-BEAUCHÊNE
Hautes-Alpes

★★**Bermond-Gauthier** (N75) ☎92580352
Feb—20 Dec
rm20 (🛁🚿10) ⌂ **P**12 sB71—104
sB🛁🚿101—108 dB97—101
dB🛁🚿138—186 M50—160 ≈ mountains
Credit card [1]

ST-JULIEN-EN-GENEVOIS
Haute-Savoie

★***Savoyarde* (DPn)** 15 rte de Lyon ☎50492579
rm10 (🛁1) **P**

ST-JULIEN-LES-VILLAS See **TROYES**

ST-JUNIEN
Haute-Vienne

★★**Concorde** LF 49 av H-Barbusse (n.rest) ☎55021708
🛁🚿26 **P**16 sB🛁🚿116—213
dB🛁🚿145—290
Credit cards [1] [2] [3]

★★**Relais de Comodoliac** LF (FAH) 22 av S-Carnot ☎55022726 tx590336
🛁28 **P** ☾ sB🛁207—221 dB🛁246—287
M57—124

ST-LARY-SOULAN
Hautes-Pyrénées

★★**Terrasse Fleurie** ☎62394026 tx520360
15 Dec—15 Apr & 15 May—15 Sep
rm28 (🛁🚿16) **P**20 sB93—163
sB🛁🚿fr163 dB144 dB🛁🚿172—264
Mfr56 mountains
Credit card [2]

ST-LAURENT-DE-COGNAC See **COGNAC**

ST-LAURENT-DU-VAR See **NICE**

ST-LAURENT-SUR-SÈVRE

At **TRIQUE (LA)** (1km N)

★★★**Baumotel La Chaumière (DPn)** ☎51678812 tx710705
🛁🚿20 ⌂ **P** sB🛁🚿197—372
dB🛁🚿259—454 M49—260 ≈

ST-LÉONARD See **BOULOGNE-SUR-MER**

ST-LÉONARD-DES-BOIS
Sarthe

★★★**Touring** (MAP) (n.rest) ☎43972803 tx722006
Feb—15 Dec
🛁🚿33 ⌂ **P** Lift ☾ sB🛁🚿167—237
dB🛁🚿259—314 M65—170 mountains
Credit cards [1] [2] [3] [5]

ST-LIEUX-LES-LAVAUR See **LAVAUR**

ST-LÔ
Manche

★★**Marignan (DPn)** pl Gare ☎33051515
Closed 7—22 Feb
rm18 (🛁🚿12) ⌂ **P** sBfr70 sB🛁🚿fr115
dB🛁🚿fr150 M90—250
Credit cards [1] [3] [5]

★★**Terminus** LF 3 av Briovère ☎33575754
rm15 (🛁🚿13) ⌂ sB96 sB🛁🚿126—156
dB142—152 dB🛁🚿152—192 M60—85
Credit cards [1] [3]

★★***Univers*** LF **(DPn)** 1 av Briovère ☎33051084
rm24 (🛁🚿18) **P**20
Credit cards [2] [3]

★***Armoric*** 15 r de la Marne (n.rest) ☎33571747
20 Feb—26 Dec
rm21 (🛁🚿7) **P** Lift

★**Cremaillére (DPn)** 27 r du Belle, pl de la Préfecture ☎33571468
rm12 (🛁🚿8) **P**12 sBfr89 sB🛁🚿fr128
dB104 dB🛁🚿143—180 M60—110
Credit card [1]

ST-LOUIS
Haut-Rhin

★★***Pfiffer*** 77 r Mulhouse (n.rest) ☎89697444
6 Jan—9 Aug & 26 Aug—20 Dec
rm36 (🛁🚿21) ⌂ **P** Lift

At **HUNINGUE** (2km E D469)

★★**Climat** 4 av de Bâle ☎89698610
🛁43 sB🛁213—233 dB🛁268—288
M52—67
Credit cards [1] [3]

ST-LOUP-DE-VARENNES See **SENNECEY-LE-GRAND**

ST-MALO
Ille-et-Vilaine

★★★**Central** (BW/MAP) 6 Grande Rue ☎98408770 tx740802
🛁🚿46 ⌂ Lift ☾ sB🛁🚿227—307
dB🛁🚿304—404 Mfr80
Credit cards [1] [2] [3] [5]

★★★**Duguesclin** 8 pl Duguesclin (n.rest) ☎99560130 tx740802
🛁🚿22 Lift sB🛁🚿181—231
dB🛁🚿262—302
Credit cards [1] [2] [3] [5]

★★★**Mecure** chassée du Sillon (n.rest) ☎99568484 tx740583
🛁70 ⌂ **P**30 Lift sB🛁240—410
dB🛁302—490 sea
Credit cards [1] [2] [3] [5]

★★**Ibis** r Gl-de-Gaulle, qtr de la Madeleine ☎99821010 tx730626
🛁73 **P**73 sB🛁212 dB🛁250—274
Credit cards [1] [3]

★★**Louvre** 2—4 r de Marins (n.rest) ☎99408662
15 Feb—Dec
rm45 (🛁🚿39) **P**15 Lift sB103—235
sB🛁🚿153—235 dB139—271
dB🛁🚿189—271

★Noguette 9 r de la Fosse ☎99408357
🛁🚿12 **P** dB🛁🚿166—216 M46—190
Credit card [3]

🚗 **Corsaires** 2 av L-Martin ☎99567866
Closed Sat pm & Sun For

At **GOUESNIÈRE (LA)** (12km SE on D4)

★★Gare (1.5km N on D76 à la Gare)
☎99891046 tx740896

rm55 (🛁🚿51) A29rm ⛍ **P**50 sB92—102
sB🛁🚿122—172 dB124—144
dB🛁🚿154—244 M85—185 🎾
Credit cards [2] [5]

At **PARAMÉ** (1km E)

★★*Rochebonne* 15 bd Châteaubriand
☎99560172 tx740802

🛁🚿39 Lift
Credit cards [1] [3]

ST-MARTIN-BELLEVUE
Haute-Savoie

★★★*Novotel Val Thorens* ☎79080726
tx980230

🛁104 **P** Lift

ST-MARTIN-EN-BRESSE
Saône-et-Loire

★★Au Puits Enchante ☎85427083

Feb—Dec
🛁🚿12 ⛍ **P** Lift dB🛁🚿124—170
M65—126

ST-MAURICE-SUR-MOSELLE
Vosges

★★Relais des Ballons LF rte Bénélux-Bâle (N66) ☎29251109

rm17 (🛁🚿14) ⛍ **P**20 sB100—130
sB🛁🚿150 dB130—175 dB🛁🚿200 ≈
mountains
Credit cards [1] [2] [3] [5]

★Bonséjour LF ☎29251233

rm15 (🛁2) **P** sB93 sB🛁145 dBfr108
dB🛁fr145 M42—120

ST-MAXIMIN-LA-STE-BAUME
Var

🚗 **Auto Real** X-rd Mont Fleury ☎94780358
Closed Winter & Sun All Makes

🚗 **STP** av d'Estienne d'Orves ☎94780089
For

ST-MICHEL-DE-MAURIENNE
Savoie

★★Savoy LF 25 r Gl-Ferrié ☎79565512

rm18 (🛁14) ⛍ **P**6 sB98—118 sB🛁158
dB136—156 dB🛁199—241 M60—150
Credit cards [1] [2] [3]

ST-MICHEL-SUR-ORGE
Essonne

★★★*Delfis-Bois-des-Roches*
17 r Berlioz ☎62571455 tx290532

🛁88 **P** Lift
Credit card [3]

ST-NABORD See **REMIREMONT**

ST-NAZAIRE
Loire-Atlantique

★★Dauphin 33 r J-Jaurès (n.rest)
☎40665961

rm20 (🛁🚿16) **P** sB94—114
sB🛁🚿114—138 dB154—174 dB🛁🚿211
Credit cards [1] [2] [5]

🚗 **J Barbelion** 79 r de la Ville-Huard
☎40222542 M/c

ST-NICHOLAS See **ARRAS**

ST-OMER
Pas-de-Calais

★★Bretagne LF 2 pl Vainquai
☎21383578 tx133290

rm41 (🛁39) **P**25 sB🛁158 dB🛁186—296
Credit cards [2] [3]

★★Ibis St-Omer r H-Dupuis ☎21931111
tx135206

🛁43 **P**27 Lift sB🛁218—236
dB🛁259—272 M54—120
Credit cards [1] [3]

★★St-Louis 25 r d'Arras (n.rest)
☎21383521

🛁🚿20 ⛍ **P**13 sB🛁🚿fr74 dB🛁🚿fr103
Credit cards [1] [3]

At **TILQUES** (4km NW on N43)

★★Vert Mesnil (FAH) (1.5km E of N43)
☎21932899 tx133360

3 Jan—20 Dec
🛁🚿40 **P**120 sB🛁🚿226—446
dB🛁🚿292—472 M70—200 🎾
Credit cards [1] [2] [3] [5]

ST-OUEN-L'AUMONE See **PONTOISE**

ST-PALAIS-SUR-MER
Charente-Maritime

★★★*Courdouan* av Pontaillac
☎46221033

Jun—15 Sep
🛁🚿35 **P**12 sea

ST-PARDOUX L'ORTIGIER See **DONZENAC**

ST-PAUL
Alpes-Maritimes

★★★★Mas d'Artigny (DPn) (Relais et Châteaux) rte de la Colle (D7) ☎93328454
tx470601

🛁83 ⛍ **P** Lift ☾ sB🛁405—1160
dB🛁550—1350 M230—300 🎾 ≈ 📺

★★Climat rte de la Colle ☎93329424

🛁19 **P**19 sB🛁211—224 dB🛁231—247
M50—86 ≈ sea

ST-PAUL-DE-LOUBRESSAC
Lot

★Relais de la Madeleine LF ☎65219808

10 Jan—6 Dec
rm16 (🛁🚿7) **P** sBfr90 sB🛁🚿114 dB104
dB🛁🚿128 M45 & alc 🎾

ST-PÉE-SUR-NIVELLE
Pyrénées-Atlantiques

★★Pyrénées Atlantiques (N618)
☎59540222

🛁🚿35 **P**40 dB🛁🚿156—190 M65—75 🎾
mountains
Credit card [2]

ST-PIERRE-DE-CHARTREUSE
Isère

★★Beau Site LF ☎76886134

15 Dec—15 Apr & 15 May—Sep
rm33 (🛁28) sB155—245 sB🛁245—265
dB290—310 dB🛁290—310 M70 ≈
mountains
Credit cards [1] [2] [3]

ST-PIERRE-DU-VAUVRAY See **LOUVIERS**

ST-PIERRE-QUIBERON See **QUIBERON**

ST-POL-DE-LÉON
Finistère

🚗 **E Charetteur** pl du Creisker ☎98690208
Closed 1—21 Sep, Sat & Sun Ren

ST-POL-SUR-TERNOISE
Pas-de-Calais

★*Lion d'Or* LF (FAH) 68 r Hesdin
☎21031293

rm30 (🛁🚿23) **P**
Credit cards [1] [2] [3] [5]

ST-PONS
Hérault

★★Château de Ponderach (Relais et Châteaux) (1.2km S) rte de Narbonne
☎67970257

Etr—10 Oct
rm11 (🛁9) ⛍ **P**40 Lift sB🛁342 dB🛁434
Mfr150 mountains

★*Pastre* LF (at the station) ☎67970054

15 Jan—15 Dec
rm20 (🛁🚿7)
Credit card [1]

ST-POURÇAIN-SUR-SIOULE
Allier

★Chêne Vert (FAH) 35 bd Ledru-Roulin
☎70454065

rm35 (🛁🚿27) A15rm ⛍ sB🛁🚿fr183
dB111—144 dB🛁🚿229 M80—200
Credit cards [1] [2] [3] [5]

★Deux Ponts LF (FAH) **(DPn)** Ilot de Tivoli
☎70454114

rm28 (🛁🚿16) ⛍ **P**50 sB89 sB🛁🚿169
dB113—128 dB🛁🚿128—218 M55—150
lake
Credit cards [1] [2] [3] [5]

ST-PRIEST See **LYON**

ST-QUAY-PORTRIEUX
Côtes-du-Nord

★★Gerbot d'Avoine LF **(DPn)**
2 bd Littoral ☎96704009

Closed 23 Nov—12 Dec & 6—21 Jan
rm26 (🛁🚿12) **P** sB65 sB🛁🚿110 dB95
dB🛁🚿165

★Bretagne (DPn) 36 quai de la République
☎96704091

rm15 (🚿6) sB107—117 sB🚿127—142
dB134—154 dB🚿154—164 M65—120 t%
sea

ST-QUENTIN
Aisne

★★**Campanile** ZAC de la Vallée, r Ct-Naudin ☎23092122 tx150596

🛁40 **P** sB🛁217—238 dB🛁240—261 M61—82
Credit card 3

★★**Grand** 6 r Dachery ☎23626977 tx140225

🛁41 **P**16 sB🛁193—281 dB🛁306
Credit cards 1 3 5

★★**Paix Albert 1er** (Inter) 3 pl du 8 Octobre ☎23627762 tx140225

rm82 🚗 **P**12 Lift sB144 sB🛁🚿250 dB168 dB🛁🚿274—318
Credit cards 1 4 5

C Corbizet 128 r d'Epargenmailles ☎23626854 Closed Sun AR

ST-QUENTIN-EN-YVELINES
Yvelines

★★***Fimotel*** Parc d'Activités de Bois-d'Arcy ☎34605024

🛁62 **P**65 Lift
Credit cards 2 3 5

ST-RAMBERT-D'ABLON
Drôme

★★**Ibis** 'La Champagnière' (RN7) ☎75030400 tx345958

🛁39 **P**36 sB🛁201—231 dB🛁246—276 Mfr65 mountains
Credit cards 1 2 3

ST-RAPHAËL
Var

★★★***Continental*** prom du Prés-Coty (n.rest) ☎94950014 tx970809

rm49 (🛁🚿34) **P** Lift ☾ sea

★★**Beau-Séjour** prom Prés-Coty (n.rest) ☎94950375

20 Mar—1 Nov
🛁40 Lift sB🛁195 dB🛁350 sea
Credit card 1

★★***Provençal*** **(DPn)** 197 r de la Garonne (n.rest) ☎94950152

Closed 15 Dec—15 Jan
rm29 (🛁🚿24) ☾
Credit card 1

🚗 **R Bacchi** 658 av de Verdun ☎94522736 Closed Sat pm & Sun Peu

Leruste (N98) ☎94952620 Closed Sun Ren

ST-RÉMY-DE-PROVENCE
Bouches-du-Rhône

★★★**Antiques** 15 av Pasteur (n.rest) ☎90920302

22 Mar—15 Oct
🛁27 A2rm **P**50 sB🛁fr236 dB🛁342—392 ⩯
Credit cards 2 3 5

★★**Castelet des Alpilles** **(DPn)** pl Mireille ☎90920721

20 Mar—10 Nov
rm20 (🛁🚿16) sB99—152 sB🛁🚿216—299 dB178 dB🛁🚿242—325 M68—153 mountains
Credit cards 2 3 5

ST-SATUR
Cher

★★***Laurier*** **LF** **(DPn)** r du Commerce ☎48541720

Closed Feb
rm10 (🚿5) **P**8
Credit card 3

ST-SERNIN-SUR-RANCE
Aveyron

★★**Carayon** **LF** (Inter) pl du Fort ☎65996026

rm23 (🛁21) **P**12 dB111 dB🛁169—255 M53—190
Credit cards 1 2 3 5

ST-TROJAN-LES-BAINS See **OLÉRON (ILE D')**

ST-TROPEZ
Var

★★★★**Byblos** av P-Signac ☎94970004 tx470235

17 Apr—Oct
🛁105 🚗 **P**30 Lift ☾ sB🛁846—1306 dB🛁1077—1942 M alc ⩯ sea
Credit cards 2 3 5

★★★**Coste** (Inter) Port Du Pilon (n.rest) ☎94970064

15 Mar—3 Nov
rm30 (🛁🚿25) **P** sB🛁🚿fr100 dBfr100 dB🛁🚿fr150 sea
Credit cards 1 2 3 4 5

★★★**Ermitage** av P-Signac (n.rest) ☎94975233

Closed 7 Nov—14 Dec
🛁🚿29 **P**15 ☾ sB🛁🚿275—430 dB🛁🚿350—430 sea
Credit card 5

🚗 **Auto Service des Salins** rte des Salins ☎94970955 Closed 6 Oct—3 Nov, Sat & Sun Fia Lan

ST-VAAST-LA-HOUGUE
Manche

★★**France et des Fuschias** **LF** **(DPn)** 18 r Ml-Foch ☎33544226

15 Feb—Dec
rm32 (🛁🚿27) sB121—271 sB🛁🚿231—271 dB127—272 dB🛁🚿227—272 M85
Credit cards 1 3 5

ST-VALERY-EN-CAUX
Seine-Maritime

★★★**Agora** av Clemenceau ☎35973548 tx172308

🛁157 **P** Lift sB🛁235—255 dB🛁290—310 M85—130

ST-VALLIEZ
Drôme

🚗 **Brassière** av Buissonet ☎75230265 Closed Sun & Mon Cit

🚗 **Martin** 15 av Buissonet ☎752311334

🚗 **Paradis du Plein Air** La Croix des Mailles (3km N on N7) ☎75230666 Closed Sun All makes

ST-WITZ See **SURVILLIERS-ST-WITZ**

STE-ADRESSE See **HAVRE (LE)**

STE-ANNE-LA-PALUD
Finistère

★★★***Plage*** (Relais et Châteaux) la Plage ☎98925012

Apr—10 Oct
rm30 (🛁🚿29) A6rm **P** Lift 🎾 ▭ sea

STE-CATHÉRINE See **BRIANÇON**

STE-ENIMIE
Lozère

★★**Commerce** (FAH) (N586) ☎66485001

Apr—10 Oct
rm20 (🛁🚿12) A12rm 🚗 dB130 dB🛁🚿142—195 M54—87&alc Beach
Credit cards 1 2 3

STE-FOY-LES-LYONS See **LYON**

STE-MAXIME
Var

See also **BEAUVALLON**

★★★**Beau Site** 6 bd des Cistes ☎94961963 tx970080

15 Mar—15 Oct
🛁🚿40 🚗 **P**40 Lift ☾ sB🛁🚿265—389 dB🛁🚿300—500 Mfr80 🎾 ⩯ ▭ sea mountains
Credit cards 1 2 3 5

★★★***Belle Aurore*** 4 bd J-Moulin ☎94960245

Mar—Oct
🛁🚿18 A4rm **P** ☾ Beach sea

🚗 **Arbois** av Gl-Leclerc ☎94961403 Closed Nov & Sun Ren

STE-MENEHOULD
Marne

🚗 **J Garet** 47—49 r Florion ☎26608138 Closed alternate wk-ends Ope

🚗 **Relais L-Champagne** Esso & Total 50 Station, 52 av V-Hugo ☎26608270 Closed Jun also Wed & Sat All makes

SAINTES
Charente-Maritime

★★★**Commerce Mancini** r des Messageries ☎46930661 tx791012

rm40 (🛁🚿31) 🚗 ☾ sB111—123 sB🛁🚿193—233 dB156—199 dB🛁🚿276—306 M70—250
Credit cards 1 2 3 5

★★★**Relais du Bois St-George** r de Royan (D137) ☎46935099 tx790488

🛁21 🚗 **P**80 ☾ sB🛁219—319 dB🛁378—488 M105 & alc ▭
Credit cards 1 3

★★**Messageries** (Inter) r des Messageries (n.rest) ☎46936499

rm37 (🛁🚿30) 🚗 ☾ sB118—128 sB🛁🚿168—178 dB145 dB🛁🚿210
Credit cards 1 2 3 5

★★***Terminus*** esp de la Gare (n.rest) ☎46743503
rm36 (⇌ 🚿 14) 🚗 P ☾

SAINTES-MARIES-DE-LA-MER (LES)
Bouches-du-Rhône

★★***Mirage*** 14 r C-Pelletan (n.rest) ☎90978043
25 Apr—15 Oct
🚿 27

SALBRIS
Loire-et-Cher

★★★**Parc** LE (MAP) (**DPn**) 10 av d'Orléans ☎54971853 tx751164
⇌ 🚿 27 🚗 **P** sB ⇌ 🚿 146—316
dB ⇌ 🚿 172—342 M75—110
Credit cards [1] [2] [3] [5]

★**Dauphin** LE (**DPn**) 57 bd de la République ☎54970483
Closed 16—29 Jan
rm10 (⇌ 🚿 6) **P**15 sB111—200
sB ⇌ 🚿 122—220 dB131—220
dB ⇌ 🚿 142—220 M80—160
Credit cards [1] [3]

SALERS
Cantal

★***Beffroi*** r du Beffroi ☎71407011
Apr—Oct
⇌ 🚿 10 **P**15 mountains

SALIERS See **ST-GILLES**

SALLANCHES
Haute-Savoie

★★**Ibis** av de Genève ☎50581442 tx385754
⇌ 60 **P** Lift sB ⇌ 178—182 dB ⇌ 233—238 mountains
Credit cards [1] [3]

SALON-DE-PROVENCE
Bouches-du-Rhône

★***Grand Poste*** 1 r Prés-Kennedy ☎90560194
Feb—Oct
rm28 (⇌ 🚿 17) **P**

🚘 **Bagnis** 35 r D-Kinet ☎90535507 Closed Sat pm Alf

At **BARBEN (LA)** (8km SE)

★***Touloubre*** ☎90551685
15 Jan—15 Nov
rm16 (⇌ 🚿 8) **P**100
Credit cards [2] [3]

At **LANÇON-PROVENCE** (9km SE on A7)

★★★**Mercure** (A7) ☎90539070 tx440183
Rest Mar—Oct
⇌ 100 **P**20 Lift sB ⇌ 258—308
dB ⇌ 326—366 M alc ≈ mountains
Credit cards [1] [2] [3] [5]

SALSES
Pyrénées-Orientales

★★★**Relais Rousillon** (N9) ☎68386067
⇌ 56 **P** ≈ mountains

France

SANARY-SUR-MER
Var

★★**Tour** (**DPn**) 24 quai Gl-de-Gaulle ☎94741010
⇌ 🚿 28 **P**4 sB ⇌ 🚿 200—230 M65—135 sea
Credit cards [3] [5]

🚘 **Maria** quartier des Prats ☎94740324 Closed Sat pm & Sun Alf Fia Mer Ope Peu

SANCÉ-LES-MÂCON See **MÂCON**

SANCERRE
Cher

★★**Rempart** LE Rempart des Dames ☎48541018
⇌ 12 🚗 **P**40 sB ⇌ 122—139
dB ⇌ 161—177 Mfr85
Credit cards [2] [3] [5]

SANNOIS
Val-d'Oise

★★**Campanile** ZUP d'Ermont-Sannois, av de la Sadernaude ☎34137957 tx697841
⇌ 49 **P** sB ⇌ 204—225 dB ⇌ 226—247 M61—82
Credit card [3]

SANTENAY
Côte-d'Or

★★★**Santana** (BW/MAP) av des Sources ☎80206211 tx350190
Apr—Oct
⇌ 65 **P**65 Lift ☾ sB ⇌ 220 dB ⇌ 273 M78 🔑 ≈
Credit cards [1] [2] [3] [5]

SARAN See **ORLÉANS**

SARLAT-LA-CANÉDA
Dordogne

★★★**Hostellerie de Meysset** (**DPn**) rte des Eyzies ☎53590829
26 Apr—4 Oct
⇌ 🚿 26 **P**30 sB ⇌ 🚿 280—315 dB ⇌ 🚿 345 M145—230
Credit cards [1] [2] [3] [5]

★★★**Madeleine** (**DPn**) 1 pl de la Petite-Rigaudie ☎53591240 tx550689
Mar—15 Nov
⇌ 🚿 22 sB ⇌ 🚿 239—268
dB ⇌ 🚿 285—353 M72—200
Credit cards [1] [2] [3] [5]

★★★***Salamandre*** r Abbé Surguier (n.rest) ☎53593598 tx550059
Apr—Oct
⇌ 23

★★***St-Albert*** LE 2 pl Pasteur ☎53590109
rm50 (⇌ 🚿 35) A24rm

★***Lion d'Or*** 48 av Gambetta ☎53590083
Mar—Dec
rm25 (⇌ 🚿 7)

🚘 **Castan** av de la Dordogne ☎53593679 Closed Sun & Mon Tal

🚘 **Fournet** rte de Vitrac ☎53590523 M/c For

🚘 **Pechauriol** rte de Brive ☎53590530 Toy

🚘 **Sariat Auto** rte de Vitrac ☎53591064 Closed Sun & Mon Cit

SARREGUEMINES
Moselle

🚘 **Schwindt** 62 rte de Nancy ☎8982677 Ren

SATOLAS AIRPORT See **LYON**

SAULCE-SUR-RHÔNE
Drome

★★***Ibis Montelimar Nord*** (N7) quartier Fraysse ☎75630960 tx345960
⇌ 29 **P**60 ≈
Credit cards [1] [3]

🚘 **J P Frey** (N7) ☎75610038 Closed Sun Cit

SAULIEU
Côte-d'Or

★★★**Poste** LE (Inter) 2 r Grillot ☎80640567 tx350540
rm48 (⇌ 42) 🚗 **P**35 ☾ sB100
sB ⇌ 210—260 dBfr120 dB ⇌ 230—325 M100—225
Credit cards [1] [2] [3]

🚘 **J Baut** r Grillot ☎80640345 Closed Sun & Mon Ren

SAUMUR
Maine-et-Loire

★★**Londres** 48 r Orléans (n.rest) ☎41512398
rm26 (⇌ 🚿 17) **P** sB104—108 sB ⇌ 🚿 127 dB188 dB ⇌ 🚿 185—231

★**Croix-Verte** 49 r de Rouen ☎41673931
Feb—15 Dec
rm18 (⇌ 🚿 5) **P**12 sB98—103
sB ⇌ 🚿 118—128 dB121—131
dB ⇌ 🚿 144—196 M50—150
Credit cards [1] [3]

At **BAGNEUX** (1.5km SW)

★★**Campanile** Côte de Bournan ☎41501440 tx720183
⇌ 43 **P** sB ⇌ 204—225 dB ⇌ 226—247 M61—82
Credit card [3]

At **CHÊNEHUTTE-LES-TUFFEAUX** (8km NW)

★★★***Prieuré*** (Relais et Châteaux) ☎41501531 tx720379
Mar—Jan
rm35 (⇌ 🚿 34) A15rm **P** ☾ 🔑 ≈

SAUSHEIM See **MULHOUSE**

SAUT-DES-CUVES See **GÉRARDMER**

SAUZET See **MONTÉLIMAR**

SAVERNE
Bas-Rhin

★★**Geiswiller** LE 17 r Côte ☎88911851
rm38 (⇌ 🚿 36) 🚗 **P**15 Lift sB100—210
sB ⇌ 🚿 170—190 dB ⇌ 🚿 220—290
M60—190 ≈ mountains
Credit cards [1] [2] [3] [5]

★**Boeuf-Noir** LE (**Pn**) 22 Grande Rue ☎88911053
rm20 (🛁 🚿 13) 🚗 **P**8 sB63—77 sB 🛁 🚿 89 dB101 dB 🛁 🚿 151—161 M39—135 mountains
Credit cards [1] [3]

★**Chez Jean** LE (**DPn** in season) 3 r de la Gare ☎88911019
Closed Jan
rm22 (🛁 🚿 18) 🚗 **P**25 Lift sB102 sB 🛁 🚿 167 dB 🛁 🚿 184—194 M45—150 mountains
Credit cards [1] [3] [5]

SAVIGNAC-LES-ÉGLISES
Dordogne

★★**Parc** LE (**Pn**) ☎53050811
Mar—8 Jan
rm14 (🛁 🚿 13) 🚗 **P**20 ☾ dB390—640 dB 🛁 🚿 560—640 M180—265 🎾
Credit cards [1] [2] [3] [5]

SAVIGNY-SUR-CLAIRIS
Yonne

🔧 **Chapuls** les Dornets ☎86863348 Ren

SAVONNIÈRES See **TOURS**

SÉES
Orne

★**Cheval Blanc** LE (**DPn**) 1 pl St-Pierre ☎33278048
rm9 (🚿 2) sB69—87 sB🚿 83—87 dB82—132 dB🚿 fr96 M52—165
Credit cards [1] [3]

★**Dauphin** LE (**DPn**) 31 pl Halls ☎33278007
rm19 **P** dBfr75 M95

🔧 **Hugeron** 60 r de la République ☎33278013 Cit

SELLIÈRES
Jura

See also **POLIGNY**

At **PASSENANS** (6km SE)

★★**Domaine Touristique du Revermont** LE (**DPn**) ☎84446102
Mar—Dec
🛁 🚿 28 🚗 **P**50 Lift sBfr148 sB 🛁 🚿 148—186 dB 🛁 🚿 204—235 M63—145 🎾 ♒
Credit cards [1] [3] [5]

SEMUR-EN-AUXOIS
Côtes-d'Or

★★**Lac** LE (3km S on D1036 at Lac de Pont) ☎80971111
Feb—14 Dec
rm23 (🛁 🚿 19) 🚗 **P**30 sB122—142 sB 🛁 🚿 182—192 dB164—184 dB 🛁 🚿 214—234 M60—120 lake
Credit cards [1] [3] [5]

★**Côte d'Or** LE (**DPn**) 3 pl G-Gaveau ☎80970313
Closed Feb
rm15 (🛁 🚿 10) 🚗 **P**12 sBfr68 dB102—117 dB 🛁 🚿 127—232 M60—125
Credit cards [1] [2] [3] [5]

★**Gourmets** (**Pn**) 4 r Varenne ☎80970941
Jan—15 Nov & Tues
15rm (🚿 3) A6rm 🚗 sB71 sB🚿 148 dB102 dB🚿 172 M60—120
Credit card [3]

🔧 **Delaveau** 3 r de Paris ☎80970261 Closed Sun For

🔧 **Renault** 21 r du Cours ☎80970510 Closed Sun & Mon Ren

SÉNAS
Bouches-du-Rhône

★**Luberon** (**DPn**) 17 av A-Aune (N7) ☎90572010
15 Dec—15 Oct
rm7 (🛁 🚿 4) **P**5 dB118 dB 🛁 🚿 128—176 M51—75
Credit cards [1] [3]

🔧 **Testud** 31 av A-Aune ☎90572018 Closed Sat pm & Sun All makes

SENLIS
Oise

★★**Campanile** r E-Gazeau ☎600507
🛁 49 sB 🛁 217—238 dB 🛁 239—260 M61—82

★★***Ibis*** (N324) ☎44537050 tx104101
🛁 50 **P**50 Lift
Credit cards [1] [3]

🔧 **Delacharlery** 3-5 av Foch ☎44530968 Ren

Gare 6 16 cours Boutteville ☎44530253 Closed 3 wks Aug, Sat & Sun AR

SENNECEY-LE-DIJON See **DIJON**

SENNECEY-LE-GRAND
Saône-et-Loire

★**Lion d'Or** r de la Gare ☎85448375
rm11 (🚿 4) 🚗 **P**10 sB🚿 76 dB97 dB🚿 107 M51—120

At **ST-LOUP-DE-VARENNES** (10km N on N6)

🔧 **Desmaris** ☎85442076 Closed 3 wks Aug, Sat & Sun Ren

SENONCHES
Eure-et-Loir

★**Forêt** LE (**DPn**) pl Champ de Foire ☎37377850
Closed Feb
rm14 (🛁 🚿 6) 🚗 **P**50 sB91—104 sB 🛁 🚿 117 dBfr116 dB 🛁 🚿 129—169 Mfr60
Credit card [1]

SENS
Yonne

★★★**Paris & Poste** (BW/MAP) 97 r de la République ☎86651743 tx801831
🛁 🚿 32 🚗 **P** ☾ sB 🛁 🚿 248—288 dB 🛁 🚿 296—436 M148—260
Credit cards [1] [2] [3] [4] [5]

🔧 **Sens Bourgogne Autos** 5 bd de Verdun ☎86655123 Closed Sat pm & Sun For

🔧 **Vanne** 184 rte de Lyon ☎86651218 Closed Sat pm & Sun Aud VW

SEPT-SAULX
Marne

★★**Cheval Blanc** (**DPn**) r du Moulin ☎26616027 tx830885
15 Feb—15 Jan
🛁 🚿 22 **P** sB 🛁 🚿 220—265 dB 🛁 🚿 295—310 M150—400 🎾
Credit cards [1] [2] [3] [5]

SERRES
Hautes-Alpes

★**Alpes** av Grenoble (n.rest) ☎92670018
Apr—Nov
rm20 (🛁 🚿 9) 🚗 **P**12 sB92—102 sB 🛁 🚿 127—167 dB 🛁 🚿 149—151 mountains

SÈTE
Hèrault

★★★**Grand** 17 quai Ml-Lattre-de-Tassigny ☎67747177 tx480225
Jan—23 Dec
🛁 🚿 51 🚗 **P**30 Lift ☾ sB 🛁 🚿 194—350 dB 🛁 🚿 219—375 sea
Credit cards [1] [2] [3] [5]

★★★**Imperial** (BW/MAP) pl E-Herriot (n.rest) ☎67532832 tx480046
🛁 🚿 43 🚗 **P**14 Lift ☾ sB 🛁 🚿 258—380 dB 🛁 🚿 279—410 t% sea
Credit cards [1] [2] [3] [5]

🔧 **14 Juillet** 27 av V-Hugo ☎67488282 Closed Sep, Sat & Sun All Makes

SEVRAN
Seine-et-Marne

★★***Climat*** av R-Dautry, ZAC de Sevran ☎43834560 tx692844
🛁 43 **P**50
Credit cards [1] [3]

SEVRIER
Haute-Savoie

★**Robinson** ☎50465411
Apr—Oct
rm12 (🛁 4) 🚗 **P** dB164—176 dB 🛁 264—296 M55—60 🎾 ♒ lake mountains
Credit cards [1] [2] [5]

SEYSSEL
Aine

★★**Rhône** LE ☎50592030
Jan—15 Nov
🛁 🚿 10 A5rm 🚗 sB92—128 sB 🛁 🚿 117—208 dB124—134 dB 🛁 🚿 144—284 M85—260 mountains
Credit cards [1] [2] [3] [4]

SÉZANNE
Marne

★★**Croix d'Or** LE (**DPn**) 53 r Notre-Dame ☎26806110
Closed 1—14 Jan
🛁 🚿 13 🚗 **P**12 sB 🛁 🚿 116 dB 🛁 🚿 171
Credit cards [1] [2] [3] [4] [5]

SIGEAN
Aude

★**Ste-Anne** (**DPn**) ☎68482438

rm12 (🚿3) **P** sB75 dB100 dB🚿120—140 Mfr50

SIORAC-EN-PÉRIGORD
Dordogne

★**Scholly** LE r de la Poste ☎53316002

rm32 (🛁🚿27) **P**40 dB155—299 dB🛁🚿245—334 M85—300 Credit cards [2] [3] [4] [5]

SISTERON
Alpes-de-Hautes-Provence

★★★**Grand du Cours** av de la Libération, pl de l'Église (n.rest) ☎92610451

15 Mar—15 Nov
🛁🚿50 🏠**P**30 Lift ☾ sB🛁🚿162—242 dB🛁🚿234—314 mountains
Credit cards [1] [2] [3] [5]

🚗 **Provence** av J-Jaurès ☎92611228 Closed Sat pm & Sun Cit

SOISSONS
Aisne

★★**Lions** rte de Reims, ZI Soissons (3km E via N31) ☎23732983 tx140568

🛁28 **P**35 sB🛁202—218 dB🛁285—316 M68—120 S%
Credit cards [1] [2] [3] [5]

★★**Picardie** 6 r Neuve St-Martin ☎23532193 tx145633

🛁33 **P**40 Lift sB🛁210—230 dB🛁275—295 M75—180
Credit cards [1] [2] [3] [5]

★**Rallye** 10 bd de Strasbourg (n.rest) ☎23530047

rm12 (🛁🚿5) 🏠**P** sB99—199 sB🛁🚿140—198 dB129—242 dB🛁🚿169—242

SOLESMES See **SABLÉ-SUR-SARTHE**

SOSPEL
Alpes-Maritimes

★★**Étrangers** LE (**DPn**) 7 bd Verdun ☎93040009 tx970439

26 Jan—25 Nov
rm35 (🛁🚿32) A5rm **P**15 Lift sB137—207 sB🛁🚿137—207 dB174—264 dB🛁🚿204—284 M65—110 ▭ 🏊 mountains
Credit cards [1] [3]

SOUILLAC
Lot

★★**Ambassadeurs** LE 7-12 av Gl-de-Gaulle ☎65327836

28 Nov—28 Sep
rm28 (🛁🚿24) A10rm 🏠**P**20 sB104—108 sB🛁🚿127—173 dB122—173 dB🛁🚿189—225 M43—140 mountains
Credit cards [1] [3]

★★**Périgord** LE (FAH) 31 av Gl-de-Gaulle ☎65327828

May—5 Oct
🛁🚿58 A18rm 🏠**P**20 sB🛁🚿149—229 dB🛁🚿168—268 M55—105 🏊
Credit cards [1] [3]

★★**Renaissance** LE (FAH) (**DPn**) 2 av J-Jaurès ☎65327804

Apr—2 Nov
🛁🚿30 🏠**P**20 Lift sB🛁🚿162—188 dB🛁🚿194—245 M55—120 🏊
Credit cards [1] [3]

★★**Roseraie** LE 42 av de Toulouse ☎65378269

20 Apr—15 Oct
🛁🚿26 🏠**P** Lift sB🛁🚿92—131 dB🛁🚿127—182

★★**Auberge du Puits** LE ☎65378032

Jan—Oct
rm16 (🛁🚿7) **P**40 sB83—150 sB🛁🚿100—150 dB98—165 dB🛁🚿115—165 Mfr42

★**Nouvel** 21 av Gl-de-Gaulle ☎65327958

rm30 (🛁🚿21) **P**30 sB79—160 sB🛁🚿92—167 dB94—175 dB🛁🚿107—182 M45—145
Credit cards [1] [2] [3] [5]

🚗 **M Cadier** rte de Sarlat ☎65378272 Closed Sat & Sun Tal

SOUPPES-SUR-LOING
Seine-et-Marne

🚗 **Cornut Osmin** 7 av Ml-Leclerc ☎64297032 Closed Sat pm, Sun & Mon am Ren

SOURCE (LA) See **ORLÉANS**

SOUSCEYRAC
Lot

★***Déjeuner de Sousceyrac*** LE (**DPn**) ☎65330056

Apr—Nov
rm10 (🛁🚿9) A4rm
Credit cards [2] [3] [5]

SOUSTONS
Landes

★★***Bergerie*** (**DPn**) av du Lac ☎58480143

Apr—15 Oct
🛁29 A17rm **P**

STAINVILLE
Meuse

★★★**Grange** LE ☎29786015

15 Mar—15 Dec
rm9 (🛁🚿8) 🏠**P**6 sB🛁🚿fr132 dB🛁🚿fr192 M63—130
Credit cards [1] [5]

STRASBOURG
Bas-Rhin

★★★★**Grand** 12 pl de la Gare (n.rest) ☎88324690 tx870011

rm88 (🛁🚿85) **P** Lift ☾ sB332—412 sB🛁🚿362—412 dB404—514 dB🛁🚿444—514
Credit cards [1] [2] [3] [5]

★★★★**Hilton International** av Herrenschmidt ☎88371010 tx890363

🛁253 **P**90 Lift ☾ sB🛁540—650 dB🛁640—745 mountains
Credit cards [1] [2] [3] [4] [5]

★★★★**Holiday Inn** 20 pl de Bordeaux ☎88357000 tx890515

🛁🚿170 **P**150 Lift sB🛁🚿515—585 dB🛁🚿635—720 Mfr100 ▭
Credit cards [1] [2] [3] [5]

★★★★**Sofitel** pl St-Pierre-le-Jeune ☎88329930 tx870894

🛁🚿180 🏠**P**50 Lift ☾ sB🛁🚿497—727 dB🛁🚿604—814 Mfr125
Credit cards [1] [2] [3] [4] [5]

★★★***France*** 20 r du Jeu des Enfants (n.rest) ☎88323712 tx890084

🛁🚿70 🏠 Lift

★★★***Hannong*** (FAH) 15 r du 22 Novembre ☎88321622 tx890551

🛁🚿70 **P**18 Lift
Credit cards [1] [2] [3] [5]

★★★**Monopole-Métropole** LE 16 r Kuhn (n.rest) ☎88321194 tx890366

🛁🚿94 🏠 Lift ☾ sB🛁🚿255—345 dB🛁🚿320—410
Credit cards [1] [2] [3] [4] [5]

★★★**Novotel Centre Halles** quai Kléber ☎88221099 tx880700

🛁🚿97 **P** Lift sB🛁🚿fr416 dB🛁🚿fr501
Credit cards [1] [2] [3] [5]

★★★**PLM Pont de l'Europe** Parc du Rhin ☎88610323 tx870833

🛁93 sB🛁312—332 dB🛁384—404 Mfr48
Credit cards [1] [2] [3] [4] [5]

★★★***Terminus-Gruber*** (BW/MAP) 10 pl de la Gare ☎88328700 tx870998

rm78 (🛁🚿70) 🏠**P**500 Lift ☾
Credit cards [1] [2] [3] [5]

★★**Arcade** 7 r de Molsheim ☎88223000 tx880147

🚿245 **P**80 Lift sB🚿197—252 dB🚿233—268 Mfr70
Credit cards [1] [3] [4]

★★***Climat*** pl A-Maurios, Maille Irène, ZUP Hautepierre ☎88285923 tx612241

🛁38 **P**40
Credit cards [1] [2]

★★***Ibis*** 1 r Sebastopol, quai Kléber ☎88221499 tx880399

🛁97 **P** Lift
Credit cards [1] [3] [5]

★★**Vendôme** (Inter) (n.rest) 9 pl de la Gare ☎88324523 tx890850

🛁🚿48 Lift sB🛁🚿fr190 dB🛁🚿220
Credit cards [1] [2] [3] [5]

🚗 **Straub** 34 r de la Ganzau, Neuhof ☎88397160 Closed Aug, Sat & Sun AR

At **GEISPOLSHEIM** (12km SE on RN83)

★★**Campanile** 20 r de l'Ill (N83) ☎88667477 tx890797

🛁50 **P** Lift sB🛁217—238 dB🛁239—260 M61—82
Credit card [3]

At **ILKIRCH-GRAFFENSTADEN** (7km S)

★★★**Mercure Strasbourg Sud** r du 23 Novembre, Ostwald ☎88662156 tx890142
➡76 **P**100 sB➡331 dB➡387 M90 ≈
Credit cards [1] [2] [3] [5]

★★★***Novotel Strasbourg Sud*** rte de Colmar (N83) ☎88662156 tx890142
➡76 **P** ≈
Credit cards [1] [2] [3] [5]

SULLY-SUR-LOIRE
Loiret

★★**Grand Sully** **LE** **(Pn)** 10 bd Champ de Foire ☎38362756
15 Jan—20 Dec
rm12 (➡10) ⌂ **P**12 sBfr112 sB➡198 dBfr302 dB➡fr302 Mfr130
Credit cards [1] [2] [3] [5]

★★**Poste** **(Pn)** 11 r fbg St-Germain ☎38362622
Mar—25 Jan
rm27 (➡⫛13) A10rm **P**25 sBfr97 sB➡⫛132—202 dBfr144 dB➡⫛154—264 M75—150
Credit cards [1] [2] [3]

SURESNES
Hauts-de-Seine

★★***Ibis*** 6 r de Bourets ☎45068844 tx614484
➡62 ⌂ **P** Lift ☾

SURVILLIERS-ST-WITZ
Val-d'Oise

★★★**Mercure Paris St-Witz** r J-Noulin ☎34682828 tx695917
➡115 **P**400 Lift sB➡290—325 dB➡340—375 M120—200 ≈
Credit cards [1] [2] [3] [5]

★★★***Novotel Paris Survilliers*** Autoroute A1—D16 ☎34686980 tx695910
rm79 **P** ≈

TAIN L'HERMITAGE
Drôme

★★★**Commerce** (Inter) 69 av J-Jaurès ☎75086500 tx345573
➡⫛41 ⌂ **P**50 Lift ☾ dB➡⫛282—342 M84—260 ≈ mountains
Credit cards [1] [2] [3] [4] [5]

⛟ **45e Parallele** Pont de l'Isère ☎75586004 M/c Closed 28 Oct—15 Nov, Sat pm & Sun All makes

⛟ **Vullierme** 126 av J-Jaurès ☎75083501 Closed Sat pm & Sun F..n

TALANGE See **METZ**

TALLOIRES
Haute-Savoie

★★★**Cottage** **(Pn)** rte G-Bise ☎50607110
Mar—Oct
➡⫛36 ⌂ **P**50 Lift ☾ sB➡⫛430—550 dB➡⫛500—800 M150 ⚲ ⊟ mountains lake
Credit cards [2] [5]

★★***Beau Site*** ☎50607104
23 May—5 Oct

France

rm38 (➡⫛30) A28rm ⌂ **P**40 ⚲ lake mountains
Credit cards [1] [2] [3] [5]

★★***Vivier*** ☎50607054
Apr—Oct
➡⫛30 ⌂ **P**

TAMNIÈS
Dordogne

★★**Laborderie** **LE** ☎53296859
15 Mar—15 Nov
rm32 (➡⫛31) A16rm dB130—172 dB➡⫛160—272 M55—200 ≈

TARARE
Rhône

★**Mère Paul** **(DPn)** (2km on N7) ☎74631457
rm10 (➡⫛9) **P**10 sB113—153 sB➡⫛113—153 dB146—176 dB➡⫛146—176 M40—120
Credit cards [1] [3]

TARASCON-SUR-ARIÈGE
Ariège

★★***Poste*** **LE** **(DPn)** 16 av V-Pilhès ☎61646041
Closed Mon (Oct—Jun only)
rm30 (➡⫛18) **P** mountains

TARASCON-SUR-RHÔNE
Bouches-du-Rhône

★★***Terminus*** pl du Colonel-Berrurier ☎90911895
Closed 15 Jan—15 Feb
rm23 (➡⫛14)
Credit cards [1] [3]

★**Provençal** 12 cours A-Briand ☎90911141
Mar—Oct
➡⫛22 ⌂ **P**10 ☾ sB➡⫛92—146 dB➡⫛132—162 M45—120
Credit cards [1] [2] [3] [4] [5]

TARBES
Hautes-Pyrénées

★★★**Président** (BW/MAP) 1 r G-Faure ☎62939840 tx530522
➡⫛57 ⌂ Lift sB➡⫛237 dB➡⫛299 ≈ mountains
Credit cards [1] [2] [3] [4] [5]

★★**Campanile** (4km SW on N21) Lotissement Longchamp, rte de Lourdes ☎62938320 tx530571
➡42 **P** sB➡204—225 dB➡226—247 M61—82
Credit card [3]

★★**Croix Blanche** pl Verdun (n.rest) ☎62930854
rm32 (➡⫛13) sB89—154 sB➡⫛142—154 dB103—168 dB➡⫛146—168
Credit card [3]

★***Henri IV*** (Inter) 7 bd B-Barère (n.rest) ☎62340168
➡⫛24 ⌂ **P** Lift ☾

⛟ **SA Auto Selection** 15 r F-Marque ☎62936930 Closed Sun & Mon am Ren Toy Vol

THÉOULE-SUR-MER
Alpes-Maritimes

★★**Guerguy la Galère** la Galère ☎93754454
Feb—Nov
➡14 ⌂ **P** dB➡610—790 Mfr200 S15% sea

★***Hermitage Jules César*** 1 av C-Dahon ☎93499612
15 Mar—15 Oct
rm18 (➡⫛16) sea mountains

THIERS
Puy-de-Dôme

★★**Fimotel** rte de Clermont-Ferrand (N89) ☎73806440 tx392000
➡42 **P** Lift sB➡fr217 dB➡fr244 M56 & alc mountains
Credit cards [2] [5]

⛟ **Sauvagnat** 90 r de Lyon ☎73800374 Closed Aug, Sat pm & Sun Cit

THIONVILLE
Moselle

⛟ **R Dillmann** 81 rte de Garche ☎82533081 Closed 12 Jul—4 Aug & Sun Cit

THOISSEY
Ain

★★★***Chapon Fin*** (Relais et Châteaux) **(DPn)** r du Champ de Foire ☎74040474
15 Feb—4 Jan
➡⫛25 ⌂ **P**100 Lift ☾
Credit Cards [3] [5]

★**Beau-Rivage** **(Pn)** av Port ☎7404016
15 Mar—15 Oct
⫛10 **P** sB⫛109 dB⫛125—171 M mountains

THOUARS
Deux-Sèvres

★★***Climat*** les Moulins à Vent ☎49681321
➡24 **P**20
Credit cards [1] [3]

THURY-HARCOURT
Calvados

★**Relais de la Poste** **(DPn)** rte Caen ☎31797212
20 Mar—20 Dec
➡⫛11 ⌂ **P** dB➡⫛200—350 M95—180
Credit cards [1] [2] [3] [4] [5]

TILQUES See **ST-OMER**

TINQUEUX See **REIMS**

TONNERRE
Yonne

★★★**Abbaye St-Michel** **LE** (Relais et Châteaux) **(DPn)** Montée St-Michel ☎86550599 tx801356
Feb—20 Dec
➡11 **P**30 sB➡466 dB➡622—792

M250—350
Credit cards 2 3 5

Carrosserie Auto rte de St-Martin ☎86550009 Closed Xmas, New Year & Mon All makes

TORCY See **CREUSOT (LE)**

TOULON
Var

★★★★**Frantel Tour Blanche** bd Amiral Vence ☎94244157 tx400347

93 **P**70 Lift sB 308—393 dB 401—466 Mfr110 sea
Credit cards 1 2 3 4 5

★★***Urbis*** 51 r J-Jaurès ☎94923219 tx400479

30 Lift
Credit cards 2 3 5

Carrefour Auto 49 av Gl-Pruneau ☎94415986 Closed Sat Toy

Soleil 31 r A-Chenièr ☎94272556

At **CAMP ST-LAURENT** (7.5km W via B52-exit Ollioules)

★★★**Novotel** ☎94630950

86 **P**90 Lift
Credit cards 1 2 3 5

★★**Ibis** Autoroute B52 ☎94632121 tx400759

60 **P** Lift

At **FARLÈDE (LA)** (8.5km NE)

★★***Climat*** quartier de l'Auberte ☎94487427

39 **P**40
Credit cards 1 3

At **VALETTE-DU-VAR (LA)** (7km NE)

★★**Campanile** ZA des Espaluns ☎94211301 tx430978

50 **P** sB 217—238 dB 239—260 M61—82
Credit card 3

Azur av de 1 Université ☎94233648 Closed Sat & Sun For

TOULOUSE
Haute-Garonne

★★★**Caravelle** (BW/MAP) 62 r Raymond IV (n.rest) ☎61627065 tx530438

30 Lift sB 319—339 dB 368—408
Credit cards 1 2 3 4 5

★★★**Compagnie du Midi** Gare Matabiau ☎61628493 tx530171

65 Lift sB 240—310 dB 280—350 M100—120
Credit cards 2 5

★★★***Concorde*** 16 bd Bonrepos (n.rest Sun & Aug) ☎61624860 tx531686

97 **P** Lift

★★★**Diane** 3 rte de St-Simon ☎61075952 tx530518

35 **P**35 sB 295—335 dB 340—390 M125
Credit cards 1 2 3 5

France

★★★**Mercure** r St-Jérome ☎61231177 tx520760

170 **P** Lift

★★**Ibis** les Raisins, 27 bd des Minimes ☎61226060 tx530437

130 **P**75 Lift sB 196—212 dB 215—232 Mfr75&alc
Credit cards 1 3

★★**Voyageurs** (Inter) 11 bd Bonrepos (n.rest) ☎61628979

34 Lift sB 158—198 dB 186—226
Credit cards 1 2 3 5

Vie 57—59 allées C-de-Fitte ☎61429911 Closed Sat pm & Sun Tal

At **LABÈGE** (11km SE)

★★**Campanile** ☎61340189 tx532007

49 dB 240—261 M61—82

At **MIRAIL (LE)**

★★**Climat** av du Mirail, 2 r A-Coutét ☎61448644 tx521980

43 **P**43 sB 250 dB 270 M80
Credit cards 1 3

★★**Ibis** r J-Babinet ☎61408686 tx520805

89 **P**80 Lift sB 185—208 dB 199—222
Credit cards 1 3

Smeca St-Michel 123 r Vauquelin ☎61401010 Closed Sat & Sun AR

At **ROQUES-SUR-GARONNE** (6km SW)

★★**Campanile** Carrefour RN117 ☎61725151 tx521426

50 **P** sB 217—238 dB 239—260 M61—82
Credit card 3

TOULOUSE AIRPORT

★★★★**Frantel Wilson** 7 r de Labéda (n.rest) ☎61212175 tx530550

95 Lift sB 477—557 dB 579—669 M alc
Credit cards 1 2 3 4 5

★★★**Novotel Toulouse Purpan** 23 r de Maubec ☎61493410 tx520640

123 **P** Lift sB 337—386 dB 384—442 M alc
Credit cards 1 2 3 5

At **BLAGNAC** (7km NE)

★★**Campanile** av D-Daurat 3 ☎61710340 tx530915

42 **P** sB 217—238 dB 239—260 M61—82
Credit card 3

TOUQUES See **DEAUVILLE**

TOUQUET-PARIS-PLAGE (LE)
Pas-de-Calais

★★★**Côte d'Opale** (**DPn**) 99 bd Dr J-Pouget, bd de la Mer ☎21050811

15 Mar—15 Nov
rm28 (22) sB172 sB 327 dB199 dB 354 M110 sea
Credit cards 1 2 3 5

★★★***Novotel-Thalamer*** La Plage ☎21052400 tx160480

104 **P** Lift

★★★**Westminster** (Inter) av Verger ☎21051966 tx160439

Mar—Nov
145 **P**200 Lift **DPn**460—515 M120—160 S15%
Credit cards 1 2 3 4 5

★★***Forêt*** 73 r de Moscou (n.rest) ☎21050988

10
Credit card 2

★★**Ibis** Front de Mer ☎21053690 tx134273

71 Lift sB 253—322 dB 299—368 Mfr74 sea
Credit cards 1 3

★★**Plage** 13 bd de la Mer (n.rest) ☎21050322

15 Mar—15 Nov
rm26 (21) sB111—146 sB 214—241 dB130—160 dB 233—260 sea
Credit cards 1 3

★★**Windsor-Artois** 7 r St-Georges (off r de la Paix) ☎21053087

rm49 (35) A6rm Lift sB95—235 dB120—260 dB 120—260 M65—75

★**Chalet** 15 r de la Paix ☎21845565

Apr—15 Nov
rm15 (9) sBfr102 sB 166—229 dB118—156 dB 217—268 Mfr75 sea
Credit card 3

★**Robert's** (**DPn**) 66 r de Londres ☎21051198

Apr—Sep
rm14 (3) sB73—83 sB 113 dB96—116 dB 126 M55—80

★**Touquet** 17 r de Paris (n.rest) ☎21052254

rm16 (10) sB95 sB 165 dB110 dB 180

At the **GOLF LINKS** (3km S)

★★★**Manoir** av du Golf ☎21052022 tx135565

15 Mar—15 Nov
rm44 (42) A6rm **P**60 sB 365—620 dB 590—690 M155 &alc
Credit cards 1 2 3

TOURCOING
Nord

★★★***Novotel Neuville*** Autoroute Lille-Grand (N near Halluin interchange) ☎20940770 tx131656

118 **P** Lift M alc

★★**Ibis** centre Gl-de-Gaulle, r Carnot ☎20248458 tx132695

102 Lift sB 194—224 dB 230—260 M58—88
Credit cards 1 3

TOUR-DU-PIN (LA)
Isère

At **FAVERGES-DE-LA-TOUR** (10km NE)

★★★★**Château de Faverges** ☎74974252 tx300372

7 May—19 Oct
🛁 🚿 46 A26 **P**20 Lift ☾ sB 🛁 🚿 455—1155 dB 🛁 🚿 560—1560 M275 ⚲ ≈ ▣
Credit cards [2] [3] [5]

TOURETTES See **FAYENCE**

TOURNUS
Saône-et-Loire

★★★**Rempart** 2 & 4 av Gambetta (N6) ☎85511056 tx351019

🛁 30 ⌂ **P**16 Lift sB 🛁 277—362 dB 🛁 289—484 M150—300
Credit cards [1] [2] [3] [5]

★★★**Sauvage** (BW/MAP) pl du Champ de Mars ☎85511445 tx800726

15 Dec—15 Nov
🛁 🚿 31 ⌂ **P**10 Lift ☾ sB 🛁 🚿 212 dB 🛁 🚿 237—260 M75
Credit cards [1] [2] [3] [5]

★**Terrasses** LE (**DPn**) 18 av du 23 Janvier ☎85510174

5 Feb—5 Jan
rm12 (🛁 🚿 6) ⌂ sB89—108 sB 🛁 🚿 128—168 dB106—126 dB 🛁 🚿 146—186 M50—140
Credit card [3]

🚗 **M Pageaud** 3 rte de Paris ☎85510705 Closed Sat pm & Sun Ren

🚗 **Scavardo** (N6, exit Sud) ☎85510320 Closed Sat pm & Sun Cit

TOURS
Indre-et-Loire

See also **JOUÉ-LÈS-TOURS**

★★★**Armor** LE 26 bis bd Heurteloup (n.rest) ☎47052960 tx752020

rm41 (🛁 🚿 34) A9rm ⌂ **P**7 Lift ☾ sB112—138 sB 🛁 🚿 151—225 dB130—156 dB 🛁 🚿 169—263
Credit cards [1] [2] [3] [5]

★★★**Bordeaux** LE 3 pl du Ml-Leclerc ☎47054032 tx750414

🛁 🚿 52 **P** Lift ☾ sB 🛁 🚿 238—288 dBfr150 dB 🛁 🚿 260—310 ⚲ ▣
Credit cards [1] [2] [3] [5]

★★★**Central** (FAH) 21 r Berthelot (n.rest) ☎47054644 tx751173

rm42 (🛁 🚿 32) ⌂ **P**50 Lift sB135—168 sB 🛁 🚿 265 dB170—200 dB 🛁 🚿 310
Credit cards [1] [2] [3] [5]

★★★**Château de la Loire** 12 r Gambetta (n.rest) ☎47051005 tx750008

Mar—Nov
rm32 (🛁 🚿 30) Lift sB107 sB 🛁 🚿 144—207 dB140 dB 🛁 🚿 177—245
Credit cards [1] [2] [3] [5]

★★★**Meridien** 292 av de Grammont ☎47280080 tx750922

🛁 125 **P**100 Lift ☾ sB 🛁 387—482 dB 🛁 479—594 Mfr110 ⚲ ≈
Credit cards [1] [2] [3] [4] [5]

France

★★★**Royal** 65 av de Grammont (n.rest) ☎47647178 tx752006

🛁 35 ⌂ Lift ☾ sB 🛁 256—262 dB 🛁 319—324
Credit cards [1] [2] [3] [5]

★★★**Univers** 5 bd Heurteloup ☎47053712 tx751460

🛁 🚿 91 ⌂ **P** Lift ☾ sB 🛁 🚿 282—340 dB 🛁 🚿 331—414 M110—130
Credit cards [1] [2] [3] [5]

★★***Arcade*** 1 r G-Claude ☎47614444 tx751201

🚿 139 **P**28 Lift

★★***Climat*** ZI les Granges Galand (N76), St-Avertin ☎47277117 tx37170

🛁 38 **P**35
Credit cards [1] [3]

★★***Cygne*** 6 r du Cygne (off r Colbert) (n.rest) ☎47666641

rm20 (🛁 🚿 12)
Credit card [3]

★★**Ibis** a Petite Arche, av A-Maginot ☎47543220 tx751592

🛁 49 **P** sB 🛁 193—219 dB 🛁 237—263 M alc
Credit cards [1] [3]

★★***Mondial*** LE 3 pl de la Résistance (n.rest) ☎47056268

rm17 (🛁 🚿 12) **P**
Credit card [3]

★**Balzac** 47 r de la Scellerie (n.rest) ☎47054087 tx750008

rm20 (🛁 🚿 14) sB67—108 sB 🛁 🚿 137—185 dB164—212 dB 🛁 🚿 224—254
Credit cards [1] [2] [3] [5]

★**Choiseul** 12 r de la Rôtisserie (n.rest) ☎47208576

🛁 🚿 16 sB 🛁 🚿 178—188 dB 🛁 🚿 215—235
Credit cards [1] [3]

★***Colbert*** 78 r Colbert (n.rest) ☎47666156

rm17 (🛁 🚿 12)

★**Foch** 20 r Ml-Foch (n.rest) ☎47057059

🛁 🚿 16 A2rm sB109—143 sB 🛁 🚿 fr123 dBfr161 dB 🛁 🚿 181—191
Credit cards [1] [2] [3]

🚗 **Autotouraine** 151 av A-Maginot ☎47411515

🚗 **Nouveau Tours** 16 r Constantine ☎47057492 Closed Sat & Sun Maz

🚗 **G Pont** ZI du Menneton ☎47392533 Closed Aug 2—24 & Sat For

At **CHAMBRAY-LES-TOURS** (6km S)

★★★**Novotel Tours Sud** N10—ZAC de la Vrillonerie ☎47274138 tx751206

🛁 125 Lift sB 🛁 328—345 dB 🛁 408—420 ≈
Credit cards [1] [2] [3] [5]

★★**Ibis** (N10) La Vrillonnerie ☎47282528 tx751297

🛁 60 **P**80 sB 🛁 200—231 dB 🛁 243—272 M60—80 ≈
Credit cards [1] [3]

At **SAVONNIÈRES** (10km W D7)

★**Faisan** ☎47500017

Closed Nov
rm13 (🛁 🚿 9) **P** sB75—93 sB 🛁 🚿 fr93 dBfr126 dB 🛁 🚿 fr126 M58—95

TRANS-EN-PROVENCE
Var

★★***Climat*** quai de Cognet ☎94708211 tx692844

🛁 34 **P**

TRÉBEURDEN
Côtes-du-Nord

★★★**Manoir de Lan Kerellec** (Relais et Châteaux) allée de Lan-Kerellec ☎96235009 tx741172

Mar—Nov
🛁 15 **P**20 sB 🛁 400—480 dB 🛁 480—630 M120—220 ⚲ Beach sea
Credit cards [1] [2] [3] [4] [5]

★★**Family** LE (Inter) 85 r des Plages ☎96235031

15 Mar—Sep
rm25 (🛁 21) **P**15 sB128—143 sB 🛁 🚿 203—243 dB151—166 dB 🛁 🚿 226—266 Mfr60 sea
Credit card [2]

★★**Ker an Nod** LE r Pors Termen ☎96235021

Mar—Nov
rm20 (🛁 🚿 14) **P**20 sB128—228 sB 🛁 🚿 228 dB256 dB 🛁 🚿 276 M87 sea
Credit cards [1] [2] [3] [5]

TRÉGASTEL-PLAGE
Côtes-du-Nord

★★★**Belle Vue** LE (FAH) 20 r des Calculots ☎96238818

May—Sep
🛁 🚿 33 **P**35 sB 🛁 🚿 171—219 dB 🛁 🚿 246—352 M90—240 sea
Credit cards [1] [3]

★★**Beau Séjour** LE (Inter) (**DPn**) ☎96238802

20 Mar—Sep
rm18 (🛁 14) **P**10 sB103—123 sB 🛁 203—223 dB146—166 dB 🛁 246—286 M80—150 sea
Credit cards [1] [2] [3] [4] [5]

★★**Mer et Plage** ☎96238803

Apr—Oct
rm40 (🛁 🚿 25) **P**15 sB125—145 dB170—210 dB 🛁 🚿 210—270 M66—250 sea
Credit cards [1] [2] [3] [5]

TRÉGUIER
Côtes-du-Nord

★★**Kastell Dinec'h** LE (FAH) ☎96924939

Mar—15 Oct & Nov—Dec
🛁 🚿 15 **P**30 dBfr225 dB 🛁 🚿 260 M70—150
Credit card [3]

TRÉPORT (LE)
Seine-Maritime

★***Rex*** 50 quai François-1er ☎35862655 rm17 (➡ ⋒ 4) **P** sea

TRETS
Bouches-du-Rhône

⛟ **Rosso** 3 C-Mirabeau ☎42292031 Closed Sat pm & Sun For

TRÉVOL
Allier

★★**Relais d'Avrilly** (N7) ☎70426143 tx990638

➡ 42 **P**200 Lift sB ➡ 257—283 Mfr70
Credit cards 1 2 3 4

TRIGNAC
Loire-Atlantique

★★**Campanile** ☎40904444 tx701243

➡ 49 **P** sB ➡ 217—238 dB ➡ 239—260 M61—82

★★**Ibis** 5 r de la Fontaine au Brun ☎40903939 tx701231

➡ 45 **P** sB ➡ 233 dB ➡ 271

TRIMOUILLE (LA)
Vienne

★**Paix (Pn)** pl Église et de la Mairie ☎49916050

15 Mar—Oct
rm12 (➡ ⋒ 9) ☾ sB86 sB ➡ ⋒ 136—166 dB152—202 dB ➡ ⋒ 152—202 M50—175 ⚲ ▭
Credit card 3

TRINITÉ-SUR-MER (LA)
Morbihan

★★**Rouzic** LF 17 cours de Quais ☎97557206

15 Dec—15 Nov
➡ ⋒ 32 Lift sB ➡ ⋒ 149—240 dB ➡ ⋒ 167—258 M74—143 sea
Credit cards 1 2 3 5

TRIQUE (LA)
See **ST-LAURENT-SUR-SÈVRE**

TROIS-ÉPIS (LES)
Haut-Rhin

★★★★**Grand** (BW/MAP) ☎89498065 tx880229

➡ 48 **P**35 Lift ☾ sB ➡ 545—625 dB ➡ 590—1790 M alc ▭ mountains
Credit cards 1 2 3 5

TROUVILLE-SUR-MER
Calvados

★★★***Flaubert*** r G-Flaubert ☎31883723

Mar—15 Nov
rm33 (➡ ⋒ 26) Lift ☾
Credit cards 1 2 3 5

★★**Reynita** 29 r Carnot (n.rest) ☎31881513

Closed Jan
rm24 (➡ ⋒ 19) sB ➡ ⋒ 120 dB136—210 dB ➡ ⋒ 210
Credit cards 1 2 3 5

TROYES
Aube

★★★***Grand*** (Inter) 4 av Ml-Joffre (opp station) ☎25799090 tx840582

➡ 95 **P** Lift
Credit cards 1 2 3 5

★★**Fimotel** bd G-Pompidou ☎42615014 tx215269

➡ 42 **P** Lift
Credit cards 1 2 3 5

★★**Paris** (Inter) 54 r R-Salengro (n.rest) ☎25731170

rm27 (➡ ⋒ 13) ⌂ sB95—137 dB120 dB ➡ ⋒ 150—226

⛟ **Contant Autos** 15 bd Danton ☎25434819 Closed Sat & Sun Ren

At **BUCHÈRES** (6km SW)

★★**Campanile** Haut de Caurgerennes (RN71) ☎25496767 tx840840

➡ 42 **P** sB ➡ 217—238 dB ➡ 239—260 M61—82
Credit card 3

At ST-ANDRÉ-LES-VERGERS (4km SW)

⛟ **SARL Juszak** 37 rte d'Auxerre ☎25824655 Closed Sat pm & Sun AR

At **ST-JULIEN-LES-VILLAS** (2km SE)

⛟ **Sud Auto** 139 bd de Dijon ☎25820376 Closed Sat pm & Sun BMW

TROYES AIRPORT

At **BARBEREY** (6km NW on N19)

★★★***Novotel Troyes Aéroport*** (N19) ☎25745995 tx840759

➡ 84 **P** ⛱
Credit cards 1 2 3 5

TULLE
Corrèze

★★★**Limouzi** 19 quai République ☎55264200 tx590140

➡ 50 ⌂ **P** Lift ☾ sB ➡ 152—197 dB ➡ 194—249
Credit cards 1 2 3 5

ULIS (LES)
Essonne

★★**Campanile** ZA de Courtaboeuf ☎69286060 tx603094

➡ 50 **P** sB ➡ 217—238 dB ➡ 239—260 M61—82
Credit card 3

★★**Climat** av des Andes ☎64460506

➡ ⋒ 42

URY See **FONTAINEBLEAU**

UZERCHE
Corréze

★★**Ambroise** av de Paris ☎55731008

Closed Nov
➡ ⋒ 20 ⌂ **P**20 sB ➡ ⋒ 93 dB ➡ ⋒ 106—160 M43—110
Credit cards 1 3

★★**Teyssier** r Pont-Turgot ☎55731005

Mar—Nov
rm17 (➡ 10) ⌂ **P**25 sB98—113 sB ➡ 148—193 dB131—146 dB ➡ 181—216 M75—200
Credit card 3

⛟ **Renault** rte de Limoges ☎55731575 Ren

UZÈS
Gard

★**Provençale** 3 r Grande Bourgade ☎66221106

⋒ 10
Credit card 1

VAIRES-SUR-MARNE
Seine-et-Marne

⛟ **Central Service** 73 r de la Gare ☎60201518 All makes

VAISON-LA-ROMAINE
Vaucluse

★★**Beffroi (Pn)** r de l'Évêche ☎90340471

15 Mar—15 Nov & 15 Dec—5 Jan
rm21 (➡ ⋒ 14) A10rm **P**11 sB134—343 sB ➡ ⋒ 241—343 dB235—269 dB ➡ ⋒ 269—371 M86—125
Credit cards 1 2 3 5

★★**Logis de Château** LF (FAH) les Hauts de Vaison ☎90360998 tx431389

15 Mar—Oct
➡ 40 ⌂ **P** Lift dB ➡ 220—320 ⚲ ⛱

VAL-ANDRÉ (LE)
Côtes-du-Nord

★***Bains*** 7 pl Gl-de-Gaulle ☎96722011

20 May—20 Sep
rm26 **P**7 sea

VALBONNE
Alpes-Maritimes

★★★***Novotel Sophia Antipolis*** ☎93333800 tx970914

➡ 97 **P** Lift ⚲ ⛱ mountains

★★**Ibis Sophia Antipolis** r A-Caquot ☎93653060 tx461363

➡ 99 **P**80 Lift sB ➡ 235—265 dB ➡ 279—309 M60—100 mountains
Credit cards 1 2 3

VALDAHON
Doubs

★★**Relais de Franche Comté** LF (Inter) **(Pn)** ☎81562318

15 Jan—20 Dec
➡ 20 ⌂ **P**100 sB ➡ 162—180 dB ➡ 199—230 M48—170
Credit cards 1 2 3 5

VAL D'ISÈRE
Savoie

★★★★***Sofitel*** ☎79060830 tx980557

Dec—May & Jul & Aug
➡ 53 ⌂ **P** Lift ☾ ⛱ mountains
Credit cards 1 2 3 5

★★★**Aiglon** ☎79060405

Dec—5 May →

➜ ⌂ 21 sB ➜ ⌂ 328—418
dB ➜ ⌂ 406—446 M100—150 mountains

★★***Savoie*** ☎79060630
rm36 (➜ ⌂ 34) Lift mountains

★**Vieux Village** LF (**DPn** in season)
☎79060379
Dec—Apr & Jul—Aug
➜ 24 **P**10 sB ➜ 185 dB ➜ 290 M89
mountains

VALENÇAY
Indre

★★★***Espagne*** (Relais et Châteaux) 8 r du Château ☎54000002 tx751675
Mar—Nov
➜ 18 **P**

★★**Lion d'Or** pl Marché ☎54000087
Rest. closed Jan & Feb
rm15 (➜ ⌂ 8) **P**12 sB92—109
sB ➜ ⌂ 112—129 dB118—147
dB ➜ ⌂ 133—157 M48—135
Credit cards [1] [2] [3] [5]

VALENCE
Drôme

★★ ★**Novotel Valence Sud** 217 av de Provence (N7) ☎75422015 tx345823
➜ 107 **P**150 Lift sB ➜ 309 dB ➜ 366
Mfr68 &alc ≈
Credit cards [1] [2] [3] [5]

★★**Ibis** 355 av de Provence ☎75444254
tx345384
➜ 78 **P**78 Lift sB ➜ 202—232
dB ➜ 264—296 M50—120 ≈
Credit cards [1] [3]

★★**Park** (Inter) 22 r J Bouin (n.rest)
☎75433706
➜ ⌂ 21 🚗 sB ➜ ⌂ 163—190
dB ➜ ⌂ 195—254
Credit cards [2] [3] [5]

★★**Pic** (Relais et Châteaux) (**DPn**) 285 av V-Hugo ☎75441532
Closed Aug
➜ 4 🚗 **P**18 dB ➜ 430—680 M190—390 & alc
Credit cards [2] [5]

🚙 **Anayan** 170 r du Châteauvert
☎75441685 Cit

🚙 **Brun Valence Motors** 73 & 79 av de Verdun ☎75430791 Closed Sat pm & Sun Ope Vau

🚙 **Costechareyre** 31 av des Auréates
☎75440109 Closed 2 wks Sep, Sat pm & Sun All makes

J Jaurès 410 av de Chabeuil ☎75421266
Closed Sat pm & Sun Aud VW

🚙 **Minodier** rte de Beauvallon, ZI
☎75443124 Cit

🚙 **Royal** av de Provence ☎75421200
Closed Sat & Sun Mer

At **BOURG-LÈS-VALENCE** (1km N)

★★**Balladins** Montée du Long (RN7)
☎75560229 tx649394
➜ 36 🚗 **P**36 sB ➜ 166 dB ➜ 182 M56—77
Credit cards [1] [2] [3]

France

★★***Climat*** rte de Châteauneuf-sur-Isère (CD67) ☎75427746 tx692844
➜ 42 **P**

★★**Seyvet** LF (Inter) 24 av M-Urtin
☎75432651
Closed 7—26 Jan
➜ ⌂ 34 🚗 **P**35 Lift ☾ sB ➜ ⌂ 167—225
dB ➜ ⌂ 200—265 M58 mountains
Credit cards [1] [2] [3] [5]

At **PORTES-LÈS-VALENCE** (5km S)

🚙 **Pietri** r J-Jaurés ☎75570564 Closed Sat pm All makes

VALENCE-D'AGEN
Tarn-et-Garonne

★★**Tout-Va-Bien** 35—39 r de la République ☎63395483
Closed Jan
rm21 (➜ ⌂ 20) 🚗 sB78—129 sB ➜ ⌂ fr138
dB136—187 dB ➜ ⌂ fr186 M65—190
Credit card [2]

VALENCIENNES
Nord

★★★**Grand** (BW/Inter/MAP) 8 pl de la Gare ☎27463201 tx110701
➜ ⌂ 96 Lift ☾ sB ➜ ⌂ 244—319
dB ➜ ⌂ 264—321 M75—160
Credit cards [1] [2] [3] [5]

★★★**Novotel Valenciennes Ouest**
Autoroute Paris—Bruxelles, ZI No2
☎27442080 tx120970
➜ 75 **P** sB ➜ fr308 dB ➜ fr368 ≈
Credit cards [1] [2] [3] [5]

★★***Ibis*** Autoroute A2 (Valenciennes Ouest exit) ☎27445566 tx160737
➜ 65 **P** sB ➜ 183—214 dB ➜ 199—227
Credit cards [1] [2] [3] [4] [5]

VALETTE-DU-VAR (LA) See **TOULON**

VALLOIRE
Savoie

★★***Grand de Valloire et Galibier*** (Inter)
☎79643266 tx980553
15 Jun—15 Sep & 20 Dec—15 Apr
rm43 (➜ ⌂ 41) **P** Lift mountains

VALOGNES
Manche

★**Louvre** 28 r Réligieuses ☎33400007
5 Jan—Nov
rm20 (➜ ⌂ 6) 🚗 **P**10 sB74—89
sB ➜ ⌂ 104—154 dB97—117
dB ➜ ⌂ 127—167 M42—65

VALS-LES-BAINS
Ardèche

★★★**Vivarais** (BW/MAP) 5 r C-Expilly
☎75946585 tx345866
Jan—15 Nov
➜ ⌂ 40 **P** Lift ☾ sB ➜ ⌂ 234—324
dB ➜ ⌂ 298—368 M80—180
Credit cards [1] [2] [3] [5]

★★**Europe** LF (FAH) 86 r J-Jaurès
☎75374394 tx346256
rm35 (➜ ⌂ 29) 🚗 Lift dB160—205
dB ➜ ⌂ 230—260 M75—100
Credit cards [1] [2] [3] [5]

VAL-SUZON
Côte-d'Or

★★★**Hostellerie Val Suzon** (**DPn**) (N71)
☎80356015
Closed Jan
➜ ⌂ 8 A10rm sB ➜ ⌂ 205—235
dB ➜ ⌂ 260—300 M130 mountains
Credit cards [1] [2] [3] [5]

VANDOEUVRE-LES-NANCY See **NANCY**

VANNES
Morbihan

★★★**Marebaudière** 4 r A-Briand
☎97473429
6 Jan—19 Dec
➜ ⌂ 40 **P**60 sB ➜ ⌂ 220—250
dB ➜ ⌂ 275—305 M63—215
Credit cards [1] [2] [3] [5]

★★**Ibis** r E-Jourdan, ZI de Ménimur Est
☎97636111 tx950521
➜ 59 sB ➜ fr193 dB ➜ 237—253 Mfr66
Credit cards [1] [3]

★★**Image Ste-Anne** (FAH) 8 pl de la Libération ☎97367633 tx950352
Rest. closed Sun pm Oct—Mar
rm32 (➜ ⌂ 27) A4rm **P**12 Lift sB94—111
sB ➜ ⌂ 210—226
Credit cards [1] [3]

★**Marée Bleue** (**Pn**) 8 pl Bir-Hakeim
☎97472429
6 Jan—19 Dec
rm16 (⌂ 8) **P**60 sB103 sB⌂ 150 dB167
dB⌂ 167 M63—215
Credit cards [1] [2] [3] [5]

🚙 **Beauséjour** rte de Vannes ☎97418412
Closed Sun & Mon Ren

🚙 **Benelux** rte de Ste-Anne ☎97631376
Aud VW

🚙 **Poulichet** 13 r A-Briand ☎97474546
Closed Sat & Sun Tal

VARCES
Isère

★★***Escale*** (Relais et Châteaux) (**DPn**) pl de la République ☎76728019
Closed Jan
➜ 11 **P**10 ᑫ mountains
Credit cards [1] [2]

VARENGEVILLE-SUR-MER
Seine-Maritime

★★**Terrasse** LF (**DPn**) ☎35851254
Mar—Oct
rm28 (➜ ⌂ 18) **P**20 **DPn**fr115 Mfr55 ᑫ sea

VARENNES-VAUZELLES See **NEVERS**

VARETZ See **BRIVE-LA-GAILLARDE**

VATAN
Indre

🚙 **R Monière** av de la Libération
☎54497529 M/c Closed Sun Dat

VAUDREUIL (LES) See **LOUVIERS**

VAULX-EN-VELIN
Rhône

★★**Fimotel** 9 r N-Carmellino ☎78807226 tx305964

🛁 42 **P**20 Lift sB🛁 232—251 dB🛁 283—293 Mfr70
Credit cards [1] [2] [3] [5]

VENCE
Alpes-Maritimes

★★★★**Domaine St-Martin** (Relais et Châteaux) rte de Coursegoules ☎93580202 tx470282

Mar—Nov
🛁 13 A12rm 🅿 **P**25 ☾ dB🛁 1330—1780 M300—350 St% 🎾 ⛱ sea
Credit cards [1] [2] [3] [5]

★★**Diana** av Poilus (n.rest) ☎93582856

🛁 25 🅿 **P**25 Lift sB🛁 255—275 dB🛁 280—300 mountains
Credit cards [1] [2] [3] [5]

VENDIN-LE-VIEL See **LENS**

VENDÔME
Loir-et-Cher

★★**Vendôme** LF (FAH) 15 fbg Chartrain ☎54770288 tx750383

🛁🚿 35 🅿 Lift sB🛁🚿 210—300 dB🛁🚿 255—325 M70—210
Credit cards [1] [3]

VENIZY See **ST-FLORENTIN**

VERDUN
Meuse

🚗 **Capucins** 8 r L-Maury ☎29860453 Closed Jul or Aug & Sat Peu

🚗 **M Carré** 41 av de Paris ☎29862097 Dat Tal

🚗 **F Martin** 61 bis r du Coulmier ☎29841087 Closed Aug & Sat pm Fia For Mer

🚗 **M Rochette** r V-Schleiter ☎29865049 Closed Sun For

At **CHATTANCOURT** (14km NW on D38)

🚗 **M Riboizi** ☎29861513 Closed Mon am Ren

VERDUN-SUR-LE-DOUBS
Sâone-et-Loire

🚗 **M Geunot** av G-d'Estaing ☎8542517 Closed Mon Cit

VERETZ
Indre-et-Loire

★**St-Honoré** (**DPn**) ☎47503006

rm9 (🛁🚿 6) sB85—172 sB🛁🚿 172 dB97—184 dB🛁🚿 184 M52—155
Credit cards [1] [2] [3] [5]

VERNET-LES-BAINS
Pyrénées-Orientales

★★**Angleterre** (**DPn**) 9 av de Burnay ☎68055058

2 May—26 Oct
rm20 (🛁🚿 11) sB87 dB99—109 dB🛁🚿 139—149 Mfr70
Credit card [3]

VERNEUIL-SUR-AVRE
Eure

★★**Clos** (Relais et Châteaux) (**DPn**) 98 Ferté Vidame ☎32322181 tx172770

Feb—15 Dec
🛁🚿 11 🅿 **P**11 sB🛁🚿 420—490 dB🛁🚿 460—530 M150—300
Credit cards [1] [2] [3] [5]

★★**Saumon** LF (FAH) (**DPn**) 89 pl de la Madeleine ☎32320236 tx172770

rm20 (🛁🚿 16) A10rm sB99 sB🛁🚿 176—216 dB115 dB🛁🚿 192—232 M65—150
Credit cards [1] [3]

VERRIÈRES-LE-BUISSON
Essonne

★★**Climat** ZAC des Prés Houts, av G-Pompidou ☎69307070

🛁 38 **P**80 sB🛁 235 dB🛁 254 M68
Credit card [1]

VERSAILLES
Yvelines

★★★**Trianon Palace** 1 bd de la Reine ☎39503412 tx698863

rm130 (🛁🚿 124) **P**200 Lift ☾ sB🛁🚿 490—778 dB🛁🚿 670—1020 M162—220
Credit cards [1] [2] [3] [4] [5]

★★**Clagny** 6 Impasse Clagny (n.rest) ☎39501809

rm20 (🛁🚿 18) sB94 dB161 dB🛁🚿 180—203
Credit cards [1] [2]

★★**St-Louis** 28 r St-Louis (n.rest) ☎39502355 tx698958

🛁🚿 27 sB🛁🚿 136—176 dB🛁🚿 212—262

★★**Cheval Rouge** (**DPn**) 18 r A-Chenier ☎39500303

15 Jan—20 Dec
rm40 (🛁🚿 22) 🅿 **P**18 sB111—149 sB🛁🚿 184—194 dB159—167 dB🛁🚿 212—332 M69—85

VERT-ST-DENIS See **MELUN**

VERVINS
Aisne

★★★**Tour du Roy** (**DPn**) 45 r Gl-Leclerc ☎23980011 tx140542

Feb—15 Jan
🛁🚿 15 **P**15 sB🛁🚿 145—325 dB🛁🚿 250—400 M120—250 🎾
Credit cards [1] [2] [3] [4] [5]

★**Cheval Noir** 33 r de la Liberté ☎23980416

Closed Xmas & New Year
rm16 (🛁🚿 7) 🅿 **P** sB78—120 sB🛁🚿 108—120 dB136—140 dB🛁🚿 166—170 M50—90

VESOUL
Haute-Saône

★★**Nord** 7 r Aigle Noir ☎84750256

rm33 (🛁🚿 32) 🅿 **P** Lift ☾ sB🛁🚿 fr175 dBfr216 dB🛁🚿 fr216 M70—150

★★**Relais N19** (Inter) rte de Paris (N19) ☎84764242

12 Jan—21 Dec
🛁🚿 22 🅿 **P**40 sB🛁🚿 224—274 dB🛁🚿 268—308 M110—190
Credit cards [1] [2] [3] [5]

🚗 **Vesoul Auto Service** av Pasteur, Echenoz la Méline ☎84752801 Closed Sun All makes

VEURDRE (LE)
Allier

★★**Pont Neuf** LF (FAH) rte de Lurcy Lévis ☎70664012 tx392978

rm25 (🛁🚿 20) 🅿 **P**25 sB103 sB🛁🚿 172—182 dB120—144 dB🛁🚿 190—209 M65—140
Credit cards [1] [2] [3] [5]

VEYRIER-DU-LAC
Haute-Savoie

★**Auberge du Colvert** ☎50601023

Etr—15 Nov
🛁 10 **P** sB🛁 235—285 dB🛁 320—370 M150—300 lake mountains
Credit cards [1] [3]

VICHY
Allier

★★★***Albert-1er*** av P-Doumer (n.rest) ☎70318110

Etr—Nov
rm33 (🛁🚿 26) 🅿 **P** Lift ☾

★★★**Pavillion Sévigné** (BW/MAP) 10 pl Sévigné ☎70321622 tx990393

🛁🚿 40 **P** Lift sB🛁🚿 360—510 dB🛁🚿 460—680 M145—260
Credit cards [1] [2] [3] [5]

🚗 **St-Blaise** 2—6 rte de Lisbonne ☎70986371 Closed Sat pm & Sun AR

VIC-SUR-CÈRE
Cantal

★★**Beauséjour** LF av du Parc ☎71475027

15 May—Sep
rm75 (🛁🚿 64) A16rm **P**60 Lift sB85—117 sB🛁🚿 125—197 dB140—164 dB🛁🚿 150—234 M55—85 mountains
Credit card [1]

At **COL DE CUREBOURSE** (6km SE on D54)

★**Auberge des Monts** (**DPn**) ☎71475171

🛁🚿 30 🅿 **P**30 ☾ sB🛁🚿 fr160 dB🛁🚿 fr250 mountains
Credit card [1]

VIENNE
Isère

★★***Nord*** (Inter) 11 pl Miremont ☎74857711

🛁🚿 43 🅿 **P**22 Lift ☾
Credit cards [1] [2] [3] [5]

🚘 **Avignon** 20 av du Gl-Leclerc ☎74534825 Closed 15—30 Aug, Sat pm & Sun Alf AR Mer

🚘 **Fréty** rte du 11 Novembre ☎74531040 M/c Closed Sun All makes

🚘 **Ménender** le Péage du Vizille ☎74680541 Closed Sat am Peu

At **CHONAS-L'AMBALLAN** (9km S on N7)

★★**Relais 500 de Vienne** (N7) ☎74588144 tx380343
rm36 (🛁 🚿 34) ⌂ **P**100 sB 🛁 🚿 193—217 dB 🛁 🚿 210—239 M45—120 ≈
Credit cards [1] [2] [3] [5]

VILLARS
Loire

★★**Campanile** r de l'Artisanat ☎77935248 tx307101
🛁 41 **P** sB 🛁 217—238 dB 🛁 239—260 M61—82
Credit card [3]

VILLEDIEU-LES-POÊLES
Manche

★★**St-Pierre & St-Michel** LF (**DPn**) 12 pl de la République ☎33610011
20 Jan—25 Dec
rm24 (🛁 🚿 19) ⌂ **P**10 sB72—89 sB 🛁 🚿 114—206 dB91—103 dB 🛁 🚿 128—220 M40—100
Credit cards [1] [3]

VILLEFRANCHE-DU-PERIGORD
Dordogne

★★**Bruyères** LF ☎53299797
🛁 10 A4rm dB 🛁 186—220 M50—160
Credit cards [1] [3]

VILLEFRANCHE-SUR-MER
Alpes-Maritimes

★★★**Provençal** 4 av Ml-Joffre ☎93017142 tx970433
rm45 (🛁 🚿 42) Lift ☾ sB126—204 sB 🛁 🚿 176—204 dB141—219 dB 🛁 🚿 191—219 M60—85 sea
Credit cards [1] [2] [3] [4] [5]

★★★**Welcome** (BW/MAP) 1 quai Courbet ☎93552727 tx470281
Closed Nov—15 Dec
rm32 (🛁 28) ⌂ Lift sB 🛁 260—490 dB 🛁 260—550 sea
Credit cards [1] [2] [3] [5]

★★**Coq-Hardi** LF 8 bd de la Corne d'Or ☎93017106
Closed Nov
🛁 🚿 20 ⌂ **P** sB 🛁 🚿 215—245 dB 🛁 🚿 170—260 Mfr60 ≈ sea

VILLEFRANCHE-SUR-SAÔNE
Rhône

★★★**Plaisance** (FAH) 96 av de la Libération ☎74653352 tx375746
Closed Xmas & New Year
🛁 🚿 68 A6rm ⌂ **P**20 Lift sB 🛁 🚿 203—263 dB 🛁 🚿 236—301 M72—255
Credit cards [1] [2] [3] [5]

★★**Climat** rte de Riottier-le-Peace ☎74629955

France

🛁 43 **P**50 sB 🛁 236—256 dB 🛁 257—277 Mfr54
Credit cards [1] [3]

★★**Campanile** r G-Mangin 210 ☎74680758 tx310208
🛁 43 **P** sB 🛁 204—225 dB 🛁 226—247 M61—82
Credit card [3]

★★**Ecu de France** 35 r d'Anse ☎74683448
🚿 30 ⌂ **P**12 sB🚿 fr155 dB🚿 170—210
Credit cards [2] [3]

★**Ibis** Le Péage-Commune de Limas ☎74682223 tx370777
🛁 🚿 113 **P**130 Lift sB 🛁 🚿 186—190 dB 🛁 🚿 244—250 M55—80
Credit cards [1] [3]

Europe r Ampère ☎74655059 Closed Sat pm & Sun Aud VW

M Thivolle 695 av T-Braun ☎74652710 Closed Sat Cit

VILLENEUVE D'ASCQ See **ROUBAIX**

VILLENEUVE-DE-MARSAN
Landes

★**Europe** LF (**Pn**) 1 pl Foirai ☎58452008
rm15 (🛁 🚿 12) **P**15 sB125—175 sB 🛁 🚿 205 dB150—200 dB 🛁 🚿 230 M75—200 ≈
Credit card [3]

VILLENEUVE-DE-RIVIÈRE See **ST-GAUDENS**

VILLENEUVE-LÈS-AVIGNON
Gard

★★★**Magnanerale** 37 r Camp de Bataille ☎90251111
🛁 🚿 20 ⌂ **P**15 ☾ sB 🛁 🚿 282—482 dB 🛁 🚿 394—514 Mfr150 ⚲ ≈
Credit cards [1] [2] [3] [5]

★★★**Prieuré** 7 pl Chapitre ☎90251820 tx431042
Mar—Nov
🛁 35 **P**60 Lift ☾ sB 🛁 410—750 dB 🛁 750—1000 M180—220 ⚲ ≈
Credit cards [1] [2] [3] [5]

VILLENEUVE-LA-GARENNE See **PARIS**

VILLENEUVE-LOUBET-PLAGE See **CAGNES-SUR-MER**

VILLENEUVE-SUR-LOT
Lot-et-Garonne

★★★**Parc** (BW/MAP) 13 bd de la Marine ☎53700106 tx550379
🛁 🚿 46 ⌂ Lift ☾ sB 🛁 🚿 229—384 dB 🛁 🚿 289—445
Credit cards [1] [2] [3] [5]

★★***Prune d'Or*** pl de la Gare ☎5390050
rm17 (🛁 🚿 11) ⌂ **P**20
Credit cards [2] [3] [5]

VILLENEUVE-SUR-YONNE
Yonne

★**Dauphin** (**DPn**) 14 r Carnot ☎86871855
Seasonal
🛁 11 ⌂ **P**10 sB 🛁 147—229 dB 🛁 240—248

VILLERS-COTTERÉTS
Aisne

★★**Ibis** rte de Vivières (CD81) ☎23962680 tx145363
🛁 62 **P**100 sB 🛁 fr232 dB 🛁 fr274 M alc
Credit cards [1] [3]

VILLERS-LES-POTS See **AUXONNE**

VILLIERS-SEMEUSE See **CHARLEVILLE-MÉZIÈRES**

VILLERS-SUR-MER
Calvados

★★★**Bonne Auberge** LF (**DPn**) 1 r du Ml-Leclerc ☎31870464
15 Mar—3 Nov
🛁 🚿 24 **P**20 Lift dB 🛁 🚿 250—315

🚘 **Méridien** 13 r du Gl-Leclerc ☎31870213 Closed Wed in Winter Tal

VINAY See **ÉPERNAY**

VINCENNES See **PARIS**

VINEUIL See **BLOIS**

VIRE
Calvados

★★**Cheval Blanc** LF (FAH) 2 pl du 6 Juin 1944 ☎31680021 tx170428
Closed Fri & Sat Oct—May & Xmas
rm21 (🛁 11) A15rm sB117—165 sB 🛁 214—249 dB136—184 dB 🛁 233—268 M80—250
Credit cards [1] [2] [3] [5]

VIRONVAY See **LOUVIERS**

VIRY-CHÂTILLON
Essonne

★★***Climat*** r Octave-Longuet ☎69442121 tx612241
🛁 38 **P**

VITRAC
Dordogne

★**Plaisance** LF au Port (N703) ☎53283304
Feb—17 Nov
rm38 (🛁 🚿 35) **P**30 sB97—217 sB 🛁 🚿 127—217 dB144—234 dB 🛁 🚿 144—234 M50—160 ⚲
Credit cards [2] [3]

VITRÉ
Ille-et-Vilaine

★**Chêne Vert** (**DPn**) 2 pl du Gl-de-Gaulle ☎99750058
Closed 22 Sep—22 Oct & Sat
rm22 (🛁 🚿 8) ⌂ sB79 sB 🛁 🚿 126 dB116 dB 🛁 🚿 225 M52—150

VITROLLES See **MARSEILLE AIRPORT**

VITRY-LE-FRANÇOIS
Marne

★**Bon Séjour** 4 fbg L-Bourgeois ☎26740236

rm25 (🛁3) A15rm 🚗 **P** sB88 sB 🛁 108 dB106 dB 🛁 126 M40 🔧

★**Cloche** 34 r A-Briand ☎26740384

rm24 (🛁🚿11) 🚗 **P**16 sB66—140 sB 🛁🚿168—210 dB175—189 dB 🛁🚿226—230 M73—84 Credit cards 1 3

★**Nancy** 22 Grand Rue de Vaux ☎26740937

rm14 (🛁🚿7) 🚗 sBfr87 sB 🛁🚿139—168 dB197 dB 🛁🚿149—185 M47—67

VIZILLE
Isère

★***Parc*** 25 av A-Briand ☎76680301

rm24 (🛁🚿16) **P**4 mountains Credit cards 2 3

VOGELGRUN See **NEUF-BRISACH**

VOREPPE See **GRENOBLE**

VOUVRAY
Indre-et-Loire

★**Grand Vatel** LF **(Pn)** av Brûlé ☎47527032

Jan—Nov
🛁🚿7 🚗 sB 🛁🚿170 dB 🛁🚿215—220 M98—175 Credit cards 2 3

WALHEIM See **ALTKIRCH**

Monaco

WAST (LE)
Pas-de-Calais

★★**Château de Tourelles** ☎21333478

Closed Jan
🛁16 **P** sB 🛁159—242 dB 🛁218—288 Mfr70

WIMEREUX
Pas-de-Calais

★★**Atlantic** Digue le Mer ☎21324101

Closed Feb
rm11 (🛁🚿10) 🚗 **P**16 Lift sB185—245 sB 🛁🚿225—265 dB270—290 dB 🛁🚿270—290 Mfr165 sea

★★**Paul et Virginie** 19 r Gl-de-Gaulle ☎21324212

20 Jan—21 Dec
rm18 (🛁🚿16) sB 🛁🚿164 dB 🛁🚿183—263 Mfr65

★**Centre** 78 r Carnot ☎21324108

rm25 (🛁🚿18) 🚗 **P**20 sBfr106 sB 🛁🚿146 dBfr142 dB 🛁🚿201 M60—120 & alc Credit cards 1 3

WITTENHEIM See **MULHOUSE**

WOIPPY See **METZ**

YENNE
Savoie

★**Logis Savoyard** pl C-Dullin ☎79367038

rm13 A4rm 🚗 **P**3 sB81 dB94 Mfr43

YFFINIAC See **ST-BRIEUC**

Monaco

Prices are in French Francs.

MONTE CARLO

★★★★★***Paris*** pl du Casino ☎93508080 tx469925

🛁300 **P** Lift ☾ 🔧 Pool ⊡ sea

★★★★**Hermitage** sq Beaumarchais ☎93506731 tx479432

🛁260 **P**30 Lift ☾ sB 🛁675—1275 dB 🛁900—1550 M215 S15% ⊡ sea Credit cards 1 2 4 5

★★★**Alexandra** 35 bd Princesse Charlotte (n.rest) ☎93506313 tx489286

rm55 (🛁🚿49) Lift sB188 sB 🛁🚿354 dB263 dB 🛁🚿418—454 Credit cards 2 3 5

🔧 **Bristol** 48 r Grimaldi ☎93300376 Closed Sat pm & Sun BMW

At **MONTE-CARLO BEACH**

★★★★**Beach** ☎93309880 tx479617

🛁🚿313 **P**120 Lift ☾ sB 🛁🚿475—1080 dB 🛁🚿620—1135 ⛱ Beach sea mountains
Credit cards 1 2 3 5

Germany

International distinguishing sign

Area (Federal Republic)
95,965 sq miles
Population
61,400,000
Local time *GMT + 1 (Summer GMT + 2)*

National flag *Horizontal stripes of even width starting from top, black, red and gold*

How to get there

If you use one of the short-crossing Channel ferries and travel via Belgium, the German Federal Republic is just within a day's drive. The distance from Calais to Köln (Cologne) is just under 260 miles.

By driving through northern France and entering Germany near Strasbourg, the journey usually takes two days. This entry point is also used if travelling by the longer Channel crossings: Cherbourg, Caen, Dieppe or Le Havre to southern Germany. The distance from Le Havre to Strasbourg is 425 miles, a journey which will take at least one or two days. The longer crossing ferries operating across the North Sea to the Netherlands can be an advantage if visiting northern Germany. Alternatively, it is possible to use the ferry operating between Harwich and Hamburg.

Motoring regulations and general information

This information should be read in conjunction with the general content of the European ABC (pages 4-26). **Note** As certain regulations and requirements are common to many countries they are covered by one entry in the ABC and the following headings represent some of the subjects dealt with in this way:

AA Agents
Crash or safety helmets
Customs regulations for European countries
Drinking and driving
Fire extinguisher
First-aid kit
Insurance
International distinguishing sign
Medical treatment
Mirrors
Overtaking
Police fines
Radio telephones/Radio transmitters
Seat belts
Tyres
Visitors' registration

Accidents

Dial 112 for **fire,** 110 **police** and **ambulance** in most areas.

You are generally required to call the police when individuals have been injured or considerable damage has been caused. Not to give aid to anyone injured will render you liable to a fine. Callboxes with two luminous red stripes contain an emergency telephone which can be used without inserting money. By lifting the receiver and pulling the emergency lever you are automatically connected with fire or police. See also *Accidents* page 5.

Accommodation

There is a good selection of hotels, many of which are listed in the official Hotel Guide. This is obtainable from the Tourist Office in London, which can also provide details of accommodation in castles and stately homes. Regional and local tourist organisations also have details of inns and boarding houses.

For a nominal charge, tourist information offices will usually assist in finding hotel accommodation (see page 205). Enquiries by post should be accompanied by an international reply coupon (obtainable from the post office).

There is also a reservations service operated by the ADZ (Allgemeine Deutsche Zimmer-reservierung). This organisation will make instantly confirmed bookings at hotels throughout the country. Full information about this service, including details of the hotels concerned, may be obtained from ADZ, Beethovenstrasse 61, 6000 Frankfurt/Main 1 ☏ (069)740767; tx416666. Reduced prices apply to children under ten years of age sharing a room with their parents. Reservations are not normally held after 18.00hrs.

Automatic hotel reservation facilities are available in Frankfurt at the airport, the main railway station and at the ADAC office, Frankfurt West, by the Wiesbaden-Frankfurt autobahn.

Berlin

Documents required for travel through the German Democratic Republic to West Berlin.

Be sure you have a valid standard passport (children over 16 years of age must have a separate passport), national driving licence and vehicle registration document. The Green Card is now accepted, but make sure that it covers you for the GDR (DDR) before you depart from the United Kingdom. Third party insurance can be arranged at the border crossings. Transit visas for journeys to West Berlin can be obtained at the frontier crossings at a cost of *DM*5 per person (each way). Tourists travelling directly between the German Federal Republic and West Berlin are exempt from paying road tax.

Customs crossings The main frontier Customs Houses between the German Federal Republic and the German Democratic Republic officially open for transit from the Federal Republic to West Berlin are listed below. The names printed in italics are within the GDR (DDR), the others outside it.

Frankfurt *Wartha*; Herleshausen
Hamburg *Zarrentin*; Gudow
Hannover *Marienborn*; Helmstedt
München *Hirschberg*; Saalebrücke; Rudolphstein

Hours: Crossings are open day and night.

Entry to West Berlin is possible at Drewitz/Dreilinden on the routes from Frankfurt, Hannover and Munich and at Staaken on the route from Hamburg.

Entry to East Berlin for day visits from West Berlin is at Kochstrasse (Checkpoint Charlie) and Friedrichstrasse. There are no restrictions for tourists of non-German nationality who wish to make a day trip from West to East Berlin, but make sure that this is mentioned on the insurance policy. A minimum exchange (25 marks) of local currency is necessary. Entry visa for a day trip to East Berlin is *DM*5 per person.

A booklet entitled *Motoring in Eastern Europe* is available to AA members.

Boats

Boat registration documentation is recommended in respect of boats temporarily imported into the German Federal Republic. See page 6 for further information.

Breakdown

If your car breaks down, try to move it to the verge of the road so that it does not obstruct traffic flow. A warning triangle must be placed to the rear of the vehicle and hazard warning lights, if fitted to the vehicle, must be used. See also *Breakdown* page 6 and *Warning triangle* page 205.

The ADAC operates a breakdown service, similar to that run by the AA, called the *Strassenwacht*. Patrol cars operate on motorways, on the more important roads and in urban areas. On motorways, patrols are notified by the Motorway Authorities, whom you can contact by using the emergency telephones. The direction of the nearest telephone is indicated by the point of the black triangle on posts alongside the motorways.

In addition, the Deutscher Touring Automobil Club (DTC), with which the AA is allied, also has a patrol service. The Automobil Club of Germany (AvD) and the Auto Club Europa (ACE) operate patrol services, but the AA is not associated with these clubs and details are not available.

British Army of the Rhine (BAOR)

Service personnel posted to Germany should consult their Standing Orders or Commanding Officer before taking a car to Germany or using it there. Although enjoying some privileges they will be regarded to some extent as residents in the country and tourist regulations (as outlined in this section) may not apply. For example, a tourist can use a warning triangle not strictly to the German regulations, but a service man will break local regulations unless his conforms.

A leaflet entitled *'Importation of Motor Vehicles into Germany by Members of the British Forces'* is available to AA members.

British Embassy/Consulates

(See also page 6)

The British Embassy is located at *5300 Bonn 1* Friedrich-Ebert-Allee 77 ☏ (0228)234061, but the Embassy has no consular section. There are British Consulates in Berlin, Dusseldorf,

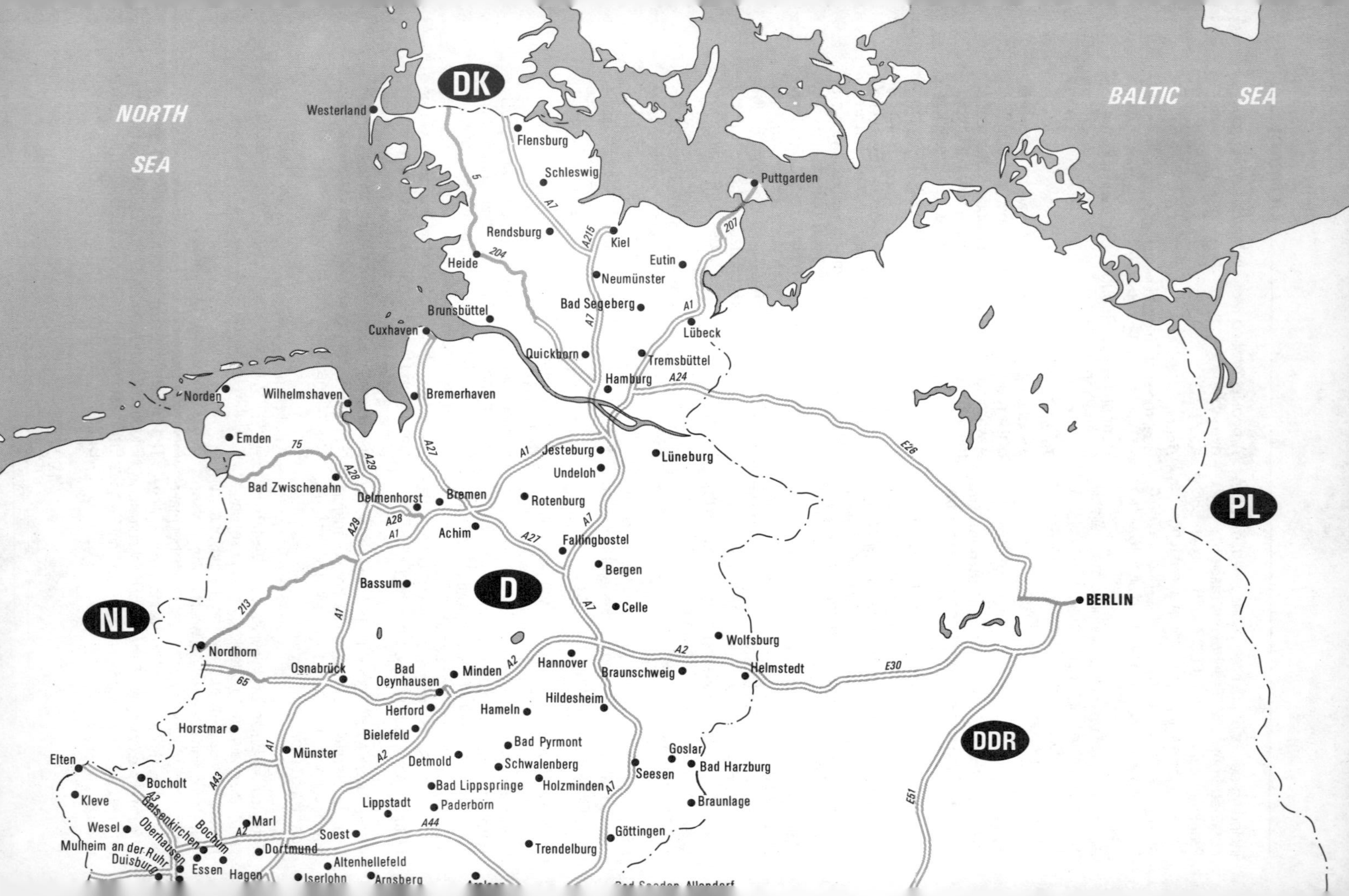
NORTH SEA
BALTIC SEA
DK
PL
D
NL
DDR
Westerland
Flensburg
Schleswig
Rendsburg
Kiel
Heide
Eutin
Neumünster
Bad Segeberg
Puttgarden
Brunsbüttel
Cuxhaven
Quickborn
Lübeck
Tremsbüttel
Hamburg
Norden
Wilhelmshaven
Bremerhaven
Emden
Bad Zwischenahn
Delmenhorst
Bremen
Jesteburg
Undeloh
Lüneburg
Rotenburg
Achim
Fallingbostel
Bergen
Bassum
Celle
BERLIN
Wolfsburg
Nordhorn
Osnabrück
Bad Oeynhausen
Minden
Hannover
Braunschweig
Helmstedt
Herford
Hameln
Hildesheim
Horstmar
Bielefeld
Bad Pyrmont
Münster
Detmold
Schwalenberg
Goslar
Bad Harzburg
Seesen
Elten
Bocholt
Bad Lippspringe
Holzminden
Kleve
Lippstadt
Paderborn
Braunlage
Marl
Wesel
Gelsenkirchen
Oberhausen
Bochum
Soest
Mulheim an der Ruhr
Duisburg
Dortmund
Göttingen
Trendelburg
Essen
Hagen
Altenhellefeld
Iserlohn
Arnsberg
5
A7
A215
207
204
A1
A24
A27
A29
A28
75
A2
E26
E30
E51
213
65
A43
A3
A44

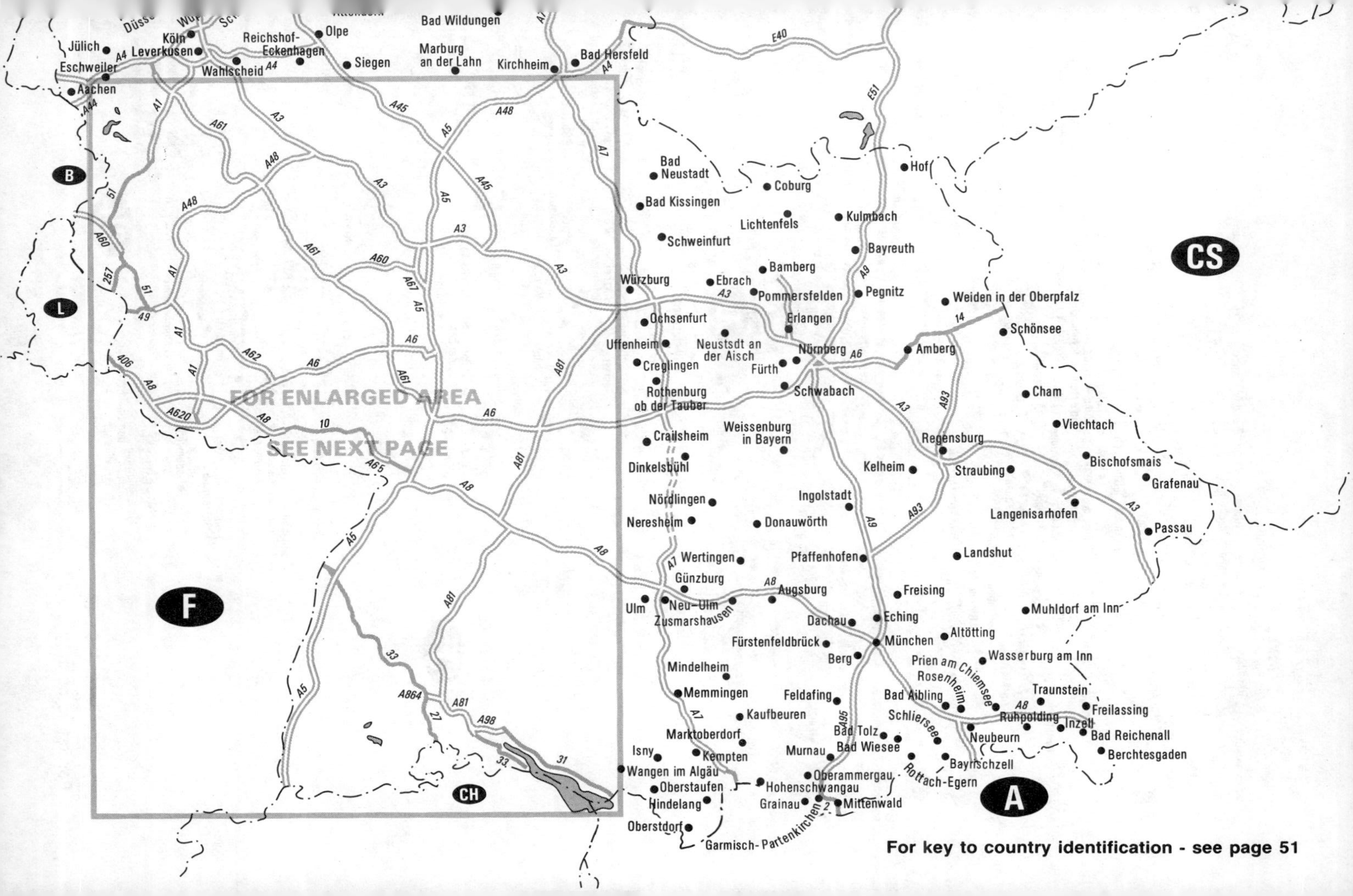
FOR ENLARGED AREA
SEE NEXT PAGE
CS
F
A
CH
B
L
Jülich
Köln
Leverkusen
Eschweiler
Aachen
Reichshof-Eckenhagen
Wahlscheid
Olpe
Siegen
Bad Wildungen
Marburg an der Lahn
Kirchheim
Bad Hersfeld
Hof
Bad Neustadt
Coburg
Bad Kissingen
Lichtenfels
Kulmbach
Schweinfurt
Bayreuth
Bamberg
Würzburg
Ebrach
Pommersfelden
Pegnitz
Weiden in der Oberpfalz
Ochsenfurt
Erlangen
Schönsee
Uffenheim
Neustsdt an der Aisch
Nürnberg
Amberg
Creglingen
Fürth
Rothenburg ob der Tauber
Schwabach
Cham
Viechtach
Crailsheim
Weissenburg in Bayern
Regensburg
Bischofsmais
Dinkelsbühl
Kelheim
Straubing
Grafenau
Nördlingen
Ingolstadt
Langenisarhofen
Neresheim
Donauwörth
Passau
Wertingen
Pfaffenhofen
Landshut
Günzburg
Augsburg
Freising
Ulm
Neu-Ulm
Zusmarshausen
Muhldorf am Inn
Dachau
Eching
Fürstenfeldbrück
München
Altötting
Berg
Prien am Chiemsee
Wasserburg am Inn
Mindelheim
Rosenheim
Traunstein
Memmingen
Feldafing
Bad Aibling
Freilassing
Kaufbeuren
Schliersee
Ruhpolding
Inzell
Marktoberdorf
Bad Tolz
Neubeurn
Bad Reichenall
Isny
Kempten
Murnau
Bad Wiesee
Berchtesgaden
Bayrischzell
Wangen im Algäu
Oberammergau
Rottach-Egern
Oberstaufen
Hohenschwangau
Hindelang
Grainau
Mittenwald
Oberstdorf
Garmisch-Partenkirchen
E40
E51
A1
A3
A4
A5
A6
A7
A8
A9
A44
A45
A48
A60
A61
A62
A65
A67
A81
A93
A95
A98
A620
A864
10
14
27
31
33
49
51
257
406
For key to country identification - see page 51

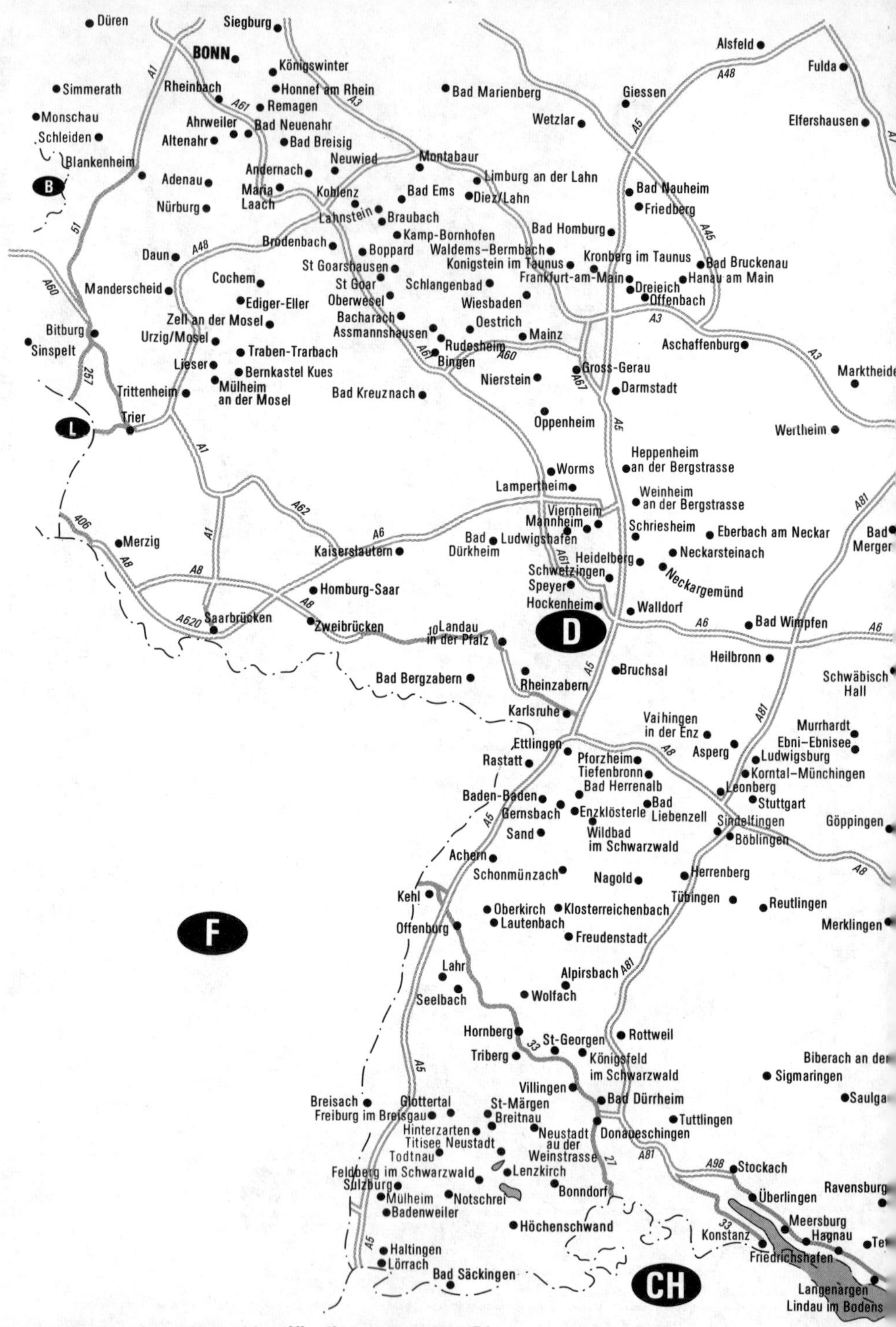

For key to country identification - see page 51

Frankfurt/Main, Hamburg and Munich; there are British Consulates with Honorary Consuls in Bremen, Frieburg, Hanover, Nurembourg and Stuttgart.

Currency including banking hours

(See also page 9)
The unit of currency is the Deutsche Mark (*DM*) divided into 100 *Pfennigs*.. At the time of going to press £ = *DM*3.04. Denominations of bank notes are *DM* 5, 10, 20, 100, 500, 1,000; standard coins are *DM* 1, 2, 5 and *Pfennigs* 1, 2, 5, 10, 50. There are no restrictions on the amount of foreign or Germany currency that a bona fide tourist may import or export.

Most banks are open from Monday to Wednesday and Friday 08.30-12.00hrs and 14.00-15.30hrs and Thursday 08.30-12.00hrs and 14.00-17.30hrs; closed on Saturdays. Exchange offices of the Deutsche-Verkehrs-Kredit-Bank are located at main railway stations, and road and rail frontier crossing points. Generally they are open from early morning until late at night.

Dimensions and weight restrictions

Private **cars** and **trailers** or **caravans** are restricted to the following dimensions — height: 4 metres; width: 2.50 metres; length: 12 metres. The maximum permitted overall length of vehicle/trailer or caravan combination is 18 metres.

A fully-laden trailer without an adequate braking system must not weigh more than 50% of the towing vehicle. A fully-laden trailer with an adequate braking system must not weigh more than the towing vehicle.

Driving licence

(See also page 11)
A valid British driving licence is acceptable in the German Federal Republic. The minimum age at which a visitor may drive a temporarily imported car or motorcycle is 17 years.

Emergency messages to tourists

(See also page 11)
Emergency messages to tourists are broadcast daily on German Radio.

Deutschlandfunk transmitting on 396.8 metres medium wave broadcasts these messages in German after the news at 16.00 and 23.00hrs between May and September.

Saarländischer Rundfunk transmitting on 211 metres medium wave broadcasts the messages in German at 05.00 and 01.00hrs throughout the year.

Emergency messages are also broadcast by a variety of regional radio stations transmitting on ultra short wavelengths.

Lights

(See also page 14)
Driving on sidelights only is prohibited. When fog, falling snow, or rain substantially affect driving conditions, dipped headlights or fog lamps should be used even during daylight. The use of two fog lamps together with dipped headlamps in such conditions is required by law. However, rear fog lights may only be used when visibility is less than 50 metres (55yds).

Motoring clubs

The principal German motoring clubs are the **Allgemeiner Deutscher Automobil Club** (ADAC) which has its headquarters at *8000 München 70* Am Westpark 8, ☎ (089)76760 and the **Deutscher Touring Automobil Club** (DTC) whose headquarters are at *8000 München 60* Amalienburgstrasse 23 ☎ (089)8111048. Both clubs have offices in the larger towns and office hours are from 08.00-17.00hrs Mon-Fri. The ADAC also has offices at major frontier crossings. See also page 16 and *Town Plan of Central München* pages 226-227.

Motorways

A comprehensive motorway (Autobahn) network dominates the road system and takes most of the long distance traffic. It is considered negligent to run out of petrol on a motorway and the police can fine offending motorists up to *DM*60.

Orange badge scheme for disabled drivers

(See also page 16)
In the German Federal Republic special parking places reserved for disabled drivers are indicated by parking sign (white letter on blue panel) with international disabled symbol added. Provided no other parking facilities are available within the immediate vicinity badge holders may:
a park for a maximum of three hours where parking prohibited sign (red ring and bars on blue background) is displayed. The time of arrival must be shown on the parking disc;

b park beyond the permitted time where a limited duration zone sign (white panel, red ring and diagonal bar on blue background) is displayed;
c park beyond the permitted time where a parking sign (white letter on blue panel) is displayed with an additional panel restricting parking time;
d park during the permitted periods for loading and unloading in pedestrian zones;
e park without charge or time limit at parking meters.

Parking

(See also page 17)
When parking make sure you do not contravene regulations and park in the direction of the traffic flow. Parking is forbidden in the following places: on a main road or one carrying fast-moving traffic; on or near tram lines; within 15 metres (49ft) of a bus or tram stop; above man-hole covers; on the left hand side of the road (unless the road is one-way). A vehicle is considered to be parked if the driver has left it so that it cannot be immediately removed if required or if it is stopped for more than 3 minutes. When stopping is prohibited under all circumstances, this is indicated by an international sign. Parking meters and special areas where parking discs are used, are indicated by signs which also show the permitted duration of parking. Disabled drivers may be granted special parking concessions; application should be made to the local traffic authority. Spending the night in a vehicle is tolerated for one night, provided there are no signs to the contrary and the vehicle is lit and parked in a lay-by. The sign showing an eagle in a green triangle (wild-life reserve) prohibits parking outside parking lots.

Passengers

(See also page 18)
Children under 12 are not permitted to travel in a vehicle as front seat passengers when rear seating is available.

Petrol

(See also page 18)
Credit cards Few petrol stations will accept credit cards.
Duty-free petrol In addition to the petrol in the vehicle tank up to 10 litres in a can may be imported free of customs duty and tax.
Petrol (leaded) Normal benzin (91 octane) and Super benzin (98 octane) grades.
Petrol (unleaded) is sold in Germany as the Normal benzin (91 octane) and Super benzin (95 octane) grades. These octane ratings are not indicated on the pumps, but in most cases the pumps dispensing unleaded petrol are marked *bleifrei* (lead free).

Postal information

Mail Postcards *DM*0.70, letters up to 20gm *DM*1.00.
Post offices There are 15,000 post offices in the German Federal Republic. Opening hours are from 08.00-18.00hrs Monday to Friday and 08.00-14.00hrs Saturday. In some large towns the Head Post Office is open 24hrs a day. Some small offices close for a break at noon.

Postcheques

(See also page 20)
Postcheques may be cashed at all post offices for any amount up to a maximum of *DM*250 per cheque. Counter positions are identified by the words *Auskunft, Auszahlungen* or *Post giro checks*. See *Postal information* for post office opening hours.

Priority

On pedestrian crossings (zebra crossings) pedestrians have the right of way over all vehicles except trams. Buses have priority when leaving public bus stops and other vehicles must give way to a bus driver who has signalled his intention to leave the kerb. See also *Priority including Roundabouts* page 21.

Public holidays

Official public holidays in the German Federal Republic for 1987 are given below. Epiphany, Corpus Christi, Assumption and All Saints Day are not holidays throughout the Federal Republic. See also *Public holidays* page 21.
January 1 (New Year's Day)
January 6 (Epiphany)
April 17 (Good Friday)
April 20 (Easter Monday)
May 1 (May Day)
May 28 (Ascension Day)
June 8 (Whit Monday)
June 17 (Berlin Day)
June 18 (Corpus Christi)
August 15* (Assumption)
November 1† (All Saints Day)
November 18 (Repentance Day)
December 25 (Christmas Day)
December 26* (Second day of Christmas)

*Saturday †Sunday

Roads including holiday traffic

The *Bundesstrassen* or state roads vary in quality.

In the north and in the touring areas of the Rhine Valley, Black Forest and Bavaria the roads are good and well graded.

Traffic at weekends increases considerably during the school holidays which are from July to mid September. In order to ease congestion, heavy lorries are prohibited on all roads at weekends from approximately mid June to the end of August and generally on all Sundays and public holidays. See also *Road conditions* page 22.

Road signs

(See also page 22)
A blue rectangular sign with, for example, '70/110km' in white — indicates a recommended speed range.

A blue rectangular sign with a white arrow pointing upwards and 'U' and a figure in white — indicates a diversion for motorway traffic.

Shopping hours

Generally these are: *food shops* from Monday to Friday 07.00-13.00/14.00-18.30hrs, Saturdays 07.00-13.00hrs; *department stores* from Monday to Friday 09.00-18.00hrs, Saturdays 09.00-14.00hrs. Some shops close for lunch between 13.00 and 15.00hrs.

Speed limits

(See also page 22)
The speed limit in built-up areas is 50kph (31mph) unless otherwise indicated by signs. The beginning of a built-up area is indicated by the placename sign. Outside built-up areas the limit for private cars is 100kph (62mph) unless otherwise signposted. Motorways (*Autobahnen*), dual carriageways and roads with at least two marked lanes in each direction, which are not specifically signposted have a recommended speed limit of 130kph (81mph). Vehicles towing a caravan or trailer are limited to 80kph (49mph). All lower limits must be adhered to. Anyone driving so slowly that a line of vehicles has formed behind him must permit the following vehicles to pass. If necessary he must stop at a suitable place to allow this.

Note Outside built-up areas, motor vehicles to which a special speed limit applies, as well as vehicles with trailers with a combined length of more than 7 metres (23ft), must keep sufficient distance from the preceding vehicle so that an overtaking vehicle may pull in.

Spiked or studded tyres

The use of *spiked tyres* is not permitted on German registered vehicles. However, foreign registered vehicles may use them in a restricted zone near the German/Austrian border, but only on ordinary roads not motorways. See also *Cold weather touring* page 8.

Tourist information

(See also page 24)
The UK office of the German National Tourist Office is in London at 61 Conduit Street, W1R 0EN ☏ 01-734 2600 (recorded message service Monday to Friday 10.00-13.00hrs and 14.00-17.00hrs). In the Federal Republic there are regional tourist associations — (DFV) whilst in most towns there are local tourist offices, usually situated near the railway station or town hall. Any of these organisations will be pleased to help tourists with information and hotel and other accommodation. The offices are usually open from 08.30 to 18.00hrs but in larger towns until 20.00hrs.

Traffic lights

(See also page 24)
At some intersections with several lanes going in different directions, there are lights for each lane; watch the light arrow for your lane.

Using the telephone

(See also page 24)
Insert coin **after** lifting receiver, dialling tone continuous tone. When making calls to subscribers within the German Federal Republic precede number with relevant area code (shown in parentheses against town entry in gazetteer). Use three 10 Pfennig coins (two in some callboxes) for local calls and *DM*1 or 5 coins for national and international calls.
International callbox identification Green sign.
Telephone rates Charges are based on units of time, 1 unit = 10.667 seconds, the cost is *DM*0.23. Many hotels and garages provide, as a service, direct line telephones but charges are likely to be up to double the public rate.
What to dial for the Irish Republic 00 353.
What to dial for the UK 00 44.

Warning triangle

The use of a warning triangle is compulsory for all vehicles except two-wheelers. The triangle must be placed on the road behind the vehicle to warn following traffic of any obstruction, 100 metres (109yds) on ordinary roads and 200 metres (219yds) on motorways. Vehicles over 2,500kg (2 tons 9cwt 24lbs) must also carry a yellow flashing light.

Although the warning triangle sold by the AA does not correspond exactly to the type prescribed for Germany, it is legally acceptable for use by *bona fide* tourists. See also *Warning triangles/Hazard warning lights* page 25.

Wheel chains

These must not be used on snow free roads. In winter months the ADAC hires out chains for cars and caravans. Chains can only be returned to ADAC offices and only during the hours of opening. On production of a valid AA membership card, chains may be hired at the following reduced charges.

Deposit	*members (DM)*	*non-members (DM)*
Matic	100	100

Hire charge per day (days of collection and return are both counted as whole days)

	members (DM)	*non-members (DM)*
Matic	5.00	7.00

If the chains are used a fee of *DM*10.00 (members) and *DM*20.00 (non-members) is payable. If chains are lost or damaged, or their wear exceeds the normal, the full selling price is charged. If the deposit receipt is lost, the chains can be returned only to the station from which they were hired.

Chains are considered to have been used if the seal on the packaging has been removed in which case the hire charge is calculated on the basis of the fees for used chains for the whole period of hire, irrespective of the actual number of days in use. The maximum period of hire is 60 days. Reservations are not possible and the ADAC does not dispatch the chains by post. Chains are made in several sizes, but as foreign-made tyres may be different, it is not guaranteed that the appropriate size will be available; in this case alternative arrangements must be made. Further details may be obtained from the ADAC Head Office, department 'Strassendienste Schneekettenverleih', 8 München 70, Am Westpark 8 ☎ (089)76760. (No wheel chains are actually hired out from head office.) Speed must be restricted by 50kph (31mph) when using chains. See also *Cold weather touring* page 8.

Prices are in German Marks (Deutschmarks)
Abbreviations:
pl platz
str strasse

AACHEN
Nordrhein-Westfalen (☎0241)

★★★★**Quellenhof** (SRS) Monheimsallee 52 ☎152081 tx832864
➡200 ⌂ **P**50 Lift ☾ sB➡155–225 dB➡238–308
Credit cards [1] [2] [3] [5]

★★★***Novotel*** am Europapl ☎164091 tx832435
➡119 **P**170 Lift ☾ ⩊
Credit cards [1] [2] [3] [4] [5]

★★**Benelux** Franzstr 21–23 ☎22343
➡fh30 ⌂ **P**15 Lift ☾ sB➡fh fr98 dB➡fh 120–160
Credit cards [1] [2] [3] [5]

★★**Brabant** Stolberger Str 42 ☎500025
rm24 (fh 17) ⌂ **P**12 Lift ☾ sBfr57 sBfh 67–92 dBfr94 dBfh 104–124 M9–28

★★**Buschhausen** Adenauerallee 215 ☎63071 tx832897
➡fh83 ⌂ **P** Lift sB➡fh 68–125 dB➡fh 98–175 M15–30 ▭
Credit cards [1] [2] [3] [5]

★★**Marschiertor** Wallstr 1–7 (n.rest) ☎31941
2 Jan–23 Dec
rm45 (➡fh 40) **P**30 Lift ☾ sB➡fh 66–94 dB88–92 dB➡fh 125–135
Credit cards [2] [3] [4] [5]

★★**Stadt Koblenz** Leydelstr 2 (n.rest) ☎22241
10 Jan–20 Dec
fh 16 ☾ sBfh 95–110 dBfh 135
Credit cards [2] [3]

★**Braun** Lütticher Str 517 ☎74535
rm13 (➡fh 6) ⌂ **P**15 sB46 sB➡fh 57 dB77 dB➡fh 89 M9–25

★***Lousberg*** Saarstr 108 ☎20332
rm26 (fh 10) ⌂ **P** Lift

⛟ **Kuckartz** Dresdener Str 20 ☎503083 M/c **P** Ren

ACHERN
Baden-Württemberg (☎07841)

★★★**Götz Sonne-Eintracht** Hauptstr 112 ☎6450 tx752277
➡fh 55 **P**50 Lift ☾ sB➡fh 82–133 dB➡fh 123–225 M18–45 ▭ mountains
Credit cards [1] [2] [3] [5]

★★★**Seehotel** ☎3011 tx752240
Jan–Nov
rm58 (➡fh 57) ⌂ **P**100 Lift ☾ sB➡fh 66–76 dB➡fh 108–128 ⩊ lake
Credit cards [1] [2] [3] [4] [5]

ACHIM
Niedersachsen (☎04202)

At **ACHIM-UPHUSEN** (5.5km NW)

★★★**Novotel Bremer Kreuz** zum Klümoor ☎6086 tx249440
➡116 **P**130 Lift ☾ sB➡97–130 dB➡117–153 Malc ⩊
Credit cards [1] [2] [3] [5]

ADENAU
Rheinland-Pfalz (☎02691)

★***Wilden Schwein*** Haupstr 117 ☎2055
fh 18 ⌂ **P**

AHRWEILER
Rheinland-Pfalz (☎02641)

★**Stern** Marktpl 9 ☎34738
Seasonal
rm16 (fh 3) **P** sB34–35 sBfh 55–60 dB60–70 dBfh 90 M14–17

AIBLING (BAD)
Bayern (☎08061)

★★**Lindner** Marienpl 5 ☎4050
rm32 (➡fh 22) ⌂ **P**18 Lift sB50 sB➡fh 60–70 dB90–100 dB➡fh 120–140 M9–29
Credit cards [1] [2] [5]

★★**Schuhbräu** Rosenheimer Str 6–8 ☎2020
rm58 (➡37) **P**40 Lift sB58–72 sB➡81–99 dB105–143 dB➡129–187 M10–30 S12% t14% ▭ mountains
Credit cards [1] [2] [5]

ALPIRSBACH
Baden-Württemberg (☎07444)

⛟ **K Jautz** Haupstr 29 ☎2345 For

At **EHLENBOGEN** (4km N)

★★**Adler** Hauptstr 1 ☎2215
rm21 (fh 9) ⌂ **P**20 sB30–33 sBfh 33–36

dB60 dB🚿66—76 M5—20 U
Credit cards [1] [2] [4] [5]

ALSFELD
Hessen (☎06631)

★**Schwalbennest** Pfarrniesenweg 14 ☎5061
🚿31 🅿︎ **P**

🚘 ***Hartman*** Hersfelder Str 81 ☎4044 Ope

ALTENAHR
Rheinland-Pfalz (☎02643)

★★**Post** Brückenstr 2 ☎2098
rm55 (🛁 🚿38) 🅿︎ **P**20 Lift ☾ sB30—35 sB🛁 🚿45—55 dB60—70 dB🛁 🚿80—105 M10—24 📺 mountains
Credit cards [1] [2] [3] [5]

At **MAYSCHOSS** (2km NE)

★★**Lochmühle** (BW) Bundesstr 62 ☎1345 tx861766
rm64 (🛁 🚿62) 🅿︎ **P**100 Lift ☾ sB🛁 🚿76—123 dB🛁 🚿122—186 M22 📺
Credit cards [1] [2] [3] [5]

ALTENHELLEFELD
Nordrhein-Westfalen (☎02934)

★★★**Gut Funkenhof** ☎1012 tx84277
🛁 🚿42 A8rm **P**60 sB🛁 🚿75—95 dB🛁 🚿110—145 M25&alc ⚲ 📺 mountains
Credit cards [1] [2] [5]

ALTÖTTING
Bayern (☎08671)

★★★**Post** (ROM) Kapellpl 2 ☎5040 tx56962
🛁 🚿90 **P**10 Lift sB🛁 🚿96 dB🛁 🚿136 M23—40 📺
Credit cards [1] [2] [3] [4] [5]

AMBERG
Bayern (☎09621)

★**Goldeness Lamm** Rathausstr 6 ☎21041
rm24 (🚿5) 🅿︎ **P**15 sB29 sB🚿38 dB52 dB🚿58
Credit cards [1] [2] [4] [5]

Weiss Bayreuther Str 26 ☎62120 M/c **P** For

ANDERNACH
Rheinland-Pfalz (☎02632)

★★**Rhein** Rheinpromenade ☎42240
15 Mar—1 Nov
🛁 🚿25 **P** Lift sB🛁 🚿45—48 dB🛁 🚿75—90 M15—18
Credit cards [1] [2] [3] [5]

★**Anker** K-Adenauer Allee 21 ☎42907
March—15 Dec
rm28 (🚿24) **P**4 sB39 sB🚿54 dB77 dB🚿97 lake
Credit cards [1] [2]

🚘 ***Autohandel & Service*** Werftstr 24 ☎43824 **P** AR Vol

🚘 **R Heinemann** Koblenzerstr 56 ☎43016 **P** For

🚘 **E Kirsch** Fullscheuerweg 36 ☎492401 **P** Ren

Germany

ARNSBERG
Nordrhein-Westfalen (☎02931)

★★★**Dorint-Sauerland** Zu den drei Bänken ☎2001 tx847122
🛁163 🅿︎ **P**100 Lift ☾ sB🛁85—118 dB🛁134—172 📺
Credit cards [1] [2] [3] [5]

AROLSEN
Hessen (☎05691)

★★★**Dorint Schlosshotel Arolsen** (GS) Grosse Allee 1 ☎3091 tx994521
🛁 🚿55 🅿︎ **P**70 Lift ☾ sB🛁 🚿94—109 dB🛁 🚿158—182 📺
Credit cards [1] [2] [3] [5]

ASCHAFFENBURG
Bayern (☎06021)

★★★**Aschaffenburger Hof** Frohinnstr 11 ☎214411 tx4188736
🛁 🚿65 🅿︎ **P**100 Lift ☾ sB🛁 🚿70—120 dB🛁 🚿90—148 M12—40
Credit cards [1] [2] [3] [5]

★★★***Romantik Hotel-Post*** Goldbacherstr 19 ☎21333 tx04188736
🛁 🚿75 🅿︎ **P** Lift ☾ ≈

🚘 **Amberg** Würzburger Str 67 ☎91018 **P** Alf AR DJ Fia LR Lan

K Grundhoefer Wuerzburgerstr 101 ☎91028 Col

🚘 **P Thomas** Würzburger Str 97 ☎91021 **P** For

ASENDORF See **JESTEBURG**

ASPERG
Baden-Württemberg (☎07141)

★★★**Adler** Stuttgarter Str 2 ☎63001 tx7264603
🛁 🚿65 🅿︎ **P**60 Lift sB🛁 🚿110—139 dB🛁 🚿166—220 M23—78 📺
Credit cards [1] [2] [3] [5]

ASSMANNSHAUSEN
Hessen (☎06722)

See also **RÜDESHEIM**

★★**Anker** Rheinstr 5 ☎2912
Etr—Oct
🛁 🚿51 A20rm **P**25 Lift sB🛁 🚿60 dB🛁 🚿85—125 M12—40
Credit card [2]

★★**Café Post** Rheinuferstr 2A ☎2326
Mar—15 Nov
rm17 (🛁 🚿9) 🅿︎ **P**8 sB49—54 sB🛁 🚿69 dB68—83 dB🛁 🚿93—118 M20—25 mountains
Credit cards [2] [3] [5]

★★**Krone** Rheinuferstr 10 ☎2036
21 Mar—15 Nov
rm82 (🛁 🚿48) 🅿︎ **P**100 Lift ☾ sB52—62 sB🛁 🚿fr107 dB104—114 dB🛁 🚿134—249 M alc ≈ mountains
Credit cards [1] [2] [3] [5]

ATTENDORN
Nordrhein-Westfalen (☎02722)

★★**Burghotel Schnellenberg** (GS) (3.5km W) ☎6940 tx876732
1 Feb—2 Jan
🛁43 🅿︎ **P**80 sB🛁90—130 dB🛁140—190 ⚲
Credit cards [1] [2] [3] [5]

AUGSBERG
Bayern (☎0821)

★★★★**Holiday Inn Turmhotel** Wittelsbacher Park ☎577087 tx533225
🛁185 **P**400 Lift ☾ sB🛁153—168 dB🛁196—216 M17—40 📺
Credit cards [1] [2] [3] [4] [5]

★★★**Drei Mohren** (SRS) Maximillianstr 40 ☎510031 tx053710
🛁 🚿110 🅿︎ **P** Lift ☾

★★**Ost** Fuggerstr 4—6 (n.rest) ☎33088 tx0533576
3 Feb—20 Dec
rm54 (🚿50) **P**5 Lift ☾ sB46—53 sB🚿76—90 dB🚿120—135
Credit cards [1] [2] [3] [5]

★**Post** Fuggerstr 7 ☎36044
rm50 (🛁 🚿40) A1rm 🅿︎ **P**20 Lift ☾ sB40—90 sB🛁 🚿70—100 dB75—90 dB🛁 🚿90—160 M18—22 S15% t14%
Credit cards [1] [2]

🚘 **Listle** Kriegshaberstr 58 ☎403055 **P** Ren

BACHARACH
Rheinland-Pfalz (☎06743)

★★**Altköinischer Hof** Blücherstr 2 ☎1339
Jan—25 Mar & Nov—Dec
rm45 (🛁 🚿24) 🅿︎ **P**10 Lift sB48—49 sB🛁 🚿65—70 dB84 dB🛁 🚿99—114 M12—28
Credit cards [3] [5]

BAD Each place preceded by 'Bad' is listed under the name that follows it.

BADEN-BADEN
Baden-Württemberg (☎07221)

★★★★★**Brenner's Park** Schillerstr 6 ☎3530 tx781261
🛁 🚿108 A28rm 🅿︎ **P**80 Lift ☾ sB🛁 🚿187—407 dB🛁 🚿244—684 📺

★★★★**Badischer Hof** (SRS) Lange Str 47 ☎22827 tx781121
🛁140 🅿︎ **P**70 Lift ☾ sB🛁155—225 dB🛁234—384 ≈ 📺
Credit cards [1] [2] [3] [5]

★★★★**Europälscher Hof** (SRS) Kaiserallee 2 ☎23561 tx781188
🛁 🚿135 🅿︎ **P**50 Lift ☾ sB🛁 🚿155—225 dB🛁 🚿264—384
Credit cards [1] [2] [3] [5]

★★★★**Holiday Inn Sporthotel** Falkenstr 2 ☎33011 tx781255
🛁121 **P**80 Lift ☾ sB🛁148—270 dB🛁170—318 M22—40&alc 📺 mountains
Credit cards [1] [2] [3] [4] [5]

★★★**Golf** (2km SW) Fremersbergstr 113 ☎23691 tx781174
Apr—Oct
🛁🚿85 🏠 **P** sB🛁🚿98—155
dB🛁🚿140—230 t% ✂ ≈ 📺 mountains

★★★**Hirsch** Hirschstr 1 ☎23896 tx781193
🛁🚿56 A20rm 🏠 Lift sB🛁🚿103—145
dB🛁🚿170—240

★★★**Waldhotel Fischkultur** Gaisbach 91 ☎71025
Feb—7 Jan
rm38 (🛁🚿28) 🏠 **P**30 Lift sB81—105
dB100—124 dB🛁🚿131—170 M18—35
St% mountains
Credit cards [1] [2]

★★**Allee-Hotel Bären** Haupstr 36 ☎71046 tx781291
🛁81 🏠 **P**60 Lift ☾ sB🛁98—140
dB🛁155—240 M alc
Credit cards [1] [2] [5]

★★**Markt** Marktpl 17 ☎22747
rm27 (🛁🚿12) **P**8 Lift sB36—40
sB🛁🚿50—55 dB72—75

★**Bischoff** Römerpl 2 (n.rest) ☎22378
Feb—20 Nov
🛁🚿21 **P**5 Lift sB🛁🚿60 dB🛁🚿90—100
Credit cards [1] [2] [3] [4] [5]

★**Römerhof** Sofienstr 25 (n.rest) ☎23415
Feb—15 Dec
rm27 (🚿19) 🏠 Lift sB35—45 sB🚿60 dB80
dB🚿95—100
Credit cards [1] [2] [3] [4] [5]

🚗 ***H Burkle*** Malschbacher Str 4—6 ☎7418 **P** For

E Scheibel Hubertustr 19 ☎62005 For

At **MUMMELSEE** (29km S on Schwarzwaldhochstr)

★★***Berghotel Kandel*** ☎1088
20 Dec—10 Nov
rm25 (🛁🚿15) **P** ≈ lake

BADENWEILER
Baden-Württemberg (☎07632)

★★★★**Römerbad** Schlosspl 1 ☎700 tx772933
🛁112 🏠 **P** sB🛁160—210
dB🛁250—310 M50—55

★★★**Park** (BW)E-Eisenlohrstr 6 ☎710 tx17763210
Mar—15 Nov
rm75 (🛁🚿73) A25rm 🏠 **P**40 Lift ☾ sBfr115
sB🛁🚿150—180 dB🛁🚿246—288 📺 ≈
Credit cards [1] [2] [3]

★★★**Sonne** (ROM) Moltkestr 4 ☎5053
8 Feb—10 Nov
🛁🚿40 🏠 **P**20 sB🛁🚿72—90
dB🛁🚿122—170
Credit cards [1] [2] [3] [5]

BAMBERG
Bayern (☎0951)

★★★***Bamberger Hof-Bellevue*** Schönleinspl 4 ☎22216 tx662867
🛁🚿50 🏠 **P**13 Lift ☾
Credit cards [1] [2] [3] [5]

★★★**National** Luitpoldstr 37 ☎24112 tx662916
🛁🚿41 🏠 **P** Lift ☾ sB🛁🚿70—130
dB🛁🚿100—150 M20—35
Credit cards [1] [2] [3] [5]

★★**Messerschmitt** (ROM) Langestr 41 ☎27866
🛁🚿12 🏠 **P**4 sB🛁🚿56—85
dB🛁🚿110—145 M20—36
Credit cards [1] [2] [3] [5]

★***Straub*** Ludwigstr 31 (n.rest) ☎25838
rm38 (🛁🚿7) 🏠 **P** ☾

🚗 ***Schuberth*** Siechenstr 87 ☎62253 M/c **P** Ren

At **BUG** (4km S)

★★***Buger Hof*** am Regnitzufer 1 ☎56054
rm32 (🚿14) 🏠 **P**

BASSUM
Niedersachsen (☎04241)

H Holtorf Bremer Str 47 ☎2356 **P** For

BAYREUTH
Bayern (☎0921)

★★★***Bayerischer Hof*** Bahnhofstr 14 ☎22081 tx642737
rm62 (🛁🚿52) 🏠 **P** Lift ☾ M alc

BAYRISCHZELL
Bayern (☎08023)

★★**Alpenrose** Schlierseestr 100 ☎620
🛁🚿40 A10rm 🏠 **P**100 sB🛁🚿56—68
dB🛁🚿91—146 M15—35 mountains

BERCHTESGADEN
Bayern (☎08652)

★★★**Geiger** (Relais et Châteaux) Stanggasse ☎5055 tx56222
🛁🚿49 🏠 **P**50 Lift sB🛁🚿80—150
dB🛁🚿130—220 📺 ≈ mountains
Credit cards [1] [2] [5]

★★**Königliche Villa** (GS) Kalbersteinstr 4 ☎5097
🛁20 **P**30 sB🛁85—125 dB🛁125—210
M26—45 📺 mountains
Credit cards [1] [2] [3] [4] [5]

H Buchwinkler Bahnhofstr 21 ☎4087 **P** Aud Por VW

G Köppl Hindenburg Allee 1 ☎2615 **P** Aud VW

BERG
Bayern (☎08151)

At **LEONI** (1km S)

★★★**Dorint Starnberger See** ☎5911 tx0526483
🛁71 **P**40 Lift ☾ sB🛁107—120
dB🛁164—176 📺 lake
Credit cards [1] [2] [3] [5]

BERGEN
Niedersachsen (☎05051)

★**Kohlmann** Lukenstr 6 ☎3014
🛁🚿15 🏠 **P**50 sB🛁🚿48 dB🛁🚿85
M15—45
Credit cards [1] [2] [5]

BERGZABERN (BAD)
Rheinland-Pfalz (☎06343)

★★★**Park** Kurtalstr 83 ☎2415
Mar—7 Jan
🛁🚿40 🏠 **P**60 Lift sB🛁🚿55—88
dB🛁🚿108—165 M15—50 📺
Credit cards [1] [5]

BERLIN
(☎030)

★★★★★**Bristol Kempinski Berlin** Kurfürstendamm 27 ☎881091 tx183553
🛁336 **P**150 Lift ☾ sB🛁230—330
dB🛁280—400 M45—50 📺
Credit cards [1] [2] [3] [4] [5]

★★★★★**Inter-Continental Berlin** Budapester Str 2 ☎26020 tx184380
🛁🚿600 🏠 **P**300 Lift ☾ sB🛁🚿181—296
dB🛁🚿257—382 Mfr33 📺
Credit cards [1] [2] [3] [4] [5]

★★★★**Ambassador** (ETAP) Bayreuther Str 42 ☎21902 tx184259
🛁120 **P**40 Lift ☾ sB🛁118—160
dB🛁150—190 M17—35 📺
Credit cards [1] [2] [3] [4] [5]

★★★★**Berlin** (ETAP) Kurfürstenstr 62 ☎269291 tx184332
🛁🚿255 **P**200 Lift ☾ sB🛁🚿105—145
dB🛁🚿168—195 M20—25
Credit cards [1] [2] [3] [4] [5]

★★★★**Berlin Plaza** Knesebeckstr 63 ☎88413 tx184181
🛁🚿131 **P**60 Lift ☾ sB🛁🚿fr98
db🛁🚿124—144 M18—36
Credit cards [1] [2] [3] [5]

★★★★**Franke** A-Achilles Str 57 ☎8921097 tx184857
rm69 (🛁🚿65) sB🛁🚿96—102
dB🛁🚿fr155 M alc 📺

★★★★**Ibis** Messendamm 10 ☎302011 tx182882
🛁🚿191 **P**100 Lift ☾ sB🛁🚿98
dB🛁🚿135 M17—34
Credit cards [1] [2] [3] [5]

★★★★**Savoy** (BW) Fasanenstr 9—10, Charlottenburg ☎310654 tx184292
🛁🚿118 **P**200 Lift ☾ sB🛁🚿168
dB🛁🚿240—280 Mfr30
Credit cards [1] [2] [3] [5]

★★★★**Schweizerhof Berlin** Budapesterstr 21—31 ☎26960 tx185501
🛁430 **P**65 Lift ☾ **DPn**46—48 M28—30 📺
Credit cards [1] [2] [3] [5]

★★★**Alsterhof** Augsburger Str 1 ☎219960 tx183484
🛁🚿140 **P**20 Lift ☾ sB🛁🚿133—159
dB🛁🚿178—198 M22—80 📺
Credit cards [1] [2] [3] [5]

★★★**Arosa** Lietzenburgerstr 79—81 ☎880050 tx183397
🛁🚿90 **P**24 Lift ☾ sB🛁🚿125—160 dB🛁🚿200—235 M20—70 🏊
Credit cards [1] [2] [3] [5]

★★★**Crest (See page 50)** am ADAC Haus, Güntzelstr 14 (n.rest) ☎870241 tx182948
🛁🚿110 🚗 Lift ☾ sB🛁🚿147 dB🛁🚿194
Credit cards [1] [2] [3] [4] [5]

★★★**Hamburg** Landgrafenstr 4 ☎269161 tx184974
🛁240 🚗 **P** Lift sB🛁122—129 dB🛁148—174 M20—30
Credit cards [1] [2] [3] [5]

★★★**Lichtburg** Paderbornerstr 10 ☎8918041 tx184208
🛁63 🚗 **P**7 Lift ☾ sB🛁92—113 dB🛁143—181 M18—22&alc ⛱
Credit cards [1] [2] [3] [5]

★★★**Novotel** Ohmstr 4—6 ☎381061 tx181415
🛁119 **P**65 Lift ☾ sB🛁132—142 dB🛁142—152 M21—42
Credit cards [1] [2] [3] [4] [5]

★★★**Zoo** Kurfürstendamm 25 (n.rest) ☎883091 tx183835
rm143 (🛁136) 🚗 **P**80 Lift ☾ sB🛁110—138 dB🛁170—240
Credit cards [1] [2] [3] [5]

★★***Astrid*** Bleibtreustr 20, Charlottenburg (n.rest) ☎8815959
rm11 (🚿6) Lift

★★**Stephanie** Bleibtreustr 38—39, Charlottenburg (n.rest) ☎8818073 tx0184216
rm40 (🛁🚿18) **P** Lift ☾ sB55—60 sB🛁🚿75—90 dB80 dB🛁🚿110—120

★***Charlottenburger Hof*** Stuttgarter pl 14 ☎3244819
rm35 (🚿6) **P** ☾

🚙 **W Hinz** Naumannstr 79 ☎7843051 AR DJ Hon

Butenuth Forckenbeckstr 94 ☎82051 M/c For

W Lautenschlaeger Neuendorfer Str 2—4 ☎3332513 **P** Peu

🚙 ***B Luckow*** Stettiner Str 10 ☎4938967 **P** AR

🚙 ***H Richtzenhaln*** Kantstr 126 ☎3122020 **P** AR

BERNKASTEL-KUES
Rheinland-Pfalz (☎06531)

★★***Burg-Landshut*** Gestade 11, Bernkastel ☎3019 tx466422
Mar—15 Nov & 20 Dec—3 Jan
rm35 (🛁🚿22) 🚗 **P** ☾ mountains

★★**Drel Könige** Bahnhofstr 1, (n.rest) ☎2327
15 Mar—15 Nov
🛁🚿40 🚗 **P**18 Lift sB🛁🚿75—95 dB🛁🚿120—140 lake
Credit cards [1] [2]

★★**Post** Gestade 17 ☎2022 tx4721569
rm39 (🛁🚿29) 🚗 **P**6 Lift sB40—42 sB🛁🚿65—88 dB58—62 dB🛁🚿88—130 M alc
Credit cards [1] [2] [3] [5]

★★**Sonnenlay** Haupt Str 47, Wehlen (4km NW) ☎6496
🛁🚿11 **P**12 sB🛁🚿38—47 dB🛁🚿66—104 M9—24

★***Graacher Tor*** ☎2566
Apr—Oct
rm33 (🛁🚿12) A12rm **P**

BIBERACH AN DER RISS
Baden-Württemberg (☎07351)

★★★***Reith*** Ulmer Str ☎7828
rm40 (🛁🚿28) 🚗 **P**18 Lift
Credit cards [2] [5]

Schwaben Steigmühlstr 34 ☎7878 M/c **P** For Hon

BIELEFELD
Nordrhein-Westfalen (☎0521)

★★★**Novotel** am Johannisberg 5 ☎124051 tx932991
🛁119 **P**200 Lift ☾ sB🛁108—143 dB🛁156—189 M18—28 S15% t14% 🏊
Credit cards [1] [2] [3] [4] [5]

★★***Waldhotel Brand's Busch*** Furtwänglerstr 52 ☎24093 tx532835
🛁60 🚗 **P** Lift
Credit cards [1] [2] [3] [5]

🚙 **S Tiekotter** Detmolder Str 661 ☎80158 **P** For

BIERSDORF See **BITBURG**

BIESSENHOFEN See **KAUFBEUREN**

BINGEN
Rheinland-Pfalz (☎06721)

★★★**Rheinhotel Starkenburger Hof** Rheinkai 1 ☎14341
20 Jan—1 Dec
rm30 (🛁🚿20) 🚗 **P**4 ☾ sB32 sB🛁🚿45—51 dB64 dB🛁🚿90—102
Credit cards [1] [2] [3] [4] [5]

★★***Rheinterrassen*** Museumstr ☎12021
🛁11 🚗 **P**

🚙 **Pieroth** Mainzerstr 439 ☎17355 **P** For

BISCHOFSMAIS
Bayern (☎09920)

★★★**Wastlsäge** (BW) L-Mueller-Weg 3, ☎216 tx69158
15 Dec—31 Oct
🛁🚿90 Lift sB🛁🚿55—75 dB🛁🚿100—145 🎾 ⛱

BITBURG
Rheinland-Pfalz (☎06561)

★**Mosella** Karenweg 11 ☎3147
rm11 (🚿4) 🚗 **P**4 sB29—33 sB🚿33 dB52—58 dB🚿58

🚙 **Auto Jegen** Saarstr 46 ☎1054 **P** Maz

🚙 **C Metzger** Mötscherstr 49 ☎7004 Alf AR LR

At **BIERSDORF** (12km NW)

★★★**Dorint Sporthotel Südeifel** am Stausee ☎(06569)841 tx 4729607
🚿106 **P**400 Lift ☾ sB🚿80—106 dB🚿130—172 🎾 ⛱ lake
Credit cards [1] [2] [3] [5]

BLANKENHEIM
Nordrhein-Westfalen (☎02449)

★★**Schlossblick** Nonnenbacher Weg 2—4 ☎238 tx833631
20 Dec—1 Nov
rm34 (🛁🚿24) 🚗 **P**20 sB30 sB🛁🚿40 dB60 dB🛁🚿76 M6—26 ⛱ lake
Credit cards [1] [2] [3] [5]

BÖBLINGEN
Baden-Württemberg (☎07031)

★★★**Novotel** O-Lilienthal Str 18 ☎23071 tx7265438
🛁118 **P**150 Lift ☾ sB🛁130—150 dB🛁163—173 Mfr20 🏊
Credit cards [1] [2] [3] [5]

BOCHOLT
Nordrhein-Westfalen (☎02871)

🚙 **Tepasse & Co** Dinxperloer str 285 ☎43989 M/c **P** Dat

BOCHUM
Nordrhein-Westfalen (☎0234)

★★★***Novotel*** am Stadionsring 22 ☎594041 tx825429
🛁118 **P**400 Lift ☾ 🏊
Credit cards [1] [2] [3] [5]

★★**Arcade** Universitätstr 3 ☎33311 tx825447
🚿168 **P** Lift sB🚿78 dB🚿98
Credit card [1]

BONN
Nordrhein-Westfalen (☎0228)

★★★★**ETAP Königshof** Adenauerallee 9—11 ☎26010 tx886535
🛁138 🚗 **P**120 Lift ☾ sB🛁140—170 dB🛁190—240 M alc
Credit cards [1] [2] [3] [4] [5]

★★★★**Bristol** Poppelsdorfer Allee, Ecke Prinz Albert Str ☎20111 tx8869661
🛁🚿120 🚗 **P**140 Lift ☾ sB🛁🚿189—240 dB🛁🚿240—340 M30—60 ⛱
Credit cards [1] [2] [3] [5]

★★★**Novotel** Bonn Hardtberg, Pascalstr Ecke ☎52010 tx886743
🛁142 **P**100 Lift ☾ sB🛁117—137 dB🛁137—147 M11—98 🏊
Credit cards [1] [2] [3] [5]

★★★**Sternhotel** Markt 8 ☎654455 tx886508
🛁🚿70 **P** Lift ☾ sB🛁🚿89—109 dB🛁🚿119—149
Credit cards [1] [2] [3] [4] [5]

★★**Beethoven** Rheingasse 26 ☎631411 tx886467
rm62 (🛁🚿49) 🚗 **P**10 Lift ☾ sB52—82 →

sB 🛁 🚿 102—132 dB132 dB 🛁 🚿 152 M11—25
Credit cards 1 2 3 5

★★**Bergischer Hof** Münsterpl 23 ☎633441
rm28 (🛁 🚿 11) Lift sB46—56 sB 🛁 🚿 66—76 dBfr92 dB 🛁 🚿 107—115 M10—18

★★***Mozart*** Mozartstr 1 (n.rest) ☎635198
rm32 (🛁 🚿 25) **P** Lift ☾

★★***Savoy*** Berliner Freiheit 17 (n.rest) ☎651356
rm25 (🛁 🚿 17) **P** Lift ☾
Credit cards 1 2 3 5

🚗 ***Auto-Hessel*** Pützchen Chaussee 43—53 ☎462088 **P** AR Hon

Auto-Kumpel Bonner Talweg 319—325 ☎232061 **P** AR Dat DJ LR

Mahlberg K-Frowein Str 2 ☎636656 AR

At **GODESBERG (BAD)** (7km SW on road No9)

★★★**Godesberg** auf den Godesberg 5 ☎316071 tx885503
🛁 🚿 22 **P** ☾ sB 🛁 🚿 80—120 dB 🛁 🚿 110—150
Credit cards 1 2 3 5

★★★**Insel** Theaterpl 5—7 ☎364082 tx885592
🛁 🚿 66 **P**32 Lift ☾ sB 🛁 🚿 85—110 dB 🛁 🚿 155—175 M15—25
Credit cards 1 2 5

★★★**Park** am Kurpark 1 (n.rest) ☎363081 tx885463
rm52 (🛁 47) 🚘 **P**15 Lift ☾ sB65 sB 🛁 95—120 dB 🛁 145—190
Credit card 1

★★★**Rheinhotel Dressen** Rheinstr 45—49 ☎82020 tx885417
🛁 🚿 68 🚘 **P**70 Lift ☾ sB 🛁 🚿 89—163 dB 🛁 🚿 152—190 Mfr25 mountains
Credit cards 1 2 3 5

★★**Rheinland** Rheinallee 17 ☎353087
🛁 🚿 25 A12rm 🚘 **P**50 ☾ sB 🛁 🚿 51—94 dB 🛁 🚿 133—153 M25—30

★**Sonnenhang** Mainzerstr 275 (n.rest) ☎346820
🚿 13 🚘 **P**14 ☾
sB🚿 39—45 dB🚿 69—80 lake mountains

At **RÖTTGEN** (7km S on 257)

★★★**Bonn** Reichsstr 1 ☎251021 tx8869505
🛁 🚿 48 **P**120 ☾
Credit cards 1 2 3 5

BONN AIRPORT See **KÖLN — BONN** under **KÖLN**

BONNDORF
Baden-Württemberg (☎07703)

★★**Schwarzwald** Rothausstr 7 ☎421
15 Dec—15 Nov
rm41 (🛁 🚿 40) A26rm 🚘 **P**30 Lift sB37 sB 🛁 🚿 44—51 dB70—78 dB 🛁 🚿 84—98 🏊
Credit cards 1 2 3 4 5

Germany

★**Germania** Martinstr 66 ☎281
rm8 (🛁 🚿 4) **P**20 sB36 sB 🛁 🚿 43 dB72 dB 🛁 🚿 86 M17—28

🚗 ***O Jung*** Rathausstr 10 ☎588 **P** For

BOPPARD
Rheinland-Pfalz (☎06742)

★★★**Bellevue** (BW) Rheinallee 41—42 ☎1020 tx426310
🛁 🚿 95 🚘 **P**80 Lift ☾ sB 🛁 🚿 90—130 dB 🛁 🚿 120—180 M30—48 🎾 🏊 mountains
Credit cards 1 2 3 5

★★★**Klostergut Jakobsberg** (GS) (12km N via B9 to Spay) ☎3061 tx426323
🛁 🚿 110 **P**200 Lift ☾ sB 🛁 🚿 95—160 dB 🛁 🚿 150—260 M alc 🎾 🏊
Credit cards 1 2 3 5

★★**Ebertor** Heerstr (B9) ☎2081 tx426310
Apr—Oct
🚿 63 🚘 **P**100 ☾ sB🚿 fr69 dB🚿 fr96 Mfr28 🎾 mountains
Credit cards 1 2 3 4 5

★★**Günther** Rheinallee 40 (n.rest) ☎2335
15 Jan—16 Dec
rm19 (🛁 18) **P** Lift sB27—33 sB 🛁 34—43 dB 🛁 60—86 t%

★★**Rheinkrone** Mainzer Str 4 ☎5088
Apr—Oct
🛁 36 **P**30 sB 🛁 50—70 dB 🛁 75—120 M10—30 mountains
Credit cards 1 2 3 5

★★**Rheinlust** Rheinallee 27—30 ☎3001 tx426319
18 Apr—Oct
rm91 (🛁 🚿 74) A38rm 🚘 **P**20 Lift ☾ sB37—39 sB 🛁 🚿 47—78 dB66—73 dB 🛁 🚿 88—135 M18—68
Credit cards 1 2 3 5

★**Hunsrücker Hof** Steinstr 26 ☎2433
15 Mar—30 Oct
rm23 (🛁 🚿 17) A2rm **P**2 sB30—35 sB 🛁 🚿 35—40 dB56—66 dB 🛁 🚿 60—70 M7—22

BRAUBACH
Rheinland-Pfalz (☎02627)

★**Hammer** Untermarkstr 15 ☎336
Closed Jan
rm11 (🛁 🚿 5) A1rm 🚘 **P**3 sB30—35 sB 🛁 🚿 35—37 dB58—62 dB 🛁 🚿 64—70 M9—27
Credit cards 1 2 3 5

BRAUNLAGE
Niedersachsen (☎05520)

★★★★**Maritim Berghotel** Am Pfaffensteig ☎3051 tx96261
🛁 🚿 300 🚘 **P**400 Lift ☾ sB 🛁 102—177 dB 🛁 162—278 🎾 🏊 🏊 mountains
Credit cards 1 2 3 5

★★**Tanne** (ROM) Herzog-Wilhelm-Str 8 ☎1034
🛁 🚿 22 A10rm **P**25 sB 🛁 🚿 60—90 dB 🛁 🚿 90—165 M15—85 mountains
Credit cards 1 2 3 4 5

BRAUNSCHWEIG (BRUNSWICK)
Niedersachsen (☎0531)

★★★★**Mercure Atrium** Berliner Pl 3 ☎73301 tx952576
🛁 🚿 130 🚘 **P**250 Lift sB 🛁 🚿 115—135 dB 🛁 🚿 165—205 M14—50
Credit cards 1 2 3 5

★★★***Forsthaus*** Hamburgerstr 72 ☎32801
rm48 (🛁 🚿 25) 🚘 **P**40 Lift ☾ lake
Credit cards 1 2 5

★★★**Mövenpick** Welfenhof ☎48170 tx952777
🛁 30 🚘 **P**1100 Lift ☾ sB 🛁 150—170 dB 🛁 85—450 🏊
Credit cards 1 2 3 5

★★**Frühlings** Bankpl 7 ☎49317
rm60 (🛁 🚿 39) **P**40 Lift ☾ sB36—46 sB 🛁 🚿 55—80 dBfr75 dB 🛁 🚿 80—110
Credit cards 1 2 5

🚗 **Opel-Dürkop** Helmstedter Str 60 ☎7031 Ope Vau

BREDENEY See **ESSEN**

BREISACH
Baden-Württemberg (☎07667)

★★★**Münster** Münsterbergstr 23 ☎7071 tx772687
Closed 7—20 Jan
🛁 🚿 42 🚘 **P**20 Lift sB 🛁 🚿 80—104 dB 🛁 🚿 138—172 M19—93 🏊 mountains
Credit cards 1 2 3 5

BREISIG (BAD)
Rheinland-Pfalz (☎02633)

★**Vater & Sohn** Zehnerstr 78 ☎9148
rm8 (🛁 🚿 3) **P**50 sB38—45 sB 🛁 🚿 48—55 dB75—89 dB 🛁 🚿 95—109 M10—30
Credit cards 1 2 5

BREITNAU
Baden-Württemberg (☎07652)

★★★***Kreuz*** Dorfstr 1 ☎1388
20 Dec—2 Nov
🛁 🚿 17 🚘 **P**

BREITSCHEID See **DÜSSELDORF**

BREMEN
Bremen (☎0421)

★★★★**Park** im Bürgerpark ☎34080 tx244343
rm150 (🛁 🚿 137) A52rm 🚘 **P**200 Lift ☾ sB 🛁 🚿 213—253 dB 🛁 🚿 286—316
Credit cards 1 2 3 5

★★★**Mercure Columbus** Bahnhofspl 5—7 ☎14161 tx244688
🛁 🚿 153 **P**90 Lift ☾ sB 🛁 🚿 115—145 dB 🛁 🚿 155—175 M alc
Credit cards 1 2 3 5

★★★***Crest* (See page 50)** A-Bebel Allee 4 ☎23870 tx244560
🛁 147 **P**100 Lift ☾
Credit cards 1 2 3 4 5

★★★Überseehotel (ETAP) Am Markt-Wachstr 27—29 ☎320197 tx246501
🛁🚿126 🏠 **P**80 Lift ☾ sB🛁🚿85—120 dB🛁🚿125—160 Mfr9
Credit cards [1] [2] [5]

🚘 **Auto-Handelshaus** Stresemannstr 9 ☎499040 **P** For

🚘 ***Deutschland*** Hastedter Heer Str 303—305 ☎492074

At **BRINKUM** (4km S)

★★Atlas G-Daimler Str 3 ☎874037
🚿30 **P** sB🚿55 dB🚿80

BREMERHAVEN
Bremen (☎0471)

★★★Nordsee-Hotel-Naber T-Heusspl ☎48770 tx238881
🛁🚿101 🏠 **P** Lift sB🛁🚿139 dB🛁🚿190—210 M22—27

★★Haverkamp Pragerstr 34 ☎48330 tx238679
🛁🚿108 🏠 **P**45 Lift ☾ sB🛁🚿90—160 dB🛁🚿140—210 ▭
Credit cards [1] [2] [3] [5]

BRINKUM See **BREMEN**

BRODENBACH
Rheinland-Pfalz (☎02605)

★★Peifer Moselstr 69 (1.5km W) (n.rest) ☎756
15 Jan—20 Dec
🚿30 🏠 ☾ sB🚿32—48 dB🚿64—96

★★Post Rhein-Mosel Str 21 ☎3048
15 Mar—15 Nov
rm28 (🛁🚿14) A10rm 🏠 **P**30 sB25—30 sB🛁🚿38—40 dB50—58 dB🛁🚿60—80 M alc lake
Credit cards [1] [2] [5]

BRUCHSAL
Baden-Württemberg (☎07251)

Hetzel Murgstr 12 ☎2283 **P** AR

BRÜCKENAU (BAD)
Bayern (☎09741)

★★★Dorint Kurhotel H-von-Bibra Str 13 ☎850 tx17974
Seasonal
🛁🚿113 🏠 **P**40 Lift ☾ sB🛁🚿91—113 dB🛁🚿140—182 ⚲ ▭
Credit cards [1] [2] [3] [5]

BRUNSBÜTTEL
Schleswig-Holstein (☎04852)

At **ST MICHAELISDONN** (13km N)

★★★Gardels Westerstr 15—19 ☎(04853) 566 tx28625
rm88 (🛁🚿65) 🏠 **P**96 ☾ sB46—50 sB🛁🚿62—86 dB91—95 dB🛁🚿121—153 M20—80 ▭
Credit cards [1] [2] [3] [5]

BÜDELSDORF See **RENDSBURG**

BUG See **BAMBERG**

CARTHAUSEN See **HALVER**

Germany

CELLE
Niedersachsen (☎05141)

★★★Celler Hof Stechbahn 11 ☎28061 tx925117
rm61 (🛁🚿56) 🏠 **P**25 Lift ☾ sB48—69 sB🛁🚿89—148 dB88—118 dB🛁🚿128—196 M15—68
Credit cards [1] [2] [5]

★★*Hannover* Wittinger str 56 ☎35014
🛁🚿13 🏠 **P**15
Credit card [1]

🚘 **Von Maltzan & Trebeljahr** Hohe Wende 3 ☎3921 For

🚘 **W Friedrich** Wiesenstr 22 ☎1057 M/c **P** AR Col DJ

CHAM
Bayern (☎09971)

★★Randsberger Hof Randsbergerhofstr 15 ☎1266
🛁🚿85 🏠 **P**80 Lift ☾ sB🛁🚿41—45 dB🛁🚿81—89 M9—40
Credit cards [1] [2] [3] [4] [5]

COBBENRODE See **ESLOHE**

COBURG
Bayern (☎09561)

★★Blankenburg Rosenstr 30 ☎75005
🛁38 🏠 **P** Lift sB🛁65—95 dB🛁105—125

★★Goldener Anker Rosengasse 14 ☎95027
🛁🚿60 🏠 **P**18 Lift sB🛁🚿55—90 dB🛁🚿95—135 ▭
Credit cards [1] [2] [3] [5]

COCHEM
Rheinland-Pfalz (☎02671)

★★Alte Thorschenke (GS) Brückenstr 3 ☎7059
15 Mar—5 Jan
rm55 (🛁🚿40) 🏠 **P** Lift ☾ sB50—62 sB🛁🚿57—75 dB81—121 dB🛁🚿103—171 M17—65 ▭

★★Brixlade Uferstr 13 ☎3015
🛁🚿40 **P**10 Lift sB🛁🚿40—65 dB🛁🚿70—95 M14—28 mountains
Credit card [2]

★★Germania Moselpromenade 1 ☎261 tx869422
6 Feb—6 Jan
rm28 (🛁🚿17) 🏠 **P**10 Lift sB62—72 sB🛁🚿67—77 dB104—114 dB🛁🚿134—142
Credit cards [1] [2] [3] [5]

★★Hafen Uferstr & Zehnthausstr ☎8474
🛁🚿16 A15rm 🏠 **P**20 sB🛁🚿40—55 dB🛁🚿60—90 M10—25
Credit cards [1] [2] [3] [5]

★*Hendriks* Jahnstr 8 (n.rest) ☎7361
rm16 **P**8

🚘 **Autohof Cochem** Sehler Anglagen 53 ☎8426 **P** Ope

🚘 **M J Schneider** Industriegebiet ☎4078 M/c **P** For

CÖLBE See **MARBURG AN DER LAHN**

COLOGNE See **KÖLN**

CONSTANCE See **KONSTANZ**

CRAILSHEIM
Baden-Württemberg (☎07951)

★★Post-Faber Langestr 2—4 ☎8038
rm68 (🛁🚿64) 🏠 **P**12 Lift sB40 sB🛁🚿50—68 dB🛁🚿82—106 M11—26
Credit cards [1] [2] [3] [4] [5]

CREGLINGEN
Baden-Württemberg (☎07933)

★★Krone Haupstr 12 ☎558
Feb—20 Dec
rm25 (🚿12) A11rm 🏠 **P**10 sB27—30 sB🚿31—33 dB54—60 dB🚿62—68 M7—18

CUXHAVEN
Niedersachsen (☎04721)

★★★*Donners* am Seedeich 2 ☎37014
🛁🚿85 🏠 **P** Lift ☾ ⛱ sea

DACHAU
Bayern (☎08131)

★★★Götz Pollnstr 6 ☎21061
🚿38 🏠 **P**16 Lift sB🚿78—92 dB🚿90—130 M17—28 ▭

DARMSTADT
Hessen (☎06151)

★★★★Maritim Rheinstr 105 ☎80041 tx419625
🛁🚿312 **P**150 Lift ☾ sB🛁🚿141—231 dB🛁🚿192—308 M24—38 ▭
Credit cards [1] [2] [3] [5]

★★Weinmichel Schleiermacherstr 10—12 ☎26822 tx419275
rm75 (🛁🚿74) **P**20 Lift sB🛁🚿72—104 dB🛁🚿118—134 M18—28
Credit cards [1] [2] [3] [5]

🚘 ***G Pöche*** Eschollbrücker Str 16 ☎33234 For

🚘 **J Wiest** Riedstr 5 ☎8640 Aud Por VW

DAUN
Rheinland-Pfalz (☎06592)

★★★Kurfürstliches Amtshaus (BW) auf dem Burgberg ☎3031 tx4729310
🛁42 **P**60 Lift ☾ sB🛁88—98 dB🛁138—288 M29—118 ▭ mountains
Credit card [2]

★★Hommes Wirichstr 9 ☎538
20 Dec—15 Nov
🛁🚿42 🏠 **P** Lift ☾ sB🛁🚿56—75 dB🛁🚿96—134 M16—35 ▭ mountains
Credit cards [1] [2] [3] [4] [5]

★★Stadt Daun Leopoldstr 14 ☎3555
🛁27 **P**30 Lift sB🛁55—66 dB🛁110—119 Mfr18 ▭
Credit cards [1] [2] [3] [5]

🚘 **M Gessner** Bitburger Str ☎692 **P** Aud VW

DECHSENDORF See **ERLANGEN**

DELMENHORST
Niedersachasen (☎04221)

★★***Annenriede*** Annenheider Damm 129 ☎6871
🛁🚿60 ⌂ **P**80 ☾
Credit cards [1] [2] [3] [5]

★★**Central** am Bahnhof (n.rest) ☎18019
rm44 (🛁🚿15) **P** ☾ sB30–45 sB🛁🚿45 dB55–79 dB🛁🚿79

⛟ **O Funke** Wildeshauser Str 19 ☎81300 **P** Dat

⛟ ***Hohsmer*** Syker Str 11 ☎70035 **P** For

DETMOLD
Nordrhein-Westfalen (☎05231)

★★**Detmolder Hof** Langestr 19 ☎28244 tx935850
🛁39 A18rm **P**7 Lift sB🛁80–154 dB🛁118–208 ⚲
Credit cards [1] [2] [3] [5]

★**Friedrichshöhe** Paderbornestr 6, Heiligenkirchen (3km S) ☎47053
rm15 (🚿12) ⌂ **P**30 sB45–49 sB🚿45–49 dB84–94 dB🚿84–94 M9–30 mountains

⛟ **British Cars** Paderborner Str 52 ☎47556 **P** AR LR

⛟ **H Stein** Am Gelskamp 23 ☎66880 **P** Peu

⛟ ***M Wagner*** Grünstr 34 ☎28222 **P** Ren

DIEZ/LAHN
Rheinland-Pfalz (☎06432)

⛟ **Auto-Müller** Wilhelmstr 44 ☎2622 **P** For

DINKELSBÜHL
Bayern (☎09851)

★★***Goldene Kanne*** Segringerstr 8 ☎2363
rm24 (🛁🚿10) ⌂ **P**

★★**Goldene Rose** Marktpl 4 ☎831 tx61123
Mar–8 Jan
🛁20 ⌂ **P**12 sB🛁45–60 dB🛁69–109
Credit cards [1] [2] [3] [4] [5]

DONAUESCHINGEN
Baden-Württemberg (☎0771)

★★★**Oschberghof** ☎841 tx792717
🛁53 ⌂ **P** Lift ☾ sB🛁fr105 dB🛁fr145 Mfr25 ⛱ ⛳

★★**Sonne** ☎3144
Closed 15 Dec–20 Jan
🛁🚿20 ⌂ **P**14 sB🛁🚿51–53 dB🛁🚿101–105 M10–29

⛟ ***P Greuner*** Raiffeisenstr 60 ☎4730 **P** AR

DONAUWÖRTH
Bayern (☎0906)

★★**Traube** Kapellstr 14 ☎6096 tx51331
rm35 (🛁🚿17) A18rm ⌂ **P**22 Lift sB39–43 sB🛁🚿55–67 dB72–76 dB🛁🚿100–110 M7–25
Credit cards [1] [2] [3] [5]

⛟ **J Schlicker** Berger Allee 11 ☎3001 **P** For

DORTMUND
Nordrhein-Westfalen (☎0231)

★★★★**Römischer Kaiser** (GT) Olpestr 2 ☎54321 tx822441
🛁🚿160 **P** Lift ☾ sB35–50 sB🛁🚿114–128 dB60 dB🛁🚿157–175
Credit cards [1] [2] [3] [4] [5]

⛟ ***E Eickmann*** Dorfstr 34 ☎593718 **P** Peu

⛟ **H Peters** Juchostr 25 ☎596021 **P** For

⛟ ***Tremonia-Auto*** Eisenstr 50 ☎818811 **P** Peu

At **OESPEL** (6km W)

★★★★**Novotel Dortmund-West** Brennaborstr 2 ☎65485 tx8227007
🛁104 **P**160 Lift ☾ sB🛁110–130 dB🛁143–163 M alc ⛱
Credit cards [1] [2] [3] [5]

DREIEICH
Hessen (☎06103)

★★★**Dorint Kongress** Eisenbahnstr 200 ☎6060 tx417954
🛁🚿96 **P**70 Lift ☾ sB🛁🚿139–178 dB🛁🚿198–246 ⛶
Credit cards [1] [2] [3] [5]

DUISBURG
Nordrhein-Westfalen (☎0203)

★★★**Duisburger Hof** (SRS) Neckarstr 2 König-Heinrich-Pl ☎331021 tx855750
rm110 (🛁🚿90) ⌂ **P**300 Lift ☾ sB🛁🚿149–189 dB🛁🚿228–268
Credit cards [1] [2] [3] [4] [5]

★★**Ibis** Hercator str 15 ☎300050 tx855872
🚿95 **P** Lift sB🚿78–88 dB🚿108–118 M alc

DÜREN
Nordrhein-Westfalen (☎02421)

★★★**Germania** J-Schregel Str 20 ☎15000
rm58 (🛁🚿45) ⌂ **P**30 Lift ☾ sBfr40 sB🛁🚿55–90 dB60 dB🛁🚿70–120 M13–32
Credit card [1]

★**Nachtwächter** Kölner Landstr 12 ☎74031
Closed 20 Dec–6 Jan
rm36 (🚿31) A10rm **P**20 sB32–42 sB🚿36–42 dBfr60 dB🚿75 M6–28

At **MARIAWEILER** (3km NW)

★★**Mariaweiler Hof** an Gut Nazareth 45 ☎87900
rm10 (🚿6) ⌂ **P**22 sBfr32 sB🚿50 dBfr62 dB🚿80 M7–25
Credit cards [1] [2]

DÜRKHEIM (BAD)
Rheinland-Pfalz (☎06322)

★★★***Crest*** **(See page 50)** Kurbrunnenstrasse ☎601 tx454694
🛁101 **P** Lift ☾
Credit cards [1] [2] [3] [4] [5]

★★★**Kur Parkhotel** (BW) Schlosspl 1–4 ☎7970 tx454818
🛁109 **P**140 Lift ☾ sB🛁65–118 dB🛁130–172 ⛶
Credit cards [1] [2] [3] [5]

DÜRRHEIM (BAD)
Baden-Wurttemberg (☎07726)

★★★**Waldeck** Waldstr 18 ☎8001 tx7921315
🛁🚿65 A18rm ⌂ **P**56 Lift sB🛁🚿75–87 dB🛁🚿118–146 ⛶
Credit cards [1] [2] [3] [5]

DÜSSELDORF
Nordrhein-Westfalen (☎0211)

★★★★★**Park** (SRS) Corneliuspl 1 ☎8651 tx8582331
🛁🚿160 **P**50 Lift ☾ sB🛁🚿219–310 dB🛁🚿280–400 M alc
Credit cards [1] [2] [3] [5]

★★★★***Hilton International*** G-Glock Str 20 ☎434963 tx8584376
🛁379 **P**350 Lift ☾ ⛶
Credit cards [1] [2] [3] [4] [5]

★★★★**Holiday Inn** G-Adolf pl 10 ☎38370 tx8586359
🛁120 **P**25 Lift ☾ sB🛁210 dB🛁255 M25–45 ⛶
Credit cards [1] [2] [3] [4] [5]

★★★**Börsen** Kreuzstr 19A (n.rest) ☎363071 tx8587323
🛁🚿76 Lift ☾ sB🛁🚿130–160 dB🛁🚿190–240
Credit cards [1] [2] [3] [5]

★★★**Novotel** am Schonenkamp 9 ☎741092 tx8584374
🛁120 **P**100 Lift sB🛁140–160 dB🛁173–183 M20–25 ⛱
Credit cards [1] [2] [3] [5]

★★★**Ramada** am Seestern 16 ☎591047 tx8585575
🛁222 **P**120 Lift ☾ sB🛁182–232 dB🛁244–329 M28–55 ⛶
Credit cards [1] [2] [3] [4] [5]

⛟ ***Birkelbach & Unkruer*** Hoffeldstr 51 ☎671094 **P** AR Saa

At **BREITSCHEID** (12km N on A52 near Mülheim exit)

★★★**Novotel Breitschelder Kreuz** Lintorfer Weg 75 ☎(02102) 17621 tx8585272
🛁120 **P**160 Lift ☾ sB🛁135–155 dB🛁168–178 Mfr22 ⚲ ⛱
Credit cards [1] [2] [3] [5]

At **RATINGEN** (5km N. Follow signs from exit Ratingen/Kaiserwerth on A52)

★★★★***Crest*** Broichhofstr 3 **(See page 50)** ☎(02102)46046 tx8585235
🛁200 **P**150 ☾ ⛱ ⛶
Credit cards [1] [2] [3] [4] [5]

Germany

EBERBACH AM NECKAR
Baden-Württemberg (☎06271)

★★**Krone-Post** Haupstr 1 ☎2310
Mar—Dec
rm48 (🛁🚿33) **P**20 Lift sB🛁🚿50—75
dB65 dB🛁🚿85—105
Credit cards [1] [2] [3] [5]

EBNI-EBNISEE
Baden-Wûrttemberg (☎07184)

★★★***Landgasthof Hirsch*** ☎811
tx17718410
Feb—10 Jan
🛁🚿37 ⛟ **P**50 Lift ⚲ ⛱ 🖃
Credit cards [1] [5]

EBRACH
Bayern (☎09553)

★***Klosterbräu*** Marktpl 6 ☎212
Closed 10 Jan—10 Feb
rm19 (🚿17) ⛟ **P**50

ECHING
Bayern (☎089)

★★**Olymp** Wielandstr 3 ☎3195073
tx5214960
6 Jan—22 Dec
🛁🚿33 ⛟ **P**15 sB🛁🚿75—85
dB🛁🚿108 Mfr11 🖃
Credit cards [1] [2] [3] [5]

EDIGER-ELLER
Rheinland-Pfalz (☎02675)

★★**Weinhaus Oster** Moselweinstr 61
☎232
Mar—15 Nov
rm12 (🛁🚿8) **P**12 sB38—40
sB🛁🚿46—49 dB71—75 dB🛁🚿79—98
M8—12
Credit cards [1] [2]

EHLENBOGEN See **ALPIRSBACH**

EICHERSCHEID See **SIMMERATH**

ELFERSHAUSEN
Bayern (☎09704)

★★★**Ullrich** Aug—Ullrich 42 ☎281
tx672807
rm71 (🛁🚿67) ⛟ **P**150 Lift sB47
sB🛁🚿80—82 dB75 dB🛁🚿104—119
M20—22 🖃
Credit cards [1] [2] [5]

ELTEN
Nordrhein-Westfalen (☎02828)

★★**Wald** Lindenallee 34 ☎2091
tx8125286
🚿21 **P**40 Lift sB🚿85 dB🚿150 M35—90 🖃
mountains
Credit cards [1] [2] [4] [5]

EMDEN
Niedersachsen (☎04921)

★**Goldener Adler** Neutorstr 5 ☎24055
🚿16 **P**5 ☾ sB🚿93 dB🚿141 M13—32
Credit cards [1] [2] [5]

EMS (BAD)
Rheinland-Pfalz (☎02603)

★★★**Staatliches Kurhaus** (BW)
Römerstr 1—3 ☎3016 tx869017
rm108 (🛁🚿102) **P**50 Lift ☾ sB106—110
sB🛁🚿106—110 dB150—160
dB🛁🚿150—160 M24—42 🖃
Credit cards [1] [2] [3] [5]

★★***Russischer Hof*** Römerstr 23 ☎4462
rm22 (🛁🚿15) **P** Lift

ENNEPETAL
Nordrhein-Westfalen (☎02333)

★★***Burgmann*** ☎71517
🚿11 **P** Lift

ENZKLÖSTERLE
Baden-Württemberg (☎07085)

★★***Parkhotel Hetschelhof*** ☎273
Dec—Oct
rm18 (🛁🚿16) ⛟ **P**

ERFTTAL See **NEUSS**

ERLANGEN
Bayern (☎09131)

★★★★**Transmar Kongress** (GT)
Beethoven Str 3 ☎8040 tx629750
🛁🚿138 ⛟ **P** Lift ☾ sB🛁🚿149—196
dB🛁🚿179—259 🖃

★★★***Grille*** Bunsenstr 35 ☎6136
tx629839
🛁🚿65 ⛟ **P**30 Lift ☾
Credit cards [1] [2] [3] [5]

★★**Luise** Pfalzerstr 15 (n.rest) ☎1220
🛁75 ⛟ **P**20 Lift ☾ sB🛁69—99
dB🛁99—125 🖃
Credit cards [1] [5]

Auto Winter Resenscheckstr 10 ☎38888
Peu Tal

At **DECHSENDORF** (5km NW)

★**Rasthaus am Heusteg** Heusteg 13
☎41225
rm20 (🚿4) ⛟ **P**50 sB35 sB🚿40—48 dB62
dB🚿70—78 M10—35
Credit card [1]

At **TENNENLOHE** (3km S)

★★★***Transmar Motor*** (GT)
Wetterkreuzstr 7 ☎6080 tx629912
🛁126 **P**120 Lift ☾ 🖃
Credit cards [1] [2] [3] [5]

⛟ **Konrad** P-Gossen Str 116 ☎31025 **P** For

ESCHBORN See **FRANKFURT AM MAIN**

ESCHWEILER
Nordrhein-Westfalen (☎02403)

★***Schwan*** ☎26810
rm11 (🚿2) **P**10 mountains

H Adenau Tulpenweg 6 ☎4162 **P** AR Maz

ESLOHE
Nordrhein-Westfalen (☎02973)

At **COBBENRODE** (7km S)

★★**Hennemann** Olperstr 28 (☎02970)236
🛁🚿23 ⛟ **P**30 sB🛁🚿50 dB🛁🚿42—57
M10—25 ⚲ 🖃 mountains

ESPENAU See **KASSEL**

ESSEN
Nordrhein-Westfalen (☎0201)

★★★**Handelshof** (Mövenpick) am
Hauptbahnhof 2 ☎17080 tx857562
🛁195 Lift ☾ sB🛁130—145
dB🛁150—165

★★**Arcade** 50 Hollestr ☎24280
tx8571133
🚿144 **P**50 Lift sB🚿85—109 dB🚿118
M14—25
Credit cards [1] [3]

At **ESSEN-BREDENEY** (7km S on 224)

★★★**Bredeney** (BW) T-Althoff Str 5
☎714081 tx0857597
🛁🚿293 ⛟ **P**170 Lift ☾ sB🛁🚿140—155
dB🛁🚿200—220 M26—32 🖃
Credit cards [1] [2] [3] [4] [5]

At **ESSEN-RÜTTENSCHEID** (3km S on 224)

★★★**Arosa** Rüttenscheider Str 149
☎72280 tx857354
🛁🚿68 A16rm ⛟ **P**21 Lift ☾ sB89
sB🛁🚿115—150 dB🛁🚿195—230 M20
Credit cards [2] [3] [5]

ETTLINGEN
Baden-Württemberg (☎07243)

★★★***Erbprinz*** (Relais et Châteaux)
Rheinstr 1 ☎12071 tx782848
🛁🚿50 ⛟ **P** Lift ☾

EUTIN
Schleswig-Holstein (☎04521)

★**Wittler** Bahnhofstr 28 ☎2347
rm29 (🛁🚿17) ⛟ **P**20 sB35—45
sB🛁🚿50—65 dB60—70 dB🛁🚿90—110
M15—20
Credit cards [1] [2] [3] [5]

FALLINGBOSTEL
Niedersachsen (☎05162)

★★**Berlin** Düshorner Str 7 ☎3066
🚿18 ⛟ **P**30 sB🚿51 dB🚿88 M10—35 ⚲
Credit cards [1] [2] [3] [5]

FELDAFING
Bayern (☎08157)

★★★**Kaiserin Elisabeth** Tutzinger Str 2
☎1013 tx526408
rm67 (🛁🚿48) A17rm ⛟ **P** Lift ☾ sB65—95
sB🛁🚿95—145 dB130—160
dB🛁🚿170—260 M35—50 ⚲ mountains
lake
Credit cards [1] [2] [3] [5]

FELDBERG IM SCHWARZWALD
Baden-Württemberg (☎07655)

★★★**Dorint Feldberger Hof** Seebück 12
☎(07676) 311 tx7721124
🛁🚿70 ⛟ **P**100 Lift ☾ sB🛁🚿70—80
dB🛁🚿110—160 🖃 mountains
Credit cards [1] [2] [3] [5]

FINTHEN See **MAINZ**

Germany

FLENSBURG
Schleswig-Holstein (☎0461)

★★**Europa** Rauthausstr 1—5 ☎17522
rm70 (🛁🚿31) ⌂ ☾ sB40—42 sB🛁🚿67 dBfr72 dB🛁🚿fr98 M12—15
Credit cards 1 2 3 4 5

★★**Flensburger Hof** Süderhofenden 38 ☎17320 tx22594
rm28 (🛁🚿24) ⌂ **P**25 Lift sB65—70 sB🛁🚿110—125 dB🛁🚿145—155 M17—31
Credit cards 1 2 3 5

C Christiansen Nordstr, Engelsby ☎6031 **P** Peu Tal

At **HARRISLEE** (5km N)

★★**Grenze** ☎7020 tx461108
rm200 (🛁190) **P**500 Lift ☾ sB50—158 dB68—168 dB🛁68—168 Mfr15
Credit cards 1 2 3 4 5

FRANKFURT AM MAIN
Hessen (☎069)

Electronic room reservation facilities are available at the airport, the main railway station and the ADAC Service Centre, autobahn ext 'Frankfurt West'. These facilities are not operative during Trade Fairs.

★★★★★**Frankfurt Intercontinental** W-Leuschner-Str 43 ☎230561 tx413639
🛁800 **P**500 Lift ☾ sB🛁295—335 dB🛁360—400 M34—37
Credit cards 1 2 3 4 5

★★★★***Crest* (See page 50)** Isenburger Schneise 40, Niederad (6km S) ☎67840 tx416717
🛁281 **P**150 ☾
Credit cards 1 2 3 4 5

★★★★**Frankfurter Hof** (SRS) am Kaiserpl 9 ☎20251 tx411806
🛁400 **P**100 Lift ☾ sB🛁189—349 dB🛁270—380
Credit cards 1 2 3 4 5

★★★★**Hessischer Hof** (GT) F-Ebert-Anlage 40 ☎75400 tx411776
🛁🚿160 **P**100 Lift ☾ sB🛁🚿150—375 dB🛁🚿260—430 M alc
Credit cards 1 2 3 4 5

★★★★**Holiday Inn** Mailänder Str 1 ☎68020 tx411805
🛁404 **P**400 Lift ☾ sB🛁186—246 dB🛁244—304 M alc
Credit cards 1 2 3 4

★★★★**Parkhotel Frankfurt** (Mövenpick) Wisenhüttenpl 28—38 ☎26970 tx412808
🛁🚿280 **P**70 Lift ☾ sB🛁🚿265—305 dB🛁🚿369—399 M29&alc
Credit cards 1 2 3 4 5

★★★★**Savigny** (BW) Savignystr 14—16 ☎75330 tx412061
🛁🚿129 A40rm Lift ☾ sB🛁🚿120—190 dB🛁🚿230—300 M23—75
Credit cards 1 2 3 5

★★★**Excelsior Monopol** Mannheimer Str 7—13 ☎230171 tx413061
🛁🚿298 Lift ☾ sB🛁🚿85—130 dB🛁🚿99—230 M22—45
Credit cards 1 2 3 5

★★★**National** (BW) Baseler Str 50 ☎234841 tx412570
🛁🚿70 ⌂ **P**20 Lift ☾ sB🛁🚿131—151 dB🛁🚿207—230
Credit cards 1 2 3

★★★**Ramada Caravelle** Oeserstr 180 ☎39050 tx416812
🛁236 **P**50 Lift ☾ sB🛁163—196 dB🛁232—284 Mfr28
Credit cards 1 2 3 4 5

B Kneifel Praunheimer Landstr 21 ☎780925 **P** AR Dat DJ LR

British Car Services Sulzbacher Str 10—14 ☎734306 AR Sko

At **ESCHBORN** (12km NW)

★★★**Novotel Frankfurt Eschborn** P-Helfmann Str 10 ☎(06196)42812 tx4072842
🛁227 **P**300 Lift sB🛁138—162 dB🛁175—185 Mfr20
Credit cards 1 2 3 5

At **SULZBACH** (14km W via A648)

★★★★**Holiday Inn** am Main Taunus Zentrum 1 ☎(06196) 7878 tx410373
🛁291 **P**300 Lift ☾ sB🛁180—224 dB🛁240 M21
Credit cards 1 2 3 4 5

FRANKFURT AM MAIN AIRPORT
Hessen (☎0611)

★★★**Novotel** am Weiher 20 ☎75050 tx4170101
🛁🚿151 **P**200 Lift ☾ sB🛁🚿150—172 dB🛁🚿185—195 M20 lake
Credit cards 1 2 3 5

FREIBURG IM BREISGAU
Baden-Württemberg (☎0761)

★★★★**Colombi** (SRS) Rotteckring 16 ☎31415 tx772750
🛁🚿101 ⌂ **P**50 Lift ☾ sB🛁🚿158—185 dB🛁🚿210—245
Credit cards 1 2 3 5

★★★**Novotel** am Karlspl 1 ☎31295 tx772774
🛁112 ⌂ **P**400 Lift ☾ sB🛁150 dB🛁173 mountains
Credit cards 1 2 3 4 5

★★★**Rappen** Münsterpl 13 ☎31353
rm20 (🛁🚿13) A3rm **P** Lift sB48—68 sB🛁🚿73—98 dB105—145 dB🛁🚿145 M10—35
Credit cards 1 2 5

★★★**Victoria** Eisenbahnstr 54 ☎31881 tx17761103
rm70 (🛁🚿60) A32rm ⌂ **P**22 Lift ☾ sB72—77 sB🛁🚿102—122 dB114 dB🛁🚿174—184 Mfr11&alc
Credit cards 1 2 3 5

★★**Roten Bären** Oberlinden 12 (adj to Schwabentor Gateway) ☎36913 tx7721574
rm33 (🛁🚿32) **P**7 Lift sBfr75 sB🛁🚿95—115 dBfr120 dB🛁🚿130—180
Credit cards 1 2 3 5

F Speck Habsburgerstr 99 ☎31131 M/c **P** AR

FRIELASSING
Bayern (☎08654)

★★***Krone*** Hauptstr 26 ☎9057
🛁40 ⌂ **P** Lift mountains

FREISING
Bayern (☎08161)

★★**Bayerischer Hof** Untere Hauptstr 3 ☎3037
rm70 (🛁🚿69) ⌂ **P**18 Lift sB🛁🚿47—49 dB🛁🚿86—94 M14—22

FREUDENSTADT
Baden-Württemberg (☎07441)

★★★**Steigenberger** (SRS) K-von-Hahn Str 129 ☎81071 tx764266
🛁🚿136 **P**120 Lift ☾ sB🛁🚿94—129 dB🛁🚿148—218
Credit cards 1 2 3 5

★★★**Schwarzwald Hof** Hohenrieder Str 74 ☎7421 tx0764371
🛁🚿40 ⌂ **P**10 Lift sB🛁🚿78—89 dB🛁🚿143—172 M alc
Credit cards 1 2 3 5

★★★**Sonne am Kurpark** Turnhalle Str 63 ☎6044 tx764388
26 Dec—Nov
rm49 (🛁🚿42) ⌂ **P**25 Lift ☾ sB55—59 sB🛁🚿85—135 dBfr92 dB🛁🚿148—212 M22—49
Credit cards 1 2 3 5

★★**Krone** Marktpl 29 ☎2007
rm30 (🚿10) ⌂ **P** sB45—50 sB🚿50—55 dB90—100 dB🚿100—110 M9—24

★★**Württemberger Hof** Lauterbadstr 10 ☎6047 tx764388
18 Dec—18 Nov
rm22 (🛁🚿13) ⌂ **P**25 Lift ☾ sB45—49 sB🛁🚿65—69 dB76 dB🛁🚿108—128
Credit cards 1 2 3 5

★**See** Forststr 17 ☎2688
Dec—Oct
rm11 (🚿7) A6rm ⌂ **P**7 sB38—45 dB76—86 dB🚿90—104 M14—30
Credit cards 1 2 5

Autohaus Baum & Keinadh Stuttgarter Str 92/94 ☎7494 **P** Cit Hon

Hornberger & Schilling Jetzt Deutzstr 2 ☎7084 M/c **P** Ope Vau

Oberndorfer & Hillier Alte Poststr 3 ☎2278 For

At **LAUTERBAD** (3km SE)

★★**Gruner Wald** Kinzigtalstr 23 ☎2427
rm40 (🛁🚿34) ⌂ **P**50 sB30 sB🛁🚿42—53 dB60 dB🛁🚿84—106 M9—25 mountains
Credit card 1

FRIEDBERG
Hessen (☎06031)

🚚 ***Kögler*** Gilessener Str 19—21 ☎4661 M/c **P** For

FRIEDRICHSDORF See **HOMBURG (BAD)**

FRIEDRICHSHAFEN
Baden-Württemberg (☎07541)

★★**Buchorner Hof** Friedrichstr 33 ☎25041 tx734210

16 Jan—20 Dec
🛁🚿65 🚗**P**10 Lift ☾ sB🛁🚿75—85
dB🛁🚿110—180 M alc
Credit cards [1] [2] [3] [5]

Frank Meisterhofener Str 9 ☎2117 M/c **P** For Hon

O Muller Donaustr 5 ☎55038 **P** AR DJ

FULDA
Hessen (☎0661)

★★★***Lenz*** Leipzigerstr 122 ☎601041 tx49733

rm48 (🛁🚿37) A22rm **P** Lift ☾

🚚 **W Fahr** Langebrücke Andreasberg 4 ☎8161 Ope Vau

🚚 **E Sorg** Kreuzbergstr 44 ☎41075 **P** For

FÜRSTENFELDBRÜCK
Bayern (☎08141)

★**Post** Hauptstr 7 ☎24074

rm43 (🛁🚿33) 🚗**P**30 Lift sB🛁🚿65
dB🛁🚿80—95 M10—28
Credit cards [1] [2] [3] [5]

Auto Wolff Am Fohlenhof 7 ☎91626 M/c AR Saa

FÜRTH
Bayern (☎0911)

★★★**Novotel Fürth** Lauberweg 6 ☎791010 tx622214

🛁129 **P**110 Lift sB🛁117—137
dB🛁137—147 Mfr20 ♒
Credit cards [1] [2] [3] [4] [5]

GAIMERSHEIM See **INGOLSTADT**

GARMISCH-PARTENKIRCHEN
Bayern (☎08821)

★★★★**Holiday Inn** Mittenwalderstr 2 ☎7561 tx592415

🛁🚿117 **P**80 Lift ☾ sB🛁🚿187—197
dB🛁🚿239—249 M22—25 ⛳ ▭ mountains
Credit cards [1] [2] [3] [4] [5]

★★★**Bernriederhof** von Müller Str 12 ☎71074 tx592421

🛁🚿41 🚗**P**15 ☾ sB🛁🚿fr164
dB🛁🚿198—288 M20 mountains
Credit cards [1] [2] [3] [5]

★★★**Dorint** Mittenwalderstr 59 ☎7060 tx592464

🛁156 🚗**P**150 Lift ☾ sB🛁90—240
dB🛁130—280 ⛳ ▭ mountains
Credit cards [1] [2] [3] [5]

★★★**Grand Sonnenbichl** Burgstr 97 ☎7020 tx059632

🛁🚿90 **P**80 Lift ☾ sB🛁🚿120—165

dB🛁🚿200—270 t% ▭ mountains
Credit cards [1] [2] [3] [4] [5]

★★★**Wittelsbach** von Brugstr 24 ☎53096 tx59668

20 Dec—20 Oct
🛁🚿60 🚗**P**25 Lift ☾ sB🛁🚿84—108
dB🛁🚿130—180 M23—35 ▭ mountains
Credit cards [1] [2] [3] [5]

★★**Garmischer Hof** Bahnhofstr 51 (n.rest) ☎51091

rm41 (🛁🚿28) **P**20 Lift ☾ sB36—44
sB🛁🚿52—67 dB65—77 dB🛁🚿92—115
t% mountains
Credit cards [1] [2] [5]

★★**Partenkirchner-Hof** Bahnhofstr 15 ☎58025 tx592412

15 Dec—15 Nov
🛁80 🚗**P** ☾ sB🛁77—122
dB🛁🚿124—174 M22—36 ▭ mountains
Credit cards [1] [2] [5]

🚚 **Maier** Unterfeldstr 3 ☎50141 Fia Lan

GELSENKIRCHEN
Nordrhein-Westfalen (☎0209)

★★★★**Maritim** Stadtgarten 1 ☎15951 tx824636

🛁250 🚗**P**150 Lift ☾ sB🛁104—166
dB🛁174—234 ▭
Credit cards [1] [2] [3] [5]

★★**Ibis** Bahnhofsvorpl 12 ☎17020 tx824705

🚿104 **P** Lift sB🚿78—88 dB🚿108—118
M &alc

🚚 **A Stork** Ringstr 50—56 ☎21941 M/c **P** For Hon

GERNSBACH
Baden-Württemberg (☎07224)

★**Ratsstuben** Hauptstr 34 ☎2141

🛁21 **P**15 sB🛁29 dB🛁58 mountains

GIESSEN
Hessen (☎0641)

★★★**Kübel** Bahnhofstr 47 ☎77070 tx4821754

rm45 (🛁🚿44) **P**30 ☾ sBfr50
sB🛁🚿60—120 dB🛁🚿98—180
Credit cards [1] [2] [3] [4]

★**Lahn** Lahnstr 21 ☎73516

rm14 (🚿5) 🚗**P** sB33—34 sB🚿50—65
dB80—85 dB🚿75—80

GLOTTERTAL
Baden-Württemberg (☎07684)

★★**Hirschen** Rathausweg 2 ☎810 tx772349

🛁🚿31 A10rm **P**100 Lift sB🛁🚿74—104
dB🛁🚿148—204 M13—45 ⛳ mountains
Credit card [1]

GODESBERG (BAD) See **BONN**

GÖGGLINGEN See **ULM**

GÖPPINGEN
Baden-Württemberg (☎07161)

★★**Hohenstaufen** Obere Freihofstr 64 ☎70077 tx727619

🛁🚿21 A12rm 🚗**P** sB🛁🚿69—89
dB🛁🚿120—130 M18—35
Credit cards [1] [2] [3] [4] [5]

Schwabengarage Pfingstwasen 2 ☎71091 M/c For

GOSLAR
Niedersachsen (☎05321)

At **GRAUHOF BRUNNEN** (4km NE)

★★**Grauhof Landhaus** ☎84001

rm30 (🛁20) 🚗**P**50 Lift sB46 sB🛁70 dB92
dB🛁130 M alc
Credit cards [1] [2] [3] [5]

At **HAHNENKLEE** (15km SW)

★★★**Dorint Harzhotel Kreuzeck** am Kreuzeck ☎741 tx953721

🛁🚿96 🚗**P** 160 Lift ☾ sB🛁🚿65—109
dB🛁🚿136—176 ⛳ ▭ lake
Credit cards [1] [2] [3] [5]

GÖTTINGEN
Niedersachsen (☎0551)

★★**Sonne** Paulinerstr 10—12 ☎56738 tx96787

5 Jan—20 Dec
🛁🚿41 🚗**P**10 Lift ☾ sB🛁🚿63—80
dB🛁🚿94—110 Mfr15
Credit cards [1] [3] [5]

GRAFENAU
Bayern (☎08552)

★★★**Sonnenhof** (SRS) Sonnenstr 12 ☎2033 tx57413

🛁🚿196 🚗**P**100 Lift sB🛁🚿64—92
dB🛁🚿118—174 Mfr26 ⛳ ▭
Credit cards [1] [2] [3] [5]

GRAINAU
Bayern (☎08821)

★★★***Alpenhotel Waxenstein*** Eibseestr 16 ☎8001 tx59663

🛁49 🚗**P** Lift ☾ ♒ mountains

★★**Post** Postgasse 10 ☎8853

20 Dec—15 Oct
🛁🚿35 🚗**P**30 sB🛁🚿60—68
dB🛁🚿119—135 Mfr20 mountains
Credit cards [2] [5]

GRAUHOF BRUNNEN See **GOSLAR**

GRIMLINGHAUSEN See **NEUSS**

GROSS-GERAU
Hessen (☎06152)

★★**Adler** Frankfurter Str 11 ☎2286

rm68 (🛁🚿59) 🚗**P** Lift sB49
sB🛁🚿74—89 dB88 dB🛁🚿116—138
M8—70
Credit cards [1] [2] [3]

Autohaus Fritsch Gernsheimer Str 60 ☎58016 For

GRÖTZINGEN See **KARLSRUHE**

Germany

GÜNZBURG
Bayern (☎08221)

★★**Goldene Traube** Marktpl 22 ☎5510
rm34 (🛁 🚿 20) 🏠 **P**12 sB37—60
sB 🛁 🚿 43—60 dB64—85 dB 🛁 🚿 79—85
M12—25
Credit cards [1] [2] [3] [5]

★★**Hirsch** Marktpl 18 ☎5610
🛁 🚿 14 A12rm 🏠 **P**10 sB 🛁 🚿 35—56
dB 🛁 🚿 70—82 M15—50
Credit card [2]

HAGEN
Nordrhein-Westfalen (☎02331)

★★★**Crest (See page 50)** Wasserloses
Tal 4 ☎3910 tx823441
🛁 🚿 148 🏠 **P**100 Lift ☾ sB 🛁 🚿 127—157
dB 🛁 🚿 198—214 📺
Credit cards [1] [2] [3] [4] [5]

★★**Deutsches Haus** Bahnhofstr 35
☎21051 tx0823640
rm38 (🛁 🚿 37) 🏠 **P**6 Lift ☾ sB49—54
sB 🛁 🚿 75—90 dB92—98
dB 🛁 🚿 104—135

HAGNAU
Baden-Württemberg (☎97532)

★**Landhaus Maessmer** Meersburgerstr 12
(n.rest) ☎6227
Mar—Oct
rm14 (🛁 🚿 13) **P**14 sB50—70
sB 🛁 🚿 50—70 dB 🛁 🚿 90—140 mountains
lake

HAHNENKLEE See **GOSLAR**

HALTINGEN
Baden-Württemberg (☎07621)

★***Rebstock*** Grosse Gasse 30 ☎62257
rm19 (🚿 10) A4rm 🏠 **P** ☾

HALVER
Nordrhein-Westfalen (☎02353)

At **CARTHAUSEN** (4km NE)

★★★**Frommann** ☎611
🛁 🚿 22 A16rm 🏠 **P**40 sB 🛁 🚿 80—90
dB 🛁 🚿 131—143 📺
Credit cards [1] [2] [3] [5]

HAMBURG
Hamburg (☎040)

★★★★★**Vier Jahreszeiten** Neuer
Jungfernstieg 9—14 ☎34941 tx211629
🛁 175 🏠 **P** Lift ☾ sB 🛁 250—315
dB 🛁 374—464 M alc lake
Credit cards [2] [3] [4] [5]

★★★★**Atlantic Kempinski Hamburg**
an der Alster 72 ☎248001 tx2163297
🛁 282 🏠 **P**100 Lift ☾ sB 🛁 283—303
dB 🛁 356—426 📺 lake
Credit cards [1] [2] [3] [4] [5]

★★★★**Hamburg Plaza** Marseiller Str 2
☎35020 tx214400
🛁 🚿 570 🏠 **P**300 Lift ☾ sB 🛁 🚿 180—250
dB 🛁 🚿 220—290 📺 lake
Credit cards [1] [2] [3] [4] [5]

★★★**Berlin** Borgfeldstr 1—9 ☎251640
tx213939
🛁 🚿 93 **P**50 Lift ☾ sB 🛁 🚿 100—120
dB 🛁 🚿 130—150 M alc
Credit cards [1] [2] [3] [5]

★★★***Crest* (See page 50)** Mexikoring 1
City Nord ☎6305051 tx2174155
🛁 185 **P**100 Lift ☾
Credit cards [1] [2] [3] [4] [5]

★★★**Europäischer Hof** (GT) Kirchenallee
45 ☎248171 tx2162493
🛁 🚿 350 **P**100 Lift ☾ sB 🛁 🚿 120—190
dB 🛁 🚿 160—240 M15

★★★**Novotel Hamburg Nord** Oldesloer
Str 166, Schnelsen ☎5502073 tx212923
🛁 124 **P**176 Lift ☾ sB 🛁 122—142
dB 🛁 142—152 Mfr19 ⛱
Credit cards [1] [2] [3] [5]

★★★**Oper** Drehbahn 15 ☎35601
tx212475
🛁 🚿 112 🏠 **P**1000 Lift ☾ sB 🛁 🚿 105—130
dB 🛁 🚿 135—170 Mfr15
Credit cards [1] [2] [3] [5]

★★★**Reichshof** (SRS) Kirchenallee 34
☎248330 tx2163396
🛁 🚿 310 🏠 Lift ☾ sB 🛁 🚿 130—180
dB 🛁 🚿 190—260 M alc
Credit cards [1] [2] [3] [5]

★★★**Smolka** Isestr 98, Harvestehude
☎475057 tx215275
🛁 🚿 40 🏠 **P**6 Lift ☾ sB 🛁 🚿 115—165
dB 🛁 🚿 186—215 M alc
Credit cards [1] [2] [3] [5]

★★**Ibis** Wandsbeker Zollstr 25—29
☎6829021 tx2164929
🚿 144 **P**500 Lift sB🚿 100—106
dB🚿 141—147
Credit cards [1] [2] [3] [5]

★★**Pacific** Neuer Pferdemarkt 30 (n.rest)
☎4395094
rm60 (🛁 🚿 30) **P**30 Lift ☾ sB55
sB 🛁 🚿 65—75 dB85 dB 🛁 🚿 95—105

★**Hamburg** Hoheluftshaussee 119 (n.rest)
☎204141
rm36 (🛁 🚿 17) 🏠 **P**12 ☾ sB 🛁 🚿 97
dB 🛁 🚿 139
Credit cards [1] [2] [3] [5]

○**Holiday Inn** Graumannsweg 10
☎2277091 tx2165287
Due to open Summer 1987
🛁 290 **P**200 Lift ☾ sB 🛁 186—216
dB 🛁 237—282 M16—38 📺
Credit cards [1] [2] [3] [4] [5]

🚗 ***BMC Autohandelsgesellschaft***
Stormaner Str 26 ☎683344 **P** AR Saa

🚗 ***A Dannmeyer*** Grossiohering 66
☎6724569 AR

🚗 ***Dethlefs Automobile*** Neuländer Str 6
☎774775 **P** AR

🚗 **Nemeth** Koppel 65 ☎244849 AR DJ Peu
RR

P Nitzschke Steinbeker Hauptstr 84
☎7128459 **P** AR LR

🚗 **Vidal** Angerstr 20—22 ☎257900 **P** DJ LR

HAMELN
Niedersachsen (☎05151)

★★★**Dorint Weserbergland** 164 er Ring
3 ☎7920 tx924716
🛁 🚿 103 🏠 **P**40 ☾ sB 🛁 🚿 91—116
dB 🛁 🚿 152—168 📺
Credit cards [1] [2] [3] [5]

★★**Zur Börse** Osterstr 41a ☎7080
Closed Xmas & New Years Day
🛁 🚿 36 🏠 **P**25 Lift sB 🛁 🚿 43—49
dB 🛁 🚿 76—92 M12—20
Credit cards [1] [2] [5]

H Struck Hastenbeckerweg 50 ☎12052 **P**
For

HANAU AM MAIN
Hessen (☎06181)

🚗 **Zentralgarage-Bommersheim** Hernstr
21—23 ☎29060 **P** For

HANNOVER
Niedersachsen (☎0511)

★★★**Crest (See page 50)** Tiergartenstr
117 ☎523092 tx922748
🛁 🚿 108 🏠 **P**100 Lift ☾
Credit cards [1] [2] [3] [4] [5]

★★★**Kastens Luisenhof** (SRS) Luisenstr
1—3 ☎1244 tx922325
🛁 🚿 180 🏠 **P**120 Lift ☾ sB 🛁 🚿 129—215
dB 🛁 🚿 192—340 M25—60
Credit cards [1] [2] [3] [4] [5]

★★★**Parkhotel Kronsberg** (BW)
Messeschnellweg ☎861086 tx923448
🛁 🚿 109 🏠 **P**400 Lift ☾ sB 🛁 🚿 105—150
dB 🛁 🚿 160—200 M alc
Credit cards [1] [2] [3] [4] [5]

★★**Central Kaiserhof** E-August-Platz 4
☎327811 tx922810
🛁 🚿 81 **P**20 Lift ☾ sB 🛁 🚿 96—168
dB 🛁 🚿 136—256
Credit cards [1] [2] [3] [5]

★★**Föhrenhof** (BW) Kirchhorster Str 22
☎61721 tx923448
🛁 🚿 78 **P**150 Lift ☾ sB 🛁 🚿 110—150
dB 🛁 🚿 170—200 M alc
Credit cards [1] [2] [3] [4] [5]

🚗 **British Cars** Constantinstr 90c ☎691150
M/c **P** AR DJ

Deisterstrasse Deisterstr 33—37 ☎444016
P For

HANNOVER AIRPORT

★★★★**Holiday Inn** Petzelstr 60,
Flughafen ☎730171 tx0924030
🛁 🚿 145 **P**250 Lift ☾ sB 🛁 🚿 155—185
dB 🛁 🚿 195—235 📺
Credit cards [1] [2] [3] [4] [5]

HARRISLEE See **FLENSBURG**

HARZBURG (BAD)
Niedersachsen (☎05322)

★★★**Bodes** Stadtpark 48 ☎2041
rm90 (🛁 🚿 81) 🏠 **P**60 Lift ☾ sB35—45
sB 🛁 🚿 46—72 dB70—80 dB 🛁 🚿 90—150
Credit cards [2] [5]

Germany

★★**Braunschweiger Hof** H-Willhelm Str 54 ☎7035 tx957821
🛁🚿69 🏠**P**45 Lift sB🛁🚿69—98 dB🛁🚿118—158 M10—42 ▣ mountains
Credit cards [1] [2] [3] [5]

HEIDELBERG
Baden-Württemberg (☎06221)

See also **WALLDORF**

★★★**Alt Heidelberg** Rohrbacher Str 29 ☎15091 tx461897
🛁80 A20rm 🏠**P**22 Lift ☾ sB🛁125—145 dB🛁165—195 M23
Credit cards [1] [2] [3] [4] [5]

★★★***Anlage*** F-Ebert Anlage 32 ☎26425
rm20 (🛁🚿19) **P** Lift ☾

★★★**Crest (See page 50)** Pleikartsförsterstr 101, Kirchheim ☎71021 tx461650
🛁🚿112 🏠**P**150 ☾ sB🛁🚿142—169 dB🛁🚿179—214
Credit cards [1] [2] [3] [4] [5]

★★★**Europälsche Hof** (SRS) F-Ebert Anlage 1 ☎27101 tx461840
🛁🚿127 🏠**P**150 Lift ☾ sB🛁🚿139—219 dB🛁🚿250—310 M45—58
Credit cards [1] [2] [3] [5]

★★★**Ritter** (ROM) Haupstr 178 ☎24272 tx461506
rm34 (🛁🚿26) **P**30 Lift ☾ sB60—65 sB🛁🚿75—140 dB85—90 dB🛁🚿140—250 M20—25
Credit cards [1] [2] [3] [5]

★★**Central** (n.rest) ☎20672 tx461566
rm52 (🛁🚿44) 🏠**P**20 Lift ☾ sB46 sB🛁🚿67 dB🛁🚿118
Credit card [2]

★**Kohler** Goethestr 2 (n.rest) ☎24360
12 Jan—19 Dec
rm43 (🛁🚿32) **P** Lift ☾ sB49—54 sB🛁🚿62—75 dB72—84 dB🛁🚿89—112

★**Vier Jahreszeiten** Haspelgasse 2, an der alten Brücke ☎24164
23 Jan—21 Dec
rm24 (🛁🚿16) A2rm 🏠**P**10 ☾ sB55—85 sB🛁🚿95—135 dB95—100 dB🛁🚿145—185 mountains

Auto-Bahr In der Neckarhelle 41 ☎800181 **P** Peu Tal

🚙 **Auto-Kunz** Pleikartsförster Str 13 ☎71055 M/c **P** BMW Hon Peu Tal

Bosch-Dienet Karl Benz Str 2 ☎22171 Lucas

🚙 **Raichle & Baur** Hebelstr 12 ☎24954 AR DJ LR

HEILBRONN
Baden-Württemberg (☎07131)

★★★**Insel** F-Ebert Brücke ☎6300 tx728777
🛁120 **P**100 Lift ☾ sB🛁94—178 dB🛁178—228 M29 ▣
Credit cards [3] [5]

★★**Kronprinz** Bahnhofstr 29 ☎83941 tx728561
rm35 (🛁🚿20) 🏠**P**6 Lift sB52—54 sB🛁🚿62—71 dB93—102 dB🛁🚿111—121 M12—32

🚙 **ASG Auto-Service** Weipertstr 17 ☎161850 **P** AR DJ LR

HEILIGENROTH See **MONTABAUR**

HELMSTEDT
Niedersachsen (☎05351)

★★**Petzold** Schöninger Str 1 ☎6001
rm28 (🛁🚿21) 🏠**P**17 sB39 sB🛁🚿46—50 dB64 dB🛁🚿78 M12—26 & alc

🚙 **Wagner** K-Adenauer-Pl 3 ☎31007 **P** Aud VW

HEPPENHEIM AN DER BERGSTRASSE
Hessen (☎06252)

★**Goldenen Engel** Grosser Markt 2 ☎2563
rm35 (🛁🚿18) 🏠**P**10 sBfr40 sB🛁🚿44—59 dBfr69 dB🛁🚿74—94 M9—25 mountains

HERFORD
Nordrhein-Westfalen (☎05221)

Niebaum & Hamacher Liebig Str 3—6 ☎72069 **P** For

🚙 ***P Wiegers*** Waltgeriststr 71 ☎2086 **P** M/c AR DJ Hon

HERRENALB (BAD)
Baden-Württemberg (07083)

★★★★**Mönchs Posthotel** (Relais et Châteaux) Dobler Str 2 ☎7440 tx7245123
🛁🚿50 🏠**P**40 Lift ☾ sB🛁🚿115—135 dB🛁🚿200—245 M35—45 🏊 ▤ mountains
Credit cards [2] [5]

HERRENBERG
Baden-Württemberg (☎07032)

★**Neue Post** Wilhelmstr 48 ☎5156
13 Jan—23 Dec
rm7 (🚿4) **P**9 sB37 sB🚿43 dB74 dB🚿86 M8—17

HERSFELD (BAD)
Hessen (☎06621)

★★**Parkhotel Rose** am Kurpark 9 ☎14454
🛁🚿20 🏠**P**24 Lift sB🛁🚿90—95 dB🛁🚿159 M25—95&alc mountains
Credit cards [1] [2] [3] [5]

★★**Stern** (ROM) Lingg Pl 11 ☎72007
🛁🚿49 A19rm 🏠**P**30 Lift sB🛁🚿65—90 dB🛁🚿110—140 M18—32 ▣
Credit cards [1] [2] [3] [5]

HILDESHEIM
Niedersachsen (☎05121)

Felske Automobile Porschestr 2 ☎515077 **P** AR DJ

HINDELANG
Bayern (☎08324)

★★★**Prinz-Luitpold-Bad** A-Gross Weg ☎2011
🛁🚿115 🏠**P**80 Lift ☾ sB🛁🚿71—118 dB🛁🚿116—242 M16—28 🔧 ▣ 🏊 mountains

HINTERZARTEN
Baden-Württemberg (☎07652)

★★★★**Parkhotel Adler** (Relais et Châteaux) Adlepl ☎711 tx772692
🛁🚿74 A15rm 🏠**P**200 Lift ☾ sB🛁🚿110—195 dB🛁🚿180—345 M38—85 🔧 ▣ Ʊ mountains
Credit cards [1] [2] [3] [4] [5]

HÖCHENSCHWAND
Baden-Württemberg (☎07672)

★★★**Kurhaus** Kurhauspl 1 ☎4111 tx7721212
rm50 (🛁🚿41) 🏠**P**60 Lift ☾ sB40—52 sB🛁🚿56—81 dB🛁🚿52—77 🔧 ▣ mountains
Credit cards [1] [2] [3] [5]

HÖCHSTADT AN DER AISCH
Bayern (☎09193)

★★**Kapuzinerbräu** Hauptstr 28 (n.rest) ☎8327
🛁🚿15 🏠**P**25 Lift sB🛁🚿53—63 dB🛁🚿86—96

HOCKENHEIM
Baden-Württemberg (☎06205)

★★**Luxhof** an der Speyerer Brücke ☎32333
🛁🚿50 A8rm 🏠**P** sB🛁🚿70—99 dB🛁🚿120—152 M15—30

HOF
Bayern (☎09281)

🚙 **Autoveri** C-Benz Str 4 ☎9067 **P** For

HOHELEYE See **WINTERBERG**

HOHENSCHWANGAU
Bayern (☎08362)

★★**Lisl und Jägerhaus** Neuschwansteinstr 1 ☎81006 tx541332
Jan—Mar
rm56 (🛁🚿49) A20rm Lift ☾ sB38—48 sB🛁🚿68-78 dBfr86 dB🛁🚿86—176 M3—60
Credit cards [1] [2] [3] [5]

HOLZMINDEN
Niedersachsen (☎05531)

H Friedrich Bülte 3 ☎7820 **P** Cit

HOMBURG (BAD)
Hessen (☎06172)

At **FRIEDRICHSDORF** (5km NE on 455, Exit Friedberg from autobahn A5 E4)

★★★***Crest Im Taunus* (See page 50)** Im Dammwald 1 ☎171 tx415892
🛁134 **P**100 Lift ☾
Credit cards [1] [2] [3] [4] [5]

HOMBURG SAAR
Saarland (☎06841)

★★★**Stadt Homburg** (BW) Ringstr 80 ☎1331 tx44683
🛁🚿40 A10rm 🏠**P**50 Lift ☾ sB🛁🚿85 dB🛁🚿130—170 ▣
Credit cards [1] [2] [3] [5]

HONNEF AM RHEIN (BAD)
Nordrhein-Westfalen (☎02224)

🚗 ***P Reuffel*** Bahnhofstr 2B ☎2406 **P** Alf AR

At **ZWINDHAGEN-REDERSCHEID** (8km SE)

★★★**Golfhotel Waldbrunnen** Brunnenstr 7 ☎(02645) 150 tx863020

🛁🚿50 ⌂ **P**100 Lift ☾ sB🛁🚿99—145 dB🛁🚿180—210 ⚲ ⛶ ▣ ∪ ▣
Credit cards 1 2 3 5

HORNBERG
Baden-Württemberg (☎07833)

★★**Schloss Hornberg** auf dem Schlossberg 1 ☎6841

Feb—22 Dec
rm43 (🛁🚿36) **P**30 sBfr35 sB🛁🚿45—65 dBfr55 dB🛁🚿65—100 M12—45 mountains
Credit cards 1 2 3 5

HORSTMAR
Nordrhein-Westfalen (☎02558)

★**Crins** Münsterstr 11 ☎7370

rm12 (🚿1) A6rm ⌂ sB33 dB65 M7—22
Credit cards 1 2 3 4 5

INGOLSTADT
Bayern (☎0841)

★★★★**Holiday Inn** Goethestr 153 ☎2281 tx55710

🛁123 **P**120 Lift sB🛁125—166 dB🛁170—226 M20—35 ▣
Credit cards 1 2 3 4 5

★★**Rappensberger** Harderstr 3 ☎1625 tx55834

3 Jan—24 Dec
rm95 (🛁🚿64) ⌂ Lift ☾ sB46—48 sB🛁🚿78—88 dB80—85 dB🛁🚿120—155 M9—25
Credit cards 1 2 5

★**Adler** Theresienstr 22 ☎35107

Feb—23 Dec
rm45 ⌂ **P**20 ☾ sBfr36 dBfr64

Bacher Goethestr 56 ☎2261 **P** For

🚗 **F Querfurt** Esplanade 3 ☎32603 **P** AR

🚗 ***E Willner*** Goethestr 61 ☎2205 **P** Ope Vau

At **GAIMERSHEIM** (8km NW)

★★**Heidehof** Ingolstädter Str, 121, Friedrichshofen ☎(08458)711 tx55688

🛁56 ⌂ **P**109 Lift sB🛁79—93 dB🛁125—145 ▣
Credit cards 1 2 3 5

INZELL
Bayern (☎08665)

★★★**Dorint Inzell** Lärchenstr 5 ☎6051 tx866580

🛁🚿88 **P**120 Lift ☾ sB🛁🚿59—75 dB🛁🚿98—160 ▣ mountains
Credit cards 1 2 3 5

ISERLOHN
Nordrhein-Westfalen (☎02371)

🚗 **Sportcar Centre** Baarstr 119 ☎40048 **P** Alf AR LR

Germany

ISNY
Baden-Württemberg (☎07562)

★★**Hohe Linde** Lindauerstr 75 ☎2066

rm30 (🛁🚿18) ⌂ **P** sB36 sB🛁🚿46 dB74 dB🛁🚿88 ▣

JESTEBURG
Niedersachsen (☎04183)

At **ASENDORF** (4.5km SE)

★★**Heidschnucke** zum Auetal 14 ☎2094-99

rm53 (🛁🚿49) **P**100 sB53—63 sB🛁🚿73—89 dB90—108 dB🛁🚿122—154 M15—60 ▣
Credit cards 1 2 3 5

KAISERSLAUTERN
Rheinland-Pfalz (☎0631)

★★★**Dorint Pfalzerwald** St-Quentin Ring 1 ☎28071 tx45614

🛁🚿150 ⌂ **P**140 Lift ☾ sB🛁🚿86—116 dB🛁🚿132—168 ▣
Credit cards 1 2 3 5

🚗 **Schicht** Kaiserstr 74 ☎54060 **P** BMW

KAMP-BORNHOFEN
Rheinland-Pfalz (☎06773)

★**Anker** Rheinuferstr 46 ☎215

Apr—Oct
rm16 (🛁🚿10) ⌂ **P**8 sB38—40 sB🛁🚿41—44 dB69—75 dB🛁🚿77—89 M12—25
Credit card 5

KARLSRUHE
Baden-Württemberg (☎0721)

★★★**Berliner Hof** Douglasstr 7 (n.rest) ☎23981

rm55 (🛁🚿54) ⌂ **P**12 Lift ☾ sBfr59 sB🛁🚿69—88 dB🛁🚿125
Credit cards 1 2 3 5

★★★**Kaiserhof** Marktpl ☎26616 tx7825600

rm40 (🛁36) **P**20 Lift sB60 sB🛁🚿90—110 dB🛁🚿110—160 M alc
Credit cards 1 2 3 4 5

★★★***Park*** (Mövenpick) Etlingerstr 23 ☎60461 tx7825443

🛁🚿126 **P**160 Lift ☾
Credit cards 1 2 3 5

★★★**Ramada Renaissance** Mendelsohnpl ☎3717-0 tx7825699

🛁215 **P**107 Lift ☾ sB🛁165—205 dB🛁205—265 M alc
Credit cards 1 2 3 4 5

★★★**Schloss** Bahnhofpl 2 ☎3540 tx7826746

🛁96 **P**30 Lift ☾ sB🛁145—160 dB🛁225—260 M15—30
Credit cards 1 2 3 4 5

★★**Eden** Bahnhofstr 17—19 ☎28718 tx7826415

🛁🚿68 ⌂ **P**6 Lift ☾ sB🛁🚿80—115 dB🛁🚿110—168
Credit cards 1 2 3 5

★★**Hasen** Gerwigstr 47 ☎615076

rm37 (🛁🚿36) ⌂ **P** Lift ☾ sB58 sB🛁🚿68—75 dB🛁🚿fr95 M15—30
Credit cards 1 2 3 5

★★**Markt** Kaiserstr 76 (n.rest) ☎27777

rm31 (🛁🚿28) ⌂ **P** Lift ☾ sBfr60 sB🛁🚿70—90 dB90—99 dB🛁🚿110—125
Credit cards 1 2 3 5

🚗 ***Autohaus Badenia*** Industriegebiet Westbahnhof Ziegelstr 1 ☎590070 **P** Dat

🚗 **Böhler** Ottostr 6 ☎409090 **P** Vol

Autohaus Jurgen Kussmaulstr 15 ☎751099 **P** AR Col DJ

F Opel Herman Billing Str 8—12 ☎1301 Ope

Vollmer & Sack Gottesauerstr 37 ☎60471 **P** For

Zentral Blumenstr 4 ☎27141 **P** Peu Tal

At **GRÖTZINGEN** (8km E)

★★★**Schloss Augustenburg** (GS) Kirchstr 20 ☎48555 tx7826647

🛁🚿27 A12rm **P**40 sB🛁🚿95—120 dB🛁🚿140—160
Credit cards 1 3 5

KASSEL
Hessen (☎0561)

★★★★**Holiday Inn** Hellingenrödestr 61 ☎52151 tx99814

🛁141 **P**200 Lift sB🛁109—161 dB🛁138—210 M alc ▣
Credit cards 1 2 3 4 5

★★★**Dorint Reiss** W-Hilpert Str 24 Hauptbahnhof ☎78830 tx099740

rm101 (🛁🚿78) ⌂ **P**100 Lift ☾ sB🛁🚿59—118 dB🛁🚿148—168
Credit cards 1 2 3 5

★★★**Park-Hotel Hessenland** Obere Königsstr 2, am Rathaus ☎14974 tx99773

rm94 (🛁🚿80) **P** Lift ☾ sB48 sB🛁🚿73 dB86 dB🛁🚿106 M10
Credit cards 1 2 5

🚗 ***Auto Rössler*** Raiffeisenstr 1 ☎21063 **P** For

Autohaus Stadhallengarage Breitscheidstr 37 ☎103831 Peu

Kuhlborn-Fahrzeuge Sternbergstr 3 ☎21322 AR Saa

F Richter Schillerstr 46—48 ☎700030 For

At **ESPANAU** (10km NW)

★★**Waldhotel Schäferberg** Wilhelmsthaler Str 14 ☎(05673)7971

🛁🚿60 ⌂ **P**100 Lift sB🛁🚿58—83 dB🛁🚿98—126 M12—30
Credit cards 1 2 3 4 5

KAUFBEUREN
Bayern (☎08341)

🚗 **Langer** Neugablonzer Str 88 ☎8448 For

At **BIESSENHOFEN** (6.5km S)

★★**Neue Post** Füssener Str 17 ☎8525
20 P150 sB 37—70
dB 66—130 M20—50 mountains
Credit cards 1 2 3 5

KEHL
Baden-Württemberg (☎07851)

Geiger Strassburger Str 11 ☎5046 **P** Aud Por VW

Zipperer Königsberger Str 10 ☎8077 For

KELHEIM
Bayern (☎09441)

★★**Ehrnthaller** Donaustr 22 ☎3333
rm69 (55) **P** Lift sB33
sB 41—61 dB50—60 dB 68—98
Credit cards 1 2 3 5

KEMPTEN (ALLGÄU)
Bayern (☎0831)

★★★**Fürstenhof** (BW) Rathauspl 8
☎23050 tx541535
76 A21rm **P** Lift sB 95—140
dB 150—200 M alc
Credit cards 1 2 3 5

★★★***Peterhof*** Salzstr 1 ☎25525
51 **P** Lift ☾ M alc

KIEL
Schleswig-Holstein (☎0431)

★★★**Conti-Hansa** (BW) Schlossgarten 7
☎5115-0 tx282913
167 **P90** Lift ☾ sB 159—209
dB 203—263 M30 lake
Credit cards 1 2 3 4 5

Inter-Car Hamburg Chaussee ☎686441
P All makes

Paulsen & Thoms Stormarnstr 35
☎680191 **P** For

KIRCHHEIM
Hessen (☎06625)

★★★**Motel Center** (1.5km S near Autobahn exit) ☎631 tx0493337
140 **P200** sB 65—80
dB 90—110 M12—30
mountains
Credit cards 1 2 3 5

KISSINGEN (BAD)
Bayern (☎0971)

★★★**Bristol** Bismarckstr 8—10 ☎4031
Mar—Oct
rm101 (83) **P20** Lift ☾ sB85—93
sB 99—110 dB170—180
dB 190—200 M20—25

★★★**Dorint** Prühlingstr 1 ☎3050
tx672910
94 **P30** Lift ☾ sB 79—88
dB 128—146
Credit cards 1 2 3 5

★★**Fürst Bismarck** Euerdorfer Str 4
☎1277
Feb—Nov
rm36 (31) **P35** Lift ☾ sB44—49
sB 64—79 dB86—98 dB 132—168

Germany

M9—20
Credit cards 1 3 4

K H Fürsch Kapellenstr 31 ☎61413 AR

KLEVE
Nordrhein-Westfalen (☎02821)

Arden Automobile Kalkarer Str 21—23
☎29200 **P** AR

KLOSTERREICHENBACH
Baden-Württemberg (☎07442)

★★**Sonne-Post** ☎2277
Closed 1—21 Dec
rm28 (19) **P30** sB37—51
sB 49—61 dB74—102
dB 98—122 M10—35 t% mountains

KOBLENZ
Rheinland-Pfalz (☎0261)

★★★**Diehl's Rheinterrasse**
Ehrenbreitstein ☎72010 tx862663
65 **P54** Lift ☾ sB 75—95
dB 130—200 M18—36
Credit cards 1 2 5

★★★***Kleiner Riesen*** Rheinanlagen 18
(n.rest) ☎32077 tx862442
27 **P** Lift ☾

★★**Scholz** Moselweisser Str 121 ☎42488
30 **P** sB 48 dB 85
M8—23
Credit cards 1 2 3 5

G Schilling Andernacher Str 232
☎85003 Ren

P Wirtz Andernacher Str 201 ☎83028
Ope

KÖLN (COLOGNE)
Nordrhein-Westfalen (☎0221)

See plan page 220

★★★★★**Excelsior Hotel-Ernst** (SRS)
Dompl ☎2701 tx8882645 Plan **1**
146 Lift ☾ sB 208—255
dB 260—380 M39—45
Credit cards 1 2 5

★★★★★**Dom** (THF) Domkloster 2A
☎233751 tx8882919 Plan **2**
126 **P** Lift ☾ sB 235—275
dB 355—405 Mfr40
Credit cards 1 2 3 5

★★★**Augustinerplatz** Hohestr 30 (n.rest)
☎236717 tx2214040 Plan **3**
57 **P** Lift ☾ sB 100—155
dB 190—245
Credit cards 1 2 3 5

★★★**Haus Lyskirchen** am Filzengraben
26—32 ☎234891 tx08885449 Plan **5**
2 Jan—23 Dec
95 **P40** Lift ☾ sB 90—136
dB 165—196
Credit cards 1 2 3 5

★★★**Mondial** (ETAP) Berchergasse 10
☎219671 tx8881932 Plan **6**
204 **P120** Lift ☾ sB 140—160
dB 185—200
Credit cards 1 2 3 5

★★★**Rheingold** Engelbertstr 33—35
(n.rest) ☎236531 tx8882923 Plan **8**
48 **P** Lift ☾ sB 115 dB 185
Credit cards 1 2 3 5

★★**Ariane** Hohe Pforte 19—21 (n.rest)
☎236033 Plan **9**
rm44 (41) **P4** Lift ☾sB48—63
sB 73—126 dB94—134
dB 144—194

★★**Berlin** Domstr 10 ☎123051 tx8885123
Plan **10**
rm78 (76) **P14** Lift ☾ sB53—83
sB 83—110 dB110—165
dB 135—200
Credit cards 1 2 3 4 5

★★***Conti*** Brüsseler Str 42 ☎219262
tx8881644 Plan **12**
5 Jan—19 Dec
43 Lift ☾
Credit cards 1 2 3

★★**Intercity Ibis** Bahnhofvorpl (n.rest)
☎132051 tx8881002 Plan **12A**
66 Lift sB 99 dB 129
Credit cards 1 2 3 5

★★***Panorama*** Siegburgesrstr 37
☎884041 Plan **13**
30 **P** Lift ☾

At **KÖLN-BONN AIRPORT** (17km SE)

★★★★**Holiday Inn** Waldstr 255 ☎5610
tx8874665 Not on plan
112 **P100** Lift ☾ sB 181 dB 238
Credit cards 1 2 3 4 5

At **KÖLN-LINDENTHAL**

★★★***Crest* (See page 50)** Dürener Str
287 ☎463001 tx8882516 Plan **4**
154 **P150** Lift ☾ lake
Credit cards 1 2 3 4 5

★★**Bremer** Dürenerstr 225 ☎405013
tx8882063 Plan **11**
5 Jan—22 Dec
rm69 (58) A16rm **P30** Lift ☾
sB65—90 sB 95—115 dB100—115
dB 140—170 M28—55
Credit cards 1 2 3 5

At **KÖLN-MARSDORF**

★★★***Novotel*** Horbellerstr 1 ☎16081
tx8886355 Plan **6A**
140 **P120** Lift ☾
Credit cards 1 2 3 5

At **KÖLN-MÜLHEIM**

★★★**Kaiser** Genovevastr 10—14 (n.rest)
☎623057 tx8873546 Plan **7**
40 **P20** Lift ☾ sB 95—175
dB 125—220
Credit cards 1 2 3 5

KÖNIGSFELD IM SCHWARZWALD
Baden-Württemberg (☎07725)

★★★**Schwarzwald** H-Voland Str 10
☎7093 tx792426
rm56 (47) **P32** Lift sB56—64 →

KÖLN (COLOGNE)

1 ★★★★★ Excelsior Hotel-Ernst
2 ★★★★★ Dom
3 ★★★ Augustinerplatz
4 ★★★ Crest (At Köln-Lindenthal)
5 ★★★ Haus Lyskirchen
6 ★★★ Mondial
6A ★★★ Novotel (At Köln-Marsdorf)
7 ★★★ Kaiser (At Köln-Mülheim)
8 ★★★ Rheingold
9 ★★ Ariane
10 ★★ Berlin
11 ★★ Bremer (At Köln-Lindenthal)
12 ★★ Conti
12A ★★ Intercity Ibis
13 ★★ Panorama

sB🛁🚿69–75 dB96 dB🛁🚿112–152 ✂ ▭
Credit cards 1 2 3 5

KÖNIGSTEIN IM TAUNUS
Hessen (☎06174)

★★★**Sonnenhof** Falkensteiner Str 9 ☎3051 tx410636
rm44 (🛁🚿38) ⌂ ☾ sB76–96
sB🛁🚿fr124 dB108–158
dB🛁🚿184–204 M 21–78 ✂ ▭
Credit cards 1 2 5

★★**Parkhotel Bender** Frankfurterstr 1 ☎1005
rm36 (🛁🚿22) ⌂ **P**20 sB42–57
sB🛁🚿72–97 dB69–84
dB🛁🚿104–134
Credit cards 1 2 3 5

KÖNIGSWINTER
Nordrhein-Westfalen (☎02223)

★**Siebengebirge** Haupstr 342 ☎21359
Feb–15 Dec
rm10 (🚿8) ⌂ **P**7 sB40–44 sB🚿43–48
dB73–80 dB🚿85–100 M12–25
Credit cards 1 2 3 5

KONSTANZ (CONSTANCE)
Baden-Württemberg (☎07531)

★★★**Insel** (SRS) auf der Insel 1 ☎25011 tx733276
rm113 (🛁112) A2rm **P** Lift ☾
sB🛁115–160 dB🛁170–230 lake

★★**Deutsches Haus** Markstätte 15 (n.rest) ☎27065
rm42 (🛁🚿34) ⌂ Lift ☾ sB45
sB🛁🚿55–60 dB75 dB🛁🚿115–130
Credit cards 1 2 5

KORNTAL-MÜNCHINGEN
Baden-Württemberg (☎07150)

★★★**Mercure** Siemensstr 55 ☎130 tx723589
🛁209 **P**250 Lift sB🛁fr151 dB🛁fr185 ▭
Credit cards 1 2 3 4 5

KREFELD
Nordrhein-Westfalen (☎02151)

★★★**Parkhotel Krefelder Hof** (BW) Uerdinger Str 245 ☎590191 tx853748
🛁148 ⌂ **P**180 Lift ☾ sB🛁150–180 →

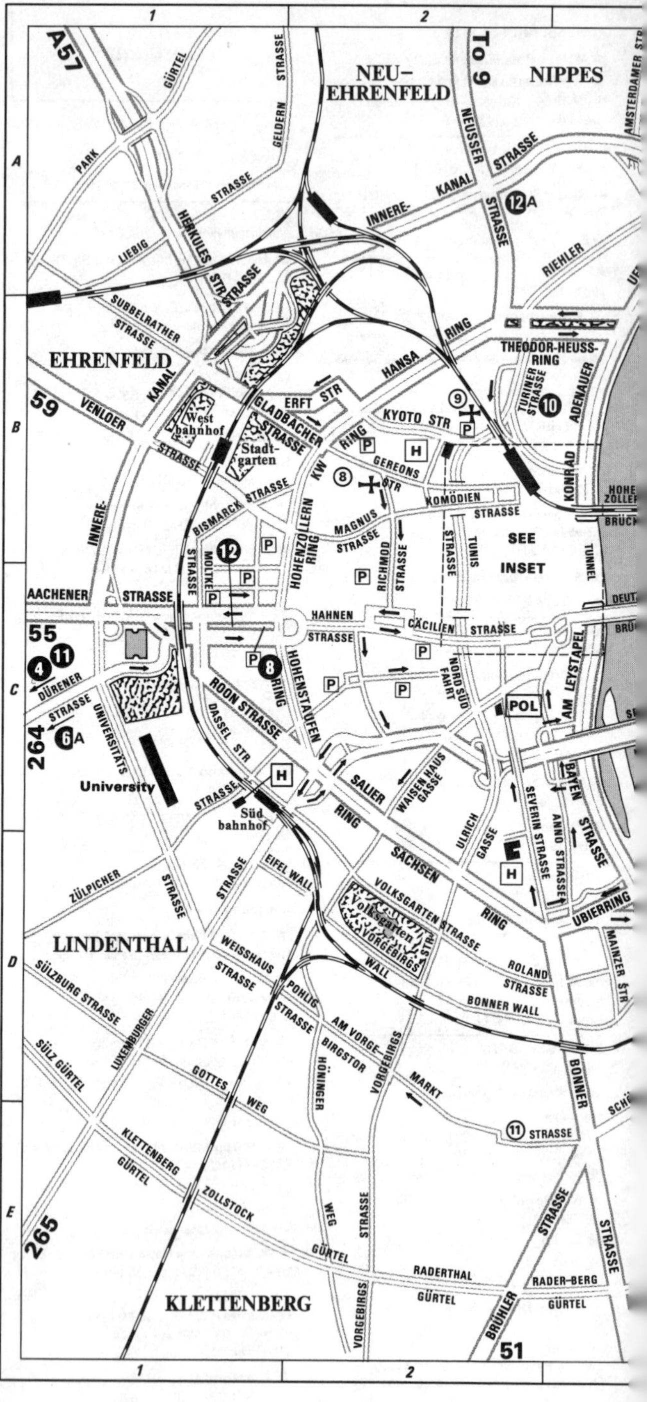

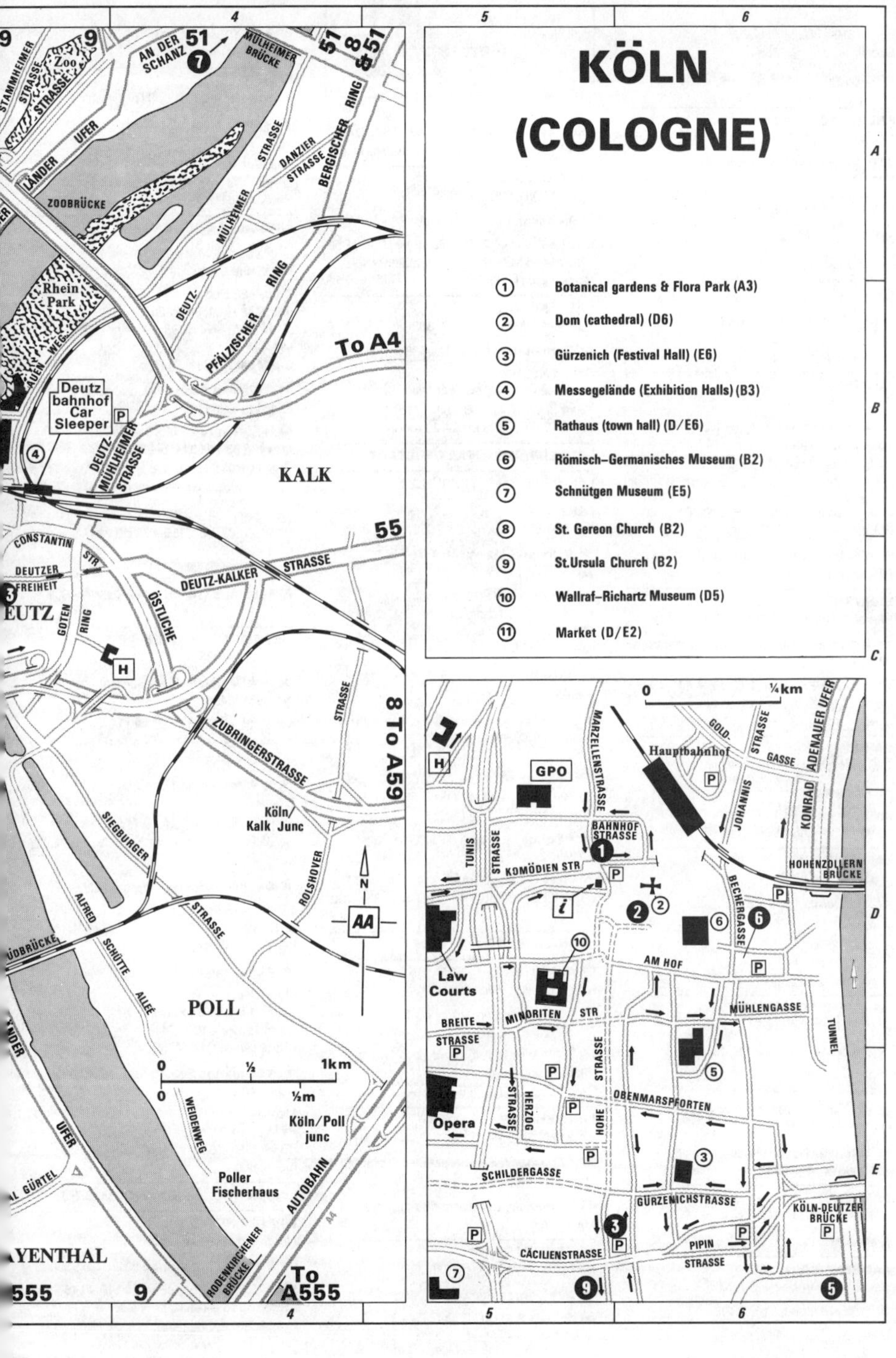

KÖLN
(COLOGNE)
① Botanical gardens & Flora Park (A3)
② Dom (cathedral) (D6)
③ Gürzenich (Festival Hall) (E6)
④ Messegelände (Exhibition Halls) (B3)
⑤ Rathaus (town hall) (D/E6)
⑥ Römisch-Germanisches Museum (B2)
⑦ Schnütgen Museum (E5)
⑧ St. Gereon Church (B2)
⑨ St.Ursula Church (B2)
⑩ Wallraf-Richartz Museum (D5)
⑪ Market (D/E2)
KALK
POLL
Zoo
Rhein Park
Deutz bahnhof Car Sleeper
To A4
To A59
To A555
Köln/Kalk Junc
Köln/Poll junc
Poller Fischerhaus
Hauptbahnhof
GPO
Law Courts
Opera

dB 210—252 M38
Credit cards 1 2 3 5

Preckel Virchowstr 140—146 ☎37110 **P** Ren

KREUZNACH (BAD)
Rheinland-Pfalz (☎0671)

E Holzhäuser Mannheimerstr 183—185 ☎30031 For

KREUZWERTHEIM See **WERTHEIM**

KRONBERG IM TAUNUS
Hessen (☎06173)

★★★**Schloss** Hainstr 25 ☎7011 tx415424

rm54 (52) **P**60 Lift sB 200—225 dB 310—355 M alc
Credit cards 1 2 3 4 5

KULMBACH
Bayern (☎09221)

★★★**Hansa-Hotel-Hönsch** Weltrichstr 2A (n.rest) ☎7995

rm29 (25) **P** Lift sB42—48 sB 50—58 dB90—98 dB 98—110

A Dippold Kronacher Str 2 ☎2017 Aud Por VW

W Schubarth Kronacher Str 29 ☎5660 AR DJ

LAHNSTEIN
Rheinland-Pfalz (☎02621)

★★★**Rhein-Lahn** (Dorint) Im Kurzentrum 14 ☎151 tx8698275

220 **P**420 Lift sB 88—104 dB 150—180 mountains
Credit cards 1 2 3 5

LAHR
Baden-Württemberg (☎07821)

★★**Schulz** Alte Bahnhofstr 6 ☎22674

rm37 (16) **P**21 Lift sB54—110 sB 54—110 dB60—150 dB 60—150

LAMPERTHEIM
Hessen (☎06206)

★★★***Deutsches Haus*** Kaiserstr 47 ☎2022

6 Jan—22 Dec
31 **P**25 Lift
Credit cards 1 2 3 5

LANDAU IN DER PFALZ
Rheinland-Pfalz (☎06341)

★★**Körber** Reiterstr 11 ☎4050

15 Jan—20 Dec
rm40 (35) **P**20 sB40—45 sB 48—65 dBfr80 dB fr100
Credit card 2

Autohaus Nesper Wieslauterstr 61 ☎80066 M/c **P** Col Tal

LANDSHUT
Bayern (☎0871)

K Meusel Ottostr 15 ☎72048 For

LANGENARGEN
Baden-Württemberg (☎07543)

★★**Schiff** Marktpl 1 ☎2407

Mar—Oct

Germany

rm42 (35) **P**2 Lift sB 60—74 dB 90—146 M16—30 mountains lake

LANGENISARHOFEN
Bayern (☎09938)

★**Buhmann** Kreuzstr 1 an der B8 ☎277

rm10 (7) **P**30 sB29 sB 36 dB58 dB 66 M8—30 mountains
Credit cards 1 2 5

LAUTENBACH
Baden-Württemberg (☎07802)

★**Sternen** Hauptstr 47 ☎3538

Closed Nov
rm42 (40) **P**40 Lift sB40—42 sB 51—54 dB80—84 dB 102—108 M10—32 mountains

LAUTERBAD See **FREUDENSTADT**

LENGFELD See **WÜRZBURG**

LENZKIRCH
Baden-Württemberg (☎07653)

★★**Ursee** Grabenstr 18 ☎781

15 Dec—3 Nov
rm49 (45) **P**50 Lift sBfr50 sB 62—68 dBfr92 dB 110—150 M20—50 mountains
Credit card 3

LEONBERG
Baden-Württemberg (☎07152)

★★★**Eiss** Neue Ramtelstr 28 (near the Autobahn) ☎20041 tx724141

rm100 (75) A20rm **P**150 Lift sB56—60 sB 85—140 dBfr90 dB 150—220 M23—45
Credit cards 1 2 3 5

★★**Sonne** Stuttgarterstr 1 ☎27626 tx724127

rm40 (28) A17rm **P**40 sB40—46 sB 55—85 dB70—75 dB 85—130 M9—35

LEONI See **BERG**

LEVERKUSEN
Nordrhein-Westfalen (☎0214)

★★★**Ramada** am Büchelter Hof 11 ☎41012 tx8510238

202 **P**150 Lift sB 160—200 dB 200—290 M22
Credit cards 1 2 3 5

LICHTENFELS
Bayern (☎09571)

H Eberhardt Bamberger Str 57 ☎5006 M/c **P** Fia Peu

Szymansky Bamberger Str 125 ☎3654 M/c **P** AR

LIEBENZELL (BAD)
Baden-Württemberg (☎07052)

★★★**Kronen** Badweg 7 ☎2081

60 **P**30 Lift sB 69—80

dB 105—154 M18—62
Credit card 4

LIESER
Rheinland-Pfalz (☎06531)

★★**Mehn** Moselstr 2 ☎6019

Feb—20 Dec
rm35 (32) A9rm **P**60 sB38 sB 42—49 dB 80—115 M10—26
Credit card 1

LIMBURG AN DER LAHN
Hessen (☎06431)

★★**Dom** Grabenstr 57 ☎24077

7 Jan—23 Dec
rm59 (51) **P**22 Lift sB52 sB 78—94 dB98 dB 130—146 M9—25
Credit cards 1 2 3 5

★★**Zimmermann** Blumenröderstr 1 ☎4611 tx0484702

25 A5rm **P**16 sB 75—90 dB 98—168 M15—56
Credit cards 1 2 3 5

★**Huss** Bahnhofpl 3 ☎25087 tx4821614

rm35 (24) **P**50 Lift sB39—44 sB 58—66 dB65—76 dB 85—112 M13—25
Credit cards 1 2 3 5

Autohaus Tritsch Industriestr ☎4601 **P** For

LINDAU IM BODENSEE
Bayern (☎08382)

★★★**Bayrischer Hof** Seepromenade ☎5055 tx54340

195 **P** Lift sB 94—163 dB 188—290 M37—43 &alc mountains lake

★★★**Reutemann** Seepromenade ☎5055 tx54340

37 **P** Lift sB 84—114 dB 160—220 Mfr35&alc mountains lake

★★**Kellner** Alwindstr 7 (n.rest) ☎5686

15 May—15 Sep
rm12 (6) **P** sB38—40 sB 45 dB76—80 dB 86—92

★★**Lindauer Hof** Seehafen ☎4064

Mar—Dec
21 **P** Lift sB 58—79 dB 122—168 lake
Credit cards 1 2 3 5

★★**Seegarten** Seepromenade ☎5055 tx054340

Mar—Nov
29 **P** Lift sB 78—99 dB 119—185 Mfr35&alc lake mountains

LINDENTHAL See **KÖLN (COLOGNE)**

LIPPSPRINGE (BAD)
Nordrhein-Westfalen (☎05252)

★★★**Bad Lippspringe** ☎2010 tx936933

75 **P**120 Lift sB 115—145 dB 165—195 M25
Credit cards 1 2 3 5

LIPPSTADT
Nordrhein-Westfalen (☎02941)

Mertens Planckstr 12 ☎14041 For

LÖRRACH
Baden-Württemberg (☎07621)

★★★**Binoth am Markt** Baslerstr 169 ☎2673
rm22 (🛁 🚿 18) 🏠 **P** Lift sB45—50 sB 🛁 🚿 60—70 dB65—80 dB 🛁 🚿 90—100
Credit cards [1] [2] [3] [5]

🚗 ***Badenia*** Brühlerstr 8 ☎2420 For

🚗 ***Büche & Tröndle*** Tumringer Str 290 ☎8502 Aud Por VW

LÜBECK
Schleswig-Holstein (☎0451)

★★★**Lysia** (Mövenpick) auf der Wallhalbinsel ☎15040 tx26707
🛁 🚿 129 A60rm **P**120 Lift sB 🛁 🚿 138—168 dB 🛁 🚿 166—196 M19—24
Credit cards [1] [2] [3] [5]

★★**Kaiserhof** Kronsforder Allee 13 ☎791011
rm55 (🛁 🚿 53) A16rm 🏠 **P**30 Lift ☾ sB80—120 sB 🛁 🚿 80—120 dB 🛁 🚿 105—156 M alc
Credit cards [1] [2] [3] [5]

★★**Lindenhof** Lindenstr 1A ☎84015
rm55 (🛁 41) 🏠 **P**15 Lift ☾ sB44—48 sB 🛁 68—75 dB80—85 dB 🛁 105—125 Mfr12
Credit cards [1] [3] [4] [5]

🚗 ***Albrecht & Wirth*** Ratzeburger Allee 127 ☎501031 For

🚗 **Jäckel** Travemunder Allee 15—17 ☎33088 **P** Ren

🚗 **N Köster** Heiligen-Geist-Kamp 6—8 ☎32031 **P** Cit

LÜDENSCHEID
Nordrhein-Westfalen (☎02351)

★★★***Crest* (see page 50)** Parkstr 66 ☎1561 tx826644
🛁 195 **P**100 Lift ☾ 📺
Credit cards [1] [2] [3] [4] [5]

Märkischer Automobil Nottebohm Str 2 ☎45066 For

LUDWIGSBURG
Baden-Württemberg (☎07141)

At **MONREPOS (SCHLOSS)** (5km NW)

★★★★***Schlosshotel Monrepos*** (BW) ☎30101 tx7264720
🛁 🚿 83 **P** Lift ☾ ≈ lake

LUDWIGSHAFEN
Rheinland-Pfalz (☎0621)

★★★**City Europa** Ludwigspl 5—6 ☎519011 tx464701
🛁 🚿 90 🏠 **P**11 Lift sB 🛁 🚿 118—128 dB 🛁 🚿 156—170 Mfr18&alc 🎾 📺
Credit cards [1] [2] [3] [5]

★★★**Excelsior** (BW) Lorientallee 16 ☎519201 tx464540
🛁 160 **P** Lift ☾ sB 🛁 fr135 dB 🛁 fr180 M10—70 alc 📺
Credit cards [1] [2] [3] [4] [5]

Germany

LÜNEBURG
Niedersachsen (☎04131)

★★**Landwehr** Hamburgerstr 15 ☎121024
20 Jan—20 Dec
🛁 🚿 35 🏠 **P**40 ☾ sB 🛁 🚿 55—85 dB 🛁 🚿 92—160 M14 ≈
Credit cards [1] [5]

🚗 **F Anker** Vor dem Bardowicker Tore 44 ☎31066 M/c **P** For

MAINZ
Rheinland-Pfalz (☎06131)

★★★★***Hilton International*** Rheinstr 68 ☎2450 tx4187570
🛁 🚿 435 🏠 **P** Lift ☾

★★★**Central** Bahnhofspl 8 ☎674001 tx4187794
🛁 🚿 64 **P** Lift ☾ sB 🛁 🚿 82—105 dB 🛁 🚿 130—200
Credit cards [1] [2] [3] [5]

★★★**Europa** Kaiserstr 7 ☎3650 tx4187702
rm87 (🛁 🚿 86) 🏠 **P** Lift ☾ sB 🛁 🚿 110—150 dB 🛁 🚿 180—210 M25
Credit cards [2] [3] [5]

★★★**Mainzer Hof** (ETAP) Kaiserstr 98 ☎233771 tx4187787
🛁 🚿 73 **P** Lift ☾ sB 🛁 🚿 117—138 dB 🛁 🚿 160—190 M alc
Credit cards [1] [2] [3] [4] [5]

★★★**Novotel Mainz Süd** Essenheimer Str ☎361054 tx4187236
🛁 🚿 121 **P**200 Lift sB 🛁 🚿 130 dB 🛁 🚿 163 M22—122 ≈
Credit cards [1] [2] [3] [5]

Heinz am Bismarckpl ☎676011 For

At **FINTHEN** (7km W)

★★**Kurmainz** Flugplatzstr 44 ☎40056 tx4187001
5 Jan—21 Dec
🛁 70 🏠 **P**40 Lift sB 🛁 🚿 98—145 dB 🛁 128—180 M19—65 🎾 📺 mountains
Credit cards [1] [2] [3] [5]

MANDERSCHEID
Rheinland-Pfalz (☎06572)

★★**Zens** Kurfürstenstr 35 ☎769
2 Dec—1 Jan & 15 Feb—5 Nov
rm47 (🛁 🚿 28) **P**15 Lift sB39 sB 🛁 🚿 70 dB98 dB 🛁 🚿 136 📺

MANNHEIM
Baden-Württemberg (☎0621)

★★★★**Mannheimer Hof** (SRS) A-Anlage 4—8 ☎45021 tx462245
🛁 🚿 170 **P** Lift ☾ sB 🛁 🚿 135—185 dB 🛁 🚿 190—240 Mfr30
Credit cards [1] [2] [3] [5]

★★★**Augusta** (BW) A-Anlage 43—45 ☎408001 tx462395
🛁 🚿 105 🏠 **P**40 Lift ☾ sB 🛁 🚿 148—153 dB 🛁 🚿 215—235 Mfr25
Credit cards [1] [2] [3] [4] [5]

★★★***Novotel*** auf dem Friedenspl ☎402071 tx463694
🛁 🚿 180 **P**120 Lift ☾
Credit cards [1] [2] [3] [4] [5]

★★***Intercity Mannheim*** Hauptbahnhof ☎22925 tx463604
🛁 🚿 48 **P** Lift ☾
Credit cards [1] [2] [3] [5]

★★**Kaiserring** Kaiserring 18 (n.rest) ☎23931
rm52 (🛁 🚿 46) **P**6 Lift ☾ sB36 sB 🛁 🚿 48—52 dB72 dB 🛁 🚿 92—129
Credit cards [1] [2] [3] [5]

★★**Mack** Mozartstr 14 (n.rest) ☎23888 tx0462116
6 Jan—8 Aug & 25 Aug—20 Dec
rm60 (🛁 28) A6rm 🏠 **P**8 Lift ☾ sB38—40 sB 🛁 48—68 dB66 dB 🛁 76—115
Credit cards [1] [3] [4] [5]

🚗 **H Kohlhoff** Obere Riedstr 117—119 ☎737005 **P** For

🚗 ***Kurpfalz*** Schwetzinger Str 148—152 ☎441031 For

At **SANDHOFEN** (10km N)

★★**Weber** Frankenthaler Str 85 ☎38080 tx463537
🛁 🚿 100 🏠 **P**80 Lift ☾ sB 🛁 🚿 69—125 dB 🛁 🚿 107—165 M alc
Credit cards [1] [2] [3] [5]

MARBURG AN DER LAHN
Hessen (☎06421)

★★**Europälscher Hof** Elisabethstr 12 ☎64044 tx482636
rm107 (🛁 🚿 92) A40rm 🏠 **P**75 Lift ☾ sB43—48 sB 🛁 🚿 50—80 dB70—80 dB 🛁 🚿 95—135 M alc
Credit cards [1] [2] [3] [5]

At **CÖLBE** (7km N)

🚗 **M Feeser** Erlenring 9 ☎23038 **P** For

MARIA LAACH
Rheinland-Pfalz (☎02652)

★★**Seehotel** ☎4241
rm70 (🛁 🚿 46) 🏠 **P**60 Lift ☾ sB39—46 sB 🛁 🚿 50—60 dB70—90 dB 🛁 🚿 105—115 M12—36 📺 mountains
Credit cards [1] [2]

MARIA WEILER See **DÜREN**

MARIENBERG (BAD)
Rheinland-Pfalz (☎02661)

★★★***Knelpp-Kurhotel Wildpark*** Kurallee 1 (1km W) ☎7069
20 Dec—15 Nov
rm45 (🛁 🚿 40) 🏠 **P** Lift ≈ mountains

MARKTHEIDENFELD
Bayern (☎09391)

★★**Schöne Aussicht** Brückenstr 8 ☎3455
🛁 🚿 57 🏠 **P**30 Lift sB 🛁 🚿 44—50 dB 🛁 🚿 76—80

★**Anker** Obertorstr 6–8 ☎4041 tx689608
🛁🚿37 ⌂ **P** Lift ☾ sB🛁🚿65–75
dB🛁🚿110–150 Mfr35
Credit card 2

MARKTOBERDORF
Bayern (☎08342)

★★**Sepp** Bahnhofstr 13 ☎2048
🛁🚿60 ⌂ **P**55 ☾ sB🛁🚿38–55
dB🛁🚿70–90 M10–20 mountains
Credit cards 1 5

MARL
Nordrhein-Westfalen (☎02365)

★★★**Novotel** E-Weitsch Weg 2 ☎1020 tx829916
🛁🚿96 **P**50 Lift ☾ sB🛁🚿110–130
dB🛁🚿143–153 M17–36 〽 lake
Credit cards 1 2 3 5

MAYSCHOSS See **ALTENAHR**

MEERSBURG
Baden-Württemberg (☎07532)

★★**Bären** Marktpl 11 ☎6044
15 Mar–10 Nov
🚿16 ⌂ **P**2 sB🚿49 dB🚿78–96 M15–25

★★**3 Stuben** Winzergasse 1 ☎6019
Feb–Dec
🛁🚿20 ⌂ **P** sB🛁🚿70–80
dB🛁🚿95–130 M16–29

★★**Weinstube Löwen** Marktpl 2 ☎6013
🛁14 ⌂ **P**12 sB🛁55–60
dB🛁🚿110–132 M12–35

MEMMINGEN
Bayern (☎08331)

★★★**Adler** Maximillianstr 3 ☎87015
rm55 (🛁40) ⌂ **P**20 Lift ☾ sB35
sB🛁🚿48–55 dB70 dB🛁🚿95–98
M10–25
Credit cards 1 4

Draxler Birkenweg 1 ☎4717 **P** Dat

C Schenk Donaustr 29 ☎86048 Ope Vau

MERGENTHEIM (BAD)
Baden-Württemberg (☎07931)

★★★★**Victoria** Poststr 2–4 ☎5930 tx74224
🛁🚿90 ⌂ **P**100 ☾ sB🛁🚿84–104
dB🛁🚿158–178 M25–40 ♨ 〽
Credit cards 1 2 3 4 5

MERKLINGEN
Baden-Württemberg (☎07337)

★**Ochsen** Hauptstr 12 ☎283
Closed Nov
rm19 (🚿12) ⌂ **P**20 sBfr38 sB🚿fr50 dB65
dB🚿80 M10–35

MERZIG
Saarland (☎06861)

Auto-Industrie Trierer Str 197–199 ☎5025
P For

MINDELHEIM
Bayern (☎08261)

E Schragl Kanzelwandstr 5 ☎8021 Aud VW

Germany

MINDEN
Nordrhein-Westfalen (☎0571)

★★**Kruses Park** Marienstr 108 ☎46033 tx97986
rm40 (🚿32) ⌂ **P**150 sB61 sB🚿93–103
dB104 dB🚿156–166 M18–28 lake
Credit cards 1 2 3 4 5

★★**Silke** Fischerglacis 21 (n.rest) ☎23736
🛁22 ⌂ **P**20 sB🛁86 dB🛁135 ♨

MITTENWALD
Bayern (☎08823)

★★**Post** Obermarkt 9 ☎1094
rm96 (🛁🚿68) ⌂ **P** Lift ☾ ⚲ ♨ mountains

★**Zerhoch** H-Barth-Weg 7 (n.rest) ☎1508
15 Dec–25 Oct
🛁15 ⌂ **P**8 sB🛁36–43 dB🛁56–78
mountains

MÖHRINGEN See **STUTTGART**

MÖNCHENGLADBACH
Nordrhein-Westfalen (☎02161)

★★★★**Dorint Mönchengladbach**
Hohenzollernstr 5 ☎86060 tx852656
🛁🚿102 **P**250 Lift ☾ sB🛁🚿125–135
dB🛁🚿165–240 ♨
Credit cards 1 2 3 5

★★★★**Holiday Inn** am Geropl ☎3070 tx852363
🛁127 **P**150 Lift sB🛁142–160
dB🛁172–190 Mfr23 ♨
Credit cards 1 2 3 4 5

A Moers Kölner Str 345 ☎601631 M/c **P**

R Rankin Druckerstr 17 ☎129128 AR DJ

W Reipen Am Gerstacker 160 ☎2940 **P**
Ope Vau

At **RHEYDT** (4km S)

★★★**Besch Parkhotel** H-Junkers Str 2
☎(02166)44011 tx8529143
🛁🚿33 ⌂ **P** Lift sB🛁🚿111
dB🛁🚿176–186 M28
Credit cards 1 2 3 4 5

★★**Coenen** Giesenkirchener Str 41–45
☎(02166)10088
🛁55 ⌂ **P**35 Lift sB🛁90–110
dB🛁130–170 Mfr20
Credit cards 1 2 3 4 5

MONREPOS (SCHLOSS) See **LUDWIGSBURG**

MONSCHAU
Nordrhein-Westfalen (☎02472)

★★**Aquarium** Heidgen 34 ☎693
🛁🚿10 A3rm **P**14 sB🛁🚿48–54
dB🛁🚿76–94 M17–30 〽 mountains
Credit card 5

★★**Horchem** Rurstr 14 ☎490
15 Mar–Feb
rm14 (🛁🚿10) ⌂ **P**4 ☾ sB🛁🚿57
dB60–64 dB🛁🚿68–72 M14–35

mountains
Credit cards 1 2 5

★★**Lindenhof** Laufenstr 77 ☎686
15 Dec–5 Nov
rm12 (🚿9) A4rm **P**12 sB45 sB🚿70 dB80
dB🚿110 Mfr12 mountains
Credit card 2

★**Burgau** St-Vither Str 16 (n.rest) ☎2120
rm13 (🚿9) **P**10 sB33 sB🚿48 dB🚿90
mountains
Credit card 2

★**Haus Herrlichkeit** Haagweg 3A (n.rest)
☎3190
🚿6 ⌂ **P**10 sB🚿35–38 dB🚿66–70
mountains
Credit card 1

MONTABAUR
Rheinland-Pfalz (☎02602)

★***Post*** Bahnhofstr 30 ☎3361
rm23 (🛁🚿7) ⌂ **P**9 Lift

★**Schlemmer** Kirchstr 18 ☎5022
6 Jan–20 Dec
rm25 (🛁🚿11) ⌂ **P**6 sB35 sB🛁🚿44–60
dB60 dB🛁🚿75–120 M10–26

At **HEILIGENROTH** (250 m from Montabaur exit Frankfurt-Köln Autobahn)

★★**Heiligenroth** ☎5044 tx869675
🚿28 ⌂ **P**40 Lift ☾ sB🚿59–62 dB🚿88–98
M14–30
Credit cards 1 2 3 5

MÜHLDORF AM INN
Bayern (☎08631)

★**Jägerhof** Stadpl 3 ☎4004
7 Jan–23 Dec
rm27 (🚿20) **P**20 sB29 sB🚿49 dB70 dB🚿82
Credit cards 1 2 3 5

MÜLHEIM See **KÖLN (COLOGNE)**

MÜLHEIM AN DER MOSEL
Rheinland-Pfalz (☎06534)

★★**Moselhaus Selzer** Moselstr 7 ☎707
Mar–Nov
rm14 (🛁13) ⌂ **P**30 sB43 sB🛁58 dB76
dB🛁101 M10–25 lake

MÜLHEIM AN DER RUHR
Nordrhein-Westfalen (☎0208)

★★★**Noy** Schlosstr 28–30 ☎44671 tx208358
rm60 (🛁🚿58) ⌂ **P** Lift ☾ sB60–72
sB🛁🚿110–160 dB🛁🚿181–221 M alc
Credit cards 1 2 3 5

MÜLLHEIM
Baden-Württemberg (☎07631)

★★★***Euro-Hotel Alte Post*** (On road B3 near Autobahn exit) ☎5522 tx772916
rm57 (🛁🚿48) A42rm ⌂ **P**50 ☾
Credit cards 1 2 5

★★***Markgraf*** Marzellerweg 18 ☎3026
rm13 (🛁7) ⌂ **P** mountains

MUMMELSEE See **BADEN-BADEN**

MÜNCHEN (MUNICH)
Bayern (☎089)
See Plan page 226

★★★★★**Vier Jahreszeiten** (Intercont) Maxilmilionstr 17 ☎230390 tx523859 Plan **5**
⇌⋒365 A172rm ⌂ **P** Lift ☾
sB⇌⋒249—279 dB⇌⋒383—478 Mfr45
⚲ ≋
Credit cards 1 2 4 5

★★★★**Bayerischer Hof** (SRS) Promenadepl 2—6 ☎21200 tx523409 Plan **1**
⇌⋒440 **P** Lift ☾ sB⇌⋒170—225
dB⇌⋒290—380 M38—46 ▣
Credit cards 1 2 3 4 5

★★★★***Excelsior*** Schützenstr 11 ☎557906 tx522419 Plan **2**
⇌⋒105 ⌂ **P** Lift ☾

★★★★**Hilton International** am Tucherpark 7 ☎3845 Plan **2A**
⇌480 ⌂ **P**300 Lift ☾ sB⇌173—263
dB⇌215—355 M30 ▣
Credit cards 1 2 3 4 5

★★★★**Holiday Inn München** Leopoldstr 194 ☎340971 tx5215439 Plan **3**
⇌363 **P**200 Lift ☾ sB⇌218—253
dB⇌296—316 ▣
Credit cards 1 2 3 4 5

★★★***Crest* (See page 50)** Effnerstr 99 ☎982541 tx524757 Plan **5A**
⇌155 Lift ☾
Credit cards 1 2 3 4 5

★★★**Deutscher Kaiser** Arnulfstr 2 ☎558321 tx522650 Plan **6**
⇌⋒157 ⌂ **P**15 Lift ☾ sB⇌⋒130—140
dB⇌⋒185—205 M25
Credit cards 1 2 3 5

★★★**Eden-Wolff** (SRS) Arnulfstr 4—8 ☎558281 tx523564 Plan **7**
⇌⋒214 ⌂ **P** Lift ☾ sB⇌⋒140—200
dB⇌⋒180—290
Credit cards 1 2 3 4 5

★★★***Penta*** (Forum) Hochstr 3 ☎4485555 tx529046 Plan **8**
⇌⋒583 ⌂ **P** Lift ☾ ≋

★★**Daniel** Sonnenstr 5 (n.rest) ☎554945 tx523863 Plan **10**
rm80 (⇌⋒76) **P** Lift ☾ sB71—78
sB⇌⋒89—105 dB96—108
dB⇌⋒125—155 M21
Credit cards 2 5

★★**Drei Löwen** (BW) Schillerstr 8 ☎595521 tx523867 Plan **11**
⇌⋒130 ⌂ **P**40 Lift ☾ sB⇌⋒118—126
dB⇌⋒174—192 M alc
Credit cards 1 2 3 4 5

★★**Leopold** Leopoldstr 119, Schwabing ☎367061 tx5215160 Plan **12**
rm82 (⇌⋒69) A52rm ⌂ **P**50 Lift ☾
sB⇌⋒99—120 dB90 dB⇌⋒135—150
M20—30
Credit cards 1 2 3 4 5

★★**Platzl** Münzstr 8—9 ☎237030 tx0522910 Plan **13**
rm100 (⇌⋒52) **P**80 Lift ☾ sB66—72
sB⇌⋒76—92 dB88—96

Germany

dB⇌⋒106—155 M23
Credit cards 1 2

○**Holiday Inn München Sud** Kistlerhofstr 142 ☎780020 tx5218645 Not on plan
Opening 1 Feb 1987
⇌⋒320 **P**200 Lift ☾ sB⇌⋒160—185
dB⇌⋒200—250 M25 ▣
Credit cards 1 2 3 4 5

🚗 ***Auto-Frühling*** Klarastr 20 ☎187081 AR Maz

🚗 **Auto König Personenwagen** Eggenfeldener Str 100 ☎930004 AM AR Alf DJ LR Lot RR

🚗 ***Corso-Behnke*** Zielstattstr 63 ☎786087 Lot Maz Peu

🚗 ***Recknagel & Niedermeier Automobile*** Landsberger Str 328 ☎5806011 AR Hon

🚗 ***Wolf*** Mullerstr 50 ☎265488 **P** AR

MÜNSTER
Nordrhein-Westfalen (☎0251)

★★★**Kaiserhof** Bahnhofstr 14 (n.rest) ☎40059 tx892141
⇌⋒110 **P** Lift ☾ sB⇌⋒99—135
dB⇌⋒151—185

★★★**Mövenpick** Kardinal-von-Galen Ring 65 ☎89020 tx17251104
⇌120 **P**100 Lift sB⇌⋒125—145
dB⇌⋒145—165
Credit cards 1 2 3 5

★★★**Schloss Wilkinghege** (GS) Steinfurterstr 374 (4km NW on B54) ☎213045
⇌⋒37 A18rm ⌂ **P** ☾ ⚲ ▣

★★**Conti** Berlinerpl 2A ☎40444 tx892113
⇌⋒60 ⌂ **P**35 Lift ☾ sB62
sB⇌⋒82—102 dB109 dB⇌⋒124—184
M14
Credit cards 1 2 3 4 5

Ing W Brandes Altenbergerstr 32 ☎(02533)534 **P** Alf AR DJ

🚗 ***W Eitz*** Soltauer Strabe 61 ☎3406 **P** Peu

🚗 **Auto Hartmann** Alberloher Weg 668 ☎616033 **P** Peu Tal

Lich Weser-Ecke-Oder-Str ☎230613 Dat

MURNAU
Bayern (☎08841)

★★★**Alpenhof Murnau** (Relais et Châteaux) Ramsachstr 8 ☎1045
⇌48 **P**55 Lift ☾ sB⇌115—175
dB⇌155—245 M alc ≋ mountains

MURRHARDT
Baden-Württemberg (☎07192)

★★**Sonne Post** Karlstr 6—9 ☎8081 tx7245910
⇌⋒37 A10rm ⌂ **P**40 Lift ☾ sB39—43
sB⇌⋒75—83 dB72—76
dB⇌⋒112—144 Mfr19 ▣
Credit cards 1 2 3 4 5

NAGOLD
Baden-Württemberg (☎07452)

★★**Post** (ROM) Bahnofstr 2—4 ☎4048
rm24 (⇌⋒23) A7rm **P**22 Lift
sB⇌⋒82—92 dB⇌⋒133—160 M18—45
Credit cards 1 2 3 4 5

NAUHEIM (BAD)
Hessen (☎06032)

★★★**Park Hotel am Kurhaus** Nördlicher Park 16 ☎3030 tx415514
⇌99 ⌂ **P**250 Lift ☾ sB⇌126—162
dB⇌206—276 Mfr27 ▣
Credit cards 1 2 3 5

NECKARELZ See **MOSBACH**

NECKARGEMÜND
Baden-Württemberg (☎06223)

★★**Ritter** (GS) Neckarstr 40 ☎7035 tx461837
rm40 (⇌⋒38) **P**70 ☾ sB66—88
sB⇌⋒66—88 dB⇌⋒95—145 M18—35
Credit cards 1 2 3 4

NECKARSTEINACH
Hessen (☎06229)

★★**Schiff** Neckargemünderstr 2 ☎324
25 Jan—14 Dec
rm40 (⇌⋒22) **P**15 Lift sB40 sB⇌⋒fr42
dB⇌⋒84—88 M6—30

NERESHEIM
Baden-Württemberg (☎07326)

★***Klosterhosplz*** ☎6282
Mar—Dec
rm50 (⋒20) A15rm ⌂ **P**300 Lift

NEUASTENBERG See **WINTERBERG**

NEUBEURN
Bayern (☎08035)

★★**Burg** Marktpl 23 ☎2456
⋒13 ⌂ **P**10 Lift sB⋒52—85 dB⋒86—130
M7—32 mountains

NEUENAHR (BAD)
Rheinland-Pfalz (☎02641)

★★★**Dorint** am Dahliengarten ☎8950 tx861805
⇌172 ⌂ **P**100 Lift ☾ sB⇌115—128
dB⇌176—192 ▣
Credit cards 1 2 3 5

★★★**Kurhotel** (SRS) Kurgartenstr 1 ☎2291 tx861812
⇌⋒245 **P** Lift ☾ sB⇌⋒127—155
dB⇌⋒186—230 Mfr33 ▣
Credit cards 1 2 3 5

★★**Giffels Goldener Anker** Mittelstr 14 ☎2385 tx861768
rm85 (⇌82) ⌂ **P**50 Lift ☾ sB⇌69—85
dB⇌130—190 M15—40
Credit cards 1 2 3 4 5

★★***Hamburger Hof*** Jesuitenstr 11 (n.rest) ☎26017
rm36 (⇌27) ⌂ **P** ☾

🚗 ***J Waldecker*** Heerstr 115 ☎2366 For

MÜNCHEN (MUNICH)

1 ★★★★ Bayerischer Hof
2 ★★★★ Excelsior
2A ★★★★ Hilton International
3 ★★★★ Holiday Inn München
5 ★★★★★ Vier Jahreszeiten
5A ★★★ Crest
6 ★★★ Deutscher Kaiser
7 ★★★ Eden-Wolff
8 ★★★ Penta
10 ★★ Daniel
11 ★★ Drei Lôwen
12 ★★ Leopold
13 ★★ Platzl

NEUMÜNSTER
Schleswig-Holstein (☎04321)

★★**Lenz** Gasstr 11—12 (n.rest) ☎45072
14 **P**30 sB 47—57
dB 73—88

E Landschoof Rungestr 5 ☎53518 **P** Dat

NEUSS
Nordrhein-Westfalen (☎02101)

At **ERFTTAL** (5km SE off A57)

★★★**Novotel Neuss** am Derikumer Hof 1 ☎17081 tx8517634
116 **P**150 Lift sB 71—142
dB 71—152 M12—25
Credit cards 1 2 3 4 5

At **GRIMLINGHAUSEN** (4.5km SE on B9)

★★**Landhaus** Hüsenstr 17 ☎37030 tx8517891
29 **P**20 Lift sB 120—160
dB 193—249 M14—30
Credit card 1

NEUSTADT See TITISEE-NEUSTADT

NEUSTADT AN DER AISCH
Bayern (☎09161)

★★**Römerhof** R-Wagnerstr 15 ☎3011
rm23 (12) **P**30 sB28—38
sB 40—50 dB55—70 dB 75—90
M10—35
Credit cards 1 2 3 5

NEUSTADT AN DER SAALE (BAD)
Bayern (☎09771)

★★★***Schwan & Post*** am Hohntor ☎5038
22 **P**10

NEUSTADT AN DER WEINSTRASSE
Rheinland-Pfalz (☎06321)

At **SCHÖNTAL** (3km W)

★***Konigsmühle*** Schöntalstr 10 ☎83031
rm38 (15) A13rm **P** Lift mountains

NEU-ULM
Bayern (☎0731)

★★★**Mövenpick** Silcherstr 40 ☎80110 tx712539
109 **P**250 Lift sB 143—153
dB 171—181
Credit cards 1 2 3 4 5

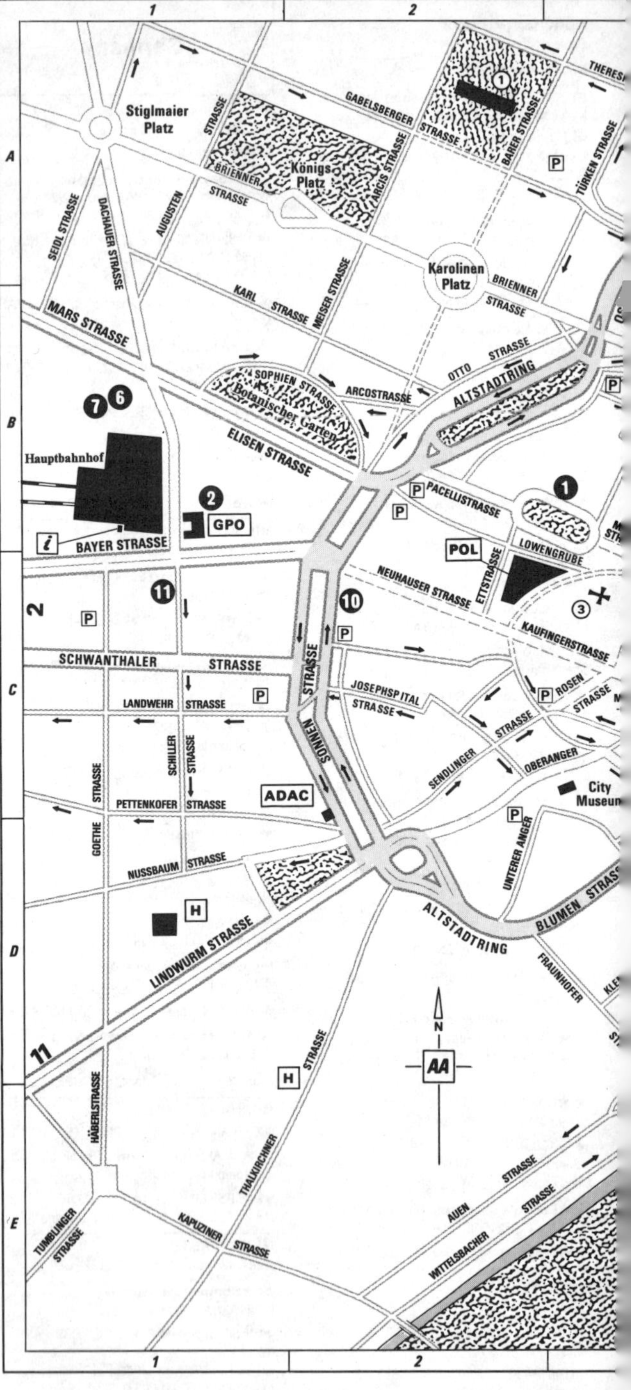

MÜNCHEN (MUNICH) CENTRAL
Englischer Garten
State Gallery of Modern Art
National Museum
Hof Garten
Ethnological Museum
MAX JOSEPH BRÜCKE
PRINZREGENTEN BRÜCKE
MAXIMILIAN BRÜCKE
LUDWIGS BRÜCKE
BOSCHE BRÜCKE
CORNELIUS BRÜCKE
ISAR
MONTGELAS STRASSE
MÖHL STRASSE
OETTINGEN STRASSE
EMIL-RIEDEL-STRASSE
WIDENMAYER STRASSE
MARIA-THERESIA-STRASSE
ISMANINGER STRASSE
KÖNIGIN STRASSE
LUDWIG STRASSE
VON-DER-TANN STRASSE
GALERIE STRASSE
LERCHENFELD STRASSE
PRINZREGENTEN STRASSE
ALTSTADTRING
KARL-SCHARNAGL-RING
HOFGARTEN STRASSE
SEITZ STRASSE
WAGMÜLLER STRASSE
LIEBIG STRASSE
MARSTALL STRASSE
RESIDENZSTRASSE
MAXIMILIAN STRASSE
TRIFT STRASSE
STERN STRASSE
HILDEGARD STRASSE
SPARKASSENSTRASSE
THOMAS-WIMMER-RING
THIERSCHSTRASSE
STEINSDORF STRASSE
EINSTEIN STRASSE
FRAUEN STRASSE
ZWEIBRÜCKEN STRASSE
INNERE WIENER STRASSE
KLENZE STRASSE
KOHL STRASSE
BAADER STRASSE
ERHARDT STRASSE
CORNELIUS STRASSE
ZEPPELIN STRASSE
LILIEN STRASSE
ROSENHEIMER STRASSE
SCHWEIGER STRASSE
OHLMÜLLER STRASSE
FALKEN STRASSE
GEBSATTEL STRASSE
BALAN STRASSE
AUERFELD STRASSE
ORLEANS STRASSE
Ostbahnhof
Car Sleeper
A94
304
To A8
11 & 13
0 ½km
0 ½m
ALTSTADTRING (RING ROAD)
4 5 6
A B C D E

NEUWIED
Rheinland-Pfalz (☎02631)

🚗 **Sportwagen Service** Königsberger Str 12 ☎53018 Dat

NIEFERN-ÖSCHELBRONN See **PFORZHEIM**

NIERSTEIN
Rheinland-Pfalz (☎06133)

★★**Alter Vater Rhein** ☎5628

Closed Xmas
rm11 (🚿10) **P**5 sB28 sB🚿35 dB🚿70 M8—31

★**Rheinhotel** Mainzerstr 16 ☎5161 tx4187784

9 Jan—9 Dec
🛁🚿13 ⛫ **P**13 sB🛁85—110 dB🛁119—160 M15—100
Credit cards [1] [2] [3] [5]

NORDEN
Niedersachsen (☎04931)

★★**Deutsches Haus** Neuer Weg 26 ☎4271

rm41 (🛁🚿39) ⛫ **P**40 Lift sB36—40 sB🛁🚿48—52 dB67—71 dB🛁🚿89—119 M10—33
Credit cards [1] [2] [3] [5]

NORDHORN
Niedersachen (☎05921)

★***Eureglo*** Dortmunder Str 20 ☎5077

rm26 (🚿24) ⛫ **P** ☾

NÖRDLINGEN
Bayern (☎09081)

★★**Sonne** Marktpl 3 ☎5067 tx051749

rm40 (🛁🚿30) ⛫ **P**20 sB32—35 sB🛁🚿50—55 dB64—72 dB🛁🚿80—110 M alc

NOTSCHREI
Baden-Württemberg (☎07602)

★★**Waldhotel am Notschrei** ☎219

rm40 (🛁🚿35) ⛫ **P**150 Lift sB40—45 sB🛁🚿52—55 dB72—84 dB🛁🚿90—124 M20—42 📺 mountains
Credit cards [2] [5]

NÜRBURG
Rheinland-Pfalz (☎02691)

At **NÜRBURGRING** (1km SW)

★★**Sporthotel Tribüne** ☎3020 tx863919

🛁🚿27 ⛫ **P**300 ☾ sB🛁🚿54—62 dB🛁🚿99—109 M18—45
Credit cards [1] [3] [5]

NÜRNBERG (NUREMBERG)
Bayern (☎0911)

★★★★★**Grand** Bahnhofstr 1 ☎203621 tx622010

🛁185 ⛫ **P**30 Lift ☾ sB🛁140—180 sB🛁175—215
Credit cards [1] [2] [3] [4] [5]

★★★★**Carlton** (BW) Eilgutstr 13 ☎203535 tx622329

🛁🚿130 **P**25 Lift ☾ sB🛁🚿125—170 dB🛁🚿185—225 M30—50
Credit cards [1] [2] [3] [5]

Germany

★★★★***Crest*** **(See page 50)** Münchener Str 283 ☎49441 tx622930

🛁143 ⛫ **P**100 Lift ☾
Credit cards [1] [2] [3] [4] [5]

★★★**Atrium** (BW) Münchener Str 25 ☎49011 tx626167

🛁200 ⛫ **P**200 Lift ☾ sB🛁153—163 dB🛁180—210 M alc 📺
Credit cards [1] [2] [5]

★★★**Bayerischer Hof** Gleissbühlstr 15 (n.rest) ☎209251 tx626547

🚿80 ⛫ **P**30 Lift ☾ sB🚿79—85 dB🚿118—124 M alc
Credit cards [1] [2] [3] [5]

★★★**Novotel Nürnberg Süd** Münchener Str 340 ☎86791 tx626449

🛁117 **P**120 Lift sB🛁130—155 dB🛁163—183 ≈
Credit cards [1] [2] [3] [5]

★★★**Sterntor** Tafelhofstr 8—14 ☎2358 tx622632

rm120 (🛁95) **P**50 Lift ☾ sB55—70 sB🛁90—120 dB80—95 dB🛁145—180 M17—25
Credit cards [1] [2] [3] [4] [5]

★★★**Victoria** Königstr 80 (n.rest) ☎203801 tx0622825

7 Jan—22 Dec
rm64 (🛁🚿59) **P**75 Lift ☾ sB55 sB🛁🚿75—85 dB🛁🚿120—140
Credit cards [1] [2] [5]

★★**Drei Linden** Äussere Sulzbacherstr 1 ☎533233

🛁🚿28 ⛫ **P**25 ☾ sB🛁🚿80—95 dB🛁🚿130—150 M17—35
Credit cards [1] [2] [3] [5]

🚗 **E Kaiser** H-Kolb Str 35 ☎835221 **P** Saa

🚗 **Auto Pieper** Eibacher Haupstr 34 ☎643042 **P** Vol

🚗 **Autohaus Motus GmbH** Cuxhavenerstraße 2 ☎34915 **P** AR DJ LR Vol

🚗 **Auto Wuestner** Leyher Str 23 ☎327211 **P** Dat

OBERAMMERGAU
Bayern (☎08822)

★★**Alte Post** Dorfstr 19 ☎6691

mid Dec—Oct
rm32 (🛁🚿25) A5rm ⛫ **P**14 sB35 sB🛁🚿50 dB70—90
Credit cards [1] [2] [4] [5]

★★**Böld** König-Ludwig-Str 10 ☎520 tx592406

🛁🚿57 ⛫ **P**50 Lift sB🛁🚿87—107 dB🛁🚿134—154 M20—30 mountains
Credit cards [1] [2] [3] [5]

★★**Friedenshöhe** König-Ludwig-Str 31 ☎598

20 Dec—26 Oct
🛁11 **P**50 sB🛁45—75 dB🛁96—123

M12—26 t% mountains
Credit cards [1] [2] [3]

★★***Schilcherhof*** Bahnhofstr 17 ☎4740

Closed Dec—9 Jan
rm17 (🛁🚿12) A10rm ⛫ **P** mountains

OBERHAUSEN
Nordrhein-Westfalen (☎0208)

★★★**Ruhrland** Berlinerpl 2 ☎805031 tx856900

rm60 (🛁🚿45) ⛫ **P** Lift ☾ sB60—70 sB🛁🚿80—130 dB120—130 dB🛁🚿160—200 M20—30
Credit cards [1] [2] [3] [5]

🚗 **P Gerstmann** Wehrstr 17—33 ☎870045 M/c **P** For Hon

OBERKIRCH
Baden-Württemberg (☎07802)

★★★**Obere Linde** (ROM) Hauptstr 25—27 ☎3038 tx752640

rm44 (🛁🚿41) ⛫ **P**75 Lift ☾ sB50—90 sB🛁🚿90—120 dB80—100 dB🛁🚿130—190 🎾 mountains
Credit cards [1] [2] [3] [4] [5]

At **ÖDSBACH** (3km S)

★★★**Grüner Baum** Almstr 33 ☎2801 tx752627

🛁🚿50 A6rm ⛫ **P**80 Lift sB🛁🚿65—98 dB🛁🚿98—190 🎾 📺 mountains
Credit cards [1] [2] [3] [4] [5]

OBERSTAUFEN
Bayern (☎08386)

★★**Kurhotel Einsle** Kalzhoferstr 4 (n.rest) ☎2032

rm27 (🛁🚿21) **P**15 sB🛁🚿43—52 dB🛁🚿98 mountains

OBERSTDORF
Bayern (☎08322)

★★★**Wittelsbacher Hof** Prinzenstr 24 ☎1018 tx541905

18 Dec—10 Apr & 15 May—20 Oct
rm90 (🛁🚿86) ⛫ **P**40 Lift ☾ sB50—60 sB🛁🚿78—95 dB🛁🚿110—176 M28—30 t% ≈ 📺 mountains
Credit cards [2] [5]

🚗 ***Nebelhorn*** Nebelhornstr 59 ☎4669 **P** Fia

OBERWESEL
Rheinland-Pfalz (☎06744)

★★**Auf Schönburg** (GS) Schönburg (1.5km SE) ☎7027

Mar—30 Nov
rm20 (🛁🚿19) **P**10 Lift sB🛁🚿80—90 dB80 dB🛁🚿120—180 M35—90
Credit cards [2] [3]

★**Goldner Pfropfenzieher** ☎207

15 Mar—Oct
rm18 (🛁🚿10) A2rm ⛫ **P**10 sB30—32 sB🛁🚿36 dB60 dB🛁🚿78—84 M7—24

★★**Römerkrug** (GS) Marktpl 1 ☎8176

Feb—15 Dec
🛁🚿7 **P**10 sB🛁🚿50—80 dB🛁🚿90—130 M15—40 ≈ mountains lake

OCHSENFURT
Bayern (☎09331)

★**Bären** Hauptstr 74 ☎2282

Feb—22 Dec
rm28 (🛁 🚿 15) 🚗 **P**20 sB35—40
sB 🛁 🚿 40—55 dB65—75 dB 🛁 🚿 80—120
M9—29
Credit cards [1] [2] [5]

ÖDSBACH See **OBERKIRCH**

OESPEL See **DORTMUND**

OESTRICH
Hessen (☎06723)

★★★**Schwan** (ROM) Rheinallee 5—7
☎3001 tx42146

Mar—Nov
🛁 🚿 66 A20rm **P**20 Lift sB 🛁 🚿 95—165
dB 🛁 🚿 180—230 Mfr30 lake
Credit cards [1] [2] [3] [5]

OEYNHAUSEN (BAD)
Nordrhein-Westfalen (☎05731)

★★**Hahnenkamp** (2.5km NE) Alte
Reichsstr 4 ☎5041

Closed 23 & 24 Dec
🛁 🚿 18 **P**50 sB 🛁 🚿 102—132
dB 🛁 🚿 146—186 M13—45
Credit cards [1] [2] [3] [5]

OFFENBACH
Hessen (☎069)

★★★**Novotel** Strahlenberger Str 12
☎818011 tx413047

🛁 130 **P**120 Lift ☾ sB 🛁 125—149
dB 🛁 149—159 Mfr20 ⛱

Credit cards [1] [2] [3] [5]

★★**Graf** Berliner str/Ecke Schlosstr (n.rest)
☎811702

5 Jan—21 Dec
🛁 🚿 28 🚗 **P**4 sB 🛁 🚿 70—95
dB 🛁 🚿 98—135
Credit cards [1] [2] [3]

OFFENBURG
Baden-Württemberg (☎0781)

★★★**Dorint** Messeplatz ☎5050 tx752889
🛁 132 **P**100 Lift ☾ sB 🛁 120—140
dB 🛁 155—250 📺
Credit cards [1] [2] [3] [5]

★★★**Palmengarten** Okenstr 13—17
☎25031 tx752849

15 Jan—24 Dec
🛁 🚿 70 🚗 **P**60 Lift ☾ sB 🛁 🚿 95—195
dB 🛁 🚿 155—255 ⛱
Credit cards [2] [5]

★**Sonne** Hauptstr 94 ☎71039

rm34 (🛁 🚿 20) A16rm 🚗 **P** sB52—56
sB 🛁 🚿 60—64 dB72—78 dB 🛁 🚿 84—130
M16—25
Credit cards [1] [2] [3]

A Fandrich C-Benz Str 6 ☎25200 AR

🚘 **A Linck** Freiburger Str 26 ☎25005 Ope

At **ORTENBERG** (4km SE)

★**Glattfelder** Kinizigtalstr 20 ☎31219
rm14 (🛁 🚿 11) 🚗 **P**30 sB30—42 sB 🛁 🚿 42
dB50 dB 🛁 🚿 70 mountains
Credit cards [2] [5]

OLPE
Nordrhein-Westfalen (☎02761)

★★**Tillmanns** Kölnerstr 15 ☎2607

Closed 22 May—14 Jun
rm15 (🛁 🚿 11) **P**20 sB45 sB 🛁 🚿 58—75
dBfr80 dB 🛁 🚿 98—118 M13—35
Credit card [2]

OPPENHEIM
Rheinland-Pfalz (☎06133)

★★**Kurpfalz** Wormser Str 2 ☎2291
tx4187784

9 Jan—9 Dec
🛁 🚿 20 🚗 **P**4 sB 🛁 🚿 41—85
dB 🛁 🚿 85—119 M15—45
Credit cards [1] [2] [3] [5]

★**Oppenheimer Hof** F-Ebert-Str 84 ☎2495
rm25 (🛁 🚿 23) **P**25 sB 🛁 🚿 65—75
dB 🛁 🚿 95—115
Credit cards [1] [2] [5]

🚘 ***Heinz*** Gartenstr 15—19 ☎2055 For

ORTENBERG See **OFFENBURG**

OSNABRÜCK
Niedersachsen (☎0541)

★★★★**Parkhotel** Edinghausen 1
☎46083 tx94939

🛁 80 🚗 **P**200 Lift ☾ sB 🛁 🚿 60—105
dB 🛁 🚿 115—155 M12—40 📺
Credit cards [2] [3]

★★★**Hohenzollern** H-Heine Str 17
☎33170 tx094776

rm100 (🛁 🚿 91) **P**35 Lift ☾ sB68—93
sB 🛁 🚿 88—173 dBfr125 dB 🛁 🚿 145—285
M30 📺
Credit cards [1] [2] [3] [4] [5]

★★**Ibis** Blumenheller Kleg 152 ☎40490
tx94831

🚿 96 **P** Lift ☾ sB🚿 88—98 dB🚿 131 Mfr18
Credit cards [1] [2] [3] [5]

🚘 **Autohaus Beinke** Schuetzenstr 27
☎73520 **P** Peu Tal

🚘 ***H Van Beers*** Bahlweg 16 ☎73596 Alf

G Clupka Pferdestr 2 ☎572629 **P** AR

🚘 **K Meierrose** Pagenstecherstr 74
☎691110 M/c **P** BMW

PADERBORN
Nordrhein-Westfalen (☎05251)

★★**Arosa** (BW) Westernmauer 38 ☎2000
tx936798

🛁 🚿 100 🚗 **P**160 Lift ☾ sB 🛁 🚿 99—129
dB 🛁 🚿 180—195 M22—42 📺
Credit cards [1] [2] [3] [5]

★★**Ibis** am Paderwall 1—5 ☎25031
tx936972

🚿 90 🚗 **P**60 Lift sB🚿 88—93 dB🚿 123
M10—48
Credit cards [1] [2] [3] [4] [5]

🚘 **F Kleine** Rathenaustr 79—83 ☎208 For

PASSAU
Bayern (☎0851)

★★**Weisser Hase** Ludwigstr 23 ☎34066
🛁 🚿 117 🚗 **P**40 Lift ☾ sB 🛁 🚿 75
dB 🛁 🚿 110

🚘 **F Hofbauer** Neuburgerstr 141 ☎6017
Ope

PEGNITZ
Bayern (☎09241)

★★★★**Pflaum's Posthotel** (Relais et
Châteaux) Nürnberger Str 14 ☎7250
tx642433

🛁 58 **P**60 Lift sB 🛁 110—220
dB 🛁 130—280 M35—89 📺 U mountains
Credit cards [1] [2] [3] [5]

PFAFFENHOFEN
Bayern (☎08441)

🚘 **F X Stigimayr** Scheyererstr 70 ☎9894 **P**
BMW

PFORZHEIM
Baden-Württemberg (☎07231)

★★★**Ruf am Schlossberg** ☎16011
tx783843

🛁 53 **P**35 Lift ☾ sB 🛁 95—120
dB 🛁 140—180 M19—95
Credit cards [1] [2] [3] [4] [5]

🚘 **Autosalon R Schweickert** Karlsruher Str
40 ☎16364 **P** AR DJ Vol

Autohaus Hartmann Luisenstr 59 ☎12888
P Peu

At **NIEFERN-ÖSCHELBRONN** (6km E at
Pforzheim East exit on E11)

★★★***Crest* (See page 50)** Pforzheimer
Str ☎(07233)1211 tx783905

🛁 72 **P**75 Lift ☾
Credit cards [1] [2] [3] [4] [5]

POMMERSFELDEN
Bayern (☎09548)

★★**Schloss** ☎488

rm64 (🛁 🚿 58) A14rm 🚗 **P**100 sB48—58
sB 🛁 🚿 58—68 dB71—76 dB 🛁 🚿 86—106
M15—50 🎾 📺
Credit cards [1] [2]

PRIEN AM CHIEMSEE
Bayern (☎08051)

★★**Bayerischer Hof** Bernauerstr 3
☎1095

15 Dec—15 Nov
rm47 (🛁 42) 🚗 **P**40 Lift sB45 sB 🛁 53—55
dB78—80 dB 🛁 92—98 M12—20
mountains
Credit card [1]

PUTTGARDEN
Schleswig-Holstein (☎04371)

★★**Dänia** am Fährbahnhof ☎3016
tx29814

1 Apr—Oct
🚿 72 **P**100 Lift ☾ sB🚿 108 dB🚿 168 M12
sea

PYRMONT (BAD)
Niedersachsen (☎05281)

★★**Kurhaus** Heiligenangerstr 4 ☎151
tx931636 →

Germany

Mar—7 Jan
rm102 (🛁 🚿 85) **P**15 Lift ☾ sB88—108
sB 🛁 🚿 108—127 dB155 dB 🛁 🚿 212—224
M20—60
Credit cards [1] [2] [3] [5]

QUICKBORN
Schleswig-Holstein (☎04106)

★★★**Jagdhaus Waldfriden** (ROM) Kieler Str 1 (On B4 3km N) ☎3771

rm17 (🚿 15) **P**60 sB🚿 88—113
dB🚿 140—200 Mfr39
Credit cards [1] [2] [3] [5]

RASTATT
Baden-Württemberg (☎07222)

★★***Blume*** Kaiserstr 38 ☎32222

rm40 (🛁 🚿 14) 🚗 **P** ☾

★***Katzenberger's Adler*** Jonefstr 7 ☎32103

Closed Jul
rm6 🚗 **P**

RATINGEN See **DÜSSELDORF**

RAVENSBURG
Bayern (☎0751)

★★**Waldhorn** Marienpl 15 ☎16021 tx732311

🛁 🚿 40 A25rm 🚗 **P**15 Lift sB 🛁 🚿 68—98
dB 🛁 🚿 110—190 M28—58
Credit cards [1] [2] [3] [5]

REGENSBURG
Bayern (☎0941)

★★★**Avia** Frankenstr 1—3 ☎42093 tx65703

🛁 🚿 81 🚗 **P**150 Lift ☾ sB 🛁 🚿 119—134
dB 🛁 🚿 129—144 M12
Credit cards [1] [2] [3] [5]

★★**Karmeliten** Dachaupl 1 ☎54308 tx65170

20 Jan—20 Dec
rm80 (🛁 🚿 60) **P**20 Lift ☾ sBfr55
sB 🛁 🚿 79—86 dBfr88 dB 🛁 🚿 120—128
M18—25
Credit cards [1] [2] [5]

★★**Straubinger Hof** A-Schmetzer Str 33 ☎59075

7 Jan—20 Dec
rm64 (🛁 🚿 49) 🚗 **P**22 Lift sB45—49
sB 🛁 🚿 55—67 dB 🛁 🚿 87—104 M alc
Credit cards [1] [2] [3] [4] [5]

★**Wiendl** Universitätstr 9 ☎90416

rm26 (🚿 22) 🚗 **P**50 sB32 sB🚿 40—45 dB54
dB🚿 65—75 M9—19

🚘 ***Auto Bindig*** Vilsstr 28 ☎47015 **P** Cit Peu

🚘 **Kellnberger** Kirchmeierstr 24 ☎35091 M/c **P** Ren

O Seltz Alte Straubinger Str 19 ☎793377 AR DJ

REICHENHALL (BAD)
Bayern (☎08651)

★★★**Axelmannstein** (SRS) Salzburgerstr 2—6 ☎4001 tx56112

🛁 155 🚗 **P**80 Lift ☾ sB 🛁 132—192
dB 🛁 192—420 M42—48 ⚲ 📺 mountains
Credit cards [1] [2] [3] [5]

★★★**Kurhotel Luisenbad** Ludwigstr 33 ☎5011 tx56131

20 Dec—Oct
rm84 (🛁 🚿 71) 🚗 **P**30 Lift ☾ sB113—123
sB 🛁 🚿 135—149 dB 🛁 🚿 230—286
M29—42 📺 mountains
Credit cards [1] [2] [3] [5]

★★**Panorama** Baderstr 6 ☎61001 tx56194

🛁 83 **P**50 Lift ☾ sB 🛁 79—115
dB 🛁 132—204 M alc 📺 mountains
Credit cards [1] [2] [3] [5]

Prechter Innsbrücker Str Angerl 6 ☎2078 For

REICHSHOF-ECKENHAGEN
Nordrhein-Westfalen (☎02265)

★★★**Haus Leyer** am Aggerberg 33 ☎9021

🛁 16 **P**20 sB 🛁 70—85 dB 🛁 130—150
M9—29 📺 mountains
Credit cards [2] [5]

REMAGEN
Rheinland-Pfalz (☎02642)

★★**Fürstenberg** Rheinpromenade 41 ☎23020

rm14 (🛁 🚿 12) **P** sB35—60 sB 🛁 🚿 50—60
dB70—105 dB 🛁 🚿 55—105
Credit cards [1] [2] [3] [5]

★**Fassbender** Mark Str 78 ☎23472

rm23 (🚿 3) 🚗 **P**4 sB28—32 sB🚿 32—35
dB56—64 dB🚿 60—68 M13—18

RENDSBURG
Schleswig-Holstein (☎04331)

★**Germania** Paradepl 3 ☎22997

15 Jan—22 Dec
rm20 🚗 **P**

At **BÜDELSDORF** (2km N)

J Suhr Hollerstr 9 ☎3406 For

REUTLINGEN
Baden-Württemberg (☎07121)

★★**Ernst** Leonhardspl ☎44081 tx729898

rm67 (🛁 🚿 63) A52rm 🚗 **P**8 Lift sB62—67
sB 🛁 🚿 70—97 dB98—104
dB 🛁 🚿 110—150 M9—31 📺
Credit cards [1] [2] [3] [5]

Auto-Specht Weissdornweg 2 ☎54775 **P** AR Cit

RHEINBACH
Nordrhein-Westfalen (☎02226)

★★★**Ratskeller** vor dem Voigttor 1 ☎4978

🛁 🚿 26 **P**20 sB 🛁 🚿 68—75
dB 🛁 🚿 108—118 M13—42
Credit cards [1] [2] [3] [4] [5]

R Schulz Meckenheimer Str 17—19 ☎4500 **P** For

RHEINZABERN
Rheinland-Pfalz (☎07272)

★**Goldenes Lamm** Hauptstr 53 ☎2377

6 Jan—20 Dec
rm10 (🛁 4) 🚗 **P**15 sB23 sB 🛁 30
dB 🛁 60—70 M8—21

RHEYDT See **MÖNCHENGLADBACH**

ROSENHEIM
Bayern (☎08031)

★★★**Goldener Hirsch** Münchner Str 40 ☎12029

rm39 (🛁 🚿 12) **P**10 Lift sB39—42
sB 🛁 🚿 58—68 dB78—80 dB 🛁 🚿 95—110
Credit cards [1] [2] [3] [5]

🚘 **G Rupp** Innstr 34 ☎13970 M/c **P** AR

ROTENBURG (WÜMME)
Niedersachsen (☎04261)

★**Deutsches Haus** Grosse Str 51 ☎3300

rm8 **P**20 sB31 dB62

🚘 **G Bassen** Industriestr 15 ☎5050 **P** Toy

🚘 ***K Lengen*** Harburger Str 67 ☎5409 **P** M/c Peu Tal

ROTHENBURG OB DER TAUBER
Bayern (☎09861)

★★★★**Eisenhut** (Relais et Châteaux/SRS) Hermgasse 3 ☎2041 tx61367

Mar—6 Jan
🛁 80 🚗 **P**22 Lift ☾ sB 🛁 140—155
dB 🛁 195—270 M48—96
Credit cards [1] [2] [3] [5]

★★★**Burg** Klostergasse 1 (n.rest) ☎5037 tx61315

1 Dec—1 Nov
🛁 16 🚗 **P**10 sB 🛁 105—125
dB 🛁 140—220 mountains
Credit cards [1] [2] [3] [4] [5]

★★★**Goldener Hirsch** Untere Schmiedgasse 16 ☎2051 tx61372

Feb—Nov
rm80 (🛁 🚿 66) A20rm 🚗 **P**50 Lift ☾ sB80
sB 🛁 🚿 95—160 dB145 dB 🛁 🚿 145—260
M34—55
Credit cards [1] [2] [3] [5]

★★**Glocke** Plönlein 1 ☎3025

rm26 (🛁 🚿 22) A12rm 🚗 **P**30 Lift sB43—49
sB 🛁 🚿 57—83 dB68 dB 🛁 🚿 98—126
M14—36
Credit cards [1] [2] [3] [5]

★★**Markusturm** (ROM) Rödergasse 1 ☎2370 tx986180

15 Mar—10 Jan
🛁 🚿 26 🚗 **P**30 sB 🛁 🚿 115—125
dB 🛁 🚿 160—230
Credit cards [1] [2] [4] [5]

★★**Reichsküchenmeister** Kirchpl 8 ☎2046

rm31 (🛁 🚿 27) 🚗 **P**20 Lift sBfr40
sB 🛁 🚿 65—85 dBfr80 dB 🛁 🚿 95—130
M9—30
Credit cards [1] [2] [4] [5]

★★**Tilman Riemenschneider** Georgengasse 11—13 ☎5061 tx61384

🛁 65 🚗 **P**15 Lift ☾ sB 🛁 92—132

dB 114—224 M11—48
Credit cards 1 2 3 5

Central Schutzenstr 11 3088 **P** DJ Mer

Döhler Ansbacherstr 38—40 2084 **P** Ope Vau

ROTTACH-EGERN
Bayern (08022)

★★★★**Bachmair am See** Seestr 47 6444 tx526920
230 **P**150 Lift sB 135—190 dB 230—350 M35—80 lake mountains
Credit cards 2 5

RÖTTGEN See **BONN**

ROTTWEIL
Baden-Württemberg (0741)

★★**Johanniterbad** Johannsergrasse 12 6083 tx762705
rm26 (24) **P** Lift sB 57—73 dB 104—116
Credit cards 1 2 3 5

RUDESHEIM
Hessen (06722)

See also **ASSMANNSHAUSEN**

★★★**Waldhotel Jagdschloss Niederwald** (GS) 1004 tx42152
Mar—10 Dec
47 A20rm **P**150 Lift sB 98—135 dB 180—198 M21—42&alc mountains

Rüdesheim Geisenheimerstr 18 1085 **P** Ope

RUHPOLDING
Bayern (08663)

★★**Sporthotel am Westernberg** am Wundergraben 4 1674
15 Dec—31 Oct
33 **P**40 sB 49—95 dB 96—152 M14—34 mountains
Credit cards 1 2 3 4 5

RÜTTENSCHEID See **ESSEN**

SAARBRÜCKEN
Saarland (0681)

★★★★**Residence** (ETAP) Faktoreistr 2 33030 tx4421409
rm73 (20) **P**200 Lift sB 85—130 dB 150—180 Mfr20
Credit cards 1 2 3 5

★★★**Kongress** (ETAP) Hafenstr 8 30691 tx04428942
150 **P** Lift sB 129 dB 175 M25
Credit cards 1 2 3 4 5

★★★**Novotel** Zinzergerstr 9 58630 tx4428836
99 **P**120 Lift sB 101 dB 129 M12—45
Credit cards 1 2 3 5

★★**Christine** Gersweilerstr 39 55081 tx4428736
27 Dec—23 Dec
rm65 (40) **P**50 Lift sB46—53

Germany

sB 64—108 dB84—90 dB 118—148
Credit cards 1 2 3 4 5

★★**Wien** Gutenbergstr 29 (n.rest) 55088
6 Jan—20 Dec
27 **P**10 Lift sB 49—53 dB 82

O Muller Kaiserstr 32 811118 **P** AR DJ LR

Ritz Sulzbachstr 33—35 36529 **P** AR

SÄCKINGEN (BAD)
Baden-Wurttemberg (07761)

★**Kater Hiddigeigel** Tanzenpl 1 4055
rm15 (12) **P** sB32 sB 52—58 dB60 dB 76—90
Credit cards 1 2

ST-GEORGEN
Baden-Wurttemberg (07724)

★★**Hirsch** Bahnhofstr 70 7125
22 **P**10 sB 62—66 dB 106—108 M10—33
Credit cards 1 2 3 5

ST-GOAR
Rheinland-Pfalz (06741)

★★**Goldenen Löwen** Heerstr 82 1674
Mar—3 Nov
rm15 (14) **P** sB45 sB 66 dB65 dB 120 river

★★**Schneider** am Markt 1 1689
Mar—Dec
rm18 (9) **P**10 sB37—54 sB 44—54 dB73—77 dB 97—107 M9—30 mountains

★**Hauser** Heerstr 77 333
Feb—15 Dec
rm15 (12) **P**15 sBfr33 sB fr50 dBfr66 dB fr81 M9—28 mountains
Credit cards 1 2 3 5

ST-GOARSHAUSEN
Rheinland-Pfalz (06771)

★★**Erholung** Nastatterstr 161 2684
Restaurant closed Nov—14 Mar
56 **P**50 sB 46—48 dB 87—91 M10—12 mountains

ST-MÄRGEN
Baden-Württemberg (07669)

★★**Hirschen** Feldberg Str 9 201
42 A22rm **P** Lift sB 32—52 dB 60—103 M10—35 mountains
Credit cards 1 2 5

ST MICHAELISDONN See **BRUNSBÜTTEL**

SAND
Baden-Wurttemberg (07226)

★★**Plättig** (1.5km N) 226
rm66 (49) **P**80 Lift sBfr35 sB fr70 dBfr70 dB 110—170 M19—42 mountains
Credit cards 1 2 3 5

SANDHOFEN See **MANNHEIM**

SAULGAU
Baden-Württemberg (07581)

★★**Kieber-Post** Hauptstr 100 3051
35 **P**25 sB 55—65 dB 95—120 M18—42
Credit cards 1 2 3 5

SCHACKENDORF See **SEGEBERG (BAD)**

SCHLANGENBAD
Hessen (06129)

★★★**Staatliches Kurhaus** Rheingauer Str 47 420
rm96 (93) **P** Lift sB 92—131 dB 144—202 M20—30

SCHLEIDEN
Nordrhein-Westfalen (02445)

★**Schleidener Hof** Gemünder Str 1 216
rm15 (11) **P** sB26 sB 30 dB50 dB 60 M6—30 mountains
Credit card 1

SCHLESWIG
Schleswig-Holstein (04621)

★★**Strandhalle** am Jachthafen 22021
rm28 (25) **P**28 Lift sB39—41 sB 65—71 dB 90—120 M10—35
Credit cards 1 2 3 5

★**Weissen Schwan** Gottorfstr 1 32712
rm17 (10) A4rm **P**20 sB41—48 sB 48 dB82—96 dB 92—105 M10—23

A Wriedt Flensbunger Str 88 25087 **P** Ren

SCHLIERSEE
Bayern (08026)

★★★**Schliersee** Kirchbichlweg 18 4086 tx526497
91 A33rm **P**50 Lift sB fr92 dB 134—164 M22—44 mountains
Credit cards 1 2 3 5

SCHÖNBERG See **SEELBACH**

SCHÖNMÜNZACH
Baden-Württemberg (07447)

★★***Kurhotel Schwarzwald*** Murgtalstr 657 1088
rm26 (19) **P** Lift mountains

SCHÖNSEE
Bayern (09674)

★★**St-Hubertus** am Lauberberg 415 tx0631825
rm92 (81) **P**150 Lift sB48—53 sB 53—73 dB76—86 dB 91—121 M9—24
Credit cards 2 5

SCHÖNTAL See **NEUSTADT AN DER WEINSTRASSE**

SCHRIESHEIM
Baden-Württemberg (06203)

★★**Luisenhöhe** Eichenweg 10 65617
28 **P**50 sB 47—62 dB 104—124 Mfr16 mountains

SCHWABACH
Bayern (☎09122)

🚗 **Auto-Buhl** Nürnberger Str 43 ☎78479 **P** Toy Saa

🚗 **W Feser** Limbacher Str 26 ☎1503 **P** Aud VW

SCHWÄBISCH HALL
Baden-Württemberg (☎0791)

★★★**Hohenlohe** Weilertor 14 ☎6116 tx74870
26 Dec—23 Dec
🛁🚿98 🏠 **P**80 Lift sB🛁🚿98—130 dB🛁🚿166—220 ▭ ≋
Credit cards 1 2 3 5

★★***Goldener Adler*** am Markt 11 ☎6364
18 Jan—30 Dec
rm18 (🛁🚿11) 🏠 **P**

SCHWALENBERG
Nordrhein-Westfalen (☎05284)

★★**Schloss Burg Schwalenberg** (GS) ☎5167
Closed 6 Jan—25 Feb
🛁🚿16 🏠 **P**50 sB🛁🚿50—75 dB🛁100—150 M25—50 mountains
Credit cards 1 2

SCHWEINFURT
Bayern (☎09721)

★★★**Dorint Panorama** (n.rest) ☎1481 tx673358
🛁🚿77 🏠 **P**100 Lift ☾ sB🛁🚿68—76 dB🛁🚿106—116
Credit cards 1 2 3 5

★★**Central** Zehntstr 20 (n.rest) ☎1325 tx673349
🛁40 🏠 **P** Lift sB🛁52—63 dB🛁85—95
Credit cards 1 2 3 5

SCHWELM
Nordrhein-Westfalen (☎02336)

★★**Prinz Von Preussen** Altmarkt 8 ☎13444
🚿15 **P**18 sB🚿50 dB🚿95 M13—36
Credit card 5

SCHWETZINGEN
Baden-Württemberg (☎06202)

★★**Adler Post** Schlosstr 3 ☎10036
rm32 (🛁🚿25) 🏠 **P**10 sB62 sB🛁🚿90—106 dB169—189 dB🛁🚿169—189 M15—35
Credit cards 1 2 3 5

SEELBACH
Baden-Württemberg (☎07823)

At **SCHÖNBERG** (6km E)

★★**Pass Höhen** ☎2044
rm26 (🚿25) 🏠 **P**120 sB44—46 sB🚿61—64 dB81—89 dB🚿110—119 M15—35 ▭ mountains
Credit cards 1 2 5

SEESEN
Niedersachsen (☎05381)

★★**Goldener Löwe** Jacobsonstr 20 ☎1201 tx957316
rm22 (🛁🚿15) A9rm 🏠 **P** sB58—60 sB🛁🚿74—84 dB82—86

Germany

dB🛁🚿102—132 M8—35
Credit cards 1 2 3 5

🚗 **Hoffman** Autobahnizubringestr ☎1215 For

SEGEBERG (BAD)
Schleswig-Holstein (☎04551)

At **SCHACKENDORF** (5km NW on B404)

★★**Stefanie & Motel B404** ☎3600
rm36 (🛁🚿22) 🏠 **P**100 sB28—35 sB🛁🚿38—46 dB52—61 dB🛁🚿55—66 M8—30
Credit cards 1 2 3 5

SIEGBURG
Nordrhein-Westfalen (☎02241)

M Bässgen Frankfurterstr 1—5 ☎66001 Ope

SIEGEN
Nordrhein-Westfalen (☎0271)

★★★***Crest* (See page 50)** Kampenstr 83 ☎54072 tx872734
🚿102 **P**60 Lift ☾ ▭
Credit cards 1 2 3 4 5

★★★**Johanneshöhe** Wallhausenstr 1 ☎310008
rm26 (🛁🚿25) 🏠 **P**40 ☾ sB49 sB🛁🚿70—85 dB🛁🚿110—140 M19—38 mountains
Credit cards 1 2 5

SIGMARINGEN
Baden-Württemberg (☎07571)

🚗 **J Zimmermann** in der Burgwiesen 18 ☎1696 **P** Ope

SIMMERATH
Nordrhein-Westfalen (☎02473)

At **EICHERSCHEID** (4km S)

★**Haus Gertud** Bachstr 4 ☎1310
🚿8 A3rm **P**20 sB🚿25—30 dB🚿44—54 ⚲ mountains

SINDELFINGEN
Baden-Württemberg (☎07031)

★★★★**Crest (See page 50)** W-Haspel Str 101 ☎6150 tx07265778
🛁🚿146 **P**100 Lift ☾ sB🛁🚿195 dB🛁🚿254
Credit cards 1 2 3 4 5

★★★★**Holiday Inn** Schwertstr 65 ☎6196—0 tx7265569
🛁185 🏠 **P**200 Lift ☾ sB🛁185—195 dB🛁233—235 ▭
Credit cards 1 2 3 4 5

SINSPELT
Rheinland-Pfalz (☎06522)

★★**Altringer** Nevenburger Str 4 ☎812
Mar—15 Nov
🛁21 A3rm **P**30 sB🛁36—40 dB🛁65—73 M10—40 ⚲
Credit card 1

SOEST
Nordrhein-Westfalen (☎02921)

★★**Andernach Zur Börse** Thomästr 31 ☎4019
rm16 (🚿10) 🏠 **P**80 sB39—42 sB🚿48 dB72 dB🚿84
Credit cards 1 2 5

★★**Pilgrim-Haus** Jakobistr 75 ☎1828
🛁7 **P**3 sB🛁68 dB🛁120
Credit cards 1 2 3 4 5

🚗 **H Sledler** Riga Ring 15 ☎70138 For

SOODEN-ALLENDORF (BAD)
Hessen (☎05652)

★★**Kurhaus Kurpark** ☎3031
🛁🚿40 **P** Lift sB🛁🚿62—101 dB🛁🚿102—172 M12—30 ▭
Credit cards 1 2 3 4 5

SPEYER
Rheinland-Pfalz (☎06232)

★★**Goldener Engel** Mühlturm Str 1A ☎76732
6 Jan—23 Dec
🛁🚿38 **P**15 Lift sB🛁🚿57—69 dB🛁🚿89—105
Credit cards 1 2 3 5

STAMMHEIM See **STUTTGART**

STOCKACH
Baden-Württemberg (☎07771)

★★***Linde*** Goethestr 23 ☎2226
rm26 (🛁18) 🏠 **P** Lift

STRAUBING
Bayern (☎09421)

★★**Seethaler** Theresienpl 25 ☎12022
🛁25 🏠 **P**25 sB🛁68 dB🛁98 M alc

★★**Wittelsbach** Stadtgraben 25 ☎1517
rm41 (🛁🚿30) 🏠 **P**25 Lift sB40 sB🛁🚿45—55 dB🛁🚿78—98 M10—20
Credit cards 1 2 5

STUTTGART
Baden-Württemberg (☎0711)

★★★★**Graf Zeppelin** (SRS) A-Klett-Pl 7 ☎299881 tx722418
🛁🚿280 **P** Lift ☾ sB🛁🚿199—249 dB🛁🚿320—380 ▭
Credit cards 1 2 3 5

★★★★**Schlossgarten** Schillerstr 23 ☎299911 tx722936
🛁🚿125 🏠 **P**70 Lift ☾ sB🛁🚿165—200 dB🛁🚿250—270 M15—50
Credit cards 1 2 3 4 5

★★★**Europe** (BW) Siemensstr 26—38, Feuerbach ☎815091 tx723650
rm158 (🛁🚿48) 🏠 **P**200 Lift ☾ sB🛁🚿145—160 dB🛁🚿190 Mfr30
Credit cards 1 2 3 5

★★★**Intercity** A-Klett Pl 2 (n.rest) ☎299801 tx723543
rm104 (🛁🚿95) **P** Lift ☾ sB73—84 sB🛁🚿110—115 dB🛁🚿130—165

★★★**Parkhotel** Villastr 21 ☎280161 tx723405
🛁🚿80 **P**80 Lift ☾ sB🛁🚿150—190

dB 200—250 M30—36
Credit cards [1] [2] [3] [5]

★★★*Rieker* Friedrichstr 3 (n.rest) ☎221311
63 Lift

★★★**Waldhotel Degerloch** Guts-Muths-Weg 18 ☎765017 tx7255728
50 **P**35 Lift ☾ sB 103—148
dB 166—216 M9—32
Credit cards [1] [2] [3] [5]

★★*Ketterer* Marienstr 3 ☎294151 tx722340
rm80 (72) **P** Lift ☾

A V G Auto-Verkaufs Chemnitzer Str 7 ☎722094 AR DJ

At **MÖHRINGEN** (7km S on rd 27)

Schwaben Vaihingerstr 131 ☎7800585 For

At **STAMMHEIM** (8km N)

★★★**Novotel Stuttgart Nord** Korntaler Str 207 ☎801065 tx7252137
117 **P**85 Lift ☾ sB 130—150
dB 163—173 M16—30
Credit cards [1] [2] [3] [5]

STUTTGART AIRPORT

★★★*Flughafen* (Mövenpick) Randstr ☎7907-0 tx7245677
128 **P**150 Lift ☾
Credit cards [1] [2] [3] [5]

SULZBACH See **FRANKFURT AM MAIN**

SULZBURG
Baden-Württemberg (☎07634)

★★**Waldhotel Bad Sulzburg** Badstr 67 ☎8270 tx763411
7 Feb—7 Jan
rm40 (22) A22rm **P**80 Lift sB38
sB 70—75 dB60—72
dB 120—124 M28—65
mountains
Credit cards [1] [5]

TENNENLOHE See **ERLANGEN**

TETTNANG
Baden-Württemberg (☎07542)

★★**Rad** Lindauerstr 2 ☎6001 tx734245
70 **P**100 Lift sB 69—75
dB 100—108 M15
Credit cards [1] [2] [3] [5]

TIEFENBRONN
Baden-Württemberg (☎07234)

★★**Ochsen Post** F-J-Gall Str 13 ☎279 tx783485
Feb—Dec
18 **P**60 sB 69—98
dB 89—138 M12—49
Credit cards [1] [2] [5]

TITISEE-NEUSTADT
Baden-Württemberg (☎07651)

At **NEUSTADT**

★★★**Adler-Post** (ROM) Hauptstr 16 ☎5066
rm30 (26) **P**32 sB48—58
sB 68—95 dB90—110

Germany

dB 130—170 M28—58 mountains
Credit cards [1] [2] [3] [5]

At **TITISEE**

★★★**Brugger** Strandbadstr 14 ☎8238 tx7722332
68 **P**100 Lift ☾ sB 55—110
dB 110—200 M26 mountains lake
Credit cards [1] [2] [3] [5]

★★★**Schwarzwaldhotel am See** Seestr 12 ☎8111 tx7722341
20 Dec—Nov
86 **P**130 Lift ☾ sB 110—140
dB 140—210 M40 lake mountains
Credit cards [1] [2]

★★**Rauchfang** Bärenhofweg 2 ☎8255
17 **P**15 sB 50—64
dB 94—126 mountains
Credit cards [1] [3] [5]

★★**Seehof am See** Seestr 47 (n.rest) ☎8314
24 Dec—Oct
rm25 (24) **P**25 Lift sB56—61
sB 58—77 dB92—122
dB 136—154 lake mountains
Credit cards [1] [2] [3] [4] [5]

★**Seerose** Seestr 21 (n.rest) ☎8274
20 Dec—Oct
rm10 (2) **P**10 sB23 dB46—52 dB 60 mountains
Credit cards [1] [2] [3] [5]

TODTNAU
Baden-Württemberg (☎07671)

★★**Waldeck** Poche 6 ☎216
Dec—Oct
27 A13rm **P**40 sB 54—59
dB 97—112 M10—30
mountains
Credit cards [1] [2] [3] [5]

TÖLZ (BAD)
Bayern (☎08041)

★★**Galssacher Haus** an der Umgehungsstr ☎9583
Dec—Oct
rm22 (18) A10rm **P**3 sB31—34
sB 38—46 dB56—63 dB 70—90
M9—22 mountains
Credit cards [1] [2]

★★**Post-Hotel Kolberbräu** Marktstr 29 ☎9158
21 **P**20 Lift sB 45—60
dB 85—110 Mfr12 mountains

TRABEN-TRARBACH
Rheinland-Pfalz (☎06541)

★★**Clauss-Feist** Moselufer ☎6431
15 Mar—5 Nov
rm24 (11) **P**15 sB30—32
sB 35—42 dB50—60 dB 64—80
M12—24&alc

★★**Krone** an der Mosel 93 ☎6363
23 **P**30 sB 68—75
dB 98—110 M20—32 mountains
Credit cards [1] [2] [5]

TRAUNSTEIN
Bayern (☎0861)

★★**Parkhotel Traunsteiner Hof** Bahnhofstr 11 ☎69041
rm60 (54) **P**10 Lift ☾ sB46—50
sB 58—70 dB 106—122 M14—21
Credit cards [1] [2] [5]

TREMSBÜTTEL
Schleswig-Holstein (☎04532)

★★★**Schloss** (GS) ☎6544
Closed 12 Jan—10 Feb
rm20 (16) **P**300 ☾ sB80—170
sB 100—170 dB130—450
dB 180—450
Credit cards [1] [2] [5]

TRENDELBURG
Hessen (☎05675)

★★**Burg** (GS) ☎1021 tx994812
23 **P**60 sB 70—110
dB 100—160 Mfr28 mountains
Credit cards [1] [2]

TRIBERG
Baden-Württemberg (☎07722)

★★★★**Parkhotel Wehrle** (Relais et Châteaux/ROM) Gartenstr 24 ☎4081 tx792609
rm60 (55) A30rm **P**32 Lift ☾ sB52
sB 75—111 dB103 dB 145—205
M30—48 mountains
Credit cards [1] [2] [3] [4] [5]

TRIER
Rhineland-Pfalz (☎0651)

★★★★**Holiday Inn** Zurmaienerstr 164 ☎23091 tx472808
212 **P**150 Lift ☾ sB 102—122
dB 125—165 M25—55
Credit cards [1] [2] [3] [4] [5]

★★★**Dorint Porta Nigra** Porta Nigra Pl 1 ☎27010 tx472895
107 **P**400 Lift ☾ sB 106—116
dB 162
Credit cards [1] [2] [3] [5]

★★★*Europa Parkhotel* (BW) Kaiserstr 28—29 ☎40011 tx472858
85 **P** Lift ☾

★★**Hügel** Bernhardstr 14 (n.rest) ☎33066
25 **P**15 sB 55—68 dB 90—115
Credit cards [1] [2] [3]

★★**Petrisberg** Sickingenstr 11 (n.rest) ☎41181
30 A10rm **P**30 sB 65—75
dB 95—105

J Arweiler am Verteilerring ☎20080 Ope

Daewel Im Siebenbom ☎87063 Alf AR DJ

TRITTENHEIM
Rheinland-Pfalz (☎06507)

★**Moselperle** Moselweinstr 42 ☎2221
6 Jan—22 Dec →

rm14 (🛁 🚿 9) ⌂ **P**11 sB30—35 sB 🛁 🚿 35 dB55—60 dB 🛁 🚿 60—65 M9—25 📺 mountains

TÜBINGEN
Baden-Württemberg (☎07071)

★★★**Bad** am Freibad 2 ☎73071
10 Jan—20 Dec
🛁 🚿 35 ⌂ **P**50 sB 🛁 🚿 61—76
dB 🛁 🚿 85—110 Mfr16 🎾 ≈
Credit cards 1 2 3

★***Stadt Tübingen*** Stuttgarterstr 97 ☎31071
rm39 (🛁 🚿 27) ⌂ **P** ☾

TUTTLINGEN
Baden-Württemberg (☎07461)

★★**Schlack** Bahnhofstr 59 ☎72081 tx762577
🛁 🚿 37 A14rm ⌂ **P**42 sB 🛁 🚿 61—116
dB 🛁 🚿 104—164 M10—48
Credit cards 1 2 3 4 5

★**Ritter** Königstr 12 ☎8855
rm19 (🚿 9) ⌂ **P** sB29—32 sB🚿 35—40
dB56 dB🚿 68—76 mountains

ÜBERLINGEN
Baden-Württemberg (☎07551)

★★★**Parkhotel St-Leonard** Obere St-Leonhardstr 83 ☎8080 tx733983
🛁 🚿 114 ⌂ **P**160 Lift ☾ sB 🛁 🚿 87—130
dB 🛁 🚿 160—194 M8—32 🎾 📺 lake mountains
Credit card 2

★★**Alpenblick** ☎4559
rm26 (🚿 25) ⌂ **P**20 sB🚿 45—54
dB🚿 88—102 M16 ≈ lake

★★**Bad** Christophstr 2 ☎61055 tx0733909
Closed 20 Nov—20 Dec & 15 Jan—1 Feb
🛁 🚿 50 **P**20 Lift ☾ sB 🛁 🚿 65—115
dB 🛁 🚿 110—180 M15—35 lake
Credit cards 1 2 3 5

★★**Hecht** Munsterstr 8 ☎63333
🛁 🚿 14 ⌂ **P**8 sB 🛁 🚿 83—103
dB 🛁 🚿 166—186 M11—120
Credit cards 1 2 3 5

★★**Seegarten** Seepromenade 7 ☎63498
Feb—Nov
🛁 🚿 28 **P**4 Lift sB 🛁 🚿 72—97
dB 🛁 🚿 144—184 M17—26 ≈ lake
Credit card 1

UFFENHEIM
Bayern (☎09842)

★**Traube** am Marktpl 3 ☎8288
Feb—20 Dec
rm16 (🛁 🚿 8) ⌂ **P**5 sB22—25 sB 🛁 🚿 30
dB45—50 dB 🛁 🚿 55 M8—15

ULM
Baden-Württemberg (☎0731)

★★**Goldenes Rad** Neue Str 65 (n.rest) ☎67048
rm22 (🛁 🚿 13) Lift ☾ sB44—58
sB 🛁 🚿 80—82 dB75—85
dB 🛁 🚿 103—105
Credit cards 1 2 3 5

Germany

★★**Ibis** Neutorstr 12 ☎619001 tx712927
🚿 90 ⌂ **P** Lift sB🚿 90—100 dB🚿 130—140
M alc

★★**Intercity Ulm** Bahnhofspl 1 ☎61221 tx712871
rm111 (🛁 🚿 92) **P**120 Lift ☾ sB59—73
sB 🛁 🚿 86—99 dB119 dB 🛁 🚿 147—161
M15—40
Credit cards 1 2 3 4 5

★★***Neutor Hospiz*** Neuer Graben 23 ☎15160 tx712401
rm92 (🛁 🚿 85) ⌂ **P**20 Lift ☾
Credit cards 1 2 3 5

★★**Roter Löwe** Ulmer Gasse 8 ☎62031
6 Jan—23 Dec
rm30 (🛁 🚿 24) ⌂ **P** Lift ☾ sB44—46
sB 🛁 🚿 50 dB84 dB 🛁 🚿 94 M8—26&alc

★★**Stern** Sterngasse 17 ☎63091 tx712923
🛁 🚿 62 ⌂ **P** Lift ☾ sB 🛁 🚿 80—90
dB 🛁 🚿 115—125 M20
Credit cards 1 2 5

🚗 ***Auto Schiegel*** Lukasstr 1 ☎381435 **P** Dat Saa

Schwabengarage Marchtaler Str 23 ☎1621 M/c **P** For Hon

At **GÖGGLINGEN** (8km SW)

★★**Ritter** ☎7365
rm16 (🚿 10) ⌂ **P** sB26—39 sB🚿 39
dB50—52 dB🚿 56—70 M9—30

UNDELOH
Niedersachsen (☎04189)

★***Witte's*** in der Nordheide ☎267
Feb—15 Dec
🛁 🚿 20 ⌂ **P**100

ÜRZIG/MOSEL
Rheinland-Pfalz (☎06532)

★**Moselschild** Hauptstr 12—14 ☎3001 tx4721542
🛁 14 ⌂ **P**30 sB 🛁 69—85 dB 🛁 98—130
M17—35 lake mountains
Credit cards 1 2 3 5

★**Rotschwänzchen** Moselufer 18 ☎2183
1 Apr—15 Dec
🚿 11 A4rm **P**4 sB🚿 25—28 dB🚿 56—60
mountains
Credit cards 1 2

VAIHINGEN AN DER ENZ
Baden-Württemberg (☎07042)

★**Post** Franckstr 23 ☎4071
rm21 (🛁 🚿 12) ⌂ **P**4 Lift sB45
sB 🛁 🚿 60—65 dB70 dB 🛁 🚿 85—90
M9—18&alc
Credit cards 1 2 3 4 5

VIECHTACH
Bayern (☎09942)

★★**Sporthotel Schmaus** Stadtpl 5 ☎1627
🛁 48 ⌂ **P**22 Lift sB 🛁 41—65
dB 🛁 84—110 📺
Credit cards 1 2 3 5

VIERNHEIM
Hessen (☎06204)

★★★★**Holiday Inn** Bürgermeister Neff Str 12 ☎5036 tx465452
🛁 🚿 121 **P**150 Lift ☾ sB 🛁 🚿 154—159
dB 🛁 🚿 213—218 M22 📺
Credit cards 1 2 3 4 5

VILLINGEN
Baden-Württemberg (☎07721)

★★**Ketterer** Brigachstr 1 ☎22095 tx792554
🛁 🚿 38 **P**20 Lift ☾ sB 🛁 🚿 60—90
dB 🛁 90—150 M20—70
Credit cards 1 2 5

WAHLSCHEID
Nordrhein-Westfalen (☎02206)

★★★**Schloss Auel** (GS) Lohmar (1.5km NE) ☎2041 tx887510
rm23 (🛁 19) **P**90 sB62—72 sB 🛁 107—122
dB94—104 dB 🛁 154—194 Mfr35 🎾 📺
Credit cards 1 2 5

WALDEMS-BERMBACH
Hessen (☎06126)

★★***Hahnberg*** ☎2777
Feb—10 Jan
rm15 (🛁 🚿 11) **P**

WALLDORF
Baden-Württemberg (☎06227)

See also **HEIDELBERG**

★★★★**Holiday Inn** Roterstr (1.5km SW near autobahn exit) ☎62051 tx466009
🛁 127 ⌂ **P**150 Lift ☾ sB 🛁 162—182
dB 🛁 209—229 M alc 🎾 ≈ 📺
Credit cards 1 2 3 4 5

★★**Vorfelder** Bahnhofstr ☎2085 tx466016
rm38 (🛁 🚿 30) ⌂ **P** Lift ☾ sB40—50
sB 🛁 🚿 80—95 dBfr90 dB 🛁 🚿 120—150
Mfr29
Credit cards 1 2 5

WANGEN IM ALLGÄU
Baden-Württemberg (☎07522)

★★**Alte Post** (ROM) Postpl 2 ☎4014 tx732774
🛁 🚿 28 A10rm **P** sB 🛁 🚿 60—65
dB 🛁 🚿 110—125 M12—60 mountains

WASSEBURG AM INN
Bayern (☎08071)

★★**Fletzinger** Fletzingergasse 1 ☎8010
15 Jan—15 Dec
🛁 🚿 38 ⌂ Lift sB 🛁 🚿 55—69
dB 🛁 🚿 90—118
Credit cards 1 2 5

WEIDEN IN DER OBERPFALZ
Bayern (☎0961)

🚗 **Friederich** Bahnhofstr 17 ☎42081 BMW

🚗 **Stegmann** Obere Bauscherstr 16 ☎43055 Aud VW

WEINHEIM AN DER BERGSTRASSE
Baden-Württemberg (☎06201)

★★**Fuchs'sche Mühle** Birkenauer Talstr 10 ☎61031

rm28 (🛁🚿21) 🚗 **P**50 Lift sB35
sB🛁🚿85—95 dB🛁🚿95—105 M20—40
📺

WEISSENBURG IN BAYERN
Bayern (☎09141)

★★**Rose** (ROM) Rosenstr 6 ☎2096

🛁🚿29 🚗 **P**10 sB🛁🚿58—120
dB🛁🚿90—160
Credit cards [1] [2] [3] [5]

WERTHEIM
Baden-Württemberg (☎09342)

★★**Schwan** Mainpl 8 ☎1278

Closed Jan
rm38 (🛁🚿28) A10rm 🚗 **P**12 ☾ sB38—42
sB🛁🚿55—75 dBfr72 dB🛁🚿85—120
M15—170
Credit cards [1] [2] [3] [5]

At **KREUZWERTHEIM**

★**Herrnwiesen** Herrnwiesen 4 ☎37031

🛁🚿17 🚗 **P**20 sB🛁🚿45 dB🛁🚿68—70
mountains

WERTINGEN
Bayern (☎08272)

★**Hirsch** Schulstr 7 ☎2055

rm29 (🚿21) A17rm 🚗 **P** sB35 sB🚿43 dB61
dB🚿77 M7—17
Credit cards [2] [5]

WESEL
Nordrhein-Westfalen (☎0281)

★★★**Kaiserhof** Kaiserring 1 ☎21972

🛁🚿37 🚗 **P**40 Lift sB🛁🚿50 dB🛁🚿96
M5—35
Credit cards [1] [2] [3] [5]

WESTERLAND (Island of Sylt)
Schleswig-Holstein (☎04651)

No road connection exists between the mainland and the Island of Sylt; however there is a rail connection between Niebül and Westerland. Cars are loaded onto trains by ramps.

★★★**Stadt Hamburg** (Relais et Châteaux)
Strandstr 2 ☎858

rm75 (🛁🚿63) **P**40 Lift ☾ sB53—83
sB🛁🚿75—159 dB86—112
dB🛁🚿120—320 M29—36

WETZLAR
Hessen (☎06441)

★★★**Mercure** Bergstr 41 ☎48031
tx483739

🛁🚿154 🚗 **P**50 Lift sB🛁🚿111—143
dB🛁🚿151—191 M17—32 📺
Credit cards [1] [2] [3] [5]

★★**Eulerhaus** Buderuspl 1 (n. rest)
☎47016 tx483763

rm24 (🛁🚿15) **P**6 Lift sB40 sB🛁🚿55
dB70 dB🛁🚿90
Credit cards [1] [2] [5]

WIESBADEN
Hessen (☎06121)

★★★★★**Nassauer Hof** (SRS) Kaiser Friedrich-Pl 3-4 ☎1330-0 tx4186847

🛁209 🚗 Lift **P**85 ☾ sB🛁235—295
dB🛁340—400 Mfr35 📺
Credit cards [1] [2] [3] [5]

★★★**Forum** A-Lincoln Str 17 ☎77811
tx4186369

🛁157 **P**150 Lift ☾ sB🛁145—210
dB🛁175—260 M alc 📺
Credit cards [1] [2] [3] [4] [5]

★★★**Fürstenhof-Esplanade**
Sonnenberger Str 32 ☎522091 tx4186447

rm74 (🛁🚿52) 🚗 **P**10 Lift ☾ sB48—68
sB🛁🚿85—120 dB95—120
dB🛁🚿120—190 M10—28
Credit cards [1] [2] [5]

★★★**Schwarzer Bock** Kranzpl 12
☎3821 tx4186640

🛁🚿160 **P** Lift ☾ sB🛁🚿140—195
dB🛁🚿200—300 M alc 📺
Credit cards [1] [2] [3] [5]

★★**Central** Bahnhofstr 65 (n.rest)
☎372001 tx4186604

rm70 (🛁🚿45) 🚗 **P**10 Lift ☾ sBfr58
sB🛁🚿fr95 dB75—85 dB🛁🚿120—140
Credit cards [1] [2] [3] [5]

★**Oranien** Platter Str 2 ☎525025
tx4186217

🛁🚿85 🚗 **P**70 Lift ☾ sB🛁🚿79—89
dB🛁🚿120—130
Credit cards [1] [2] [3] [5]

Heine Mainzer Str 141 ☎719780 **P** Alf Peu

🚘 ***Wiesbaden*** Stresemannring (nr main rly station) ☎145-0 **P** Ope

At **WIESBADEN-DOTZHEIM**

H Hell Stegerwaldstr 35 ☎422088 AR Maz

At **WIESBADEN-SONNENBERG**
(6.5km NE)

★***Köhler*** König-Adolf Str 6 ☎540804
rm11 **P**20

WIESSEE (BAD)
Bayern (☎08022)

★★★**Hubertus** Sonnenfeldweg 29
☎82774 tx526188

20 Dec—20 Oct
rm105 (🛁🚿78) A30rm **P**58 Lift ☾ sB50—56
sB🛁🚿68—93 dB90—104
dB🛁🚿124—174 M14—22 ⛱ lake
mountains
Credit cards [1] [2] [3] [4] [5]

WILDBAD IM SCHWARZWALD
Baden-Württemberg (☎07081)

★★★★***Sommerberg*** Heermannsweg 5
(2.5km W) ☎1641 tx724015

🛁100 🚗 **P** Lift ☾ 🎾 📺 mountains

WILDUNGEN (BAD)
Hessen (☎05621)

★★★**Staatliches Badehotel** Dr Marc Str 4 ☎860 tx0994612

rm117 (🛁🚿75) 🚗 **P**60 Lift ☾
sB🛁🚿71—108 dB🛁🚿133—192 🎾 ⛱
📺 🅸
Credit cards [1] [5]

WILHELMSHAVEN
Niedersachsen (☎04421)

★★**Loheyde** Eberstr 104 ☎43048

rm112 (🛁🚿43) A15rm 🚗 **P** Lift ☾

🚘 ***August Hillmann*** Banter Weg 5 ☎20010
M/c For

WILLINGEN
Hessen (☎05632)

★★**Waldhotel Willingen** am Köhlerhagen 3 ☎6016

Closed 1—20 Dec
🛁42 **P**120 sB🛁73 dB🛁142 M20—24
St% 🎾 📺 mountains
Credit cards [1] [5]

WIMPFEN (BAD)
Baden-Württemberg (☎07063)

★★**Blauer Turm** Burgviertel 5 ☎225

rm33 (🚿14) **P**60 sB45—52 sB🚿65—72
dB80—89 dB🚿100—144 M7—25

★★**Weinmann** Marktpl 3 ☎7710

Mar—Nov
🚿15 🚗 **P**60 sB🚿50 dB🚿100

WINDHAGEN See **HONNEF AM RHEIN (BAD)**

WINTERBERG
Nordrhein-Westfalen (☎02981)

At **NEUASTENBERG** (6km SW)

★★★**Dorint Ferienpark** ☎2033 tx84539

🛁136 **P**150 Lift ☾ sB🛁87—115
dB🛁124—200 🎾 📺 lake
Credit cards [1] [2] [3] [5]

At **WINTERBERG-HOHELEYE** (10km SE)

★★★**Hochsauerland** ☎(02758)313
tx875629

🛁🚿90 **P**50 Lift sB🛁🚿69—139
dB🛁🚿125—199 M12—38&alc 🎾 📺
mountains

WOLFACH
Baden-Württemberg (☎07834)

★★**Krone** Marktpl 33 ☎350

rm23 (🛁🚿14) A9rm 🚗 **P**4 sB40—42
sB🛁🚿42—46 dB80—84 dB🛁🚿84—88
M15—20 t% mountains

WOLFSBURG
Niedersachsen (☎05361)

★★★★**Holiday Inn** Rathausstr 1
☎12081 tx958457

🛁207 **P**250 Lift sB🛁96—165
dB🛁133—198 M13—50 📺
Credit cards [1] [2] [3] [4] [5]

WORMS
Rheinland-Pfalz (☎06241)

★★★**Dom** Obermarkt 10 ☎6913 tx467846
🛁 🚿 60 🏠 **P**25 Lift ☾ sB 🛁 🚿 73—89 dB 🛁 🚿 122—167 M28
Credit cards 1 2 3 5

🚗 ***Betriebe Berkenkamp*** Speyerer Str 88 ☎6343 **P** For

WUPPERTAL
Nordrhein-Westfalen (☎0202)

At **WUPPERTAL II-BARMEN**

H Wilke Kohlenstr 19 ☎606052 AR DJ Lan Saa

At **WUPPERTAL I-ELBERFELD**

★★★★**Kaiserhof** (PLM) Döppersberg 50 ☎459081 tx8591405
🛁 🚿 130 **P**300 Lift ☾ sB 🛁 🚿 90—195 dB 🛁 🚿 190—295 M10—33
Credit cards 1 2 3

★★***Post*** Postr 4 (n.rest) ☎450131
2 Jan—24 Dec
rm54 (🛁 🚿 53) **P** Lift ☾

★★**Rathaus** Wilhelmstr 7 (n.rest) ☎450148 tx8592424
2 Jan—23 Dec
🛁 🚿 35 **P**15 Lift ☾ sB 🛁 🚿 85 dB 🛁 🚿 120
Credit cards 1 3

At **WUPPERTAL XXI-RONSDORF**

🚗 **Automobile Vosberg** Remscheider Str 192 ☎468066 **P** AR Hon

At **WUPPERTAL XXII-LANGERFELD**

★**Neuenhof** Schwelmer Str 246—8 ☎602536
rm25 (🛁 🚿 12) 🏠 **P**20 Lift sB40—70 sB 🛁 🚿 60—80 dB80—140 dB 🛁 🚿 120—140 M10—30

Germany

WÜRZBURG
Bayern (☎0931)

★★★**Bahnhofhotel Excelsior** Haugerring 2—3 (n.rest) ☎50484 tx68435
rm54 (🛁 🚿 40) **P5** Lift ☾ sB45 sB 🛁 🚿 70—90 dB80—90 dB 🛁 🚿 130—160 mountains
Credit cards 1 2 3 5

★★★**Rebstock** (BW) Neubaustr 7 ☎50075 tx68684
🛁 🚿 81 **P**300 Lift sB 🛁 🚿 108—147 dB 🛁 🚿 177—271 M22—40
Credit cards 1 2 3 5

★★**Central** Koelikerstr 1 (n.rest) ☎56952
6 Jan—20 Dec
rm23 (🚿 9) 🏠 **P**10 Lift ☾ sB40—65 sB🚿 60—65 dB88—100 dB🚿 95—100
Credit cards 1 2

★★**Franziskaner** Franziskanerpl 2 ☎50360
rm47 (🛁 🚿 7) **P**20 Lift ☾ sB57—74 sB 🛁 🚿 79—89 dB93—118 dB 🛁 🚿 123—133 M11—25
Credit cards 1 2 3 5

★★**Walfisch** am Pleidenturm 5 ☎50055 tx068499
🛁 40 🏠 **P** Lift ☾ sB 🛁 104—119 dB 🛁 157—177 M alc
Credit cards 1 2 3 5

At **LENGFELD** (4km NE on 19)

🚗 **Autohaus Stoy** Industriestr 1 ☎27646 Dat Tal

ZELL AN DER MOSEL
Rheinland-Pfalz (☎06542)

★★**Post** Schlossstr 25 ☎4217
🛁 🚿 16 **P**14 Lift sB 🛁 🚿 49 dB 🛁 🚿 97
Credit cards 1 2 5

ZUSMARSHAUSEN
Bayern (☎08291)

★★**Post** Augsberger Str ☎302
rm27 (🛁 🚿 13) 🏠 **P**30 sB35 sB 🛁 🚿 40 dB58 dB 🛁 🚿 70
Credit cards 1 2 5

ZWEIBRÜCKEN
Rheinland-Pfalz (☎06332)

★★★**Fasanerie** (ROM) Fasaneriestr ☎44074 tx451182
🛁 🚿 50 **P**80 sB 🛁 🚿 85—115 dB 🛁 🚿 125—165
Credit cards 1 2 3 4 5

★★**Rosen** von Rosen Str 2 (n.rest) ☎6014
rm42 (🛁 🚿 32) **P**10 Lift sB41—44 sB 🛁 🚿 51—57 dB 🛁 🚿 78—86
Credit cards 1 2 3 5

Carbon Zweibrückerstr 4 ☎6048 **P** For

ZWISCHENAHN (BAD)
Niedersachsen (☎04403)

★***Ferien-Motel*** am Schlart 1 (2km E) ☎2005 tx254713
rm30 (🛁 🚿 26) A4rm **P**

D Mengers Windmühlenstr 2 ☎3378 **P** AR

The historic city of Cologne

Gibraltar

International distinguishing sign

Area *2.5 sq miles*
Population *28,843*
Local time *GMT + 1 (Summer GMT + 2)*

National flag *Union Jack*

How to get there

Gibraltar is normally approached overland through France and Spain via the Bayonne-San Sebastian route at the western end of the Pyrenees. The promontory itself is entered via the La Linea customs post and is open to pedestrian and vehicular traffic of all nationalities. The distance from Calais to Gibraltar is 1,420 miles and would normally require three or four night stops.

Motoring regulations and general information

This information should be read in conjunction with the general content of the European ABC (pages 4-26). **Note** As certain regulations and requirements are common to many countries they are covered by one entry in the ABC and the following headings represent some of the subjects dealt with in this way:

Crash or safety helmets
Customs regulations for European countries
Drinking and driving
Fire extinguisher
First-aid kit
International distinguishing sign
Medical treatment
Mirrors
Overtaking
Police fines
Priority
Radio telephones/Radio transmitters
Road signs
Traffic lights
Tyres

AA Agents

Gibraltar J Lucas Imossi & Sons Ltd, 1-5 Irish Town, PO Box 167 ☏ 73500/73525/73550. See also *AA Agents* page 5.

Accidents

Fire ☏ 190 **police** and **ambulance** ☏ 199. There are no firm rules of procedure after an accident; the recommendations under *Accidents* page 5 are advised.

Accommodation

The Tourist Office produces a complete list of hotels giving full details of facilities offered. Hotels provide an international cuisine; fish and seafoods are predominant but there are restaurants offering continental food, as well as Chinese, Italian, Spanish and Indian dishes. There are a number of establishments providing the atmosphere of an English pub selling familiar beers.

Breakdown

If your car breaks down, try to move it to the side of the road so that it obstructs the traffic flow as little as possible and contact a local garage for assistance. See also *Breakdown* page 6 and *Warning triangle* page 239.

British Embassy/Consulate

(See also page 6)
There is no Embassy or Consulate in Gibraltar; as a Crown Colony the Governor is the British representative.

Caravans and luggage trailers

(See also page 6)
The temporary importation of trailer caravans into Gibraltar is restricted and an import licence is necessary; luggage trailers however do not require an import licence.

Currency including banking hours

(See also page 9)
The unit of currency is the Gibraltar pound which is at par with the pound Sterling; British coins are legal tender. There is no restriction on the amount of currency which may be imported, but large amounts which are to be subsequently re-exported should be declared on entry.

Banks are open Monday to Friday between

09.00—15.30hrs and from 16.30—18.00hrs on Friday.

Dimensions and weight restrictions

On some specified roads vehicles must not exceed — height: 4.22 metres; width: 2.51 metres; length: 15.54 metres. In the city and Upper Rock vehicles must not exceed — height: 3.66 metres; width: 2.13 metres; length: 15.54 metres. The combined weight of car/caravan combinations must not exceed 3.500kg (3tons 8cwt 100lbs). See also *Caravan and luggage trailers* above.

Driving licence

A valid British driving licence is acceptable in Gibraltar. The minimum age at which a visitor may drive a temporarily imported car or motorcycle is 18 years.

Emergency messages to tourists

(See also page 11)
Emergency messages to tourists are broadcast by the Gibraltar Broadcasting Corporation (GBC) throughout the year. The messages are transmitted once only as soon as air time is available on 1458KHz medium wave, 91.3MHz and 100.5MHz VHF.

Horn, use of

The use of car horn is not permitted within the city limits.

Lights

(See also page 14)
Parking lights should be used in badly lit areas and when visibility is poor. It is compulsory to drive with dipped headlights in the hours of darkness. The use of full headlights is prohibited in built-up areas.

Parking

(See also page 17)
It is prohibited to park by a bus stop, loading/unloading bay, taxi stand, traffic sign or in any position which is likely to cause unnecessary obstruction.

Passengers

(See also page 18)
There are no restrictions on the ages of front seat passengers, but it is recommended that children do not travel in a vehicle as front seat passengers.

Petrol

(See also page 18)
Credit cards Petrol stations do not accept credit cards.
Duty-free petrol The petrol in the vehicle tank may be imported free of customs duty and tax.
Petrol cans Petrol may only be imported in a purpose made steel container. Duty will be charged and the lead content of the petrol must be 0.15grammes.
Petrol (leaded) Super (98 octane) grade only.
Petrol (unleaded) is not sold in Gibraltar.

Postal information

Mail Postcards 19*p*; letters up to 20gm 22*p*.
Post offices The General Post Office is located at 104 Main Street. There are also two sub-Post Offices one in the North District and one in the South District. Opening hours are 09.00—17.00hrs Monday to Friday and 09.00—13.00hrs on Saturday.

Postcheques

(See also page 20)
Postcheques may be cashed at the General Post Office up to a maximum of £50. Counter positions are identified by a *Postcheque* window sticker. See *Postal information* for opening hours.

Public holidays

Official public holidays in Gibraltar for 1987 are given below. See also *Public holidays* page 21.
January 1 (New Year's Day)
March 9 (Commonwealth Day)
April 17 (Good Friday)
April 20 (Easter Monday)
May 1 (May Day)
May 25 (Spring Bank Holiday)
June 15 (Queen's Birthday)
August 31 (Late Summer Bank Holiday)
December 25 (Christmas Day)
December 28 (Boxing Day)

Roads

Generally the roads are in good condition although most tend to be very narrow. Those on the Rock are steep whilst in the town there are sharp bends.

Shopping hours

Shops are open Monday to Friday from 09.00—13.00hrs and 15.00—19.30hrs and 09.00—13.00hrs on Saturday.

Speed limits

(See also page 22)
The standard legal limit for cars and motorcycles within the City of Gibraltar is 32kph (20mph) and 48kph (30mph) outside the city; car/caravan combinations are restricted to 32kph (20mph) both inside and outside the city.

Tourist information

(See also page 24)

The Gibraltar Government Tourist Office has an office at Arundel Great Court, 179 The Strand, London WC2R 1EH ☏ 01—836 0777/8. Within Gibraltar local information is available from the Government Tourist Office in Cathedral Square, The Piazza Main Street and at the frontier.

Using the telephone

(See also page 24)

Insert coin **after** lifting receiver (instructions in English in all callboxes). Use 5*p* coins for local calls and 20*p* or 50*p* coins for international calls.

International callbox identification All coin boxes within the town area have IDD facilities.

Telephone rates A telephone call to the UK costs 70*p* per minute. Cheap rate calls costing 60*p* per minute may be made between 24.00hrs on Friday to 12.00hrs on Saturday and between 24.00hrs on Saturday to 12.00hrs on Sunday.

What to dial for the Irish Republic 00 353.

What to dial for the UK 00 44.

Visitors' registration

British subjects in transit or staying in Gibraltar as temporary visitors are automatically issued with a permit enabling them to stay for one month; if necessary the permit can be renewed.

Warning triangle

The use of a warning triangle is not compulsory but strongly recommended. See also *Warning triangles/Hazard warning lights* page 25.

Prices are in Sterling

Abbreviations
Pde Parade
Rd Road
St Street

GIBRALTAR

★★★★**Caleta Palace** Catalan Bay ☏76501 tx2345
🛁 200 🏠 **P**40 Lift ☾ sB 🛁 22—28 dB 🛁 37—41 M6—7 ⛱ sea
Credit cards 1 2 3 5

★★★★**Holiday Inn** Governor's Pde ☏70500 tx2242
🛁 120 **P** Lift sB 🛁 42—48 dB 🛁 49—55 M7—8 ⛱ sea mountains
Credit cards 1 2 3 5

★★★★**Rock** Europa Rd ☏73000 tx2238
🛁 160 **P**50 Lift ☾ sB 🛁 35—41 dB 🛁 46—51 Mfr10 ⛱ sea
Credit cards 1 2 3 5

★★★**Montarik** Main St ☏77065 tx2226
🛁 🚿 65 Lift sB 🛁 🚿 14—15 dB 🛁 🚿 20—21
Credit cards 2 3

★★★**Queen's** Boyd St ☏74000 tx2269
rm64 (🛁 52) **P**40 Lift ☾ sB14 sB 🛁 18 dB20 dB 🛁 22—34 Mfr5&alc sea mountains
Credit cards 1 3

🚗 **Central** 20 Line Wall Road ☏75149 **P** AR Mer

🚗 **J Lucas Imossi** Waterport Circle ☏75627 For

North Garage West Place of Arms ☏78205 **P** Peu Tal

International distinguishing sign

Area *mainland 40,674 sq miles, islands 9,860 sq miles*
Population *9,740,000*
Local time *GMT + 2 (Summer GMT + 3)*

National flag *Five horizontal blue stripes on white background with a white cross on blue background in the top left hand corner*

A leaflet entitled *'Motoring in the Greek Islands'* is available to AA members.

How to get there

The usual and most direct route for the motorist is through Belgium, West Germany (Köln/Cologne and München/Munich), Austria (Salzburg) and Yugoslavia (Belgrade). The alternative road route is via France or Switzerland, Italy (Milan and Trieste), and Yugoslavia. The third way of reaching Greece is to drive to southern Italy and use the direct ferry services. The distance to Athínai (Athens) is just under 2,000 miles and would normally require four to five overnight stops. Car-sleeper services operate during the summer from Brussels and 's-Hertogenbosch to Ljubljana; from Boulogne, Brussels and Paris to Milan; and from Milan to Bari and Brindisi.

Motoring regulations and general information

This information should be read in conjunction with the general content of the European ABC (pages 4-26). **Note** As certain regulations and requirements are common to many countries they are covered by one entry in the ABC and the following headings represent some of the subjects dealt with in this way:

AA Agents
Crash or safety helmets
Customs regulations for European countries
Drinking and driving
Insurance
International distinguishing sign
Medical treatment
Mirrors
Overtaking
Police fines
Radio telephones/Radio transmitters
Seat belts
Traffic lights
Tyres
Visitors' registration

Accidents

Fire in Athínai ☏ 199. In other cities the numbers are given in the local telephone directories. **Police** in Athínai and most big cities ☏ 100; elsewhere local telephone directories should be consulted. **Tourist police** ☏ 171. **Ambulance** in Athínai ☏ 166; in other cities consult local telephone directories. In the case of accidents in which private property is damaged or persons injured the police should be called. They should also be called to minor incidents that cannot be settled amicably on the spot. Your own insurance company should be informed as well as the Motor Insurers Bureau in Athínai. The Motoring Club (ELPA) should also be informed preferably at their Head Office (see under *Motoring club* for address). See also *Accidents* page 5.

Accommodation

The Hellenic Chamber of Hotels issues a comprehensive guide to hotels, which includes details of some 4,000 establishments in categories de-luxe, A, B and C, Prices, which should be exhibited in rooms, are controlled by the National Greek Tourist Office. ATV, stamp duty and local taxes are not included in quoted rates. Additional charges are sometimes made for air-conditioning.

Boats

Boat registration documentation is recommended in respect of boats temporarily imported into Greece. See page 6 for further information.

Breakdown

The Automobile and Touring Club of Greece (ELPA) provides a breakdown service in most big cities and assistance can be obtained by dialling

104. See also *Breakdown* page 6 and *Warning triangle* page 244.

British Embassy/Consulates

The British Embassy is located at *10675 Athínai* 1 Ploutarchou Street ☎ (01)7236211. There is a British Consulate in Salonika; there are British Vice-Consulates in Kríti and Kérkira; British Vice-Consulates with Honorary Consuls in Kavala, Pátrai, Rodhos and Samos. See also page 6 and *Town Plan of Athínai* pages 246-247.

Currency including banking hours

(See also page 9)
The unit of currency is the Greek Drachma (*Dr*) divided into 100 *Lepta*. At the time of going to press £=*Dr*200.45. Denominations of bank notes are *Dr* 50, 100, 500, 1,000, 5,000; standard coins are *Dr* 1, 2, 5, 10, 20, 50. The maximum amount of Greek currency which may be taken into or out of Greece is *Dr*3,000 in notes of *Dr*50 and *Dr*100 denominations. There are no formalities concerning the import and export of foreign currency not exceeding the equivalent of US $500. However, if the amount is in excess of this it must be declared to the Currency Control Authorities upon arrival.

Banks are open from 08.00-14.00hrs Monday to Friday. Some foreign exchange offices are open in the afternoon.

Dimensions and weight restrictions

Private **cars** and towed **trailers** or **caravans** are restricted to the following dimensions — height: 4 metres; width: 2.50 metres; length (including any coupling device): up to 2,500kg 8 metres, over 2,500kg 10 metres. The maximum permitted overall length of vehicle/trailer or caravan combination is 18 metres.

Trailers without brakes may have a total weight of up to 50% of the unladen weight of the towing vehicle and of the driver whose weight is considered equal to 70kg. The maximum permitted total weight of trailer and towing vehicle must not exceed 3,500kg.

Driving licence

A valid British driving licence is acceptable in Greece. The minimum age at which a visitor may drive a temporarily imported car or motorcycle (over 50cc) is 17 years. However, an International Driving Permit is required by the holder of a licence issued in the Republic of Ireland. See under *Driving licence* and *International Driving Permit* page 11 for further information.

Emergency messages to tourists

(See also page 11)
Emergency messages to tourists are broadcast daily by the National Broadcasting Institute of Greece.

ERT1 transmitting on 411 metres medium wave broadcasts these messages in English, French, German and Arabic at 07.40hrs daily throughout the year.

ERT2 transmitting on 305 metres medium wave broadcasts the messages in English and French at 14.25 and 21.15hrs daily throughout the year.

Fire extinguisher

(See also page 12)
It is compulsory for all vehicles to be equipped with a fire extinguisher.

First-aid kit

(See also page 12)
It is compulsory for all vehicles to be equipped with a first-aid kit.

Lights

(See also page 14)
Driving on sidelights only is not permitted. It is recommended that *motorcyclists* use dipped headlights during the day.

Motoring club

The **Automobile and Touring Club of Greece** (ELPA) has its head office at *11527 Athínai* 2 Messogion Street ☎ (01)779 1615 and branch offices are maintained in major towns throughout the country and on Kérkira and Kriti. Office hours are 09.30—19.00hrs Monday to Friday; Saturday and Sunday 09.30—13.00hrs. The club is able to provide general touring information and this may be obtained by telephoning 174 in Athínai and ☎ (01)174 throughout the country, Monday to Saturday 08.00—22.00hrs. See also page 16 and *Town plan of Athínai* pages 246-247.

Motorways

The motorways are usually only single-carriageway with some dual carriageway sections. Tolls are charged on most sections. Thessaloniki (Salonica)—Athínai (Athens) *Dr*230 Athínai—Pátrai (Patras) *Dr*130.

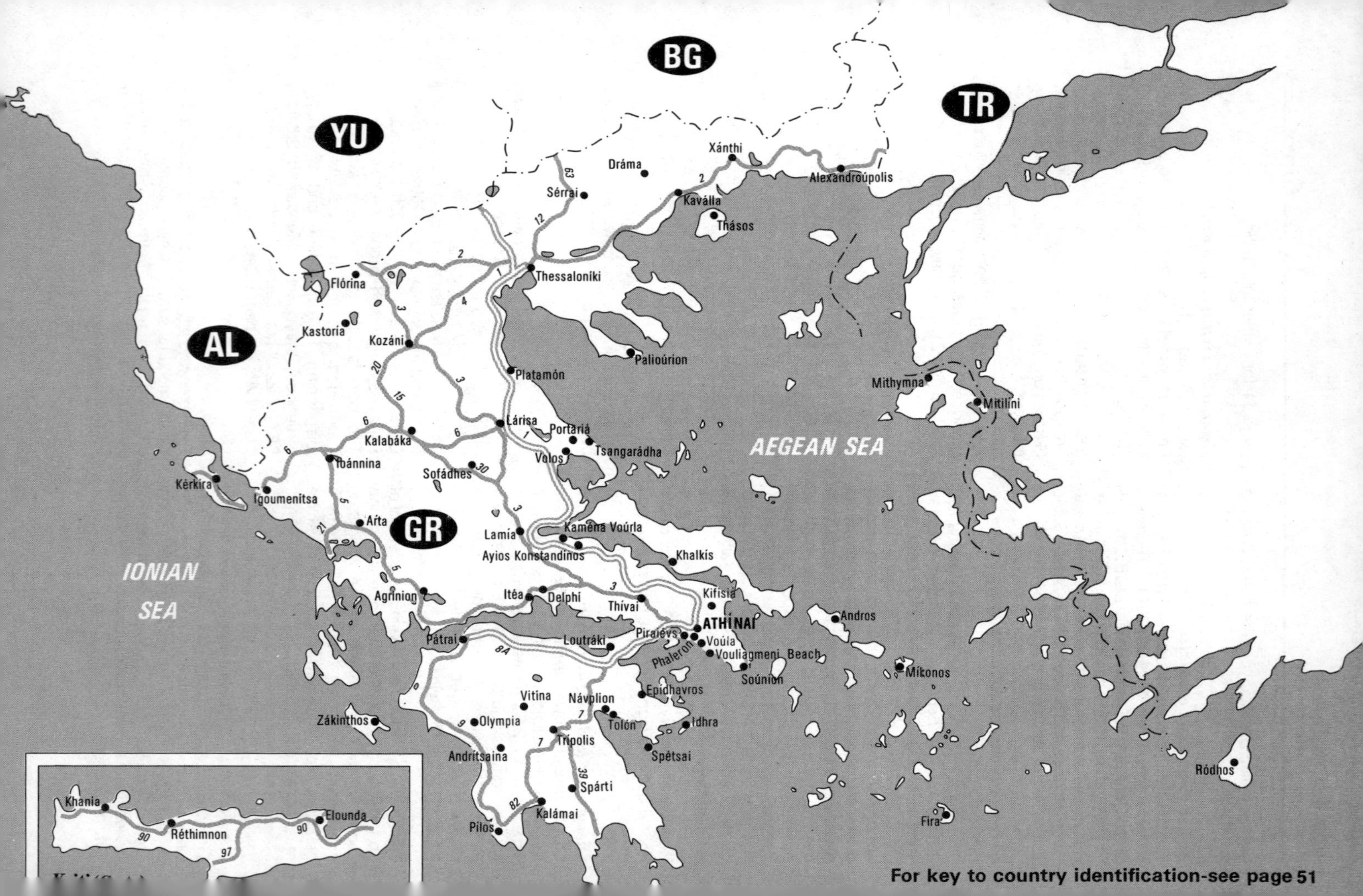

For key to country identification-see page 51

Parking

(See also page 17)
According to Greek law parking is prohibited within 5 metres (16½ft) of an intersection; within 15 metres (49ft) of a bus stop or a level crossing; within 3 metres (10ft) of a fire hydrant; and where there is a continuous central white line unless there are two lanes in each direction.

Parking in Athínai can be difficult, and some garages charge high rates. It is forbidden to park in the *Green Zone* except where parking meters have been installed. *Warning* The police in Athínai are empowered to confiscate and detain the number plates from visitors' cars which are illegally parked. A heavy fine will also be imposed upon offenders and visitors are reminded that it is illegal to drive a vehicle without number plates.

Passengers

(See also page 18)
Children under 10 are not permitted to travel in a vehicle as front seat passengers.

Petrol

(See also page 18)
Credit cards Few petrol stations will accept credit cards.
Duty-free petrol The petrol in the vehicle tank may be imported free of customs duty and tax.
Petrol cans It is **forbidden** to carry petrol in cans in a vehicle.
Petrol (leaded) Venzini Apli (91—92 octane) and Venzini Super (96-98 octane) grades.
Petrol (unleaded) is sold in Greece as Super (95 octane). Stations selling unleaded petrol will display a special sign.

Postal information

Mail Postcards *Dr*35, letters — up to 20gm *Dr*35.
Post offices There are 850 post offices in Greece. Opening hours are from 07.30—20.30hrs Monday to Friday in large towns and 07.30—15.00hrs Monday to Friday in small ones. Post offices in central Athínai are located in Syntagma Square, Omonia Square and at Eolou Street 100.

Postcheques

(See also page 20)
Postcheques may be cashed at all post offices for any amount up to a maximum of *Dr*12,000 per cheque in multiples of *Dr*1,000 per cheque. Counter positions are identified by the words *Mandats* or *Orders*. See *Postal information* for post office opening hours.

Priority

At crossroads outside cities traffic on a main road has priority. See also *Priority including Roundabouts* page 21.

Public holidays

Official public holidays in Greece for 1987 are given below. See also *Public holidays* page 21.
January 1 (New Year's Day)
January 6 (Epiphany)
March 2 (First Day of Lent)
March 25 (National Holiday)
April 17 (Good Friday)
April 20 (Easter Monday)
May 1 (May Day)
June 8 (Whit Monday)
August 15* (Assumption)
October 28 (National Holiday)
December 25 (Christmas Day)
December 26* (Boxing Day)

*Saturday

Roads

Although the road system is reasonably comprehensive, surfaces vary and secondary roads may be poor. On long drives a good average speed is between 30 and 40 miles an hour. The islands are best visited by sea or air. Only the larger islands — Kríti (Crete), Kérkira (Corfu) and Rodhos (Rhodes) — have reasonably comprehensive road systems. Roads on the smaller islands are generally narrow and surfaces vary from fairly good to rather poor. A leaflet entitled *Road conditions in Greece* is available to AA members.

Road signs

(See also page 22)
The signposting is fairly good, both Greek and English lettering are used.

Shopping hours

Generally shops and stores are open from 08.00—15.00hrs on Monday, Wednesday and Saturday; on Tuesday, Thursday and Friday from 08.00—14.00hrs and 17.30—20.30hrs.

Speed limits

(See also page 22)
Unless otherwise indicated by signs, private cars with or without trailers are subject to the following restrictions: 50kph (31mph) in built-up areas; 80kph (49mph) outside built-up areas; 100kph (62mph) on motorways.

Spiked or studded tyres
There are no special regulations regarding the use of *spiked tyres*. See also *Cold weather touring* page 8.

Tourist information
(See also page 24)
The National Tourist Organisation of Greece at 195-197 Regent Street, London W1R 8DL ☎ 01—734 5597 will be pleased to help tourists before their departure. The organisation has offices in main towns throughout Greece.

Tourist Police
On duty in all resorts and at major frontier crossings. They all speak English and their job is to assist tourists in any way they can.

Using the telephone
(See also page 24)
Insert coin **after** lifting receiver, dialling tone same as UK. When making calls to subscribers within Greece precede number with relevant area code (shown in parentheses against town entry in gazetteer). Use *Dr*5 coin for local calls (blue/grey callbox) and *Dr*10 or *Dr*20 coins for national and international calls, but all coins must be dated 1976 or later.
International callbox identification (and national out of town calls) Orange sign round top.
Telephone rates The cost of a call between Athínai and London is *Dr*135 per minute.
What to dial for the Irish Republic 00 353.
What to dial for the UK 00 44.

Warning triangle
The use of a warning triangle is compulsory for all vehicles except two-wheelers. The triangle must be placed 20 metres (22yds) behind the vehicle in built-up areas and 50 metres (55yds) outside built-up areas. See also *Warning triangles/Hazard warning lights* page 25.

Prices are in Greek Drachmae
Abbreviations:
Av Avenue
Pl Place
Sq Square
St Street

AGRÍNION
Central Greece (☎0641)

★★***Soumells*** 3 Ethniki Odos ☎23473
rm20 (🛁 4) **P**

ALEXANDROÚPOLIS
Thrace (☎0551)

★★**Astir** 280 Av Komotinis ☎26448
🛁 56 **P**100 ☾ sB🛁 2590—3120
dB🛁 3450—4250 Mfr1000 ≈ Beach sea
Credit cards [1] [2] [3] [5]

★★***Egnatia*** ☎28661
🛁 96 🚗 **P** 🎾 Beach sea

ANDRÍTSAINA
Peloponnese (☎0626)

★***Theoxenia*** ☎22219
Mar—Oct
rm17 (🛁 🚿 9) **P**

ANDROS
(Island of Andros) (☎0282)

★★***Xenia*** ☎22270
Apr—Oct
🛁 26 **P**

ÁRTA
Epirus (☎0681)

★★***Xenia*** Frourion ☎27413
rm22 (🚿 11) **P** 🎾

ATHÍNAI (ATHENS)
Attica (☎01)
See plan pages 246 and 247

★★★★★**Acropole Palace** 51 28th Octovriou ☎5223851 tx15909 Plan **1**
🛁 107 sB🛁 fr4070 dB🛁 fr6200

★★★★★**Astir Palace** Athens Centre ☎3643112 tx222380 Plan **1A**
🛁 86 Lift ☾ sB🛁 14750
dB🛁 16875—19490 Mf1700
Credit cards [1] [2] [3] [5]

★★★★★***Athénée Palace*** 1 Kolokotroni ☎3230791 tx6188 Plan **2**
🛁 150 🚗 **P** Lift ☾
Credit cards [2] [5]

★★★★★***Athens Hilton*** 46 Vassilissis Sofias Av ☎7220201 tx215808 Plan **2A**
🛁 🚿 473 🚗 **P**150 Lift ☾ ≈ sea mountains
Credit cards [1] [2] [4] [5]

★★★★★**Grande Bretagne** Platia Syntagmatos ☎3230251 tx219615 Plan **3**
🛁 400 Lift ☾ sB🛁 13830—20703
dB🛁 18129—26439 Mfr1800
Credit cards [1] [2] [3] [4] [5]

★★★★★***King George*** Constitution Sq ☎3230651 tx215296 Plan **4**
🛁 140 🚗 **P** Lift ☾
Credit cards [1] [2] [3] [4] [5]

★★★★★**St George Lycabettus** 2 Kleomenous ☎7290711 tx214253 Not on plan
🛁 150 🚗 **P** Lift ☾ sB🛁 5995—7230
dB🛁 9130—10425 M1325 ≈
Credit cards [1] [2] [3] [4] [5]

★★★★**Amalia** 10 Amalias Av ☎3237301 tx215161 Plan **6**
🛁 98 Lift ☾ sB🛁 6800 dB🛁 8800 M1200
Credit cards [1] [2] [3] [4] [5]

★★★★**Esperia Palace** 22 Stadiou ☎3238000 tx0215773 Plan **8**
🛁 185 Lift ☾ sB🛁 4560 dB🛁 6000 M1100
Credit cards [1] [2] [3] [4] [5]

★★★★**Holiday Inn** Michalakopoulou 50, Ilissia 612 ☎7248322 tx218870 Plan **9**
🛁 188 🚗 Lift ☾ sB🛁 9640—12610
dB🛁 15290—23340 Mf1300 ≈
Credit cards [1] [2] [3] [4] [5]

★★★★***King Minos*** 1 Pireos ☎5231111 tx215339 Plan **10**
🛁 175 🚗 **P** Lift ☾
Credit cards [2] [3] [5]

★★★★**Olympic Palace** 16 Philellinon ☎3237611 tx215178 Plan **11**
🛁 90 **P** Lift sB🛁 fr5500 dB🛁 fr6900 M900

★★★**Acadimos** 58 Acadimias St ☎3629221 Plan **12**
🛁 🚿 130 Lift sB🛁 🚿 1851—2104
dB🛁 🚿 2796—3160 M700 mountains

★★★***Adrian*** 74 Adrianou Pl (n.rest) ☎3250454 Plan **13**
15 Mar—5 Nov
🛁 22 Lift

★★★**Asty** 2 Pireos ☎5230424 Plan **15**
rm 128(🛁 🚿 120) Lift ☾ sB1700—2000
sB🛁 🚿 2200—2400 dB🛁 🚿 3200—3400
t%
Credit cards [1] [2] [5]

★★★***El Greco*** 65 Athinas ☎3244553 tx219682 Plan **18**
🛁 🚿 92

★★★**Omonia** 4 Platia Omonias ☎5237210 Plan **20**
🛁 🚿 275 Lift sB🛁 🚿 1398—1796
dB🛁 🚿 1885—2397 M700

★★★**Stadion** 38 Vassileos Konstantinou ☎7226054 tx215838 Plan **21**

rm70(🛁🚿56) Lift ☾ sB1433—1935
sB🛁🚿1998—2710 dB2230—2980
dB🛁🚿2548—3769 M900 mountains
Credit cards [2] [5]

★★★**Stanley** 1—5 Odysseos St
☎5241611 tx216550 Plan **22**

rm396 (🛁🚿395) 🏠 **P** Lift ☾ sB🛁🚿fr4532
dB🛁🚿fr6108 M1250 ≈

★★***Diomia*** 5 Diomias St, Constitution Sq
☎3238034 tx214265 Plan **23**

🛁🚿71 Lift ☾
Credit cards [1] [2] [3] [4] [5]

★★**Imperial** 46 Mitropoleos St (n.rest)
☎3227617 Plan **24**

rm21 (🚿18) A5rm **P** Lift sB1400—2200
sB🚿1700—2700 dB2200—3500
dB🚿2300—3780

★★**Kronos** 18 Aghiou Dimitriou (n.rest)
☎3211601 Plan **25**

rm56 (🛁🚿38) Lift

J E Condellis Orfeos 154, Argyroymois
☎3425031 For

G Maglaras Velvendous 127, Kipseli
☎8624891 Toy

🚗 ***Tzen*** 101 Syngrou Av ☎9221870
P Saa

At **GLIFÁDHA** (17km S)

★★★**Astir** 58 Vassileos Georgiou B, Astir Beach ☎8946461 tx215925 Plan **14**

15 Apr—Oct
🛁114 **P**200 ☾ sB🛁6400—9400
dB🛁7300—28600 Mfr1100 Q ≈ Beach sea
Credit cards [1] [2] [3] [4] [5]

★★★***Florida*** 33 L-Metaxa ☎8945254
Plan **19**

rm86 (🛁27) **P** Lift

AYIOS KONSTANDÍNOS
Central Greece (☎0235)

★★**Levendi** ☎31808 tx222391

🛁28 ☾ sB🛁1960—3330
dB🛁3220—4320 M600—750 St% Beach sea

CHALKIS See **KHALKÍS**

CORFU See **KÉRKIRA**

CRETE See **KRÍTI**

DELPHÍ
Central Greece (☎0265)

★★★**Amalia** Apollonos ☎82101
tx215161

🛁185 **P**100 Lift ☾ sB🛁5400 dB🛁7600
M1200 sea mountains
Credit cards [2] [3] [4] [5]

★★★**Delphi-Xenia** ☎82151

🛁45 **P**30 ☾ sB🛁3407 dB🛁5108 M1000
sea mountains
Credit cards [2] [5]

★★★***Europa*** ☎82353

🛁🚿46 **P** sea

Greece

★***Dionyssos*** 34 Vassileos Pavlou & Frideriks (n.rest) ☎82257

Apr—Sep
rm12 sea

DRÁMA
Macedonia (☎0521)

★★***Xenia*** 10 Ethnikis Amynis ☎23195

rm32 (🛁20) **P**

ELOUNDA See **KRÍTI (CRETE)**

EPÍDHAVROS (EPIDAURUS)
Peloponnese (☎0753)

★★**Xenia** ☎22003

rm24 (🚿12) ☾ mountains

FALERON See **PHALERON**

FIRA See **THÍRA (SANTORINI)**

FLÓRINA
Macedonia (☎0385)

★★★**King Alexander** 68 Leoforos Nikis
☎23501

🛁🚿38 **P**60 Lift sB🛁🚿1995—2145
dB🛁🚿3240—3390 Malc mountains

★★★***Tottis*** ☎22645

rm32 **P**

GLIFÁDHA See **ATHÍNAI (ATHENS)**

IDHRA (HYDRA)
Island of Hydra (☎0298)

★★**Hydroussa** (n.rest) ☎52217 tx219338

Apr—Oct
🚿36 ☾ sB🚿2530—3529 dB🚿3373—4619
sea
Credit cards [1] [2] [5]

★★***Miramare*** Mandraki ☎52300

Etr—Oct
🚿28 Beach sea
Credit card [1]

IGOUMENITSA
Epirus (☎0665)

★**Xenia** 2 Vassileos Pavlou ☎22282

Apr—Oct
🚿72 🏠 **P**36 ☾ sB🚿fr2126 dB🚿fr2946
Mfr718 Beach sea
Credit cards [1] [2] [3] [4] [5]

IOÁNNINA (JANINA)
Epirus (☎0651)

★★★**Palladion** 1 Pan Scoumbourdi & 28th Octovriou ☎25856 tx322212

🛁🚿135 Lift ☾ sB🛁🚿1480—2540
dB🛁🚿2010—3590 M800 lake mountains
Credit card [2]

★★***Acropole*** 3 Vassileos Georgiou A (n.rest) ☎26560

rm33 (🛁🚿20) Lift ☾ lake

★★***Xenia*** (**DPn** in summer) 33 Vassileos Georgiou B ☎25087

🛁🚿60 **P** Lift ☾ mountains lake

ITÉA
Central Greece (☎0265)

★***Xenia*** ☎32263

Apr—Oct
🚿18 **P** beach

JANINA See **IOÁNNINA**

KALABÁKA
Thessaly (☎0432)

★**Xenia** ☎22327 tx295345

Apr—Oct
🛁22 **P**11 ☾ **DPn**3477 mountains

KALÁMAI (KALAMATA)
Peloponnese (☎0721)

★★★***Rex*** 26 Aristomenous ☎22334

rm51 (🛁30) Lift
Existence unconfirmed

KAMÉNA VOÚRLA
Central Greece (☎0235)

★★★★**Astir Galini** ☎22327 tx296140

🛁131 **P**300 Lift ☾ **DPn**3400—9000
Mfr1100 Q 🖵 ≈ Beach sea mountains
Credit cards [1] [2] [3] [4] [5]

KASTORÍA
Macedonia (☎0467)

★★***Xenia du Lac*** pl Dexamenis ☎22565

🛁🚿26 🏠 **P**

KAVÁLLA
Macedonia (☎051)

★★***Galaxy*** 51 El Venizelou ☎224605
tx452207

🛁🚿150 Lift ☾ sea

★**Panorama** 32C El Venizelou ☎224205

rm51 (🛁🚿11) **P**10 Lift sB1600—1937
sB🛁🚿1937—2275 dB2356—2727
dB🛁🚿2609—3031 sea mountains

🚗 **D Hionis-G Vardavoulias** E Venizelou 77 St ☎25058 **P** AR Maz Mer

KÉRKIRA (CORFU)
(Island of Corfu) (☎0661)

CORFU

★★★★★**Corfu Palace** L-Democratias
☎39485 tx332126

Apr—Oct
🛁115 **P** Lift ☾ ≈ 🖵 sea
Credit cards [1] [3] [4] [5]

KOMENO BAY (10km N of Corfu town)

★★★★**Astir Palace** ☎91490 tx332169

Apr—Oct
🛁308 A124rm **P**500 Lift ☾
DPn4960—18020 Mfr1680 Q 🖵 ≈
Beach sea
Credit cards [1] [2] [3] [4] [5]

KHALKIS (CHALKIS)
Euboea (☎0221)

★★★**Lucy** 10 L-Voudouri ☎23831

rm92 (🛁🚿80) **P** Lift sB🛁🚿fr2610
dB🛁🚿fr3410 Beach sea

KHANIÁ See **KRÍTI (CRETE)**

ATHINAI (ATHENS)

1 ★★★★★ Acropole Palace
1A ★★★★★ Astir Palace
2 ★★★★★ Athénée Palace
2A ★★★★★ Athens Hilton
3 ★★★★★ Grande Bretagne
4 ★★★★★ King George
6 ★★★★ Amalia
8 ★★★★ Esperia Palace
9 ★★★★ Holiday Inn
10 ★★★★ King Minos
11 ★★★★ Olympic Palace
12 ★★★ Acadimos
13 ★★★ Adrian
14 ★★★ Astir (At Glifádha 17km S)
15 ★★★ Asty
18 ★★★ El Greco
19 ★★★ Florida (At Glifádha 17km S)
20 ★★★ Omonia
21 ★★★ Stadion
22 ★★★ Stanley
23 ★★ Diomia
24 ★★ Imperial
25 ★★ Kronos

KIFISIÁ
Attica (☎01)

★★★**Cecil** 7 Xenias, Kefalari ☎8013836
Apr—Oct
🛁 🚿 85 **P**100 Lift ☾ sB 🛁 🚿 3150
dB 🛁 🚿 4750—5560 M1500 mountains
Credit cards [2] [3]

KOMENO BAY See **KÉRKIRA (CORFU)**

KOZÁNI
Macedonia (☎0461)

★★***Hermionion*** 7 Platia Nikis ☎36007
rm20 (🛁 🚿 8)

KRÍTI (CRETE)

ELOUNDA (☎0841)

★★★★**Astir Palace** ☎41580 tx262215
Apr—Oct
🛁 220 A80rm **P**500 Lift ☾ **DPn**
6450—15800 Mfr1650 Beach sea mountains
Credit cards [1] [2] [3] [4] [5]

KHANIÁ (☎0821)

★★★**Kydon** Platia Agoras ☎26190
tx291146
🛁 115 **P**20 Lift ☾ sB 🛁 3200 dB 🛁 5600
sea mountains
Credit cards [1] [2] [4] [5]

★★***Xenia*** Theotokopoulou ☎24561
🛁 🚿 44 **P**

RÉTHIMNON (☎0831)

★★***Xenia*** 30 N Pasrrou ☎29111
🛁 🚿 25 **P** ☾ Beach sea

LAMÍA
Central Greece (☎0231)

★★***Apollionian*** 25 Hatzopoulou, Platia Parkou (n.rest) ☎22668
rm36 (🛁 🚿 24) **P** Lift

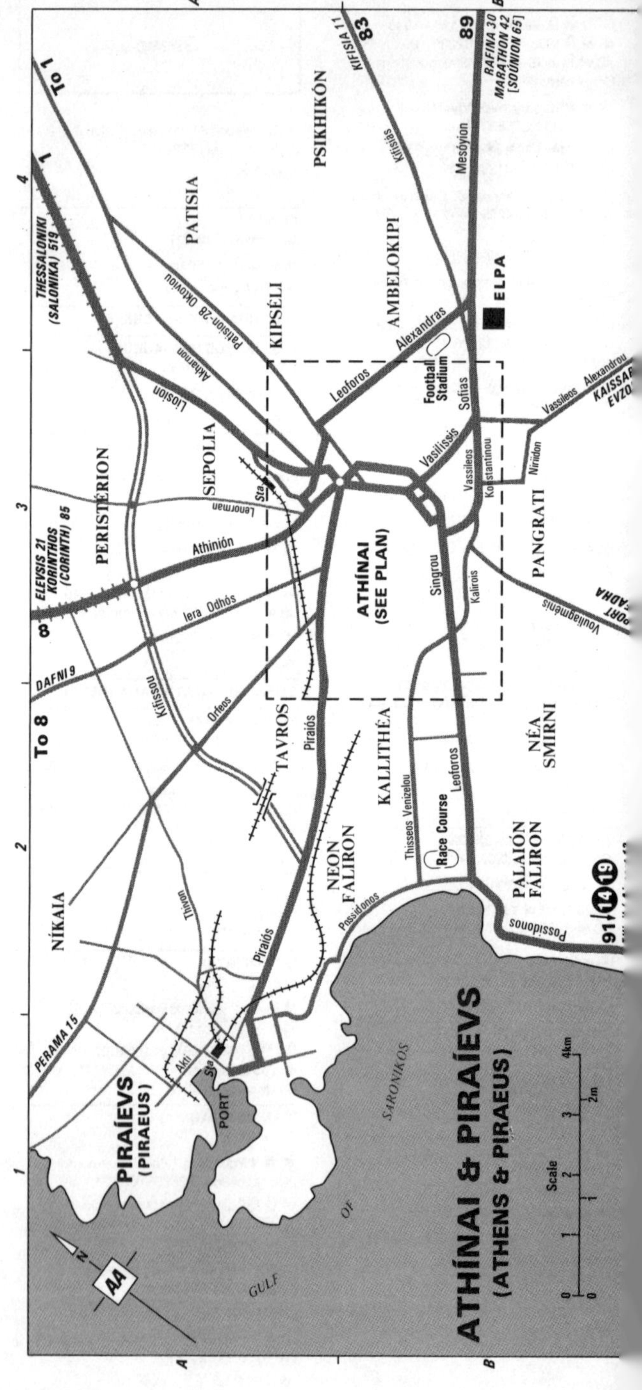

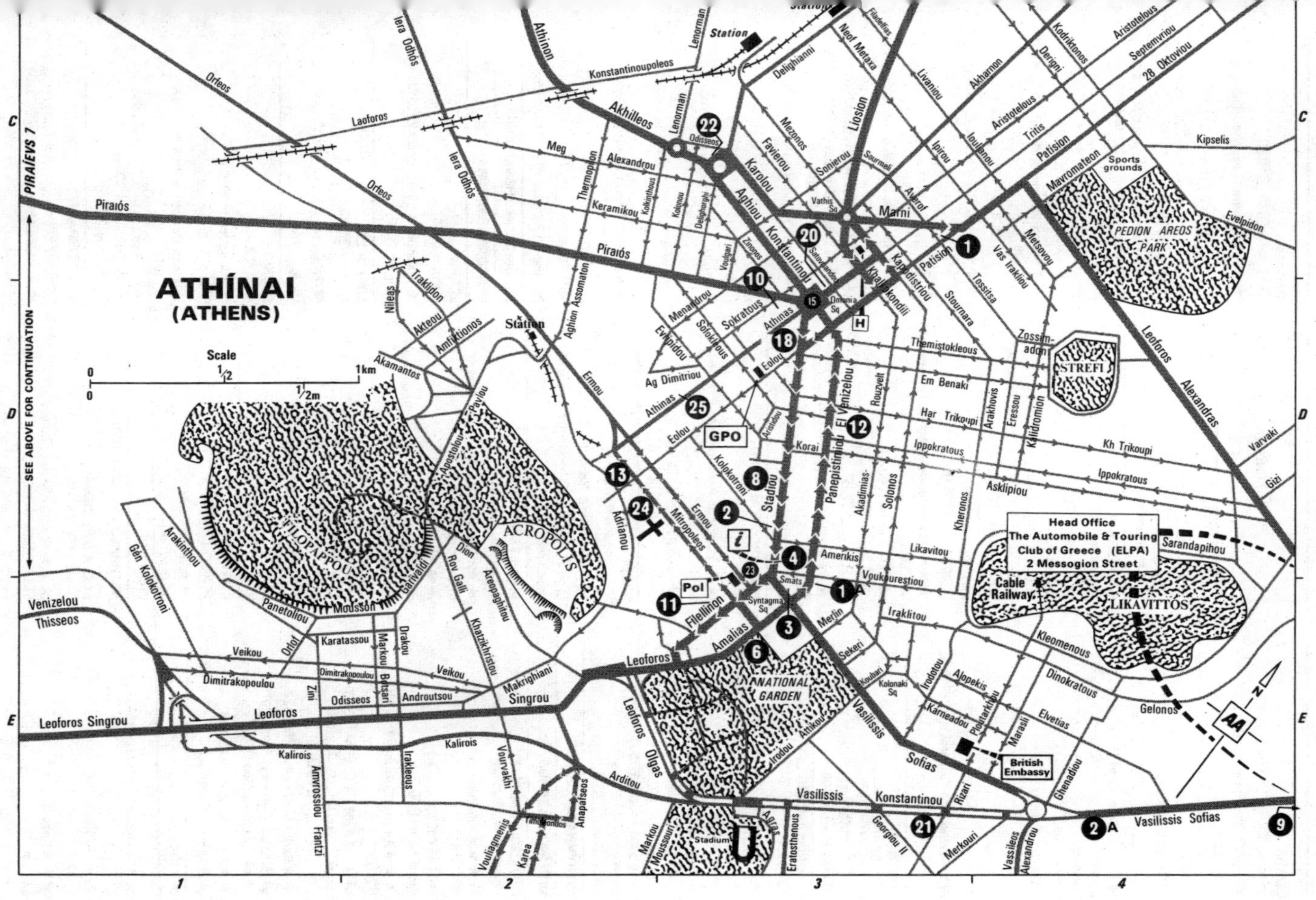

ATHÍNAI
(ATHENS)
Scale
0
1/2
1km
0
1/2m
SEE ABOVE FOR CONTINUATION
PIRAIÉVS 7
Head Office
The Automobile & Touring
Club of Greece (ELPA)
2 Messogion Street
Cable
Railway
LIKAVITTÓS
PEDION AREOS
PARK
Sports
grounds
STREFI
NATIONAL
GARDEN
ACROPOLIS
FILOPAPPOU
Stadium
British
Embassy
GPO
Pol
AA
Station
Leoforos Alexandras
Vasilissis Sofias
Vasilissis Konstantinou
Leoforos Olgas
Leoforos Singrou
Panepistimiou El Venizelou
Stadiou
Akadimias
Aghiou Konstantinou
Patision
Piraiós
Athinas
Ermou
Mitropoleos
Amalias
Filellinon
Akhilleos
Iera Odhós
Orfeos
Syntagma Sq
Omonia Sq

Greece

LÁRISA
Thessaly (☎041)

★***Xenia*** 135 Farsalon ☎239002
🚿130 ⌂ ☾

LESBOS

MITHYMNA (☎0253)

★★**Delphinia 1** ☎71315 tx297116
🛁 🚿99 ☾ (**DPn**) sB🛁 🚿2970–3709
dB🛁 🚿4790–5890 M843–935 🎾 📺
Beach sea
Credit cards [2] [5]

MITILINI (☎0251)

★★★***Xenia*** ☎22713
Apr–Oct
🛁74 **P** Lift ☾ ≈ sea mountains

⚙ **Vamvakoula** A-Gianareli 50 ☎27091
M/c **P** Toy

LOUTRÁKI
Attica (☎0741)

★★★***Karelion*** 23 G-Lekka ☎42347
🛁 🚿40 **P** ≈ Beach

MÍKONOS (ISLAND OF)
(☎0289)

★★★**Leto** ☎22207 tx293201
🛁 🚿25 **DPn**2290–4150 M850–1000 sea
Credit cards [1] [2] [3]

★★★**Theoxenia** ☎22230 tx239201
Apr–Oct
rm57 (🛁33) ☾ sB2600–3100
sB🛁3200–4300 dB3500–4100
dB🛁4200–5700 sea
Credit cards [1] [2] [3]

MITHYMNA See **LESBOS**

MITILÍNI See **LESBOS**

NÁVPLION (NAUPLIA)
Peloponnese (☎0752)

★★★★***Amphityron*** Akti Miaouli
☎27366
🛁 🚿48 **P**30 Lift ☾ ≈ sea
Credit cards [1] [4] [5]

★★★**Amaila** 93 Argous ☎24400
tx215161
🛁 🚿172 **P**200 Lift ☾ sB🛁 🚿5400
dB🛁 🚿7600 M1200 ≈ sea
Credit cards [1] [2] [3] [4] [5]

★★**Park** 1 Dervenaklon ☎27428
🛁 🚿70 Lift ☾ sB🛁 🚿1802–2075
dB🛁 🚿2410–2755 M760

★★***Xenia*** Acronafplia ☎28981
🛁 🚿58 **P** Lift Beach sea

OLYMPIA
Peloponnese (☎0624)

★★★**Amalia** ☎22190 tx215161
🛁 🚿147 **P**150 Lift ☾ sB🛁 🚿5400
dB🛁 🚿7600 M1200 ≈ mountains
Credit cards [1] [2] [3] [4] [5]

★★★***Spap*** ☎22514
🛁51 **P**
Credit cards [1] [2] [3] [4] [5]

★★***Xenia*** ☎22510
Apr–Oct
🚿36 **P** ☾ mountains

PALIOÚRION
Macedonia (☎0374)

★★**Xenia** ☎92277
Jun–Sep
🚿72 **P** ☾ sB🚿1818–3032
dB🚿2420–3980 M700–770 🎾 Beach sea
Credit cards [1] [2] [5]

PÁTRAI (PATRAS)
Peloponnese (☎061)

★★★**Méditérranée** 18 Aghiou Nicolaou
☎279602
🛁100 Lift sB🛁2090–2275
dB🛁2996–3248 Mfr850 sea
Credit cards [2] [3] [5]

★★***Majestic*** 67 Aghiou Andreou
☎272002
🛁73 **P** Lift Beach sea

PHALERON (FALERON)
Attica (☎01)

★★★**Coral** 35 Possidonos Av ☎9816441
tx210879
🛁90 ⌂ **P**10 Lift ☾ ≈ sea
Credit cards [1] [2] [3] [4] [5]

PÍLOS
Peloponnese (☎0723)

★★**Miramare** 3 Tsamadou ☎22226
🚿20 ⌂ **P**20 ☾ sB🚿2200 dB🚿3400 M600
Beach sea

PIRAIÉVS (PIRAEUS)
Attica (☎01)

★★***Arion*** 109 Vassileos Pavlou, Kastella
(n.rest) ☎4121425
rm36 (🛁2) **P** Lift sea

★★***Phedias*** 189 Kountourioti, Passalimani
(n.rest) ☎4170552
rm26 ⌂ **P** Lift ☾

PLATAMÓN
Macedonia (☎0352)

★***Olympos*** 18 Frouriou ☎41380
Jul–Sep
rm23 **P** Beach sea

PORTARIA
Thessaly (☎0421)

★★***Xenia*** ☎25922
🛁 🚿76 Lift mountains
Credit cards [1] [5]

RÉTHIMNON See **KRÍTI (CRETE)**

RÓDHOS (RHODES)
(Island of Rhodes) (☎0241)

★★★★★**Grand Astir Palace** Akti
Miaouli ☎26284 tx292121
🛁376 **P**500 Lift ☾ (**DPn**) sB🛁5100–8950
dB🛁8000–14920 Mfr1500 🎾 ≈ 📺
Beach sea
Credit cards [1] [2] [3] [4] [5]

★★★★**Ibiscus** 17 Nissyrou ☎24421
tx222131
Apr–Oct
🛁207 **P** Lift ☾ **DPn**3000–7200 sea
Credit cards [1] [4]

★★★**Elafos & Elafina** (Astir) Mount
Profitis Elias ☎(0246) 21221 tx292121
Apr–Oct
🛁68 **P**100 Lift sea mountains
Credit cards [1] [2] [3] [4] [5]

★★★**Mediterranean** 35–37 Ko ☎24661
tx292108
🛁 🚿154 Lift ☾ **DPn**3815–7880 sea

★★★***Park*** 12 Riga Ferreou ☎24611
tx292137
Apr–Oct
🛁 🚿90 **P** Lift ☾ ≈

★★★**Spartalis** 2 N-Plastira (n.rest)
☎24371
🛁 🚿79 Lift sB🛁 🚿2544–3932
dB🛁 🚿3883–5816 sea
Credit cards [1] [2] [5]

★★***Arion*** 17 Ethnarhou Makariou (n.rest)
☎20006
May–Oct
🚿85 ☾ sea

★★***Soleil*** 2 Democratias ☎24190
July–20 Sep
rm90 (🛁41) Lift
Credit card [2]

★***Achillion*** 14 Platia Vassileos Pavlou
(n.rest) ☎24604
Mar–Oct
🛁 🚿50 Lift

Zuvalas 10 Afstralias ☎23281 M/c Ope

SALONICA See **THESSALONÍKI**

SANTORINI See **THÍRA**

SÉRRAI
Macedonia (☎0321)

★★***Xenia*** 1 Aghias Sophias ☎22931
rm32 **P**

SOFÁDHES
Thessaly (☎0443)

⚙ ***G Popotas*** 7 St-George's ☎22341
M/c **P**

SOÚNION
Attica (☎0292)

★★***Aegalon*** ☎39200
🚿44 **P** Lift Beach sea

★**Mount Belvedere Park** ☎39102
tx223914
🛁94 sB🛁2861–3387 dB🛁3666–4329
M740–840 t9% 🎾 ≈ sea
Credit cards [2] [3] [4] [5]

SPÁRTI (SPARTA)
Peloponnese (☎0731)

★★★**Lida** Atreidon-Ananiou ☎23601
15 Mar–Oct
🛁 🚿40 **P** Lift mountains

★★★***Xenia*** Lofos Dioskouron ☎26524
🛁🚿33 **P**

★★***Dioskuri*** 95 Lykourgou-Atreidon
☎28484
🛁34 Lift mountains

SPÉTSAI
(Island of Spétsai) (☎0298)

★★★**Kastell** ☎72311 tx214531
15 Mar—15 Dec
🛁🚿90 **P** ☾ sB🛁3565—4267
dB🛁🚿5667—7306 M1100 🎾 Beach 📺 ⛱
sea
Credit cards [2] [5]

THÁSOS
(Island of Thásos) (☎0593)

★★**Xenia** ☎22105
Apr—Oct
rm27 (🛁🚿19) **P**

THEBES See **THÍVAI**

THESSALONÍKI (SALONICA)
Macedonia (☎031)

★★★★**Makedonia Palace** L-Megalou Alexandrou ☎837520 tx412162
🛁287 **P** Lift ☾ sB🛁6000—8400
dB🛁7560—10560 Mfr1500 t% sea
Credit cards [1] [2] [3] [5]

★★★**Capsis** 18 Monastiriou ☎521321 tx412206
🛁428 **P** Lift ☾ sB🛁2675—7140
dB🛁3926—10730 ⛱
Credit cards [1] [2] [3] [4] [5]

★★★**City** 11 Komninon ☎269421 tx412208
rm105 (🛁🚿101) 🚗 Lift
sB🛁🚿3150—3750 dB🛁🚿4700—6100
M1200
Credit cards [2] [5]

★★★***Olympic*** 25 Egnatia ☎522131
rm52 (🛁39) 🚗 **P** Lift ☾

★★★***Rotonda*** 97 Monastiriou ☎517121 tx412322
🛁🚿79 🚗 **P** Lift ☾ mountains

★★★***Victoria*** 13 Langada ☎522421 tx412145
🛁🚿68 **P** Lift ☾
Credit card [2]

G Anastassiades 2—4 Vassileos Georgiou ☎515209 For

🚗 **ETEA** 142 Grammou-Bitsi, Phoenix ☎417421 **P** Aud VW

Ioannidis 136-138 Vassilisis Olgas ☎844412 **P** Vau

🚗 ***Saracakis*** 5 Kilom Monastriou Str ☎764802 **P** Hon Vol

Sinis 18 Grammou Vitsi ☎417127
Ope

Tasta 7th KM Thessveria, Diavata ☎763623
Mer

THIRA (SANTORINI)
(Island of Thira) (☎0286)

FIRA

★★***Atlantis*** ☎22232 tx293113
Apr—Oct
🛁🚿25 ☾ sea mountains

THÍVAI (THEBES)
Attica (☎0262)

★★***Dionyssion Melathron*** 71 Metaxa & Kadmou ☎27855
rm34 (🛁🚿4) **P**

TOLÓN
Peloponnese (☎0752)

★★**Minoa** 56 Atkis ☎59207 tx098157
15 Mar—Oct
🛁🚿44 A18rm Lift sB🛁🚿2200—2585
dB🛁🚿2955—3355 M700 📺 Beach sea
Credit cards [1] [2] [3] [4]

★***Solon*** ☎59204
15 Mar—Oct
🛁🚿28 **P** sea mountains

TRÍPOLIS
Peloponnese (☎071)

★★★***Menalon*** Platia Areos ☎222450
🛁🚿40 **P** Lift

TSANGARÁDHA
Thessaly (☎0423)

★★***Xenia*** ☎49205
rm46 (🛁🚿42) **P**

VITÍNA
Peloponnese (☎0795)

★★***Xenia*** ☎21218
Apr—Sep
🛁🚿20 **P** ☾ mountains

VÓLOS
Thessaly (☎0421)

★★★***Xenia*** 1 N Plastira, Aghios Konstantinos ☎24825
🛁🚿48 Lift Beach

★★***Aegil*** 17A Argonafton (n.rest) ☎25691
rm40 (🛁14) **P** sea

★★***Pallas*** 44 Lassonos & Argonafton (n.rest) ☎23510
rm50 (🛁🚿12) **P** Lift sea

VOÚLA
Attica (☎01)

★★★***Atlantis*** 6 Aphroditis ☎8958443
🛁🚿15 P

★***Miramare*** 4 Vassileos Pavlou (n.rest) ☎8958446
rm20 **P**

VOULIAGMENI BEACH
Attica (☎01)

★★★★★**Astir Palace Aphrodite** ☎8960211 tx22304
Apr—Oct
🛁🚿167 **P**200 Lift ☾ **(DPn)**
sB🛁🚿11000—13600
dB🛁🚿16500—19500 t% 🎾 ⛱ Beach
sea
Credit cards [1] [2] [3] [4] [5]

★★★★★**Astir Palace Arion** ☎8960211 tx215013
🛁154 A77rm **P**200 Lift ☾ **(DPn)**
sB🛁8300—14500 dB🛁13200—21000
Mfr2300 🎾 ⛱ 📺 Beach sea
Credit cards [1] [2] [3] [5]

★★★★★**Astir Palace Nafsika** ☎8960211 tx210712
Apr—Oct
🛁🚿165 **P** Lift ☾ **(DPn)**
sB🛁🚿13500—16000
dB🛁🚿17700—20500 M2500 🎾 ⛱ 📺
Beach sea
Credit cards [1] [2] [3] [4] [5]

XÁNTHI
Thrace (☎0541)

★★***Xenia*** 9 Vassilissis Sophias ☎24135
🚿24 **P**

ZÁKINTHOS
(Island of Zákinthos) (☎0695)

★★***Xenia*** 66 D-Roma ☎22232
🚿39 **P** Lift Beach

Ireland

International distinguishing sign

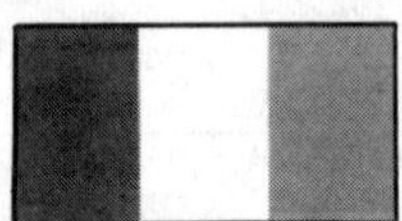

Area *27,136 sq miles*
Population *3,443,405*
Local time *GMT (Summer GMT + 1)*

National flag
Vertical tricolour of green, white and orange

How to get there

Car-carrying services operate from Britain to both the Republic and the Northern counties. The services to the Republic are Fishguard to Rosslare; Holyhead to Dun Laoghaire; Holyhead to Dublin; Liverpool to Dublin. To the north the services are from Cairnryan to Larne; Stranraer to Larne; Liverpool to Belfast. There are also services to and from France: Le Harvre and Cherbourg to Rosslare and Roscoff and Le Havre to Cork.

Motoring regulations and general information

Politically, Ireland is divided into two, the Republic which is a sovereign independent state and Northern Ireland which forms part of the United Kingdom. Motoring conditions and regulations in the North are almost the same as in Great Britain and therefore the *Country information section* will apply only to the Republic except where some notes concerning the North are considered necessary.

This information should be read in conjunction with the general content of the European ABC (pages 4-26) with special reference to *Rule of the Road* (page 22). **Note** as certain regulations and requirements are common to many countries they are covered by one entry in the ABC and the following headings represent some of the subjects dealt with in this way:

Crash or safety helmets
Customs regulations for European countries
Drinking and driving
Fire extinguisher
First-aid kit
International distinguishing sign
Medical treatment
Mirrors
Overtaking
Police fines
Radio telephones/Radio transmitters
Seat belts
Tyres
Visitors' registration

Accidents

Fire, police, ambulance ☏ 999.
A driver who is involved in an accident must stop immediately and exchange particulars with the other party. If this is not possible the occurrence must be reported to a member of the Garda Siochana or at the nearest Garda station. See also *Accidents* page 5.

Accommodation

There is excellent accommodation of all types available from first-class luxury hotels to more modest but nevertheless comfortable hotels. Guesthouse, town and country homes accommodation is widely available and fuller information can be obtained from the AA or from the Irish Tourist Board who can also supply details of self-catering accommodation. In the gazetteer for Ireland hotels are by star classification as in Great Britain. The AA's full-time highly qualified team of inspectors regularly visit all listed establishments in Ireland.

Breakdown

If your car breaks down, try to move it to the side of the road so that it obstructs the traffic flow as little as possible. The AA's Breakdown Service is available to members, on terms similar to those in Britain. Patrols operate throughout the country and their services are complemented by garages. See also *Breakdown* page 6 and *Warning triangle* page 254.

British Embassy/Consulate

(See also page 6)
The British Embassy together with its consular section is located at 33 Merrion Road *Dublin 4* ☏ (01)695211.

Currency including banking hours

(See also page 9)
The unit of currency is the Irish Pound or Punt (*IR£*) divided into 100 *Pence*. At the time of going to press £ = *IR£*1.10. There is no restriction on the amount of foreign and Irish currency or travellers cheques which may be imported, but large amounts which are to be re-exported should be declared on entry. Visitors and residents leaving the Irish Republic may only export up to *IR£*100 in Irish currency and up to *IR£*500 in foreign currency, together with the imported amount declared on entry.

Banks are open Monday to Friday between 10.00—12.30hrs and 13.30—15.00hrs. Dublin banks remain open on Thursday until 17.00hrs; in other parts of the country most banks have one late opening evening but this varies from town to town.

Dimensions and weight restrictions

Private **cars** and towed **trailers** or **caravans** are restricted to the following dimensions — height: no restriction; width: 2.50 metres; length: 12 metres. The maximum permitted overall length of vehicle/trailer or caravan combination is 18 metres.

Trailers without brakes may weigh up to 762kg or may have a total weight of up to 50% of the towing vehicle.

Driving licence

(See also page 11)
A valid British licence is acceptable in the Republic of Ireland. The minimum age at which a visitor may drive a temporarily imported car or motorcycle (exceeding 150 cc) is 17 years.

Emergency messages to tourists

(See also page 11)
Emergency messages to tourists are broadcast on Irish radio (RTE). These messages are transmitted in English on 529 metres medium wave at 08.00—09.00, 13.30 and 18.30hrs.

Horn, use of

On roads where a permanent speed limit is in force the use of a horn is prohibited between 23.30—07.00hrs.

Insurance

(See also page 13)
Short-term third-party insurance cover cannot be arranged at the frontier or point of entry.

Lights

(See also page 14)
As the rule of the road in the Republic is drive on the left, the general advice regarding adjustment of headlights for driving on the right should be ignored.

Motoring club

The Automobile Association has its regional headquarters in the Republic of Ireland at 23 Suffolk Street *Dublin* ☎ (01)779481 and an AA centre at 9 Bridge Street *Cork* ☎ (021)505155. In Northern Ireland there is an AA centre at 108—110 Great Victoria Street *Belfast* ☎ (0232)44538. The offices are open Monday to Friday 09.00—17.00hrs and 09.00—12.30hrs on Saturday (09.30—13.00hrs in Belfast). The AA centre in Cork closes for lunch between 13.00—14.00hrs.

Motorways

The Republic has two stretches of motorway, the 5 miles which bypass the town of Naas on the N7 and 3 miles north of Dublin on N1.

Orange badge scheme for disabled drivers

(See also page 16)
In the Republic of Ireland badge holders may park without payment of fees at parking meters and in areas where parking discs are in operation. They are not entitled to park on single or double yellow lines or in areas where they are likely to cause an obstruction.

Parking

(See also page 17)
Parking is prohibited both where there are yellow lines on the roadway and within the boundary of a bus stop as defined by roadway markings. The offence of dangerous parking carries heavy penalties, particularly if committed in the hours of darkness.

Parking meters are in use in the central zones of Dublin and operate Monday to Friday 08.00—18.30hrs. The parking disc system is used in central Cork and Limerick and is zoned to limit parking from 1 to 3 hours.

Passengers

(See also page 18)
Children under 12 are not permitted to travel in a vehicle as front-seat passengers unless they are using special seats or safety belts suitable for children.

For key to country identification-see page 51

Petrol
(See also page 18)
Credit cards Petrol stations generally accept recognised credit cards.
Duty-free petrol The petrol in a vehicle tank may be imported free of customs duty and tax. Up to 10 litres in a can may also be imported duty and tax free if crossing into the Republic from Northern Ireland.
Petrol (leaded) Regular (90 octane) and Super (99 octane) grades.
Petrol (unleaded) is not sold in the Republic of Ireland.

Postal information
Mail Postcards 24*p*; letters up to 20gm 28*p*.
Post offices There are some 250 main and sub post offices in the Republic, opening hours are from 09.00—17.30hrs Monday to Friday.

Postcheques
(See also page 20)
Postcheques may be cashed at sub post offices displaying a Postcheque sticker and all main post offices for any amount up to a maximum of *IR*£75 per cheque. Counter positions are identified by the words *Money orders*. See *Postal information* for post office opening hours.

Priority
At uncontrolled road junctions where both roads are principal roads, or alternatively, where neither road is a principal road, drivers must give way to vehicles approaching from the right. Principal roads are indicated by authorised signs at uncontrolled road junctions.

Public holidays
Official public holidays in the Republic of Ireland for 1987 are given below. See also *Public holidays* page 21.
January 1 (New Year's Day)
March 17 (St Patrick's Day)
April 17† (Good Friday)
April 20 (Easter Monday)
June 8 (Whit Monday)
August 3 (Bank Holiday)
October 26 (Public Holiday)
December 25 (Christmas Day)
December 26* (St Stephens day)

*Saturday
†Not official but banks, government offices and most businesses close.

Roads
The road numbering system in the Republic of Ireland has been changed and new direction signs are gradually being brought into use. Roads are divided into three main categories. These are National Primary, National Secondary and Regional. The National Primary roads have the prefix N and a number between 1 and 25. National Secondary roads also have the prefix N but a number above 50. Regional roads have the prefix R.

Shopping hours
Generally shops are open 09.00—17.30hrs Monday-Saturday with some supermarkets open until 21.00hrs on Thursday or Friday. Most shops have one early closing day each week and this is usually 13.00hrs on Wednesday or Saturday.

Speed limits
(See also page 22)
In built-up areas 48kph (30mph); outside built-up areas between 64/88kph (40/55mph) as indicated by signs. Vehicle/trailer combinations 56kph (35mph).

Tourist information
(See also page 24)
The Irish Tourist Board has an office at 150 New Bond Street, London W1Y 0AQ ☏ 01-493 3201 and regional offices at 6-8 Temple Row, Birmingham B2 5HG ☏ 021-236 9724; 28 Cross Street, Manchester M2 3NH ☏ 061-832 5981 and 19 Dixon Street, Glasgow G1 4AJ ☏ 041-221 2311. In the Republic the Irish Tourist Board offices are located at Baggot Street Bridge, Dublin ☏ (01)765871; tourist information 747733.

The Northern Ireland Tourist Board has an office at 11 Berkeley Street, London W1 ☏ 01-493 0601 and regional offices at PO Box 26, Sutton Coldfield, West Midlands ☏ 021-353 7604 and Olympia House, 142 Queen Streeet, Glasgow G1 3BU ☏ 041-221 5115. In Northern Ireland the Northern Ireland Tourist Board offices are located at High Street, Belfast BT1 2DS ☏ 231221.

Traffic lights
(See also page 24)
Traffic lights are used in most large towns and follow the red, green, amber sequence.

Using the telephone
(See also page 24)
Insert coin **after** lifting the reciever, dialling tone same as the UK. When making calls within the

Republic precede number with relevant area code as necessary (shown in parentheses against town entry in gazetteer where applicable). Use 5*p* and 10*p* coins for local calls and 5*p*, 10*p* and 50*p* coins for national and international calls.
International callbox identification Payphone or Telefón.
Telephone rates A direct call to the UK from a payphone between 08.00—18.00hrs costs 60*p* per minute.
What to dial for the UK 03*
*Calls may be dialled direct to all exchanges in Britain except from old-style coin-box telephones.

Warning triangle

The use of a warning triangle is only compulsory in respect of vehicles with an unladen weight of 1524kg (1½ tons). See also *Warning triangles/Hazards warning lights* page 25.

Prices are in Irish pounds or punts, except for Northern Ireland when prices are in pound sterling. The counties of Northern Ireland are: Co. Antrim, Co. Armagh, Co. Down, Co. Fermanagh, Co. Londonderry and Co. Tyrone.

According to our information garages with no specific service will handle any make of car.

Abbreviations:
Av Avenue
Pl Place
Rd Road
Sq Square
St Street
m mile

ABBEYFEALE
Co Limerick (☎068)

★Leen's ☎31121
Closed 24—31 Dec
rm14 (🚿3)
Credit cards [1] [3]

🚗 **O'Leary's** Convent Rd ☎31137

ACHILL ISLAND
Co Mayo (☎098)

★McDowell's Slievemore Rd ☎43148
18 Mar—Oct
rm10 (🚿4) **P**20 sB10—12 sB🚿12—14 dB18—20 dB🚿21—23 M10—11

🚗 **Henry's** Achill Sound ☎45246

🚗 **E T Sweeney & Son** Achill Sound ☎45243

ADARE
Co Limerick (☎061)

★★★Dunraven Arms ☎86209 tx70202
🛁🚿24 **P**22 ☾ sB🛁🚿25—29 dB🛁🚿50—60 M8—18 &alc
Credit cards [1] [2] [3] [5]

AHERLOW
Co Tipperary (☎062)

★★★Glen ☎56146
rm24 (🛁🚿21) **P**150
Credit cards [1] [2] [3]

★★Aherlow House ☎56153
rm10 (🛁🚿8) **P**20 sB🛁🚿17—20 dB🛁🚿34—40 M12alc
Credit cards [1] [2] [3] [5]

ANTRIM
Co Antrim (☎08494)

🚗 **Hugh Tipping Mtrs** 23 Crosskennnan Rd ☎62225

ARDEE
Co Louth (☎041)

McCabes 1 Castle St ☎53291 Sko Toy

ARDMORE
Co Waterford (☎024)

★Cliff House ☎94106
24 May—24 Sep
rm16 (🛁🚿7) **P**20 M&alc
Credit cards [2] [3] [5]

ARKLOW
Co Wicklow (☎0402)

★★Arklow Bay ☎32309
rm28 (🛁🚿19) 🏠 **P**100 ☾ sB16—20 sB🛁🚿19—23 dB26—34 dB🛁🚿32—40 M6—12&alc
Credit cards [1] [2] [3] [5]

ARMAGH
Co Armagh (☎0861)

🚗 **Mallview S/Sta** (JJ Andrews) Mall View ☎523415

ASHBOURNE
Co Meath (☎01)

🚗 **Rath Service Station** ☎350218

ASHFORD
Co Wicklow (☎0404)

★★Cullenmore ☎4108
Closed 25—26 Dec
rm13 (🛁10) **P**200
Credit cards [1] [2] [3] [5]

ATHLONE
Co Westmeath (☎0902)

★★★Prince of Wales ☎72626 tx53068
Closed 25—26 Dec
🛁🚿42 **P**40 ☾
Credit cards [1] [2] [3] [4] [5]

★★Royal Hoey ☎72924
Closed Xmas
rm47 (🛁🚿30) **P**50 Lift ☾ sB18 sB🛁🚿22 dB38 dB🛁🚿42 M6—10alc
Credit cards [1] [3] [5]

Kenna Motors Dublin Rd ☎72726 AR

🚗 **Kenny & O'Brien** Cornafulla ☎37103

Kilmartin Dublin Rd ☎75426 For

AUGHRIM
Co Wicklow (☎0402)

🚗 **Aughrim Car Sales** ☎6257

BAILIEBOROUGH
Co Cavan (☎042)

★★Bailie ☎65334
Closed 25 Dec
rm21 (🛁🚿5) **P**10

BALLINA
Co Mayo (☎096)

★★★Downhill ☎21033 tx33796
Closed 16—27 Dec
🛁🚿54 **P**200 ☾ sB🛁🚿24—37 dB🛁🚿48—69 M9—18 📺
Credit cards [1] [2] [3] [5]

🚗 **Finmax of Ballina** Dublin Rd ☎21288 For

🚗 **Judges Auto Svc** Sligo Rd ☎21864

BALLINASCARTY
Co Cork (☎023)

★★★Ardnavaha House ☎49135 tx75702
16 Mar—14 Oct
🛁36 **P**30 ☾ sB🛁25—29 dB🛁38—46 M9—22&alc 🎾 ♨ U
Credit cards [1] [2] [3] [4] [5]

BALLINASLOE
Co Galway (☎0905)

★★★Hayden's Dunloe St ☎42347
Closed 24—27 Dec
rm55 (🛁🚿41) **P** Lift ☾ sB14—15 sB🛁🚿20—21 dB27—30 dB🛁🚿39—42 M7—14&alc
Credit cards [1] [2] [3] [5]

🚗 **Louis Bannerton** Galway Rd ☎42420

Fred Kilmartin Athlone Rd ☎42204 For

BALLINROBE
Co Mayo

★Lakelands ☎20 tx53703
Closed 23—30Dec
rm18 (🛁5) **P**7 sB16—17 sB🛁20—21 dB32—34 dB🛁36—38 M5—12
Credit cards [2] [3] [5]

BALLINSPITTAL
Co Cork (☎021)

🚗 **O'Regans** ☎73120

Ireland

BALLYBUNION
Co Kerry (☎068)

★★**Marine** ☎27139
Etr—Oct
rm17 (🛁🚿6) **P**50 ☾ sB14—16
sB🛁🚿17—19 dB27—31 dB🛁🚿27—31
M15
Credit cards [1] [3]

BALLYCANEW
Co Wexford (☎055)

🚗 **Kinsellas** ☎27108

BALLYCOTTON
Co Cork (☎021)

★★**Bay View** ☎646746
rm20 (🛁5) ⛺ **P**40 sB17 dB34 dB🛁37
M6—14
Credit cards [2] [3]

BALLYGALLY
Co Antrim (☎057483)

★★★**Ballygally Castle** 274 Coast Rd
☎212
🛁🚿29 **P**40 sB🛁🚿25 dB🛁🚿40 M7—9
🔑
Credit cards [1] [2] [3] [5]

BALLYHAUNIS
Co Mayo (☎0907)

★**Central** ☎30030
Closed Xmas week & Good Fri
rm15 **P**10 sB12—13 dB20—23 M6—7
Credit cards [1] [3]

BALLYLICKEY
Co Cork (☎027)

★★**Sea View** ☎50462
Apr—Oct
rm12 (🛁🚿10) A2rm ⛺ **P**40
sB🛁🚿18—20 dB🛁🚿40 M8&alc

BALLYLIFFEN
Co Donegal

★★**Strand** ☎Clonmany 7
Closed Good Fri & 24—26 Dec
🛁🚿10 **P**70 sB🛁🚿16—20
dB🛁🚿24—28 M6—15
Credit cards [1] [3]

BALLYMAHON
Co Longford (☎0902)

🚗 **Finnegan's** ☎32229

BALLYMENA
Co Antrim (☎0266)

★★★**Adair Arms** Ballymoney Rd ☎3674
🛁🚿40 **P**60 ☾
Credit cards [1] [2] [3] [5]

R G McBurney & Sons 1—21 Railway St
☎46014 Aud VW

BALLYMONEY
Co Antrim (☎02656)

🚗 **Curragh S/Sta** (J A W Murphy) 93
Forcess Rd ☎62071

GMG 4 Portrush Rd ☎64761 Col

🚗 **Lexie Kerr** 16a Victoria Rd ☎62343

Weybridge Mtr Cycles 95 Parkview
☎62984 M/c

BALLYNAHINCH
Co Down (☎0238)

R Gibb & Sons 41 Main St ☎562519 For

BALLYNAHINCH
Co Galway (☎0849)

★★★**Ballynahinch Castle** ☎21269
tx28809
4 Apr—Oct
🛁🚿20 **P** sB🛁🚿40—45 dB🛁🚿68—78
M11—18 🔑
Credit cards [1] [2] [3] [5]

BALLYSHANNON
Co Donegal (☎072)

★★**Dorrian's Imperial** ☎51147
Closed 25 Dec
🛁🚿26 **P**12 ☾ sB🛁🚿19—23
dB🛁🚿31—36 M5—13&alc

🚗 **Abbey** Donegal Rd ☎51246

BALLYVAUGHAN
Co Clare (☎065)

★★**Gregan's Castle** ☎77005 tx70130
Etr—Oct
rm14 (🛁11) A2rm **P**30 sB30—39
sB🛁35—44 dB41—51 dB🛁52—63
M8—21
Credit card [3]

★★**Hyland's** ☎77037
Etr—Sep
rm12 (🛁🚿9) **P**50 sB17—19
sB🛁🚿20—21 dB30—37 dB🛁🚿36—42
M14&alc
Credit cards [1] [3] [5]

BALTIMORE
Co Cork (☎028)

★★**Baltimore House** ☎20164
Etr—Sep
rm15 (🛁3) **P**20 sB15—17 sB🛁17—19
dB30—34 dB🛁34—38 M8&alc

BANGOR
Co Down (☎0247)

★★**Ballyholme** 256—262 Seacliff Rd
☎472807
rm36 (🚿7) ⛺ **P**12 sB15—16 sB🚿18—19
dB27—30 dB🚿36—38 M5—9
Credit cards [1] [2] [3]

★★**Winston** 19—23 Queens Pde
☎454575
rm46 (🛁28) ⛺ **P**6 ☾ sB11—12 sB🛁20
dB30 dB🛁30 M4—8
Credit cards [1] [2] [3] [5]

Ballyrobert Cars 402 Belfast Rd ☎852262
Ope Vau

🚗 **Bangor Auto Recovery** 32—34 Belfast
Rd ☎457428

🚗 **Car & Commercial Repair Svcs**
521 Belfast Road ☎450200

🚗 **P W Gethin & Sons** 16 Belfast Rd
☎465881 Sko

S Mellon & Sons 40 Bingham St ☎457525
Maz

BANGOR-ERRIS
Co Mayo

🚗 **Erris Mtrs** ☎3

BANTRY
Co Cork (☎027)

★★★**Westlodge** ☎50360 tx28477
🛁🚿104 **P**500 ☾ sB🛁🚿26—30
dB🛁🚿43—48 M5—16 🔑 📺
Credit cards [1] [2] [3] [4] [5]

🚗 **Hurley Bros** Bridge St ☎50092

🚗 **O'Learys** ☎50127

BELFAST
(☎0232)

★★★★**Forum** Great Victoria St
☎245161 tx74491
🛁200 **P**80 Lift ☾ sB🛁fr55 dB🛁fr70
M8—13alc
Credit cards [1] [2] [3] [4] [5]

★★★**Stormont** 587 Upper Newtonards
Rd ☎658621
Closed Xmas Day
🛁🚿67 **P**300 Lift ☾ sB🛁🚿38 dB🛁🚿52
M8—10&alc
Credit cards [1] [2] [3] [5]

A S Baird Boucher Rd ☎661811 Peu Tal

Charles Hurst Mtrs 10—18 Adelaide St
☎230566

Charles Hurst Mtr Cycles 201—207
Castlereagh Rd ☎732393 M/c

T H Clarke & Co 441A Beersbridge Rd
☎650328

J E Coulter 58—82 Antrim Rd ☎744744 For

🚗 **Finaghy** (W G Creighton) 87—89 Upper
Lisburn Rd ☎626711

GMG (City Cars) 182—184 Shore Rd
☎772054 Col Sko

🚗 **GMG Mtrs** (G McKeown) 2a Ardmore Av,
Finaghy Rd North ☎622063

MB Mtr Cycles 79—85 Ravenhill Rd
☎56084 M/c

Noel Orr Mtr Cycles 78—80 Castlereagh Rd
☎58622 M/c

Parkgate 86 Parkgate Av ☎655149 Peu Tal

Sydney Pentland 17—29 Ravenhill Rd
☎51422 Ope Vau

SMW Volvo (Stanley Mtr Wks) 59—75 Latas
Dr ☎703666 Vol

Ulster Boucher Rd ☎681721 Ren

G Wright Mtrs 73-77 Ravenhill Rd ☎56697

BIRR
Co Offaly (☎0509)

★★**County Arms** ☎20791
🛁🚿18 **P**100 ☾
Credit cards [1] [2] [3] [5]

🚗 **P L Dolan & Sons** Main St ☎20006

Ireland

BLACKROCK
Co Dublin (☎01)

Carroll & Kinsella Motors Rock Rd ☎888624 Toy

BLARNEY
Co Cork (☎021)

★★★***Hotel Blarney*** ☎85281 tx75262

Closed 24—27 Dec
🛁🚿74 **P**400 ☾
Credit cards 1 2 3 4

BLESSINGTON
Co Wicklow (☎045)

★★★**Downshire House** ☎65199

Closed mid Dec—mid Jan
🛁🚿18 A7rm P25 ⚷

🚗 **Hughes** ☎65156 Ren

BORRIS-IN-OSSORY
Co Laois (☎0505)

★★**Leix County** ☎41213

rm19 (🚿2) **P** ☾ sB17—20 sB🚿17—20 dB32—34 dB🚿32—34 M6—15&alc
Credit cards 1 2 3

BOYLE
Co Roscommon (☎079)

★★**Royal** ☎62016

Closed 25—26 Dec
🛁16 **P**100 sB🛁21—23 dB🛁38—39 M6—15
Credit cards 1 2 3 5

🚗 **Carty's** ☎62318

BRAY
Co Wicklow (☎01)

★★**Royal** ☎862935

rm53 (🛁🚿51) **P**200 Lift ☾ sB24—30 sB🛁🚿24—30 dB43—50 dB🛁43—50 M6—8
Credit cards 1 2 3

BUNRATTY
Co Clare (☎061)

★★★**Fitzpatrick's Shannon Shamrock** ☎61177 tx26214

Closed 25 Dec
🛁106 **P**300 ☾ sB🛁36—43 dB🛁49—61 M7—14&alc ♒ ▭
Credit cards 1 2 3 4 5

BUSHMILLS
Co Antrim (☎02657)

J C Halliday & Sons 206 Straid Rd ☎31452 Cit

CAHERDANIEL
Co Kerry (☎0667)

★★**Derrynane** ☎5136

Apr—Oct
🛁🚿62 **P** ☾ sB🛁🚿15—20 M4—12 ⚷ ♒
Credit cards 1 2 3 5

CALEDON
Co Tyrone (☎0861)

Donnelly Bros Armagh Rd ☎58235

CARLOW
Co Carlow (☎0503)

★★**Royal** ☎31621 tx24858

rm35 (🛁25) ⌂ **P**25 sB16—18 sB🛁24—28 dB26—30 dB🛁36—40 M5—12
Credit cards 1 2 3 5

🚗 **Deerpark Service Station** Dublin Rd ☎31414

🚗 **Statham Sheridan** Court Pl ☎31665 For

CARNAROSS
Co Meath (☎046)

🚗 **Clarkes** ☎41903

CARNLOUGH
Co Antrim (☎0574)

★★**Londonderry Arms** ☎85255

🛁🚿12 **P**16 sB🛁🚿fr18 dB🛁🚿fr32 M7—10
Credit cards 1 2 3 5

CARRAROE
Co Galway (☎091)

★★**Hotel Carraroe** (BW) Ostan Cheathru Rua ☎95116 tx28871

20 Apr—Sep
🛁🚿20 **P**200 ☾ ⚷ ♒

CARRICK
Co Donegal

🚗 **McLoughlins**

CARRICKFERGUS
Co Antrim (☎09603)

★★**Coast Road** 28 Scotch Quarter ☎61021

Closed Xmas Day
🛁🚿20 ☾ sBfr17 sB🛁🚿fr19 dBfr27 dB🛁🚿fr27 M5—9
Credit cards 3 5

★**Dobbins Inn** 6—8 High St ☎63905

Closed Xmas
🛁🚿13 ☾ sB🛁🚿17 dB🛁🚿32 M2—8
Credit cards 1 3

CARRICKMACROSS
Co Monaghan (☎042)

🚗 **Meegans** ☎61068

CARRICKMORE
Co Tyrone (☎066273)

🚗 **Rockview S/Sta** 351 Drumnakilly Rd ☎244

CARRICK-ON-SHANNON
Co Leitrim (☎078)

★★**Bush** ☎20014 tx40394

3 Mar—18 Oct
rm25 (🛁🚿20) **P**25 ☾ sB16—20 sB🛁🚿28—32 dB🛁🚿44—52 M8—12
Credit cards 1 2 3 5

★★**County** ☎20042 tx40395

Closed 24—27 Dec
rm17 (🛁🚿14) ☾ sB16—18 sB🛁🚿16—18 dB32—34 dB🛁🚿32—36 M6—13
Credit cards 1 2 3

🚗 **William Cox & Sons** Main St ☎20217

CASHEL
Co Galway (☎095)

★★★**Cashel House** (Relais et Châteaux) ☎21252 tx28812

12 Mar—Oct
🛁🚿32 **P**40 sB🛁🚿28—32 dB🛁🚿56—64 M12—19 ⚷
Credit cards 1 2 3 5

★★★**Zetland** ☎31011 tx28853

20 Apr—20 Oct
🛁🚿20 ⌂ **P**25 sB🛁🚿25—45 dB🛁🚿50—66 M20
Credit cards 1 2 3 5

CASHEL
Co Tipperary (☎062)

★★★**Cashel Palace** ☎61411 tx26938

🛁20 **P**100 ☾ sB🛁35—69 dB🛁70—99 M22&alc
Credit cards 1 2 3 5

CASTLEBAR
Co Mayo (☎094)

★★★***Breaffy House*** (BW) ☎22033 tx53790

Feb—20 Dec
🛁🚿40 **P**200 Lift ☾ sB🛁🚿25—32 dB🛁🚿50—56 M6—14
Credit cards 1 2 3 5

★**Traveller's Friend** ☎23111 tx53790

Closed 24—26 Dec
rm11 **P** ☾ sB16—19 dB28—30 M3—10&alc
Credit cards 1 3

★**Welcome Inn** ☎22054

Closed 24—26 Dec
rm26 (🛁🚿6) **P**10 ☾
Credit cards 1 2 3

CASTLEBLAYNEY
Co Monaghan (☎042)

🚗 **Trunk Road** ☎40041

CASTLEDERMOT
Co Kildare (☎0503)

M Hennessy & Sons ☎44114 Cit

CASTLEGREGORY
Co Kerry (☎066)

★★**Tralee Bay** ☎39138

Etr—Sep
rm13 (🛁6) **P**300
Credit cards 1 2 3 5

CASTLE ISLAND
Co Kerry (☎066)

McElligotts Limerick Rd ☎41284 Fia La

CASTLEREA
Co Roscommon (☎0907)

🚗 **Lavins** The Demesne ☎20096

CASTLETOWNBERE
Co Cork (☎027)

🚗 **Oakmount** (Peter Hanley) ☎70264

CAVAN
Co Cavan (☎049)

★★★**Hotel Kilmore** Dublin Rd ☎32288

🛁40 **P**600 ☾ sB🛁23—25 dB🛁44—46
Credit cards 1 2 3

Brady's Dublin Rd ☏31833 Ren

Jackson's Farnham St ☏31700 For

CHARLESTOWN
Co Mayo (☏094)

Walsh's Auto Svc Bellaghy ☏54131

CLAREMORRIS
Co Mayo (☏094)

Duggan's Convent Rd ☏71610

CLIFDEN
Co Galway (☏095)

★★★**Abbeyglen Castle** ☏21070 tx28366
Closed last three weeks Jan
40 P100 sB 20—30 dB 40—60 M6—16
Credit cards 1 2 3 5

★★★**Ardagh** ☏21384
Apr—Oct
rm22 (17) P60 sB17—22 sB 24—29 dB 33—43 M13&alc
Credit cards 1 2 3

★★★**Rock Glen** ☏21035
mid Mar—Oct
30 P40 sB 30—35 dB 45—57 M18
Credit cards 1 2 3 5

Brian Walsh Mtrs Galway Rd ☏21037

CLOGHER
Co Tyrone (☏06625)

R Armstrong Augher Rd ☏48661

CLONAKILTY
Co Cork (☏023)

Western Western Rd ☏33327

CLONMEL
Co Tipperary (☏052)

★★★**Clonmel Arms** (Inter) ☏21233 tx80263
rm35 (25) Lift sB25—29 sB 32—37 dB 48—52 M8—13&alc
Credit cards 1 2 3 4 5

★★★**Minella** ☏22388
30 P400 sB 22—29 dB 40—50 M10—15
Credit cards 1 2 3 4 5

★★**Hearn's** ☏21611
Closed 24—31Dec
rm25 (12 4) P40
Credit cards 1 3

Blue Star Cashel Rd ☏21177 Toy

Central Dungarvan Rd ☏22399 Dat

National Garages 22 Thomas St ☏22600 Ren

CLOUGHEY
Co Down

★★**Roadhouse** 204—208 Main Rd ☏Portavogie(02477)71500
Closed Xmas Day
9 P30 sB 17—18 dB 28—30
Credit cards 1 3

Ireland

COLERAINE
Co Londonderry (☏0265)

Coleraine 2 Castlerock Rd ☏51311

JKC Specialist Cars 7—9 Millburn Rd ☏55222 BMW

Macfarlane Autos Gateside Rd, Loughanmill Ind Est ☏3153

CONG
Co Mayo

★**Ryan's** ☏4
Apr—Sep
rm13 (7)

CONVOY
Co Donegal (☏074)

McGlincheys ☏47174

COOKSTOWN
Co Tyrone (☏06487)

R A Patrick 21—23 Orritor Rd ☏63601

R Turkington 45 Killmoon St ☏62675 Ren

COOTEHILL
Co Cavan (☏049)

★★**White Horse** ☏52124
rm30 (24) P200 sB 19—21 dB 35—39 M8—18
Credit cards 1 3

CORK
Co Cork (☏021)

★★★★**Jury's** Western Rd ☏966377 tx26073
140 P500 sB fr58 dB fr72 M12—14
Credit cards 1 2 3 4 5

★★★**Metropole** (BW) McCurtain St ☏508122 tx75077
rm120 (93) Lift sB36 sB 47 dB50 dB 61 M4—15
Credit cards 1 2 3 4 5

★★★**Silver Springs** Lower Glanmire Rd ☏507533 tx26111
Closed 25 Dec—3 Jan
72 P300 Lift sB 40—45 dB 60—70 M7—15&alc
Credit cards 1 2 3 5

★★**Moore's** Morrison Island ☏271291
Closed 25—26 Dec
rm38 (34)
Credit cards 1 3

Lee Model Farm Rd ☏42933 Fia Lan

COURTMACSHERRY
Co Cork (☏023)

★★**Courtmacsherry** ☏46198
Etr—Sep
rm16 (5) P60 sB17—19 dB34—37 dB 38—40 M13—15

COURTOWN HARBOUR
Co Wexford (☏055)

★★**Bay View** ☏25307
17 Mar—Sep
rm19 (3) P
Credit cards 1 3

★★**Courtown** ☏25108
Etr—Oct
rm26 (16)
Credit cards 1 2 3 5

Doyles ☏27318

CRAIGAVON
Co Armagh (☏0762)

Irish Rd Mtrs Highfield Heights, Highfield Rd ☏42424 For

CRAUGHWELL
Co Galway (☏091)

Craughwell Motors ☏46018

CRAWFORDSBURN
Co Down

★★★**Ye Olde Inn** 15 Main St ☏Helens Bay (0247)853255
Closed Xmas Day & Boxing Day
21 sB 32 dB 52 M4—9&alc
Credit cards 1 3 5

CROSSHAVEN
Co Cork (☏021)

★***Helm*** ☏831400
Jun—7 Sep
rm19 (2) P60

CROSSMAGLEN
Co Armagh (☏0693)

Donaghy Bros Newry St ☏861228

CROSSMOLINA
Co Mayo (☏096)

Connor Mtrs Main St & Erris St ☏31377

Park Motors Erris Rd ☏31331

CULLYBACKEY
Co Antrim (☏0266)

Albert Wylie 46 Craigs Rd ☏880554

CUSHENDALL
Co Antrim (☏02667)

★★**Thornlea** 6 Coast Rd ☏71223
rm13 P20 sB13 dB24 M4—7&alc
Credit cards 1 2 3 5

DERRYGONELLY
Co Fermanagh (☏036564)

Derrygonelly Autos Main St ☏217

DINGLE
Co Kerry (☏066)

★★★**Sceilig** ☏51144 tx26900
Apr—Oct & Dec
79 P
Credit cards 1 2 3 4 5

DOAGH
Co Antrim

Colin Agnew 49 Station Rd ☏Ballyclare (09603) 40462

DONABATE
Co Dublin (☎01)

🚚 **Matt Halpin Mtrs** Beaverstown ☎453580

DONEGAL
Co Donegal (☎073)

★★★**Hyland's Central** (BW) The Diamond ☎21027 tx40522
Closed Xmas
🛁🚿57 **P**18 Lift ☾ sB🛁🚿26–30 dB🛁🚿38–44 M8–16&alc
Credit cards [1] [2] [3]

★★**Abbey** ☎4
Closed 25–27 Dec
rm40 (🛁🚿26) **P**80 Lift ☾ sB19–21 sB🛁🚿23–25 dB32–36 dB🛁🚿36–40 M8–14
Credit cards [1] [2] [3] [4] [5]

🚚 **R E Johnston** Quay St ☎21039 BL LR

🚚 **J Owen Car Sales** Derry Rd ☎21791 Dat

DOWNPATRICK
Co Down (☎0396)

Charles Keown Mtrs 9A Ballynagross Rd ☎3755 Ren

DROGHEDA
Co Louth (☎041)

★★★**Boyne Valley** ☎37737 tx91880
🛁🚿20 **P**400 ☾ sB🛁🚿22–24 dB🛁🚿40–45 M7–14&alc
Credit cards [1] [2] [3] [5]

★**Rossnaree** ☎37673
Closed 25 Dec
🛁20 **P**200 ☾
Credit cards [1] [3]

Boyne Cars North Rd ☎38566 Dat

N Smith North Rd ☎31106 For

Tara Motors North Rd ☎38785 Fia Lan

DUBLIN
Co Dublin (☎01)

★★★★**Burlington** Leeson St ☎605222 tx25517
🛁🚿439 🏠 **P**400 Lift ☾ sB🛁🚿fr55 dB🛁🚿fr70 M8–16
Credit cards [1] [2] [3] [4] [5]

★★★★**Jury's** Ballsbridge ☎605000 tx25304
🛁🚿300 **P**320 Lift ☾ sB🛁🚿fr76 dB🛁🚿fr90 M11–15&alc ⛱ 📺
Credit cards [1] [2] [3] [4] [5]

★★★★**Shelbourne** St-Stephen's Green ☎766471 tx25184
🚿171 🏠 Lift ☾ sB🚿fr68 dB🚿fr88 M18–21&alc
Credit cards [1] [2] [3] [4] [5]

★★★**Ashling** Parkgate St ☎772324 tx32802
Closed Xmas
🛁🚿56 🏠 **P**70 Lift ☾ sB🛁🚿33–36 dB🛁🚿51–54 M5–16&alc
Credit cards [1] [2] [3] [4] [5]

★★★**Blooms** Anglesea St ☎715622 tx31688
🛁🚿86 **P**20 Lift ☾ sB🛁🚿fr55 dB🛁🚿fr66 M12
Credit cards [1] [2] [3] [4] [5]

★★★**Dublin International** Dublin Aiport (6m N on N1) ☎379211 tx24612
🛁🚿190 **P**300 ☾ sB🛁🚿53 dB🛁🚿63 M8–12&alc 📺
Credit cards [1] [2] [3] [4] [5]

★★★**Green Isle** Clondalkin (6m S on N7) ☎593476 tx90280
🛁50 **P**300 ☾ sB🛁🚿36–39 dB🛁🚿52–56
Credit cards [1] [2] [3] [4] [5]

★★★**Marine** Sutton (Inter) (8m N on coast rd R106) ☎322613 tx24858
Closed 25–26 Dec
🛁🚿27 **P**100 ☾
Credit cards [1] [2] [3] [5]

★★★**Montrose** Stillorgan Rd ☎693311 tx91207
🛁180 **P**200 Lift ☾
Credit cards [1] [2] [3] [4] [5]

★★★**Royal Dublin** O'Connell St ☎733666 tx24288
5 Jan–24 Dec
rm103 (🛁🚿101) Lift ☾ sB🛁🚿43–54 dB🛁🚿56–73 M9–15&alc
Credit cards [1] [2] [3] [5]

★★★***Sach's*** ☎680995 tx31667
Closed 25 Dec
🛁20 **P**200 Lift ☾
Credit cards [1] [2] [3] [5]

★★★**Skylon** ☎379121
🛁🚿88 **P**150 Lift ☾
Credit cards [1] [2] [3] [4] [5]

★★★**Tara Tower** Merrion Rd ☎694666 tx25517
🛁🚿82 **P**300 Lift ☾ sB🛁🚿36–39 dB🛁🚿52–55
Credit cards [1] [2] [3] [4] [5]

Bagenal Fagan & Sons 8/12 Terenure Pl ☎901840 Cit Dat

Ballsbridge Motors 162 Shelbourne Rd ☎689651 Aud Maz MB VW

🚚 **Borrowman's Breakdown Service** 17 Gortmore Rd ☎694766

Cahill Mtrs Howth Rd, Raheny ☎314066 Dat

Callow Gilmore (Mtrs) Bluebell Av ☎516877 Dat

Carroll & Kinsella Upper Churchtown Rd ☎983166 Sko

Carroll & Kinsella Mtrs 164 Walkinstown Rd ☎508142 Sko Toy

🚚 **Cheeverstown** Naas Rd, Clondalkin ☎514089

Clonskeagh Mtrs Clonskeagh Rd ☎694142

Dublin Automotive Svcs Kilbarrack Ind Est, Kilbarrack Rd ☎390281

J Duffy Ballygall Rd ☎342577 BMW Col

🚚 **Emergency Breakdown Svcs** 55 Clonskea Rd ☎697985

Fairlane Mtr Co Greenhills Rd, Tallaght ☎515200 For

Huet Motors 78–84 Townsend St ☎779177 Lot RR Vol

🚚 **T Kane** 17A Rear Fairview Av, Fairview ☎338143

G Kellett Services 44 South Dock St, South Lotts Rd ☎689177

Kenilworth Motors Harolds Cross Rd ☎975757

Linders of Smithfield Smithfield Sq ☎721222 Toy

🚚 **McCarville Mtrs** 5 Old Bawn Rd, Tallaght ☎516685

E P Mooney & Co Longmile Rd ☎552416 Dat

Park Mtrs 218 North Circular Rd ☎792011

Sweeney & Forte 54 Howth Rd ☎332301 Fia Lan

Walden Motor Co 171–5 Parnell St ☎747831 For

DUNADRY
Co Antrim (☎08494)

★★★★**Dunadry Inn** ☎Templepatrick (08494)32474 tx747245
Closed 25–28 Dec
🛁64 **P**350 ☾ sB🛁44 dB🛁55 Mfr5&alc
Credit cards [1] [2] [3] [4] [5]

DUNDALK
Co Louth (☎042)

★★★**Ballymascanlon House** (BW) ☎71124 tx43735
Closed Xmas
🛁🚿36 **P**400 ☾ sB🛁🚿26–30 dB🛁🚿42–50 M9–14&alc 🔑 📺
Credit cards [1] [2] [3] [5]

★★★**Imperial** ☎32241 tx33860
Closed Xmas Day
🛁🚿50 **P**100 Lift ☾ sB🛁🚿25–28 dB🛁🚿35–39 M4–11
Credit cards [1] [2] [3] [5]

🚚 **Nursery** Mullararlin Rd ☎35088

DUNFANAGHY
Co Donegal (☎074)

★★**Arnold's** ☎36208
Apr–Sep
rm36 (🛁26) 🏠 **P**50 sB13–17 sB🛁15–19 dB26–34 dB🛁30–38 M6–12&alc 🔑
Credit card [3]

★★**Carrig Rua** ☎36133
Etr–Sep
🛁22 **P**20 sB🛁14–20 dB🛁27–35 M7–13
Credit card [3]

DUNGANNON
Co Tyrone (☎08687)

Donnelly Bros 14–18 Georges St ☎22887

🚚 **Park Rd S/Sta** (H Corrigan) 1–7 Park Rd ☎24929

DUNGARVAN
Co Waterford (☎058)

🚗 **Donnellys** Youghal Rd ☎42288

DUNGLOE
Co Donegal (☎075)

★★**Ostan Na Rosann** ☎21088
🛁 48 **P**150 ☾ sB🛁 17–20 dB🛁 30–36
M5–14 ▭
Credit cards [1] [2] [3] [5]

🚗 **Greenes** Carnmore Rd ☎21021

DUN LAOGHAIRE
Co Dublin (☎01)

★★★**Royal Marine** ☎801911
rm115 (🛁 90) **P**100 Lift ☾
Credit cards [1] [2] [3] [5]

★★★**Victor** (BW) ☎853555 tx24434
Closed Xmas Day
🛁🚿 60 **P**300 Lift ☾ sB🛁🚿 28–35
dB🛁🚿 40–48 M6–17 ⚲
Credit cards [1] [2] [3] [4] [5]

JPS Mtrs Ashgrove Ind Est, Kill Av
☎805727 BMW

DUNMORE EAST
Co Waterford (☎051)

★★**Haven** ☎83150
May–Sep
rm17 (🛁🚿 10) **P**30 sB16–22
sB🛁🚿 16–22 dB31–43 dB🛁🚿 31–43
M9&alc
Credit cards [1] [2] [3]

DUNMURRY
Co Antrim

★★★★**Conway** Kingsway
☎Belfast(0232)612101
🛁 77 **P**250 Lift ☾ sB🛁 45 dB🛁 57 M4–8
≈
Credit cards [1] [2] [3] [4] [5]

Saville Mtrs 101 Kingsway ☎Belfast (0232)
614211

EDENDERRY
Co Offlay (☎0405)

🚗 **McNelis** Rathangan Rd ☎31480

EDERNEY
Co Fermanagh

🚗 **McIlhills** Market St ☎Kesh (03656)
31294

EDGEWORTHSTOWN
Co Longford (☎043)

🚗 **Kane's** ☎71044

EGLINTON
Co Londonderry

★★***Glen House*** 9 Main St ☎Londonderry
(0504)810527
🛁🚿 16 **P**55 ☾
Credit cards [1] [2] [3] [5]

EMO
Co Laois (☎0502)

★★★**Montague** ☎26154 tx33272
🛁🚿 78 **P**200 ☾ sB🛁🚿 29 dB🛁🚿 48
M5–16
Credit cards [1] [2] [3] [5]

Ireland

ENNIS
Co Clare (☎065)

★★★**Auburn Lodge** Galway Rd ☎21247
Closed 25–26 Dec
🛁🚿 22 **P**200 sB🛁🚿 25–28
dB🛁🚿 35–40 M7–12 ⚲
Credit cards [1] [2] [3] [5]

★★★**Old Ground** ☎28127 tx28108
🛁🚿 60 **P**150 ☾ sB🛁🚿 44–46
dB🛁🚿 62–66
Credit cards [1] [2] [3] [4] [5]

★★★**West County Inn** (BW) ☎28421
🛁🚿 110 **P**500 Lift ☾
Credit cards [1] [2] [3] [5]

ENNISCORTHY
Co Wexford (☎054)

★★**Murphy-Floods** Town Centre ☎33413
Closed 25 Dec
rm22 (🛁 18) **P**2 ☾ sB17–19 sB🛁 20–23
dB30–32 dB🛁 33–35 M7–12&alc
Credit cards [1] [2] [3]

ENNISCRONE
Co Sligo (☎96)

★**Killala Bay** ☎36239
rm18 (🛁🚿 6) **P** sB11–15 sB🛁🚿 14–18
dB21–27 dB🛁🚿 25–31 M10

ENNISKILLEN
Co Fermanagh (☎0365)

★★★**Kyllyhelvin** ☎23481
🛁🚿 25 **P**200 ☾
Credit cards [1] [2] [3] [5]

★***Railway*** ☎22084
Closed Xmas
rm17 (🚿 14) A6rm ☾
Credit card [3]

Erne Eng Co Queens St ☎3721 For

🚗 **Leo McGrory & Sons** Tempo Rd
☎24351

Modern Mtrs 74 Forthill St ☎22974 Aud VW

Patrick McNulty & Sons Mtrcycles 24–26
Belmore St ☎22423 M/c

ENNISTYMON
Co Clare (☎065)

★★**Falls** ☎71004
rm30 (🛁🚿 16) **P**30 sB16–18
sB🛁🚿 17–19 dB30–34 dB🛁🚿 32–36
Credit cards [1] [2] [3] [5]

FERBANE
Co Offaly

🚗 **Freddie Vaugh Car Sales** Ballycumber
Rd ☎Ferbane 202

FERMOY
Co Cork (☎025)

Cavanaghs Ashe Quay ☎31211 For

Fermoy Autos Court House Rd ☎32328
Ren

Harry O'Sullivan 41–43 McCurtain St
☎31797 Aud Maz VW

FINTONA
Co Tyrone (☎0662)

🚗 **Irwins** 12–14 King St ☎841208

FOXFORD
Co Mayo (☎094)

★★***Pontoon Bridge*** ☎56120 tx92194
May–14 Oct
rm16 (🛁 8) **P**50 ⚲
Credit cards [1] [3]

🚗 **Reape's Auto Svc** ☎56119

GALWAY
Co Galway (☎091)

★★★★**Great Southern** Eyre Sq
☎64041 tx28364
🛁 120 Lift ☾ sB🛁 40–50 dB🛁 58–79
Credit cards [1] [2] [3] [5]

★★★***Ardilaun House*** (Inter) Taylor's Hill
☎21433 tx28873
Closed 20–31 Dec
🛁🚿 85 **P**220 Lift ☾
Credit cards [1] [2] [3] [5]

★★★**Corrib Great Southern** ☎55281
tx28844
🛁🚿 113 **P**200 Lift ☾ sB🛁🚿 41–46
dB🛁🚿 62–71 ▭
Credit cards [1] [2] [3] [4] [5]

★★★**Flannery's** (BW) Dublin Rd
☎55111 tx28976
🚿 100 **P**200 Lift ☾ sB🚿 22–33 dB🚿 39–55
Credit cards [1] [2] [3] [4] [5]

★★★**Anno Santo** Threadneedle Rd,
Salthill ☎22110
Closed 21–31 Dec
rm13 (🚿 10) **P**12
Credit cards [1] [2] [3]

★★**Galway Ryan** Dublin Rd ☎53181
tx28349
Closed 24–25 Dec
🚿 96 **P**100 Lift ☾ sB🚿 36–45 dB🚿 42–62
Credit cards [1] [2] [3] [4] [5]

★★**Skeffington Arms** Eyre Sq ☎63173
Closed 1 wk Xmas
🛁🚿 21 **P**25 sB🛁🚿 21–28
dB🛁🚿 38–45 M6–16
Credit cards [1] [3] [4]

★★**Warwick** Salthill ☎21244
Etr–15 Oct
rm50 (🛁 30) **P**50 ☾
Credit cards [1] [2] [3]

★**Atlanta** ☎62241
Closed 25 Dec
rm20 **P**6

★**Lochlurgain** 22 Monksfield, Upper Salthill
☎22884
Closed Jan–27 Mar & 28 Oct–Dec
rm17 (🛁🚿 5) **P**8 sB17–20 sB🛁🚿 21–24
dB28–33 dB🛁🚿 35–40 M8–15
Credit cards [1] [2] [3]

★**Rockbarton Park** Salthill ☎22018
Closed Xmas
rm11 (🛁🚿 9) **P**12
Credit cards [1] [2] [3] [5]

🚗 **Higgins** Headford Rd ☎61263 For

J J Fleming Tuam Rd ☎55451 Ope

J Kelleher Salthill Service Station, Salthill ☎22418 Vol

GARRETTSTOWN
Co Cork (☎021)

★★**Coakley's Atlantic** ☎73215

Closed Xmas
🛁 22 **P**60 ☾ sB🛁 21–24 dB🛁 30–36 M8–15&alc
Credit cards 1 2 3

GARRISON
Co Fermanagh

Melvin (A & S Rasdale) ☎Belleek (036586)246

GARRYVOE
Co Cork (☎021)

★★**Garryvoe** ☎646718

Closed 25 Dec
rm19 (🛁🚿 17) **P**10
Credit cards 1 2 3 5

GLENDALOUGH
Co Wicklow (☎0404)

★★**Royal** ☎5135

14 Mar–Oct
🛁 13 **P**20 Lift sB🛁 24–26 dB🛁 40–44 M7–16&alc
Credit cards 1 2 3

GLENGARRIFF
Co Cork (☎027)

★★**Eccles** ☎63003

May–Sep
🛁🚿 35 **P**30 ☾ sB🛁🚿 17–20 dB🛁🚿 30–36 M13&alc
Credit cards 1 2 3 5

GLENGORMLEY
Co Antrim (☎02313)

🚗 **Dencourt Mtrs** Rush Pk, Mallusk Rd ☎48221 Vau

🚗 **Glengormley S/Sta** (L Morrow) 333 Antrim Rd ☎2186

GLEN O' THE DOWNS
Co Wicklow (☎01)

🚗 Glen ☎874932

GLOUNTHAUNE
Co Cork (☎021)

★★**Ashbourne** ☎353319

🛁🚿 27 🏠 **P**200 sB🛁🚿 30–32 dB🛁🚿 44–46 M7–15 &alc 🔑 ♨
Credit cards 1 2 3 5

GOREY
Co Wexford (☎055)

★★★***Marfield House*** ☎21124 tx80757

Closed 15 Nov–15 Dec
🛁🚿 12 **P** Lift ☾ 🔑

🚗 **O'Sullivans** Scarnagh, Coolgreany ☎7127

GORT
Co Galway (☎091)

★★**Glynn's** Main St ☎31047

🛁🚿 14 **P**6 sB🛁🚿 15–18 dB🛁🚿 30–35 M5–13

GORTAHORK
Co Donegal (☎074)

★★***McFadden's*** ☎35267

Mar–Oct
rm28 (🛁🚿 7) **P**50
Credit cards 1 2 3 4 5

GOUGANE BARRA
Co Cork

★★**Gougane Barra** ☎Ballingeary 69

Apr–Sep
rm32 (🛁 18) **P**30 sB14–15 sB🛁 15–16 dB25–27 dB🛁 28–30 M11
Credit cards 1 3

HEADFORD
Co Galway (☎093)

★**Angler's Rest** ☎35528

5 Jan–20 Dec
rm14 (🛁🚿 7) sB14 sB🛁🚿 fr15 dBfr28 dB🛁🚿 fr30

HOLYWOOD
Co Down (☎02317)

★★★★**Culloden** ☎5223 tx74617

🛁🚿 74 **P**450 Lift ☾ 🔑
Credit cards 1 2 3 4 5

🚗 **R Henderson & Sons** New Rd, Redburn Sq ☎3795

HOWTH
Co Dublin (☎01)

★★**Howth Lodge** ☎390288

2 Jan–22 Dec
🛁🚿 14 **P**200 ☾ sB🛁🚿 fr20 dB🛁🚿 fr28
Credit cards 1 2 3 5

INCHIGEELA
Co Cork

★**Creedon's** ☎12

rm20 (🛁🚿 7) **P**20 ☾ sB🛁🚿 11 dB19 dB🛁🚿 21
Credit cards 1 2 3 4 5

★**Lake** ☎10

rm10 (🛁 2) 🏠 **P**20 sB10 sB🛁 12 dB20 dB🛁 22 M5–7

INNISHANNON
Co Cork (☎021)

★★**Innishannon** ☎75121 tx75398

Closed Xmas
🛁🚿 13 **P**100 ☾ sB🛁🚿 22–24 dB🛁🚿 36–40 M9–14&alc
Credit cards 1 2 3 5

IRVINESTOWN
Co Fermanagh (☎03656)

★★**Mahons** ☎21656

rm22 (🛁🚿 10) 🏠10 **P**30 sBfr14 sB🛁🚿 fr15 dBfr28 dB🛁🚿 fr30 M5–7 St%
Credit cards 1 3

🚗 **Killadeas S/Sta** Drummall, Lisnarick ☎21530

JULIANSTOWN
Co Meath (☎041)

★★**Glenside** Smithstown ☎29049

Closed 18–31 Dec
🛁🚿 14 **P**25
Credit cards 1 2 3 5

KENMARE
Co Kerry (☎064)

★★★★**Park** ☎41200 tx70005

Closed mid Nov–Xmas
🛁🚿 50 **P**80 Lift ☾ sB🛁🚿 54–62 dB🛁🚿 93–128 🔑 ▣
Credit cards 1 3

★★★***Kenmare Bay*** ☎41300

Apr–Oct
🛁🚿 100 **P**200 ☾
Credit cards 1 2 3 4 5

Randles Bros Shelbourne Rd ☎41355 AR Dat

KESH
Co Fermanagh (☎03656)

★★**Lough Erne** Main St ☎31275

Closed Xmas Day
rm14 (🛁 3) **P**100 sBfr11 sB🛁 fr12 dBfr21 dB🛁 fr24 M6–8
Credit cards 1 3 5

KILCOCK
Co Kildare

🚗 **Dermot Keily** Dublin Rd ☎287311 For

🚗 **McGeeneys** Church St ☎287375

KILDARE
Co Kildare (☎045)

🚗 **T & A Boyle** Cherryville ☎21898

KILFENORA
Co Clare (☎065)

🚗 **Connole's** ☎88008

KILKEE
Co Clare

★**Halpins** Erin St ☎32

rm11 (🛁🚿 3) sB15–17 sB🛁🚿 17–19 dB26–31 dB🛁🚿 30–35 M5–12&alc
Credit cards 1 2 3 5

KILKEEL
Co Down (☎06937)

★★**Kilmorey Arms** ☎62220

rm17 (🛁🚿 16) 🏠12 **P** ☾

KILKENNY
Co Kilkenny (☎056)

★★★**Hotel Kilkenny** College Rd ☎62000

🛁🚿 60 **P**200 ☾ 🔑 ▭

★★★***Newpark*** ☎22122 tx80080

🛁 44 **P**200 ☾ 🔑
Credit cards 1 2 3 5

★★**Springhill Court** Waterford Rd ☎21122

🛁🚿 44 **P**140 ☾
Credit cards 1 2 3

🚗 **Kilkenny S/Sta** Carlow Rd ☎22528

🚗 **W Tallis** 1 Johns Quay ☎65384

KILLARNEY
Co Kerry (☎064)

★★★★**Great Southern** ☎31262 tx26998
Feb—23 Dec
🛁🚿184 **P**100 Lift ☾ sB🛁🚿42—53 dB🛁🚿64—84 M10—17&alc 🎾 ▭
Credit cards [1] [2] [3] [4] [5]

★★★**Aghadoe Heights** (Inter) ☎31766 tx26942
20 Jan—20 Dec
🛁🚿60 **P**180 ☾ sB🛁🚿26—50 dB🛁🚿49—76 🎾
Credit cards [1] [2] [5]

★★★**Cahernane** Muckross Rd ☎31895 tx28123
Closed Nov & Jan—Mar
🛁🚿16 **P**30 ☾
Credit cards [1] [2] [3] [4] [5]

★★★**Glen Eagle** ☎31870 tx70023
mid Mar—Jan
🛁🚿96 ☾ 🎾
Credit cards [1] [2] [3] [4] [5]

★★★**International** (BW) ☎31816 tx28125
Mar—Oct
🛁88 ☾ sB🛁27—32 dB🛁39—50
Credit cards [1] [2] [3] [5]

★★★**Lake** ☎31035
28 Mar—27 Oct
🛁🚿64 **P**150 ☾ sB17—19 sB🛁🚿25—26 dB28—30 dB🛁🚿36—38 M14 🎾
Credit cards [1] [2] [3] [5]

★★★**Torc Great Southern** ☎31611 tx28207
25 Apr—12 Oct
🛁🚿96 **P**150 ☾ sB🛁🚿45 dB🛁🚿68 M9—12 🎾
Credit cards [1] [2] [3] [5]

★★**Arbutus** ☎31037
Feb—Nov
🛁🚿35 ☾ sB🛁🚿20—24 dB🛁🚿31—35
Credit cards [1] [2] [3]

★★**Grand** ☎31159
Etr—Oct
rm27 (🛁🚿26) **P** ☾ sB15—17 sB🛁🚿17—19 dB28—32 dB🛁🚿30—34 M5—10&alc
Credit card [2]

★★**Killarney Ryan** ☎31555 tx26950
🛁🚿168 **P**100 Lift ☾ 🎾
Credit cards [1] [2] [3] [4] [5]

🚗 **Coffeys** (Glem Mtrs) Coolbane, Ballyhar ☎(066)64217

Killarney Motor Works New Rd ☎31087 For

🚗 **Murphys** Clohane Iron Mills, Cork Rd ☎Headford 6

🚗 **Randles** Muckross Rd ☎31237

Ireland

KILLEAGH
Co Cork (☎024)

🚗 **Fiztgibbons** ☎95113

KILLINCHY
Co Down (☎0238)

H A McBriar & Son 64 Comber Rd ☎541261 Toy

KILLINEY
Co Dublin (☎01)

★★★**Court** ☎851622 tx33244
🛁🚿34 **P**200 Lift ☾ sB🛁🚿45—52 dB🛁🚿52—73 M6—14&alc
Credit cards [1] [2] [3]

★★★**Fitzpatrick's Castle** ☎851533 tx30353
🛁🚿48 **P**300 ☾ sB🛁🚿48—72 dB🛁🚿68—106 M7—17&alc 🎾 ≈ ▭
Credit cards [1] [2] [3] [5]

KILLYLEAGH
Co Down (☎0396)

T M Martin & Son 6—8 Cross St ☎828203

KILMACANOGUE
Co Wicklow (☎01)

🚗 **Gerard Conroy Mtrs Svcs** ☎860618

KILMEADEN
Co Waterford (☎051)

🚗 **Hennessys** ☎84129

KILRUSH
Co Clare

★★**Inis Cathaig** ☎36
rm16 (🛁🚿10) **P**40
Credit cards [1] [3] [5]

🚗 **Kilrush Mtrs** Ennis Rd ☎48

KINAWLEY
Co Fermanagh

🚗 **V G Brennan** Enniskillen Rd ☎(036574)314

KINGSCOURT
Co Cavan (☎042)

★**Mackin's** ☎67164
rm14 (🛁🚿4) **P**6 sB10—12 sB🛁🚿10—12 dB20—24 dB🛁🚿20—24

KINSALE
Co Cork (☎021)

★★★**Acton's** ☎772135 tx75443
rm58 (🛁46) **P**80 sB20—32 sB🛁26—40 dB34—46 dB🛁40—58 M7—14 &alc ≈
Credit cards [1] [2] [3] [4] [5]

KINSALEBEG
Co Waterford (☎024)

🚗 **McGraths** ☎92588

KINVARRA
Co Galway (☎091)

🚗 **P O'Loughlin** ☎37135

LAHINCH
Co Clare (☎065)

★★★**Aberdeen Arms** (Inter) ☎81100 tx70132
Etr—6 Oct
🛁🚿48 **P**48 Lift sB🛁🚿27—32 dB🛁🚿40—50 M alc
Credit cards [1] [2] [3] [5]

LARNE
Co Antrim (☎0574)

★★★**Magheramorne House** 59 Shore Rd, Magheramorne (3m S on A2) ☎79444
🛁23 **P**60 Lift ☾
Credit cards [1] [2] [3]

GMG 96—98 Glenarm Rd ☎(08494)77328 Col Dat

🚗 **Rock Mtr Wks** 52 Ballymena Rd ☎73122

Wilsons of Rathenny 39 Glynn Rd ☎5411 For

LAYTOWN
Co Meath (☎041)

🚗 **Clarke's** ☎27278

LETTERFRACK
Co Galway (☎095)

★★★***Rosleague Manor*** ☎21420 tx28906
Etr—Oct
🛁🚿15 **P**20
Credit cards [1] [3]

LETTERKENNY
Co Donegal (☎074)

★★**Gallagher's** ☎22066
Closed 25—30 Dec
rm26 (🛁22) **P**20 ☾ sB14—16 sB🛁19—21 dB26—28 dB🛁32—34 M7—12
Credit cards [1] [2] [3] [5]

🚗 **Patrick Doherty & Sons** Pluck ☎57116

🚗 **Hegarty's** Ballymacool ☎21282

LIMAVADY
Co Londonderry (☎05047)

🚗 **T A Kerr** Rascahan ☎64903

LIMERICK
Co Limerick (☎061)

★★★**Jury's** Ennis Rd ☎55266 tx28266
25—26 Dec
🛁🚿95 **P** ☾ sB🛁🚿fr42 dB🛁🚿fr51
Credit cards [1] [2] [3] [4] [5]

★★★**Limerick Inn** Ennis Rd ☎51544 tx28121
Closed Xmas Day
🛁🚿153 **P**500 Lift ☾ sB🛁🚿49—54 dB🛁🚿64—74 M8—19&alc 🎾 ▭
Credit cards [1] [2] [3] [4] [5]

★★★**Limerick Ryan** Ennis Rd ☎53922 tx26920
🛁🚿184 **P**200 Lift ☾ sB🛁🚿30—39 dB🛁🚿39—50 M7—12&alc
Credit cards [1] [2] [3] [5]

★★★**New Green Hills** Caherdavin ☎53033 tx70246
🛁55 **P**400 ☾
Credit cards [1] [2] [3] [4] [5]

★★★**Two Mile Motor Inn** (BW) Ennis Rd ☎53122 tx70157
Closed 24—25 Dec
🛁🚿125 **P**200 ☾
Credit cards [1] [2] [3] [5]

★★**Royal George** O'Connell St ☎44566 tx26910
Closed 25 Dec
🛁58 Lift ☾ sB🛁26—29 dB🛁44—47 M5—13&alc
Credit cards [1] [2] [3] [4] [5]

Elm Motors Coonagh Cross, Ennis Rd ☎51577 AR Vol

Gleeson Bros Ellen St ☎45567 Tal

F Hogan Dublin Rd ☎46000 Aud Maz Mer Por VW

P Keogh Castle St ☎43133 BMW Dat

LISBURN
Co Antrim (☎08462)

J Hanna Mtrs 1 Queens Rd ☎72416 Hon

LISCANNOR
Co Clare

★★**Liscannor Golf** ☎81186
Closed Apr—Nov
🛁26 **P**120 ☾ sB🛁🚿26—28 dB🛁🚿36—38 M8—15&alc
Credit cards [1] [2] [3] [5]

LISDOONVARNA
Co Clare (☎065)

★★**Imperial** ☎74015
Mar—Oct
🛁🚿42 **P**500 ☾ sB🛁🚿12—15 dB🛁🚿24—30 M5—10&alc
Credit card [1]

★★**Keane's** ☎74011
May—10 Oct
rm12 (🛁🚿7) **P**8
Credit cards [1] [3]

★★**Lynch's** ☎74010
Jun—5 Oct
rm16 (🛁🚿8) **P**10 ☾ sB12—14 sB🛁🚿14—16 dB24—28 dB🛁🚿28—32
Credit cards [1] [3]

★★**Spa View** ☎74026
14 Mar—Nov
rm15 (🚿2) **P**20 sB🚿19—20 dB🚿29—32 M4—15 ⚲
Credit cards [1] [3]

LISMORE
Co Waterford (☎058)

★★**Ballyrafter House** ☎54002
Apr—Sep
rm12 (🛁4) ⌂ **P**20

LISNASKEA
Co Fermanagh (☎03657)

★★**Ortine** ☎21206
Closed Xmas Day
rm20 (🚿17) **P**50 sB17—20 sB🚿19—20 dB26—30 dB🚿29—30 M5—9&alc
Credit cards [1] [3]

🚗 **Monaghan Bros** Drumhaw ☎21354

Ireland

LIXNAW
Co Kerry

🚗 **O'Keeffes** ☎32157

LONDONDERRY
Co Londonderry (☎0504)

★★★★**Everglades** Prehan Rd ☎46722 tx748005
Closed Xmas
🛁38 **P**250 ☾
Credit cards [1] [2] [3] [5]

Desmond Mtrs 173 Strand Rd ☎267613 For

Eakin Bros Maydown Rd ☎860601 Vau

🚗 **A McGeady & Sons** 43 Barry St ☎261255

🚗 **Tullyally Car Breakers** Tullyally Rd, Ardmore ☎49395

LONGFORD
Co Longford

🚗 **Longford Auto Svc** Little Water St ☎41046

LOUGH ARROW
Co Sligo (☎079)

★**Rock House** Castle Baldwin ☎66073
Mar—Nov
rm7 (🛁🚿5) **P**50 sB13—15 sB🛁🚿15—17 dB26—30 dB🛁🚿30—34 M8—12&alc
Credit cards [1] [2] [3] [5]

LOUGHBRICKLAND
Co Down

🚗 **Frank McGrath** Main St ☎Banbridge (08206) 22396

MACROOM
Co Cork (☎026)

★★**Castle** ☎41074
Closed Xmas
rm18 (🚿16) ⌂ **P**20 ☾ sB11—13 sB🚿12—15 dB22—25 dB🚿24—26 M5—10&alc
Credit cards [1] [3] [4] [5]

★**Victoria** ☎41082
rm22 (🛁4) sB9 🛁11 dB17 dB🛁18 M6—9
Credit cards [1] [2] [3] [5]

Kellehers Lower Main St ☎41029 For

MAGHERA
Co Londonderry (☎0648)

🚗 **Danny Otterson** Fairhill ☎42651

MALAHIDE
Co Dublin (☎01)

★★**Grand** ☎450633
rm48 (🛁🚿43) Lift ☾
Credit cards [1] [2] [3] [5]

Heeley Mtrs Main St ☎452044 For

MALIN
Co Donegal (☎077)

★**Malin** ☎70606
Closed Good Fri & 25 Dec
rm12 (🛁2) sB10—12 sB🛁13—14 dB20—24 dB🛁25—28 M6
Credit card [1]

MALLOW
Co Cork (☎022)

🚗 **Blackwater Mtrs** Ballydaheen ☎21436

MIDLETON
Co Cork (☎021)

Lee Broderick St ☎631306 Fia

MILLTOWN MALBAY
Co Clare (☎065)

🚗 **McCarthy's** Flag Rd ☎84039

MITCHELSTOWN
Co Cork (☎025)

🚗 **Murphys** Church St ☎24611

MONAGHAN
Co Monaghan (☎047)

★★★***Hillgrove*** ☎81288
rm46 (🛁🚿35) **P**700 ☾ ⚲
Credit cards [1] [3] [5]

🚗 **Gerry Mullin Mtrs** North Rd ☎81396

MONASTEREVIN
Co Kildare (☎045)

M A Finlay & Sons ☎25331 Fia Lan

MONEYMORE
Co Londonderry (☎06487)

🚗 **Thomas James Boyce** 43 Lawford St ☎48257

MONEYREAGH
Co Down

🚗 **Todds** Milligan Cross ☎Castlereagh (023123)576

MOVILLE
Co Donegal

★★**McNamara's** ☎10
rm15 (🛁🚿7) sB14—16 sB🛁🚿14—16 dB30—32 dB🛁🚿30—32 M6—14&alc

★**Foyle** ☎25
rm20 (🛁1)
Credit cards [2] [3]

MOY
Co Tyrone (☎08687)

🚗 **McMullan Bros** 17 Dungannon St ☎84252

MULLINGAR
Co Westmeath (☎044)

★★★**Bloomfield House** ☎40894
Restricted service 25 Dec
🛁33 **P**200 ☾ sB🛁24—27 dB🛁39—42 M7—12&alc ⚲
Credit cards [1] [2] [3] [5]

🚗 **Conlon Mtrs** Dublin Bridge ☎40731

Mullingar Autos Dublin Bridge ☎41241 Aud Maz Peu Tal VW

🚗 **Westmeath Motors** Dublin Rd ☎48806 Fia Lan

Ireland

NAAS
Co Kildare (☎045)

🚗 **T Hennessy** Sallins Rd ☎9251 Aud Maz VW

NEWCASTLE
Co Down (☎03967)

★★★**Slieve Donard** ☎23681
rm118 (🛁🚿110) **P**300 Lift ☾ 🎾 ▭
Credit cards ① ② ③ ⑤

★★**Enniskeen** 98 Bryansford Rd ☎22392
Mar—Oct
🛁🚿12 sB16—17 sB🛁🚿19—21
dB27—30 dB🛁🚿31—34 M6—8
Credit cards ① ③

NEWCASTLE WEST
Co Limerick (☎069)

★***River Room Motel*** ☎62244
🛁🚿15 **P** 🎾
Credit cards ① ② ③

NEWMARKET-ON-FERGUS
Co Clare (☎061)

★★★★**Dromoland Castle** (Relais et Châteaux) ☎71144 tx26854
Apr—Oct
🛁🚿67 **P**100 ☾ sB🛁🚿fr75 dB🛁🚿fr95
M10—25&alc
Credit cards ① ② ③ ④ ⑤

★★★**Clare Inn** ☎71161 tx24025
Mar—Dec
🛁🚿121 **P** Lift ☾ 🎾 ▣
Credit cards ① ② ③ ④ ⑤

NEWPORT
Co Mayo (☎098)

★★**Newport House** ☎41222 tx53740
20 Mar—Sep
🛁🚿12 A8rm **P**30 ☾ sB🛁🚿26—32
dB🛁🚿44—56 M10—18&alc
Credit cards ② ③ ⑤

NEW ROSS
Co Wexford (☎051)

★★**Five Counties** ☎21703 tx80577
Feb—24 Dec
🛁🚿37 **P**150 ☾ sB🛁🚿25—35
dB🛁🚿45—55 M3—13&alc
Credit cards ① ② ③ ④ ⑤

🚗 **D P Services** The Rookery, Stokestown ☎22114

🚗 **Priory Lane** Priory Lane ☎21844

NEWTOWNABBEY
Co Antrim

★★★**Chimney Corner** 630 Antrim Rd ☎Glengormley (02313) 44925 tx748158
Closed Xmas wk
🛁🚿63 **P**320 ☾ sB🛁🚿34 dB🛁🚿47 🎾 U
Credit cards ① ② ③ ⑤

Adair Smith Mtrs 581 Doagh Rd, Mossley ☎Glengormley (02313)49401 Dat

NEWTOWNARDS
Co Down (☎0247)

M Ferguson Regent House, Regent St ☎812626 For

OMAGH
Co Tyrone (☎0662)

★★**Royal Arms** 51 High St ☎3262
Closed Xmas Day
rm21 (🛁🚿19) **P**200 ☾ sBfr14 sB🛁🚿fr15
dB🛁🚿fr26 M6—8

🚗 **Sean Duncan** Brookmount Rd ☎44161

Johnston King Mtrs 82 Derry Rd ☎41520 For

OMEATH
Co Louth (☎042)

★**Park** ☎75115
rm10 **P**200 sB16 dB31 M6—12

OUGHTERARD
Co Galway (☎091)

★★★**Connemara Gateway** ☎82328 tx28905
🛁🚿64 **P**70 sB🛁🚿26—37
dB🛁🚿45—58 M7—17 🎾 ⛆
Credit cards ① ② ③ ④ ⑤

★★**Corrib** ☎82329
rm17 (🛁🚿4) A5rm **P**50 sB15—19
dB29—37 M14 alc
Credit cards ① ② ③ ⑤

★★**Egan's Lake** ☎82205
Closed Xmas
rm24 (🛁16) **P** sB🛁fr14 dB🛁fr28 Mfr13

PARKNASILLA
Co Kerry (☎064)

★★★★**Great Southern** ☎45122 tx26899
27 Mar—1 Jan
🛁57 **P**80 ☾ sB🛁63—66 dB🛁93—102
M11—20&alc 🎾 ▭ ▣ U
Credit cards ① ② ③ ④ ⑤

PORTADOWN
Co Armagh (☎0762)

🚗 **T A Bryans** 111 Harford St ☎336347

PORTBALLINTRAE
Co Antrim

★★**Bayview** 2 Bayhead Rd ☎Bushmills (02657) 31453
rm16 (🛁🚿14) **P**50 ☾ sB20 sB🛁🚿20
dB33 dB🛁🚿33 M6—10&alc
Credit cards ① ③ ⑤

★★**Beach** ☎Bushmills (02657) 31214
rm28 (🛁14) **P**40 ☾

PORTLAOISE
Co Laois (☎0502)

★★★**Killeshin** Dublin Rd ☎21663 tx33272
🛁50 **P**400 ☾ sB🛁25—30 dB🛁36—46
M7—15
Credit cards ① ② ③ ④ ⑤

Frosts of Portlaoise Dublin Rd ☎22333 For

Laois Mtrs Dublin Rd ☎21392 Fia

🚗 **Portlaoise S/Sta** Dublin Rd ☎22048

PORTMARNOCK
Co Dublin (☎01)

🚗 **Dan Fay** 8 Portmarnock Walk ☎463982

PORT-NA-BLAGH
Co Donegal (☎074)

★★★**Port-Na-Blagh** ☎36129
Etr—Sep
rm45 (🛁28) **P**80 ☾ sB16—19 sB🛁19—22
dB32—37 dB🛁37—44 M13&alc 🎾

★★★**Shandon** Marble Hill Strand ☎36137
Mar—5 Oct
🛁🚿55 **P**100 Lift ☾ sB🛁🚿20—25
dB🛁🚿35—40 M13—15 🎾 ▣

PORTSTEWART
Co Londonderry (☎026583)

🚗 **Cahore Mtrs** (Charlie Troland) Station Rd ☎2221

PORTUMNA
Co Galway (☎0509)

★★**Westpark** ☎41112
Apr—Sep
🛁🚿29 **P**200 ☾ sB🛁🚿23
dB🛁🚿33—36 🎾
Credit cards ① ② ③ ⑤

🚗 **G A Claffey** Clonfert Av ☎41009

RAPHOE
Co Donegal (☎074)

★**Central** ☎45126
Closed 23—30 Dec
rm10 (🚿3) **P**8 sB13—14 sB🚿14—16
dB25—27 dB🚿27—28 M6—10alc

RATH LUIRC (CHARLEVILLE)
Co Cork (☎063)

🚗 **Park** Smiths Rd ☎367

RATHMULLAN
Co Donegal (☎074)

★★★**Rathmullan House** (Relais et Châteaux) ☎58188
Etr—Sep
rm20 (🛁🚿15) **P**50 sB15—17
sB🛁🚿22—25 dB30—34 dB🛁🚿34—38
M13—15 🎾
Credit cards ① ② ③ ⑤

★★**Fort Royal** ☎58100
Etr—Sep
rm16 (🚿1) A5rm **P**50 sB17—23
sB🛁🚿22—28 dB35—47 dB🛁🚿41—53
M15 🎾 ▣
Credit cards ① ② ③

★**Pier** ☎58178
2 Mar—30 Sep
rm16 (🛁🚿11)

RATHNEW
Co Wicklow (☎0404)

★★**Hunter's** ☎4106
rm18 (🛁🚿10) 🏠 **P**50

RENVYLE
Co Galway

★★★**Renvyle House** Tully Cross ☎21122 tx28896 →

16 Mar—Oct & 21—31 Dec
🛁 70 **P**75 ☾ sB 🛁 21—36 dB 🛁 41—50 ⚲
◪ ∪
Credit cards [1] [3]

ROSCOMMON
Co Roscommon (☎0903)

★★★**Abbey** ☎6505 tx53816
Closed Xmas Day
🛁 🚿 25 **P**40 ☾ sB 🛁 🚿 26—32
dB 🛁 🚿 52—53 M6—16
Credit cards [1] [2] [3] [5]

🚗 **P Casey** Athlone Rd ☎6101 For

ROSCREA
Co Tipperary (☎0503)

★★**Racket Hall** ☎21748
Closed 24—27 Dec
rm10 (🛁 🚿 3) **P**30 sB20—23
sB 🛁 🚿 25—28 dB34—39 dB 🛁 🚿 39—44
M5—13&alc
Credit cards [1] [2] [3]

★**Pathe** ☎21301
Closed 25 Dec
rm22 (🛁 9) **P**8 sB13—14 sB 🛁 16—17
dB20—22 dB 🛁 23—24 M5—11&alc
Credit cards [1] [2] [3] [5]

Spooners Glebe View ☎21063 Aud Maz VW

ROSMUCK
Co Galway (☎091)

🚗 **Mannion's** ☎74113

ROSSCAHILL
Co Galway (☎091)

★★**Ross Lake House** ☎80109
rm12 (🛁 🚿 6) **P**100 M&alc ⚲
Credit cards [1] [3]

ROSSES POINT
Co Sligo (☎071)

★★**Yeats Country Ryan** ☎77211
tx40403
Apr—Oct
🛁 🚿 79 **P**100 Lift ☾ sB 🛁 🚿 40—45
dB 🛁 🚿 50—60 M9—12&alc ⚲
Credit cards [1] [2] [3]

ROSSLARE
Co Wexford (☎053)

★★★**Kelly's** ☎32114 tx80111
22 Feb—6 Dec
🛁 🚿 93 **P**100 Lift ☾ sB 🛁 🚿 26—30
dB 🛁 🚿 50—56 M8—17 ⚲ ⛽

★★★**Casey's Cedars** (Inter) ☎32124
tx80237
Closed 2—31 Jan
🛁 34 **P**100 sB 🛁 28—36 dB 🛁 44—56
M7—16
Credit cards [1] [2] [3] [5]

★★**Golf** ☎32179
Mar—4 Nov
rm25 (🛁 🚿 13) **P**20 sB19—21
sB 🛁 🚿 23—25 dB37—41 dB 🛁 🚿 43—48
M8—14 ⚲
Credit cards [1] [2] [3]

Ireland

ROSSLARE HARBOUR
Co Wexford (☎053)

★★★**Great Southern** ☎33233 tx80788
May—Oct
🛁 98 **P**120 ☾ ⚲ ▭
Credit cards [1] [2] [3] [4] [5]

★★★**Hotel Rosslare** ☎33110 tx80772
Closed 25 Dec
rm25 (🛁 🚿 22) **P**40 ☾ sB15—23
sB 🛁 🚿 18—25 dB38—46 dB 🛁 🚿 42—50
M5—13&alc
Credit cards [1] [2] [3]

ROSSNOWLAGH
Co Donegal (☎072)

★★★**Sand House** (Inter) ☎51777
tx40460
Etr—4 Oct
🛁 🚿 40 **P**60 sB 🛁 🚿 25—38
dB 🛁 🚿 50—70 M9—18 ⚲
Credit cards [1] [2] [5]

ROSTREVOR
Co Down (☎06937)

J C Campbell Shore Rd ☎38691

ROUNDSTONE
Co Galway

★**Seal's Rock** ☎15
Closed mid Sep—Mar
rm17 **P**15

SCARIFF
Co Clare

★★**Clare Lakelands** ☎18
Closed Good Fri & Xmas day
🛁 18 **P**20 ⚲

SHANKILL
Co Dublin

🚗 **Riverside S/Sta** Ballybrack Rd ☎824672

SHILLELAGH
Co Wicklow (☎055)

🚗 **Shillelagh Mtrs** ☎29127 Fia

SKIBBEREEN
Co Cork (☎028)

🚗 **Hurley Bros** Glen St ☎21555

SLANE
Co Meath (☎041)

★**Conyngham Arms** ☎24155
Closed 24—30 Dec
rm12 (🛁 🚿 11) **P**15
Credit cards [1] [2] [3] [5]

SLIGO
Co Sligo (☎071)

★★★**Ballincar House** Ballincar ☎5361
Closed 24 Dec—20 Jan
🛁 🚿 20 **P**100 sB 🛁 🚿 29—35
dB 🛁 🚿 47—58 M8—15
Credit cards [1] [2] [3]

★★★**Sligo Park** Cornageeha ☎60291
tx40397
🛁 60 **P**300 ☾ sB 🛁 35—40 dB 🛁 47—52
M5—14&alc
Credit cards [1] [2] [3] [5]

★★**Silver Swan** ☎3231
Closed 25 & 26 Dec
rm24 (🛁 🚿 13) **P**40 ☾ sB17—20
sB 🛁 🚿 19—22 dB29—35 dB 🛁 🚿 33—39
M6—12
Credit cards [1] [2] [3] [5]

Henderson Motors Bundoran Rd ☎5286 For

SNEEM
Co Kerry (☎064)

🚗 **Sneem Mtrwks** ☎45101

SPIDDAL (Spiddle)
Co Galway (☎091)

★★**Bridge House** ☎83118
6 Jan—23 Dec
rm14 (🛁 🚿 8) **P**20 ☾ sB17—18
sB 🛁 🚿 19—20 dB33—35 dB 🛁 🚿 35—38
M8—15
Credit cards [1] [3]

★★**Park Lodge** ☎83159
Closed Nov—Feb
🛁 🚿 25 **P**50 sB 🛁 🚿 20 dB 🛁 🚿 30
M8—10&alc
Credit cards [1] [2] [3]

STRABANE
Co Tyrone (☎0504)

★★★**Fir Trees Lodge** Melmount Rd
☎883003
🛁 🚿 26 **P**100 ☾
Credit cards [1] [2] [3] [4] [5]

🚗 **J Sayers Ltd** 107 Melmout Rd, Sion Mills
☎58232

R A Wallace & Sons 85 Fyfin Rd, Victoria Bridge ☎58334 Ren

STRANORLAR
Co Donegal (☎074)

★★★**Kee's** ☎31018
Closed 24—27 Dec
🛁 🚿 25 **P**100 sB 🛁 🚿 16—18
dB 🛁 🚿 27—29 M6—11&alc
Credit cards [1] [2] [3]

STROKESTOWN
Co Longford (☎078)

🚗 **Greenes Car & Tractor Sales** 'Tiernan House' Elphin St ☎21044

THURLES
Co Tipperary (☎0504)

★★**Hayes** ☎22122
rm37 (🛁 20) ⌂ **P**40 ☾ sB20 sB 🛁 23 dB37
dB 🛁 42 M8—12
Credit cards [1] [3]

🚗 **Eamonn Hayden** Loughbeg ☎22403

TIPPERARY
Co Tipperary (☎062)

★**Royal** ☎51204
Closed 25 Dec
rm18 (🛁 2) **P**100 ☾ sB13—15 sB 🛁 15—17

dB22—25 dB 🛁 28—30 M6—12&alc
Credit cards 2 3

🚗 **Sean Crowe Mtrs** Limerick Rd ☎51219

🚗 **Galtee S/Sta** Limerick Rd ☎51689

TRALEE
Co Kerry (☎066)

★★★**Earl of Desmond** ☎21299 tx26964
🛁 🚿 52 **P**120 ☾ sB 🛁 🚿 25—27
dB 🛁 🚿 33—37 M7—12&alc 🔑
Credit cards 1 2 3

★★★**Mount Brandon** ☎21311 tx28130
🛁 🚿 162 **P**500 Lift ☾
Credit cards 1 2 3 4 5

🚗 **Ruane's** 13 Prince's St ☎21838

TRAMORE
Co Waterford (☎051)

★★**Sea View** ☎81244
Mar—Oct
rm11 (🛁 🚿 6) ☾ sB20—23 sB 🛁 🚿 22—26
dB39—45 dB 🛁 🚿 44—51 M13&alc
Credit cards 1 2 3 5

VIRGINIA
Co Cavan (☎049)

★★★**Park** (BW) ☎47235
Mar—Dec
rm19 (🛁 🚿 16) A6rm **P**100 ☾ 🔑
Credit cards 1 2 3 5

WATERFORD
Co Waterford (☎051)

★★★**Ardree** ☎32111 tx80684
Closed 25 & 26 Dec
🛁 100 **P**250 Lift ☾ 🔑
Credit cards 1 2 3 4 5

★★★**Granville** (Inter) The Quay ☎55111 tx80188
Closed 25 & 26 Dec
🛁 🚿 66 Lift ☾ sB 🛁 🚿 30—32
dB 🛁 🚿 51—56 M6—14&alc
Credit cards 1 2 3 5

Ireland

★★★**Tower** The Mall ☎75801 tx80699
🛁 🚿 81 **P**150 Lift ☾ sB 🛁 🚿 32—38
dB 🛁 🚿 51—59 M7—14
Credit cards 1 2 3 5

★★**Dooley's** 30 The Quay ☎73531
Closed 25—27 Dec
rm36 (🛁 33)
Credit cards 1 2 3

C J Deevy & Co 48 Parnell St ☎55719

McConnell Bros William St ☎74037 Toy

T Murphy Morgan St ☎76614 Aud Maz MB VW

Sheridan Cork Rd ☎72891 For

WATERVILLE
Co Kerry (☎0667)

★**Bay View** ☎4122 tx26974
May—Aug
rm29 (🛁 🚿 9) **P** sB8—12 sB 🛁 🚿 11—16
dB16—24 dB 🛁 🚿 22—32 M7—12&alc
Credit cards 2 3

WESTPORT
Co Mayo (☎098)

★★★**Hotel Westport** ☎25122 tx53846
🛁 🚿 49 **P**150 ☾ sB 🛁 🚿 17—28
dB 🛁 🚿 37—45 M12—14&alc
Credit cards 1 2 3 5

★★**Clew Bay** ☎25438
Closed Xmas
rm32 (🛁 🚿 23) sB12—16 sB 🛁 🚿 15—20
dB23—28 dB 🛁 🚿 23—30 M5—10
Credit cards 1 2 3 5

★★**Railway** The Mall ☎25090
🛁 🚿 21 🏠 **P**15 sB 🛁 🚿 16—18
dB 🛁 🚿 28—32 M6—9
Credit cards 1 2 3 5

★★**Westport Ryan** ☎25811 tx53757
🛁 🚿 57 **P**100 ☾ 🔑
Credit cards 1 2 3 4 5

🚗 **Duffy's** Mill St ☎25942

WEXFORD
Co Wexford (☎053)

★★★**New White's** (BW) George's St ☎22311 tx80630
Closed 25 Dec
🛁 🚿 75 **P**80 Lift ☾ sB 🛁 🚿 27—34
dB 🛁 🚿 39—52 M7—13&alc
Credit cards 1 2 3 4 5

★★★**Talbot** Trinity St ☎22566 tx80658
🛁 106 **P**60 Lift ☾
Credit cards 1 2 3 4 5

★★**Ferrycarrig** Ferrycarrig Bridge ☎22999 tx80147
Apr—Oct
🛁 40 **P**50 Lift ☾ sB 🛁 25—28 dB 🛁 44—47
M11 🔑
Credit cards 1 2 3 5

Ferry Bank Motors Ferry Bank ☎22107 Ope

🚗 **Rocklans Service Station** ☎43372

WICKLOW
Co Wicklow (☎0404)

🚗 **Vartry Service** New St ☎3127 Aud Maz VW

WOODENBRIDGE
Co Wicklow (☎0402)

★★**Woodenbridge** ☎5146
rm15 (🛁 🚿 14) **P**100 sB18—25
sB 🛁 🚿 18—25 dB35 dB 🛁 🚿 35
M7—9&alc
Credit cards 1 3

The Customs House, Dublin

Italy and San Marino

International distinguishing signs

San Marino *See page 272*
Area *116,280 sq miles*
Population *57,426,000*
Local time *GMT + 1 (Summer GMT + 2)*

National flag
Vertical tricolour of green, white and red

Leaflets entitled *Motoring in Sicily* and *Motoring in Sardinia* are available to AA members.

How to get there

Although there are several ways of getting to Italy, entry will probably be by way of France or Switzerland. The major passes which are closed in winter, are served by road or rail tunnels. The distance to Milan from the channel ports is approximately 650—700 miles, requiring one or two night stops. Rome is 360 miles further south. Car-sleeper services operate during the summer from Boulogne, Brussels, 's-Hertogenbosh or Paris to Milan.

Motoring regulations and general information

This information should be read in conjunction with the general content of the European ABC (pages 4-26). **Note** as certain regulations and requirements are common to many countries they are covered by one entry in the ABC and the following headings represent some of the subjects dealt with in this way:

AA Agents
Crash or safety helmets
Customs regulations for European countries
Drinking and driving
Fire extinguisher
First-aid kit
Insurance
International distinguishing sign
Medical treatment
Mirrors
Overtaking
Police fines
Radio telephones/Radio transmitters
Road signs
Traffic lights
Tyres
Visitors' registration

Accidents

Fire, police, ambulance (Public emergency service) ☏ 113. No particular procedure is required following an accident, excepting that a report must be made to the insurance company. If the accident involves personal injury it is obligatory that medical assistance is sought for the injured party, and that the incident is reported to the police. On some *autostrade* there are emergency telephones as well as emergency push-button call boxes. See also *Accidents* page 5.

Accommodation

Hotels are classified into categories from *4* to *de luxe*, and there are three categories of pensions. All charges must be agreed by the Provincial Tourist Board (*Ente provinciali per il Turismo*) and they will provide details of hotels in their area. The Italian State Tourist Office publishes an official list of Italian hotels and pensions (*Annuario Alberghi*) which can be consulted at its London office or major travel agents.

Boats

Boat registration documentation is recommended in respect of boats temporarily imported into Italy. See page 6 for further information.

Third party insurance is compulsory in Italian waters for craft with engines of more than 3hp and an Italian translation of the insurance certificate should be carried.

Breakdown

Try to move the car to the verge of the road and place a warning triangle to warn following traffic of the obstruction. The Italian motoring club Automobile Club d'Italia (ACI) provides a breakdown service operated by the Breakdown Service Company of the ACI using its own staff on motorways and authorised repair garages on ordinary roads. The service can be used by any visiting motorist driving a foreign registered vehicle. It provides free towage from the breakdown location to the nearest ACI affiliated garage, but a charge is made if the vehicle is towed elsewhere. Visiting motorists who have purchased Italian petrol coupons (see page 270) will find a '*carte carburante*' coupon included in the tourist booklet which entitles them to receive emergency on-the-spot roadside assistance free of charge. Assistance can be obtained by using the little telephone columns placed along motorways (every 2km) or by dialling 116 from any part of the country on ordinary roads. Any additional services must be paid for. See also *Breakdown* page 6 and *Warning triangle* page 272.

British Embassy/Consulates

The British Embassy together with its consular section is located at *00187 Roma* Via XX Settembre 80A ☎ (06) 4755441/4755551. There are British Consulates in Florence, Genoa, Milan, Naples, and Venice; there are British Consulates with Honorary Consuls in Trieste and Palermo (Sicily) and a Vice-Consulate with Honorary Consul in Cagliari (Sardinia). See also page 6 and *Town Plan of Roma* pages 288-289.

Currency including banking hours

(See also page 9)
The unit of currency is the Italian Lira (*Lit*). At the time of going to press £ = *Lit* 2,446. Denominations of bank notes are *Lit* 1,000, 2,000, 5,000, 10,000, 50,000, 100,000; standard coins are *Lit* 5, 10, 20, 50, 100, 200, 500. The maximum amount of Italian currency which may be taken into or out of Italy is *Lit* 400,000. There are no restrictions on the amount of foreign currency that may be imported and amounts up to *Lit* 5,000,000 may be exported without formality. However, in order to export amounts in excess of *Lit* 5,000,000 it is necessary to declare the amount on entry using the special form (V2) obtainable at frontier Customs posts. This form is then shown to the Customs when leaving Italy.

Most banks are open from Monday to Friday 08.30 to 13.00hrs and from 13.00 to 16.30hrs.

Dimensions and weight restrictions

Private cars and towed trailers or caravans are restricted to the following dimensions — **car** height: 4 metres; width: 2.50 metres; length: with one axle 6 metres, with two or more axles 12 metres. **Trailer/caravan** height: 4 metres; width: 2.30 metres; length: with one axle 6 metres, with two axles 7.50 metres. The maximum permitted overall length of vehicle/trailer or caravan combination is 18 metres.

Trailers with an unladen weight of over 750kg or 50% of the weight of the towing vehicle must have service brakes on all wheels.

Driving licence

(See also page 11)
A valid British driving licence is acceptable in Italy if accompanied by an official Italian translation which may be obtained free from the AA. The minimum age at which a visitor may drive a temporarily imported car is 18 years. However, visitors under 21 years are not permitted to drive vehicles which have a top speed in excess of 180kph (112mph). The minimum ages at which visitors may drive temporarily imported motorcycles are 17 (not exceeding 125cc), 18 (between 125cc—350cc) and 21 (exceeding 350cc).

Emergency messages to tourists

(See also page 11)
Emergency messages to tourists are broadcast daily by the ACI through the Italian radio-television network (RAI).

RAI first channel transmitting on medium wave broadcasts these messages in English, German, French and Spanish at 06.57, 07.57, 09.57, 11.57, 12.57, 13.56, 14.57, 16.57, 18.57, 20.57, 22.57 and 00.27hrs daily throughout the year. *RAI third channel* transmitting on medium wave broadcasts the messages in Italian at 10.00 and 12.00hrs Monday to Saturday.

Fiscal receipt

In Italy the law provides for a special numbered fiscal receipt (ricevuta fiscale) to be issued after paying for a wide range of goods and services including meals and accommodation. This receipt indicates the cost of various goods and services obtained and the total charge after adding VAT. Tourists should ensure that this receipt is issued as spot checks are made by the authorities and both the proprietor and consumer are liable to an on-the-spot fine if the receipt cannot be produced.

Horn, use of

In built up areas the use of the horn is prohibited except in cases of immediate danger. At night flashing headlights may be used instead of the

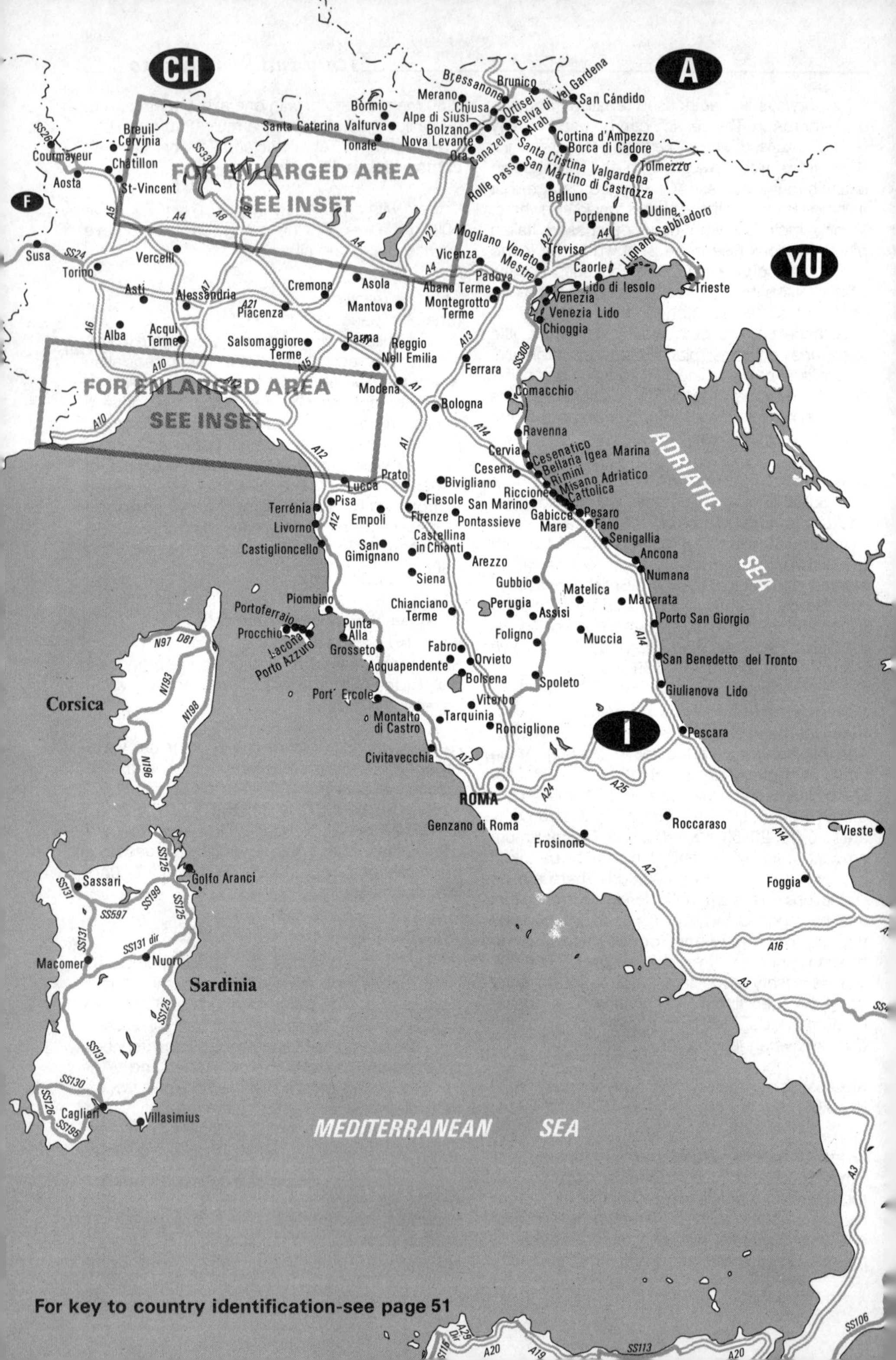

For key to country identification-see page 51

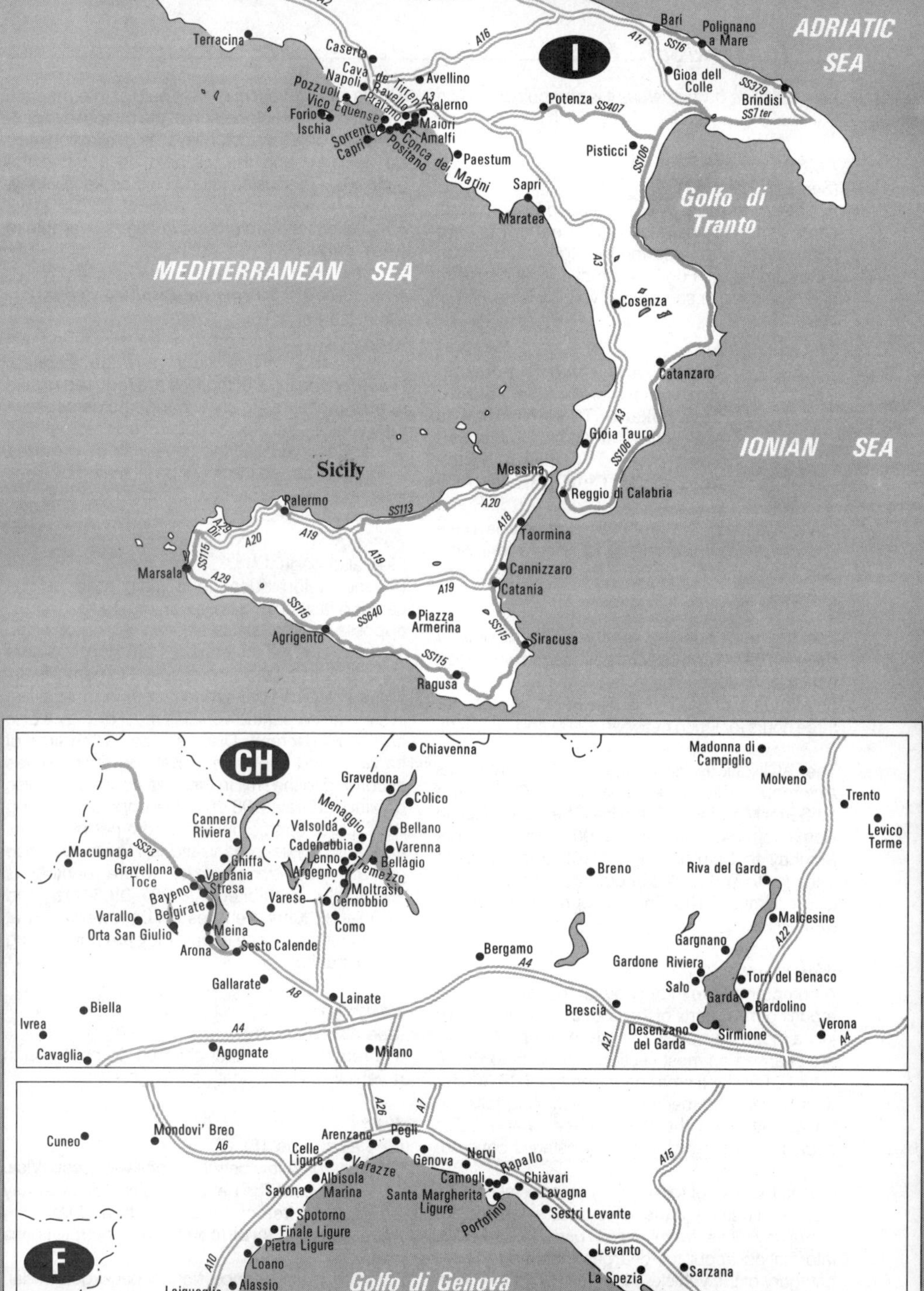

Campobasso
ADRIATIC SEA
Terracina
Caserta
Bari
Polignano a Mare
Cava de' Tirreni
Avellino
Napoli
Pozzuoli
Ravello
Praiano
Salerno
Vico Equense
Forio
Ischia
Maiori
Amalfi
Sorrento
Capri
Positano
Conca dei Marini
Gioa dell Colle
Brindisi
Potenza
Pisticci
Paestum
Sapri
Maratea
Golfo di Tranto
MEDITERRANEAN SEA
Cosenza
Catanzaro
Gioia Tauro
IONIAN SEA
Sicily
Messina
Reggio di Calabria
Palermo
Taormina
Marsala
Cannizzaro
Catania
Piazza Armerina
Agrigento
Siracusa
Ragusa
I
CH
Chiavenna
Madonna di Campiglio
Gravedona
Molveno
Còlico
Trento
Menaggio
Cannero Riviera
Valsoldà
Bellano
Levico Terme
Cadenabbia
Varenna
Macugnaga
Ghiffa
Lenno
Bellàgio
Gravellona Toce
Verbania
Argegno
Tremezzo
Breno
Riva del Garda
Baveno
Stresa
Moltrasio
Varese
Cernobbio
Varallo
Belgirate
Malcesine
Orta San Giulio
Meina
Como
Gargnano
Arona
Sesto Calende
Bergamo
Gardone Riviera
Torri del Benaco
Salo
Gallarate
Garda
Lainate
Bardolino
Biella
Brescia
Ivrea
Desenzano del Garda
Sirmione
Verona
Cavaglia
Agognate
Milano
Cuneo
Mondovi' Breo
Arenzano
Pegli
Celle Ligure
Varazze
Genova
Nervi
Rapallo
Albisola Marina
Camogli
Chiàvari
Savona
Lavagna
Santa Margherita Ligure
Portofino
Sestri Levante
Spotorno
Finale Ligure
Pietra Ligure
F
Levanto
Loano
Sarzana
Golfo di Genova
La Spezia
Alassio
Laigueglia
Lerici
Marina di Carrara
San Bartolomeo al Mare
Marina di Massa
Forte dei Marmi
Diano Marina
Imperia
Ventimiglia
Montecatini Terme
San Remo
Marina di Pietrasanta
Bordighera
Ospedaletti
Lido di Camaiore
Viareggio

horn. *Outside built up areas* it is compulsory to use the horn when warning of approach is necessary.

Lights

(See also page 14)
Full beam headlights can be used only outside cities and towns. Dipped headlights are compulsory when passing through tunnels even if they are well lit. Fog lamps may be used in pairs and only in fog or snow when visibility is restricted.

Motoring clubs

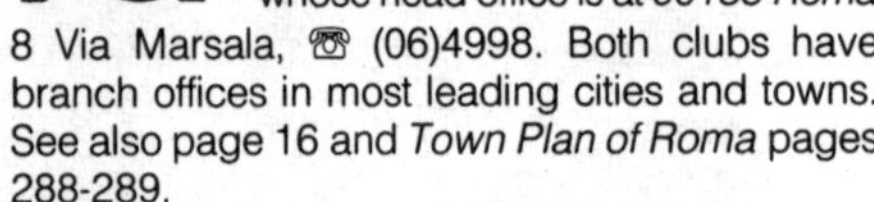

There are two motoring organisations in Italy the **Touring Club Italiano** (TCI) which has its head office at *20122 Milano* 10 Corso Italia. ☎ (02)8526 and the **Automobile Club d'Italia** (ACI) whose head office is at *00185 Roma* 8 Via Marsala, ☎ (06)4998. Both clubs have branch offices in most leading cities and towns. See also page 16 and *Town Plan of Roma* pages 288-289.

The hours of opening for the TCI are usually between 09.00 and 19.00hrs although some open earlier and close later. A few are closed all day on Mondays or Saturdays. However, all close for three hours for lunch between 12.00 and 16.00hrs.

The ACI offices and those of the Provincial Automobile Clubs open between 08.30 and 13.30hrs Monday to Saturday. The head office in Roma opens between 08.00 and 14.00hrs Monday to Saturday and 15.00 and 19.00hrs Tuesday to Friday. A 24-hour information service is in operation. The Roma telephone number is (06)4212.

Motorways

A comprehensive motorway (autostrada) system reaching most parts of the country is available. To join a motorway follow the green signposts. Tolls are charged on most sections *eg* Milan to Rome is *Lit* 18,050 for a small car rising to *Lit* 39,800 for a large car. The methods of calculating tolls are based either on the wheel base or the cubic capacity of the vehicle, and the distance covered.

On the majority of toll motorways a travel ticket is issued on entry and the toll is paid on leaving the motorway. The travel ticket gives all relevant information about toll charges including the toll category of the vehicle. At the exit point the ticket is handed in. On some motorways, notably A8, A9, A11, A14 (Pescara—Lanciano) and A12 (Roma—Civitavecchia) toll is paid at intermediate toll stations for each section of the motorway used. However, on a few motorways the destination must be declared and the toll paid on entering the motorway. There is no refund on a broken journey.

A leaflet entitled *Motorways in Italy* is available to AA members.

Orange badge scheme for disabled drivers

(See also page 16)
In Italy public transport is given priority in town centres and private cars may be banned. However, the local authorities are required to take special measures to allow badge holders to take their vehicles into social, cultural and recreational areas. Reserved parking bays may be provided in some areas and these will be indicated by signs featuring the international disabled symbol.

Parking

(See also page 17)
Parking is forbidden on a main road or one carrying fast moving traffic, on or near tram lines, opposite another stationary vehicle, on or within 12 metres (39½ft) of a bus or tram stop. Violators of parking regulations are subject to heavy fines. There is a *blue zone* (*zona disco*) in most cities; in such areas parked vehicles must display a disc on the windscreen. Discs are set at the time of parking, and show when parking time expires according to the limit in the area concerned. Disc parking operates 08.00—20.00hrs on working days. Discs can be obtained from petrol stations and automobile organisations. There are also *green zones* (*zona verde*) where parking is absolutely prohibited 08.00—09.30hrs and 14.30—16.00hrs. Vehicles will be towed away at the owner's expense even if they are not causing an obstruction.

Passengers

(See also page 18)
It is recommended that children do not travel in a vehicle as front seat passengers.

Petrol

(See also page 18)
Credit cards A few petrol stations will accept Visa.
Duty-free petrol The petrol in the vehicle tank may be imported free of customs duty and tax.
Petrol cans It is **forbidden** to carry petrol in cans in a vehicle.
Petrol coupons A concessionary package of Italian petrol coupons and motorway toll vouchers may be purchased from most AA Travel Agencies and

AA Centres. An additional benefit of the package is a free breakdown and replacement car concession, but see also *Breakdowns* page 6 for details of the 5-Star Service. The package is available to personal callers only and a passport and vehicle registration document must be produced at the time of application. Further information may be obtained from any AA Centre. The package **cannot** be purchased inside Italy but may be obtained from ACI offices at main crossing points and also many ACI offices in port areas if arriving by ship.
Petrol (leaded) Benzina Normale (85—88 octane) and Benzina Super (98—100 octane) grades.
Petrol (unleaded) is sold in Italy as Super Senza Piombo (95 octane). Pumps dispensing unleaded petrol are marked in English Super unleaded.

Postal information
Mail Letters first 20gm *Lit* 550, postcards *Lit* 450 (max 5 words). Express surcharge *Lit* 1,500.
Post offices There are 14,000 post offices in Italy. Opening hours are from 08.15—13.00hrs Monday to Friday and 08.15—12.00hrs Saturday. On the last day of the month offices close at 12.00hrs.

Postcheques
(See also page 20)
Postcheques may be cashed at all post offices for a fixed sum of *Lit* 150,000 per cheque. Counter positions are identified by the *Postcheque* window sticker. See *Postal information* for post office opening hours.

Priority
Traffic on state highways (*Strade Statali*), which are all numbered and indicated by signs, has right of way, as do public service vehicles and, on postal routes, buses belonging to the service. These bus routes are indicated by a special sign. See also *Priority including Roundabouts* page 21.

If two vehicles are travelling in opposite directions and the drivers of each vehicle want to turn left, they must pass in front of each other (not drive round as in the UK).

Public holidays
Official public holidays in Italy for 1987 are given below. Many towns have local public holidays on the Feast Day of their Patron Saint. See also *Public holidays* page 21.
January 1 (New Year's Day)
January 6 (Epiphany)
April 20 (Easter Monday)
April 25 (Liberation Day)
May 1 (Labour Day)
August 15* (Assumption)
November 1† (All Saints' Day)
December 8 (Immaculate Conception)
December 25 (Christmas Day)
December 26 *(Boxing day)
*Saturday †Sunday

Roads
Main and secondary roads are generally good and there are an exceptional number of bypasses. Mountain roads are usually well engineered; see pages 37-48 for details of mountain passes. See also *Road conditions* page 22.

Seat Belts
The wearing of seat belts is not compulsory in Italy. However, if your car is fitted with seat belts it is strongly recommended that you wear them in the interests of safety.

Shopping hours
Generally *food shops* are open Monday to Saturday 08.00—13.00hrs and 16.00—20.00hrs, but close at 13.00hrs on Thursday. Most *other shops* are open Monday to Saturday 09.00—13.00hrs and 16.00—19.30hrs, but only open at 16.00hrs on Monday.

Speed limits
(See also page 22)
The maximum speed limit in built-up areas, unless otherwise indicated is 50kph (31mph). Mopeds are restricted to 40kph (24mph) on all roads unless there is a lower limit. On normal roads limits are 80kph to 110kph; motorways 90kph to 140 kph depending on the cc of the vehicle's engine. Limits are signposted. Any infringement of speed regulations can result in punitive fines of up to £300, and these penalties have been enforced.

Spiked or studded tyres
Spiked or studded tyres may be used provided that:
a they are used between 15 November and 15 March;
b they do not exceed 120 kph (74 mph) on motorways, and 90 kph (56 mph) on other roads. All signed lower limits must not be exceeded;
c they must not exceed a total weight of 3,500kg;
d they are fitted to all wheels, including those of a trailer (if any).

Additionally visiting motorists are advised to have mud flaps fitted behind the rear wheels. Spiked tyres may be used on roads where wheel chains are compulsory, provided they are used on all four wheels. See also *Cold weather touring* page 8.

Tourist Information

(See also page 24)
The Italian State Tourist Office (ENIT) has an office in London at 1 Princess street, W1R 8AY ☏ 01-408 1254. It will be pleased to assist you with any information regarding tourism. In Italy there are three organisations the *Ente Nazionale Italiano per il Turismo* (ENIT) with offices at frontiers and ports: the *Assessorati Regionali per il Turismo* (ART) and the *Ente Provinciale per il Turismo* (EPT) who will assist tourists through their regional and provincial offices. The *Aziende Autonome di Cura Soggiorno e Turismo* (AACST) have offices in places of recognised tourist interest and concern themselves exclusively with matters of local interest.

Using the telephone

(See also page 24)
Insert coins **before** lifting receiver, dialling tone short and long tones. When making calls to subscribers within Italy precede number with relevant area code (shown in parentheses against town entry in gazetteer). Use *Lit* 200 *gettoni* tokens available at bars, tobacconists and slot machines or coins in new payphones.
International callbox identification Yellow sign.
Telephone rates The cost of a call to the UK if dialled direct is twelve tokens per minute.
What to dial for Irish Republic 00 353.
What to dial for the UK 00 44.

Warning triangle

The use of a warning triangle is compulsory for all vehicles except two-wheelers. It should be used to give advance warning of a stationary vehicle which is parked on a road in fog, near a bend, on a hill or at night when the rear lights have failed. The triangle must be placed on the road not less than 50 metres (55yds) behind the vehicle. Motorists who fail to do this are liable to an administrative fine of between *Lit* 5,000 and *Lit* 20,000. See also *Warning triangles/Hazard warning lights* page 25.

Wheel chains

Roads where these are compulsory are marked by a national sign. Chains cannot be hired in Italy but can be purchased at garages or vehicle accessory shops everywhere. Approximate prices per pair are as follows: iron *Lit* 10,000—30,000, steel/iron, *Lit* 20,000—40,000. Drivers of vehicles proceeding without wheel chains on roads where they are compulsory are liable to prosecution. See also *Cold weather touring* page 8.

Winter conditions

(See also page 26)
It is possible to approach northern Italy, Milan and Turin by road or train tunnels.

From Switzerland via Simplon rail tunnel; via the Grand St Bernard road tunnel; via the St Gotthard road tunnel; via the San Bernardino road tunnel; also via the Julier and Maloja passes.

From France via the Mont Blanc road tunnel; via the Fréjus road tunnel; in favourable weather, via the Lautaret and Montgenèvre passes; also via the French Riveria coast, entering at Ventimiglia.

From Austria via the Resia and Brenner passes; wheel chains may be necessary in severe weather. The Plöcken pass is occasionally closed in winter, but the roads entering Italy at Dobbiaco and Tarvisio are normally free from obstruction.

Roads within the country, apart from those in the Dolomites, are not seriously affected in winter although during January and February certain highways across the Apennines may be obstructed. Touring in the Dolomites is generally confined to the period from early May to mid October.

San Marino

National flag *White over blue in two strips of equal breadth*

A small Republic with an area of 23 sq miles and a population of 21,500 situated in the hills of Italy near Rimini. The official information office in the UK is the Italian State Tourist Office at 1 Princes Street, London W1R 8AY. The chief attraction is the city of San Marino on the slopes of Monte Titano. Its laws, motoring regulations and emergency telephone number are the same as Italy.

Prices are in Italian Lire

Abbreviations
Gl Generale
pza piazza

ABANO TERME
Padova (☎409)

★★★★**Trieste & Victoria** (SRS) via Pietro d'Abano ☎669101 tx430250
Mar—Nov
113 **P**80 Lift ☾ sB 75000—90000 dB 110000—140000

★★★**Bristol Buja** via Monteortone 2 ☎669390 tx430210
rm144 (139) **P**80 Lift ☾ sB 57500—88500 dB 86000—126000 M30000—40000
Credit cards 1 2 3 5

★★★***Terme Milano*** viale Delle Terme 169 ☎669139
9 Mar—6 Jan
rm101 (73) **P**70 Lift ☾
Credit cards 1 2 3 5

ACQUAPENDENTE
Viterbo (☎0763)

★**Roma** viale del Fiore 13 ☎74016
rm26 (10) **P**50 sB17500 dB33200 dB 390000 M16000

ACQUI TERME
Alessandria (☎0144)

Carrara corso Divisione Acqui 7 ☎53733 **P** Aud VW

AGOGNATE
Novara (☎0321)

★★***Meridiana*** Autostrade Torino ☎23156
Closed 9—22 Aug
17 **P** Lift ☾ Pool

AGRIGENTO See **SICILIA (SICILY)**

ALASSIO
Savona (☎0182)

★★★★**Diana** via Garibaldi 110 ☎42701 tx270655
25 Mar—23 Nov & 21 Dec—1 Feb
77 **P**45 Lift ☾ sB 51000—78000 dB 92000—136000 M32000—37000&alc Beach sea
Credit cards 1 2 3

★★★★**Spiaggia** via Roma 78 ☎43403 tx271617
83 Lift ☾ sB 65000—75000 dB 110000—140000 M28000—36000 Beach sea
Credit cards 1 3

★★★**Flora** Lungomare Cadorna 22 ☎40336
Mar—Oct
rm45 (29) **P**7 Lift ☾ sB36500—45500 sB 45500—58500 dB58000—65000 dB 65000—78000 M28000 Beach sea
Credit cards 1 2 3 5

★★★**Majestic** via L-da-Vinci 300 ☎42721
28 Apr—4 Oct
77 Lift ☾ sB 30000—40000

dB 50000—68000 M12000—16000 Beach sea

★★★**Méditerranée** via Roma 63 ☎42564
Apr—Oct
rm80 (75 4) A24rm Lift ☾ **DPn**53000—100000 Beach sea
Credit cards 1 2 3

★★***Mare*** via Boselli 24 ☎40635
rm49 (48) Lift Beach sea
Credit cards 1 3

★★**Toscana** via L-da-Vinci ☎40657
65 **P**15 Lift ☾ sB 39000—48000 dB 70000—76000 M20000 Beach

★★**Villa Carlotta** via Adelasia 11 ☎40463
Apr—Oct
rm16 (8) **P** sB16000—26000 sB 18500—31000 dB32000—52000 dB 37000—62000 M20000—25000 Beach sea

ALBA
Cuneo (☎0173)

★★**Savona** pza Savona ☎42381
106 **P**25 Lift ☾ sB 40000 dB 60450 M20000—22000
Credit cards 1 2 3 5

ALBISOLA MARINA
Savona (☎019)

★★★***Corallo*** via M-Repetto 116 ☎41784
rm22 (19) **P**13 sea
Credit cards 2 3 5

ALESSANDRIA
Alessandria (☎0131)

★★**Europa** via Palestro ☎446228
33 **P**10 Lift ☾ sB 46500 dB 81000 M25000 S15%
Credit cards 1 3 4 5

ALPE DI SIUSI
Bolzano (☎0471)

★★★***Eurotel*** ☎72928 tx400181
Xmas—Etr & Jul—mid Sep
84 **P**50 ☾ mountains
Credit cards 2 5

AMALFI
Salerno (☎089)

★★★★**Santa Caterina** via Statale ☎871012 tx770093
70 A9rm **P**30 Lift ☾ sB 95000—115000 dB 160000—200000 M40000—45000 Beach sea
Credit cards 1 2 3 5

★★★**Aurora** pza dei Prontontini 7 ☎871209
Apr—15 Oct
30 **P** Lift ☾ sB 35000—46500 dB 64500—80500 Beach sea
Credit cards 1 2 3 5

★★★**Luna** Lungomare ☎871002 tx770161
45 **P**25 Lift ☾ sB 54000—68000 dB 88000—100000 M35000 Beach sea
Credit cards 1 2 3 4 5

★★★**Miramalfi** ☎871588
rm44 (32) **P**40 Lift ☾ sB31000—37000 sB 37000—43500 dB58000—68000 dB 63500—78000 M24000 Beach sea
Credit cards 1 2 3 4 5

★★**Bellevue** via Nazionale 163 (n.rest) ☎871846
Apr—Sep
23 **P**15 ☾ dB 55000 sea

★★***Marina Riviea*** via F-Gioia 22 ☎871104
15 Mar—Oct
rm18 (16) **P**3 Lift Beach sea

At **LONE** (2.5km W)

★★★***Caleidoscopio*** via P-Leone X6 ☎871220
Apr—10 Oct
24 A7rm **P**35 ☾ Beach sea

At **MINORI** (3km E)

★★***Caporal*** ☎877408
43 A18rm **P** ☾ Beach

★★***Santa Lucia*** via Nazionale 44 ☎877142
Mar—Oct
rm29 (27) Lift
Credit cards 2 3

ANACAPRI See **CAPRI (ISOLA DI)**

ANCONA
Ancona (☎071)

★★★***AGIP*** Palombina Nuova (SS 16 Adriatic km293) ☎888241 tx611627
50 **P** Lift ☾

★★★**Jolly** Rupi di via XXIX Settembre 14 ☎201171 tx560343
89 **P** Lift ☾ sB 75000 dB 115000
Credit cards 1 2 3 4 5

At **PORTONOVO** (14km SE)

★★***Fortino Napoleonico*** via Poggio ☎801124
30 **P**50 ☾ Beach sea
Credit card 2

SAMET via de Gasperi 80 ☎31568 M/c For

AOSTA
Aosta (☎0165)

★★★***Ambassador*** via Duca degli Abruzzi ☎42230
rm43 (40) **P** Lift ☾ mountains

★★★**Motelalp** (n.rest) ☎40007
52 **P**50 ☾ sB 33500—48000 dB 51000—72500 mountains
Credit card 2

★★★**Valle d'Aosta** corso Ivrea 146 ☎41845 tx212472 →

Italy

🛁 104 🚗 **P**100 Lift ☾ sB🛁 50500—90500 dB🛁 77000—126000 mountains
Credit cards 1 2 3 5

★★**Gran Paradiso** via L'Binel 12 ☎40654
🛁 33 **P** ☾ sB🛁 35000—38000 dB🛁 56000—62000 M16000 mountains

★★**Mignon** viale Gran San Bernardo 7 ☎40980 tx215013
🛁 22 🚗 **P**30 ☾ sB🛁 39000—42500 dB🛁 65000—73000 mountains
Credit cards 1 2 3 4 5

★★**Rayon de Soleil** viale Gran St-Bernardo ☎362247
15 Mar—Oct
🛁 39 🚗 **P**30 Lift ☾ sB🛁 39500—49500 dB🛁 59000—77000 M18000 ≋ mountains
Credit cards 2 3

★★**Turin** via Torino 14 ☎44593
20 Dec—15 Nov
🛁🚿 51 🚗 **P**11 Lift ☾
sB🛁🚿 32500—48000
dB🛁🚿 51000—73000 M16500 mountains
Credit cards 1 2 3 5

🚙 **F Gal** via Monte Emilius 9 ☎2353 AR

ARABBA
Belluno (☎0436)

★***Posta*** ☎79105
Dec—Apr & Jun—Sep
🛁🚿 13 🚗 **P** mountains

ARENZANO
Genova (☎010)

★★★***Miramare*** ☎9127325
rm42 (🛁 25) 🚗 Lift ☾ sea
Credit cards 2 3 5

★**Europa** ☎9127384
May—Sep
rm13 (🛁 3) 🚗 **P**20 sB17500 dB32000 dB🛁 38000 M13500 sea
Credit cards 1 2 3 4 5

AREZZO
Arezzo (☎0575)

★★★**Continentale** pza G-Monaco 7 ☎21251
🛁 78 **P** Lift ☾ sB🛁 44000 dB🛁 73000 M17000
Credit cards 1 2 3 5

🚙 **Magi Ezio di Piero & Corrado Magi** via M-Perennio 24 ☎21264 AR

ARGEGNO
Como (☎031)

★***Belvedere*** ☎82116
Apr—Oct
rm17 (🛁🚿 11) **P** ☾ lake

ARONA
Novara (☎0322)

★★★***Antares*** via Gramsci 9 (n.rest) ☎3438
🛁🚿 51 🚗 **P**25 Lift ☾ lake
Credit cards 1 2 3 5

Italy

ASOLO
Treviso (☎0423)

★★★★**Villa Cipriani** (CIGA/Relais et Châteaux) ☎55444 tx411060
🛁🚿 32 🚗 **P**45 Lift ☾
sB🛁🚿 210000—240000
dB🛁🚿 300000—360000 Mfr75000&alc t% mountains
Credit cards 1 2 3 4 5

ASSISI
Perugia (☎075)

★★★**Giotto** via Fontabella 41 ☎812209 tx660122
15 Mar—15 Nov
rm72 (🛁🚿 62) 🚗 **P**20 ☾ sB32800 sB🛁🚿 45300 dB50600 dB🛁🚿 69000 M26000
Credit cards 1 2 3 5

★★★**Subasio** via Frate Elia 2 ☎812206 tx662029
🛁🚿 66 🚗 **P**100 Lift ☾ sB🛁🚿 70000 dB🛁🚿 100000 M20000 mountains
Credit cards 1 2 3 4 5

★★★**Windsor Savola** porta San Francesco 1 ☎812210 tx660122
🛁 33 🚗 Lift ☾ sB🛁 45000 dB🛁 67000 M20000
Credit cards 1 2 3 5

★★**Umbra** via degli Archi 2 ☎812240
rm27 (🛁🚿 22) ☾ sB29800 sB🛁🚿 42300 dB44600 dB🛁🚿 63000 mountains
Credit cards 1 2 3 5

ASTI
Asti (☎0141)

★★★***Salera*** via M-Marello 19 ☎211815
🛁 54 🚗 **P** Lift ☾

🚙 **G Vignetti** via Ticino 1 ☎55016 M/c **P**

AVELLINO
Avellino (☎0825)

★★★**Jolly** via Tuoro Cappuccini 97A ☎32191 tx722584
rm74 (🛁 57) **P** Lift ☾ sB🛁 65000 dB🛁 106000
Credit cards 1 2 3 4 5

BADIA (LA) See **ORVIETO**

BARBARANO See **GARDONE RIVIERA**

BARDOLINO
Verona (☎045)

★★★**Vela d'Or** 22 Cisano ☎7210067
Apr—Sep
🛁 50 **P**30 ☾ sB🛁 35000—44500 dB🛁 58000—77000 M18000 🎾 ≋ lake

🚙 **A Tortella** via Marconi 26 ☎7210053

BARI
Bari (☎080)

★★★★**Grand Ambasciatori** via Omodeo 51 ☎410077 tx810405
🛁 177 🚗 **P**120 Lift ☾ sB🛁 136100 dB🛁 194500 M31000 ≋
Credit cards 1 2 3 5

★★★★**Palace** via Lombardi 13 ☎216551 tx810111
🛁🚿 210 🚗 **P** Lift ☾
sB🛁🚿 113000—150500
dB🛁🚿 202500—241000

★★★**Boston** (BW) via Piccinni 155 (n.rest) ☎216633
🛁🚿 70 🚗 **P**15 Lift ☾
sB🛁🚿 54000—72000
dB🛁🚿 91000—121000
Credit cards 1 2 3 4 5

★★★**Jolly** via G-Petroni 15 ☎364366 tx810274
🛁 164 🚗 Lift ☾ sB🛁 95000—103000 dB🛁 145000—156000
Credit cards 1 2 3 4 5

🚙 **Autoservizio** traversa 65 Japigia 44 ☎330158 **P** For

At **TORRE A MARE** (12km E)

★★★***AGIP*** SS 16km 816 ☎300001 tx611627
🚿 95 **P** Lift ☾

BAVENO
Novara (☎0323)

★★★**Lido Palace** Strada Statale Sempione 30 ☎24444 tx200697
🛁🚿 100 🚗 **P**60 Lift ☾
sB🛁🚿 63000—70000
dB🛁🚿 96000—130000 M30000—35000 🎾 ≋ mountains lake
Credit cards 1 2 3 4 5

★★**Beau Rivage** viale della Vittoria 36 ☎24534
Apr—Sep
rm80 (🛁🚿 50) A8rm **P**50 Lift ☾ sB24500—34500 sB🛁🚿 29000—41000 dB35000—46000 dB🛁🚿 45000—58000 M15000 lake
Credit cards 1 2 3 4 5

★★**Simpson** via Garibaldi 52 ☎24112 tx200217
20 Mar—Oct
🛁 100 🚗 **P**100 Lift ☾ sB🛁 57000—75000 dB🛁 73000—91000 t% 🎾 ≋ lake
Credit cards 1 2 3 5

★★**Splendid** via Sempione 12 ☎24583 tx200217
20 Mar—Oct
🛁 100 🚗 **P**100 Lift ☾ sB🛁 54500—84500 dB🛁 79000—117000 M25000—40000 T% ≋ lake
Credit cards 1 2 3 5

At **FERIOLO** (3km NW)

★★**Carillon** Strada Nazionale del Sempione 2 ☎28115
Apr—Sep
🛁🚿 26 **P**30 sB🛁🚿 34500—44500 dB🛁🚿 55000—62000 M18000 lake
Credit cards 1 2 3 5

BELGIRATE
Novara (☎0322)

★★★**Milano** (BW) via Sempione 4 ☎76525 tx200490

60 P40 Lift sB 36500—56500 dB 68000—88000 M13000—22000 lake
Credit cards 1 2 3 4 5

★★★**Villa Carlotta** via Sempione 119 76461 tx200490

120 P6 Lift sB 56500—73500 dB 92000—112000 M17000—21000 lake
Credit cards 1 2 3 4 5

BELLAGIO
Como (031)

★★★★**Villa Serbelloni** via Roma 1 950216 tx380330

mid Apr—mid Oct
82 P100 Lift
sB 165000—185000
dB 240000—270000 M55000—65000 lake
Credit cards 2 3

★★★***Lac*** pza Mazzini 950320

4 Apr—10 Oct
rm50 (49) P3 Lift lake
Credit cards 1 2 3 5

★★★***Ambassadeur Metropole*** pza Mazzini 5 950409 tx380861

Mar—Oct
rm46 (40) Lift lake
Credit card 2

★★**Belvedere** via Valassina 33 950410

Apr—10 Oct
rm50 (45) P30 Lift sB33500 sB 50500 dB56000 dB 69000—77000 M19000 lake
Credit cards 2 3

★★**Florence** pza Mazzini 950342

20 Apr—10 Oct
rm48 (28) P Lift sB36000—38000 sB 60000 dB 81000—82000 M19000 mountains lake
Credit cards 1 2 3 5

BELLANO
Como (0341)

★★**Meridiana** via C-Alberto 19 821126

rm40 (36) A5rm P20 Lift sB30000 sB 40000 dB52000 dB 65000 M18000 mountains lake
Credit card 5

BELLARIA IGEA MARINA
Forli (0541)

At **IGEA MARINA**

★★★***Touring Spiaggia*** via la Pinzoni 217 630419

20 May—20 Sep
31 P20 Lift Beach sea

BELLUNO
Belluno (0437)

B Mortti via T-Veccellio 117 30790 Alf

BERGAMO
Bergamo (035)

★★★**Excelsior San Marco** pza Repubblica 6 232132 tx301295

151 Lift sB 92800 dB 148100 M35000
Credit cards 2 3

Italy

★★**Agnelo d'Oro** via Gombito 22 249883

20 Lift sB 32500 dB 56000 M30000
Credit cards 2 3 5

BIELLA
Vercelli (015)

★★★**Astoria** viale Roma 9 (n.rest) 20545 tx214083

50 P Lift sB 88000 dB 126000
Credit cards 1 2 3 5

BIVIGLIANO
Firenze (055)

★★**Giotto Park** 406608 tx574316

Mar—20 Oct
rm36 (32) A18rm P40 sB41000—52000 sB 51000—88000 dB61000—86000 dB 81000—136000 M22000—24000 mountains
Credit cards 1 2 5

BOLOGNA
Bologna (051)

★★★★★***Royal Carlton*** (SRS) via Montebello 8 554141 tx510356

250 P400 Lift
Credit cards 2 3

★★★★**Jolly** pza XX Settembre 2 264405 tx510076

176 Lift sB 114000 dB 165000
Credit cards 1 2 3 4 5

★★★***AGIP*** via EM Lepido 203/4 401130

60 P Lift

★★★***Crest* (see page 50)** pza della Constituzione 372172 tx510676

164 P150 Lift
Credit cards 1 2 3 4 5

★★★***Garden*** via Lame 109 522222

83 P Lift

AMM via Po 2A 492552 M/c Ren

C Cesari via della Grada 9 554554 VW

Cisa Via A-di-Vincenzo 6 370434 AR

BOLSENA
Viterbo (0761)

★★**Columbus** Lungo Lago 27 98009

15 Mar—15 Oct
42 P16 Lift sB 36000—47000 dB 54000—72000 M20000—24000 lake
Credit cards 2 5

BOLZANO-BOZEN
Bolzano (0471)

★★★★**Alpi** via Alto Adige 35 970535 tx400156

110 Lift sB 81000 dB 132000 M22000 mountains
Credit cards 1 2 3 4 5

★★★**Grifone** pza Walther 7 977056 tx400081

rm132 (101) P80 Lift sB50500 sB 98500 dB101000 dB 141000 M23000 mountains
Credit cards 1 2 3 4 5

★★**Luna** via Piave 15 975642 tx400309

rm95 (86) P100 Lift sB37000 sB 62000 dB69000 dB 109000 M19500
Credit cards 1 2 4 5

★**Citta di Bolzano** pza Walther 21 9755221 tx401434

rm102 (79) P Lift sB35000 sB 53000 dB61000 dB 86000
Credit cards 1 2 3 4 5

★**Scala** via Brennero 11 41111

60 P50 Lift sB 53000—57000 dB 79000—89000 M alc mountains
Credit cards 1 2 3 5

M Mattevi 6 via Roma 96 48070 AR Cit

Mich via Galileo Galilei 6 41119 M/c **P** AR DJ Hon

1000 Miglia via Macello 13 26340 Ope Vau

SAS Motor via Macello 54 25373 BMW

E Tasini via Roma N61B 916465

BORCA DI CADORE
Belluno (0435)

At **CORTE DI CADORE** (2km E)

★★★***Bolte*** 82001 tx440072

15 Jun—21 Sep & 22 Dec—16 Mar
84 P100 Lift mountains
Credit cards 1 2 3 5

BORDIGHERA
Imperia (0184)

★★★★**Grand del Mare** Portico della Punta 34 262201 tx270535

22 Dec—Oct
103 P70 Lift sB 84000—109000 dB 138000—196500 M45000 Beach sea
Credit cards 2 3

★★***Excelsior*** via Gl-Biamonti 30 262979

20 Dec—20 Oct
rm43 (30) P50 Lift sea

★★**Villa Elisa** via Romana 70 261313

20 Dec—15 Oct
32 P20 Lift sB 35000—50000 dB 51000—76000 M20000—25000 Beach sea
Credit cards 1 2 3 4

BÒRMIO
Sondrio (0342)

★★***Posta*** via Roma 66 904753 tx321425

Dec—Apr & Jul—Sep
55 Lift
Credit cards 2 3 5

BRENO
Brescia (☎0364)

★★**Giardino** ☎22376

rm40 (36) P100 Lift sB14500—19500 sB 19500—23500 dB28000—35000 dB 33000—37000 M12000 mountains
Credit card 2

BRESCIA
Brescia (☎030)

★★★***AGIP*** viale Bornata 42 (SS 11km 236) ☎361654

42 P ☾

Brescia Motori via L-Appollonio 17A ☎50051 AR

BRESSANONE-BRIXEN
Bolzano (☎0472)

★★★**Elefante** Rio Bianco 4 ☎22288

Mar—Nov
43 A14rm P40 ☾ sB 70000—80000 dB 140000—160000 M25000 mountains

★★★**Gasser** via Giardini 19 ☎22105

22 Mar—19 Oct
30 P30 Lift ☾ sB 37000—50000 dB 74000—100000 M13000—14000 mountains
Credit cards 1 2 4 5

★★**Corona d'Oro-Goldene Krone** via Fienili 4 ☎24154

27 Feb—15 Nov & 20 Dec—10 Jan
36 P18 Lift sB 32000—36000 dB 56000—64000 M13000—18000 mountains
Credit card 2

F I Lanz via Stazione 32 ☎22226 **P** Aud VW

A Pecora via V-Veneto 57 ☎23277

BREUIL-CERVINIA
Aosta (☎0166)

★★**Valdôtain** Lac Bleu ☎949428 tx211822

Dec—Apr & Jun—Sep
35 P15 Lift ☾ sB 30000—45000 dB 50000—75000 M30000 mountains lake
Credit cards 1 2

BRINDISI
Brindisi (☎0831)

★★★***Internazionale*** Lungomare Regina Margherita ☎23475

87 P Lift ☾ sea

Biagio via Cappuccini 70 ☎23037 M/c Ope

T Marino via E-Fermi 7, Zone Industriale ☎24094 M/c **P** For

BRUNICO-BRUNECK
Bolzano (☎0474)

★★★***Posta*** Greben 9 ☎85127 tx400530

rm64 (59) **P** ☾ mountains

CADENABBIA
Como (☎0344)

★**Beau-Rivage** via Regina 87 (n.rest) ☎40426

Apr—Oct

Italy

rm20 (9) P20 sB22000—26500 sB 30000—32500 dB35000—37000 dB 52000—53000 S10% mountains lake
Credit cards 1 2

CAGLIARI See **SARDEGNA (ISOLA) (SARDINIA)**

CAMAIORE (LIDO DI)
Lucca (☎0584)

L Galletti via del Termine 2 ☎90024 DJ Vol

CAMOGLI
Genova (☎0185)

★★★★**Cenobio dei Dogi** via Cuneo 34 ☎770041 tx211116

Jun—Jan
88 P80 Lift ☾ sB 97000—103500 dB 175000—259000 M55000 Beach sea mountains
Credit card 2

★★**Casmona** via Garibaldi 103 ☎770015

rm34 (22) ☾ sB30000—36000 sB 35000—41000 dB55000—60000 dB 60000—67000 M18000 sea mountains
Credit cards 1 2 3 4 5

CAMPOBASSO
Campobasso (☎0874)

P Vitale via XXIV Maggio 95 ☎61069 Aud Mer Por VW

CANAZEI
Trento (☎0462)

★★**Croce Bianca** via Roma 3 ☎61111

15 Jun—10 Oct
41 P35 Lift ☾ DPn45000—64000 mountains
Credit cards 1 2 3 5

CANDELI See **FIRENZE (FLORENCE)**

CÀNNERO RIVIERA
Novara (☎0323)

★★★**Cannero** Lungolago 2 ☎788046

20 Mar—30 Oct
32 P20 Lift sB 42000—45000 dB 62000—74000 M20000—22000 lake
Credit cards 1 2 3

CANNIZZARO See **SICILIA (SICILY)**

CAORLE
Venezia (☎0421)

★★**Excelsior** viale Vespucci 11 ☎81515

15 May—28 Sep
55 P40 Lift ☾ sB 38500—45500 dB 77000—91000 M17000 Beach sea
Credit cards 2 3

G Cecotto via Strada Nuova 64 ☎81315 M/c

CAPRI (ISOLA DI)
Napoli (☎081)

CAPRI

★★★★★**Grand Quisiana** (CIGA) via Camerelle 2 ☎8370788 tx710520

Apr—Oct
150 Lift ☾ DPn162800—261800 sea
Credit cards 1 2 3 5

At **ANACAPRI** (3.6km W)

★★★**San Michele** via G-Orlandi 1 ☎8371427

60 P50 Lift ☾ sB 41000—60000 dB 66000—81000 M26000 sea
Credit cards 1 3

CARRARA (MARINA DI)
Massa Carrara (☎0585)

★★***Mediterraneo*** via Genova 2 bis ☎635222

rm50 (48) P30 Lift ☾ sea

CASERTA
Caserta (☎0823)

★★★**Jolly** viale V-Veneto 9 ☎325222 tx710548

92 **P** Lift ☾ sB 72000 dB 105000
Credit cards 1 2 3 4 5

Colombo via Colombo 56 ☎25268 **P** Cit Lan Mer Ren

M Masulio via Roma 78—92 ☎26441 AR

CASTELLINA IN CHIANTI
Siena (☎0577)

★★**Villa-Casalecchi** (**DPn**) (1km S) ☎740240

Apr—Oct
19 A3rm P30 DPn110000 mountains
Credit cards 2 3 5

At **RICAVO** (4km N)

★★★**Tenuta di Ricavo** ☎740221

Apr—mid Oct
25 A16rm P30 Pn75000—140000 mountains

CASTIGLIONCELLO
Livorno (☎0586)

★★★***Miramare*** via Marconi 8 ☎752435

Etr—15 Sep
rm64 (60) A6rm **P** Lift ☾ sea

★★***Guerrini*** via Roma 12 ☎752047
Closed Nov & public hols
rm22 (12) P2 sea
Credit cards 2 3 5

CATANIA See **SICILIA (SICILY)**

CATANZARO
Catanzaro (☎0961)

★★★***AGIP*** exit Strada due Mari ☎51791

76 **P** Lift ☾

Autosabim Nuova Bellavista 35—37 M/c **P** For

CATTOLICA
Forlì (☎0541)

★★★★***Victoria Palace*** via Carducci 24 ☎962921 tx550459

15 May—28 Sep
🛁98 **P** Lift ☾ Beach sea

★★★**Diplomat** via del Turismo 9 ☎962200

31 May—15 Sep
🛁80 **P**40 Lift ☾ sB🛁28000—34000 dB🛁45000—62000 M12000—15000 ✂ Beach sea

★★★**Europa-Monetti** via Curiel 33 ☎961159

May—Sep
rm77 (🛁🚿72) 🚗 **P**50 Lift ☾ sB23000—29000 sB🛁🚿23000—29000 dB48000—64000 dB🛁🚿48000—64000 M17000—20000 ✂ ⛴ Beach

★★★***Gambrinus*** via Carducci 86 ☎961347

May—Oct
rm42 (🚿33) **P** Lift Beach sea

★★★**Maxim** via Facchini 7 ☎962137 tx551084

15 May—20 Sep
🚿55 **P**40 Lift ☾ sB🚿25000—29000 dB🚿46000—54000 M12000—16000

★★★**Moderno-Majestic** viale d'Annunzio 13 ☎961169

15 May—22 Sep
🛁60 **P**40 Lift ☾ sB🛁25000—35000 dB🛁45000—55000 M15000—16000 Beach sea
Credit card [2]

★★★**Rosa** via Carducci 80 ☎963275

20 May—20 Sep
🛁🚿53 **P**40 Lift ☾ **Pn**36000—47000 sea

★★**Senior** viale del Prete ☎963443

May—Sep
🛁🚿43 **P**12 Lift ☾ sB🛁🚿16000—24500 dB🛁🚿30000—44000 Mfr15000 ⛴

★**Bellariva** via Fiume 10 ☎961609

5 Apr—Sep
rm26 (🛁🚿16) A12rm **P**10 ☾ sB20500—28500 sB🛁🚿24500—32500 dB21000—22500 dB🛁🚿23000—24500 M10000—14000 ✂ Beach

🚘 **A Fernando** via del Prete 4 ☎961055 M/c **P** Aud VW

CAVA DE TIRRENI
Salerno (☎089)

★★**Victoria** corso Mazzini 4 ☎465048
🛁🚿61 🚗 **P**40 Lift ☾ sB🛁🚿29500—35500 dB🛁🚿50000—55000 M15000 ✂ mountains
Credit cards [2] [3] [5]

At **CORPO DI CAVA** (4km SW)

★★**Scapolatiello** ☎463911
🛁54 🚗 **P** Lift ☾ sB🛁32000—34500 dB🛁56000—59000 M15000—18000 ⛴ mountains
Credit cards [3] [5]

Italy

CAVAGLIA
Vercelli (☎0161)

★★***Prateria*** ☎96115

Mar—Nov
🛁32 🚗 **P** mountains

CAVI See **LAVAGNA**

CELLE LIGURE
Savona (☎19)

★★★***San Michele*** via Monte Tabor 26 ☎990017

Jun—Sep
rm57 (🛁51) **P**38 Lift ☾ ⛴ sea

CERNOBBIO
Como (☎031)

★★★★★**Villa d'Este** via Regina 40 ☎511471 tx380025

Apr—Oct
🛁🚿180 A40rm **P**150 Lift ☾ sB🛁🚿280000 dB🛁🚿450000 M alc ✂ ⛴ 🏊 mountains lake
Credit cards [2] [3] [5]

★★★***Regina Olga*** via Regina 18 ☎510171 tx380821
🛁🚿67 🚗 **P** Lift ☾ ⛴ mountains lake

★**Asnigo** pza San Stefano (n.rest) ☎510062

16 Mar—Nov
rm25 (🚿19) **P**20 sB25500 sB🚿38500 dB45000 dB🚿60000 lake
Credit cards [1] [3] [4]

CERVIA
Ravenna (☎0544)

★★**Buenos Aires** Lungomare G-Deledda 130 ☎973174 tx550394

Apr—Oct
🚿62 🚗 **P**38 Lift ☾ sB🚿32000—40000 dB🚿50000—61000 M15000—19600 Beach sea
Credit cards [1] [2] [3] [5]

🚘 **Opel-Cervia** via Oriani 67 ☎991390 M/c Ope

At **MILANO MARITTIMA** (3km N)

🚘 **Europa** viale 2 Giugno 15 ☎92276 **P** Fia

CERVINIA-BREUIL See **BREUIL-CERVINIA**

CESENA
Forlì (☎0547)

★★★**Casali** via Benedetto Croce 81 ☎22745 tx550480
🛁🚿40 🚗 **P**20 Lift ☾ sB🛁🚿39000—42500 dB🛁🚿60000—74000 M19000—25000
Credit card [3]

CESENATICO
Forlì (☎0547)

★★★**Britannia** viale Carducci 129 ☎80041 tx550036

24 May—15 Sep
🛁44 🚗 **P**20 Lift ☾ sB🛁43000—53000 dB🛁72000—94000 M22000 ⛴ Beach sea
Credit cards [1] [2] [3] [4] [5]

★★★**Internazionale** via Ferrara 7 ☎80231

Jun—Sep
🛁50 **P**40 Lift ☾ sB🛁40000—58000 dB🛁62000—88000 M20000 ✂ ⛴ Beach sea
Credit card [1]

★★★**Torino** viale Carducci 55 ☎80044

15 May—Sep
🚿45 **P**50 Lift **DPn**30000—50000 Mfr16500 ⛴ sea

Internazionale viale Carducci 95 ☎81418 Ope

🚘 **Luciano** via A-Saffi 91 ☎81347 BMW Mer

CHÂTILLON
Aosta (☎0166)

★★**Marisa** via Pellissier 10 ☎61845

Mar—Oct
🛁🚿28 🚗 **P**30 Lift sB🛁🚿29000—34000 dB🛁🚿46000—53000 M15000 mountains
Credit cards [3] [5]

CHIANCIANO TERME
Siena (☎0578)

★★★**Grand Capitol** viale della Libertà 492 ☎64681

Apr—Oct
🛁68 🚗 **P**30 Lift ☾ sB🛁50000 dB🛁80000 M25000 ⛴
Credit cards [2] [3] [5]

CHIAVARI
Genova (☎0185)

★★**Santa Maria** via T-Groppo ☎309621
🛁34 🚗 **P**30 Lift ☾ sB🛁38000 dB🛁63000 Mfr25000 sea
Credit cards [2] [3] [5]

Cantero corso Dante 90 ☎307018 **P**

G Ughini via Nazario Sauro 13—15 ☎308278 Aud Mer VW

CHIAVENNA
Sondrio (☎0343)

★★★**Conradi** pza Verdi 10 ☎32300
rm34 (🛁🚿26) 🚗 **P**20 Lift ☾ sB23500 sB🛁🚿27500 dB43500 dB🛁🚿52000 M16000 mountains
Credit card [5]

CHIOGGIA
Venezia (☎041)

★★**Grande Italia** pza Vigo (n.rest) ☎400515
rm50 (🛁🚿

CIVITAVECCHIA
Roma (☎0766)

SAC Lungomare Garibaldi 42 ☎21830 AR

CÒLICO
Como (☎0341)

★★**Risi** Lunge L-Polti 1

Mar—Oct
🛁45 **P**20 Lift sB🛁29000 dB🛁58000 →

M18000
Credit cards 2 4

★**Gigi** ☎940268

rm12 (⛆ 9) 🚘 **P**8 sB28000 sB⛆ 38000 dB48000 dB⛆ 63000 M22000—26000 mountains
Credit card 3

COLLE DI VAL D'ELSA See **SIENA**

COMACCHIO
Ferrara (☎0533)

At **LIDO DEGLI ESTENSI** (7km SE)

★★**Conca del Lido** viale G-Pascoli 42 ☎327459 tx216149

15 May—Sep
⛆ 59 **P**30 Lift ☾ sB⛆ 34500 dB⛆ 45500 M25000 ⛱ sea
Credit cards 2 5

COMO
Como (☎031)

★★★**Como** via Mentana 28 (n.rest) ☎266173

🛁 72 🚘 **P**50 Lift ☾ sB🛁 76500 dB🛁 111000 ⛱ lake mountains
Credit cards 2 5

★★★**Flori** via per Cernobbio 12 (n.rest) ☎557642

🛁⛆ 49 🚘 **P**10 Lift ☾ sB🛁⛆ 82500 dB🛁⛆ 115000 lake mountains
Credit cards 1 2 3 5

★★★**Metropole Suisse** pza Cavour 19 (n.rest) ☎269444

🛁⛆ 70 🚘 **P**20 Lift ☾ sB🛁⛆ 77500 dB🛁⛆ 110000 lake mountains
Credit cards 1 2 3 5

★★**Engadina** viale Rosselli 22 (n.rest) ☎550415

Mar—15 Nov
🛁⛆ 21 **P**6 Lift ☾ sB🛁⛆ 40000—45000 dB🛁⛆ 55000—70000

★★**Park** viale Rosselli 20 ☎556782

🛁⛆ 42 🚘 **P**4 Lift ☾ sB32000—55000 sB🛁⛆ 55000—59000 dB55000—61000 dB🛁⛆ 84000—90000 lake
Credit cards 1 2 5

★★**San Gottardo** pza Volta ☎263531

rm60 (🛁⛆ 32) 🚘 **P**4 Lift ☾ sB34000 sB🛁⛆ 50500 dB57900 dB🛁⛆ 83500 M18000 mountains
Credit cards 1 2 3 4 5

🚗 **Autorimessa Dante** via Dante 59 ☎272545 **P** Ren

Grassi & Airoldi via Napoleona 50 ☎266027 AR

CONCA DEI MARINI
Salerno (☎089)

★★★**Belvedere** (SS 163) ☎871266

Apr—Oct
🛁 36 🚘 **P**36 Lift ☾ sB🛁 44000—56000 dB🛁 79000—97000 M34000 ⛱ Beach sea
Credit card 2

CORPO DI CAVA See **CAVA DE'TIRRENI**

Italy

CORTE DI CADORE See **BORCA DI CADORE**

CORTINA D'AMPEZZO
Belluno (☎0436)

★★★★**Corona** corso C-Battisti ☎3251 tx440004

20 Dec—Mar & Jul—15 Sep
rm57 (🛁⛆ 46) A11rm 🚘 **P**30 Lift ☾ sB34000—62000 sB🛁⛆ 52000—95000 dB62000—99000 dB🛁⛆ 89000—164000 M25000—30000 mountains
Credit cards 2 3 5

★★★★**Grand Savola** via Roma 62 ☎3201 tx440811

🛁 142 🚘 **P**100 Lift ☾
sB🛁 110000—160000
dB🛁 160000—270000 M44000—55000 🎾 ⛱ mountains
Credit cards 1 2 3 4 5

★★★***AGIP*** via Roma 70 (SS 51km 102) ☎61400

⛆ 28 Lift

★★★**Ancora** corso Italia 62 ☎3261 tx440004

20 Dec—Etr & Jul—15 Sep
🛁⛆ 71 🚘 **P**20 Lift ☾
sB🛁⛆ 45000—88000
dB🛁⛆ 75000—158000 M30000—40000
Credit cards 2 3 5

★★★***Concordia Parc*** corso Italia 28 ☎4251 tx440004

22 Dec—20 Mar & 10 Jul—Aug
🛁⛆ 58 🚘 **P**30 Lift ☾ mountains
Credit cards 1 2 3

★★★**Cortina** corso Italia 94 ☎4221 tx440004

20 Dec—15 Apr & 15 Jun—15 Sep
🛁 48 🚘 **P**15 Lift ☾ sB🛁 84000—145000 dB🛁 127000—250000 M35000—45000 mountains
Credit cards 1 2 3 4 5

★★★***Cristallo*** (CIGA) via R-Mandardi 42 ☎4281 tx440090

25 Jun—15 Sep & 20 Dec—31 Mar
🛁 102 🚘 **P** Lift ☾ 🎾 ⛱ ▣ mountains

★★★**Europa** corso Italia 207 ☎3221 tx440004

Closed Nov
🛁⛆ 52 **P**40 Lift ☾
sB🛁⛆ 105000—130000
dB🛁⛆ 180000—230000 M40000 mountains
Credit cards 1 2 3 4 5

★★★**Poste** pza Roma 14 ☎4271 tx440044

20 Dec—20 Oct
🛁 80 🚘 **P**75 Lift ☾ sB🛁 130000—178000 dB🛁 180000—256000 M45000—58000 mountains
Credit card 2

★★**Alpes** via la Verra 2 ☎2021

20 Dec—Mar & Jul—Sep
rm32 (🛁⛆ 16) **P**32 sB26000—43500 sB🛁⛆ 31000—54200 dB48000—78400 dB🛁⛆ 58000—95500 M16000—25000 mountains

★★**San Marco** pza Roma 6 ☎866941

Xmas—Etr & Jun—Oct
rm25 (🛁⛆ 22) **P**15 sB30000—68000 sB🛁⛆ 42000—86000 dB50000—97000 dB🛁⛆ 68000—152000 M22000—30000 mountains
Credit cards 2 5

🚗 **Dolomiti** corso Italia 182 ☎61077 **P** Fia Lan

COSENZA
Cosenza (☎0984)

At **RENDE** (6km NW off SS 107)

★★★***AGIP*** (SS 19—Bivio SS 107) ☎839101

⛆ 65 **P** Lift ☾

🚗 **AMC** via S-Pellico ☎39598 M/c BMW

COURMAYEUR
Aosta (☎0165)

★★★★★**Royal & Golf** via Roma 87 ☎843621 tx214312

Dec—Apr & Jul—Aug
🛁⛆ 100 A4rm 🚘 **P**30 Lift ☾
sB🛁⛆ 90000—150000
dB🛁⛆ 146000—265000 M50000 ⛱ ▣ mountains
Credit cards 2 3

★★★★**Palace Bron** (2km E) Verso Plan Gorret ☎842545 tx211085

20 Dec—10 Apr & Jul—Aug
🛁 30 **P** Lift ☾ sB🛁 80000—95000 dB🛁 138000—170000 M32000—38000 mountains
Credit cards 1 2 3 5

★★★★**Pavilion** Strada Regionale 60 ☎842420 tx210541

Dec—Apr & Jun—Oct
🛁 40 🚘 **P**36 Lift ☾ sB🛁 85000—125000 dB🛁 150000—230000 Mfr40000 ▣ mountains
Credit cards 1 2 3 5

CREMONA
Cremona (☎0372)

🚗 **General Cars** via Catelleone 77—79 ☎20343 Ope Vau

At **SAN FELICE** (5km E)

★★★***AGIP*** (exit Autostrade Piscenza/Brescia) ☎43101

⛆ 77 **P** Lift ☾

CUNEO
Cuneo (☎0171)

🚗 **Cunicar** via Torino ☎66442 AR

DESENZANO DEL GARDA
Brescia (☎030)

★★★**Mayer & Splendid** pza del Porto ☎9141409

Apr—mid Nov
🛁⛆ 60 🚘 **P**20 Lift sB🛁⛆ 30000—40000

dB 🛁 🚿 50000—55000 M15000 lake
Credit cards [1] [2] [3] [5]

★★★ ***Ramazzotti*** viale Dal Molin 78 (n.rest) ☎9141808 tx300395
Apr—Sep
rm22 (🛁 10) 🚗 P

★★ ***Europa*** ☎9142333
Mar—Oct
rm37 (🛁 31) 🚗 P Lift lake

★★ ***Vittoria*** Portovecchio 4 ☎9108117
🛁 🚿 35 P ☾ lake

DIANO MARINA
Imperia (☎0183)

★★★★ **Diana Majestic** via Degli Oleandri 15 ☎495445 tx271025
25 Mar—20 Oct
🛁 🚿 80 A20rm 🚗 P60 Lift ☾
sB 🛁 🚿 79000—99000
dB 🛁 🚿 123000—205000 M40000 ⛱
Beach sea

★★★ **Bellevue & Méditerranée** via Gl-Ardoine 2 ☎495089
20 Dec—30 Sep
🛁 🚿 71 🚗 P50 Lift ☾
sB 🛁 🚿 53000—58000
dB 🛁 🚿 86000—93000 M25000 ⛱ Beach sea
Credit card [2]

🚘 **G Ghiradi** via G-Ardoino 127 ☎45334 M/c **P** Alf

ELBA (ISOLA D')
Livorno (☎0565)

LACONA

★★★ **Capo Sud** ☎964021
10 May—Sep
🛁 🚿 39 **P**40 ☾ **DPn**43000—68000 🎾
Beach sea

PORTO AZZURRO

★★★ **Elba International** ☎968611 tx590669
Apr—Oct
🛁 🚿 242 **P**250 Lift ☾
sB 🛁 🚿 46000—51000
dB 🛁 🚿 74000—83000 M14000—40000 🎾
⛱ Beach sea

★ **Belmare** ☎95012 tx95076
🛁 25 **P** ☾ sB 🛁 30000—41000
dB 🛁 50000—62000 M15000—20000 sea
Credit cards [1] [2] [3] [5]

PORTOFERRAIO

★★★ **Hermitage** ☎969932 tx500219
May—Sep
🛁 🚿 100 **P**70 Lift ☾ **DPn**72000—165000 🎾
⛱ Beach sea
Credit card [2]

PROCCHIO

★★★★ ***Golfo*** ☎907565 tx590690
24 May—Sep
🛁 🚿 95 🚗 **P** Lift ☾ 🎾 ⛱ Beach sea

At **SPARTAIA**

★★★ **Desirée** ☎907502 tx590649
May—6 Oct
🛁 🚿 69 **P**12 ☾ dB 🛁 🚿 fr96000 🎾 ⛱

Italy

Beach sea
Credit cards [1] [2] [3] [4] [5]

EMPOLI
Firenze (☎0571)

★★ **Tazza d'Oro** via del Papa 46 ☎72129 tx570378
rm56 (🛁 🚿 49) 🚗 **P**14 Lift ☾ sB39000
sB 🛁 🚿 42000 dB58000 dB 🛁 🚿 63000
M16000
Credit cards [2] [3] [5]

FABRO
Umbria (☎0763)

★★ **Fabro** Contrada della Stazione 70 ☎82063
rm15 (🛁 10) **P**30 ☾ sB28000 sB 🛁 40000
dB43000 dB 🛁 60000 M20000—25000

FANO
Pesaro & Urbino (☎0721)

★★ ***Excelsior*** Lungomare Simonetti 17 ☎82558
5 Jun—15 Sep
rm30 (🚿 27) **P** Beach sea

FERIOLO See **BAVENO**

FERRARA
Ferrara (☎0532)

★★★ **Astra** viale Cavour 55 ☎26234 tx226150
rm79 (🛁 🚿 68) 🚗 **P**8 Lift ☾ sB51000
sB 🛁 🚿 61000 dB 🛁 🚿 104000 M15000
Credit cards [1] [2] [3] [5]

🚘 **SIRA** via Bologna 306 ☎93275 M/c For

FIESOLE
Firenze (☎055)

★★★★ **Villa San Michele** (Relais et Châteaux) via Doccia 4 ☎59451 tx570643
Mar—16 Oct
🛁 28 **P**20 ☾ **DPn**280000—690000
Credit cards [1] [2] [3] [5]

★★ **Villa Bonelli** via F-Poeti 1 ☎59513
rm23 (🛁 🚿 14) 🚗 Lift ☾ sB35000
sB 🛁 🚿 43000 dB50000 dB 🛁 🚿 67000
M10000—23000 mountains
Credit cards [1] [2] [3]

FINALE LIGURE
Savona (☎019)

At **VARIGOTTI** (6km SE)

★★★ **Nik-Mehari** via Aurelia 104 ☎698096
🛁 🚿 36 🚗 **P** Lift ☾ sB 🛁 🚿 94000
dB 🛁 🚿 128000 M45000 Beach sea
Credit cards [1] [2] [3] [5]

FIRENZE (FLORENCE)
Firenze (☎055)

★★★★★ **Excelsior Italia** (CIGA) pza Ognissanti 3 (off Lungarno A-Vespucci) ☎264201 tx570022
🛁 205 🚗 **P** Lift ☾ sB 🛁 248000—278000
dB 🛁 396000—446000 t%
Credit cards [1] [2] [3] [4] [5]

★★★★★ **Savoy** pza della Repubblica 7 ☎283313 tx570220
🛁 101 Lift ☾ sB 🛁 259000—320000
dB 🛁 390000—440000 M70000
Credit cards [1] [2] [3]

★★★★★ **Villa Medici** (SRS) via il Prato 42 ☎261331 tx570179
🛁 107 **P** Lift sB 🛁 282000 dB 🛁 484000
M alc ⛱

★★★★ **Grandhotel Baglioni** (BW) pza Unita Italiana 6 ☎218441 tx570225
🛁 🚿 195 🚗 Lift ☾ sB 🛁 🚿 179000
dB 🛁 🚿 255000 M33000
Credit cards [1] [2] [3] [5]

★★★★ **Jolly** pza V-Veneto 4A ☎2770 tx570191
🛁 167 **P** Lift ☾ sB 🛁 130000
dB 🛁 185000—204000 ⛱
Credit cards [1] [2] [3] [4] [5]

★★★★ **Londra** (GT) via Jacopo da Diacceto 16—20 ☎262791 tx571152
🛁 🚿 105 🚗 **P**10 Lift ☾ sB 🛁 🚿 164000
dB 🛁 🚿 228000 M39000&alc
Credit cards [1] [2] [3] [5]

★★★★ **Minerva** pza Santa Maria Novella 16 ☎284555 tx570414
🛁 🚿 112 🚗 **P** Lift ☾
sB 🛁 🚿 96000—164000
dB 🛁 🚿 147000—228000 M39000 ⛱
Credit cards [1] [2]

★★★ **Adriatico** via Maso Finiguerra 9 ☎261781 tx572265
🛁 114 **P**30 Lift ☾ sB 🛁 73000
dB 🛁 113000 M25000
Credit cards [1] [2] [3] [5]

★★★ ***AGIP*** Autostrade del Sole Raccordo Firenze-Mare (12km NW) ☎440081 tx570263
🚿 156 **P** Lift ☾

★★★ ***Crest*** **(See page 50)** viale Europa 205 ☎686841 tx570376
🛁 92 **P** Lift ☾ ⛱
Credit cards [1] [2] [3] [5]

★★★ **Croce di Malta** via della Scala 7 ☎282600 tx570540
🛁 100 Lift ☾ sB 🛁 164000 dB 🛁 225000
M35000 ⛱
Credit cards [2] [3]

★★★ ***Kraft*** via Solferino 2 ☎284273 tx571523
🛁 66 Lift ☾ ⛱
Credit cards [1] [2] [3] [5]

★★★ **Pierre** via Lamberti 5 (n.rest) ☎216218 tx573175
🚿 39 Lift ☾ dB 🚿 168000—223000
Credit cards [2] [3] [5]

★★★ **Regency** (Relais et Châteaux) pza d'Azeglio 3 ☎245247 tx571058
🛁 🚿 38 🚗 ☾ sB 🛁 🚿 240000—309000
dB 🛁 🚿 340000—437000 M alc
Credit cards [1] [2] [3] [5]

★★★**Roma** pza Santa Maria Novella 8 (n.rest) ☎210366 tx573175
🛁70 ⌂P6 Lift ☾
Credit cards [1] [2] [3] [5]

★★★**Villa Belvedere** via Benedetto Castelli 3 (n.rest) ☎222501
Mar—Nov
🛁🚿27 **P**30 Lift ☾ sB🛁🚿fr112000
dB🛁🚿164000—184000 🎾 ♒

★★**Basilea** via Guelfa 41 ☎214587 tx571698
rm52 (🛁50) ⌂P7 Lift ☾ sB59000
sB🛁73000 dB🛁113000
Credit cards [1] [2] [3] [5]

★★**Liana** via V-Alfieri 18 (n.rest) ☎245303
rm20 (🛁🚿11) ⌂P15 ☾ sB37000
sB🛁🚿45000 dB60000 dB🛁🚿72000

★★**Rapallo** via Santa Caterina d'Allessandria 7 ☎472412 tx574251
rm40 (🛁🚿25) ⌂P10 Lift ☾ sB59000
sB🛁🚿73000 dB91000 dB🛁🚿113000
M25000
Credit cards [1] [2] [3] [5]

🚗 **Europa** Borgognissanti 96 ☎260846 **P** Ope Vol

🚗 **M Ronchi** via Crimea 8 ☎489855 For

🚗 **Zaniratti** viale Fratelli Rosselli 55 ☎471465 AR Vol

At **CANDELI** (6km SE on road to Bagno a Ripoli)

★★★★***Villa Massa*** ☎630051 tx573555
rm56 (🛁42) A14rm **P** Lift ☾

At **SESTO FIORENTINO** (9km NW)

★★**Villa Villoresi** ☎4489032
🛁🚿30 **P** sB🛁🚿88500
dB🛁🚿39000—194000 M35000 ♒

FOGGIA
Foggia (☎0881)

★★★**Cicolella** viale 24 Maggio 60 ☎3890 tx810273
🛁🚿125 Lift ☾ sB🛁🚿77000—83000
dB🛁🚿153000—163000 Mfr28000
Credit cards [1] [2] [3] [4] [5]

FOLIGNO
Perugia (☎0742)

★★★**Umbria** via C-Battisti 3 ☎52821
🛁🚿47 **P**25 Lift ☾ sB🛁🚿35000—41000
dB🛁🚿54000—62000 M15000—23000
mountains
Credit cards [1] [2] [3] [4] [5]

FORIO See **ISCHIA (ISOLA D')**

FORTE DEI MARMI
Lucca (☎0584)

★★★★***Augustus*** viale Morin 169 ☎80202 tx590673
15 May—Sep
🛁🚿70 A27rm **P** Lift ☾ 🎾 Beach sea

★★★***Alcione*** viale Morin 137 ☎89952
Jun—Sep
rm45 (🛁40) **P**30 Lift ☾ Beach sea
Credit cards [2] [3]

★★★**Astoria Garden** via L-da-Vinci 10 ☎80754
May—Sep
🛁30 **P**20 ☾ sB🛁36000—45000
dB🛁60000—70000 Beach
Credit cards [1] [2] [3] [5]

★★★**Byron** viale Morin 46 ☎80087
May—Oct
🛁🚿40 A5rm **P**25 ☾
sB🛁🚿60000—90000
dB🛁🚿90000—160000 M35000 ♒ sea
Credit cards [2] [5]

★★★**Raffaelli Park** (BW) via Mazzini 37 ☎81494 tx590239
🛁🚿28 A6rm **P**50 Lift ☾
sB🛁🚿80000—108000
dB🛁🚿111000—156000 M35000 🎾 ♒
Beach
Credit cards [1] [2] [3]

★★★**Raffaelli Villa Angela** via G-Mazzini 64 ☎80652 tx590239
May—Oct
🛁🚿33 A15rm **P**50 Lift ☾ sB🛁🚿54000
dB🛁🚿77000 M30000—35000 🎾 ♒
Beach
Credit cards [1] [2] [3]

★★**Adams Villa Maria** Lungomare 110 ☎80901
24 May—Sep
🛁41 **P**50 Lift ☾ sB🛁50000—80000
dB🛁80000—140000 M25000—35000 ♒
mountains sea
Credit cards [1] [2] [3] [5]

FROSINONE
Frosinone (☎0775)

★★***Palace Hasser*** via Brighindi 1 ☎852747
🛁60 ⌂P Lift ☾

GABBICE MARE
Pesaro & Urbino (☎0541)

★★★**Alexander** via Panoramica 35 ☎961166 tx550535
May—Sep
🛁🚿46 **P**35 Lift ☾ sB🛁🚿31000—37000
dB🛁🚿50000—58000 Mfr16000 ♒
Beach sea

★★**Club de Bona** via Panoramica 33 ☎962622 tx550535
May—Sep
🛁🚿50 ⌂P8 Lift sB🛁🚿32000—39000
dB🛁🚿56000—64000 M20000 🎾 ♒
Beach sea
Credit cards [3] [5]

★★***Valbruna*** via Redipuglia 1 ☎961843
20 May—20 Sep
rm36 (🛁🚿30) **P** Lift ☾

GALLARATE
Varese (☎0331)

★★**Astoria** pza Risorgimento 9A ☎791043 tx351005
🛁🚿50 ⌂P50 Lift ☾ sB🛁🚿57000
dB🛁🚿73000 M30000
Credit cards [2] [3] [5]

GARDA
Verona (☎045)

★★★★***Eurotel*** via Gardesana 18 ☎7255107 tx431299
🛁🚿150 ⌂P Lift ☾ ♒ lake

★★★**Regina Adelaide Palace** via 20 Settembre ☎7255013 tx341078
🛁🚿54 **P**30 Lift ☾ sB🛁🚿58000—70000
dB🛁🚿96000—115000 M20000—24000
lake
Credit cards [1] [2] [3]

★★**Tre Corone** via Lungolago 44 ☎624033
Mar—Oct
🛁25 **P** Lift ☾ sea lake

GARDONE RIVIERA
Brescia (☎0365)

★★★★**Grand** via Zanardelli 72 ☎20261 tx300254
15 Apr—10 Oct
🛁🚿180 **P** Lift ☾ sB🛁🚿63000—100000
dB🛁🚿106000—170000 M34000 ♒ lake
Credit cards [1] [2] [3] [5]

★★★***Lac*** corso Repubblica 58 ☎20124
Apr—15 Oct
rm30 (🛁17) Lift lake

★★★**Monte Baldo** ☎20951
20 May—Sep
rm46 (🛁🚿36) A15rm **P**30 Lift ☾
sB🛁🚿47000 dB76000—82000
dB🛁🚿76000—82000 M22000 ♒
Credit cards [2] [3]

★★***Bellevue*** via Zanardelli 44 ☎20235
Apr—10 Oct
🛁🚿31 ⌂P3 Lift lake

At **BARBARANO** (1km W)

★★★**Astoria** ☎20761 tx301088
🛁🚿85 ⌂P30 Lift ☾
sB🛁🚿62000—72000
dB🛁🚿119000—134000 M25000 t% 🎾
♒ lake
Credit cards [1] [2] [3] [4] [5]

★★★**Spiaggia d'Oro** ☎20764 tx301088
🛁🚿42 ⌂P30 Lift ☾
sB🛁🚿77000—89000
dB🛁🚿144000—169000 M25000 t% ♒
lake
Credit cards [1] [2] [3] [4] [5]

GARGNANO
Brescia (☎0365)

★**Europa** ☎71191
Apr—30 Oct
🛁🚿20 **P** lake

GENOVA (GENOA)
Genova (☎010)

★★★★★**Colombia** (CIGA) via Balbi 40 ☎261841 tx270423
🛁172 **P**15 Lift ☾ sB🛁151000—196000
dB🛁227000—272000 M alc t%
Credit cards [1] [2] [3] [4] [5]

Italy

★★★★**Plaza** via M-Piaggio 11 ☎893641 tx213142
🛁 🚿97 🚗 **P**20 Lift ☾ sB 🛁 🚿 121000 dB 🛁 🚿 186000 M35000
Credit cards [2] [3] [5]

★★★★**Savoia Majestic** (SRS) via Arsenale de Terra 5, Stazione Centrale Principle ☎261641 tx270426
🛁 🚿 120 **P**15 Lift ☾ sB 🛁 🚿 126000 dB 🛁 🚿 182000 M40000
Credit cards [1] [2] [3] [5]

🚗 **ARA** via Marsilio de Padova 6 ☎317388

Dilia viale Carlo-E-Mello Rosselli 18 ☎300430 For

🚗 **B Koelliker** corso Euopa 810 ☎3993241 AR

🚗 ***Oram*** via G-Bandi 10 Quarto ☎384653 DJ Vol

XX-Settembre via D-Fiasella 19 ☎511941 **P** Cit

GENZANO DI ROMA
Roma (☎06)

★★**Villa Robinia** viale Frattelli Rosselli 19 ☎9396409
🛁 30 **P**20 Lift ☾ sB 🛁 24000 dB 🛁 38000 M16000
Credit card [5]

GHIFFA
Novara (☎0323)

★★**Ghiffa** via Belvedere 88—90 ☎59285 tx200285
Apr—Oct
rm24 (🛁 🚿 19) 🚗 **P** Lift sB31000—39000 sB 🛁 🚿 39000—59000 dB48000—68000 dB 🛁 🚿 68000—78000 M26000 lake
Credit cards [1] [2] [3]

GIOIA DEL COLLE
Bari (☎080)

🚗 **Auto Carrozzeria** via Santeramo 120 ☎830417 M/c **P** Ren

GIOIA TAURO
Reggio di Calabria (☎0966)

★★★**Mediterraneo** via Nazionale ☎51854
🛁 55 🚗 **P** Lift ☾ sB 🛁 29000—33000 dB 🛁 46000—50000 M14000—16000
Credit cards [1] [2] [3] [5]

GIULIANOVA LIDO
Teramo (☎085)

🚗 **Ubaldo & Forlini** via G-Galilei 180 ☎862771 M/c Ope Vau

GOLFO ARANCI See **SARDEGNA (ISOLA) (SARDINIA)**

GRAVEDONA
Como (☎0344)

★**Turismo** ☎85227
Mar—Nov
rm12 (🛁 5) 🚗 **P**20 sB29000 sB 🛁 31000 dB49000 dB 🛁 49000 M15000

GRAVELLONA TOCE
Novara (☎0323)

★**Helios** ☎848096
rm19 (🛁 11) **P**15 sB23500—27000 sB 🛁 28500—32000 dB 🛁 49000—54000 M15000—17000 mountains

GRIGNANO See **TRIESTE**

GROSSETO
Grosseto (☎0564)

★★★***AGIP*** (SS 1km 179 exit Roma) ☎24100
🚿 32 **P**

★★★***Lorena*** via Trieste 3 ☎25501
🛁 🚿 66 🚗 **P** Lift ☾

🚗 **Morelli** via Privata dei Curiazi 13 ☎23000 AR Vol

GUBBIO
Perugia (☎075)

★★***Tre Ceri*** via Benamati 6 ☎9272853
🚿 30 🚗 **P**10 Lift ☾
Credit cards [2] [3] [5]

IESOLO (JESOLO) (LIDO DI)
Venezia (☎0421)

★★★★***Las Vegas*** via Mascagni 3 ☎971515 tx223535
Apr—Oct
🛁 🚿 110 **P**70 Lift ☾ ⛱ Beach sea

★★★***Anthony*** via Padova 25 ☎971711 tx410433
May—Sep
🛁 🚿 68 **P** Lift ☾ 🎾 ⛱ Beach sea

★★★***Cesare Augustus*** ☎90971 tx410423
May—Sep
🛁 🚿 120 **P** Lift ☾ ⛱ Beach sea

★★★***London*** via Dalmazia 64 ☎90988
May—Sep
rm84 (🛁 🚿 82) **P** Lift ☾ Beach sea

★★★**Ritz** via Zanella 2 ☎90861
May—25 Sep
🛁 🚿 48 **P**30 Lift ☾ sB 🛁 🚿 48000—70000 dB 🛁 🚿 76000—110000 M25000—30000 ⛱ Beach sea
Credit card [2]

★★**Regina** via Bafile 115 ☎90383
Apr—Sep
🛁 🚿 50 **P**35 Lift ☾ sB 🛁 🚿 36000—41000 dB 🛁 🚿 72000—82000 M19000 Beach

★★**Termini** via Altinate 32 ☎962312 tx223491
Apr—10 Dec
🛁 45 **P**35 Lift ☾ sB 🛁 30000—45000 dB 🛁 60000—90000 M25000 ⛱ Beach sea

🚗 **Brusa** pza Mazzini ☎91344 For

At **IESOLO PINETA** (6km E)

★★★**Bellevue** via Oriente 100 ☎961233 tx410433
15 May—15 Sep
🛁 🚿 64 **P** Lift ☾ sB 🛁 🚿 95000—115000 dB 🛁 🚿 190000—230000 M30000 🎾 Beach sea

★★**Danmark** via Oriente 170 ☎961013 tx410433
May—Sep
rm56 (🛁 🚿 50) 🚗 **P**48 ☾ sB25000—35000 sB 🛁 🚿 35000—45000 dB60000—70000 M12000 ⛱ Beach sea

IGEA MARINA See **BELLARIA IGEA MARINA**

IMPERIA
Imperia (☎0183)

🚗 **Riviera Motori** viale Matteotti 175 ☎20297 AR

ISCHIA (ISOLA D')
Napoli (☎081)

FORIO

★★***Splendid*** (1km N) ☎987374
20 Mar—30 Oct
🛁 🚿 45 **P**30 ☾ ⛱ sea
Credit cards [2] [5]

ISCHIA

★★★★**Jolly** via A-de-Luca 42 ☎991744 tx710267
Mar—Oct
🛁 208 **P** Lift ☾ sB 🛁 83000—121000 dB 🛁 143000—214000 ⛱ 🏊
Credit cards [1] [2] [3] [4] [5]

IVREA
Torino (☎0125)

★★**Eden** (n.rest) ☎424741
🛁 🚿 36 🚗 **P**10 Lift ☾ sB 🛁 🚿 51000 dB 🛁 🚿 67000—70000 mountains
Credit cards [3] [5]

🚗 **M Peroni** via S Lorenzo 10 ☎422022 VW

JESOLO See **IESOLO**

LACONA See **ELBA (ISOLA D')**

LAIGUEGLIA
Savona (☎0182)

★★★***Aquillia*** via Asti 1 ☎49040
Apr—Oct
🛁 40 🚗 **P**25 Lift Beach sea

★★**Mariolina** via Concezione 15 ☎49024
🛁 21 **P** sB 🛁 20000—26000 dB 🛁 36000—38000 M13000—18000 Beach sea
Credit card [3]

★★***Splendid*** pza Badaro 4 ☎49325
Etr—Sep
🛁 🚿 50 **P** Lift ☾ ⛱ Beach

★★**Windsor** pza 25 Aprile 7 ☎49000
May—Oct
🛁 🚿 53 Lift ☾ sB 🛁 🚿 28000—41000 dB 🛁 🚿 42000—62000 M16000 Beach sea

LAINATE
Milano (☎02)

★**Italmotel** via Manzoni 43 ☎9370869 tx324354
🛁 34 **P**34 ☾ dB 🛁 112000 M27000 🎾 ⛱ 🏊
Credit cards [2] [5]

LAVAGNA
Genova (☎0185)

★★**Tiguillo** via Matteotti 3 ☎392965
28 Mar—Oct
rm42 (🛁🚿30) 🚗 **P**6 Lift sB21400—23900 sB🛁🚿28000—30200 dB42000—46000 dB🛁🚿54000—58000 M17000—24000 sea

At **CAVI** (3km SE)

★***Scogliera*** (n.rest) ☎390072
Jun—Sep
🚿21 🚗 **P**21 Beach sea

🚘 **G Cordano** corso Buenos Aires ☎301101 **P** Fia

LEGHORN See **LIVORNO**

LENNO
Como (☎0344)

★★***San Giorgio*** via Regina 81 ☎40415
Apr—Sep
rm29 (🛁🚿24) 🚗 **P**30 Lift ☾ ⚲ lake
Credit cards [1] [3]

LERICI
La Spezia (☎0187)

★★★**Doria** via A-Doria (n.rest) ☎967124
rm42 (🛁🚿30) **P**60 Lift ☾ sB48700 sB🛁🚿50500 dB50000 dB🛁🚿75000 sea

★★***Italia*** ☎967108
🚿16 **P** sea

LEVANTO
La Spezia (☎0187)

★★★***Crystal*** via Vallesanta ☎808261
15 Jun—Sep
rm16 (🛁🚿14) A9rm **P** ☾ sea mountains

★★**Carla** via M-della-Liberta 28 ☎808275
🚿36 Lift sB🚿21500—23500 dB🚿44000 M19000
Credit card [1]

★**Garden** corso Italia 6 ☎808173
Apr—Sep
rm15 sB19000 dB35000 M18000 sea
Credit cards [1] [2] [3] [5]

LEVICO TERME
Trento (☎0461)

★★★**Grand Bellavista** via V-Emanuele 7 ☎706136 tx400856
May—Sep
🛁🚿78 **P**50 Lift sB🛁🚿35000—41000 dB🛁🚿60000—70000 M25000 🏊 lake
Credit card [5]

LIDO DEGLI ESTENSI See **COMACCHIO**

LIDO DI CAMAIORE See **CAMAIORE (LIDO DI)**

LIDO DI IESOLO (JESOLO) See **IESOLO (JESOLO) (LIDO DI)**

LIGNANO SABBIADORO
Udine (☎0431)

At **LIGNANO PINETA** (5km SW)

★★★***Medusa Splendid*** Arco dello Scirocco 13 ☎422211
15 May—15 Sep
🛁🚿56 **P**45 🏊 U Beach
Credit card [3]

At **LIGNANO RIVIERA** (7km SW)

★★★**Eurotel** calle Mendelssohn 13 ☎428992 tx450193
May—Sep
🛁🚿66 **P** Lift ☾ sB🛁🚿38000—64000 dB🛁🚿75000—104000 M21000 🏊
Credit cards [1] [2] [3] [5]

Italy

LIVORNO (LEGHORN)
Livorno (☎0586)

★★★**Giappone** via Grande 65 ☎24751
rm60 (🛁🚿58) **P** Lift ☾ sB🛁🚿47000 dB54500 dB🛁🚿69500 M17000
Credit cards [1] [2] [3] [5]

At **STAGNO** (5km N on SS1)

★★★***AGIP*** (SS 1km 320) ☎943067 tx611627
🚿50 **P** Lift ☾

LOANO
Savona (☎019)

★★★**Garden Lido** Lungomare N-Sauro 9 ☎669666 tx213178
🛁🚿95 🚗 **P** Lift sB🛁🚿64000—67000 dB🛁🚿93000—97000 M29000—35000 🏊 Beach sea
Credit cards [1] [2] [3] [5]

LONE See **AMALFI**

LUCCA
Lucca (☎0583)

At **MASSA PISANA** (4.5km S on SS12R)

★★★**Villa la Principessa** (Relais et Châteaux) ☎370037 tx590068
21 Feb—Nov
🛁44 **P**50 Lift ☾ sB🛁133000—163000 dB🛁256000—276000 M35000—70000 🏊
Credit cards [1] [2] [3] [5]

MACERATA
Macerata (☎0733)

★★★***AGIP*** via Roma 149B (SS 77km 89) ☎34248 tx611627
🚿51 **P** Lift ☾

MACOMER See **SARDEGNA (ISOLA) (SARDINIA)**

MACUGNAGA
Novara (☎0324)

★★**Cristallo** Franzione Pecetto ☎65139
Jun—Sep & Dec—Apr
rm21 (🛁17) 🚗 **P**25 mountains
Credit cards [1] [2] [3] [5]

MADONNA DI CAMPIGLIO
Trento (☎0465)

★★★**Savoia** ☎41004 tx300254
Dec—10 Apr
🛁🚿57 🚗 **P**25 Lift ☾ sB🛁🚿74000—79000 dB🛁🚿134000—145000 M34000 mountains
Credit cards [2] [5]

★★***Golf*** ☎41003 tx400882
23 Dec—12 Apr
🛁🚿125 **P**100 Lift ☾ 📺 mountains
Credit cards [1] [2] [3]

MAIORI
Salerno (☎089)

★★★***San Francesco*** via S-Tecla 54 ☎877070
15 Mar—15 Oct
🛁44 🚗 **P**40 Lift ☾ Beach sea

MALCESINE
Verona (☎045)

★★★**Lac** via Gardesana 18 ☎7400156
May—10 Oct
🛁41 🚗 **P**10 Lift ☾ **DPn**38000—58000 M20000 lake mountains

★★**Vega** via Roma 10 ☎7400151 tx480448
Apr—Oct
🛁🚿19 **P**20 Lift sB🛁🚿33000—47000 dB🛁🚿53500—74000 M18000 lake mountains
Credit cards [1] [2] [3]

MANTOVA
Mantova (☎0376)

★★**Apollo** pza Don Leoni 17 (n.rest) ☎350522
🛁35 🚗 **P** Lift ☾ sB🛁49000 dB🛁83000 lake mountains
Credit cards [1] [2] [3] [5]

★★**Broletto** via Accademia 1 (n.rest) ☎326784
🛁16 Lift ☾ sB🛁43500—47000 dB73500—79000
Credit cards [1] [2] [3]

Filipini via Curtatone & Montanara 58 ☎29696 Aud Por VW

MARATEA
Potenza (☎0973)

★★★★***Santavenere*** ☎876160
Mar—Oct
🛁🚿49 A5rm **P** ☾ ⚲ 🏊 Beach sea

MARGHERA See **MESTRE**

MARINA DI CARRARA See **CARRARA (MARINA DI)**

MARINA DI MASSA See **MASSA (MARINA DI)**

MARINA DI PIETRASANTA See **PIETRASANTA (MARINA DI)**

MARSALA See **SICILIA (SICILY)**

MASSA (MARINA DI)
Massa Carrara (☎0585)

★★★***Marina*** viale Magliano 3 ☎20192
15 May—Sep
🛁32 **P**18 ☾
Credit card [3]

MATELICA
Macerata (☎0737)

★★★***AGIP*** (SS256 Muccese km29)
☎82381 tx611627

🚿16 **P**

MAZZARÒ See **TAORMINA** under **SICILIA (SICILY)**

MEINA
Novara (☎0322)

★***Bel Sit*** via Sempione 76 ☎6483

Dec—Oct
🛁🚿12 🚗 **P**

MENAGGIO
Como (☎0344)

★★★**Bella Vista** via IV Novembre 9
☎32136

20 Mar—10 Oct
rm38 (🛁🚿37) 🚗 **P**15 Lift sB30000—35000
sB🛁🚿40000—45000 dB50000—56000
dB🛁🚿60000—70000 Mfr16500 lake
mountains
Credit cards [1] [2] [3] [5]

★★**Loveno** via N-Sauro 37 ☎32110

Apr—Oct
rm13 (🛁10) A5rm 🚗 **P**10 sB29000—36000
sB🛁34000—42000 dB43000—54000
dB🛁56000—68000 M16000—36000 lake
mountains
Credit card [3]

At **NOBIALLO** (1km N)

★★**Miralago** via Diaz 26 ☎32363

Apr—Oct
rm28 (🛁23) 🚗 **P** sB25000 sB🛁27000
dB🛁50000 M16000 lake

MERANO-MERAN
Bolzano (☎0473)

★★★★***Grand Bristol*** via O-Huber 14
☎49500 tx400662

15 Mar—Oct
🛁🚿146 🚗 **P**40 Lift ☾ ≈ mountains
Credit cards [1] [2] [3] [5]

★★★**Adria** via Gilm 2 ☎36610 tx401011

Mar—Nov
🛁40 A9rm **P**30 Lift ☾ sB🛁50000—68000
dB🛁100000—136000 M17000—22000
▣ ≈ mountains

★★★**Augusta** via O-Huber 2 ☎49570
tx400632

20 Mar—Oct
🛁26 🚗 **P**17 Lift ☾ sB🛁46000—53000
dB🛁87000—97000 M21000—23000
mountains
Credit card [3]

★★★***Eurotel Merano*** via Garibaldi 5
☎34900 tx400471

Mar—Oct
🛁🚿125 🚗 Lift ☾ mountains
Credit cards [1] [2] [3] [4] [5]

★★★***Mirabella*** via Garibaldi 35 ☎36512

23 Mar—3 Nov
🛁🚿30 🚗 Lift ☾ ≈ ▣ mountains

★★★**Palace** via Cavour 2 ☎34734
tx400256

16 Mar—15 Nov & 20 Dec—6 Jan
🛁110 **P**80 Lift ☾ sB🛁99000—145000
dB🛁170000—240000 M40000 ≈ ▣
mountains
Credit cards [1] [2] [3] [5]

★★★**Savoy** via Rezia 1 ☎47600
tx400632

Mar—Nov
🛁54 **P**50 Lift ☾ sB🛁63000—92000
dB🛁100000—138000 M22000—25000
≈ mountains
Credit cards [1] [2] [3] [4] [5]

★★**Irma** via Belvedere 17 ☎30124
tx401089

Mar—Nov
🛁🚿50 A2rm **P**30 Lift ☾
sB🛁🚿39000—66000
dB🛁🚿78000—132000 M12000—25000
⚲ ▣ ≈ mountains

★★**Regina** via Cavour 101 ☎33432
tx401595

Mar—Oct
rm80 (🛁🚿74) **P**25 Lift ☾ sB52000
sB🛁🚿58000 dB82000 dB🛁🚿92000 ≈
mountains
Credit cards [1] [2] [3] [5]

★**Westend** ☎47654 tx401606

Mar—Nov
🛁🚿22 **P**12 ☾ sB🛁🚿27000—40000
dB🛁🚿54000—70000 M12000—15000
mountains

🚘 **Merano** via Roma 288 ☎32074 M/c Ren

MESSINA See **SICILIA (SICILY)**

MESTRE
Venezia (☎041)
See also **VENEZIA (VENICE)**

★★★**Ambasciatori** corso del Popolo 221
☎5310699 tx410445

🛁🚿104 🚗 **P**60 Lift ☾
sB🛁🚿70000—98000
dB🛁🚿110000—147000 M32000
Credit cards [1] [2] [3] [4] [5]

★★★**Bologna & Stazione** pza Stazione,
via Piave 214 ☎931000 tx410678

🛁🚿128 **P**42 Lift ☾ sB🛁🚿68000
dB🛁🚿110000 M25000
Credit cards [1] [2] [3] [5]

★★★**Plaza** pza Stazione ☎929388
tx410490

🛁🚿227 🚗 Lift ☾ sB🛁🚿66250
dB🛁🚿107100 M27500
Credit cards [1] [2] [3] [5]

★★★**President** via Forte Marghera 99
(n.rest) ☎985655

🛁🚿51 🚗 **P**30 Lift ☾ sB🛁🚿67500
dB🛁🚿110000
Credit card [2]

★★★***Sirio*** via Circonvallazione 109
☎984022 tx410626

🚿100 **P** Lift ☾

★★★**Tritone** pza Stazione 16 ☎938454
tx411188

Feb—15 Nov
🛁🚿67 Lift ☾ sB🛁🚿61000
dB🛁🚿102000 M20000
Credit cards [2] [3]

★★**Aurora** pza G-Bruno 15 (n.rest)
☎989832

rm33 (🛁🚿19) **P**10 Lift ☾ sB26000—35000
sB🛁🚿36000—46000 dB47000—60000
dB🛁🚿57000—72000

★★**Venezia** pza XXVII Ottobre ☎985533
tx410693

🛁🚿100 🚗 **P**60 Lift ☾ sB🛁🚿43000
dB🛁🚿72000 M21000
Credit cards [1] [2] [3] [4] [5]

Autolambro SAS corso del Popolo 7
☎929922 Cit

Crivellari via le Stazione 34 ☎929225 **P** Fia

🚘 **Damiami & Giorgio** via Torino 40
☎932844 M/c For

🚘 **S Lorenzo** via Giustizia 27 ☎926722 **P**
Ope Vau

Roma/Caldera via Piave 182 ☎929611 Fia

At **MARGHERA** (1km S)

★★**Lugano** via Rizzardi 11 ☎936777
tx411155

🛁🚿62 🚗 **P**20 Lift ☾
sB🛁🚿54000—64000
dB🛁🚿87000—102000 M16000—20000
≈
Credit cards [1] [2] [3] [5]

MILANO (MILAN)
Milano (☎02)

★★★★★**Excelsior-Gallia** (SRS) pza
Duca d'Aosta 9 ☎6277 tx311160

🛁265 Lift ☾ sB🛁191200—223000
dB🛁253200—307000 t18%
Credit cards [1] [2] [3] [5]

★★★★★***Palace*** (CIGA) pza della
Repubblica 20 ☎6336 tx311026

🛁199 🚗 **P** Lift ☾

★★★★★**Principe di Savoia** (CIGA) pza
della Repubblica 17 ☎6230 tx310052

🛁302 🚗 **P** Lift ☾ sB🛁217000—302000
dB🛁319000—444000 t18%
Credit cards [1] [2] [3] [4] [5]

★★★★★**Diána Majestic** (CIGA) viale
Piáve 42 (n.rest) ☎203404 tx333047

🛁94 **P**20 Lift ☾ sB🛁129500—174500
dB🛁189000—249000 t%
Credit cards [1] [2] [3] [5]

★★★★**Duomo** via San Raffaele 1 ☎8833
tx312086

🛁160 **P**6 Lift ☾ sB🛁186000
dB🛁274000 M45000
Credit cards [1] [2] [3]

★★★★**Hilton International** via Galvani
12 ☎6983 tx330433

🛁🚿347 **P**360 Lift ☾
sB🛁🚿245500—315500
dB🛁🚿321000—409000 M45000
Credit cards [2] [3]

★★★★**Jolly President** Largo Augusto 10 ☏7746 tx312054
🛁 220 ⌂ Lift ☾ sB 🛁 195000 dB 🛁 230000
Credit cards [1] [2] [3] [4] [5]

★★★★**Jolly Touring** via U-Tarchetti 2 ☏6335 tx320118
🛁 277 Lift ☾ ⌂ sB 🛁 160000 dB 🛁 205000
Credit cards [1] [2] [3] [4] [5]

★★★★**Select** (BW) via Baracchini 12 (n.rest) ☏8843 tx312256
🛁 🚿 140 ⌂ Lift ☾
sB 🛁 🚿 135000—150000
dB 🛁 🚿 210000—250000 St%
Credit cards [1] [2] [3] [4]

★★★***AGIP*** Milano Tangenziale Ovest, Assago (14km SW) ☏8463441 tx320132
🚿 222 **P** Lift ☾ Pool

★★★**American** (BW) via Finocchiaro Aprile 2 ☏6315
🛁 400 ⌂ **P** Lift ☾ sB 🛁 110000 dB 🛁 145000 Mfr30000
Credit cards [1] [2] [3] [4] [5]

★★★**Concorde** (BW) via Monza 132 (n.rest) ☏2895853 tx315805
🛁 84 ⌂ **P**30 Lift ☾ sB 🛁 130000 dB 🛁 170000—190000
Credit cards [1] [2] [3]

★★★**Manin** via Manin 7 ☏6596511 tx320385
🛁 110 **P**20 Lift ☾ sB 🛁 146000 dB 🛁 197000 M40000
Credit cards [1] [2] [3] [4]

★★**Eur** via L-da-Vinci 36A (n.rest) ☏4451951
🚿 39 ⌂ **P**30 Lift ☾ sB🚿 80000 dB🚿 105000—120000
Credit cards [1] [2] [3] [5]

★★***Fini*** via del Mare 93 (n.rest) ☏8464041
rm98 (🛁 🚿 72) ⌂ **P** Lift ☾

★★***Gamma*** via V-Peroni 85 (n.rest) ☏2141116
🛁 🚿 55 ⌂ Lift ☾

🚗 **Forlanini** via Mecenate 84 ☏5060340 Fia

At **SAN DONATO MILANESE** (8km SE on road N9)

★★★***AGIP*** Ingresso Autostrada del Sole ☏512941 tx320132
🚿 270 **P** Lift ☾

At **SEGRATE** (6km E)

★★★★**Jolly Milano 2** via Flli Cervi ☏21606 tx321266
🛁 149 **P** Lift ☾ sB 🛁 156000 dB 🛁 177000
Credit cards [1] [2] [3] [4] [5]

MILANO MARITTIMA See **CERVIA**

MINORI See **AMALFI**

MISANO ADRIATICO
Forli (☏0541)

★★**Gala** via Pascoli 8 ☏615109
15 May—15 Sep
🛁 27 **P**27 Lift ☾ sB 🛁 30000—50000

Italy

dB 🛁 50000—90000 M25000—35000 sea
Credit cards [1] [2] [3] [5]

MODENA
Modena (☏059)

★★★★**Fini** via E-Est 441 ☏238091 tx510286
🛁 🚿 93 ⌂ **P**50 Lift ☾ sB 🛁 🚿 106600 dB 🛁 🚿 163500 M alc
Credit cards [1] [2] [3] [4] [5]

★★★***AGIP*** (SS 9 via Tre Olmi-Autosole Raccordo Brennero) ☏518221 tx611627
🚿 184 **P** Lift ☾

🚗 **Barbieri Auto** via E-Est 1040 ☏360260 **P** AR

Bellei via E-Est 1127 ☏366271 For

MOGLIANO VENETO
Treviso (☏041)

★★★★***Villa Condulmer*** via Zermanese 1 ☏457100
🛁 🚿 54 **P** ☾ ⚲ ≋ ▣ ∪

MOLTRASIO
Como (☏031)

★★**Caramazza** via Besana 50 ☏290050
3 Mar—30 Oct
🛁 20 ⌂ **P**20 Lift sB 🛁 57000 dB 🛁 84000 M23000 lake

MOLVENO
Trento (☏0461)

★★**Cima Tosa** via Scuole 5 ☏586928
Jun—Sep
🛁 🚿 36 **P**20 Lift sB 🛁 🚿 24000—32000 dB 🛁 🚿 42000—62000 M15000—17000 lake mountains
Credit cards [2] [3]

★★**Miralago** pza Scuole 4 ☏586935
Jul—Sep & 20 Dec—30 Mar
🛁 35 **P**30 Lift sB 🛁 32000—34000 dB 🛁 58000—63000 M20000 ≋ lake mountains
Credit cards [2] [3]

MONDOVI' BREO
Cuneo (☏0174)

🚗 **F Govone** via Piava 4 ☏40355 **P** Cit Fia

MONTALTO DI CASTRO
Viterbo (☏0766)

★★★***AGIP*** via Aurelia (SS 1km 108) ☏89090
🚿 32 **P** ☾

MONTECATINI TERME
Pistoia (☏0572)

★★★★**Croce di Malta** (SRS) via IV Novembre 18 ☏75871 tx574041
🛁 🚿 115 ⌂ **P**20 Lift ☾
sB 🛁 🚿 82500—102500
dB 🛁 🚿 155000—185000 M30000 ≋
Credit cards [1] [2] [3] [4]

★★★***Astoria*** via Fedeli ☏71191
Apr—Oct
rm65 (🛁 🚿 62) A10rm **P**50 Lift ☾ ≋ mountains
Credit card [2]

★★**Lido Palace Risorgimento** via IV Novembre 14 ☏70731
15 Mar—Oct
🛁 56 Lift ☾ sB 🛁 38000 dB 🛁 62000 M17000

MONTEGROTTO TERME
Padova (☏049)

★★★★***International Bertha*** Largo Traiano ☏793100 tx430277
🛁 126 ⌂ **P**100 Lift ☾ ⚲ ▭ ≋ ▣ mountains
Credit cards [1] [2] [3] [4] [5]

MONTESILVANO MARINA See **PESCARA**

MUCCIA
Macerata (☏0737)

★★★***AGIP*** Bivio Maddalena (SS 77km 44) ☏43138
🚿 37 **P** Lift ☾

NAPOLI (NAPLES)
Napoli (☏081)

★★★★★***Excelsior*** (CIGA) via Partenope 48 ☏417111 tx710043
🛁 137 ⌂ Lift ☾ sea

★★★★**Vesuvio** (SRS) via Partenope 45 ☏417044 tx710127
🛁 174 ⌂ Lift ☾ sB 🛁 111000—152000 dB 🛁 160000—215000 M36000 t% sea
Credit cards [1] [2] [3] [4] [5]

★★★**Jolly Ambassador's** via Medina 70 ☏416000 tx720335
rm280 (🛁 251) ⌂ Lift ☾ sB 🛁 120000 dB 🛁 154000
Credit cards [1] [2] [3] [4] [5]

★★★**Royal** via Partenope 38 ☏400244 tx710167
🛁 🚿 287 ⌂ **P** Lift ☾ sB 🛁 🚿 131700 dB 🛁 🚿 206600 M45500 ≋ sea
Credit cards [1] [2] [3] [5]

🚗 **S Luigi** via G-Francesco Pinto 59 ☏514865 Ren

🚗 **SVAI** via S-Veniero 17—20 ☏611122 For

At **SECONDIGLIANO** (8km N)

★★★***AGIP*** (SS7 bis km 24) ☏7540560
🚿 57 **P** Lift ☾

NERVI
Genova (☏010)

★★★***Giardino Rivera*** Passegiata a Mare ☏328581
rm30 (🛁 🚿 25) **P**20 Lift ☾ sea
Credit card [2]

★★**Milano** via Somma Donato 39 ☏328292
rm50 (🛁 🚿 37) A19rm ⌂ **P** Lift ☾ sB39500 sB 🛁 🚿 45000 dB 🛁 🚿 80000 M13000—19000 sea
Credit card [1]

NOBIALLO See **MENAGGIO**

NOVA LEVANTE-WELSCHNOFEN
Bolzano (☎0471)

★★★**Posta Cavallino Bianco** via Carezza 30, Strada Dolomiti ☎613113 tx400555

20 Dec—20 Apr & 20 May—2 Nov
46 P40 Lift
sB 43000—63000
dB 76000—101000 M15000
mountains
Credit cards 1 2 3 5

NUMANA
Ancona (☎071)

★★★***Numana Palace*** via Litoranea 10 ☎930155

May—Sep
rm9 (110) P100 lake
Credit cards 1 2 3 4 5

NUORO See **SARDEGNA (ISOLA) (SARDINIA)**

ORA-AUER
Bolzano (☎0471)

★★**Elefant** pza Principale 45 ☎80129

32 P Lift sB 27000—29500
dB 43000—46000 M13000—19000
mountains

ORTA SAN GIULIO
Novara (☎0322)

★★★***San Rocco*** via Gippini de Verona 11 (n.rest) ☎90222

37 P40 mountains

ORTISEI-ST ULRICH
Bolzano (☎0471)

★★★**Aquila** via Rezia 7 ☎76203

Dec—Apr & Jun—Oct
rm86 (70) P130 Lift
sB46500—83000 sB 59500—98000
dB79000—146000 dB 105000—176000
M17000—21500 mountains
Credit cards 1 2 3 5

ORVIETO
Terni (☎0763)

★★★***Maitani*** via L-Maitani 5 ☎33001

43 P15 Lift
Credit cards 1 2 3 5

At **BADIA (LA)** (5km S)

★★★**Badia** ☎90359

Mar—Dec
24 P100 sB 90000—100000
dB 34000—154000 M40000
Credit cards 1 2 3

OSPEDALETTI
Imperia (☎0184)

★★★**Floreal** corso R-Margherita 83 ☎59638

Closed Nov
26 Lift sB 22000—32000
dB 42000—55500 M18000—20000 sea
Credit cards 2 3 5

★★★***Rocce de Capo*** Lungomare C-Columbo (n.rest) ☎59733

Dec—Sep
22 Lift Beach sea

Italy

★★**Petit Royal** via Regina Margherita 86 ☎59026

15 Dec—Sep
rm30 (24) P15 Lift
sB24000—32000 sB 30000—41000
dB47000—62000 sB 54000—73000
M20000—25000

PADOVA (PADUA)
Padova (☎049)

★★★★***Park Hotel Villa Altichiero*** Altichiero (6km N on SS47) ☎615111

70 P Lift

PAESTUM
Salerno (☎0828)

★★**Calypso** via Licinella 35, Zona Pineta ☎811031

40 A5rm P100 sB 35000—46000
dB 60000—72000 M20000—27000
Beach sea mountains
Credit cards 2 5

PALERMO See **SICILIA (SICILY)**

PALLANZA See **VERBANIA**

PARMA
Parma (☎0521)

★★★**Palace Maria Luigia** viale Mentana 140 ☎21032 tx531008

100 P Lift sB 104000
dB 163000 M40000
Credit cards 1 2 3 5

★★**Button** via S-Vitale 7 (n.rest) ☎33177

41 P Lift sB 43800 dB 69800
Credit cards 1 2 3 5

★★**Milano** viale Ponte Bottego 9 ☎773031

rm47 (44) P30 Lift sB25800
sB 37800 dB44000 dB 57800
M17000—25000
Credit cards 2 3 5

Bottesini via Golese 30 ☎24219 M/c Hon Vol

PASSO DEL TONALE
See **TONALE (PASSO)**

PASSO DI ROLLE See **ROLLE**

PEGLI
Genova (☎010)

★★★***Mediterranée*** Lungomare 69 ☎683041

72 P75 Lift sea

PERUGIA
Perugia (☎075)

★★★***Rosetta*** pza Italia 19 ☎20841

rm108 (82) P Lift

Negri & Ricci via Romana 35, Piscille di Perugia (strada de P S Giov) ☎395044 M/c BMW

PESARO
Pessaro & Urbino (☎0721)

★★★**Mediterraneo Ricci** viale Trieste 199 ☎31556 tx560062

42 A4rm Lift sB 37000
dB 58000 M12000—15000 Beach
Credit cards 2 3 5

★★★**Savoy** viale Repubblica ☎67440 tx561624

54 P30 Lift sB 53000—78000
dB 91000—106000 M20000—25000
Credit cards 1 2 3 5

★★★**Vittoria** pza della Libertá 2 ☎34343 tx561624

36 P30 Lift sB 91000—109000
dB 131000—158000 M25000—30000
sea
Credit cards 1 2 3 5

★★**Atlantic** viale Trieste 365 ☎61911 tx560062

17 May—20 Sep
40 P32 Lift sB 31000—38000
dB 52000—60000 M22000 Beach sea
Credit cards 2 3

A Gabellini Strada Romagna 119 ☎39124 Aud Por VW

Paolo del Monte via Porta Rimini ☎32919 AR

PESCARA
Pescara (☎085)

★★★***AGIP*** Autostrada Adriatica Casello Pescara Nord (SS 16) ☎95321

85 P Lift

★★★***Carlton*** via Riviera 35 ☎26373

71 P Lift sea

MADA via Tiburtina Valeria ☎51342 For

At **MONTESLIVANO MARINA** (8km NW on SS16)

★★★★***Grand Montesilvano*** via Riviera 28 ☎838251 tx600118

140 P200 Lift Beach sea mountains
Credit cards 2 5

★★★**Serena Majestic** viale Kennedy ☎835142 tx600186

15 May—15 Oct
210 P100 Lift
sB 34000—55000
dB 57000—86000 M20000—30000
Beach sea

PIACENZA
Piacenza (☎0523)

★★★**Grande Albergo Roma** via Cittadella 14 ☎23201 tx530874

90 Lift sB 68000—73000
dB 101000—111000 M25000—30000
st%
Credit cards 1 2 3 4 5

Agosti & Lunardi via Perletti 5 ☎28920 AR

Mirani & Toscani via E-Parmense 6 ☎62721 M/c For

PIETRA LIGURE
Savona (☎019)

★★★★***Royal*** via Don Bado 129 ☎647192
105 **P** Lift ☾ Beach sea

PIETRASANTA (MARINA DI)
Lucca (☎0584)

★★★**Palazzo della Spiaggia** Lungomare Roma-Faocette ☎21195 tx501383
May—Sep
47 **P**20 Lift ☾ sB 92500—120000 dB 120000—175000 Beach sea
Credit cards [1] [2] [3] [5]

★★★**Battelli** viale Versilia 189, Motrone ☎20010 tx590403
15 May—30 Aug
42 **P**8 Lift ☾ sB 44500—53500 dB 65000—84000 M30000—35000 Beach sea

★★**Esplanade** viale Roma 235, Tonfano ☎21151 tx590403
33 **P**30 Lift ☾ dB 55000—77350 M23000—26000 sea
Credit card [1]

★★***Venezia*** via Firenze 48 ☎20731
34 **P** Lift ☾ sea

PINETA (LIGNANO) See **LIGNANO SABBIADORO**

PIOMBINO
Livorno (☎0565)

★★**Centrale** pza Verdi 2 ☎32581
rm38 (33) Lift ☾ sB47500 sB 68000 dB 111000 M25000—40000

E Blanchetti pza Constituzione 54 ☎33017 For

PISA
Pisa (☎050)

★★★★**Cavalieri** (CIGA) pza Stazioine 2 ☎43290 tx590663
100 Lift ☾ sB 24500—154500 dB 179000—234000 M50000 t9%
Credit cards [1] [2] [3] [4] [5]

★★**California Park** via Aurelia (4km NW on SS67) ☎890726 tx500119
16 Mar—Oct
74 **P**100 ☾ sB 48000—62000 dB 81000—101000 M25000
Credit cards [1] [2] [3] [5]

G Finocchi via Galcesana ☎86147 Aud VW

PISTICCI
Matera (☎0835)

★★★***AGIP*** (SS407 Basentana km 137) ☎462007 tx611627
64 **P** ☾

POLIGNANO A MARE
Bari (☎080)

★***Grotta Palazzese*** Via Narciso 59 ☎740261
14 **P**6 sea
Credit cards [1] [2] [3] [4] [5]

Italy

PONTASSIEVE
Firenze (☎055)

★★★**Moderno** (n.rest) ☎8315541 tx574381
120 **P**50 Lift ☾
sB 64000—79000
dB 98000—125000 st%
Credit cards [2] [3] [5]

PORDENONE
Pordenone (☎0434)

Automobile viale Grigoletti ☎32591 AR

Cossetti & Vatta viale Venezia ☎31474 Ren

PORT' ERCOLE
Grosseto (☎0564)

★★★★**Pelicano** (Relais et Châteaux) Cale del Santi (4.5km SW on Strada Panoramica) ☎833801 tx500131
10 Mar—10 Jan
34 A16rm **P**60 ☾ sB 150000—270000 dB 150000—410000 M65000 Beach sea
Credit cards [2] [3] [5]

★***Don Pedro*** via Panoramica ☎833914
Mar—Sep
44 **P** Lift ☾ sea

PORTO AZZURRO See **ELBA (ISOLA D')**

PORTOFERRAIO See **ELBA (ISOLA D')**

PORTOFINO
Genova (☎0185)

★★★★**Splendido** (Relais et Châteaux) viale Baratta 13 ☎69551 tx331057
30 Mar—Oct
67 **P**67 Lift ☾ sB 243000 dB 386000 M70000 St% sea
Credit cards [1] [2] [3]

★★***Piccolo*** via Duca degli Abruzzi 31 ☎69015
Mar—2 Nov
rm27 (25) **P** ☾ Beach sea

PORTONOVO See **ANCONA**

PORTO SAN GIORGIO
Ascoli Piceno (☎0734)

★★**Terrazza** via Castelfidaro 2 ☎3790005
32 **P**20 Lift sB16000—22000 sB 20000—25500 dB34000—38500 dB 44000—48000 M17000 Beach

Petracci via Nazionale Adriatica 235 ☎4248

POSITANO
Salerno (☎089)

★★★**Savola** via C-Colombo 73 (n.rest) ☎875003
15 Apr—15 Oct
rm44 (39) Lift ☾
sB 26000—38000 dB48000—60000 dB 64000—78000 sea

★★**Buca di Bacco & Buca Résidence** via Rampa Teglia 8 ☎875699 tx722574
22 Mar—14 Oct
55 Lift ☾ sB 52000—58000 dB 93000—113000 M35000 sea
Credit cards [1] [2] [3] [5]

★★***Maresca*** ☎825140
Jan—30 Oct
20rm (12) **P** mountains sea
Credit cards [1] [2] [3] [4] [5]

POTENZA
Potenza (☎0971)

L Olita via del Gallitello ☎26477 **P** Ope Vau

POZZUOLI
Napoli (☎081)

Pelli via E-Scarfoglio ☎7605322 M/c Ope Vau

PRAIANO
Salerno (☎089)

★★***Grand Tritone*** via Campo 1 ☎874333 tx770025
Apr—Oct
70 **P** Lift ☾ Beach sea
Credit cards [2] [3]

★★**Tramonto d'Oro** via G-Capriglione 119 ☎874008 tx770073
50 **P**25 Lift ☾
dB 58000—96000 M20000—25000 sea
Credit cards [1] [2] [3] [5]

PRATO
Firenze (☎0574)

★★★***President*** via Simintendi 20 ☎30251 tx571587
78 **P**40 Lift ☾
Credit cards [1] [2] [3] [4] [5]

★★**Flora** via Cairoli 31 (n.rest) ☎20021 tx571358
31 Lift ☾ sB 64000—69000 dB 98000—109000
Credit cards [1] [2] [3] [5]

PROCCHIO See **ELBA (ISOLA D')**

PUGNOCHIUSO See **VIESTE**

PUNTA ALA
Grosseto (☎0564)

★★★★**Gallia Palace** (Relais et Châteaux) via delle Sughere ☎922022 tx590454
18 May—Sep
98 **P**80 Lift ☾
sB 137000—197000
dB 184000—324000 M39000—47000 Beach sea
Credit card [2]

RAGUSA See **SICILIA (SICILY)**

RAPALLO
Genova (☎0185)

★★★**Eurotel** via Aurelia Ponente 22 ☎60981 tx213851
65 **P**80 Lift sB 68000—77000 dB 111000—124000 M30000—35000 sea
Credit cards [1] [2] [3] [5]

★★★***Grand Italia & Lido*** Lungomare Castello 1 ☎50492
🛁 50 **P** Lift ☾ Beach ⊡ ∪ sea
Credit cards [2] [3] [5]

★★★***Miramare*** via V-Veneto 27 ☎50293
rm28 (🛁 🚿 23) **P** Lift ☾ sea

★★★***Riviera*** pza IV Novembre 2 ☎50248
Closed 2 Nov—20 Dec
🛁 🚿 25 Lift ☾ sea
Credit cards [2] [5]

★**Brandoni** via Marsala 24 ☎50423
rm12 (🛁 4) Lift ☾ sB16500—18500 dB33000—37000 dB 🛁 34000—39000 M12000 sea
Credit card [2]

🚗 **E Massa** via G-Mameli 182 ☎50689 AR

🚗 **Ratto & Cordano** via Arpinati 33 ☎51419 M/c **P**

RAVELLO
Salerno (☎089)

★★★**Caruso Belvedere** via Toro 52 ☎857111
rm26 (🛁 🚿 22) **P**30 ☾ sB33500—37500 sB 🛁 🚿 43500—53500 dB52000—68000 dB 🛁 🚿 82000—92000 M32000 sea
Credit card [2]

★★★**Palumbo** via Toro 28 ☎857244 tx770101
🛁 🚿 22 A7rm ⌂ **P** ☾
sB 🛁 🚿 178000—208000
dB 🛁 🚿 256000—336000 M45000 sea
Credit cards [1] [2] [3] [5]

★★**Parsifal** via d'Anna 5 ☎857144
15 Mar—10 Oct
rm19 (🛁 16) ⌂ **P**8 Lift ☾ sB25000—31000 sB 🛁 35000—37000 dB42000—47000 dB 🛁 56000—60000 M25000 sea
Credit cards [1] [2] [3] [4] [5]

RAVENNA
Ravenna (☎0544)

★★★★**Jolly** pza Mameli 1 ☎35762 tx550575
🛁 75 Lift ☾ sB 🛁 90000 dB 🛁 134000
Credit cards [1] [2] [3] [4] [5]

★★★**Bisanzio** via Salara 30 (n.rest) ☎27111 tx551070
🛁 36 Lift ☾ sB 🛁 72000 dB 🛁 114000
Credit cards [1] [2] [3] [5]

★★**Centrale Byron** via IV Novembre 14 (n.rest) ☎33479 tx551070
rm57 (🛁 54) Lift ☾ sB 🛁 41500 dB 🛁 67000
Credit cards [1] [2] [3] [5]

★**Romea** (2.5km S on SS16) ☎61247
🛁 🚿 39 **P**100 Lift ☾ sB 🛁 🚿 41000—45000 dB 🛁 🚿 68000—74000 M22000
Credit cards [1] [2] [3] [5]

🚗 **C Ravennate** via M-Perilli 40 ☎421579 **P** Fia Ren

REGGIO DI CALABRIA
Reggio di Calabria (☎0965)

C Mazzone via San Caterina 12 ☎48600 M/c Aud Por VW

REGGIO NELL 'EMILIA
Reggio Nell 'Emilia (☎0522)

★★★★**Grand Astoria** via L-Nobili 4 ☎35245 tx530534
🛁 112 ⌂ **P** Lift ☾ sB 🛁 94000 dB 🛁 134000 M30000
Credit cards [1] [2] [3] [5]

★★★***Posta*** pza C-Battisti 4 (n.rest) ☎32944
rm69 (🛁 🚿 60) ⌂ Lift ☾
Credit cards [1] [2] [3] [5]

RENDE See **COSENZA**

RICAVO See **CASTELLINA IN CHIANTI**

RICCIONE
Forli (☎0541)

★★★★**Atlantic** Lungomare della Libertá 15 ☎601155 tx550192
Apr—15 Oct
🛁 🚿 65 ⌂ **P**50 Lift ☾
sB 🛁 🚿 60000—100000
dB 🛁 🚿 100000—140000 M35000 ≋ Beach sea
Credit cards [1] [2] [3] [4] [5]

★★★★**Savioli Spiaggia** via G-d'Annunzio 2—6 ☎43252 tx551038
May—Sep
🛁 🚿 100 ⌂ **P**80 Lift ☾
sB 🛁 🚿 73000—92000
dB 🛁 🚿 120000—160000 M35000 t% ≋ sea
Credit cards [1] [2] [3] [5]

★★★**Abner's** Lungomare Repubblica 7 ☎600601 tx550153
🛁 50 **P**15 Lift ☾ sB 🛁 71000—101000 dB 🛁 112000—152000 M20000—35000 ୧ ≋ Beach sea
Credit card [2]

★★★**Arizona** via G-d'Annunzio 22 ☎48520
May—Sep
🛁 64 **P**30 Lift ☾ sB 🛁 36500—46000 dB 🛁 60500—80500 M20000—25000 Beach sea
Credit cards [2] [5]

★★★**Lungomare** viale Milano 7 ☎41601 tx550561
25 Mar—20 Sep
🛁 🚿 58 **P**40 Lift ☾ sB 🛁 🚿 25000—50000 dB 🛁 🚿 35000—70000 M19000—30000 Beach sea
Credit cards [2] [3] [5]

★★★**Vienna & Touring** viale Mirano 78c ☎601700 tx550153
May—Sep
🛁 85 ⌂ **P**15 Lift ☾ sB 🛁 64000—79000 dB 🛁 98000—128000 M20000—35000 ୧ ≋ Beach sea
Credit card [2]

★★**Alexandra Plaza** viale Torino 61 ☎610541 tx550330
Apr—Sep
🛁 60 **P**40 Lift ☾ sB 🛁 43000—70000 dB 🛁 66000—95000 M22000—35000 ≋ Beach sea
Credit cards [2] [3]

★★**Nevada** via Milano 54 ☎601245 tx551245
15 May—Sep
🛁 🚿 50 ⌂ **P**30 Lift ☾ sB 🛁 🚿 32000 dB 🛁 🚿 58000 M17000 Beach sea

🚗 **Morelli & Mucciollo** via R-Molari 26 ☎600806 M/c **P** VW

RIMINI
Forli (☎0541)

★★★**Ambasciatori** viale Vespucci 22 ☎27642 tx550132
🛁 🚿 66 **P**40 Lift ☾ sB 🛁 🚿 75000—99000 dB 🛁 🚿 120000—182000 M35000 ≋ Beach sea
Credit cards [1] [2] [3] [4] [5]

★★★**President** via Tripoli 270 ☎25741
May—Sep
🛁 50 ⌂ Lift ☾ sB 🛁 27000—32000 dB 🛁 47000—56000 M12000
Credit cards [1] [2] [3] [5]

★★***Alpen*** viale Regina Élena 203 ☎80662
May—Sep
🛁 🚿 56 **P** Lift ☾ sea

🚗 **Grattacielo** viale P-Amedeo 11 ☎24610 **P** Ope

🚗 **Sartini** viale P-Amedeo 13 ☎27548 **P** Fia

At **RIVAZZURRA** (4km SE)

★★★**Grand Meeting** viale Regina Margherita 46 ☎32123
May—Sep
🛁 🚿 50 **P**30 Lift ☾ sB 🛁 🚿 20500—44500 dB 🛁 🚿 29500—62000 M18000 Beach sea

★★★**Little** via Gubbio 16 ☎33258
May—Oct
🚿 50 **P**15 Lift ☾ sB🚿 19500—28500 dB🚿 39000—52000 M13000
Credit cards [1] [2] [3] [5]

RIVA DEL GARDA
Trento (☎0464)

★★★**Lac & Parc** (BW) viale Rovereto 38 ☎520202 tx400258
22 Mar—20 Oct
🛁 🚿 177 ⌂ **P**150 Lift ☾
sB 🛁 🚿 62000—72000
dB 🛁 🚿 114000—164000 M25000—28000 ୧ ⊡ ≋ lake mountains
Credit cards [1] [2] [3] [5]

RIVAZZURRA See **RIMINI**

RIVIERA (LIGNANO) See **LIGNANO SABBIADORO**

ROCCARASO
L'Aquila (☎0864)

★★★***AGIP Roccaraso*** (SS17 dell'Appennino l'Abruzzese km 136) ☎62443
🚿 57 **P** Lift ☾ mountains

ROLLE (PASSO DI)
Trento (☎0439)

★***Passo Rolle*** ☎68216
rm27 (🛁 7) **P** mountains

ROMA (ROME)

Roma (☎06)

See Plan page 000

★★★★★**Cavalieri Hilton** via Cadlolo 101 ☎3151 tx610296 Plan **1**
🛁387 ⌂ **P**100 Lift ☾
sB🛁240000—280000
dB🛁360000—400000 M alc 🔑

★★★★★**Excelsior** (CIGA) via V-Veneto 125 ☎4708 tx610232 Plan **1A**
🛁394 ⌂ **P** Lift ☾ sB🛁254000—330000
dB🛁353000—501000

★★★★★**Grand** (CIGA) via Vittorio E-Orlando 3 ☎4709 tx610210 Plan **2**
🛁171 ⌂ **P** Lift ☾ sB🛁213500—293500
dB🛁297000—427000 M alc t18%

★★★★★***Grand Flora*** via V-Veneto 191 (n.rest) ☎497821 tx680494 Plan **2A**
🛁200 ⌂ Lift ☾

★★★★★**Hassler** pza Trinità dei Monti 6 ☎6782651 tx610208 Plan **3**
🛁102 ⌂ Lift ☾ sB🛁280000—330000
dB🛁420000—500000 M alc t%

★★★★★**Jolly — Leonardo da Vinci** via dei Gracchi 324 ☎39680 tx611182 Plan **3A**
🛁245 ⌂ Lift ☾ sB🛁145000
dB🛁200000
Credit cards [1] [2] [3] [4] [5]

ROMA (ROME)

1 ★★★★★ Cavalieri Hilton
1A ★★★★★ Excelsior
2 ★★★★★ Grand
2A ★★★★★ Grand Flora
3 ★★★★★ Hassler
3A ★★★★★ Jolly-Leonardo da Vinci
4 ★★★★★ Jolly V-Veneto
6 ★★★★ Eliseo
6A ★★★★ Holiday Inn Parco del Medici
8 ★★★★ Quirinale
8A ★★★★ Holiday Inn St Peter's
8B ★★★★ Sheraton
9 ★★★★ Ville
10 ★★★ AGIP (6km W on SS1)
10A ★★★ Bernini-Bristol
10B ★★★ Boston
11 ★★★ Britannia
12 ★★★ Columbus
13 ★★★ Commodore
15 ★★★ Lord Byron
16 ★★★ Nord-Nuova Roma
19 ★★★ Regina-Carlton
20 ★★★ Rivoli
21 ★★★ Savoy
25 ★ Bela (At La Storta 16km NW on SS2)
29 ★ Scalinata di Spagna

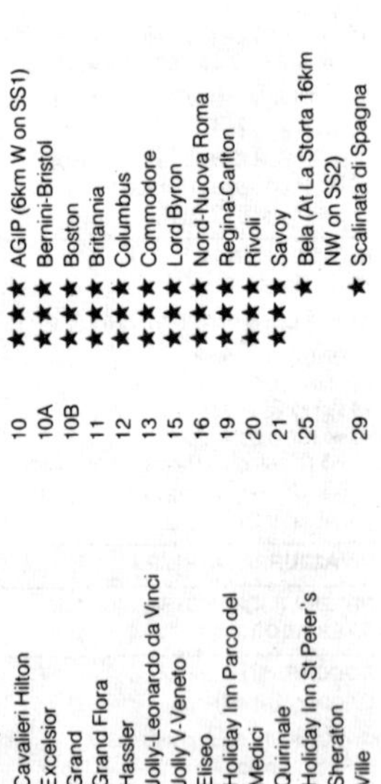

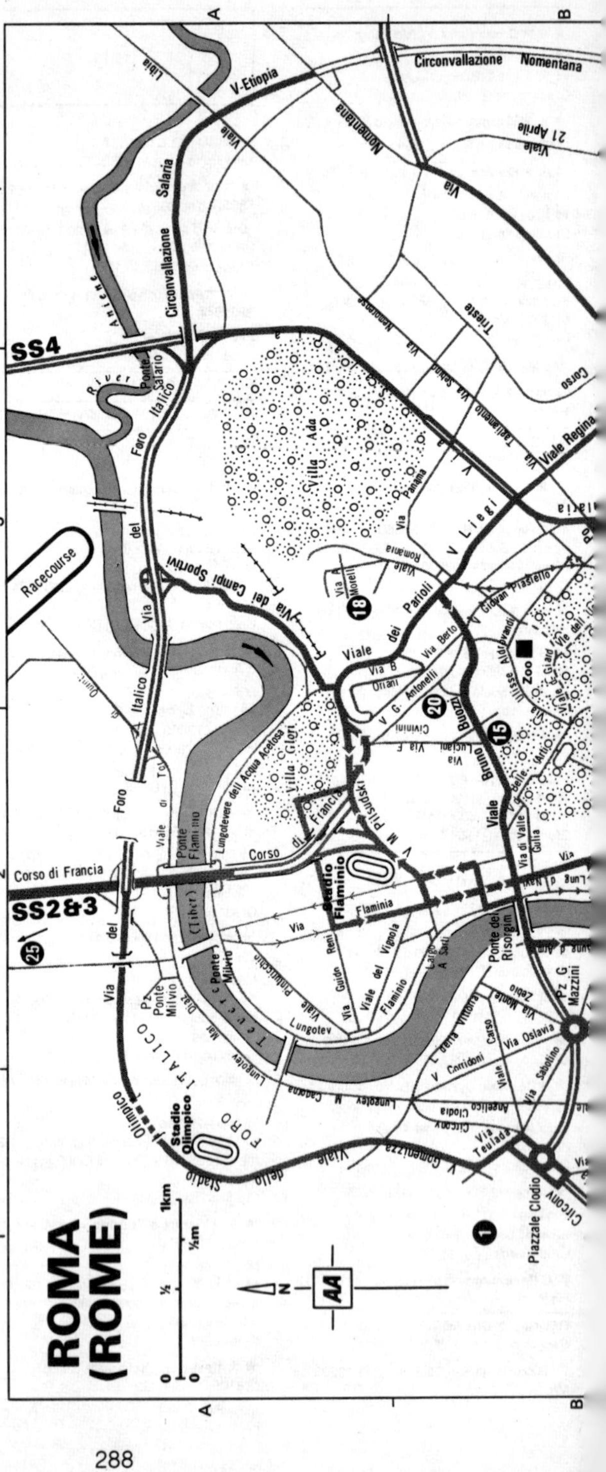

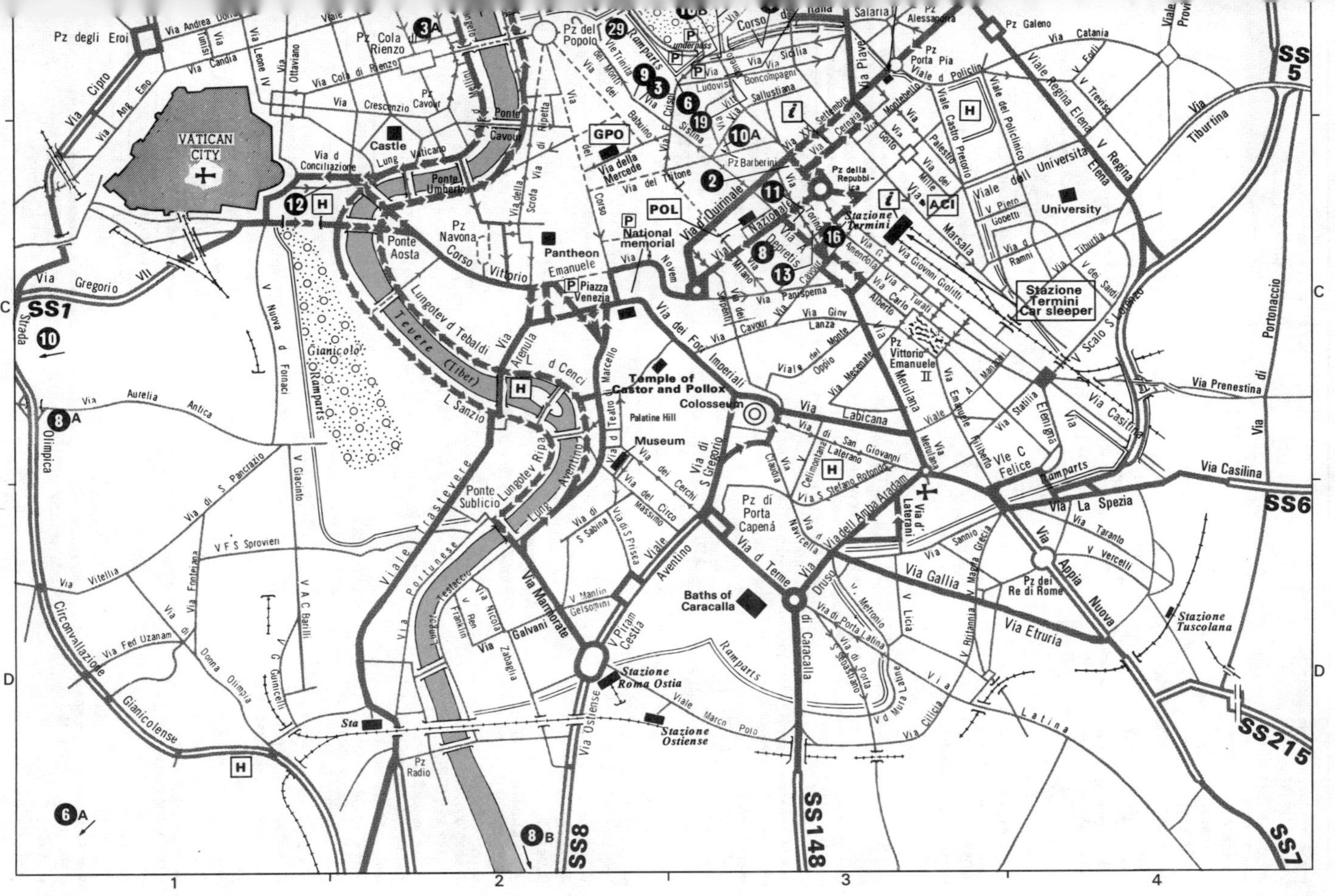

SS5
SS6
SS215
SS7
SS148
SS8
SS1
Via Prenestina
Via Casilina
Stazione Tuscolana
Via Tiburtina
Viale Regina Elena
V Regina Elena
Viale dell Università
University
Viale del Policlinico
Viale Castro Pretorio
Stazione Termini Car sleeper
Scalo S Lorenzo
Via La Spezia
Via Appia Nuova
Pz dei Re di Rome
Via Etruria
Via Gallia
Via Latina
Ramparts
Vle C Felice
Via Merulana
Via d' Laterani
Pz Vittorio Emanuele II
Via Labicana
Via Giovanni Giolitti
Stazione Termini
Pz della Repubblica
Via Nazionale
Via A Depretis
Via Cavour
Via dei Fori Imperiali
Colosseum
Temple of Castor and Pollox
Palatine Hill
Museum
Via di S Gregorio
Pz di Porta Capená
Baths of Caracalla
Via d Terme di Caracalla
Viale Aventino
Via del Circo Massimo
Via dei Cerchi
Via d Teatro di Marcello
Stazione Roma Ostia
Stazione Ostiense
Viale Marco Polo
V Piram Cestia
Via Ostiense
Via Marmorate
Via Galvani
Via Zabaglia
Lungotev Aventino
Lungotev Ripa
Ponte Sublicio
Viale Trastevere
Via Portuense
Pz Radio
Sta
Via d'Quirinale
Via Sistina
Pz Barberini
Via Piave
Salaria
Pz Porta Pia
Pz Alessandria
Pz Galeno
Via XX Settembre
POL
National memorial
GPO
Via della Mercede
Via del Tritone
Via del Babuino
Vle Trinità dei Monti
Pz del Popolo
Corso
Pantheon
Piazza Venezia
Corso Vittorio Emanuele
Pz Navona
Ponte Aosta
Lungotev d Tebaldi
Tevere (Tiber)
L Sanzio
Via Arenula
L d Cenci
Ponte Umberto
Ponte Cavour
Castle
Pz Cavour
Via Crescenzio
Via Cola di Rienzo
Pz Cola di Rienzo
Ottaviano
Via d Conciliazione
Gianicolo
V Giacinto
V A C Barilli
V Nuova d Fornaci
V G Guinicelli
V F S Sprovieri
Via di S Pancrazio
Via Aurelia Antica
Via Fonteiana
Via Fed Uzanam
Via Vitellia
Circonvallazione Gianicolense
Strada Olimpica
Via Gregorio VII
VATICAN CITY
Via Leone IV
Via Candia
Via Andrea Doria
Pz degli Eroi
Via Cipro
Via Ang Emo
Portonaccio
C
D
1
2
3
4

★★★★★**Jolly V-Veneto** corso d'Italia 1 ☏8495 tx612293 Plan **4**

🛁 200 🚗 Lift ☾ sB🛁 160000 dB🛁 220000
Credit cards 1 2 3 4 5

★★★★**Eliseo** (BW) via di Porta Pinciana 30 ☏460556 tx610693 Plan **6**

🛁 53 🚗 Lift ☾ sB🛁 159000 dB🛁 250500 M37000
Credit cards 1 2 3 5

★★★★***Holiday Inn Parco del Medici*** viale Castello della Magliana 65 (10km W of autostrada to Fiumicino [Airport]) ☏5475 tx613302 Plan **6A**

🛁 331 **P** Lift ☾ Pool

★★★★**Holiday Inn St-Peter's** via Aurelia Finntica 415 ☏5872 tx625434 Plan **8A**

🛁 334 **P**400 Lift ☾ sB🛁 130000 dB192000 t%
Credit cards 1 2 3 5

★★★★**Quirinale** (SRS) via Nazionale 7 ☏4707 tx610332 Plan **8**

🛁 200 🚗 Lift ☾ sB🛁 fr160000 dB🛁 fr220000 Mfr40000
Credit cards 1 2 5

★★★★**Sheraton** viale del Pattinaggio ☏5453 tx614223 Plan **8B**

🛁 623 🚗 **P**200 Lift ☾ sB🛁 176500—221000 dB🛁 241500—306500
Credit cards 1 2 3 4 5

★★★★**Ville** (Forum) via Sistina 69 ☏6733 tx620836 Plan **9**

🛁 197 **P** Lift ☾ sB🛁 168000 dB🛁 252000
Credit cards 2 3 4 5

★★★***AGIP*** via Aurelia (6km W on SS1) ☏6379001 tx613699 Plan **10**

222 **P** Lift ☾

★★★**Bernini Bristol** (SRS) pza Barberini 23 ☏463051 tx619554 Plan **10A**

🛁 127 Lift ☾ sB🛁 245000—265000 dB🛁 350000—380000 M alc
Credit cards 1 2 5

★★★**Boston** (ETAP) via Lombardia 47 ☏473951 tx680460 Plan **10B**

🛁 125 🚗 **P** Lift ☾ sB🛁 105000—135000 dB🛁 165000—215000 M25000—27000
Credit cards 1 2 3 5

★★★**Britannia** via Napoli 64 (n.rest) ☏465785 tx611292 Plan **11**

🛁 32 **P**6 Lift ☾ sB🛁 140000 dB🛁 175000
Credit cards 1 2 3 5

★★★**Columbus** via della Concillazione 33 ☏6565435 tx620096 Plan **12**

107rm (🛁 68) **P**30 Lift ☾ sB55000—60000 sB🛁 80000—90000 dB90000—100000 dB🛁 130000—140000 Mfr35000 St%
Credit cards 1 2 3 5

★★★***Commodore*** via Torino 1 (n.rest) ☏4754112 tx612170 Plan **13**

🛁 65 🚗 Lift ☾
Credit cards 1 2 5

Italy

★★★***Lord Byron*** (Relais et Châteaux) via G-de-Notaris 5 ☏3609541 tx611217 Plan **15**

🛁 50 🚗 **P** Lift ☾
Credit cards 1 2 3 5

★★★**Nord-Nuova Roma** via G-Amendola 3 ☏465441 tx610556 Plan **16**

🛁 159 🚗 Lift ☾ sB🛁 86000 dB🛁 130000 M26000
Credit cards 1 2 3 5

★★★**Regina-Carlton** via V-Veneto 72 ☏476851 tx620863 Plan **19**

🛁 134 🚗 Lift ☾ sB🛁 165000 dB🛁 244000 Mfr45000
Credit cards 1 2 3 5

★★★**Rivoli** via Torquato Taramelli 7, Parioli ☏870141 tx614615 Plan **20**

🛁 50 Lift sB🛁 90000 dB🛁 110000

★★★**Savoy** via Ludovisi 15 ☏4744141 tx611339 Plan **21**

🛁 115 Lift ☾ sB🛁 170000 dB🛁 265000 M30000
Credit cards 1 2 3 4 5

★★**Hiberia** via 24 Maggio 7 ☏6782662 Not on plan

rm25 (🛁 23) Lift ☾ sB36500—40500 sB🛁 42500—46500 dB69000—73000 dB🛁 73000—83000
Credit cards 1 2 3 5

★***Scalinata di Spagna*** pza Trinita dei Monti 17 (n.rest) ☏6793006 Plan **29**

🛁 14 **P**3 ☾

Marchir Orlando Circonvallazione Trionfale 133 ☏3599893 M/c DJ Sko Toy

At **STORTA (LA)** (16km NW on SS2)

★***Bela*** via Cassia 1801 ☏3790232 Plan **25**

🛁 44 **P** ☾

RONCIGLIONE
Viterbo (☏0761)

★★★**Rio Vicano** via Cassia Cuimna (km19) ☏626366 tx616083

20 Mar—6 Nov
🛁 50 🚗 **P**50 ☾ sB🛁 33000—39000 dB🛁 57000—66300 M15000—17000 lake
Credit cards 1 2 3 4 5

ST-VINCENT
Aosta (☏0166)

★★★★***Billia*** viale Piemonte 18 ☏3446 tx212144

🛁 134 🚗 **P** Lift ☾ mountains

Fabris pza Zerbion ☏2619 **P** Cit

SALERNO
Salerno (☏089)

★★★★**Jolly** Lungomare Trieste 1 ☏225222 tx770050

rm105 (🛁 102) **P** Lift ☾ sB🛁 84000 dB🛁 128000
Credit cards 1 2 3 4 5

G Jannone via Picenza 12 ☏351229 AR DJ

At **VIETRI SUL MARE** (3km W)

★★★★**Lloyd's Baia** (SRS) via de Marinis ☏210145 tx770043

🛁 120 🚗 **P**100 Lift ☾ sB🛁 91000 sB🛁 127000 M35000 Beach sea
Credit cards 1 2 3 5

SALÓ
Brescia (☏0365)

★★★**Duomo** via Duomo 18 ☏21026 tx303028

🛁 22 🚗 **P** Lift ☾ sB🛁 60000—80000 dB🛁 98000 M alc lake
Credit cards 1 2 3 5

SALSOMAGGIORE TERME
Parma (☏0524)

★★★★**Porro** via Porro 10 ☏78221 tx530639

8 Mar—Dec
rm85 (🛁 79) **P**100 Lift ☾ sB67000—73000 sB🛁 79500—85500 dB105000—114500 dB🛁 119500—132500 M35000
Credit cards 1 2 5

SAN BARTOLOMEO AL MARE
Imperia (☏0183)

★★★***Mayola*** ☏400739

15 Mar—15 Oct
🛁 80 🚗 **P**20 Lift ☾ Beach sea
Credit cards 1 2 3 4 5

SAN BENEDETTO DEL TRONTO
Ascoli Piceno (☏0735)

E G Tomassini corso Mazzini 249 ☏5608 Aud VW

SÁN CÁNDIDO-INNICHEN
Bolzano (☏0474)

★★**Park Sole Paradiso** via Sesto 11 ☏73120 tx400329

20 Dec—5 Apr & 30 May—5 Oct
🛁 45 🚗 **P**30 Lift sB🛁 25000—50000 dB🛁 50000—100000 M13000—25000 S10% mountains
Credit cards 2 5

SAN DONATO MILANESE
See **MILANO (MILAN)**

SAN FELICE See CREMONA

SAN GIMIGNANO
Siena (☏0577)

★★**Cisterna** pza della Cisterna 23 ☏940328

10 Mar—10 Nov
🛁 46 Lift ☾ sB🛁 35000—42000 dB🛁 68000—76000 M22000—35000
Credit cards 1 2 3 5

SAN MAMETE See VALSOLDA

SAN MARINO follows ITALY

SAN MARTINO DI CASTROZZA
Trento (☏0439)

★★★***San Martino*** ☏680011 tx44043

20 Dec—20 Apr & Jul—20 Sep
🛁 46 🚗 **P** ☾ mountains

★★***Savoia*** via Passo Rolle 233 ☎68094 tx401543

20 Dec—1 Apr & Jul—1 Sep
🛁 🚿 73 🚗 **P**50 Lift ☾ mountains
Credit cards [2] [5]

★**Belvedere** via Passo Rolle 247 ☎68000 tx401543

20 Dec—5 Apr & 25 Jun—10 Sep
🛁 33 **P**30 Lift sB 🛁 49000—60000
dB 🛁 74000—124000 M25000—27000 mountains
Credit cards [1] [2] [3]

SAN REMO
Imperia (☎0184)

★★★★★**Royal** corso Imperatrice 80 ☎79991 tx270511

20 Dec—20 Oct
🛁 138 🚗 **P**90 Lift ☾
sB 🛁 144000—164000
dB 🛁 258000—288000 M50000 🎾 ≈ sea
Credit cards [1] [2] [3] [5]

★★★★***Miramare*** corso Matuzia 9 ☎882381 tx270620

20 Dec—22 Sep
🛁 🚿 57 **P**60 Lift ☾ 🎾 ▭ sea
Credit cards [1] [2] [3] [5]

★★★**Astoria West End** corso Matuzia 8 ☎70791 tx213834

🛁 112 🚗 **P**35 Lift ☾ sB 🛁 75000—92000
dB 🛁 130000—170000 M40000 ≈ Beach sea
Credit cards [2] [5]

★★★**Europa** corso Imperatrice 27 ☎70605

rm76 (🛁 🚿 49) 🚗 Lift ☾ sB47000—51000
sB 🛁 🚿 65500—70000 dB88000—95000
dB 🛁 🚿 105000—121000 M260000 sea
Credit cards [1] [2] [3] [5]

★★★**Paradiso** corso Imperatrice ☎85112 tx270620

20 Dec—Oct
🛁 🚿 41 🚗 **P**28 Lift ☾
sB 🛁 🚿 52500—57500
dB 🛁 🚿 74000—93000 M20000—28000 Beach sea
Credit cards [1] [2] [3] [4] [5]

★★★***Residence Principe*** via Asquasciati 48 (n.rest) ☎83565 tx216390

🛁 52 🚗 **P**25 Lift ☾ ≈ ▭ sea
Credit cards [4] [5]

★★**Beaurivage** corso Trieste 49 ☎85146 tx270620

🛁 🚿 29 Lift ☾ sB 🛁 🚿 33700
dB 🛁 🚿 63000 M18500 sea

★★**Bobby Motel** via Marconi 208 (2.5km W on SS1) ☎60255

22 Dec—20 Oct
🛁 75 A10rm 🚗 **P**55 Lift ☾ sB 🛁 51000
dB 🛁 87000 sea

★★***King*** corso Cavallotti 92 ☎880167

🛁 🚿 26 **P**25 ☾ sea

★★***Morandi*** corso Matuzia ☎73686

🛁 🚿 32 🚗 **P** Lift ☾ sea

Italy

SANTA CATERINA VALFURVA
Sondrio (☎0342)

★★**Sobretta** ☎935510

Dec—Apr & Jul—10 Sep
rm26 (🛁 🚿 20) 🚗 **P**25 sB20000—24000
dB26000—36000 dB 🛁 🚿 30000—46000
M16000 mountains

SANTA CRISTINA VAL GARDENA-ST CHRISTINA IN GRÖDEN
Bolzano (☎0471)

★★**Posta** ☎76678

🛁 🚿 74 A16rm 🚗 **P** Lift ☾
sB 🛁 🚿 23000—35000
dB 🛁 🚿 46000—70000 M18000—22000 🎾 ≈ mountains

SANTA MARGHERITA LIGURE
Genova (☎0185)

★★★★★**Imperial Palace** via Pagana 19 ☎88991 tx271398

15 Mar—6 Nov
🛁 🚿 106 **P**80 Lift ☾
sB 🛁 🚿 138000—198000
dB 🛁 🚿 244000—364000 M60000 ≈ Beach sea
Credit cards [2] [5]

★★★★**Miramare** (SRS) via M-Ignoto 30 ☎87014 tx270437

🛁 82 🚗 **P**25 Lift ☾ sB 🛁 116000—146000
dB 🛁 212000—272000 M60000 ≈ Beach U sea
Credit cards [2] [3]

★★★**Continental** via Pagana 8 ☎86512 tx271601

🛁 76 A6rm 🚗 **P**50 Lift ☾
sB 🛁 60000—96000
dB 🛁 104000—169000 M32000—42000 Beach sea
Credit cards [1] [2] [3] [5]

★★★**Laurin** corso Marconi 3 (n.rest) ☎289971 tx583043

🛁 🚿 41 Lift ☾ sB 🛁 🚿 78000—116000
dB 🛁 🚿 109000—158000 sea
Credit cards [1] [2] [3] [5]

★★★**Metropole** via Pagana 2 ☎286134

Closed Nov
🛁 48 A12rm 🚗 **P27** Lift ☾
sB 🛁 62000—66000 dB 🛁 96000—110000
M26000—38000 Beach sea
Credit cards [1] [2] [3] [5]

★★★**Park Suisse** via Favale 31 ☎289571 tx271549

🛁 🚿 83 **P** sB 🛁 🚿 79000—104000
dB 🛁 🚿 138000—193000 M29000—36000 ≈ sea

★★★**Regina Elena** Lungomare M-Ignoto 44 ☎287003 tx271563

🛁 🚿 86 A22rm **P**60 Lift ☾
sB 🛁 🚿 80000—92000
dB 🛁 🚿 144000—158000 M31000—40000 Beach sea
Credit cards [1] [2] [3] [4] [5]

★★**Villa Anita** viale Minerva ☎86543

21 Dec—21 Oct
rm20 (🛁 🚿 14) A5rm 🚗 **P**7
sB 🛁 🚿 33000—35700 dB47000
dB 🛁 🚿 50700—57700 M18000—20000 sea
Credit card [3]

★**Europa** via Trento 5 ☎87187

rm16 (🛁 10) dB42000—45000
dB 🛁 50000—55000 M20000 sea
Credit cards [1] [3] [5]

SAPRI
Salerno (☎0973)

🚘 **Comisso** via Pisacane 22 ☎31370 **P** For

SARDAGNA See **TRENTO**

SARDEGNA (ISOLA) (SARDINIA)

CAGLIARI
Cagliari (☎070)

★★★***AGIP*** Circonvallazione Nuova ☎561645 tx611627

🚿 57 **P** Lift ☾

GOLFO ARANCI
Sassari (☎0789)

★★**Margherita** ☎46906

🛁 🚿 26 🚗 **P**14 ☾ sB 🛁 🚿 36000—53000
dB 🛁 🚿 59000—82000 sea
Credit cards [1] [2] [3] [5]

MACOMER
Nuoro (☎0785)

★★★***AGIP*** corso Umberto 1 (SS131 di C-Felice km 145) ☎71066 tx611627

🚿 96 **P** Lift ☾

NUORO
Nuoro (☎0784)

★★★***AGIP*** via Trieste ☎34071

🚿 51 **P** Lift ☾

SASSARI
Sassari (☎079)

★★★***AGIP*** Serra Secca ☎271440 tx611627

🚿 57 **P** Lift ☾

VILLASIMIUS
Cagliari (☎070)

★★★***Timi Ama*** (3km S) ☎791228

5 Jun—20 Sep
🛁 65 **P** ☾ 🎾 Beach

SARZANA
Le Spezia (☎0187)

★★★***AGIP*** Circonvallazione Aurelia 32 ☎621491 tx611627

🚿 51 **P** Lift ☾

SASSARI See **SARDEGNA (ISOLA) (SARDINIA)**

SAVONA
Savona (☎019)

★★★**AGIP** via Nizza, Zinola ☎801961 tx611627

🚿 60 **P** Lift ☾

★★★**Riviera-Suisse** via Palesocapa 24 (n.rest) ☎20683

rm70 (🛁 64) **P**10 Lift ☾ sB39500 →

sB 60500 dB 90000
Credit cards 1 2 3 4 5

M Spirito corso Viglienzoni 8F ☎806860

SECONDIGLIANO See **NAPOLI (NAPLES)**

SEGRATE See **MILANO (MILAN)**

SELVA DI VAL GARDENA-WOLKENSTEIN IN GRÖDEN
Bolzano (☎0471)

★★**Solaia** via Centro 142 ☎75104 tx400359

15 Jun—15 Oct & Dec—15 Apr
28 **P**30 ☾ sB 40000—50000
dB 80000—100000 M15000—30000
mountains

SENIGALLIA
Ancona (☎071)

★★★***City*** Lungomare Dante Alighieri 12 ☎63464

60 **P** Lift ☾ Beach sea

★★★**Ritz** Lungomare Dante Alighieri 142 ☎63563 tx560044

Jun—14 Sep
150 **P**200 Lift ☾ Beach sea

G E Luzi & Figli via Podesti 156 ☎62035
P Aud Por VW

SESTO CALENDE
Varese (☎0331)

★★***Tre Re*** pza Garibaldi 25 ☎924229

Mar—Nov
36 **P** Lift ☾ lake

SESTO FIORENTINO See **FIRENZE (FLORENCE)**

SESTRI LEVANTE
Genova (☎0185)

★★★★**Villa Balbi** viale Rimembranze 1 ☎42941

24 Apr—5 Oct
100 **P**45 Lift ☾ sB 80000—90000
dB 130000—150000 M38000—45000

Credit cards 1 2 3 5

★★★***Vis à Vis*** via della Chuisa 28 ☎42661

50 **P**40 Lift ☾
Credit cards 1 2 3 5

★★**Helvetia** via Cappuccini 17 ☎41175

Mar—Aug
28 **P**12 Lift ☾ sB 45000
dB 55000 M35000

SETTIMO See **TORINO (TURIN)**

SICILIA (SICILY)

AGRIGENTO
Agrigento (☎0922)

★★★**Jolly del Templi** Parco Angeli, Villaggio Mosè (SS115) ☎76144 tx910086

146 **P** Lift ☾ sB 72500 dB 112000

Credit cards 1 2 3 4 5

P Capizzi viale della Vittoria 115 ☎65854
M/c AR

Italy

CANNIZZARO
Catania (☎095)

★★★**Grand Baia Verde** (BW) via della Scogliera 8—10 ☎491522 tx970285

121 **P**50 Lift ☾ sB 120000
dB 200000 M35000
Credit cards 1 2 3 4 5

CATANIA
Catania (☎095)

★★★***AGIP*** Ognina (SS114 km92) (n.rest) ☎492233 tx611627

56 **P** Lift ☾

★★★**Jolly** pza Trento 13 ☎316933 tx970080

159 **P** Lift ☾ sB 86500—92000
dB 130000—140000
Credit cards 1 2 3 4 5

MARSALA
Trapani (☎0923)

★★★***AGIP*** Uscita per Mazara del Vallo (SS115 km31) ☎951611

32 **P** Lift ☾

MESSINA
Messina (☎090)

★★★★**Jolly** via Garibaldi 126 ☎43401 tx980074

99 Lift ☾ sB 72500 dB 115000 sea
Credit cards 1 2 3 4 5

PALERMO
Palermo (☎091)

★★★★**Jolly** Foro Italico ☎6165090 tx910076

290 **P** Lift ☾ sB 90000 dB 130000

Credit cards 1 2 3 4 5

★★★***AGIP*** via della Regione Sicillana 2620 ☎552033 tx611627

100 **P** Lift ☾

RAGUSA
Ragusa (☎0932)

CAI via R-Morandi ☎24047 Cit

SIRACUSA (SYRACUSE)
Siracusa (☎0931)

★★★★**Grand Villa Politi** via M-P-Laudlen 3 ☎32100 tx970205

94 **P**120 Lift ☾ sB 48500
dB 76500 sea
Credit cards 1 3

★★★***AGIP*** viale Teracati 30—32 ☎66944 tx611627

76 **P** Lift ☾

★★★**Jolly** corso Gelone 43 ☎64744 tx970108

102 **P** Lift ☾ sB 78000 dB 120000
Credit cards 1 2 3 4 5

TAORMINA
Messinia (☎0942)

★★★**Jolly** via Bagnoli Croce 75 ☎23312 tx980028

103 **P** Lift ☾ sB 96000 dB 150000
sea
Credit cards 1 2 3 4 5

★★***Villa Paradiso*** via Roma 2 ☎23922 tx980062

21 Dec—Oct
33 **P** Lift ☾ sea
Credit cards 1 2 3 5

At **MARRARÒ** (4.5km NE)

★★★★***Mazzarò Sea Palace*** (SRS) via Nazionale 16 ☎24004 tx980041

Apr—Oct
81 Lift ☾ Beach sea
Credit cards 2 3 5

★★★★**Villa Sant'Andrea** via Nazionale Santandrea 137 ☎23125 tx980077

36 A15rm **P**20 ☾ sB 75000
dB 150700 Beach sea mountains
Credit cards 1 2 3 5

SIENA
Siena (☎0577)

★★★★**Jolly Excelsior** pza della Lizza ☎288448 tx573345

126 Lift ☾ sB 98500—116500
dB 58500—194500
Credit cards 1 2 3 4 5

★★★★***Park*** (CIGA) via Marciano 16 ☎44803 tx571005

69 **P**100 Lift ☾
Credit cards 1 2 3 4 5

★★★**Palazzo Ravizza** Piano dei Mantellini 34 ☎280462

rm28 (20) **P**150 Lift ☾ sB37000
sB 47000 dB66000 dB 80000
M23000
Credit cards 1 2 3 5

★★★**Villa Scacciapensieri** ☎41441 tx573390

15 Mar—4 Nov
30 A10rm **P**25 Lift ☾
sB 78000—101000 dB 174000
M35000—40000
Credit cards 1 2 3 5

At **COLLE DI VAL D'ELSA** (22km NW)

★★***Arnolfo*** via F-Campana 8 ☎922020

28 **P** Lift ☾

SIRACUSA (SYRACUSE) See **SICILIA (SICILY)**

SIRMIONE
Brescia (☎030)

★★★**Florida** via Colombare ☎919018 tx300395

10 Mar—Oct
28 **P**25 ☾ sB 41000 dB 62000
M20000 lake

★★★**Grand Terme** viale Marconi 1 ☎916261 tx300395

Apr—Oct
57 **P**80 Lift ☾ sB 120000
dB 90000—210000 M38000—43000
lake mountains

★★★***Sirmione*** pza Castello ☎916331 tx300395

Apr—6 Nov
rm76 (71) A24rm Lift lake

★★Lac via XXV Aprile 60 916026

Apr—26 Oct
28 A7rm **P**30 sB 49000
dB 78000 M29000 lake
Credit card [3]

SORRENTO
Napoli (081)

★★★★Excelsior Vittoria pza Tasso 34
8781900 tx720368

115 **P**50 Lift sB 90000—116000
dB 138000—175000 M38000 sea

★★★★*Imperial Tramontano* via V-Veneto 1 8781940 tx710345

104 Lift Beach

★★★Aminta Grand via Nastro Verde 7
8781821

Apr—Oct
73 **P**30 Lift
sB 45000—60000
dB 80000—100000 M38000—40000
sea
Credit card [5]

★★★Cocumella via Cocumella 7
8782933 tx720370

50 **P** Lift sB 70000—88000
dB 65000—78000 M25000 Beach
Credit cards [2] [5]

★★★*Eden* via Correale 25 8781909

Apr—Oct
60 **P** Lift Beach sea

★★★Grand Ambasciatori via Califano 16 8782025 tx710645

103 **P**20 Lift
sB 53500—63000
dB 94500—118000 M33000
Beach sea
Credit cards [2] [3]

★★★Grand Capodimonte via del Capo 14 8784076 tx710645

Mar—Oct
131 **P**50 Lift sB 53500—63000
dB 89000—112500 M33000 sea
Credit cards [2] [3]

SPARTAIA See **ELBA (ISOLA D')** under **PROCCHIO**

SPEZIA (LA)
La Spezia (1087)

★★★★Jolly via XX Settembre 2 27200
tx331047

110 Lift sB 82000 dB 125000
Credit cards [1] [2] [3] [4] [5]

Cozzani & Rossi pza Caduti per La Liberta 6 25386 AR

SPOLETO
Perugia (0743)

★★★*AGIP* Uscita per Foligno (SS3 km127) 49340 tx611627

57 **P** Lift

SPOTORNO
Savona (019)

★★★Royal Lungomare Kennedy
745074 tx213867

Italy

May—10 Oct
100 **P**65 Lift
sB 62000—82000
dB 94000—143000 M35000
Beach sea
Credit card [2]

★★*Ligure* pza della Vittoria 745118

Apr—Oct
rm37 (30) **P**10 Beach sea

★*Villa Teresina* via Imperia 745160

Apr—Sep
rm22 (20) **P**15 Lift

STAGNO See **LIVORNO (LEGHORN)**

STORTA (LA) See **ROMA (ROME)**

STRESA
Novara (0323)

★★★★★Grand des Iles Borromées (CIGA) Lungolago Umberto 1er63 30431
tx200377

164 **P** Lift sB 197000
dB 304000 t% lake mountains
Credit cards [1] [2] [3] [5]

★★★★Bristol via Nazionale del Sempione 73 32601 tx200217

15 Mar—15 Nov
210 A30rm **P** Lift
sB 80000—108500
dB 100000—147000 M25000—40000
lake
Credit cards [1] [2] [3] [4] [5]

★★★★Regina Palace Lungolago Umberto 1er27 30171 tx200381

Apr—Nov
176 **P**100 Lift
sB 116080—155080
dB 152200—192200 M38000 lake

★★★Astoria Lungolago Umberto 1er31
32566 tx200085

28 Mar—20 Oct
107 A9rm **P**30 Lift
sB 74000—114000
dB 90000—157000 M30000 lake
Credit cards [1] [2] [3] [4] [5]

★★★Palma Lungolago Umberto 1er
32401 tx200541

Mar—Nov
128 A11rm **P**65 Lift
sB 69000—97000
dB 92000—149000 M25000—30000
lake mountains
Credit cards [1] [2] [3] [4] [5]

★★Italia & Svizzera pza Imbarcadero
30540

15 Mar—15 Nov
rm36 (24) **P** Lift sB26500—29000
sB 36500—40000 dB44000—50000
dB 57000—62000 M17000—20000
lake mountains
Credit cards [1] [2] [3] [5]

★★Lido la Peria Nera pza Stazione Funivia 30384 tx200396

Apr—10 Oct
rm27 (25) **P**15 sB36000—41000
sB 46000—51000 dB57000—67000
dB 72000—84000 M22000 lake
Credit cards [1] [2] [3] [5]

★★Milano & Speranza au Lac pza Imbarcadero 31190 tx200113

20 Mar—Oct
171 **P** Lift sB 48000—68000
dB 80000—100000 M25000—28000
lake
Credit cards [1] [2] [3] [5]

★★*Parc* via Gignous 1 30335

Apr—Oct
rm38 (35) A16rm Lift lake

★★Royal via Nazionale del Sempione
32777 tx200396

Apr—Oct
45 **P**30 Lift
sB 46000—56000
dB 62000—82000 M20000 lake
mountains

SUSA
Torino (0122)

★★Napoleon via Mazzini 44 2704

45 **P**30 Lift sB 44000 dB 64000
M18000—20000 St% mountains

SYRACUSE See **SIRACUSA** under **SICILIA (SICILY)**

TAORMINA See **SICILIA (SICILY)**

TARQUINIA
Viterbo (0766)

★★*Tarconte* via Tuscia 19 856585
tx612172

53 **P**25 Lift
Credit cards [2] [5]

TERRACINA
Latina (0773)

★★Palace Lungomare Matteotti 2
752585

73 **P**60 Lift
sB 36000—40000
dB 54000—59000 M18000 Beach sea
Credit cards [2] [3] [4] [5]

TIRRENIA
Pisa (050)

★★★Golf via dell'Edera 29 37545

77 **P**15 Lift sB 77000—92000
dB 114000—154000 M25000
Beach sea

TOLMEZZA
Udine (0433)

Automezzi Tolmezzo via Paluzza 3
2151 Fia

TONALE (PASSO)
Brescia (0364)

★★*Redivalle* 91349

rm52 (49) **P** mountains

TORINO (TURIN)
Torino (011)

★★★★★Jolly Principi di Piemonte via P-Gobetti 15 519693 tx221120 →

🛁 107 Lift ☾ sB 🛁 168000 dB 🛁 214000
Credit cards [1] [2] [3] [4] [5]

★★★★**Jolly Ambasciatori** corso V-Emanuele 104 ☎5752 tx221296

🛁 197 🚗 Lift ☾ sB 🛁 138000
dB 🛁 170000
Credit cards [1] [2] [3] [4] [5]

★★★★**Jolly-Ligure** pza C-Felice 85 ☎55641 tx220167

🛁 156 **P** Lift ☾ sB 🛁 153000 dB 🛁 195000
Credit cards [2] [3] [4] [5]

★★★★***Turin Palace*** (SRS) via Sacchi 8 ☎515511 tx221411

🛁 125 **P**44 Lift ☾
Credit cards [1] [2] [3] [4] [5]

★★★**Patria** via Cernaia 42 (n.rest) ☎519903

rm108 (🛁 🚿 86) 🚗 Lift ☾

★★**Alexandra** Lungo Dora Napoli 14 (n.rest) ☎858327 tx221562

🛁 🚿 50 🚗 **P**10 Lift ☾ sB 🛁 🚿 85000
dB 🛁 🚿 110000
Credit cards [1] [2] [3] [5]

B Koeliker via Barletta 133—135 ☎353632 AR DJ

At **SETTIMO** (8km NE on Autostrada A4)

★★★***AGIP*** ☎8001855 tx611627

🚿 100

TORRE A MARE See **BARI**

TORRI DEL BENACO
Verona (☎045)

★★***Continental*** via Gardesana, San Felice (2.5km N on SS249) (n.rest) ☎7225195

Apr—15 Oct
🛁 🚿 30 🚗 **P** Beach lake

TREMEZZO
Como (☎0344)

★★★**Bazzoni** via Regina ☎40403 tx323231

20 Mar—15 Nov
🛁 🚿 120 **P**10 Lift ☾ sB 🛁 🚿 59000—71000
dB 🛁 🚿 92000—105000 M22000
Credit cards [1] [2] [3] [4] [5]

★★★**Grand Tremezzo** via Regina 8 ☎40446 tx380128

Etr—Oct
🛁 🚿 100 🚗 **P**10 Lift ☾ sB 🛁 🚿 71500
dB 🛁 🚿 110000—140000 M30000 St% ⛳
⛱ lake mountains
Credit cards [2] [3] [5]

TRENTO
Trento (☎0461)

★★***Venezia*** pza Duomo 45 ☎26335

rm80 (🛁 🚿 75) **P** Lift ☾

🚘 **E Franceschi** via Brennero 264 ☎980110 Ope Vau

At **SARDAGNA** (4km W)

★★★***AGIP*** via Brennero, 168 Uscita per Bolzano (SS12) ☎981117 tx611627

🚿 45 **P** Lift ☾

TREVISO
Treviso (☎0422)

★★★**Continental** via Roma 16 (n.rest) ☎57216 tx311814

🛁 82 Lift ☾ sB 🛁 82000 dB 🛁 124000
Credit cards [1] [2] [3] [4] [5]

Bobbo via della Repubblica 270 ☎62396 AR DJ

Sile Motori viale della Repubblica 278 ☎62743 M/c AR

SOCAART viale della Repubblica 19 ☎63725 M/c For

🚘 **Trevisauto** viale Felissent 58 ☎63265 Ope Vau

TRIESTE
Trieste (☎040)

★★★★***Duchi d'Aosta*** (CIGA) via dell'Orologio 2 ☎62081 tx460358

🛁 52 **P** Lift ☾

★★★★**Jolly** corso Cavour 7 ☎7694 tx460139

🛁 177 🚗 Lift ☾ sB 🛁 101000
dB 🛁 140000
Credit cards [1] [2] [3] [4] [5]

★★★***AGIP*** Duino Service Area (On Autostrada A424km NW via SS14) ☎208273

🚿 80 **P** Lift ☾

🚘 **F Antonucci** via Villan de Bacchino 2 ☎414396 Peu

Filotecnica Guilliana via F-Severo 42—48 ☎569121 AR Vol

A Grandi viale Flavia 120 ☎817201 Fia

🚘 **Regina** via Raffineria 6 ☎725345 M/c **P** BMW Ope Vau

At **GRIGNANO** (8km NW)

★★★★***Adriatico Palace*** ☎224241 tx460449

Apr—12 Oct
🛁 🚿 102 🚗 **P**200 Lift ☾ ⛳ ⛱
Credit cards [1] [2] [3] [4] [5]

TURIN See **TORINO**

UDINE
Udine (☎0432)

★★★**Astoria Italia** pza XX Settembre 24 ☎207091 tx450120

🛁 80 🚗 **P**40 Lift ☾ sB 🛁 81000—87000
dB 🛁 130000—140000 M30000
Credit cards [1] [2] [3] [4] [5]

★★★**Cristallo** piazzale G-d'Annunzio 43 ☎205951

🛁 🚿 81 🚗 **P**12 Lift ☾ sB 🛁 🚿 42500
dB 🛁 🚿 69000 M17000
Credit cards [2] [3] [5]

Autofriuiana viale Europa Unita 33 ☎266330 **P** AR

🚘 **Edera** via della Cisterna 18 ☎204422

🚘 **Furgiuele & Baidell** viale Venezia 383 ☎32168 **P** For

🚘 **Nord** viale L-da-Vinci ☎55669 Ren

VALSOLDA
Como (☎0344)

At **SAN MAMETE**

★★★**Stella d'Italia** ☎68139

Apr—Oct
🛁 35 🚗 **P**14 Lift sB 🛁 39000—47000
dB 🛁 56000—66000 M22000 lake
Credit cards [1] [2] [3]

VARALLO
Vercelli (☎0163)

★★★***AGIP*** (SS299 d'Alagna—km26) ☎52447

🚿 38 **P** Lift ☾ mountains

VARAZZE
Savona (☎019)

★★**Delfino** via Colombo 48 ☎97073

🛁 🚿 25 A14rm 🚗 **P** Lift ☾ dB🚿 57000
M18000 St% Beach sea
Credit cards [1] [2] [3] [5]

VARENNA
Como (☎0341)

★★**Olivedo** ☎830115

Closed 7 Nov—5 Dec
rm22 (🛁 6) sB25000—30000
sB 🛁 33000—40000 dB50000
dB 🛁 55000—65000 M22000 lake

VARESE
Varese (☎0332)

★★★***Palace*** via L-Manara 11 ☎312600 tx380163

Mar—Oct
🛁 🚿 110 **P** Lift ☾ ⛳ lake

VARIGOTTI See **FINALE LIGURE**

VENEZIA (VENICE)
Venezia (☎041)
See also **MESTRE**

No road communications in city. Vehicles may be left in garages in piazzale Roma at the mainland end of the causeway or at open parking places on the mainland approaches. Garages will not accept advance bookings. Transport to hotels by waterbus, etc, for which there are fixed charges for fares and porterage. Hotel rooms overlooking the Grand Canal normally have a surcharge.

★★★★★**Danieli** (CIGA) Riva degli Schiavoni 4191 ☎26480 tx410077

🛁 230 Lift ☾ sB 🛁 258000—298000
dB 🛁 710000—760000 t18%
Credit cards [1] [2] [3] [5]

★★★★★***Gritti Palace*** (CIGA) campo Santa Maria del Giglio 2467 ☎26044 tx410125

🛁 101 Lift ☾ ⛱ 📺 U

★★★★***Europa & Regina*** (CIGA) Canal Grande-San Marco 2159 ☎700477 tx410123

🛁 200 Lift ☾ ⛳ ⛱ Beach 📺 U sea

★★★**Cavalletto** calle de Cavelletto, pza San Marco ☎700955 tx410684

🛁🚿79 Lift ☾ sB🛁🚿115000—170000 dB🛁🚿205000—295000 M60000
Credit card [2]

★★★**Concordia** (GT) calle Larga, San Marco 367 (n.rest) ☎706866 tx411069

🛁🚿60 Lift ☾ sB🛁🚿80000—116000 dB🛁🚿115000—183000
Credit cards [2] [3]

★★★**Gabrielli-Sandwirth** Riva degli Schiavoni 4110 ☎31580 tx410228

15 Mar—15 Nov
rm120 (🛁100) Lift sB105000 sB🛁195000 dB150000 dB🛁320000 sea

★★★**Metropole** Riva degli Schiavoni 4149 ☎705044 tx410340

🛁64 Lift ☾ sB🛁120000—190000 dB🛁155000—293000 M45000
Credit cards [1] [2] [3] [4] [5]

★★★**Saturnia & International** via XXIII Marzo San Marco 2399 ☎708377 tx410355

🛁🚿98 Lift ☾ sB🛁🚿180000—200000 dB🛁🚿270000—325000 M alc
Credit cards [1] [2] [3] [4] [5]

★★**Flora** via XXII Marzo 2283A (n.rest) ☎705844

Feb—15 Nov
🛁44 Lift ☾ sB🛁98000 dB🛁138400
Credit cards [1] [2] [3] [5]

★★***Giorgione*** Santa Apostoli 4587 ☎25810

🛁56 Lift ☾
Credit cards [1] [2] [3]

★★**Panada** (GT) calle Larga San Marco 656 (n.rest) ☎709088 tx410153

🛁🚿46 Lift ☾ sB🛁🚿80000—105000 dB🛁🚿115000—161000
Credit cards [1] [2] [3] [5]

★**Basilea** S. Croce-Rio Marin 817 (n.rest) ☎718477

rm30 (🛁🚿27) ☾ sB37900 sB🛁🚿48800 dB68100 dB🛁🚿87000
Credit card [3]

VENEZIA LIDO
Venezia (☎0041)

There is a car ferry service from Venice (piazzala Roma).

★★★★★**Excelsior** (CIGA) Lungomare Marconi 41 ☎5260201 tx410023

Apr—Nov
🛁230 🚗 Lift ☾ sB🛁217000—317000 dB🛁324000—424000 M alc t18% ✂ ≈ Beach ▣ U sea
Credit cards [1] [2] [3] [4] [5]

★★★★**Bains** (CIGA) Lungomare Marconi 17 ☎765921 tx410142

15 Apr—Oct
🛁🚿243 P Lift ☾ sB🛁🚿156000—216000 dB🛁🚿252000—582000 M alc t9% ✂ ≈ Beach sea
Credit cards [1] [2] [3] [5]

★★★**Adria-Urania & Villa Nora & Ada** viale Dandolo 24, 27 & 29 ☎5260120 tx410666

Apr—20 Oct
🛁92 **P**20 Lift ☾ sB🛁75000—100000 dB🛁140000—150000 M30000 Beach
Credit cards [2] [5]

VENTIMIGLIA
Imperia (☎0184)

★★**Posta** Sottocon vento 15 ☎351218

Mar—5 Jan
🛁18 Lift ☾ sB🛁29000 dB🛁52000

🚘 **G Revelli** via Nervia 2 ☎352459 BMW Saa

VERBANIA
Novara (☎0323)

At **PALLANZA** (1km SW)

★★★**Majestic** via V-Veneto 32 ☎504305 tx200644

22 Mar—15 Oct
🛁119 **P**50 Lift ☾ sB🛁95720 dB🛁146440 ✂ ▭ Beach sea
Credit cards [1] [2] [3] [5]

★★***Belvedere*** pza IV-Novembre 10 ☎503202 tx200269

Apr—Oct
rm58 (🛁🚿47) A40rm Lift ☾ lake

★★**San Gottardo** viale delle Magnolie 4 ☎503202 tx200269

15 Mar—15 Oct
🛁🚿40 **P**20 Lift ☾ sB🛁🚿46000—49500 dB🛁🚿68000—74000 M18000—20000 lake
Credit cards [2] [3]

VERCELLI
Vercelli (☎0161)

★★★**Viotti** via Marsala 7 ☎61602

🛁🚿61 **P**10 Lift ☾ sB🛁🚿39000—47000 dB🛁🚿77000—79000 M20000—25000
Credit cards [1] [2] [3] [5]

VERONA
Verona (☎045)

★★★★***Colomba d'Oro*** via C-Cattaneo 10 (n.rest) ☎595300 tx480872

🛁🚿52 🚗 **P** Lift ☾
Credit cards [1] [2] [3] [5]

★★★★***Due Torri*** (SRS) pza Sant'Anastasia 4 ☎595044 tx480524

🛁🚿100 🚗 **P** Lift ☾

★★★**Accademia** via Scala 12 ☎596222 tx480874

🛁🚿116 🚗 **P**30 Lift ☾
sB🛁🚿80000—90000
dB🛁🚿110000—130000 M30000
Credit cards [1] [2] [3] [4] [5]

★★★***AGIP*** via Unità d'Italia 346 (SS1 1km 307) ☎972033 tx611627

🚿68 **P** Lift ☾

★★★**San Pietro** via Santa Teresa 1 (n.rest) ☎582600 tx480523

🛁🚿58 🚗 **P**20 Lift ☾ sB🛁🚿87000 dB🛁🚿130000
Credit cards [1] [3]

★★**Capuleti** via del Pontiere 26 ☎32970 tx351609

Closed 23 Dec—10 Jan
🛁🚿36 Lift ☾ sB🛁🚿58000 dB🛁🚿89000 M18000—22000
Credit cards [1] [2] [5]

★★**Italia** via G-Mameli 54 ☎918088 tx431064

🛁🚿50 🚗 **P**20 Lift ☾ sB🛁🚿51500 dB🛁🚿80300 M20000
Credit cards [1] [2] [3]

🚘 **Auto Motor** Stradone Santa Lucia 21 ☎500344 Aud Por VW

🚘 **SVAE** via Torricelli-Z.A.I. ☎508088 For

VIAREGGIO
Lucca (☎0584)

★★★★**Palace** via F-Gioia 2 ☎46134 tx624044

🛁🚿68 🚗 Lift ☾ sB🛁🚿100000—115000 dB🛁🚿150000—190000 M35000 ≈ Beach sea
Credit cards [1] [2] [3] [5]

★★★**Plaza & de Russie** Longomare Manin 1 (n.rest) ☎46546

🛁50 Lift ☾ sB🛁65500—85500 dB🛁111000—146000 sea
Credit cards [1] [2] [3] [5]

★★**Garden** ☎44025 tx590403

rm43 (🛁40) 🚗 Lift ☾ sB38000—43000 sB🛁43000—53000 dB🛁71000—81000 M25000
Credit cards [1] [2] [3] [4] [5]

Autosalone Lupori via Galvani 9 ☎42266 **P** Cit

F Fazioli via Buonarroti 67 ☎42580 **P** Ope Vau

🚘 **Pecchia** viale del Tigli 8 ☎443312 Cit

VICENZA
Vincenza (☎0444)

★★★***AGIP*** via degli Scoligerri, Fiera ☎564711 tx611627

🚿123 **P** Lift ☾

Americana viale San Lazzaro 15 ☎463101 M/c Ope Vau

Sabema viale della Pace 50 ☎500348 M/c **P** BMW

VICO EQUENSE
Napoli (☎081)

★★**Oriente** ☎8798143 tx721050

🛁77 🚗 **P** ☾ sB🛁20000—30000 dB🛁30000—40000 sea
Credit cards [2] [3]

VIESTE
Foggia (☎0884)

★★★★**Pizzomunno Vieste Palace** ☎78741 tx810267

26 Mar—11 Oct
🛁183 A41rm 🚗 **P**300 Lift ☾
sB🛁90000—118000
dB🛁164000—204000 M50000—65000 ✂ ≈ Beach U sea
Credit cards [1] [2] [3] [5]

At **PUGNOCHIUSO** (22km S)

★★★***Ulivi*** ☎79061 tx810122
🚿202 **P** Lift 🎾 ⛱ Beach

VIETRI SUL MARE See **SALERNO**

VILLASIMUS See **SARDEGNA (ISOLA) (SARDINIA)**

VITERBO
Viterbo (☎0761)

★★**Leon d'Oro** via della Cava 36 ☎31012
15 Feb—20 Dec
rm44 (🛁 36) 🚗 **P**9 Lift ☾ sB27500
sB🛁 33550 dB🛁 58300 M15000
Credit cards [2] [3] [5]

🚚 **Tedeschi** via L-Garbini 84 ☎32109 M/c For

San Marino

Prices are in Italian Lire

SAN MARINO (☎0541)

★★★**Grand** via Antonio Onofri 31 ☎992400 tx505555
20 Mar—20 Nov
🛁🚿54 🚗 **P**25 Lift ☾ sB🛁🚿53500
dB🛁🚿74000 M14000—40000 mountains
Credit cards [1] [2] [3] [5]

★★★**Titano** Contrada del Collegio 21 ☎991007 tx505444
15 Mar—15 Nov
🛁🚿50 🚗 **P**6 Lift ☾ sB🛁🚿41000
dB🛁🚿59000 M13000—16000 mountains
Credit cards [1] [2] [3] [5]

★★***Excelsior*** via J-Istriani ☎991163
🛁🚿24 🚗 **P** Lift mountains

★**Tre Penne** via Lapidici Marini ☎992437
Closed 10 Nov—6 Dec
🛁🚿12 **P** Lift dB🛁🚿45000—52000
M12500 mountains
Credit cards [1] [2] [3] [5]

Villa Pisani, Venice

Luxembourg

International distinguishing sign

Area *999 sq miles*
Location map *See page 76*
Population *365,500*
Local time *GMT + 1 (Summer GMT + 2)*

National flag
Horizontal tricolour of red, white and blue

How to get there

Luxembourg is easily approached through either Belgium or France. Luxembourg City is just over 200 miles from Oostende or Zeebrugge, about 260 miles from Boulogne, Calais or Dunkerque, and is therefore within a day's drive of the Channel coast.

Motoring regulations and general information

This information should be read in conjunction with the general content of the European ABC (pages 4-26). **Note** As certain regulations and requirements are common to many countries they are covered by one entry in the ABC and the following headings represent some of the subjects dealt with in this way:
AA Agents
Crash or safety helmets
Drinking and driving
Fire extinguisher
First-aid kit
Insurance
International distinguishing sign
Medical treatment
Mirrors
Police fines
Radio telephones/Radio transmitters
Road signs
Seat belts
Traffic lights
Tyres
Visitors' registration

Accidents

Fire, police, ambulance ☏ 012—Civil Defence emergency services (*Secours d'urgence*).

There are no firm rules to adopt following an accident, however anyone requested to give assistance must do so, in most cases the recommendations under *Accidents* on page 5 are advisable.

Accommodation

A national guide to hotels, inns, restaurants, and boarding houses in the Grand Duchy can be obtained free of charge from the National Tourist Office. Details of holiday flats and chalets are also available from this source.

Boats

When temporarily importing boats into Luxembourg, documentation, in addition to the *Customs regulations* referred to below, may be required if your route takes you through France. See *Boats* page 6 for further information.

Breakdown

The Automobile Club de Grand-Duché de Luxembourg (ACL) operates a 24-hour road assistance service throughout the whole country. The vehicles of the ACL are yellow in colour and bear a black inscription '*Automobile Club Service Routier*'. This service should not be confused with the '*Depannages Secours Automobiles*' or '*DSA*' which is a commercial enterprise not connected with the AA or any other organisation. See also *Breakdown* page 6 and *Warning triangle* page 300.

British Embassy/Consulate

(See also page 6)
The British Embassy together with its consular section is located at *Luxembourg Ville* 28 Boulevard Royal ☏ 29864/66.

Currency including banking hours

(See also page 9)
The unit of currency is the Luxembourg Franc (*LFr*) divided into 100 *Centimes*. At the time of going to press £ = *LFr*62.85. Denominations of bank notes are *LFr* 50, 100, 1,000; standard coins are *LFr* 1, 5, 10, 20 and *Centimes* 25, 50. There are no restrictions on the amount of foreign or local

currency which can be taken into or out of the country but because of the limited market for Luxembourg notes in other countries, it is advisable to change them before leaving. Belgian currency is also used in Luxembourg.

Banks are open Monday to Friday from 08.30/09.00—12.00hrs and 13.30/14.00—16.30/17.00hrs.

Customs regulations

A *Customs Carnet de Passages en Douane* is required for all temporarily imported boats unless entering and leaving by water. See also *Customs regulations for European countries* page 9 for further information.

Dimensions and weight restrictions

Private **cars** and towed **trailers** or **caravans** are restricted to the following dimensions — height: 4 metres; width: 2.50 metres; length: 12 metres. The maximum permitted overall length of vehicle/trailer or caravan combination is 18 metres.

The weight of a caravan must not exceed 75% of the weight of the towing vehicle.

Driving licence

(See also page 11)
A valid British licence is acceptable in Luxembourg. The minimum age at which a visitor may drive a temporarily imported car or motorcycle is 17 years.

Emergency messages to tourists

(See also page 11)
Emergency messages to tourists are broadcast during the summer on the German *RTL* programme. These messages are transmitted on 208 metres medium wave and may be given at any time between 06.00—01.00hrs.

Horn, use of

In built-up areas it is prohibited to use the horn except to avoid an accident. *Outside built-up areas* use the horn instead of the lights only, during the day, to warn of approach.

Lights

(See also page 14)
It is prohibited to drive on sidelights only. At night and also during the day when necessary, vehicles parked on a public road must have their side lights on if the public lighting does not enable them to be seen from a sufficient distance. Vehicles equipped with a side parking light may use this instead of sidelights. Should fog or snow reduce visibility to less than 100 metres, vehicles stopped or parked outside a built-up area must be illuminated by dipped headlights or fog lamps. Two fog lamps may be used at the same time as dipped headlights but full headlights together with fog or spot lamps may not be used at the same time. At night it is compulsory to flash one's headlights before overtaking another vehicle, at places where visibility is restricted, and whenever road safety requires it. It is compulsory for *motorcyclists* to use dipped headlights during the day.

Motoring club

(See also page 16)

The **Automobile Club du Grand-Duché de Luxembourg** (ACL) has its head office at *8007 Bertrange* (Luxembourg), 13 Route de Longwy ☎ 311031. ACL office hours are 08.30—12.00hrs and 13.30—18.00hrs from Monday to Friday; closed Saturday and Sunday.

Motorways

Only short sections totalling 64km (40 miles) are at present open, but a future network of 160km is planned.

Orange badge scheme for disabled drivers

(See also page 16)
In Luxembourg parking places reserved for disabled drivers are indicated by a parking sign (white letter on a blue panel) or a parking prohibited sign (red ring and bars with blue background) both with the international disabled symbol added. However, badge holders are not permitted to exceed the parking time limit.

A disabled driver may obtain special concessions for parking if he/she applies to the Administration Communale or police station.

Overtaking

(See also page 17)
Outside built-up areas at night it is compulsory to flash one's headlights before overtaking another vehicle. During the day use the horn instead of lights.

Parking

(See also page 17)
Park on the right hand side of the road in the direction of the traffic flow unless parking is prohibited on this side. Spending the night in a

vehicle or trailer on the roadside is prohibited.

In towns parking is controlled by parking discs, parking meters and persons who issue tickets. Discs are available from the ACL, the Administration Communale, principle banks, petrol companies and other firms. Discs must be displayed on the windscreen and are set at the time of parking and show when parking time expires.

Passengers

(See also page 18)
Children under 10 years are not permitted to travel in a vehicle as front seat passengers when rear seating is available.

Petrol

(See also page 18)
Credit cards Many petrol stations will accept Visa.
Duty-free petrol In addition to the petrol in the vehicle tank up to 10 litres in a can may be imported free of customs duty and tax.
Petrol (leaded) Normal (90—93 octane) and Super (98 octane) grades.
Petrol (unleaded) is sold in Luxembourg where it is known as *2085*. It has an octane rating of 93 and the pumps dispensing unleaded petrol are marked *essence sans plomb* (lead free petrol).

Postal information

Mail Postcards *LFr*7, letters up to 20gm *LFr*10.
Post offices There are 100 post offices in Luxembourg. Opening hours are from 08.00—12.00hrs and 14.00—17.00hrs Monday to Friday. The post office at Luxembourg station is open every day from 06.00—22.00hrs, and the airport post office every day from 07.00—21.30hrs. The Esch-sur-Alzette office is open on Saturdays. Small offices are open for shorter hours which are shown at the entrance to the post office.

Postcheques

(See also page 20)
Postcheques may be cashed at all post offices for any amount of up to a maximum of *LFr*5,000 per cheque. Counter positions are identified by the words *Chèques* or *Postcheques*. See *Postal information* for post office opening hours.

Priority

All road users must yield right of way to other road users when entering a public road, starting from the kerb or reversing. See also *Priority including Roundabouts* page 21.

Public holidays

Official public holidays in Luxembourg for 1987 are given below. See also *Public holidays* page 21.
January 1 (New Year's Day)
April 20 (Easter Monday)
May 1 (Labour Day)
May 28 (Ascension Day)
June 7† (Pentecost)
June 8 (Whit Monday)
June 23 (National Day)
August 15* (Assumption)
November 1† (All Saints' Day)
December 25 (Christmas Day)
December 26* (Boxing day)
*Saturday †Sunday

Roads

There is a comprehensive system of good main and secondary roads.

Shopping hours

Some shops close on Monday mornings but the usual hours of opening for *food shops* are from Monday to Saturday 08.00—12.00hrs and 14.00—18.00hrs. However, *supermarkets* open from 09.00-20.00hrs but close at 18.00hrs on Saturdays.

Speed limits

(See also page 22)
The placename indicates the beginning and the end of a built-up area. The following speed limits for cars are in force if there are no special signs: built-up areas 60kph (37mph); main roads 90kph (56mph); Motorways 120kph (74mph). All lower signposted speed limits must be adhered to.

Spiked or studded tyres

Spiked tyres may be used between December and March, however they must be fitted to all four wheels and speeds must not exceed 60kph (37mph) on ordinary roads and 90kph (56mph) on motorways. Vehicles registered in Luxembourg and equipped with spiked tyres must display a disc bearing the figure '60' in black; foreign registered vehicles only need to comply if obligatory in country of registration. See also *Cold weather touring* page 8.

Tourist information

(See also page 24)
The National Tourist Office in London is at 36-37 Piccadilly (entrance Swallow Street), W1V 9PA ☎ 01-434 2800 (recorded message service out of office hours). In Luxembourg the Office National du Tourisme (National Tourist Office),local

authorities and tourist information societies (*Syndicats d'Initiatives*) organise information offices and will be pleased to assist you with information regarding tourism.

Using the telephone

(See also page 24)
Insert coin **after** lifting reciever, dialling tone same as in the UK. Use *LFr*5 coins for local calls and *LFr*5 or *LFr*20 for national and international calls. Belgian coins may also be used.
International callbox identification Roadside callboxes.

Telephone rates A telephone call to the UK costs *LFr*75 for three minutes and *LFr*25 for each additional minute.
What to dial for the Irish Republic 00 353
What to dial for the UK 00 44.

Warning triangle

The use of a warning triangle is compulsory for all vehicles except two-wheelers. The triangle must be placed on the road about 100 metres (109yds) behind the vehicle to warn following traffic of any obstruction. See also *Warning triangles/Hazard warning lights* page 25.

Prices are in Belgian Francs
See French section for abbreviations

BEAUFORT

★★**Meyer** Grand r 120 ☎86262 tx1524
Closed 16 Jan—1 Mar
🛁🚿40 🚗 **P** Lift sB🛁🚿1100—1200
dB🛁🚿1800—2200

BERDORF

★★**Ermitage** rte de Grundhof 44 ☎79184
27 Mar—28 Sep
🛁🚿16 🚗 **P** sB🛁🚿1370
dB🛁🚿2230—2300

CLERVAUX

★★**Abbaye** r Principale 80 ☎91049 tx1522
24 Mar—30 Oct & 20—30 Dec
rm50 (🛁🚿35) 🚗 **P** Lift sB800—950
sB🛁🚿1100—1325 dB1100—1525
dB🛁🚿1400—2000

★★**Claravallis** r de la Gare 3 ☎91034 tx3134
Apr—Dec
rm28 (🛁🚿24) **P** Lift sB1500 dB2100
dB🛁🚿2400

★★**Grand Central** pl Princessa Maria Theresa 9 ☎91105
15 Mar—Dec
rm17 (🛁🚿15) Lift sB800 dB🛁🚿1500

E Wagener-Heuts Grand-rue 52 ☎91080 Toy

DIEKIRCH

★**Beau Séjour** Esplanade 10—12 ☎803403
Closed 11—23 Oct
rm28 (🚿14) Lift sB630—840 dB920—1170

DOMMELDANGE

★★★**Novotel Luxembourg** rte d'Echternach (E42) ☎435643 tx1418
🛁173 **P** 🔑

ECHTERNACH

★★★**Bel Air** (Relais et Châteaux) rte Berdorf 1 ☎729383 tx2640
🛁24 🚗 **P** Lift sB🛁1900—3100
dB🛁2800—4400 🔑

★★**Commerce** pl du Marché 16 ☎72301
Mar—15 Nov & 20 Dec—1 Jan
rm56 (🛁🚿52) 🚗 **P** Lift sB650—800
sB🛁🚿1150 dB970—1200
dB🛁🚿1300—1550

★★**Parc** rue de l'Hôpital 9 ☎729481 tx60455
25 Mar—15 Nov
🛁🚿27 **P** sB🛁🚿1300—1600
dB🛁🚿1800—2200

★**Marmann** r de Luxembourg 7 (n.rest) ☎72188
Mar—mid Oct
rm16 (🚿6) 🚗

★**Universel & Cheval Blanc** r de Luxembourg 40 ☎729991
Apr—Oct
rm35 (🛁🚿30) **P** Lift sB1000—1300
sB🛁🚿1300 dB1300 dB🛁🚿1700—1800

Schneiders r de Luxembourg 17 ☎729045 Ren

EHNEN

★***Moselle*** rte du Vin 131 ☎76717
17 Jan—Nov
rm18 (🛁🚿13) 🚗 **P** Lift

ESCH-SUR-ALZETTE

Euro-Motor Esch bd Kennedy 108 ☎540134 For

Muller Esch bd Kennedy 122—4 ☎544844 Ope

C Reding r de Belvaux 109 ☎352323 Peu Tal

ETTELBRUCK

Grand Garage P Wengler av des Alliés 36 ☎82157 For

FINDEL See **LUXEMBOURG**

GREVENMACHER

★***Poste*** 26 r de Tréves (n.rest) ☎75136
rm12 (🛁1) 🚗 **P**

GRUNDHOF

★★**Brimer** ☎86251 tx1308
15 Feb—10 Nov
🛁23 **P** Lift sB🛁1250—1800
dB🛁2000—2500

★**Ferring** rte Beaufort 4 ☎86015
25 Mar—15 Nov
rm27 (🛁🚿25) 🚗 **P** Lift sB🛁🚿1200
dB1400 dB🛁🚿1700—1900

HALLER

★★**Hallerbach** r des Romains 2 ☎86151
Closed 11 Jan—Feb & Dec
🛁18 **P** Lift sB🛁1000—1400
dB🛁1500—2200 🔑

HEINERSCHEID

★**Wagener** r de Stavelot 29 ☎98503
rm10 🚗 **P** sB450 dB900

KAUTENBACH

★**Hatz** ☎96561
Closed 17 Nov—15 Dec
rm12 (🚿6) **P** sB600 sB🚿750 dB900
dB🚿1100

KIRCHBERG See **LUXEMBOURG**

LAROCHETTE

★★**Residence** rue de Medernach 14 ☎87391 tx60529
🛁🚿22 **P** sB🛁🚿1500
dB🛁🚿1900—2000

LUXEMBOURG

★★★★**Intercontinental** r J-Engling 4 ☎43781 tx3754
🛁346 🚗 **P**100 Lift sB🛁3900—4900
dB🛁4900—5900 🔑
Credit cards 1 2 3 4 5

★★★★***Kons*** pl de la Gare 24 ☎486021 tx2306
rm141 (🛁🚿116) Lift

★★★**Central Molitor** (GT) av de la Liberté 28 ☎489911 tx2613
🛁36 🚗 Lift sB🛁1990 dB🛁2630
Credit cards 1 2 3 5

★★★**Cravat** bd. Roosevelt 29 ☎21975 tx2846
🚿60 🚗 Lift sB🚿2600—3400
dB🚿3100—3900

★**Français** pl d'Armes 14 ☎23009
rm26 (🚿23) Lift sB🚿1000—1800
dB🚿2000—2200

Grand Garage de la Pétrusse r des Jardiniers 13—15 ☎442324 AR DJ

P Lentz rte d'Arlon 257 ☎444545 Dat

M Losch rte de Thionville ☎488121 Aud Por VW

At **FINDEL** (8km NW)

★★★★**Aerogolf Sheraton** rte de Trèves ☎34571
150 **P** Lift ☾ sB 3280—3980 dB 4280—4980

At **KIRCHBERG**

★★★★**Holiday Inn** European Centre ☎437761
260 **P** Lift sB 3600—4000 dB 4600—5200
Credit cards 1 2 3 5

Euro-Motor r des Labours ☎433030 For

Luxembourg

At **STRASSEN** (2km W on N9)

★★**Dany** rte d'Arlon 72 ☎318062
17 **P** sB 1000—2000 dB 1500—2300

MERSCH

★**Marisca** pl de l'Étoile 1 ☎328456
Closed 21 Aug—14 Sep
rm18 (8) **P** sB1000—1350 dB1600—1700 dB 1800—2100

MONDORF-LES-BAINS

★★★***Grand Chef*** av des Bains 36 ☎68122 tx1840
23 Apr—20 Oct
rm46 (41) **P** Lift

STRASSEN See **LUXEMBOURG**

VIANDEN

★★***Collette*** Grand r 68—70 ☎84004
Apr—Oct
rm30 (14)

★★**Heintz** Grand r 55 ☎84155
28 Mar—4 Nov
rm30 (25) **P** Lift sB800—900 sB 900—1300 dB970—1400 dB 1600—2000

★**Oranienburg** Grand r 126 ☎84153
Closed Jan—14 Feb
rm36 (27) Lift sB780 sB 900 dB1200 dB 1500

Netherlands

International distinguishing sign

Area *15,900 sq miles*
Population
14,340,000
Local time *GMT + 1*
(Summer GMT + 2)

National flag
Horizontal tricolour of red, white and blue

How to get there

There are direct ferry services to the Netherlands. Services operate from Harwich to the Hook of Holland, Hull to Rotterdam (Europoort) and Sheerness to Vlissingen (Flushing); the sea journey can take between 7 and 14 hours depending on the port of departure. Alternatively one of the short channel crossings can be used, and the Netherlands can be easily reached by driving through France and Belgium. The distance from Calais to Den Haag is just over 200 miles and is within a day's drive.

Motoring regulations and general information

This information should be read in conjunction with the general content of the European ABC (pages 4-26). **Note** As certain regulations and requirements are common to many countries they are covered by one entry in the ABC and the following headings represent some of the subjects dealt with in this way:
AA Agents
Crash or safety helmets
Customs regulations for European countries
Drinking and driving
Fire extinguisher
First-aid kit
Insurance
International distinguishing sign
Medical treatment
Mirrors
Overtaking
Police fines
Radio telephones/Radio transmitters
Seat belts
Traffic lights
Tyres
Visitors' registration

Accidents

Police and **ambulance** Amsterdam and Den Haag ☎ 222222, Rotterdam ☎ 141414; **Fire** Amsterdam ☎ 212121, Den Haag ☎ 222333, Rotterdam ☎ 292929. Numbers for other towns are in the front of the local telephone directories. If necessary contact the State Police Emergency Centre ☎ (03438)14321.

In the event of a serious or complicated accident, especially when personal injury has been sustained, the police should be called before the vehicles are removed. See also *Accidents* page 5.

Accommodation

The official hotel guide includes details of most hotels in the Netherlands. Information on other types of accommodation such as guest houses, furnished rooms and bungalows can be obtained from tourist information offices (VVV).

Hotels are officially classified and the category is exhibited outside each. Room prices must by law be indicated in hotel receptions and in each bedroom but they are not subject to official control. The service charge amounts to 15%, and it is usual for this to be included in the charges as well as value added tax.

The National Reservation Centre is open from 08.00—20.00hrs Monday to Saturday and will secure accommodation free of charge. Applications may be made direct by post, telephone or telex to NRC Leidschendam, PO Box 404 2260KA ☎ (070)202500 (if calling this number from the UK refer to your *Telephone Dialling Codes* booklet) or telex 33755. For those already in the Netherlands the VVV offices will book a room for a small charge.

Boats

Boat registration documentation is recommended in respect of boats temporarily imported into the Netherlands. See page 6 for further information.

Breakdowns

If your car breaks down, try to move it to the verge of the road so that it obstructs the traffic flow as little as possible, and place a warning triangle behind the vehicle to warn following traffic of the obstruction. The Royal Dutch Touring Club (ANWB) maintained a 24hr road patrol service (Wegenwacht) which operates throughout the country. See also *Breakdown* page 6 and *Warning triangle* page 307.

British Embassy/Consulate

(See also page 6)

The British Embassy is located at *2514 ED Den Haag* Lange Voorhout 10 ☎ (070)645800, but the Embassy has no consular section. The British Consulate is located at *1075 AE Amsterdam* Koningslaan 44 ☎ (020)764343.

Currency including banking hours

(See also page 9)

The unit of currency is the Dutch Guilder or Florin (*Fls*) divided into 100 *Cents.* At the time of going to press £ = *Fls*3.43. Denominations of bank notes are *Fls* 5, 10, 25, 50, 100, 250, 1,000; standard coins are *Fls* 1, 2.50, and *Cents* 5, 10, 25. There are no restrictions limiting the import of currency. All imported currency may be freely exported, as well as any currency exchanged in, or drawn on an account established in, the Netherlands.

Banks are open Monday to Friday 09.00—16.00hrs and closed on Saturday. At all ANWB offices, money can be exchanged from Monday to Friday 08.45—16.45hrs, and on Saturdays 08.45—12.00hrs; there are also exchanges at the principle railway stations (*eg* Amsterdam, Arnhem, Eindhoven, Den Haag, Hoek van Holland, Maastricht, Rosendaal, Rotterdam, Utrecht and Venlo).

Dimensions and weight restrictions

Private **cars** and towed **trailers** or **caravans** are restricted to the following dimensions — height: 4 metres; width: on 'A' roads* 2.50 metres (unladen) and 2.60 metres (including load), on 'B' roads* 2.20 metres (including load); Length**: with 2 axles 11 metres. The maximum permitted overall length of vehicle/trailer or caravan combination is 18 metres.

Maximum weight of caravan/luggage trailers without brakes 750kg or 75% of towing vehicle; with brakes 100% of weight of towing vehicle.

*'A' roads are main roads, 'B' roads are secondary roads. 'B' roads are indicated by signs bearing the capital letter 'B', roads which do not have these signs may be considered 'A' roads. **Trailers with single axle and manufactured before 1967—10 metres, after 1967—8 metres.

Driving licence

(See also page 11)

A valid British driving licence is acceptable in the Netherlands. The minimum age at which a visitor may drive a temporarily imported car or motorcycle is 18 years.

Emergency messages to tourists

(See also page 11)

Emergency messages to tourists are broadcast daily on Dutch radio.

Radio Hilversum 1 transmitting on 298 metres medium wave broadcasts these messages in Dutch, German and English as necessary at 17.55hrs on Sunday throughout the year.

Emergency messages are also broadcast in Dutch by a variety of regional local radio stations.

Firearms

The Dutch laws concerning the possession of firearms are the most stringent in Europe. Any person crossing the frontier with any type of firearm will be arrested. The law applies also to any object which on superficial inspection, shows resemblance to real firearms (*eg* plastic imitations etc). If you wish to carry firearms, real or imitation, of any description into the Netherlands, seek the advice of the Netherlands Consulate.

Lights

(See also page 14)

Driving on sidelights only is prohibited. Dipped headlights must be used at all times in built-up areas. In fog or falling snow, fog lamps may be used in pairs in conjunction with sidelights only. Headlights should be flashed as a warning of approach at night provided that they do not inconvenience other traffic. All vehicles parked on a public road must have their sidelights on if not within 30 metres (33yds) of a street lamp.

Motoring club

(See also page 16)

The **Koninklijke Nederlandse Toeristenbond** (ANWB) has its headquarters at *2596 EC Den Haag* Wassenaarseweg 220 and offices in numerous provincial towns. They

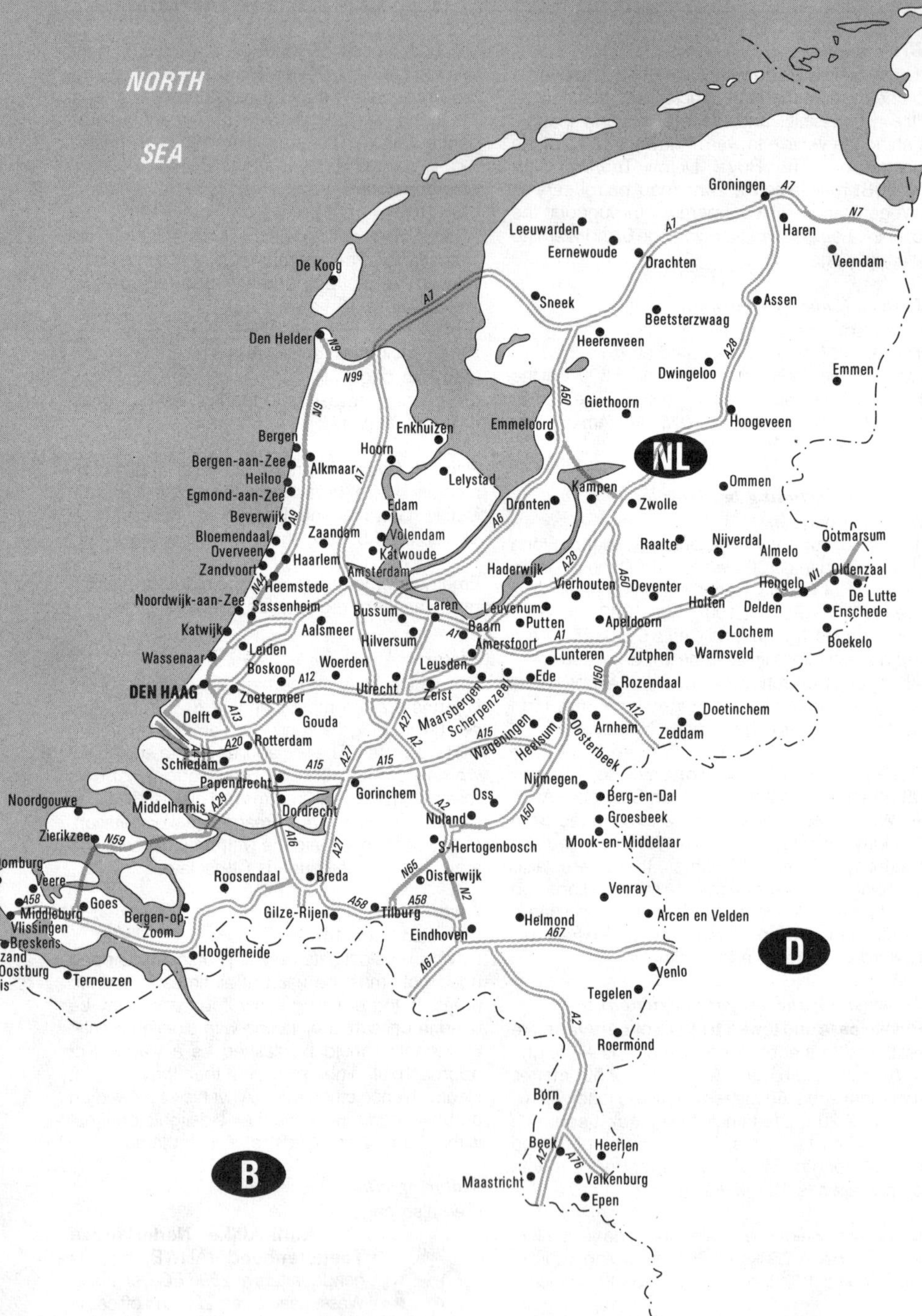

For key to country identification-see page 51

will assist motoring tourists generally and supply road and touring information. Offices are usually open between 08.45 and 16.45hrs Monday to Friday, and 08.45 to 12.00hrs on Saturdays. Traffic information can be obtained from the ANWB by phoning (070)313131 (24hrs service).

Motorways

There is a network of Motorways (*Autosnelweg*) carrying most inter-city and long-distance traffic. Nearly all motorways are part of the European international network, and carry an 'E' number (Green and white sign with the prefix 'E'), as well as the national number (red and white sign with the prefix 'A').

Recently a new numbering system of the European international network was introduced. Below is a list of the old and new 'E' numbers:

Old No	**Route**	**New No**
E3	Belgian Frontier — Eindhoven — Venlo	E 34
E8	Hoek van Holland — Den Haag — Utrecht — Oldenzaal	E 30
E9	Utrecht — Eindhoven — Maastricht	E 25
E9	Amsterdam — Utrecht	E 35
E10	Amsterdam — Rotterdam — Breda	E 19
E10	Amsterdam — Groningen	E 22
E35	Amsterdam — Amersfoort	E231
E35	Amersfoort — Groningen	E232
E35	Groningen — German Frontier	E 22
E36	Hoek van Holland — Rotterdam — Utrecht	E 25
E36	Utrecht — Arnhem — German Frontier	E 35
E37	Breda — Utrecht	E311
E38	Vlissingen — Breda — Eindhoven	E312
—	Rotterdam — Nijmegen	E 31

Orange badge scheme for disabled drivers

(See also page 16)

In the Netherlands badge holders may:
a park in special car parks set aside for the handicapped where there is no time limit;
b park for an indefinite period in blue zones;
c park for an indefinite period where parking sign (white letter on blue panel with additional panel stating parking times) is displayed;
d park for a maximum of two hours where parking prohibited (red ring and bars on blue background) or alternative parking (red ring and bars on blue background with white upright 'line' symbol) signs appear. A handicapped person's parking disc must be used. However, this concession does not apply when other parking facilities are to be found within a reasonable distance.

Parking

(See also page 17)

You can stop provided that you keep to the extreme right of the road and do not interfere with other traffic. You are allowed to stop to let passengers in and out at bus stops. Spending the night in a vehicle or trailer on the roadside is **not** permitted.

Parking meters and/or parking discs are used in many towns. Discs can be obtained from police stations, ANWB offices and many tobacco shops and must be displayed on the windscreen. They must be set at the time of parking and show when parking time lapses according to the limit in the area concerned. Failure to observe zonal regulations could result in a fine or the vehicle being towed away.

Passengers

(See also page 18)

Children under 12 are not permitted to travel in a vehicle as front seat passengers with the exception of children under 4 using a safety seat of approved design and children over 4 able to wear a safety belt.

Petrol

(See also page 18)

Credit cards The use of credit cards to obtain petrol is not available to visiting motorists.
Duty-free petrol In addition to the petrol in the vehicle tank up to 10 litres in a can may be imported free of customs duty and tax.
Petrol (leaded) Super Benzine (98—100 octane) grade.
Petrol (unleaded) is sold in the Netherlands as the Normal Benzine (92—95 octane) grade. The octane rating is not indicated on pumps dispensing unleaded petrol, but the pumps may be coloured green.

Postal information

Mail Postcards *Fls*0.55, letters up to 20gm *Fls*0.75.
Post offices There are 2,600 post offices in the Netherlands. Opening hours of main post offices are from 08.30—19.00hrs Monday to Friday and 09.00—12.00hrs Saturday. Smaller offices are open from 08.30—17.00hrs Monday to Friday.

Postcheques

(See also page 20)

Postcheques may be cashed at all post offices for any amount up to a maximum of *Fls*250 per cheque. Counter positions are identified by the words *Alle Geldhandelingen* or *Postbank*. See *Postal information* for post office opening hours.

Priority

Regulations in the Netherlands take account of the very large numbers of cyclists for whom special tracks are provided on a number of roads. Motor vehicles generally have priority over this slower moving traffic except when controlled with the appropriate road signs. However, cyclists proceeding straight ahead at intersections have priority over all turning traffic. Visitors should be extremely alert. See also *Priority including Roundabouts* page 21.

Public holidays

Official public holidays in the Netherlands for 1987 are given below. See also *Public holidays* page 21.
January 1 (New Year's Day)
April 17 (Good Friday)
April 20 (Easter Monday)
April 30 (The Queen's Birthday)
May 5 (Liberation Day)
May 28 (Ascension Day)
June 8 (Whit Monday)
December 25 (Christmas Day)
December 26* (Boxing Day)
*Saturday

Religious services

(See also page 22)

The Intercontinental Church Society welcomes visitors from any denomination to English language services in the following centres:
1011 HW Amsterdam The Revd Brian Eaves, Christ Church, Groenburgwal 42 ☎ 248877.
2585 HA Den Haag The Revd Canon Alan Lindsay, 2 Riouwstraat ☎ 555359.
3024 Rotterdam The Revd Canon John Taylor, 113 Pieter de Hoochweg ☎ 4765025.
Utrecht The Revd Douglas Beukes, Holy Trinity Church, Van Hogendorpstraat 26 ☎ 513424.

Roads

Main roads usually have only two lanes but they are well surfaced. The best way to see the countryside is to tour along minor roads, often alongside canals.

Road signs

(See also page 22)

Signposting is good; in some places there are special by-way tours signposted by the ANWB. In residential areas the sign '*woonerven*' indicates that bumps (silent policemen) have been installed across the roads to oblige drivers to reduce speed.

Shopping hours

Generally food shops are open 08.00—18.00hrs Monday—Saturday. Most food shops close for one half day per week, but this varies according to location. Most other shops including department stores are open from 13.00—17.30 hrs on Monday, from 09.00—17.30 hrs Tuesday—Friday, from 09.00—16.00hrs Saturday.

Speed limits

(See also page 22)

The placename indicates the beginning and end of a built-up area. The following speed limits for cars are in force if there are no special signs. Built-up areas 50kph (31mph). Outside built-up areas it is 100kph (62mph) on motorways and 80kph (49mph) on other roads. Car/trailer combinations are limited to 80kph (49mph).

Spiked or studded tyres

Although residents are not permitted to use *spiked tyres*, visitors may do so provided that they do not exceed 80kph (49mph), and only if spikes are allowed in their home country. See also *Cold weather touring* page 8.

Toll bridges and tunnels

Toll bridges: **Zeeland** (Oosterschelde) bridge; car *Fls*4.00 car/caravan *Fls*6.00 **Waalbrug** (near Tiel); car *Fls*2.90 car/caravan *Fls*3.50.

Toll tunnels: **Kiltunnel** ('s-Gravendeel-Dordrecht); car *Fls*3.50 car/caravan *Fls*10.

Tourist information

(See also page 24)

The Netherlands Board of Tourism, 25-28 Buckingham Gate, London SW1E 6LD ☎ 01-630 0451 will be pleased to assist you with any information regarding tourism and has branch offices (VVV) in all towns and large villages in the Netherlands. They can be recognised by the sign illustrated on the left (Blue with white lettering).

There are three types of these branch offices: Travel offices giving detailed information about the whole of the Netherlands; Information Offices giving general information about the Netherlands and detailed information about their own region, and Local Information offices giving detailed information about that locality.

Using the telephone

(See also page 24)
Insert coin **after** lifting receiver (instructions in English in all public callboxes). When making calls to subscribers within the Netherlands precede number with relevant area code (shown in parentheses against town entry in gazetteer). Use 25 cent coin for local calls and *Fls*2.50 coins for national and international calls.
International callbox identification All callboxes.
Telephone rates The cost of a call to the UK is *Fls*0.95 for each minute. Local calls cost 25 cents. The cheap rate operates from 18.00—07.00hrs on Saturday and Sunday, the charge being *Fls*0.70 per minute.
What to dial for the Irish Republic 09 *353.
What to dial for the UK 09 *44.
*Wait for a second dialling tone.

Warning triangle

The use of a warning triangle is compulsory for all vehicles except two-wheelers. The triangle must be used to warn following traffic of any obstruction and also if a parked vehicle is insufficiently illuminated either by its own or street lighting. See also *Warning triangles/Hazard warning lights* page 25.

Prices are in Dutch Florins (Guiden or Guilder)
Abbreviations:
pl plein
st straat

AALSMEER
Noord-Holland (☎02977)

★★**Schouwsehof** Raadhuispl 16 ☎25551
🛁 🚿 11 sB 🛁 🚿 80 dB 🛁 🚿 110 M13—65

🚗 **Boom** Oosteindweweg 220 ☎25667 **P** AR

ALKMAAR
Noord-Holland (☎072)

★★★**Alkmaar Ladbroke Inn** Arcadialaan 2 ☎120744 tx57658
🛁 🚿 90 **P**150 ☾ sB 🛁 🚿 56—67 dB 🛁 🚿 96—120 M18—85
Credit cards 1 2 3 4 5

🚗 **Klaver** Helderseweg 29—30 ☎127033 **P** AR

🚗 **N Schmidt** Nassaupl 1 ☎113545 For

ALMELO
Overijssel (☎05490)

★★**Postiljon** (BW) Aalderinkssingel 2 ☎26655 tx44817
🛁 🚿 50 **P** sB 🛁 🚿 73—107 dB 🛁 🚿 83—117
Credit card 1

🚗 **Autobedrijf** Wierdensestr 107 ☎12472 M/c Col For

🚗 **Konink** H-R-Holst Laan 1 ☎11064 Aud Por VW

AMERSFOORT
Utrecht (☎033)

★★★**Witte** Utrechtseweg 2 ☎14142
rm17 (🛁 🚿 15) **P** sB58 sB 🛁 🚿 82 dB110 dB 🛁 🚿 125

★★**Golden Tulip Berg** (GT) Utrechtseweg 225 ☎620444 tx79213
🛁 🚿 52 🏠 **P** Lift sB 🛁 🚿 85—98 dB 🛁 🚿 126—170
Credit cards 1 2 3 5

🚗 **Stam Amersfoort** Kapelweg 12 ☎635104 Ren

AMSTERDAM
Noord-Holland (☎020)

See plan on page 308

★★★★★**Amstel** (Intercont) Prof-Tulppl 1 ☎226060 tx11004 Plan **1**
🛁 111 🏠 **P** Lift sB 🛁 295—395 dB 🛁 395—500 M60

★★★★★**Amsterdam Hilton** Apollolaan 138—140 ☎780780 tx11025 Plan **2**
🛁 274 **P** Lift sB 🛁 250—360 dB 🛁 310—450 M13—65
Credit cards 1 2 3 4 5

★★★★★**Apollo** (THF) Apollolaan 2 ☎735922 tx14084 Plan **3**
🛁 225 **P** Lift sB 🛁 220—320 dB 🛁 270—370
Credit cards 1 2 3 5

★★★★★**Europe** (ETAP/Relais et Châteaux) Nieuwe Doelenstr 2—4 ☎234836 tx12081 Plan **4**
🛁 🚿 79 **P** Lift ☾ sB 🛁 🚿 275—375 dB 🛁 🚿 375—475 M55—150
Credit cards 1 2 3 5

★★★★★**American** (Forum) Leidsekade 97 ☎245322 tx12545 Plan **5**
🛁 185 Lift sB 🛁 238 dB 🛁 310
Credit cards 1 2 3 5

★★★★**Amsterdam Marriott** Stadhouderskade 19—21 ☎835151 tx15087 Plan **5A**
🛁 395 🏠 **P** Lift sB 🛁 370—410 dB 🛁 430—470

★★★★**Caransa** (Crest **See page 50**) Rembrandtspl 19 ☎229455 tx13342 Plan **6**
🛁 66 Lift ☾ sB 🛁 225 dB 🛁 295 M33
Credit cards 1 2 3 4 5

★★★★**Carlton** (Jolly) Vijzelstr 2—18 (n.rest) ☎222266 tx11670 Plan **7**
🛁 157 Lift ☾ sB 🛁 197 dB 🛁 275
Credit cards 1 2 3 4 5

★★★★**Crest** (**See page 50**) de Boellelaan 2 ☎462300 tx13647 Plan **8**
🛁 260 **P**100 Lift ☾ sB 🛁 225 dB 🛁 275
Credit cards 1 2 3 4 5

★★★★**Doelen** (Crest **See page 50**) Nieuwe Doelenstr 24 ☎220722 tx14399 Plan **9**
🛁 🚿 85 Lift ☾ sB 🛁 🚿 215—235 dB 🛁 🚿 285—315 M33
Credit cards 1 2 3 4 5

★★★★**Ladbroke Park** Stadhouderskade 25—29 ☎717474 tx11412 Plan **10A**
🛁 184 🏠 Lift ☾ sB 🛁 198—228 dB 🛁 280—325 M35
Credit cards 1 2 3 4 5

★★★★**Memphis** de Lairessestr 87 ☎733141 tx12450 Not on plan
🛁 81 Lift sB 🛁 150—175 dB 🛁 215—260 M30
Credit cards 1 2 3 5

★★★★**Port van Cleve** (ETAP) N.Z. Voorburgwal 178 ☎244860 tx13129 Plan **11**
🛁 110 Lift sB 🛁 129—152 dB 🛁 156—257
Credit cards 1 2 3 5

★★★★**Pulitzer** (GT) Prinsengracht 315—331 ☎228333 tx16508 Plan **12**
🛁 🚿 189 Lift sB 🛁 🚿 195—225 dB 🛁 🚿 255—275 M75—110
Credit cards 1 2 3 5

★★★★**Victoria** Damrak 1—6 ☎234255 tx16625 Plan **12A**
🛁 🚿 160 Lift ☾ sB 🛁 🚿 184—214 dB 🛁 🚿 270
Credit cards 1 2 3 5

★★★**Apollofirst** Apollolaan 123—125 ☎730333 tx13446 Plan **13**
rm32 (🛁 31) Lift sB 🛁 145 dB 🛁 200 M47—86

★★★**Barbizon Centre** (GT) Stadhouderskade 7 ☎851351 tx12601 Plan **14**
🛁 241 🏠 **P** Lift sB 🛁 220—350 dB 🛁 270—400 M40
Credit cards 1 2 3 5

★★★**Delphi** Apollolaan 101—105 ☎795152 tx16659 Plan **15**

rm48 (🛁 ⛲ 44) Lift sB120 sB 🛁 ⛲ 130 dB165 dB 🛁 ⛲ 180

★★★**Euromotel E9** (ETAP) J Muyskenweg 10 ☎658181 tx13382 Plan **16**

rm140 (⛲ 128) **P** sB83 sB⛲ 100 dB110 dB⛲ 130
Credit cards 1 2 3 5

★★★**Euromotel E10** (ETAP) Oude Haagseweg 20 ☎179005 tx15524 Plan **17**

🛁 ⛲ 157 **P** Lift sB 🛁 ⛲ 115 dB 🛁 ⛲ 145 M25
Credit cards 1 2 3 5

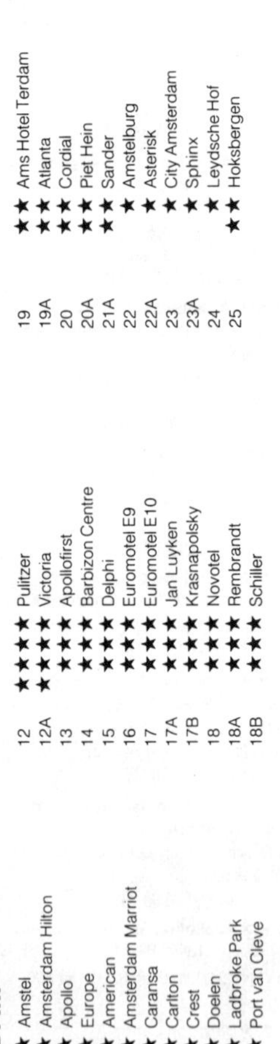

AMSTERDAM

1 ★★★★★ Amstel
2 ★★★★★ Amsterdam Hilton
3 ★★★★★ Apollo
4 ★★★★★ Europe
5 ★★★★★ American
5A ★★★★ Amsterdam Marriot
6 ★★★★ Caransa
7 ★★★★ Carlton
8 ★★★★ Crest
9 ★★★★ Doelen
10A ★★★★ Ladbroke Park
11 ★★★★ Port van Cleve
12 ★★★★ Pulitzer
12A ★★★★ Victoria
13 ★★★ Apollofirst
14 ★★★ Barbizon Centre
15 ★★★ Delphi
16 ★★★ Euromotel E9
17 ★★★ Euromotel E10
17A ★★★ Jan Luyken
17B ★★★ Krasnapolsky
18 ★★★ Novotel
18A ★★★ Rembrandt
18B ★★★ Schiller
19 ★★ Ams Hotel Terdam
19A ★★ Atlanta
20 ★★ Cordial
20A ★★ Piet Hein
21A ★★ Sander
22 ★ Amstelburg
22A ★ Asterisk
23 ★ City Amsterdam
23A ★ Sphinx
24 ★ Leydsche Hof
25 ★★ Hoksbergen

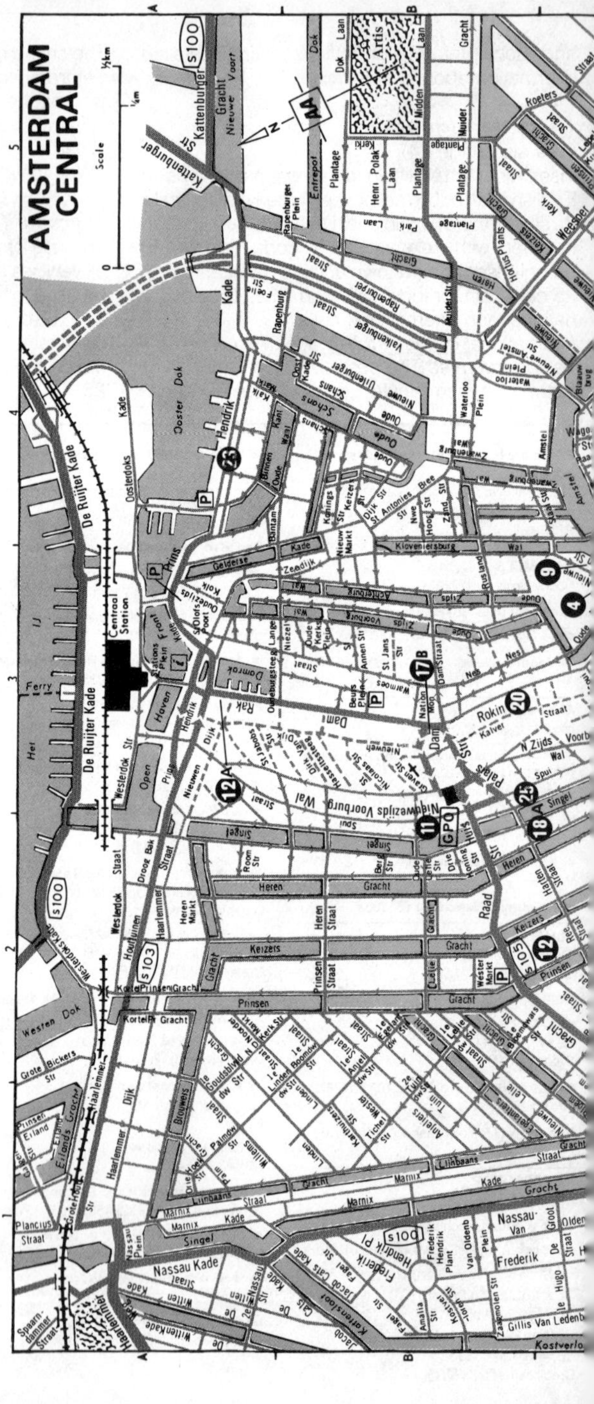

AMSTERDAM CENTRAL

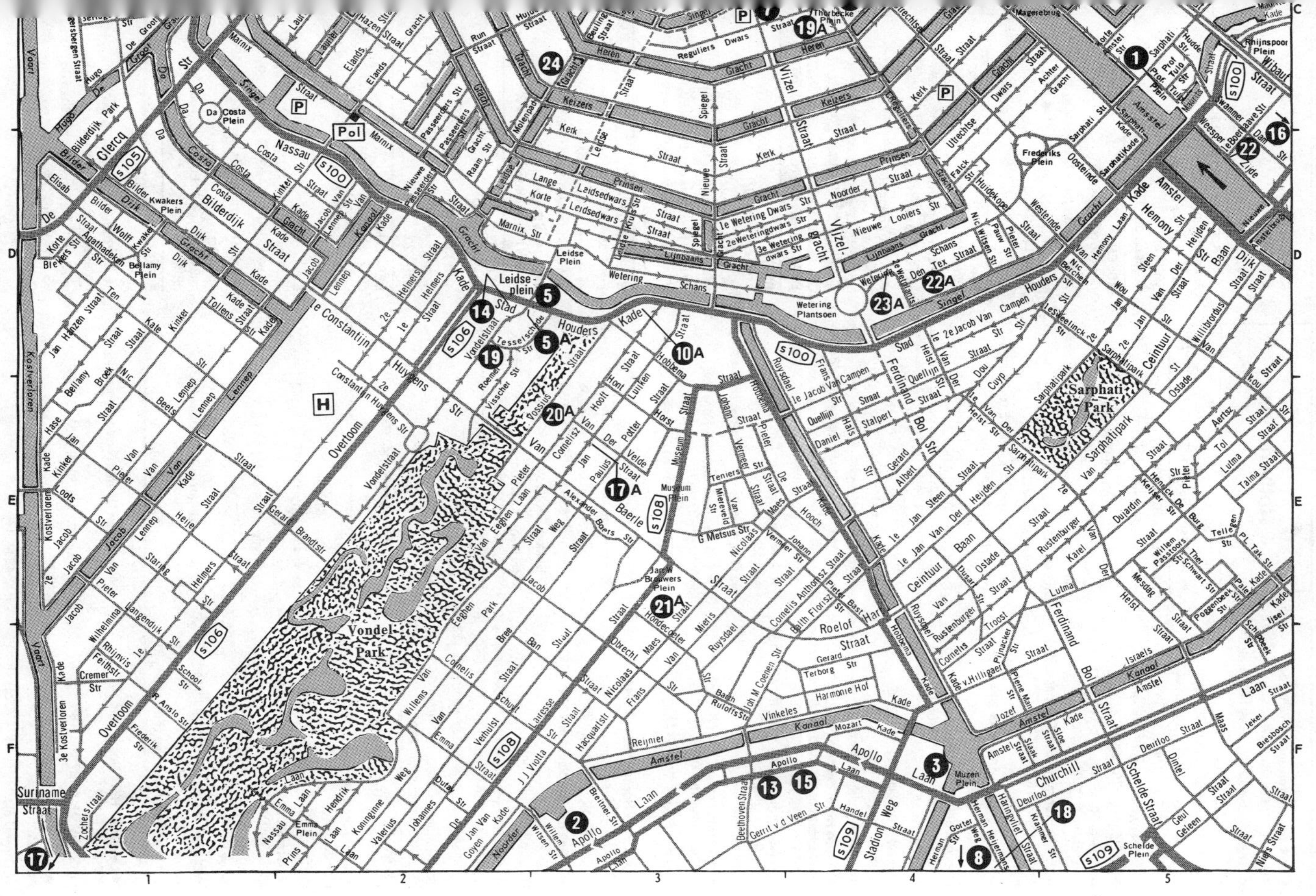
Vondel Park
Sarphati Park
Museum Plein
Leidse-plein
Leidse Plein
Frederiks Plein
Wetering Plantsoen
Vijzel-gracht
Ferdinand Bol Str
Overtoom
Stadhouders Kade
Singel
Kostverloren Vaart
Apollo Laan
Churchill Laan
Schelde Straat
Schelde Plein
Muzen Plein
Amstel Kanaal
Van Baerle Str
Jan W Brouwers Plein
Da Costa Plein
Bellamy Plein
Kwakers Plein
Thorbecke Plein
Rhijnspoor Plein
Suriname Straat
Ruysdael Kade
Hobbema Kade
s 100
s 105
s 106
s 108
s 109
C
D
E
F
1
2
3
4
5

★★★**Jan Luyken** Jan Luykenstr 58 ☎764111 tx16254 Plan **17A**

🛁🚿63 Lift sB🛁🚿190 dB🛁🚿210—240

★★★**Krasnapolsky** (SRS) Dam 9 ☎5549111 tx12262 Plan **17B**

rm364 (🛁🚿332) ⌂ Lift sB190 sB🛁🚿275 dB275 dB🛁🚿350 M45

★★★**Novotel** Europa Boulevard 10 ☎5411123 tx13375 Plan **18**

🛁600 **P** Lift ☾ sB🛁225 dB🛁275 M30 Credit cards [2] [3] [5]

★★★**Rembrandt** (Crest **See page 50**) Herengracht 255 (n.rest) ☎221727 tx15424 Plan **18A**

🛁111 Lift ☾ sB🛁195 dB🛁240 Credit cards [1] [2] [3] [4] [5]

★★★**Schiller** (Crest **See page 50**) Rembrandtspl 26—36 ☎231660 tx14058 Plan **18B**

rm97 (🛁🚿92) Lift ☾ sB🛁🚿235 dB🛁🚿315 M38—45 Credit cards [1] [2] [3] [4] [5]

★★**Ams Hotel Terdam** (BW) Tesselschadestr 23—29 ☎831811 tx14275 Plan **19**

rm54 (🛁🚿52) Lift sB93 sB🛁🚿142 dB136 dB🛁🚿198 M23—29 Credit card [2]

★★**Atlanta** Rembrandtspl 8—10 (n.rest) ☎253585 Plan **19A**

rm30 (🛁🚿17) sB45 sB🛁🚿95 dB75 dB🛁🚿125

★★**Cordial** Rokin 62—64 ☎264411 tx15621 Plan **20**

🚿44 Lift sB🚿76—110 dB🚿99—140

★★**Hoksbergen** Singel 301 ☎266043 Plan **25**

🚿14 sB🚿95 dB🚿125

★★**Piet Hein** Vossiusstr 53 ☎628375 tx10869 Plan **20A**

rm31 (🛁🚿23) sB58 sB🚿88 dB98 dB🚿128

★★**Sander** J-Obrechstr 69 (n.rest) ☎735429 tx18456 Plan **21A**

15 Jan—10 Dec
🚿15 sB🚿95—120 dB🚿115—135

★**Amstelburg** Weesperzijde 28 ☎946407 Plan **22**

rm15 sB40 dB70

★**Asterisk** Den Texstr 14—16 (n.rest) ☎262396 Plan **22A**

rm19 (🛁🚿13) sB45 sB🛁🚿62 dB65 dB🛁🚿125

★**City Amsterdam** Prins Hendrikkade 130 (n.rest) ☎230836 Plan **23**

rm18 (🛁🚿7) sB45 sB🛁🚿60 dB80 dB🛁🚿120

★**Leydsche Hof** Leidsegracht 14 ☎232148 Plan **24**

rm12 (🚿5) sB45 dB75 dB🚿85

★**Sphinx** Weteringschans 82 ☎273680 Plan **23A**

rm17 (🛁🚿8) sB45 sB🛁🚿70 dB63 dB🛁🚿105

Netherlands

🚗 **Asmoco** J-Rebelstr ☎195444 **P** BMW

AMSTERDAM AIRPORT

At **SCHIPHOL** (10km SW)

★★★★**Schiphol** (GT) Kruisweg 495 ☎(02503)15851 tx74546 Not on plan

🛁168 **P** Lift ☾ sB🛁200—240 dB🛁235—260 Credit cards [1] [2] [3] [5]

★★**Ibis** Schipholweg 181 ☎(02968)1234 tx16491 Not on plan

🛁396 **P** Lift ☾ Credit cards [1] [2] [3] [5]

APELDOORN
Gelderland (☎055)

★★★**Bloemink** (ETAP) Loolaan 56 ☎214141 tx49253

rm90 (🛁🚿83) **P** Lift sB42 sB🛁🚿272 dB69 dB🛁🚿282 ⛳ Credit cards [1] [2] [3] [5]

★★★**Cantharel** Van Golsteinlaan 20 ☎414455 tx49550

🛁🚿48 **P** Lift sB🛁🚿55 dB🛁🚿55—88

★★★**Keizerskroon** (GT) Koningstr 7 ☎217744 tx49221

🛁🚿67 **P** Lift sB🛁🚿175—185 dB🛁🚿220—270 ⛳ Credit cards [1] [2] [3] [5]

★★**Berg en Bos** Aquamarijnstr 58 ☎552352

🛁🚿17 sB🛁🚿45 dB🛁🚿73—102

🚗 **Bakker** Gazellestr 21 ☎214208 **P** Ren

🚗 **Nefkens-Apeldoorn** Wagenhakershoek 2/Edisonlaan 270 ☎414222 Peu

ARCEN-EN-VELDEN
Limburg (☎04703)

★**Maas** Schans 18 ☎1556

6 Mar—Nov
rm15 (🛁🚿13) ⌂ **P** sB43 sB🛁🚿75 dB100 dB🛁🚿125 ≋

ARNHEM
Gelderland (☎085)

★★★**Haarhuis** (BW) Stationspl 1 ☎427441 tx45357

🛁🚿96 **P** Lift sB🛁🚿85—95 dB🛁🚿119—133 Credit card [2]

★★★**Postiljon** (BW) Europaweg 25 ☎453741 tx45028

🚿30 **P** sB🚿88 dB🚿59—98 Credit card [2]

★★**Leeren Doedel** Amsterdamseweg 467 ☎332344

rm9 (🛁🚿4) **P** sB38 sB🛁🚿48 dB70 dB🛁🚿95

🚗 **J Reymes** Amsterdamseweg 5A ☎423204 **P**

🚗 **Rosler & Meljer** Boulevard Heuvelink 5a ☎435984 For

At **VELP** (2km NE)

★★★★**Crest** (**See page 50**) Pres-Kennedylaan 102 ☎649849 tx45527

🛁🚿74 **P**150 ☾ sB🛁🚿165 dB🛁🚿205 M17—48 Credit cards [1] [2] [3] [4] [5]

ASSEN
Drenthe (☎05920)

★★★**Overcingel** Stationspl 10 ☎11333

rm36 (🛁🚿32) **P** Lift sB48 sB🛁🚿58 dB95 dB🛁🚿150 M30

🚗 **AZA** Europaweg ☎55944 **P** Mer

BAARN
Utrecht (☎02154)

★**Prom** Amalialaan 1 ☎12913

🛁🚿43 sB🛁🚿66 dB🛁🚿91

🚗 **M Kooy** Eemnesser 57a ☎12619 All makes

🚗 **Splinter Eemland** Eemneserweg 16—22 ☎15555 **P** For

BEATRIXHAVEN See **MAASTRICHT**

BEEK
Limburg (☎04402)

★★★**Euromotel Limburg** (ETAP) Vliegveldweg 19 ☎72462 tx56059

🛁🚿64 **P** sB🛁🚿85—90 dB🛁🚿120—125 M19 Credit cards [1] [2] [3] [5]

BEETSTERZWAAG
Friesland (☎05126)

★★★★**Lauswolt** (Relais et Châteaux) Van Harinxmaweg 10 ☎1245 tx46241

🛁🚿34 ⌂ **P** sB🛁🚿100—185 dB🛁🚿105—240 M70—98 🎾

BERGEN
Noord-Holland (☎02208)

★★**Park** Breelaan 19 ☎12223

rm26 (🚿17) **P** sB45 sB🚿55 dB90 dB🚿110 M15—30

BERGEN-AAN-ZEE
Noord-Holland (☎02208)

★★★**Nassau-Bergen** van der Wyckpl 4 ☎97541

5 Jan—22 Dec
rm42 (🛁🚿41) **P** sB85 sB🛁🚿135 dB150 dB🛁🚿200 M45—53 ≋

★**Prins Maurits** van Hasseltstr 7 ☎12364

Apr—Oct
rm24 (🚿22) ⌂ **P** sB63 sB🚿93 dB86 dB🚿115

BERG-EN-DAL
Gelderland (☎08895)

★★★**Park Val Monte** (GT) Oude Holleweg 5 ☎1704 tx48428

rm92 (🛁🚿90) **P** sB87 sB🛁🚿126 dB113 dB🛁🚿150 M33 🎾 ≋ Credit cards [1] [2] [3] [5]

BERGEN-OP-ZOOM
Noord-Brabant (☎01640)

★★★**Gouden Leeuw** Fortuinstr 14 ☎35000 tx78265
🛁🚿29 Lift sB🛁🚿65—100 dB🛁🚿125—135

★**Draak** Grote Markt 37—38 ☎33661
rm32 (🛁🚿18) Lift sB45 sB🛁🚿53 dB150 dB🛁🚿200 M35

🚗 **Difoga** Bredasestr 25 ☎50200 For

🚗 **Swagemakers P** Alf

🚗 **Vos** Ravelstr 10—12 ☎42050 Cit

BEVERWIJK
Noord-Holland (☎02510)

🚗 **Admiraal & Zn** Laan der Nederlanden 1 ☎360510 **P** Cit

Wijkeroog Bullerlaan 6 ☎41664 **P** AR

BLOEMENDAAL
Noord-Holland (☎023)

★★**Iepenhove** Hartenlustlaan 4 ☎258301
rm44 (🛁🚿35) **P** Lift sB44 sB🛁🚿75 dB110 dB🛁🚿120 M25—85

🚗 **Van Loon's** Korte Kleverlaan 30—44 ☎259311 **P** Lan Ren Saa

BOEKELO
Overijssel (☎05428)

★★★★**Boekelo** Oude Deldenerweg 203 ☎1444 tx44301
rm80 (🛁🚿78) **P** Lift ☾ sB🛁🚿160 dB🛁🚿189 🎾 ⛱ 🖭
Credit cards [1] [2] [3] [4] [5]

BORN
Limburg (☎04498)

★★★**Crest (See page 50)** Langereweg 21 ☎51666 tx36048
🛁🚿50 **P** ☾ sB🛁🚿110 dB🛁🚿145
Credit cards [1] [2] [3] [4] [5]

BOSKOOP
Zuid-Holland (☎01727)

★★**Neuf** Barendstr 10 ☎2031
🛁🚿12 **P** sB🛁🚿40—78 dB🛁🚿70—98

🚗 **Eerste Boskoops** Plankier 2—6 ☎2110 **P** Mer Ope

BREDA
Noord-Brabant (☎076)

★★★**Brabant** (ETAP) Heerbaan 4—6 ☎224666 tx54263
🛁🚿80 **P** Lift sB🛁🚿90—95 dB🛁🚿100—105 🖭
Credit cards [1] [2] [3] [5]

★★★**Novotel** Dr-Batenburglaan 74 ☎659220 tx74016
🛁80 **P** Lift ☾ sB🛁116 dB🛁130 🎾 ⛱
Credit cards [2] [3] [5]

★★**Breda** (ETAP) Roskam 20 ☎222177 tx54126
🛁🚿130 🏠 **P** Lift sB🛁🚿31—115 dB🛁🚿97—125 M18 🖭
Credit cards [1] [2] [3] [5]

🚗 **Nefkens-Breda** Loevesteinstr 20 ☎659211 **P** Peu

Netherlands

🚗 **Tigchelaar** Boeimersingel 6 ☎224400 **P** For

🚗 **Van Nunen** Haagweg 442—444 ☎224920 **P** AR

🚗 **Valkenberg** Spinveld 74 ☎222371 Cit

At **GINNEKEN** (2km S)

★★★**Mastbosch** (GT) Burg-Kerstenslaan 20 ☎650050 tx54406
rm40 (🛁🚿39) **P** Lift sB60 sB🛁🚿117 dB160 dB🛁🚿177
Credit cards [1] [2] [3] [5]

BRESKENS
Zeeland (☎01172)

★★**Wapen van Breskens** Grote Kade 33 ☎1401
rm20 (🚿6) **P** sB38 sB🚿55 dB75 dB🚿110

🚗 **Van de Ree** Mercurivsstr 11—13 ☎1729 **P** For

BUNNIK See **UTRECHT**

BUSSUM
Noord-Holland (☎02159)

★**Gooiland** Stationsweg 16—22 ☎43724
rm12 (🚿4)

🚗 **Hogguer Bussum** Vlietlaan 58—66 ☎18651 For

🚗 **Van Meurs** Huizerweg 84—86 ☎34047 Ope

🚗 **Van Meurs** Noorderweg 2 ☎30024 **P** Ren

CADZAND
Zeeland (☎01179)

★★★**Schelde** Scheldestr 1 ☎1720
🛁🚿26 **P** sB🛁🚿75 dB120 dB🛁🚿140 M25—35 🖭

DELDEN
Overijssel (☎05407)

★★**Zwaan** Langestr 2 ☎1206
rm13 (🛁🚿9) 🏠 **P** sB55 sB🛁🚿85 dB95 dB🛁🚿115 ⛱

DELFT
Zuid-Holland (☎015)

★★**Leeuwenbrug** Koornmarkt 16 (n.rest) ☎134640 tx33756
🛁🚿34 Lift sB🛁🚿95—130 dB🛁🚿125—150

★**Central** Wijnhaven 6—8 ☎123442
rm38 (🛁🚿27) sB53 sB🛁🚿95 dB103 dB🛁🚿125

🚗 **Kinesis** Vulcenusweg 281 ☎616464 For

DEN HAAG See **HAAG (DEN) (HAGUE, THE)**

DEN HELDER See **HELDER (DEN)**

DEVENTER
Overijssel (☎05700)

★★★**Postiljon** (BW) Deventerweg 121 ☎24022 tx49028
🛁🚿103 **P** Lift sB🛁🚿78—103 dB🛁🚿88—113 M17—50
Credit card [2]

🚗 **Hardonk's** Gl-Gibsonstr 6 ☎13945 Fia Mer Vau

DOETINCHEM
Gelderland (☎08340)

🚗 **Martens** Edison Str 1 ☎33250 **P** For

DOMBURG
Zeeland (☎01188)

★★**Duinheuvel** Badhuisweg 2 ☎1282
rm17 (🛁🚿13) **P** sB46 dB74 dB🛁🚿121 M28

DORDRECHT
Zuid-Holland (☎078)

★★★**Bellevue Groothoofdspoort** Boomstr 37 ☎137900
🛁🚿19 **P** sB🛁🚿65—88 dB🛁🚿115—125 M25

★★★**Postiljon** Rijksstraatweg 30 ☎184444 tx20478
🛁🚿96 **P** Lift ☾ sB🛁🚿90—123 dB🛁🚿125—133

🚗 **Dubbeesteyn** Dubbelsteynlaan 51 ☎161155 **P** BMW

🚗 **Kern's** Copernicusweg 1 ☎171633 Ren

🚗 **J Van den Berg** Blekersdijk 96 ☎143088 For

🚗 **H W Van Gorp & Zonnen** A-Cuypsingel 296 ☎142044 Peu

DRACHTEN
Friesland (☎05120)

★★★**Crest (See page 50)** Zonnedauw 1 ☎20705 tx46693
🛁🚿48 **P** Lift ☾ sB🛁🚿125 dB🛁🚿160
Credit cards [1] [2] [3] [4] [5]

🚗 **Siton** de Knobben 25 ☎14455 Ope

DRONTEN
Gelderland (☎03210)

🚗 **Visser** de Ketting 1 ☎3114 Ope Vau

DWINGELOO
Drenthe (☎05219)

At **LHEE** (1.5km SE)

★★**Borken** ☎7200
Closed 31 Dec—1 Jan
rm24 (🛁🚿15) 🏠 **P** dB70 dB🛁🚿110 🖭

EDAM
Noord-Holland (☎02993)

★**Dam** Keizersgracht 1 ☎71766
rm12 (🚿8) sB45 dB75 dB🚿85

🚗 **Evodam** D-Poschlaan ☎65551 Ren

EDE
Gelderland (☎083380)

🚗 **Van der Kolk** Klaphekweg 30 ☎30201 For

Van Silthout Proosdijveldweg 1 ☎36710 **P** Ren

At **VEENENDAAL** (8km W)

★★**Ibis** Vendelier 8 ☎(08385)22222 tx45599

41 Lift ☾ sB 80 dB 95 M17—25
Credit cards 1 2 3 5

EEMNES See **LAREN**

EERNEWOUDE
Friesland (☎05117)

★★★**Princenhof** P-Miedemaweg 15 ☎9206

15 Mar—Oct
rm45 (38) **P** sB43 sB 75 dB85 dB 140

EGMOND-AAN-ZEE
Noord-Holland (☎02206)

★★★**Bellevue** Boulevard Noord (A7) ☎1025

rm51 (48) Lift sB42 sB 77 dB93 dB 170

J A Karels Trompstr 17 ☎1250 AR

EINDHOVEN
Noord-Brabant (☎040)

★★★★★**Cocagne** (SRS) Vestdijk 47 ☎444755 tx51245

207 **P** Lift sB 160—185 dB 200—220 M25—100

★★★★**Holiday Inn** Veldmaarschalk Montgomerylaan 1 ☎433222 tx51775

200 **P** Lift sB 155—175 dB 210—225 M25

★★★**Eindhoven** Aalsterweg 322 ☎123435 tx51999

180 **P** Lift sB 70—95 dB 70—95

Driessen Pieterbergweg 31 ☎413701 Saa

Van Laarhoven's Auto Hondsruglaan 99 ☎413615 **P** AR

L Lang Pisanostr 49 ☎433887 Fia Lan

OBAM Aalsterweg 135 ☎116444 For

EMMELOORD
Overijssel (☎05270)

Gorter Kampwai 50 ☎3541 AR Ope Vau

EMMEN
Drenthe (☎05910)

Jong Statenweg 5—7 ☎22330 Cit

Misker Odoornerweg 4 ☎18288 AR

ENKHUIZEN
Noord-Holland (☎02280)

★★**Wapen van Enkhuizen** Breedstr 59 ☎13434

rm27 (11) **P** sB33 sB 45 dB61 dB 75 M19

Watses Westerstr 273—275 ☎12708 For

ENSCHEDE
Overijssel (☎053)

★★★**Memphis** M-H-Tromplaan 55 ☎318244 tx44702

Netherlands

rm37 (35) **P** Lift sB38 sB 90 dB74 dB 135 M26

Auto Fischer Oldenzaalsestr 137 ☎354555 For

Oldenhof Europalaan 23 ☎310961 BMW

Ruinemans de Reulver 30 ☎770077 Hon

EPEN
Limburg (☎04455)

★**Gerardushoeve** Julianastr 23 ☎1793

2 Jan—Nov
6 **P** Lift sB 44 dB 88

FLUSHING See **VLISSINGEN**

GIETHOORN
Overijssel (☎05216)

★★★**Giethoorn** Beulakerweg 128 ☎1216

20 **P**

GILZE-RYEN
Noord-Brabant (☎01615)

★★★**Gilze Rijen** Klein Zwitserland 8 ☎2051 tx54800

138 **P** Lift dB 65—200

GINNEKEN See **BREDA**

GOES
Zeeland (☎01100)

★**Ockenburgh** van de Spiegelstr 104 ☎16303

Closed Sunday
rm7 (5) **P**

Adria West Havendyk 150 ☎20440 **P** For

Van Frassen Voorstad 79 ☎27353 M/c **P** Cit

B Oeveren A-Plasmanweg 2 ☎12730 **P** Mer

Van Strien Van de Spiegelstr 92 ☎14840 **P** Aud VW

GORINCHEM
Zuid-Holland (☎01830)

★★★**Gorinchem** Van Hogendorpweg 8—10 ☎22400

15 **P** sB 87 dB 133

Van Mill Banneweg 1—3 ☎32344 Fia Ope Vau

GOUDA
Zuid-Holland (☎01820)

J L Hulleman Burg Jamessingel 2 ☎12977 **P** For

GROESBEEK
Gelderland (☎08891)

★★**Wolfsberg** Mooksebaan 12 ☎1327

Mar—Oct & 23 Dec—2 Jan
rm20 (15) **P** sB41 sB 43 dB78 dB 101 M25—35&alc

GRONINGEN
Groningen (☎050)

★★★**Crest** (**See page 50**) Donderslaan 156 ☎252040 tx53394

59 **P** ☾ sB 102 dB 145
Credit cards 1 2 3 4 5

★★★**Euromotel Groningen** (ETAP) Expositielaan 7 ☎258400 tx53795

159 **P** Lift sB 100—110 dB fr134 M20—65
Credit cards 1 2 3 5

A—Z Friesestraatweg 22 ☎120012 **P** Hon

Geba Flemingstr 1 ☎250015 AR

Gronam Rijksstraatweg 130, Oosterhoogeburg ☎411552 For

B Oosterhuis Prontonstr ☎182223 Toy

HAAG (DEN) (HAGUE, THE)
Zuid-Holland (☎070)

★★★★★**Promenade** Van Stolkweg 1 ☎525161 tx31162

100 **P** Lift sB 190—220 dB 220—250 Malc

★★★★**Bel Air** (GT) J-de-Wittlaan 30 ☎502021 tx31444

350 **P** Lift sB 125 dB 168
Credit cards 1 2 3 5

★★★★**Indes** (Crest **See page 50**) Lange Voorhout 54—56 ☎469553 tx31196

77 **P**16 Lift ☾ sB 335 dB 435
Credit cards 1 2 3 4 5

★★★★**Sofitel** Koningin Julianapl 35 ☎814901 tx34001

144 Lift ☾ sB 239—264 dB 322—372 M48

★★★**Corona** Buitenhof 40—42 ☎637930 tx33027

26 Lift sB 135—150 dB 155—175

★★★**Parkhotel de Zalm** Molenstr 53 ☎624371 tx33005

rm132 (109) Lift sB59 sB 104 dB172 dB 187

★**Esquire** Van Aerssenstr 59—61 ☎522341 tx34329

rm20 (12) sB55 sB 80 dB80 dB 130

Auto Haag Calandpl 2 ☎889255 Ren

Case Pletterijstr 6 ☎858780

Central Auto Bedrijf Prinses Megrietplantsoen 10 ☎814131 For

National Automobiel Bedrijf Scheldestr 2 ☎47617 Hon

Zoet Meteorstr 87—89 ☎880855

At **RIJSWIJK**

★★★**Hoornwijk** J-Thijssenweg 2 ☎903130 tx32538

70 **P** sB 85 dB 115

At **SCHEVENINGEN**

★★★★**Europa** (Crest **See page 50**) Zwolsestr 2 ☎512651 tx33138

🛁🚿174 🏠 Lift ☾ sB🛁🚿189 dB🛁🚿243 🏞 sea
Credit cards [1] [2] [3] [4] [5]

★★★**Badhotel** Gevers Deynootweg 15 ☎512221 tx31592

🛁🚿96 Lift sB🛁🚿80—115 dB🛁🚿130—150

★★★**Flora Beach** Gevers Deynootweg 63 ☎543300

🛁🚿82 **P** Lift sB🛁🚿80 dB🛁🚿216

★★**Aquarius** Zeekat 107—110 (n.rest) ☎543543

🛁🚿23 **P** sB🛁🚿65—125 dB🛁🚿85—145

★★**Bali** Badhuisweg 1 ☎502434

rm34 (🛁🚿8) **P** sB40 sB🛁🚿55 dB75 dB🛁🚿100 Malc

HAARLEM
Noord-Holland (☎023)

★★★**Lion d'Or** (GT) Kruisweg 34—36 ☎321750 tx71101

rm34 (🛁🚿33) Lift sB130 sB🛁🚿150 dB150 dB🛁🚿170 M33—35
Credit cards [1] [2] [3] [5]

🚗 **Kimman** Zijlweg 35 ☎339069 M/c **P** AR DJ

HAGUE (THE) See **HAAG (DEN)**

HARDERWIJK
Gelderland (☎03410)

★★**Baars** Smeepoortstr 52 ☎12007

rm17 (🛁🚿15) **P** sB40 sB🛁🚿65 dB65 dB🛁🚿100 M20

🚗 **Gelderse Auto Service** Handelsweg 4 ☎13800 **P** For

HAREN
Groningen (☎050)

★★★**Postiljon** Emmalaan 33 ☎347041 tx53688

🛁🚿97 **P** Lift sB🛁🚿80—105 dB🛁🚿93—118 M19

HEELSUM
Gelderland (☎08373)

★★★**Klein Zwitserland** Klein Zwitserlandlaan 5 ☎19104 tx45627

rm62 (🛁🚿61) **P** Lift sB120 sB🛁🚿155 dB192 dB🛁🚿192 M45 🔑 🏞 ⛶

HEEMSTEDE
Noord-Holland (☎023)

🚗 **Barnhoorn** Roemer Visscherspl 21 ☎242250 Toy

HEERENVEEN
Friesland (☎05130)

★★★**Postijon** (BW) Schans 65 ☎24041 tx46591

🛁🚿61 **P** Lift sB🛁🚿78—103 dB🛁🚿88—113
Credit card [2]

HEERLEN
Limburg (☎045)

★★★**Grand** (GT) Groene Boord 23 ☎713846 tx56920

Netherlands

🛁🚿106 🏠 **P** Lift sB🛁🚿fr120 dB🛁🚿180—250 M35—75&alc 🔑
Credit cards [1] [2] [3] [5]

★★★**Heerlen** Terworm 10 ☎719450 tx56759

🛁🚿78 **P** Lift sB🛁🚿65 dB🛁🚿70 M18

🚗 **Canton-Reiss** Valkenburgerweg 34 ☎718040 AR

🚗 **Van Haaren** Schandelerboord 25 ☎721152 For

🚗 **Heijnen Heerlen** Frankenlaan 1 ☎713600 **P** Ren

🚗 **Sondagh** ☎223300 **P** Cit

🚗 **Vencken** Heesbergstr 60—64 ☎412641 **P** Aud VW

HEILOO
Noord-Holland (☎02205)

★★★**Heiloo** Kennemerstraatweg 425 ☎2244

🛁22 **P** sB🛁🚿60 dB🛁🚿90 🏞

HELDER (DEN)
Noord-Holland (☎02230)

🚗 **Ceres** Baljuwstr 139 ☎30000 Peu

At **NIEUW DEN HELDER** (2km SW)

★★**Den Helder** Marsdiepstr 2 ☎22333

🚿75 **P** sB🚿48 dB🚿70 M23—42

HELMOND
Noord-Brabant (☎04920)

★★★**West Ende** Steenweg 1 ☎24151

rm47 (🛁🚿43) **P** Lift sB44 sB🛁🚿90 dB86 dB🛁🚿135 M24

🚗 **Alards** Gerwenseweg 31 ☎42645 **P** AR

🚗 **J Gorp** Engelseweg 220 ☎39670 Cit

HENGELO
Overijssel (☎074)

★★★**Lansink** C-T-Storkstr 14—18 ☎910066

🛁🚿24 **P** sB🛁🚿60—80 dB🛁🚿95—108 Malc

★★**Ten Hoopen** Burg Jansenpl 20 ☎910265

🚿20 sB🚿50—85 dB🚿105—135

🚗 **G Ter Haar** Braemarsweg 140 ☎913901 AR

🚗 **W Noordegraaf** Oldenzaalsestr 19—23 ☎914444 M/c For

'S-HERTOGENBOSCH
Noord-Brabant (☎073)

★★★**Eurohotel** (BW) Hinthamerstr 63 ☎13777 tx50014

🛁47 🏠 Lift sB🛁80—85 dB🛁100—105
Credit card [2]

🚗 **Rietvelden** Rietvelderweg 34 ☎211355 Fia

HILVERSUM
Noord-Holland (☎035)

★★**Hilfertsom** Koninginneweg 28—30 ☎232444

rm37 (🛁🚿28) **P** sB58 sB🛁🚿85 dB85 dB🛁🚿135

★★**Hof van Holland** (BW) Kerkbrink 1—7 ☎46141 tx43399

🛁🚿59 **P** Lift sB🛁🚿115—129 dB🛁🚿150—275 M23
Credit card [2]

🚗 **H Koster** Langestr ☎41156 BMW

🚗 **J K Poll** Zoverijnstr 2 ☎47841 For

HOLTEN
Overijssel (☎05483)

★★**Hoog Holten** Forthaarsweg 7 ☎61306 Feb—29 Dec

rm22 (🛁🚿13) **P** ☾ sB44 sB🛁🚿55 dB88 dB🛁🚿110 Malc 🔑

★★**Losse Hoes** Holterbergweg 14 ☎61353 tx30405

rm12 (🚿8) **P** sB53 dB85 M57 🏞

HOOGERHEIDE
Noord-Brabant (☎01646)

★★**Pannenhuis** Antwerpsestraatweg 100 ☎4552

rm21 (🚿12) **P** sB38 sB🚿65 dB75 dB🚿95 M28—45&alc

HOOGEVEEN
Drenthe (☎05280)

★★★**Hoogeveen** (ETAP) Mathijsenstr 1 ☎63303

🛁🚿39 **P** sB🛁🚿38—65 dB🛁🚿80 Malc
Credit cards [1] [2] [3] [5]

🚗 **Europagarage** van Limburg Stirumstr ☎66666 **P** For

HOORN
Noord-Holland (☎02290)

★**Keizerskroon** Breed 31—33 ☎12717

🛁🚿20 sB🛁🚿60 dB🛁🚿95 M19

🚗 **Koopmans** Dampten 5 ☎17644 **P** Hon

🚗 **Van der Linden & Van Sprankhuizen** Berkhouterweg 11 ☎36464 **P** Ope Vau Vol

KAMPEN
Overijssel (☎05202)

★★**Van Dijk** IJsselkade 30—31 ☎14925

rm22 (🛁🚿9) sB50 sB🛁🚿60 dB75 dB🛁🚿95

🚗 **J H R Van Noort** Nijverheidsstr 35 ☎12241 For

KATWIJK AAN ZEE
Zuid-Holland (☎01718)

★★**Noordzee** Boulevard 72 ☎13450
Closed Dec—Feb. Rest Closed Nov—Mar

🛁🚿42 Lift sB🛁🚿63—73 dB🛁🚿95—135

🚗 **Rijnland West** Kon Wilhelminastr 16 ☎72743 For

KATWOUDE
Noord-Holland (☎02993)

★★★**Katwoude** Rijksweg S 11 ☎65656 tx16025
🛁🚿86 **P** Lift sB🛁🚿55 dB🛁🚿65 M20–55 🎾 🏊

KOOG (DE)
Texel (☎02228)

★★★**Opduin** Ruyslaan 22 ☎445 tx57555
Closed 5 Jan–1 Mar
rm52 (🛁🚿43) ⌂ **P** Lift sB65 sB🛁🚿130 dB130 dB🛁🚿260 M19 🎾 🏊

LAREN
Noord-Holland (☎02153)

At **EEMNES** (2km E)

★★★**Witte Bergen** Rijksweg A1 ☎86754 tx73041
🛁🚿62 **P** sB🛁🚿58–70 dB🛁🚿63–75

LEEUWARDEN
Friesland (☎058)

★★★**Oranje** (GT) Stationsweg 4 ☎126241 tx46528
🛁78 ⌂ Lift sB🛁133 dB🛁173 M35–48
Credit cards 1 2 3 5

★★**Eurohotel** Europapl 20 ☎131113 tx46674
rm56 (🛁🚿46) **P** Lift sB47 sB🛁🚿80 dB🛁🚿120

🚗 **Molenaar** Keidam 2 ☎(058)661115 **P** Toy

🚗 **Nagelhout** Brandemeer 2 ☎(058)663633 Dat Toy

🚗 **Zeeuw** Valerinsstr 2–11 ☎(058)131444 M/c For

LEIDEN
Zuid-Holland (☎071)

★★★★**Holiday Inn** (GT) Haagse Schouwweg 10 ☎769310 tx39213
🛁🚿192 **P** Lift sB🛁🚿165–180 dB🛁🚿220–235 🎾 🏊 ⛳
Credit cards 1 2 3 5

🚗 **Br Automobiel** Bedr Oldenbamereldstr 37 ☎172679 AR

🚗 **Rijnland** Vijf Meilaan 7 ☎310031 For

At **LEIDERDORP** (2km SE)

★★**Ibis Leiderdorp** Elisabethhof 4 (exit Hoogmade off Motorway) ☎414141 tx30251
🛁70 **P** Lift sB🛁98 dB🛁125 M20–27

LELYSTAD
Flevoland (☎03200)

★★★**Congre Scentrum Lelystad** (ETAP) Agoraweg 11 ☎42444 tx70311
🛁86 ⌂ Lift ☾ sB🛁88–93 dB🛁116–128 M18–30
Credit cards 1 2 3 5

LEUSDEN
Utrecht (☎03498)

★★**Hulze den Treek** Trekerweg 23 ☎1425
Closed Xmas & New Year
rm20 (🛁🚿12) **P** Lift sB48 sB🛁🚿55 dB95 dB🛁🚿140 M35–113

Netherlands

LEUVENUM
Gelderland (☎05770)

★★**Roode Koper** Jhr-Sandbergweg 82 ☎7393 tx49633
🛁🚿25 **P** sB🛁🚿58–84 dB🛁🚿113–161 M24–95 🎾 🏊

LHEE See **DWINGELOO**

LOCHEM
Gelderland (☎05730)

★★**Lochemse Berg** Lochemseweg 42 ☎1377
🚿15 **P** Lift sB🚿45–47 dB🚿94

🚗 **Van de Straat** Tramstr 36 ☎1652 M/c **P** AR

LUNTEREN
Gelderland (☎08388)

★★★**Lunterse Boer** Boslaan 87 ☎3657
🛁🚿18 **P** sB🛁🚿80–90 dB🛁🚿115–135 M40

★★**Wormshoef** Dorpsstr 192 ☎4241
rm35 (🛁🚿24) **P** sB48 sB🛁🚿63 dB90 dB🛁🚿110 M17–43

LUTTE (DE)
Overijssel (☎05415)

★★★**Bloemenbeek** Beuningerstr 6 ☎1224
🛁🚿20 **P** sB🛁🚿90 dB🛁🚿135–150 🎾 🏊

MAARSBERGEN
Utrecht (☎03433)

★★**Maarsbergen** Woudenbergseweg 44 ☎341 tx47986
🚿11 **P** sB🚿60 dB🚿75 M17

MAASTRICHT
Limburg (☎043)

★★★★★**Maastricht** De Ruiterij 1 ☎254171 tx56822
🛁111 **P** Lift sB🛁170–205 dB🛁238–292 M43

★★★**Casque** Vrijthof 52 Helmstr 14 ☎214343 tx56657
rm40 (🛁🚿35) ⌂ Lift sB60 sB🛁🚿175 dB120 dB🛁🚿150 M33

🚗 **Straten** via Regia 170 ☎434500 Aud VW

At **BEATRIXHAVEN** (4km N)

🚗 **Feyts Autos** Korvetweg 20–22 ☎16755 **P** For

MIDDELBURG
Zeeland (☎01180)

★★★**Commerce** Loskade 1 ☎36051
rm40 (🛁🚿39) Lift sB70 sB🛁🚿85 dB115 dB🛁🚿125

★★★**Nieuwe Doelen** Loskade 3–7 ☎12121
Closed Xmas & New Year
rm27 (🚿13) Lift sBfr48 sB🚿fr65 dBfr95 dB🚿130

★**Huifkar** Markt 19 ☎12998
🚿4 sB🚿58–65 dB🚿87–89

🚗 **Louisse** Kalverstr 1 ☎25851 Ope

MIDDLEHARNIS
Zuid-Holland (☎01870)

🚗 **Auto Service** Kastanjelaan 41–43 ☎3094

🚗 **Knöps** Langeweg 113 ☎2222 Ope Vau

MOOK-EN-MIDDELAAR
Limburg (☎08896)

★★★**Plasmolen** Rijksweg 170 ☎1444
rm29 (🛁🚿18) **P** sBfr45 sB🛁🚿95 dB108 dB🛁🚿125 M38–88 🎾

NIEUW DEN HELDER See **HELDER (DEN)**

NIJMEGEN
Gelderland (☎080)

★★★**Nijmegen** (ETAP) Stationspl 29 ☎238888 tx48670
🛁100 **P** Lift ☾ sB🛁fr102 dB🛁fr125 M28
Credit cards 1 2 3 5

🚗 **Jansen & Ederveen** Winkelsteegseweg 150 ☎563664 Ren

🚗 **W Peeters** Kronenburgersingel 207 ☎239300

NIJVERDAL
Overijssel (☎05486)

🚗 **Blokken** Bergleidingweg 27 ☎12959 AR

NOORDGOUWE
Zeeland (☎01112)

🚗 **Akkerdaas** Kloosterweg 2 ☎1347 **P** Ope Vau

NOORDWIJK AAN ZEE
Zuid-Holland (☎01719)

★★★★**Ladbroke Noordzee** Kon-Wilhelmina Boulevard 8 ☎19205 tx39206
🛁🚿88 **P**10 Lift sB🛁🚿139 dB🛁🚿225–266 M22–30 sea 🏊
Credit cards 1 2 3 5

★★★**Noordwyk** Parallelboulevard 7 ☎19231 tx39116
🚿36 Lift sB🚿75–100 dB🚿85–125 M23–28

★★**Alwine** Jan van Henegouwenweg 7 ☎12213
🚿28 Lift sB🚿60–70 dB🚿110–120 M13 🏊

★★**Clarenwijck** Kon-Astrid Boulevard 46 ☎12727
15 Jan–20 Dec
rm25 (🛁🚿18) **P** sB40 sB🛁🚿50 dB80 dB🛁🚿110 M30

★**Duinlust** Koepelweg 1 ☎12916
Mar–Oct
rm25 **P** sB30–55 dB60–100 M20

🚗 **Beuk** Golfweg 19 ☎19213 Fia Lan

🚗 **Rijnland West** Beeklaan 5 ☎14300 For

NULAND
Noord-Brabant (☎04102)

★★★**Nuland** Rijksweg 25 ☎2231 tx50448

→ 80 **P** Lift dB→ 60—90 M18—70 ⊟

OISTERWIJK
Noord-Brabant (☎04242)

★★★**Swaen** de Lind 47 ☎19006 tx52617

Closed 9—29 Jul & 30 Dec—12 Jan
→⋒ 19 **P** Lift sB→⋒ fr175 dB→⋒ fr225 M85

🚗 **Spoormaker** Kerkstr 80 ☎84683 Fia

OLDENZAAL
Overijssel (☎05410)

🚗 **Munsterhuis** Oliemolenstr 4 ☎15661 Ren

🚗 **Olde Monnikhof** Vos de Waelstr 20 ☎14451 Ope

OMMEN
Overijssel (☎05291)

★★**Zon** Voorbrug 1 ☎1141

Closed 1—10 Jan
→⋒ 16 **P** sB→⋒ 65 dB→⋒ 95

🚗 **Leerentveld** Hammerweg 1 ☎2500 Dat

OOSTBURG
Zeeland (☎01170)

★***Commerce*** Markt 24 ☎2912

→⋒ 20

OOSTERBEEK
Gelderland (☎085)

★★★**Bilderberg** Utrechtseweg 261 ☎340843 tx45484

→ 146 **P** Lift sB→ 115—150
dB→ 197—210 ⊟

★★**Strijland** Stationsweg 6—8 ☎343034

→⋒ 31 **P** sB→⋒ 59—79 dB→⋒ 89—138 M28—38 ⊟

★**Dreyeroord** Gr-van Rechterenweg 12 ☎333169

rm28 (→⋒ 25) **P** Lift sB→⋒ 51—86
dB→⋒ 101—107 M30

OOTMARSUM
Overijssel (☎05419)

★★★★★**Wiemsel** (Relais et Châteaux) Winhofflaan 2 ☎2155 tx44667

→⋒ 31 **P** sB→⋒ 95—130
dB→⋒ 150—190 M69—115 ⚲ ⊟

★★**Wapen Von Ootmarsum** Almelosestr 20 ☎1500

Closed 31 Dec & 1 Jan
rm16 (⋒ 15) **P** sBfr41 dB⋒ 81—85 M18—31

OSS
Noord-Brabant (☎04120)

★**Alem** Molenstr 81 ☎22114

rm12 (→ 11) **P** sB35 sB→ 75 dB→ 110 M18

🚗 **J Putters** Hertogensingel 38 ☎23600 **P** Alf Mer

Netherlands

OVERVEEN
Noord-Holland (☎023)

★★**Roozendaal** Bloemendaalseweg 260 ☎277457

→⋒ 12 **P** sB→⋒ 65—75
dB→⋒ 100—135 M30—45

PAPENDRECHT
Zuid-Holland (☎078)

★★★**Crest** (**See page 50**) Lange Tiendweg 2 ☎152099 tx29331

→⋒ 83 **P**160 Lift ☾ sB→⋒ 149
dB→⋒ 196
Credit cards [1] [2] [3] [4] [5]

🚗 **Hoog en Laag** Hoeklandsestr, Patten ☎334757 Toy

PUTTEN
Gelderland (☎03418)

★★★**Postiljon** Strandboulevard 3 ☎56464 tx47867

→⋒ 38 **P** Lift sB→⋒ 78 dB→⋒ 88—113

RAALTE
Overijssel (☎05720)

★★★**Zwaan** Kerkstr 2 ☎53122

rm20 (→⋒ 16) **P** sB46 sB→⋒ 65 dB78
dB→⋒ 97 M20—45 ⊟

RIJSWIJK See **HAAG (DEN) (HAGUE, THE)**

ROERMOND
Limburg (☎04750)

🚗 **Nedam** Maasbrug ☎23351 **P** Ope Vau

🚗 **Opheij** II Singel 29—31 ☎12125 AR Hon

ROOSENDAAL
Noord-Brabant (☎01650)

★★**Central** Stationspl 9 ☎35657 tx78192

rm20 (→⋒ 17) sB59 sB→⋒ 79 dB106
dB→⋒ 136

🚗 **Hennekam** Amri-Lonckestr 1 ☎26924 For

🚗 **Van Poppel** Van Beefhovenlaan 9 ☎36566 AR

ROTTERDAM
Zuid-Holland (☎010)

See also **SCHIEDAM**

★★★★★**Hilton International** Weena 10 ☎4144044 tx22666

→⋒ 259 ⌂ Lift ☾ sB→⋒ 255—328
dB→⋒ 300—370
Credit cards [1] [2] [3] [4] [5]

★★★★**Atlanta** (GT) Aert van Nesstr 4 ☎4110420 tx21595

rm170 (→⋒ 165) ⌂ Lift sB100 sB→⋒ 150
dB125 dB→⋒ 200
Credit cards [1] [2] [3] [5]

★★★★**Central** Kruiskade 12 ☎4140744 tx24040

→⋒ 64 Lift sB→⋒ 115—160
dB→⋒ 160—205

★★★★**Park** (BW) Westersingel 70 ☎4363611 tx22020

→⋒ 157 **P** Lift sB→⋒ 117—200
dB→⋒ 190—235
Credit card [2]

★★★★**Rijn** Schouwburgpl 1 ☎4333800 tx21640

→⋒ 140 ⌂ **P** Lift sB→⋒ 110—200
dB→⋒ 208—225 M38

★★★**Savoy** (GT) Hoogstr 81 ☎4139280 tx21525

→⋒ 94 Lift sB→⋒ 90—120
dB→⋒ 110—140
Credit cards [1] [2] [3] [5]

★★**Baan** Rochussenstr 345 ☎47700555

Closed 16 Dec—14 Jan
rm14 (⋒ 9) sB55 sB⋒ 65 dB70 dB⋒ 90

★★**Pax** Schiekade 658 ☎4663344

rm44 (→⋒ 40) **P** Lift sB50 sB⋒ 87 dB107 dB⋒ 115

★★**Walsum** Mathenesserlaan 199 ☎4363275 tx20010

Closed 31 Dec
rm29 (→⋒ 26) sB60 sB→⋒ 90 dB90
dB→⋒ 120 M25

★**Holland** Provenierssingel 7 ☎4653100

rm24 sB50 dB85

🚗 **Dunant** Dunantstr 22—40 ☎760166 Toy

🚗 **Vliet** Kleiweg 35 ☎225029 AR

🚗 **Gam Rotterdam** Smirnoffweg 21—23 ☎298844 Aud VW

🚗 **Hoogenboom** Geissendorfferweg 5—15 ☎298844 **P** Aud VW

At **VLAARDINGEN**

★★★★**Delta** (Crest **See page 50**) Maasboulevard 15 ☎4345477 tx23154

→⋒ 78 **P** Lift ☾ sB→⋒ 165 dB→⋒ 205 Malc ⊟
Credit cards [1] [2] [3] [5]

ROZENDAAL
Gelderland (☎085)

★★★**Residence Roosendael** Beekhuizenseweg 1 ☎629123

Closed 28 Dec—3 Jan
→ 10 ⌂ **P** sB→ 85—100 dB→ 125—175 M55

SASSENHEIM
Zuid-Holland (☎02522)

★★★**Sassenheim** Warmonderweg 8 ☎19019 tx41688

→ 57 **P** Lift ☾ dB→ 70

SCHEVENINGEN See **HAAG (DEN) (HAGUE, THE)**

SCHIEDAM
Zuid-Holland (☎010)

See also **ROTTERDAM**

★★★**Novotel** Hargalaan 2 ☎4713322 tx22582

→ 138 **P** Lift sB→ fr123 dB→ fr136 ≈
Credit cards [1] [3] [5]

SCHIPHOL See **AMSTERDAM AIRPORT**

SLUIS
Zeeland (☎01178)

★**Sanders de Pauw** Kade 44 ☎1224
Closed 29—31 Dec
rm10 (🚿5) **P** dB80 dB🚿100

SNEEK
Friesland (☎05150)

★★**Wijnberg** Markstr 23 ☎12421
rm22 (🛁🚿19) sBfr39 sB🛁🚿fr75 dB90 dB🛁🚿113 M19&alc

★**Bonnema** Stationsstr 62—66 ☎13175
Closed New Years Day
rm14 (🚿10) **P** sB40 sB🚿55 dB65 dB🚿98 M19

🚗 **Deinum** Edisonstr 1 ☎22055 M/c Ope Vau

🚗 **F Ozinga's** Akkerwinde ☎13344 For

🚗 **H de Vries** Oosterkade 26 ☎13291 **P** Ren

TEGELEN
Limburg (☎077)

🚗 **Linssen** Roermondseweg 139 ☎31421 M/c **P** Fia

TERNEUZEN
Zeeland (☎01150)

★★**Milliano** Nieuwstr 11 (n.rest) ☎12342
🛁🚿20 **P**

TEXEL (ISLAND OF) See **KOOG (DE)**

TILBURG
Noord-Brabant (☎013)

★★★**Heuvelpoort** (ETAP) Heuvelpoort 300 ☎354675 tx52722
🛁63 ⌂ Lift ☾ sB🛁110 dB🛁150—250
Credit cards [1] [2] [3] [5]

★★**Postelse Hoeve** Dr-Deelenlaan 10 ☎636335 tx52788
🛁🚿22 **P** sB🛁🚿83—100
dB🛁🚿100—125 M20—50&alc

🚗 **W A Holland** Hart Van Brabanlaan 110 ☎422600 **P** AR DJ

UTRECHT
Utrecht (☎030)

★★★★**Holiday Inn** Jaarbeurspl 24 ☎910555 tx47745
🛁280 ⌂ Lift sB🛁215—235
dB🛁260—280 Malc 📺

★★★**Pays Bas** (GT) Janskerkhof 10 ☎333321 tx47485
🛁47 Lift sB🛁95—115 dB🛁167—210 M48—95
Credit cards [1] [2] [3] [5]

★★★**Smits** (ETAP) Vredenburg 14 (n.rest) ☎331232 tx47557
rm46 (🛁🚿42) Lift ☾ sB🛁🚿98
dB🛁🚿98—123 Malc
Credit cards [1] [2] [3] [5]

★★**Hes** Maliestr 2 ☎316424 tx70870
Closed 21 Dec—1 Jan
rm19 (🛁🚿18) Lift sB55 sB🛁🚿95 dB100 dB🛁🚿110

🚗 **Van Meeuwen's** Weerdsingel 42—44 ☎719111 Alf Hon Vau

🚗 **Stichtse** Leidseweg 128 ☎931744 For

At **BUNNIK** (7km SE)

★★★**Postiljon** (BW) Kosterijland 8 ☎(03405)69222 tx70298
🛁🚿84 **P** Lift sB🛁🚿90—100
dB🛁🚿115—125
Credit card [2]

VALKENBURG
Limburg (☎04406)

★★★★**Prinses Juliana** (Relais et Châteaux) Broekhem 11 ☎12244 tx56351
🛁🚿27 ⌂ **P** Lift sB🛁🚿110—150
dB🛁🚿130—225 M70—110

★★★**Atlanta** Neerhem 20 ☎12193
25 Mar—Oct & 20—31 Dec
rm36 (🛁🚿30) **P** Lift sB40 sB🛁55 dB80
dB🛁🚿90 M26—50

★★**Apollo** Nieuweweg 7 ☎15341
Closed 3 Jan—15 Mar
🛁🚿32 **P** sB🛁🚿35—40 dB🛁🚿60—70

★★**Tourotel** Wilhelminlaan 28—34 ☎13998 tx56714
Closed Nov—18 Dec & 3 Jan—Feb
rm42 (🚿27) ⌂ **P** sB38 sB🚿67 dB76
dB🚿114 M19—35

🚗 **Auto-Caubo** Neerham 25 ☎15041

🚗 **Nerum** Neerham 25 ☎15041 **P** Aud VW

VEENDAM
Groningen (☎05987)

🚗 **Bakker** Dr-Bossaan 21 ☎12288 **P** Alf

VEENENDAAL See **EDE**

VEERE
Zeeland (☎01181)

★**Campveerse Toren** Kade 2 ☎291
rm18 (🛁🚿13) **P** sB40 sB🛁🚿85 dB65
dB🛁🚿140

VELP See **ARNHEM**

VENLO
Limburg (☎077)

★★★★**Bovenste Molen** Bovenste Molenweg 12 ☎41045 tx58393
🛁🚿63 **P** sB🛁🚿130—230
dB🛁🚿185—285 📺

★★★**Novotel** Nijmeegseweg 90 ☎544141 tx58229
🛁88 **P** Lift ☾ sB🛁103—108
dB🛁113—118 Mfr30 🏊
Credit cards [2] [3] [5]

★★**Wilhelmina** Kaldenkerkerweg 1 ☎16251
Closed Xmas Day
🛁🚿34 **P** Lift sB🛁🚿70—90
dB🛁🚿110—135

★**Groisch Quelle** Eindhovensestr 3—8 ☎13560
rm20 sB30—45 dB60 M23

🚗 **AML** Wezelseweg 53E ☎96666 **P** Mer

🚗 **Van Gorp** Ferd Bolstr 10 ☎16752 Cit

🚗 **L Van den Hombergh** Straelseweg 18 ☎11441 For

🚗 **J B Nefkens & Zonen** Staelseweg 52 ☎12474 Peu

🚗 **Peters** Burg Bloemartsstr 30 ☎10455 Vol

VENRAY
Limburg (☎04780)

🚗 **J Gop** Horsterweg 10a ☎86825 Cit

🚗 **Van Haren** Raadhuisstr 38 ☎85300 **P** For

VIERHOUTEN
Gelderland (☎05771)

★★★**Mallejan** Nunspeterweg 70 ☎241
Closed 5 Dec
🛁42 ⌂ **P** Lift sB🛁70 dB🛁120 🎾

VLAARDINGEN See **ROTTERDAM**

VLISSINGEN (FLUSHING)
Zeeland (☎01184)

★★★**Britannia** bd Evertsen 244 ☎13255 tx36219
🛁35 **P** Lift sB🛁100—110 dB🛁133—140

★★★**Strand** (GT) bd Evertsen 4 ☎12297 tx37878
🛁🚿40 **P** Lift sB🛁🚿75—105
dB🛁🚿135—150
Credit cards [1] [2] [3] [5]

🚗 **Dÿkwel Vlissingen** Pres-Rosseveltlaan 745 ☎12008 Peu

VOLENDAM
Noord-Holland (☎02993)

★★**Van Diepen** Haven 35 ☎63705
16 Mar—2 Nov
rm18 (🛁🚿11) **P** sB43 sB🛁🚿48 dB80
dB🛁🚿100 M23—100&alc

WAGENINGEN
Gelderland (☎08373)

🚗 **Van der Kolk** Station Str 2 ☎19055 For

WARNSVELD
Gelderland (☎05750)

★**Het Jachthuis** Vordenseweg 2 ☎23328
rm8 (🛁🚿6) **P** sB38 sB🛁🚿48 dB85
dB🛁🚿95 M25 🎾

WASSENAAR
Zuid-Holland (☎01751)

★★**Duinoord** Wassenaarse Slag 26 ☎19332 tx34383
🛁🚿20 **P** sB🛁🚿62—108
dB🛁🚿105—129

🚗 **A Blankespoor** Oostdorperweg 29—31 ☎12405 AR DJ

🚗 **Jansen** Rijksstraatweg 773 ☎79941 Aud VW

WOERDEN
Zuid-Holland (☎03480)

★★★**Eenhoorn** (GT) Utrechtsestraatweg 33 ☎12515 tx76151

🛁🚿66 ⌂ P ☾ sB🛁🚿104 dB🛁🚿137 M27
Credit cards [1] [2] [3] [5]

ZAANDAM
Noord-Holland (☎075)

Verenigde Zeemanstr 43 ☎172751 For

ZANDVOORT
Noord-Holland (☎02507)

★★★**Bouwes** (GT) Badhuispl 7 ☎12144 tx41096
🛁🚿58 P Lift sB🛁🚿85—135 dB🛁🚿145—170
Credit cards [2] [3] [5]

★★★**Palace** Burg van Fenemapl 2 ☎12911 tx41812
🚿45 P Lift sB🚿55—75 dB🚿110—135 M25—30

★★**Hoogland** Westerparkstr 5 ☎15541 tx71222
Closed 16 Dec—14 Jan
rm26 (🛁🚿25) sBfr50 sB🛁🚿75 dBfr80 dB🛁🚿fr135 M23—35

ZEDDAM
Gelderland (☎08345)

★★**Aaldering** s'Heerenbergseweg 1 ☎1273
rm24 (🛁🚿14) P sBfr35 dBfr80

ZEIST
Utrecht (☎03404)

★★★**Hermitage** Het Rond 7 ☎24414
Closed 1 Jan
🚿14 P Lift sB🚿78—100 dB🚿110—150 M43—73

J Molenarr's 2e Hogeweg 109 ☎18041 P Alf

A F Phillippo Laan Van Cattenbroeck 23 ☎14529 Toy

ZIERIKZEE
Zeeland (☎01110)

★★**Mondragon** Havenpark 21 ☎3051
🛁🚿9 sB🛁🚿70 dB🛁🚿90—140

ZOETERMEER
Zuid-Holland (☎079)

★★★**City** Boerhaavelaan ☎219228 tx36726
🛁60 P Lift sB🛁90—126 dB🛁100—173 M25—75

ZUTPHEN
Gelderland (☎05750)

★★**Gravenhof** Kuiperstr 11 ☎18222
🛁🚿12 P sB🛁🚿70—83 dB🛁🚿fr120 M38—78

★★**Inntel Zutphen** de Stoven 14 ☎25555 tx49701
🛁65 P250 Lift ☾ sB🛁fr100 dB🛁fr110 Mfr19
Credit cards [1] [2] [3] [5]

H Nijendijk Spittaalstr 32—34 ☎15257 AR

Welmers H-Dunentweg 2 ☎12537 P Fia

ZWOLLE
Overijssel (☎038)

★★★**Postiljon** Hertsenbergweg 1 ☎216031 tx42180
🛁🚿72 P Lift sB🛁🚿78—103 dB🛁🚿88—113

★★★**Wientjes** (GT) Stationsweg 7 ☎211200 tx42640
🛁🚿47 ⌂ P Lift sB🛁🚿75—125 dB🛁🚿110—160
Credit cards [1] [2] [3] [5]

A typical scene in Holland

Norway

International distinguishing sign

Area *125,000 sq miles*
Population *4,070,000*
Local time *GMT + 1 (Summer GMT + 2)*

National flag
Red with a white-bordered blue upright cross.

How to get there

Norway can be reached direct by ferry. Services operate from Newcastle to Bergen or Stavanger, or from Harwich to Kristiansand and Oslo. Crossing times vary between approximately 21 and 36 hours. Another way of reaching Norway is by using one of the short Channel crossings to France or Belgium, then driving through the Netherlands and northern Germany to Denmark, then either using one of the direct ferry links to southern Norway or travelling via Sweden. Crossing from Harwich to Hamburg gives a shorter overland journey via Germany and Denmark.

The distance from the Channel ports to Oslo via Sweden is about 1,000 miles, and would normally require three night stops.

Motoring regulations and general information

This information should be read in conjunction with the general content of the European ABC (pages 4-26). **Note** As certain regulations and requirements are common to many countries they are covered by one entry in the ABC and the following headings represent some of the subjects dealt with in this way:
AA Agents
Crash or safety helmets
Customs regulations for European countries
Drinking and driving
Fire extinguisher
First-aid kit
Insurance
International distinguishing sign
Medical treatment
Mirrors
Overtaking
Police fines
Radio telephones/Radio transmitters
Road signs
Seat belts
Traffic lights
Tyres
Visitors' registration

Accidents

In Oslo emergency telephone numbers are **Fire** 001, **Police** 002, **Ambulance** 003. For other towns see inside front cover of the local telephone directory.

There are no firm rules of procedure, except when personal injuries are sustained, in which case, the police must be called. Under such circumstances you should obtain medical assistance for the injured person. It is also obligatory to place a warning triangle on the road to notify following traffic of the obstruction. See also *Accidents* page 5.

Accommodation

There is no official classification of hotels, but all establishments offering overnight accommodation must be officially authorised. Such establishments must be easily recognisable as hotels and must have adequate amenities.

Establishments mainly catering for international tourist traffic which must satisfy the more rigorous requirements may qualify for the description of 'tourist' and 'mountain' hotels (turist — and høyfjells — hoteller). In most towns of any size there is a range of hotels from the simple to the more luxurious. Higher standards are required of these hotels than is generally the case with country hotels.

Lists of establishments which are members of the Norway Travel Association are available from the National Tourist Board. Full details of prices and facilities are given.

Pensionater and *hospitser* are too small to be classed as hotels but they provide electricity, modern sanitation and, frequently, hot and cold water in bedrooms. *Turiststasjoner* (tourist stations) and *fjellstuer* (mountain inns) provide comfortable rooms but often there is no electricity or modern sanitation. Nevertheless, they are scrupulously clean.

Breakdown

The Norwegian Motoring Club (NAF) operates a limited road patrol service between about 20 June and 1 September. The service operates from 10.00 to 19.00hrs daily but in view of its limitations a local garage may offer help more quickly. See also *Breakdown* page 6 and *Warning triangle* page 323.

British Embassy/consulates

The British Embassy together with its consular section is located at *Oslo 2* Thomas Heftyesgate 8 ☏ 563890/7. There are British Consulates with Honorary Consuls in Ålesund, Bergen, Harstad, Haugesund, Kristiansund(N), Kristiansand(S), Narvik, Stavanger, Tromsø and Trondheim. See also page 6 and *Town Plan of Oslo* pages 330-331.

Currency including banking hours

(See also page 9)
The unit of currency is the Norwegian Krone (*NKr*) divided into 100 *Ore*. At the time of going to press £ = *NKr*10.84. Denominations of bank notes are *NKr* 10, 50, 100, 500, 1,000; standard coins are *NKr* 1, 5, 10 and *Ore* 10, 50. There are no restrictions on the import of foreign or Norwegian currency, but it is recommended that any large amounts be declared on arrival in case of subsequent re-exportation. No more than *NKr*5,000 in notes not higher than *NKr*1,000 may be exported.

Banks are open 08.30—15.00hrs Monday to Friday and closed on Saturday. Currency may usually be exchanged at railway stations and airports. Their opening hours vary, but are usually 08.00—21.00hrs from Monday to Friday and 08.00—14.00hrs Sunday. At Bogstad Camping (a well-equipped NAF site near Oslo) there is an exchange office open from June to August on weekdays with opening hours as ordinary banks, closed on Saturday and Sunday.

Dimensions

(See also page 10)
Private cars and towed trailers or caravans are restricted to the following dimensions — **car** height: no restriction; width: 2.50 metres; length: 12.40 metres. **Trailer/caravan** height: no restriction; width: 2.30* metres; length: 12.40 metres. The maximum permitted overall length of vehicle/trailer or caravan combination is either 15 or 18 metres depending on the category of State Highway. However, some roads are closed to vehicle/trailer or caravan combinations.

Trailers without brakes may weigh up to 750kg and may have a total weight of up to 50% of the towing vehicle.

*A special permit can be granted for caravans exceeding 2.30 metres but not 2.35 metres, on condition that the difference in width between the motor vehicle and caravan does not exceed 30cm. Applications for the permit should be sent to Vegdirektoratet, Postboks 8109, Oslo 1.

Driving licence

(See also page 11)
A valid British licence is acceptable in Norway. The minimum age at which a visitor may drive a temporarily imported car or motorcycle is 17 years.

Emergency messages to tourists

(See also page 11)
Emergency messages to tourists are broadcast in English by Norwegian State Radio (NRK) in the programme *Reiseradio* (Travel Radio). The messages are transmitted in medium wave on 228 metres and 1376 metres at 09.00hrs Monday to Friday.

Lights

(See also page 11)
Dipped headlights should be used in towns and built-up areas.

Motoring clubs

The **Norwegian Motoring Club** (NAF) which has its headquarters at *0155 Oslo 1* Storgaten 2 ☏ (02)429400 has offices or agents in main towns. Office hours are generally 08.30—16.00hrs Monday to Friday and 08.30—13.00hrs on Saturday. See also page 16 and *Town Plan of Oslo* pages 330-331.

Motorways

Several main roads incorporate stretches of motorway (*motorvei*), mainly around Oslo, with short stretches at Bergen, Stavanger, and Moss. Motorways are divided into two classes, Motorvei

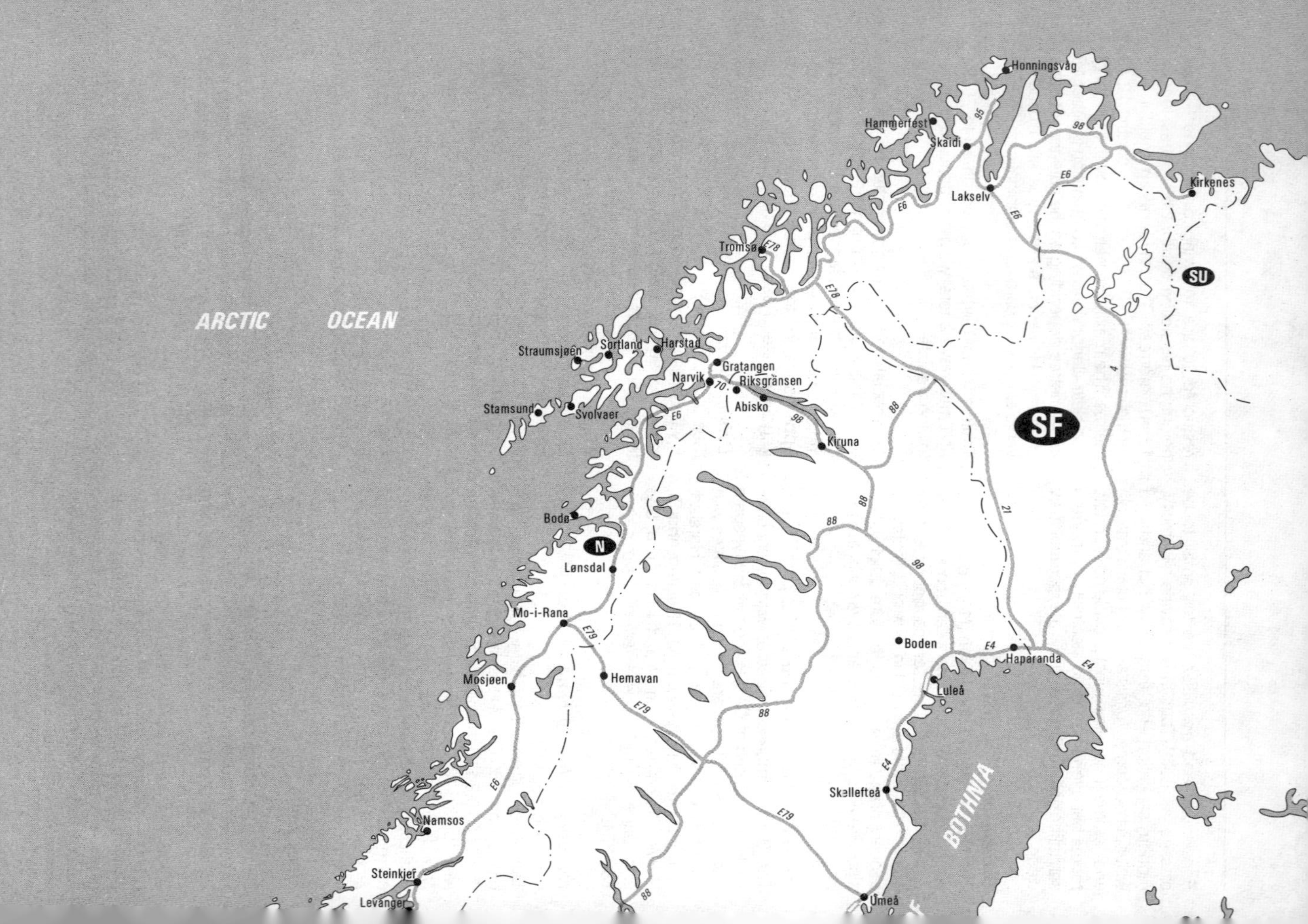

Honningsvåg
Hammerfest
Skaidi
Lakselv
Kirkenes
SU
ARCTIC OCEAN
Tromsø
SF
Straumsjøen
Sortland
Harstad
Gratangen
Narvik
Riksgränsen
Abisko
Stamsund
Svolvaer
Kiruna
Bodø
N
Lønsdal
Mo-i-Rana
Hemavan
Mosjøen
Boden
Haparanda
Luleå
Skellefteå
BOTHNIA
Namsos
Steinkjer
Levanger
Umeå

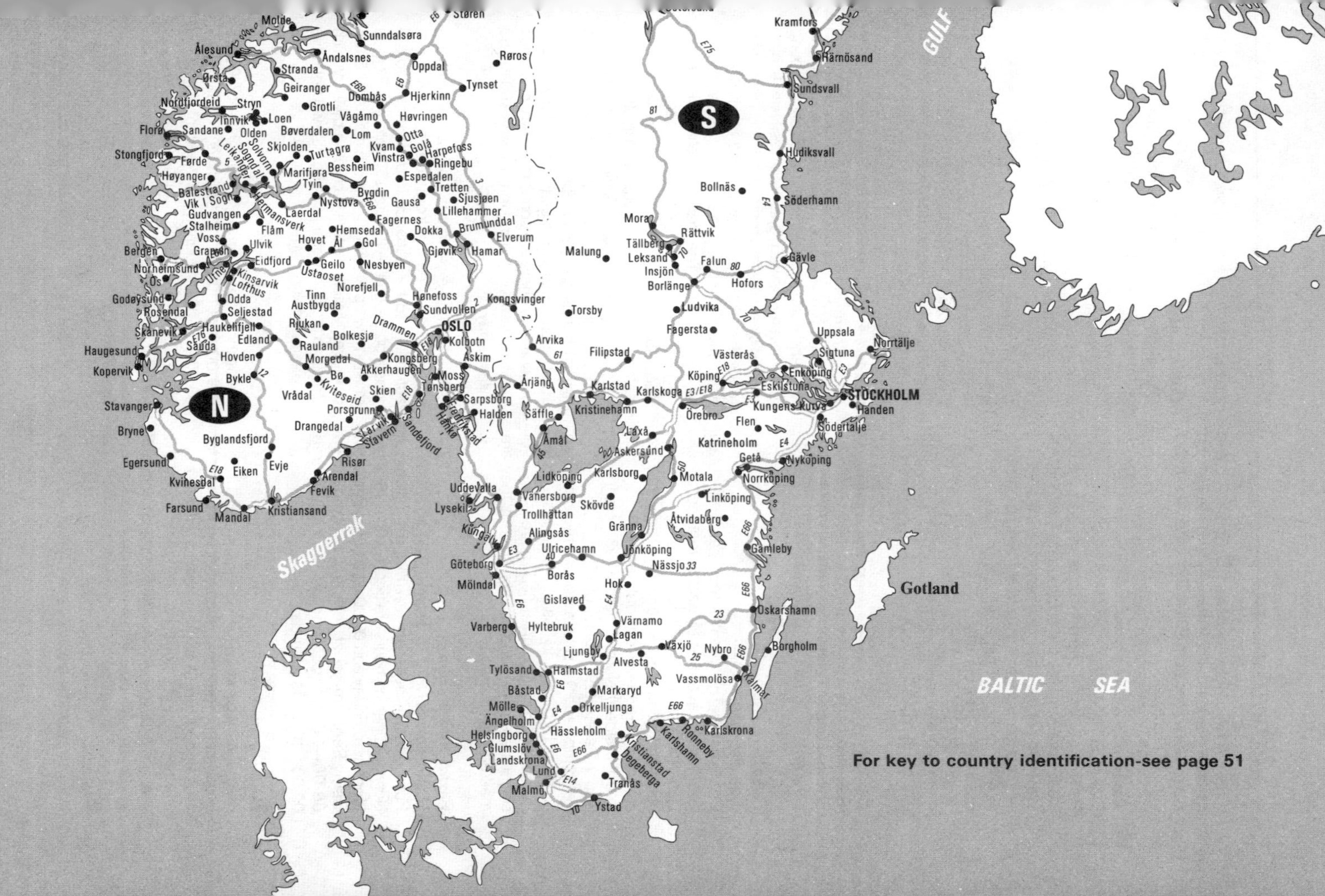

For key to country identification-see page 51

Klasse A and Motorvei Klasse B. The first is the usual two-lane dual carriageway and the second is a two-lane road from 20ft to 25ft wide with limited access points.

Parking

(See also page 17)

Parking places and no parking areas in towns are clearly marked with the appropriate international signs. Do not park by signs bearing the inscription *All stans forbudt* which means stopping prohibited. Spending the night in a vehicle or trailer on the roadside is **not** permitted.

Parking meters are in use in main towns. The free use of unexpired time on meters is authorised.

Passengers

(See also page 18)

Children under 12 are not permitted to travel in a vehicle as a front seat passengers.

Petrol

(See also page 18)

Credit cards The use of credit cards to obtain petrol is not available to visiting motorists.
Duty-free petrol In addition to the petrol in the vehicle tank up to 15 litres in a can may be imported free of custom duty and tax.
Petrol (leaded) Normal Benzin (93 octane) and Super Benzin (99 octane) grades.
Petrol (unleaded) is sold in Norway by some Esso and Norol stations and has an octane rating of 95. Pumps dispensing unleaded petrol in Norol stations are green and in Esso stations they are marked with a green sign.

Postal information

Mail Postcards *NKr*2.75, letters 5—20gm *NKr*3.00.
Post offices There are 2,700 post offices in Norway. Opening hours are from 09.00—16.00hrs Monday to Friday and 09.00—13.00hrs Saturday. Oslo Sentrum post office is open from 08.00—20.00hrs Monday to Friday and 09.00—15.00hrs Saturday.

Postcheques

(See also page 20)

Postcheques may be cashed at all post offices for any amount up to a maximum of *NKr*600 per cheque. Counter positions are identified by the words *Postgiro* or *Inn-og Utbetalinger*. See *Postal information* for post office opening hours.

Priority

In Norway trams always have right of way. See also *Priority including Roundabouts* page 21.

Public holidays

Official public holidays in Norway for 1987 are given below. See also *Public holidays* page 21.
January 1 (New Year's Day)
April 16 (Maundy Thursday)
April 17 (Good Friday)
April 20 (Easter Monday)
May 1 (Labour Day)
May 17† (National Day)
May 28 (Ascension Day)
June 8 (Whit Monday)
December 25 (Christmas Day)
December 26* (Boxing day)
*Saturday †Sunday

Roads

In southern and eastern Norway, the most important routes have modern surfaces. In the west and north, some road surfaces are oil bound (partly water-bound) grit. Vehicles with a high ground clearance are more suitable on mountain roads than those with low ground clearance. As a courtesy to other road users, you should fit mudguard flaps. The roads sometimes have soft edges — a great inconvenience to motorcyclists. Watch for warning signs *Løse Veikanter* and *Svake Kanter*. In the fjord district and often in other areas, careful and confident driving is necessary, although gradients are seldom excessive and hairpin bends can usually be easily negotiated. The region is mainly unsuitable for large vehicles or caravans. There are sometimes ferry crossings and a reasonable touring maximum is 100 to 150 miles a day.

Bergen tollring experiment A pay-and-display toll system has been introduced by the local authorities to help finance improvements to the roads of Bergen. All motorists entering Bergen must now pay *NKr*5 (approximately 50p). However, visiting motorists coming by ferry from Britain to the Skoltegrunnskaien pier will not have to pay any toll on arrival.

Shopping hours

Monday to Friday 08.30—17.00hrs (09.00—19.00hrs Thursdays). Saturday 08.30—14.00hrs. During the month of July some shops restrict their opening times to 09.00—15.00hrs.

Speed limits

(See also page 22)

In built-up areas all vehicles are restricted to 50kph

(31mph) unless there are signs to the contrary. Outside built-up areas private vehicles are restricted to 80kph (49mph) and on certain motorways the speed limit is 90kph (56mph). Vehicles towing caravans are limited to 80kph (49mph) if the trailer is equipped with a braking system, 60kph (37mph) if not.

Spiked or studded tyres

These may be used from 15 October to 30 April. If *spiked tyres* are used, they must be fitted to all four wheels. See also *Cold weather touring* page 9.

Tourist Information

(See also page 24)
The Norwegian Tourist Board maintains an information office in London at 20 Pall Mall (entrance St James's Square), SW1Y 5NE ☎ 01-839 6255 (recorded message service between 09.00—11.00hrs and 14.00—17.00hrs). Local tourist information is available from tourist offices and kiosks throughout Norway.

Trams

(See also page 24)
Stationary trams may be overtaken on the right at moderate speed, or on the left where there is no room on the right. Moving trams may normally be overtaken only on the right, but overtaking is permitted on the left in one-way streets or where there is no room on the right.

Using the telephone

(See also page 24)
Insert coins **after** lifting receiver (instructions in English in many callboxes). When making calls to subscribers within Norway precede number with relevant area code (shown in parentheses against town entry in gazetteer). Use *NKr*1 coins for local calls and *NKr*5 coins for national and international calls.
International callbox identification Most callboxes.
Telephone rates The cost of a direct dialled call to the UK is *NKr*0.90 for 9 seconds. An operator assisted call costs *NKr*12.60 for 3 minutes and *NKr*4.80 for each additional minute. An extra charge of *NKr*9.60 is made for a personal call. Local calls cost *NKr*1.
What to dial for Irish Republic 095 353.
What to dial for the UK 095 44.

Warning triangle

The use of a warning triangle is compulsory for all vehicles except two-wheelers. See also *Warning triangles/Hazard warning lights* page 25.

Wheel chains

Chains may be necessary if tyre equipment is not adequate for driving under winter conditions. See also *Cold weather touring* page 8.

Winter conditions

Roads to the Swedish frontier (leading to Stockholm and Göteborg) are kept clear. The western fjord district is generally unsuitable for motoring between mid October and late May, and in places until mid June. During this period, the road from Bergen to Oslo via Haukeli remains open but the road via Eidfjord and Geilo is obstructed. It is possible to take cars by train between Voss and Ål (see below) or to motor via Voss, Gudvangen (ferry to Revsnes), Laerdal, and Fagernes. On this stretch it is necessary to use spiked tyres or chains during the winter.

The road from Stavanger to Oslo and the Oslo-Trondheim-Mo-i-Rana road is always open. The possibility of motoring further north depends on the weather. Ålesund and Kristiansund can be approached from Dombås and Oppdal. A map showing roads passable in winter can be obtained from the Norwegian Tourist Board in London.

In winter only, cars may be conveyed by the Bergen railway between Voss and Ål, provided space is booked at least 24 hours in advance. Cars must be available at the station at least three hours before departure. Vehicle rates are calculated at time of booking.

Prices are in Norwegian Kroner
In Norwegian ø is the equivalent to œ.
The Norwegian alphabet differs from the English one in that the last letters after Z are Æ, Ø, Å; this must be borne in mind when using Norwegian reference books.
According to our information garages with no specific service agencies will handle any make of car.
Abbreviations:
gt gaten
pl plads

AKKERHAUGEN
Telemark (☎036)

★★**Norsjø Turisthotel** ☎66211
➡ ⩇50 A10rm **P**65 Lift ☾ sB➡ ⩇fr320 dB➡ ⩇fr490 M80—100

ÅL
Buskerud (☎067)

★★★**Bergjøstølen** ☎84618
Feb—Apr & 20 Jun—20 Oct
rm35 (⩇25) sB185—235 sB⩇235—335 dB270—370 dB⩇370—470 M75—100 lake mountains
Credit card 3

★★***Sundre*** (n.rest) ☎81100
rm28 (➡12) **P** mountains

ÅLESUND
Møre-og-Romsdal (☎071)

★★**Noreg** Kongensgate 27 ☎22938 tx40440
➡ ⩇107 **P**10 Lift ☾ sB➡ ⩇495—745 dB➡ ⩇735—895
Credit cards 1 2 3 5

Ødegårds Karosserifabrikk ☎42079

Vestlandske Auto Vaagav 27 ☎25500 For

ÅNDALSNES
Møre-og-Romsdal (☎072)

I Sylte ☎21477

ARENDAL
Aust-Agder (☎041)

★★★***Phönix*** Tyholmen ☎25160
➡83 **P** Lift ☾
Credit cards 1 2 3 5

Josephsens Auto ☎26200

ASKIM
Østfold (☎02)

Martiniussen Bilservice ☎887776

BALESTRAND
Sogn-og-Fjordane (☎056)

★★★**Kvikne's** Balholm ☎91101 tx42858
10 May—Sep
rm210 (➡189) **P** Lift ☾ sB310 sB➡410 dB400 dB➡600 M140&alc Beach sea mountains
Credit cards 1 2 3 4 5

★★***Kringsjå*** ☎91303
5 Jan—28 Aug
rm30 (➡17) **P** sea

★★**Midtnes Pensionat** ☎91133
rm38 (➡ ⩇30) **P**20 Lift sB175 sB➡ ⩇240 dB255 dB➡ ⩇335 M75—80 Beach sea

Norway

★***Balestrand Pensionat*** ☎91138
rm35 (➡20) A10rm **P**20 Lift Beach sea
Credit card 5

BERGEN
Hordaland (☎05)

★★★★**SAS Royal** Bryggen ☎318000 tx40640
➡300 **P** Lift ☾ sB➡fr790 dB➡fr940
Credit cards 1 2 3 5

★★★**Grand Terminus** Kong Oscarsgt 71 ☎311655 tx42262
rm126 (➡45) **P**15 Lift ☾ sB➡565—650 dB➡685—770 M100
Credit cards 1 2 3 4 5

★★★**Norge** (SRS) Ole Bulls Pl 4 ☎210100 tx42129
➡ ⩇350 **P**30 Lift ☾ sB➡ ⩇650—715 dB➡ ⩇705—930 M115—145 lake mountains
Credit cards 1 2 3 5

★★★**Orion** Bradbenken 3 (n.rest) ☎318080 tx42442
➡ ⩇199 **P** Lift ☾ sB➡ ⩇510—550 dB➡ ⩇590—700
Credit cards 1 2 3 5

★★★***Scandic*** Kokstadflaten 2, Koustad ☎227150
➡148 **P**150 Lift ☾ mountains
Credit cards 1 2 3 4 5

★★**Hordaheimer** C-Sundtsgt 18 ☎232320 tx40926
rm75 (➡ ⩇60) A6rm **P** Lift ☾ sB230 sB➡ ⩇390—440 dB380 dB➡ ⩇520 M70—90
Credit cards 1 2 3

★★**Neptun** Walckendorffsgt 8 ☎326000 tx40040
➡99 **P**14 Lift ☾ sB➡585—655 dB➡685—750 M alc
Credit cards 1 2 3 5

★★**Rosenkrantz** Rosenkrantzgt 7 ☎315000 tx42427
➡118 **P**4 Lift ☾ sB➡595—775 dB➡800—880 M115—150
Credit cards 1 2 3 5

★★**Hanseaten** Sandbrogt 3 ☎316155
rm31 (➡23) **P**4 Lift ☾ sB280 sB➡380 dB460 dB➡560 M50—70 sea
Credit cards 1 2 3 5

★**Park** H-Hårfagresgt 35 (n.rest) ☎320960
Closed Xmas—Etr
rm38 (➡28) **P**8 sB➡340 dB➡470 mountains

Vikingservice ☎292222 AR Cit DJ

BESSHEIM
Oppland (☎062)

★***Fjellstue*** ☎38913
Feb—Sep
rm170 (➡13) **P**80 mountains lake
Credit card 3

BØ
Telemark (☎036)

★★***Bø*** ☎60111 tx21119
➡65 **P** ☾ lake mountains

★★**Lifjell Turist** (8km N of railway station) ☎60011 tx21119
rm70 (➡68) **P**150 ☾ **DPn**345—440 M120—150 lake mountains
Credit cards 1 2 5

BODØ
Nordland (☎081)

★★★**Grand** Storgt 3 ☎20000
2 Jan—24 Dec
rm52 (➡48) **P**20 ☾ sB290 sB➡490—570 dB➡655—680 M alc mountains
Credit cards 1 2 3 4

★★★**SAS Royal** Storgt 2 ☎24100 tx64031
➡184 **P**100 Lift sB➡695 dB➡900 M80—90 sea
Credit cards 1 2 3 5

BOLKESJØ
Telemark (☎036)

★★★***Bolkesjø*** ☎18600 tx21007
➡123 **P** Lift ☾ sea

BØVERDALEN
Oppland (☎062)

★**Jotunhelmen Fjellstue** ☎12910 tx71954
15 Feb—15 Oct
rm39 (➡ ⩇24) A6rm **P**40 sB210—250 sB➡ ⩇290—310 dB350—380 dB➡ ⩇460—500 M65—80 lake mountains

At **ELVESETER** (4km SW)

★★★**Elveseter Turist** ☎12000
Jun—27 Sep
➡95 **P** Lift sB➡138—178 dB➡276—326 M80 mountains

BRUMUNDDAL
Hedmark (☎065)

★★★**Hedemarken** ☎40011
➡57 ☾ sB➡425—495 dB➡575—650 M100—125
Credit cards 1 3 5

BRYNE
Rogaland (☎04)

★★***Jæren Turist Rica*** ☎482488
➡51 **P** ☾

BYGDIN
Oppland (☎061)

★★**Bygdin Hoyfjellshotell** ☎41213
25 Jun—15 Sep
rm50 (➡22) **P**100 ☾ sB235 sB➡250 dB290 dB➡310 M80—90 mountains

BYGLANDSFJORD
Aust-Agder (☎043)

★★**Revsnes Turisthotell** ☎34105
mid Jan—mid Dec
➡43 **P**50 sB➡275—290 dB➡440—470

M95 lake mountains
Credit cards 2 5

BYKLE
Aust-Agder (☎043)

★***Bykle*** ☎38120
rm15 A10rm **P** Lift M alc mountains

DOKKA
Oppland (☎061)

★★★***Spatind Høyfjellshotell*** ☎19506
96 A12rm **P** mountains lake

Dokka Bilberging ☎10558

DOMBÅS
Oppland (☎062)

★★★**Dombås Turisthotell** ☎41001 tx19959
100 **P**50 Lift sB 420 dB 520 mountains
Credit cards 1 2 3

★★★**Dovrefjell** ☎41005 tx76573
rm89 (86) sB 345 dB 590 M100 mountains
Credit cards 1 2 3

Storrusten ☎41009

DRAMMEN
Buskerud (☎03)

★★★★**Park** Gamie Kirkpl 3 ☎838280 tx74278
103 **P**50 Lift sB 380—650 dB 490—760 M100—105
Credit cards 1 2 3

Bilberging ☎824930

DRANGEDAL
Telemark (☎036)

★★★***Gautefall*** ☎36600 tx21756
75 **P**80 mountains
Credit cards 1 2 3 5

Drangedal ☎36255

EDLAND
Telemark (☎036)

★★**Vågslid** ☎70532 tx21441
48 **P** sB 425 dB 595 M75—130 lake mountains
Credit cards 1 2 3 5

EGERSUND
Rogaland (☎04)

★★***Elger*** J-Feyers gt 3 ☎491811
27 **P**
Credit cards 1 3

EIDFJORD
Hordaland (☎054)

★★***Voringfoss*** ☎65184
rm57 (43) A27rm **P**50 Beach sea mountains
Credit cards 1 2 3 5

EIKEN
Vest-Agder (☎043)

★★★**Eiken Feriesenter** ☎48200
48 **P**40 Lift sB 360 dB 510 M80—90 lake mountains
Credit cards 1 2 3 5

Norway

ELVERUM
Hedmark (☎064)

E Kristiansen ☎11827 & 12738

ELVESETER See **BØVERDALEN**

ESPEDALEN
Oppland (☎062)

★★**Dalseter Høyfjellshotell** ☎99910 tx76722
26 Dec—1 Jun & 15 Jun—Sep
90 **P** Lift sB 320—385 dB 515—585 M140 lake mountains
Credit card 1

★***Espedalen Fjellstue*** (n.rest) ☎99912
18 Dec—23 Apr & Jun—Sep
29 lake mountains

EVJE
Aust-Agder (☎043)

★★**Grenaderen** ☎30400
30 A2rm **P**75 sB 250—270 dB 300—340 M45—105 mountains
Credit cards 1 2 3

Lanz Auto ☎043-30301

FAGERNES
Oppland (☎061)

★★★**Fagernes** ☎31100 tx76562
109 **P**4 Lift sB 555—640 dB 710—810 M100—110
Credit cards 1 2 3 5

★★★***Sanderstolen*** (28km SW on road to Gol) ☎34000 tx19061
lake

★***Fagerlund*** ☎30600
rm25 (6) A8rm **P** lake mountains

Autoservice ☎32266

FARSUND
Vest-Agder (☎043)

★★★**Fjordhotel** ☎91022 tx21678
63 **P**80 Lift sB 355—615 dB 510—750 M90—120 Beach sea
Credit cards 1 2 3 5

Kjell Ore Bill & Oljesenter ☎93111

FEVIK
Aust-Agder (☎041)

★★**Strand** ☎47322 tx21854
40 **P**150 sB 380—475 dB 575—625 M alc Beach sea
Credit cards 1 2 3 5

FLÅM
Sogn-og-Fjordane

★★★***Fretheim*** ☎(056)32200
10 May—25 Sep
rm85 (54) A16rm sea

FLORØ
Sogn-og-Fjordane (☎057)

★★***Victoria*** ☎41033 tx42186
rm85 (63) **P**20 Lift sea mountains
Credit cards 1 2 3 4 5

FØRDE
Sogn-og-Fjordane (☎057)

★★***Sunnfjord*** ☎21622 tx42217
161 **P** Lift

Autoservice ☎25311 Fia

FREDRIKSTAD
Østfold (☎032)

★★★***City*** ☎17750 tx17072
104 **P** Lift

Fredrikstad Automobil-Forr Mosseveien 3 ☎11260 For

GAUSA
Oppland (☎062)

★★★**Gausdal Højfjellshotell** ☎28500 tx71805
115 **P**100 sB 300—400 dB 500—700 M90—110 mountains
Credit cards 1 2 3 5

★★★**Skeikampen Høyfjellshotell** ☎28505 tx78601
rm60 (54) **P**60 Lift sB140—165 sB 240—265 dB300—320 dB 400—420 M90—120 mountains
Credit cards 1 2 3 5

GEILO
Buskerud (☎067)

★★★★**Bardøla** ☎85400 tx18771
rm102 (100) Lift sB fr540 dB fr820 M150—170 mountains
Credit cards 1 2 3 5

★★★★***Highland*** ☎85600 tx18401
92 **P**

★★★**Vestlia Hoyfjellshotell & Sportell** ☎85611 tx19874
75 A37rm **DPn**330—480 mountains lake
Credit cards 1 2 3 5

★★**Alpin** ☎85544
Closed May
27 **P**30 sB 220 dB 345 sea mountains
Credit cards 1 2 3 5

★★**Geilo** ☎85511 tx74919
73 **P**70 sB 435 dB 650 M110 lake mountains
Credit cards 1 2 3 5

★★**Haugen** (n.rest) ☎85644
rm50 (36) **P** mountains lake

Geilo Auto ☎85790

GEIRANGER
Møre-og-Romsdal (☎071)

★★★**Geiranger** ☎63005 tx40760
May—Oct
69 **P**30 Lift sB 650—750 →

dB 🛁 510—610 M95—135 ⛱ sea
Credit cards 1 2 3 4 5

★★★ ***Union*** ☎63000 tx42339
Mar—20 Dec
🛁 140 ⌂ P4 Lift ☾ 📺
Credit cards 1 2 3 4 5

★★ **Grande** ☎63067
May—Sep
🛁 🚿 15 **P**40 dB 🛁 🚿 320—355
M90—100&alc Beach sea

★★ **Meroks Fjord** ☎63002 tx40670
10 May—20 Sep
🛁 55 **P** Lift ☾ sB 🛁 370—405
dB 🛁 490—540 M85—135 ⛱ lake
Credit cards 1 2 3 5

GJØVIK
Oppland (☎061)

★★★ ***Strand Rica*** ☎72120 tx71610
rm87 (🛁 73) **P**25 Lift ☾ 📺 lake
Credit cards 1 2 3 5

★★ **Grand** Jernbanegt 5 ☎72180
🛁 34 A22rm **P**10 ☾ sB 🛁 380—460
dB 🛁 565—665 M75—110
Credit cards 1 2 3 5

🚗 **Carhos Bilberging** ☎73386

GODØYSUND
Hordaland (☎054)

★★ **Godøysund Fjord** ☎31404
20 Apr—Oct
🛁 50 **P**20 ☾ 🎾 Beach sea
Credit cards 2 3 4 5

GOL
Buskerud (☎067)

★★★ ***Oset Høyfjellshotell*** (20km N)
☎77920
🛁 105 **P**80 ☾ 🎾 📺 Beach sea mountains
Credit cards 1 3

★★★ **Pers** ☎9102 tx78472
🚿 54 **P** sB🚿 575 dB🚿 790 M140 mountains
Credit cards 1 2 3 4 5

★★ **Eldsgard** ☎74955
rm48 (🛁 🚿 30) **P**40 sBfr200
sB 🛁 🚿 300—350 dBfr250
dB 🛁 🚿 400—450 M90—105 U mountains
Credit cards 1 2 5

★★ ***Storefjell Høyfjellshotel*** ☎77930 ⛱

★ ***Thorstens*** (n.rest) ☎74062
🛁 26 **P**

GOLÅ
Oppland (☎062)

★★★ ***Golå Høifjellshotell***
Gudbrandsdalen ☎98109 tx18601
Jun—Oct
🛁 🚿 37 **P**100 ☾ 🎾 ⛱ Beach U mountains
lake
Credit card 1

GRANVIN
Hordaland (☎055)

★★ ***Granvin Fjordhotell*** ☎25106
rm40 (🛁 25) ⌂ **P** ☾ sea mountains

Norway

GRATANGEN
Troms (☎082)

★ ***Gratangen*** ☎20108

GROTLI
Oppland (☎062)

★★ **Grottli Høyfjellshotell** ☎13912
15 Feb—Sep
rm55 (🛁 52) **P**250 ☾ sB 🛁 423—498
dBfr491 dB 🛁 491—646 M60—80 lake
mountains
Credit cards 1 2 3 5

GUDVANGEN
Sogn-og-Fjordane (☎05)

★★ **Gudvangen** ☎531929
Jun—15 Sep
rm28 (🛁 🚿 9) A7rm **P**40 sB250 sB 🛁 🚿 300
dB340 dB 🛁 🚿 410 M90&alc lake mountains

HALDEN
Østfold (☎031)

🚗 **H Thanstrøm** Augustaborg ☎81122 Maz
Vau

HAMAR
Hedmark (☎065)

★★★ **Oirud Rica** ☎50100 tx72834
🛁 🚿 176 ⌂ **P** Lift ☾ sB 🛁 🚿 295—595
dB 🛁 🚿 420—795 M alc 📺 ⛱
Credit cards 1 2 3 5

★★★ ***Victoria*** Strandgt 21 ☎30500
tx78568
🛁 🚿 118 **P**

🚗 **Furnes Bil** ☎50300

HAMMERFEST
Finnmark (☎084)

★★ **Grand Rica** ☎11333 tx75814
rm76 (🛁 65) ☾ sBfr392 sB 🛁 fr637
dB 🛁 fr779 M70—85 sea
Credit cards 1 2 3 4 5

HANKØ
Østfold (☎032)

★★ ***Hankø Nye Fjord*** ☎32105 tx74950
Mar—20 Dec
🛁 🚿 67 **P** ☾ 🎾 ⛱ Beach

HARPEFOSS
Oppland (☎062)

★★★ **Wadahl Høyfjellshotell** (5km S of
railway station) ☎98300 tx72534
Dec—Apr & Jun—Sep
🛁 🚿 95 ⌂ **P**100 Lift ☾ sB 🛁 🚿 360—440
dB 🛁 🚿 560—640 M110—130 🎾 📺 ⛱ U
lake mountains
Credit cards 1 3

HARSTAD
Troms (☎082)

★★★ ***Grand Nordic*** ☎62170 tx64152

★★★ **Viking Nordic** ☎64080 tx64322
🛁 🚿 93 A7rm **P**20 Lift ☾ sB 🛁 🚿 595

dB 🛁 🚿 695 M80—95 📺 sea
Credit cards 1 2 3 5

HAUGESUND
Rogaland (☎047)

★★★ **Maritim** Asbygt 3 ☎11100 tx42691
🚿 180 **P**120 Lift ☾ sB🚿 400—600
dB🚿 500—800 M alc
Credit cards 1 2 3 5

★★★ **Saga** Skippergt 11 ☎11100 tx42691
rm90 (🛁 85) ⌂ **P**25 Lift ☾ sB 🛁 625—725
dB 🛁 725—825
Credit cards 1 2 3 5

★★ ***Haugaland*** Rutebilstasjonen (n.rest)
☎13466 tx42691
rm22 (🚿 16) **P** ☾

★★ **Imi** (n.rest) ☎23699
rm22 (🛁 18) **P**11 ☾ sB200—230 sB 🛁 310
dBfr330 dB 🛁 420
Credit cards 1 2 3

★★ ***Park*** ☎12000 tx42921
🛁 114 ⌂ **P**150 Lift ☾ 📺 sea
Credit cards 1 2 3 5

🚗 **Førland Bilberging** ☎31000

HAUKELIFJELL
Telemark (☎036)

★ ***Haukeliseter Fjellstue*** (n.rest) ☎70515
rm38 (🚿 6) A23rm **P**50 sea mountains lake

HEMSEDAL
Buskerud (☎067)

★★ **Hemsedal** ☎74500 tx78472
🛁 135 Lift ☾ sB 🛁 445 dB 🛁 620 M125 📺
⛱ mountains
Credit cards 1 2 3 4 5

★★ **Skogstad** ☎78333 tx72400
🛁 80 Lift ☾ sB 🛁 430 dB 🛁 570 M80—100
lake mountains
Credit cards 1 2 3 5

HERMANSVERK
Sogn-og-Fjordane (☎056)

★★ ***Sognefjord Turist*** ☎53444 tx40654
🛁 38 **P** Lift ☾ ⛱ Beach sea

HJERKINN
Oppland (☎062)

★ ***Hjerkinn Fjellstue*** ☎42927
Jun—Sep
rm34 (🛁 7) A23rm **P** M alc mountains lake

HØNEFOSS
Buskerud (☎067)

★★ **Grand** (n.rest) ☎22722
rm47 (🛁 28) A7rm ⌂ **P** ☾ sB190—200
sB 🛁 300—310 dB340 dB 🛁 400—420
Credit card 3

At **KLEKKEN** (3km E)

★★★ **Klaekken** ☎32200 tx78838
Closed 5—28 Jul
🛁 🚿 82 **P** Lift ☾ sB 🛁 🚿 265—285
dB 🛁 🚿 560—600 M110—115 🎾 📺 ⛱ ▣
mountains
Credit cards 1 2 3 5

HONNINGSVÅG (MAGERØYA ISLAND)
Finnmark (☎084)
(Access by ferry from KÅFJORD)

★★★**SAS Nordkapp** ☎72333 tx64346
rm174 (🛁58) A32rm Lift ☾ sB400
sB🛁565—635 dB780—875
dB🛁780—875 M75—80 sea mountains
Credit cards [1] [2] [3] [5]

HOVDEN
Aust-Agder (☎043)

★★**Hovden Høyfjellshotell** ☎39600 tx21968
🛁82 **P**100 Lift ☾ sB🛁350 dB🛁480 🎾 ▭ ∪ lake mountains
Credit cards [1] [2] [3] [5]

★★★**Hovdestøylen** ☎39552 tx21257
🛁🚿41 A26rm 🏠 **P**50 Lift ☾ sB🛁🚿430 dB🛁🚿650 M85—150 🎾 ▭ ▣ ∪ lake
Credit cards [1] [2] [3] [5]

HOVET
Buskerud (☎067)

★★★***Hallingskarvet*** ☎88525
rm38 (🛁36) A4rm 🏠 **P**150 ☾ ▭ ▣ ∪ mountains lake
Credit cards [1] [2] [5]

HØVIK See **OSLO**

HØVRINGEN
Oppland (☎062)

★★***Brekkeseter Fjellstue*** ☎33711 tx11954
15 Feb—20 Apr & 20 Jun—Sep
rm66 (🛁🚿54) **P**

★★***Hovringen Høyfjellshotell*** (n.rest) ☎33722 tx11954
24 Jun—Sep
rm82 (🛁62) **P** ☾ mountains

HØYANGER
Sogn-og-Fjordane (☎057)

★★***Øren*** ☎12606

INNVIK
Sogn-og-Fjordane (☎057)

★★**Misjonshelmen** ☎74252
rm24 (🛁🚿19) A3rm **P**30 Lift sB200 sB🛁🚿240 dB270 dB🛁🚿295 M55—70 Beach sea

KINSARVIK
Hordaland (☎054)

★★★**Kinsarvik Fjord** ☎63100 tx42292
15 Jan—20 Dec
rm75 (🛁62) **P** Lift ☾ sB220 sB🛁325—355 dB330 dB🛁450—510 M105—130 sea
Credit cards [1] [2] [3] [5]

KIRKENES
Finnmark (☎085)

★★★**Kirkenes Rica Turist** ☎911491
rm64 (🛁50) A6rm **P**30 Lift ☾ sB420—605 sB🛁595—605 dB620 dB🛁800—850 M90—105 🎾 sea mountains

KLEKKEN See **HØNEFOSS**

Norway

KOLBOTN
Oslo (☎02)

★★★**Müller** Lienga 1 ☎807500 tx74260
🛁🚿145 **P**100 Lift ☾ sB🛁🚿295—655 dB🛁🚿395—795
Credit cards [1] [2] [3] [5]

KONGSBERG
Buskerud (☎03)

★★★***Grand*** Kristian Augustsgt 2 ☎732029 tx72991
🛁94 🏠 **P**

★★★**Gyldenløve** ☎731744 tx74908
🛁🚿43 **P**30 Lift ☾ sB🛁🚿350—550 dB🛁🚿450—650 M75—100 mountains
Credit cards [1] [2] [5]

KONGSVINGER
Hedmark (☎066)

★★**Vinger** ☎17222
Closed Etr
🛁🚿63 A11rm **P**100 Lift ☾ sB🛁🚿245—570 dB🛁🚿440—740 M65—105 ▭
Credit cards [1] [2] [3] [5]

🚗 **Kristiansen Bilberging** ☎15180

KOPERVIK
Rogaland (☎047)

★★★**Karmøy** ☎50400
🛁55 **P** Lift ☾ sB🛁405—425 dB🛁520—580 M57—68 sea
Credit cards [1] [2] [3]

KRISTIANSAND S
Vest-Agder (☎042)

★★★**Caledonien** V-Strandgt 7 ☎29100 tx21222
Mar—Dec
🛁🚿205 🏠 **P**400 Lift ☾ sB🛁🚿695 dB🛁🚿795 M alc sea
Credit cards [1] [2] [3] [4] [5]

★★★**Christian Quart** ☎22210 tx21126
🛁🚿110 🏠 **P**40 Lift ☾ sB🛁🚿330—640 dB🛁🚿500—785 M alc
Credit cards [1] [2] [3] [4] [5]

★★★**Ernst** Rådhusgt 2 ☎21400 tx21104
🛁69 🏠 **P**12 Lift ☾ sB🛁475—595 dB🛁605—800 M165—170
Credit cards [1] [2] [3] [5]

★★★***Fregatten Rica*** Dronningensgt 66 ☎21500 tx21792
rm50 (🛁45) 🏠 **P** Lift ☾ M alc

★★★**Norge** Dronningensgt 5—9 ☎23320 tx21369
🛁65 **P**65 Lift sB🛁290—395 dB🛁420—460 M52—95
Credit cards [1] [2] [3] [5]

🚗 **Nygaards Auto** ☎23810

KRISTIANSUND N
Møre-og-Romsdal (☎073)

★★★***Grand*** Bernstorffredet 1 ☎73011 tx55488
🛁🚿115 **P**

🚗 **Moblistasjonen** ☎74680 & 75218

KVAM
Oppland (☎062)

★★**Vertshuset Sinclair** ☎94024
🚿16 **P**100 sB🚿266—321 dB🚿347—422 M40—80 mountains
Credit cards [1] [2] [3] [5]

KVINESDAL
Vest-Agder (☎043)

★★★***Utsikten Turist*** ☎50444

★★**Rafoss** ☎50388
Closed Xmas & Easter
rm18 (🛁🚿16) **P**12 sB🛁🚿290—320 dB🛁🚿390—420 M90 mountains
Credit cards [2] [5]

KVITESEID
Telemark (☎036)

★★**Kviteseld** ☎53222
rm34 (🛁🚿20) A7rm **P**40 sB210—260 sB🛁🚿fr260 dB360—460 dB🛁🚿fr460 M70—80 sea lake mountains
Credit cards [1] [2] [3] [5]

LAERDAL
Sogn-og-Fjordane (☎056)

★★★**Lindstrøm Turisthotell** ☎66202 tx40689
Apr—15 Oct
🛁🚿90 A40rm **P**100 Lift ☾ sB🛁🚿250—430 dB🛁🚿390—630 M110—150 mountains
Credit cards [1] [2] [3] [5]

LAKSELV
Finnmark (☎084)

★★**Banak** ☎61377
🛁🚿22 A4rm **P**15 ☾ sB🛁🚿340—460 dB🛁🚿480—680 M alc mountains
Credit cards [1] [3] [5]

🚗 **Lakselv Bilberging** ☎61744

LARVIK
Vestfold (☎034)

★★★**Grand** Storgt 38 ☎83800 tx21024
rm114 (🛁90) **P**100 Lift ☾ sB255—355 sB🛁430—530 dB460 dB🛁595—635 M85&alc
Credit cards [1] [2] [3] [5]

🚗 **Latas** Nansetgt 36/38 ☎81212 For

LEIKANGER
Sogn-og-Fjordane (☎056)

★★**Leikanger Fjord** ☎53622
rm45 (🛁42) **P**50 sB🛁370—410 dB🛁500—580 Beach sea
Credit cards [1] [3]

LEVANGER
Nord-Trøndelag (☎076)

★★***Backlund*** Kirkegt 41 ☎81600
rm60 (🚿57) Lift ☾

Nilsen Bilberging ☎82522

LILLEHAMMER
Oppland (☎062)

★★★**Lillehammer** ☎54800 tx19592

65 **P**400 Lift ☾ sB 535—585 dB 690 M120—125
Credit cards 1 2 3 5

★★★**Oppland** ☎58500 tx74869

75 A8rm **P**100 Lift ☾ sB 320—550 dB 470—700 M95—110 lake mountains
Credit cards 1 2 3 5

★★★***Victoria Rica*** Storgt 82 ☎50049 tx19806

94 **P** Lift ☾

★★**Ersgaard** ☎50684

rm29 (16) A9rm ☾ sBfr170 sBfr230 dB300—320 dBfr380 M70—90 U lake
Credit card 2

★**Breiseth** Jerbanegt 5 ☎50060 tx16384

rm35 (2) **P**25 sB145 dB265 dB 325 M55—65

Furnes Bil & Karosseriverkstad ☎51016

At **NORDSETER** (14km NE)

★★★**Nevra** ☎64001 tx19598

rm70 (50) **P**20 ☾ sB180—365 sB 225—465 dB320—606 dB 510—800 M85 lake mountains
Credit cards 1 2 3 5

★★★**Nordseter Høyfjeilshotell** ☎64004 tx19706

46 **P**40 ☾ sB 325 dB 550 M75—100 lake mountains
Credit cards 1 2 3 5

LOEN
Sogn-og-Fjordane (☎057)

★★★★**Alexandra** ☎77660 tx42665

207 **P**100 Lift ☾ sB 485—545 dB 390—800 M110—170 sea
Credit cards 1 2 3 5

★★**Richards** ☎77657

Apr—Oct
25 **P**30 ☾ sB fr340 dB fr480 Mfr50alc sea mountains
Credit cards 1 2 3 5

★***Rake*** ☎Stryn 1534

LOFTHUS
Hordaland (☎054)

★★★**Ullensvang** ☎61100 tx42659

130 **P**90 Lift ☾ sB 485—640 dB 670—980 M125—165 Beach sea mountains
Credit cards 1 2 3 5

LOM
Oppland (☎062)

★★**Fossberg Turiststasjon** ☎11073

rm42 (29) A17rm **P**50 sB135—140 sB 175—185 dB220—240 dB 270—280 mountains

Norway

★★***Fossheim*** ☎11005

Feb—Nov
rm55 (42) A22rm **P** mountains

S Skaansar ☎11041

LONSDAL
Nordland (☎081)

★★**Polarsirkelen Høyfjeilshotell** ☎94122

rm43 (13) A2rm **P**50 ☾ sB315 sB 360 dB505 dB 585 M85—95 mountains
Credit cards 1 2 3 4 5

MANDAL
Vest-Agder (☎043)

★★★**Solborg Turisthotell** ☎61311 tx21992

rm65 (62) **P**70 Lift ☾ sB 270—500 dB500—700 dB 500—700 M85—120 sea
Credit cards 1 2 3 4 5

★***Bondehelmen*** Elvegt 23A ☎61422

Viking Bilservice ☎65005

MARIFJØRA
Sog-og-Fjordane (☎056)

★★**Tørvis** ☎87200

43 A8rm **P** ☾ sB 205—295 dB 320—420 M85—95 Beach sea mountains
Credit card 2

MO-I-RANA
Nordland (☎087)

★★★**Meyergården** ☎50555 tx55649

rm125 (100) **P** Lift ☾ sB550—600 dB 650—700 Mfr70 alc sea
Credit cards 1 2 3 5

Rana Transportservice ☎52220

MOLDE
Møre-og-Romsdal (☎072)

★★★**Alexandra** Storgt 1—7 ☎51133 tx42847

129 **P** Lift ☾ sB fr615 dB fr755 sea mountains
Credit cards 1 2 3 5

★**Knausen** ☎51577

18 A18rm **P** Lift ☾ sB 430—490 dB 540—630 M60—65 sea mountains
Credit cards 1 2 3

Bj-Rødseth ☎56755 & 52767

MORGEDAL
Telemark (☎036)

★★**Morgedal** ☎54144 tx21712

70 **P**80 Lift ☾ sB 310—390 dB 460—540 M105—145 lake mountains
Credit cards 1 2 3 5

MOSJØEN
Nordland (☎087)

★★***Fru Haugans*** ☎70477

rm54 (41) A31rm **P**15 ☾
Credit cards 1 3

★★***Lyngengården*** ☎70622

rm29 (20) **P** ☾ mountains

Sparby Bilberging ☎71023

MOSS
Østfold (☎032)

★★★***Refsnes-Gods*** Godset 5 Jeløy ☎70411

Closed Xmas & Etr
60 **P**60 Lift ☾ Beach
Credit cards 1 2

Moss Bilberging Oreveien 37 ☎55433 Hon Vau

NAMSOS
Nord-Trøndelag (☎077)

★★***Grand Bondehelmen*** Kirkegt 7—9 ☎73155

rm48 (12)

Bugge ☎72150

NARVIK
Nordland (☎082)

★★★**Grand Royal** Kongensgt 64 ☎41500 tx64032

110 **P**30 Lift ☾ sB 280—630 dB 390—750 M75—95 sea mountains
Credit cards 1 2 3 5

A Olsen Bil & Kranservice ☎44208

NESBYEN
Buskerud (☎067)

★★★**Østenfor Turisthotell** ☎71530 tx78398

63 **P**50 Lift ☾ sB 295—330 dB 470—540 Mfr125 lake mountains
Credit cards 1 2 5

★★**Ranten Fjelistue Mykingstølen** ☎73445

Closed May
34 sB 215 dB 375 lake mountains
Credit cards 1 3 5

★★**Smedsgarden Pensonat** (n.rest) ☎73125

5 May—Sep
rm40 (20) A2rm sB125 sB 165 dB250 dB 290 M60—70 Beach sea mountains

★★**Svenkerud** ☎71260

51 **P**40 Lift ☾ sB 260 dB 355 M85 mountains
Credit cards 2 3

Nesbyen Auto ☎71066 Aud VW

NORDFJORDEID
Sogn-og-Fjordane (☎057)

★★★***Nordfjord Turist*** ☎60433

55 **P**200 ☾ sea
Credit cards 1 2 3 5

NORDSETER See **LILLEHAMMER**

NOREFJELL
Buskerud (☎067)

★★***Fjellhvil*** ☎46174
rm59 (🛁 32) A8rm ☾ mountains lake

★***Sandum Seter*** ☎46155

NORHEIMSUND
Hordaland (☎05)

★★★**Norheimsund Fjord** ☎551522 tx42757
Feb—20 Dec
🛁 🚿 36 **P**50 sB🛁 🚿 350—400 dB🛁 🚿 540—630 M140 Beach sea
Credit cards [1] [2] [3] [5]

★★***Sandven*** ☎51911
15 Jan—15 Dec
rm46 (🛁 🚿) **P** mountains

NYSTOVA
Oppland (European Highway E68/5) (☎061)

★★★**Nystuen Fjellhotell** ☎37710
rm50 (🚿 45) A22rm **P**75 ☾ sB🚿 200—250 dB🚿 300—400 M45—95&alc Beach sea lake mountains
Credit cards [1] [2] [3]

ODDA
Hordaland (☎54)

★★★**Hardanger** ☎42133 tx42245
🛁 🚿 50 **P**15 Lift sB🛁 🚿 480—580 dB🛁 🚿 755—830 M50—150 ⊡ sea
Credit cards [1] [2] [3] [5]

🚗 **Moe Motor** ☎42364 Fia

🚗 **Nå Auto** ☎42700

OLDEN
Sogn-og-Fjordane (☎057)

★★★***Yris Turisthotell*** ☎73240
May—Sep
rm39 (🛁 34) ☾ ⏖ sea mountains

★★**Olden Fjord** ☎73235 tx40560
May—Oct
🛁 40 **P**40 ☾ sB🛁 fr425 dB🛁 fr590 M95 Beach sea mountains
Credit cards [1] [2] [3] [5]

★***Olden Krotell*** ☎73296
🚿 13 **P** ⊡ sea
Credit cards [1] [2] [3]

OPPDAL
Sør-Trøndelag (☎074)

★★***Müllerhotel Oppdal*** ☎21611
rm52 (🛁 50) **P** ☾ mountains

★★**Oppdal Turishotell** ☎21111
rm74 (🛁 64) **P**100 Lift sBfr235 sB🛁 320—555 dBfr330 dB🛁 475—665 M110—150 ⊡ mountains
Credit cards [1] [2] [3] [5]

★**Fagerhaug** ☎23601
🛁 16 **P**200 sB🛁 fr285 dB🛁 fr425 M25—80 mountains
Credit card [5]

🚗 **Prøven Bil** 21888 Peu

ØRSTA
Møre-og-Romsdal (☎070)

★★**Viking Fjord** ☎66800
rm42 (🛁 🚿 40) **P**60 Lift ☾ sB🛁 🚿 475 dB🛁 🚿 550—600 Mfr95 sea mountains
Credit cards [1] [2] [3]

🚗 **Mur Bil** ☎66514 & 66094

OS
Hordaland (☎05)

★★★***Solstrand*** ☎300099 tx42050
🛁 115 **P**100 ☾ Lift 🎾 ⊡ Beach sea
Credit cards [1] [2] [3] [5]

OSLO
Oslo (☎02)

See plan pages 330 and 331

★★★★**Bristol** Kristian IV-des gt 7 ☎415840 tx71668 Plan **1**
🛁 🚿 143 ⌂ **P**6 Lift ☾ sB🛁 🚿 720—780 dB🛁 🚿 920 M alc
Credit cards [1] [2] [3] [5]

★★★★**Continental** Stortingsgt 24 ☎419060 tx71012 Plan **2**
🛁 170 ⌂ Lift ☾ sB🛁 810 dB🛁 950
Credit cards [1] [2] [3] [5]

★★★★**Grand** (SRS) K-Johansgt 31 ☎429390 tx71683 Plan **3**
🛁 308 ⌂ Lift ☾ sB🛁 fr850 dB🛁 910—1350
Credit cards [1] [2] [3] [4] [5]

★★★★**KNA** (GT) Parkveien 68 ☎446970 tx71763 Plan **3A**
Closed Etr & Jul
🛁 152 ⌂ **P**13 Lift ☾ sB🛁 795—850 dB🛁 975—1900 Mfr140alc
Credit cards [1] [2] [3] [5]

★★★★**SAS Scandinavia** Holbergstgt 30 ☎113000 tx79090 Not on plan
🛁 500 ⌂ **P**170 Lift ☾ sB🛁 955—1025 dB🛁 1190—1250 ⊡ sea
Credit cards [1] [2] [3] [4] [5]

★★★***Ambassadeur*** C-Colletsvej 15 ☎441835 tx71446 Not on plan
🛁 33 Lift ☾ M alc ⊡
Credit cards [1] [2] [3] [5]

★★★***Astoria*** Akersgt 21 ☎426900 tx18754 Plan **5**
rm99 (🛁 91) Lift ☾ M alc

★★★***Carlton Rica*** Parkveien 78 ☎563090 tx17902 Plan **4**
🛁 50 Lift ☾

★★★***SAS Globetrotter*** Fornebuparken ☎120220 tx18745 Plan **6**
🛁 150 **P** Lift ☾ Beach sea

★★★***Smestad*** Sørkedalsveien 93 ☎146490 Plan **7**
🛁 31 A2rm **P**30 ☾
Credit cards [1] [2] [3] [5]

★★★**Triangel** Holbergsplass 1 ☎208855 tx19413 Plan **7A**
🛁 144 ⌂ **P**15 Lift ☾ sB🛁 590 dB🛁 690 M85—125 ⊡
Credit cards [1] [2] [3] [4] [5]

★★★**Voksenåsen** (SARA) Ullveien 4, Voksenkollveien ☎143090 Plan **8**
🛁 🚿 72 **P**80 ☾ sB🛁 🚿 405—635 dB🛁 🚿 630—960 M125 ⏖ sea
Credit cards [1] [2] [3] [5]

★★***Forbunds*** (Temperance) Holbergs Plass 1 ☎208855 tx19413 Plan **9**
rm107 (🛁 100) ⌂ **P** Lift ☾

★★**IMI** (Temperance) Staffeldtsgt 4 ☎205330 tx78142 Plan **10A**
🛁 🚿 60 A72rm ⌂ **P**10 Lift ☾ sB🛁 🚿 345—570 dB🛁 🚿 540—740 Mfr65
Credit cards [1] [2] [3] [5]

★★**Nye Helsfyr** Strømsveien 108 ☎654110 tx76776 Plan **10**
🛁 115 **P**120 Lift ☾ sB🛁 fr790 dB🛁 fr1005 Mfr120
Credit cards [1] [2] [3] [5]

★★***Panorama*** Sognsveien 218 ☎187080 tx18432 Plan **11**
Jun—Aug
rm414 Lift ☾ mountains lake

★★**Sara Oslo** (SARA) Biskop Gunnerusgt 3 ☎429410 tx71342 Plan **14**
🛁 309 **P** Lift ☾ sB🛁 740—890 dB🛁 935—995 Mfr125&alc
Credit cards [1] [2] [3] [4] [5]

★★**Stefan** Rosenkrantzgt 1 ☎429250 tx19809 Plan **12**
🛁 131 ⌂ **P**10 Lift ☾ sB🛁 410—815 dB🛁 670—970 M120—145
Credit cards [1] [2] [3] [5]

★**Ansgar** (Temperance) Møllergt 26 (n.rest) ☎204735 tx19602 Plan **15**
rm58 (🛁 14) ⌂ Lift ☾ sB250—350 sB🛁 300—450 dB300—490 dB🛁 400—560
Credit cards [1] [2] [3] [4] [5]

At **HØVIK** (10km W)

★★★***Scandic*** Ramstadsletta 12—14 (E18) ☎121740 tx72430 Not on plan
🛁 103 **P**100 Lift ☾
Credit cards [1] [2] [3] [4] [5]

OTTA
Oppland (☎062)

★★★***Otta Turist*** ☎30033
🛁 🚿 85 ⌂ **P** Lift ☾ ⏖

🚗 **Otta Auto** ☎30111

PORSGRUNN
Telemark (☎035)

★★**Vic** Skelegt 1 ☎55580 tx21450
🛁 95 **P** Lift ☾ sB🛁 525—550 dB🛁 575—625
Credit cards [1] [2] [3] [5]

🚗 **A Goberg** ☎97499

RANDABERG See **STAVANGER**

RAULAND
Telemark (☏036)

★★★**Rauland Høgfjellshotell** ☏73222 tx21580
116 A6rm **P**60 ☾ sB 350—380 dB 620—660 M135 mountains
Credit cards 1 2 3 5

★***Rauland Fjellstoge*** ☏73425
Jun—7 Oct & 22 Dec—Apr
rm33 (22) ☾ mountains lake

Rauland Servicesenter ☏73103

RINGEBU
Oppland (☏062)

★★**Venabu Fjellhotell** ☏84055
56 **P** Lift sB 380 dB 540—650 M120 mountains lake
Credit cards 1 2 3 5

RISØR
Aust-Agder (☏041)

★★★**Risør** ☏50700
33 A3rm **P**30 ☾ sB 400—610 dB 560—900 M85 Beach sea
Credit cards 1 2 3 5

RJUKAN
Telemark (☏036)

★★★**Gaustablikk Høyfjellshotell** ☏91422 tx21677
94 **P**50 ☾ sB 415 dB 630 M125—140 mountains lake
Credit cards 1 2 3 5

OSLO

1 ★★★★ Bristol
2 ★★★★ Continental
3 ★★★★ Grand
3A ★★★★ KNA
4 ★★★ Carlton Rica
5 ★★★ Astoria
6 ★★★ SAS Globetrotter
7 ★★★ Smestad
7A ★★★ Triangel
8 ★★★ Voksenåsen
9 ★★ Forbunds
10 ★★ Nye Helsfyr
10A ★★ IMI
11 ★★ Panorama
12 ★★ Stefan
14 ★★ Sara Oslo
15 ★ Ansgar

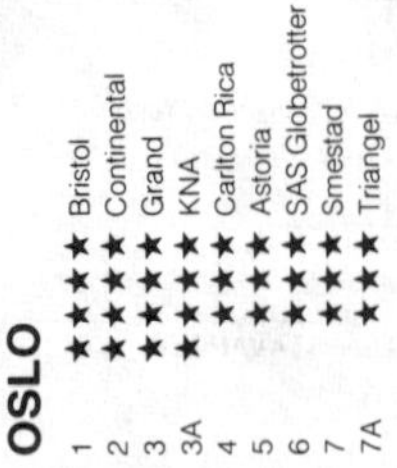

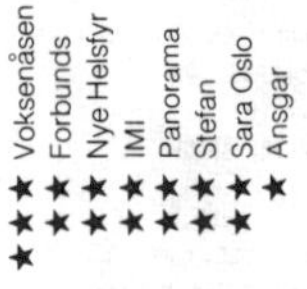

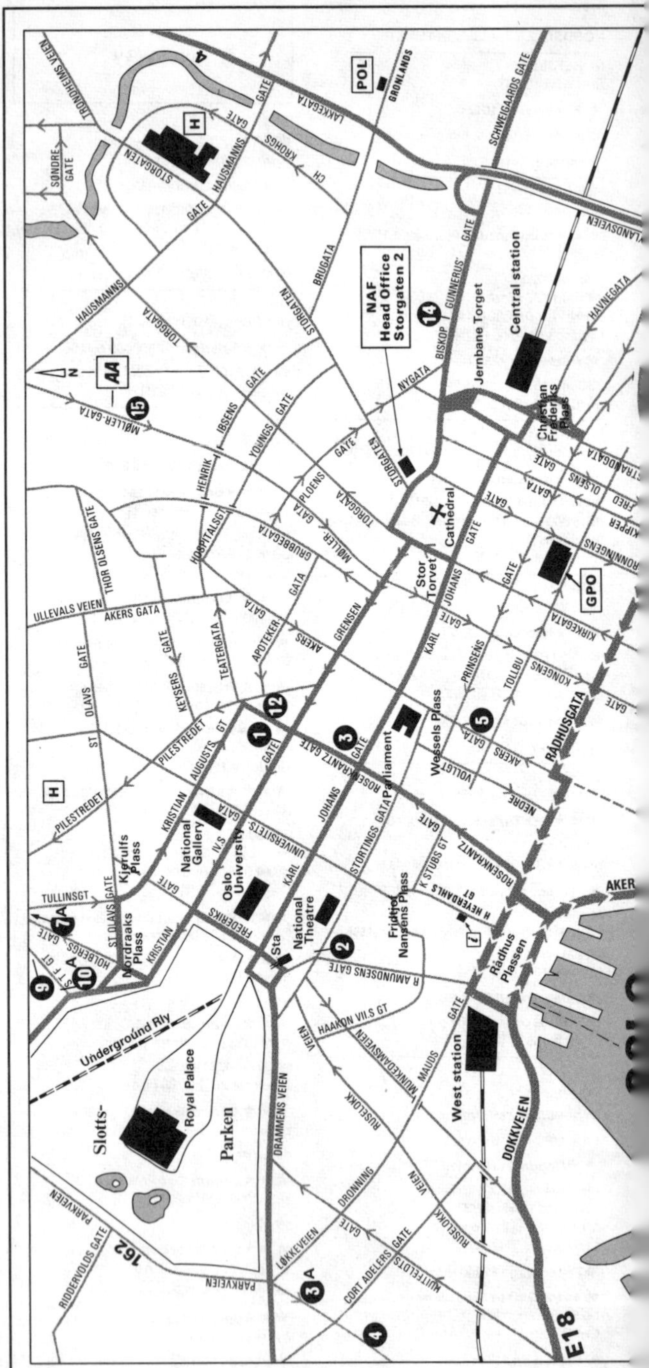

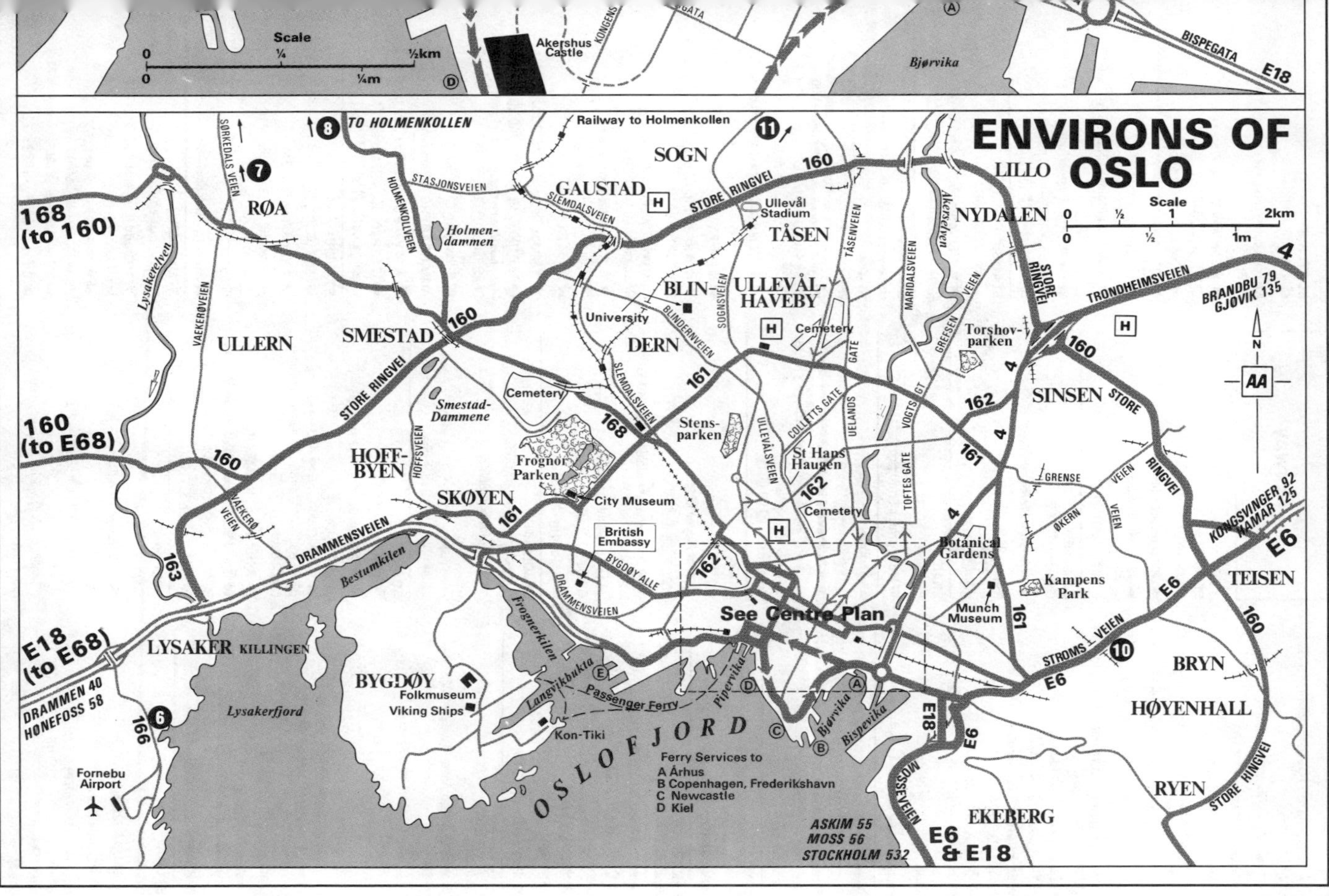

ENVIRONS OF OSLO
Scale
0 ½ 1 2km
0 ½ 1m
AA
N
BRANDBU 79
GJØVIK 135
KONGSVINGER 92
HAMAR 125
E6
TEISEN
BRYN
HØYENHALL
RYEN
STORE RINGVEI
LILLO
NYDALEN
SINSEN
TRONDHEIMSVEIEN
Torshov-parken
Kampens Park
Munch Museum
Botanical Gardens
EKEBERG
E6 & E18
MOSSEVEIEN
ASKIM 55
MOSS 56
STOCKHOLM 532
Akerselven
MARIDALSVEIEN
TÅSENVEIEN
TOFTES GATE
ULLEVÅL-HAVEBY
TÅSEN
Ullevål Stadium
St Hans Haugen
Cemetery
ULLEVÅLSVEIEN
See Centre Plan
Bjørvika
Bispevika
Pipervika
OSLOFJORD
Ferry Services to
A Århus
B Copenhagen, Frederikshavn
C Newcastle
D Kiel
Railway to Holmenkollen
SOGN
GAUSTAD
BLIN-DERN
University
Stens-parken
SLEMDALSVEIEN
City Museum
British Embassy
Frogner Parken
BYGDØY ALLE
DRAMMENSVEIEN
Frognerkilen
Langvikbukta
Passenger Ferry
Kon-Tiki
Folkmuseum
Viking Ships
BYGDØY
TO HOLMENKOLLEN
Holmen-dammen
HOLMENKOLLVEIEN
STASJONSVEIEN
SMESTAD
Smestad-Dammene
SKØYEN
HOFFSVEIEN
HOFF-BYEN
Bestumkilen
RØA
SØRKEDALS VEIEN
ULLERN
VAEKERØVEIEN
Lysakerelven
LYSAKER
KILLINGEN
Lysakerfjord
Fornebu Airport
168 (to 160)
160 (to E68)
E18 (to E68)
DRAMMEN 40
HØNEFOSS 58
Scale
0 ¼ ½km
0 ¼m
Akershus Castle
Bjørvika
BISPEGATA
E18

★★★***Skinnarbu Høyfjellshotell*** Mosvatn ☎95461 tx21633
rm60 (🛁 50) ⛵ mountains lake

★***Rjukan Fjellstue*** ☎95162
rm46 A35rm **P**70 mountains

🚗 **B Berge Bilforretning** Sam Ejdesgate 265 ☎94422 Vol

RØROS
Sør-Trøndelag (☎074)

★★★**Bergstadens Turisthotell** ☎11111 tx55617
🛁 🚿 65 **P**50 ☾ 📺 mountains
Credit cards [1] [2] [3] [4] [5]

★★★**Røros Turisthotell** An-Magrittsv ☎11011 tx55570
🛁 🚿 108 A10rm Lift ☾ sB 🛁 🚿 465—580 dB 🛁 🚿 505—740 M95—125 🎾 📺 mountains
Credit cards [1] [2] [3] [5]

🚗 **Nye Røros Auto** ☎11855 For

ROSENDAL
Hordaland (☎054)

★★***Fjord*** ☎81511
🛁 40 **P**80 ☾ Beach sea
Credit card [3]

SANDANE
Sogn-og-Fjordane (☎057)

★***Firdahelmen*** ☎66177

SANDEFJORD
Vestfold (☎4734)

★★★★***Park*** ☎65550 tx21055
🛁 🚿 163 🏠 Lift ☾ 📺
Credit cards [1] [2] [3] [5]

★★***Kong Carl*** ☎63117
🛁 27 🏠 **P** ☾

🚗 **Kjell's Bilhejlp** ☎75792

SARPSBORG
Østfold (☎031)

★★★**Saga** Sannesundsveien 1 ☎54044 tx78544
🛁 67 🏠 **P**8 Lift sB 🛁 395—570 dB 🛁 570—690 M alc
Credit cards [1] [2] [3] [5]

★★**St-Olav** ☎52055 tx78744
rm72 (🛁 64) 🏠 **P**25 Lift ☾ sB325 sB 🛁 350—450 dB400 dB 🛁 475—525 M75alc
Credit cards [1] [2] [3] [5]

★***Victoria*** ☎54500
rm18 (🛁 🚿 8) **P**

🚗 **Bilservice** Astridsgt 42 ☎53000

SAUDA
Rogaland (☎047)

At **SAUDASJØEN** (5km SW)

★★**Sauda Fjord** ☎91211
rm28 (🛁 14) A4rm **P**50 ☾ sB315 sB 🛁 415—510 dB500 dB 🛁 600—670 Mfr90 🎾 sea
Credit cards [1] [2] [3] [5]

Norway

SELJESTAD
Hordaland (☎054)

★★**Seljestad** ☎45155
🛁 43 sB 🛁 fr370 dB 🛁 fr580 Mfr70 mountains
Credit cards [1] [3] [5]

SJUSJØEN
Oppland (☎065)

★★***Rustad Fjellstue*** (n.rest) ☎63408
8 Jun—24 Sep
rm47 (🛁 28) ∪ Beach sea mountains lake
Credit card [5]

SKAIDI
Finnmark (☎084)

🚗 **Holmgrens Transport** ☎16145

SKÅNEVIK
Hordaland (☎047)

★★**Skånevik Fjord** ☎65255
🛁 49 **P** ☾ sB 🛁 390 dB 🛁 540—565 Mfr90 Beach sea mountains
Credit cards [1] [2] [3] [5]

SKIEN
Telemark (☎035)

★★★***Høyer*** ☎20540
rm73 **P** Lift ☾

★★★***Ibsen*** Kuerndalen 10 ☎24990 tx21136
🛁 🚿 118 🏠 Lift ☾ 📺
Credit cards [1] [2] [3] [5]

🚗 **A Goberg** ☎97500

SKJOLDEN
Sogn-og-Fjordane (☎056)

★★**Skjolden** ☎86606
May—Sep
rm51 (🛁 47) **P**80 Lift ☾ sB 🛁 287 dB344 dB 🛁 409 M100 Beach sea

SOGNDAL
Sogn-og-Fjordane (☎056)

★★★**Sogndal** ☎72311 tx42727
6 Jan—22 Dec
🛁 110 **P**40 Lift ☾ sB 🛁 420—475 dB 🛁 630—740 Mfr85 ⛵ sea mountains
Credit cards [1] [2] [3] [5]

★★**Hofslund Fjord** ☎71022
🛁 🚿 45 **P**30 ☾ sB 🛁 🚿 281 dB 🛁 🚿 414 Mfr85 ⛵ Beach sea mountains

🚗 **SMS Maskin** ☎72230

SOLVORN
Sogn-og-Fjordane (☎056)

★★**Walaker** ☎84207
10 May—30 Sep
rm25 (🛁 20) **P**20 Lift sB180—220 sB 🛁 260—300 dB280—340 dB 🛁 320—500 M50—120 Beach sea mountains

SORTLAND
Nordland (☎088)

No road connection: rail services from HARSTAD

★★***Sortland Nordic*** Vesterålsgt 59 ☎21833 tx75845
rm65 (🛁 🚿 60) **P** Lift ☾ sea

STALHEIM
Hordaland (☎05)

★★★★**Stalheim** ☎520122 tx40536
10 May—Sep
🛁 130 **P**30 Lift ☾ sB 🛁 385 dB 🛁 650—800 Mfr135 mountains
Credit cards [1] [2] [3] [5]

STAMSUND
Nordland (☎088)

★★★***Lofoten*** ☎89300 tx64011
rm38 (🚿 26) A10rm 🏠 **P** Lift ☾ ⛵ sea

STAVANGER
Rogaland (☎04)

★★★★**Atlantic** Jernbaneveien 1 ☎527520 tx33095
🛁 362 🏠 **P**90 Lift ☾ sB 🛁 345—990 dB 🛁 440—1055 M alc
Credit cards [1] [2] [3] [4] [5]

★★★***KNA*** (GT) Lagårdsvegen 61 ☎562690 tx71763
🛁 🚿 148 **P**

★★★***St-Svithun*** (Temperance) Klubbgt 3 ☎533020 tx73646
rm70 (🛁 🚿 50) **P**60 Lift ☾ lake
Credit cards [1] [2] [3] [5]

★★★***Scandic*** Elganesveien 181 ☎526500 tx33144
🛁 🚿 154 **P** Lift ☾ ⛵

★★**Alstor** Tjensvoll 4 ☎527020 tx40756
🛁 78 **P**100 ☾ sB 🛁 400—760 dB 🛁 fr760 M alc 📺 🏊 lake mountains
Credit cards [1] [2] [3] [4] [5]

🚗 **Bilberging** ☎582900

At **RANDABERG** (8.5km NW)

★★★***Viste Strand*** ☎597022 tx73694
🛁 🚿 53 **P**100 ☾ 🎾 Beach sea
Credit cards [1] [2] [3] [4] [5]

STAVERN
Vestfold (☎034)

★★**Wassilioff** ☎98311
rm48 (🛁 47) ☾ sB 🛁 370—410 dB 🛁 470—540 🎾 sea
Credit cards [1] [5]

🚗 **Stavern Auto** ☎99489

STEINKJER
Nord-Trøndelag (☎077)

★★**Grand** Kongenstgt 37 ☎64700 tx55111
🛁 🚿 90 **P**3 Lift ☾ sB 🛁 🚿 560—660 dB 🛁 🚿 750—870 Mfr90
Credit cards [1] [2] [3] [5]

🚗 **Stortvik og Øyen** ☎61472

STONGFJORD
Sogn-og-Fjordane (☎057)

🚗 **Stongfjord Auto** ☎31675 Hon

STØREN
Sør-Trøndelag (☎074)

★★★**Støren** ☎31118

🛁 32 **P** Lift ☾ sB🛁 fr395 dB🛁 490—590 M80—110 mountains

STRANDA
Møre-og-Romsdal (☎071)

★★★**Müllerhotell Stranda** ☎60000

rm70 (🛁🚿55) **P**40 Lift ☾ sB185 sB🛁🚿210—365 dB370 dB🛁🚿520 M75—100 ⛳ ≈ sea mountains
Credit cards [1] [2] [3] [5]

STRAUMSJØEN
Nordland (☎088)

🚗 **K Strømme** ☎38259 Vau

STRYN
Sogn-og-Fjordane (☎057)

🚗 **Karstad** ☎71011 Maz

SUNDVOLLEN
Buskerud (☎067)

★★**Sundvolden** ☎39140 tx72960

🛁 130 **P**400 Lift ☾ sB🛁 fr340 dB🛁 fr520 ▭ mountains lake
Credit cards [1] [2] [3] [5]

SUNNDALSØRA
Møre-og-Romsdal (☎073)

★★***Müllerhotell Sunndalen*** ☎91655

rm65 (🛁🚿47) 🏠 **P** Lift ☾ ⛳ mountains

SURNADAL
Møre-og-Romsdal (☎073)

★★**Surnadal** ☎61544

rm71 (🛁56) **P**100 ☾ sB180—315 sB🛁 245—465 dB220—365 dB🛁 350—620 M85—110 mountains
Credit cards [1] [2] [3] [5]

SVOLVÆR
Nordland (☎088)

★★★***Lofoten Nordic*** ☎71200 tx64451
rm68 (🛁63) Lift ☾ sea mountains

TINN AUSTBYGDA
Telemark (☎036)

🚗 **Marumsrud Bilverksted** ☎97166

TØNSBERG
Vestfold (☎033)

★★***Grand*** ☎12203 tx72400

🛁🚿43 A8rm **P**40 Lift ☾
Credit cards [1] [2] [3] [5]

🚗 **Bergans Auto** ☎14999

TRETTEN
Oppland (☎062)

★★★***Gausdal*** ☎28500 tx71805

rm125 (🛁120) 🏠 **P**100 ☾ ⛳ ▭ U mountains
Credit cards [1] [2] [3] [5]

★***Glomstad Gard*** (n.rest) ☎76257

16 Dec—Apr & Jun—10 Oct
rm27

Norway

TROMSØ
Troms (☎083)

★★★**SAS Royal** Sjogt 7 ☎56000 tx64260

🛁🚿192 **P**20 Lift ☾ sB🛁🚿695—725 dB🛁🚿820—850 M115—175 sea mountains
Credit cards [1] [2] [3] [5]

★★**Grand Nordic** Storgt 44 ☎85500 tx64204

🛁 106 🏠 **P**20 Lift ☾ sB🛁 675—790 dB🛁 830—975 Mfr95&alc sea
Credit cards [1] [2] [3] [5]

🚗 **Bilredningstjenesten** ☎70700

TRONDHEIM
Sør-Trøndelag (☎07)

★★★***Astoria*** Nordregt 24 ☎529550 tx55154

rm52 (🛁48) Lift ☾

★★★***Britannia*** Dronningensgate 5 ☎530040 tx55451

rm120 (🛁112) **P** Lift ☾ M alc

★★★**Prinsen** Kongensgt 30 ☎530650 tx55324

🛁 66 **P**25 Lift ☾ sB🛁 fr690 dB🛁 790 M90—120
Credit cards [1] [2] [3] [5]

★★★**Royal Garden** Kjoepmannsgate 73 ☎521100 tx55060
🛁 297 🏠 **P**20 Lift ☾ sB🛁 405—790 dB🛁 590—980 ▭
Credit cards [1] [2] [5]

★★★***Scandic*** Brøsetveien 186 ☎939500 tx55420

🛁 153 **P**200 Lift ☾ M alc
Credit cards [1] [2] [3] [5]

★★***Larssens*** T-Angellsgt 106 ☎528851

🛁 30 **P**4 Lift ☾
Credit cards [1] [2] [3] [5]

🚗 **Prøven Bil** ☎935540

TURTAGRØ
Sogn-og-Fjordane

★★**Turtagrø** ☎Skjolden 86616

Seasonal
rm29 (🛁4) **P**30 sBfr180 sB🛁 fr210 dBfr300 dB🛁 fr360 Mfr110 mountains

TYIN
Oppland (☎061)

★★★***Tyin Høyfjelshotell*** (**DPn** in winter) ☎37712

Jan—Oct
🛁🚿100 Lift ☾ ≈ mountains lake

TYNSET
Hedmark (☎064)

★★**Tynset** 80600

rm42 (🛁12) **P**40 ☾ sBfr285 sB🛁 fr385 dBfr400 dB🛁 fr485 M alc mountains
Credit cards [1] [2] [3] [5]

ULVIK
Hordaland (☎05)

★★★***Brakanes*** ☎526105 tx42955

1 Mar—20 Dec
🛁 105 🏠 **P**100 Lift ☾ ⛳ Beach ▣ sea
Credit cards [1] [2] [3] [5]

★★***Strand*** ☎526305

May—15 Oct
🛁🚿57 **P**15 ☾ ▭ sea
Credit cards [1] [2] [3] [5]

★★***Ulvik Turist*** ☎26200

Closed Jan
rm63 (🛁🚿51) Lift ☾ sea

★***Bjotvelt*** ☎26300

sea

USTAOSET
Buskerud (☎067)

★***Ustaoset Fjellstue*** ☎87123

15 Jun—Sep
rm26 (🚿7) **P** mountains

UTNE
Hordaland (☎054)

★★**Utne** ☎66983

rm23 (🛁🚿19) A7rm **P**10 ☾ sBfr260 sB🛁🚿fr350 dBfr410 dB🛁🚿fr520 Mfr95
Credit cards [1] [2] [5]

VÅGÅMO
Oppland (☎062)

★★★***Villa*** ☎37071 tx18876

🛁 63 **P** ☾ ≈ mountains

VIKI I SOGN
Sogn-og-Fjordane (☎056)

★★**Hopstock** ☎95102

🛁🚿34 **P**25 ☾ sB🛁🚿345—440 dB🛁🚿510—610 M135&alc ≈ Beach sea
Credit cards [1] [2] [3] [5]

VINSTRA
Oppland (☎062)

★★★**Fefor Høyfjellshotell** ☎90099 tx72849

🛁🚿115 **P**120 Lift ☾ sB🛁🚿345 dB🛁🚿510 M105—125 ⛳ ≈ ▣ U Beach mountains lake
Credit cards [1] [2] [3] [5]

★★**Sødorp Gjestgivengård** ☎91000 tx18601

🛁 27 A12rm **P**100 sB🛁 270—335 dB🛁 350—415 M65—75 mountains
Credit cards [1] [2] [3] [5]

★★***Vinstra*** ☎90199

VOSS
Hordaland (☎05)

★★★**Fleischer's** ☎511155 tx40470

🛁 71 Lift ☾ sB🛁 520—560 dB🛁 690—710 M130 ⛳ ▭
Credit cards [1] [2] [3] [5]

★★★***Park Voss*** ☎511322

🛁 48 🏠 **P** Lift ☾ mountains lake

★★★***Voss*** ☎512006 tx42748

🛁🚿20 **P**30 mountains
Credit cards [1] [3] [5]

★★**Jarl** ☏511933 tx42748

➡ ⋒55 **P**20 Lift ☾ sB ➡ ⋒380—475 dB ➡ ⋒480—750 M60—110 ▭ Credit cards 1 2 3 5

★***Nøring Pensjonat*** ☏511211

➡ 23 **P** M alc mountains lake

Motor Service ☏512700 For Ren

Norway

VRÅDAL
Telemark (☏036)

★★★**Straand** ☏56100 tx21762

➡ 113 A12rm **P**130 Lift ☾ sB ➡ 300—390 dB ➡ 440—600 M125 ▭ Beach U mountains lake
Credit cards 1 2 3 4 5

★★***Vrådal*** 56127

rm70 (➡ ⋒51) **P** Lift ☾ mountains lake

Bergen, part of the old town

Portugal

International distinguishing sign

Area *34,700 sq miles*
Location map *See pages 348 and 349*
Population *10,100,000*
Local time *GMT (Summer GMT + 1)*

National flag *Divided vertically, green in the hoist, red in the fly with the arms of the former monarchy superimposed on the gold armillary in the centre.*

How to get there

The usual approach to Portugal is via France and Spain, entering Spain on the Biarritz to San Sebastian road at the western end of the Pyrénées. The distance from the Channel ports to Lisboa (Lisbon), the capital, is about 1,300 miles, a distance which will require three or four night stops. The driving distance can be shortened by using one of the car-sleeper services from Boulogne or Paris to Biarritz, or Paris to Madrid. Alternatively you can ship your vehicle to Spain by the Plymouth to Santander car ferry, then travel onwards by road. Santander to Lisboa is about 550 miles and this will require one or two night stops.

Motoring regulations and general information

This information should be read in conjunction with the general content of the European ABC (pages 4-26). **Note** As certain regulations and requirements are common to many countries they are covered by one entry in the ABC and the following headings represent some of the subjects dealt with in this way:

AA Agents
Crash or safety helmets
Customs regulations for European countries
Drinking and driving
Fire extinguisher
First-aid kit
Insurance
International distinguishing sign
Medical treatment
Mirrors
Police fines
Radio telephones/Radio transmitters
Road signs
Seat belts
Traffic lights
Tyres
Visitors' registration

Accidents

Fire, police, and **ambulance** Public emergency service ☎ 115. There are no firm rules of procedure after an accident; however, the recommendations under *Accidents* on page 5 are advised.

Accommodation

A list of hotels by regions is available from the Tourist Office in London. Hotels are officially approved and classified by the office of the Secretary of State for Information and Tourism. Details of officially authorised charges and the classification of the hotel must be exhibited in every bedroom. The cost of meals served in bedrooms, other than breakfast, is subject to an increase of 10%. Children under eight years of age are granted a discount of 50% on prices of meals.

While commendations and complaints about hotels are an important source of information to us, members may also like to know that an official complaint book, which must be kept in all establishments, enables guests to record their comments.

Complaints may also be made to local Tourism Delegations and Boards or to the State Tourism Department, Palácio Foz, Praça dos Restaudores, Lisboa. The Government has encouraged the building of well-equipped hotels, particularly in the Algarve region. Tourist inns known as *pousadas* and *estalagens* are controlled by the *Direcçao General de Turismo*, the official Portuguese tourist organisation; details of most of these are included in the gazetteer.

Pousadas are Government-owned but privately run. They have been specially built or converted, and are often located in the more remote touring areas where there is a lack of other hotels. Visitors may not usually stay more than five nights.

Estalagens are small, well-equipped wayside inns (although there are some in towns), privately-owned and run, and normally in the one- or two-star category.

Breakdown

The Portuguese motoring club Automóvel Club de Portugal (ACP) operates a breakdown service and breakdown assistance may be obtained by telephoning Porto 29271 in the north and Lisboa 736121 in the south. See also *Breakdown* page 6 and *Warning triangle* page 338.

Should you break down or need assistance on the Ponte 25 de Abril (on the southern approach to Lisboa), keep the vehicle as near to the right-hand side of the bridge as possible, remain in the vehicle and hang a white handkerchief out of the window. You must wait inside the vehicle until the road patrol arrives. Vehicles must not be towed, except by purpose-built towing vehicles, or pushed by hand on the bridge. If you run out of petrol on the bridge you will be fined *ESc*600 and have to buy 10 litres (2gal 1½pt) of petrol from the bridge authorities at the official price.

British Embassy/Consulates

The British Embassy together with its consular section is located at *1296 Lisboa Cedex* 35-37 Rua de Sao Domingos à Lapa ☏ 661122/47/91. There are British Consulates in Oporto and Portimão. See also page 6 and *Town Plan of Central Lisboa* pages 342-343.

Currency including banking hours

(See also page 9)
The unit of currency is the Escudo (*ESc*) divided into 100 *Centavos*. It is sometimes written with the dollar sign *eg* 1$50 (one escudo fifty centavos). One thousand escudos are known as 1 *Conto*. At the time of going to press £ = *ESc*216.60. Denominations of bank notes are *ESc* 20, 50, 100, 500, 1,000, 5,000; standard coins are *ESc* 1, 2½, 5, 25 and *Centavos* 50. There are no restrictions on the import of foreign currency, but amounts in excess of *ESc*100,000 must be declared on arrival. It is prohibited to import more than *ESc*30,000 in Portuguese currency. Any amount of foreign currency may be exported provided it was declared on entry, but no more than *ESc*30,000 in Portuguese currency may be exported.

Banks are open Monday to Friday from 08.30—11.45hrs and 13.00—14.45hrs. During the summer currency exchange facilities are usually provided throughout the day in main tourist resorts, at frontier posts, airports and in some hotels.

Dimensions and weight restrictions

Private **cars** and towed **trailers** or **caravans** are restricted to the following dimensions — height: 4 metres; width: 2.50 metres; length: 12 metres. The maximum permitted overall length of vehicle/trailer or caravan combination is 18 metres.

There are no weight restrictions governing the temporary importation of trailers into Portugal. However, it is recommended that the following be adhered to — weight (unladen): up to 750kg if the towing vehicle's engine is 2,500cc or less; up to 1,500kg if the towing vehicle's engine is between 2,500cc and 3,500cc; up to 2,500kg if the towing vehicle's engine is more than 3,500cc.

Driving licence

A valid British driving licence is acceptable in Portugal. The minimum age at which a visitor may drive a temporarily imported car or motorcycle (over 50cc) is 17 years. See also page 11 and *Speed limits* page 338.

Emergency messages to tourists

(See also page 11)
Emergency messages to tourists are broadcast all year by Portuguese Radio.

Radiodifusão Portuguesa (RDP1) transmitting on 383 metres and 451 metres medium wave broadcasts these messages in English, French, German, Italian, Portuguese and Spanish every hour during the news Monday to Saturday.

Radiodifusão Portuguesa (RDP2) transmitting on 290 metres and 397 metres medium wave broadcasts the messages as RDP1 above.

Lights

(See also page 14)
The use of full headlights is prohibited in built-up areas.

Motoring club

The **Automovel Club de Portugal** (ACP) which has its headquarters at *Lisboa 1200* rua Rosa Araújo 24 ☏ 563931 has offices in a number of provincial towns. They will assist motoring tourists generally and supply information on touring and other matters. ACP offices are normally open 09.00—12.45 and 13.00—17.00hrs Monday to Friday; English and French are spoken. Offices are closed on Saturday and Sunday. See also page 16 and *Town Plan of Central Lisboa* pages 342-343.

Motorways

About 113 miles of motorway (Auto-Estrada) are open, and more stretches are under construction. A 200 mile network is planned. Tolls are charged on most sections. A leaflet entitled *Motorways in Portugal* is available to AA members.

Orange badge scheme for disabled drivers

(See also page 16)
In Portugal parking places reserved for disabled drivers are indicated by signs displaying the international disabled symbol. However, badge holders are not allowed to park in places where parking is otherwise prohibited.

Overtaking

(See also page 17)
Vehicles more than 2 metres wide must stop, if need be, to facilitate passing.

Parking

(See also page 18)
Parking is forbidden, except where parking signs are displayed, and on a main road outside a built-up area, also on a road carrying fast-moving traffic. At night, parking is prohibited on all roads outside built-up areas. Always park in the direction of the traffic flow except where regulations decree otherwise or where parking is allowed on only one side of the road. Parking lights must be used in badly-lit areas and when visibility is poor. Spending the night in a vehicle by the roadside is not advisable.

Passengers

(See also page 18)
It is recommended that children do not travel in a vehicle as front seat passengers.

Petrol

(See also page 18)
Credit cards Petrol stations do not accept credit cards.
Duty-free petrol In addition to the petrol in the vehicle tank an unlimited quantity in cans may be imported free of customs duty and tax.
Petrol (leaded) Gasolina Normal (85 octane) and Gasolina Super (98 octane) grades.
Petrol (unleaded) is not sold in Portugal.

Postal information

Mail Postcards *ESc*52.50, Letters 5-220gm *ESc*52.50.
Post offices There are 1,045 post offices in Portugal. Opening hours are from 09.00—19.00hrs Monday to Friday, with the smaller offices closing between 12.30—14.00hrs.

Postcheques

(See also page 20)
Postcheques may be cashed at all post offices for any amount up to a maximum of *ESc*13,000 per cheque. Counter positions are identified by the *Postcheque* sign. See *Postal information* for post office opening hours.

Priority

Vehicles on motorways have right of way over all vehicles approaching from the respective slip roads. See also *Priority including Roundabouts* page 21.

Public holidays

Official public holidays in Portugal for 1987 are given below. See also *Public holidays* page 21.
January 1 (New Year's Day)
March 3 (Carnival Day)
April 17 (Good Friday)
April 25 (Revolution Day)
May 1 (Labour Day)
June 10 (Portugal Day)
June 18 (Corpus Christi)
August 15* (Assumption)
October 5† (Republic Day)
November 1† (All Saints' Day)
December 1 (Independence Day)
December 8 (Immaculate Conception)
December 24 (Christmas Eve)
December 25 (Christmas Day)
*Saturday †Sunday

Registration document

If the vehicle is not registered in your name a special certificate is required authorising you to use it. This certificate is available free from the AA. See also page 21.

Roads

Main roads and most of the important secondary roads are good as are the mountain roads of the north-east. A leaflet entitled '*Road conditions in Spain and Portugal*' is available to AA members.

Shopping hours

Shops are usually open Monday to Friday

09.00—13.00hrs and 15.00—19.00hrs and Saturdays 09.00—13.00hrs.

Speed limits

(See also page 22)

The beginning of a built-up area is marked by a sign bearing the placename; there are no signs showing the end — the only indication is the sign for the beginning of the area (on the other side of the road) for motorists coming from the other direction. In built-up areas the limit is 60kph (37mph), or 50kph (31mph) for vehicles towing trailers. Outside built-up areas private vehicles must not exceed 120kph (74mph) on motorways and 90kph (56mph) on other roads; private vehicles towing trailers must not exceed 90kph (56mph) on motorways and 70kph (43mph) on other roads. There is a minimum speed limit of 40kph (24mph) on motorways, except where otherwise signposted.

Visitors to Portugal who have held a full driving licence for less than one year are restricted to driving at a top speed of 90kph (56mph). They must also display a yellow disc bearing the figure '90' at the rear of their vehicle (obtainable from ACP frontier office at Valenca, Vilar Formoso and Caia). Leaflets giving details in English are handed to visitors at entry points.

Spiked or studded tyres

The use of *spiked tyres* is prohibited in Portugal. See also *Cold weather touring* page 8.

Toll bridges

Lisbon Tagus Bridge	*ESc*
Cars	65
Cars with caravans/trailers	110-150
Motorcycles — over 50cc	30
under 50cc not permitted	

Pedestrians, bicycles, and bicycles with auxiliary motors of less than 50cc, are prohibited. Drivers must maintain a speed of 40—70kph (24—43mph) on the bridge. Speed is checked by radar. Heavy vehicles must keep at least 20 metres (66ft) behind the preceding vehicle. Toll payable in one direction only, when travelling from Lisbon to the south. There are no charges for vehicles travelling northbound, into Lisbon.

Tourist Information

(See also page 24)

The Portuguese National Tourist Office, New Bond Street House, 1/5 New Bond Street (above National Westminster Bank, entrance in Burlington Gardens opposite Burlington Arcade), London W1Y 0NP ☎ 01-493 3873, will be pleased to assist you with information regarding tourism. There is an office of the Direccão Geral de Turismo in Lisboa and local information offices will be found in most provincial towns under this name or one of the following; Comissão Municipal de Turismo, Junta de Turismo or Cãmara Municipal.

Using the telephone

(See also page 24)

Insert coin **after** lifting receiver, dialling tone same as UK. When making calls to subscribers within Portugal precede number with relevant area code as necessary (shown in parentheses against town entry in gazetteer). Use *ESc*2.50 or *ESc*5 coins for local calls and *ESc*25 for national and international calls.

International callbox identification Selected boxes in Lisbon and Porto.

Telephone rates Calls to the UK cost *ESc*7.50 per 2.8 seconds. Local calls cost *ESc*5.50.

*What to dial for Irish Republic** 00 353.

*What to dial for the UK** 00 44.

*or see local instructions.

Visas

(See also page 25)

Visitors wishing to stay in Portugal for more than 60 days must either obtain a visa or pay a fine of *ESc*750 when leaving the country.

Warning triangle

The use of a warning triangle is compulsory for all vehicles except two-wheeled vehicles. The triangle must be placed on the road 30 metres (33yds) behind the vehicle and must be clearly visible from 100 metres (109yds). See also *Warning triangles/Hazard warning lights* page 25.

Wheel chains

The use of wheel chains is permitted when weather conditions make them necessary. See also *Cold weather touring* page 8.

Prices are in Portuguese Escudos. According to our information garages with no specific service agencies will handle any make of car.

Abbreviations:

av avenida
Capt Capitão
esp esplanada
Gen General
r rua

ABRANTES
Ribatejo (☎041)

★★★**Turismo** Largo de Santo António ☎21261 tx43626
42 **P**100 ☾ sB 3520–4220 dB 4640–5440 M1400 mountains lake
Credit cards 1 2 3 4 5

A Ferreira r Brito Capelo 482 ☎129 AR

Sosepor Largo de Chafariz ☎22127 Cit

AGUEDA
Costa de Prata (☎034)

At **SEREM** (11km N)

★★**Pousada San Antonio** ☎521230 tx37150
12 **P**18 sB 2700–5900 dB 3600–6850 M1300–2100 mountains
Credit cards 1 2 3 5

ALBERGARIA A VELHA
Beira Litoral (☎034)

★**Alameda** Estrada Naciónal 1 ☎521402
18 **P**20 ☾ sB 1160–1560 dB 2070–2720 M600–1500 mountains

ALBUFEIRA
Algarve (☎089)

★★★★★***Balaia*** (SRS) Praia M-Luisa ☎52681 tx56278
193 **P**150 Lift ☾ Beach sea

★★★**Sol Marr** J-Bernardino de Sousa ☎52121 tx56217
74 A10rm Lift ☾ sB 3350–7550 dB 4900–8700 Mfr1450 sea
Credit cards 1 2 3 5

★★**Estalagem do Cerro** r B-Cerro da Piedade ☎52191 tx56211
83 Lift ☾ sB 3300-6400 dB 4600–9300 M1500–2000&alc sea

★★***Estalagem Mar á Vista*** Cerro da Piedade ☎52154
29 Lift

ALCÁCER DO SAL
Baixo Alentejo (☎065)

★★**Estalagem da Berrosinha** Estrada Naciónal 5 ☎62363
rm10 (9) **P** mountains

ALJCOBAÇA
Estremadura (☎044)

T Marques Praça 25 de Abril 48 ☎42175 AR

Portugal

ALPEDRINHA
Beira Baize (☎052)

★**Estalagem São Jorge** ☎57154
Closed Oct
rm12 (10) ☾ sB1600–1800 sB 1600–1800 dB2700–3000 dB 2700–3000 M600–700
Credit cards 1 2 3 5

AMARANTE
Douro Litoral (☎055)

At **SERRA DO MARÃO** (25km E on N15 to Vila Real)

★**Pousada de São Gonçalo** ☎461113 tx26321
15 **P**16 ☾ sB 3030–6400 dB 4260–7850 M1300–2100 mountains
Credit cards 1 2 3 4 5

ARMAÇÃO DE PÊRA
Algarve (☎082)

★★★***Estalagem Algar*** av Beira-Mar ☎32353
Mar—Oct
19

★★★**Garbe** av Marginal ☎32188 tx57485
109 **P** Lift ☾ sB 3900–8000 dB 4600–8900 M1500–2000 sea mountains
Credit cards 1 3

AVEIRO
Beira Litoral (☎034)

★★**Arcada** r Viana do Castelo 4 (n.rest) ☎23001 tx37460
52 Lift ☾ sB 1900–3200 dB 2900–4200
Credit cards 1 2 3 4 5

Riauto av 5 de Outubro 18 ☎22031 AR

AZEITÃO
Estremadura

★**Estalagem Quintas das Torres** Quinta das Torres ☎2080001
13 A2rm **P** sB 3075 dB 4830 mountains

BARCELOS
Minho (☎053)

Castro r F-Borges ☎82008 AR

BEJA
Baixo Alentejo (☎084)

Acall av M-Fernandes 27 ☎22191 AR BMW

J Pinto Caeiro av de Boavista 1 & 7 ☎23031 For

BRAGA
Minho (☎053)

Ranhada & Taixeira Largo 1 de Dezembro 20 ☎22912 For

BRAGANÇA
Tras-Os-Montes Alto Douro (☎0503)

★★***Pousada de São Bartolomeu*** Estrada de Turismo ☎22493
12 **P** mountains

Chamauto r A-Herculano ☎22478 Dat

CALDAS DA RAINHA
Estremadura (☎062)

★***Central*** Largo do Dr J-Barbosa 22 (n.rest) ☎22078
rm40 (9) **P** ☾

Auto-Leiria r Capt Filipe de Sousa 89 ☎22561

Auto-Mechânica das Caldas r P-Proença ☎22947 Cit

CANAS DE SENHORIM
Beira Atla (☎032)

At **URGEIRÇA** (1km NE on N234)

★★★**Urgeiriça** ☎67267 tx53535
53 **P**200 ☾ sB 2200–2800 dB 3100–3700 M800–900 mountains
Credit cards 1 2 3 5

CANIÇADA
Minho

★★**Pousada de São Bento** Cerdeirinhas-Soengas ☎57190 tx32339
20 A8rm **P**25 ☾ sB 5250–9350 dB 5600–9750 M1400–2200 mountains lake
Credit cards 1 2 3 4 5

CARCAVELOS
Estremadura (☎01)

★★★**Praia-Mar** r do Gurué 16 ☎2473131 tx42283
158 **P**10 Lift ☾ sB 5100–5600 dB 6000–6700 Mfr1700 sea
Credit cards 1 2 3 5

CASCAIS
Estremadura (☎01)

★★★★★**Estoril Sol** Estrada Marginal ☎282831 tx15102
400 **P**120 Lift ☾ sB 10500–11600 dB 11800–13500 M2500 sea
Credit cards 1 2 3 4 5

★★★**Baia** Estrada Marginal ☎281033 tx43468
87 Lift ☾ sB 2050–4800 dB 3100–6600 M1100 sea
Credit cards 1 2 3 5

★★★***Estalagem Albatroz*** r F-Aronca 100–102 ☎282821 tx16052
40 **P** Lift ☾ sea

★★★***Nau*** r Dr Iracy Doyle Lote 14 ☎282861 tx42289
56 Lift sea mountains
Credit cards 1 2 3 5

★★***Estalagem Solar do Carios*** r Latino Coelho 8 ☎2868463
rm8

J Jorge av E-Navarro 32 ☎280112

Reparadora de Cascais r das Amendoeiras-Torre ☎289045 AR

At **PRAIA DO GUINCHO** (4km W)

★★★★**Guincho** ☎2850491 tx43138

🛁 39 A3rm Lift ☾ sB🛁 6400—10000 dB🛁 9300—14550 M2600 ▣ sea mountains
Credit cards [1] [2] [3] [5]

★★**Estalagem Mar do Guincho** Praia do Guincho ☎2850251

🛁 13 A1rm **P**30 ☾ dB🛁 3000—5100 M900—1500 sea
Credit cards [1] [2] [3] [4] [5]

CASTELO BRANCO
Beira Baixa (☎072)

🚗 **Avenida de Castelo Branco** av Gen H-Delgado 75—79 ☎421 AR

🚗 **S Cristóvão** av Gen H-Delgado ☎283

CASTELO DO BODE See **TOMAR**

CHAVES
Tras-Os-Montes Alto Douro (☎0506)

★★***Estalagem Santiago*** r do Olival (n.rest) ☎22545

🛁 31

Império de Chaves av 5 de Outubro ☎22133 Dat

COIMBRA
Beira Litoral (☎039)

★★★***Bragança*** Largo das Ameias 10 ☎22171

🛁 83 **P**9 Lift ☾
Credit cards [1] [3]

Brinca & Morais r do Arnadod 19—21 ☎29096 Dat

P Irmãos r de Sofia 171 ☎25493 For

S José av Fernão de Magalhães 216 ☎25578 AR

COLARES
Estremadura (☎01)

★**Estalagem do Conde** Quinta do Conde ☎2991652

Closed Nov—Dec
🛁 10 **P**20 sB🛁 3500—4000 dB🛁 4000—4500 M1000—1200 mountains
Credit cards [1] [3] [4]

At **PRAIA DAS MACÁS** (4km NW by N375)

★★★**Miramonte** ☎9291230 tx13221

🛁 89 **P**8 ☾ dB🛁 6600 M1500 ≋ mountains

COSTA DA CAPARICA
Estremadura (☎01)

★★**Estalagem Colobri** ☎2900776

🛁 🚿 25 **P** Lift sea mountains
Credit cards [1] [2] [3]

COVILHÃ
Beira Baixa (☎075)

Auto Representações de Covilhã Largo das Forças Armadas ☎22048 Cit

---

CURIA
Beira Litoral (☎031)

★★★**Palace** ☎52131

Portugal

15 Apr—15 Oct
🛁 125 **P**70 Lift ☾ sB🛁 4100—5000 dB🛁 5500—6000 Mfr1600 ⛳ ≋

ELVAS
Alto Alentejo (☎068)

★★**Estalagem D Sancho II** Praça da Sancho II ☎62684

🛁 🚿 26 Lift ☾ sB🛁 🚿 2300—3000 dB🛁 🚿 3450—4400 Malc
Credit cards [1] [2] [3] [4] [5]

★**Pousada de Santa Luzia** (outside town on Borba-Badajoz road) ☎62194 tx12469

rm11 (🛁 🚿 9) **P**50 ☾ sB🛁 🚿 fr6350 dB🛁 🚿 fr7750 Mfr2000
Credit cards [1] [2] [3] [4] [5]

Antunes & Guerra av de Badajoz ☎170

ERICEIRA
Estremadura (☎061)

★★**Estalagem Morais** r M-Bombarda 3 (n.rest) ☎62611 tx44938

1 Dec—31 Oct
🛁 40 Lift ☾ sB🛁 1170—1950 dB🛁 1750—4150 ≋ ▣ sea
Credit cards [1] [2] [3] [4] [5]

ESPINHO
Douro Litoral (☎02)

★★★**Praia Golfe** r 6 ☎721630 tx23727

🛁 119 **P**20 Lift ☾ sB🛁 4800 dB🛁 6200 M1400—1800 ⛳ ≋ ▣ ▣ U sea
Credit cards [1] [2] [4] [5]

ESPOSENDE
Minho (☎053)

★★**Suave-Mar** av E-Duarto Pacheco ☎961445 tx32362

🛁 🚿 59 **P**25 ☾ sB🛁 🚿 3000 dB🛁 🚿 5000 Malc ⛳ ≋ sea mountains
Credit cards [1] [3]

ESTORIL
Estremadura (☎01)

★★★★★**Palacio Estoril** Parque Estoril ☎2680400 tx12757

🛁 167 **P**100 Lift ☾ sB🛁 8000—14000 dB🛁 9500—15000 Malc ≋ ▣ sea
Credit cards [1] [2] [3] [4] [5]

★★★★**Cibra** ☎2681811 tx16007

🛁 85 A7rm Lift ☾ sB🛁 5800 dB🛁 7500 M1150 ⛳ sea
Credit cards [2] [3]

★★**Founder's Inn (Albergaria do Fundador)** r D-A-Henriques 161 ☎2682221

🛁 7 **P**5 sB🛁 3200—4700 dB🛁 3900—6400 ≋ sea mountains
Credit cards [1] [2] [3] [5]

ESTREMOZ
Alto Alentejo (☎068)

★★★**Pousada Rainha Santa Isabel** Castelo de Estremoz ☎22618 tx43885

🛁 23 **P**16 Lift ☾ sB🛁 8900—10900 dB🛁 10750—12800 M1750—2500
Credit cards [1] [2] [3] [4] [5]

Ago Comercial Estremoz av de Santo António, Estrada Nacional 4 & Rossió Marquês de Pombal 33 ☎22215 Cit

---

ÉVORA
Alto Altentejo (☎066)

★★★★**Pousada dos Lois** ☎24051 tx43288

🛁 32 ☾ sB🛁 9000—11000 dB🛁 10500—13000 M2000—2600
Credit cards [1] [2] [3] [5]

★★★**Planicle** r M-Bombarda 40 ☎24026 tx13500

🛁 33 **P** Lift ☾ sB🛁 3310—3700 dB🛁 4220—4800 M1200—1400
Credit cards [1] [2] [3] [4] [5]

R Cruz r do Raimundo 99C ☎24096 Cit

FARO
Algarve (☎089)

★★★★***Eva*** av da República ☎24054 tx56524

🛁 🚿 150 Lift ☾ ≋ sea
Credit cards [1] [2] [3] [5]

★★★**Faro** Praça D F-Gomes 2 ☎22076 tx56108

🛁 🚿 52 Lift ☾ sB🛁 🚿 3900—6350 dB🛁 🚿 3400—6800 M1200 lake
Credit cards [1] [2] [3] [5]

★★**Albacor** r Brites de Almeida 25 (n.rest) ☎22093

🛁 🚿 38 **P**50 Lift ☾ sB🛁 🚿 2250—3825 dB🛁 🚿 2900—4000 sea mountains
Credit cards [1] [2] [3] [5]

A Baptista r do Alportel 121A ☎23071 Cit

FIAAL Largo do Mercado 2—6 ☎23061 For Vol

At **PRAIA DE FARO** (8km SW)

★★***Estalagem Aeromar*** ☎23542

Feb—Nov
🛁 20

FÁTIMA
Beira Litoral (☎049)

★★★**Fatima** r Jacinta Marto ☎52351 tx43750

🛁 76 **P** Lift ☾ sB🛁 3000 dB🛁 4500 M1200
Credit cards [1] [2] [3] [5]

★★**Trés Pastorinhas** Cova da Iria ☎52429

🛁 92 **P** Lift ☾ sB🛁 2400 dB🛁 3700 M270—800
Credit cards [1] [2] [3] [4] [5]

FIGUEIRA DA FOZ
Beira Litoral (☎033)

★★★★**Figueira** av 25 de Abril ☎22146 tx53086

🛁 91 Lift ☾ sB🛁 2350—4150 dB🛁 3600—6800 Mfr1300 ≋ sea
Credit cards [1] [2] [3] [4] [5]

FUNDÁO
Beira Baixa (☏075)

Industrias do Fundão Estrada Nacional 18 ☏52375

GUARDA
Beira Alta (☏071)

★★★***Turismo*** Largo de São Francisco ☏22206 tx18760
105 P Lift ☾ mountains

★★**Alicança** r V-da-Gama ☏22135
rm31 (16) P34 sB1200 sB 1580 dB1740 dB 2520 Malc
Credit cards 2 3

★★***Filipe*** r V-de-Gama 9 ☏22659
rm25 (7) Lift ☾ mountains

Auto Neofor r 31 de Janeiro 20 ☏21348 For

D José r Batalha Reis 2 ☏22947 Cit

GUIMARAES
Costa Verde (☏53)

★★**Pousada Sta Maria Oliveira** Largo de Oliveria ☏412157 tx32875
16 P10 Lift ☾ sB 4060—8260 dB 5620—9670 M2000—2300
Credit cards 1 2 3 5

LAGOS
Algarve (☏082)

★★★***Meaia Praia*** Meia Praia (4km NE) ☏62001 tx57497
Apr—Oct
66 P Lift ☾ sea
Credit cards 1 2 3 4 5

★★***Pensão Dona Ana*** Praia de Dona Ana ☏62322
Apr—Oct
rm11 (5)

★★**Residential Mar Azul** r 25 de Abril 13 (n.rest) ☏62181
rm18 (14) ☾ sB1050—1650 sB 1350—2800 dB1650—2500 dB 1750—3100 sea
Credit cards 1 3

LECA DO BALIO
Douro Litoral

★★★**Estalagem via Norte** Estrada via Norte ☏9480294 tx26617
12 P20 ☾ sB 4790 dB 5880 M1300
Credit cards 1 2 3 5

LEIRIA
Beira Litoral (☏044)

★★★**Euro Sol** r D J-Alves da Silva (n.rest) ☏24109 tx42031
92 P70 Lift ☾ sB 3300 dB 5400 M1150 mountains
Credit cards 1 2 3 4 5

Auto-Leiria r Machado Santos 10B ☏24191 For

Lubrigaz r Capt Mousinho Albuquerque 38—42 ☏22135

Portugal

LISBOA (LISBON)
Estremadura (☏01)

See plan pages 342 and 343

★★★★★**Ritz** (Intercont) r R-da-Fonseca 88A ☏684146 tx12589 Plan **1**
300 P100 Lift ☾ sB 13500—17000 dB 16500—21000 Malc
Credit cards 1 2 3 4 5

★★★★★**Sheraton** r L-Coelho 1 ☏575757 tx12774 Plan **1A**
400 P Lift ☾ sB 12000—16000 dB 15000—19000
Credit cards 1 2 3 4 5

★★★★**Avenida Palace** r 1 de Dezembro 123 ☏360151 tx12815 Plan **2**
96 P Lift sB 5500—10000 dB 7000—12000 Malc

★★★★**Eduardo VII** av Fontes Pereira de Mello 5 ☏530141 tx18340 Plan **3**
111 Lift ☾ sB 4300—5400 dB 5200—6800 M1400—1700
Credit cards 1 2 3 4 5

★★★★***Fénix*** Praça Marques de Pombal 8 ☏535121 tx12170 Plan **4**
117 Lift ☾ Malc
Credit cards 1 2 3 5

★★★★**Florida** (ETAP) r Duque de Palmela 32 ☏567145 tx12256 Plan **5**
120 Lift ☾ sB 4800—5500 dB 5900—6900
Credit cards 1 2 3 4 5

★★★★**Mundial** r D-Duarte 4 ☏863101 tx12308 Plan **6**
147 P60 Lift ☾ sB 6100 dB 7500 M1600
Credit cards 1 2 3 5

★★★★**Novotel Lisboa** av J-Malhoa 1642 ☏7262610 Not on plan
246 Lift ☾ sB 7300—9200 dB 9100—11400 M1950

★★★★**Plaza** Travessa do Salitre 7 (Off av da Liberdade) ☏363922 tx16402 Plan **7**
100 P30 Lift ☾ sB 6500—7500 dB 7500—9000 M1600
Credit cards 1 2 3 4 5

★★★★**Tivoli** (SRS) av da Liberdade 185 ☏530181 tx12588 Plan **8**
342 P200 Lift ☾ sB fr9982 dB 12449 Mfr2170
Credit cards 1 2 3 5

★★★**Flamingo** (GT) r Castilho 41 ☏532191 tx14736 Plan **9**
39 Lift ☾ sB 5300—7300 dB 5900—7900 M1500
Credit cards 1 2 3 5

★★★**Miraparque** av Sidonio Pais 12 ☏578070 tx16745 Plan **9A**
100 P Lift ☾ sB 3850—4150 dB 4800—5500 Mfr1300

★★★**Torre** r dos Jeronimos 8 ☏636262 Plan **10**
49 Lift ☾ sB 2840 dB 4280 M850 sea
Credit cards 1 2 3 4 5

★★**Borges** r Garrett 108 ☏361951 tx15825 Plan **12**
100 P Lift ☾ sB 3050 dB 4200 M700
Credit cards 1 2 3 4

★★***Jorge V*** r Mouzinho da Silveira 3 ☏562525 Plan **13**
52 P Lift ☾

★★**Principe** av Duque d'Avila 201 ☏536151 tx43565 Plan **15**
67 P25 Lift ☾ sB 3250—4250 dB 4000—5500 M1050
Credit cards 1 2 3 4 5

Auto Montes Claros av Marconi 6A ☏801066

Auto Palma Estrada das Larenjeira 196—198 ☏786914

Auto Rail r C-Mardel 12 ☏562061 For

Fernandes & Santos av Duque de Loulè 56 ☏42807

Flamingo r L-Cordeiro 4A ☏534627

Sorel r F-Folque 12A ☏563441 Cit

LUSO
Beira Litoral (☏031)

★★★★**Termas** r dos Banhos ☏93450 tx53042
Apr—Nov
157 P100 Lift ☾ sB 4145—4745 dB 5490—6190 M1600 mountains lake
Credit cards 1 3

MACEDO DE CAVALAIEROS
Tras-Os-Montes Alto Douro (☏0508)

★**Estalagem Caçador** Largo Pinto de Azevedo ☏42354
25 Lift ☾ sB 3115—3685 dB 6610 M1350

MANGUALDE
Beira Alta (☏032)

★★***Estalagem Cruz de Mata*** Estrada Nacional ☏62556
13

MANTEIGAS
Beira Alta (☏075)

★★**Pousada de São Laurenco** (13km N on road to Gouveia) ☏47150 tx53992
14 P sB 2700—5900 dB 3600—6850 M1300—2100 mountains
Credit cards 1 2 3 4 5

MIRANDA DO DOURO
Tras-Os-Montes Alto Douro (☏0503)

★★***Pousada de Santa Catarina*** ☏42255
12 P

MONTE GORDO
Algarve (☏081)

★★★**Das Caravelas** r Diogo Cão ☏44458 tx56020 →

LISBOA (LISBON)

1	★★★★★	Ritz
1A	★★★★★	Sheraton
2	★★★★	Avenida Palace
3	★★★★	Eduardo VII
4	★★★★	Fénix
5	★★★★	Florida
6	★★★★	Mundial
7	★★★★	Plaza
8	★★★★	Tivoli
9	★★★	Flamingo
9A	★★★	Miraparque
10	★★★	Torre
12	★★	Borges
13	★★	Jorge V
15	★★	Principe

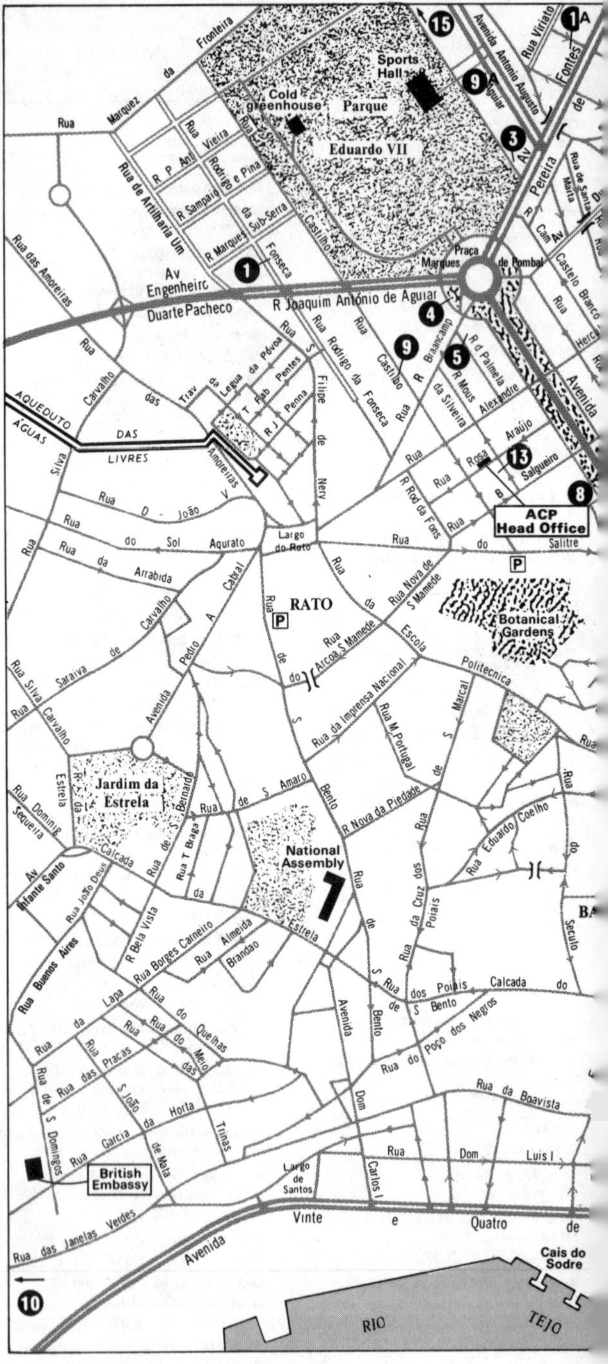

🛁 🚿84 **P**20 Lift ☾ sB 🛁 🚿1620–2600 dB 🛁 🚿2550–4200 M1700 ✂ ⛱ Beach sea
Credit cards [1] [2] [3] [4] [5]

★★★***Dos Navegadores*** r Gancaiso Velho ☏42490 tx56054
🛁 103 Lift ☾ ⛱ sea

★★★**Vasco da Gama** av Infante D-Henrique ☏44321 tx56020
🛁 170 **P**50 Lift ☾ sB 🛁 3070–5070 dB 🛁 5420–11000 M1870 ✂ ⛱ Beach sea
Credit cards [1] [2] [3] [5]

MONTES DE ALVOR See **PORTIMÃO**

NAZARÉ
Estremadura (☏062)

★★★**Dom Fuas** Estrada Dom Fuas ☏51351 tx13889
🛁 40 **P**20 Lift ☾ sB 🛁 2500–3000 dB 🛁 3500–4000 Mfr1000 sea mountains
Credit cards [1] [2] [5]

★★★**Nazaré** Largo A-Zuquete ☏51311 tx16116
🛁 52 **P** Lift ☾ sB 🛁 2900 dB 🛁 4060 M1090 sea
Credit cards [1] [2] [3] [4] [5]

★★★**Praia** av V-Guimaraes 39 (n.rest) ☏51423 tx16329
Closed Dec
🛁 40 🏠 Lift ☾ sB 🛁 3000–5000 dB 🛁 3600–5600 sea mountains
Credit cards [1] [2] [3] [4] [5]

ÓBIDOS
Estremadura (☏062)

★★**Estalagem do Convento** r Dr-J-de-Ornelas ☏95217 tx44906
🛁 23 **P**30 ☾ sB 🛁 3600–5100 dB 🛁 3900–5400 M1100–1750 mountains
Credit cards [1] [3]

★**Pousada do Castelo** (on the Caldas da Rainhatorres Vedras-Lisbon rd) ☏95105 tx15540
🛁 9 ☾ sB 🛁 5650–11000 dB 🛁 7800–13000 M1650–2600
Credit cards [1] [2] [3] [5]

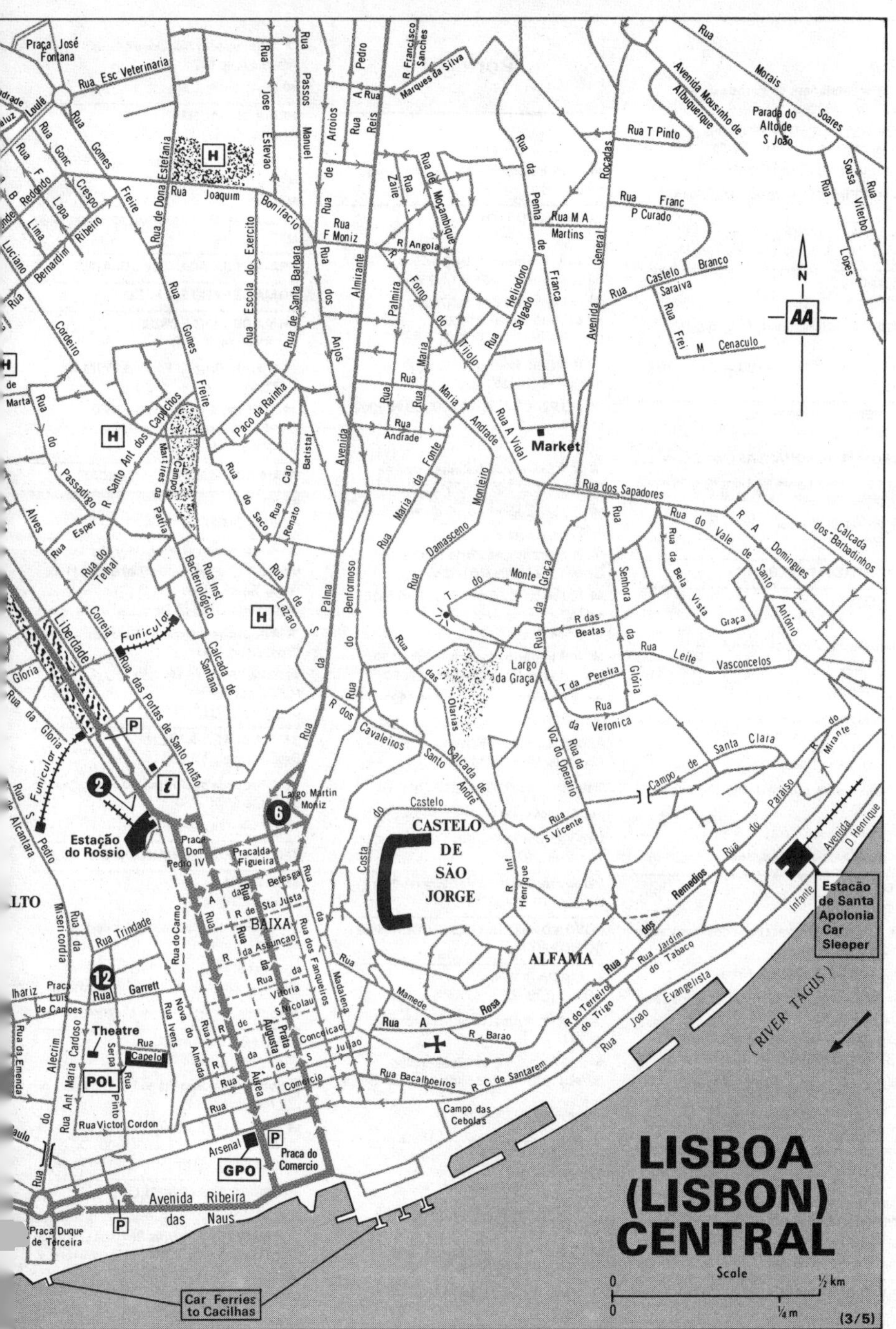
LISBOA
(LISBON)
CENTRAL
Scale
0
½ km
0
¼ m
(3/5)
N
AA
CASTELO
DE
SÃO
JORGE
ALFAMA
BAIXA
Estação
do Rossio
Estacão
de Santa
Apolonia
Car
Sleeper
Car Ferries
to Cacilhas
GPO
POL
Theatre
Market
Praca do
Comercio
Arsenal
Praca Duque
de Terceira
Avenida Ribeira
das Naus
(RIVER TAGUS)
Largo Martin
Moniz
Largo
da Graça
Praca José
Fontana
Rua Esc Veterinaria
Rua dos Sapadores
Rua do Vale de Santo António
Calcada
dos Barbadinhos
Funicular
Liberdade
Rua das Portas de Santo Antão
Rua Bacalhoeiros
R C de Santarem
Rua Jardim
do Tabaco
Rua Joao Evangelista
Campo das
Cebolas
Rua Trindade
Rua Garrett
Praca
Luis
de Camoes
Rua Victor Cordon
Rua Ivens
Rua Nova do Almada
Rua do Carmo
Rua Augusta
Rua Prata
Rua dos Fanqueiros
Rua Áurea
Rua do Comercio
Rua da Madalena
Rua Conceicao
Rua S Julião
Praca
Dom
Pedro IV
Pracalda
Figueira
Rua Betesga
R de Sta Justa
R da Assuncao
Rua da Vitoria
Rua S Nicolau
Rua Capelo
Rua Serpa Pinto
Rua Ant Maria Cardoso
Rua Alecrim
Rua da Emenda
Rua da Misericordia
Rua S Pedro de Alcantara
Rua da Gloria
Rua Mamede
Rua A Rosa
R Barao
Rua Remedios
Rua dos Remedios
R do Terreiro
do Trigo
Avenida Infante D Henrique
Rua do Paraiso
R do Mirante
Campo de Santa Clara
Rua S Vicente
R Inf Henrique
Costa do Castelo
Rua da Voz do Operario
Rua da Veronica
T da Pereira
Rua da Glória
Rua Leite Vasconcelos
R das Beatas
Rua da Senhora da Glória
Rua da Penha de Franca
Rua da Graça
Rua da Beta Vista Graça
R A Domingues
Rua do Monte
Rua Damasceno Monteiro
Rua das Olarias
Calcada de Santo André
R dos Cavaleiros
Rua da Palma
Rua do Benformoso
Avenida Almirante Reis
Rua Maria Andrade
Rua Maria da Fonte
Rua A Vidal
Rua Andrade
Rua Heliodoro Salgado
Rua Forno do Tijolo
Rua Palmira
R Angola
Rua de Moçambique
Rua Zaire
Rua F Moniz
Rua dos Anjos
Rua de Arroios
Rua A Pedro
Rua A Reis
R Francisco Sanches
Marques da Silva
Rua Passos Manuel
Rua Jose Estevão
Rua de Dona Estefania
Rua Joaquim Bonifacio
Rua Escola do Exercito
Rua de Santa Barbara
Rua Gomes Freire
Rua Paco da Rainha
Rua Cap Renato Batista
Rua do Saco
Rua de S Lazaro
Rua Inst Bacteriológico
Calcada de Santana
Campo Martires da Patria
R Santo Ant dos Capuchos
Rua do Passadigo
Rua Esper
Rua do Telhal
Rua Alves Correia
Rua Cordeiro
Rua Bernardim Ribeiro
Rua Luciano
Rua Gomes Freire
Rua Crespo
Rua Lapa
Rua Gonc
Rua F Redondo
Loulé
Rua T Pinto
Avenida Mousinho de Albuquerque
Rua Morais Soares
Parada do
Alto de
S João
Rua Sousa Viterbo
Rua Lopes
Rua Franc
P Curado
Rua Castelo Branco
Saraiva
Rua Frei
M Cenaculo
Avenida General Rocadas
Rua M A
Martins
Rua da Penha de Franca
ALTO

Portugal

OFIR
Minho

★★★**Estalagem do Parque do Rio** ☎961521 tx32066

🛁36 **P**50 Lift ☾ sB🛁2520—3590 dB🛁3910—5680 M1180 🎾 ≈
Credit cards [1] [2] [3] [4] [5]

★★★**Pinhal** Estrada do Mar ☎961473 tx32857

🛁🚿90 Lift sB🛁🚿1500—8125 dB🛁🚿1875—8750 M1000—1250 🎾 ≈

OLHÃO
Algarve

★**Ria-Sol** r Gl-Humberto Delgado, 37 ☎72167 tx56923

🛁53 sB🛁2000—2700 dB🛁3000—3800 sea

OLIVEIRA DO HOSPITAL
Beira Alta (☎038)

At **POVOA DAS QUARTAS** (7km E on N17)

★★**Pousada Santa Bàrbara** ☎52252 tx53794

🛁16 🚗 **P**80 ☾ sB🛁4500—6700 dB🛁5900—8950 M1500—2300 mountains

OPORTO See **PORTO**

PAREDES
Douro Litoral

Ruão Serpa Pinto ☎22164 AR

PENAFIEL
Douro Litoral

Egas Moniz av Egas Moniz 155 ☎22032 Vol

PORTALEGRE
Alto Alentejo (☎045)

★***Alto Alentejo*** 19 de Junho 59 (n.rest) ☎22290

rm15 (🛁10) ☾

🚗 **Auto-Portalegre** r de Maio 94 ☎23540

PORTIMÃO
Algarve (☎082)

★★★★***Alvor Praia*** Praia dos Tres Irmaos ☎24021 tx57399

🛁241 **P** Lift ☾ ≈ Beach sea

★★**Miradoiro** r Machado dos Santos 13 (n.rest) ☎23011

🛁26 **P** ☾ sB🛁1650—3600 dB🛁2100—3900

★***Estalagem Mira-Foia*** r V-Vaz das Vacas 33 ☎22011

🛁23 Lift

J F C Alexandre av D-A-Henriques AR

At **MONTES DE ALVOR** (5km W on N125)

★★★★***Penina Golf*** Montes de Alvor ☎22051 tx57307

🛁209 **P** Lift ☾ 🎾 ≈ ⛳ mountains
Credit cards [2] [3] [5]

PORTINHO DA ARRÁBIDA
Estremadura (☎01)

★★**Residencia de Santa Maria de Arrábida** (n.rest) ☎2080527

Apr—Sep
🛁33 🚗 **P**60 ☾ dB🛁3750—4675 sea mountains

PORTO (OPORTO)
Douro Litoral (☎02)

★★★★**Infante de Sagres** Praça Filipa de Lencastre 62 ☎28101 tx26880

🛁84 Lift ☾ sB🛁6600—7900 dB🛁7100—8500 M1900
Credit cards [1] [2] [3] [4] [5]

★★★**Dom Henrique** r Guedes de Azevedo ☎25755 tx22554

🛁113 **P**20 Lift ☾ sB🛁8000 dB🛁9000 M1400
Credit cards [1] [2] [3] [5]

★★★**Grande da Batalha** Praça da Batalha 116 ☎20571 tx25131

🛁150 Lift ☾ sB🛁fr5100 dB🛁fr6000 Malc

★★★**Grande do Porto** r da Santa Catarina 197 ☎28176 tx22553

🛁100 🚗 Lift ☾ sB🛁4700 dB🛁5850 M1250
Credit cards [1] [2] [3] [5]

★★★**Império** Praça da Batalha 130 (off r São Lidefosa) ☎26861 tx26060

🛁95 sB🛁2800—3300 dB🛁3500—4000 M1500

Almerindo F de A-Ferreira av dos Combatentes 627 ☎485258

Batalha r A-Herculano ☎23024 Vol

Filinto Mota r do Godim ☎562202 Cit

Lab-Vitorino Fer da Silva r Nau Trindade 154 ☎482782

Pereira de Castro & Ferreira r Antero Quental 591 ☎480759

POVOA DAS QUARTAS See **OLIVEIRA DO HOSPITAL**

PRAIA DA ROCHA
Algarve (☎082)

★★★★★**Algarve** at T-Cabreira ☎24001 tx57347

🛁220 **P** Lift ☾ sB🛁9765—12586 dB🛁11935—14105 Mfr2604 🎾 ≈ Beach sea
Credit cards [1] [2] [3] [5]

★★★***Estalagem Mira Sol*** r E-F-Bivar ☎24046

rm38

★★***Belavista*** av T-Cabreira (n.rest) ☎24055 tx57395

🛁27 A10rm **P** ☾ sea
Credit cards [1] [2] [3] [4] [5]

★★***Estalagem Alcaia*** av Marginal ☎24062

🛁20 sea

★★***Estalagem São José*** r A-de-Albuquerque ☎24037

🛁25 A14rm **P** ☾ sea

PRAIA DA SALEMA
Algarve (☎082)

★★**Estalagem Infante do Mar** ☎65137 tx57451

Mar—Oct
🛁30 sB🛁3000—4680 dB🛁3600—5280 M850 ≈ sea

PRAIA DAS MACÀS See **COLARES**

PRAIA DE FARO See **FARO**

PRAIA DE SANTA CRUZ
Estremadura (☎063)

★★**Santa Cruz** r J-P Lopes ☎97148 tx42509

🛁32 **P**5 Lift ☾ sB🛁1250—3050 dB🛁2000—4000 M700—1000
Credit cards [1] [2] [3] [5]

PRAIA DO GUINCHO See **CASCAIS**

SAGRES
Algarve (☎082)

★★★**Baleeira** ☎64212 tx57467

🛁118 **P** ☾ sB🛁4200 dB🛁5400 M1200 🎾 ≈ Beach U sea
Credit cards [1] [2] [3] [5]

★★**Pousada do Infante** Ponta da Atalaia ☎64222 tx57491

🛁23 🚗 **P**50 ☾ sB🛁10500 dB🛁12000 M2500 sea
Credit cards [1] [2] [3] [4] [5]

SANTA CLARA-A-VELHA
Baixo Alentejo (☎083)

★★***Pousada de Santa Clara*** Barragem de Santa Clara ☎52250

🛁6 **P** ≈ mountains lake

SANTA LUZIA See **VIANA DO CASTELO**

SANTARÉM
Ribatejo (☎043)

★★**Abidis** r Guilherme de Azevedo 4 ☎22017

rm28 (🛁6) 🚗 ☾ sB1312—1500 dB2000—2375 dB🛁3126—3625 M1260

Autogirar r P-de Santarém 47 ☎24077 Dat

SANTIAGO DO CACÉM
Baxio Alentejo (☎069)

★**Pousada de São Tiago** Estrada National ☎22459 tx16166

🛁107 A3rm **P**15 sB🛁3150—6400 dB🛁4500—7850 M1300—1600 ≈
Credit cards [1] [2] [3] [5]

SÃO BRAS DE ALPORTEL
Algarve (☎089)

★***Pousada de São Bras*** Serro do Caldeirao (5km N on main road) ☎42305 tx56945

🛁23 A8rm **P**30 ☾ mountains
Credit cards [1] [2] [3] [5]

SEREM See **AGUEDA**

SERPA
Baixo Alentejo (☏084)

★★**Pousada de São Gens** Alto de São Gens ☏90327 tx43651

rm18 (➡12) **P**100 sB➡3150—6400 dB➡4500—7850 M1300—1800 Credit cards 1 2 3 4 5

SERRA DO MARÃO See **AMARANTE**

SESIMBRA
Estremadura (☏01)

★★★★**Do Mar** ☏2233326 tx13883

➡119 Lift ☾ sB➡3250—6050 dB➡5100—9600 M1700 sea Credit cards 1 2 3 4 5

★★★★**Espadarte** Esplanada do Atlantico ☏2233189 tx14699

➡ 80 **P** Lift ☾ sea Credit cards 1 2 3 5

SETÚBAL
Estremadura (☏065)

★★★★**Esperança** av L-Todi 220 ☏25151 tx17158

➡76 Lift ☾ sB➡2250—4150 dB➡3000—4900 M900—1250 sea mountains Credit cards 1 2 3 5

★★**Pousada de São Filipe** ☏23844

➡ 14 sB➡ 8500—10500 dB➡ 9950—12000 M1750—2350

Setubauto av dos Combatentes da Grande Guerra 81 ☏23131 For

SINES
Baixo Alentejo (☏069)

★★★***Malhada*** do Farol ☏62105

➡27

SINTRA
Estremadura (☏01)

★★★★**Palàcio de Seteais** r Barbosa do Bocage 8 ☏9233200 tx14410

➡18 **P**50 Lift ☾ sB➡10000—14000 dB➡11000—15000 M2350—2600 sea mountains Credit cards 1 2 3 5

Sintra av DF de Almeido 1 ☏2932353 For

TAVIRA
Algarve (☏081)

★★★***Eurotel-Tavira*** Quinta das Oliverias ☏22042 tx56218

➡79 **P**100 Lift ☾ sea mountains

Portugal

TOMAR
Ribatejo (☏049)

J Antunes Oliveira & Alves av D Nuno Alvares Pereira, Loto 8 & 9 ☏33637 Dat

Auto Mecânica Tomarense av D Nuno Alvares Pereira 15 ☏33144 For

At **CASTELO DO BODE** (14km SE, near Dam)

★★***Pousada de São Pedro*** ☏38159

➡15 A7rm **P** mountains lake

TORRES VEDRAS
Estremadura (☏061)

Auto-Torreense r Santos Bernardes ☏22021

Foroestre Parque do Choupal ☏23115 For

URGEIRIÇA See **CANAS DE SENHORIM**

VALE DO LOBO
Algarve (☏089)

★★★★**Dona Filipa** (THF) ☏94141 tx56848

➡ 135 **P**100 Lift ☾ sea Credit cards 1 2 3 4 5

VALENÇA DO MINHO
Minho (☏051)

★★**Pousada de São Teotónio** ☏22242 tx32837

➡12 A4rm **P** ☾ Credit cards 1 2 3 4 5

VIANA DO CASTELO
Minho (☏058)

★★★★**Parque** Azenhas do D-Prior ☏24151 tx32511

➡124 **P**100 Lift ☾ sB➡3125—4325 dB➡4400—6250 M1300—1500 sea mountains Credit cards 1 2 5

★★★**Alfonso III** av Alfonso III 494 ☏24123 tx32599

➡89 Lift ☾ sB➡2800—5400 dB➡3850—8800 M1000—1800 sea

★★***Allanca*** av dos Combatentes da Grande Guerra ☏23001

rm29 (➡15) **P** ☾ sea

★★**Rali** av Afonso III 180 (n.rest) ☏22176

➡39 **P** Lift ☾ sB➡1700—3200 dB➡3000—4200 mountains Credit cards 1 2 3

Auto-Vianense av Camões 25—27 ☏22092 VW

At **SANTA LUZIA** (2km NW: also funicular connection)

★★★★**Santa Luzia** ☏22192 tx32420

➡47 **P** Lift ☾ sB➡4500—6700 dB➡5900—7750 M1500—2300 sea mountains Credit cards 1 2 3 5

VILA DO CONDE
Douro Litoral (☏052)

★★**Estalagem do Brasão** r J-M-de Melo ☏624016

➡28 **P**28 sB➡1600—2200 dB➡2400—3400 Mfr1200 Credit cards 1 2 3 4 5

VILA FRANCA DE XIRA
Ribatejo (☏063)

Auto Nascimento r A-L-Batista 2 ☏23122 Cit

Auto-Vilafranquense r Curado 8 ☏22830

VILA REAL
Tras-Os-Montes Alto Douro (☏059)

★★***Tocalo*** av Carvalho Araujo 45 ☏23106

➡52 Lift ☾ mountains

A Camilo Fernandes r Visconde de Carnaxide 26 ☏22151 For

VILA REAL DE SANTO ANTÓNIO
Algarve (☏081)

★★★**Eurotel** Praia da Altura ☏95450 tx56068

Apr—Oct

➡ 135 **P**80 Lift sB➡ 2250—5000 dB➡ 2750—6150 M900 Beach sea Credit cards 1 2 3 4 5

VISEU
Beira Alta (☏032)

★★★**Grão Vasco** r G-Barreiros ☏23511 tx53608

➡ 88 **P**70 Lift ☾ sB➡ 5150 dB➡ 6700 M1300alc mountains Credit cards 1 2 3 5

GAVIS av E-Navarro ☏22966 Aud BMW VW

Lopes & Figueiredo av da Bélgica 52 ☏25151 AR

Spain and Andorra

International distinguishing sign

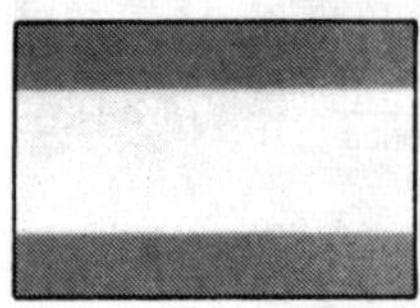

Andorra
See page 353
Area *mainland*
189,950 sq miles
Balearic Islands
1,935 sq miles
Population
37,100,000
Local time *GMT + 1*
(Summer GMT + 2)

National flag
Horizontal tricolour of red, yellow and red

Leaflets entitled '*Motoring in the Balearics*' and '*Motoring in the Canary Islands*' are available to AA members.

How to get there

From the Channel ports, Spain is approached via France. The two main routes are at either end of the Pyrenean mountains, the Biarritz to San Sebastiàn-Donostia road, or motorway, at the western end for central and southern Spain, or the Perpignan to Barcelona road, or motorway, at the eastern end for the Costa Brava. The distance from Calais to Madrid is about 990 miles and usually requires two or three night stops. It is possible to shorten the journey by using the car sleeper services between Boulogne or Paris and Biarritz or Narbonne, or Paris to Madrid. There is also a direct ferry service from Plymouth to Santander which takes about 24 hours.

Motoring regulations and general information

This information should be read in conjunction with the general content of the European ABC (pages 4-26). **Note** As certain regulations and requirements are common to many countries they are covered by one entry in the ABC and the following headings represent some of the subjects dealt with in this way:
Crash or safety helmets
Drinking and driving
Fire extinguisher
First-aid kit
Insurance
International distinguishing sign
Medical treatment
Mirrors
Police fines
Radio telephones/Radio transmitters
Seat belts
Tyres
Visitors' registration

AA Port agent

Santander Viajes Ecuador SA, Calle Lealtad 21 ☎ (942)215708. See also *AA Agents* page 5 and *Town Plan of Santander* page 368.

Accidents

Fire, police, ambulance. In all cities dial 091 for **police** and 2323232 for **fire** service in Madrid and Barcelona; in other towns call the operator, There are no firm rules of procedure after an accident; however, in most cases the recommendations under *Accidents* on page 5 are advisable.

There is an assistance service for victims of traffic accidents which is run by the Central Traffic Department. At the moment the service operates day and night on the N1 Madrid-Irún road, on the N11 road, in the province of Lerida, on some roads in the provinces of Valencia (N111, N340, N332, and N430) and Vizcaya (N625, N634, N240, C639, C6211, C6315, C6318, and C6322).

There is an SOS telephone network on these roads; motorists in need of help should ask for *auxillio en carretera* (road assistance). The special ambulances used are in radio contact with the hospitals participating in the scheme.

Accommodation

Spain has some of the most attractively furnished hotels in Europe—especially luxury hotels converted from former monasteries or palaces. Provincial hotels are pleasantly old-fashioned; usually the plumbing and lavatories are just about adequate, and do not compare with those in modern hotels in coastal resorts. Hotels are officially classified, and the category exhibited outside each. Establishments are now permitted to charge for breakfast whether taken or not.

While commendations or complaints about hotels are an important source of information to us, AA members may also like to know that Spanish hotels must keep official complaint forms and if these are unobtainable at the hotel, they are available from Tourist Information offices.

Paradores are fully-appointed tourist hotels, usually on the outskirts of towns or in the country. Some are newly built, but others are converted country houses, palaces, or Moorish castles. They offer very good value for money. A stay must normally be limited to ten days. Bookings for Paradores should be addressed to: Central de Reservas de los Paradores del Esta do Apartado de Correos 50043, Madrid 1 ☏ (91)4359700 (if calling this number from the UK refer to your *Telephone Dialling Codes* booklet) or telex 46865. Alternatively, you may contact their London Office on ☏ (01)402 8182.

Bail Bond

An accident in Spain can have very serious consequenses, including the impounding of the car, and property, and the detention of the driver pending bail. A Bail Bond can often facilitate release of person and property, and you are advised to obtain one of these from your insurer, for a nominal premium, together with your Green Card. A Bail Bond is a written guarantee that a cash deposit of usually up to £1,500 will be paid to the Spanish Court as surety for bail, and as security for any fine which may be imposed, although in such an event you may have to reimburse any amount paid on your behalf. In very serious cases the Court will not allow bail and it has been known for a minor Spanish court to refuse Bail Bonds, and to insist on cash being paid by the driver. Nevertheless, motorists are strongly advised to obtain a Bail Bond and to ensure that documentary evidence of this (in Spanish) is attached to the Green Card.

Boats

Boat registration documentation is compulsory for all craft over approximately 10ft in length. See page 6 for further information.

Breakdown

If your car breaks down, try to move it to the verge of the road so that it obstructs the traffic flow as little as possible and place a warning triangle 30 metres behind the vehicle to warn following traffic. A 24-hour breakdown service is run by the Spanish Motorway Club (RACE). To obtain assistance in the Madrid area or elsewhere in Spain call the Real Automovil Club de España (RACE) national breakdown centre in Madrid ☏ (91)4412222 which provides an English speaking service. See also *Breakdown* page 6 and *Warning triangles* page 352.

British Embassy/Consulates

The British Embassy together with its consular section is located at *Madrid 4* Calle de Fernando et Santo 16 ☏ (91)4190200. There are British Consulates in Algeciras, Alicante, Barcelona, Bilbao, Malaga, Seville and Palma; there are British Consulates with Honorary Consuls in Santander, Tarragona and Vigo. There is a British Vice-Consulate in Ibiza and a British Vice-Consulate with Honorary Consul in Menorca. See also page 6 and *Town Plan of Central Madrid* pages 362-363.

Currency including banking hours

(See also page 9)
The unit of currency is the Spanish Peseta (*Ptas*) divided into 100 Centimos. At the time of going to press £ = *Ptas*199.03. Denominations of bank notes are *Ptas* 100, 500, 1,000, 2,000, 5,000; standard coins are *Ptas* 1, 5, 25, 50, 100. Visitors may import unlimited amounts of foreign and Spanish currency, but amounts over *Ptas*100,000 and *Ptas* 500,000 must be declared on arrival. No more than *Ptas*100,000 in Spanish currency may be exported, but there are no restrictions on the export of foreign currency provided the amount does not exceed the amount declared on arrival.

In the summer banks are usually open 08.30—13.30hrs Monday to Friday and 08.30—12.30hrs on Saturday. There are also exchange offices at travel agents which are open 09.00—13.00hrs and 16.00—19.00hrs from Monday to Friday, and 09.00—13.00hrs on Saturday.

Customs regulations

A television set, radio, pocket calculator or tape recorder may be temporarily imported but only against a deposit of duty and a permit valid for three months issued by the Spanish Customs. See also *Customs regulations for European countries* page 9 for further information.

Dimensions and weight restrictions

Private **cars** and towed **trailers** or **caravans** are restricted to the following dimensions — height: 4 metres; width: 2.50 metres; length: 11 metres.

Golfo de Cadiz

1 Colares
2 Cascais
3 Estoril
4 Carcavelos
5 Costa da Caparica

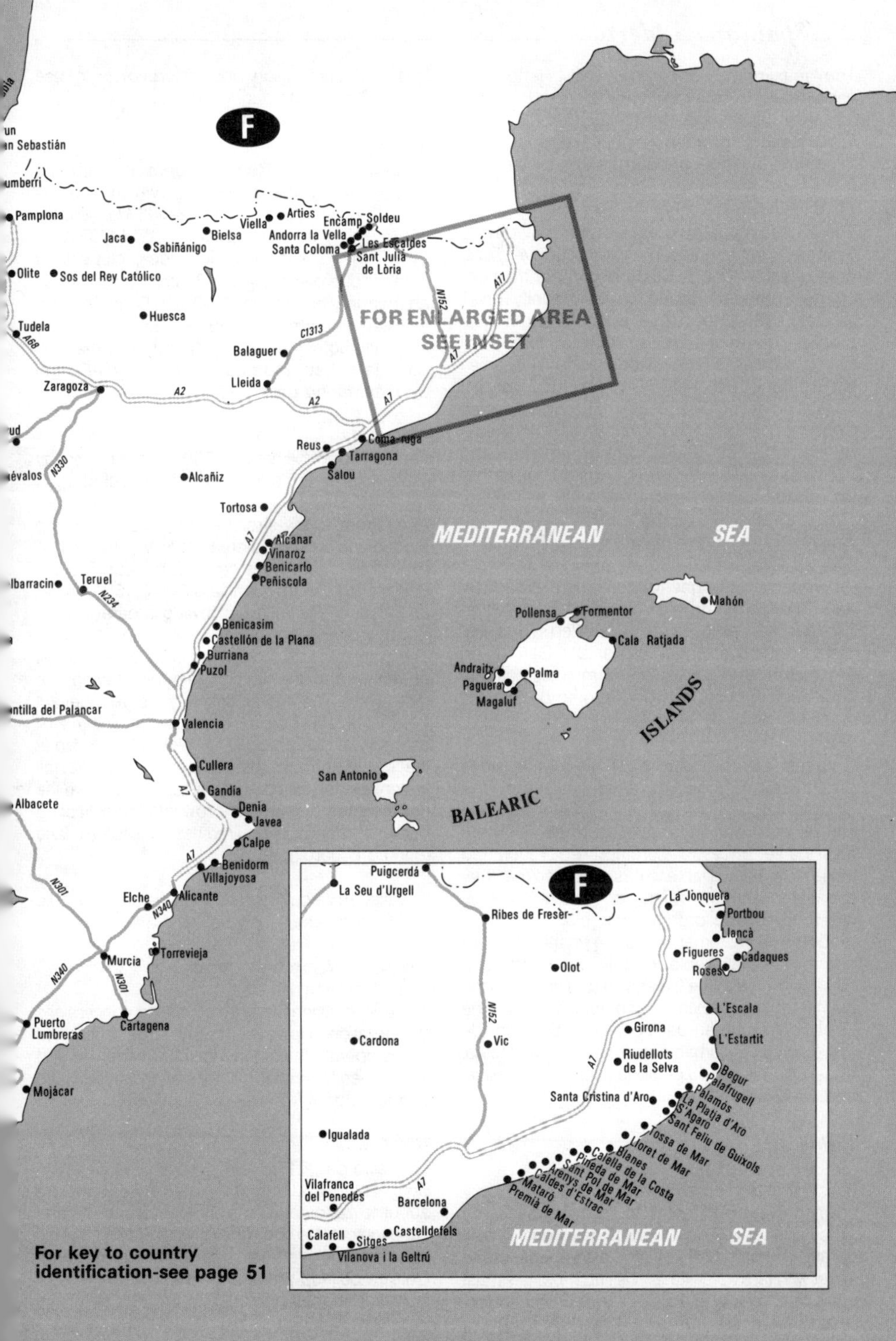
F
San Sebastián
Pamplona
Jaca
Sabiñánigo
Bielsa
Viella
Arties
Encamp
Soldeu
Andorra la Vella
Les Escaldes
Santa Coloma
Sant Julià de Lòria
Olite
Sos del Rey Católico
Huesca
Tudela
A68
Balaguer
C1313
N152
A17
FOR ENLARGED AREA SEE INSET
Zaragoza
A2
Lleida
A7
Reus
Coma-ruga
Tarragona
Salou
N330
Alcañiz
Tortosa
MEDITERRANEAN SEA
Alcanar
Vinaroz
Benicarlo
Peñiscola
Teruel
N234
Mahón
Pollensa
Formentor
Cala Ratjada
Benicasim
Castellón de la Plana
Burriana
Puzol
Andraitx
Paguera
Palma
Magaluf
ISLANDS
Valencia
Cullera
San Antonio
Gandía
BALEARIC
Albacete
Denia
Javea
Calpe
Benidorm
Villajoyosa
N301
Elche
Alicante
N340
Torrevieja
Murcia
Puerto Lumbreras
Cartagena
Mojácar
Puigcerdá
La Seu d'Urgell
Ribes de Freser
La Jonquera
Portbou
Llancà
Figueres
Cadaques
Roses
Olot
L'Escala
Girona
Cardona
Vic
L'Estartit
Riudellots de la Selva
Begur
Palafrugell
Santa Cristina d'Aro
Pálamos
La Platja d'Aro
S'Agaro
Sant Feliu de Guixols
Igualada
Tossa de Mar
Lloret de Mar
Blanes
Calella de la Costa
Pineda de Mar
Sant Pol de Mar
Arenys de Mar
Caldes d'Estrac
Mataró
Premià de Mar
Vilafranca del Penedés
Barcelona
Castelldefels
Calafell
Sitges
Vilanova i la Geltrú
MEDITERRANEAN SEA

For key to country identification-see page 51

The maximum permitted overall length of vehicle/trailer or caravan combination is 18 metres.

Trailers with an unladen weight exceeding 750kg must have an independant braking system.

Driving licence

The minimum age at which a visitor may drive a temporarily imported car or motorcycle (over 75cc) is 18 years. Although Spain became a member of the European Economic Community on 1 January 1986 it has not yet adopted Community practice on mutual recognition of temporary visitors' domestic driving licences. Until Spanish law is modified either an IDP (or an official Spanish translation of your licence stamped by a Spanish Consulate, which costs more than an IDP) should be carried. See under *Driving Licence* and *International Driving Permit* page 11 for further information.

Emergency messages to tourists

(See also page 11)
Emergency messages to tourists are broadcast daily throughout the year by *Radio Nacional de España*. The messages are transmitted in Spanish, French and occasionally English and German on 513 metres medium wave at 5 minutes past the hour begining 05.05hrs and ending 00.05hrs.

Garages

Garages are officially classified. Blue signs displayed outside garages indicate the classification I to III as well as the type of work that can be dealt with, by means of symbols. There must be set prices for common repair jobs and these must be available to customers so that they may authorise repairs. They are also required by law to keep and produce complaint forms on request by a customer. If you are unable to obtain one they are available from Tourist Information offices, or write to the Delegado de Turismo in the capital of the province concerned, or to the Dirección General de Servicios, Sección de Inspeción y Reclamaciones enclosing all factual evidence. This should be done as soon as possible and whilst still in Spain.

Lights

(See also page 14)
Passing lights (dipped headlights) are compulsory on motorways and fast dual carriageways even if they are well lit. The use of full headlights in built up areas is prohibited but it is also an offence to travel with faulty sidelights. Visiting motorists must equip their vehicle with a set of replacement bulbs. It is also compulsory for *motorcyclists* to use dipped headlights during the day.

Motoring club

The **Real Automovil Club de España** (RACE) which has its headquarters at *28003 Madrid* Calle José Abascal 10 ☎ 4473200 is associated with local clubs in a number of provincial towns. Motoring club offices are normally open from 09.00—14.00hrs Monday to Friday and are closed on Sundays and public holidays. Some, including Madrid are closed on Saturdays. See also page 16 and *Town Plan of Central Madrid* pages 362-363.

Motorways

There are approximately 1,230 miles of motorway (Autopista) open, and more are projected.

Apart from a few stretches of motorway in the Madrid and Barcelona areas, tolls are charged on most of the motorways *eg* La Jonquera (French-Spanish border) to Valencia is *Ptas* 3,465 for a car and *Ptas* 4,785 fór a car towing a caravan.

The majority of toll motorways issue a travel ticket on entry and the toll is paid on leaving the motorway. The travel ticket gives all relevant information about the toll charges including the toll category of the vehicle. The ticket is handed in at the exit point and the toll paid. On some toll motorways the toll collection is automatic; have the correct amount ready to throw into the collecting basket. If change is required use the separate lane marked accordingly.

A leaflet entitled *Motorways in Spain* is available to AA members.

Orange badge scheme for disabled drivers

(See also page 16)
There is no national system of parking concessions in operation. However, many large cities and towns operate their own individual schemes and it is understood that consideration is shown to badge holders from other countries.

Overtaking

(See also page 17)
Both at night and during the day, drivers who are about to be overtaken must operate their right-hand indicator to show the driver following that his intention to overtake has been understood. Outside built-up areas drivers about to overtake must sound their horn during the day and flash

their lights at night. Stationary trams must not be overtaken while passengers are boarding or alighting.

Parking

(See also page 18)
Parking is forbidden in the following places: within 5 metres (16½ft) of cross-roads or an intersection; near a level crossing; within 5 metres of the entrance to a public building; on a main road or one carrying fast-moving traffic; on or near tram lines; within 7 metres (23ft) of a tram or bus stop. You must not park on a two-way road if it is not wide enough for three vehicles. In one-way streets, vehicles are parked alongside buildings with even numbers on even dates and on the opposite side on odd dates; any alteration to this system is anounced by signs or notices in the press. Drivers may stop their vehicles alongside another parked vehicle if there is no space free nearby and the flow of traffic is not obstructed, but only long enough to let passengers in or out or to load or unload goods.

A special parking zone has been established in the centre of Madrid and motorists wishing to park in this zone may obtain tickets from tobacconists. The tickets must be displayed on the windscreen and cost *Ptas*25 for ½hr, *Ptas*50 for 1 hr and *Ptas*75 for 1½hrs.

Passengers

(See also page 18)
It is recommended that children do not travel in a vehicle as front seat passengers.

Petrol

(See also page 18)
Credit cards The use of credit cards to obtain petrol is not available to visiting motorists.
Duty-free petrol In addition to the petrol in the vehicle tank up to 5 litres in a can may be imported free of customs duty and tax.
Petrol (leaded) Gasolina Normal (92 octane) and Gasolina Super (97 octane) grades.
Petrol (unleaded) is sold in Spain as Gasoline Normal (95 octane) grade.

Postal information

Mail Postcards *Ptas*35, letters up to 20gm *Ptas*34.
Post offices There are 1,550 post offices in Spain. Opening hours are from 08.00—14.00hrs Monday to Saturday.

Postcheques

(See also page 20)
Postcheques may be cashed for any amount up to *Ptas*13,000 per cheque in multiples of *Ptas* 1,000, but only at main post offices. Counter positions are identified by the words *Caja Postal de Ahorros* or *Reintegros*. See *Postal information* for post office opening hours.

Priority

Drivers on secondary roads must give way to vehicles in both directions when entering a main road. See also *Priority including Roundabouts* page 21.

Public holidays

Official public holidays in Spain for 1987 are given below. In addition there are many local and regional holidays throughout mainland Spain. See also *Public holidays* page 21.
January 1 (New Year's Day)
January 6 (Epiphany)
March 19 (Saint Joseph)
April 16 (Maundy Thursday)
April 17 (Good Friday)
May 1 (May Day)
June 18 (Corpus Christi)
July 25 (St James the Apostle)
August 15* (Assumption)
October 12 (Day of our Lady of El Pilar)
November 1† (All Saints' Day)
December 8 (Immaculate Conception)
December 25 (Christmas Day)
*Saturday †Sunday

Religious services

(See also page 22)
The Intercontinental Church Society welcomes visitors from any denomination to English language services in the following centres:
Barcelona 08022 The Revd Ben Eaton, San Juan de la Salle 41, Horacio 38 ☎ 478867;
Ibiza The Revd Joe Yates-Round, Aptdo 6, San Antonio Abad, Ibiza, Baleares ☎ 343383.

Roads including holiday traffic

The surfaces of the main roads vary, but on the whole are good. The roads are winding in many places and at times it is not advisable to exceed 30—35mph. Secondary roads are often rough, winding, and encumbered by slow, horse-drawn traffic. A leaflet entitled *Road conditions in Spain and Portugal* is available to AA members.

Holiday traffic, particularly on the coast road to Barcelona and Tarragona and in the San Sebastián—Donostia area, causes congestion which may be severe at weekends.

Road signs

(See also page 22)
All main roads are prefixed 'N', six of those radiating from Madrid are numbered in Roman numerals, Secondary roads are prefixed 'C'.

In the Basque area local versions of some placenames appear on signposts together with the national version used in current AA gazetteers and maps. Some local names differ considerably from the national spelling — *eg* San Sebastián = Donostia. In the Catalonia area some local spellings are used exclusively on signposts but most of these are recognisable against the national version — *eg* Gerona = Girona, Lérida = Lleida.

Shopping hours

Generally shops are open Monday to Saturday from 09.00—13.00hrs and 15.00—19.30hrs with a two hour break for lunch; department stores may open at 10.00hrs and close at 20.00hrs.

Speed limits

(See also page 22)
In built-up areas all vehicles are limited to 60kph (37mph) except where signs indicate a lower limit. Outside built-up areas cars are limited to 120kph (74mph) on motorways and *90kph (56mph) or **100kph (62mph) on other roads. Vehicles towing a caravan or trailer are limited to 80kph (49mph) on motorways and *70kph (43mph) or **80kph (49mph) on other roads.
*On ordinary roads.
**On roads with more than one lane in each direction, a special lane for slow moving vehicles or wide lanes.

Spiked or studded tyres

Spikes on tyres must be 10mm in diameter and not more then 2mm in length. See also *Cold weather touring* page 8.

Tourist information

(See also page 24)
The Spanish National Tourist Office, Metro House, 57-58 St James's Street London SW1A 1LD ☎ 01-499 0901, will be pleased to assist you with information regarding tourism and there are branch offices in most of the leading Spanish cities, towns and resorts. Local offices are normally closed at lunchtime.

Traffic lights

(See also page 24)
In some cases the green light remains on with the amber light when changing from green to red. Two red lights,one above the other mean 'no entry'. Usually lights on each side of crossroads operate independently and must be obeyed independently. A policeman with a whistle may over-ride the traffic lights, and he must be obeyed.

Turning

Unless there is a 'turning permitted', sign three-point turns and reversing into side streets are prohibited in towns.

Using the telephone

(See also page 24)
Insert coin **before** lifting reciever. When making calls to subscribers within Spain precede number with relevant area code (shown in parentheses against town entry in gazetteer). Use *Ptas*5, 25 or 50 coins for local calls (Min 2x5) and *Ptas*50 for national and international calls. The international telephone system connects all principal towns, but long delays on trunk calls are not unusual.
International callbox identification Light green sign.
Telephone rates A call to the UK costs *Ptas*261 for the first 3 minutes and *Ptas*97 for each additional minute. The cost of local calls is determined by the distance (within the town limits) and the time taken. Hotels, restaurants etc., usually make an additional charge.
What to dial for the Irish Republic 07 *353.
What to dial for the UK 07 *44.
*Wait for second dialling tone.

Warning triangles

The use of two warning triangles is compulsory for vehicles weighing more than 3,500kg (3 tons 8cwt 100lbs) and passenger vehicles with more than nine seats (including the driver's). The triangles must be placed on the road in front of and behind the vehicle at a distance of 30 metres (33yds) and be visible from at least 100 metres (109yds). However, it is recommended that all other vehicles except two-wheelers carry a warning triangle. See also *Warning triangles/Hazard warning lights* page 25.

Winter conditions

(See also page 26)
Most roads across the Pyrénées are either closed or affected by winter weather, but the roads or motorways to Biarritz and Perpignan in France avoid the mountains. The main routes into Portugal are unaffected. Within the country, motoring is not severely restricted although certain roads may be temporarily blocked, particularly in January and February. The most important roads likely to be affected are San Sebastián (Donostia)—Burgos—

Madrid, Madrid—Granada, Zaragoza—Teruel and Granada—Murcia, but these are swept immediately there is a snowfall. On the Villacastin—Madrid road there is a tunnel under the Guadarrama Pass. Roads likely to be affected by heavy snowfall are:

Pass	*Road*
Pajares	León—Gijon
Reinosa	Santander—Palencia
Escudo	Santander—Burgos
Somosierra	Burgos—Madrid
Orduña	Bilbao (Bilbo) — Burgos
Barazar	Bilbao (Bilbo) — Vitoria (Gasteiz)
Piqueras	Logroño—Madrid
Navacerrada	Madrid—Le Granja

The Real Automóvil Club de España will give you up-to-date information about road conditions. See also *Major road tunnels* pages 34-35, and *Major rail tunnels* page 36.

Andorra

National flag *Vertical tricolour blue, yellow and red*

Andorra is an independent Principality covering 190 sq miles with a population of 32,700. It is situated high in the Pyrénées between France and Spain and jointly administered by the two co-princes (the president of France, the Bishop of La Seu d'Urgell) and the Andorrans. French and Spanish are both spoken and the currency of either country is accepted. General regulations for France and Spain apply to Andorra with the following exceptions.

Accidents

Fire and **ambulance** ☎ 18 **police** ☎ 17. There are no firm rules of procedure after an accident; however, in most cases the recommendations under *Accidents* on page 5 are advisable.

Breakdown

The Automobile Club d'Andorra ☎ (078)20890 will offer advice and assistance in the event of a breakdown. However, owing to many unnecessary journeys made in the past, the motorist is now asked to go to the garage and personally accompany the mechanic or breakdown vehicle to his car. See also *Breakdown* page 6.

British Consulate

(See also page 6)
Andorra comes within the Consular District of the British Consul-General at Barcelona.

Dimensions

The maximum height for vehicles where tunnels are involved is 3.5m.

Motoring club

(See also page 16)

The Automobil Club d'Andorra has its head office at *Andorra la Vella* Carrer Babot Camp 4 ☎ (078)20890.

Passengers

(See also page 18)
Children under 10 years of age are not permitted to travel in a vehicle as front seat passengers.

Roads

Andorra can be approached from France via the Pas de la Casa (6,851ft), then from the frontier over the Envalira Pass (7,897ft). Roads may occasionally be closed for short periods between November and April. The approach from Spain via La Seu d'Urgell is always open. The three main roads radiating from the town are prefixed N and numbered; side roads are prefixed V.

Speed limits

(See also page 22)
The following speed limits apply to Andorra. Car, car/caravan combination. *Built-up areas* 40kph (25mph); *Other roads* 70kph (43mph). Some villages have a speed limit of 20kph (12mph).

Weather information

(See also page 26)
The condition of the Envalira pass may be obtained by ☎ 21166 or 21055.

Wheel chains

These must be used on the Envalira pass whenever conditions require it. See also *Cold weather touring* page 8.

Prices are in Spanish Pesetas
Abbreviations:
av avenida
c calle
Cdt Commandant
Cpt Capitán
ctra carretera
Gl Generalisimo
pl plaza
ps paseo

AIGUA-BLAVA See **BEGUR**

ALARCÓN
Cuenca (☎966)

★★**Parador del Marques de Villena** ☎331350
Jan–9 Dec & 3 Nov–Dec
→11 🏠 **P**40 Lift ☾ sB→4510–5925 dB→6700–8700 M1800 t% mountains
Credit cards [1] [2] [3] [5]

ALBACETE
Albacete (☎967)

★★★***Parador Nacional de la Mancha*** ☎229450
→70 **P** Lift ☾ 🎾 ≈

ALBARRACIN
Teruel (☎974)

★★★***Albarracin*** Azagra ☎710011
→36 **P** ≈ mountains

ALCANAR
Tarragona (☎977)

★★**Biarritz** (n. rest) ☎737025
15 Jun–15 Sep
→24 **P**25 sB→2075 dB→3250 🎾 Beach sea
Credit cards [2] [5]

ALCAÑIZ
Teruel (☎974)

★★★**Parador Nacional de la Concordia** ☎830400
Closed 10 Jan–28 Feb
→12 Lift ☾ sB→5800–6600 dB→7700–8700 M1800 mountains
Credit cards [1] [2] [3] [5]

Agullo S.L. Rondas de Castelseras 4 ☎830777 Mer

ALGECIRAS
Cádiz (☎956)

★★★★**Reina Cristina** (THF) ps de las Conferencias ☎650061 tx78057
→135 **P**250 Lift ☾ sB→6150–7800 dB→10750–13350 M1250 🎾 ≈ sea
Credit cards [1] [2] [3] [4] [5]

★★★**Alarde** Alfonso XI–4 (n.rest) ☎660408 tx78009
→68 🏠 **P**6 Lift ☾ sB→2480–2675 dB→4515–5060 t6%
Credit cards [1] [2] [3] [5]

Automoción Baltanas ctra Cádiz-Málaga 21 ☎660950 LR

🚗 **Villalobos** crtra N340 ☎656361 All makes

Spain

ALICANTE
Alicante (☎965)

★★★***Meliá Alicante*** Playa de El Postiguet ☎205000 tx66131
→545 **P** Lift ☾ ≈ sea

★★★**Palas** pl del Ayuntamiento 6 ☎206690
→53 🏠 **P**30 Lift ☾ sB→2720–3395 dB→4460–5515 M900–1100
Credit cards [1] [2] [3] [4] [5]

★★***Gran Sol*** Méndez Núñez 3 ☎203000
→150 Lift ☾ sea

Nuevo C/Tomas Aznar Domenech 7 ☎283932 All makes

ALMAGRO
Ciudad Real (☎926)

★★★**Parador Nacional** Ronda de San Francisco ☎860100
→🚿55 **P**40 ☾ sB→🚿4120–6200 dB→🚿6700–8200 M1800 ≈ t%
Credit cards [1] [2] [3] [4] [5]

ALMERÍA
Almería (☎951)

★★★★**Gran** av Reina Regente 4 (n.rest) ☎238011 tx75343
→124 🏠 Lift ☾ sB→4275–4625 dB→7150–7750 t6% ≈ sea
Credit cards [1] [2] [3] [5]

★★★**Costasol** Generalisimo 58 ☎234011
→🚿55 🏠 **P**25 Lift ☾ sB→🚿3326–3986 dB→🚿4615–5502 Mfr700 t6%
Credit cards [1] [2] [3] [5]

★★★**Perla** pl del Carmen 1 ☎238877
→44 **P**4 sB→2210–2550 dB→3560–4020 Mfr500 t6%
Credit cards [2] [3] [5]

Automecanica Almeriense Paraje los Callejones N340 KM117.4 ☎237033 **P** For

ALMURADIEL
Cuidad Real (☎926)

★★★**Podencos** ctra NIV–Km232 ☎339000
→64 🏠 **P** ☾ sB→fr2670 dB→fr4540 Mfr1115 t6% ≈ mountains
Credit cards [1] [3]

ALSASUA
Navarra (☎948)

★★**Alaska** ctra Madrid–Irún Km402 ☎562802
→29 🏠 **P** ☾ sB→2775–3075 dB→3750–4350 M1000 t% ≈ mountains

🚗 **P Celaya Urrestarazu** ctra Gl-Irún Madrid ☎560233 Vol

ANTEQUERA
Málaga (☎952)

★★**Parador Nacional** Parque M-Christina ☎840901

→55 **P**70 ☾ dB→5500–6500 M1800 t6% ≈ mountains
Credit cards [1] [2] [3] [5]

ARANDA DE DUERO
Burgos (☎947)

★★★**Bronces** ctra Madrid–Irún Km161 ☎500850
→🚿29 A17rm 🏠 **P**12 ☾ sBfr3100 sB→🚿fr2865 dBfr5260 dB→🚿fr5260 Mfr1200 t6%
Credit cards [1] [2] [3] [5]

★★★**Montehermoso** ctra Madrid–Irún Km163 ☎501550
→52 🏠 **P**50 Lift ☾ sB→2375–2575 dB→3850–4150 M1300 t6% mountains
Credit cards [2] [3] [5]

★★**Area Tudanca** ☎506011
→20 🏠 **P**50 ☾ dB→3550 t% mountains
Credit cards [2] [3] [5]

★★**Tres Condes** ☎502400
→37 🏠 **P**12 ☾ sB→2125 dB→3800 M1100 t6% mountains
Credit card [3]

Electro-Sanz av Castilla 49 ☎501134 AR

ARCOS DE LA FRONTERA
Cádiz

★★★***Parador Nacional Casa del Corregidor*** pl d'España ☎700460
→21 Lift

ARENAS DE CABRALES
Asturias

★***Naranjo de Buines*** ctra General ☎845119
rm38 (→🚿22) A18rm mountains

ARENYS DE MAR
Barcelona (☎93)

★★★**Raymond** ps Xifré 1 ☎7921700
→🚿33 🏠 **P** Lift ☾ sea

★★**Floris** Playa Cassá 78 ☎7920384
Mar–Oct
→30 Lift ☾ sB→1350–1650 dB→2700–3100 M900 sea
Credit cards [1] [2] [3] [5]

★***Impala*** Apartado 20 (n.rest) ☎7921504
→🚿52 **P** ☾ sea

ARGOMANIZ
Alava

★★★**Parador Nacional de Argomaniz** ☎282200
→48 **P**50 Lift ☾ sB→4600 dB→6200 Mfr1800 mountains
Credit cards [1] [2] [3] [5]

ARTIES
Lleida (☎973)

★★★**Parador Nacional Don Gaspar de Portola** ☎640801 tx46865
→40 A9rm 🏠 **P**35 Lift ☾ sB→5800–6200 dB→7700–8200 M1800 t6% mountains
Credit cards [1] [2] [3] [4] [5]

ASTORGA
León (☎987)

🚗 **Automoviles Melchor** ctra Madrid–Coruña 186 ☎615259 **P** For LR

ÁVILA
Ávila (☎918)

★★★★***Palacio Valderrabanos*** pl Catedral 9 ☎211023
🛁 73 **P** Lift ☾
Credit cards [1] [2] [3] [4] [5]

★★★***Parador Nacional Raimundo de Borgona*** Marques de Canales de Chozas 16 ☎211340
🛁 62 🏠 **P** Lift

★★**Cuatro Postes** ctra Salamanca 23 ☎220000
🛁 36 🏠 **P** Lift ☾ sB🛁 2680 dB🛁 4460 M1050 t6%
Credit cards [1] [2] [3] [4] [5]

AYAMONTE
Huelva (☎955)

★★★***Parador Nacional Costá de la Luz*** ☎320700
🛁 20 🏊 sea

BADAJOZ
Badajoz (☎924)

★★★**Gran Zurbaran** ps Castelar ☎223741 tx28818
🛁 215 🏠 **P**100 Lift ☾ sB🛁 3880–4269 dB🛁 6560–7200 M1500–1650 S6% t6% 🎾 🏊
Credit cards [1] [2] [3] [4] [5]

BAGUR See **BEGUR**

BAILEN
Jaén (☎953)

★★★**Don Lope de Sosa** Km295 ctra Madrid–Cádiz ☎670058 tx28311
🛁 27 **P**40 ☾ dB🛁 3820–4040 M1045 t6%
Credit cards [1] [2] [3] [4] [5]

★★★**Parador Nacional** (1km S on N1) ☎670100
🛁 86 **P** sB🛁 4500–5000 dB🛁 6000–6700 M1600–1800 t6%
Credit cards [1] [2] [3] [5]

BAIONA
Pontevedra (☎986)

★★★**Parador Nacional Conde de Gondomar** ☎355000
🛁 128 🏠 **P**100 ☾ sB🛁 4325–6100 dB🛁 7700–10200 M1950 t6% 🎾 🏊 Beach sea
Credit cards [1] [2] [3] [5]

BALAGUER
Lleida (☎973)

★★★***Parador Colaborador Conde Jaime de Urgel*** c Urgel 2 ☎445604
🛁 60 🏠 **P** Lift ☾ 🏊

BALEARES (ISLAS DE)
IBIZA SAN ANTONIO (☎971)

★★★***Tanit*** Cala Gracio ☎341300 tx69221

Spain

Apr–Oct
🛁 386 **P** Lift ☾ 🎾 🏊 sea

MALLORCA (MAJORCA)
CALA RATJADA (☎971)

★★★***Son Moll*** Playa Son Moll ☎563100
Apr–Oct
🛁 🚿 118 Lift ☾ 🏊 sea
Credit cards [3] [5]

FORMENTOR (☎971)

★★★★★**Formentor** ☎531300 tx68523
🛁 🚿 131 🏠 **P** Lift ☾ 🎾 🏊 Beach U sea

MAGALUF (☎971)

★★★★***Magaluf Playa Sol*** ☎681050 tx69175
🛁 242 **P** Lift 🎾 🏊 sea

PAGUERA (☎971)

★★★★***Villamil*** (THF) ☎686050 tx68841
🛁 102 **P** Lift ☾ 🎾 🏊 sea mountains

PALMA DE MALLORCA (☎971)

★★★★★***Son Vida Sheraton*** ☎451011 tx68651
🛁 171 **P**80 Lift ☾ 🎾 🏊 ⊟ ◪ U sea mountains
Credit cards [1] [2] [3] [4] [5]

★★★★★**Victoria-Sol** av J-Miró 21 ☎234342 tx68558
🛁 171 **P** Lift ☾ sB🛁 9300 dB🛁 14600 t12% 🏊 sea

★★★★**Maricel** C'as Catala Beach ☎402712
🛁 🚿 55 A8rm **P**20 Lift ☾ sB🛁 🚿 2850–3850 dB🛁 🚿 5700–7700 M1600 t6% 🏊 sea mountains
Credit cards [1] [2] [3] [4] [5]

★★★★***Meliá Mallorca*** c de Monseñor Palmer 2 ☎205000 tx68538
🛁 240 **P** Lift Pool sea

★★★**Nixe-Palace** av J-Miró 269 ☎403811 tx68569
🛁 130 🏠 **P**35 Lift ☾ sB🛁 4550–8550 dB🛁 6200–11100 Mfr1900 t6% 🏊 Beach sea mountains
Credit cards [1] [2] [3] [4] [5]

★★★***Paso*** Alvaro de Bazán 3 ☎237602 tx232740
🛁 260 **P** Lift 🏊 ⊟

🚗 **T Minaco** Gran via Asima 11 ☎200111 Cit LR

🚗 **T Oliver** G-Llabre 12–14 ☎275503 All makes

At **PLAYA DE PALMA (CA'N PASTILLA)**

★★**Oasis** B-Riutort 25 ☎260150 tx69103
🛁 110 🏠 **P**5 Lift ☾ sB🛁 2046–2646 dB🛁 3492–4692 M825 🏊 Beach sea mountains
Credit cards [1] [2] [3] [4] [5]

At **PLAYA DE PALMA NOVA** (16km SW)

★★★**Hawaii** ☎681150 tx68670
Jan–Oct
🛁 230 **P**15 Lift ☾ sB🛁 2450–3050 dB🛁 4100–5300 M900 🏊 sea

POLLENSA (☎971)

At **CALA SAN VINCENTE**

★★★★***Molins*** ☎530200
🛁 🚿 100 **P**8 Lift ☾ 🎾 🏊 sea

At **PUERTO DE POLLENSA** (6km NE)

★★★**Miramar** ps de Anglada Camarasa 39 ☎531400
Apr–Oct
🛁 🚿 70 **P**10 Lift ☾ sB🛁 🚿 2200–4050 dB🛁 🚿 3300–4600 M1150 🎾 Beach
Credit cards [2] [3] [5]

SON SERVERA (☎971)

At **COSTA DE LOS PINOS** (7.5km NE)

★★★★***Eurotel Golf Punta Rotja*** ☎567600 tx68666
29 Mar–Oct
🛁 190 **P** Lift ☾ 🎾 🏊 ◪ Beach sea
Credit cards [2] [3] [4] [5]

MENORCA (MINORCA)
MAHÓN (☎971)

At **VILLACARLOS** (3km W)

★★★★***Agamenon*** Fontanillas ☎362150
Apr–Oct
🛁 76 **P**30 Lift ☾ 🏊 sea

BARAJAS See **MADRID**

BARCELONA
Barcelona (☎93)

★★★★★***Avenida Palace*** (SRS) av Gran via des les Corts Catalones 605–607 ☎3019600 tx54734
🛁 229 **P** Lift ☾

★★★★★**Ritz** av Gran via de les Corts Catalones 668 ☎3185200 tx52739
🛁 204 **P**3 Lift ☾ sB🛁 11975 dB🛁 18450 M4945 t12%
Credit cards [1] [2] [3] [5]

★★★★**Condado** Aribau 201 ☎2002311 tx54546
🛁 89 Lift ☾ sB🛁 3155–3500 dB🛁 5510–6195 Mfr1295 t6%
Credit cards [2] [3] [5]

★★★★**Diplomatic** (GT) carrer de Pau Claris ☎3173100 tx54701
🛁 215 🏠 **P**80 Lift ☾ sB🛁 fr12060 dB🛁 fr15750 M3200 t12% 🏊
Credit cards [1] [2] [3] [4] [5]

★★★★**Majestic** (BW) ps de Gracia 70 ☎2154512 tx52211
🛁 355 **P** Lift ☾ sB🛁 10282 dB🛁 13250 🏊

★★★★**Manilla** Rambla Estudios III ☎3186200 tx54634
🛁 200 🏠 **P** Lift ☾ sB🛁 6250–6650 dB🛁 8100–8500 Mfr1600 t6%

★★★★**Presidente** av Diagonal 570 ☎2002111 tx52180
🛁 160 ⌂ **P** Lift ☾ sB🛁 7500—9500 dB🛁 fr11900 Mfr2500 t% ≈

★★★★***Princesa Sofia*** pl Papa Pio XII ☎3307111 tx51032
🛁 496 ⌂ **P** Lift ☾ ≈

★★★★**Regente** Rambla de Cataluña 76 ☎2152570 tx51939
🛁 78 Lift ☾ sB🛁 5900 dB🛁 7000—9050 Mfr1650 t6% ≈
Credit cards [1] [2] [3] [5]

★★★**Arenas** Capitan Arenas 20 (n.rest) ☎2040300 tx54990
🛁 62 ⌂ Lift ☾ sB🛁 6400 dB🛁 9600

★★★**Astoria** (BW) c de Paris 203 (n.rest) ☎2098311 tx97429
🛁 🚿 114 Lift ☾ sB🛁 🚿 3919—5114 dB🛁 🚿 6108—7208 t6%
Credit cards [1] [2] [3] [4] [5]

★★★**Calderón** (BW) Rambla de Cataluña 26 ☎3010000 tx51549
🛁 244 ⌂ **P**65 Lift ☾ sB🛁 8904 dB🛁 11130 t5% ≈
Credit cards [1] [2] [3] [4] [5]

★★★**Cristal** Diputación 257 ☎3016600 tx54560
🛁 🚿 150 ⌂ **P** Lift ☾ sB🛁 🚿 5900—7000 dB🛁 🚿 9050 t%

★★★**Dante** c Mallorca 181 ☎3232254 tx52588
🛁 🚿 81 ⌂ **P**20 Lift ☾ sB🛁 4575—4975 dB🛁 5850—6250 t6%
Credit cards [1] [2] [3] [4] [5]

★★★**Derby** (BW) c de Loreto 21 ☎3223215 tx97429
🛁 116 ⌂ **P**200 Lift ☾ sB🛁 6266 dB🛁 10082
Credit cards [1] [2] [3] [4] [5]

★★★**Expo** (GT) c Mallorca 1 ☎3251212 tx54147
🛁 🚿 432 Lift ≈

★★★***Gaudi*** ctra Nou de la Rambla 12 ☎3179032 tx50111
🛁 73 **P** Lift ☾
Credit cards [1] [2] [3] [4] [5]

★★★**Regina** (BW) c Vergara 4 ☎3013232 tx59380
🛁 103 ⌂ **P** Lift sB🛁 3900 dB🛁 6400

★★★**Wilson** av Diagonal 568 (n.rest) ☎2092511 tx52180
🛁 55 ⌂ Lift ☾ sB🛁 4350—5150 dB🛁 6700 t6%

★★**Park** av Marques Argentera 11 ☎3196000
rm95 (🛁 🚿 75) ⌂ Lift sB2000—2300 sB🛁 🚿 2350—3000 dB🛁 🚿 3550—4200 M950 t6%
Credit cards [2] [3] [5]

British Motors Paseo Reina E Montcada nr 13 ☎2048352 AR DJ

⛟ **British Motors** Floridablanca 133 ☎2230882 AR

California c Mallorca 419 ☎2363545 **P**

Spain

⛟ **Auto-Layetana** c Infanta Carlota 2 ☎3216150 For

⛟ **F Roca** Diputación 43 ☎3251550 M/c AR Aud Chy DJ RR VW

⛟ **Romagosa** c Bolivia 243—245 ☎3071957 LR

⛟ **Romagosa** c Padilla 318 ☎2566300 Ope

⛟ **Ryvesa** Aragón 179 ☎2531600 Mer

BARCO DE ÁVILA (EL)
Ávila (☎918)

★★★***Manila*** ctra de Plasencia Km 69 ☎340844
🛁 50 ⌂ **P** Lift ☾ mountains

BEGUR
Girona (☎972)

★★★***Bagur*** De Coma y Ros 8 ☎622207
Apr—Sep
🛁 🚿 35 **P**10 ☾ mountains

★★**Sa Riera** Playa de Sa Riera ☎623000
15 Mar—15 Oct
🛁 🚿 41 **P**55 sB🛁 🚿 2250—2630 dB🛁 🚿 3920—4570 M1000 t6% ≈ sea

At **AIGUA BLAVA** (3.5km SE)

★★★***Aigua-Blava*** Playa de Fornells ☎622058
29 Mar—21 Oct
🛁 🚿 85 ⌂ **P** ☾ 🎾 ≈ sea
Credit card [3]

★★★**Parador Nacional Costa Brava** ☎622162
🛁 77 A10rm **P**72 Lift ☾ sB🛁 5400—6100 dB🛁 8700—9700 Mfr1950 t6% ≈ sea mountains
Credit cards [2] [3] [5]

BÉJAR
Salamanca (☎923)

★★★**Colón** c Colón 42 ☎400650 tx26809
🛁 54 Lift sB🛁 1950—2750 dB🛁 3400—4100 M1300 t6% mountains
Credit cards [1] [2] [3] [4] [5]

BENALMÁDENA
Málaga (☎952)

★★★★**Riviera** ctra Cádiz-Málaga Km288 ☎441240 tx77041
🛁 189 **P**50 Lift ☾ sB🛁 4450—6450 dB🛁 6900—9900 M1600 t6% 🎾 ≈ sea
Credit cards [1] [2] [3] [5]

★★★**Siroco** ctra de Cádiz Km228 ☎443040 tx77135
🛁 261 **P**40 Lift sB🛁 2120—4250 dB🛁 3250—6500 M1460—1585 t6% 🎾 ≈ sea
Credit cards [1] [2] [3] [4] [5]

★★***Puerto Benalmádena*** ctra de Cádiz Km229 ☎441640
🛁 78 Lift ≈ sea

BENAVENTE
Zamora (☎988)

★★★**Parador Nacional** ☎630304
🛁 30 ⌂ **P** ☾ sB🛁 4900—6200 dB🛁 7000—8200 M1600—1800 t6%
Credit cards [1] [2] [3] [4] [5]

BENICARLO
Castellón (☎964)

★★★***Parador Costa del Azahar*** ctra de Peñiscola ☎470100
🛁 108 **P** ☾ 🎾 ≈ sea

★★**Sol** av Magallanes 90 ☎471349
🛁 22 ⌂ **P**50 ☾ sB🛁 1900—2200 dB🛁 2600—3000 M800 sea mountains

BENICASIM
Castellón (☎964)

★★★★**Azor** ps Maritimo ☎300350 tx65503
Mar—Oct
🛁 88 **P**80 Lift ☾ sB🛁 3170—3570 dB🛁 4540—4840 M1500 🎾 ≈ sea mountains
Credit cards [1] [3] [4] [5]

★★★**Voramar** ☎300150
Easter—15 Oct
🛁 55 ⌂ **P**30 sB🛁 2150—2650 dB🛁 3300—4100 M775—925 t6% 🎾 Beach sea

★★**Bonaire** ps Maritimo ☎300600 tx65503
Mar—Oct
🛁 78 **P**78 ☾ sB🛁 2475—2825 dB🛁 3950—4250 M1300 🎾 ≈ sea mountains

BENIDORM
Alicante (☎965)

★★★★**Gran Delfin** Playa de Poniente ☎853400
22 Mar—1 Oct
🛁 99 **P**37 Lift ☾ sB🛁 5475—5925 dB🛁 9350—10150 M2300 🎾 ≈ sea
Credit cards [1] [2] [3] [5]

★★***Presidente*** av Filipinas ☎853950
🛁 🚿 228 Lift ☾ 🎾 ≈
Credit cards [1] [2] [3] [5]

⛟ **Autonautica** ctra Alicante-Valencia Km116.700 ☎853562 For

BIELSA
Huesca (☎974)

At **VALLE DE PINETA** (14km NW)

★★★***Parador Nacional Monte Perdido*** ☎501011
🛁 16 **P** Lift ☾ mountains

BILBAO (BILBO)
Vizcaya (☎94)

★★★★★**Villa de Bilbao** Gran Via 87 ☎4416000 tx32164
🛁 142 ⌂ **P** Lift ☾ sB🛁 10280 dB🛁 fr13300 Mfr1700 t12%
Credit cards [2] [5]

★★★★**Aránzazu** R-Arias 66 ☎4413100 tx32164
🛁 172 ⌂ **P** Lift ☾ sB🛁 6770 dB🛁 8840

M1000 t%
Credit cards 1 2 3 5

★★★★***Avenida*** av H-de-Saracho 2 ☎4124300 tx32164
rm16

★★★★***Carlton*** pl F-Moyua 2 (n.rest) ☎4162200 tx32233
🛁150

★★★★**Ercilla** (GT) Ercilla 37 ☎4438800 tx32449
🛁350 🚗 P80 Lift sB🛁6800 dB🛁10800 M1000 t6%
Credit cards 1 2 3 5

BLANES
Girona (☎972)

★★★★**Park** ☎330250
May–Oct
🛁131 P100 Lift ☾ sB🛁3355–4265 dB🛁5510–6960 M1240 🎾 ⛱ Beach sea

★★**Horitzo** ps Maritimo 11 ☎330400
15 Apr–Oct
🛁🚿122 Lift ☾ sB🛁🚿1975–2675 dB🛁🚿3450–5250 M1100

★★***San Antonio*** ps del Mar 63 ☎331150
May–Sep
🛁🚿156 Lift ☾

★★**San Francisco** ps del Mar 27 ☎330477
May–Oct
🛁🚿32 🚗 P20 Lift ☾ sB🛁🚿1425–1825 dB🛁🚿2550–2950 M675–700 sea

BURGOS
Burgos (☎947)

★★★★**Aimiranté Bonifaz** Vitoria 22–24 (n.rest) ☎206943 tx39430
🛁79 Lift ☾ sB🛁3145–3670 dB🛁5740–6690 t6%
Credit cards 1 2 3 4 5

★★★★**Landa Palace** (Relais et Châteaux) (2km S on N1) ctra de Madrid–Irún Km230 ☎206343
🚿39 🚗 P Lift ☾ sB🚿fr8350 dB🚿fr11200 Mfr3600 t12% ⛱

★★★***Asubio*** Carmen 6 (n.rest) ☎203445
🛁30 Lift ☾ sB🛁2700–2900 dB🛁3600–4200

🚘 **J Barrios** c de Vitoria 109 ☎224900 Fia Lan

🚘 **Mecanico 'Sulzo'** San Agustin 5–7 ☎202364 P Aud VW

🚘 **Pedro** ctra Madrid/Irún Km247 ☎224528 P Peu Tal

BURRIANA
Castellón (☎964)

★★★***Aloha*** (2.5km E) av Mediterraneo 75 ☎510104
Mar–Sep
🛁30 P Lift ☾ ⛱ sea mountains

CABRERA (LA)
Madrid (☎91)

★★**Mavi** ctra de Madrid–Irún 58 ☎8688000

Spain

🛁🚿43 P ☾ sB🛁🚿1640–1790 dB🛁🚿2880–3030 Mfr1050 mountains

CÁCERES
Cáceres (☎927)

★★★**Alcántara** av Virgen de Guadalupe 14 ☎228900
🛁67 🚗 Lift ☾ sB🛁2910–3160 dB🛁4845–5220 t6%
Credit cards 1 2 3 5

★★***Alvarez*** Moret 20 ☎246400
🛁🚿37 P4 Lift ☾
Credit cards 2 3 5

CADAQUES
Girona (☎972)

★★★**Playa-Sol** (n.rest) ☎258100
Closed Jan
🛁🚿50 🚗 P50 Lift ☾ sB🛁🚿3850–4250 dB🛁🚿7100–8300 🎾 ⛱ sea
Credit cards 1 5

CÁDIZ
Cádiz (☎956)

★★★**Atlantico** Parque Genovés 9 ☎212301
🛁153 ⛱
Credit cards 1 2

🚘 **Saina** Ronda del Puente ☎253285 Ren

CALAFELL
Tarragona (☎977)

★★★**Kursaal** av San J-de-Dios ☎692300
Etr–Oct
🛁39 🚗 P14 Lift ☾ sB🛁2900–3400 dB🛁5300–6800 M1500 t6% sea
Credit cards 1 2 3 5

★★★***Miramar*** Rambia Costa Dorada 1 ☎690700
26 Mar–15 Oct
🛁🚿200 🚗 P Lift ☾ ⛱

CALAHORRA
La Rioja (☎941)

★★★**Parador Nacional Marco Fablo Quintiliano** av Generalisimo ☎130358
🛁63 P50 Lift ☾ sB🛁4500–5000 dB🛁6000–6700 M1600–1800 t6%
Credit cards 1 2 3 5

CALA RATJADA See **BALEARES (ISLAS DE)** under **MALLORCA**

CALA SAN VICENTE See **BALEARES (ISLAS DE)** under **POLLENSA, MALLORCA**

CALATAYUD
Zaragoza (☎976)

★★***Calatayud*** (2km NE on N11 at Km237) ☎881323
🛁🚿63 🚗 P ☾ mountains
Credit card 3

CALDES D'ESTRAC
Barcelona (☎93)

★★★★**Colón (DPn)** ps 16 ☎7910351
Mar–Oct
🛁83 🚗 P12 Lift ☾ sB🛁3250–3950 dB🛁5900–7100 M1350 🎾 ⛱ sea mountains
Credit cards 1 2 3

CALELLA DE LA COSTA
Barcelona (☎93)

★★★★**Las Vegas** ctra de Francia ☎7690850
May–Oct
🛁🚿110 P35 Lift ☾ sB🛁🚿1425–2875 dB🛁🚿2350–5275 M650 ⛱ sea mountains
Credit cards 1 2 3 5

★★★★**Mont-Rosa** ps de las Rocas ☎7690508
May–Oct
🛁120 P Lift ☾ sB🛁2250–4090 dB🛁3580–6310 M1150 t12% ⛱ sea

★★***Fragata*** ps de las Rocas ☎7692112
15 May–15 Oct
🛁72 P Lift ☾ sea

CALELLA DE PALAFRUGELL See **PALAFRUGELL**

CALPE
Alicante (☎965)

★★★**Paradero Ifach** Explanada del Puerto 50 ☎830300
Mar–Dec
🛁29 P60 sB🛁2225 dB🛁4450 t6% 🎾 Beach sea

★★**Venta la Chata** (4km N) ☎830308
18 Nov–18 Dec
🛁17 🚗 P50 ☾ sB🛁2025–2440 dB🛁3730–4930 M1180 🎾 sea mountains
Credit cards 2 5

🚘 **Autocrats** av Diputación ☎832803 P Toy

CAMBADOS
Pontevedra (☎986)

★★★**Parador Nacional del Albariño** ps de Cervantes ☎542250
🛁63 P70 Lift ☾ sB🛁3675–5050 dB🛁6700–8200 M1800 t6%
Credit cards 1 2 3 5

CARDONA
Barcelona (☎93)

★★★**Parador Nacional Duques de Cardona** ☎8691275
🛁61 P60 Lift ☾ sB🛁5000 dB🛁6700 M1800 t6% mountains
Credit cards 1 2 3 5

CARMONA
Sevilla (☎954)

★★★★**Parador Nacional Alcázar Rey Don Pedro** ☎141010 tx72992
🛁🚿59 P100 Lift ☾ sB🛁🚿4600–6600 dB🛁🚿8700–10000 M1950 t6% ⛱
Credit cards 1 2 3 4 5

CAROLINA (LA)
Jaén (☎953)

★★★**Perdiz** (ctr a N IV) ☎660300 tx28315

🛁 89 ⌂ **P**80 ☾ sB🛁 3660—4160 dB🛁 5020—5670 M1500 t6% ≈ mountains
Credit cards [1] [2] [3]

CARTAGENA
Murcia (☎968)

★★★***Cartagonova*** Marcos Redondo 3 ☎504200 tx67771

🛁 🚿 126 ⌂ **P** Lift ☾ sea

CASTELLCIUTAT See **SEU D'URGELL (LA)**

CASTELLDEFELS
Barcelona (☎93)

★★★**Neptuno** ps Garbi 74 ☎6651450

🛁 42 **P** Lift ☾ sB2800 sB🛁 3100 dB4500 dB🛁 5100 ⚲ ≈

★★★**Rancho** ps de la Marina 212 ☎6651900

🛁 🚿 60 Lift ☾ sB🛁 🚿 3900 dB🛁 🚿 5300 ⚲ ≈ mountains
Credit card [5]

CASTELLÓN DE LA PLANA
Castellón (☎964)

★★★**Mindoro** Moyano 4 ☎222300 tx65413

🛁 114 **P**60 Lift ☾ sB🛁 4990 dB🛁 7780 M1350 t6% sea
Credit cards [1] [2] [3] [4] [5]

🚗 **Tagerbaf** Hños Vilafana 13 ☎216653 **P** All makes

At **GRAO DE CASTELLÓN** (5km E)

★★★★**Golf** Playa del Pinar ☎221950

Mar—Oct
🛁 127 ⌂ **P** Lift ☾ sB🛁 3550—3825 dB🛁 5100—5650 M950—1000 t6% ⚲ ≈ Beach [▣] sea
Credit cards [1] [3] [5]

CASTILLO DE SANTA CATALINA
See **JAÉN**

CAZORLA
Jaén (☎953)

★★***Parador Nacional el Adelantado*** (25km SE) ☎721075

rm30 (🛁 16) A8rm ⌂ ⟲

CERVERA DE PISUERGA
Palencia (☎988)

★★★***Parador Nacional de Fuentes Carrionas*** ☎870075

25 Dec—2 Nov
🛁 80 ⌂ **P** Lift ☾ mountains lake

CESTONA
Guipúzcoa (☎943)

★★★★**Arocena** ☎867040

10 Jul—10 Oct
🛁 109 ⌂ **P**60 Lift ☾ sB🛁 2930 dB🛁 4785 M1400 t6% ⚲ ≈ mountains
Credit cards [1] [2] [3]

Spain

CHINCHÓN
Madrid (☎91)

★★★**Parador Nacional** av Generalisimo 1 ☎8940836

🛁 38 ☾ sB🛁 5700—7000 dB🛁 7500—9200 M1800—1950 t6% ≈ mountains
Credit cards [1] [2] [3] [5]

CIUDAD RODRIGO
Salamanca (☎923)

★★★**Parador Nacional Enrique II** pl del Castillo 1 ☎460150

🛁 27 **P** ☾ sB🛁 5000—6600 dB🛁 6700—8700 M1800 t6% mountains
Credit cards [1] [2] [3] [5]

🚗 **Vicente** Salamanca Km320 ☎461426 All makes

COMA-RUGA
Tarragona (☎977)

★★★**Gran Europa (Pn)** av Palfurina ☎680411 tx56681

Apr—Nov
🛁 160 ⌂ **P**70 Lift ☾ sB🛁 3050—5800 dB🛁 5500—11000 ⚲ ≈ Beach sea
Credit cards [1] [3] [5]

COMILLAS
Cantabria (☎942)

★★★**Casal del Castro** San Jeronimo ☎720061

Apr—Sep
🛁 45 **P**40 Lift sB🛁 2600—2800 dB🛁 3600—4600 M1400 ⚲ sea mountains
Credit cards [2] [3]

CÓRDOBA
Córdoba (☎957)

★★★★***Gran Capitan*** av America 3—5 ☎470250

🛁 97 ⌂ **P** Lift ☾

★★★★***Meliá Córdoba*** Jàrdines de la Victoria ☎298066 tx76591

🛁 106 **P** Lift ☾ ≈

★★★★**Parador Nacional de la Arruzafa** av de la Arruzafa ☎275900

🛁 🚿 62 ☾ ≈ mountains

★★**Marisa** Cardenal Herrero 6 ☎474142

🛁 28 sB🛁 2200 dB🛁 3850
Credit cards [2] [3] [5]

★***Brilliante*** av del Brilliante 97 ☎475800

rm27 (🛁 🚿 18) mountains
Credit cards [1] [3]

CORUÑA (LA) (CORUÑA A)
La Coruña (☎981)

★★★★**Finisterre** ps del Parrote 2 ☎205400 tx86086

🛁 127 **P** Lift ☾ sB🛁 4600 dB🛁 7800 ⚲ ≈ Beach sea

COSTA DE LOS PINOS See **BALEARES (ISLAS DE)** under **SON SERVERA, MALLORCA**

COVARRUBIAS
Burgos (☎947)

★★★**Arlanza** pl de Doña Urraca ☎403025

15 Mar—15 Dec
🛁 40 Lift ☾ sB🛁 2400—2600 dB🛁 4850—4450 M1100 t6% mountains
Credit cards [1] [2] [3] [5]

CUENCA
Cuenca (☎966)

★★★**Cueva del Fraile** (BW) ☎211571

Mar—13 Jan
🛁 40 **P** ☾ sB🛁 2680—2980 dB🛁 4160—4510 M1200 t6% ⚲ ≈ mountains
Credit cards [1] [2] [3] [4] [5]

★★★**Torremangana** San Ignacio de Loyola 9 ☎223351 tx23400

🛁 115 ⌂ Lift ☾ sB🛁 3425—3975 dB🛁 6150—6850 M1350 t6%
Credit cards [1] [2] [3] [5]

CULLERA
Valencia (☎96)

★★★***Sicania*** ctra El Faro, Playa del Raco ☎1520143 tx64774

🛁 117 ⌂ **P** Lift ☾ Beach sea

DENIA
Alicante (☎965)

At **PLAYA DE LES MARINAS** (1km N)

★★**Angeles** Playa de las Marinas 649 ☎780458

15 Mar—30 Nov
🛁 60 **P**50 ☾ sB🛁 1850—2250 dB🛁 3100—3850 M1000 ⚲ Beach sea
Credit cards [1] [3] [5]

EL Each name preceded by 'El' is listed under the name that follows it.

EJIDO (EL)
Almeria (☎951)

★★★★**Golf Almerimar** ☎480950 tx78933

🛁 38 A20rm **P**16 Lift ☾ sB🛁 5375—7355 dB🛁 6750—8750 M600 t6% ⚲ ≈ sea
Credit cards [1] [2] [3] [4] [5]

ELCHE
Alicante (☎965)

★★★**Huerto del Cura** F-G-Sanchiz 14 ☎458040 tx66814

🛁 59 ⌂ **P**50 ☾ sB🛁 5575—5925 dB🛁 8100—8600 M1750 t6% ⚲ ≈
Credit cards [1] [2] [3] [5]

ESCALA (L')
Girona (☎972)

★★★***Barca*** E-Serra 25 ☎770162

Jun—Sep
🛁 26 ☾ sea

ESCORIAL (EL) See **SAN LORENZO DE EL ESCORIAL**

ESTARTIT (L')
Girona (☎972)

★★**Amer** ☎757212
May—Oct
🛁 54 A11rm ☾ sB🛁 1715—2200
dB🛁 2630—3800 ≈

★***Vila*** Santa Ana 34 ☎758113
Jun—Sep
rm58 (🛁 🚿 35) A20rm ☾

ESTEPONA
Málaga (☎952)

★★★★***Robinson Clubhotel Atalaya Park*** (SRS) ☎781300 tx77210
🛁 446 **P**86 Lift ☾ 🎾 ≈ ▣ Beach ◳ sea mountains
Credit cards [1] [2] [3] [4] [5]

★★★***Santa Marta*** Apartado 2 ☎780716
Apr—Sep
🛁 37 ☾ ≈ Beach sea mountains

★**Buenavista** ps Maritimo ☎800137
🛁 38 ⌂ Lift ☾ sB🛁 1200—1800
dB🛁 2400—3600 M800 t6% sea
Credit card [3]

FERROL
La Coruña (☎981)

🚗 **Castelos** ctra a la Gándara 11/17
☎313365 For

FIGUERES
Girona (☎972)

★★★★**President** crte Nacional 11 de Madrid-Francia ☎501700
🛁 🚿 75 ⌂ **P**60 Lift ☾ sB🛁 🚿 2890—3990
sB🛁 🚿 4460—5890 M1375
Credit cards [1] [2] [3] [5]

★★★**Ampurdan** ctra Madrid-Francia Km763 ☎500562
🛁 39 ⌂ **P**50 Lift ☾
Credit cards [1] [2] [3] [5]

★★★***Durán*** c Lasuaca 5 ☎501250
🛁 65 ⌂ Lift ☾
Credit cards [1] [2] [3]

★★**Muriscot** ☎505151
🛁 🚿 20 ⌂ **P**40 Lift sB🛁 🚿 1600—1900
dB🛁 🚿 2500—2900 mountains
Credit cards [1] [2] [3] [5]

🚗 **Central** Carrer Nou s/n, Zona Rally Sud
☎500667 For

Victoria ctra de Rosas ☎500293 LR

FORMENTOR See **BALEARES (ISLAS DE)** under **MALLORCA**

FORNELLS DE LA SELVA
See **GIRONA (GERONA)**

FUENGIROLA
Málaga (☎952)

★★★★**Mare Nostrum** ctra de Cádiz
☎471100 tx27578
Jul—15 Oct
🛁 242 ⌂ **P**100 Lift sB🛁 3340—4040
dB🛁 4680—5680 M1000 t6% 🎾 ≈ sea
Credit cards [1] [2] [3] [4]

★★★★***Palmeras*** ps Maritimo ☎472700
tx77202
🛁 428 ⌂ **P** Lift 🎾 ≈ sea mountains
Credit card [2]

★★★★**Piramides** ps Maritimo ☎470600
tx77315
🛁 320 ⌂ **P**50 Lift ☾ sB🛁 5400—6950
dB🛁 7400—9550 M2000 t6% 🎾 ≈ sea mountains
Credit cards [1] [2] [3] [4] [5]

★★★**Florida** Playa Florida ☎476100
tx77791
🛁 116 **P**15 Lift ☾ sB🛁 2150—2900
dB🛁 3950—4850 M1125 t6% ≈ Beach sea
Credit cards [2] [3] [5]

FUENTE DÉ
Cantabria (☎942)

★★***Parador Nacional del Rio Deva***
☎730001
Nov—15 Dec
🛁 78 **P** ☾ mountains

FUENTERRABÍA (HONDARRIBIA)
Guipúzcoa (☎943)

★★**Guadalupe** Punta de Espana (n.rest)
☎641650
Jun—Sep
🛁 🚿 35 **P**15 ☾ sB🛁 🚿 2225—2450
dB🛁 🚿 3800—5250 t6% ≈

★★***Parador Nacional el Emperador*** pl de Armas del Castillo (n.rest) ☎642140
🛁 16

At **JAIZKÍBEL** (8km SW)

★★★***Jaizkibel*** Monte Jaizkibel ☎641100
🛁 🚿 13

GANDÍA
Valencia (☎96)

★★**Ernesto** ctra de Valencia 40
☎2864011
🛁 🚿 86 **P** Lift ☾ sB🛁 🚿 1275
dB🛁 🚿 2350 M750

GERONA See **GIRONA**

GIJÓN
Asturias (☎985)

★★★★***Robledo*** A-Trúan 2 (n.rest)
☎355940
🛁 138 Lift ☾

★★***Parador Nacional Molino Viejo*** Parc de Isabel la Catolica 19 ☎370511
🛁 6 **P** ☾

GIRONA (GERONA)
Girona (☎972)

★★**Europa** J-Garreta 23 (n.rest) ☎202750
🛁 🚿 26 **P** Lift ☾ sB🛁 🚿 1675—2075
dB🛁 🚿 3050—3550

At **FORNELLA DE LA SELVA** (5km S off N11)

★★★**Fornella Park** ☎476125
🛁 31 **P**100 Lift ☾ sB🛁 3080—3580
dB🛁 5210—5260 M1500 t6% ≈ mountains
Credit cards [1] [2] [3] [5]

🚗 **Blanch** ctra N11 Km718 ☎476028 Ope

GRANADA
Granada (☎958)

★★★★**Alhambra Palace** Peña Partida 2
☎221466 tx78400
🛁 🚿 136 **P** Lift ☾ sB🛁 🚿 7100
dB🛁 🚿 9300 M1950 t6% mountains
Credit cards [1] [2] [3] [4] [5]

★★★★**Brasilia** Recogidas 7 (n.rest)
☎258450
🛁 69 ⌂ **P** Lift ☾ sB🛁 2950—3350
dB🛁 4700—5300 t6%
Credit cards [3] [5]

★★★★***Carmen*** av J-Atonio 62 ☎258300
tx78546
🛁 207 ⌂ **P** Lift ☾

★★★★**Meliá Granada** A-Garnivet 7
☎227400 tx78429
🛁 211 Lift ☾ sB🛁 4350—6050
dB🛁 6800—7900 M1600

★★★**Guadalupe** av de los Alijares
☎223423
🛁 43 **P**15 Lift sB🛁 3250 dB🛁 6200
M1300 t6% mountains
Credit cards [1] [2] [3] [5]

★★★**Kenia** Molinas 65 ☎227506
🛁 19 **P**15 ☾ sB🛁 2550 dB🛁 4900 M1400 t6%
Credit cards [1] [2] [3] [4] [5]

★★★***Parador Nacional de San Francisco*** (in the Alhambra) ☎221462
🛁 32 **P** ☾ mountains

★★**Inglaterra** Cetti Merien 4 (off Gran Via de Colon) ☎221559
rm40 (🛁 36) Lift ☾ sB2500 dB🛁 3900 t6%
Credit cards [2] [5]

★**América** Real Alhambra 53 ☎227471
Mar—Oct
rm14 (🛁 13) ☾ sB🛁 2750 dB🛁 4600
M1300 t6% mountains

🚗 **Autiberia** av Andalucia ☎205602 LR Ope

🚗 **Auto Dibesa** av Andalucia Km3
☎276750 **P** Aud VW

🚗 **Rafael de los Reyes** Carril del Picón 9
☎202225 All makes

At **SIERRA NEVADA** (40km SE)
★★★★***Meliá Sierra Nevada*** Pradollano
☎480400 tx78507
Dec—Apr
🛁 221 **P** Lift ☾ ≈ mountains

★★★***Meliá Sol y Nieve*** Pradollano
☎480300 tx78507
Dec—May
🛁 178 **P** Lift ☾ ≈ mountains

★★★***Parador Nacional Sierra Nevada***
☎480200
Closed Nov
🛁 🚿 32 ⌂ **P** ☾ 🎾 mountains

GRAO DE CASTELLÓN See **CASTELLÓN DE LA PLANA**

GREDOS
Avila (☎918)

★★★**Parador Nacional de Gredos** ☎348048

🛁77 🚗 **P**150 Lift ☾ sB🛁3500—5100 dB🛁6000—7700 M1300—1800 t6% U mountains
Credit cards [1] [2] [5]

GUADALAJARA
Guadalajara (☎911)

★★★***Husa*** ctra Madrid—Barcelona Km57 ☎221800

🛁61 🚗 **P** Lift ☾ 🎾 ≈

🔧**R Aguilera** Ferial 7 — Ingeniero Marina 44 ☎220029 All makes

GUADALUPE
Cáceres (☎927)

Hospederiá de Real Monasterio (Monastery where accommodation is provided by the monks) pl J-Carlos 1 ☎367000

🛁40 **P**30 Lift ☾ sB🛁2560 dB🛁4020 M1380 t6% mountains
Credit cards [1] [3]

★★**Parador Nacional de Zurbarian** Marques de la Romana 10 ☎367075

🛁20 **P** ☾ dB🛁5500—6500 ≈ mountains

HUELVA
Huelva (☎955)

★★★★**Luz Huelva** av Sundheim 26 (n.rest) ☎250011 tx75527

🛁105 🚗 **P**16 Lift sB🛁5490 dB🛁7950 🎾 📺
Credit cards [1] [2] [3] [5]

★★★**Tartessos** av M-A-Pinzon 13—15 ☎245611

🛁112 Lift ☾ sB🛁2750 dB🛁4900 t6%
Credit cards [1] [2] [3] [5]

HUESCA
Huesca (☎974)

★★★**Pedro I de Argagón** ps de Gl-Franco 34 ☎220300 tx58626

🛁52 🚗 **P**12 Lift ☾ sB🛁3475 dB🛁5550 M1200 t6%
Credit cards [1] [3] [5]

🔧**Tumasa** ctra Zaragoza ☎243294 LR Peu Tal

IBIZA See **BALEARES (ISLAS DE)**

IGUALADA
Barcelona (☎93)

★★★***América*** ctra N11 Km557 ☎8031000

🚿52 **P**40 Lift ☾ ≈ mountains
Credit cards [1] [3] [5]

IRÚN
Guipúzcoa (☎943)

★★★**Alcázar** av Iparralde 11 ☎620900

🛁48 Lift ☾ sB🛁2625—2975 dB🛁4550—5150 M1200 t6%
Credit card [2]

★★***Lizaso*** Marires de Guadalupe 5 (n.rest) ☎611600

rm20 (🛁🚿10) ☾

★***Paris*** ps de Colón 94—96 (n.rest) ☎616545

rm22 (🛁🚿7)

JACA
Huesca (☎974)

★★★**Gran** ps del Gl-Franco 1 ☎360900

🛁🚿80 🚗 **P** Lift ☾ 🎾 ≈ mountains

★★**Conde Aznar** Gl-Franco 3 ☎361050

🛁🚿23 ☾ sB🛁🚿2225—2725 dB🛁🚿2950—3550 M990 St%

JAÉN
Jaén (☎953)

🔧**López** Sta Tomás 2 ☎228501 Sko

At **CASTILLO DE SANTA CATALINA** (4km W)

★★★★**Parador Nacional** ☎264411

🛁43 Lift ☾ sB🛁5800—6600 dB🛁7700—8700 M1800 t6% ≈ mountains
Credit cards [1] [2] [3] [5]

JAIZKÍBEL See **FUENTERRABIA**

JARANDILLA DE LA VERA
Cáceres (☎927)

★★★★***Parador Nacional de Carlos-V*** ☎560117

🛁6 **P** ☾ ≈ mountains

JÁVEA
Alicante (☎965)

★★★***Parador Nacional Costa Blanca*** ☎790200

🛁65 🚗 **P** Lift ☾ ≈ sea

🔧**Auto Jávea** av de Ondara 11 ☎790178 For

JEREZ DE LA FRONTERA
Cádiz (☎956)

★★★★***Jerez*** (CIGA) av A-Domecq 41 ☎330600 tx75059

🛁120 **P** Lift ☾ ≈

★★***Aloha*** (On western bypass) ☎332500

🛁30 🚗 **P** ≈

JONQUERA (LA)
Girona (☎972)

★★★***Porta Catalana*** (2km SW on A17-service area) ☎540640

🛁80 **P** Lift ☾ mountains

★★★***Puerta de España*** ctra Nacional II ☎540120

🛁26 **P** ☾ mountains

LA Each name preceded by 'La' is listed under the name that follows it.

LAREDO
Cantabria (☎942)

★★★**Cosmopol** av de la Victoria ☎605400

15 Jun—15 Sep
🛁60 **P**60 Lift sB🛁3465 dB🛁5680 M1500 t% ≈ sea
Credit cards [1] [2] [3]

★***Ramona*** av J-Antonio 4 ☎607189

rm13 **P**35 ☾

LECUMBERRI
Navarra (☎948)

★★***Ayestaran*** ctra San Juan 64 ☎504127

rm120 (🛁🚿65) A94rm 🚗 **P** Lift ≈ mountains lake

LEÓN
León (☎987)

★★★★**Conde Luna** Indepencia 7 ☎206512 tx89888

🛁150 🚗 Lift sB🛁3100—3400 dB🛁6200—6700 M800 t6% 📺
Credit cards [1] [2] [3] [4] [5]

★★★★**San Marcos** pl San Marcos ☎237300 tx89809

🛁215 Lift sB🛁6800—7250 dB🛁10600—11700 M2000 t12%
Credit cards [1] [2] [3] [5]

★★★★***Oliden*** Playa de Santo Domingo 4 ☎227500

rm50 (🛁🚿45) **P** Lift ☾

★★★**Riosol** av de Palencia 3 ☎223650

🛁141 Lift ☾ sB🛁2305—2620 dB🛁3790—4290 M1050 t6% mountains
Credit cards [1] [2] [3] [4] [5]

★★**Quindos** av J-Antonio 24 ☎236200

🛁96 **P** Lift ☾ sB🛁2550—2800 dB🛁3950—4250 M1100 t6%
Credit cards [1] [2] [3] [4] [5]

LÉRIDA See **LLEIDA**

LLANÇÁ
Girona (☎972)

At **PUERTO DE LLANÇÁ** (2km NE)

★★★**Mendisol** Playa de Grifeu ☎380100

15 Jun—15 Sep
🛁35 🚗 **P** ☾ sB🛁3500—5350 dB🛁5000—6600 M1400 sea mountains
Credit card [3]

★★***Berna*** ps Marítimo 5 ☎380150

15 May—Sep & Xmas wk
🛁38 **P** ☾ Beach sea

★***Miramar*** ps Marítimo 23 ☎380132

Apr—Sep
rm31

LLANFRANCH See **PALAFRUGELL**

LLANES
Asturias (☎985)

★★***Peñablanca*** Pidal 1 (n.rest) ☎400166

15 Jun—15 Sep
🛁31 ☾
Credit cards [1] [3]

LLANSA See **LLANÇÁ**

LLEIDA (LÉRIDA)
Lleida (☎973)

★★★**Condes de Urgel** av de Barcelona 17—27 ☎202300

105 P Lift ☾ sB 3925 dB 6050
Credit cards 1 2 3 5

Dalmau ctra Nacional 2 Km463 ☎261611 Aud VW

LLORET DE MAR
Girona (☎972)

★★★★**Monterry** ctra de Tossa ☎364050 tx57374
Mar—5 Nov
228 P Lift ☾ sB 4300—5300 dB 8600—10600 M2100 t6% sea
Credit cards 1 2 3 5

★★★★**Rigat Park** Playa de Fanals ☎365200 tx57015
Mar—Oct
96 P120 Lift ☾ sB 5450—7450 dB 7900—9900 M2000 sea
Credit cards 1 3 5

★★★★**Santa Marta** (Relais et Châteaux) Playa de Santa Cristina ☎364904
20 Jan—15 Dec
78 A18rm P200 Lift ☾ sB 5000—7700 dB 8800—13800 M3500 t6% sea mountains
Credit cards 1 2 3 5

★★★**Anabel** Feliciá Serra 10 ☎364108
Mar—Oct
230 P10 Lift ☾ sea mountains

★★**Excelsior** ps M-J-Verdaguer 16 ☎364137 tx97061
24 Mar—Oct
45 Lift ☾ sB 2050—2800 dB 4000—5400 M950—1000 sea
Credit cards 1 2 3 5

★★**Fanals** ctra de Blanes ☎364112 tx57362
Apr—Oct
80 P40 Lift ☾ sB 2460—2960 dB 4920—5620 M1300 mountains
Credit card 5

Celler av Vidreras 22—26 ☎365397 Peu Tal

LOGROÑO
Rioja (☎941)

★★★★**Carlton Rioja** av Rey-J-Carlos 5 ☎242100
120 P19 Lift ☾ sB 3910—4135 dB 6470—6720 t6%
Credit cards 1 2 3 5

★★***El Cortijo*** ctra del Cortijo Km2 ☎225050
40 P ☾ mountains

LOS Each name preceded by 'Los' is listed under the name that follows it.

Spain

LUARCA
Asturias (☎985)

★***Gayoso*** ps de Gómez 4 ☎640054
28 P Lift ☾

LUGO
Lugo (☎982)

★★**Méndez Nuñez** Reina 1 ☎230711
100 Lift ☾ sB 2800—3300 dB 4600—5100 t6%

MADRID
Madrid (☎91)

See plan pages 362 and 363

★★★★★***Meliá Madrid*** c de la Princesa 27 ☎2418200 tx22537 Plan **2**
266 P Lift ☾

★★★★★**Palace** pl de la Cortes 7 ☎4297551 tx22272 Plan **3**
510 P Lift ☾ sB 13400 dB 18300 M3750 t12%
Credit cards 1 2 3 4 5

★★★★★**Princesa Plaza** (SRS) Serrano Jover 3 ☎2422100 tx44378 Plan **4A**
406 P400 Lift ☾ sB 12070 dB 15680 M3650 t12%
Credit cards 1 2 3 4 5

★★★★★**Ritz** (THF) pl de la Lealtad 5 ☎2212857 tx43986 Plan **5**
155 P Lift ☾ sB 23250—29250 dB 30500—42500 M alc t12%
Credit cards 2 3 5

★★★★★**Villa Magna** ps e la Castellana 22 ☎2614900 tx22914 Plan **6**
194 P350 Lift ☾ sB 20200 dB 28400 M6000 t12%
Credit cards 2 5

★★★★**Alcalá** (BW) c de Alcalá 66 ☎4351060 tx48094 Plan **7**
153 Lift ☾ sB 5490 dB 8700 M1750 t6%
Credit cards 1 2 3 4 5

★★★★**Castellana Inter-Continental** ps de la Castellana 49 ☎4100200 tx27686 Plan **8**
311 P Lift ☾ sB 16000 dB 20000 t6%
Credit cards 1 2 3 4 5

★★★★**Emperador** Gran Via 53 ☎2472800 tx46261 Plan **9**
232 P Lift ☾ sB 6780 dB 8820—10810 M1690 t6%
Credit cards 1 2 3 5

★★★★**Emperatriz** Lópe de Hoyos 4 ☎4136511 tx43640 Plan **10**
170 Lift ☾ sB 5415 dB 8980 M1575 t6%

★★★★***Meliá Castilla*** Cpt Haya 43 ☎2708000 tx23142 Plan **11**
1000 P Lift ☾

★★★★**Plaza** (SRS) pl de España 8 ☎2471200 tx27383 Plan **11A**
306 Lift ☾ sB 8950 dB 11660 Mfr1920 t6%
Credit cards 1 2 3 4 5

★★★★**Sanvy** c de Goya 3 ☎2760800 tx44994 Plan **12**
141 Lift ☾ sB 6900 dB 9500 t6%
Credit cards 1 2 3 5

★★★★**Velázquez** Velázquez 62 ☎2752800 tx22779 Plan **13**
144 P10 Lift ☾ sB 6450 dB 8400 M1775 t6%
Credit cards 2 3 4 5

★★★**Atlantico** Gran Via 38 (n.rest) ☎2226480 Plan **13A**
62 Lift ☾ sB 3560 dB 5350
Credit cards 1 2 3 4 5

★★★**Carlos V** c Maetro Vitoria 5 (n.rest) ☎2314100 tx48547 Plan **14**
70 P Lift ☾ sB 4025 dB 5500 t6%
Credit cards 1 2 3 5

★★★**Carlton** ps de las Delicias 26 ☎2397100 Plan **15**
133 P Lift ☾ sB 4400—6200 dB 8400—9600
Credit cards 1 2 3 5

★★★**Centro Norte** Mauricio Ravel 10 ☎7333400 tx42598 Not on plan
179 P1400 Lift ☾ sB 4625 dB 6050 M700—750 t6%
Credit cards 2 3 5

★★★***Gran Via*** Gran Via 25 (n.rest) ☎2221121 tx44173 Plan **15A**
162 Lift

★★★**Lope de Vega** Gran Via 59 (n.rest) ☎2477000 Plan **16**
47 P Lift ☾ sB 2250—2750 dB 3900—4500 t6%
Credit cards 2 5

★★★***Miguel Angel*** c de Miguel Angel 29—31 ☎4428199 tx44235 Plan **17**
305 ☾

★★★**Principe Pio** ps de Onesimo Redondo 16 ☎2478000 tx42183 Plan **18**
157 P Lift ☾ sB 3975 dB 5900 M1225 t6%
Credit cards 1 2 3

★★★**Residenciá Madrid** Carretas 10 (off Puerto del Sol) (n.rest) ☎2216520 Plan **19**
Closed 2 wks Dec
71 Lift ☾ sB 3250—3850 dB 5000
Credit cards 1 2 3 4 5

★★★**Tirol** Marqués de Urquijo 4 (n.rest) ☎2481900 Plan **20**
rm92 (84) Lift sB 3580 dB 4475
Credit card 3

★★**Mercator** c de Atocha 123 ☎4290500 tx46129 Plan **21**
90 P Lift ☾ sB 3205 dB 4985 t6%
Credit cards 1 2 3 4 5

MADRID

2	★★★★★	Meliá Madrid
3	★★★★★	Palace
4A	★★★★★	Princesa Plaza
5	★★★★★	Ritz
6	★★★★★	Villa Magna
7	★★★★	Alcalá
8	★★★★	Castellana Inter-Continental
9	★★★★	Emperador
10	★★★★	Emperatriz
11	★★★★	Meliá Castilla
11A	★★★★	Plaza
12	★★★★	Sanvy
13	★★★★	Velázquez
13A	★★★	Atlántico
14	★★★	Carlos-V
15	★★★	Carlton
15A	★★★	Gran Via
16	★★★	Lope de Vega
17	★★★	Miguel Angel
18	★★★	Principe Pio
19	★★★	Residenciá Madrid
20	★★★	Tirol
21	★★	Mercator

At **BARAJAS** (15km N on N1)

★★★★★**Barajas** (GT) av Logroño 305 ☎7477700 tx22255 Not on plan

🛁230 **P** Lift ☾ sB🛁8525—10135 dB🛁13110 M2375 t12% 🏊 📺
Credit cards 1 2 3 4 5

★★★***Eurotel*** Galéon 27 ☎7471355 tx45688 Not on plan

🛁271 **P** Lift

MAGALUF See **BALEARES (ISLAS DE)** under **MALLORCA**

MAHÓN See **BALEARES (ISLAS DE)** under **MENORCA**

MÁLAGA
Málaga (☎952)

★★★★**Málaga Palacio** av Cortina del Muelle 1 (n.rest) ☎215185 tx77021

🛁223 Lift sB🛁5500—7000 dB🛁6900—9000 t12% 🏊 sea
Credit cards 2 5

★★★**Las Vegas** ps de Sancha 28 ☎217712

🛁🚿73 **P**20 Lift sB🛁🚿2450—2750 dB🛁🚿3700—4000 🏊 sea
Credit cards 2 3 5

★★★***Naranjos*** ps Sancha 35 ☎224317 tx77030

🛁🚿41 🚗 **P** Lift ☾ sea

★★**Parador Nacional de Gibralfaro** ☎221902

🛁12 **P** ☾ dB🛁7700—8700 M1800 t6% sea
Credit cards 1 2 3 5

MALLORCA See **BALEARES (ISLAS DE)**

MANZANARES
Ciudad Real (☎926)

★★**Parador Nacional** (2km S) ☎610400

🛁🚿50 **P**250 Lift ☾ sB🛁🚿4600 dB🛁🚿6200 M1400 t6% 🏊
Credit cards 1 2 3 4 5

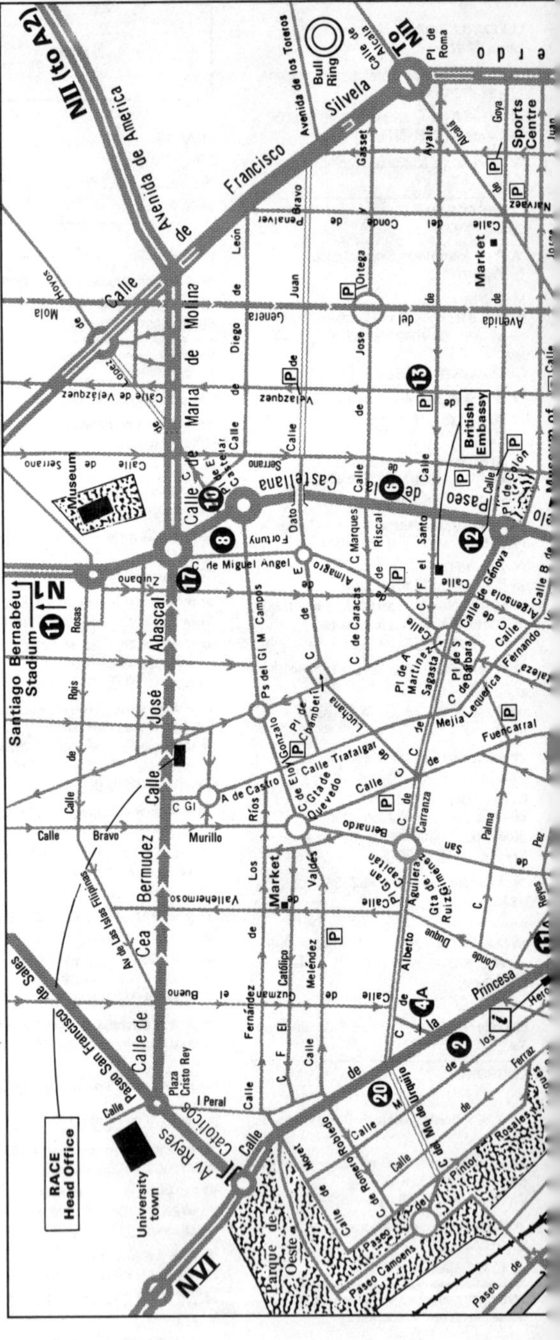

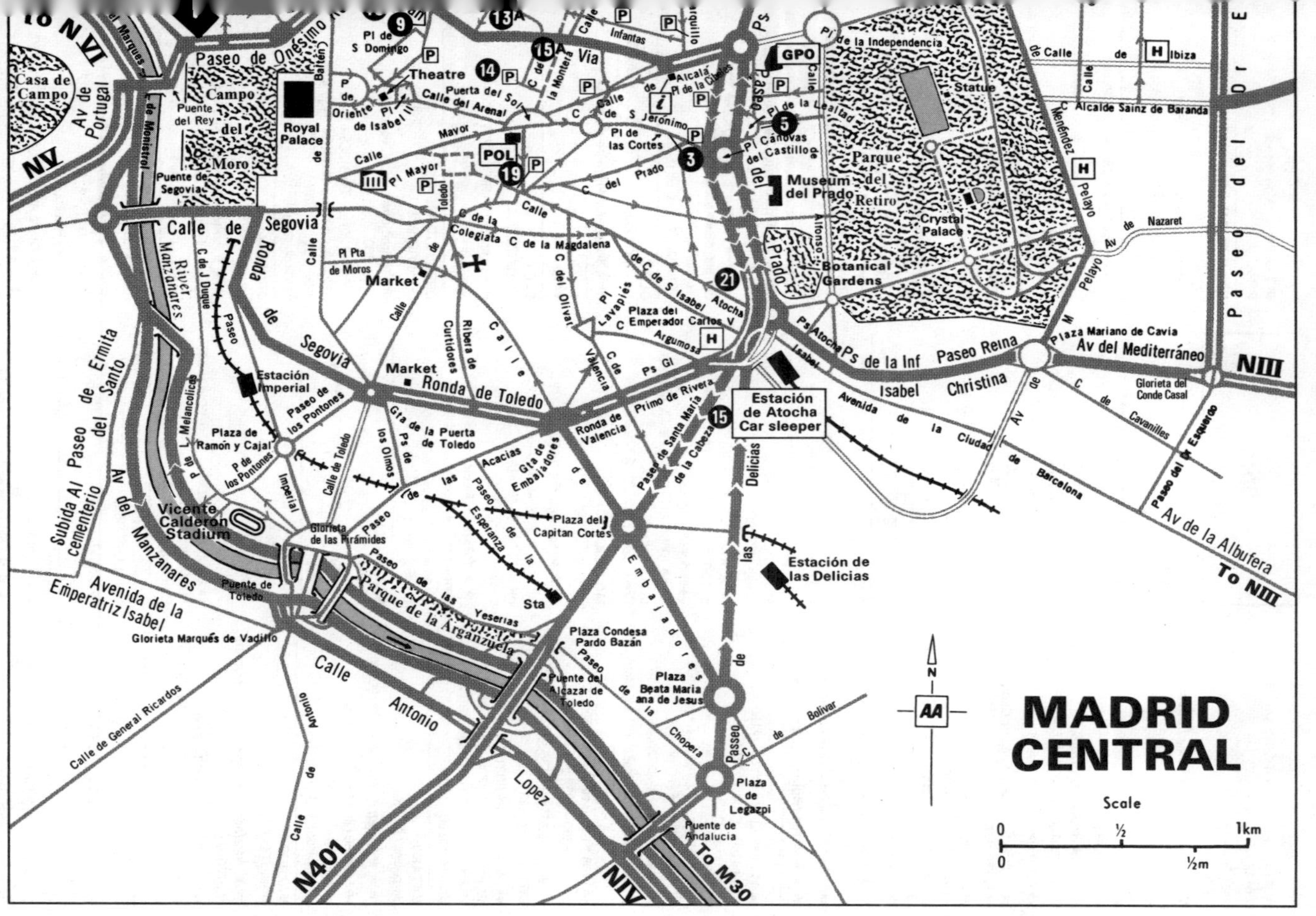

MADRID
CENTRAL
Scale
0
½
1km
0
½m
To NIII
NIII
Av de la Albufera
Paseo del Dr Esquerdo
Glorieta del Conde Casal
Av del Mediterráneo
Plaza Mariano de Cavia
C de Cavanilles
Av de la Ciudad de Barcelona
Paseo Reina Christina
Ps de la Inf Isabel
Avenida de la Ciudad
Menéndez Pelayo
Av Pelayo
Av de Nazaret
C Alcalde Sainz de Baranda
Calle de Ibiza
Pl de la Independencia
Statue
Parque del Retiro
Crystal Palace
Botanical Gardens
Museum del Prado
Prado
Alfonso
Ps Atocha
Estación de Atocha Car sleeper
Estación de las Delicias
Paseo de las Delicias
Plaza de Legazpi
Paseo C de Bolivar
Chopera
To M30
NIV
Puente de Andalucia
Plaza Beata Maria ana de Jesus
Embajadores
Plaza Condesa Pardo Bazán
Puente del Alcazar de Toledo
Paseo de la Chopera
Lopez
Calle Antonio
N401
Calle de Antonio
Yeserias
Parque de la Arganzuela
Paseo de la Esperanza
Plaza del Capitan Cortes
Sta
Gta de Embajadores
Acacias
Ronda de Valencia
Ronda de Toledo
Primo de Rivera
Paseo de Santa Maria de la Cabeza
Calle de Embajadores
Ribera de Curtidores
Market
Gta de la Puerta de Toledo
Ps de los Olmos
Paseo de las Pirámides
Glorieta de las Pirámides
Calle de Toledo
Paseo de los Pontones
P de los Pontones
Imperial
Estación Imperial
Plaza de Ramon y Cajal
Vicente Calderon Stadium
Puente de Toledo
Glorieta Marqués de Vadillo
Calle de General Ricardos
Avenida de la Emperatriz Isabel
Av del Manzanares
Subida Al Paseo de Ermita del Santo
cementerio
River Manzanares
P de L Melancolicos
C de J Duque
Paseo
Ronda de Segovia
Calle de Segovia
Puente de Segovia
Campo del Moro
Puente del Rey
Paseo de Onésimo
Royal Palace
Bailén
Casa de Campo
Av de Portugal
To N VI
NV
del Marques de Monistrol
Pl de Oriente
Pl de Isabel II
Pl de S Domingo
Theatre
Calle del Arenal
Puerta del Sol
Calle Mayor
Pl Mayor
Toledo
POL
C de la Colegiata
C de la Magdalena
C del Olivar
C de Valencia
Pl Lavapiés
de C de S Isabel
Atocha
Plaza del Emperador Carlos V
C Argumosa
Ps Gl
C del Prado
Pl de las Cortes
C de S Jerónimo
Calle de la Montera
Via
Infantas
Alcalá
Pl de la Cibeles
Paseo del Prado
Pl Cánovas del Castillo
Pl de la Lealtad
GPO
Pl Pta de Moros
Paseo del Dr E

★★*Cruce* ctra Madrid-Cádiz Km173 ☎611900
🛁37 **P**
Credit card 3

Serrano-Calvillo ctra Madrid-Cádiz Km171 ☎611192
P Ope

MARBELLA
Málaga (☎952)

★★★★★***Meliá Don Pepe*** ctra de Cádiz-Málaga Km186 ☎770300 tx770555
🛁218 **P** Lift ☾ Beach sea

★★★★★**Monteros** ctra de Cádiz ☎771700 tx77059
🛁🚿163 **P**300 Lift ☾ sB🛁🚿10000—15000 dB🛁🚿12800—18900 Beach sea
Credit cards 1 2 3 5

★★★★***Chapas*** ctra de Cádiz ☎831375 tx77057
🛁🚿117 **P** Lift ☾ sea mountains

★★★★**Guadalpin** ctra Cádiz-Málaga Km186 ☎771100
🛁110 **P**49 ☾ sB🛁2750—4150 dB🛁4100—6200 M1175 t6%
Credit cards 1 2 3 5

★★★***Artola*** (SRS) ctra de Cádiz Km201 ☎831390 tx77654
🛁18 **P** Lift ☾ sea

★★★***Estrella del Mar*** ctra Cádiz-Málaga Km191 ☎831275 tx79669
🛁🚿98 **P** Lift sB🛁🚿4755—5515 dB🛁🚿6300—7250 sea

★★★**Fuerté** Castillo de Sans Luis ☎771500 tx77523
🛁146 A116rm **P**80 Lift ☾ sB🛁5550—6050 dB🛁7900—9200 M1850 t6% Beach sea
Credit cards 2 3 5

MATARÓ
Barcelona (☎093)

★★★***Castell de Mata*** (N11) ☎7905807
🛁52 **P**150 Lift ☾ Beach sea mountains
Credit cards 1 2 3 4 5

MAZAGÓN
Huelva (☎955)

★★★**Parador Nacional Cristóbal Colón** ☎376000
🛁23 **P**50 ☾ sB🛁5200—6000 dB🛁6500—7500 Mfr1800 t6% sea
Credit cards 2 3 5

MEDINACELI
Soria (☎975)

★★***Duque de Medinaceli*** rte N11 ☎326111
rm13 (🛁🚿5) **P**100
Credit cards 1 2 3 5

★★***Nico*** Carret Genl Km151 ☎326011
🛁21 A9rm **P** ☾ mountains
Credit cards 1 3

MENORCA See **BALEARES (ISLAS DE)**

Spain

MÉRIDA
Badajoz (☎924)

★★★**Emperatriz** pl España 19 ☎313111
🛁41 ☾ sB🛁2300—2500 dB🛁4300—4600 M1250

★★★**Parador Nacional 'Via de la Plata'** pl de Queipo de Llano 3 ☎313800
🛁50 ☾ sB🛁6600 dB🛁8700 M1800 t6%
Credit cards 1 2 3 5

★★**Zeus** ctra Madrid Km341 (n.rest) ☎318111
🛁44 **P**44 Lift ☾ sB🛁2075—2175 dB🛁3150—3350 t6%
Credit cards 3 5

MIERES
Asturias

Tunon Poligno Industrial ☎463323 Peu Tal

MIJAS
Málaga (☎952)

★★★**Mijas** (BW) Tamisa ☎485800 tx77393
🛁100 **P**40 ☾ sB🛁7325—7975 dB🛁10650—11550 t6% mountains
Credit cards 1 2 3 5

MOJÁCAR
Almeria (☎951)

★★★**Moresco** ☎478025 tx77342
🛁147 Lift ☾ sB🛁3910—4665 dB🛁7396—8140 M1840 sea
Credit cards 2 3 5

★★★**Parador Nacional Reyes Catolicos** ☎478250
🛁98 **P**200 ☾ sB🛁5000—6600 dB🛁6700—8700 M1800 t6% sea

MOLAR (EL)
Madrid (☎91)

M Sato Ctra Burgos Km42-3 ☎8410081
P Ren

MONTILLA DEL PALANCAR
Cuenca (☎966)

★★★**Sol** ctra Madrid-Valencia 11 ☎331025
🛁🚿37 **P**17 sB🛁🚿1850 dB🛁🚿3000 M1100 mountains
Credit cards 1 2 3 4 5

MOTRIL
Granada (☎958)

Litoral ctra de Almeria Km1.4 ☎601950 Peu Tal

MURCIA
Murcia (☎968)

★★★***7 Coronas Meliá*** Ronda de Garay 3 ☎217771
🛁121 **P** Lift ☾

T Guillen ctra de Alicante 119 ☎241212
P Peu Tal

NAVALMORAL DE LA MATA
Cáceres (☎927)

★***Moya*** Apartado 110 ☎530500
rm40 (🛁🚿21) **P**10 mountains
Credit cards 2 5

NAVARREDONDA DE LA SIERRA See **GREDOS**

NERJA
Málaga (☎952)

★★★★***Parador Nacional*** ☎520050
🛁60 **P** Lift ☾ sea

NUÉVALOS
Zaragoza (☎976)

★★★**Monasterio de Piedra** (3km S) ☎849011
🛁🚿61 **P**500 ☾ sB🛁🚿3275 dB🛁🚿4550 M1150 mountains
Credit cards 2 5

OJÉN
Málaga (☎952)

★**Refugio N de Juanar** Sierra Blanca (10km NW) ☎881000
rm19 (🛁17) **P**60 ☾ sB3700 sB🛁3700 dB4800 dB🛁5300 M1450 mountains
Credit cards 1 2 3 4 5

OLITE
Navarra (☎948)

★★★***Parador Principe de Viana*** ☎740000
🛁39 **P** Lift ☾

OLOT
Girona (☎972)

Ferran ctra de Ripoll ☎261546 All makes

Maso av Gerona 7 ☎262340 AR

ORENSE (OURENSE)
Orense (☎988)

★★**Barcelona** av Pontevedra 13 ☎220800
rm50 (🛁20) Lift ☾ sB1365—1465 dB2430—2580 dB🛁3230—3430 M900 t6%
Credit cards 1 3 5

OROPESA
Toledo (☎925)

★★★***Parador Nacional de Virrey Toledo*** pl del Palacio 1 ☎430000
🛁44 **P** Lift ☾ mountains

OVIEDO
Asturias (☎985)

★★★★★***Reconquista*** Gil de Jaz 16 ☎241100 tx87328
🛁141 **P** Lift ☾

★★★**Gruta** Alto de Buenavista ☎232450
🛁55 **P**400 Lift ☾ sB🛁3885 dB🛁6166 t6% mountains
Credit cards 1 2 3 5

★★***Principado*** San Francisco 6 ☎217792
🛁🚿55 Lift ☾ mountains

PAGUERA See **BALEARES (ISLAS DE)** under **MALLORCA**

PAJARES (PUERTO DE)
Asturias (☎985)

★★***Parador Nacional Puerto de Pajares*** ☎496023
rm29 (🛁 🚿 10) ⌂

PALAFRUGELL
Girona (☎972)

🚗 **Mato Suquet** Bagur 19 ☎300248 Cit

At **CALELLA DE PALAFRUGELL** (5km SE)

★★★★**Alga** ☎300058 tx57077
Seasonal
🛁 54 **P**30 Lift ☾ sB🛁 2775–5650 dB🛁 3650–7950 Mfr1000 🎾 🏊 sea mountains
Credit cards [1] [3]

★★★**Garbi** ☎300100
24 Mar–15 Oct
🛁 30 A6rm **P**80 Lift ☾ sB🛁 3875–5575 dB🛁 3950–5550 M800–1200 🏊 sea
Credit cards [1] [3]

★★**Mediterráneo** Playa Baños ☎300150
Jun–Sep
🛁 🚿 38 **P**40 ☾ sB🛁 🚿 1990–2460 dB🛁 🚿 3410–4920 M1050 t6% 🎾 sea

At **LLAFRANCH** (6km E)

★★★**Paraiso** ☎300450
Apr–Oct
🛁 55 **P**40 Lift ☾ dB🛁 4550–5700 M1200 🎾 🏊 mountains
Credit cards [1] [2] [3] [5]

★★★**Terramar** ps de Cypsele 1 ☎300200
18 May–1 Oct
🛁 🚿 56 ⌂ Lift ☾ sB🛁 🚿 3100–3950 dB🛁 🚿 5500–6300 M1500–1700 t6% sea
Credit cards [1] [2] [3] [4] [5]

★★**Llafranch** ps Cypsele 16 ☎300208
rm28 (🛁 24) sB1475–2125 sB🛁 1875–2775 dB🛁 3200–4750 M1050 t6% sea
Credit cards [1] [3] [5]

★**Llevante** Francesc de Blanes 5 ☎300366
Closed 27 Oct–11 Dec
🛁 🚿 20 sB🛁 🚿 2200–2875 dB🛁 🚿 4120–6140 M1000–1100 t6% sea

At **TAMARIU** (4km SE)

★★★**Hostalillo** Bellavista 22 ☎300158 tx54136
20 Jun–21 Sep
🛁 70 ⌂ **P**15 Lift ☾ sB🛁 4550–5650 dB🛁 5700–7200 M1300 sea

★★★**Tamariu** ps del Mar 3 ☎300108
15 May–Sep
🛁 🚿 46 A22rm ⌂ **P**15 Lift ☾ sB🛁 🚿 1950–2150 dB🛁 🚿 3600–4000 M1150–1200 sea
Credit card [1]

PALAMÓS
Girona (☎972)

★★★**Trias** ps del Mar ☎314100
22 Mar–10 Oct

Spain

🛁 🚿 80 ⌂ **P**35 Lift ☾ sB3050–3620 sB🛁 🚿 3250–3820 dB6100–7240 dB🛁 🚿 6900–8040 M1800–2200 🏊 Beach sea
Credit cards [1] [3]

★★**Marina** av 11 de Septembre 48 ☎314250
🛁 🚿 62 ⌂ **P**7 Lift ☾ sB🛁 🚿 2575–2825 dB🛁 🚿 3900–4150 M925 t6%
Credit cards [1] [2] [3] [5]

★★**San Juan** av de la Victoria ☎314208 tx57077
Apr–Sep
🛁 🚿 31 ☾ sB🛁 🚿 2330–2710 dB🛁 🚿 3360–3820 M980 🏊 sea
Credit cards [1] [3]

🚗 **Central** ctra a San Feliú 6 ☎650635 Aud VW

At **SAN ANTONIO DE CALONGE** (2.5km S)

★★★***Lys*** ctra de San Feliú ☎314150
Jun–Sep
🛁 70 ⌂ **P** Lift ☾ Beach sea

★★★**Rosa dels Vents** ps del Mar ☎651311 tx57077
24 May–Sep
🛁 70 ⌂ **P**200 Lift ☾ sB🛁 2800–5000 dB🛁 4600–8000 M850 🎾 Beach sea
Credit cards [3] [5]

★★★**Rosamar** ps del Mar 33 ☎650548
May–15 Oct
🛁 64 ⌂ **P**40 Lift ☾ sB🛁 1800–3500 dB🛁 3000–6500 sea
Credit cards [2] [4]

PALENCIA
Palencia (☎988)

★★★***Rey Sancho de Castilla*** av Ponce de Leon ☎725300
🛁 100 ⌂ **P** Lift ☾ 🎾 🏊

PALMA DE MALLORCA See **BALEARES (ISLAS DE)** under **MALLORCA**

PAMPLONA
Navarra (☎948)

★★★★**Tres Reyes** Jardines de la Taconera ☎226600 tx37720
🛁 176 ⌂ **P** Lift ☾ sB🛁 6700–7700 dB🛁 9400–104000 🏊
Credit cards [1] [2] [3] [5]

★★★**Yoldi** av San Ignacio 11 ☎224800
🛁 🚿 46 ⌂ **P**30 Lift ☾ sB🛁 🚿 2770 dB🛁 🚿 4040–4340 t6%
Credit cards [1] [3] [4] [5]

★***Valerio*** av de Zaragoza 5 (n.rest) ☎245466
rm16 (🛁 1) Lift

PANCORBO
Burgos (☎947)

★★★**El Molino** ctra G-Madrid-Irún Km306 ☎354050

🛁 48 ⌂ **P** ☾ sB🛁 2200–2500 dB🛁 4000–4600 🎾 🏊 mountains
Credit cards [1] [2] [3] [5]

PEÑISCOLA
Castellón (☎964)

★★★**Hosteria del Mar** ctra de Benicarló Km6 ☎480600
🛁 85 **P**100 Lift ☾ sB🛁 2935–4035 dB🛁 4270–6070 🎾 🏊 Beach sea
Credit cards [1] [2] [3] [4] [5]

PINEDA DE MAR
Barcelona (☎93)

★★**Mont Palau** c Mayor 21 ☎7623387
Mar–Nov
rm109 (🛁 🚿 99) A17rm **P**14 Lift ☾ sB🛁 🚿 1385–1625 dB🛁 🚿 2070–2850 M550–650 sea
Credit card [3]

★★**Sorrabona** ps Maritimo 10 ☎7623250
May–Oct
🛁 🚿 100 **P**20 Lift ☾ dB🛁 🚿 1950–3850 M650 🏊 sea

PLASENCIA
Cáceres (☎927)

★★★**Alfonso VIII** c Alfonso VIII 32 ☎410250 tx28960
🛁 56 ⌂ Lift ☾ sB🛁 3050–3350 dB🛁 5150–5575 M1425 t6%
Credit cards [2] [3]

PLATJA D'ARO (LA)
Girona (☎972)

★★★**Cliper** ☎817000
🛁 40 **P** ☾ sB🛁 1700–1900 dB🛁 2800–3100 Mfr700 mountains
Credit cards [1] [2]

★★★***Miramar*** Verge del Carme N12 ☎817150
15 May–Sep
🛁 45 ⌂ **P** Lift ☾ Beach sea

★★★**Rosamar** pl Mayor ☎817304
15 May–15 Oct
🛁 60 ⌂ **P**8 Lift ☾ sB🛁 2350 dB🛁 4200 M800 mountains

★★★***Xaloc*** Playa de Rovira ☎817300 tx57219
Apr–Oct
🛁 45 **P**15 Lift Beach sea
Credit card [3]

★★**Els Pins** ☎817219
22 Mar–Oct
🛁 🚿 70 ⌂ Lift ☾ sB🛁 🚿 2040–3250 dB🛁 🚿 2840–5590 M740 sea
Credit cards [1] [2] [3] [4] [5]

★★**Residencia Japet** ctra de Palamós 18–20 ☎817366
Closed 10 Oct–7 Dec
🛁 48 **P**50 ☾ sB🛁 1200–2450 dB🛁 2000–4000 M1000 t6%
Credit cards [1] [2] [3]

PLAYA DE GANDÍA See **GANDÍA**

PLAYA DE PALMA (CA'N PASTILLA) See **BALEARES (ISLAS DE)** under **PALMA DE MALLORCA, MALLORCA**

PLAYA DE PALMA NOVA See **BALEARES (ISLAS DE)** under **PALMA DE MALLORCA, MALLORCA**

POLLENSA See **BALEARES (ISLAS DE)** under **MALLORCA**

PONFERRADA
Léon (☎987)

★★**Madrid** J-Antonio 50 ☎411550
➡ 🚿 54 **P** Lift sB ➡ 🚿 1500—1700
dB ➡ 🚿 3200 M750 t6%

PONTEVEDRA
Pontevedra (☎986)

★★**Parador Nacional Casa del Barón** Maceda S/n ☎855800
➡ 47 **P**10 Lift ☾ sB ➡ 4600—5300
dB ➡ 6000—7000 M1800 t6%
Credit cards [1] [2] [3] [5]

PORTBOU
Girona (☎972)

★**Costa Brava Costa Blava** Cerbere 20—26 ☎390003
Jun—Sep
rm30 (➡ 6) sB1250—1450 dB2100—2500
dB ➡ 2700—2900 M950
Credit cards [1] [3]

PORTOMARÍN
Lugo (☎982)

★★★***Parador Nacional de Puertomarin*** ☎545025
➡ 10 **P** ☾ mountains lake

PREMIÀ DE MAR
Barcelona (☎93)

★★***Premia*** c San Miguel 46 ☎7510336
🚿 23 ☾ sea mountains
Credit cards [1] [3]

PUEBLA DE SANABRIA
Zamora (☎988)

★★**Parador Nacional de Puebla de Sanabria** ☎620001
rm24 (➡ 18) ⌂ sB ➡ 4100—5100
dB ➡ 6000—7700 M1600—1800 t6%

PUERTO DE LLANÇA See **LLANÇA**

PUERTO DE POLLENSA See **BALEARES (ISLAS DE)** under **POLLENSA, MALLORCA**

PUERTO DE SANTA MARIA (EL)
Cádiz (☎956)

★★★★***Meliá el Caballo Blanca*** Playa de Valdelagrana (2.5km S on ctra de Cádiz) ☎863745 tx76070
➡ 94 **P** ☾ ≋ U

PUERTO LUMBRERAS
Murca (☎968)

★★**Parador Nacional de Puerto Lumbreras** ☎402025
➡ 60 ⌂ **P**30 Lift ☾ sB ➡ 3600 dB ➡ 6200
M1800 t6% ≋ mountains
Credit cards [1] [2] [3] [4] [5]

PUIGCERDÁ
Girona (☎972)

★★**Maria Victoria** Florenza 9 ☎880300

Spain

➡ 🚿 50 **P**8 Lift ☾ sB ➡ 🚿 1985—2535
dB ➡ 🚿 3470—3970 M1250—1350 t6%
mountains
Credit cards [1] [2] [3] [5]

★★***Martinez*** ctra de Llivia (n.rest) ☎880250
➡ 15 **P** ☾ ≋ mountains

PUZOL
Valencia (☎96)

★★★★**Monte Picayo** Paraje Denominado Monte Picayo (Autoroute 7, Exit 6) ☎1420100 tx62087
➡ 82 ⌂ **P**350 Lift ☾ sB ➡ 9560
dB ➡ 12400 M1800 t12% Q ≋ sea mountains
Credit cards [1] [2] [3] [5]

RASCAFRIA
Madrid (☎91)

★★★★**Santa Maria de el Paular** (CIGA) ☎8693200 tx23222
➡ 🚿 58 **P**30 ☾ sB ➡ 🚿 4600—7800
dB ➡ 🚿 10050—13850 M2650 St6% Q ≋
U mountains
Credit cards [2] [3] [5]

REINOSA
Cantabria (☎942)

★★★***Vejo*** av Cantabria 15 ☎751700
➡ 71 ⌂ **P** Lift ☾ mountains
Credit cards [2] [3] [5]

★★***Fontibre-Iberia*** Nestares ☎750450
➡ 🚿 51 ⌂ **P** Lift ☾ mountains

Partes av Cantabria 26 ☎750334 Aud VW

REUS
Tarragona (☎977)

★★**Gaudi** Arrabal Robuster 49 (n.rest) ☎305545
➡ 71 Lift ☾ sB ➡ 2125—2405
dB ➡ 3470—3910 sea
Credit cards [1] [3] [5]

Petrubial c Rosér 25 ☎304605 AR

RIBADEO
Lugo (☎982)

★★**Eo** av de Asturias 5 (n.rest) ☎110750
24 Mar—Sep
➡ 24 **P**20 ☾ sB ➡ 2750—3250
dB ➡ 3800—4500 t6% ≋ sea mountains
Credit cards [1] [3]

★★**Parador Naciónal** ☎110825
➡ 47 ⌂ **P**40 Lift ☾ sB ➡ 5000—6200
dB ➡ 6700—8200 M1600—1800 t6% sea
Credit cards [2] [5]

RIBADESELLA
Asturias (☎985)

★★★**Gran del Sella** la Playa ☎860150
Apr-Sep
➡ 74 **P** Lift ☾ sB ➡ 4335—5735
dB ➡ 6470—8070 M1850 t6% Q ≋ sea
lake mountains
Credit cards [1] [2] [3] [5]

RIBES DE FRESER
Girona (☎972)

★★**Prats** San Quintin 20 ☎727001
➡ 30 **P**25 ☾ sB ➡ 1325—1725
dB ➡ 2550—2950 M800—950 t6% ≋
mountains

★★**Terralta** El Baiell ☎727350
27 Jun—Sep
➡ 30 sB ➡ 2000 dB ➡ 3000 M1100 t6%
≋ mountains

RUIDELLOTS DE LA SELVA
Girona (☎72)

★★★**Novotel Gerona** Autopista A17—Salida 8 ☎477100 tx57238
➡ 82 **P**100 ☾ sB ➡ 6600—7100
dB ➡ 7800—9400 t6% Q ≋
Credit cards [1] [2] [3] [5]

RONDA
Málaga (☎952)

★★★***Reina Victoria*** c Jerez 39 ☎871240
➡ 🚿 88 **P** Lift ☾ ≋ mountains
Credit cards [3] [5]

ROSES
Girona (☎972)

★★★★**Almadraba Park** Playa de Almadraba ☎256550
Apr—14 Oct
➡ 66 ⌂ **P**120 Lift ☾ Q ≋ sea
Credit cards [1] [2] [3] [4] [5]

★★★***Coral Playa*** ctra Playa ☎256250 tx57191
Apr—Oct
➡ 🚿 133 **P** Lift ☾

★★★***Vistabella*** Playa de Cañyellos Petites ☎256008
15 Dec—15 Oct
➡ 43 ⌂ **P** ☾ Q ≋ Beach sea

★★***Terraza*** Playa ☎256154
Mar—Nov
➡ 🚿 110 ⌂ **P** Lift ☾ Q ≋ sea

SABIÑANIGO
Huesca (☎974)

★★***Pardina*** ☎480975
➡ 64 **P**60 Lift ☾ ≋ mountains

S'AGARÓ
Girona (☎972)

★★★★★**Gavina** (Relais et Châteaux) ☎321100 tx57132
Apr—Oct
➡ 🚿 74 **P**100 Lift ☾ sB ➡ 🚿 16325
dB ➡ 🚿 21150 M3575 t12% Q ≋ ⊡ sea
mountains
Credit cards [1] [2] [3] [4] [5]

★★★**Caleta Park** Platja de Sant Pol ☎320012 tx57566
22 Mar—20 Oct
➡ 🚿 105 ⌂ **P**80 Lift ☾ sB ➡ 🚿 2800—3800
dB ➡ 🚿 5600—8100 M1300—1500 t6% Q
≋ sea
Credit cards [1] [3] [4] [5]

Spain

SALAMANCA
Salamanca (☎923)

★★★**Monterrey** Azafranal 21 ☎214400 tx26809
➡89 Lift sB➡3950—6050 dB➡5900—8400 M1700 t6%
Credit cards [1] [2] [3] [5]

★★★**Parador Nacional** ☎228700
➡108 ⌂ **P** Lift ☾ sB➡5600 dB➡7700—8200 M1800 t6% 🏊
Credit cards [1] [2] [3] [4] [5]

🚗 **Vicente Sanchez Marcos** av de las Comuneros 30 ☎222450 Cit

At **SANTA MARTA DE TORMES** (4km E)

★★★**Jardin Regio** ☎200250 tx22895
➡🚿118 ⌂ **P**300 Lift ☾ sB➡🚿3175—3675 dB➡🚿5250—6250 M1500 t6% 🎾 🏊 mountains
Credit cards [1] [2] [3] [5]

SALER (EL) See **VALENCIA**

SALOBREÑA
Granada (☎958)

★***Salambina*** (1km W) ☎610037
➡14 **P**12 sea
Credit cards [1] [2] [3] [5]

SALOU
Tarragona (☎977)

★★★***Calaviña* (DPn)** ctra Tarragona—Salou Km10 ☎380848 tx56501
15 May—15 Oct
➡🚿70 **P** Lift ☾ 🏊 sea

★★★***Picnic*** ctra Salou-Reus Km1 ☎380158
➡45 **P** ☾ 🏊 sea

★★★***Salou Park*** Burselas 35, Cala Capellens ☎380208
➡102 **P** Lift ☾ 🏊 sea
Credit cards [1] [2] [3] [4] [5]

★★***Planas*** pl Bonet 2 ☎380108
Apr—Oct
➡100 Lift ☾ sea

🚗 **Internaciónal** c P-Martel ☎380614 **P** All makes

SAN ANTONIO See **BALEARES (ISLAS DE)** under **IBIZA**

SAN ANTONIO DE CALOGNE See **PALAMÓS**

SAN LORENZO DE EL ESCORIAL
Madrid (☎91)

★★★★***Victoria Palace*** J-de-Toledo 4 ☎8901511
➡🚿90 **P** Lift ☾ 🏊 mountains

SAN PEDRO DE ALCÁNTARA
Málaga (☎952)

★★★★**Golf Guadalmina** ☎781400 tx77058
➡90 **P**40 ☾ sB➡5140—8400 dB➡7210—11100 M2150—2600 🎾 🏊 ⛳ sea
Credit cards [1] [2] [3] [5]

SAN SEBASTIÁN (DONOSTIA)
Guipúzcoa (☎943)

★★★★**Costa Vasca** av Pio Baroja 9 ☎211011 tx36551
➡203 ⌂ **P**80 Lift ☾ sB➡7300 dB➡9500 M2000 t6% 🎾 🏊
Credit cards [1] [2] [4] [5]

★★★**Gudamendi** (4km W) ☎214000
➡20 **P**300 sB➡3400—4300 dB➡4600—6600 M1500 sea mountains
Credit cards [2] [3]

★★★**Monte Igueldo** ☎210211
➡121 ⌂ **P** Lift ☾ sB➡4500—6900 dB➡8200—9000 t6% 🎾 🏊 sea

🚗 **Gruas España** av Isabel II 15 ☎458352 **P**

🚗 **Ingels** av A-Elosegui 108 ☎396516 Ope

SANTA CHRISTINA D'ARO
Girona (☎972)

★★★★**Costa Brava Golf** ☎837052 tx57252
20 Mar—15 Oct
➡91 **P**60 Lift ☾ sB➡3450—5450 dB➡5900—8900 M1400 t6% 🎾 🏊 ⛳ mountains
Credit cards [1] [2] [3] [4] [5]

SANTA CRUZ DE MUDELA
Ciudad Real

🚗 **Izquiredo** ctra Madrid-Cádiz Km217 ☎342022 **P** All makes

SANTA MARIA DE HUERTA
Soria (☎975)

★★★**Parador Nacional de Santa Maria de Huerta** ☎327011
➡40 ⌂ **P**26 ☾ sB➡4600 dB➡6200 M1800 t6%
Credit cards [1] [2] [3] [4] [5]

SANTA MARTA DE TORMES
See **SALAMANCA**

SANTANDER
Cantabria (☎942)

See plan page 368

★★★★***Bahia*** av de Alfonso XIII 6 ☎221700 tx35859 Plan **1**
➡🚿181 Lift ☾ sea mountains

★★**Colón** pl de las Brisas 1 (n.rest) ☎272300 Plan **3**
Jul—15 Sep
rm33 (➡23) ☾ sB1330 dB2260 dB➡3260 t6% sea mountains

★★**Romano I** c F-Vial 3 Not on plan
➡34 ⌂ **P**15 ☾ sB➡2750 dB➡4700 M800 St%

Sancho Motor c Castilla 62 ☎370017 For

At **SARDINERO (EL)** (3.5km NE)

★★★**Rhin** Reina Victoria 155 ☎274300 Plan **2**
➡🚿95 ⌂ Lift ☾ sB➡2870—3785 dB➡2145—2940 sea
Credit cards [1] [2] [3] [4] [5]

★★★**Santemar** Joaquin Costa 28 (n.rest) ☎272900 tx35963 Plan **4**
➡350 ⌂ **P**150 Lift sB➡4170—6765 dB➡6140—9665 t6% 🎾 sea
Credit cards [1] [2] [3] [5]

★★★***Sardinero*** pl Italia 1 ☎271100 tx35795 Plan **5**
➡112 Lift ☾ sea
Credit cards [1] [2] [3] [4] [5]

SANT FELIÚ DE GUIXOLS
Girona (☎972)

★★★★***Muriá Park*** ps Dels Guixols 21—23 (n.rest Nov—Mar) ☎320450 tx57364
➡🚿86 Lift ☾ 🏊 sea

★★★***Montecarlo*** Montaña de San Elmo ☎320000
Jun—Sep
➡61 **P** Lift ☾ sea

★★★**Montjol** San Elmo ☎320300 tx94442
May—Oct
➡64 **P**20 Lift ☾ 🏊 sea
Credit cards [2] [3] [5]

★★★**Rex** Rambla Portalet 18 (n.rest) ☎320312
Jun—15 Sep
➡🚿25 Lift ☾ sB➡🚿1280—1920 dB➡🚿2780—3160
Credit cards [1] [3] [5]

★★**Noles** Rambla J-Antonio 10 ☎320400
Apr—Oct
➡60 ⌂ **P**30 Lift ☾ sB➡2148 dB➡3395 M975
Credit cards [1] [2] [3] [5]

★★**Turist** San Ramón 39 ☎320841
15 May—Sep
➡🚿24 A11rm ⌂ **P**10 Lift ☾ sB➡🚿1225—1725 dB➡🚿2150—3250 M825 sea
Credit cards [1] [2] [3] [4] [5]

🚗 **Metropol Comercial** ctra Gerona 7 ☎320982 Ren

SANTIAGO DE COMPOSTELA
La Coruña (☎981)

★★★★★**Los Reyes Catolicos** pl de España 1 ☎582200 tx86004
➡🚿157 ⌂ **P**60 Lift ☾ sB➡🚿6250—11640 dB➡🚿8450—15000 M2650 t12% mountains
Credit cards [1] [2] [3] [5]

★★★**Peregrino** av R-de-Castro ☎591850 tx82352
➡150 **P**50 Lift ☾ sB➡2850—3650 dB➡5000—6450 M1600 t% 🏊 mountains
Credit cards [1] [2] [3] [5]

SANTILLANA DEL MAR
Cantabria (☎942)

★★★**Los Infantes** av le Dorat 1 ☎818100
➡30 **P**20 ☾ sB➡2625—4325 dB➡3950—6150 M1300 t6%
Credit cards [1] [2] [3]

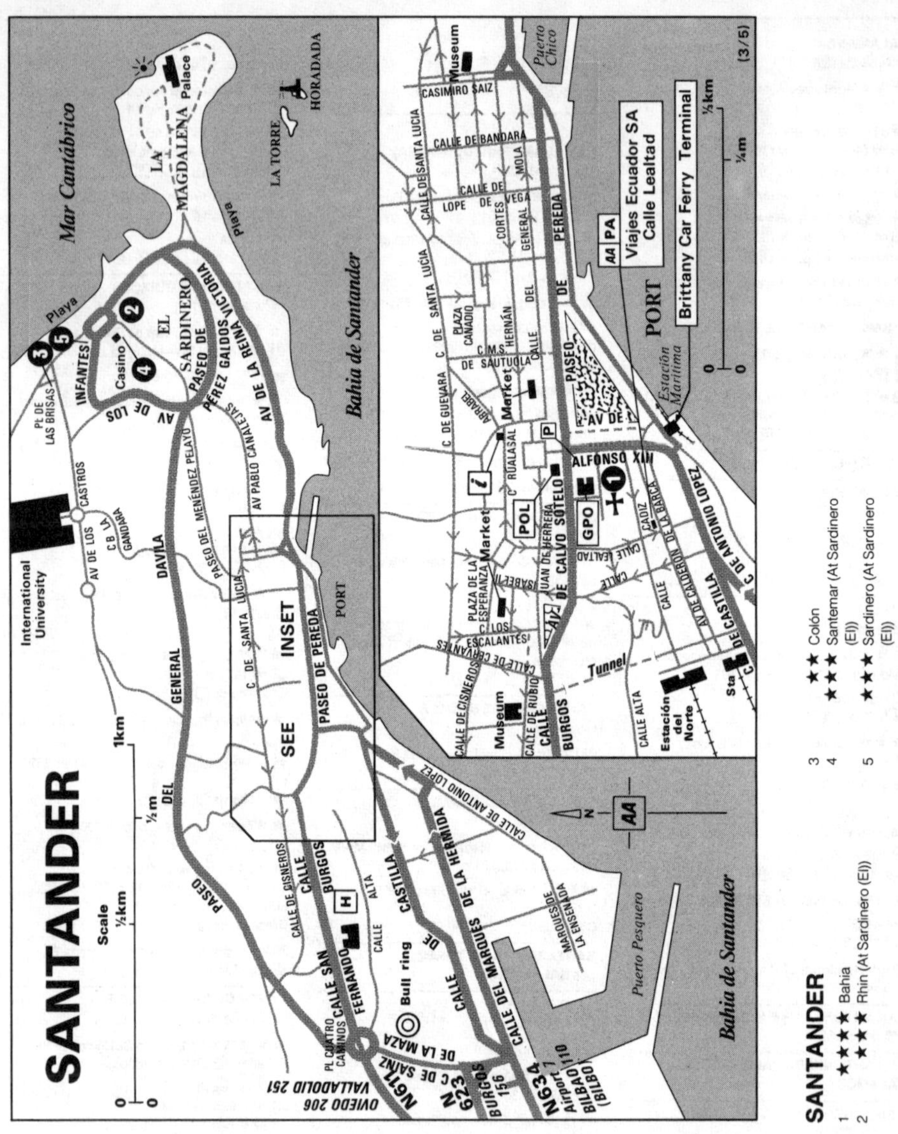

★★★**Parador de Gil Blas** ☎818000
🛁28 ☾ sB🛁5500–6600
dB🛁7500–8700 M1800–1950 t6%
Credit cards 1 2 3 5

★★**Altamira** Cantón 1 ☎818025
🛁30 **P**20 ☾ sB🛁2700–3300
dB🛁3400–4600 M925 t6% mountains
Credit cards 2 5

SANT POL DE MAR
Barcelona (☎93)

★★★**Gran Sol** ctra de Francia Km670
☎7600051
🛁 🚿41 **P** Lift ☾ sB🛁 🚿2500–3600
dB🛁 🚿3900–5300 M1300 t6% sea
Credit cards 1 3 4 5

SANTO DOMINGO DE LA CALZADA
Rioja (☎941)

★★***Parador Nacional*** ☎340300
🛁20 **P** ☾

SAN VICENTE LA BARQUERA
Cantabria (☎942)

★★**Miramar** La Barquera (1km N)
☎710075
Mar–15 Dec
🛁15 A15rm **P**150 ☾ sB🛁2550–2950
dB🛁3500–4200 M1100 t6% sea
mountains
Credit cards 2 3

SARDINERO (EL) See **SANTANDER**

SEGOVIA
Segovia (☎911)

★★★**Linajes** Dr-Velasco 9 (n.rest)
☎431712
🛁55 🏠 **P**40 Lift ☾ sB🛁3225–3950

dB 🛁 5450—6725 t6% mountains
Credit cards [1] [2] [3] [5]

★★★**Parador Nacional de Segovia**
☎430462
🛁 80 🚗 P30 Lift ☾ sB 🛁 6600—7400
dB 🛁 8700—9700 M1950 t6% ≈ ⊠
mountains
Credit cards [1] [2] [3] [4] [5]

★★★***Puerta de Segovia*** ctra de Soria (N110) ☎437161
🛁 100 **P** Lift ☾ % ≈ mountains

★★★***R Las Sirenas*** J-Bravo 30 (n.rest)
☎434011
🛁 🚿 39 **P**10 Lift ☾ mountains
Credit cards [2] [3] [5]

SEU D'URGELL (LA)
Lleida (☎973)

★★***Parador Nacional*** Santo Domingo
☎352000
🛁 86 🚗 **P** Lift ☾ ≈ mountains

★**Avenida** av Gl-Franco 18 ☎350104
rm40 (🛁 🚿 30) Lift ☾ sB1300—1500
sB 🛁 🚿 1300—1460 dB2620—2970
dB 🛁 🚿 2700—3075 M740 t6% mountains
Credit cards [1] [3] [5]

At **CASTELLICIUTAT** (1km SE)

★★★**Castell** (Relais et Châteaux) ctra C1313 ☎350704 tx93610
🛁 40 **P**100 sB 🛁 6000 dB 🛁 8000 M2750
t6% ≈ mountains
Credit cards [1] [2] [3] [5]

SEVILLA (SEVILLE)
Sevilla (☎954)

★★★★★***Alfonso XIII*** (CIGA) San Fernando 2 ☎222850 tx72725
🛁 148 **P** Lift ☾ ≈

★★★★***Colón*** J-Canalejas 1 ☎222900
tx72726
rm268 Lift ☾

★★★★**Inglaterra** (BW) pl Nueva 7
☎224970 tx72244
🛁 120 🚗 Lift ☾ sB 🛁 5989—8586
dB 🛁 9010—13038
Credit cards [1] [2] [3] [5]

★★★**Becquer** (BW) Reyes Catolicos 4
(n.rest) ☎228900 tx72884
🛁 🚿 126 🚗 Lift ☾ sB 🛁 🚿 2775—4775
dB 🛁 🚿 5050—7300 M alc t6%
Credit cards [1] [2] [3] [5]

★★**Doña Maria** Don Remondo 19 (n.rest)
☎224990
🛁 61 🚗 **P** Lift sB 🛁 4400—7400
dB 🛁 7800—12300 t6% ≈
Credit cards [2] [3] [5]

SIERRA NEVADA See **GRANADA**

SIGÜENZA
Guadalajara (☎911)

★★★**Parador Nacional Castillo de Sigüenza** ☎390100
🛁 76 **P** Lift ☾ sB 🛁 5000—6200
dB 🛁 6700—8200 M1800 t6% ≈
mountains
Credit cards [1] [2] [3] [4] [5]

SITGES
Barcelona (☎93)

★★★★**Calipolis** ps Maritimo ☎8941500
tx53067
🛁 🚿 175 Lift ☾ sB 🛁 🚿 4450—5550
dB 🛁 🚿 7100—8850 M1375—1500 t6% sea
Credit cards [1] [2] [3] [5]

★★★★**Terramar** ps Calvo Sotelo
☎8940050 tx53186
May—3 Nov
🛁 209 Lift ☾ sB 🛁 3725—5325
dB 🛁 5850—8850 M1500 t6% % ≈ Beach
⊠ sea
Credit cards [1] [2] [3] [4] [5]

★★★**Antemare** av Nuestra Señora de Montserrat ☎8940600 tx52962
Apr—Nov
🛁 72 🚗 **P**100 Lift ☾ sB 🛁 3850—4950
dB 🛁 5700—7800 M1500 t6% ≈ sea
Credit cards [1] [3] [4] [5]

★★★***Platjador*** ps Ribera 35 ☎89405054
May—Oct
🛁 44 Lift ☾ sea

★★**Arcadia** c Socias 22—24 (n.rest)
☎8940900 tx52962
Apr—15 Nov
🛁 37 **P**30 Lift ☾ sB 🛁 2500—3550
dB 🛁 3800—6000 t6% ≈
Credit cards [1] [3] [4] [5]

★★***Luna Playa*** Puerto Alegre 51
☎89040430
🛁 12 **P** Lift ☾ sea

★★**Sitges Residencia** San Gaudencio 5
(n.rest) ☎8940072 tx52962
Jun—Sep
rm52 (🛁 🚿 28) Lift ☾ sB1200—1500
dB2100—2600 dB 🛁 🚿 2400—3350 t6%

★**Romantic** San Isidro 23 ☎8940643
tx52962
23 Apr—15 Oct
rm55 (🛁 🚿 50) ☾ sB2250—2350
sB 🛁 🚿 2450—2550 dB4100—4300
dB 🛁 🚿 4500—4700 M600—700

SON SERVERA See **BALEARES (ISLAS DE)** under **MALLORCA**

SORIA
Soria (☎975)

★★★**Caballero** E-Saavedra 4 ☎220100
🛁 84 **P** Lift ☾
Credit cards [2] [3] [5]

★★★**Mesón Leonor** ps del Mirón
☎220250
🛁 32 🚗 **P**4 ☾ sB 🛁 2250—2700
dB 🛁 4000—4800 M1100 t6% mountains
Credit cards [1] [2] [3] [5]

★★***Les Heras*** pl Ramóny Cajal 5
☎213346
rm24 (🛁 🚿 17) **P** ☾

★★***Parador Nacional Antonio Machado***
Parque del Castillo ☎213445
🛁 14

SOS DEL REY CATÓLICO
Zaragoza (☎948)

★★★***Parador Nacional Fernando de Aragón*** ☎888011
🛁 66 🚗 **P** Lift ☾ mountains

SUANCES-PLAYA
Cantabria (☎942)

★***Lumar*** ctra de Tagle ☎810214
Jun—15 Sep
rm29 (🛁 🚿 27) **P** sea mountains

TALAVERA DE LA REINA
Toledo (☎925)

★★**Auto-Estacion** av Toledo 1 ☎800300
🛁 🚿 40 🚗 ☾ sB 🛁 🚿 1380—1480
dB 🛁 🚿 2360—2560 M590 t6%
Credit cards [1] [3] [5]

TAMARIU See **PALAFRUGELL**

TARIFA
Cádiz (☎956)

★★★**Mesón de Sancho** ctra Cádiz-Málaga ☎684900
🛁 50 🚗 **P** ☾ dB 🛁 2950—3700 M1250
t6% % ≈ sea mountains
Credit cards [1] [2] [3] [4] [5]

★★**Balcón de España** ctra Cádiz
☎684326
Apr—Oct
🛁 38 **P**40 sB 🛁 3350—3650
dB 🛁 5200—6000 M1750 % ≈ U
mountains
Credit card [2]

★★***Dos Mares*** ctra Cádiz-Málaga Km78
☎684035
Apr—Oct
🛁 19 **P**50 ☾ % ≈ Beach U sea

TARRAGONA
Tarragona (☎977)

★★★★***Imperial Tarraco*** Rambla de San Carlos ☎233040 tx50441
🛁 170 🚗 **P** Lift ☾ % ≈ sea

★★★***Astari*** via Augusta 95 ☎236911
May—Oct
rm83 (🛁 🚿 73) 🚗 **P**50 Lift ☾ ≈ sea

★★★**Lauria** Lauria 4 ☎236712
🛁 🚿 72 🚗 **P**20 Lift ☾ sB 🛁 🚿 3585
dB 🛁 🚿 4670 t6% ≈ sea
Credit cards [1] [2] [3] [4] [5]

★★**Nuria** via Augusta 217 ☎235011
Apr—Sep
🛁 61 A11rm 🚗 **P** Lift sB 🛁 1725—2075
dB 🛁 2650—3200 M880 sea

🚘 **Minicar Pons** c Gasometro 40—42
☎216169 All makes

🚘 **Tarrauto** ctra de Valencia Km246.8
☎540870 Peu Tal

TERUEL
Teruel (☎974)

★★★**Parador Nacional** ☎601800
🛁 60 **P** Lift ☾ sB 🛁 5400–6200 dB 🛁 7200–8200 M1800 t5% 🎾 ≈ mountains
Credit cards [1] [2] [3] [4] [5]

J Z Coll ctra Sagunto-Burgos Km 123 ☎601061 For

TOJA (ISLA DE LA)
Pontevedra (☎986)

★★★★★**Gran** ☎730025 tx88042
🛁 201 **P** Lift ☾ sB 🛁 6200–11400 dB 🛁 9200–15600 M2500 t12% 🎾 ≈ Beach ▣ sea
Credit cards [1] [2] [3] [4] [5]

TOLEDO
Toledo (☎925)

★★★**Parador Conde de Orgaz** ☎221850 tx47998
🛁 76 **P**120 Lift ☾ sB 🛁 4800 dB 🛁 8300–10800 M1950 t6% ≈
Credit cards [1] [2] [3] [5]

★★***Maravilla*** Barrio Rey 5–7 ☎223300
🛁 18 Lift ☾ sB 🛁 2300 dB 🛁 3950 M900–1100

TORDESILLAS
Valladolid (☎983)

★★★**Montico** ctra N122 Km 145 ☎770551 tx26575
🛁 34 ⌂ **P** ☾ sB 🛁 2400–3300 dB 🛁 4100–5300 M1500 t6% ≈
Credit cards [1] [2] [5]

★★★**Parador Nacional de Tordesillas** ctra N620 Km 153 ☎770051
rm72 (🛁 65) ⌂ **P**100 Lift ☾ sB 🛁 3100–4100 dB 🛁 6200–7700 M1800 t6%
Credit cards [1] [2] [3] [4] [5]

TORREMOLINOS
Málaga (☎952)

★★★★***Meliá Torremolinos*** av de C-Alessandri 109 ☎380500 tx77060
Mar–Oct
🛁 284 **P** Lift ☾ 🎾 ≈

★★★★***Parador Nacional del Golf*** ☎381255
🛁 40 **P** ☾ 🎾 ≈ Beach ▣ sea

★★★★***Pez Espada*** via Imperial ☎380300 tx77655
Apr–Oct
🛁 149 **P**50 Lift ☾ 🎾 ≈ Beach sea
Credit cards [1] [2] [3] [5]

★★★***Isabel*** ps Maritimo 97, Playa del Lido ☎381744
Mar–Oct
🛁 40 **P**4 Lift ☾ ≈ Beach sea
Credit cards [1] [2] [3]

★★★***Meliá Costa del Sol*** ps Marítimo, Playa de Bajondilla ☎386677 tx77326
🛁 540 **P** Lift ☾ ≈ sea

★★★**Nidos** c Los Nidos ☎380400 tx77151
Jun–Sep
🛁 70 **P** ☾ sB 🛁 3550 dB 🛁 5500 🎾 ≈

★★★**Tropicana** Trópico 2 ☎386600 tx77107
🛁 86 Lift ☾ sB 🛁 4050–5250 dB 🛁 5700–7800 M1650 t6% ≈ sea
Credit cards [1] [2] [3] [5]

🚗 **Salamanca** av C-Allessandri 27 ☎381151 AR

TORREVIEJA
Alicante (☎965)

★★**Berlin** Torre del Moro ☎711537
🛁 🚿 50 **P**13 Lift ☾ sB 🛁 2100–2700 dB 🛁 3350–4200 ≈ sea
Credit cards [1] [2] [3] [5]

TORTOSA
Tarragona (☎977)

★★★**Parador Nacional Castillo de la Zuda** Castillo de la Zuda ☎444450
🛁 82 **P** Lift ☾ sB 🛁 4600–5800 dB 🛁 6200–7700 M1800 t6% ≈ mountains
Credit cards [1] [2] [3] [5]

TOSSA DE MAR
Girona (☎972)

★★★★**Gran Reymar** Playa de Mar Menuda ☎340312 tx57094
Mar–Oct
🛁 131 **P**80 Lift ☾ sB 🛁 3800–7300 dB 🛁 3600–8600 M2100 t6% 🎾 ≈ sea mountains

★★★**Ancora** av de la Palma 4 ☎340299
Jun–Sep
rm65 (🛁 🚿 60) ⌂ **P**40 ☾ sB1110–1230 sB 🛁 🚿 1255–1500 dB2220–2400 dB 🛁 🚿 2520–2800 M 🎾 sea

★★★**Florida** av de Palma 21 ☎340308
May–Oct
🛁 45 **P** Lift ☾ sB 🛁 1900–2550 dB 🛁 3200–4600 🎾

★★★**Mar Menuda** Playa de Mar Menuda ☎341000
Etr–Oct
🛁 40 ⌂ **P**40 Lift ☾ sB 🛁 3010–3210 dB 🛁 4520–6020 M1550 t6% 🎾 ≈ Beach sea mountains
Credit cards [1] [3] [5]

★★**Corsico** ps del Mar (n.rest) ☎340174
Mar–Sep
🛁 🚿 28 **P** Lift ☾ sB 🛁 🚿 1775–2275 dB 🛁 🚿 3550–4010 t6% sea
Credit cards [3] [5]

🚗 **Nautica** ctra San Feliú ☎341021 Aud VW

TUDELA
Navarra (☎948)

★★**Morase** ps de Invierno 2 ☎821700
🛁 10 **P**10 Lift ☾ sB 🛁 3075–3275 dB 🛁 4050–4400 M1500
Credit cards [1] [2] [3] [5]

★***Tudela*** ctra de Zaragoza ☎820558
🛁 🚿 16 **P**13 ☾
Credit cards [1] [3]

TUI
Pontevedra (☎986)

★★★**Parador Nacional San Telmo** ☎600300
🛁 22 **P**40 ☾ sB 🛁 5000–6200 dB 🛁 6700–8200 M1800 t6% ≈ lake
Credit cards [1] [2] [3] [4] [5]

ÚBEDA
Jaén (☎953)

★★★***Parador Nacional Condestable Dávalos*** pl Váquez de Molina 1 ☎750345
🛁 25 ⌂

VALDEPEÑAS
Ciudad Real (☎926)

★★★**Meliá el Hildalgo** ctra National IV ☎323254 tx48136
🛁 🚿 54 ⌂ **P** sB 🛁 🚿 4030–4350 dB 🛁 🚿 5300–5700 ≈

VALENCIA
Valencia (☎96)

★★★★**Reina Victoria** c de las Barcas 4 ☎3520487 tx64755
🛁 100 ⌂ Lift ☾ sB 🛁 5200 dB 🛁 8850 M2000 t6%
Credit cards [1] [2] [5]

★★★★***Rey Don Jaima*** av Baleares 2 ☎3607300 tx64252
🛁 314 **P** Lift ☾ ≈

★★★**Dimar** Gran via Marqués del Turia 80 (n.rest) ☎3341807 tx62952
🛁 95 **P** Lift ☾ dB 🛁 4650–8025

★★★**Excelsior** Barcelonina 5 ☎3514612
🛁 🚿 65 Lift ☾ sB 🛁 🚿 3090 dB 🛁 🚿 5380 M700 t6%
Credit cards [2] [3] [5]

★★**Bristol** Abadia de San Martin 3 (n.rest) ☎3521176
15 Jan–Dec
🛁 🚿 40 Lift ☾ sB 🛁 🚿 2650–2950 dB 🛁 🚿 4500–5000 t6% sea mountains
Credit cards [1] [2] [3] [5]

🚗 **Auto-Montalt** c San Vicente 118 ☎3703150 For

🚗 **Jocar** E-Bosca 22 ☎3627707 All makes

At **SALER (EL)** (12km S)

★★★**Parador Nacional Luis Vives** ☎1611186
🛁 58 **P**60 Lift ☾ sB 🛁 6600–7400 dB 🛁 8700–9700 M1950 t6% 🎾 ≈ Beach ▣ sea mountains
Credit cards [1] [2] [3] [5]

VALLADOLID
Valladolid (☎983)

★★★★***Olid Meliá*** pl San Miguel 10 ☎357200 tx26312
🛁 237 **P** Lift ☾

★★★***Conde Ansurez*** Maria de Molina 9 (n.rest) ☎351800
→ 76 Lift ☾

★★★***Meliá Parque*** Joaquin-Garaia-Morato 17 ☎470100 tx26355
→ 300 ⌂ **P** Lift

VALLE DE PINETA See **BIELSA**

VERÍN
Orense (☎988)

★★**Parador Nacional de Monterrey** ☎410075
→ 23 ⌂ **P** ☾ sB→ 4600—5800 dB→ 6200—7700 M1800 t6% ≋ mountains
Credit cards [2] [3] [5]

VIC
Barcelona (☎93)

★★★**Parador Nacional** (15km NE) ☎8887211
→ 37 ⌂ **P**30 Lift ☾ sB→ 5400—6600 dB→ 7200—8700 M1800 t6% ℓ ≋ lake
Credit cards [1] [2] [3] [4] [5]

★★***Colón*** Rambla ps 1 ☎8860220
rm40 (→ ⋒ 34) ⌂ **P** ☾

VIELLA
Lleida (☎973)

★★★***Parador Nacional Valle de Ara'n*** Estación de la Tūca ☎640100
→ 135 ⌂ **P** Lift ☾

VILAFRANCA DEL PENEDÉS
Barcelona (☎93)

⛟ **Romeu** av Barcelona 56 ☎8900592 **P** All makes

VILLACARLOS See **BALEARES (ISLES DE)** under **MAHÓN, MENORCA**

VILLACASTÍN
Segovia (☎911)

★★★***Parador Nacional*** ☎107000
→ 13 **P** ☾

VILLAFRANCA DEL BIERZO
León (☎987)

★★★**Parador Nacional Villafranca del Bierzo** ☎540175
→ 40 ⌂ **P**20 ☾ sB→ 3500 dB→ 6200 M1800 t6% mountains
Credit cards [1] [2] [3] [5]

VILLAJOYOSA
Alicante (☎965)

★★★★**Montiboll** (Relais et Châteaux) ctra N332, Km108.6 ☎890250 tx68288
Mar—Oct
→ 49 ⌂ **P**30 Lift ☾ sB→ 5600—7600 dB→ 10200—13200 M2400 t6% ℓ ≋ Beach sea
Credit cards [1] [2] [3] [5]

VILLALBA
Lugo (☎982)

★★**Parador Nacional Condes de Villalba** ☎510011
→ 6 **P** Lift ☾ sB→ 6600 dB→ 8700 M1800 t6% mountains
Credit cards [1] [2] [3] [5]

VILANOVA I LA GELTRÚ
Barcelona (☎93)

★**Solvi 70** ps Ribes Roges 1 ☎8151245
8 Oct—8 Nov
→ ⋒ 30 ⌂ **P**12 sB→ ⋒ 1750—2050 dB→ ⋒ 2800—3000 M825—900 t6% U sea
Credit card [2]

VINAROZ
Castellón (☎964)

★★**Duc de Vendôme** ctra N340 Km144 ☎450944
→ 12 ⌂ **P**15 ☾ sB→ 2435—2635 dB→ 3595—3790 M1215 t6%
Credit cards [2] [3] [5]

★★**Roca** ctra Valencia-Barcelona Km140.7 ☎450350
→ 36 ⌂ **P**200 ☾ sB→ 1800—2000 dB→ 2800—3200 M750 t6% ℓ sea

⛟ **Automecanica López** c Convento 29 ☎451022 All makes

VITORIA (GASTEIZ)
Alva (☎945)

★★★★**Canciller Ayala** Ramón y Cajal 6 ☎220800 tx35441
→ ⋒ 185 ⌂ **P**50 Lift ☾ sB→ ⋒ 4750—5450 dB→ ⋒ 8200—10900 t6%
Credit cards [1] [2] [3] [4] [5]

★★★**General Álava** av de Gasteiz 53 ☎222200 tx35468
→ 105 ⌂ **P** Lift sB→ 2850—3450 dB→ 4700—5700 t6%
Credit cards [1] [2] [4] [5]

★★★***Parador Nacional*** Apartado 601 ☎282200
→ 47 **P**100 Lift ☾ mountains lake
Credit cards [1] [2] [3] [5]

ZAFRA
Badajoz (☎924)

★★★***Parador Nacional Hernán Contés*** pl de Maria Cristina ☎550200
16 Dec—Oct
rm28 (→ ⋒ 28) ☾ ≋

On **N432 Badajoz road** (16km NW)

⛟ **F Alvarez Ruiz** ctra Badajoz-Granada Km73.6 ☎551160 **P** Cit

ZAMORA
Zamora (☎988)

★★**Cuatro Naciones** av Alfonso IX ☎512275
→ ⋒ 40 Lift ☾ sB→ ⋒ 1970—2170 dB→ ⋒ 3040—3790 M875 t6%
Credit cards [2] [3] [5]

★★***Parador Nacional Condes de Alba & Aliste*** pl de Cánovas 1 ☎514497
→ 19 ⌂ **P** ☾ ≋

ZARAGOZA
Zaragoza (☎976)

★★★**Goya** Cinco de Marzo 5 (off ps de la Independencia) ☎229331 tx58680
→ 150 ⌂ **P**20 ☾ sB→ 3725 dB→ 6400 M1400 t6%
Credit cards [1] [2] [3] [5]

★★**Conde Blanco** Predicadores 84 (n.rest) ☎441411
→ 83 ⌂ **P**40 Lift ☾ sB→ 2105—2435 dB→ 3330—3750 t6%

On **N11 Madrid road** (8km SW)

★★**Cisne** ctra Madrid, Barcelona Km309 ☎332000
rm61 (→ 51) **P** ☾ sB1260 sB→ 2260 dB→ 4670 ≋ mountains

ZARAUZ (ZARAUTZ)
Guipúzcoa (☎943)

★★★**Zarauz** av de Navarra 4 ☎830200
15 Jan—15 Dec
→ 82 **P** Lift ☾ sB→ 3220—4170 dB→ 4490—5490 M1250 t6% sea mountains
Credit card [3]

★★**Alameda** Travesia Alameda ☎830143
Apr—Sep
rm26 (⋒ 4) **P**14 ☾ sB2090 dB3240 dB⋒ 3760 M840 t6% mountains
Credit cards [1] [3]

Andorra

Prices are in Spanish pesetas
(☎ from France 16078 ☎ from Spain 9738)

ANDORRA LA VELLA

★★★**Andorra Center** ctra Dr-Nequi 12 ☎24999 tx377
→ 150 ⌂ **P**75 Lift ☾ sB→ 4650 dB→ 5870 M1475 ℓ ≋ ☐ mountains
Credit cards [1] [2] [3] [4] [5]

★★★***Andorra Palace*** Prat de la Creu ☎21072 tx208
→ 140 ⌂ **P**100 Lift ☾ ℓ ☐ mountains
Credit cards [1] [2] [3] [5]

★★★**Andorra Park** (MAP) ☎20979 tx203
→ ⋒ 35 A35rm **P** ☾ sB3100 sB→ ⋒ 6350 dB5000 dB→ ⋒ 7800 M2100 ℓ ≋ mountains
Credit cards [1] [2] [3] [4] [5]

★★★***Mercure*** av Méritxell 58 ☎20773 tx208
→ 70 ⌂ **P**100 Lift ☾ ℓ ☐ mountains
Credit cards [1] [2] [3] [5]

★★★**Sasplugas** av del Princep Iglesias ☎20311
→ 26 ⌂ **P**25 Lift sB→ 2950—4050 dB→ 5100—5900 M1500—2000 mountains
Credit cards [1] [3] [4]

★★***Internacional*** ctra Mossen Tremosa 2 ☎21422
→ ⋒ 50 Lift

★★**Pyrénées** av Princep Benlloch 20 ☎20508 tx209

rm84 (🛁🚿54) ⌂ **P**30 Lift ☾ sB1550 sB🛁🚿2200 dB1900 dB🛁🚿3000 M1000 🎾 🏊 🏊 mountains

Credit cards 1 2 3

🚗 **CIMEX** av Dr Mitjavila 5 ☎23190 **P** Fia

ENCAMP

★**Residencia Belvedere** ctra Bellavista ☎31263

15 Dec—15 Oct

rm10 (🛁1) **P**8 sB1684—1789 dB3157—3368 dB🛁3578—3789 M1473—1579 mountains

ESCALDES (LES)

★★★**Roc Blanc** (MAP) pl dels Co-Princeps 5 ☎21486 tx224

🛁240 ⌂ **P**68 Lift ☾ sB🛁5775

dB🛁10150 M2200 S15% 🎾 🏊 🏊 mountains

Credit cards 1 2 3 4 5

★★***Pia*** (n.rest) ☎21432

Jul—25 Aug

rm32 (🛁15) Lift mountains

Becier 105 av Charlemagne ☎21462 Ren

SANTA COLOMA

★★★***Roureda*** av d'Enclar 18 ☎20681

Jun—Sep

🚿36 **P**30 ☾ 🏊 mountains

🚗 **Becier** Av d'Enclar ☎20672 Ren

SANT JULIÀ DE LÒRIA

★★★***Co-Princeps*** ctra de Hué 1 ☎41002

Apr—Oct

🛁80 **P** Lift ☾ mountains

★★**Sardana** pl Major 2—4 ☎41018

Apr—Sep

🛁🚿25 mountains

SOLDEU

At TARTER (EL) (3km W)

★★★**Tarter** ☎51165

Dec—15 Oct

🛁37 ⌂ **P**30 ☾ sB🛁2260 dB🛁3720 M900—1300 mountains

Credit cards 1 3 5

Plaza Tipica, Salamanca

Sweden

International distinguishing sign

Area *173,624 sq miles*
Location map *See page 320*
Population *8,342,621*
Local time *GMT + 1 (Summer GMT + 2)*

National flag *Gold cross on a blue field*

How to get there

Sweden can be reached by direct ferry services operating from Harwich or Newcastle to Göteborg (Gothenburg). The crossing takes 23—26 hours. It is also possible to reach Sweden via Denmark, using the Newcastle or Harwich to Esbjerg car ferry services; sailing time is about 20 hours. Alternatively you can take one of the short Channel crossings to France or Belgium, then drive through the Netherlands, northern Germany, and Denmark to Sweden, using the ferry connections between Puttgarden—Rødbyhavn, and Helsingør—Helsingborg. Crossing from Harwich to Hamburg gives a shorter overland journey via Germany or Denmark. The distance from Calais to Stockholm, the capital, is about 1,000 miles and would normally require three night stops.

Motoring regulations and general information

This information should be read in conjunction with the general content of the European ABC (pages 4-26). **Note** As certain regulations and requirements are common to many countries they are covered by one entry in the ABC and the following headings represent some of the subjects dealt with in this way:

AA Agents
Crash or safety helmets
Customs regulations for European Countries
Drinking and driving
Fire extinguisher
First-aid kit
Insurance
International distinguishing sign
Medical treatment
Mirrors
Overtaking
Police fines
Radio telephones/Radio transmitters
Road signs
Seat belts
Traffic lights
Tyres
Visitors' registration

Accidents

Fire, police and **ambulance** ☎ 90000. The emergency telephone number should only be used in the case of personal injury or illness.

In the case of an accident it is not necessary to call the police, but the driver is required to give information regarding his name and address to other persons concerned. He is not allowed to leave the scene of the accident before this is done, no matter how slight the damage. If a driver goes away he may be sentenced to imprisonment or be fined. However, as a general rule, report the matter to the police in your own interests. See also *Accidents* page 5.

Accommodation

Swedish hotels have a particularly good reputation for cleanliness. A full list is published by the Swedish Tourist Board, but there is no official classification. The Swedish equivalent of VAT is included in all prices, as is the service charge. In many places summer chalets can be rented. In the south it is possible to holiday on a farm or as paying guest at a manor house. The Swedish Touring Club has over fifty lodges at which families can be accommodated. They provide from 4 to 6 beds, hot and cold water, and showers.

Breakdown

The Swedish motoring organisation Motormännens Riksförbund (M) operates a road service on main roads (E-roads) during the summer months. There are also alarm centres organised by Larmtjanst AB (Alarm Services Ltd) or garages which are open day and night to help motorists in difficulties. The service is restricted to breakdowns and accidents and is not free. See also *Breakdown* page 6 and *Warning triangles* page 376.

British Embassy/Consulates

The British Embassy together with its consular section is located at *11527 Stockholm* Skarpögatan 6-8 ☎ (08)670140. There are British Consulates with Honorary Consuls in Gävle, Göteborg and Malmö. See also page 6 and *Town Plan of Stockholm* pages 382-383.

Currency including banking hours

(See also page 9)
The unit of currency is the Swedish Krona (*SKr*) divided into 100 *Öre*. At the time of going to press £ = *SKr*10.24. Denominations of bank notes are *SKr* 5, 10, 50, 100, 500, 1,000, 10,000; standard coins are *SKr* 1, 5 and *Öre* 10, 50. There are no restrictions on the amount of foreign or Swedish currency that a bona fide tourist may import in the country. No more than *SKr*6,000 in local currency notes of less than *SKr*1,000 may be exported, but there are no restrictions on the export of foreign currency provided it was obtained outside Sweden.

In towns, banks are generally open 09.30—15.00hrs but some may be open until 18.00hrs Monday to Thursday. In the country banks are usually open from 10.00hrs to 14.00hrs Monday to Friday.

Dimensions and weight restrictions

(See also page 10)
Private **cars** and towed **trailers** or **caravans** are restricted to the following dimensions — height: no restriction; width: 2.60 metres; length: 24 metres which is also the maximum permitted overall length of vehicle/trailer or caravan combination.

Trailers without brakes must not exceed twice the maximum weight of the towing vehicle.

Driving licence

(See also page 11)
A valid British driving licence is acceptable in Sweden. The minimum age at which a visitor may drive a temporarily imported car is 18 years and a temporarily imported motorcycle 17 years.

Emergency messages to tourists

(See also page 11)
Emergency messages to tourists are broadcast daily throughout the year by Swedish Radio. *Sveriges Radio* (Programme 1) transmitting on medium wave 245 metres, 255 metres, 306 metres, 388 metres, 417 metres and 506 metres broadcasts these messages in English, French, German and Swedish at 08.10, 13.10, 16.45 and 21.50hrs. *Sveriges Radio* (Programme 3) transmitting as above, but messages broadcast at 11.55 and 19.02hrs.

Lights

(See also page 14)
It is compulsory for all motorists including motorcyclists to use dipped headlights during the day.

Motoring clubs

The **Motormännens Riksförbund** (M) has its headquarters at *10248 Stockholm* Sturegatan 32 ☎ (08)7823800 and the **Svenska Turistforeningen** (STF) at *10120 Stockholm* Vasagatan 48 ☎ (08)7903100. Both have branch offices and agents in main towns.

See also page 16 and *Town Plan of Stockholm* pages 382-383 for location of Motormännens Riksförbund.

Motorways

Several main roads, mainly E3, E4, E6 and E18 incorporate stretches of motorway (motorväg) and semi-motorway (motortrafikled). There are 844 miles open in all and further sections are under construction or in the planning stage. No tolls are charged.

Orange badge scheme for disabled drivers

(See also page 16)
Although concessions are available to disabled drivers in Sweden, they have not yet been extended to include visiting disabled drivers. However, foreign parking permits for the disabled may be recognised in some areas at the discretion of local traffic wardens.

Overtaking

(See also page 17)
On roads where the hard shoulder is separated from the driving lane(s) with a continuous white line it is strongly recommended not to use it other than in the case of emergency. In other cases the hard shoulder may also be used by vehicles travelling at more than 30kph (18mph) to facilitate overtaking and traffic flow. However, priority must be given to all other traffic when leaving the hard shoulder. These hard shoulders may also be used

by cyclists and vehicles with a maximum speed of 30kph.

Parking

(See also page 18)
In Stockholm and a few of the larger towns there are parking restrictions which are connected with road cleaning and are decided locally. A sign (blue disc with red border and red diagonal) is placed under the street name and gives the day and times when parking is prohibited. The restriction applies only to the side of the street on which the sign is displayed.

Passengers

(See also page 18)
It is recommended that children do not travel in a vehicle as front seat passengers unless seated in a special child restraint.

Petrol

(See also page 18)
Many petrol stations are equipped with 24-hour filling automats where payment is made with 10, 50 or 100 Kroner bank notes.
Credit cards International credit cards are becoming more widely accepted at petrol stations.
Duty-free petrol The petrol in the vehicle tank may be imported free of custom duty and tax. However, as an additional concession, the customs authorities generally allow a reasonable quantity of petrol to be imported in a spare can.
Petrol (leaded) Premium (96—98 octane) grades.
Petrol (unleaded) is sold in Sweden. It has an octane rating of 95 and pumps dispensing unleaded petrol are marked *Blyfri*.

Postal information

Mail Postcards *SKr*2.30; letters up to 20gm *SKr*2.90.
Post offices There are 2,500 post offices in Sweden. Opening hours of the larger offices are from 09.00—18.00hrs Monday to Friday and 09.00—13.00hrs Saturday. Smaller offices open 10.00—16.00hrs Monday to Friday and 10.00—13.00hrs Saturday. In Stockholm the Head Post Office is open from 08.00—21.00hrs and 11.00—13.00hrs on Sunday. The Central Station post office is open from 07.00—22.00hrs on weekdays.

Postcheques

(See also page 20)
Postcheques may be cashed for any amount up to a maximum of *SKr*600 per cheque at all post offices except those in smaller villages. A local charge of *SKr*2 is made for each encashment on a Saturday. All counter positions will cash *Postcheques*. See *Postal information* for post office opening hours.

Priority

Buses have priority when leaving bus stops in areas where speed is restricted to 50kph (32mph). See also *Priority including Roundabouts* page 20.

Public holidays

Official public holidays in Sweden for 1987 are given below. See also *Public holidays* page 21.
January 1 (New Year's Day)
January 6 (Epiphany)
April 17 (Good Friday)
April 19 (Easter Sunday)
April 20 (Easter Monday)
May 1 (May Day)
May 28 (Ascension Day)
June 7 (Whit Sunday)
June 8 (Whit Monday)
June 20 (Midsummer Day)
November 1† (All Saints' Day)
December 25 (Christmas Day)
December 26* (Boxing day)

*Saturday †Sunday

Roads

There is a comprehensive network of numbered, well-signposted highways but minor roads are not numbered. Although many roads in the south are being improved, others — particularly in central and northern Sweden — are still surfaced with loose gravel.

In various parts, chiefly along the Baltic coast, there are protected areas where only certain roads are open to motorists, and in these areas visitors may stay only at certain places and for a limited time. The two areas likely to concern visitors are around Boden and Kalix in the provinces of Norrbotten. Warning notices are displayed in English and other languages on the boundaries of these areas.

Road number changes Road numbers have been revised and changes to the classification and numbering of some roads throughout the country have taken place during 1986. 910 kilometres of national roads have been *downgraded* to county roads, and 1750 kilometres of county roads were *upgraded* to national roads.

Shopping hours

Shopping hours vary, especially in large cities, but most are open 09.00—18.00hrs from Monday to

Friday, and 09.00—14.00hrs or 16.00hrs on Saturday.

Speed limits

(See also page 22)
There are maximum speed limits indicated by signs on all roads in Sweden. In built-up areas 50kph (31mph); on all minor roads and roads with a high traffic density 70kph (43mph); on all other roads 90kph (56mph) and 110kph (68mph) on motorways. Cars towing caravans fitted with brakes 70kph (43mph); without brakes 40kph (24mph).

Spiked or studded tyres

Spiked tyres are permitted from 1 October to 30 April. They may be used during the rest of the year if weather conditions require their use, and if the relevant special decision is announced by the authorities. When spiked tyres are used they must be fitted on all wheels. If a vehicle with spiked tyres tows a trailer, the trailer must be fitted with spiked tyres. See also *Cold weather touring* page 0.

Tourist Information

(See also page 24)
Local tourist information is available from tourist offices throughout Sweden. Persons requiring information in the UK should contact the Swedish National Tourist Office, 3 Cork Street, London W1X 1HA ☎ 01-437 5816.

Trams

(See also page 24)
Trams should be overtaken on the right if the position of the tracks permits this. If there is no refuge at a tram stop, drivers should stop and give way to passengers alighting from and boarding the tram. All road users must give way to trams.

Using the telephone

(See also page 24)
Insert coin **after** lifting receiver (instructions in English in most callboxes). When making calls to subscribers within Sweden precede number with relevant area code (shown in parentheses against town entry in gazetteer). Use *SKr*1 coin for local calls and *SKr*1 or 5 coins for national and international calls.
International callbox identification Callboxes with 1/3 slots.
Telephone rates A call to the UK costs *SKr*5.35 per minute. Local calls cost a minimum of *SKr*1.
What to dial for Irish Republic 009 353*.
What to dial for the UK 009 44*.
*Wait for second dialling tone

Warning triangle

The use of a warning triangle is compulsory for all vehicles except two-wheelers. See also *Warning triangles/Hazard warning lights* page 25.

Winter conditions

During winter there is usually no difficulty in driving to Stockholm from Göteborg, Oslo or Denmark. Farther north, motoring is also possible subject to prevailing conditions, as the main roads are cleared as quickly as possible. Generally, however, the touring season is from May to September.

Prices are in Swedish Kroner
Abbreviations
gt gatan

ABISKO
Lappland (☎0980)

★★**Abisko Turistation** ☎40000
Mar—15 Sep
🚿30 A35rm dB🚿390—430 M45—75 lake mountains
Credit card [1]

ALINGSÅS
Västergötland (☎0322)

★★★***Scandic*** Bankgt 1 ☎14000
🛁🚿66 **P** ☾

🚗 **Allbärgning** Ölandsgt 15 ☎36300

ALVESTA
Småland (☎0472)

★★★***Scandic*** Stargt ☎11350
🛁48 ⌂ **P**10 Lift ☾
Credit cards [1] [2] [3] [4] [5]

ÅMÅL
Dalsand (☎0532)

★★***Stadshotellet*** Kungsgt 9 ☎12020
rm49 (🛁🚿39) A12rm ⌂ **P** Lift 🎾 ≋

🚗 **Dalslands** Industrigt ☎11045 VW

ÄNGELHOLM
Skåne (☎0431)

★***Erikslunds*** N Varalov ☎22114
rm15 (🛁🚿7) ⌂ **P**30 Lift
Credit cards [1] [2]

ÅRE
Jämtland (☎0647)

★★***Diplomat Åre-Aregarden*** ☎50265 tx44050
🛁85 **P**50 🎾 📺 mountains lake
Credit cards [1] [2] [3] [5]

ÅRJÄNG
Värmland (☎0573)

★★★***Scandic*** Arikavägen ☎11070 tx12636
🛁🚿40 **P** ☾ ≋

ARLÖV See **MALMÖ**

ARVIKA
Värmland (☎0570)

★★★***Bristol*** Kyrkogt 25 (n.rest) ☎13280
🛁🚿40 ⌂ **P** Lift

★★**Oscar Statt** Torggt 9 ☎19750
🚿43 ⌂ **P**43 Lift ☾ sB🚿270—475 dB🚿370—575
Credit cards [1] [2] [3] [5]

🚗 **Ola By Bilbärgning** Mossebergsgt 3 ☎11057

ASKERSUND
Närke (☎0583)

★★★***Scandic*** Marieborg Sundsbrogt ☎12010 tx12636
🛁🚿36 **P** ☾ ≋

★★**Vättern** Torgparken 3 ☎11155
rm24 (🛁🚿18) **P** sB285 sB🛁🚿285 dB290 dB🛁🚿325
Credit card [1]

Sweden

ÅTVIDABERG
Östergötland (☎0120)

★★★**Stallet** Östantorpsvägen 2 ☎11940 tx5586
68 P75 ☾ sB 315—500 dB 430—680 M30—250
Credit cards 1 2 3 5

BÅSTAD
Skåne (☎0431)

★★**Enehall** Stationsterrassen 10 ☎75015
Etr—Nov
rm60 (50) A50rm sB150—180 sB 200—255 dB300—360 dB 350—440 M35—75
Credit cards 1 2 3 5

★★**Hallandsås** ☎(0430) 24270
rm22 (17) ☾ sB 150—250 dB 340
Credit cards 1 2 3 5

BODEN
Norrbotten (☎0921)

★★★**Bodensia** (Inter S) Medborgarplatsen ☎17710
97 P Lift ☾ sB 595 dB 695

BOLLNÅS
Hälsingland (☎0278)

★★***Frimurarehotellet*** Stationsgt 15 ☎13220 tx17930
rm67 (42) Lift

BORÅS
Västergötland (☎033)

★★★**Grand** (SARA) Hallbergsgt 14 ☎108200 tx36182
166 P Lift ☾ sB 540—580 dB 705—725 M70—110
Credit cards 1 2 3 5

★★★***Scandic*** Hultasjögt 7 ☎157000
95 P Lift ☾

BORGHOLM
Öland (☎0485)

Lundgren Långgt ☎10068 Dat

BORLÄNGE
Dalarna (☎0243)

★★★**Galaxen** Jussi Björlings Väg 25 ☎80010 tx74270
129 P40 Lift ☾ sB 305—550 dB 410—710 M30—100 mountains
Credit cards 1 2 3 5

★★★***Scandic*** Stationsgt 21—23 ☎28120
111 P Lift ☾

★★**Brage** (SARA) Sationsgt 1 ☎24150
96 P32 Lift ☾ sB 245—500 dB 350—650 M34—75
Credit cards 1 2 3 5

DEGEBERGA
Skåna (☎0450)

Degeberga-Auto Tingsvägen 48 ☎50002 AR

ENKÖPING
Uppland (☎0171)

★★***Stadshotellet*** Stora Torget ☎20010
rm67 (63) P Lift ☾

ESKILSTUNA
Södermanland (☎016)

★★★***Eskilstuna*** (SARA) Hamngt 11 ☎137225 tx460465
228 P Lift ☾

FAGERSTA
Västmanland (☎0223)

★★★***Scandic*** Blomstervägen ☎17060
49 P85 Lift ☾
Credit cards 1 2 3 5

FALUN
Dalarna (☎023)

★★★***Grand*** (SARA) Trotzgt 9—11 ☎18700
182 P100 Lift ☾ mountains
Credit cards 2 3 5

★★★***Scandic Norslund*** ☎22160 tx74137
107 P100 Lift ☾
Credit cards 1 2 3 4 5

Borlänge Bilbägning H-Hedströssväg ☎19630

FILIPSTAD
Värmland (☎0590)

★★★***Scandic*** Lasarettsgt 2 ☎12530
47 P ☾ lake mountains
Credit cards 1 2 3 4 5

FLEN
Södermanland (☎0157)

★★★***Scandic*** Brogt 5 ☎13940
48 P100 ☾
Credit cards 1 2 3 4 5

FLENINGE See **HELSINGBORG**

GAMLEBY
Smårland (☎0493)

★**Tjust** ☎11550
rm17 (7) P50 ☾ sB175—310 sB 375—455 dB 425—585 M30—60 lake mountains
Credit cards 1 2 3 5

GÅVLE
Gästrikland (☎026)

★★★***Scandic*** (3km S on E4) Hemmlingby ☎188060 tx47355
202 P200 Lift
Credit cards 2 3 4 5

Dahlboms Bomhusvägen 55 ☎100400 Alf Ren

GETÅ
Östergötland (☎011)

★★**Getå** ☎62050
48 P50 ☾ sB 382 dB 545 M77 Beach sea mountains

GISLAVED
Småland (☎0371)

★★★***Scandic*** Riksväg 26 ☎11540 tx12636
54 P Lift ☾

GLUMSLÖV
Skåne (☎0418)

★★★**Örenäs Slott** ☎70250 tx72759
128 Lift ☾ sB 310—525 dB 420—625
Credit cards 1 2 3 5

GÖTEBORG (GOTHENBURG)
Bohuslän (☎031)

★★★★★***Park Avenue*** (SRS) Kungsports Avenyn 36—38 ☎176520 tx2320
320 P Lift ☾
Credit cards 1 2 3 5

★★★★***Europa*** (SARA/THF) Köpmansgt 38 ☎801280 tx21374
480 P Lift ☾

★★★★**Opalen** Engelbrektsgt 73 ☎810300 tx2215
237 P20 Lift ☾ sB 590—690 dB 800 M65—85

★★★**Eggers** Drottningtorget 1 ☎171570 tx27273
90 P Lift ☾ sB 520 dB 645
Credit cards 1 2 3 5

★★★**Ekoxen** (Inter S) N Hamngt 38 (n.rest) ☎805080 tx21993
75 P Lift ☾ sB 345—740 dB 430—890
Credit cards 1 2 3 4 5

★★★**Gothia** (SARA) Mässans Gata 24 ☎409300 tx21941
292 P800 Lift ☾ sB 910 dB 1030 M55—200
Credit cards 1 2 3 4 5

★★★**Novotel** Klippen 1 ☎149000 tx28181
150 P Lift ☾ sB 350—715 dB 450—815 sea

★★★***Rubinen*** Kungsports Avenyn 24 ☎810800 tx20837
189 P Lift ☾
Credit cards 1 2 3 5

★★★***Scandic*** Bäckobolsvägen ☎520060 tx27767
180 P Lift ☾

★★★**Scandinavia** (THF) Kustgt 10 ☎427000 tx21522
323 P150 Lift ☾ sB 290—695 dB 330—845 sea
Credit cards 1 2 3 4 5

★★★**Windsor** Kungsportsavenyn 6 ☎176540 tx21014
83 P Lift ☾ sB 600 dB 775

★★**Frälsningsarméns Ritz** Burggrevegt 25 ☎175260 tx21283
rm107 (100) P8 Lift ☾ sB260 sB 280—380 dB430 dB 580—660
Credit cards 1 2 3 5

★★**Örgryte** Danska Vagen 68 ☎197620 tx27565
🛁 🚿 74 🏠 **P**70 Lift ☾ sB 🛁 🚿 415 dB 🛁 🚿 515 M35—50 📺
Credit cards [1] [2] [3] [4] [5]

★**Liseberg Heden** Sten Sturegt ☎200280 tx27450
🛁 160 **P** Lift ☾ sB 🛁 460—520 dB 🛁 600—680
Credit cards [1] [2] [3] [4] [5]

★***Örnen*** Lorensbergsgt 6 (off Vasagt) (n.rest) ☎182380
rm30 Lift
Credit cards [1] [2] [3]

🚗 **Motorverken** Fröfästegt 68 ☎289560 For

GRÄNNA
Småland (☎0390)

★★★***Scandic*** Gyllene Uttern ☎10800
🛁 🚿 56 **P** Lift ☾ lake

HÄGERSTEN See **STOCKHOLM**

HALMSTAD
Halland (☎035)

★★★★**Hallandia** Rädhusgt 2 ☎118800 tx38030
🛁 132 **P**80 Lift ☾ sB 🛁 450 dB 🛁 530 sea
Credit cards [1] [2] [3] [5]

★★★**Grand** Stationsgt 44 ☎119140 tx38210
🚿 120 **P**200 Lift ☾ sB🚿 380—645 dB🚿 520—800 M40&alc
Credit cards [1] [2] [3] [4] [5]

★★★**O K Motor** Strandvallen 3 ☎104300 tx38279
🛁 117 **P**200 Lift sB 🛁 485 dB 🛁 580 ⚲ ≈
Credit cards [1] [2] [3] [5]

★★★**Mårtenson** Storgt 52 ☎118070
🛁 🚿 70 **P** Lift ☾ sB 🛁 🚿 280—520 Malc
Credit cards [1] [2] [3] [5]

HANDEN
Stockholm (☎08)

★★★**Najaden** Rudsjoterrassen 3 ☎7457400 tx16726
🛁 🚿 72 🏠 **P**70 Lift ☾ sB 🛁 🚿 280—520 dB 🛁 🚿 300—620 M60—120 📺 lake
Credit cards [1] [2] [3] [4]

HAPARANDA
Norrbotten (☎0922)

★★***Stadshotellet*** Torget 7 ☎11490
rm40 (🛁 🚿 28) 🏠 Lift ≈

HÄRNÖSAND
Ångermanland (☎0611)

★★★***Scandic*** Ådalsvägen ☎19560
🛁 🚿 51 **P** ≈

HÄSSLEHOLM
Skåne (☎0451)

★★***Göingehof*** Frykholmsgt 23 ☎14330
🛁 🚿 44 Lift
Credit cards [1] [2] [3]

Sweden

HELSINGBORG
Skåne (☎042)

★★★**Grand** (Inter S) Stortorget 8—12 ☎120170 tx72271
🛁 130 🏠 **P** Lift ☾ sB 🛁 640—700 dB 🛁 675—820

★★★**Horisont** Gustaf Adolfs Gata 47 ☎149260 tx72739
🚿 171 **P**130 Lift ☾ sB🚿 610—630 dB🚿 715—785 M50—100 📺 sea
Credit cards [1] [2] [3] [5]

★★★***Scandic*** Florettgt 41 ☎151560 tx72149
🛁 🚿 175 **P** ☾ ≈

★★***Kronan*** Ängelholmsvagen 35 ☎127965
rm43 (🚿 40)
Credit cards [1] [2] [3] [5]

★★**Mollberg** Stortorget 18 (Off Södra Storgt) ☎120270 tx72234
🛁 🚿 115 🏠 **P**75 Lift ☾ sB 🛁 🚿 600—660 dB 🛁 🚿 700—770 M34—48
Credit cards [1] [2] [3] [5]

🚗 **Scania** Muskötgt 1 ☎151410 VW

At **FLENINGE** (10km NE)

★★***Fleninge*** ☎205155
rm27 (🛁 26) **P**27 ☾
Credit cards [1] [3]

HEMAVAN
Lappland (☎0954)

★★***Hemavans Fjällhotell*** ☎30150
26 Dec—13 May & 10 Jun—16 Sep
rm72 (🛁 10) A12rm **P** ☾ mountains lake

HOFORS
Gästrikland (☎0290)

★★★***Scandic*** R80 Skolgt 11 ☎23010 tx12636
🛁 🚿 40 **P** Lift ☾

HOK
Småland (☎0393)

★★★**Hook Manor** (Relais et Châteaux) ☎21080 tx70419
rm100 (🛁 90) **P** sB90—495 sB 🛁 490—595 dB550—690 dB 🛁 650—1340 M90—200 ⚲ ≈ ▣
Credit cards [1] [2] [3] [5]

HUDIKSVALL
Hålsingland (☎0650)

★★★**Stadshotellet** (Inter S) Storgt 36 ☎15060 tx71534
🛁 144 🏠 **P** Lift ☾ sB 🛁 610—625 dB 🛁 710—725 ≈

HYLTEBRUK
Småland (☎0345)

🚗 **Hylte Bilverkstad** Gamia Nissastigen ☎10206 Ope

INSJÖN
Dalarna (☎0247)

★★★***Insjön*** Hotellvägen ☎41050
🚿 28 A8rm **P**12 Lift mountains
Credit cards [1] [2] [3] [5]

JÖNKÖPING
Småland (☎036)

★★★★**Portalen** Västra Storgt 9 ☎118200 tx70037
🛁 179 🏠 **P**155 Lift ☾ sB 🛁 550—665 dB 🛁 710 📺 lake mountains
Credit cards [1] [2] [3] [4] [5]

★★★**City** Västra Storgt 25 ☎119280 tx70611
rm67 (🛁 🚿 57) 🏠 **P**20 Lift ☾ sB380 sB 🛁 🚿 450—525 dB 🛁 🚿 610—665 M60—70
Credit cards [1] [2] [3] [5]

★★★***Savoy*** Brunnsgt 15 ☎119480
rm60 (🛁 33)

★★★***Scandic*** Rosenlund ☎119160
🛁 174 **P** Lift ☾ 📺
Credit cards [1] [2] [3] [4] [5]

★★★**Stora** (Inter S) ☎119300 tx70057
🛁 111 🏠 **P** Lift ☾ sB 🛁 590—725 dB 🛁 690—825 lake
Credit cards [1] [2] [3] [5]

★★***Grand*** Hovrättstorget ☎119600
rm60 (🛁 16) 🏠 **P** Lift mountains lake

🚗 **Atteviks** J-Bauersgt 1 ☎169100 Aud Por VW

🚗 **Autolarm Börje Linden** Ö Stradt 5 ☎114048 All makes

KALMAR
Småland (☎0480)

★★★***Scandic*** (3km W) Dragonvagen 7 ☎22360 tx43007
🛁 🚿 149 **P** ☾ ≈ ▣

★★★**Stads** (Inter S) Stortorget 14 ☎15180 tx43109
🛁 150 Lift ☾ sB 🛁 600—775 dB 🛁 800—1050

★★★**Witt** (SARA) Södra Langgt 42 ☎15250 tx43133
Closed 23—26 Dec
🛁 112 🏠 Lift ☾ sB 🛁 505—645 dB 🛁 800—1000 M60—90 📺
Credit cards [1] [2] [3] [5]

KARLSBORG
Västergotland (☎0505)

★★★**Kanalhotellet** Storgt 94 ☎12130
rm25 (🛁 🚿 19) A19rm **P**40 ☾ sB200 sB 🛁 🚿 300 dB300 dB 🛁 🚿 340 M35—100&alc lake mountains
Credit cards [1] [2] [3] [5]

KARLSHAMN
Blekinge (☎0454)

★★★***Scandic*** Strömmavägen ☎16660
🛁 🚿 100 **P** Lift ☾ 📺
Credit cards [1] [2] [3] [4] [5]

Sweden

KARLSKOGA
Värmland (☏0586)

★★★***Scandic*** Hyttåsen ☏50460
➡⋒80 **P** Lift ☾ ▭
Credit cards [1] [2] [3] [4] [5]

KARLSKRONA
Blekinge (☏0455)

★★★**Statt** (Inter S) Ronnebygt 37 ☏19250 tx43187
➡105 ⌂ **P** Lift ☾ sB➡600–900 dB➡900–1250 St%

KARLSTAD
Värmland (☏054)

★★★***OK Motor*** Höjdgt 3 ☏131000 tx66083
➡⋒165 **P** Lift ☾ ≏
Credit cards [1] [2] [3] [4] [5]

★★★***Scandic*** Sandbäcksgt 6 ☏1871200 tx66379
➡⋒146 **P** Lift ☾ ▭ lake
Credit cards [1] [2] [3] [4] [5]

★★★**Stads** (Inter S) Kungsgt 22 ☏115220 tx66024
➡130 **P** Lift ☾ sB➡510–550 dB➡600–660 ≏

★★★**Winn** (SARA) Norra Strandgt 9–11 ☏102220 tx66120
➡⋒177 ⌂ **P**40 Lift ☾ sB➡⋒605 dB➡⋒740
Credit cards [1] [2] [3] [5]

★★**Gösta Berling** Drottninggt 1 ☏150190
➡⋒75 ⌂ **P**25 Lift ☾ sB➡⋒200–400 dB➡⋒300–500 M30–85
Credit cards [1] [2] [3] [4] [5]

★★**Ritz** Västra Torggt 20 (n. rest) ☏115140
Closed Xmas and New Year
➡62 **P** Lift ☾

★***Drott*** Järnvägsgt 1 ☏115635 tx66329 rm38 (➡⋒6) Lift

KATRINEHOLM
Södermanland (☏0150)

★★★**Stads** (Inter S) Storgt 20 ☏50440 tx64055
➡92 Lift ☾ sB➡530–560 dB➡630–670

KIRUNA
Lappland (☏0980)

★★★**Ferrum** Köpmansgt 1 ☏18600 tx8746
➡⋒170 ⌂ **P**37 Lift ☾ sB➡⋒581–601 dB➡⋒717–762 Malc mountains
Credit cards [1] [2] [3] [5]

KÖPING
Västmanland (☏0221)

★★★**Scheele** Hultgrensgt 10 ☏18120 tx40423
➡⋒112 **P**112 Lift ☾ sB➡⋒525 dB➡⋒690
Credit cards [1] [2] [3] [5]

KRAMFORS
Ångermanland (☏0612)

★★★**Kramm** Torggt 14 ☏13160 tx71325
➡109 **P**50 Lift ☾ sB➡346 dB➡492 M75
Credit cards [1] [2] [3] [5]

KRISTIANSTAD
Skåne (☏044)

★★**Grand** V Storgt 15 ☏103600 tx48234
➡⋒150 ⌂ **P**35 Lift ☾ sB➡⋒545–730 dB➡⋒740–830 M87–218
Credit cards [1] [2] [3] [5]

Kristianstads Bilcentrum Blekringevägen 2 ☏115890 Aud VW

KRISTINEHAMN
Värmland (☏0550)

E Andersson Bil & Maskin 1a Indstrigt 3 ☏15540 BWM For RR

KUNGÄLV
Bohuslän (☏0303)

★★★**Fars Hatt** ☏10970 tx2415
➡⋒123 A28rm **P**400 Lift ☾ sB➡⋒565–585 dB➡⋒730–770 M90–120 St% ≏ mountains
Credit cards [1] [2] [3] [4] [5]

KUNGENS KURVA
Stockholm (☏08)

★★★***Scandic*** Ekgardsvågen 2 ☏7100460 tx13830
➡⋒276 **P** Lift ☾ ▭
Credit cards [1] [2] [3] [5]

LAGAN
Småland (☏0372)

★★★**Scandic** Laganland ☏35200
➡32 **P**100 sB➡310–405 dB➡395–530 M45–125
Credit cards [1] [2] [3] [5]

LANDSKRONA
Skåne (☏0418)

★★★**Öresund** Kungsgt 15 ☏29000 tx72327
➡138 **P**70 Lift ☾ sB➡265–560 dB➡370–700 ▭
Credit cards [1] [2] [3] [5]

LAXA
Närke (☏0584)

★★★***Scandic*** ☏11540
➡⋒43 **P** ☾
Credit cards [1] [2] [3] [4] [5]

LEKSAND
Dalarna (☏0247)

★★***Tre Kullor*** Hjortnäsu 2 ☏11350 rm40 (➡⋒13) ⌂

LIDKOPING
Västergötland (☏0510)

Per Bengtsson Wennerbergsvägen 27 ☏22470 Hon Ope Vau

E Bjöstig Wennerbergsvägen 33 ☏22480 Por

LINKÖPING
Östergötland (☏013)

★★★**Ekoxen** Klostergt 68 ☏146070 tx50142
➡⋒95 A23rm ⌂ Lift ☾ sB➡⋒230–760 dB➡⋒280–950 ▭
Credit cards [1] [2] [3] [5]

★★★**Frimurarehotellet** St-Larsgt 14 ☏129180 tx50053
➡⋒210 **P**100 Lift ☾ sB➡⋒590 dB➡⋒690
Credit cards [1] [2] [3] [5]

★★★***Rally*** (SARA) Storgt 72 ☏130200 tx50055
2 Jan–23 Dec
➡⋒135 ⌂ **P**28 Lift ☾
Credit cards [1] [2] [3] [4] [5]

★★★***Scandic*** Rydsvagen ☏171060
➡⋒94 **P** ☾ ▭
Credit cards [1] [2] [3] [4] [5]

★★★**Stora** Stora Torget 9 ☏129630 rm110 (⋒95) **P**19 Lift ☾ sB⋒495–700 dB⋒600–850
Credit cards [1] [2] [3] [5]

LJUNGBY
Småland (☏0372)

★★★**Terraza** (Inter S) Stora Torget 1 ☏13560 tx52046
Closed Jul
➡⋒95 ⌂ **P**20 Lift ☾ sB➡⋒600–650 dB➡⋒800–850
Credit cards [1] [2] [3] [5]

LUDVIKA
Västmanland (☏0240)

★★★**Grand** (Inter S) Eriksgt 6 ☏18220 tx74023
➡105 ⌂ **P** Lift ☾ sB➡560–640 dB➡660–760
Credit cards [1] [2] [3]

LULEÄ
Norrbotten (☏0920)

★★★★**SAS Luleä** Storgt 17 ☏94000
➡211 ⌂ **P**35 Lift ☾ sB➡650 dB➡740 ▭
Credit cards [1] [2] [3] [5]

★★★***Scandic*** Mjölkudden ☏28360 tx80253
➡⋒158 **P** Lift ☾ ≏

★★★**Stads** (Inter S) Storgt 15 ☏10410 tx80413
➡120 ⌂ sB➡595–785 dB➡695–885 sea

LUND
Skåne (☏046)

★★★**Grand** (Inter S) Bantorget 1 ☏117010 tx33484
➡87 ⌂ **P** Lift ☾ sB➡690–820 dB➡775–900
Credit cards [1] [2] [3]

★★★**Lundia** (Inter S) Knut den Stores Gata 2 ☎124140 tx32761

27 Dec—23 Dec
🛁97 **P** Lift ☾ sB🛁695—820
dB🛁840—980
Credit cards [1] [3] [4] [5]

LYSEKIL
Bohuslän (☎0523)

★★**Lysekil** Rosvikstorgt 1 ☎11860
🛁🚿50 A20rm **P**60 Lift ☾
sB🛁🚿240—395 dB🛁🚿340—550
M55—76 sea
Credit cards [1] [2] [3] [4] [5]

🚗 **Winthers** Landsvägsgt 50 ☎15050 VW

MALMÖ
Skåne (☎040)

★★★★**Savoy** (Inter S) N Vallgt 62 ☎70230 tx32383
🛁80 🏠 **P** Lift ☾ sB🛁700—750
dB🛁800—850 sea

★★★★**Scandinavia** (Inter S) Drottninggt 1F ☎936700 tx32235
🛁215 🏠 **P** Lift ☾ sB🛁625—760
dB🛁780—850

★★★***Kramer*** Stortorget 7 ☎70120 tx32159
rm100 (🛁85) **P** Lift ☾

★★★**St-Jörgen** Stora Nygt 35 ☎77300 tx32404
🛁🚿285 🏠 **P**100 Lift ☾ sB🛁🚿385—790
dB🛁🚿850—920
Credit cards [1] [2] [3] [4] [5]

★★***Tunnein*** Adelgt 4 ☎101930
🛁🚿49 🏠 **P**4 Lift ☾
Credit cards [1] [2] [3] [5]

★★***Winn*** (SARA) Jörgen Kocksgt 3 (n.rest) ☎101800 tx33295
3 Jan—21 Dec
🛁101 🏠 **P**100 Lift ☾
Credit cards [1] [2] [3] [5]

🚗 **Auto-Linden** Nya Agnesfridsg 129 ☎223030 Fia

🚗 **Malmö Scanauto** Lundavägen 72 ☎934630 AR DJ

At **ARLÖV** (7km NW)

★★★***Scandic*** Kronetorpsvägen ☎433620
10 Jan—23 Dec
rm76 (🛁🚿72) **P**76 ☾ 📺
Credit cards [1] [2] [3] [4] [5]

At **SEGEVÅNG** (5km E)

★★★***Scandic*** Segesvängen ☎180120 tx33478
26 Dec—23 Dec
rm170 (🛁🚿162) **P** Lift ☾ 📺
Credit cards [1] [2] [3] [4] [5]

MALUNG
Dalarna (☎0280)

★**Nya Skinnargården** Grönlandsvägen ☎11750
🛁51 **P**60 sB🛁153 dB🛁306—570
M35—65 mountains
Credit cards [1] [2] [3]

Sweden

MARKARYD
Småland (☎0433)

★★***Stora*** ☎10730
rm44 (🛁🚿41) A20rm **P**

MÖLLE
Skåne (☎042)

★***Grand*** Bökebolsv 11 ☎47280
Etr—Sep
rm50 (🛁30) **P** ☾ sea mountains

MÖLNDAL
Västergötland (☎031)

★★★***Scandic*** Abro ☎275060 tx12636
🛁🚿172 **P** Lift ☾ 🏊

🚗 **Bilexa** Mölndalsvägen ☎813560 Ope Maz Vau

MORA
Dalarna (☎0250)

★★★**Mora** (Inter S) Strandgt 12 ☎11750 tx74220
🛁91 🏠 **P** Lift ☾ sB🛁570—600
dB🛁650—690 📺 lake
Credit cards [1] [2] [3]

★★★***Scandic*** Kristinebergsgt ☎15070
🛁🚿79 A32rm **P** ☾ 🏊

MOTALA
Östergötland (☎0141)

★★★**Stads** (Inter S) Stora Torget ☎16400 tx5561
🛁🚿79 **P**15 Lift ☾ sB🛁🚿545—580
dB🛁🚿645—680 lake
Credit cards [1] [2] [3] [4] [5]

🚗 **Jansen Motor** Vadstenavägen 30—34 ☎16230 For

🚗 **Wahistedts** Vintergt 17 ☎16030 VW

NÄSSJÖ
Småland (☎0380)

★★★***Högland*** (SARA) Esplanaden 4 ☎13100 tx35289
🛁105 🏠 **P** Lift ☾

🚗 **Höre Bil** Höregt 12 ☎11005 AR

NORRKÖPING
Östergötland (☎011)

★★★***Scandic*** (3km N) Järngt ☎100380 tx64115
🛁🚿156 **P** ☾ ⚲ 📺
Credit cards [1] [2] [3] [4] [5]

★★★***Standard*** (SARA) Slottsgt 99 ☎129220 tx64171
🛁176 🏠 **P** Lift ☾

🚗 **Automobilf** Frekriksdalsgt 45 ☎186290 Dat Peu

🚗 **Zetterbloms** Grundverksgt ☎100440 Alf AR Fia

NORRTÄLJE
Uppland (☎0176)

🚗 **Norrtälje Bilcentral** Trädgårdsgt 3 ☎12510 For

NYBRO
Småland (☎0481)

★★***Stora*** Stadshusplan ☎11935 tx17930
rm32 (🛁🚿8) Lift

NYKÖPING
Södermandland (☎0155)

★★★***Scandic*** Gumsbacken ☎89000
🛁🚿100 **P** Lift ☾ 📺
Credit cards [1] [2] [3] [4] [5]

🚗 **E Källander** Industrigt 10 ☎17170 Ope Vau

ÖREBRO
Närke (☎019)

★★★**Grev Rosen** Södra Grev Rosengt 2 ☎130240 tx73557
Closed Xmas
rm73 🏠 **P**62 Lift ☾ sB190—380
dB350—540
Credit cards [1] [2] [3] [5]

★★★**Grand** Fabriksgt 21—25 ☎150200 tx73362
🛁227 🏠 **P**80 Lift ☾ sB🛁580—660
dB🛁720—825 📺 mountains
Credit cards [1] [2] [3] [5]

★★★***Scandic*** Västhagagt 1 ☎130480 tx73581
🛁🚿205 **P** Lift ☾ 🏊

★★★***Stora*** Drottninggt 1 ☎124360 tx73230
rm108 (🛁🚿69) 🏠 **P** Lift ☾

★★***Bergsmannen*** Drottninggt 42 ☎130320
Closed Jul
rm66 (🛁36) 🏠 **P** Lift ☾

ÖRKELLJUNGA
Skåne (☎0435)

★★★***Scandic*** ☎51442
🚿29 **P**60
Credit cards [1] [2] [3] [4] [5]

ÖRNSKÖLDSVIK
Ångemanland (☎0660)

★★★***Scandic*** Häsmarksvägen 4 ☎82870
🛁🚿173 🏠 **P** Lift 🏊

★★***Statt*** (SARA) Lasarettsgt 2 ☎10110
rm110 🏠 **P** Lift ☾ lake

OSKARSHAMN
Småland (☎0491)

🚗 **Ekelunds** Ringplatsen 11 ☎14330 AR Fia Vau

🚗 **C E Holström** Nygråd 13 ☎15050 BMW Cit

ÖSTERSUND
Jämtland (☎063)

★★★**Östersund** (Inter S) Kyrkgt 70 ☎117640 tx44065

🛁 129 🚗 P Lift ☾ sB 🛁 525 dB 🛁 650
Credit cards [1] [2] [3]

★★★***Scandic*** Krondikesvagen 97
☎127560

🛁 🚿 12 P ☾ ⛱

★★**Winn** (SARA) Prästgt 16 ☎127740
tx44038

rm198 🚗 P Lift ☾ sB520—620 dB620—720
📺 lake
Credit cards [1] [2] [3] [4] [5]

RÄTTVIK
Dalarna (☎0248)

★★***Rättvikshästen*** Nyäkersvägen
☎11015

rm40 (🚿 20) P50 ✂ ⛱
Credit cards [1] [2] [3] [4] [5]

RIKSGRÄNSEN
Lappland (☎0980)

★★★**Riksgränsen** (SARA) ☎40080
tx8767

15 Feb—15 Dec
🛁 🚿 144 Lift sB 🛁 🚿 455—675
dB 🛁 🚿 660—1220 M60—110 lake
mountains
Credit cards [1] [2] [3] [5]

★***Lapplandia Sporthotel*** ☎43120

🛁 🚿 95 A9rm lake

RONNEBY
Blekinge (☎0457)

★★★**Ronneby Brunn** ☎12750 tx43505

🛁 🚿 301 A34rm Lift ☾ sB 🛁 🚿 366—631
dB 🛁 🚿 512—812 Mfr75 ✂ ⛱
Credit cards [1] [2] [3]

SÄFFLE
Värmland (☎0533)

★★★***Scandic*** O-Trätäljagt 2 ☎12660

🛁 🚿 67 P ☾ 📺
Credit cards [1] [2] [3] [4] [5]

SALTSJÖBADEN See **STOCKHOLM**

SEGEVÅNG See **MALMÖ**

SIGTUNA
Uppland (☎0760)

★★***Stads*** St Nygt 3 ☎50100

rm26 (🛁 🚿 24) P Lift ☾ lake
Credit cards [1] [2] [3] [5]

SKELLEFTEÅ
Västerbotten (☎0910)

★★★**Malmia** (Inter S) Torget 2 ☎77300
tx65201

🛁 140 🚗 P Lift ☾ sB 🛁 610—640
dB 🛁 710—740
Credit cards [1] [2] [3]

★★***Statt*** (SARA) Stationsgt 8—10 ☎14140

rm110 🚗 P Lift ☾

SKÖVDE
Västergötland (☎0500)

★★★**Billingehus** (SARA)
Asbotorpsvägen ☎83000 tx67006

🛁 🚿 244 P300 Lift ☾ sB 🛁 🚿 350—700
dB 🛁 🚿 500—900 M50—85 ✂ 📺 ⛱
Credit cards [1] [2] [3] [5]

Sweden

★★**Billingen** (SARA) Trädgårdgt 10
☎10790

🛁 92 🚗 P5 Lift ☾ sB 🛁 590—630
dB 🛁 785 M75—115
Credit cards [1] [2] [3] [5]

SÖDERHAMN
Hälsingland (☎0270)

★★★***Scandic*** Montörsbacken ☎18020

🛁 🚿 87 P90 Lift ☾ 📺
Credit cards [1] [2] [3] [4] [5]

SÖDERTÄLJE
Södermanland (☎0755)

★★★***Scandic*** Verkstadsvägen ☎34260
tx16682

🛁 125 P100 Lift ☾ 📺
Credit cards [1] [2] [3] [4] [5]

★★★**Skogshöjd** (Inter S) Täppgt 15
☎32670 tx13672

🛁 230 🚗 P Lift ☾ sB 🛁 570 dB 🛁 640 📺
Credit cards [1] [2] [3]

SOLNA See **STOCKHOLM**

STOCKHOLM
Stockholm (☎08)

See plan pages 382 and 383

★★★★★**Grand** Södra
Blasieholmshamnen 8 ☎221020 tx19500
Plan **2**

🛁 331 P Lift ☾ sB 🛁 720—1050
dB 🛁 1030—1430 sea
Credit cards [1] [2] [3] [5]

★★★★★**Strand** (BW) Nybrokajen 9
☎22900 tx10504 Plan **3**

🛁 134 🚗 P Lift ☾ sB 🛁 800—1125
dB 🛁 1100—1280 M60—110 sea
Credit cards [1] [2] [3] [5]

★★★★**Mornington** (Inter S) Nybrogt 53
☎631240 tx10145 Plan **5**

🛁 137 🚗 P12 Lift ☾ sB 🛁 655 dB 🛁 840
Malc
Credit cards [1] [2] [3] [4] [5]

★★★***Amaranten*** (THF) Kungsholmsgt 31
☎541060 tx17498 Plan **7**

🛁 🚿 415 🚗 P60 Lift ☾ 📺
Credit cards [1] [2] [3] [5]

★★★**Bromma** Brommaplan 1 ☎252920
tx13125 Plan **8**

2 Jan—23 Dec
🛁 🚿 141 P50 Lift ☾ sB 🛁 🚿 550
dB 🛁 🚿 650—750 Malc
Credit cards [1] [2] [3] [5]

★★★**Continental** Vasagt ☎244020
tx10100 Plan **9**

🛁 250 🚗 Lift ☾ sB 🛁 750—950
dB 🛁 890—1300 Malc
Credit cards [1] [2] [3] [5]

★★★**Diplomat** Strandvägen 7C
☎635800 tx17119 Plan **10**

🛁 🚿 132 P Lift ☾ sB 🛁 🚿 800—975

dB 🛁 🚿 975—1100
Credit cards [1] [2] [3] [4] [5]

★★★**Malmen** Götgt 49—51 ☎226080
tx519489 Plan **11**

🛁 🚿 280 🚗 P100 Lift ☾ sB 🛁 🚿 590—630
dB 🛁 🚿 760—860
Credit cards [1] [2] [3] [4] [5]

★★★***Palace*** St-Eriksgt 115 ☎241220
tx19877 Plan **12**

Closed Xmas & New Year
🛁 214 🚗 P65 Lift
Credit cards [1] [2] [3] [4] [5]

★★★***Reisen*** (THF) Skeppsbron 12—14
☎223260 tx17494 Plan **13**

🛁 125 Lift ☾ ⛱ sea

★★★**Sjöfartshotellet** Katarinavagen 26
☎226960 tx19020 Plan **14**

rm184 (🛁 🚿 182) 🚗 Lift sB 🛁 🚿 570—630
dB 🛁 🚿 675—750
Credit cards [1] [2] [3] [5]

★★★**Terminus** (Inter S) Vasagt 20
☎222640 tx11749 Plan **15**

Closed Xmas
🛁 155 🚗 P Lift ☾ sB 🛁 665—690
dB 🛁 840—890

★★★**Wellington** (Inter S) Storgt 6
☎670910 tx17963 Plan **15A**

🛁 50 Lift ☾ sB 🛁 630 dB 🛁 800
Credit cards [1] [2] [3]

★★***Adlon*** Vasagt 42 (n.rest) ☎245400
tx11543 Plan **16**

rm58 (🛁 🚿 38) 🚗 P10 Lift ☾
Credit cards [1] [2] [3] [4] [5]

★★**City** ☎222240 tx12487 Plan **17**

🛁 🚿 300 P Lift ☾ sB 🛁 🚿 545—645
dB 🛁 🚿 615—745
Credit cards [1] [2] [3] [5]

★★**Eden** Sturegt 10 ☎223160 tx10570
Plan **18**

🛁 🚿 60 🚗 P Lift ☾ dB 🛁 🚿 450—890
Credit cards [1] [2] [3] [5]

★**Kung Car** Birger Jarlsgt 23 (n.rest)
☎221240 tx12262 Plan **21**

🛁 🚿 87 🚗 P30 Lift ☾ sB 🛁 🚿 575—795
dB 🛁 🚿 770—895
Credit cards [1] [2] [3] [5]

🚘 **W Kindwall** Roslagsgt 4 Järfälla
☎970820 All makes

🚘 **Phillipsons Norr** Regeringsgt 109
☎340000 Mer

At **HÄGERSTEN** (15km SW on E3)

★★★**Attaché** Cedergrensugen 16
☎181185 tx16726 Plan **19**

🛁 🚿 56 P30 Lift ☾ sB 🛁 🚿 280—525
dB 🛁 🚿 300—630
Credit cards [1] [2] [3] [4] [5]

★★***Scandic*** Vantörsvägen 285, Gyllene
Ratten ☎462660 Plan **20**

rm125 (🛁 114) ☾

At **SALTSJÖBADEN** (20km SE road No
228)

★★★★**Grand** ☎7170020 tx10210 Plan **4**

🛁 🚿 103 P200 Lift ☾ sB 🛁 🚿 417—842 →

STOCKHOLM

2 ★★★★★ Grand
3 ★★★★★ Strand
4 ★★★★ Grand (At Saltsjöbaden 20km SE on road no. 228)
5 ★★★★ Mornington
7 ★★★ Amaranten
8 ★★★ Bromma
9 ★★★ Continental
10 ★★★ Diplomat
10A ★★★ Flamingo (At Solna 5km N)
11 ★★★ Malmen
12 ★★★ Palace
13 ★★★ Reisen
13A ★★★ Scandic (At Täby)
14 ★★★ Sjöfartshotellet
15 ★★★ Terminus
15A ★★★ Wellington
16 ★★ Adlon
17 ★★ City
18 ★★ Eden
19 ★★★ Attaché (At Hägersten)
20 ★★ Scandic (At Hägersten)
21 ★★ Kung Carl

dB 🛁 🚿 574—1214 M84—118 🎾 Beach sea
Credit cards 1 2 3 5

At **SOLNA** (5km N)

★★★**Flamingo** Hotellgt 11 ☎830800 tx10060 Plan **10A**
🛁 🚿 130 🚗 **P** Lift ☾ sB 🛁 🚿 390—583 dB 🛁 🚿 610—696 M27—100
Credit cards 1 2 3 5

★★★***Scandic*** Jarva Krog, Uppsalar Ullriksdale ☎850360 tx13767 Not on plan
rm215 (🛁 205) 🚗 **P**190 Lift ☾ 📺
Credit cards 1 2 3 4 5

At **TÄBY** (15km N)

★★★***Scandic*** ☎7680580 tx16630 Plan **13A**
🛁 🚿 121 **P**100 Lift ☾
Credit cards 1 2 3 4 5

STORLIEN

Jämtland (☎0647)

★★***Storliens Högfjällshotellet*** ☎70170 tx44051
rm189 (🛁 140) **P**100 Lift ☾ 🎾 📺 mountains
Credit cards 1 2 3 4 5

SUNDSVALL

Medelpad (☎060)

★★★**Bore** (Inter S) Trädgårdsgt 31—33 ☎150600 tx71280
🛁 🚿 145 🚗 **P**15 Lift ☾ sB 🛁 🚿 595 dB 🛁 🚿 695 📺
Credit cards 1 2 3 4 5

★★★**Sundsvall** Esplanaden 29 ☎171600 tx71254
🚿 201 🚗 **P**160 Lift ☾ sB🚿 550 dB🚿 690 lake mountains
Credit cards 1 2 3 4 5

★★★***Scandic*** Vardshusbacken 6 ☎566860 tx71092
🛁 🚿 160 **P** ☾ ⛵

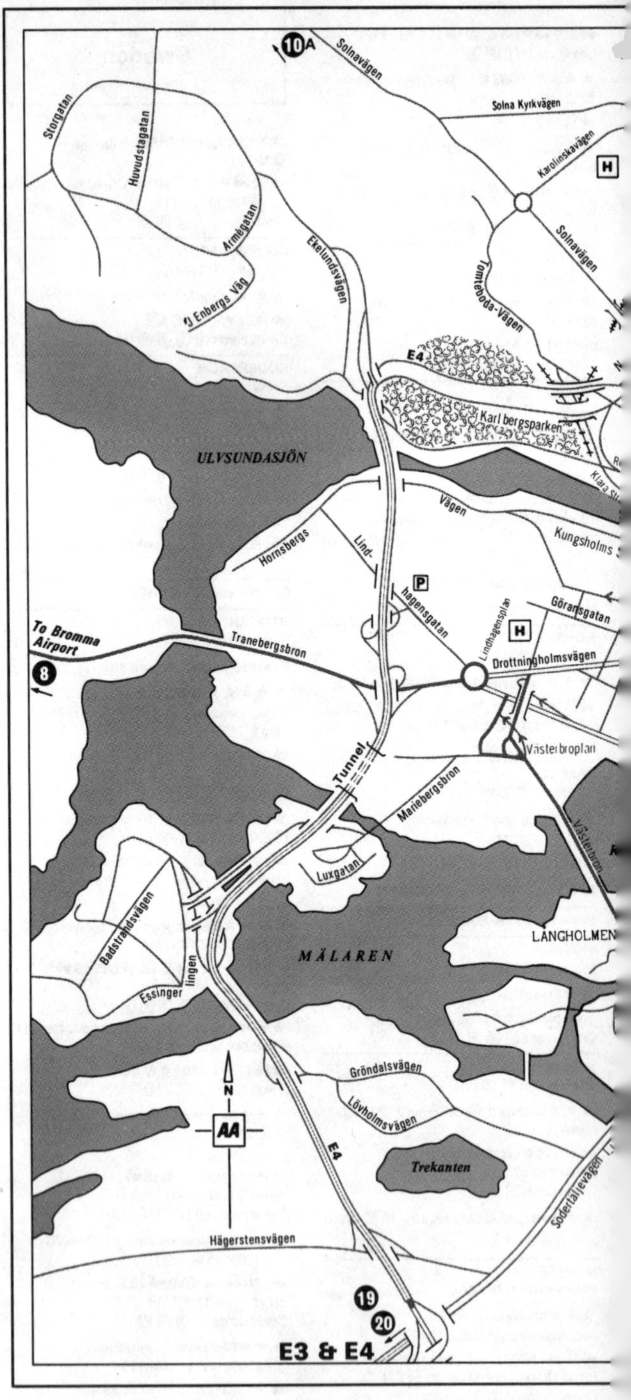

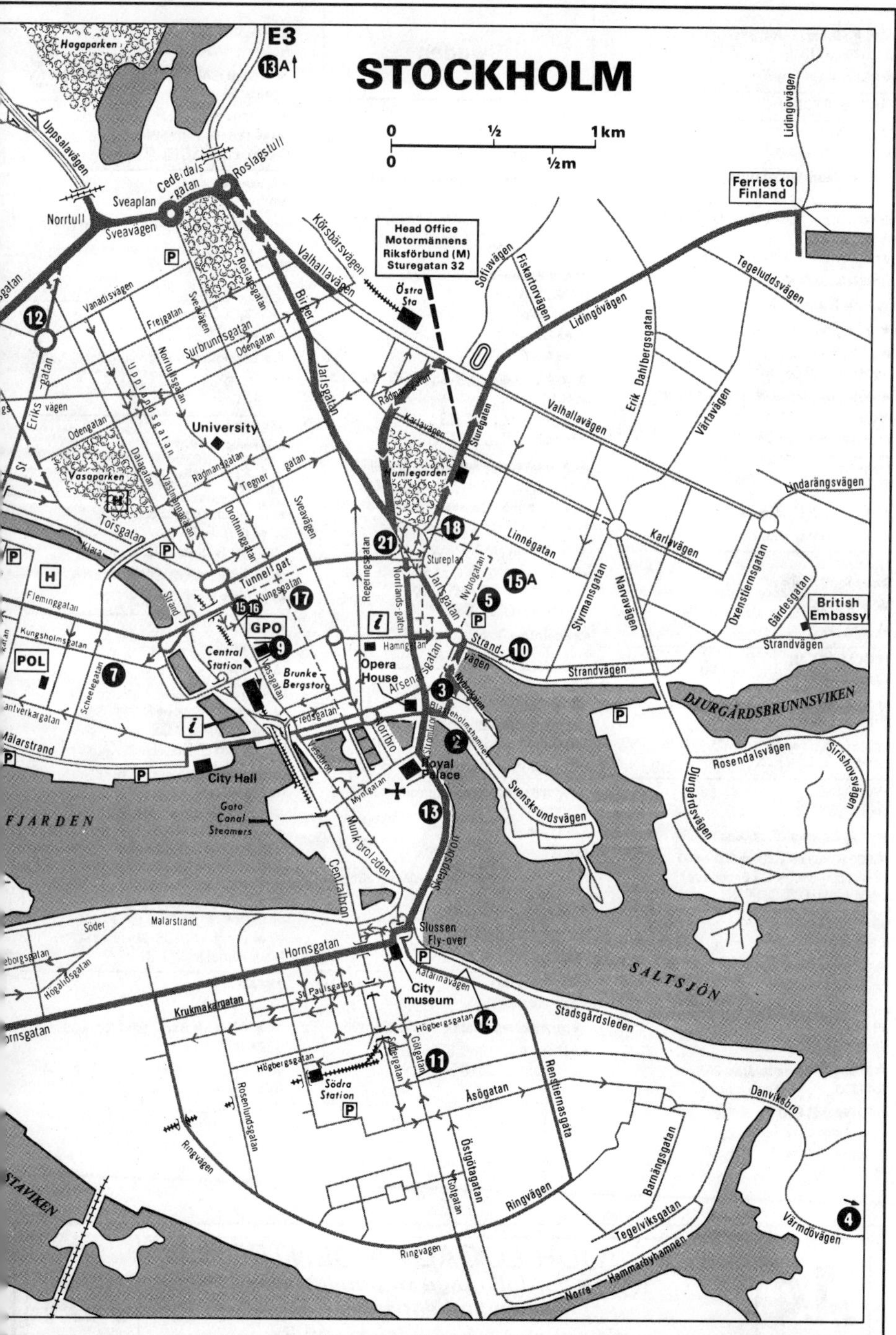
STOCKHOLM
0 ½ 1km
0 ½m
E3
Hagaparken
Uppsalavägen
Norrtull
Sveaplan
Sveavägen
Cedeidalsgatan
Roslagstull
Körsbärsvägen
Valhallavägen
Head Office
Motormännens
Riksförbund (M)
Sturegatan 32
Östra Sta
Ferries to
Finland
Lidingövägen
Tegeluddsvägen
Sofiavägen
Fiskartorpvägen
Erik Dahlbergsgatan
Värtavägen
University
Vasaparken
Torsgatan
Humlegården
Sturegatan
Jarlsgatan
Birger
Odengatan
Surbrunnsgatan
Karlavägen
Linnégatan
Stureplan
Lindarängsvägen
Narvavägen
Styrmansgatan
Oxenstiernsgatan
Gärdesgatan
British
Embassy
Strandvägen
Kungsgatan
Tunnelgat
GPO
Central
Station
Brunke-
Bergstorg
Opera
House
Hamngatan
Kungsholmsgatan
POL
Fleminggatan
City Hall
Mälarstrand
FJARDEN
Goto
Canal
Steamers
Royal
Palace
Skeppsbron
Svensksundsvägen
DJURGÅRDSBRUNNSVIKEN
Rosendalsvägen
Djurgårdsvägen
Sirishovsvägen
Centralbron
Munkbrolåden
Slussen
Fly-over
Hornsgatan
City
museum
Katarinavägen
Krukmakargatan
St Paulsgatan
Högbergsgatan
Götgatan
Södra
Station
Åsögatan
Renstiernasgatan
Stadsgårdsleden
SALTSJÖN
Danviksbro
Rosenlundsgatan
Ringvägen
Östgötagatan
Barnängsgatan
Tegelviksgatan
Värmdövägen
Norra Hammarbyhamnen
STAVIKEN

★★★**Strand** (SARA) Strandgt 10
☎121800 tx71340
202 P Lift ☾ sea

TÄBY See **STOCKHOLM**

TÅLLBERG
Dalarna (☎0247)

★★★**Green** ☎50250 tx74188
100 P100 sB 235—435
dB 370—1270 M100—125 lake
Credit card 1

★★**Dalecarlia** ☎50255
rm50 (15) lake

★★**Långbers** ☎50290
60 P120 Lift lake mountains
Credit cards 1 3

★★**Siljansgården** ☎50040 tx74088
22 Dec—Sep
rm25 (12) A18rm P lake

TORSBY
Värmland (☎0560)

★★**Björnidet** Kyrkogt 2 ☎11910
rm26 (17) P ☾ mountains lake

TRANÅS
Småland (☎0140)

★★★**Scandic** Storgt 22 ☎14160
73 Lift ☾

TROLLHÄTTAN
Västergötland (☎0520)

★★★★**Swania** (Inter S) Storg 49
☎12570 tx42225
56 Lift sB 645—675
dB 745—790

TYLÖSAND
Halland (☎035)

★★**Tylösands** ☎30500 tx38209
230 P190 Lift ☾ sB 500—600
dB 750—850 Beach sea
Credit cards 1 2 3 4 5

UDDEVALLA
Bohuslän (☎0522)

★★★**Carlia** N-Drottninggt 20—22
☎14140 tx42224
rm66 (64) P15 Lift ☾ sB 285—485
dB 410—640 M35—100
Credit cards 1 2 3 5

★**Viking** Strömstadsvägen 25 (n.rest)
☎14550
rm20 (2) P10 ☾
Credit cards 1 2 3 5

Sweden

ULRICEHAMN
Västergötland (☎0321)

★★★**Scandic** Nyboholm ☎12040
58 P ☾

UMEÅ
Västerbotten (☎090)

★★★**Blå Aveny** Rådhusesplanaden 14
☎132300 tx54010
165 P Lift ☾ sB 645—695
dB 750—840
Credit cards 1 2 3

★★★**Scandic** Yrkesvägen 8 ☎135250
tx54012
162 P200 Lift ☾
Credit cards 1 2 3 4 5

★★★**Strand** V-Strandgt 11 (n.rest)
☎129020
Closed Xmas & New Year
44 Lift

★★★**Winn** (SARA) Skolgt 64 ☎122020
148 P20 Lift ☾ sB 545—585
dB 625—670 M35—300
Credit cards 1 2 3 5

Edströms Rothoffsvägen 16 ☎118470
For

UPPSALA
Uppland (☎018)

★★★★**Uplandia** (Inter S)
Dragarbrunnsgt 32 ☎102160 tx76125
133 P Lift ☾ sB 595 dB 745

★★★**Scandic** Gamla Uppsalagt 50
☎100280
rm157 (152) P130 ☾
Credit cards 1 2 3 4 5

★★**Gillet** (SARA) Dragarbrunnsgt 23
☎155360 tx76028
170 P Lift ☾ sB 335—590
dB 530—750
Credit cards 1 2 3 5

VÄNERSBORG
Västergötland (☎0521)

★★★**Scandic** Nabbensberg ☎62120
119 P400 Lift ☾ lake
Credit cards 1 2 3 4 5

VARBERG
Halland (☎0340)

★★**Statt** (SARA) Kungsgt 24—28 ☎16100
tx3481
126 Lift ☾ sB 480—550
dB 645—960 M45—250 sea
Credit cards 1 2 3 5

VÄRNAMO
Småland (☎0370)

★★★**Värnamo** (SARA) Storgt 20 ☎11530
125 P100 Lift ☾ sB 535—565
dB 710—760
Credit cards 1 2 3 5

VASSMOLÖSA
Småland (☎0480)

★**Wassmolösa Gästgivaregård** ☎32065
Jan—22 Dec
rm9 P

VÄSTERÅS
Västmanland (☎021)

★★★**Park** (Inter S) Gunnibogt 2 ☎110120
tx40477
141 Lift sB 590—660
dB 700—770
Credit cards 1 2 3 5

★★★**Scandic** ☎180280 tx40765
133 P Lift ☾

VÄXJÖ
Småland (☎0470)

★★★**Park** Sandviksvägen 1 ☎29050
tx52277
147 Lift ☾ sB 275—550
dB 350—700
Credit cards 1 2 3 4 5

★★★**Scandic** Hejaregt 15 ☎22070
tx52150
rm112 (106) P Lift ☾
Credit cards 1 2 3 4 5

★★★**Statt** (SARA) Kungsgt 6 ☎13400
tx52139
Seasonal
rm139 (137) P Lift ☾ sB445
sB 495—570 dB720 dB 720
Credit cards 1 2 3 5

YSTAD
Skåne (☎0411)

★★★**Ystads Saltsjöbad** ☎13630
tx32342
109 P500 ☾ sB 350 dB 500
M65—85 Beach sea
Credit cards 1 2 3 5

Switzerland and Liechtenstein

Switzerland Liechtenstein

International distinguishing signs

Liechtenstein See page 391
Area *15,953 sq miles*
Population *6,500,000*
Local time *GMT + 1 (Summer GMT + 2)*

National flag *A white cross on a red field*

How to get there

From Great Britain, Switzerland is usually approached via France. The distance from the Channel ports to Bern, the capital, is approximately 470 miles, a distance which will normally require only one night stop.

Motoring regulations and general information

This information should be read in conjunction with the general content of the European ABC (pages 4-26). **Note** As certain regulations and requirements are common to many countries they are covered by one entry in the ABC and the following headings represent some of the subjects dealt with in this way:

AA Agents
Crash or safety helmets
Customs regulations for European countries
Drinking and driving
Fire extinguisher
First-aid kit
Insurance
International distinguishing sign
Medical treatment
Mirrors
Overtaking
Police fines
Radio telephones/Radio transmitters
Road signs
Seat belts
Traffic lights
Tyres
Visitors' registration

Accidents

Fire ☎ 118 **police** and **ambulance** ☎ 117 (144 for ambulance in Aarau, Baden, Basel, Bern, Olten, Schwytz, Winterthur, Wohlen, Zürich and Zug). The most important principle is that all persons involved in an accident should ensure, as far as is possible, that the traffic flow is maintained. Should the accident have caused bodily injuries, the police must be called immediately. Those injured should be assisted by the persons at the scene of the accident until the arrival of medical help. It is not necessary to call the police if the accident has only caused material damage, although the driver(s) concerned should immediately report the incident to the owner of the damaged property and exchange particulars. If this is not possible, the police must be informed. See also *Accidents* page 5.

Accommodation

Hotel classifications are indicated in the *Guide to Swiss Hotels,* published annually by the Swiss Hotel Association. The guide, which also contains details of spas and facilities for sports, is available from the Swiss National Tourist Office in London and local tourist offices issue hotel guides on a regional basis.

Prices generally include continental breakfast, all service and taxes. Some hotels offer reduced prices for children not requiring separate rooms.

The Swiss Hotel Association operates a service for dealing with complaints which should be addressed to them at PO Box 2657, 3001 Berne and marked *Complaints Service.*

Boats

Boat registration documentation is recommended in respect of boats temporarily imported into Switzerland. See page 6 for further information.

Breakdown

The major motoring club, Touring Club Suisse, operates a patrol service and a day and night breakdown service but it is likely that you will be charged for any service. The service (*Secours routier*) operates from several centres throughout

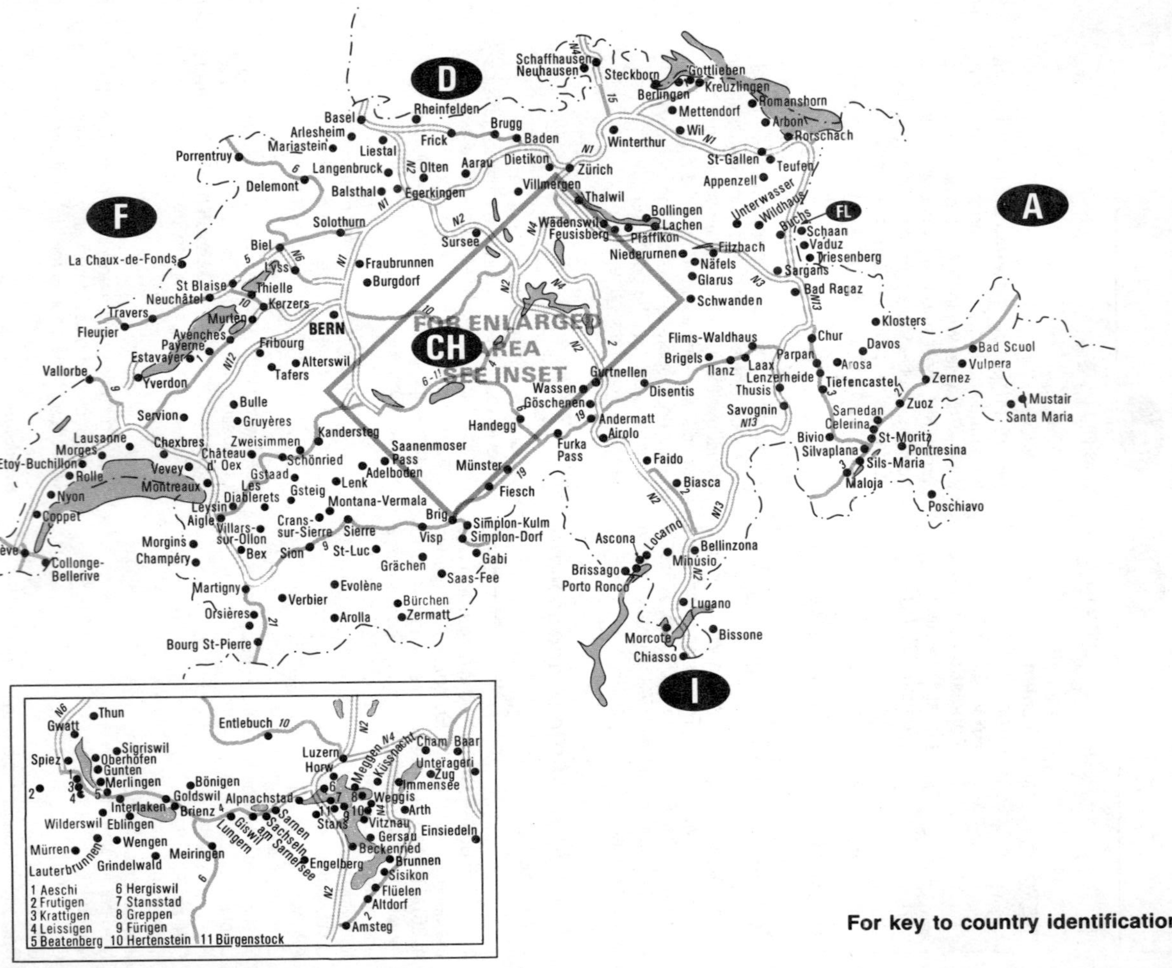

For key to country identification - see page 51

the country and can be summoned by telephone. When calling, give the operator the password *Touring Secours, Touring Club Suisse,* and state your location and if possible the nature of the trouble. The operator will state within a short time whether it will be a black and yellow patrol car or garage assistance, and how soon help can be expected. See also *Breakdown* page 6. *Motorways* page 388 and *Warning triangle* page 390.

British Embassy/Consulates

(See also page 6)
The British Embassy together with its consular section is located at *3005 Berne* Thunstrasse 50 ☎ (031)445021/6. There are British Consulates in Genève and Zürich and British Consulates with Honorary Consuls in La Tour de Peilz and Lugano.

Currency including banking hours

(See also page 9)
The unit of currency is the Swiss Franc (*SFr*) divided into 100 *Centimes* or *Rappen*. At the time of going to press £ = *SFr*2.45. Denominations of bank notes are *SFr* 10, 20, 50, 100, 1,000; standard coins are *SFr* 1, 2, 5 and *Centimes* or *Rappen* 5, 10, 20, 50. There are no restrictions on the import or export of foreign or Swiss currency.

Banks are open Monday to Friday and closed on Saturday. The opening hours in Basel are 08.15—17.00 (Wednesday 18.30); Bern 08.00—16.30 (Thursday 18.00); Genève 08.30—16.30/17.30; Lausanne 08.30—12.00 and 13.30—16.30 (Friday 17.00); Lugano 09.00—12.00/12.30 and 13.00/13.30—16.00; Zürich 08.15/09.00—16.30/17.00 (Thursday 18.00). There are exchange offices in nearly all TCS offices open during office hours. At railway stations in large towns and at airports, exchange offices are open 08.00—20.00hrs although these hours may vary slightly from place to place.

Dimensions and weight restrictions

Private cars and towed trailers or caravans are restricted to the following dimensions — **car** height: 4 metres; width: 2.30 metres; length: up to 3,500kg 8 metres, over 3,500kg 12 metres. **Trailer/caravan** height: 4 metres; width*: 2.10 metres; length*: 6 metres (including tow bar). The maximum permitted overall length of vehicle/trailer or caravan combination is 18 metres.

It is dangerous to use a vehicle towing a trailer or caravan on some mountain roads; motorists should ensure that roads on which they are about to travel are suitable for the conveyance of vehicle/trailer or caravan combinations.

The fully-laden weight of trailers which do not have an independent braking system should not exceed 50% of the unladen weight of the towing vehicle, but trailers which have an independent braking system can weigh up to 100% of the unladen weight of the towing vehicle.

*The Swiss Customs authorities can authorise slightly larger limits for foreign caravans for direct journeys to their destination and back *ie* caravans up to 2.20 metres (7ft 2in) in width and up to either 6.50 metres (21ft 4in) or 7 metres (23ft) in length depending on whether Alpine passes are used. A charge is made for these special authorisations. Caravans up to 2.50 metres (8ft 2in) in width may also enter Switzerland if towed by a four-wheel-drive vehicle or one exceeding 3.5 tonnes, but no special authorisation is required.

Driving licence

(See also page 11)
A valid British driving licence is acceptable in Switzerland. The minimum age at which a visitor may drive a temporarily imported car is 18 years and a temporarily imported motorcycle (exceeding 125cc) 20 years.

Emergency messages to tourists

(See also page 11)
Emergency messages to tourists are broadcast daily throughout the year by Swiss Radio. Any messages broadcast in English will be grouped together after the last news bulletin.
Radio Suisse Romande transmitting on 392 metres medium wave broadcast these messages in French at 12.25 and 18.30hrs.
Radio der deutschen und rätoromanischen Schweiz transmitting on 192 metres medium wave broadcasts the messages in German at 18.40hrs and on 567.1 metres medium wave at 12.25 and 18.40hrs.
Radio della Svizzera Italiana transmitting on 538 metres medium wave broadcasts the messages in Italian at 12.25 and 18.55hrs.
Radio Suisse Internationale transmitting on short wave broadcasts in Italian at 14.30hrs on 31.46 metres, in French at 12.30 and 13.30hrs on 48.66 metres and in German at 13.00 and 14.00hrs on 75.28 metres.

Lights

(See also page 14)

Driving on sidelights only is prohibited. Spotlights are forbidden. Fog lamps can be used only in pairs of identical shape, brilliance and colour, dipped headlights must be used in cities and towns. Dipped headlights must be used at all times in tunnels, whether they are lit or not, and failure to observe this regulation can lead to a fine. Switzerland has a '*tunnel*' road sign (a red triangle showing a tunnel entrance in the centre) which serves to remind drivers to turn on their dipped headlights. In open country, headlights must be dipped: at least 200 metres (220yds) in front of any pedestrian or oncoming vehicle (including trains parallel to the road); when requested to do so by the driver of an oncoming vehicle flashing his lights; or when reversing, travelling in lines of traffic or stopping. Dipped headlights must be used when waiting at level crossings, or near roadworks. They must also be used in badly-lit areas when visibility is poor. It is recommended that *motorcyclists* use dipped headlights during the day.

Motoring club

The **Touring Club Suisse** has branch offices in all important towns and has its head office at *1211 Genève* 3 rue Pierre-Fatio 9 ☎ (022)371212. The TCS will extend a courtesy service to all motorists but their major services will have to be paid for. TCS offices are usually open from 08.30 to 12.00hrs and 13.30 to 17.00hrs, during the week and between 08.00 and 11.30hrs on Saturday mornings (summer only). They are not open on Sunday. See also page 16 and *Town Plan of Central Genève* pages 398-399.

Motorways

There are approximately 880 miles of motorways (Autobahn or Autoroute) and more are under construction. A network of 1,143 miles is planned.

Motorways are numbered N (national road) and are divided into classes 1, 2 and 3; they vary from the usual two-lane (sometimes three) dual carriageway to 25ft wide two-lane roads with limited access points. To join a motorway follow the green and white signposts or signposts with the motorway symbol.

Motorway telephones are placed 2km (1¼m) apart along all motorways, and give an automatic connection with the motorway control police. Ask for TCS patrol assistance. A patrol will normally be sent, but if one is not available, help will be sent from a TCS affiliated office.

Motorway tax The Swiss authorities levy an annual motorway tax. A vehicle sticker, costing *SFr*30 for vehicles up to 3.5 tonnes (unladen) and known locally as a *vignette*, must be displayed by vehicles using Swiss motorways including motorcycles, trailers and caravans. Motorists may purchase the stickers from AA Centres and AA Port Service Centres or at the Swiss frontier. Vehicles over 3.5 tonnes (unladen) are taxed on all roads in Switzerland; a licence for one day, 10 days, one month and one year periods can be obtained. There are no stickers and the tax must be paid at the Swiss frontier.

Orange badge scheme for disabled drivers

(See also page 16)

In Switzerland badge holders may:

a park without time limit at parking places where time limits are in force or within a blue or red zone;
b park without time limit at parking meters on payment of the minimum charge;
c park where parking is otherwise banned, provided no obstruction or danger is caused and that no other parking spaces are available. Parking is not allowed where stopping is prohibited;
d park at reserved parking places indicated by parking sign (white on blue panel) displaying the international disabled symbol.

Parking

(See also page 18)

Parking restrictions are indicated by international signs or by broken yellow lines or crosses at the side of the road, or yellow markings on pavements or poles. Parking is forbidden where it would obstruct traffic or view on a main road or one carrying fast-moving traffic, and on or within 1.5 metres (5ft) of tram lines. Stopping is forbidden, even for passengers to get in or out of a vehicle, for unloading goods, in places marked by a continuous yellow line at the side of the road or red markings on pavements or poles. When parked on a slope or incline, use the handbrake and place chocks or wedges under the wheels. If you have to stop in a tunnel you must immediately switch off your engine. Spending the night in a vehicle or trailer on the roadside may be tolerated in some Cantons but make sure you do not contravene local regulations.

In some large towns, there are short-term parking areas known as *blue zones*. In these areas parked vehicles must display a disc on the windscreens; discs are set at the time of parking, and show when parking time expires. Restrictions apply 08.00—19.00hrs on weekdays throughout the year. Discs can be obtained from the TCS, the police, some large shops, or tobacconists' shops. Failure to observe zonal regulations could result in a fine or the vehicle being towed away.

In Lausanne, a *red zone* system is in operation; for this, adjustable discs entitling up to 15 hours' parking are available from the local TCS office or the tourist information office. These discs may be used for either *red* or *blue zones*, one side of the disc to be used for the *blue zone* and the other side for the *red zone*. Failure to observe zonal regulations could result in a fine or in the vehicle being towed away.

Passengers

(See also page 18)
Children under 12 are not permitted to travel in a vehicle as front seat passengers when rear seating is available.

Petrol

(See also page 18)
Credit cards It is unlikely that garages will accept credit cards in payment for petrol.
Duty-free petrol In addition to the petrol in the vehicle tank up to 25 litres in a can may be imported free of custom duty and tax.
Petrol (leaded) Super (98—99 octane) grade.
Petrol (unleaded) is sold in Switzerland as the Medium (95 octane) grade. Pumps dispensing unleaded petrol may have either a green hose or a green strip on the side, but the octane rating is marked on the pumps.

Postal information

Mail Postcards *SFr*0.70; letters 5-20gm *SFr*0.90.
Post offices There are 4,000 post offices in Switzerland. Opening hours are from 07.30—12.00hrs and 13.30—18.00hrs Monday to Friday and 07.30—11.00hrs Saturday.

Postcheques

(See also page 20)
Postcheques may be cashed at all post offices for any amount up to a maximum of *SFr*200 per cheque in multiples of *SFr*10. Counter positions are identified by the words *Payments/ Auszahlungen/Pagamenti*. See *Postal information* for post office opening hours.

Priority

When the road is too narrow for two vehicles to pass, vehicles towing trailers have priority over other vehicles; heavy vehicles over light vehicles. If two vehicles of the same category cannot pass, the vehicle nearest to the most convenient stopping point or lay-by must reverse. On mountain roads if there is no room to pass, the descending vehicle must manoeuvre to give way to the ascending vehicle — unless the ascending vehicle is obviously near a lay-by. If two vehicles are travelling in opposite directions and the driver of each vehicle wants to turn left, they must pass in front of each other (not drive round). Drivers turning left may pass in front of traffic islands in the centre of an intersection. See also *Priority including Roundabouts* page 21.

Lanes reserved for buses have been introduced; these are marked with either a continuous or broken yellow line and the word 'bus'. Bus lanes may be supplemented with the sign 'Bus lane only — *Voie réservée aux bus*' (a circular blue sign with the white silhouette of a bus superimposed on it). Only the broken yellow line may be crossed, either at a junction when turning or to enter the premises of a company.

Public holidays

Official public holidays throughout Switzerland for 1987 are given below. There are other official public holidays such as Epiphany, Corpus Christi and All Saints' Day, but they vary from canton to canton. See also *Public holidays* page 21.
January 1 (New Year's Day)
April 17 (Good Friday)
April 20 (Easter Monday)
May 28 (Ascension Day)
June 8 (Whit Monday)
December 25* (Christmas Day)

*Saturday

Religious services

(See also page 22)
The Intercontinental Church Society welcomes visitors from any denomination to English language services in the following centres:
4051 Basel The Revd Canon Tom Roberts, Chaplain's Flat, Henric Petri Strasse 26 ☎ (061)235761
1807 Blonay (near Vevey) The Revd David Ritchie, La Parsonage, Champsavoux ☎ (021)532239

Roads including holiday traffic

The road surfaces are generally good, but some main roads are narrow in places. Traffic congestion may be severe at the beginning and end of the German school holidays (see page 204).

On any stretch of mountain road, the driver of a private car may be asked by the driver of a postal bus, which is painted yellow, to reverse, or otherwise manoeuvre to allow the postal bus to pass. Postal bus drivers often sound a distinctive three note horn and no other vehicles may use this type of horn in Switzerland.

Shopping hours

Generally shops are open from 08.00/09.00—18.30/18.45hrs Monday to Friday and 08.00/09.00—16.00/17.00hrs on Saturday. In large towns some shops close on Monday morning; in suburban areas and small towns shops normally close on Wednesday or Thursday afternoons.

Speed limits

(See also page 22)

Because the country is mountainous with many narrow and twisting roads, it is not safe to maintain a high speed. Built-up areas are indicated by signs bearing the placename and in these areas the speed limit is 50kph (31mph) for all vehicles.

Outside built-up areas the limit of 80kph (49mph) except on motorways where vehicles are subject to a limit of 120kph (74mph). Car/caravan or luggage trailer combinations are restricted to 80kph* (49mph) on all roads outside built-up areas. These limits do not apply if another limit is indicated by signs or if the vehicle is subject to a lower general speed limit.

*If the weight of the caravan or luggage trailer exceeds 1,000kg a speed limit of 60kph (37mph) applies on roads outside built-up areas, but 80kph (49mph) is still permissible on motorways.

Spiked or studded tyres

Spiked or studded tyres may be used on light vehicles and on trailers drawn by such vehicles from 1 November to 31 March provided they are fitted to all four wheels and a speed of 80kph (49mph) is not exceeded. They are prohibited on motorways and semi-motorways with the exception of the N13 between Thusis and Mesocco and between Göschenen and Airolo on the N2 (St Gothard road tunnel). Spiked or studded tyres may not be substituted for wheel chains when these are compulsory. On-the-spot fines of *SFr*30 are imposed for the use of spiked or studded tyres after 31 March. See also *Cold weather touring* page 8.

Tourist Information

(See also page 24)

The Swiss Government maintains an excellent information service in London at the Swiss National Tourist Office, 1 New Coventry Street, W1V 8EE ☏ 01-734 1921. In all provincial towns and resorts throughout the country there are tourist information offices who are pleased to help tourists with local information and advice.

Using the telephone

(See also page 24)

Insert coin **after** lifting receiver, dialling tone continuous tone. When making calls to subscribers within Switzerland precede number with relevant area code (shown in parentheses against town entry in gazetteer). Use coins to the value of 40 cents for local calls and *SFr*1 or *SFr*5 coins for national and international calls.

International callbox identification All callboxes.

Telephone rates A direct dial call to the UK costs *SFr*1.80 per minute. Local calls are cheaper at weekends.

What to dial for Irish Republic 00 353.

What to dial for the UK 00 44.

Warning triangle/Hazard warning lights

The use of a warning triangle is compulsory for all vehicles except two-wheelers. The triangle must be placed on the road at least 50 metres (55yds) behind the vehicle on ordinary roads and at least 150 metres (164yds) on motorways. If the vehicle is in an emergency lane the triangle must be placed on the right of the emergency lane. Hazard warning lights may be used in conjunction with the triangle on ordinary roads, but on motorways and semi-motorways they must be switched off as soon as the warning triangle is erected. If this is not done the police may impose an *on-the-spot* fine (see page 20). See also *Warning triangles/ Hazard warning lights* page 25.

Weather services

The Touring Club Suisse operates a weather service to give up-to-the-minute conditions of mountain passes. The information appears on notices placed at strategic points along the roads leading up to the passes. When the weather is exceptional, special bulletins are issued by the TCS through the press and broadcasting services. You can also get road/weather reports in French, German or Italian, according to the canton from which the call is made on the national telephone system by dialling 162 (weather) or 163 (road conditions).

Wheel chains

These are generally necessary on journeys to places at high altitudes. Roads with a sign 'chains compulsory' (a tyre with chains on it drawn on a white board which also includes the name of the road) are closed to cars without wheel chains. It is a punishable offence to drive without this equipment. See also *Cold weather touring* page 8.

Winter conditions

(See also page 26)
Entry from France and Germany: the main entries are seldom affected, although the Faucille pass on the Dijon—Genève road, and also minor routes through the Jura, Vosges, and Black Forest may be obstructed.

To Italy: from western Switzerland — during the winter months this is via the Grand St Bernard road tunnel or the Simplon rail tunnel (see page 00); wheel chains are sometimes necessary on the approach to the Grand St Bernard road tunnel. From central Switzerland use the St Gotthard road tunnel. From eastern Switzerland, the San Bernardino tunnel (see page 35) or the Julier or Maloja passes can be used.

To Austria: the route across northern Switzerland via Liechtenstein is open all the year.

Within the country: the main highways linking Basel, Zürich, Luzern, Bern, Lausanne, and Genève are unaffected. The high passes are usually closed in the winter months but it is generally possible to drive within reasonable distance of all winter sports resorts. According to weather conditions, wheel chains may be compulsory or spiked tyres necessary.

Liechtenstein

National flag *Blue over red in two strips of equal breadth*

The principality of Liechtenstein has a population of 26,500 and an area of 65 sq miles. Although it is an independent state it is represented in diplomatic and other matters by Switzerland. Vaduz is the capital.

Traffic regulations, insurance laws, and the monetary unit are the same as for Switzerland and prices are adjusted to match those in the major country.

Prices are in Swiss Francs
Abbreviations:
pl place, platz
pza piazza
r rue
rte route
str strasse

AARAU
Aargau (☎064)

F Brack Buchserstr 17–25 ☎221851 **P** For

F Glaus Entfelderstr 8 ☎221332 Dat

ADELBODEN
Bern (☎033)

★★★★**Nevada Palace** ☎732131 tx922184
15 Dec–15 Apr & 15 Jun–15 Sep
rm72 (62) **P**60 Lift sB55–110 sB 70–130 dB110–220 dB 140–260 M35–60 mountains

★★***Parkhotel Bellevue*** ☎731621
Dec–Apr & Jun–Oct
rm60 (45) **P** Lift mountains

★**Alpenrose** ☎731161
Dec–Etr & Jun–25 Sep
rm35 (11) A5rm **P**12 sB39–47 sB 51–61 dB77–93 dB 101–121 M19–28 mountains
Credit cards 1 3 4 5

★***Bären*** ☎732151
rm12

ADLISWIL See **ZÜRICH**

AESCHI
Bern (☎033)

★★**Baumgarten** ☎544121
rm20 (19) **P**20 sB39–45 sB 49–56 dB73–83 dB 92–105 M15–18 mountains
Credit cards 1 2 3 5

AIGLE
Vaud (☎025)

★★**Nord** r Colomb 4 ☎261055 tx456105
19 Lift sB 80 dB 110–130 mountains
Credit cards 2 3 4 5

AIROLO
Ticino (☎094)

Airolo ☎881765 Alf Cit

S Gottardo ☎881177 **P** Toy

Wolfisberg via San Gottardo ☎881055 M/c AR Vol

ALPNACHSTAD
Obwalden (☎041)

★★**Rössli** ☎961181
Mar–Nov
48 **P**50 sB 48–58 dB 85–105 M15–30 lake mountains
Credit cards 1 2 3

ALTDORF
Uri (☎044)

★***Schwarzer Löwen*** Gothardstr ☎21007
rm19 (5) Lift mountains

Musch Bruno Gothardstr 54 ☎21120 M/c **P** Cit Dat Vol

ALTERSWIL
Fribourg (☎037)

A Piller Hofmatt ☎441237 AR

AMSTEG
Uri (☎044)

★★★***Stern & Post*** (ROM) Gothardstr ☎64440 tx866385
rm40 (20) **P** Lift mountains

ANDERMATT
Uri (☎044)

★★★**Badus** ☎67286
6 Jun–20 Oct & Dec–15 May
23 **P**17 Lift sB 44–51 →

dB 🛁 🚿 88—102 M12—20 mountains
Credit cards [2] [5]

★★*Helvetia* ☎67515 tx868608
rm33 (🛁 🚿 30) **P**10 Lift mountains
Credit cards [1] [2] [3] [5]

★★*Ideal Krone* ☎67206 tx868605
15 Nov—15 Oct
🛁 🚿 48 **P**20 Lift mountains
Credit cards [1] [2] [3] [5]

★★**Monopol Metropol** ☎67575 tx868606
15 Dec—Apr & Jun—15 Oct
🛁 🚿 31 ⌂ **P**20 Lift sB 🛁 🚿 49—75
dB 🛁 🚿 98—150 M24—30 ▭ mountains
Credit cards [1] [2] [3] [5]

🚗 **L Loretz** Gotthardstr 38 ☎67243 **P** Ren

APPENZELL
Appenzell (☎071)

★★★**Hecht** (Amb) Hauptgasse 9
☎871026 tx719267
Closed 20 Nov—23 Dec
rm43 (🛁 🚿 18) Lift sB42—57
sB 🛁 🚿 57—82 dB79—89 dB 🛁 🚿 99—134
mountains
Credit cards [1] [2] [3] [5]

★★*Mettien* ☎871246
rm44 (🚿 29) A15rm **P** mountains

★★**Santis** (ROM) ☎878722 tx71826
Closed 8 Jan—20 Feb
🛁 🚿 33 **P**20 Lift sB 🛁 🚿 75—90
dB 🛁 🚿 110—150 M25—40 mountains
Credit cards [1] [2] [3] [4] [5]

🚗 **W Baumann** Weissbadstr 11 ☎871466
M/c Cit Dat Peu

ARBON
Thurgau (☎071)

★★★*Metropol* (Amb) Bahnhofstr 49
☎463535 tx77247
🛁 🚿 42 **P**100 Lift ☾ ▭ lake mountains
Credit cards [1] [2] [3] [5]

★★**Rotes Kreuz** ☎461914
rm20 (🛁 🚿 14) **P**10 Lift sB30—45
sB 🛁 🚿 35—45 dB 🛁 🚿 70—90 M14 lake
Credit card [3]

ARLESHEIM
Basel (☎061)

★**Ochsen** ☎725225
rm26 (🛁 🚿 13) ⌂ **P**10 sB35—37
sB 🛁 🚿 55—60 dB68—73 dB 🛁 🚿 88—95
Credit cards [1] [2] [3] [5]

AROLLA
Valais (☎027)

★★*Grand Hotel & Kurhaus* ☎831161
Jul—Aug & 20 Dec—20 Apr
rm72 (🛁 🚿 60) **P**80 Lift mountains
Credit cards [1] [2] [3] [5]

AROSA
Graubünden (☎081)

★★★★**Kulm** ☎310131 tx74279
Dec—Apr & Jul—Sep
🛁 🚿 146 ⌂ **P** ☾ sB 🛁 🚿 80—320
dB 🛁 🚿 130—540 ℘ ▭ mountains
Credit cards [2] [3] [5]

Switzerland

★★★*Alexandra-Palace* ☎310111
tx74261
🚿 163 ⌂ **P** Lift ☾ ≈ mountains

★★★*Cristallo* ☎312261 tx74270
15 Jul—10 Oct & Dec—20 Jun
🛁 40 **P** Lift ☾ mountains

★★★**Sporthotel Valsana** (Amb)
☎310275 tx74232
Dec—Apr & Jun—Oct
🛁 86 ⌂ **P**30 Lift ☾ sB 🛁 80—160
dB 🛁 170—340 M15—35 ℘ ≈ ▭
mountains
Credit cards [1] [2] [3] [5]

★★**Seehof** ☎311541 tx74277
Dec—Apr
🛁 🚿 70 ⌂ **P**32 Lift ☾ sB 🛁 🚿 70—130
dB 🛁 🚿 140—260 M25—35 mountains
Credit cards [1] [2] [3] [5]

🚗 **Grand Dosch** Seebodenpl ☎312222 M/c
P Alf Mer Ope Vau

ARTH-AM-SEE
Schwyz (☎041)

🚗 **Rigi** Zugerstr 17—23 ☎821223 M/c **P**
Peu

ASCONA
Ticino (☎093)

★★★★**Acapulco au Lac** Lago di
Maggiore ☎354521 tx846135
Mar—Oct
rm42 (🛁 🚿 41) **P** Lift ☾ sB 🛁 🚿 76—143
dB 🛁 🚿 120—208 M alc ▭ lake
Credit cards [1] [2] [3] [5]

★★★★**Eden Roc** via Albarelle ☎350171
tx846164
Closed 14 Mar 18 Nov
🛁 45 ⌂ **P**40 Lift ☾ sB 🛁 140—300
dB 🛁 260—380 M34—46 ≈ ▭ lake
Credit cards [1] [2] [3] [5]

★★★**Ascona** (Amb) via Collina ☎351135
tx846035
Mar—Dec
🛁 🚿 75 ⌂ **P**50 Lift ☾ sB 🛁 🚿 100—150
dB 🛁 🚿 190—280 M35&alc ≈ lake
mountains
Credit cards [1] [2] [3] [5]

★★★**Schweizerhof** via Locarno
☎351214 tx846217
7 Mar—Oct
🛁 🚿 43 **P**17 Lift sB 🛁 🚿 60—84
dB 🛁 🚿 100—168 Mfr29&alc ≈ U
mountains
Credit cards [2] [3] [5]

★★★**Tamaro au Lac** (ROM) ☎350282
tx846132
Mar—Nov
🛁 🚿 51 Lift sB 🛁 🚿 65—70
dB 🛁 🚿 120—150 M20—30 ≈ lake
Credit cards [1] [2] [3]

★*Plazza au Lac* ☎351181
Mar—Nov
🚿 10 A5rm **P** mountains lake

🚗 **C Buzzini** via Locarno 124 ☎352414 Aud
VW

🚗 **Cristallina** via Circonvallazione ☎351320
P Alf AR Maz

🚗 **Storelli** via Cantonale ☎352196 Mer Toy

AVENCHES
Vaud (☎037)

🚗 **J P Divorne** rte de Berne 6 ☎751263 **P**
Ope

BAAR
Zug (☎042)

★★**Lindenhof** Dorfstr ☎311220
🛁 🚿 5 **P**20 Lift sB 🛁 🚿 48—50
dB 🛁 🚿 60—72
Credit cards [1] [2] [3] [5]

BADEN
Aargau (☎056)

★★★**Parc** (Amb) Romerstr 24 ☎201311
tx825013
2 Jan—23 Dec
🛁 🚿 73 ⌂ **P**60 Lift ☾ sB 🛁 🚿 105—120
dB 🛁 🚿 140—160
Credit cards [1] [2] [3] [4] [5]

★★★**Verenahof** Kurpl ☎225251
rm132 (🛁 🚿 73) **P** Lift ☾ sB70—80
sB 🛁 🚿 90—100 dB140—160
dB 🛁 🚿 180—200 M30—40 ▭ ≈ lake
mountains

🚗 **Müller J Kappelerhof** ☎227326 **P** Aud
VW

BAD Each name preceded by 'Bad' is listed under the name that follows it.

BÂLE See **BASEL**

BALSTHAL
Solothurn (☎062)

★★**Kreuz** Hauptstr ☎713412 tx680149
rm48 (🛁 🚿 45) A32rm ⌂ **P**100 sB30
sB 🛁 🚿 45—55 dB60 dB 🛁 🚿 80 M alc
mountains
Credit cards [1] [2] [3] [5]

★*Rössli* ☎715858
🚿 6 **P**

BASEL (BÂLE) (☎061)

★★★★★**Basel Hilton** Aeschengraben
31 ☎226622 tx962555
🛁 226 **P**100 Lift ☾ sB 🛁 135—190
dB 🛁 199—269 ▭
Credit cards [1] [2] [3] [4] [5]

★★★★★**Drei Könige** Blumenrain 8
☎255252 tx962937
🛁 90 **P**30 Lift ☾ sB 🛁 162—227
dB 🛁 254—379
Credit cards [1] [2] [3] [4] [5]

★★★★★**Euler** Centralbahnpl 14
☎234500 tx962215
🛁 66 ⌂ **P**18 Lift ☾ sB 🛁 147—177
dB 🛁 214—249 M6—35
Credit cards [1] [2] [3] [4] [5]

★★★★**International** (Amb) Steinentorstr
25 ☎221870 tx962370
🛁 🚿 200 ⌂ **P**40 Lift ☾ sB 🛁 🚿 135—190

dB🛁🚿190—260 M15—30 📺
Credit cards [1] [2] [3] [4] [5]

★★★★**Schweizerhof** Centralbahnpl 1 ☎222833 tx962373

🛁75 **P**16 Lift ☾ sB🛁107—125 dB🛁165—180 M alc
Credit cards [1] [2] [3] [4] [5]

★★★**Admiral** (Amb) Rosentalstrasse 5 ☎267777 tx963444

rm130 (🛁🚿120) ⌂ **P**1400 Lift ☾ sB40—55 sB🛁🚿58—85 dB78—95 sB🛁🚿88—140 M14 ≈
Credit cards [1] [2] [3] [4] [5]

★★★**Bernina Basel** Innere Margarethenstr 14 (n.rest) ☎237300 tx963813

🛁🚿35 **P**1500 Lift sB🛁🚿80—120 dB🛁🚿120—190
Credit cards [1] [2] [3] [4] [5]

★★★**Cavalier** Reiterstr 1 ☎392262

🛁🚿27 **P** Lift sB🛁🚿58—85 dB🛁🚿88—130
Credit cards [1] [2] [3] [5]

★★★***Drachen*** Aeschenvorstadt 24 ☎239090 tx62346

rm38 (🛁🚿35) ⌂ **P** Lift ☾

★★★**Europe** (ETAP) Clarastr 35—43 ☎268080 tx64103

🛁🚿172 Lift ☾ sB🛁🚿130 dB🛁🚿190
Credit cards [1] [2] [3] [5]

★★★**Excelsior** Aeschengraben 13 (n.rest) ☎225300 tx962303

🛁24 **P**20 Lift sB🛁70—80 dB🛁110—150
Credit cards [1] [2] [3] [5]

★★★***Merian am Rhein*** Rheingasse 2 ☎259466 tx63537

rm53 (🛁🚿47) ⌂ **P** ☾ Lift
Credit cards [1] [2] [3] [5]

★★★**Victoria am Bahnhof** Centralbahnpl 3—4 ☎225566 tx962362

rm115 (🛁🚿99) ⌂ **P**24 Lift ☾ sB55—70 sB🛁🚿88—105 dB90—110 dB🛁🚿140—165 M alc
Credit cards [1] [2] [3] [4] [5]

★★**Greub** Centralbahnstr 11 ☎231840

rm56 (🛁🚿15) Lift sB40—50 sB🛁🚿65—75 dB70—90 dB🛁🚿90—120
Credit cards [1] [2] [3] [5]

★★**Jura** Centralbahnpl 11 ☎231800

rm80 (🛁🚿37) **P**6 Lift ☾ sB40—55 sB🛁🚿65—80 dB70—90 dB🛁🚿100—140
Credit cards [1] [2] [3] [4] [5]

★★**Krafft** Rheingasse 12 ☎268877 tx64360

rm52 (🛁🚿45) ⌂ **P**8 Lift ☾ sB40—57 sB🛁🚿64—90 dB70—100 dB🛁🚿97—145
Credit cards [1] [2] [3] [5]

★★***Rochat*** Petersgraben 23 ☎258140

rm48 (🛁🚿30) **P**10 Lift ☾

★★**St-Gotthard-Terminus** Centralbahnstr 13 ☎225250

rm60 (🛁🚿14) ⌂ **P**2 Lift ☾ sB58—68

Switzerland

sB🛁🚿78—88 dB95—105 dB🛁🚿115—135 M10—25
Credit cards [1] [2] [3] [4] [5]

★**Bristol** Centralbahnstr 15 ☎223822

rm32 (🛁🚿6) **P**10 Lift ☾ sB45—60 sB🛁🚿75—95 dB70—90 dB🛁🚿90—105 M8—12
Credit cards [1] [2] [3] [4] [5]

🚗 **Autavia** Hardstr 14 ☎427878 For

🚗 **Delta** Grabenackerstr 10 ☎466288 Hon

Dreispitz Reinacherstr 28 ☎501550 AR

🚗 **Dufour** Dufourstr 36 ☎231214

🚗 **Grosspeter** Grosspeterstr 12 ☎507000 **P** Ope

🚗 **Olympic** Viadukstr 45 ☎230126 BMW

🚗 **St-Johann** Ryffstr 16 ☎438450 AR Fia

🚗 **C Schlotterbeck** Viaduktstr 40 ☎220050 AR Cit

🚗 **Settelen** Turkheimerstr 17 ☎383800 AR Toy

🚗 **G Uecker** Nafelserstr 19 ☎385076

BEATENBERG
Bern (☎036)

★***Beauregard*** ☎411341
Dec—Apr & May—Oct
rm22 (🛁6)

★***Jungfraublick*** ☎411581

rm13 (🚿10) mountains lake

BECKENRIED
Nidwalden (☎041)

★★**Edelweiss** ☎641252

rm25 (🛁🚿17) ⌂ **P**20 sB42—52 sB🛁🚿53—63 dB73—93 dB🛁🚿95—115 Mfr13 ≈ lake mountains
Credit cards [1] [2] [3] [5]

★***Mond*** ☎641204

rm30 (🚿22) **P**20 Lift lake
Credit cards [2] [3] [5]

★***Sonne*** ☎641205

rm34 **P** mountains lake

BELLINZONA
Ticino (☎092)

★★★***Unione*** Gl-Guisan ☎255577 tx846277

10 Jan—20 Dec
rm35 (🛁🚿29) **P**30 Lift mountains
Credit cards [1] [2] [3] [5]

🚗 **Ferrari** via Lugano 31 ☎251668 **P** Toy

🚗 **Gottardo** viale Portone 6 ☎252818 AR Hon

🚗 **Pedrini** via Lugano 18 ☎255274 Peu

BERLINGEN
Thurgau (☎054)

★***Seestern*** ☎611404

rm9 (🚿4) ⌂ **P**50 lake

BERN (BERNE)
Bern (☎031)

★★★★★**Bellevue Palace** Kochergasse 3—5 ☎224581 tx911524

🛁155 ⌂ **P** Lift ☾ sB🛁155—175 dB🛁230—280 M alc mountains
Credit cards [1] [2] [3] [5]

★★★★★***Schweizerhof*** (Amb) Bahnhofpl 11 (Nr Station) ☎224501 tx32188

🛁90 **P** Lift ☾

★★★★**City Mövenpick** (Amb) Bubenbergpl 7 ☎225377 tx912049

🛁🚿47 Lift ☾ sB🛁🚿99—112 dB🛁🚿129—142
Credit cards [1] [2] [3] [4] [5]

★★★**Astor Touring** Eigerplatz/Zieglerstr 66 ☎458666 tx912834

🛁🚿63 **P**20 Lift ☾ sB🛁🚿61—80 dB🛁🚿90—115 M15—25
Credit cards [1] [2] [3] [5]

★★★***Bären*** (Amb) Schauplatzgasse 4 ☎223367 tx33199

🛁🚿57 **P** Lift ☾
Credit cards [1] [2] [3] [5]

★★★**Bern** Zeughausgasse 9 ☎211021 tx911555

🛁🚿100 Lift ☾ sB🛁🚿95—115 dB🛁🚿130—160 M20
Credit cards [1] [2] [3] [5]

★★★***Bristol*** Schauplatzgasse 10 (off Bärenpl) (n.rest) ☎220101 tx33199

rm83 (🛁🚿52) **P** Lift ☾

★★★**Savoy** Neuengasse 26 (n.rest) ☎224405 tx911683

🛁🚿56 **P** Lift ☾ sB🛁🚿90—115 dB🛁🚿130—155
Credit cards [1] [2] [3] [4] [5]

★★★**Wächter** (Mövenpick) Neuengasse 44 ☎220866 tx912230

rm44 (🛁🚿35) Lift sB54—65 sB🛁🚿95—115 dB🛁🚿145—155 M alc
Credit cards [1] [2] [3] [5]

★★**Continental** Zeughausgasse 27 (n.rest) ☎222626 tx912222

🛁🚿37 Lift ☾ sB🛁🚿70—90 dB🛁🚿100—130
Credit cards [1] [2] [3] [5]

★***Goldener Schlüssel*** Rathausgasse 72 ☎220216

rm29 **P** Lift ☾

🚗 **Auto Marti** Eigerpl 2 ☎451515 BMW

🚗 **Citroën (Suisse)** Freiburgstr 447 ☎553311 **P** Cit

🚗 **Egghölzli** Egghölzlistr 1 ☎446366 **P** Hon Peu Vau

🚗 **Schulthelss** Hofweg 5 ☎427742 **P** For

🚗 **Willy** Freiburgstr 443 ☎552511 **P** Fia For

At **GÜMLIGEN** (6km E)

🚗 **Schwarz** Worbstrasse 171 ☎523636 **P** Lan Vol

At **LYSSACH**

★★**Lyssach** ☎471601
🚿37 **P**50 Lift sB🚿58—63 dB🚿90—100 mountains
Credit cards [1] [2] [3] [4] [5]

At **MURI** (3km SE on N6)

★★**Krone** ☎521666
rm28 (🛁🚿13) **P** sB45—65 sB🛁🚿86—110 dB70—100 dB🛁🚿110—130 M16—35
Credit cards [1] [2]

🚘 **Bigler & Bürki** Thunstr 25 ☎521600 **P** AR

At **WABERN** (2km S)

🚘 **F Waeny** Seftigenstr 198 ☎542622 **P** AR Maz

BEX-LES-BAINS
Vaud (☎025)

★**St-Christophe** ☎652979
🚿10 A4rm **P**10 sB40—60 sB🚿60 dB70—100 dB🚿100 mountains
Credit cards [1] [2] [3] [4] [5]

🚘 **Rallye** r Servannaz ☎631225 Saa Toy

BIASCA
Ticino (☎092)

★★**Poste** via Stazione ☎722121
rm10 (🚿6) **P**20 sB44—50 sB🚿58—63 dB86—96 dB🚿114—126 M24—34 mountains
Credit cards [1] [2] [3] [4] [5]

🚘 **Maggetti** via San Gottardo ☎721266

BIEL (BIENNE)
Bern (☎032)

★★★★**Élite** pl Gl-Guisan ☎225441 tx34101
🛁🚿60 **P**10 Lift ☾ sB🛁🚿105—120 dB🛁🚿180—320 M25
Credit cards [1] [2] [3] [4] [5]

★★★**Continental** (Amb) r d'Aarberg 29 ☎223255 tx34440
🛁🚿80 **P**50 Lift ☾ sB🛁🚿95—105 dB🛁🚿130—150
Credit cards [1] [2] [3] [4] [5]

🚘 **W Mühle** Heilmannstr 16 ☎222201 M/c **P** AR Ren

🚘 **Progress** Portstr 32 ☎259666 Alf Hon

BISSONE
Ticino (☎091)

★★★**Lago di Lugano** ☎688591 tx79378
10 Mar—2 Jan
🛁90 **P**60 Lift ☾ sB🛁88—173 dB🛁146—242 M35&alc 🏊 lake mountains
Credit cards [1] [2] [3] [4] [5]

BIVIO
Graubünden (☎081)

★★★**Post** ☎751275
rm42 (🛁🚿33) **P**30 ☾ sB43—58 sB🛁🚿53—83 dB96—136 dB🛁🚿116—166 M25—45 mountains
Credit cards [1] [2] [3] [5]

Switzerland

BOLLINGEN
St-Gallen (☎055)

★★**Schiff** am Oberen Zürichsee ☎283888
🚿18 🏠 **P** Lift sB🚿53 dB🚿90 M9—28 🏊 lake
Credit cards [1] [2] [3]

BÖNIGEN
Bern (☎036)

★★★**Seller au Lac** (Amb) ☎223021 tx923164
Dec—Oct
🛁🚿50 🏠 **P**40 Lift ☾ sB🛁🚿79—124 dB🛁🚿157—247 M20—45 lake mountains
Credit cards [1] [2] [3] [4] [5]

BOURG ST PIERRE
Valais (☎026)

🚘 **Tunnel du Grand St-Bernard** ☎49124

BRÉ See **LUGANO**

BRIENZ
Bern (☎036)

★★**Bären** ☎512412
Mar—Dec
rm35 (🛁🚿10) 🏠 **P**11 Lift sBfr32 sB🛁🚿45 dB64—80 dB🛁🚿90—110 M20&alc 🏊 lake mountains
Credit cards [1] [2] [3] [5]

★★***Gare*** ☎512712
rm10 (🚿3) **P** mountains

★★**Schönegg** (n.rest) ☎511113
Feb—Oct
rm16 (🛁🚿9) A6rm **P**11 sB33—38 dB64—68 dB🛁🚿84—96 lake mountains
Credit card [3]

BRIG (BRIGUE)
Valais (☎028)

★★★**Viktoria-Terminus** (Amb) Bahnhofstr 2 ☎231503 tx473861
Dec—Oct
rm40 (🛁🚿34) 🏠 **P**6 Lift ☾ sB45—55 sB🛁🚿50—80 dB🛁🚿96—130 M24—36 mountains
Credit cards [1] [2] [3] [5]

★★**Brigerhof** Rhonesandstr 18 (n.rest) ☎231607
Feb—Oct
🛁🚿30 🏠 **P**15 Lift ☾ sB🛁🚿53—58 dB🛁🚿90—101 🏊 mountains
Credit cards [1] [2] [3] [5]

★★**Sporting** (n.rest) ☎232363
rm33 (🛁🚿21) 🏠 **P**15 Lift sB38—43 sB🛁🚿49—55 dB65—73 dB🛁🚿78—94 mountains
Credit cards [1] [2] [3] [5]

At **GLIS** (2km E)

🚘 **Saltina** ☎232562 Toy

BRIGELS
Graubünden (☎086)

★★★**Eurotel** La Val Breil ☎41252 tx74577
Jun—Oct & Dec—Apr
🛁🚿50 🏠 **P**40 Lift sB🛁🚿60—130 dB🛁🚿80—200 M26 🏊 mountains
Credit cards [2] [3] [5]

BRISSAGO
Ticino (☎093)

★★**Mirto au Lac** ☎651328
Apr—Oct
rm27(🛁🚿23) 🏠 **P**20 Lift ☾ sB🛁🚿50—57 dB🛁🚿100—140 lake

BRUGG
Aargau (☎056)

★★★**Rotes Haus** Haupstr 7 ☎411479 tx825105
🛁🚿24 **P** Lift sB🛁🚿45—50 dB🛁🚿85 M6—30alc
Credit cards [1] [2] [3] [5]

BRUNNEN
Schwyz (☎043)

★★★**Waldstätterhof** (Amb) ☎331133 tx866007
16 Feb—30 Jan
🛁🚿100 🏠 **P**100 Lift ☾ sB🛁🚿95—130 dB🛁🚿140—210 M25—40 🎾 lake mountains
Credit cards [1] [2] [3] [4] [5]

★★**Bellevue** Vierwaldstattersee ☎311318 tx866022
Apr—15 Oct
🛁50 🏠 **P**25 Lift sB🛁77—87 dB🛁134—154 M19—35 🏊 lake mountains
Credit cards [1] [2] [3] [4] [5]

★★**Élite & Aurora** ☎311024 tx866104
15 Oct—1 Feb
🛁🚿75 🏠 **P**12 Lift sB🛁🚿44—69 dB🛁🚿88—118 M12—35 lake mountains
Credit cards [1] [2] [3] [5]

★★★***Metropole au Lac*** ☎311039
Mar—Nov
rm21 (🛁🚿9) 🏠 Lift lake

★★**Schmid** ☎311882
Mar—Oct
rm10 (🛁8) **P** Lift dB50—70 dB🛁100—120 lake mountains
Credit cards [1] [2] [3] [5]

★★**Weisses-Rösseli** ☎311022
rm30 (🛁🚿5) **P**3 sB42—48 dB78—90 dB🛁🚿94—114 M10—20
Credit cards [1] [2] [3] [5]

★**Alpina** ☎311813
rm23 (🛁🚿12) **P** sB42 sB🛁🚿52 dB80 dB🛁🚿94 M12—15 mountains
Credit card [2]

🚘 **Inderbitzin** Gersauerstr 17 ☎311313 Aud VW

BUCHS
St-Gallen (☎085)

🚘 **Sulser** St Gallerstr 19 ☎61414 Ope Vau

BULLE
Fribourg (☎029)

★★***Rallye*** rte de Riaz 8 ☎28498 tx940017
🚿15 🏠 **P** Lift ☾ mountains

BÜRCHEN
Valais (☎028)

★★★**Bürchnerhof** ☎442434
🛁19 **P**26 sB🛁49—65 dB🛁65—114
M6—30 mountains

BURGDORF
Bern (☎034)

🚗 **Central** Gotthelfstr 21 ☎228288 **P** Cit Vau

BÜRGENSTOCK
Nidwalden (☎041)

★★***Waldheim*** ☎641306
rm60 (🛁🚿46) 🏠 **P** Lift 📺 mountains
Credit cards [2] [3]

BUSSIGNY See **LAUSANNE**

CASSARATE See **LUGANO**

CASTAGNOLA See **LUGANO**

CELERINA
Graubünden (☎082)

★★★**Cresta Palace** (Amb) ☎33564 tx74461
20 Jun—20 Sep & 15 Dec—15 Apr
rm98 (🛁🚿81) 🏠 **P**80 Lift ☾ sB67—97
sB🛁🚿77—177 dB124—184
dB🛁🚿144—184 M26—52 ♣ 📺
mountains
Credit cards [1] [2] [3] [4] [5]

★★**Cresta Kulm** ☎33373 tx74636
20 Dec—10 Apr & 20 Jun—10 Oct
rm40 (🛁🚿36) 🏠 **P**20 Lift ☾ sB75—105
sB🛁🚿80—125 dB110—190
dB🛁🚿130—240 ≋ mountains
Credit cards [1] [2] [3] [4] [5]

CHAM
Zug (☎042)

🚗 **Ettmüller** Steinhauserstr ☎363133 **P** Cit

CHAMPÉRY
Valais (☎025)

★★**Alpes** ☎791222
15 Dec—15 Apr & Jun—20 Sep
rm23 (🛁🚿18) **P**12 sB30—60
sB🛁🚿37—70 dB60—120
dB🛁🚿72—140 mountains
Credit cards [1] [2] [3] [5]

★★**Beau-Séjour** ☎791701 tx456284
Dec & 15 Apr—Sep
🛁🚿21 **P**12 Lift sB🛁🚿45—70
dB🛁🚿80—120 M22 mountains
Credit cards [1] [2] [3] [5]

★★**Parc** ☎791313
rm30 (🛁24) **DPn**75—135 ♣ ≋ 📺
mountains

CHÂTEAU-D'OEX
Vaud (☎029)

★★★***Beau-Séjour*** ☎47423 tx940022
15 Dec—Oct
rm43 (🛁🚿34) **P**10 Lift mountains
Credit cards [1] [2] [3]

★★★**Hostellerie du Bon Accueil**
☎46320
20 May—20 Oct & 20 Dec—20 Apr
🛁🚿12 **P**20 sB🛁🚿88—103
dB🛁🚿116—151 mountains
Credit cards [1] [2] [3] [5]

★★★***Victoria*** ☎46434
Dec—Apr & May—Oct
🛁🚿18 🏠 **P** Lift ≋ mountains

🚗 **Pont** Petit Pré ☎46173 M/c **P** Ope Vau

🚗 **J Yersin** ☎47539 **P** AR Cit Toy Vol

CHÂTELET (LE) See **GSTEIG**

CHAUX-DE-FONDS (LA)
Neuchâtel (☎039)

★★★***Club*** r du Parc 71 ☎235300
tx35548
🛁40 Lift

🚗 **E Frey** r F-Courvoisier 68 ☎286677

🚗 **Migrol** r du Locle 69 ☎265926 Alf AR DJ For

🚗 **Trois Rois** bd des Eplatures 8 ☎268181 For Lan

CHERNEX See **MONTREAUX**

CHEXBRES
Vaud (☎021)

★★★**Bellevue** ☎561481
🛁🚿27 **P**50 Lift sB🛁🚿65—80
dB🛁🚿90—120 M alc lake mountains
Credit cards [1] [2] [3] [4] [5]

★★★**Signal** ☎562525 tx452212
Mar—Nov
🛁🚿82 🏠 **P**50 Lift ☾ sB🛁🚿60—100
dB🛁🚿116—170 M25—36 ♣ 📺 U lake
mountains
Credit cards [1] [3]

★★**Cécil** ☎561292
rm23 (🛁🚿17) **P**50 Lift ☾ sB45—50
sB🛁🚿50—70 dB80—85
dB🛁🚿100—120 ≋ lake mountains
Credit cards [1] [2] [3] [5]

CHIASSO
Ticino (☎091)

★★★**Touring Mövenpick**
(Amb/Mövenpick) pza Indipendenza
☎445331 tx842493
🛁🚿60 **P** Lift sB🛁🚿79—118
dB🛁🚿99—138 M alc
Credit cards [1] [2] [3] [5]

CHUR (COIRE)
Graubünden (☎081)

★★★**Duc de Rohan** (Amb) Masanserstr
44 ☎221022 tx74161
rm35 (🛁🚿33) 🏠 **P** Lift ☾ sB🛁🚿60—80
dB🛁🚿98—126 📺
Credit cards [1] [2] [3] [5]

★★**A.B.C.** Bahnhofpl (n.rest) ☎226033
tx74580
🛁🚿33 🏠 **P**12 Lift sB🛁🚿65—80
dB🛁🚿105—130 mountains
Credit cards [1] [2] [3] [5]

★★**Drei Könige** Reichsgasse 18
☎221725
rm38 (🛁🚿26) 🏠 **P** Lift sB35—40
sB🛁🚿50—65 dB70—76 dB🛁🚿90—100
M16—32
Credit cards [1] [2] [3] [4] [5]

★★**Sommerau** Emserstr ☎225545
tx74172
🛁🚿88 **P**200 sB🛁🚿65—75
dB🛁🚿110—170 M8—70 mountains
Credit cards [1] [2] [3] [4] [5]

★★**Stern** (ROM) Reichsgasse 11
☎223555 tx74198
🛁🚿55 🏠 **P**28 Lift ☾ sB🛁🚿65—75
dB🛁🚿106—116 M15—25&alc
Credit cards [1] [2] [3] [5]

🚗 **Auto Center Tribolet** Rossbodendstr 14
☎221212 AR For Toy

🚗 **Calandag** Kasernenstr 30 ☎221414 Peu Tal

🚗 **Comminot** Rossbodenstr 24 ☎223737 **P** AR Maz

🚗 **Grand Garage Dosch** Kasernenstr 138
☎215171 Ope Vau

🚗 **Lidoc** St-Margrethenstr 9 ☎221313 **P** Alf Mer Vau

COLLONGE-BELLERIVE
Genève

★★***Bellerive*** ☎521420
Feb—15 Dec
rm11 (🛁8) A4rm **P** lake

COPPET
Vaud (☎022)

🚗 **Port** rte de Suisse ☎761212 AR Maz

CORNAREDO See **LUGANO**

CRANS-SUR-SIERRE
Valais (☎027)

★★★★**Alpine & Savoy** ☎412142
tx473134
15 Dec—Etr & 20 Jun—15 Sep
rm60 (🛁45) 🏠 **P**30 Lift ☾ sB50—85
sB🛁70—140 dB100—170 dB🛁160—260
M35—45 📺 mountains
Credit cards [1] [2] [3] [4] [5]

★★★***Élite*** ☎414301
🛁35 **P**30 Lift ≋ mountains
Credit cards [1] [2] [3] [5]

★★★**Robinson** ☎411353
🛁🚿16 **P**15 Lift ☾ sB🛁🚿63—88
dB🛁🚿116—156 M25 mountains
Credit cards [1] [2] [3]

★★★**Royal** ☎413931 tx473227
Seasonal
🛁🚿70 **P**40 Lift ☾ sB🛁🚿73—158
dB🛁🚿81—166 M35—45 mountains
Credit cards [1] [2] [3] [5]

★★★**Splendide** ☎412056
15 Dec—15 Apr & 15 Jun—15 Sep
31 P30 Lift sB 62—73
dB 124—146 M24—28 mountains

CULLY See **LAUSANNE**

DAVOS
Graubünden (☎083)

At **DAVOS DORF**

★★★**Alpes** Promenade 136 ☎61261
tx74341
rm57 (47) P19 Lift sB48—79
sB 58—108 dB76—138
dB 96—196 lake mountains
Credit cards 1 2 3 5

★★★***Meierhof*** Promenade ☎61285
tx74363
Dec—Apr & Jun—Oct
84 P65 Lift mountains
Credit cards 1 2 3 5

At **LARET** (8km NE)

★***Tischiery's im Landhaus*** ☎52121
Dec—Apr & Jun—Oct
rm30 (12) P mountains

At **DAVOS PLATZ**

★★★**Morosani Post** (Amb) Promenade
42 ☎21161 tx74350
Seasonal
90 P Lift sB 73—170
dB 120—390 mountains
Credit cards 1 2 3 5

★★★**Schweizerhof** (Amb) Promenade
50 ☎21151 tx74324
6 Dec—21 Apr & 28 May—28 Sep
rm103 (100) P40 Lift
sB 69—87 dB 122—158 M18—28
mountains
Credit cards 1 2 3 5

★**Belmont** Tanzbuhlstr 2 (n.rest) ☎35032
Dec—15 Apr & 15 Jun—15 Sep
rm25 P10 sB50—55 dB90—110 mountains

DELÉMONT
Jura (☎066)

★★★***National*** rte de Bâle 25 ☎229622
27 P Lift
Credit cards 1 2 3 5

★***Bonne Auberge*** r du 23 Juin 32
☎221758
Closed Feb
rm9 (6) P20
Credit cards 1 2 3 5

Mercay r de la Maltière 20 ☎221745 Fia

Gare Willemin rte de Moutier 65
☎222461 P Ren Vol

DIABLERETS (LES)
Vaud (☎025)

★★★★**Eurotel** ☎531721 tx456174
17 May—12 Oct & 21 Dec—11 Apr
rm98 (90) Lift sB41—113
sB 55—128 dB114—246 M23
mountains
Credit cards 1 2 3 5

Switzerland

DIETIKON
Zürich (☎01)

★★★**Krone** (ROM) Zürcherstr 3
☎7406011
20 P40 sB 67—75
dB 108—128 M11—49
Credit cards 1 2 3 5

DISENTIS
Graubünden (☎086)

★★★★**Park Baur** ☎74545 tx74585
Closed Nov
54 P100 Lift sB 72—80
dB 108—124 M12—45
mountains
Credit cards 1 2 3 5

DÜRRENAST See **THUN (THOUNE)**

EBIKON See **LUZERN (LUCERNE)**

EBLIGEN
Bern (☎036)

★**Hirschen** ☎511551
14 P40 sB 30—40
dB 55—95 lake mountains
Credit card 2

EGERKINGEN
Solothurn (☎062)
See also **OLTEN**

★★***AGIP*** (Autobahn crossroads N1/N2)
☎612121 tx68644
68 P200 sB 66 dB 98
M25—35
Credit cards 1 2 3 4 5

EINSIEDELN
Schwyz (☎055)

★★★**Drei Könige** ☎532441 tx875293
52 P Lift sB 57—62
dB 98—135 Mfr22 mountains

EMMENBRÜCKE See **LUZERN (LUCERNE)**

ENGELBERG
Obwalden (☎041)

★★★***Bellevue Terminus*** ☎941213
tx78555
Jan—Sep & Dec
rm90 (80) A3rm P Lift mountains

★★★**Dorint Regina Titlis** Dorfstr
☎942828 tx866272
128 P80 Lift sB 70—110
dB 120—200 mountains
Credit cards 1 2 3 5

★★★**Europäischer Hof** (Amb) Postfach
272 (n.rest) ☎941263 tx866461
15 May—Oct & 10 Dec—15 Apr
rm98 (67) P20 Lift sB54—105
sB 77—123 dB90—202
dB 130—232 M15—20 mountains
Credit cards 1 2 3 4 5

★★***Hess*** ☎941366 tx866270
Closed Nov
rm58 (44) P Lift mountains

★***Engelberg*** Dorfstr 14 ☎941168
Closed Nov
rm33 (25) A13rm P Lift mountains
Credit cards 1 2 3 5

ENTLEBUCH
Luzern (☎041)

★★***Drei Könige*** ☎721227
rm12 (7) P Lift mountains

ESTAVAYER-LE-LAC
Fribourg (☎037)

★**Lac** ☎631343
30 P50 dB 90—104 lake
Credit card 3

ETOY-BUCHILLON
Vaud (☎021)

★★**Pêchers-Etoy** rte du Lac Genève-Lausanne ☎763277
14 P sB 52—68
dB 74—85 M10—21 lake
mountains

EVOLÈNE
Valais (☎027)

★★***Hermitage*** ☎831232
Jun—Sep & Dec—Apr
rm22 (12)

★***Dent-Blanche*** ☎831105
rm50 P mountains

★***Eden*** ☎831112
Closed Nov
rm18

FAIDO
Ticino (☎094)

★★**Milan** ☎381307
15 Apr—Oct
rm39 (27) Lift sB50 sB 63 dB85
dB 105 M22—26 mountains
Credit cards 1 2 3 5

FERNEY VOLTAIRE See **GENÈVE AIRPORT**

FEUSISBERG
Zürich (☎01)

★★★**Panorama** Tagungszentrum
☎7842464 tx875825
65 P200 Lift sB 95—115
dB 150—185 M20—50 lake mountains
Credit cards 1 2 3 5

FIESCH
Valais (☎028)

★***Glacier & Poste*** ☎711301
rm35 (20) P6 mountains
Credit cards 1 2

FILZBACH
Glarus (☎058)

★**Seeblick** ☎321455
rm10 P sB28—32 dB56—64 M7—11 lake
mountains

FLEURIER
Neuchâtel (☎038)

🚗 **C Duthe** r de Temple 34 ☎611637 **P** Aud VW

🚗 **C Hotz** r de l'Industrie 19 ☎612922 Cit Peu Tal

FLIMS-WALDHAUS
Graubünden (☎081)

★★★★ ***Park-Hotels Waldhaus*** ☎390181 tx74125
Dec—Mar & Apr—Oct
🛁🚿160 🏠 **P** Lift ☾ 🎾 ≈ 📺 mountains
Credit cards [2] [3] [5]

★★★ **Alpes** Hauptstr ☎390101 tx74565
Closed 13 Apr
🛁80 🏠 **P**40 Lift ☾ sB🛁65—105 dB🛁110—190 📺 mountains
Credit cards [1] [2] [3] [5]

★★★ ***Schloss*** ☎391245
Dec—mid Apr & May—Oct
rm41 (🛁🚿36) A19rm 🏠 **P** Lift mountains

★★★ ***Segnes*** ☎391281 tx74125
Closed Nov
rm90 (🛁60) **P**50 Lift ☾ 🎾 mountains
Credit cards [2] [3] [4] [5]

★★ **Guardaval** (n.rest) ☎391119
Jun—Sep & Dec—Apr
rm10 (🛁🚿7) **P**8 sB28—36 sB🛁🚿38—52 dB58—72 dB🛁🚿68—96 mountains
Credit cards [1] [2] [3]

★★ ***National*** ☎391224
Closed May
rm24 (🛁🚿12) 🏠 **P** Lift ☾ mountains

FLÜELEN
Uri (☎044)

★ ***Weisses Kreuz*** ☎21717
Apr—Nov
rm33 (🛁🚿13) 🏠 **P** M alc mountains lake
Credit cards [1] [2] [3] [5]

🚗 **Sigrist** Axenstr 30 ☎21260 **P** Ren

FRAUBRUNNEN
Bern (☎031)

★★ ***Löwen*** ☎967219
rm5 (🛁🚿4) A1rm **P**

FRIBOURG
Fribourg (☎037)

★★★ **Eurotel** Grand-Places 14 ☎813131 tx942439
🛁🚿130 **P** Lift ☾ sB🛁🚿74—111 dB🛁🚿125—160 📺
Credit cards [1] [2] [3] [4] [5]

🚗 **Central** r de l'Industrie 7 ☎243520 For

🚗 **Gendre** rte de Villars 105 ☎240331 Aud VW

🚗 **Piller** r Guillimann 24—26 ☎223092 Cit Lan

FRICK
Aargau (☎064)

★ **Engel** ☎611314
rm20 (🚿10) 🏠 **P**100 ☾ sBfr32 sB🚿38—42 dBfr60 dB🚿65—68 M10—30 🎾
Credit cards [1] [2] [3] [5]

Switzerland

FRUTIGEN
Bern (☎033)

★ **Simplon** ☎711041
rm15 (🛁🚿4) **P**30 sB33—35 sB🛁🚿42—46 dB65—69 dB🛁🚿83—91 M12—15 mountains
Credit card [1]

🚗 **Niederfeld** ☎711414 **P** Aud VW

FÜRIGEN
Nidwalden (☎041)

★★★ **Fürigen** ☎611254 tx866257
🛁🚿70 A20rm **P** Lift ☾ sB🛁🚿70—82 dB🛁🚿120—144 🎾 ≈ lake mountains
Credit cards [1] [2] [3] [4] [5]

FURKA PASS
Uri (☎044)

★ ***Furkablick*** ☎67297
Jun—Sep
rm20 🏠 mountains

GABI
Valais (☎028)

★★ **Weissmies** Simplonstr ☎291116
rm18 (🛁🚿5) A2rm 🏠 **P**25 sB31—37 sB🛁🚿35—40 dBfr54 dB🛁🚿70 mountains
Credit cards [1] [3] [5]

GENÈVE (GENEVA) (☎022)

See plan pages 398 and 399

★★★★★ ***Bergues*** (THF) quai des Bergues 33 ☎315050 tx23383 Plan **1**
🛁117 🏠 **P**7 Lift ☾ M alc mountains lake
Credit cards [1] [2] [3] [4] [5]

★★★★★ **Noga Hilton International** quai du Mont-Blanc 19 ☎319811 tx289704 Plan **1A**
🛁🚿291 **P**250 Lift ☾ sB🛁🚿268—318 dB🛁🚿385—435 M28—42 📺
Credit cards [1] [2] [3] [4] [5]

★★★★★ **Président** quai Wilson 47 ☎311000 tx22780 Plan **2**
🛁185 🏠 **P** Lift ☾ sB🛁199—264 dB🛁308—393 M45 lake
Credit cards [1] [2] [3] [4] [5]

★★★★★ **Rhône** quai Turrettini 3 ☎319831 tx22213 Plan **3**
🛁🚿281 🏠 **P** Lift ☾ sB🛁🚿170—210 dB🛁🚿270—335 M40—80
Credit cards [1] [2] [3] [5]

★★★★★ **Richemond** (Relais et Châteaux) Jardin Brunswick ☎311400 tx22598 Plan **4**
🛁🚿98 🏠 **P**300 Lift ☾ sB🛁🚿fr270 dB🛁🚿fr450 M alc lake mountains
Credit cards [1] [2] [3] [5]

★★★★ **Beau Rivage** (Amb) quai du Mont-Blanc 13 ☎310221 tx23362 Plan **5**
🛁🚿120 **P** Lift ☾ sB🛁🚿225—265 dB🛁🚿330—430 lake mountains
Credit cards [1] [2] [3] [5]

★★★★ **Paix** quai du Mont-Blanc 11 ☎326150 tx22552 Plan **6**
🛁🚿106 **P**10 Lift ☾ sB🛁🚿165—200 dB🛁🚿320—380 M35&alc lake mountains
Credit cards [1] [2] [3] [4] [5]

★★★ **Ambassador** quai des Bergues 21 pl Chevelu ☎317200 tx23231 Plan **7**
rm90 (🛁85) 🏠 **P**10 Lift ☾ sBfr55 sB🛁78—112 dB🛁120—200 M25—50 lake mountains
Credit cards [1] [2] [3] [5]

★★★ ***Angleterre*** quai du Mont-Blanc 17 ☎328180 tx22668 Plan **8**
🛁65 **P** Lift ☾ mountains lake

★★★ **Berne** r de Berne 26 ☎316000 tx22764 Plan **9**
🛁88 Lift ☾ sB🛁128—180 dB🛁171—200
Credit cards [1] [2] [3] [4] [5]

★★★ **Century** (Amb) av de Frontenex 24 (n.rest) ☎368095 tx23223 Plan **10**
🛁🚿139 **P**20 Lift ☾ sB🛁🚿128—137 dB🛁🚿145—210
Credit cards [1] [2] [3] [5]

★★★ **Cornavin** bd J-Fazy 33 (n.rest) ☎322100 tx22853 Plan **11**
rm125 (🛁🚿115) Lift ☾ sB100—135 sB🛁🚿135 dB150—185 dB🛁🚿185
Credit cards [1] [3]

★★★ **Cristal** 4 r Pradier (n.rest) ☎313400 tx289926 Plan **11A**
🛁🚿79 Lift sB🛁🚿110—130 dB🛁🚿160—180
Credit cards [1] [2] [3] [5]

★★★ **Eden** r de Lausanne 135 ☎326540 tx23962 Plan **12**
🛁🚿54 Lift ☾ sB🛁🚿110—120 dB🛁🚿140—160 M24 lake
Credit cards [1] [2] [3] [4] [5]

★★★ **Grand Pré** r du Grand Pré 35 (n.rest) ☎339150 tx23284 Plan **13**
🛁🚿80 🏠 **P**6 Lift sB🛁🚿105—160 dB🛁🚿160—200
Credit cards [1] [2] [3] [5]

★★★ ***Lutetia*** r de Carouge 12 ☎204222 tx28845 Plan **14**
🛁42 Lift

★★★ **Warwick** (Amb) r de Lausanne 14 ☎316250 tx23630 Plan **15**
🛁169 Lift ☾ sB🛁180 dB🛁250
Credit cards [1] [2] [3] [4] [5]

★★ **Montbrillant** r de Montbrillant 2 ☎337784 Plan **19**
rm48 (🛁40) **P**6 Lift sBfr45 sB🛁fr80 dB58 dB🛁fr110 Mfr10 mountains
Credit cards [1] [2] [3] [5]

★★ **Touring-Balance** (Amb) pl Longemalle 13 ☎287122 tx427634 Plan **21**
rm56 (🛁🚿52) Lift ☾ sB🛁🚿110 dB🛁🚿140—150 lake
Credit cards [1] [2] [3] [4] [5]

★ ***Adris*** r Gevray 6—8 (n.rest) ☎315225 Plan **22**
rm22 (🛁🚿19) Lift
Credit cards [1] [2] [3] [5]

GENÈVE (GENEVA)

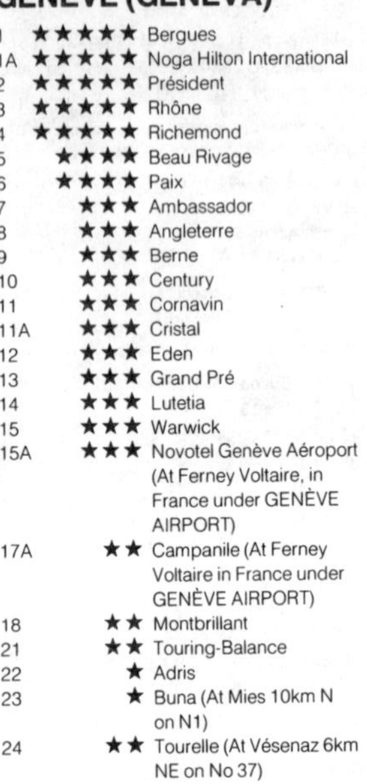

1	★★★★★	Bergues
1A	★★★★★	Noga Hilton International
2	★★★★★	Président
3	★★★★★	Rhône
4	★★★★★	Richemond
5	★★★★	Beau Rivage
6	★★★★	Paix
7	★★★	Ambassador
8	★★★	Angleterre
9	★★★	Berne
10	★★★	Century
11	★★★	Cornavin
11A	★★★	Cristal
12	★★★	Eden
13	★★★	Grand Pré
14	★★★	Lutetia
15	★★★	Warwick
15A	★★★	Novotel Genève Aéroport (At Ferney Voltaire, in France under GENÈVE AIRPORT)
17A	★★	Campanile (At Ferney Voltaire in France under GENÈVE AIRPORT)
18	★★	Montbrillant
21	★★	Touring-Balance
22	★	Adris
23	★	Buna (At Mies 10km N on N1)
24	★★	Tourelle (At Vésenaz 6km NE on No 37)

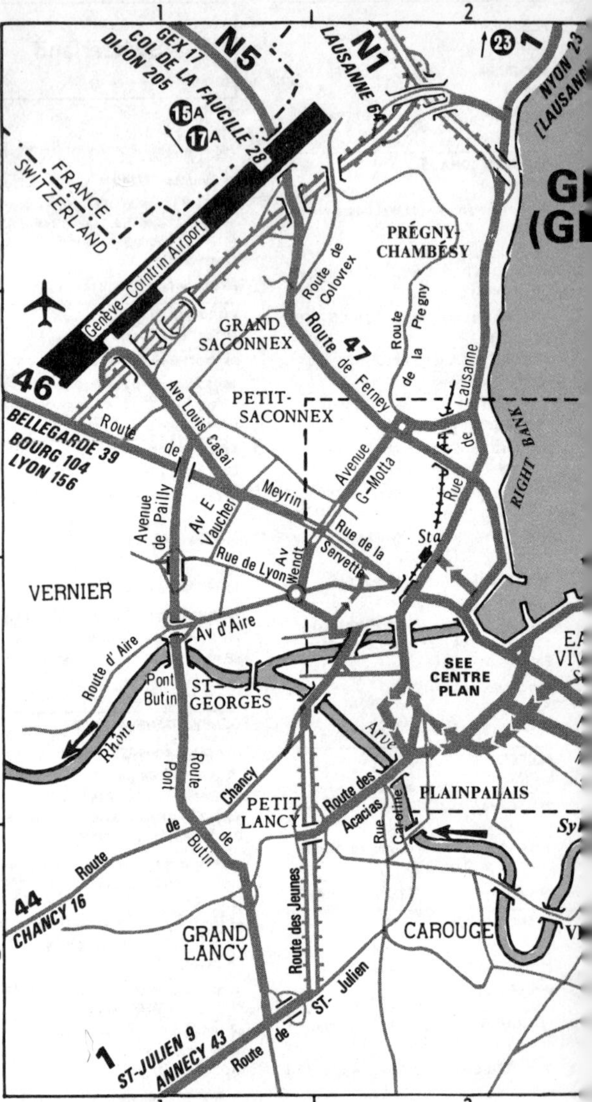

Acacias Motors r Boissonnas 11 ☎433600

Athénée rte de Meyrin 122 ☎960044 **P** BMW Mer RR

Autohall Metropole rte du Pont Butin ☎921322 For

Auto Import Viguet 1 Acacias ☎425804 **P** BMW

Bouchet rte de Meyrin 54—56 ☎968900 AR Peu

E Frey rte des Acacias 23 ☎421010 AR Mer Toy

Nouveau r Pré Jérome 21—23 ☎202111 M/c BMW

Tranches bd des Tranchées 50 ☎468911 Maz

At **MIES** (10km N on N1)

★***Buna*** ☎551535 Plan **23**

6 **P** mountains

At **VÉSENAZ** (6km NE on No 37)

★★**Tourelle** rte d'Hermance 26 ☎521628 Plan **24**

15 Jan—15 Dec
rm24 (21) A2rm **P**15 sB70—80
dB 90—125 lake mountains
Credit cards 1 2 3 5

GENÈVE AIRPORT (7km N)

At **FERNEY VOLTAIRE** (in France, 4km from airport)

★★★**Novotel Genève Aéroport** rte de Meyrin ☎(50)408523 tx385046 Plan **15A**

79 **P** sB 295—318 dB 322—345
M alc mountains
Credit cards 1 2 3 5

★★**Campanile** chemin de la Planche Brûlee ☎(50)407479 tx380957 Plan **17A**

42 **P** sB 204—225 dB 226—247
M61—82
Credit card 3

GERSAU

Schwyz (☎041)

★★★**Beau-Rivage** ☎841223 tx72588

May—Sep
rm34 (28) **P**14 Lift sB30—35
sB 35—50 dB60—70 dB 70—100
M10—30 mountains
Credit cards 1 2 3 5

★★★**Seehof du Lac** ☎841245 tx72588

Apr—Oct
18 **P**25 Lift sB 42—58 dB 84—116
M alc lake mountains
Credit cards 1 2 3 4 5

★**Bellevue** (n.rest) ☎841120

rm18 (5) **P**8 sB30—40 dB60—70
dB 80—90

GISWIL
Obwalden (☎041)

★***Krone*** Brünigstr ☎681151
rm100 (⛺ 60) ⛺ **P** Lift mountains

GLARUS
Glarus (☎058)

★★***Glarnerhof*** Bahnhofstr 2 ☎614106
rm30 (🚿 16) ⛺ **P** Lift mountains

Autocentre Buchholz Buchholzstrasse ☎611834 **P** Ope

K Enz Schweizerhofstr 7 ☎611770 Cit

GLATTBRUGG See **ZÜRICH AIRPORT**

GLION See **MONTREUX**

GLIS See **BRIG (BRIGUE)**

GOLDSWIL
Bern (☎036)

★***Park*** ☎222942
rm55 (🚿 2) A7rm **P** mountains

Burgseell Brienzerseestr ☎221043 Saa Toy

GÖSCHENEN
Uri (☎044)

★***St-Gotthard*** ☎65263
rm25 (🚿 ⛺ 4) ⛺ **P**

GOTTLIEBEN
Thurgau (☎072)

★★★***Krone*** (ROM) ☎692323
🚿 ⛺ 20 **P** Lift lake

Switzerland

GRÄCHEN
Valais (☎028)

★★***Beausite*** ☎562656
Dec—Apr & Jun—Oct
rm42 (🛁🚿9) 🚗 Lift 🏊

★***Grächerhof & Schönegg*** (Amb)
☎562515
Jun—Oct & Dec—Apr
rm35

GREPPEN
Luzern (☎041)

★**St-Wendelin** ☎811016
🛁8 🚗 **P**40 sB🛁51—61 dB🛁92—122
M13—36 🏊 lake mountains
Credit cards [1] [2] [3] [4] [5]

GRINDELWALD
Bern (☎036)

★★★★**Grand Regina** ☎545455
tx923263
Closed mid Oct—mid Dec
🛁120 🚗 **P**90 Lift ☾ sB🛁140—160
dB🛁260—300

★★★**Belvédère** ☎545434 tx923244
20 Dec—27 Sep
🛁🚿60 **P**40 Lift sB🛁🚿87—107
dB🛁🚿154—194 M32—40 &alc ▤
mountains
Credit cards [1] [2] [3] [5]

★★★**Gletschergarten** ☎531721
12 Apr—5 Oct
🛁🚿28 **P**20 Lift sB🛁🚿60—90
dB🛁🚿100—165 M22&alc mountains

★★★**Parkhotel Schönegg** ☎531853
tx923245
Closed Nov
rm60 (🛁50) 🚗 **P**70 Lift sB40—60
sB🛁70—100 dB70—110 dB🛁120—180
▤ mountains
Credit cards [1] [2] [3] [5]

★★★***Schweizerhof*** ☎532202 tx923254
20 Dec—10 Apr & 28 Jun—5 Oct
🛁40 **P**40 Lift ▤ mountains
Credit card [3]

★★★***Sunstar & Adler*** ☎545417
tx923230
May—Oct & Dec—Apr
🛁🚿180 🚗 **P** Lift ☾ M alc ▤ mountains
Credit cards [1] [2] [3] [4] [5]

★★***Derby*** ☎545461 tx923277
Closed 4 Nov—8 Dec
rm74 (🛁🚿72) **P**25 Lift mountains
Credit cards [1] [2] [3] [5]

★★***Grindelwald*** ☎532131
rm22 (🛁18) A10rm 🚗 **P** mountains

★★**Hirschen** ☎532777
rm33 (🛁🚿20) 🚗 **P**15 Lift ☾ sB40—60
sB🛁🚿60—80 dB76—110
dB🛁🚿90—140 M20—36 mountains
Credit card [3]

★**Alpenblick** (n.rest) ☎531105
rm16 **P**16 sB30—35 dB60—70 mountains
Credit cards [1] [2] [3] [5]

🚙 **Rothenegg** Rothenegg ☎531507 Aud
VW

GRUYÈRES
Fribourg (☎029)

★★★***Hostellerie des Chevaliers***
☎61933
Closed 11 Jan—9 Feb
🛁34 🚗 **P**12 M alc mountains
Credit cards [1] [2] [3] [4] [5]

★★***Hostellerie St-Georges*** ☎62246
Mar—Nov
rm14

GSTAAD
Bern (☎030)

★★★**Bellevue Grand** (Amb) ☎83171
tx922232
Dec—Apr & Jun—Sep
🛁🚿55 🚗 **P**30 Lift ☾ sB🛁🚿100—125
dB🛁🚿200—330 M25
Credit cards [1] [2] [3] [4] [5]

★★***National-Rialto*** Hauptstr ☎43474
rm33 (🛁🚿17) 🚗 **P** Lift ☾ mountains

★★***Olden*** ☎43444
🛁🚿15 🚗 **P** mountains
Credit cards [1] [2] [4] [5]

★***Rössli*** ☎43412
Closed May
rm26 (🛁🚿16) A4rm 🚗 **P**6 mountains
Credit cards [1] [3] [5]

GSTEIG (LE CHÂTELET)
Bern (☎030)

★**Viktoria** ☎51034
rm20 (🛁🚿10) 🚗 **P**20 sB🛁🚿43—50
dB🛁🚿86—94 M9—32 mountains
Credit cards [1] [3] [5]

GUMLIGEN See **BERN**

GUNTEN
Bern (☎033)

★★★**Hirschen am See** (Amb) ☎512244
tx922100
3 May—26 Oct
🛁🚿68 🚗 **P**40 Lift sB🛁🚿50—100
dB🛁🚿100—180 M25—65 lake mountains
Credit cards [1] [2] [3] [5]

★**Bellevue** ☎511121
Mar—Oct
rm22 (🚿7) **P**40 sB50—62 sB🚿70—77
dB104—128 dB🚿130—154 M18—30 lake
mountains
Credit card [1]

GURTNELLEN
Uri (☎044)

★**Gotthard** ☎65110
rm12 (🛁🚿8) 🚗 **P**20 sB28—38
sB🛁🚿38—48 dB66—76 dB🛁🚿81—96
M15—30 mountains
Credit cards [1] [2] [3] [5]

GWATT
Bern (☎033)

★***Lamm*** ☎362233
rm16 **P** mountains

HANDEGG
Bern (☎036)

★★**Handeck** ☎731131 tx923257
May—Oct
rm40 (🛁🚿20) **P**100 sB43—47
sB🛁🚿48—52 dB44—48 dB🛁🚿49—53
M14—18
Credit cards [1] [2] [3] [5]

HERGISWIL
Nidwalden (☎041)

★★★**Belvédère** (Amb) ☎951185
tx78444
🛁🚿53 **P**50 Lift ☾ sB🛁🚿70—86
dB🛁🚿96—144 M25—40 lake
Credit cards [1] [2] [3] [4] [5]

★★★***Piltaus*** ☎951555 tx72527
🛁60 🚗 **P**50 Lift ☾ 🏊 ▤ Beach
mountains lake

HERTENSTEIN
Luzern (☎041)

★★★***Hertenstein*** ☎931444 tx72284
Mar—Nov
rm70 (🛁57) Lift ☾ 🏊 lake

HORW
Luzern (☎041)

★★***Waldhaus*** (Relais et Châteaux)
☎471754
🛁🚿17 A12rm **P** 🏊 lake mountains

HÜNIBACH See **THUN**

ILANZ
Graubünden (☎086)

★**Casutt** ☎21131
rm16 (🚿10) **P**25 sB37—42 sB🚿42—47
dB74—84 dB🚿84—94 M10—20 mountains

🚙 **Spescha** via S-Clan Suta ☎21424 **P** Cit
For

IMMENSEE AM ZUGERSEE
Schwyz (☎041)

★★**Rigi-Royal** ☎813131
rm48 (🛁🚿39) A12rm 🚗 **P**50 sB30—35
sB🛁🚿60—65 dB60—70
dB🛁🚿120—130 M10—35 lake mountains
Credit cards [2] [3] [5]

INTERLAKEN
Bern (☎036)

★★★★**Beau Rivage** (Amb) Höheweg
211 ☎216272 tx923122
Dec—Oct
🛁🚿100 🚗 **P**80 Lift ☾ sB🛁🚿100—180
dB🛁🚿154—276 ▤ mountains
Credit cards [1] [2] [3] [5]

★★★★**Metropole** (Amb) Höheweg 37
☎212151 tx923191
🛁🚿100 A30rm 🚗 **P**20 Lift
sB🛁🚿90—140 dB🛁🚿140—220 ▤
lake mountains
Credit cards [1] [2] [3] [4] [5]

★★★★★*Victoria-Jungfrau* Höheweg 41 ☎212171 tx923121
Apr—Nov & Dec—Mar
220 P Lift ☾ mountains

★★★**Bellevue Garden** Marktgasse 59 ☎224431 tx923102
25 Apr—10 Oct
60 P10 Lift ☾ sB 61—93 dB 110—160 mountains
Credit cards [1] [3] [5]

★★★**Bernerhof** (Amb) Bahnhofstr 16 ☎223131 tx923138
Feb—5 Jan
30 P6 Lift sB 80—102 dB 120—172 mountains
Credit cards [1] [2] [3] [4] [5]

★★★**Carlton** Höheweg 92 ☎223821 tx923155
Apr—Oct
rm48 (33) P20 Lift sB42—60 sB 60—85 dB68—106 dB 95—143 M21—26 mountains
Credit cards [1] [2] [3] [5]

★★★**Crystal** Rugenparkstr 13 (n.rest) ☎226233 tx923362
20 Dec—31 Oct
rm38 (30) P16 Lift sB40—50 sB 55—110 dB70—80 dB 90—140 mountains
Credit cards [1] [2] [3] [5]

★★★**Eden-Nova** Bahnhofpl 45 ☎228812 tx923143
10 Dec—Oct
42 P20 Lift sB 58—74 dB 94—126 mountains
Credit cards [1] [2] [3] [5]

★★★**Goldey** Goldey 85 Unterseen ☎224445 tx923114
May—Oct
40 P20 Lift sB 66—96 dB 108—164 M20—25 lake mountains
Credit cards [1] [2] [3]

★★★**Interlaken** Höheweg 74 ☎212211 tx923120
20 Dec—Oct
61 P40 Lift sB 60—100 dB 100—180 M25 mountains
Credit cards [1] [2] [3] [4] [5]

★★★**Krebs** Bahnhofstr 4 ☎227161 tx923150
May—15 Oct
51 P15 Lift ☾ sB 85—100 dB 140—180 M30—35 mountains
Credit cards [1] [2] [3] [5]

★★★**Lac** (Amb) Höheweg 225 ☎222922 tx923100
40 P20 Lift ☾ sB 70—90 dB 130—180 lake mountains
Credit cards [1] [2] [3] [5]

★★★**Merkur** ☎226655 tx923153
36 P10 Lift ☾ sB 58—96 dB 94—164 M18—25 mountains
Credit cards [2] [3]

★★★**Royal St-Georges** Höheweg 139 ☎227575 tx923175
15 Apr—Oct

Switzerland

rm115 (110) P60 Lift ☾ sB50—67 sB 72—103 dB86—120 dB 120—180 M20—24 mountains
Credit cards [1] [2] [3] [4] [5]

★★**Beau Site** Seestr 16 ☎228181 tx923131
15 Dec—20 Oct
rm50 (36) P25 Lift ☾ sB37—43 sB 65—95 dB70—106 dB 126—164 M20—30 mountains
Credit cards [1] [2] [3] [5]

★★**Marti** Brienzstr 38 ☎222602
20 Mar—Oct
rm30 (22) P50 sB37—42 sB 47—72 dB58—72 dB 82—112 Mfr16&alc lake mountains
Credit cards [1] [2] [3] [4] [5]

★★*National* Jungfraustr 46 ☎223621 tx923187
45 P Lift ☾ mountains
Credit cards [1] [2] [3] [4] [5]

★★**Nord** Höheweg 70 ☎222631 tx923101
15 Dec—Oct
rm52 (41) P50 Lift sB38—60 sB 55—85 dB62—106 dB 88—143 mountains
Credit cards [1] [2] [3] [4] [5]

★★**Oberland** Postgasse 1 ☎229431 tx923136
58 P12 Lift sB 62—94 dB 102—161 M20 mountains
Credit cards [1] [2] [3] [5]

★★**Splendid** Höheweg 33 ☎227612 tx923189
24 Dec—30 Oct
rm35 (32) P15 Lift sB 56—76 dB70—84 dB 100—124 mountains
Credit cards [1] [2] [3] [4]

★★*Strand Hotel Neuhaus* Seestr 121 ☎228282 tx923196
Apr—Oct & Dec—Mar
57 P mountains lake

★★*Weisses Kreuz* Höheweg ☎225951 tx923166
rm100 (40) P6 Lift ☾
Credit cards [1] [2] [3] [4] [5]

★**Harder-Minerva** Harderstr 15 ☎222361 tx923361
rm26 (21) P Lift sB34—52 sB 46—78 dB55—96 dB 77—123 M10—25 mountains
Credit cards [1] [2] [3] [5]

Bohren & Urfer Rugenparkstr 34 ☎223231 **P** Cit

Hilbergarage Harderstr 25 ☎223651 Mer Vau

National Centralstr 34 ☎222143 **P**

Waldegg Waldeggstr 34a ☎221939 **P** AR

Zimmermann Seestr 109 Unterseen ☎221515 Toy Vol

JONGNY See **VEVEY**

KANDERSTEG
Bern (☎033)

★★★★★**Royal Bellvue** ☎751212 tx922192
30 May—Oct
60 P30 Lift ☾ sB 116—206 dB 192—432 M20—65 mountains

★★★*Parkhotel Gemmi* ☎751117 tx922171
12 Apr—5 Oct
rm40 (25) P70 Lift mountains
Credit cards [1] [2] [3] [5]

★★★**Schweizerhof** ☎751241 tx922118
Jun—Oct
rm50 (25) P20 Lift sB42—57 sB 47—67 dB84—94 dB 94—114 M10—13 mountains
Credit cards [1] [2] [3] [5]

★★**Adler** ☎751121 tx922169
Closed Nov
21 P18 sB 55—70 dB 90—120 M5—48 mountains
Credit cards [1] [2] [3] [4] [5]

★★**Alpenrose** ☎751170
Dec—20 Sep
rm36 (10) P15 sB39—43 dB74—80 dB 90—100 Mfr15 mountains
Credit cards [1] [3]

★*Doldenhorn* ☎751818 tx922110
Dec—Oct
28 P mountains
Credit cards [1] [2] [3] [5]

KERZERS
Fribourg (☎031)

★*Löwen* ☎955117
rm16 ( ) mountains

KLOSTERS
Graubünden (☎083)

★★★**Grand Vereina** ☎41161 tx74359
Jul—Aug & 19 Dec—21 Mar
rm100 (80) P36 Lift ☾ sB60—80 sB 90—140 dB120—150 dB 160—280 M30—40 mountains
Credit card [3]

★★★*Silvretta* ☎41353 tx74336
15 Dec—15 Apr
100 P50 Lift ☾ mountains
Credit cards [2] [3] [5]

★★*Sport Ferienzentrum* ☎42921
Dec—Apr & May—Oct
60 P30 Lift mountains

★**Waiserhof** ☎44242 tx74248
Seasonal
11 P20 Lift sB 82—162 dB 154—254 M30—92 mountains
Credit cards [1] [2] [3] [5]

KRATTIGEN BEI SPIEZ
Bern (☎033)

★★**Bellevue-Bären** ☎543929

rm18 (🛁🚿11) A8rm **P**30 Lift sB39—44 sB🛁🚿49—57 dB77—88 dB🛁🚿97—114 M10—30 lake mountains

KREUZLINGEN
Thurgau (☎072)

🔧 **Amag** Hauptstr 99 ☎722424 Aud VW

KRIENS See **LUZERN (LUCERNE)**

KÜSSNACHT AM RIGI
Schwyz (☎041)

★★**Hirschen** ☎811027

20 Jan—24 Dec
🛁🚿25 **P**15 Lift sB🛁🚿50—80 dB🛁🚿90—120 Mfr8
Credit cards [1] [2] [3] [5]

🔧 **Aebi** Hürtelstr ☎811050 Aud VW

LA Each place preceded by 'La' is listed under the name that follows it.

LAAX
Graubünden (☎086)

★★★**Sporthotel Laax** ☎20133 tx74721

Dec—mid Oct
🛁83 **P**78 Lift sB🛁65—85 dB🛁110—130 M25—45 mountains
Credit cards [1] [2] [3] [5]

LACHEN
Schwyz (☎055)

★★**Bären** ☎631602

rm16 (🛁🚿9) 🚘 **P**10 Lift sB🛁🚿47—51 dB🛁🚿92—97 M13—30 ≈
Credit cards [1] [2] [3] [5]

LANGENBRÜCK
Basel (☎062)

★**Bären** ☎601414 tx982870

🛁🚿15 A5rm 🚘 **P**100 sB🛁🚿44—63 dB🛁🚿80—95 M9—48 mountains
Credit cards [1] [2] [3] [5]

LARET See **DAVOS**

LAUSANNE
Vaud (☎021)

★★★★★**Palace** r du Grand Chêne 7—9 ☎203711 tx24171

🛁171 🚘 **P**100 Lift ☾ sB🛁176—236 dB🛁232—332 M40—50 lake mountains
Credit cards [1] [2] [3] [4] [5]

★★★★***Continental*** pl de la Gare 2 ☎201551 tx24500

🛁120 **P**20 Lift ☾
Credit cards [1] [2] [3] [4] [5]

★★★**Agora** av du Rond Point 9 ☎271211 tx25300

🛁🚿89 🚘 **P** Lift sB🛁🚿75—110 dB🛁🚿105—150 lake mountains

★★★**Alpha** r de la Petit Chêne 34 ☎230131 tx24999

🛁🚿133 🚘 **P**13 Lift ☾ sB🛁🚿75—110 dB🛁🚿105—150
Credit cards [1] [2] [3] [5]

Switzerland

★★★**Carlton** (Amb) av de Cour 4 ☎263235 tx24800

🛁50 **P**20 Lift sB🛁120—140 dB🛁130—170 M35—60 lake mountains
Credit cards [1] [2] [3] [4] [5]

★★★**City** r Caroline 5 ☎202141 tx24400

🛁🚿58 Lift sB🛁🚿60—85 dB🛁🚿100—110

★★★***Jan*** av de Beaulieu 8 ☎361161 tx24485

rm60 (🛁45) 🚘 **P** Lift ☾

★★★**Mirabeau** ☎206231 tx25030

rm65 (🛁🚿62) Lift ☾ sB🛁🚿105—110 dB140—150 dB🛁🚿160—180 Mfr30 lake
Credit cards [1] [2] [3] [5]

★★★***Paix*** av de Benjamin Constant 5 ☎207171 tx24080

🛁🚿116 🚘 **P** Lift ☾ lake
Credit cards [1] [2] [3] [5]

★★★**Victoria** av de la Gare 46 ☎205771 tx26644

rm65 (🛁🚿54) 🚘 **P**10 Lift ☾ sB50—70 sB🛁🚿95—110 dB80—85 dB🛁🚿150—180
Credit cards [1] [2] [3] [4] [5]

At **BUSSIGNY** (7km NW)

★★★***Novotel*** r des Condémines ☎892871 tx459531

🛁100 **P**120 Lift 🎾 ≈ mountains lake
Credit cards [1] [2] [3] [4] [5]

At **CULLY** (8.5km SE)

★★**Intereurop** ☎992091 tx25973

Mar—Dec
🛁61 **P**50 Lift ☾ sB🛁70—100 dB🛁100—135 mountains lake
Credit cards [1] [2] [3] [5]

At **OUCHY**

★★★★★**Beau-Rivage** chemin-de-Beau-Rivage ☎263831 tx24341

🛁204 🚘 **P**60 Lift ☾ sB🛁160—220 dB🛁200—400 M40—50 🎾 ≈ 📺 mountains lake
Credit cards [1] [2] [3] [4] [5]

★★★★**Royal Savoy** av d'Ouchy 40 ☎264201 tx24640

🛁🚿112 🚘 **P**60 Lift ☾ sB🛁🚿120—160 dB🛁🚿200—250 M24—34 ≈ mountains lake
Credit cards [1] [2] [3] [4] [5]

★★★***Aulac*** pl de la Navigation 4 ☎271451 tx25823

🛁🚿69 **P** Lift lake

★★**Angleterre** pl du Port 9 ☎264145

rm35 (🛁🚿19) **P**30 ☾ sB50—65 sB🛁🚿75—90 dB75—95 dB🛁🚿100—140 mountains lake
Credit cards [1] [2] [3] [5]

★***France*** r de Mauborget 1 (n.rest) ☎233131

rm49 **P** Lift ☾

🔧 **City** rte de Genève 60 ☎242600 AR

🔧 **Edelweiss** av de Morges 139 ☎253131 Vau

🔧 **E Frey** carrosserie chemin du Martinet 12 ☎253722

🔧 **Gare** av de la Gare 45 ☎203761 **P** AR BMW

🔧 **Jan** R. Maupas 18 ☎361921 M/c **P** AR Fia Toy

🔧 **Occidental** av de Morges 7 ☎258225

🔧 **Tivoli** av Tivoli 3 ☎203071 AR BMW DJ

At **PULLY** (2km SE)

★★★***Montillier*** av de Lavaux 35 ☎287585 tx25747

rm45 (🛁🚿30) 🚘 **P** Lift ☾ mountains lake

At **RENENS** (5km NW)

🔧 **Étolle** rte de Cossonay 101 ☎351531 Fia Lan Mer

At **ST-SULPICE** (7km SW)

★**Pierrettes** ☎254215

🚿21 **P**40 sB🚿60—75 dB🚿75—85 M12—15 ≈ mountains lake
Credit cards [1] [2] [3] [5]

LAUTERBRUNNEN
Bern (☎036)

★★***Jungfrau*** ☎553434 tx923215

rm20 (🛁15) 🚘 **P**12 📺 mountains
Credit cards [1] [2] [3] [5]

★★**Silberhorn** ☎551471

🛁🚿28 A4rm sB🛁🚿60—70 dB🛁🚿100—140 mountains
Credit cards [1] [2] [3] [5]

★★**Staubbach** ☎551381 tx923255

20 Dec—20 Oct
🛁🚿30 🚘 **P**22 Lift sB🛁🚿60—80 dB🛁🚿120—140 M35—40 mountains

★**Oberland** ☎551241 tx923285

Closed Nov
rm25 (🛁🚿22) **P**25 sB🛁🚿45—63 dB69—94 dB🛁🚿81—112 M10—30 mountains
Credit cards [1] [2] [3] [4] [5]

LE Each name preceded by 'Le' is listed under the name that follows it.

LEISSIGEN
Bern (☎036)

★★**Kreuz** ☎471231

🛁🚿30 🚘 **P**60 Lift sB🛁🚿59—63 dB🛁🚿98—106 M25—35 ≈ Beach lake mountains

LENK
Bern (☎030)

★★★**Parkhotel Bellevue** ☎31761 tx922246

15 Dec—Mar & Jun—Sep
rm58 (🛁🚿52) 🚘 **P** Lift **DPn**90—125 ≈ mountains
Credit cards [1] [2] [3] [5]

★★★**Wildstrubel** ☎31506 tx922258
25 May—5 Oct
rm51 (→ ⋒ 40) **P**20 Lift sB48—61
sB → ⋒ 65—69 dB48—61 dB → ⋒ 57—67
M24—35 ▣ mountains
Credit cards [1] [2] [3] [5]

LENZERHEIDE
Graubünden (☎081)

★★★***Palanca*** ☎343131
16 Dec—14 Apr & 2 Jun—19 Oct
rm35 (→ ⋒ 32) ⌂ **P** Lift ☾ mountains

LEYSIN
Vaud (☎025)

★★★**Central Residence** (Amb)
☎341211 tx456132
15 Dec—Apr
→ ⋒ 100 **P**80 Lift ☾ dB → ⋒ 116—166
mountains
Credit cards [1] [2] [3] [4] [5]

★**Mont-Riant** ☎341235 tx456166
Dec—Apr & Jun—Sep
rm20 (→ ⋒ 13) **P**10 Lift sB37—56
sB → ⋒ 50—70 dB68—94 dB → ⋒ 86—128
M18—25 mountains
Credit cards [1] [2] [3] [5]

LIESTAL
Basel (☎061)

★★★**Engel** (Amb) Kasernenstr 10
☎912511 tx966040
2 Jan—23 Dec
→ ⋒ 35 ⌂ **P**35 Lift ☾ sB → ⋒ 75—85
dB → ⋒ 100—125
Credit cards [1] [2] [3] [4] [5]

★★***Radackerhof*** Rheinstr 93 ☎943222
rm27 (→ ⋒ 22) ⌂ **P** Lift

⛟ **Peter Auto** Gasstr 11 ☎919140 M/c **P**
For

⛟ **Rheingarage Buser** Rheinstr 95
☎945025 **P** Cit Vol

LOCARNO
Ticino (☎093)
See also **MINÚSIO**

★★★★★**Palma au Lac** viale Verbano
29 ☎330171 tx846124
→ ⋒ 80 ⌂ **P**25 Lift ☾ sB → ⋒ 120—160
dB → ⋒ 240—320 M25—45 ▣ lake
Credit cards [1] [2] [3] [5]

★★★**Lac** pza Grande ☎312921
Closed Nov
→ ⋒ 32 Lift ☾ sB → ⋒ 58—66
dB → ⋒ 131—134 mountains lake
Credit cards [1] [2] [5]

★★★**Quisisana** via-del-Sole 17 ☎330141
tx846020
rm70 (→ ⋒ 61) **P**20 Lift ☾ sB → ⋒ 60—105
dB → ⋒ 110—200 M25—40 ▣ mountains
lake
Credit cards [1] [2] [3] [5]

★★★**Reber au Lac** via Verbano
☎330202 tx846074
rm90 (→ ⋒ 69) A19rm ⌂ **P**40 Lift ☾
sB65—100 sB → ⋒ 85—150 dB110—180
dB → ⋒ 160—270 M35—60 ⚲ ≃ lake
Credit cards [1] [2] [3] [5]

Switzerland

★★**Montaldi** pza Stazione ☎330222
Closed 1 Mar—Dec
rm58 (→ ⋒ 43) **P**15 Lift ☾ sB28—38
sB → ⋒ 42—52 dB56—76 dB → ⋒ 84—104
Credit cards [1] [2] [3] [4] [5]

⛟ **Alfa Romeo** pza 5 Vie ☎311616 Cit

Autocentro Leoni via Ciseri 19 ☎314880
Cit Fia

At **MURALTO** (1km W)

⛟ **Autostar** via Sempione 12 ☎333355 Chy

⛟ **Starnini** via Sempione 11 ☎333355 AR

LUCERNE See **LUZERN**

LUGANO
Ticino (☎091)

★★★★**Excelsior** riva-V-Vela ☎228661
tx79151
→ ⋒ 81 **P** Lift ☾ sB → ⋒ 100—120
dB → ⋒ 150—160 M35 mountains lake
Credit cards [1] [2] [3] [5]

★★★★**Splendide-Royal** riva A-Caccia 7
☎542001 tx73032
→ ⋒ 115 ⌂ **P**60 Lift ☾ sB → ⋒ 145—195
dB → ⋒ 230—360 M45—55 ▣ lake
Credit cards [1] [2] [3] [5]

★★★***Arizona*** via S. Gottardo 58
☎229343 tx79087
rm56 (→ 50) ⌂ Lift ☾ ≃ mountains lake

★★★**Bellevue au Lac** riva A-Caccia 10
☎543333 tx79440
16 Apr—20 Oct
→ ⋒ 70 **P**30 Lift ☾ sB → ⋒ 95—135
dB → ⋒ 180—210 ≃ lake
Credit cards [1] [2] [3]

★★★***Gotthard-Terminus*** via Gl-Maraini 1
☎227777 tx73761
17 Feb—13 Nov
rm40 (→ ⋒ 25) **P** Lift lake

★★★***Holiday Select*** Salita del Frati 5
☎236172 tx79131
Mar—Dec
→ 42 ⌂ **P** Lift ☾ mountains lake

★★★**International** via Nassa 68
☎227541 tx840017
22 Mar—28 Oct
rm80 (→ ⋒ 72) **P** Lift ☾ sB45—50
sB → ⋒ 80—95 dB90 dB → ⋒ 120—164
M18—24 mountains lake
Credit cards [1] [2] [3] [4] [5]

★★★**Ticino** (ROM) pza Cioccaro 1
☎227772 tx841324
Mar—Nov
→ ⋒ 23 ⌂ Lift ☾ sB → ⋒ 110—140
dB → ⋒ 160—230
Credit cards [1] [2] [3]

★★**Continental Beauregard** Basilea
28—30 ☎561112 tx79222
Mar—Nov
rm220 (→ 100) **P**30 Lift ☾ sB52—72
sB → 72—102 dB74—114 dB → 114—174
M18 mountains lake
Credit cards [1] [2] [3] [4]

★★**Everest** via Ginevra 7 (n.rest)
☎229555 tx840057
rm45 (→ 30) **P** Lift ☾ sB50—60 sB → 75
dB80—90 dB → 120—155 lake
Credit cards [1] [2] [3]

⛟ **Cencini** via Ceresio 2 ☎512826 **P** BMW
DJ

⛟ **Centro Mercedes** via Cantonale 24
☎220732 Mer

⛟ **Lugano-Sud SA** via A-Riva 6 ☎543651
Ope

At **BRÈ** (5km E)

★***Brè Paese*** ☎514761
Mar—Nov
rm16 (→ ⋒ 10) **P** mountains

At **CASSARATE**

★★★★**Villa Castagnola au Lac**
☎512213 tx841200
→ ⋒ 90 ⌂ **P** Lift ☾ sB → ⋒ 100—150
dB → ⋒ 170—255 M30—140 ⚲ ▣ lake
Credit cards [1] [2] [3]

★**Atlantico** via Concordia 12 (n.rest)
☎512921
Feb—Nov
rm18 (→ ⋒ 14) **P**8 Lift ☾ sB30—33
sB → ⋒ 38—43 dB60—66 dB → ⋒ 70—86
Credit cards [3] [5]

⛟ **M Vismara** via Concordia 2 ☎512614 For

At **CASTAGNOLA** (2km E)

★★***Carlton*** ☎513812 tx840003
Mar—Oct
rm60 (→ ⋒ 52) ⌂ **P** Lift ☾ ≃ lake
Credit cards [1] [2] [3]

At **CORNAREDO**

⛟ **R Camenisch** Pista del Ghiaccio
☎519725 M/c AR Maz

At **MELIDE** (6km S)

★★**Riviera** ☎687912
Apr—Oct
→ ⋒ 25 **P** Lift sB → ⋒ 45—55
dB → ⋒ 80—120 M10—18 ≃ lake
Credit cards [1] [3] [5]

At **PARADISO** (2km S)

★★★★**Admiral** (SRS) via Geretta 15
☎542324 tx73177
→ ⋒ 92 ⌂ **P**45 Lift ☾ sB → ⋒ 110—150
dB → ⋒ 160—240 Malc ≃ ▣
Credit cards [1] [2] [3] [4] [5]

★★★**Grand Eden** riva Paradiso 7
☎550121 tx79150
→ ⋒ 130 A55rm ⌂ **P** Lift ☾
sB → ⋒ 140—180 dB → ⋒ 230—330
M35—45 ▣ lake
Credit cards [1] [2] [3] [5]

★★★***Conca d'Oro*** riva Paradiso 7
☎543131
May—Oct
rm35 (→ 18) **P** ≃ mountains lake

★★★***Flamingo*** viale San Salvatore 10 ☎541321 (n.rest)

Feb—Oct
rm20 (12) **P** Lift mountains

★★★**Lac Seehof** ☎541921 tx79555

25 Mar—2 Jan
53 **P**50 Lift ☾ sB 85—100
dB 150—216 M25—60 lake
Credit cards [2] [5]

★★★**Meister** via San Salvatore 11 ☎541412 tx79365

7 Apr—Oct
80 **P**12 Lift ☾ sB 80—90
dB 120—180 M25—30 mountains
Credit cards [1] [2] [4] [5]

Mazzuchelli-Auto riva Paradiso 26 ☎543412 **P** Lan RR

At **VEZIA** (3km NW)

★★**Vezia** ☎563631 tx843046

Mar—Nov
rm60 (40) **P**70 sB52—57 sB 75—85
dB72—82 dB 109—129 Malc
mountains
Credit cards [1] [2] [3] [4] [5]

LUNGERN AM SEE
Obwalden (☎041)

★**Rössli** ☎691171

10 Nov—13 Oct
rm25 (18) **P**22 ☾ sB33—35
sB 43—45 dB56—60 dB 80—90
M15—36 lake mountains
Credit cards [1] [2] [3] [5]

LUZERN (LUCERNE)
Luzern (☎041)

★★★★★**Carlton-Tivoli** (Amb) Haldenstr 57 ☎513051 tx72456

Apr—Oct
100 **P**45 Lift ☾ sB 120—170
dB 220—280 M28—45
mountains lake
Credit cards [1] [2] [3] [4] [5]

★★★★★**Grand National** (SRS) Haldenstr 4 ☎501111 tx868135

80 **P**100 Lift ☾ sB 100—190
dB 150—350 M25—35 mountains lake
Credit cards [1] [2] [3] [5]

★★★★★**Palace** Haldenstr 10 ☎502222 tx865222

165 **P**20 Lift ☾ sB 120—265
dB 180—400 mountains lake
Credit cards [1] [2] [3] [5]

★★★★**Astoria** Pilatusstr 29 ☎244466 tx78220

139 Lift ☾ sB 75—110
dB 130—170 M20
Credit cards [1] [2] [5]

★★★★**Balances** (Amb) Weinmarkt 7 ☎511851 tx868148

Apr—Oct
75 **P** Lift ☾ sB 75—110
dB 135—200 lake
Credit cards [1] [2] [3] [5]

★★★★**Montana** Adligenswilerstr 22 ☎516565 tx862820

Switzerland

Apr—Oct
70 **P**15 Lift ☾ sB 92—123
dB 158—218 M30—40 mountains lake
Credit cards [1] [2] [3] [5]

★★★**Château Gütsch** (GS) Kanonenstr ☎220272 tx868699

40 **P**50 Lift ☾ sB 85—115
dB 140—206 mountains lake
Credit cards [1] [2] [3] [4] [5]

★★★**Drei Könige** Bruchstr 35/ Kloesterstr 10 ☎228833 tx72191

70 A10rm **P6** Lift sB 50—80
dB80—100 dB 90—140 M20
mountains
Credit cards [1] [2] [3] [4] [5]

★★★**Jägerhof** Baselstr 57 ☎224751

50 **P**30 Lift ☾ sB 50—65
dB 90—117 M12—45
Credit cards [2] [3]

★★★**Ilge** ☎220918 tx862876

rm40 (32) **P**20 Lift ☾ sB40—60
sB 50—90 dB65—110
dB 80—140 M15
Credit cards [1] [2] [3] [4]

★★★**Luzernerhof** Alpenstr 3 ☎514646 tx868116

rm85 (75) A22rm **P** Lift ☾ sB50—70
sB 70—100 dB95—120
dB 110—180 M22—32
Credit cards [1] [2] [3] [5]

★★★***Monopol & Métropole*** Pilatusstr 1 ☎230866 tx78192

105 **P** Lift ☾ mountain lake

★★★**Park** ☎237566 tx78553

70 Lift ☾ sB 50—82
dB 92—143 M11—25
Credit cards [1] [2] [3] [5]

★★★**Royal** Rigistr 22 ☎511233 tx862795

Apr—Oct
50 **P** Lift ☾ sB 50—80
dB 100—140 M15 mountains lake
Credit cards [1] [3] [5]

★★★***Schiller*** Sempacherstr 4 ☎235155 tx78621

70 **P** Lift ☾

★★★**Schweizerhof** Schweizerhof quai 3 ☎502211 tx868157

rm140 (100) **P**50 Lift ☾ sB70—110
sB 110—195 dB110—180
dB 185—330 mountains lake
Credit cards [1] [2] [3] [5]

★★★**Union** Löwenstr 16 ☎513651 tx868142

80 Lift ☾ sB 100—110
dB 180—200 M20—38
Credit cards [1] [2] [3]

★★★**Wilden Mann** (Amb) Bahnhofstr 30 ☎231666 tx78233

50 **P** Lift ☾ sB 85—115
dB 140—256 M17—30alc
Credit cards [1] [2] [3] [4] [5]

★★**Alpes** Rathausquai 5 ☎515825 tx868221

41 Lift sB 66—80 dB 115—138 Malc
mountains lake
Credit cards [1] [2] [3] [5]

★★**Continental** Morgartenstr 413 ☎237566 tx78553

70 **P** Lift ☾ sB 50—82
dB 92—143 M11—25
Credit cards [1] [2] [3] [5]

★★**Diana** Sempacherstr 16 ☎232623 tx868298

Mar—Oct
40 Lift ☾ sB 60—80
dB 100—140
Credit cards [1] [2] [3] [5]

★★***Eden au Lac*** Haldenstr 47 ☎513806 tx78160

rm50 (26) **P** Lift ☾ lake mountains

★★**Rothaus** Klosterstr 4 ☎224522

52 Lift ☾ sB49—65 sB 59—80
dB82—115 dB 109—146 M11—26
Credit cards [1] [2] [3] [5]

★★**Seeburg** ☎311922 tx78270

rm100 (87) A16rm **P**40 Lift ☾
sB53—58 sB 69—95 dB88—98
dB 120—164 M25—38 mountains lake
Credit cards [1] [2] [3] [5]

Epper Luzern Horwerstr 81 ☎411122 DJ Peu

Macchi Maihofstr 61 ☎363344 AR Maz Saa

Ottiger Spitalstr 8 ☎365555 Fia Mer Por

Schwerzmann Habsburgerstr 29 ☎238181 AR

Subaru Löwenstr 18 ☎502250 Lan

T Willy Obergrundstr 109 ☎402222 **P** For

At **EBIKON** (4.5km NE)

J Windin Luzernerstr 57 ☎367500 Dat Mer

At **EMMENBRÜCKE** (1km N)

★★**Landhaus** ☎531737

30 **P**40 Lift sB 68—72
dB 98—130 Malc mountains
Credit cards [2] [3] [5]

★★**St-Christoph** ☎531308

Closed Jan
rm14 (6) **P**20 sB36—46
sB 42—49 dB60—82 dB 85—100
M12—30
Credit cards [1] [2] [3]

★**Emmenbaum** Gerliswilstr 8 ☎552960

rm12 (8) **P**60 sBfr30 sB fr35
dBfr60 dB fr70 Mfr17
Credit card [2]

At **KRIENS** (5km SW)

★**Pilatusblick** Autobahn Luzern-Süd ☎413546 tx862905

37 **P**120 sB 46—69
dB 72—118 mountains
Credit cards [2] [3]

At **SEEBURG** (2km E)

★★★***Hermitage*** Seeburgstr 72 ☎313737 tx862709

rm33 (🛁🚿29) A24rm **P** Lift mountains lake

LYSS
Bern (☎032)

🚗 **Aebi** Bernstr 38–40 ☎844994 M/c **P** Cit

MALOJA
Graubünden (☎082)

★★**Maloja-Kulm** ☎43105

20 Dec–20 Oct
rm24 (🛁🚿16) 🚗 **P**74 Lift sB36–54
sB🛁🚿54–64 dB70–88 dB🛁🚿90–116
M16–30 mountains
Credit cards 1 2 3 4 5

★***Sporthotel Maloja*** ☎43126

Dec–Apr
rm18 (🛁🚿10) **P** mountains lake

MARTIGNY
Valais (☎026)

★★★***Central*** pl Centrale ☎21184 tx473841

rm30 (🛁22) **P** Lift ☾ mountains

★★★***Forclaz*** av du Léman 15 ☎22710 tx473591

rm36 (🛁22) 🚗 Lift

★★★**Porte d'Octodure** ☎27121 tx473721

🛁55 🚗 **P**100 Lift ☾ sB🛁80–105
dB🛁130–177 M5–80 🎾 mountains
Credit cards 1 2 3 5

★★★***Poste*** ☎21444

🛁🚿32 **P** Lift ☾ mountains

★★★**Rhône** (Amb) av du Grand St-Bernard ☎21717 tx473341

Dec–Oct
🛁🚿55 🚗 **P** Lift ☾ sB🛁🚿70–80
dB🛁🚿115–130 M18 mountains

★★**Kluser** ☎22641 tx473641

Feb–Dec
rm48 (🛁41) **P**10 Lift ☾ sB35–40
sB🛁50–55 dB60–75 dB🛁85–100
M12alc mountains
Credit cards 1 2 3 4 5

🚗 **Mont-Blanc** av du Grand St-Bernard ☎21181 **P** Ren

MEGGEN
Luzern (☎041)

★★**Balm** ☎371135

20 Jan–20 Dec
rm21 (🛁🚿12) **P**30 sB40–50
sB🛁🚿60–80 dB66–80
dB🛁🚿100–130 lake mountains
Credit cards 2 3 5

MEIRINGEN
Bern (☎036)

★★**Löwen** ☎711407

rm16 (🛁🚿12) **P** sB35–40 sB🛁🚿45–50
dB60–70 dB🛁🚿70–80 M15–20
mountains
Credit cards 1 2 3 5

Switzerland

★**Weisses Kreuz** ☎711216 tx923264

🛁🚿36 **P**15 Lift sB🛁🚿53–56
dB🛁🚿96–100 M16–40 mountains
Credit cards 1 3 5

🚗 **E Boss** Alpbachstrasse ☎711631 **P** For Mer

MELIDE See **LUGANO**

MERLIGEN
Bern (☎033)

★★★★***Beatus*** ☎512121 tx922147

Apr–Nov
🛁🚿78 🚗 **P**70 Lift ☾ 📺 mountains lake
Credit cards 1 2 3 4 5

★★**Mon Abri** ☎511399

rm23 (🚿20) **P** sB22 dB🚿54 mountains

🚗 **K Wittwer** Hauptstrasse ☎512222 Cit Saa

METTENDORF
Thurgau (☎054)

🚗 **W Debrunner** Hauptstr 90 ☎651119 **P** Toy

MEYRIEZ See **MÜRTEN**

MIES See **GENÉVE**

MINÚSIO
Ticino (☎093)

See also **LOCARNO**

★★★★**Esplanade** via delle Vigne ☎332121 tx846146

rm84 (🛁🚿52) 🚗 **P**40 Lift ☾ sB65–85
sB🛁🚿100–130 dB110–150
dB🛁🚿140–240 M34–44 🎾 🏊 lake
mountains
Credit cards 1 2 3 5

★★**Remorino** (n.rest) ☎331033

15 Mar–Oct
🛁🚿25 🚗 **P**25 Lift ☾ sB🛁🚿65–85
dB🛁🚿130–170 🏊 lake mountains

🚗 **Rivaplana** via R-Simen 56 ☎334056 BMW

MONTANA-VERMALA
Valais (☎027)

★★★***Mirabeau*** (Amb) ☎413912 tx473365

Dec–May & Jun–Oct
rm54 (🛁🚿46) **P** Lift ☾ mountains

★★★**St-Georges** ☎412414 tx473854

Closed May & Nov
🛁🚿45 🚗 **P**20 Lift ☾ sB🛁🚿70–130
dB🛁🚿122–224 M25–30 🏊 mountains
Credit cards 1 2 3 4 5

★★***Eldorado*** ☎411333 tx473203

15 Feb–30 Oct
rm34 (🛁25) **P**30 Lift 🎾 🏊 mountains
Credit cards 1 2 3 5

🚗 **Lac** ☎411818 **P** Alf For

MONTREUX
Vaud (☎021)

★★★★★**Eurotel Riviera** Grand Rue 81 ☎634951 tx453120

🛁🚿175 A10rm 🚗 **P**48 Lift ☾
sB🛁🚿90–140 dB🛁🚿150–190 M33
📺 mountains lake

★★★***Excelsior*** r Bon Port 21 ☎633231 tx453133

🛁80 🚗 **P**25 Lift ☾ 📺 mountains lake
Credit cards 1 2 3 5

★★★★***Palace*** (SRS) Grand Rue 100 ☎635373 tx453101

🛁230 🚗 **P** Lift ☾ 🎾 🏊 mountains lake

★★★***Eden au Lac*** (Amb) r du Théâtre 11 ☎635551 tx453151

🛁105 🚗 **P**12 Lift ☾ 🏊 mountains lake
Credit cards 1 2 3 5

★★★**Golf** r Bon Port 35 ☎634631 tx453255

🛁60 🚗 **P**16 Lift ☾ sB🛁70–99
dB🛁116–158 M26 lake mountains
Credit cards 1 2 3 4 5

★★★**Suisse & Majestic** av des Alpes 43 ☎635181 tx453126

🛁🚿150 🚗 **P**8 Lift ☾ sB🛁🚿110–160
dB🛁🚿180–230 M35 mountains lake
Credit cards 1 2 3 4 5

★★***Bon Acceuil*** Grand Rue 80 ☎630551 tx453245

🛁🚿39 🚗 Lift ☾ mountains lake

★★**Europe** av des Alpes ☎634541 tx453261

Apr–Oct
🛁🚿101 🚗 **P**3 Lift sB🛁🚿71–95
dB🛁🚿125–165 mountains lake
Credit cards 1 2 3 5

★★**Parc & Lac** Grand Rue 38 ☎633738

Mar–Nov
🛁🚿44 Lift ☾ sB🛁🚿50–65
dB🛁🚿100–130 M22–30
Credit cards 1 2 3 5

★★***Terminus*** r de la Gare ☎631071 tx453155

rm60 (🛁33) **P** Lift ☾ mountains lake

🚗 **Central** Grand Rue 106 ☎633261 Vau

🚗 **Kursaal** av du Théâtre 7 ☎633491 DJ For

At **CHERNEX** (2km NE)

★**Pension les Iris** ☎644252

Dec–Oct
rm23 (🚿5) **P**10 Lift sB35–43 sB🚿50–55
dB65–75 dB🚿85–110 M15–23
mountains lake
Credit cards 1 3

At **GLION** (3km E)

★★★***Victoria*** ☎633131 tx453102

rm55 (🛁🚿45) 🚗 **P** Lift ☾ 🎾 🏊 mountains lake

MORAT See **MURTEN**

MORCOTE
Ticino (☎091)

★***Rivabella*** ☎691314
Apr—Oct
rm15 (🛁 10) A6rm **P** mountains lake

MORGES
Vaud (☎021)

★★★**Lac** (Amb) rte de Lausanne 70, quai Igor Stravinsky ☎716371 tx458147
🛁 🚿 30 **P**50 Lift ☾ sB 🛁 🚿 90—160
dB 🛁 🚿 132—222 M35—48 mountains lake
Credit cards [1] [2] [3] [5]

MORGINS
Valais (☎025)

★***Beau-Site*** ☎771138
rm15 **P**

MÜNSTER
Valais (☎028)

🚗 **Grimsel** ☎731350 M/c **P** For

MURALTO See **LOCARNO**

MURI See **BERN**

MÜRREN
Bern (☎036)

No road connections: take funicular from **LAUTERBRUNNEN** or **STECHELBERG**

★★★**Eiger** ☎551331 tx923262
19 Dec—21 Apr & 14 Jun—21 Sep
🛁 44 Lift sB 🛁 85—130 dB 🛁 120—230
M20—30 📺 mountains
Credit cards [1] [2] [3] [5]

MURTEN (MORAT)
Fribourg (☎037)

★★**Bâteau** ☎712701
Mar—20 Nov
🛁 15 **P**50 sB 🛁 50—65 dB 🛁 100—140
M30—35 lake
Credit cards [1] [2] [3] [5]

★★**Weisses Kreuz** Rathausgasse ☎712641
Mar—16 Dec
🛁 🚿 26 ⌂ **P** Lift sB 🛁 🚿 65—80
dB 🛁 🚿 95—135 lake mountains
Credit cards [3] [5]

🚗 **P Morier** Ryffstr 66 ☎713404 **P** For

At **MEYRIEZ** (1km S)

★★★★***Vieux Manoir au Lac*** ☎711283 tx942026
Feb—Nov
rm23 (🛁 🚿 17) **P** Lift 🎾 ≈ Beach lake

MUSTAIR
Graubünden (☎082)

★★**Münsterhof** ☎85541
rm20 (🛁 🚿 12) ⌂ **P**15 sB34—38
sB 🛁 🚿 41—48 dB67—75 dB 🛁 🚿 79—95
M10—23 mountains
Credit cards [1] [3] [5]

NÄFELS
Glarus (☎058)

★★**Schwert** ☎343373
🛁 🚿 8 **P**3 Lift sB 🛁 🚿 45—55
dB 🛁 🚿 110—120 M15—40 mountains
Credit cards [1] [2] [3] [5]

🚗 **J Felber** Hauptstr ☎343440 **P** For

NEUCHÂTEL
Neuchâtel (☎038)

★★★★***Eurotel*** av de la Gare 15—17 ☎212121 tx35515
🛁 107 **P** Lift ≈

★★★**Beaulac** (Amb) quai L-Robert 2 ☎258822 tx952531
🛁 🚿 46 **P**14 Lift ☾ sB 🛁 🚿 90—125
dB 🛁 🚿 110—155 lake mountains
Credit cards [1] [2] [3] [5]

★★★**Touring** ☎255501 tx952521
rm42 (🛁 🚿 38) **P** Lift ☾ sBfr52 sB 🛁 🚿 82
dB103 dB 🛁 🚿 123 Mfr15 lake
Credit cards [1] [2] [3] [5]

★★***City*** pl Plaget 12 ☎255412
rm35 (🛁 3) Lift

🚗 **M Facchinetti** av Portes Rouges 1—3 ☎242133 Closed wknds Fia

🚗 **Trois Rois** P-A-Mazel 11 ☎258301 For Lan

At **PESEUX** (3km W)

🚗 **Waser** r de Neuchâtel 15 ☎317573 AR

NEUHAUSEN AM RHEINFALL
Schaffhausen (☎053)

★★★***Bellevue*** ☎22121
rm27 (🛁 🚿 20) **P** Lift ☾

NEIDERURNEN
Glarus (☎058)

★★**Mineralbad** Badstr 43 ☎211703
🚿 7 ⌂ **P**40 sB🚿 35—40 dB🚿 70—80
M8—50 🎾 mountains

NYON
Vaud (☎022)

★★★**Clos de Sadex** rte de Lausanne ☎612831
Closed Feb
rm18 (🛁 🚿 14) A5rm **P**50 sB55—60
sB 🛁 🚿 105—130 dB90—95
dB 🛁 🚿 150—190 Malc lake mountains
Credit cards [1] [2] [3] [5]

★★★***Nyon*** r de Rive 15 ☎611931 tx23591
Closed Nov
rm40 (🛁 🚿 25) **P** Lift mountains lake

🚗 **L Jacques** rte de Lausanne 114 ☎612902 Alf Fia Lan

Quai quai des Alpes ☎614133 Lan

OBERHOFEN
Bern (☎033)

★★★**Moy** Schneckenbühlstr 9 ☎431514
15 May—Sep
🛁 🚿 16 ⌂ **P**20 Lift sB 🛁 🚿 50—62
dB 🛁 🚿 88—124 ≈ mountains lake
Credit cards [1] [3] [5]

★★***Montana*** ☎431661
Apr—Oct
rm30 (🛁 2) ⌂ Lift

★**Kreuz** Haupstr ☎431448
Closed Feb
rm17 (🛁 🚿 14) ⌂ **P** Lift sB42—49
sB 🛁 🚿 50—57 dB74—88 dB 🛁 🚿 90—104
M10—18 mountains lake
Credit cards [1] [2] [3] [5]

OBERLIKON See **ZÜRICH**

OLTEN
Solothurn (☎062)

See also **EGERKINGEN**

★★★***Schwelzerhof*** Bahnhofquai 18 ☎214571
rm60 (🛁 10) **P** Lift 🎾

🚗 **Moser** Baslerstr 49 ☎323280 Dat

At **STARRKIRCH** (2km)

🚗 **Pilloud** Aarauerstr 235 ☎353232 For

ORSIÈRES
Valais (☎026)

★★**Catogne** ☎41230
Closed Nov
rm25 (🛁 🚿 20) **P**30 sB39—44
sB 🛁 🚿 49—54 dB67—72 dB 🛁 🚿 87—97
Malc mountains
Credit card [3]

OUCHY See **LAUSANNE**

PARADISO See **LUGANO**

PARPAN
Graubünden (☎081)

★**Alpina** Hauptstr ☎351184
15 May—15 Oct & 15 Dec—15 Apr
rm45 (🛁 🚿 35) ⌂ **P**35 Lift ☾ sB40—45
sB 🛁 🚿 50—60 dB80—90
dB 🛁 🚿 100—120 M18—24 mountains
Credit cards [1] [2] [3]

PAYERNE
Vaud (☎037)

🚗 **Promenade** pl du Gl-Guisan 1 ☎612505 **P** For

PESEUX See **NEUCHÂTEL**

PFÄFFIKON
Schwyz (☎055)

★★**Sternen** ☎481291
rm14 (🛁 🚿 12) ⌂ **P**30 sB 🛁 🚿 30—40
dB 🛁 🚿 60—70 M8—25 🎾

PONTRESINA
Graubünden (☎082)

★★★**Grand Kronenhof** ☎60111 tx74488
Jun—Dec & Sept—Mar
rm130 (🛁 🚿 100) ⌂ **P**80 Lift ☾ sB110—140
sB 🛁 🚿 140—200 dB200—260
dB 🛁 🚿 260—380 🎾 ≈ 📺 mountains
Credit cards [1] [2] [3] [4] [5]

★★★**Müller** ☎66341
19 Dec—13 Apr & 28 May—5 Oct
rm46 (🛁 🚿 36) A11rm ⌂ **P**20 Lift sB45—70
sB 🛁 🚿 65—95 dB100—130
dB 🛁 🚿 120—190 M20—24 mountains
Credit cards [2] [3] [5]

★★★**Palü** ☎66688
Jun—Oct & Dec—Apr
🛁🚿37 🏠 **P**40 sB🛁🚿66—86
dB🛁🚿114—170 M28—35 mountains
Credit cards ① ② ③ ⑤

★★★**Schweizerhof** (Amb) Berninastr ☎66412 tx74442
20 Dec—13 Apr & Jun—Oct
🛁🚿78 🏠 **P**40 Lift ☾ sB🛁🚿85—120
dB🛁🚿160—240 mountains
Credit cards ① ② ③ ⑤

PORRENTRUY
Jura (☎066)

🚗 **J Montavon** r Cuenin 21 ☎661408 **P** Ren

🚗 **Ponts** rte de Courgenay ☎661206 **P** Ope

🚗 **L Vallat** r du Jura 5 ☎661913 M/c **P** For

PORTO-RONCO
Ticino (☎093)

★***Eden*** (n.rest) ☎355142
Mar—Oct
rm14 (🛁2) **P** mountains lake

POSCHIAVO
Graubünden (☎082)

At **PRESE (LE)** (4.5km S)

★★★**Prese** ☎50333
May—Oct
rm29 (🛁🚿28) **P**40 Lift sB55—85
sB🛁🚿69—79 dB🛁🚿138—198 M22—38
🎾 🏊 lake mountains

PULLY See **LAUSANNE**

RAGAZ-PFÄFERS (BAD)
St-Gallen (☎085)

★★★**Quellenhof** ☎90111 tx855897
rm135 (🛁🚿128) 🏠 **P**100 Lift ☾
sB🛁🚿115—175 dB🛁🚿230—350
M47—75 🎾 ⊟ ⊡
Credit card ②

★★**Park** ☎92244
Apr—Nov
rm65 (🛁🚿39) A20rm 🏠 **P**45 Lift ☾
sB40—52 sB🛁🚿57—78 dB72—95
dB🛁🚿110—150 M24—32 mountains
Credit cards ① ② ③ ④ ⑤

★★***TM Schloss Ragaz*** ☎92355
20 Dec—20 Nov
rm62 (🛁🚿55) **P**100 Lift 🏊 mountains
Credit cards ① ② ③ ⑤

REGENSDORF See **ZÜRICH**

RENENS See **LAUSANNE**

RHEINFELDEN
Aargau (☎061)

★★**Schwanen** Kaiserstr 8 ☎875344
rm55 (🛁🚿36) 🏠 **P**32 Lift sB64—76
sB🛁🚿80—100 dB120—144
dB🛁🚿150—180 M25—29 ⊟
Credit cards ① ② ③ ⑤

★***Ochsen*** ☎875101
Mar—Nov
rm30 (🚿3) 🏠

🚗 **Grell** Kaiserstr 30 ☎875051 **P** For

Switzerland

ROLLE
Vaud (☎021)

★★***Tête Noir*** ☎752251
rm20 (🛁15) lake

ROMANSHORN
Thurgau (☎071)

★★**Bodan** ☎631502
🛁🚿15 **P**50 Lift sBfr38 sB🛁🚿fr50 dB65
dB🛁🚿fr80
Credit cards ① ② ③ ⑤

RORSCHACH
St-Gallen (☎071)

★★★***Anker*** Hauptstr 71 ☎414243
rm32 (🛁🚿24) **P** Lift lake mountains

🚗 **Meier** Reitbahn Str 8 ☎412222 **P** Aud VW

SAANENMOSER PASS
Bern (☎030)

★★★**Hauts de Gstaad** ☎43222 tx922220
15 Apr—Jun & 15 Oct—Dec
🛁32 🏠 **P**100 Lift ☾ sB🛁110—200
dB🛁200—370 Mfr35 🎾 ⊟ mountains
Credit cards ① ③ ⑤

SAAS-FEE
Valais (☎028)

★★**Bergfreude** ☎572137
Feb—May & Aug—Oct
rm24 (🛁🚿8) ☾ sB🛁🚿50—70
dB100—140 dB🛁🚿110—150

SACHSELN AM SARNERSEE
Obwalden (☎041)

★★★**Kreuz** ☎661466 tx866411
rm50 (🛁🚿48) A24rm **P**50 Lift ☾
sB🛁🚿69—79 dB🛁🚿103—127 M13—25
mountains
Credit cards ① ② ③ ⑤

ST-BLAISE
Neuchâtel (☎038)

★★**Cheval Blanc** Grand Rue 18 ☎333007
Feb—Dec
🛁🚿12 **P**7 sB🛁🚿40—48
dB🛁🚿80—120 M15 lake mountains
Credit cards ① ② ③ ⑤

ST-GALLEN
St-Gallen (☎071)

★★★★**Einstein** Berneggstr 2 ☎200033 tx77478
🛁🚿65 **P** Lift ☾ sB🛁🚿110—150
dB🛁🚿170—180
Credit cards ① ② ③ ④ ⑤

★★★★**Walhalla** (Amb) Poststr 27 ☎222922 tx77160
rm54 (🛁🚿50) **P** Lift ☾ sB70
sB🛁🚿95—98 dB120 dB🛁🚿160—170
Credit cards ① ② ③ ⑤

★★★**Hecht** Marktpl ☎226502 tx77173
rm58 (🛁🚿33) **P**3 Lift ☾ sB49 sB🛁🚿84
dB87 dB🛁🚿142—167
Credit cards ① ② ③ ⑤

★★★***Im Portner*** Bankgasse 12 ☎229744
🛁25 🏠 Lift

🚗 **Capitol** Rorschacherstr 239 ☎351444 Ope

🚗 **Citroën St-Gallen** Fürstenlandstr 25 ☎282121 Cit

🚗 **City** Zürcherstr 162 ☎291131 **P** Aud Por VW

🚗 **H Erb** Fürstenlandstr 149 ☎273333

Lutz Vadianstr 57 ☎232382

ST-LUC
Valais (☎027)

★★**Bella-Tola** ☎651444 tx38194
Jun—Sep & Dec—Apr
rm42 (🛁21) 🏠 **P** Lift sB37—52
sB🛁48—70 dB63—88 dB🛁82—119
M25&alc mountains
Credit cards ② ③

ST-MORITZ
Graubünden (☎082)

★★★★★**Kulm** ☎21151 tx74472
20 Dec—5 Apr & 20 Jun—10 Sep
🛁220 🏠 **P** Lift ☾ sB🛁130—340
dB🛁250—750 M40—50 🎾 ⊟ mountains
Credit cards ① ② ③

★★★★***Carlton*** (SRS) ☎21141 tx74454
Dec—Apr & Jun—Sep
🛁115 🏠 **P** Lift ☾ 🏊 mountains lake

★★★★**Crystal** ☎21165 tx74449
Closed Nov
🛁105 Lift ☾ sB🛁75—115
dB🛁140—260 M28—33
Credit cards ① ② ③ ⑤

★★★★**Suvretta House** ☎21121 tx74491
28 Jun—6 Dec & 7 Sep—29 Mar
🛁🚿230 🏠 **P**80 Lift ☾ sB🛁🚿100—345
dB🛁🚿200—690 M40—55 🎾 ⊟ lake
mountains

★★★***Bellevue*** via dal Bagn 18 ☎22161 tx74428
🛁🚿40 🏠 **P**20 Lift ☾ mountains lake
Credit cards ① ② ③ ④ ⑤

★★★**Belvédère** ☎33905 tx74435
Dec—Apr & Jun—Sep
🛁🚿75 **P**40 Lift ☾ sB🛁🚿85—135
dB🛁🚿150—260 Malc 🎾 ⊟ mountains
lake

★★★**Neues Posthotel** ☎22121 tx74430
rm83 (🛁🚿76) 🏠 **P**24 Lift ☾ sB63—98
sB🛁🚿88—118 dB61—96
dB🛁🚿86—116 M23—28 mountains lake
Credit cards ① ② ③

★★***Bären*** Hauptstr ☎33656 tx74509
Closed May
🛁🚿65 **P** Lift ⊟ mountains

★★**Margna** Bahnhofst ☎22141 tx74402
Jun—Oct & Dec—Apr
🛁🚿64 🏠 **P**50 Lift ☾ **DPn**95—165
M20—50 mountains lake
Credit cards ② ③

Dosch via Maistr 46 ☎33333 **P** Alf Mer Ope

Martin via Somplaz 37 ☎33788 Fia Lan

At **ST-MORITZ-BAD** (1km S)

★**National** ☎33274

6 Jun—Sep & 15 Dec—Apr
35 A35rm **P**20 Lift sB 47—57
dB 94—114 M10—20
Credit card 2

At **ST-MORITZ CHAMPFÈR** (3km SW)

★★★★**Europa** ☎21175 tx74458

11 Jun—29 Nov
119 **P**100 Lift sB 95—185
dB 90—185 mountains
Credit cards 1 2 3 5

ST-SULPICE See **LAUSANNE**

SAMEDAN
Graubünden (☎082)

★★★**Bernina** (Amb) Haupstr ☎65421 tx74486

15 Jun—10 Oct & 15 Dec—15 Apr
rm70 (56) **P**50 Lift sB69—117
sB 84—117 dB112—132
dB 132—158 M20—35 mountains
Credit cards 1 2 3 4 5

Gebrüder Pfister ☎65666 Toy Vol

Palü Hauptstr ☎64743 **P** AR DJ Mer For

SANTA MARIA
Graubünden (☎082)

★★**Schweizerhof** ☎85124 tx74715

15 May—31 Oct
rm30 (25) **P**40 Lift sB35—45
sB 50—80 dB70—90
dB 100—160 M15—25 mountains
Credit cards 1 2 4 5

SARGANS
St-Gallen (☎085)

★★**Post** ☎21214

rm15 (11) A11rm **P**70 sB24
sB 28—31 dB48 dB 56—62
M10—30 mountains

SARNEN
Obwalden (☎041)

At **WILEN** (2km SW)

★★***Wilerbad*** ☎661292

rm67 (28) Lift

SAVOGNIN
Graubünden (☎081)

★★***Berg*** ☎741444

20 Dec—15 Apr & 15 Jun—15 Sep
44 **P**46 mountains
Credit cards 1 2 3

SCHAFFHAUSEN
Schaffhausen (☎053)

★★**Bahnhof** Bahnhofstr 46 ☎54001 tx76800

41 **P**30 Lift sB 70—90
dB 100—130 M16—25
Credit cards 1 2 3 5

★★**Kronenhof** Kirchhofpl 7 (off Vordergasse) ☎56631 tx897068

rm33 (30) **P** Lift sB 84—91

Switzerland

dB 142—172 M15—40
Credit cards 1 2 3 4 5

★★**Parkvilla & Swiss Chalet** Parkstr 18 ☎52737

20 **P**20 Lift sB 55—90
dB 90—150
Credit cards 1 2 3 5

Auto-Ernst Schweizerbildstr 61 ☎33322 **P** BMW For

SCHÖNRIED
Bern (☎030)

★★★**Ermitage & Golf** ☎42727 tx922213

Dec—Apr & May—Oct
48 **P** Lift sB 80—180
dB 140—440 Malc
mountains

SCHWANDEN
Glarus (☎058)

★**Adler** ☎811171

29 Jan—28 Dec
11 **P**20 sB 42—49 dB 88—97
M18—26 mountains
Credit cards 1 2 3 4 5

SCUOL (BAD)
Graubünden (☎084)

★★★**Kurhotel Belvedere** ☎91041

Jun—Oct & Dec—Apr
rm63 (50) **P** Lift sB52—72
sB 67—107 dB94—134 dB 124—214
M25—50 mountains
Credit cards 1 2 3 5

SEEBURG See **LUZERN (LUCERNE)**

SERVION
Vaud (☎021)

★★***Fleurs*** ☎932054

rm31 (14) **P** mountains

SIERRE (SIDERS)
Valais (☎027)

★★***Arnold*** rte de Sion ☎551721 tx38439

rm32 (19) **P** Lift Malc

★***Victoria-Jardin*** rte de Sion 5 ☎551007

rm14 (3) **P**10 mountains
Credit cards 1 2 3 4 5

International rte de Noës ☎551436 **P** Peu Tal

Rawyl Arc Max-Huber 18 ☎550308 **P** For

SIGRISWIL
Bern (☎033)

★**Adler** ☎512424

rm28 (22) **P**30 Lift sB35—40
sB 45—55 dB70—80 dB 90—100
lake mountains
Credit cards 1 5

SILS-MARIA
Graubünden (☎082)

★★★***Waldhaus*** ☎45331 tx74444

Jun—Oct & Dec—Apr
rm150 (125) **P**40 Lift
mountains lake
Credit cards 1 3

★***Privata*** ☎45247

Dec—Apr & Jun—Oct
rm20

At **SILS-BASEGLIA**

★★★**Margna** ☎45306 tx74496

Dec—Apr & Jun—Oct
70 **P**80 Lift sB 92—132
dB 184—264 M15—50 lake
mountains

SILVAPLANA
Graubünden (☎082)

★★***Sonne*** ☎48152 tx75649 tx75649

rm50 (34) **P** Lift mountains lake

★**Corvatsch** ☎48162

15 Dec—15 Apr & 15 Jun—15 Oct
rm16 **P**20 sB38—45 dB70—84 Malc
mountains lake

SIMPLON-DORF
Valais (☎028)

★***Poste*** ☎292111

rm14 (8) **P** mountains
Credit cards 1 2 3

SIMPLON-KULM
Valais (☎028)

★★**Bellevue** Simplon Pass ☎291331

Mar—Oct
rm45 (5) **P**100 Lift sB37—55
sB 47—65 dB73—109 dB 93—119
M15—32 mountains
Credit cards 1 2 3 4 5

SION (SITTEN)
Valais (☎027)

★★★**Rhône** (Amb) r du Sex 10 ☎228291 tx38104

44 **P**400 Lift sB 68—80
dB 116—138 Malc mountains
Credit cards 1 2 3 5

★★**Continental** rte de Lausanne 116 ☎224641

24 sB 42—45 dB 68—82
M15—60 mountains
Credit cards 1 2 3 5

★★**Touring** av de la Gare 6 ☎231551

rm28 (25) **P**5 Lift sB60—80
sB 60—80 dB 98—138 M18—25
mountains
Credit cards 1 2 3

Aviation ave Mce-Troillet 84 ☎223924 Maz Vol

Hediger Batasse ☎220131 Mer

Kasper r du Tunnel 22 ☎221271 For

Nord av Ritz 35 ☎223413 Ren

Tourbillon av de Tourbillon 23 ☎222077 Maz

SISIKON
Uri (☎044)

★★★**Tellsplatte** ☎21612

45 **P**59 Lift sB40—55

sB 🛁 🚿 50—70 dB70—90 dB 🛁 🚿 80—120
≋ mountains lake
Credit cards [1] [2] [3] [5]

SOLOTHURN (SOLEURE)
Solothurn (☎065)

★★★***Krone*** (Amb) Hauptgasse 64
☎224412

rm42 (🛁 🚿 41) ⌂ **P** Lift

🚘 **Howald Otto** Engestr 13 ☎223718 Alf Ren

SPIEZ
Bern (☎033)

★★★**Eden** Seestr 58 ☎541154 tx922181

May—Oct
rm56 (🛁 🚿 47) ⌂ **P**30 Lift sB60—70
sB 🛁 🚿 65—85 dB100—120
dB 🛁 🚿 110—150 M20—30 🎾 ≋
mountains lake

★★**Alpes** Seestr 38 ☎543354 tx911513
🛁 🚿 44 ⌂ **P**18 Lift sB 🛁 🚿 53—73
dB 🛁 🚿 99—145 M20 ≋ mountains lake

★★***Terminus*** Bahnhofpl ☎543121

rm65 (🛁 30) **P** Lift lake mountains

STANS
Nidwalden (☎041)

★★***Stanserehof*** Stansstaderstr 20
☎614122

rm45 (🛁 🚿 11) Lift mountains

STANSSTAD
Nidwalden (☎041)

★★★**Freienhof** ☎613531

rm50 (🛁 🚿 35) ⌂ **P**40 Lift ☾ sB35—42
sB 🛁 🚿 42—55 dB70—84 dB 🛁 🚿 84—110
M10—30 mountains lake
Credit cards [1] [2] [3]

★★★***Schützen*** (Amb) Stanserstr 23
☎611355 tx866256

rm45 (🛁 🚿 28) ⌂ **P**60 Lift mountains
Credit cards [1] [2] [3]

STARRKIRCH See **OLTEN**

STECKBORN
Thurgau (☎054)

🚘 **Bürgi's Erben** Seestr 143 ☎611251 **P**
Dat Saa

SURSEE
Luzern (☎045)

★★***Hirschen*** Oberstadt 10 ☎211048

rm10 (🛁 🚿 7) **P**300 Lift
Credit cards [1] [2] [3] [5]

★***Bellevue*** Mariazell ☎211844

rm15 (🚿 2) A1rm **P** mountains lake

🚘 **Central** Luzernstr 16 ☎211144 For

TAFERS
Fribourg (☎037)

🚘 **Schweingruber** Mariahilfstr 283
☎441750 M/c Ope

TARASP-VULPERA See **VULPERA (TARASP)**

Switzerland

TEUFEN
Appenzell (☎071)

★***Ochsen*** ☎332188

rm13 (🛁 2) **P** mountains

THALWIL
Zürich (☎01)

★★**Thalwilerhof** Bahnhofstr 16
☎7200603

rm25 (🛁 🚿 8) **P** Lift sB48—53
sB 🛁 🚿 70—76 dB87—92
dB 🛁 🚿 100—117 M6—26 lake
Credit cards [1] [2] [3]

THIELLE
Neuchâtel (☎038)

★★★***Novotel Neuchâtel Est*** rte de Berne ☎335757 tx952799
🛁 60 **P**200 ☾ ≋ mountains
Credit cards [1] [2] [3] [5]

THUN (THOUNE)
Berne (☎033)

★★★★**Elite** Bernstr 1—3 ☎232823
tx921214
🛁 🚿 39 **P**10 Lift sB 🛁 🚿 58—98
dB 🛁 🚿 115—155 mountains lake
Credit cards [1] [2] [3] [5]

★★★**Beau Rivage** ☎222236

May—20 Oct
rm30 (🛁 🚿 23) **P**10 Lift sB35—50
sB 🛁 🚿 55—85 dB60—85 dB 🛁 🚿 90—135
≋ mountains lake
Credit cards [1] [2] [3] [5]

★★★**Frelenhof** (Amb) Freienhofgasse 3
☎215511 tx921190
🛁 🚿 63 ⌂ **P**40 Lift ☾ sB 🛁 🚿 60—80
dB 🛁 🚿 110—140 M18—20 lake
Credit cards [1] [2] [3] [5]

★**Metzgern** Rathauspl ☎222141
Closed Oct
rm8 **P**3 sB36 dB72 mountains

🚘 **City** Kyburgstr ☎229578 Cit Maz

🚘 **Moser** Gwattstr 24 ☎341515 Aud Por VW Vol

🚘 **Touring** Industriestr 5 ☎224455

🚘 **Touring** Schlossmattstr 10 ☎224455 Mer

At **DÜRRENAST** (2km S)

★★★**Holiday** Gwattstr 1 ☎365757
tx921357
🛁 🚿 57 **P**50 Lift ☾ sB 🛁 🚿 50—90
dB 🛁 🚿 100—140 M10—30&alc lake
mountains
Credit cards [1] [2] [3] [4] [5]

At **HÜNIBACH** (1km SE)

🚘 **K Schick** Staatsstr 134 ☎433131 BMW Ren

THUSIS
Graubünden (☎081)

Central ☎811154 **P** For

🚘 **Viamala** Hauptstr ☎811822 **P** For Ope Vau

TIEFENCASTEL
Graubünden (☎081)

★★***Posthotel Julier*** Julierstr ☎771415
rm50 (🛁 🚿 39) ⌂ **P** Lift mountains

★**Albula** ☎711121
🛁 🚿 30 ⌂ **P**20 Lift sB 🛁 🚿 40—46
dB 🛁 🚿 75—85 M12—25 mountains
Credit cards [1] [2] [3] [5]

TRAVERS
Neuchâtel (☎038)

★**Crêt** ☎631178

Closed Feb
🚿 6 sB🚿 47 dB🚿 fr94 Mfr20 🎾 mountains
Credit card [2]

UNTERÄGERI
Zug (☎042)

★★★**Seefeld** Seestr 8 ☎722727
tx864981
rm37 (🛁 34) **P** Lift sBfr48 sB 🛁 78—83
dBfr95 dB 🛁 135—145 M26—45 mountains
lake
Credit cards [2] [3] [5]

UNTERWASSER
St-Gallen (☎074)

★★★**Sternen** ☎52424 tx884148
15 Dec—Mar & May—Oct
🛁 🚿 57 **P**150 Lift sB 🛁 🚿 65—90
dB 🛁 🚿 110—150 ≋ mountains
Credit cards [1] [2] [3] [5]

VALLORBE
Vaud (☎021)

★**Jurats** ☎831991
🚿 16 **P**20 sB🚿 40 dB🚿 64 mountains
Credit cards [1] [3] [5]

🚘 **Moderne** r de l'Ancien Poste 61
☎831156 **P** Aud VW

VERBIER
Valais (☎026)

★★★**Farinet** ☎76626 tx473392
Closed May—Oct
rm18 (🛁 🚿 16) **P** Lift sB50—70
sB 🛁 🚿 80—100 dB 🛁 🚿 130—170
mountains
Credit cards [1] [2] [3] [5]

★★★***Grand Combin*** ☎75515 tx38795
Jun—Sep & Dec—Apr
rm35 (🛁 🚿 30) **P** Lift ☾

★★★**Rhodania** (Amb) ☎70121 tx473392
20 Dec—Apr & 10 Jun—15 Sep
🛁 🚿 43 **P**12 Lift sB 🛁 🚿 85—123
dB 🛁 🚿 130—206 mountains
Credit cards [1] [2] [3] [4] [5]

🚘 **Verbier** ☎76666

VÉSENAZ See **GENÈVE**

VEVEY
Vaud (☎021)

★★★★**Trois Couronnes** r d'Italie 49
☎513005 tx451148
🛁 90 **P** Lift ☾ sB 🛁 132—192 →

dB🛁 234—334 M50—55 ≃ mountains lake
Credit cards [1] [2] [3] [4] [5]

★★★**Lac** (Amb) r d'Italie 1 ☎511041 tx451161
rm59 (🛁 53) 🚗 P15 Lift ☾ sB50—60 sB🛁 95—145 dB80—120 dB🛁 145—220 M35—40 ≃ mountains lake
Credit cards [1] [2] [3] [5]

★★**Familie** ☎513931 tx451181
rm62 (🛁🚿 42) **P**15 Lift sB43—50 sB🛁🚿 48—61 dB80—88 dB🛁🚿 86—110 M12—18 ▭ mountains
Credit cards [1] [2] [3]

At **JONGNY** (3km N)

★★★**Léman** ☎510544 tx451198
rm60 (🛁🚿 55) A29rm 🚗 **P**60 Lift ☾ sBfr76 sB🛁🚿 78—96 dBfr136 dB🛁🚿 161—231 M22—26 mountains lake
Credit cards [1] [2] [3] [5]

VEZIA See **LUGANO**

VILLARS-SUR-OLLON
Vaud (☎025)

★★★★**Eurotel** ☎353131 tx456206
15 Dec—15 Oct
🛁🚿 170 🚗 **P**50 Lift ☾ sB🛁🚿 86—128 dB🛁🚿 134—268 M20—27 🎾 ▭ mountains
Credit cards [1] [2] [3] [4] [5]

★★**Montesano & Regina** ☎352551 tx456217
15 Dec—20 Apr & Jun—Sep
rm50 (🛁🚿 29) 🚗 **P**20 Lift sB32—37 sB🛁🚿 42—47 dB54—64 dB🛁🚿 84—94 M20—22 🎾 mountains
Credit cards [2] [5]

VILLMERGEN
Schwyz (☎057)

🔧 **R Huber** Dorfmattenstr 2 ☎221379 **P** Aud Mer VW

VISP
Valais (☎028)

🔧 **Moderne** ☎464333 **P** Fia Mer

🔧 **Touring** Kantonstr ☎461040 **P** Aud Por VW

VITZNAU
Luzern (☎041)

★★★***Kreuz*** ☎831305 tx72524
Apr—Dec
rm52 (🛁 33) **P**40 Lift ≃ mountains lake
Credit cards [1] [2] [3] [5]

★★★**Park** ☎831322 tx862482
mid Apr—mid Oct
🛁🚿 110 🚗 **P**70 Lift ☾ sB🛁🚿 190—235 dB🛁🚿 390—430 🎾 ≃ ▭ lake

★★★***Vitznauerhof*** (Relais et Châteaux) ☎831315 tx72241
10 Apr—10 Oct
rm60 (🛁🚿 54) 🚗 **P** Lift ☾ 🎾 mountains lake

★★***Terasse am See*** ☎831033 tx72501
Etr—15 Oct
rm30 (🛁 22) **P**8 Lift mountains lake
Credit card [3]

Switzerland

VULPERA (TARASP)
Graubünden (☎084)

★★★***Schweizerhof*** ☎91331 tx74427
Jun—Sep & Dec—Apr
rm116 (🛁 101) 🚗 **P**100 Lift ☾ 🎾 ▭ ≃ ⛳ mountains
Credit cards [1] [2] [3] [5]

WABERN See **BERN (BERNE)**

WÄDENSWIL
Zürich (☎01)

★★★**Lac** Seestr 100 ☎7800031
rm24 (🛁🚿 14) **P** Lift sB40—50 sB🛁🚿 65—75 dB70—85 dB🛁🚿 95—110 lake
Credit cards [1] [2] [3] [5]

🔧 **Zentrum** Seestr 114 ☎7808080

WASSEN
Uri (☎044)

★***Alpes*** ☎65233
rm12 (🛁🚿 6) 🚗 **P** Lift mountains
Credit card [2]

Gottardgarage ☎65663 **P** BMW For

WEGGIS
Luzern (☎041)

★★★**Albana** (Relais et Châteaux) ☎932141 tx78637
26 Mar—12 Oct
🛁 70 🚗 **P**50 Lift sB🛁 80—110 dB🛁 140—200 M25—35 🎾 ▭ mountains lake
Credit cards [1] [2] [3] [5]

★★★***Alexander*** ☎932222 tx72204
🛁 55 🚗 **P**30 Lift ☾ ≃ ▭ Beach sea mountains lake
Credit cards [1] [2] [3]

★★**Beau Rivage** Gottardstr ☎931422 tx862982
Apr—15 Apr
🛁🚿 46 🚗 **P**20 Lift ☾ sB🛁🚿 70—100 dB🛁🚿 130—180 M35—40 ≃ lake mountains
Credit cards [1] [2] [3] [5]

★★★***Park*** ☎931313
Apr—Oct
rm64 (🛁🚿 50) Lift ☾ 🎾 lake mountains

★★★**Waldstätten** ☎931341 tx72428
16 Feb—Jan
🛁🚿 42 🚗 **P**40 Lift sB🛁🚿 64—88 dB🛁🚿 120—167 M22—25 lake mountains
Credit cards [1] [2] [3] [4] [5]

★★**Central am See** ☎931252
1 Mar—1 Dec
rm50 (🛁🚿 40) 🚗 **P**50 Lift sB35—50 sB🛁🚿 45—75 dB70—116 dB🛁🚿 90—140 M20—25 ≃ mountains lake
Credit cards [1] [2] [3] [4] [5]

★★**Rigi** Seestr ☎932151 tx78395
May—6 Oct
rm55 (🛁🚿 27) A35rm **P**30 sB45—62sB🛁🚿 52—78 dB81—114 dB🛁🚿 96—149 M20—30 ≃ mountains lake
Credit card [1]

★★**Rössil** Seestr ☎931106 tx862931
15 Mar—15 Oct
🛁🚿 50 🚗 **P**20 Lift sB🛁🚿 50—60 dB🛁🚿 84—115 M8—30 mountains lake
Credit card [2]

★★**Seehotel du Lac** ☎931151 tx78395
Mar—Nov
rm28 (🛁🚿 21) **P**14 Lift sB38—60 sB🛁🚿 47-75 dB70—100 dB🛁🚿 82—120 M10—30 mountains lake
Credit cards [1] [2] [3] [5]

★***Frohburg*** (n.rest) ☎931022
Apr—15 Oct
🛁🚿 20 **P**30 ≃ mountains lake
Credit cards [1] [2] [3] [5]

★***National*** Seestr ☎931225 tx78292
Apr—15 Oct
rm38 (🛁🚿 36) 🚗 **P** Lift mountains lake

WENGEN
Bern (☎036)

★★★***Victoria-Lauberhorn*** ☎565151 tx923232
Dec—Apr & Jun—Sep
rm120 **P** Lift mountains

★★★**Waldrand** ☎552855 tx923240
Jun—Sep & 15 Dec—10 Apr
rm50 (🛁🚿 47) Lift sB50—100 sB🛁🚿 65—130 dB🛁🚿 120—240 M18—22 mountains
Credit cards [1] [3] [5]

WIL
St-Gallen (☎073)

🔧 **Bahnhof** Untere Bahnhofstr 9 ☎221112 AR Ren

WILDERSWIL
Bern (☎036)

★★**Bären** ☎223521 tx923137
Dec—Nov
🛁🚿 45 A9rm 🚗 **P**25 sB🛁🚿 45—70 dB🛁🚿 76—120 mountains
Credit cards [1] [2] [3] [5]

★★**Luna** ☎228414
rm30 (🛁🚿 17) **P**20 sB33—43 sB🛁🚿 fr43 dB65—75 dB🛁🚿 69—91 Mfr10 mountains
Credit cards [1] [2] [3]

★**Alpenrose** ☎221024
Dec—Oct
rm35 (🛁🚿 13) **P**20 sB42—54 sB🛁🚿 52—66 dB79—101 dB🛁🚿 95—121 M14—24 mountains

★**Viktoria** ☎221670
rm14 (🚿 5) **P**8 sB19—24 sB🚿 25—30 dB38—44 dB🚿 50—56 M10—14 mountains
Credit cards [1] [3]

WILDHAUS
St-Gallen (☎074)

★★★***Acker*** (Amb) ☎59111 tx71208

100 A50rm P ☾ Lift mountains

★★**Hirschen** ☎52252 tx884139

70 P50 Lift sB 48—68
dB 95—135 M20—24 mountains
Credit cards 1 2 3 5

WILEN See **SARNEN**

WINTERTHUR
Zürich (☎052)

★★★★**Garten** (Amb) Stadthausstr 4
☎847171 tx896201

54 P30 Lift ☾ sB 100—110
dB 152—172 M30—50
Credit cards 1 2 3 5

★★★**Krone** Marktgasse 49 ☎232521

rm39 (35) P9 Lift ☾ sBfr50
sB 55—75 dB 95—98
Credit cards 1 2 3 4

Eulach Technikumstr 67 ☎222333 Ope

Riedbach Fraumenfeldstr 9 ☎272222 **P** AR BMW Ren

A Siegenthaler Frauenfeldstr 44
☎272900

YVERDON
Vaud (☎024)

★★***Prairie*** av des Bains 9 ☎231330
tx457136

rm36 (25) **P** Lift mountains

Belair av des Sports 13 ☎213381 For

Remparts Champs Loyats 1 ☎213535
Peu Tal

ZERMATT
Valais (☎028)

No road connection; take train from **TÄSCH** or **VISP**

★★★★**Mont Cervin Seiler** Bahnhofstr
☎661121 tx472129

1 Jan—15 Oct
rm141 (130) Lift ☾ sB70—145
sB 120—220 dB 110—325
mountains
Credit cards 1 2 3 5

★★★***Julen*** (ROM) ☎672481 tx472111

34 **P** Lift mountains

★★★**Parkhotel Beau Site** ☎671271
tx472116

Dec—28 Apr & 28 May—5 Oct
75 Lift sB 65—145
dB 120—280 M20—45
mountains
Credit cards 1 2 3 4 5

★★★***Schweizerhof*** ☎661155 tx38201

Jun—Oct & Dec—Apr
104 Lift ☾ mountains

★★★***Zermatterhof*** ☎661101 tx38275

26 Nov—6 Oct
rm95 (80) Lift ☾ mountains

★★***Dom*** ☎671371

Dec—Apr & Jun—Oct
rm40 (35) **P** Lift mountains

Switzerland

ZERNEZ
Graubünden (☎082)

★★***Baer & Post*** Curtinstr ☎81141

Dec—Oct
19 A12rm

ZUG
Zug (☎042)

★★★**City Ochsen** Kolinpl ☎213232
tx865249

50 **P**10 Lift sB 90—110
dB 160—190 M28
Credit cards 1 2 3

★★***Guggital*** Zugerbergstr ☎212821
tx865134

rm33 (32) **P**50 Lift lake mountains
Credit cards 1 2 3

★**Rössli** Vorstadstr 8 ☎210394

15 Jan—20 Dec
rm18 (10) **P** Lift mountains lake

Kaiser Baarestr 50 ☎212424 Fia Lan Mer

C Keizer Grabenstr 18 ☎218148 **P** Ren

ZUOZ
Graubünden (☎082)

★★★***Engladina*** Haupstr ☎71021

Jun—Oct & Dec—Apr
rm40 (35) **P** Lift mountains

ZÜRICH
Zürich (☎01)

★★★★★**Baur au Lac** Taistr 1
☎2211650 tx813567

150 **P**150 Lift ☾ sB 212—262
dB 364—404 M51—55 mountains lake
Credit card 2

★★★★★***Dolder*** (Amb) Kurhaus Str 65
☎2516231 tx816416

190 **P** Lift ☾ lake
Credit cards 1 2

★★★★★**Eden au Lac** Utoquai 45
☎479404 tx816339

54 **P**10 Lift ☾ sB 160—200
dB 280—360 M alc mountains lake
Credit cards 1 2 3 5

★★★★★**Savoy Baur en Ville** Poststr 12
☎2115360 tx812845

112 **P**30 Lift ☾ sB 280
dB 420
Credit cards 1 3

★★★★***Ascot*** Lavaterstr 15 ☎2011800
tx52783

60 **P** Lift ☾ M alc

★★★★**Bellerive au Lac** Utoquai 47
☎2517010 tx816398

57 **P**2 Lift ☾ sB 120—150
dB 180—220 lake
Credit cards 1 2 3

★★★★***Carlton Elite*** Bahnhofstr 41
☎2116560 tx812781

72 **P**8 Lift ☾ M alc
Credit cards 1 2 3 5

★★★★**Engematthof** Engimattstr 14
2012504 tx56327

79 **P**12 Lift ☾ sB 99—134
dB 133—188 M20—30
Credit cards 2 5

★★★★**Zum Storchen** Weinpl 2
☎2115510 tx813354

77 **P**2 Lift ☾ sB 150—200
dB 210—320 M alc lake
Credit cards 1 2 3 5

★★★**Central** Central 1 ☎2515555
tx54909

99 **P**30 Lift ☾ sB 180—200
dB 250—300 M alc
Credit cards 1 2 3 5

★★★**Excelsior** (GT) Dufourstr ☎2522500
tx59295

50 **P** Lift ☾ sB 140 dB 220
Mfr21
Credit cards 1 2 3 5

★★★**Glockenhof** (Amb) Sihlstr 31
☎2115650 tx412466

106 Lift ☾ sB 110—116
dB 148—176 M11—30
Credit cards 1 2 3 4 5

★★***Burma*** Schindlerstr 26 ☎3611008

rm32 (8) **P** Lift ☾

★★**Krone** Limmatquai 88 ☎2514222

rm23 (4) Lift sB46—50 dB74—80
dB 85—95
Credit cards 1 2 3 5

AMAG Auto & Motoren Uberlandstr 166
☎412222

Canonica Albisriederstr 401 ☎4919824
P AR Hon

E Frey Badenerstr 600 ☎4952411 **P** AR DJ

J H Keller Vulkanstr 120 ☎4322410 Hon

Riedbach Dufourstr 182 ☎552211 **P** Ope

At **ADLISWIL** (4km SE on N4)

★★★**Jolie Ville Motor Inn** (Mövenpick)
Zürichstr 105 ☎7108585 tx52507

70 **P**50 ☾ sB 78—100
dB 107—129
Credit cards 1 2 3 5

At **OERLIKON** (4km N)

★★**Sternen Oerlikon** Schaffhauserstr 335
☎3117777 tx823265

rm55 (37) Lift ☾ sB50—55
sB 70—75 dB90—100
dB 110—120 M20—38
Credit cards 1 2 3 5

At **REGENSDORF** (8km NW)

★★★★**Mövenpick Hotel Holiday Inn**
Watterstr, Zentrum ☎8402520

149 **P**50 Lift sB 123—135
dB 143—155 M alc
Credit cards 1 2 3 5

ZÜRICH AIRPORT

At GLATTBRUGG (8km NE on N4)

★★★★★**Hilton International** Hohenbuhlstr 10 ☎8103131 tx825428

⇌287 ⌂ **P**250 Lift ☾ sB⇌167—187 dB⇌214—234 Mfr22 ▭
Credit cards 1 2 3 4 5

★★★★**Airport** Oberhauserstr 30 ☎8104444 tx825416

⇌ ⋔50 ⌂ **P**100 Lift ☾ sB⇌ ⋔120 dB⇌ ⋔150—160
Credit cards 1 2 3 5

★★★★**Mövenpick** W-Mittelholzerstr 8 ☎8101111 tx57979

⇌333 **P**300 Lift ☾ sB⇌156—191 dB⇌187—222 M25—40 ▭
Credit cards 1 2 3 5

ZWEISIMMEN
Bern (☎300)

★★***Krone*** Lenkstr ☎22626

Closed Nov
rm40 (⇌ ⋔36) ⌂ Lift

★***Sport*** Saanenstr ☎21431

⋔20 **P**60 mountains
Credit cards 1 3

Liechtenstein

Liechtenstein

Prices are in Swiss Francs

SCHAAN
(☎075)

★★**Linde** Feldkircherstr 1 ☎21704

⇌ ⋔23 **P**40 sB⇌ ⋔40—48 dB⇌ ⋔68—78 Mfr10—25

⛟ **Fanal** Feldkircherstr 52 ☎24604

TRIESENBERG
(☎075)

★***Masescha*** Masescha ☎22337

7rm (⇌ ⋔2) ⌂ **P**10 Lift mountains

VADUZ
(☎075)

★★★**Park Sonnenhof** (Amb/Relais et Châteaux) Mareestr 29 ☎21192 tx78881

25 Feb—10 Jan
⇌29 ⌂ **P**30 Lift sB⇌100—160 dB⇌170—270 M14—80 ▭ mountains
Credit cards 1 2 3 4 5

★★**Real** ☎22222 tx77809

⇌ ⋔11 **P**5 sB⇌ ⋔110—130 dB⇌ ⋔120—160 M alc mountains
Credit cards 1 2 3 5

★**Engel** ☎21057

rm21 (⇌ ⋔19) **P**20 Lift ☾ sB⇌ ⋔55—75 dB⇌ ⋔75—90 M alc mountains
Credit cards 1 2 3 5

★***Löwen*** Herrengasse ☎21408

11 Dec—9 Nov
rm11 (⇌1) **P** ☾ mountains

⛟ **Muhleholzgarage** Landstr 126 ☎21668
P Alf Ren

The Emmental in the Bernese Mittelland

Yugoslavia

International distinguishing sign

Area *98,766 sq miles*
Population *22,800,000*
Local time *GMT + 1 (Summer GMT + 2)*

National flag *Horizontal tricolour of blue, white and red, with a red 5-pointed star in the centre*

How to get there

Yugoslavia is usually approached via Belgium, West Germany (Köln/Cologne and München/Munich) and Austria (Salzburg), or alternatively via France or Switzerland and Italy (Milan and Trieste). The distance from Calais via Germany to Beograd (Belgrade), the capital, is just over 1,200 miles, a distance which will normally require three of four overnight stops. Car sleeper services operate during the summer from Brussels and 's-Hertogenbosch to Ljubljana; and from Boulogne, Brussels and Paris to Milan.

Motoring regulations and general information

This information should be read in conjunction with the general content of the European ABC (pages 4-26). **Note** As certain regulations and requirements are common to many countries they are covered by one entry in the ABC and the following headings represent some of the subjects dealt with in this way:
AA Agents
Crash or safety helmets
Customs regulations for European countries
Drinking and driving
Fire extinguisher
Insurance
International distinguishing sign
Medical treatment
Mirrors
Overtaking
Police fines
Radio telephones/Radio transmitters
Seat belts
Traffic lights
Tyres
Visitors' registration

Accidents

Fire ☏ 93 **Police** ☏ 92 and **ambulance** ☏ 94 in main towns, but elsewhere the number will be found in the front of the local telephone directory. It is obligatory for the driver of a passing vehicle to assist persons injured in a traffic accident. The driver of a vehicle involved in an accident should inform the traffic police (*Saobracajna Milicija*) immediately and wait for an on-the-spot investigation and the completion of a written report on the accident and damage. See also *Accidents* page 5.

Any damage to a vehicle entering Yugoslavia must be certified at the time of entry at the frontier. When leaving the country, certificates must be produced to cover any visible damage, otherwise the vehicle and driver will be detained until the circumstances of the damage have been ascertained.

Accommodation

Many good hotels will be found in the tourist centres and main towns; the majority of those on the coast are relatively new. There is also a good coverage of motels along the country's main roads. The Yugoslav National Tourist Office issues a comprehensive hotel guide.

The summer tourist season generally lasts from mid June to mid September and the winter sports season from December to March, with local differences and variations in prices. Rates normally include a service charge but a tourist tax is payable per person per day which varies according to locality and period of stay. Special reductions are allowed for children under 7 years. Accommodation in private homes is available in every resort and may be booked locally at tourist offices (*Turisticki Biro*).

Boats

Boat registration documentation is recommended in respect of boats temporarily imported into Yugoslavia. See page 6 for further information.

Breakdown

The Yugoslav motoring club Auto-Moto Savez Jugoslavije (AMSJ) operates a breakdown and

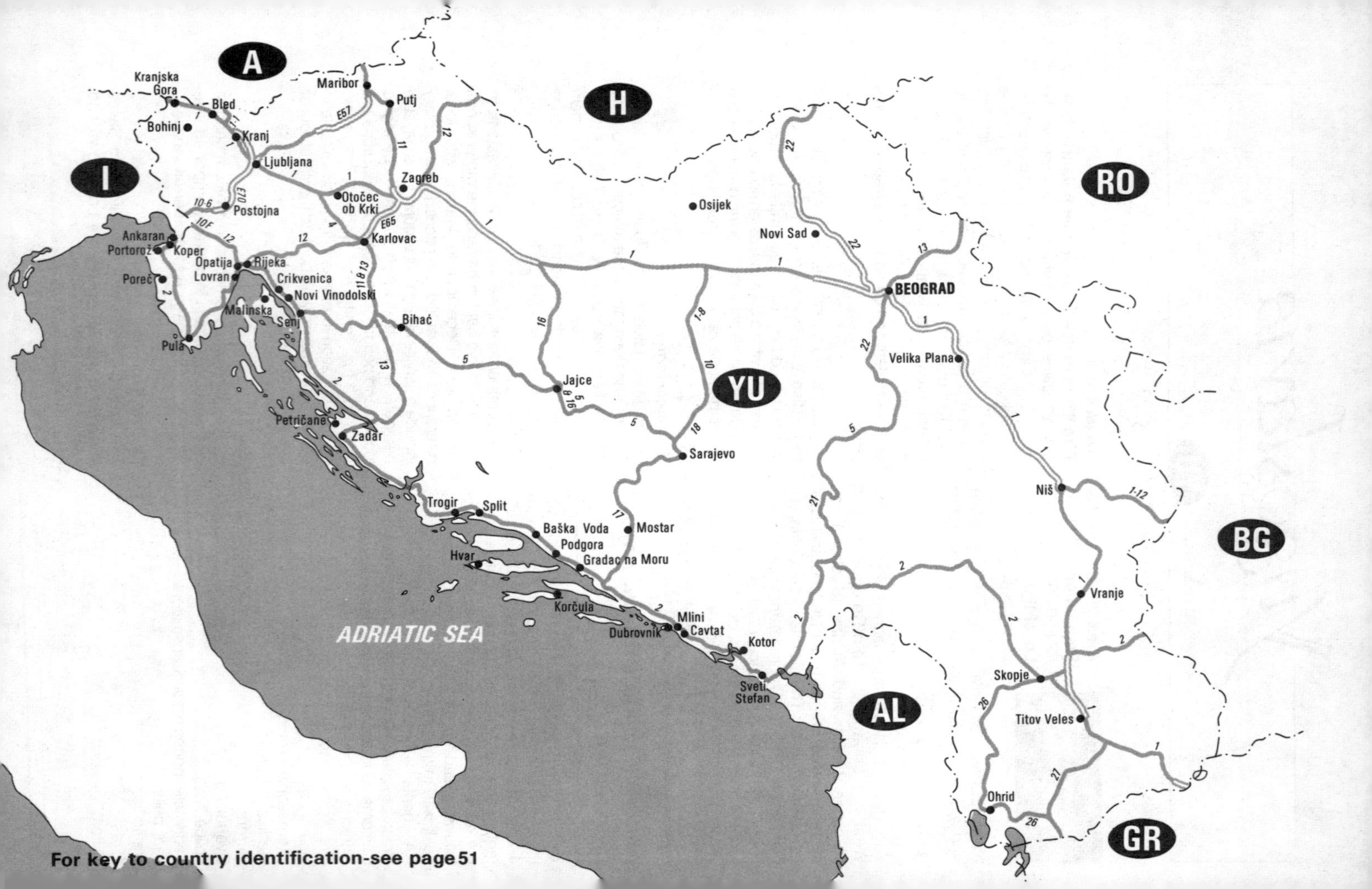

For key to country identification-see page 51

road information service which covers the whole of the country ☎ 987 for assistance. See also *Breakdown* page 6 and *Warning triangles* page 417.

British Embassy/Consulates

(See also page 6)

The British Embassy together with its consular section is located at *11000 Beograd* Generala Zdanova 46 ☎ (011)645034/43/55. There are British Consulates with Honorary Consuls in Split and Zagreb.

Currency including banking hours

(See also page 9)

The unit of currency is the Yugoslav Dinar (*Din*) divided into 100 *Para*. At the time of going to press £ = *Din*592.05. Denominations of bank notes are *Din* 10, 20, 50, 100, 500, 1,000, 5,000; standard coins are *Din* 1, 2, 5, 10, 20, 50, 100. A maximum of *Din*5,000 per person in Yugoslav currency may be imported or exported on a first journey during the course of a calendar year; for each subsequent journey during that year a maximum of *Din*2,000 is allowed. However, it is forbidden to import bank notes of a denomination larger than *Din*1,000. There are no restrictions on the import or export of foreign currency.

Visitors may exchange foreign currency at exchange offices, banks, hotels, tourist offices, and some offices of the Yugoslav motoring organisation into dinar bank notes or dinar-denominated cheques. The dinar cheques may be used to pay for certain goods and services entitling the holder to a discount. They are easily re-converted into foreign currency unlike dinar bank notes and coins. Generally banks are open Monday to Friday from 07.30—12.00hrs, but in tourist areas they remain open until 18.00hrs. All exchange receipts should be retained until you leave the country.

Dimensions

Private **cars** and towed **trailers** or **caravans** are restricted to the following dimensions — height: 4 metres; width: 2.50 metres; length*: 6 metres. The maximum permitted overall length of vehicle/trailer or caravan combination is 15 metres.

*Trailers with two axles 10 metres (including tow-bar).

Driving licence

(See also page 11)

A valid British driving licence is acceptable in Yugoslavia. The minimum age at which a visitor may drive a temporarily imported car or motorcycle (exceeding 125cc) is 18 years.

Emergency messages to tourists

(See also page 11)

Emergency messages to tourists are broadcast by the Yugoslav radio network.

Radio Beograd transmitting on 439 metres medium wave broadcasts the messages in English, French and German every day between June and September at 12.02hrs.

Radio Ljubljana transmitting on 326.8 metres medium wave broadcasts the messages in English and German between 09.35—10.00hrs Monday to Saturday from 26 May to 30 September.

Radio Yugoslavia transmitting on medium wave 881 metres, 711 metres and 1268 metres broadcasts the messages in English every day throughout the year between 15.30—16.00hrs, 18.30—19.00hrs, 20.00—20.30hrs and 22.15—22.30hrs.

First-aid kit

(See also page 12)

It is *compulsory* for visiting motorists to carry a first-aid kit in their vehicles.

Lights

(See also page 14)

Dipped headlights must be used by motorcyclists during the day when travelling outside built-up areas. It is *compulsory* for visiting motorists to equip their vehicle with a set of replacement bulbs.

Motoring club

(See also page 16)

The **Auto-Moto Savez Jugoslavije** (AMSJ) has its headquarters at 11000 Beograd Ruzveltova 18 ☎ (011)401-699 and is represented in most towns either direct or through regional and associated clubs.

Motorways

Several single and dual carriageway sections of motorway (autoput of avtocesta) are now available. There are 515 miles open in all and further stretches are under construction. Tolls are charged on most sections.

Parking

(See page 18)

Between 08.00—19.00hrs (Mon-Sat) parking meters are in use in some towns.

Passengers

(See also page 18)
Children under 12 and persons visibly under the influence of alcohol are not permitted to travel in a vehicle as front seat passengers.

Petrol

(See also page 18)
Credit cards Petrol stations do not generally have the facilities to accept credit cards.
Duty-free petrol The petrol in the vehicle tank may be imported free of customs duty and tax.
Petrol cans Petrol in cans may be imported in limited quantities but only on payment of customs duty.
Petrol coupons Tourist coupons provide a discount on pump prices and may be purchased at road border crossings, but only with freely convertible currency. They cannot be purchased in Yugoslavia. The border crossings at Škofije, Kozina, Fernatiči, Nova Gorica, Rateče, Korensko sedlo, Ljubelj, Vič, Šentilj and Gornja Radgona provide tourist services on a 24-hr basis. However visitors arriving by Motorail cannot purchase tourist petrol coupons at Jesenice, the border crossing for rail traffic, but may obtain them in Ljubljana from the Kompas agency in the airport bank.
Petrol (leaded) Normal Benzin (86 octane) and Super Benzin (98 octane) grades.
Petrol (unleaded) is sold in Yugoslavia as bezolovni benzin (95 octane). The octane rating is displayed on pumps dispensing unleaded petrol.

Postal information

Mail Postcards *Din*100, Letters *Din*150.
Post offices There are 3,500 post offices in Yugoslavia. Opening hours in major cities are 07.00—20.00hrs Monday to Friday and elsewhere 07.00—15.00hrs or 08.00—12.00hrs and 17.00—19.00hrs Monday to Friday. Most offices are open Saturdays from 07.00—15.00hrs.

Postcheques

(See also page 20)
Postcheques may be cashed at all post offices for any amount up to a maximum of *Din*25,000 per cheque. Counter positions are identified by the *Postcheque* sticker. See *Postal information* for post office opening hours.

Priority

Trams have priority over all vehicles at all times. See also *Priority including Roundabouts* page 21.

Public holidays

Official public holidays in Yugoslavia for 1987 are given below. See also *Public holidays* page 21.
January 1/2 (New Year)
April 27 (National holiday in Slovenia)
May 1/2* (Labour Day)
July 4* (Veterans' Day)
July 7 (National holiday in Serbia)
July 13 (National holiday in Montenegro)
July 22 (National holiday in Slovenia)
July 27 (National holiday in Croatia and Bosnia-Herzegovina)
August 2+ (National holiday in Macedonia)
October 11+ (National holiday in Macedonia)
November 1+ (National holiday in Slovenia)
November 25 (National holiday in Bosnia-Herzegovina)
November 29+/30 (Republic Day)
Where a two-day holiday includes Sunday, the following Monday will be a holiday.

*Saturday +Sunday

Registration documents

(See also page 21)
If the vehicle is not registered in your name you should have a letter from the owner authorising you to use it; this letter must be countersigned by a motoring organisation.

Roads

Roads have improved considerably in the last few years and many have been rebuilt. All the international transit routes are mainly in good condition, and so is the coast road from Rijeka to Dubrovnik and beyond. It is wise, when making a tour off the beaten track, to enquire at the local tourist agencies for the latest information on the next stage of the journey. Make sure your car is in good order before you go, as telephones and service stations are far apart. A leaflet entitled *Road conditions in Yugoslavia* is available to AA members.

Road signs

(See also page 22)
The words *Jedan Smer* on a blue and white arrow indicate a one-way street in the direction the arrow is pointing.

Shopping hours

Generally shops are open from 08.00—12.00hrs and 16.00—20.00hrs Monday—Friday and 08.00—15.00hrs on Saturday. Some *food shops* also open on Sunday 06.00—10.00hrs.

Speed limits

(See also page 22)

In built-up areas 60kph (37mph); outside built-up areas 80kph (49mph) but 100kph (62mph) on dual carriageways and 120kph (74mph) on motorways. Vehicle trailer combinations not exceeding 750kg in weight are restricted to 80kph (49mph) on all roads outside built-up areas.

Spiked or studded tyres

The use of *spiked tyres* is prohibited. See also *Cold weather touring* page 8.

Tourist Information

(See also page 24)
The Yugoslav National Tourist Office is located in London at 143 Regent Street, W1R 8AE ☎ 01-734 5243/8714 and 01-439 0399. They will be pleased to help tourists before their departure to Yugoslavia. Additionally, many resorts have their own tourist bureau where local information may be obtained.

Using the telephone

(See also page 24)
Insert coin **after** lifting receiver, dialling tone long and short tones. When making calls to subscribers within Yugoslavia precede number with relevant area code (shown in parentheses against town entry in gazetteer). Use *Din*5 coins for local calls and higher value coins for national and international calls (in some old style callboxes the highest value coin accepted is *Din*10).
International callbox identification Certain boxed with 3/4 coin slots.
Telephone rates A direct call to the UK costs *Din*432 per minute.
What to dial for Irish Republic 99 353.
What to dial for the UK 99 44.

Warning triangles

The use of a warning triangle is compulsory for all vehicles except two-wheelers. The triangle must be placed on the road 50 metres (55yds) behind the vehicle to warn following traffic of any obstruction. Two triangles (placed side by side) are required for vehicle/trailer combinations. See also *Warning triangles/Hazard warning lights* page 25.

Wheel chains

If summer tyres are used during winter conditions, the driving wheels must be fitted with wheel chains. See also *Cold weather touring* page 8.

In view of the fluctuation in rates of exchange, prices are shown in the currency quoted to us by the hotel i.e. US dollars ($), Deutschmarks (Dm), or £ sterling. At the time of going to press the dollar stands at 1.522 = £1. See page 203 for Deutschmark conversion.
Abbreviations:
pl plaza

The province names are as follows with their better known forms:
Bosna/Hercegovina — Bosnia and Herzegovina
Crna Gora — Montenegro
Hrvatska — Croatia
Makedonija — Macedonia
Slovenija — Slovenia
Srbija — Serbia

ANKARAN
Slovenija (☎066)

★★***Bor*** ☎51815
Apr—Oct
🛁 🚿 96 🚗 Beach

BAŠKA VODA
Hrvatska (☎058)

★★**Slavija** ☎620155
Apr—Oct
rm50 (🛁 🚿 30) sB 🛁 🚿 Dm27—51 dB 🛁 🚿 Dm45—96 sea

BEOGRAD (BELGRADE)
Srbija (☎011)

★★★★★**Beograd Inter Continental** ☎134760 tx12009
🛁 420 **P**100 Lift ☾ sB 🛁 $98 dB 🛁 $124 M$13&alc
Credit cards 1 2 3 4 5

★★★★★***Metropol*** Bulevar Revolucije 69 ☎330911 tx11777
🛁 218 🚗 **P** Lift ☾
Credit cards 1 2 3 4 5

★★★★**Excelsior** Kneza Miloša 5 ☎331381 tx12299
🛁 81 Lift ☾ sB 🛁 $40—44 dB 🛁 $53—60 t%
Credit cards 2 3 5

★★★★**Jugoslavia** (SRS) Bulevar E-Kardelja 3 ☎600222 tx11777
🛁 500 🚗 **P** Lift ☾ sB 🛁 $50 dB 🛁 $90 🏊

★★★★**Majestic** ☎636022 tx11345
🛁 92 Lift ☾ sB 🛁 $44 dB 🛁 $50—60
Credit cards 1 2 3 5

★★★***Balkan*** ☎687466
rm95 (🛁 🚿 47) Lift ☾
Credit cards 1 2 3 5

★★★**Kasina** pl Terazi 25 ☎335574 tx11865
🛁 🚿 96 Lift sB 🛁 🚿 $33 dB 🛁 🚿 $45

★★★**National** ☎601122 tx11774
🚿 70 **P** ☾ sB🚿 $30 dB🚿 $36 mountains

★★★**Putnik** ☎697221
🛁 118 Lift sB 🛁 $24—26 dB 🛁 $30—36

★★★**Slavija** Svetog Save 9 ☎450842 tx11545
🛁 509 🚗 **P**100 Lift ☾ sB 🛁 $40—50 dB 🛁 $60—90 t%
Credit cards 1 2 3 4 5

★★★***Toplice*** ☎626426
🛁 100 **P** Lift ☾

🚘 **Auto-moto Turing Društvo** Ruzveltova 19—21 ☎987 All makes

Dvadesetprvi MAJ Patrijarha Dimitrija 24 ☎592111 Fia

Interkomerc-Kontinental Omiadinskih Brigada 31 ☎154660 For Ren

Zastava-Auto Mije Kavacevića 6 ☎754899 Fia

BIHAĆ
Bosna I Hercegovina (☎077)

★★***Park*** ☎229042 tx45851
rm110 (🛁 🚿 76) 🚗 Lift sea

BLED
Slovenija (☎064)

★★★★**Golf** Cankarjeva 4 ☎77591 tx34531
🛁 150 **P** Lift ☾ sB 🛁 $25—37 dB 🛁 $40—64 🏊 mountains lake

★★★★**Grand Hotel Toplice** (SRS) ☎77222 tx34588
🛁 🚿 121 Lift sB 🛁 🚿 $22—26 dB 🛁 🚿 $38—46 🏊

★★**Jelovica** ☎77316 tx34635
rm146 (🛁 146) A30rm 🚗 **P**70 Lift ☾ sB 🛁 $19—26 dB 🛁 $28—38 M$5 lake

★★**Park** ☎77945 tx34504

86 **P** Lift ☾ sB $30–38 dB $48–66 mountains lake

★**Krim** Ljubilianska Cesta 7 ☎77418 tx34674

rm99 (69) sB$15–17 sB $20–25 dB$25–31 dB $30–36

BOHINJ
Slovenija (☎064)

★★**Zlatorog** Bohinjsko Jezero ☎76381 tx34619

74 A31rm Lift ☾ sB £17–21 dB£18–24 M£4–7 t% mountains
Credit cards 1 2 3 4 5

BORIK See **ZADAR**

CAVTAT
Hrvatska (☎050)

★★★**Cavtat** ☎78022 tx27530

Closed 5 Dec–1 Feb
485 **P** Lift ☾ sB $32–78 dB $28–62 M$10 t% Beach sea
Credit cards 1 2 3 5

★★★**Epidaurus** ☎78144 tx27523

Apr–Oct
rm192 (175) Lift Beach sea

CRIKVENICA
Hrvatska (☎051)

★★★**Esplanade** Stronsmajerovo Setalište ☎781133

Apr–Oct
89 sB Dm22–54 dB Dm38–90

★★★**International** Setalište VI Bakarica ☎781324

53 Lift sB Dm30–48 dB Dm46–72

★★**Therapia** ☎781511

115 Lift sB Dm25–45 dB Dm40–100

Automehanika Selska 1 ☎782197

DUBROVNIK
Hrvatska (☎050)

★★★★**Argentina** put Frana Supila 14 ☎23855 tx27558

121 A27rm **P**40 Lift ☾ sB $24–56 dB $43–104 Malc Beach sea
Credit cards 1 2 5

★★★★**Excelsior** put Frna Supila 3 ☎23566 tx27523

211 Lift sB $18–55 dB $22–104 Beach sea

★★★★***Libertas*** Lavceviceva 1 ☎27444 tx27588

360 **P**50 Lift ☾ Beach sea
Credit cards 1 2 3 5

★★★***Imperial*** Mise simoni 2 ☎23688 tx27523

Closed Nov–22 Dec
103 **P**15 Lift sea
Credit cards 1 2 5

Yugoslavia

★★★**Neptun** Dalmatinski put ☎23755 tx27523

Apr–Oct
220 Lift dB $22–48 Beach sea

★★★**Splendid** ☎24733

Apr–Oct
61 Lift sB $18–37 dB $26–53 Beach sea

★★★**Sumratin** (5km from Station) Aleja Ive Loie Ribara ☎24722

Apr–Oct
70 A26rm Lift sB $13–35 dB $20–46 sea

★★★**Villa Dubrovnik** Vlaha Bukovca 8 ☎22933 tx27523

Apr–Oct
56 A9rm **P** Lift sB $22–58 dB $26–88 Beach

★★***Bellevue*** put Pera Cingrie ☎25075

Apr–Oct
rm51 (47) Lift Beach sea

○**Holiday Inn** ☎28655 tx27674

209 **P**70 Lift ☾ dB $50–75 Beach sea
Credit cards 1 2 3 5

Auto-Dubrovnik put Mihaila 1 ☎23728 Cit For Ope Ren

Dubrovkinja OOUR Auto-servis Masarikov PUT 3 ☎28940 Aud VW

GORICA See **OHRID**

GRADAC NA MORU
Hrvatska (☎058)

★★**Laguna** ☎70614

70 **P** Lift sB Dm33–48 dB Dm60–90 Beach sea

HALUDOVO See **MALINSKA**

HVAR (ISLAND OF)
Hrvatska (☎058)

★★★**Adriatic** ☎74028 tx26235

63 Lift sB $15–30 dB $23–52 sea

★★**Dalmacija** ☎74120

70 sB $10–25 dB $18–44 Beach sea

★★***Pharos*** ☎74026

175

JAJCE
Bosna I Hercegovina (☎070)

★★**Turist** ☎33268

rm54 (20) sB$10 sB $12 dB$18 dB $22

KARLOVAC
Hrvatska (☎047)

Automehanika Ilovac ☎23844 VW

KOPER
Slovenija (☎066)

Trgoavto Tozd Servis is Istarska Cesta 12 ☎32201 Mer Ren

KORČULA (ISLAND OF)
Hrvatska (☎050)

★★★**Marko Polo** ☎711100 tx27556

113 **P** Lift ☾ sB $12–28 dB $18–45 Beach sea

★★★***Park*** ☎711004 tx27556

Apr–Oct
rm225 (170) A75rm **P** ☾ Beach sea

KOTOR
Crna Gora (☎082)

Autoremont put Prvoboraca 188 ☎25388 Fia Ren

KRANJ
Slovenija (☎064)

★★★***Creina*** ☎23650 tx34556

93 **P**50 Lift mountains
Credit cards 1 2 3 4 5

Gasilsko Resevaina Sluzba Oldhamska Cesta 4 ☎21060

KRANJSKA GORA
Slovenija (☎064)

★★**Kompas** (9km on Ratce-Jesenice road) ☎88661

155 Lift sB $51–81 dB $71–111

★★**Prisank** ☎88472 tx34636

64 sB Dm36–39 dB Dm50–55

LJUBLJANA
Slovenija (☎061)

★★★★**Lev** Vosnjakova 1 ☎310555 tx31350

209 **P** ☾ sB $23–34 dB $36–45 mountains

★★★★**Sion** Titova 10 ☎211232 tx31254

185 Lift sB $28–32 dB $36

★★★**Grand Union** Miklosiceva Cesta 1 ☎212133 tx31295

270 **P**10 Lift ☾ sB $29 dB $40 M$9 t%
Credit cards 1 2 3 5

★★★**Turist** Dalmationova 15 ☎322043 tx31317

rm192 (140) Lift ☾ sB $11–23 dB $22–32 t%
Credit cards 1 2 5

★★***Ilirija*** Trg Prekomorskin Brigad 4 ☎551245 tx31574

rm136 (86) **P** Lift ☾
Credit cards 1 2 5

Agrostroj Koseska 11 ☎555366 Saa

Automontaza Celovska Cesta 182 ☎556455 Alf

Autotehna Celovska 228 ☎573555 For Ope Vau

Cimos-Citroën Servis Cilenskova 13 ☎442917 All makes

PAP Autoservis Celovska 258 ☎576111 BMW

LOVRAN
Hrvatska (☎051)

★★★★**Excelsior** ☎731022
180 P90 Lift sB Dm41—65 dB Dm62—110 Malc Beach sea

★★**Beograd** ☎731022
102 A30rm P20 Lift sB Dm55—85 dB Dm90—140 Malc Beach sea

MALINSKA
Hrvatska (☎051)

At **HALUDOVO** (0.5km N)

★★★★**Palace** ☎885566 tx24142
220 Lift sB Dm41—80 dB $64—156

★★★**Tamaris** ☎885566
May—Oct
289 Lift sB Dm21—45 dB Dm39—80 Beach

MARIBOR
Slovenija (☎062)

★★**Slavija** Vita Kraigherja 3 ☎23661 tx33141
122 P200 Lift sB Dm70—75 dB Dm90—100 MDm15
Credit cards 1 2 3 4 5

★★**Orel** Grajski Trg 3 ☎26171 tx33277
rm150 (100) P Lift sBDm47 sB Dm66 dBDm74 dB Dm97 MDm15 mountains
Credit cards 1 2 3 5

Auto-Servis Cesta XIV Divizije 89 ☎513092

Ferromoto Minska Cesta 13 ☎21441 Fia

MLINI
Hrvatska (☎050)

★★**Mlini** ☎86053
90 sB $14—31 dB $18—44 Beach sea

MOSTAR
Bosna I Hercegovina (☎088)

★★**Bristol** ☎32921 tx46136
rm56 (45) Lift sB$12 sB $15 dB$20 dB $26

★★**Mostar** ☎32941 tx46136
27 P sB $15 dB $26

★★***Neretva*** ☎3230 tx46136
35 mountains
Credit cards 1 2 3 5

Auto-Moto Drustvo Splitska 66 ☎987 All makes

NIŠ
Srbija (☎018)

★★★***Ambassador*** ☎25833 tx16256
170 P25 Lift mountains
Credit cards 1 2 3 4 5

★★**Nais** ☎881270 tx16256
84 P150 Lift sB $23 dB $34 M$8 t% mountains
Credit cards 1 2 3 4 5

Yugoslavia

★★***Park 7*** Julia 4 ☎23296
93 Lift

★***Mediana*** ☎337161
rm54 (22)

Auto-Moto Drustvo Marka Oreskovića 15 ☎987 Fia

Zastava-Auto Kragujevac N Stojanovića ☎65628 Fia

NOVISAD
Srbija (☎021)

★★★**Park** Hadjuk Veljkova 2 ☎611711
315 P200 Lift sB $24 dB $40
Credit cards 1 2 3 5

Auto-Moto Drustvo Lenjinov trg 10 ☎29389 All makes

Autovojvodina Kosovska 54 ☎29168 Aud VW

NOVI VINOLDOSKI
Hrvatska (☎051)

★★**Lisanj** ☎791022 tx24468
Apr—Oct
166 A70rm P90 Lift sB £14—20 dB £24—34 M£5 Beach sea

OHRID
Makedonija (☎096)

At **GORICA** (2.5km S)

★★★**Inex Gorica** ☎22020
Apr—Oct
110 A20rm P sB $21—26 dB $32—41 Beach

OPATIJA
Hrvatska (☎051)

★★★★**Ambasador** ☎712211 tx24184
260 P300 Lift sB $22—53 dB $30—66 Beach sea
Credit cards 1 2 3 5

★★★★**Kvarner** Park 1, Maja 4 ☎711211
86 A30rm P Lift sB Dm41—91 dB Dm52—152 Beach sea

★★★***Belvedere*** Maršala Tita 89 ☎712433
May—Oct
rm171 (100) Lift Beach sea

★★★**Slavija** Maršala Tita 200 ☎711811
5 Jan—23 Dec
106 sB Dm34—70 dB Dm48—120

★★**Dubrovnik** Maršala Tita 201 ☎711611
5 Jan—23 Dec
42 Lift sB Dm29—65 dB Dm38—110 Beach sea

★★***Palme*** Maršala Tita 166 ☎711823
May—Oct
rm103 (61) Lift

40 Box Spinčićeva 21 ☎711439 Aud VW

OSIJEK
Srbija (☎054)

Remontservis Vinkovacka 7 ☎24366 Fia

OTOČEC OB KRKI
Slovenija (☎068)

★★**Grad Otočec** ☎21830 tx35740
rm21 (10) P sBDm54—68 sB Dm56—72 dBDm84—98 dB Dm69—114 MDm14—30 t% Beach
Credit cards 1 2 3 4 5

★★***Otočec*** ☎21830 tx35740
90 A61rm P100 Lift mountains Beach
Credit cards 1 2 4 5

PETRČANE
Hrvatska (☎057)

★★★**Pinija** ☎73062 tx27136
Apr—20 Oct
307 P300 Lift sB Dm30—65 dB Dm52—96 MDm10—15 sea
Credit cards 1 2 5

PODGORA
Hrvatska (☎058)

★★★**Mediteran** ☎625155 tx26322
Apr—Oct
131 sB Dm23—49 dB Dm42—76 sea

★★***Podgorka*** ☎625266
Apr—Oct
rm19

POREČ
Hrvatska (☎053)

★★***Riviera*** Obala Maršala Tita 25 ☎32433
27 Apr—Oct
rm130 (100) A30rm Lift Beach sea
Credit cards 1 2 3 5

Riviera Autoremont M Vlašića 66 ☎31344 Cit Fia Ren

PORTOROŽ
Slovenija (☎066)

★★★**Palace** ☎73541 tx34156
rm639 (609) P Lift sB£16—29 sB £16—33 dB£24—37 dB £25—52 M£4 t% Beach
Credit cards 1 2 3 5

POSTOJNA
Slovenija (☎067)

★★***Kras*** Titov Trg ☎21071 tx34181
May—Dec
rm108 (54) P Lift

PTUJ
Slovenija (☎062)

★★**Poetovio** ☎772640
rm33 (13) sBDm30 sB Dm35 dBDm54 dB Dm58

PULA
Hrvatska (☎052)

★★★***Verudela*** ☎24811
Apr—Oct
rm376 (328)) Beach sea

Auto-Servis Takop Beruda 39 22450 Aud Ren VW

RIJEKA
Hrvatska (051)

★★★**Bonavia** 33744 tx24129
161 Lift sB $25 dB $34—40

★★★***Jadran*** 421600
81 Lift sea
Credit cards [2] [3] [5]

★★**Park** 421155
rm47 (16) Lift sBDm33—35 sB Dm38 dBDm51—57 dB Dm65 Beach sea

Autoservis Barčićeva 3 30388 Cit For

SARAJEVO
Bosna I Hercegovina (071)

★★**Evropa** Vase Pelagića 5 532722 tx41219
225 Lift sB $29 dB $45

Bosna-Auto Obala 27 jula 35 43143 Mer Ren

SENJ
Hrvatska (051)

★★**Nehaj** Titova Obala 881285
rm43 (21) Lift sBDm18—28 dBDm29—54 dB Dm40—59 sea

SKOPJE
Makedonija (091)

★★**Continental** 220122 tx51318
200 P100 Lift sB $30 dB $46 M$8 t%
Credit cards [1] [2] [3] [5]

Gradska Zaednica & Auto-Moto Drustvata Ivo Lola Ribar 51 237305

SPLIT
Hrvatska (058)

★★★★**Marjan** Obala Jna 5 42866 tx26102
331 P100 Lift sea

Yugoslavia

★★★**Park** Maja 15 Setalište II 515411 tx26316
60 Lift sB $23—29 dB $29—50

Auto-Diamacija Mosorskog Odreda 1 47277 Aud Fia Mer Ren VW

STOBI See **TITOV VELES**

SVETI STEFAN
Crna Gora (086)

★★★★***Sveti Stefan*** 41005 tx61188
May—20 Oct
118 P120 Beach sea
Credit cards [1] [2] [3] [5]

★★★***Maestral*** 41333 tx61188
Apr—Oct
157 P70 Lift Beach sea
Credit cards [1] [2] [3] [5]

★★★***Milločer*** 41333 tx61188
May—Sep
72 P Beach sea
Credit cards [1] [2] [3] [5]

TITOV VELES
Makedonija (093)

At **STOBI** (26km SE)

★**Stobi** 70036
20 P Lift sB $11 dB $24 M$6—7

TROGIR
Hrvatska (058)

★★★***Medena*** 73222 tx26204
663 Lift Beach sea

VELIKA PLANA
Srbija (026)

★***Velika Plana*** 52253
32
Credit cards [2] [3] [5]

VRANJE
Srbija (017)

★★**Vranje** 26980 tx16781
70 P30 Lift sB $18 dB $48 M$4—5
Credit cards [2] [5]

ZADAR
Hrvatska (057)

At **BORIK** (On coast 4km NW)

Autorvatska Benkovacka BB 22690 Aud Cit For Mer Peu

ZAGREB
Hrvatska (041)

★★★★**Esplanade** Minhanoviceva 1 512222 tx21395
240 P Lift sB $45—61 dB $63—88 t%
Credit cards [1] [2] [3]

★★★***International*** Miramarška 511511 tx21184
420 Lift

★★**Dubrovnik** Gajeva 1 424222 tx21670
269 Lift sB frDm30 dB frDm48 MDm5
Credit cards [1] [2] [3] [4] [5]

PTT Autoradionica Folnegovičeva 6b 519868 Ope Peu

Autosanitarija Heinzelova 53 212622 AR Ren

Autoservis-Borongaj Borongajska 75 215222

Opel Servis Samoborska 222a 155343 Ope

Skolski Centar za Cestovni Saobračaj Kraljevićava 24 210320 Peu

The picturesque town of Mostar

Road report

to The Automobile Association,
Overseas Routes,
Fanum House, Basingstoke,
Hants RG21 2EA.

section of road
from | to

passing through | road no.

names shown on signposts

remarks: *ie* surface, width, estimated gradient, description of landscape

section of road
from | to

passing through | road no.

names shown on signposts

remarks: *ie* surface, width, estimated gradient, description of landscape

vehicle used | date of journey

name (block letters)

address (block letters)

membership no. | for office use only acknowledged | recorded

Road report

to The Automobile Association,
Overseas Routes,
Fanum House, Basingstoke,
Hants RG21 2EA.

section of road
from to

passing through road no.

names shown on signposts

remarks: *ie* surface, width, estimated gradient, description of landscape

section of road
from to

passing through road no.

names shown on signposts

remarks: *ie* surface, width, estimated gradient, description of landscape

vehicle used date of journey

name (block letters)

address (block letters)

membership no. for office use only
acknowledged recorded

Garage report

to The Automobile Association,
Hotel & Information Services,
Fanum House, Basingstoke,
Hants RG21 2EA.

Town, country, garage

address

telephone no.

agents for | were AIT vouchers used for payment | recommended

remarks

town, country, garage

address

telephone no.

agents for | were AIT vouchers used for payment | recommended

remarks

town, country, garage

address

telephone no.

agents for | were AIT vouchers used for payment | recommended

remarks

name (block letters)

address (block letters)

membership no. | for office use only acknowledged | recorded

Garage report

to The Automobile Association,
Hotel & Information Services,
Fanum House, Basingstoke,
Hants RG21 2EA.

Town, country, garage

address

telephone no.

agents for | were AIT vouchers used for payment | recommended

remarks

town, country, garage

address

telephone no.

agents for | were AIT vouchers used for payment | recommended

remarks

town, country, garage

address

telephone no.

agents for | were AIT vouchers used for payment | recommended

remarks

name (block letters)

address (block letters)

membership no. | for office use only acknowledged | recorded

Accommodation report

to The Automobile Association,
Hotel & Information Services,
Fanum House, Basingstoke,
Hants RG21 2EA.

town, country, hotel

your star rating | location | date of stay

food | rooms

service | sanitary arrangements | value for money

general remarks

town, country, hotel

your star rating | location | date of stay

food | rooms

service | sanitary arrangements | value for money

general remarks

town, country, hotel

your star rating | location | date of stay

food | rooms

service | sanitary arrangements | value for money

general remarks

name (block letters)

address (block letters)

membership no. | for office use only acknowledged | recorded

Accommodation report

to The Automobile Association,
Hotel & Information Services,
Fanum House, Basingstoke,
Hants RG21 2EA.

town, country, hotel

your star rating | location | date of stay

food | rooms

service | sanitary arrangements | value for money

general remarks

town, country, hotel

your star rating | location | date of stay

food | rooms

service | sanitary arrangements | value for money

general remarks

town, country, hotel

your star rating | location | date of stay

food | rooms

service | sanitary arrangements | value for money

general remarks

name (block letters)

address (block letters)

membership no. | for office use only acknowledged | recorded

Accommodation report

to The Automobile Association,
Hotel & Information Services,
Fanum House, Basingstoke,
Hants RG21 2EA.

town, country, hotel

your star rating | location | date of stay

food | rooms

service | sanitary arrangements | value for money

general remarks

town, country, hotel

your star rating | location | date of stay

food | rooms

service | sanitary arrangements | value for money

general remarks

town, country, hotel

your star rating | location | date of stay

food | rooms

service | sanitary arrangements | value for money

general remarks

name (block letters)

address (block letters)

membership no. | for office use only acknowledged | recorded

Accommodation report

to The Automobile Association,
Hotel & Information Services,
Fanum House, Basingstoke,
Hants RG21 2EA.

town, country, hotel

your star rating | location | date of stay

food | rooms

service | sanitary arrangements | value for money

general remarks

town, country, hotel

your star rating | location | date of stay

food | rooms

service | sanitary arrangements | value for money

general remarks

town, country, hotel

your star rating | location | date of stay

food | rooms

service | sanitary arrangements | value for money

general remarks

name (block letters)

address (block letters)

membership no. | for office use only acknowledged | recorded

Index

Symbols and Abbreviations

English

★★★ Hotel classification
○ Hotel likely to open during the currency of this annual guide
Private baths
Private showers
P Parking for cars
Garage and/or lock-up
☾ Night porter
Tennis court(s) (private)
Golf (private)
Riding stables (private)
Indoor swimming pool
Outdoor swimming pool
Breakdown service
☎ Telephone number. Where there is a dialling code it is shown in parentheses against the town entry
sB Single room per person per night*
sB Single with private bath/shower per person per night*
dB Double room (two persons)*
dB Double room (two persons) with private bath/shower*
M Main meal
alc à la carte
DPn Demi-pension
Pn Full pension
St% Service and/or tax charge (service and tax is included unless otherwise stated)
(n.rest) Hotel does not have own restaurant
tx Telex
rm Number of bedrooms (including annexe)
A Annexe followed by number of rooms
LF Logis de France
M/c Motorcycle repairs undertaken
Beach Hotel has private beach
Sea/mountains/lake Rooms overlook sea, mountain(s) or a lake
→ Entry continued overleaf
Plan Number gives location of hotel on town plan
Credit cards (see page 50)

*In most cases this price includes breakfast.

For a more detailed explanation refer to 'About the Gazetteer' pages 49-53.

Français

★★★ Classement des hôtels
○ Hôtels qui doivent ouvrir prochainement
Salles de bain privées
Douches privées
P Parking pour voitures
Garage et/ou garage avec serrure
☾ Portier de nuit
Court(s) de tennis (privés)
Golf (privé)
Equitation (privée)
Piscine couverte
Piscine en plein air
Service dépannage
☎ Numéro de téléphone. Lorsqu'il y a un indicatif, celui-ci est indiqué entre parenthèses à côte du nom de la ville
sB Chambre à un lit, par personne, pour un nuit*
sB Chambre à un lit avec bain/douche privé par personne, pour une nuit*
dB Chambre à deux lits (deux personnes)*
dB Chambre à deux lits (deux personnes) avec bain/douche privé*
M Repas principal
alc à la carte
DPn Demi-pension
Pn Pension complète
St% Charge pour service et/ou taxe (service et taxe sont compris sauf indication spéciale)
(n.rest) Hôtel ne fait pas restaurant
tx Télex
rm Nombre de chambres (annexes comprises)
A Annexe suivie par nombre de chambres
LF Logis de France
M/c Réparations de cyclomoteurs possibles
Beach Hôtel a une plage privée
Sea/mountains/lake Chambres avec vue sur la mer, les montagnes ou un lac
→ Suite au verso
Plan Chiffre indique l'emplacement de l'hôtel sur le plan de la ville
Cartes de credit (voir page 50)

*ce prix comprend généralement le petit-déjeuner.

Pour plus amples informations veuillez vous référer à 'About the Gazetteer' voir pages 49-53.

Deutsch

★★★ Hotelklassifzierung
○ Hotel wird wahrend de Laufzeit dieses Fuhrers eroffnet
Privatbad
Privatdusche
P Parken
Garage bzw verschliessbare Parkeinheit
☾ Nachtportier
Tennisplatz (Privat)
Golfplatz (Privat)
Reitgelegenheiten (Privat)
Hallenbad
Freibad
Pannendienst
☎ Telefonnummer. Wenn Vorwahlnummer vorhanden wird sie in Klammern zusammen mit Stadtangaben aufgeführt
sB Einzelzimmer pro Person pro Nacht*
sB Einzelzimmer mit Privatbad/Dusche pro Person pro nacht*
dB Doppelzimmer (2 Personen)*
dB Doppelzimmer (2 Personen) mit Privatbad/Dusche*
M Hauptessen
alc à la carte
DPn Demipension
Pn Vollpension
St% Dienst-bzw. Steuergebühren (Dienst-bzw. Steuergebühren sind, wenn keine Gegenangaben, einbegriffen)
(n.rest) Hotel ohne eigenes Restaurant
tx Telex

rm	Zimmeranzahl (einschliesslich Nebengebäude
A	Nebengebäude und danach Zimmeranzahl
LF	Logis de France
M/c	Motorradreparaturen
Beach	Hotel hat Privatstrand
Sea/mountains/lake	Zimmer mit einem Blick auf das Meer, die Gebirge oder einen See
→	Fortsetzung siehe umseitig
Plan	Nummer gibt den Standort des Hotels auf dem Stadtplan
Kreditkarten	(siehe Seite 50)

*in den meisten Fällen sind die Preise einschl. des Frühstücks.

Für weltere Angaben beziehen Sie sich auf 'About the Gazetteer' siehe Seites 49-53.

Italiano

★★★	Classificazione alberghi
○	Alberghi che saranno apèrti durante il periodo di validita della guida
	Bagni privati
	Docce private
P	Parcheggio macchine
	Garage e/o box
	Portiere notturno
	Campi da tennis (privati)
	Golf (privato)
	Piscina coperta
	Piscina all'aperto
	Scuola d'equitazione (privata)
	Servizio assistenza stradale
	Numero telefonico. I prefissi figurano tra parentesi vicino al norme della cittá
sB	Prezzo per persona di una camera singola (a notte)*
sB	Prezzo per persona di una camera singola con bagno/doccia privati (a notte)*
dB	Camera per due persone*
dB	Camera per due persone con bagno/doccia privati*
M	Pasto principale
alc	Alla carte
DPn	Mezza pensione
Pn	Pensione completa
St%	Servizio e/o tassa (compresi, salvo indicazione contraria)
(n.rest)	Albergo senza ristorante
tx	Telex
rm	Numero di camere (compresa la dependance)
A	Dependence, seguita dal numero di camere
LF	Logis de France
M/c	Si riparano motociclette
Beach	L'albergo è provvisto di spiaggia privata
Sea/mountains/lake	Le camere guardano sul mare/i mont/il lago
→	La lista delle voci continua a tergo
Plan	Il numero indica la posizione dell'albergo sulla cartina della cittá
Carte di credito	(vedere page 50)

*Nella maggioranza dei casi nel prezzo é inclusa la prima colazione.

Per una spiegazione plú dettagliata, consultare ia sezione 'About the Gazetteer' vedere pags 49-53.

Español

★★★	Clasificación de hoteles
○	Hoteles a ser inaugurados durante la vigencia de estaguia
	Baños en cada habitación
	Duchas en cada habitación
P	Aparcamiento para automóviles
	Garaje y/o garaje individual con cerradura
	Conserje nocturno
	Pistas de tenis (privadas)
	Golf (privado)
	Escuela hipica (privada)
	piscina cubierta
	piscina al aire libre
	Servicio de asistencia averias
	Número de teléfono. Si hay prefijo, ésta figura entre paréntesis junto al nombre de la ciudad
sB	Precio por persona de una habitación individual (por noche)*
sB	Precio por persona de una habitación individual con baño/ducha (por noche)*
dB	Precio de una habitación para dos personas*
dB	Percio de una habitación para dos personas con baño/ducha*
M	Comida principal
alc	A la carta
DPn	Media pensión
Pn	Pensión completa
St%	Servicio y/o impuesto (Ambos incluidos, a menos que se indique lo contrario)
(n.rest)	El hotel no tiene restaurante
tx	Telex
rm	Número de habitaciones (incluso el edificio anexo)
A	Edificio anexo, seguido por el número de habitaciones
LF	Logis de France
M/c	Se reparan motocicletas
Playa	El hotel tiene playa privada
Sea/mountains/lake	Las habitaciones tienen vista al mar/a las montañas/al lago
→	La lista de simbolos continúa a la vuelta
Plan	El número indica la posición del hotel en el plano de la ciudad
Tarjetas de crédito	(véase página 50)

*El la mayoria de los casos, en este precio está incluido el desayuno.

Para una explicación más detallada, consúltese la sección 'About the Gazetteer' (véase ei indice de materias) véase paginas 49-53.

Acknowledgements

All the black and white photographs in the Guide have been reproduced by courtesy of the tourist boards listed below, and the publisher would like to thank them for their help and co-operation. p.74, Austrian National Tourist Office; p.88, Belgian National Tourist Office; p.100, Danish Tourist Board; p.236, German National Tourist Office; p.265, Ireland (Bord Failte); p.296, Italian State Tourist Board; p.317, Netherlands National Tourist Office (NBT); p.334, Norwegian Tourist Board; p.372, Spanish National Tourist Office; p.412, Swiss National Tourist Office; p.420, Yugoslav National Tourist Office.